POLITICAL SERMONS OF THE AMERICAN FOUNDING ERA

1730–1805

POLITICAL SERMONS OF THE AMERICAN FOUNDING ERA

1730–1805

Edited by Ellis Sandoz

LibertyPress
INDIANAPOLIS

Liberty*Press* is a publishing imprint of Liberty Fund, Inc., a foundation established to encourage study of the ideal of a society of free and responsible individuals.

The cuneiform inscription that serves as the design motif for our endpapers is the earliest-known written appearance of the word "freedom" (*ama-gi*), or "liberty." It is taken from a clay document written about 2300 B.C. in the Sumerian city-state of Lagash.

 All inquiries should be addressed to Liberty Fund, Inc., 7440 North Shadeland Avenue, Indianapolis, Indiana 46250-2028. This book was manufactured in the United States of America.

Library of Congress Cataloging-in-Publication Data

Political sermons of the American founding era, 1730–1805 / edited by Ellis Sandoz.
p. cm.
Includes bibliographical references.
ISBN 0-86597-090-4. — ISBN 0-86597-091-2 (pbk.)
1. Christianity and politics—Sermons. 2. Sermons, American.
3. United States—History—Colonial period, ca. 1600–1775—Sources.
4. United States—History—Revolution, 1775–1783—Sources.
I. Sandoz, Ellis, 1931- .
BR115.P7P53 1991
261.7'0973'09033—dc20 90-20027
CIP

10 9 8 7 6 5 4 3 2 1

To the Pulpit, the *Puritan Pulpit*, we owe the moral force which won our independence.

John Wingate Thornton

This principle, that a whole nation has a right to do whatever it pleases, cannot in any sense whatever be admitted as true. The eternal and immutable laws of justice and morality are paramount to all human legislation. The violations of those laws is certainly within the power of a nation, but it is not among the rights of nations.

John Quincy Adams

Contents

Foreword

Inspiration for this collection of sermons came over a number of years as I did research on the American founders' political philosophy. I discovered that the "pulpit of the American Revolution"—to borrow the title of John Wingate Thornton's 1860 collection—was the source of exciting and uncommonly important material. What had passed for pamphlets in my reading of excerpted eighteenth-century American material often turned out to be published sermons. I began to realize that this material, showing the perspective of biblical faith concerning fundamental questions of human existence during our nation's formative period, was extraordinarily abundant and extraordinarily little known.

The rule of this collection has been to reprint unannotated editions of complete sermons that would permit their authors to speak fully for themselves. The genre is the political sermon, broadly construed so as to include a few pieces never preached that are *sermonic* in sense and tone—that is, hortatory and relating politics to convictions about eternal verities. The chief criterion for selection of the various pieces was their intellectual interest. I was looking especially for political theory in American sermons preached and then published from the onset of the Great Awakening to the beginning of the Second Awakening and Thomas Jefferson's second administration. An effort was made to diversify viewpoints denominationally, theologically, politically, geographically, and even nationally. Since only previously published materials have been selected—that is, nothing from manuscript sources has been included[1]—a limitation resided in the fact that the publication of sermons in America in the eighteenth century was a specialty, if not a monopoly, of New Englanders.

To permit the religious perspective concerning the rise of American nationhood to have representative expression is important because a steady attention to the pulpit from 1730 to 1805 unveils a distinctive

[1] Whether printed or manuscript sermons are more representative is a question debated in the literature; see Donald Weber, *Rhetoric and History in Revolutionary New England* (New York, 1988), 7.

rhetoric of political discourse: Preachers interpreted pragmatic events in terms of a political theology imbued with philosophical and revelatory learning. Their sermons also demonstrate the existence and effectiveness of a popular political culture that constantly assimilated the currently urgent political and constitutional issues to the profound insights of the Western spiritual and philosophical traditions. That culture's political theorizing within the compass of ultimate historical and metaphysical concerns gave clear contours to secular events in the minds of Americans of this vital era.

Religion gave birth to America, Tocqueville observed long ago.[2] On the eve of revolution, in his last-ditch attempt to stave off impending catastrophe, Edmund Burke reminded the House of Commons of the inseparable alliance between liberty and religion among Englishmen in America.[3] Mercy Otis Warren noted in her 1805 history of the American Revolution: "It must be acknowledged, that the religious and moral character of Americans yet stands on a higher grade of excellence and purity, than that of most other nations."[4] Of the Americans on the eve of the Revolution Carl Bridenbaugh has exclaimed, "who can deny that for them the very core of existence was their relation to God?"[5]

Although they present a range of viewpoints on many different problems over a period of seventy-five years, all our writers agree that political liberty and religious truth are vitally intertwined. And while the role of the clergy as the philosophers of the American founding has not received great attention from students of political theory, it was abundantly clear to contemporaries. Perhaps the best insight into the role of the ministry was expressed by a participant,

[2] Alexis de Tocqueville, *Democracy in America*, trans. George Lawrence, ed. J. P. Mayer (Garden City, N.Y., 1969), II, 432; cf. 46–47, 288–91.

[3] Edmund Burke, "Speech on Moving His Resolutions for Conciliation with the Colonies, March 22, 1775" in Burke, *Selected Writings and Speeches*, ed. Peter J. Stanlis (1963; rpr. Chicago, n.d.), 147–85, esp. 158–60.

[4] Mercy Otis Warren, *History of the Rise, Progress and Termination of the American Revolution, Interspersed with Biographical, Political and Moral Observations*, 2 vols., ed. Lester H. Cohen (Indianapolis, 1988), II, 686.

[5] Carl Bridenbaugh, *Spirit of '76: The Growth of American Patriotism Before Independence, 1607-1776* (New York, 1975), 117. The argument underlying this paragraph is stated more fully in Ellis Sandoz, *A Government of Laws: Political Theory, Religion and the American Founding* (Baton Rouge, La., 1990), esp. chaps. 3 to 6; see also the Bibliographic Note herein.

Reverend William Gordon of Roxbury, Massachusetts, who wrote the celebrated *History of the American Revolution*. "The ministers of New England being mostly congregationalists," Gordon wrote,

> are from that circumstance, in a professional way more attached and habituated to the principles of liberty than if they had spiritual superiors to lord it over them, and were in hopes of possessing in their turn, through the gift of government, the seat of power. They oppose arbitrary rule in civil concerns from the love of freedom, as well as from a desire of guarding against its introduction into religious matters. . . . The clergy of this colony are as virtuous, sensible and learned a set of men, as will probably be found in any part of the globe of equal size and equally populous. . . . [I]t is certainly a duty of the clergy to accommodate their discourses to the times; to preach against such sins as are most prevalent, and to recommend such virtues as are most wanted. . . . You have frequently remarked that though the partizans of arbitrary power will freely censure that preacher, who speaks boldly for the liberties of the people, they will admire as an excellent divine, the parson whose discourse is wholly in the opposite, and teaches, that magistrates have a divine right for doing wrong, and are to be implicitly obeyed; men professing Christianity, as if the religion of the blessed Jesus bound them tamely to part with their natural and social rights, and slavishly to bow their neck to any tyrant. . . .[6]

Whatever the differences among them, all the sermon authors take as their reality the still familiar biblical image of Creator and creation, of fallen and sinful men, striving in a mysteriously ordered existence toward a personal salvation and an eschatological fulfillment. They knew that these goals are themselves paradoxically attainable only through the divine grace of election, a condition experienced as the unmerited gift of God, discernible (if at all) in a person's faith in Christ, which yields assurance of Beatitude. The relationships are variously symbolized by personal and corporate reciprocal covenants ordering individual lives, church communities, and all of society in

[6] William Gordon, *The History of the Rise, Progress and Establishment of the United States of America, including An Account of the Late War*, 3 vols., 2d ed. (New York, 1794), I, 273–74. See the study of Gordon's *History* in Lester H. Cohen, *The Revolutionary Histories: Contemporary Narratives of the American Revolution* (Ithaca, N. Y., 1980). Apparently overlooked by Cohen is the rare and important volume by [Bernard] Hubley, *History of the American Revolution* (Northumberland, Pa., 1805). Projected as a two-volume work, only the first volume, of 606 pages, appeared, covering the years 1773 to 1775 (Evans 137105; Huntington 7593).

multiple layers productive of good works, inculcating divine truth and attentiveness to providential direction according to the "law of liberty" of the sovereign God revealed in the lowly Nazarene.[7] The picture that thus emerges is not merely parochially Puritan or Calvinistic but Augustinian and biblical.

The varieties of spiritual belief fundamental to the writers represented herein cannot be explored here, but some background can be indicated. For though our concern is with *political* sermons—and thus exceptional expressions of the faith of a people who looked to the eternal beyond for the perfect fulfillment of their pilgrimage through time in partnership with God—the *spiritual root* of that collaborative enterprise directed by Providence requires a word or two of clarification. Of course, the political background is the direct movement of disparate British colonial societies toward independent nationhood, federally organized under a Constitution that preserves the essentials of English liberty under law. It was a passage of history that involved the concerted effort of military force evinced in the Revolution and the articulation of the principles of free government; these principles inspired creation of a national community and became the grounds of a political orthodoxy called republican and constitutional government. Momentous developments crescendoed with British adoption of the Stamp Act of 1765, leading in little more than a decade to the decision for independence in 1776, which demanded eight years of fighting and formally ended with the signing of the peace treaty in Paris in 1783. The Federal Convention in 1787 provided a barely accepted Constitution, one immediately embellished by a Bill of Rights, that became the supreme law of the land in 1791. By the beginning of Jefferson's second term, the institutional arrangements had been tested and operations refined, the first party system had emerged, and the country had doubled in size thanks to the Louisiana Purchase. But another strand of history accompanies, interacts with, and gives roots to this familiar progress, one that is less known and lacks the direct line of development just rehearsed.

[7] The "law of liberty" or "perfect law of freedom (*nomon teleion eleutherias*)" of James 1:25 (cf. James 2:12 and I Peter 2:16) echoes the Johannine Christ: "Ye shall know the truth, and the truth shall make [set] you free (*eleutheroosei*)" as given in John 8:32 and reiterated in subsequent verses (8:33, 36), culminating in the great declaration: "If the Son therefore shall make you free, ye shall be free indeed."

The revolution in the spiritual life of America began within a decade of the preaching of the first sermon reprinted here, that of the celebrated Benjamin Colman in Boston in 1730. It is called the Great Awakening. There is reason to suppose that the two lines of development are intimately, even decisively, connected. Narrowly construed as occurring in the years 1739 to 1742, the Great Awakening designates the outburst of religious revival that swept the colonies in those years.[8] It reached from Georgia to New England and affected every stratum of society. Since the earthquake of 1727 that Benjamin Colman alludes to in his sermon, however, there had been a quickening of religious impulses. The Awakening was a spiritual earthquake, one that, as Alan Heimert and Perry Miller write, "clearly began a new era, not merely of American Protestantism, but in the evolution of the American mind."[9] A turning point and crisis in American society, it rumbled and echoed through the next decades.

American events could be seen as part of the general rise of religious sentiment traceable in Europe between 1730 and 1760, particularly in England, where the catalysts were the itinerant Anglican priests John and Charles Wesley, the founders of Methodism, and their compatriot George Whitefield. These men played a large part in rescuing England from the social debauchery and political corruption associated with the Gin Age, aspects of the period portrayed in Hogarth's prints and Fielding's novels.[10] Near the end of this volume's time period the so-called Second Awakening began, starting in 1800–1801 with revival camp meetings on the frontier and in the backcountry. The great political events of the American founding, thus, have a backdrop of resurgent religion whose calls for repentance and faith plainly complement the calls to resist tyranny and constitutional cor-

[8] Alan Heimert and Perry Miller, eds., *The Great Awakening: Documents Illustrating the Crisis and Its Consequences* (Indianapolis, Ind., 1967), xiii.

[9] Ibid., xiv; cf. Perry Miller, "The Great Awakening from 1740 to 1750," *Encounter* (The Divinity School, Duke University, Durham, N. C., March 1956), 5–9; also Herbert L. Osgood, *American Colonies in the Eighteenth Century*, 4 vols. (1924; rpr. Gloucester, Mass., 1958), III, 407–490; and Carl Bridenbaugh, *Cities in Revolt: Urban Life in America, 1743–1776* (New York, 1955), 64, 150–56, 404.

[10] See the biographical notes and sermons numbered 4, 13, 14, and 18 herein. On the Gin Age, see W.E.H. Lecky, *A History of England in the Eighteenth Century*, 7 vols. (London, 1892), II, chap. 5; also M. Dorothy George, *London Life in the Eighteenth Century* (1925; rpr. New York, 1964), 27–37 and *passim*; more entertainingly, see the first modern novels, Henry Fielding's *Tom Jones* (1749) and, especially, *Amelia* (1751).

ruption so as to live virtuously as God-fearing Christians, and, eventually, as responsible republican citizens.[11]

The preeminent awakener in America throughout much of this whole period was the English evangelist George Whitefield (see no. 4, herein), who first visited the colonies in 1738 and made six more preaching tours of the country, and who died in 1770 one September morning just before he was to preach in Newburyport, Massachusetts. Regarded as not only the most controversial preacher of his time but as "perhaps the greatest extemporaneous orator in the history of the English church," it is Whitefield's view of the human plight and its remedy that will best show the thrust of the Awakening as formative of the American mind. James Downey has written:

> The theme of his preaching is that of evangelicals in every age: in his natural state man is estranged from God; Jesus Christ, by his death and Atonement, has paid the price of that estrangement and made reconciliation with God possible; to achieve salvation man, with the guidance and the grace of the Holy Ghost, must repudiate sin and openly identify himself with Christ. To Whitefield religion, when properly understood, meant "a thorough, real, inward change of nature, wrought in us by the powerful operations of the Holy Ghost, conveyed to and nourished in our hearts, by a constant use of all the means of grace, evidenced by a good life, and bringing forth the fruits of the spirit." There was, of course, nothing new in this belief. Its special appeal for eighteenth-century audiences lay partly in the fact that it answered an emotional need the established Church had for too long tried to ignore, and partly in the charismatic personality of the man who revived it.[12]

It is perhaps worth stressing in a secularized age that the mystic's ascent and the evangelist's call, although conducted in different forums, have much in common. For each seeks to find the responsive

[11] A fine, concise account of the relationship of the Great Awakening to political developments is given by William G. McLoughlin in "'Enthusiasm for Liberty': The Great Awakening as the Key to the Revolution," in Jack P. Greene and William G. McLoughlin, *Preachers & Politicians: Two Essays on the Origins of the American Revolution* (Worcester, Mass., 1977), 47–73; *see also*, Donald Weber, *Rhetoric and History in Revolutionary New England* (New York, 1988).

[12] James Downey, *The Eighteenth-Century Pulpit: A Study of the Sermons of Butler, Berkeley, Secker, Sterne, Whitefield and Wesley* (Oxford, 1969), 155, 157, internal quote cited from J. Gillies, ed., *Works on Whitefield*, 6 vols. (London, 1771–1772), V, 161.

place in a person's consciousness where a vivid communion with God occurs, with the consequence that this concourse becomes the transformative core for that person, who therewith sees himself as a "new man": initially in the *conversion* experience (represented as a spiritual rebirth) and subsequently in the continuing meditative nurture of the soul, pursued by every means but chiefly, in American Protestantism, through prayer, sermons, and scriptural meditation. The great cry of the awakeners was for a converted ministry, one able to revive religious communities lacking vitality and zeal, so as to make the presence of God with his people a palpable reality. Such hortatory preaching and intent were the hallmarks of the so-called New Light, or New Side, clergy, as contrasted with their opposites (Old Light, Old Side ministers), who eschewed emotion and experimental religion. Many of the former, like Whitefield himself, had no church of their own but traveled the country preaching in homes and pastures or wherever they could four and five times in a day that often began before dawn. They were not always treated as welcome visitors by the established clergy, with whom serious conflict sometimes arose.

It is against the experiential background of such preaching that the political teaching of the ministers of the eighteenth century is to be seen as it was powerfully displayed in crisis and revolution. From their biblical perspective, it can be said that man is a moral agent living freely in a reality that is good, coming from the hand of God: "And God saw everything that he had made, and behold, it was very good."[13] With the responsibility to live well, in accordance with God's commandments and through exercise of his mind and free will, man longs for knowledge of God's word and truth and seeks God's help to keep an open heart so as to receive them. Among the chief hindrances to this life of true liberty is the oppression of men, who in service to evil deceive with untruth and impose falsehood in its place, proclaiming it to be true. Man, blessed with liberty, reason, and a

[13] Genesis 1:31. This, and Psalm 119:134 ("Deliver me from the oppression of man: So will I keep thy precepts."), were the texts for the Plymouth Anniversary Sermon by Gad Hitchcock of Pembroke, which was preached at Plymouth, Massachusetts, on December 22, 1774; it is the principal source of the summary given in this and the following paragraph; reprinted in Verna M. Hall, ed., *The Christian History of the American Revolution* (San Francisco, 1976), 30–43.

moral sense, created in the image of God, a little lower than the angels, and given dominion over the earth (Psalm 8; Hebrews 2:6–12), is the chief and most perfect of God's works.

Liberty is, thus, an essential principle of man's constitution, a natural trait which yet reflects the supernatural Creator. Liberty is God-given. The growth of virtue and perfection of being depends upon free choice, in response to divine invitation and help, in a cooperative relationship. The correlate of responsibility, liberty is most truly exercised by living in accordance with *truth.* Man's dominion over the earth and the other creatures, his mastery of nature through reason, is subject to no restraint but the law of his nature, which is perfect liberty; the obligation to obey the laws of the Creator only checks his licentiousness and abuse.

Our preachers, however, understood that this gift of freedom to do right and live truly carries another possibility, rebellion and rejection, as well. This, in turn, leads to the necessity of government to coerce a degree of right living and justice from a mankind fallen from the high road of willing obedience to the loving Father. Unfortunately, coercive law can be inflicted in ways that are not merely just and conducive to truth, righteousness, and union with God, but not infrequently to their very opposites. This biblical understanding of the human condition is reflected in the most famous passage of *The Federalist* (no. 51), which turns on the sentiments that if men were angels there would be no need for government, for what is government but the greatest of all reflections on human nature? It remains true, James Madison continued, that "Justice is the end of government. It is the end of civil society. It ever has been, and ever will be pursued, until it be obtained, or until liberty be lost in the pursuit."

A few words may now be said about the sermon as a rhetorical and symbolic form, particularly the political sermon. It was the axiom of one of the leading figures of the New Light movement and the educator of preachers, Nathanael Emmons, "Have something to say; say it." The suggestion of terseness is misleading, however, since eighteenth-century preachers had a great deal to say. The Sunday service might typically open with a prayer that lasted an hour as measured by a glass on the pulpit; it would then be turned twice during the course of the sermon. A short break for lunch would be taken, and then the preaching would continue in the afternoon. The form of Puritan sermons followed a model taught by William Perkins's *Arte of Prophysying* (1592, translated in 1607). The principle basic to his approach was, following Augustine and Calvin, that the Bible is reflexive in the sense of providing its own explanation of its meaning in a consistent whole. This literal meaning is to be found through use of the three methods of circumstance, collation,and application. Thus, it is the task of the preacher as interpreter to place any scriptural text into its circumstances and context, collating that text with similar texts elsewhere in the scriptures, to find consistent meaning, and then to finish by conforming his preaching to the "analogie of faith." This means that any statement made had to be in harmony with or contained in the Apostles' Creed.[14]

The key to finding the unity of the Bible, according to William Perkins, was to begin by first mastering Paul's Letter to the Romans; then, and only then, ought the student move to the remainder of the New Testament and subsequently to the Old Testament. The result of this, because of the emphases in Romans, will be a stress on justification, sanctification, and true faith.

The steps in writing and delivering the sermon begin with the reading of the divine text, considered as the holy Word of God and superior to or outside of the remainder of the presentation. The text is to be read aloud to the congregation by way of "opening" the Word, for (in the Calvinist conception, at least) it is the Word and the Word alone that is the proper province of preaching. The duty of the preacher, then, is merely to "open" the one clear and natural sense of scripture, so that the Holy Spirit can move through the preacher's words into the hearers' souls to effect spiritual transformation. Thus, in Perkins's formal outline, the preacher ought:

1. To read the Text distinctly out of the canonicall Scripture.
2. To give the sense and understanding of it being read by the Scripture itself.
3. To collect a few and profitable points of doctrine out of the naturall sense.
4. To applie (if he have the gift) the doctrines rightly collected to the manners of men in a simple and plain speech.

[14] My discussion at this point relies on Teresa Toulouse, *The Art of Prophesying: New England Sermons and the Shaping of Belief* (Macon, Ga., 1987), chap. 1.

This form is understood to embody the circumstances, collations, and analogies of faith previously mentioned.[15] The format of Text, Doctrine, and Application remained typical of sermons, especially on such formal occasions as the political sermons reproduced here, and in the hands of the most accomplished preachers (such as Jonathan Edwards the Elder) the old form could be effective for "sustaining rigorous analysis and dramatizing the essential relationships among the Word, human intelligence, and conduct."[16] It is no surprise that a mastery of classical rhetoric is displayed in the sermons of the eighteenth century, since this was the "golden age of the classics" in America.[17]

Of the several vehicles for expounding political theology available to American ministers, the most venerable were the election sermons preached for 256 years in Massachusetts and 156 years in Connecticut. The practice began in Vermont in 1778 and in New Hampshire in 1784 in the sermon by Samuel McClintock (no. 26, herein). These were sermons preached annually to the governor and legislature after the election of officers. To be chosen for the task was an honor, and the sermons were published and distributed to each official with an extra copy or two for the ministers of the official's home district. It is at least arguable that a published sermon is a mark of its excellence to begin with, whatever the occasion of its utterance. (In the screening of several thousand items, the intention has been that only leading clergymen putting their best foot forward on important political matters are here represented.) One index of quality is suggested by the fact that very few of the sermons preached ever were published; thus Samuel Dunbar, an Old Light minister from Stoughton, Massachu-

[15] Toulouse, *The Art of Prophesying*, 15–21, quoting William Perkins.

[16] Wilson H. Kimnach, "Jonathan Edwards's Pursuit of Reality," in Nathan O. Hatch and Harry S. Stout, eds., *Jonathan Edwards and the American Experience* (New York, 1988), 115.

[17] An idea of this can be gained from Josephine K. Piercy, *Studies in Literary Types in Seventeenth Century America (1607–1710)*, 2d ed. (Hamden, Conn., 1969), 155–67; a more elaborate treatment is George W. Hervey, *A System of Christian Rhetoric, For the use of Preachers and Other Speakers* (New York, 1873); an "index" (or glossary) of rhetorical figures from *accismus* and *addubitatio* to *votum* and *zeugma*, is given on pp. 577–628; on the classics in America, see Richard M. Gummere, *American Colonial Mind and the Classical Tradition* (Cambridge, Mass., 1963) and the books of Meyer Reinhold, who characterizes the Revolutionary period as the Golden Age of the classics, in *Classica Americana: The Greek and Roman Heritage of the United States*, (Detroit, 1984), 95.

setts, wrote out some eight thousand sermons during his long career but published only nine of them (see no. 7).

Besides the election sermon, the artillery sermon was also an annual affair in Massachusetts and dealt with civic and military matters. The Thursday or Fifth-day Lecture was begun by the Reverend John Cotton in Boston in 1633 and was practiced for 200 years; it was a popular event and was combined with Market Day for gathering and discussing matters of social and political interest. Election sermons were sometimes then repeated for a different audience. The Lecture was no Boston or Congregationalist monopoly, as can be seen from Abraham Keteltas's sermon preached during the evening Lecture in the First Presbyterian Church at Newburyport in 1777 (no. 19, herein). Convention sermons also were political in nature and grew out of election-day ceremonies.

There were many other opportunities for political discourse, such as the annual observation of January 30 as the execution day of the king-turned-tyrant, Charles I. Century sermons were preached to mark the Glorious Revolution's centenary, on November 5, 1788, the anniversary of William III's landing in England to secure it from popery and tyranny and to preserve traditional British liberties. The century sermon of Elhanan Winchester is included here (no. 33). Days of prayer, fasting, and thanksgiving were proclaimed for particular occasions throughout the eighteenth century and even earlier. Such times were nationally proclaimed ("recommended") at least *sixteen* times by the Continental Congress during the Revolutionary War; and the entire American community repaired to their various churches on such days of fasting, prayer, and humiliation to repent of sins, seek forgiveness, and implore God to lift the affliction of their suffering from them—the *jeremiad* form so central to American consciousness.[18] Days of thanksgiving were likewise proclaimed when divine favor was experienced. The end of the war brought a great outpouring of praise and gratitude, and four sermons, nos. 24 through 27, reflect these sentiments. Such proclamations became rarer under the Constitution but did not disappear during Washington's or Adams's administrations, and their suspension during Jefferson's

[18] For the text of some of these resolutions and analysis see Sandoz, *A Government of Laws*, chap. 5; for the jeremiad see Sacvan Bercovitch, *The American Jeremiad*, (Madison, Wis., 1978), 176–210 and *passim*.

administration was followed by a reinstatement under James Madison. The Fourth of July regularly occasioned political sermons as well as orations. The death of Washington evoked a universal grief and countless sermons extolling the character of the American Joseph; an example is that of Henry Holcombe, a Baptist, who preached in Savannah, Georgia (no. 49). The Boston Massacre sermons and orations commemorated the events of March 5, 1770, and the "Patriots' Day" observances, as they are now called, marked the battles of Lexington and Concord in New England each year on April 19. Not only was such preaching widely attended, repeated, and published as tracts, but it was often reprinted in the newspapers as well.

This rhetorical form expressed the philosophical mean that free government is based on liberty, and liberty is founded in truth and justice as framed by eternal laws. Republicanism and virtue were far from split apart by James Madison and his colleagues at the Federal Convention, as the clergy understood our constitutional system. For these preachers and their flocks, the two remained essentially bound together. The political culture of this country was not only all the things it is most frequently said to be (I think of Bernard Bailyn's five items), but was deeply rooted in the core religious consciousness articulated above all by the preachers; theirs were the pulpits of a new nation with a privileged, providential role in world history. What America's religious consciousness consisted of in the tumultuous and triumphant years of founding is what this book will disclose.

October 1990 Ellis Sandoz

Ellis Sandoz is a Professor of Political Science and the Director of the Eric Voegelin Institute for American Renaissance Studies, Louisiana State University, Baton Rouge.

Acknowledgments

Thanks are due, for permission to reprint materials in their collections, to the Doheny Library of the University of Southern California, Los Angeles, for one item (no. 17); to the Massachusetts Historical Society of Boston for one item (no. 19); to the American Antiquarian Society of Worcester, Massachusetts, for five items (nos. 3, 11, 12, 49, and 55); and to the Henry E. Huntington Library of San Marino, California, for the remaining forty-eight items in the book. Personal thanks go to Marcus A. McCorison, director, to John Hench, and to Keith Arbour at the American Antiquarian Society for their generous assistance. Because of two extended stays and a number of shorter visits at the Huntington Library, I owe many more debts of gratitude than I can repay here. But special thanks go to Robert Middlekauff (then director) and his wife Beverly for good counsel, assistance, and warm hospitality; also my gratitude is extended to Martin Ridge, who is director of research, and to Mary Wright, who supervises the Rare Book Reading Room. Among all the other helpful members of the Huntington staff, I especially thank Alan Jutzi, curator of rare books, and Tom Langen, who saw to the copying of over 4,000 pages of material from the rare book collection and who prepared the title-page photographs reproduced herein, except for those to nos. 3 and 11, which Marcus McCorison at the American Antiquarian Society provided. There can hardly be finer places to work than the Huntington Library and the American Antiquarian Society. Dean Charles R. Ritcheson, director of the Doheny Library, and his staff were helpful on more than one occasion with my work on this book. So also were the staffs of the New York Public Library, the Library of Congress, the Centenary College Library of Shreveport, Louisiana, and the Middleton Library and the Hill Memorial Library of Louisiana State University—and I am grateful.

I wish also to thank several institutions for financial support of my work on this book: Louisiana State University by a sabbatical leave; the Huntington Library by a Visiting Fellow's appointment; and, by research grants, the Earhart Foundation, the John M. Olin Foundation, the Armstrong Foundation, and the Wilbur Foundation.

Liberty Fund is thanked for having the courage to undertake this large publication project and to see it through to completion. Individuals too numerous to be named here deserve thanks for rendering help great and small, but I must mention Dr. Gregory T. Russell, my graduate assistant during much of the preparation period for the work and later my colleague, who was of great assistance with the details. A similar word of thanks also is due my current graduate assistant, Manuel Brieske. Not least of all I hail all the librarians, those unsung heroes of a book such as this one, and most especially the cataloguers and bibliographers, for their wonderful, anonymous labors: without them we researchers would be lost.

Lastly, my family is again thanked for continuing to tolerate my strange habits and for helping me look up this or that and to read proof as time allowed and as I could catch them: Jonathan, Erica, Lisa, and Ellis III. My wife Alverne showed hitherto unsuspected skill as bibliographer and chief assistant in organizing a mass of material. My appreciation of them rises far above mere gratitude.

I hope all these benefactors and collaborators, having helped me with this project, will cherish the book and find their expectations for it at least partly fulfilled.

E. S.

Editor's Note

The fundamental aim of this collection has been to print original, editorially unannotated editions of previously published, complete sermons that permit the authors to speak fully for themselves. The genre is the political sermon, but broadly construed so as to embrace certain essays and orations, pieces that are sermonic in sense and tone —that is, hortatory and relating politics to convictions about eternal verities. A second aim has been not to duplicate anything printed in John Wingate Thornton's fine old collection, *The Pulpit of the American Revolution* (Boston, 1860), since that volume is available in a reprint edition. With one exception, John Leland's *Rights of Conscience Inalienable* (no. 37), we also have avoided anything printed in Charles S. Hyneman and Donald S. Lutz, eds., *American Political Writing during the Founding Era, 1760–1805* (Indianapolis, 1983), still available from Liberty Press. Of other comparable collections known to us, that of Frank Moore, ed., *The Patriot Preachers of the American Revolution*, published by subscription in 1860, overlaps this collection with two items, nos. 8 and 25, but the Moore book is rare and has not been reprinted. We also avoided publishing anything contained in the first volume of Bernard Bailyn's *Pamphlets of the American Revolution* (Cambridge, Mass., 1965); we have included several pieces (nos. 8, 9, 10, 15, and 17) announced for later volumes, but the series has been suspended for over twenty-five years and appears to be defunct.

A third aim has been to provide readable and accessible texts for these sermons—accurate modern versions that scrupulously honor the integrity of the originals. Modernization has never been done for its own sake or permitted to alter meaning, and much has been done to maintain even the look of the originals. To effect our purpose, modernization rules, or guidelines, were developed over the course of several months in which the sermons were editorially analyzed—and with the assistance of the book's designer, as well. It became clear that some across-the-board standardization was needed to get the job done, but that inconsistencies between sermons were unavoidable and that homogenizing the texts was unthinkable. Applying our modernizing rules in an absolutely rigid manner, then, was impossible if we were to remain sensitive to the originals. Exceptions to the rules were made where the individual text passages cried out for them. The sermons herein remain trustworthy replicas of some unique and (at times) originally quirky texts from America's founding era.

ITALICIZATION

The original printings of the sermons, especially the earliest ones, presented us with some difficult decisions concerning the use of italics and, similarly, small capitals. To begin with, italics were used in certain texts for each proper name and for other words besides, but to say that they were used much of the time for emphasis would be incorrect. Rather, they seem to have been used for anything that might be construed as a key word *as well as* for emphasis, with the result that a large number of words appeared in italics. That this italicization could be related to oral delivery was not translatable into an editorial guideline. It was decided, then, that we would serve the reader best by not duplicating what strikes the modern eye as chaotic typography. Nevertheless, preserving the appearance of eighteenth-century typesetting also seemed desirable.

Much of the original typography was sacrificed to modern tastes, therefore, with some important exceptions. Phrases of three or four and more words in italics were kept that way, while single words and nearly all two- and three-word phrases in italic were set in roman type. With the understanding that some measure of the author's emphasis could be thus lost, we made exceptions to the rule on a case-by-case basis. It proved surprising, though, how infrequently italics had to be retained as exceptions. The rhetorical training of all the sermon authors led them to syntactical constructions that made their points of emphasis emerge (commonly by a use of parallelism) unmistakably and gracefully. Of course, they were organizing their points for the ear as much as for the eye, so their repetitions, enumerations, and references to a controlling scriptural thought, as well as other structural devices, all served to make the typographic augmentation of meaning that had once been favored much less necessary than might now be supposed.

Occasionally an italicized phrase would have in it a word or two in roman. We elected to simplify this state of affairs and italicized these words. Otherwise, no italics were introduced into the texts for any reason.

Words and phrases that were printed in small and/or large capital letters were viewed as italicized and then treated accordingly, except in the case of God, Jesus, and Christ. Here it was decided that the flavor of the early printings could be preserved. These words, where they had been entirely in capitals in the original, were uniformly presented in the large-capital/small-capital style shown here. Nowhere did we introduce this style, however, where the words had not been entirely in capitals in the original. Thus we give "GOD" as "God"; but we reproduce "God" without change, and so on.

CAPITALIZATION

Just as italicization can seem to have been too popular with early writers and printers, capitalization appears in many of the sermons to have followed only individual writers' standards. In all the texts, we have modernized capitalization as follows: If a capitalized word would be lower-cased in modern usage, we lower-cased it, but we did not capitalize any word that appeared lower-cased in the original. Thus, the reader will notice an abundant number of instances where frequently capitalized words appear lower-cased (contrary to modern usage) later on—*christian*, *king* George, *parliament*, for example—because in the later instances they had not been *originally* capitalized. We did retain the capitalizations of coinages for the Deity—"Great Benefactor," "Supreme Ruler," even "Divine Word," etc.—including the adjective if it had been originally capitalized.

SPELLING

For some sermons, errata were printed, and we made the corrections so noted without a signal to the reader. Spelling was not modernized for this edition, and spelling errors were not always corrected. The reappearance of a word in a text cued us to correct some typographical errors silently, but the hunting down of such reappearances was not engaged in. The reader will therefore detect spellings that could be construed as distorted by the original typesetter but that were not tampered with by us. Some corrections, we felt, required us to place a word or letters in brackets to signal the reader, but even these might have been silently fixed by different editors. For the most part the original spellings are preserved unless the meaning was imperiled. In no. 3, we changed *least* to *lest* because the sense dictated it. In no. 15, *precicious* was corrected to *precious*, for the error could interrupt communication. But in the same sermon, *tremenduous* was allowed to stand; in no. 17, *terrestial*; in no. 27, *impulsies*; and so forth. Who is to say that these words were not pronounced from the pulpit as they were spelled by their authors or, at least, were published? Of interest to some readers will be the spelling errors in no. 44, by the estimable Noah Webster.

As this edition makes obvious, we did modernize the long esses of eighteenth-century typography. We retained ampersands (&) and refrained from inserting missing apostrophes.

PUNCTUATION

The originals presented some interesting puzzles of punctuation. Because of the flaws in early type components and the bleed-through of inks on certain printing papers, spots and blobs occurred with frequency to seemingly alter punctuation marks, changing commas to semicolons and periods to commas, or adding commas and hyphens, and so on, wherever well-placed blobs might appear. Broken type could change a comma to a period or cause a hyphen to disappear. Many times, sentence construction pointed to the solution; other times, eighteenth-century punctuation habits made, let us say, a comma likely where an existing mark was illegible. Except in the case of some totally unintelligible words, our most difficult "calls" involved colons that looked like semicolons, for the colon then seemed to serve any number of purposes not clearly distinguishable from the semicolon's. We simply made the best determination we could from a close examination of the printed symbol when we were in doubt.

Eighteenth-century writings tend to be rife with commas, by today's standards; even so, some commas were certainly misplaced to begin with and were silently removed. In a very few instances, commas interfered with the sense and were deleted. Dashes were often used in combination with other marks,—commas, semicolons, even periods (as this sentence demonstrates). We deleted whichever mark that sense and/or syntax showed to be the extraneous one, by today's standards.

In most of the sermons an old convention of punctuation was followed that placed a punctuation mark before a parenthesis, (as this sentence demonstrates;) we modernized the punctuation in these cases. The British custom of placing a period or comma after a closing quotation mark was similarly Americanized; it now precedes the closing quotation mark.

A number of longer quotations were printed as indented extract, where originally they had been "run in" as text and set off with quotation marks. As modern convention dictates, we deleted the quotation marks from these extracted passages. There was no attempt made to standardize the uses of quotation marks in the sermons. Each author had his own approach to this and other matters of style, and many inconsistencies will be evident to the reader from sermon to sermon and within individual sermons. Sometimes quotation marks set off hypothetical responses to the author's main argument, for example, but frequently propositions of that type are merely signified by an initial capital letter in mid-sentence. These devices have not been tampered with, for in their own way they signal the reader clearly enough as to the author's meaning and intent.

The reader may also note that some authors interpolate their own words into quotations without closing and reopening quotation marks. Since it was obvious enough that this was the case, we refrained from adding the marks. Wherever quotation marks or other punctuation marks did need insertion by us, we bracketed them.

BIBLICAL QUOTES AND CITATIONS

Naturally, the sermons are replete with references to scripture. On occasion, editorial considerations led us to check on the wording of a quotation (and some few mistakes thereby detected were silently corrected, particularly in citations of chapter or verse numbers). However, no systematic checking of biblical material was done, and for all practical purposes the quotations and citations can be considered to be reproduced as they originally appeared, correct or incorrect.

OTHER MATTERS

All footnotes are the work of the sermon authors and have been edited along the same guidelines as for the sermon proper. Footnote symbols were changed as necessary to key the notes to the sermon as the material received a new paging arrangement in this edition.

Many other elements in the originals, ornamental, typographic, or idiosyncratic, have been dispensed with. Most often this involved modernizing odd arrangements of text and/or blank space.

The original pamphlets in which the sermons appeared also included announcements, legislative resolutions concerning publication, dedications, prefaces, opening prayers, and appendices that have been deleted from this volume, except where they could not be considered extraneous to the sermon's message and significance.

Not all the sermons were assigned titles by their authors, as a look at the title-page facsimiles included with each sermon will reveal. In such cases, we extracted from the pamphlet copy what we deemed appropriate as a stand-in title.

The facsimiles, while they add a visual element to this collection, also serve as testaments to the erudition and civility of the age that produced these works. They shed light on the sermons in the information and in the epigraphs they provide, the latter being an embellishing convention from the days of the Renaissance.

The facsimiles often provide two dates: the date of the sermon's delivery and that of its publication, and in many cases, these dates are not far apart. But some of the items, as previously stated, were never orally delivered though they are sermonic in tradition. The publication date was the most consistent key to the placement of the works in a time frame, therefore. We opted, then, to order the sermons according to the date of their dissemination in print. The reader may note that this results in our placing no. 20 at 1778, though apparently it was preached in 1775; moreover, no. 43 was preached in 1789, but we reprint the second edition from 1794, in which the author, David Osgood, updated his text, and which prompted a number of responses then and in 1795. Finally, no. 37 is placed with a conjectural publication date at 1791, when it was preached. Yet it may not have appeared in print until eleven years later, as indicated on the facsimile page included with it.

Bibliographic Note

No systematic bibliographic essay can be undertaken here, but some brief comments on the sources may be helpful to the reader.

A bibliography of generally relevant writings is included in Ellis Sandoz, *A Government of Laws: Political Theory, Religion and the American Founding* (Baton Rouge, La., 1990), a study that is in many respects a companion to the present volume. Extensive bibliographic information on the religious writings of the period and on pertinent secondary works can be gleaned from the notes to Harry S. Stout, *The New England Soul: Preaching and Religious Culture in Colonial New England* (New York, 1986); and to Donald Weber, *Rhetoric and History in Revolutionary New England* (New York, 1988), a work attentive to the politics–religion issues.

The Great Awakening in America, its significance and aftermath, is best presented by Alan Heimert, *Religion and the American Mind from the Great Awakening to the Revolution* (Cambridge, Mass., 1966); and by Heimert and Perry Miller, eds., *The Great Awakening: Documents Illustrating the Crisis and Its Consequences* (Indianapolis, 1967); valuable also is William G. McLoughlin, *Isaac Backus and the American Pietistic Tradition* (Boston, 1967) and the same author's "The Great Awakening as the Key to the Revolution," in Jack P. Greene and William G. McLoughlin, *Preachers & Politicians: Two Essays on the Origins of the American Revolution* (Worcester, Mass., 1977). Important also is Weber, *Rhetoric and History*, Chap. 1 and *passim*. Still fundamental is Herbert Osgood, *The American Colonies in the Eighteenth Century*, 4 vols. (New York, 1924) (see the third volume, especially at pp. 407–90); and Carl Bridenbaugh, *Mitre and Sceptre: Transatlantic Faiths, Ideas, Personalities, and Politics, 1689–1775* (New York, 1962); and the same author's *The Spirit of '76* (New York, 1976). Also, from the abundant literature on Jonathan Edwards, Sr., who was pivotal in the Awakening, may be mentioned Alan Heimert's book cited above, and Norman Fiering, *Jonathan Edwards's Moral Thought and Its British Context* (Chapel Hill, N. C., 1981); also Nathan O. Hatch and

Harry S. Stout, eds., *Jonathan Edwards and the American Experience* (New York, 1988).

The key bibliographic works for early American history utilized in making this collection include the following standard works: Joseph Sabin, Wilberforce Eames, and R.W.G. Vail, *Bibliotheca Americana. A Dictionary of Books relating to America from its Discovery to the Present Time*, 29 vols. (New York, 1868–1936); Charles Evans and Clifford K. Shipton, *American Bibliography. A Chronological Dictionary of All Books, Pamphlets and Periodical Publications Printed in the United States of America from the Genesis of Printing in 1639 down to and including the year 1820. With bibliographical and biographical notes*, 14 vols. (Chicago, New York, and Worcester, Mass., 1903–1959); Richard P. Bristol, *Supplement to Charles Evans' American Bibliography*, 2 vols. (Charlottesville, Va., 1970). The some 50,000 items listed in the Evans and Shipton and Bristol works are revised and corrected in Clifford K. Shipton and James E. Mooney, *National Index of American Imprints through 1800; the Short-title Evans*, 2 vols. (Worcester, Mass., 1969). In turn, this work serves as the index for the vast Readex microprint edition: Clifford K. Shipton, ed., *Early American Imprints, 1639–1800* (Worcester, Mass. and New York, 1955–1983), which provides copies of all extant American publications (except newspapers and broadsides) of between 1639 and 1800.

The principal sources for the biographical notes preceding each sermon are reference books which are not cited unless directly quoted. Since most of the authors included in the volume were clergymen of New England or the Middle Atlantic region and—with the notable exception of many Awakening evangelists such as the Baptists Isaac Backus and John Leland—graduates of one of the early colleges, the following reference works were relied upon especially: Frederick Lewis Weis, *New England Clergy and the Colonial Churches of New England* (Lancaster, Mass., 1936); the same author's *Colonial Churches and the Colonial Clergy of the Middle and Southern Colonies, 1607–1776* (Lancaster, Mass., 1938); John L. Sibley and Clifford K. Shipton, *Sibley's Harvard Graduates*, 17 vols. (Boston, 1873–1975); Franklin B. Dexter, *Biographical Sketches of the Graduates of Yale College*, 6 vols. (New York, 1885–1912); William B. Sprague, *Annals of the American Pulpit*, 9 vols. (New York, 1857–1869); James McLachlan and Richard A. Harrison,

Princetonians: A Biographical Dictionary, 3 vols. to date (Princeton, N.J., 1976–1981).

Of considerable help also were James A. Levernier and Douglas R. Wilmes, eds., *American Writers Before 1800*, 3 vols. (Westport, Ct., 1983); A.W. Plumstead, ed., *The Wall and the Garden: Selected Massachusetts Election Sermons, 1670–1775* (Minneapolis, 1968); Thomas R. Adams, *American Independence: The Growth of an Idea*, 2d ed. (Austin and New Haven, 1980); the same author's *The American Controversy*, 2 vols. (Providence and New York, 1980); *Encyclopedia Britannica*, 24 vols. (Chicago, 1969); Allen Johnson, Dumas Malone, et al., eds., *Dictionary of American Biography*, 22 vols. (New York, 1928–1958); Leslie Stephen and Sidney Lee, eds., *Dictionary of National Biography*, 22 vols. (Oxford, 1917–1950); and Frederick Barton, ed., *Pulpit Power and Eloquence: Or, 100 Best Sermons of the Nineteenth Century*, 3 vols. (Cleveland, 1901).

Of value for understanding the New England election sermons is the introductory and other editorial material in Thornton, *The Pulpit of the American Revolution*; also, editorial material in Plumstead, *The Wall and the Garden*. In Chapter 2 of Perry Miller, *The New England Mind: From Colony to Province* (1953; rpr. Boston, 1961), and throughout, the election sermons as *jeremiads* are the focus of the study. Miller is critiqued and his argument much expanded in Sacvan Bercovitch, *The American Jeremiad* (Madison, Wis., 1978). These sermons, and their evolution over time as a distinctive rhetorical form, are analyzed in Teresa Toulouse, *The Art of Prophesying: New England Sermons and the Shaping of Belief* (Athens, Ga., 1987). The anthology of telling extracts from the election sermons previously published by Liberty Press is indicative of this mass of material: Franklin P. Cole, ed., *They Preached Liberty* (Indianapolis, 1976). For specific identifications see R.W.G. Vail, "A Check List of New England Election Sermons," *Proceedings of the American Antiquarian Society* (Oct. 1935; rpr. Worcester, Mass, 1936), 3–36; Lindsay Swift, "The Massachusetts Election Sermons," *Publications of the Colonial Society of Massachusetts*, vol. 1: *Transactions, 1892–1894*, 388–451; Harry H. Edes, "Appendix: List of Preachers of Election Sermons," in Charles E. Grinnell, *Fanaticism: A Sermon Delivered Before the Executive and Legislative Departments of the Government of Massachusetts at the Annual Election, Wednesday, January 4, 1871* (Boston, 1871), 33–61.

In the following, keyed by number to various sermons, are sources that are supplemental to the information given in the biographical notes:

No. 1. Benjamin Colman is the subject of analysis in Toulouse, *The Art of Prophesying*, Chap. 2.

No. 3. Besides *Essential Rights and Liberties of Protestants*, only two published sermons by Elisha Williams have survived: *Death the Advantage of the Godly* and *Divine Grace Illustrious*, both dated 1728.

No. 4. The writings of George Whitefield were gathered in an incomplete edition by John Gillies in *The Works of the Reverend George Whitefield*, 6 vols. (London, 1770–72).

No. 8. Jonathan Mayhew's famous early sermon, *Discourse Concerning Unlimited Submission and Non-Resistance to the Higher Powers* (1750) is reprinted with a valuable introduction and notes in Bailyn, ed., *Pamphlets of the American Revolution* and in Thornton, ed., *Pulpit of the American Revolution;* seven sermons by Mayhew are available in a reprinted collection, Mayhew, *Sermons* (New York, 1969).

No. 9. A number of John Zubly's writings are reprinted in Randall Miller, ed., "*A Warm and Zealous Spirit* . . ." (Macon, Ga., 1982); see also the valuable biography by M. Jimmie Killingworth in *American Writers Before 1800*, 1666–69.

No. 10. A facsimile reprint of John Allen's *An Oration Upon the Beauties of Liberty*, along with an introduction by Reta A. Gilbert, can be found in G.J. Gravlee and J.E. Irvine, eds., *Pamphlets and the American Revolution: Rhetoric, Politics, Literature, and the Popular Press; Commemorative Edition, 1776–1976* (Delmar, N.Y., 1976). For the sermon's publication history, see Thomas R. Adams, *American Independence: The Growth of an Idea* (New Haven, Ct., 1980), 68–70.

No. 11. Isaac Backus's *An Appeal to the Public for Religious Liberty* is hailed as the most important of his thirty-seven published tracts and as "central to the whole movement for separation of Church and State in America" by William G. McLoughlin in *Isaac Backus*, 123; it is reprinted with valuable editorial matter in the same author's *Isaac Backus on Church, State, and Calvinism: Pamphlets, 1754–1789* (Cambridge, Mass., 1968).

No. 13. John Wesley's *A Calm Address*, its impact and the surrounding controversy, are analyzed in two articles by Frank Baker and by Donald H. Kirkham in *Methodist History*, 14 (Oct. 1975), 3–23.

No. 16. On Samuel Sherwood's *The Church's Flight into the Wilderness*, the reader is referred to Melvin B. Endy, Jr., "Just War, Holy War, and Millennialism in Revolutionary America," *William and Mary Quarterly*, 42 (Jan. 1985), 3–25 at 16; a thorough analysis of the sermon is given in Stephen J. Stein, "An Apocalyptic Rationale for the American Revolution," *Early American Literature*, 9 (1975), 211–25. Regarding the Appendix to this sermon, see Evans, *American Bibliography*, No. 13614.

No. 17. John Witherspoon's *The Dominion of Providence over the Passions of Men* is reprinted from the third volume of *The Works of the Reverend John Witherspoon*, 2d ed., 4 vols. (Philadelphia, 1802). See also the annotated edition of Witherspoon's important *Lectures on Moral Philosophy*, ed. Jack Scott (Newark, N. J., 1982); also Garry Wills, *Explaining America* (New York, 1981); B. J. Lossing, *Biographical Sketches of the Signers of the Declaration of Independence* (New York, 1848); and David C. Whitney and David S. Lovejoy, *Founders of Freedom in America* (Chicago, 1964).

No. 18. John Fletcher's *A Vindication of the Rev. Mr. Wesley's "Calm Address"* . . . (1776) may be found in *Works*, 7 vols. (London, 1774–87), reprinted in a London edition in 1815 and a New York edition in 1849.

No. 21. A chapter is devoted to Samuel Cooper in Weber, *Rhetoric and History*, 113–32; and there is a biography: Charles W. Akers, *The Divine Politician: Samuel Cooper and the American Revolution in Boston* (Boston, 1982). Some 146 sermons by Cooper are extant, the bulk of them in the Cooper Papers at the Huntington Library.

No. 30. A great many of Nathanael Emmons's sermons were collected with his theological writings and published in Jacob Ide, ed., *Works of Nathanael Emmons, D.D.*, 6 vols. (n.p., 1842–50; 2d ed., 1861–63). Ide was Emmons's son-in-law and both editions include memoirs by him and E. A. Park.

No. 32. Samuel Langdon's election sermon of 1775, entitled *Government Corrupted by Vice, and Recovered by Righteousness*, is reprinted with an introduction and editorial annotation in Plumstead, ed., *The Wall and the Garden*, 347–73.

No. 34. On the American pamphlets of Richard Price, see the annotated volume by Bernard Peach, ed., *Richard Price and the Ethical Foundations of the American Revolution* (Durham, N.C., 1979). On the debate with Edmund Burke triggered by the sermon here reprinted, see Robert B. Dishman, ed., *Burke and Paine on Revolution and the Rights of Man* (New York, 1971).

No. 36. On Israel Evans, see John Calvin Thorne, *A Monograph on the Reverend Israel Evans* (1902; rpr. New York, 1907).

No. 37. John Leland was the supposed author of *The Yankee Spy* (1794), which is reprinted in Hyneman and Lutz, eds., *American Political Writing*, II: 971–89. A collection of his works, including the present piece, is L.F. Greene, ed., *Writings of Elder John Leland* (1845; rpr. New York, 1969). Important correspondence passed between the Baptist leader and James Madison, bearing on the genesis of both the Virginia Statute of Religious Freedom and the First Amendment liberties in the Bill of Rights; see William T. Hutchinson, Robert A. Rutland, et al., eds., *The Papers of James Madison*, 17 vols. to date (Chicago and Charlottesville, Va., 1962–), VIII: 295–96; X: 516, 540–42; XI: 185, 304, 386, 408, 414, 415, 424, 442–43.

No. 42. Jonathan Edwards, Jr., is the subject of a chapter in Weber, *Rhetoric and History*.

No. 44. An excellent bibliography for Noah Webster is provided at the end of the article on him by William Vartorella in *American Writers Before 1800*. *The Webster Bible* is available in a recent reprint of the New Haven, 1833 edition (Grand Rapids, Mich., 1987).

No. 47. John Thayer's autobiographical *An Account of the Conversion of the Reverend John Thayer, lately a Protestant minister, who embraced the Roman Catholic Religion at Rome, on the 25th of May, 1783* (6th ed.: Wilmington, N.C., 1789) is of considerable interest and aroused widespread comment.

No. 52. Tunis Wortman's publications also include *An Oration on the Influence of Social Institutions Upon Human Morals and Happiness, Delivered Before the Tammany Society* (1796) and *An Address to the Republican Citizens of New York on the Inauguration of Thomas Jefferson* (1801). A good sketch of his life is given by Nelson S. Dearmont in *American Writers Before 1800*.

POLITICAL SERMONS OF THE AMERICAN FOUNDING ERA

1730–1805

Chronology

1688–1773

1688 In the Glorious Revolution, James II (House of Stuart) abdicates the throne under great pressure because of his policies and Roman Catholic faith.

1689 The Declaration of Rights (Feb. 13), Toleration Act (May 24), and English Bill of Rights (Dec. 16) are adopted.

1690 John Locke's *An Essay Concerning Human Understanding* is published, as well as his *Two Treatises of Government.*

1692 In the period of the Salem witch trials, 20 people (14 women) are executed.

1693 The College of William and Mary is started in Williamsburg, Virginia, by the Anglicans; the second oldest institution of higher education in America, it is one of nine religion-based colonial colleges.

1697 Official repentance following the Salem witch trials; an offer of compensatory indemnities to aggrieved families for unjust punishment is made by the Massachusetts General Court.

1698 Algernon Sidney's *Discourses Concerning Government*, which derives Locke's position from the Bible and religious premises, is published in London and widely read in America.

1699 John Locke's three essays on religious toleration, published separately at various times during the 1690s, are published together.

1701 Yale College is founded by conservative Congregationalists.

1702 Cotton Mather publishes the most famous of his some 400 works, *Magnalia Christi Americana; or, The Ecclesiastical History of New England.*

1706 Francis Makemie, the father of Presbyterianism in America, organizes his first American presbytery.

1707 The first session of the Baptist Association, meeting in Philadelphia, involves five churches.

1708 Members of various Calvinist sects from the German Rhineland begin to arrive in large numbers in Pennsylvania.

1709 Publication of Bishop Benjamin Hoadley's *The Origin and Institute of Civil Government* helps popularize John Locke's thinking and helps make ministers in America a major conduit for Locke's ideas.

1728 Jewish colonists erect the first American synagogue in New York.

1729 Benjamin Franklin purchases *The Pennsylvania Gazette*, the most popular newspaper of the colonial era.

1730 *GOVERNMENT THE PILLAR OF THE EARTH, Benjamin Colman

1731 Benjamin Franklin forms the Library Company in Philadelphia, the first circulating library in America—later to be used by members of the Continental Congress and the Constitutional Convention.

1733 Georgia (Savannah) is founded by General Oglethorpe. Georgia is the last of the 13 original American colonies to be settled.

1736 John and Charles Wesley, founders of Methodism, return from Georgia.

1738 George Whitefield, the great revivalist, makes his first trip to America.

1740 NINEVEH'S REPENTANCE AND DELIVERANCE, Joseph Sewall

1741 The purifying Calvinism of Jonathan Edwards, Sr., vies with a more common religious liberalism exemplified by his contemporary Benjamin Franklin. Edwards this year delivers his famous "Sinners in the Hands of an Angry God" sermon, which is widely reprinted.

1742 Whitefield makes his second trip to America. (He will return five more times to evangelize: 1744–48, 1751–52, 1754–55, 1763–65, and 1769–70.) The Great Awakening, or revival, is led by Whitefield, Gilbert and William Tennent, Joseph Bellamy, Jonathan Edwards, Sr., Jonathan Dickinson, James Davenport, and others. The Great Awakening "clearly began a new era, not merely of American Protestantism but in the evolution of the American mind" (Alan Heimert & Perry Miller).

1744 THE ESSENTIAL RIGHTS AND LIBERTIES OF PROTESTANTS, Elisha Williams

Benjamin Franklin is prominent in the formation of the American Philosophical Society, the first learned society in America.

1746 BRITAIN'S MERCIES, AND BRITAIN'S DUTIES, George Whitefield

1747 CIVIL MAGISTRATES MUST BE JUST, RULING IN THE FEAR OF GOD, Charles Chauncy

The College of New Jersey is founded by New Side Presbyterians

* Sermons are listed by year of publication and precede the events in the given year, except as noted.

in response to the Great Awakening (it is renamed Princeton in 1896).

1750 Almost a third of the people of Philadelphia, the largest city in America and the second largest in the British Empire, now owe their living to a craft of some kind.

Montesquieu's *The Spirit of Laws* is published in English.

1751 The Academy and College of Philadelphia, later to become the University of Pennsylvania, is founded by Benjamin Franklin and other laymen to be a secular institution that specializes in the teaching of utilitarian subjects.

Hume's *Enquiry Concerning the Principles of Morals* is published.

1752 Benjamin Franklin gains worldwide fame with his kite experiment.

1754 Col. George Washington, age 22, and a force of Virginians surrender to the French at Fort Necessity (July 3).

King's College (renamed Columbia in 1784) opens in New York. It is interdenominational and has no theological faculty.

On June 19, the Albany Convention meets as the first concerted effort to unite the colonies. The Albany "Plan of Union" is approved on July 10, written by Benjamin Franklin. It is rejected by the colonies and by England.

Jonathan Edwards, Sr., publishes his treatise *On the Freedom of the Will*, considered by many to be the most brilliant American theological study of the century.

1755 Francis Hutcheson's *A System of Moral Philosophy* is published in London.

The French and Indian War is the American part of the Seven Year's War (1755–63). The battles for Niagara, Ticonderoga, and Crown Point in 1759 see major contributions made by the colonists. Montreal and Quebec fall to the British. The British gain control of Detroit. During the war the American economy reaches a point of development to be internally self-sustaining.

1756 THE MEDIATORIAL KINGDOM AND GLORIES OF JESUS CHRIST, Samuel Davies

1760 THE PRESENCE OF GOD WITH HIS PEOPLE, Samuel Dunbar

George III, who will reign until 1820, takes the throne determined to "act like a king."

1762 Benjamin Franklin publishes his *Advice to a Young Tradesman*, David Hume publishes the final volume of his widely read *History of England* in London, and Jean-Jacques Rousseau publishes *A Treatise on the Social Contract* in Amsterdam.

1763 By the Treaty of Paris, Britain gains all of Canada and Louisiana east of the Mississippi River (Feb. 10).

Patrick Henry argues the "Parson's Cause" in Virginia after the British disallow a Virginia statute (Dec.).

1764 The College of Rhode Island is founded by the Baptists (it is renamed Brown University in 1804).

1765 The Stamp Act (Mar. 22) and Quartering Act (Mar. 24) are imposed. Nine of the colonies send delegates to the Stamp Act Congress in New York (Oct. 7–25).

Patrick Henry's fiery "treason" speech in the Virginia House of Burgesses is published as the influential Virginia Resolves (May 29).

1766 THE SNARE BROKEN, Jonathan Mayhew

Queens College is established by the Dutch Reformed Church (it is renamed Rutgers in 1825).

1767 The Townshend Acts (June 29) impose duties on glass, lead, paint, paper, tea, etc.

Adam Ferguson's *Essay on the History of Civil Society* is published in Edinburgh.

1768 John Dickinson of Pennsylvania arouses public opinion with his "Letters from a Farmer."

Beginning in March, merchants in Philadelphia, New York, and Boston debate and adopt nonimportation agreements.

1769 AN HUMBLE INQUIRY, John Joachim Zubly

Daniel Boone leads settlers over the mountains to Kentucky.

Blackstone publishes the last volume of his four-volume work, *Commentaries on the Laws of England.*

Dartmouth College is founded by Reverend Eleazar Wheelock.

1770 Several Americans are killed in the Boston Massacre (Mar. 5). Samuel Adams publishes a description of the event in "Innocent Blood Crying to God from the Streets of Boston." The British commander's defense attorneys John Adams and Josiah Quincy win his acquittal.

1772 The Committee of Correspondence is organized when Samuel Adams calls a Boston town meeting; other towns form similar committees (Nov. 2–Jan. 1773).

1773 AN ORATION UPON THE BEAUTIES OF LIBERTY, John Allen
AN APPEAL TO THE PUBLIC FOR RELIGIOUS LIBERTY, Isaac Backus

The Boston Tea Party: 342 casks of tea are dumped into Boston Harbor from the British ship *Dartmouth*, by men disguised as Mohawk Indians, after a meeting of 8,000 Bostonians at Old South Church, conducted by Samuel Adams (Dec. 16).

— 1 —

GOVERNMENT THE PILLAR OF THE EARTH

Benjamin Colman

BOSTON

1730

Benjamin Colman (1673–1747). One of the prominent clergymen of his day, Colman became in 1699 the first pastor of Boston's Brattle Street Church, where he found himself at odds with Increase and Cotton Mather because of certain of his views that deviated from strict Congregationalism. His B.A. and A.M. degrees were from Harvard, and he was awarded an S.T.D. by the University of Glasgow. In 1724 he declined the presidency of Harvard, but he served as one of its trustees (1717–28) and remained an overseer, in addition to his ministry at Brattle Street Church, until his death. A prolific author with more than ninety published titles to his credit, he was a supporter of the evangelical movement stirred by the Great Awakening and was a commissioner of the Society for the Propagation of the Gospel in New England and for Parts Adjacent. Thrice married, Colman was survived by his third wife, Mary Frost.

The sermon reprinted here was preached at the Thursday Lecture in Boston on August 13, 1730.

GOVERNMENT *the* Pillar *of the Earth.*

A

SERMON

Preached at the Lecture in *BOSTON*,

Before His EXCELLENCY

JONATHAN BELCHER, *Esq*;

Captain General and Commander in Chief, *&c.*

August 13th 1730.

By *Benjamin Colman.*

Isai. xxxiii. 6. *Wisdom and Knowledge shall be the Stability of thy Times, and strength of Salvation.*

BOSTON, in *New-England*

Printed for *T. Hancock*, at the Bible and Three Crowns near the Town-Dock.
1730.

For the Pillars of the Earth are the Lord's, and He hath set the World upon them.

1 Sam. ii. 8.

The words are part of a raptrous and heavenly song, utter'd by a devout, inspir'd and transported mother in Israel, upon a great and joyful occasion. If the Divine Eternal Spirit please to inspire and speak by a gracious woman, it is the same thing to us, and requires our reverend attention as much, as if he raise up a Moses or an Elias, or make his revelations by a Paul or John.

Samuel, the rare and wonderful son of inspir'd Hannah, never outspake his lovely mother in any of his prayers or acts of praise. Eli would have sat at her feet, and laid himself in the dust, at the hearing of this flowing torrent of fervent devotion from her beauteous lips; and saints thro' all ages hang on the heavenly music of her tongue.

Great things are here said of GOD, and of his government, in the families and kingdoms of men; and such wise and just observations are made, as are worthy of deep contemplation by the greatest and best of men. Had she like Deborah been the princess of the tribes of Israel, she could not have spoken with more loftiness and majesty, with more authority and command; nor better have address'd the nobles and rulers, the captains and the mighty men; to humble and lay 'em low before GOD.

"She celebrates the Lord GOD of Israel,* his unspotted purity, his almighty power, his unsearchable wisdom, and his unerring justice": In the praises of these she joys and triumphs, her heart was exalted and her mouth enlarged.

"She adores the divine sovereignty in its disposals of the affairs of the children of men; in the strange and sudden turns given to them; in the rise & fall of persons, families & countries. "She observes how the strong are soon weakned, and the weak are soon strengthned, when GOD pleases: How the rich are soon impoverish'd, and the poor inriched on a sudden: How empty families are replenish'd, and numerous families diminished["]: All this is of the Lord;

* Henry in loc.

He maketh poor and maketh rich, He bringeth low and lifteth up: He raiseth up the poor out of Dust, and lifteth up the Beggar from the Dunghill; to set them among Princes, and make them inherit the Throne of Glory; For the Pillars of the Earth are the Lord's, and He hath set the World upon them.

Thus my text is introduced as a reason for those dispensations of GOD towards a person, a family, or a people, which at any time are to us most surprising and admirable.

1. The things spoken of are great and mighty; *the Pillars of the Earth.* The earth is a vast fabrick, and in proportion to its mighty bulk must its pillars be.

The metaphor is plainly taken from architecture; as in stately, spacious and magnificent structures we often see rows of pillars, to sustain the roof and lofty towers. But whether we apply this manner of expression to the natural or moral earth, it is figurative and not literal.

The natural earth has no pillar. The will and word of GOD is its only basis. It seems to us who dwell on it fix'd and immoveable in the air. It keeps it's place and line there, as if it were set on some lasting solid pillars, and never mov'd at all.

We darkly philosophise upon the point, and talk of the poles of heaven; which are more unintelligible to a common audience than the pillars of it. We speak obscurely of the earth's being fixed on it's own center. And we discourse more intelligibly of the secret power of magnetism which is in matter; whereby bodies mutually attract or gravitate toward each other; by which the mighty globes of the universe preserve their distance, motion and order.

This seems to be the only natural pillar of the earth: The amazing work and power of GOD. And the planets which roll in the same circle with us, have all of 'em the same pillars. That is to say, all bodies thro' the whole solar system attract or gravitate toward each other, with forces according to their quantities of matter.

But after all this fine doctrine in our new philosophy, concerning the centripetal forces of the sun and planets; a plain Christian is much more edified by the simple and vulgar account which the sacred pages give us of this mysterious thing:* "*He stretcheth out the North over the empty space, and hangeth the Earth upon nothing! He hath founded it upon*

*Job xxvi. 7. Psalm xxiv. 2.

the Seas, and established it upon the Floods." Which is to say, No man knows how or where, this vast material frame finds it's basis and station.

Let us hear GOD again on the point, and say no more upon it;

> Job xxxviii. *Who is this that darkneth Counsel by Words without Knowledge? Gird up now thy Loins like a Man; for I will demand of thee, and answer thou Me. Where wast thou when I laid the Foundations of the Earth? Declare if thou hast Understanding. Who hath laid the Measures thereof, if thou knowest? Or who hath stretched the Line upon it? Whereupon are the Foundations thereof fastned? or who laid the Corner-stone thereof?*

We see then that the natural earth has no pillars, in any proper sense; Neither has the moral earth, (*i.e.* the inhabitants of it) any, but in a metaphorical sense: And so the princes and rulers of it are called it's pillars; because the affairs of the world ly upon their shoulders, and turn upon their conduct and management, in a very great degree.

And thus the text explains it self, and is to be interpreted from the scope of our context; which speaks of *the Bows of the mighty Men*, and of *the Thrones of Princes*, and then adds—*the Pillars of the Earth.* So that by pillars we are to understand governours and rulers among men; but not the persons that bear rule, so much as the order it self, government and magistracy. For the persons may be weak and slender reeds, little able of themselves to bear up any thing; and here and there they may fall; but the order stands and doth indeed uphold the world.

2. The things said of these pillars of the earth are also very great: "*They are the Lord's*, and *He has set the World upon them*.["] That is to say, The order and happiness of this lower world, the peace and weal of it, depend on the civil government which GOD has ordained in it. All this is very elegant and rhetorical, a high and noble strain of speech, upon the highest subject that belongs to this our earth.

DOCT[RINE]

The Great God has made the governments and rulers of the earth it's pillars, and has set the world upon them.

1. The governments and rulers of the earth are it's pillars.

*Judges xx.

2. These pillars of the earth are the Lord's.
3. He has set the world upon them.

I. *The governments and rulers of the earth are it's pillars.*

The pillar is a part of great use and honour in the building: So is magistracy in the world. One style in scripture for it is, foundations and corner-stones. Where we read of *the Chief* of the People*, in the Hebrew it is the corners. We read also of the † *Foundations of the Earth being out of Course.* The meaning is, the government of it was so. Kings bear up and support the inferior pillars of government, and a righteous administration restores a dissolving state: Psal. lxxv. 3. *The Earth and all the Inhabitants thereof are dissolved: I bear up the Pillars of it.*

In like manner, wise and faithful ministers are pillars in the Church: Which *is built on the Prophets and Apostles, Jesus Christ being the chief Corner-stone*, Eph. ii. 20. The prophet Jeremiah was made by God an iron pillar: And of Peter, James and John we read, that *they seemed to be Pillars:* Gal. ii. 9. They were deservedly so reputed, and truly so in the Church of Christ. Famous are the Lord's words to Peter, Matth. xvi. 18. *Thou art Peter, and on this Rock will I build my Church.* And when John had the vision of the New-Jerusalem, descending out of heaven from God, it is said that *the Wall of the City had twelve Foundations, and in them the Names of the twelve Apostles of the Lamb.*

Now the design and use of pillars in a building is one of these two, or both together: 1. For strength to uphold it, or 2. For beauty to adorn it.

1. The governments and rulers of the earth are its pillars in respect of strength to uphold and support the virtue, order and peace of it. Pillars should be made strong, and commonly are so; of stone and marble, iron and brass. And it had need be a *strong Rod to be a Sceptre to Rule*, Ezek. xix. 14. Magistrates need be strong, for government is a great weight; and it is *laid upon their shoulders.* Moses felt the weight and said, *I am not able to bear this People alone.*

2. The governments and rulers of the earth are it's pillars for ornament, to adorn it. Pillars in a fine building are made as beautiful as may be; they are plan'd and polish'd, wrought and carv'd with much art and cost, painted and gilded, for sight as well as use. As the legs

*Judges xx.
† 2. Psal. lxxxii.

are to a body, comely in it's goings: Such are pillars in a stately structure for beauty to the eye. It is the allusion of the spouse, recounting the beauties of her beloved, Cant. v. 15. *His Legs are as Pillars of Marble, set upon Sockets of fine Gold.* A bold and elegant comparison, becoming the pen of Solomon, who had built the temple of GOD with all it's pillars. They represented the strength of CHRIST and his stability, to bear the weight of the government laid upon him; and also the magnificence of *the Goings of GOD our King in the Sanctuary:* Likewise the steadiness of the divine administration. So those in power and magistracy are to be supposed, men adorn'd with superior gifts, powers and beauties of mind: Men that adorn the world wherein they live, and the offices which they sustain. And then their office adorns them also, and sets them in conspicuous places, where what is great and good in them is seen of all. To be sure, government and magistracy adorn the world as well as preserve it.

1. Magistrates uphold and adorn the world, as pillars do a fabrick, by employing their superior wisdom and knowledge, skill and prudence, discretion and judgment for the publick good. These accomplishments are to be supposed in the civil order, and they render 'em the pillars of the earth.

Wisdom is both strength and beauty, a defence and ornament. So Solomon shines among kings, for *the Wisdom of GOD was in Him. GOD gave him Wisdom and Knowledge exceeding much, and Largeness of Heart even as the Sand upon the Sea-shore.* Angels excel in strength, and rulers should be wise as the angels of GOD. The government is laid on CHRIST because in him are hid all the treasures of wisdom and knowledge. He is the wisdom of GOD and the power of GOD. As GOD at first founded the earth by his wisdom, and by his understanding established the heavens; so by the communication of wisdom and understanding to some, he preserves the order and happiness of others on it. What is said of a house is true of a state,

> *Thro' Wisdom it is builded, and by Understanding it is established, and by Knowledge shall the Chambers be filled with all precious and pleasant Riches: A wise Man is strong, yea a Man of Knowledge increaseth Strength.**

But then, Is the pillar for ornament? What is more beautiful than knowledge and wisdom? What more adorns a man, a place, a coun-

*Prov. xxiv. 3, 4, 5. 1 Cor. i. 24. Col. ii. 3. 2 Sam. xiv. 20. 1 Kings iv. 29.

try? The queen of Sheba came far to hear the wisdom of Solomon, and Huram was as much struck as she was: 2 Chron. ii. 12. *Blessed be the Lord GOD of Israel, who hath given to David the King a wise Son, endued with Prudence and Understanding, who may build a House for the Lord, and an House for the Kingdom.*

2. Integrity, uprightness, faithfulness added to knowledge and wisdom, makes men strong and beautiful pillars, whether in church or state. Every man is ready to pretend to a competency of wisdom, and as ready *to proclaim his own Goodness; but a faithful Man who can find?* Prov. xx. 6. He is a rare and beauteous spectacle, as Moses, Joshua, Samuel, Jehojada, Hezekiah and Nehemiah, in their times, and to the end of time. All that rule over men should be like to *these*, *just men ruling in the fear of the Lord*, and then they are to the world as the light and rain, without which the earth must perish. As darkness vanishes before the light, so *a King that sitteth upon the Throne of Judgment scattereth away all Evil with his Eyes.* David, that pillar of Israel, came into the government with that noble purpose and resolution, Psal. lxxv. 3. *When I shall receive the Congregation, I will judge uprightly.* So he fed them in the integrity of his heart, and led them by the skilfulness of his hands. GOD's righteousness and faithfulness, justice and judgment, are the foundation of his everlasting government, *the habitation of his throne.* See the pillars of the divine government; Psal. xxxvi. 5, 6. *Thy Faithfulness reacheth to the Clouds, thy Righteousness is as the great Mountains.* Nor can the kingdoms and provinces on the earth stand, but on the like basis of a just and righteous humane government. Psal. lxxii. 3. *The Mountains shall bring Peace to the People, and the little Hills by Righteousness.* "Both the superior and inferior magistrates shall minister abundantly to the stability and tranquility of the state.["]

3. *A publick and enlarged spirit* for the common weal and a single regard thereunto, without suffering our selves to be misled by private and selfish views. This renders men pillars to the world, in the places wherein Providence sets 'em. And so,

4. A spirit of peace and love, meekness and humility, candour and gentleness; whereby persons are ready to unite their counsels, and act in concert with one another; paying a just deference one to another and preferring one another in honour; glad to receive light from any one, and well pleased to reflect it from them; all pursuing one end, as the many pillars in a great house stand quietly near to one another,

and all help to bear it up: This *spirit of power, and of love, and of a sound mind*, render men strong and beautiful pillars of the earth. But if *the peace of God rule* not in mens hearts; if their passions shake 'em and they clash with one another; the house totters, the high arches above cleave asunder, and the roof falls in; as when Sampson bow'd the pillars of Dagons house, and buried the lewd assembly in one vast ruine.

5. A pillar implies fortitude and patience; resolution, firmness and strength of mind, under weight and burden: Not to be soon shaken in mind, nor moved away from what is right and just; but giving our reason in the meekness of wisdom, and hearing the reasons of others in the same spirit of meekness, to form an impartial judgment, and abide by it; But yet with submission to the publick judgment and determination. The unstable are as water, and more fitly likened to the *waves of the sea*, than to a pillar on shore. And the irresolute, discouraged and sinking mind is at best but a pillar built upon the sand; which falls when the wind blows and the storm beats upon it, because of its weak foundation.

There is a passive courage, ever necessary in an accomplish'd ruler, as much it may be as an active. The pillar stands regardless thro' the weather beat on it, or tho' dirt be cast on it. True it will wear under the injuries of time, but it looks still great, and stands while it wears away. The wise, the meek & strong Moses stood as many shocks, as ever man did from an impatient, murmuring, ungrateful people.

But this for the first head; the governments and rulers of the earth are its pillars.

II. These pillars of the earth *are the Lord's*.

The earth is the Lord's and the fulness thereof; the world and they that dwell therein. All are God's rightful propriety & dominion. The shields of the earth belong to him. These are the same with the pillars of it.

1. The Lord makes these pillars, forms fashions 'em, polishes and adorns 'em. He gifts, qualifies and furnishes all whom he calls out to public service. He makes the more plain and rough, and he orders the carved work and gilding in his house. He, the Father of Light & Glory, gives men their natural powers and excellencies; and all their acquired gifts are from him.

> *He looketh upon all the Inhabitants of the Earth, He fashioneth their Hearts alike, He considereth all their Works. In the Hearts of all that are wise-hearted He putteth Wisdom. Both Wisdom and Might are His: Counsel is His and sound Wisdom; He is Understanding, He is Strength; by Him Kings rule and Princes decree Judgment.**

He gave to David integrity, and to Solomon wisdom; and both were pillars of his framing.

2. Both the order & the persons are of the Lord's ordering, constituting and appointing. Civil government is of divine institution, and GOD commissions and entrusts with the administration whom he pleases. The great King of the World has order'd a government in it, and he raises up governours, supream and subordinate. *There is no Power but of GOD; the Powers that be are ordained of Him.* He puts the scepter into the hand, and the spirit of government into the heart.

3. The pillars are the Lord's, for he disposes of them as he pleases; places and fixes them where he will; rears 'em when he sees fit; and when he will removes, or takes 'em down: Or if he has no pleasure in them, breaks 'em to pieces and throws 'em away.

> *He removeth Kings, and setteth up Kings: For Promotion cometh neither from the East, nor from the West, nor from the South: But GOD is the Judge; He putteth down one and setteth up another: He leadeth Counsellors away spoiled & maketh the Judges fools: He looseth the Bond of Kings, and girdeth their Loins with a Girdle: He leadeth Princes away spoiled, and overthroweth the Mighty.*†

Thus the sovereign GOD forms the pillars of the earth, prepares 'em, sets 'em up, ordains the places and times of their standing; takes 'em down and puts others in their room. He calls, and uses whom he will, inclines and spirits how he will, and improves to what degree he will. They are his therefore, and his *is the greatness and the glory and the majesty!* And to him it must be ascribed both by the persons endowed and raised by him, and by others interested in them: 1 Chron. xxix. 12, 13. *Both Riches and Honour come of Thee, and in thy Hand is Power and Might, and in thy Hand it is to make Great, and to give Strength unto all: Now therefore, our GOD, we praise Thee, and bless thy Name for ever and ever.*

*James i. 17. Psalm xxxiii. 15. Exod. xxxi. 3. Dan. ii. 20. Prov. viii. 14.
†Dan. ii. 21. Psal. lxxv. 6, 7. Job xii, 17, 18.

But to do the utmost honour to the civil order among men, and to give yet greater glory to GOD, let us come to the third and last part of our text.

III. *GOD hath set the world* upon the governments and rulers, whom he has made the pillars of it.

The natural world is in the hand of GOD, and is upheld in it's being and order by his power. The moral world is most upon his heart, and govern'd in a way and manner suted to the nature and present state of man. And as he governs the spirits of men when he pleases by immediate impressions on them; so as more proper to the present order and happiness of mankind, he has appointed the government of men to be by men. So the peace, tranquility and flourishing of places are made to depend on the wisdom and fidelity of their rulers, in the good administration of the government. While the utmost misery and confusion befals those places where the government is ill administred. The reason is given in the text, *GOD has set the World* on this foot; it can't stand on any other bottom. The virtue and religion of a people, their riches and trade, their power, honour and reputation; and the favour of GOD toward them, with his blessing on them; do greatly depend on the pious, righteous and faithful government which they are under.

GOD hath set: As well in the nature of things, as in his word. Government is not a creature of man's lust and will, but of divine constitution, and from a necessity in the nature of things. The very being and weal of society depends thereon.

Government was not in the original of it assumed or usurped by any one man. For instance, not by Lamech before the Flood, nor by Nimrod after it. Indeed the spirit of tyranny, and the lust of dominion, seem to have began in them; but order & rule was before them. Mankind naturally went into that, and these were the men who made the first breaches on it; the one being of the race of Cain, the other of Ham; who have had some of their likeness in every place, and thro' all generations; that would turn the world upside down and overthrow the foundations which GOD has laid.

In a word, magistracy, like the other ordinances of heaven, stands by the power and blessing of GOD; who effectually owns it and works by it, establishes the earth and it abideth. He has graven it deep in the hearts of men, even as the desire of happiness and self-preservation. He has as much ordained, that while the earth remaineth civil order and government shall not cease; as he has sworn *that seed time and harvest, cold and heat, summer and winter, day and night*, shall not. Both the one and the other equally continue to the world's end, absolutely necessary to the life, comfort and welfare of mankind.

USE

I shall now make a few reflections, by way of practical inference and improvement.

1. See the divine wisdom and goodness in ordaining and establishing a magistracy and government in the world. It is one of the many great instances, wherein the Supream Governour of the world has taken care for the universal and perpetual weal of it. And they that would be lawless and ungoverned, despising dominion and speaking evil of dignity, distinction, authority and rule among men, act as madly and mischievously as one would do, that should go into a house and sap the foundation of it, till it fall upon him and crush him to death.

It is one evident mark of the Romish imposture, and of the spirit of Antichrist, that it has invaded, usurp'd upon and subverted the authority of kings and princes, governments and states, over their subjects. The popes claim of supremacy transfers the allegiance of subjects to a foreign power, and absolves 'em from their oaths. This alone is a sufficient mark of the Beast and of the man of sin. What confusion and vexation has the world suffered from this insolent & monstrous doctrine! And how strange is it that so many kingdoms and nations of Europe should so long wander after it, to their infinite misrule & distraction! But the word & dreadful judgment of GOD must be fulfilled on a wicked world.

The Reformed churches took early care to protest against this doctrine of devils. They declared for a "conscientious subjection and obedience to the laws and magistrates under which they liv'd, and by whom they were protected & defended in their just rights and liberties.["] "Every kind of magistracy (say the Helvetian churches) is instituted by GOD, for the peace and happiness of man, and all subjects should own the goodness of GOD in the institution of a magistrate, by honouring him as *the minister of GOD*.["]

These are some of the just and true principles of the Protestant religion, according to the oracles of GOD in this matter:

> Rom. xiii. 1–5. *Let every Soul be subject unto the higher Powers: For there is no Power but of GOD; the Powers that be are ordained of GOD: Whosoever therefore resisteth the Power, resisteth the Ordinance of GOD. Wherefore ye must needs be subject, not only for Wrath* (or fear of punishment) *but also for Conscience sake. Render therefore unto all their Dues, Tribute to whom Tribute is due, Custom to whom Custom, Fear to whom Fear, and Honour to whom Honour.* Tit. iii. 1. *Put them in mind to be subject to Principalities and Powers, to obey Magistrates.* 1 Pet. ii. 13, 14, 15, 16, 17. *Submit your selves to every Ordinance of Man for the Lord's sake; whether it be to the King as supream, or unto Governours as unto them that are sent by Him: For so is the Will of GOD.*

Let us very gratefully observe these precepts, for they are very graciously given us for the good of the world.

2. Are magistrates the pillars of the earth? Are they the Lord's? and has he set the world upon them? Let us then devoutly observe the governing Providence of GOD in disposing of persons and offices, both with respect unto our selves and others.

As to our selves, let GOD lead, and Providence open our way, and let us follow humbly & obediently. Let us think soberly of our selves, and not vainly pine after honour and power, or wickedly push for it like Absalom. But neither need we hide our selves like Saul, when the divine call is plain, nor insist on excuses like the meek and accomplished Moses. Or if again Providence lays us by, why should we not retire with Samuel's humility and greatness of soul.

And then as to others, Let us not think our selves neglected or overlook'd, be envious and discontent, if GOD prefer them. Suffer the Most High to rule in the kingdoms of men, and to give the provinces that belong to 'em to whomsoever he will. Let us know and keep our own place, and do our duty to those whom GOD sets over us.

Let people reverence & honour their worthy rulers, and let the highest among men be very humble before GOD. They are pillars, but of the earth. The earth and its pillars are dissolving together. Government abides, in a succession of men, while the earth endures, but the persons, however good & great, must die like other men. We must not look too much at the loftiness of any, nor lean too much on any earthly pillar: *Put not your Trust in Princes, nor in the Son of Man in whom there is no Help: His Breath goeth forth, he returneth to his Dust.* Nor may the highest among mortals behold themselves with elation & security, as the vain king of Babylon once; but let them fear and tremble before the GOD of heaven, who inherits all nations, and stands in the congregation of the mighty, and judgeth among the gods.

3. Are rulers the pillars of the earth; are they the Lord's? and has he set the world upon 'em? Let all that are in public offices consider their obligations to be pillars, in the places wherein Providence hath set 'em.

Let rulers consider what they owe to GOD, who has rear'd and set 'em up; and to the publick which GOD has set upon them. Let 'em seek wisdom & strength, grace and conduct from GOD, that they may answer the title given 'em in my text. Let 'em stand, and bear, and act for GOD; whose they are, and who has set 'em where they are. Let the publick good be their just care; that it may be seen that GOD has set the world in their heart, as well as laid it on their shoulders. Let 'em act uprightly, that they may stand secure and strong. Let 'em fear GOD, and rule by his word, that they may be approved by GOD, and accepted always by men with all thankfulness.

As government is the pillar of the earth, so religion is the pillar of government. Take away the fear of GOD's government & judgment, and humane rule utterly falls, or corrupts into tyranny. But if religion rule in the hearts and lives of rulers, GOD will have glory, and the people be made happy.

Fathers of our country, let me freely say to you, that the devotion and virtue of our humble, but illustrious ancestors (the first planters of New-England), laid the foundation of our greatness among the provinces: And it is this that must continue and establish it under the divine favour & blessing. Emulate their piety and godliness, and generous regards to the publick, and be acknowledged the pillars, the strength and ornament of your country!

But let me move you by a greater argument, even a *far more exceeding and eternal weight of glory*, which the Holy Ghost has set before you in a most illustrious promise;

> Rev. iii. 12. *Him that overcometh will I make a Pillar in the Temple of my GOD, and he shall go no more out: And I will write upon Him the Name of my GOD, and the Name of the City of my GOD, which is New-Jerusalem;*

which cometh down out of Heaven from my GOD: And I will write upon Him my New-Name.

CHRIST will erect a monumental pillar, that shall stand for ever, in honour of all them who in their station here, be they high or low, faithfully endeavour to uphold his church and kingdom.

It is a triumphant promise taken from the Roman manner of pillars rear'd to the memory of illustrious persons and patriots, on which were inscrib'd their names and worthy deeds; together with that of the empire, city or province, which they were so happy as to serve and help to save.

Infinitely more glory and honour shall be done to him who serves the Lord CHRIST, his kingdom, people and interest, in his life here on earth: When he comes into his temple above he shall have a *pillar of celestial glory* rear'd to eternize his name; and on it shall be written (O divine honour!) "*This was a faithful Servant of his GOD, and Saviour, and of the Church on Earth.*["]

There let him stand for ever, "*A monument of free grace, never to be defaced or removed.*" While the names of famous emperors, kings and generals, graven in brass or cut in marble, on stately pillars and triumphant arches, shall moulder into dust.

So the pillars in Solomon's porch were broken down, and carried away by the Chaldeans: But he that is made a pillar in the celestial temple shall *go no more out.* Yea the pillars of the literal earth and heavens will shortly tremble, and be shaken out of their place; but he that believes in CHRIST, and has his glorious name written on him, shall remain unshaken and immoveable; and remain, like his living saviour, stedfast for ever.

This infinite and eternal glory we wish to all in this worshipping assembly, the greater and the less, high and low, rich and poor together: As in the act of worship, we are all on a level before the throne of GOD. And the lowest in outward condition may be the highest in grace, and in the honours that come from above.

But in a more especial manner we wish this mercy and blessing of our GOD and king, out of his house to your Excellency our governour: Whose return to your country, and your advancement to the government of it, we cannot but congratulate in the most publick manner, with hearts full of joy, and sincere thankfulness to GOD.

The Lord GOD of our fathers, who hath *spread our heavens, and laid the foundations of our earth*, make you a pillar to us both in the state & church.

As it hath pleased him to chuse, adorn & set you up; so may he please to fix & establish you, and long continue you a father, and illustrious blessing to your people.

And may the name of CHRIST, and of these churches of our Lord JESUS, be graven deep upon your heart: And your faithful services to them be an everlasting name to you, *which shall not be cut off.*

So, not only erect your self a pillar in every pious and grateful heart, that loves our civil and religious liberties; and let their prayers and blessings come upon you; but also lay a good foundation against the world to come, for everlasting fame and renown, and *to be called great in the kingdom of heaven.*

FINIS

2

NINEVEH'S REPENTANCE AND DELIVERANCE

Joseph Sewall

BOSTON

1740

JOSEPH SEWALL (1688–1769). A Harvard graduate of 1707, Sewall spent a long and generally serene ministry at Old South Church in Boston, where he preached beyond his eightieth year. He was a strong Calvinist, yet he became a friend of George Whitefield, who preached in Sewall's pulpit during several visits to Boston. He was offered the presidency of Harvard in 1724, but he declined it after a peevish attack by Cotton Mather. He preached the artillery sermon in 1714 and the election sermon in 1724, and he was awarded a D.D. by the University of Glasgow in 1731. With his classmate Reverend Thomas Prince, he edited *The Compleat Body of Divinity* from collected papers of Samuel Willard (1726). His own papers were not collected, but *Sibley's Harvard Graduates* (vol. 5), lists twenty-nine writings by him.

Reprinted here is a fast-day sermon preached before the Massachusetts governor, the council, and the house of representatives on December 3, 1740. Always ready to look for underlying causes and strongly attached to his province, Sewall readily supported the patriot cause and permitted his meeting house to become a shrine of the American cause. In Charles Chauncy's words, Sewall "was a strenuous asserter of our civil and ecclesiastical charter-rights and priviledges. . . . He knew they were the purchase of our forefathers at the expence of much labor, blood, and treasire [*sic*]. He could not bear the thought of their being wrested out of our hands. He esteemed it our duty, in all wise, reasonable, and legal ways, to endeavour the preservation of them. . ." (Chauncy, *Discourse Occasioned by the Death of . . . Joseph Sewall* [Boston, 1769], p. 26).

Nineveh's *Repentance* and *Deliverance*.

A

SERMON

Preach'd before

His EXCELLENCY

THE

GOVERNOUR

The HONOURABLE

COUNCIL

AND

Representatives

of the Province of the

Massachusetts-Bay in *New-England*,

on a Day of FASTING and PRAYER

in the Council Chamber, *Dec.* 3. 1740.

By Joseph Sewall, D.D.

Pastor of a Church of CHRIST *in* Boston.

Jer. xviii. 7, 8. *At what instant I shall speak concerning a nation, and concerning a kingdom, to pluck up, and to pull down, and to destroy it: If that nation against whom I have pronounced, turn from their evil, I will repent of the evil that I thought to do unto them.*

BOSTON in *NEW-ENGLAND*;
Printed by J. DRAPER, Printer to His Excellency the GOVERNOUR and COUNCIL, for D. HENCHMAN in Cornhil. 1740.

And God saw their Works, that they turned from their evil Way, and God repented of the Evil that he had said that he would do unto them, and he did it not.

Jonah III. 10.

In this book we have a very memorable and instructive history. The prophet Jonah, whose name the book bears, was call'd of GOD to go to Nineveh, the capital of the Assyrian monarchy, and cry against it: He criminally attempted to fly from the presence of the Lord, by going to Joppa, and from thence to Tarshish; but that GOD whom the winds and sea obey, raised such a storm as made the heathen mariners conclude there was something very extraordinary, and accordingly they propose to cast lots, that they might know for whose cause this evil was upon them. Jonah is taken, and cast into the sea; upon which it ceased from raging: And thus, by the wonderful Providence of GOD, he became a type of our Lord and Saviour Jesus Christ, who having appeased the wrath of GOD by his obedience unto death, lay buried in the earth three days, Matth. 12. 40. *For as Jonas was three Days and three Nights in the Whale's Belly: So shall the Son of Man be three Days and three Nights in the Heart of the Earth.* Jonah having cried to GOD, as *out of the Belly of Hell,* was delivered from his dreadful confinement. Chap. 2. v. 10. *The Lord spake unto the Fish, and it vomited Jonah upon the dry Land.* Thus the brute creation, even the mighty whales, obey the word of GOD'S power, while men transgress his law. Jonah, being thus delivered from the depth of distress, obeys the second call of GOD to him, Ch. 3. v. 1. Happy is that rebuke, how sharp soever, which is sanctified to make us return to GOD and our duty. And here it is observ'd, in the third verse, that Nineveh was an exceeding great city, great to or of GOD,* "Things great and eminent have the name of GOD put upon them in scripture[,]" *of three days journey.* It is computed to have been sixty miles in compass, which may well be reckon'd three days journey for a footman, twenty miles a day, says Mr. Henry; or as the same author observeth, walking slowly and gravely, as Jonah must, when he went

* Urbs magna Dei. Calvin.

about preaching, it would take him up at least three days to go thro' all the principal streets and lanes of the city, to proclaim his message, that all might have notice of it." However, no greatness or wordly glory will be any security against GOD'S destroying judgments, if such places go on obstinately in their sins. O let not London! let not Boston, presume to *deal unjustly in the Land of Uprightness*, lest the holy GOD say of them as of his ancient people, *You have I known of all the Families of the Earth: Therefore I will punish you for all your Iniquities*, Amos 3. 2. But to return, Jonah, in obedience to the divine command, cries against this great city, *Yet forty days, and Nineveh shall be overthrown*, v. 4. In the five following verses, we have the faith and repentance of the Ninevites described, which our Lord takes particular notice of, Matth. 12. 41. *The Men of Nineveh shall rise in Judgment with this Generation, and shall condemn it, because they repented at the preaching of Jonas, and behold, a greater than Jonas is here.* Let us then attend to these words *with reverence and godly fear, lest they also rise up in judgment against us in the terrible day of the Lord.* And here I would more particularly observe, 1. *The People of Nineveh believed* GOD, v. 5. Jonah, we may suppose, declared to them the true and living GOD, who made heaven and earth, and publish'd his message in his name; and GOD wrought such a faith in them as excited a fear of his judgments, and made them deeply concern'd to put away their provoking sins, that they might escape the threatned destruction. And this impression of fear and concern was general; for we find, 2dly, *That they proclaim'd a Fast, and put on Sackcloth from the greatest of them even to the least of them.* Yea, there was a royal proclamation for this *by the Decree of the King and his Nobles*, v. 7. And this great monarch humbled himself before the Most High, who cuts off the spirit of princes, and is terrible to the kings of the earth. The king of Nineveh arose from his throne, and laid his robe from him, and cover'd him with sackcloth, and sat in ashes, v. 6. Thus did he practically confess, that he had behav'd unworthy his royal dignity, and deserv'd to have it taken from him. And the proclamation requir'd the strictest abstinence, *Let neither Man nor Beast taste any Thing.* Not as if the beasts were capable of moral good or evil; but as these had been abus'd by them, they would have their moans and cries under the want of food, further to excite penitential sorrow in themselves. And all are commanded to *cry mightily to God*, v. 8. Yea, all are exhorted to *turn every one from his evil*

Way, and from the violence that is in their hands. The Ninevites were sensible, that to outward signs and means of humiliation, they must add repentance and reformation. 3. *We have their Encouragement to attend this Duty*, in a time of impending judgment, v. 9. *Who can tell if God will turn and repent.* We may suppose that Jonah declar'd to them the grace and mercy of the GOD of Israel, and shew'd them the way of salvation thro' the then promised Messiah; that tho' their bodies should be destroy'd, their souls might be sav'd in the day of the Lord. And they might well infer some ground of hope as to their temporal deliverance from this, that the judgment was not presently executed; but the space of forty days was given them for repentance. However, as it doth not appear they had any particular promise respecting this matter, so their faith and hope are here express'd as attended with doubt and fear. Who can tell? A like expression we have, even respecting GOD'S covenant people, *Who knows if he will return and repent?* Joel 2. 14. 4. *We have an account of Nineveh's repentance, and GOD's gracious deliverance*, v. 10. *GOD saw their Works*, *i.e.* with approbation and gracious acceptance. Their works "whereby they testified the sincerity of their faith and repentance."* Our Saviour says, *they repented at the preaching of Jonas.* Luke 11. 32. We may conclude therefore that his preaching was accompanied with the powerful influences of the spirit of GOD convincing them of their many hainous transgressions, awakening them with fears of GOD'S judgments, and prevailing upon them to turn from their sins to the Lord. Had it not been for this wonderful work of grace upon them, they had been like to the sinners of the old world, who went on securely, tho' Noah was a *Preacher of Righteousness to them*, *'till the Flood came, and took them all away*. Here were some, I hope, and that not a few, who had saving repentance given them; and others were so terrified and awakened, that they engaged at least in an outward and publick reformation. And may we not suppose that in this wonderful work, GOD gave his ancient people a specimen and earnest of the call of the gentiles? Now, upon this their repentance it is said, *GOD repented of the Evil, and he did it not.* Which words must be understood in such a sense as is consistent with the divine perfections. It is not spoken of GOD, as if he could in a proper sense be griev'd for what he had done in threatn-

* Dutch annotations.

ing the Ninevites; no, this was right, and he had a gracious design in it: Nor, as if he had alter'd his counsels concerning them. He is of one mind, and who can turn him? Nor, as if he acted contrary to truth and faithfulness; no, the threatning was conditional. And accordingly when they repented GOD turned from his fierce anger, and gave them deliverance; which is agreable to that rule of his government which we have declar'd. Jer. 18. 7. 8. *At what Instant I shall speak concerning a Nation, and concerning a Kingdom, to pluck up, and to pull down, and to destroy it: If that Nation against whom I have pronounced, turn from their Evil, I will repent of the Evil that I thought to do unto them.*

From the words thus explained to you, I would observe the following doctrines,

(1.) If we would seek the Lord in a right manner, we must believe him; the threatnings and promises of his word. (2.) It is the duty of a people to cry to GOD in prayer with fasting, when he threatens to bring destroying judgments upon them; and their rulers should be ready to lead in the right discharge of this duty. (3.) Our seeking to GOD by prayer with fasting must be attended with true repentance, and sincere endeavours after reformation. (4.) When a people do thus attend their duty, GOD will repent of the evil, and not bring destruction upon them.

I. *If we would seek the Lord in a right manner under his threatned judgments, we must believe him; the threatnings and promises of his word.*

The people of Nineveh believed GOD, and proclaimed a fast. We are not told what particular credentials Jonah produc'd to prove that he was a true prophet sent from GOD. His preaching might be more full and particular than is here recorded; and GOD set it home, so that they were made sensible they had to do with the true and faithful one, whose name is Jehovah; and accordingly they set themselves to entreat his favour with great seriousness. And thus we must believe, that the Lord is that powerful, holy, faithful, and merciful GOD, which he declareth himself to be in his word. We must realise it, that his word is sure and most worthy of credit, whether he threatens evil to the impenitent, or promiseth mercy to such as confess and forsake their sins; or we shall never be concerned to seek his face in a right manner. *Without faith it is impossible to please God*, in our approaches to him: For he that cometh to GOD, *must believe that he is, and that he is a Rewarder of them that diligently seek him.* Heb. 11. 6. Agreably, in a time of danger, that pious king Jehoshaphet, said to GOD'S ancient people, *Hear me, O Judah, and ye the Inhabitants of Jerusalem, Believe in the Lord your God, so shall you be established; believe his prophets, so shall ye prosper.* 2 Chron. 20. 20. Certainly then, we who are born under the clear light of the gospel dispensation, must believe the Lord our GOD speaking to us in his word, if we would attend the duties of this day, so as to obtain mercy for ourselves, and this distressed people. We must believe that if we go on obstinately in our sins, and despite the warnings GOD has given us in his word and by his providences, we shall after our hardness and impenitent heart treasure up unto our selves wrath against the day of wrath; But if we forsake the way of sin, and return unto the Lord, he will have mercy and abundantly pardon. We must believe our Lord Jesus when he says to us, *Except ye repent, ye shall all likewise perish.* And we must also receive it as *a faithful saying, and worthy of all acceptation, that Christ Jesus came into the world to save sinners*, and will cast out none that come to him in the exercise of faith and repentance. O that there was such a faith in us! Then we should fly to GOD'S name, as to our strong tower this day, and find him our defence and refuge in the day of trouble. *By Faith Noah being warned of God of Things not seen as yet, moved with fear, prepared an Ark to the saving of his House; by the which he condemned the World, and became Heir of the Righteousness which is by Faith*, Heb. 11. 7.

II. *It is the duty of a people to cry to GOD in prayer with fasting, when he threatens to bring destroying judgments upon them; and their rulers should be ready to lead in the right discharge of this duty.*

Thus did the men of Nineveh, nor did their king refuse to humble himself and lie in the dust before that Almighty GOD, who threatned to destroy them. The order given was, "Let Man and Beast be covered with Sackcloth, and cry mightily to GOD." This then is a moral duty incumbent on all as GOD shall call. GOD'S ancient people practised it. Thus when the children of Moab and Ammon came against Jehoshaphet to battel, he feared, *and set himself to seek the Lord, and proclaimed a Fast*, 2 Chron. 20. 1–3. And we have an account in scripture of more private fasting, Mark 2. 18, 20. Where we are informed that the disciples of John, and of the pharisees used to fast. And our Lord declares that after his departure, *His Disciples should also Fast.* And we have particular direction about religious fasting, 1. Cor. 7. 5. Here then, I would be a little more particular in describing the duty of fasting and prayer, in which we are this day engaged.

1. *In religious fasting we must chasten our bodies, by abstaining from meat and drink, and other pleasures which gratify the outward man.*

Thus must we acknowledge that we have abused GOD'S good creatures, and are unworthy of the least drop and crumb even of the blessings of his common Providence. And in this way we ought to afflict and keep under our bodies, that our animal appetites may be bro't into subjection, and that our souls may be the more deeply humbled before GOD. Indeed the necessity of persons, respecting the weakness of some constitutions, is here to be regarded. However, when persons wantonly indulge their appetites, and find their own pleasures when GOD calls to weeping and mourning, is sinful and shameful. And GOD declares in his word, that this is a provoking evil, Isai. 22. 12–14. *In that Day did the Lord God of hosts call to weeping and to mourning, and to girding with sackcloth: And behold Joy and Gladness, slaying Oxen, and killing Sheep, eating Flesh, and drinking Wine; let us eat and drink, for to morrow we shall die. And it was revealed in mine Ears by the Lord of hosts, Surely this iniquity shall not be purged from you till ye die, saith the Lord God of hosts.* And surely the men of Nineveh will rise up in judgment against such, and condemn them; for we find they were very strict in attending these outward signs and means of humiliation. But then, it must be granted that this bodily abstinence will profit little, unless our hearts are broken for sin, and broken off from the pleasures of it.

2. In religious fasting we must *afflict our souls; have the heart inwardly pierced, and the spirits broken upon the account of our sins.*

That GOD who is a spirit, and forms the spirit of man within him, looks on the heart, and requireth us to worship him in spirit and truth. *The Sacrifices of God are a broken Spirit: a broken and contrite Heart, O God thou wilt not despise*, Psal. 51. 17. The call of GOD to his people on a day of solemn fasting, was that, *rent your heart*, Joel 2. 13. There must then be a deep and thorow conviction of sin, and contrition upon the account of it. We must look to Jesus whom our sins have pierced, and *mourn as one mourneth for his only Son, and be in bitterness, as one that is in bitterness for his First-born*, Zech. 12. 10. There must be hatred of sin, and indignation at it as the accursed thing which stirs up GOD'S holy displeasure against us. There must be inward grief because GOD has been dishonour'd and his law broken by our sins: *That godly Sorrow which worketh Repentance*, 2 Cor. 7. 10. There must be holy fear of GOD'S judgments. We must take shame and blame to our selves, and make that confession, Dan. 9. 8. *O Lord to us belongeth confusion of Face, to our Kings, to our Princes, and to our Fathers, because we have sinned against thee.* We must abhor our selves, lie down before GOD in deep abasement, and humble ourselves under his mighty hand: Thus must we go to GOD self-condemned, and willing to be reconcil'd to him upon his own terms; looking to Jesus as our advocate with the Father, and depending on him as the propitiation for our sins.

3. *We must cry mightily to GOD in prayer.* Earnest prayer, in this and other places of scripture, is express'd by crying to the Lord, Psal. 130. 1. *Out of the depths have I cried unto thee O Lord.* Prayer is a great part of the duty of the day; and we must take care, that it be that *effectual fervent Prayer that availeth much*, Jam. 5. 16.[,] in-wrought prayer, that prayer which is wrought in the heart by the Holy Ghost. For this end, we must ask the spirit of grace and supplication to help our infirmities, and stir up the gift of GOD in us. Thus must we pour out our hearts before GOD, and say, in most humble importunity as Jacob, *I will not let thee go, except thou bless me.* For GOD said not to the seed of Jacob, seek ye me in vain, Isa. 45. 15. And therefore, if we approve our selves the genuine sons of that patriarch, we shall also have power with GOD, and prevail thro' the merits and intercession of our Lord Jesus Christ: we shall either obtain the blessing for GOD'S people, as Elias did, tho' a man subject to like passions; or at least shall deliver our own souls. I might further set before you the prophet Daniel, who has given rulers a bright example of a publick spirit, greatly concern'd for the peace of Jerusalem. How earnest was he when he set his face to seek the Lord by prayer with fasting! Hear his repeated cries, Ch. 9. 19. *O Lord hear, O Lord forgive, O Lord, hearken and do, defer not, for thine own sake, O my God.* And when GOD call'd his people to sanctify a fast, the divine command is, Joel 2. 17.

Let the Priests, the Ministers of the Lord, weep between the Porch and the Altar, and let them say, Spare thy People, O Lord, and give not thy Heritage to Reproach; that the Heathen should rule over them: wherefore should they say among the People, Where is their God? May Moses and Aaron, lift up their hands with their hearts to GOD in prayer this day, and receive the blessing from the Lord.

4. *We must turn, each one from his evil way.* Thus when the exhortation given was to cry mightily to GOD, it follows; Yea, let them turn every one from his evil way, and *from the Violence that is in their Hands.* And indeed, unless this be our care, our sins will cry louder than our prayers, and provoke GOD to cover himself as with a cloud, Isa. 59. 1, 2. *Behold, the Lord's Hand is not shortned that it cannot save: neither his ear heavy that he cannot hear. But your Iniquities have separated between you and your God, and your Sins have hid his Face from you, that he will not hear.* And when GOD had declared to his people that he rejected their assemblies and solemn meetings, he gives them that exhortation. *Wash ye, make ye clean, put away the evil of your Doings from before mine Eyes, cease to do evil, learn to do well, seek Judgment, relieve the Oppressed, judge the Fatherless, plead for the Widow,* Isa. 1. 16, 17.

But this brings me to the 3d general head,

III. Our seeking to GOD by prayer with fasting, *must be attended with true repentance, and sincere endeavours after reformation.*

GOD saw their works, that they *turned from the evil way.* Here we may consider,

1. What is implied in this work of repentance and reformation.

2. Why we should thus engage in the work of repentance and reformation.

First, *What is implied in this work of repentance and reformation?*

A. 1. It implieth, *An holy and prevailing resolution to turn from those sins which we confess on the day of fasting.* When we appear before GOD to confess our sins and ask pardon for them; if we attend this duty in sincerity, we are convinc'd that it is an evil and bitter thing that we have forsaken GOD by transgressing his law; and we shall accordingly resolve to put away this accursed thing which separates between GOD and us, and engage to return to GOD and our duty. Thus did GOD'S people on a solemn fast. *They entred into an oath to walk in God's law,* and solemnly promis'd, that they would reform the evils which had crept in among them; in taking strange wives, in profaning the Sabbath, in their cruel exacting upon their poor brethren, *&c.* Neh. 9. 38. 10. 29–31. And it is certainly seasonable and necessary for persons on such a day to resolve, relying on GOD for grace, to put away such and such sins as have more easily beset them, to take more care to keep themselves from their own iniquity, and to reform whatever hath been contrary to GOD'S law.

Which leads me to say,

2. It intends, *That this resolution be put in practice in sincere endeavours to put away those sins and reform those evils, which have been confess'd and bewail'd before God.* This GOD requires of us. *Thus saith the Lord God, Repent and turn your selves from all your Idols, and turn away your Faces from all your Abominations*, Ezek. 14. 6. And after this manner did the children of Israel testify their repentance, when they cried to the Lord under the oppression of their enemies. *And they put away the strange gods from among them, and served the Lord and his soul was grieved for the misery of Israel.* Judg. 10. 16. Agreeably, when we have fasted and prayed, we must bring forth *fruits meet for repentance*, by engaging in a thorow reformation of all sins of omission or commission. If we have omitted religious duties, secret or family prayer, self-examination, the ordinances of GOD'S house; we must now consincienciously attend upon them. If we have neglected the duties of those relations which we sustain towards men, in publick or private life; we must now with care and diligence discharge them. If we have committed sins contrary to the laws of sobriety, righteousness and godliness; we must labour by the spirit to mortify them. In a word, we should cleanse our selves from all filthiness of the flesh and spirit, perfecting holiness in the fear of GOD. And in order to these things, we ought earnestly seek to GOD to put his laws into our minds, and write them in our hearts; for it is he alone that can work in us to will and to do, in beginning and carrying on this necessary work of reformation.

3. *That we return to God by Jesus Christ; to believe in, love and obey him.* The prophet Hosea complains, *They return, but not to the most High*, 7. 16. Whereas, when a reformation is sincere and general, we shall have a regard to the Lord our GOD in it, as to our chief good and highest end. We shall not be principally concern'd to serve a turn, and escape this or the other threatned judgment. As they, *When he*

slew them, then they sought him: and they returned and enquired early after God. And they remembered that God was their Rock, and the high God their Redeemer. Nevertheless, they did flatter him with their Mouth, and they lied unto him with their Tongues, Psal. 7. 8. 34–36. But shall make it our great business to obtain peace with GOD thro' Jesus Christ the only Mediator, who has made peace thro' the blood of his cross. And then shall we endeavour to be stedfast in his covenant. The language of our hearts must be as Hos. 6. 1. *Come and let us return unto the Lord: for he hath torn, and he will heal us; he hath smitten, and he will bind us up.* 14. 3. *Asshur shall not save us, we will not ride upon Horses, neither will we say any more to the work of our hands, Ye are our gods: for in thee the Fatherless findeth mercy.* We must return to GOD as to our Lord and lawgiver, to obey and serve him; as to the object of our desire and choice, to take our full contentment in him: Thus it is said of GOD'S people *All Judah rejoiced at the Oath: for they had sworn with all their Heart, and sought him with their whole desire, and he was found of them,* 2 Chr. 15. 15. As to particular persons, it is necessary that they thus give up themselves to the Lord, and then keep the covenant of their GOD. And as to a people, considering them collectively, this must be their prevailing desire and practice: If they are generally false & hypocritical, they will give GOD reason to complain of them, as of his ancient people, *O Ephraim, what shall I do unto thee: O Judah, what shall I do unto thee: for your goodness is as a morning cloud, and as the early dew it goeth away.* Hos. 6. 4.

Secondly, *Why should our days of fasting be thus attended with sincere endeavours after reformation?*

A. 1. *GOD demands this of us.* When that inquiry was made, Wherewith shall I come before the Lord, and bow my self before the high GOD? Shall I come before him with burnt-offerings? Will the Lord be pleased with thousands of rams or with ten thousands of rivers of oyl? The answer is, *He hath shewed thee, O Man, what is good, and what doth the Lord require of thee, but to do justly, and to love mercy, and to walk humbly with thy GOD?* Micah 6. 8. And therefore, when GOD'S people fasted in a formal customary manner, without engaging in the necessary work of reformation, GOD said to them, *Did ye at all Fast unto me, even to me?* And then it follows, *Execute true Judgment, and shew Mercy and Compassions every Man to his Brother. And oppress not the Wid-*

ow, nor the Fatherless, the Stranger, nor the Poor, and let none of you imagine Evil against his Brother in your Heart, Zech. 7. 8, 10.

2. *God makes precious promises to encourage and excite us to this duty.* Thus when God had exhorted his people to put away the evil of their doings; he adds for their encouragement, *Come now and let us reason together, saith the Lord; though your Sins be as Scarlet, they shall be white as Snow; though they be red like Crimson, they shall be as Wool. If ye be willing and obedient, ye shall eat the good of the Land.* And in the 55th Chapter we have that exhortation enforc'd with a promise of full and free pardon, v. 6, 7. *Seek ye the Lord, while he may be found, call ye upon him while he is near. Let the Wicked forsake his Way, and the unrighteous Man his Thoughts: and let him return unto the Lord, and he will have mercy upon him, and to our God, for he will abundantly pardon.* ver. 6, 7. Surely then, we must be basely ungrateful, if we are not drawn with these cords of a man, and bands of love. While we refuse to attend this great duty, we practically despise the riches of God's goodness whereby he *leads sinners to repentance.* And this is another reason why we should engage in the work of repentance and reformation.

3. If we refuse to repent and reform, *we shall be condemned out of our own mouths, and fall under the threatned judgments of God.* One considerable part of the duty of a day of religious fasting is to make an humble and penitent confession of our sins whereby we have provoked a holy God to come out in judgment against us, and to cry to him for grace that we may turn from them. Thus 'tis said of God's people on the day of solemn fasting recorded Neh. 9. *The Seed of Israel stood and confessed their Sins, and the Iniquities of their Fathers:* 2d v. But if there be no care to put away the sins which we have confess'd, we shall give our Lord and judge reason to say to us as to the wicked servant, *Out of thine own Mouth will I judge thee.* Now this will be dreadful indeed, and must aggravate our condemnation, to be thus self-condemned; and so to fall under the righteous judgment of God. We have the proof of this written for our warning in the doleful account which the Scripture gives of the sin and punishment of God's ancient convenant people. Tho' they had their days of fasting, particularly on the seventh month, when the high priest was to make an atonement for himself and the people, and enter into the holy place within the vail, Lev. 16. Notwithstanding this, God said to his people, If ye will not

be reformed, but will walk contrary to me, then will I also walk contrary to you, and will punish you seven times for your sins. And GOD fulfilled his word. *They mocked the Messengers of God, and despised his Words, and misused his Prophets, until the Wrath of the Lord arose against his People, till there was no Remedy*, 2 Chron. 36. 16. Jerusalem and the Temple were destroyed by fire, and GOD'S people led into captivity to Babylon. And after their merciful restoration, when they had filled up the measure of their sins by disobeying and crucifying the Lord of Glory, and then by rejecting the offers of the gospel made to them by his apostles; the wrath of GOD came upon them to the uttermost by the Romans, and they are made an execration and a curse unto this day.

IV. *When a people do thus turn from their evil way to the Lord, he will repent of the evil, and not bring destruction upon them.*

GOD saw their works—and *God repented of the Evil that he had said he would do unto them, and he did it not.* Judgment is GOD'S strange work; but he delighteth in mercy. And when GOD threatens, it is with a reserve of grace and favour to the penitent. *Remember therefore from whence thou art fallen & repent, and do the first Works; or else I will come unto thee quickly, and will remove thy Candlestick out of his Place, except thou repent.* Rev. 2. 5. Thus GOD said to the prophet Jeremiah,

> *Take thee a Roll of a Book, and write therein all the Words that I have spoken unto Thee against Israel, and against all the Nations, from the Day I spake unto thee, from the Days of Josiah, even unto this Day. It may be the House of Judah will hear all the evil which I purpose to do unto them; that they may return every Man from his evil Way, that I may forgive their Iniquity and their Sin*, Jer. 36. 2, 3.

GOD knew perfectly well what they would do; but then he here lets his people know how ready he was to forgive the penitent and receive them into favour: It's true, such as repent may be afflicted in this life; but then it is with the tender compassion of a father, not with the deadly wound of an enemy. The first and purest times of Christianity were times of persecution; however, while the holy martyrs overcame by the blood of the Lamb, not loving their lives unto the death; the church was preserv'd, yea increased and multiplied. And as to a people, considering them collectively, I suppose no one instance can be produc'd in which GOD pour'd out his fury to destroy them, while a spirit of repentance and reformation prevail'd. And even in times of abounding iniquity, when the glory of GOD was departing from his people, and destroying judgments breaking in like a flood; GOD was pleased to make a remarkable distinction between the penitent, and such as were hardned in sin.

> *And the Lord said unto him, Go through the midst of the City, through the midst of Jerusalem, and set a Mark upon the Foreheads of the Men that sigh and that cry for all the Abominations that be done in the midst thereof. And to the others he said in mine hearing, Go ye after him through the City and smite: let not your Eye spare, neither have ye Pity*, Ezek. 9. 4, 5.

But the time would fail me, should I attempt to speak particularly to this head; and I have in part prevented my self by what has been already said. I shall therefore only give a few hints further to confirm & illustrate the truth before us. The faithful and true GOD *declareth this in his word.*

> *When I say unto the Wicked, Thou shalt surely die: If he turn from his sin, and do that which is lawful and right; If the Wicked restore the Pledge, give again that he had robbed, walk in the Statutes of Life, without committing Iniquity; he shall surely live, he shall not die*, Ezek. 33. 14, 15.

When Ephraim bemoan'd himself and repented, GOD manifested his fatherly compassions to him.

> *I have surely heard Ephraim bemoaning himself thus, Thou hast chastised me, and I was chastised, as a Bullock unaccustomed to the Yoke: Turn thou me, and I shall be turned; for thou art the Lord my God. Surely after that I was turned, I repented; and after that I was instructed, I smote upon my thigh: I was ashamed, yea, even confounded, because I did bear the reproach of my Youth. Is Ephraim my dear Son? Is he a pleasant Child? For since I spake against him, I do earnestly remember him still: Therefore my Bowels are troubled for him; I will surely have mercy upon him, saith the Lord.* Jer. 31. 18–20.

Again, When a people do thus turn from their evil way to the Lord, *They are prepar'd to receive and improve GOD'S merciful Deliverance after a suitable manner.* While a degenerate people are impenitent they will be ready to despise the riches of GOD'S goodness and forbearance, and to wax wanton under sparing mercy. *Jeshurun waxed fat and kicked: thou art waxen fat, thou art grown thick, thou art covered with fatness; then he forsook God which made him, and lightly esteemed the Rock of his Salvation*, Deut. 32. 15. But when sin is embitter'd by the godly sorrow which worketh repentance we shall observe that caution after GOD has spoken peace, Psal. 84. 8. *Let them not turn again to Folly.* Such a people will be jealous over themselves and for the Lord of hosts, and be concern'd to improve all his gracious appearances for them to the honour of his great name. Accordingly, GOD says of his people, How shall I put thee among the children, and give thee a pleasant land? And then returns this answer, *Thou shalt call me, My Father, and shalt not turn away from me*, Jer. 3. 19. Again, this truth is evident *from the happy experience of the penitent*. We have a remarkable instance before us. Now, did GOD spare repenting Nineveh, and will he not spare his repenting covenant-people? Yes surely,

> *If their uncircumcised Hearts be humbled, and they then accept of the punishment of their Iniquity: Then will I remember my Covenant with Jacob, and also my Covenant with Isaac, and also my Covenant with Abraham will I remember; and I will remember the Land.*

And GOD was pleas'd to fulfill his promise to his people, 1 Sam. 7. and in other instances upon record in scripture. In a word, the Lord JESUS our great high priest, has offered a sacrifice of infinite value to make atonement for the congregation of his people, whether Jews or gentiles; and he lives in heaven to interceed for them: And therefore, when GOD's people look to him and mourn and turn to the Lord, he will turn from his fierce anger, and command salvation.

APPLICATION

USE 1. Learn that *true religion lays the surest foundation of a people's prosperity. Righteousness exalteth a Nation*, Prov. 14. 34. When we turn to GOD by Jesus Christ, and do works meet for repentance; we take the best way to obtain salvation from the help of his countenance, who is the Father of Lights, from whom cometh down every good & every perfect gift. It's sin that separateth between GOD and his people: When this accursed thing is therefore put away from among them, that GOD to whom belong the issues from death, will draw nigh to them with his saving health, and appear for their deliverance.

And *if* GOD *be for us, who can be against us? There is no Wisdom nor Understanding, nor Counsel against the Lord. The Horse is prepared against the Day of Battle: But Safety is of the Lord.* Prov 21. 30, 31. Certainly then, the one thing needful is to secure the presence and favour of GOD; and this we do when we return to him in hearty repentance, and then walk before him in new obedience. Blessed is that people whose GOD is the LORD: No weapon form'd against them shall prosper, and that good word shall be fulfilled unto them, *God is our Refuge and Strength, a very present Help in Trouble*, Psal. 46. 1. and v. 5. *God is in the midst of her, she shall not be moved. God shall help her, and that right early*, O that GOD would impress on our minds the firm belief of these things! O that he would affect our hearts suitably with them! That we might strive together in our prayers this day, crying to GOD with the prophet, *O Lord, revive thy Work in the midst of the Years, in the midst of the Years make known; in Wrath remember Mercy.* Hab. 3. 2.

USE 2. *Abounding iniquity will be the destruction of a people, except they repent.* If they persist and go on in the ways of sin, refusing to return to GOD, iniquity will be their ruin. *Sin is the Reproach of any People*, Prov. 14. 34. It hath both a natural and moral tendency to lay them low, and expose them to shame. Sin in the body politick, is like some foul and deadly disease in the natural body which turns the beauty of it into corruption, and weakens all it's powers. *Why should ye be stricken any more? ye will revolt more and more: the whole Head is sick, and the whole Heart is faint. From the Sole of the Foot, even unto the Crown of the Head, there is no Soundness in it; but Wounds and Bruises, and putrifying Sores: they have not been closed, neither bound up, neither molified with Ointment*, Isa. 1. 5, 6. And then, this deadly evil provokes the holy GOD to pour contempt upon a people, and lay their honour in the dust. Thus GOD threatned his people, *Thou shalt become an Astonishment, a Proverb, and a By-word, among all Nations whither the Lord shall lead thee.* Deut. 28. 37. And in the 44th and 45th [verse:] *He shall lend to thee, and thou shalt not lend to him; he shall be the Head, and thou shalt be the Tail. Moreover all these Curses shall come upon thee, and overtake thee till thou be destroyed: Because thou hearknedst not unto the Voice of the Lord thy God, to keep his Commandments and his Statutes which he commanded thee.* And the threatning was fulfilled upon them. GOD said to his people, O Israel, Thou hast fallen by thine iniquity. And the weeping prophet laments their sins and ruin, *Jerusalem hath grievously sinned: all that honoured her, despise her, because they have seen her nakedness: yea, she sigheth, and turneth backward. Her filthiness is in her skirts, she remembreth not her last end, therefore she came down wonderfully: she had no Comforter.* Yea, after this remarkable deliverance granted to Nineveh, it's suppos'd about ninety years, when they returned to their former sins, the prophet Nahum foretells their ruin, Chap. 1.

USE 3. Let us then be sensible of the *destroying evil of sin*, and the *necessity of true repentance.*

GOD speaks to us this day as to his people of old, *Thine own wickedness shall correct thee, and thy Backslidings shall reprove thee: know therefore and see, that it is an evil thing and bitter that thou hast forsaken the Lord thy God, and that my fear is not in thee, saith the Lord God of hosts*, Jer. 2. 19. And as 44. 4. *O do not this abominable thing that I hate.* Most certainly they are guilty of great folly, who make a mock at sin. This is to cast fire-brands, arrows and death; and say, Am I not sport? The wise man observes, that *One Sinner destroyeth much Good*, Eccl. 9. 18. Thus *Achan took of the accursed Thing; and the Anger of the Lord was kindled against the Children of Israel*, Josh. 7. 1. Let us then fly from sin as the most pernicious evil, and see the necessity of our turning to the Lord by sincere repentance. O let that word of the Lord sink deep into our hearts this day! *Turn ye, turn ye, Why will ye die, O House of Israel?* Ezek. 33. 11.

Which leads me to the last use;

4. Let us all be exhorted *to turn, every one from his evil way; and to engage heartily in the necessary work of reformation.*

This, this is our great duty and interest this day, as we would hope to be made instruments in GOD'S hand of saving our selves and this people. Let us then seriously consider that we have to do with that GOD who is able to save and to destroy. And settle that word in our hearts as a certain truth, *When he giveth Quietness, who then can make Trouble? and when he hideth his Face, who then can behold him? whether it be done against a Nation, or against a Man only.* Job 34. 29. And accordingly, let us turn from all sin to the Lord, and in this way hope and wait for his salvation. O let us take heed, lest there be in any of us *an evil Heart of Unbelief in departing from the living God.* To day, let us hear his voice, and not harden our hearts. May each one of us say with Job, *Now mine Eye seeth thee: Wherefore I abhor my self, and repent in Dust and Ashes.* And as it has pleased the Father to commit all judgment to the Son; let us look to him, and encourage our selves in him whom GOD hath exalted to be a *prince and a Saviour, to give repentance to Israel, and forgiveness of sins.* May our ascended JESUS, who has receiv'd of the Father the promise of the Holy Ghost, pour out this great blessing upon the whole land, and fulfill that word,

> *Then will I sprinkle clean Water upon you, and ye shall be clean: from all your filthiness and from all your Idols will I cleanse you. A new Heart also will I give you, and a new Spirit will I put within you, and I will take away the stony Heart out of your Flesh, and I will give you an Heart of Flesh. And I will put my Spirit within you, and cause you to walk in my Statutes, and ye shall keep my Judgments, and do them. And ye shall dwell in the Land that I gave to your Fathers, and ye shall be my People, and I will be your God.* Ezek. 35. 25–28.

Blessed be the Lord, his spirit has been, we hope, moving on the hearts of many to convince and awaken them. O let us not resist and quench the spirit! lest the threatning denounc'd against the sinners of the old world, should be fulfill'd on us, *My Spirit shall not always strive with Man, for that he also is Flesh.* Gen. 6. 3. Let us cherish his motions, and pray the more earnestly that he may be given in an extensive manner as a spirit of saving conversion and thorow reformation. And surely, If we duely consider the state of this sinful, distressed people, we shall be constrain'd to say with the prophet *It is Time to seek the Lord, till he come and rain Righteousness upon you.* Hos. 10. 12. And then with our fervent prayers, let us unite our best endeavours with regard to our selves, our families, and this people; that all iniquity may be put far from us, and that we may become zealous of good works. In this way we might hope GOD would say of us as of the remnant of Judah; *Then will I build you, and not pull you down, and I will plant you, and not pluck you up: for I repent me of the evil that I have done unto you.* Or as Isa. 65. 8. *Destroy it not, for a Blessing is in it.*

But the time requireth me to draw to a close. I would therefore proceed with due respect to make a particular application of what hath been said, unto our honoured rulers, who have call'd us to sanctify a fast with them; and have set apart this day to humble themselves under the sense of sin, and the tokens of the divine displeasure upon this province.

My fathers! Suffer the word of exhortation: Let GOD see your works; that you turn from every evil way; that GOD may also repent of the evil, and not bring it upon us. For how dreadful must it be if the example of the nobles and men of Nineveh should rise up in judgment against any of you: They repented at the preaching "of one Prophet sent to them by GOD, you have Moses and the Prophets"; Yea in these last days GOD has spoken to us by his Son that prince of the prophets, who is GOD manifest in the flesh. You have the sacred writings of the New-Testament, in which GOD reveals his wrath against all ungodliness and unrighteousness of men; and also his grace and mercy to the penitent by a redeemer. And as the judge of all the earth hath advanced you to rule over his people; so he declareth to you in his word, That *they who rule over Men must be just, ruling in the Fear of GOD;* and requireth you to lead in the work of reformation by your example, and by the right use of that power with which he hath betrusted you.

This people have observ'd many days of fasting and prayer, and yet there's sorrowful occasion to make that complaint; *For all this his Anger is not turned away, but his Hand is stretched out still.* You have also in this more private way sought the Lord some years past,* confessing your sins, and the sins of this people before him; notwithstanding which, the holy and faithful GOD goeth on walking contrary to us, and threatens to punish us seven times more for our sins. What means this heat of his anger? Why do we still complain, *Judgment is far from us, neither doth Justice overtake us: we wait for Light, but behold Obscurity; for Brightness, but we walk in Darkness. We grope for the Wall like the Blind, and we grope as if we had no Eyes.* Isa. 59. 9, 10. Alas! We must take up the lamentation which follows, v. 12–14.

> *Our Transgressions are multiplied before Thee, and our Sins testify against us: for our Transgressions are with us, and as for our Iniquities, we know them: In transgressing and lying against the Lord, and departing away from our God, speaking Oppression and Revolt, conceiving and uttering from the Heart, Words of Falsehood. And Judgment is turned away backward, and Justice standeth afar off: for Truth is fallen in the Street, and Equity cannot enter.*

O it is time then, high time, heartily to engage in keeping the fast

* Decemb. 10, 1736.

which God has chosen, and we have describ'd for our instruction and reproof, Isa. 58. 6, 8.

> *Is not this the Fast that I have chosen? to loose the Bands of Wickedness, to undo the heavy Burdens, and to let the Oppressed go free, and that ye break every Yoke? Is it not to deal thy Bread to the Hungry, and that thou bring the Poor that are cast out to thy House? when thou seest the Naked, that thou cover him, and that thou hide not thy self from thine own Flesh?*

Upon this God promiseth,

> *Then shall thy Light break forth as the Morning, and thine Health shall spring forth speedily: and thy Righteousness shall go before thee; the Glory of the Lord shall be thy Reward. Then shalt thou call, and the Lord shall answer; thou shalt cry, and he shall say, Here I am.* 8, 9. v.

And 12 v[:] *They that shall be of thee, shall build the old waste Places: thou shalt raise up the Foundation of many Generations; and thou shalt be called, The Repairer of the Breach, the Restorer of Paths to dwell in.* Be intreated therefore to cry to God for grace that you may cleanse your hearts and hands from all sin, and so turn to the Lord; and then, let it be your constant care and diligent endeavour to do works meet for repentance. As God has exalted you above your brethren, let your light shine before them, that others seeing your good works may glorify your heavenly Father, and be excited to follow you. Let all that behold you, see your pious regards to God's worship and ordinances, his day and house. Do your utmost that the worship of God may be maintain'd in the power and purity of it, among this people. Let all due care be taken that men may fear this *glorious and fearful name*, the Lord our God, and not presume to take it in vain; for *because of swearing the land mourns.* Let the Lord's-day be strictly observ'd; for God hath set the Sabbath as a sign between him and his people, that he is the Lord who sanctifieth them. Let the most effectual means also be used that the great abuse of taverns may be reformed; that these be not converted into tipling and gaming houses for town-dwellers, to the dishonour of God and hurt of the common-wealth. Let the fountains of justice be kept open and pure, that judgment may run down as waters; and that such as thirst after righteousness may come freely, and be refreshed. And whereas the present difficulties which embarrass our affairs, do very much arise from the want of a suitable medium of trade, and different apprehensions in the legislature about supplying the treasury, whereby the publick debts are, in part at least, left unpaid, and the country naked and defenceless, in this day of calamity and war: I can't but humbly apprehend, that this awful frown of Providence calls aloud to you further to consider, whether there has not been great injustice and oppression with relation to the bills of publick credit which have pass'd among us, from their sinking and uncertain value; and to use your best endeavours that whatever bills shall pass for time to come in lieu of money, may be a just medium of exchange; for a *false Ballance is abomination to the Lord; but a just Weight is his Delight*, Prov. 11. 1. Whatever methods may be propos'd to extricate us out of our present distress, justice and equity must be laid in the foundation; or we may expect that the Lord who loves righteousness and hates wickedness, will confound our devices, and bring them to nought. But then, I presume not in the least measure to determine whether this or that way is right. May that GOD before whom all things are open and naked, direct Your Excellency and the whole court, into such paths of righteousness as shall lead to our deliverance and safety; that we may neither oppress one another, nor become a prey to an insulting enemy! May you be filled with the most tender and fatherly compassion for your people under the present distress and danger, and do all you can to relieve them! And if there should be a difference in your opinion about the way, may you be enabled to keep the unity of the spirit in the bond of peace, that the GOD of peace may be with you, who has promis'd to guide the meek in judgment!

But in vain is salvation hoped for from the hills, and from the multitude of mountains: Truly in the Lord our GOD is the salvation of Israel!

O GOD! We know not what to do; but our eyes are unto thee. We wait upon thee O Lord, who hidest thy self from the house of Israel; confessing that we thy servants, and thy people have sinn'd. Thy ways are equal, our ways have been very unequal. O Lord, righteousness belongeth unto thee, but unto us confusion of faces, as at this day, because we have sinned against thee. To the Lord our GOD also belongeth mercies and forgivenesses, tho' we have rebell'd against him. O Lord, hear, O Lord forgive, O Lord, hearken and do, defer not, for thine own sake, O GOD! for thy city, and thy people are called by thy name. Look to the face of thine Anointed,

> O merciful Father! Behold thy Son in our nature, who on earth offer'd a sacrifice of infinite merit to atone for the sins of thy people; and now appears in heaven, as a Lamb that had been slain, interceeding for us. We are unworthy; but the name in which we now ask thy divine help, is most worthy. O hear us, for thy Son's sake, and speak peace to thy people. Give ear, O Shepherd of Israel, thou that leadest Joseph like a flock, thou that dwellest between the cherubims, shine forth. Before Ephraim and Benjamin and Manasseh, stir up thy strength, and come and save us. Turn us again O GOD; and cause thy face to shine, and we shall be saved. O remember not against us former iniquities: let thy tender mercies speedily prevent us; for we are bro't very low. Help us, O GOD of our salvation, for the glory of thy name; and deliver us, and purge away our sins for thy name's sake: So we thy people and sheep of thy pasture, will give thee thanks for ever; we will shew forth thy praise to all generations.

And would you, our honoured rulers, to whom I again address my self, have the all-wise GOD present to shew you what his people ought to do in this very critical conjuncture, and to make you the joyful instruments of our deliverance; then abide with GOD by taking his word for your rule, by making his glory your highest end, and by seeking the public-weal in all things. Ask of GOD a public spirit, and by all means labour to subdue a vicious self-love remembring the warning given us, 2 Tim. 3. 1, 2. *In the last Days perilous Times shall come. For Men shall be lovers of their own selves, covetous.* May you have the love of GOD and his people shed abroad in your hearts by his spirit; and be ready to sacrifice private views and personal interests to the publick good! Shake your hands from bribes of every kind, and when call'd to give your vote, consider seriously what is right in the sight of GOD, with whom is *no respect of persons, or taking of gifts*; and act accordingly. And if at any time you should be tempted to this great evil, as the best of men may; set that word of GOD in opposition to the temptation.

> *He that walketh righteously, and speaketh uprightly, he that despiseth the Gain of Oppression, that shaketh his Hands from holding of Bribes, that stoppeth his Ears from hearing of Blood, and shutteth his Eyes from seeing Evil: He shall dwell on high, his Place of Defence shall be the Munition of Rocks; Bread shall be given him, his Waters shall be sure.* Isa. 33. 15, 16.

In this way you shall obtain the gracious presence of GOD with you. *The Lord is with you, while ye be with him*, 2 Chron. 15. 2. And if GOD be with you and for you, who can be against you? What can harm you? What can be too hard for you, if the Almighty is pleas'd to own you as his servants, and command deliverance for his people by you? Surely the mountains shall become a plain, crooked things straight, and the night shine as the day. Let me say to you therefore as 2 Chron. 15. 7. *Be ye strong, and let not your Hands be weak: for your Work shall be rewarded.* GOD will be your shield, and exceeding great reward. You shall see the good of GOD's chosen, rejoice with the gladness of his nation, and glory with his inheritance. And when the Son of Man shall come in his glory, and all the holy angels with him, then shall he say unto you, *Inasmuch as ye have done it unto these my Brethren, ye have done it unto me: Come ye Blessed of my Father, inherit the Kingdom.*

FINIS

— 3 —

THE ESSENTIAL RIGHTS AND LIBERTIES OF PROTESTANTS

Elisha Williams

BOSTON

1744

Elisha Williams (1694–1755). As the son of Reverend William Williams (1665–1741), a great-grandson of John Cotton and of Governor Simon Bradstreet, and the younger brother of William Williams, Jr., Elisha Williams was a member of an outstanding and devout New England family. Born in Hatfield, Massachusetts, he was graduated from Harvard in 1711, studied theology with his father, read law, preached to seamen in Nova Scotia, tutored Yale students at his home for several years (including Jonathan Edwards the elder), and, in 1722, settled as pastor of a Congregational church in Wethersfield, Connecticut. There Williams remained only four years before becoming Yale University rector, a position he held until 1739. Ezra Stiles, a future Yale president who was graduated there during Williams's tenure, called him "a good classical scholar, well versed in logic, metaphysics, and ethics, and in rhetoric and oratory [who] delivered orations gracefully and with animated dignity" (John H. Harkey, *American Writers Before 1800*).

His departure from Yale was attributed to poor health, but Williams, who had also been in the Connecticut General Assembly, served there again from 1740 to 1749. Politically ambitious, he was thought to be interested in becoming governor of Connecticut. He also served as a judge on the Connecticut Supreme Court, was a chaplain during the 1745 expedition that captured Louisbourg, was appointed colonel and commander-in-chief of forces organized to invade Canada (a plan that was abandoned), and was a delegate to the Albany Congress in 1754, which devised the first American plan of union under Benjamin Franklin's leadership.

Signed "Philalethes," *The Essential Rights and Liberties of Protestants* (1744) is Williams's most famous work. It was occasioned by a 1742 Connecticut statute prompted by Standing Order clergymen's resentment of Great Awakening revivalists. It prohibited ministers from preaching outside their own parishes, unless expressly invited to do so by resident ministers. Punishment for violating this law was deprivation of support and authorization to preach, a prohibition and punishment that Williams argued violated scripture, natural rights, the social contract, and the Toleration Act of 1688. These views had so antagonized people as to prevent his reelection to the Supreme Court in the previous year, and he was abused by both Old Lights and New Lights. But the pamphlet is a triumph of political theology and

The essential Rights and Liberties of Protestants.

A seasonable PLEA

FOR

The Liberty of Conscience,

AND

The Right of private Judgment,

In Matters of RELIGION,

Without any Controul from *human Authority.*

Being a LETTER,
From a Gentleman in the *Massachusetts-Bay* to his Friend in *Connecticut.*

WHEREIN

Some Thoughts on the Origin, End, and Extent of the *Civil Power*, with brief Considerations on several late Laws in *Connecticut*, are humbly offered.

By a Lover of TRUTH *and* LIBERTY.

Matth. xxii. 21.--- *Render unto* Cæsar *the Things which are* Cæsar's; *and unto* GOD, *the Things that are* GOD's.

" If our Purses be *Cæsar*'s, our Consciences are GOD's: ---
" and if *Cæsar's* Commands interfere with GOD's, we
" must *obey* GOD *rather than Men.* --- HENRY on the Place.

BOSTON: Printed and Sold by S. KNEELAND and T. GREEN in Queenstreet. 1744.

theory. In "Williams's dazzling assault," John Dunn has written, "Locke's notions of toleration were fused with a brilliant presentation of his theory of government, and a doctrine of startling originality appeared. . . . When the cool epistemological individualism of the scholar's closet was fused with the insistent Puritan demand for emotional autonomy, the two became transmuted into a doctrine which in the radicalism of its immediate and self-conscious social vision could not have been conceived anywhere else in the eighteenth-century world" (*Political Obligation in Its Historical Context* [Cambridge, 1980]).

Sir,

I now give you my thoughts on the questions you lately sent me. As you set me the task, you must take the performance as it is without any apology for its defects. I have wrote with the usual freedom of a friend, aiming at nothing but truth, and to express my self so as to be understood. In order to answer your main enquiry concerning the extent of the civil magistrate's power respecting religion; I suppose it needful to look back to the end, and therefore to the original of it: By which means I suppose a just notion may be formed of what is properly their business or the object of their power; and so without any insuperable difficulty we may thence learn what is out of that compass.

That the sacred scriptures are the alone rule of faith and practice to a Christian, all Protestants are agreed in; and must therefore inviolably maintain, that every Christian has *a right of judging for himself* what he is to believe and practice in religion according to that rule: Which I think on a full examination you will find perfectly inconsistent with any power in the civil magistrate to make any penal laws in matters of religion. Tho' Protestants are agreed in the profession of that principle, yet too many in practice have departed from it. The evils that have been introduced thereby into the Christian church are more than can be reckoned up. Because of the great importance of it to the Christian and to his standing fast in that liberty wherewith CHRIST has made him free, you will not fault me if I am the longer upon it. The more firmly this is established in our minds; the more firm shall we be against all attempts upon our Christian liberty, and better practice that Christian charity towards such as are of different sentiments from us in religion that is so much recommended and inculcated in those sacred oracles, and which a just understanding of our Christian rights has a natural tendency to influence us to. And tho' your sentiments about some of those points you demand my thoughts upon may have been different from mine; yet I perswade my self, you will not think mine to be far from the truth when you shall have throughly weighed what follows. But if I am mistaken in the grounds I proceed upon or in any conclusion drawn from true premises, I shall be thankful to have the same pointed out: Truth being what I seek, to which all must bow first or last.

To proceed then as I have just hinted, I shall first, briefly consider *the Origin and End of Civil Government.*

First, as to the origin—Reason teaches us that all men are naturally equal in respect of jurisdiction or dominion one over another. Altho' true it is that children are not born in this full state of equality, yet they are born to it. Their parents have a sort of rule & jurisdiction over them when they come into the world, and for some time after: But it is but a temporary one; which arises from that duty incumbent on them to take care of their offspring during the imperfect state of childhood, to preserve, nourish and educate them (as the workmanship of their own almighty Maker, to whom they are to be accountable for them), and govern the actions of their yet ignorant nonage, 'till reason shall take its place and ease them of that trouble. For GOD having given man an understanding to direct his actions, has given him therewith a freedom of will and liberty of acting, as properly belonging thereto, within the bounds of that law he is under: And whilst he is in a state wherein he has no understanding of his own to direct his will, he is not to have any will of his own to follow: He that understands for him must will for him too. But when he comes to such a state of reason as made the father free, the same must make the son free too: For the freedom of man and liberty of acting according to his own will (without being subject to the will of another) is grounded on his having reason, which is able to instruct him in that law he is to govern himself by, and make him know how far he is left to the freedom of his own will. So that we are born free as we are born rational. Not that we have actually the exercise of either as soon as born; age that brings one, brings the other too. This natural freedom is not a liberty for every one to do what he pleases without any regard to any law; for a rational creature cannot but be made under a law from its Maker: But it consists in a freedom from any *superiour power on earth*, and not being under the will or legislative authority of man, and having only the law of nature (or in other words, of its Maker) for his rule.

And as reason tells us, all are born thus naturally equal, i.e. with an equal right to their persons; so also with an equal right to their preservation; and therefore to such things as nature affords for their subsistence. For which purpose GOD was pleased to make a grant of the earth in common to the children of men, first to Adam and afterwards to Noah and his sons: as the Psalmist says, Psal. 115. 16. And altho' no one has originally a private dominion exclusive of the rest of mankind in the earth or its products, as they are consider'd in this their natural state; yet since GOD has given these things for the use of men and given them reason also to make use thereof to the best advantage of life; there must of necessity be a means to appropriate them some way or other, before they can be of any use to any particular person. And every man having a property in his own person, the *labour of his body and the work of his hands* are properly his own, to which no one has right but himself; it will therefore follow that when he removes any thing out of the state that nature has provided and left it in, he has mixed his labour with it and joined something to it that is his own, and thereby makes it his property. He having removed it out of the common state nature placed it in, it hath by this labour something annexed to it that excludes the common right of others; because this labour being the unquestionable property of the labourer, no man but he can have a right to what that is once joined to, at least where there is enough and as good left in common for others. Thus every man having a natural right to (or being the proprietor of) his own person and his own actions and labour and to what he can honestly acquire by his labour, which we call property; it certainly follows, that no man can have a right to the person or property of another: And if every man has a right to his person and property; he has also a right to defend them, and a right to all the *necessary means of defence*, and so has a right of punishing all insults upon his person and property.

But because in *such a state of nature*, every man must be judge of the breach of the law of nature and executioner too (even in his own case) and the greater part being no strict observers of equity and justice; the enjoyment of property in this state is not very safe. Three things are wanting in this state (as the celebrated Lock observes) to render them safe; *viz.* an established known law received and allowed by common consent to be the standard of right and wrong, the common measure to decide all controversies between them: For tho' the law of nature be intelligible to all rational creatures; yet men being biassed by their interest as well as ignorant for want of the study of it, are not apt to allow of it as a law binding to them in the application of it to their particular cases. There wants also a *known and indifferent judge* with authority to determine all differences according to the established law: for men are too apt to be partial to themselves, and too much wanting in a just concern for the interest of others. There often wants also in a state of nature, *a power to back and support the sentence* when right, and give it due execution. Now to remedy these inconveniencies, reason teaches men to join in society, to unite together into a commonwealth under some form or other, to make a body of laws agreable to the law of nature, and institute one common power to see them observed. It is they who thus unite together, *viz.* the people, who make and alone have right to make the laws that are to take place among them; or which comes to the same thing, appoint those who shall make them, and who shall see them executed. For every man has an equal right to the preservation of his person and property; and so an equal right to establish a law, or to nominate the makers and executors of the laws which are the guardians both of person and property.

Hence then the fountain and original of all civil power is from the people, and is certainly instituted for their sakes; or in other words, which was the second thing proposed, *The great end of civil government, is the preservation of their persons, their liberties and estates, or their property.* Most certain it is, that it must be for their own sakes, the rendering their condition better than it was in what is called a state of nature (a state without such establish'd laws as before mentioned, or without any common power) that men would willingly put themselves out of that state. It is nothing but their own good can be any rational inducement to it: and to suppose they either should or would do it on any other, is to suppose rational creatures ought to change their state with a design to make it worse. And that good which in such a state they find a need of, is no other than a *greater security of enjoyment of what belonged to them.* That and that only can then be the true reason of their uniting together in some form or other they judge best for the obtaining that greater security. That greater security therefore of life, liberty, money, lands, houses, family, and the like, which may be all comprehended under that of person and property, is the sole end of all civil government. I mean not that all civil governments (as so called) are thus constituted: (tho' the British and some few other nations are through a merciful Providence so happy as to have such). There are too too many arbitrary governments in the world, where the people don't make their own laws. These are not properly speaking governments but tyrannies; and are absolutely against the law of GOD and nature. But I am considering things as they be in their own nature, what reason teaches concerning them: and herein have given a short sketch of what the celebrated Mr. Lock in his *Treatise of Government* has largely demonstrated; and in which it is justly to be presumed all are agreed who understand the natural rights of mankind.

Thus having seen what the end of civil government is; I suppose we see a fair foundation laid for the determination of the next thing I proposed to consider: Which is, *What liberty or power belonging to man as he is a reasonable creature does every man give up to the civil government whereof he is a member.* Some part of their natural liberty they do certainly give up to the government, for the benefit of society and mutual defence (for in a political society every one even an infant has the whole force of the community to protect him), and something therefore is certainly given up to the whole for this purpose. Now the way to know what branches of natural liberty are given up, and what remain to us after our admission into civil society, is to consider the ends for which men enter into a state of government. For so much liberty and no more is departed from, as is necessary to secure those ends; the rest is certainly our own still. And here I suppose with the before-mentioned noble assertor of the liberties of humane nature; *all that is given up* may be reduced to two heads.

1st. The power that every one has in a state of nature *to do whatever he judgeth fit*, for the preservation of his person and property and that of others also, within the permission of the law of nature, he gives up to be regulated by laws made by the society, so far forth as the preservation of himself (his person and property) and the rest of that society shall require.

And, 2. The power of punishing he wholly gives up, and engages his natural force (which he might before employ in the execution of the law of nature by his own single authority as he thought fit) to assist the executive power of the society as the law thereof shall require. For (he adds) being now in a new state wherein he is to enjoy many conveniencies, from the labour assistance and society of others in the same community, as well as protection from its whole strength; he is to part also with as much of his natural liberty and providing for himself, as the good and safety of the society shall require; which is not only necessary but just, since the other members of the society do the like. Now if the giving up these powers be sufficient to answer those ends for which men enter into a state of government, *viz.* the better security of their persons and properties; then no more is parted with; and therefore all the rest is ours still. This I rest on as certain, *that no more natural liberty or power is given up than is necessary for the preservation of person and property.*

I design not to mention many particulars which according to this rule I suppose are not parted with by entering into a state of government: what is reducible to one or two general heads is sufficient to our present purpose. Tho' as I pass I cannot forbear taking notice of *one point of liberty* which all members of a free state and particularly Englishmen think belonging to them, and are fond of; and that is the right that every one has *to speak his sentiments openly concerning such matters as affect the good of the whole.* Every member of a community ought to be concerned for the whole, as well as for his particular part: His life and all, as to this world is as it were embarked in the same bottom, and is perpetually interested in the good or ill success thereof: Whenever therefore he sees a rock on which there is a probability the vessel may split, or if he sees a sand that may swallow it up, or if he foresees a storm that is like to arise; his own interest is too deeply concerned not to give notice of the danger: And the right he has to his own life and property gives him a right to speak his sentiments. If the pilot or captain don't think fit to take any notice of it, yet it seems to be certain they have no right to stop the mouth of him who thinks he espys danger to the whole ships crew, or to punish the well-meaning informer. A man would scarce deserve the character of a *good member of society* who should receive to be silent on all occasions, and never mind, speak or guard against the follies or ignorance of mistakes of those at the helm. And government rather incourages than takes away a liberty, the use of which is so needful and often very beneficial to the whole, as experience has abundantly shown.

But not to detain you here,

I. The members of a civil state or society do retain their natural liberty *in all such cases* as have no relation to the ends of such a society. In a state of nature men had a right to read Milton or Lock for their instruction or amusement: and why they do not retain this liberty under a government that is instituted for the preservation of their persons and properties, is inconceivable. From whence can such a society derive any right to hinder them from doing that which does not affect the ends of that society? Should a government therefore restrain the free use of the scriptures, prohibit men the reading of them, and make it penal to examine and search them; it would be a manifest usurpation upon the common rights of mankind, as much a violation of natural liberty as the attack of a highwayman upon the road can be upon our civil rights. And indeed with respect to the sacred writings, men might not only read them if the government did prohibit the same, but they would be bound by a higher authority to read them, notwithstanding any humane prohibition. The pretence of any authority to restrain men from reading the same, is wicked as well as vain. But whether in some cases that have no relation to the ends of government and wherein therefore men retain their natural liberty; if the civil authority should attempt by a law to restrain men, people might not be oblig'd to submit therein, is not here at all the question: tho' I suppose that in such case wherein they ought to submit, the obligation thereto would arise from some other consideration, and not from the supposed law; there being no binding force in a law where a rightful authority to make the same is wanting.

II. The members of a civil state *do retain their natural liberty or right of judging for themselves in matters of religion.* Every man has an equal right to follow the dictates of his own conscience in the affairs of religion. Every one is under an indispensable obligation to search the scripture for himself (which contains the whole of it) and to make the best use of it he can for his own information in the will of GOD, the nature and duties of Christianity. And as every Christian is so bound; so he has an unalienable right to judge of the sense and meaning of it, and to follow his judgment wherever it leads him; even an equal right with any rulers be they civil or ecclesiastical. This I say, I take to be an original right of the humane nature, and so far from being given up by the individuals of a community that it cannot be given up by them if they should be so weak as to offer it. Man by his constitution as he is a reasonable being capable of the knowledge of his Maker; is a moral & accountable being: and therefore as every one is accountable for himself, he must reason, judge and determine for himself. That faith and practice which depends on the judgment and choice of any other person, and not on the person's own understanding judgment and choice, may pass for religion in the synagogue of Satan, whose tenet is that ignorance is the mother of devotion; but with no understanding Protestant will it pass for any religion at all. No action is a religious action without understanding and choice in the agent. Whence it follows, the rights of conscience are sacred and equal in all, and strictly speaking unalienable. This *right of judging every one for himself in matters of religion* results from the nature of man, and is so inseperably connected therewith, that a man can no more part with it than he can with his power of thinking: and it is equally reasonable for him to attempt to strip himself of the power of reasoning, as to attempt the vesting of another with this right. And whoever invades this right of another, be he pope or Cæsar, may with equal reason assume the other's power of thinking, and so level him with the brutal creation. A man may alienate some branches of his property and give up his right in them to others; but he cannot transfer the rights of conscience, unless he could destroy his rational and moral powers, or substitute some other to be judged for him at the tribunal of GOD.

But what may further clear this point and at the same time shew the extent of this right of private judgment in matters of religion, is this truth, That the sacred scriptures are the alone rule of faith and practice to every individual Christian. Were it needful I might easily show, the sacred scriptures have all the characters necessary to constitute a just and proper rule of faith and practice, and that they alone have them. It is sufficient for all such as acknowledge the divine authority of the scriptures, briefly to observe, that GOD the author has therein declared he has given and designed them to be our only rule of faith and practice. Thus says the apostle Paul, 2 Tim. 3. 15, 16; That *they are given by Inspiration from GOD, and are profitable for Doctrine, for Reproof, for Correction, for Instruction in Righteousness; that the Man of GOD may be perfect, thoroughly furnished unto every good Work.* So the apostle John in his gospel, Chap. 20. ver. 31. says; *These Things are written that ye might believe that JESUS is the CHRIST, the Son of GOD, and that believing ye might have Life through his Name.* And in his first epistle, Chap. 5. ver. 13. *These Things have I written, that ye may know that ye have eternal Life, and that ye may believe on the Name of the Son of God.* These passages show that what was written was to be the standing rule of faith and practice, compleat and most sufficient for such an end, designed by infinite wisdom in the giving them, containing every thing needful to be known and done by Christians, or such as believe on the name of the Son of GOD. Now inasmuch as the scriptures are the only rule of faith and practice to a Christian; hence every one has an unalienable right to read, enquire into, and impartially judge of the sense and meaning of it for himself. For if he is to be governed and determined therein by the opinions and determinations of any others, the scriptures cease to be a rule to him, and those opinions or determinations of others are substituted in the room thereof. But you will say, *The Priest's Lips should keep Knowledge, and they should seek the Law at his Mouth*, Mal. 2. 7. Yes; that is, it is their duty to explain the scriptures, and the people's duty at the same time to search the scriptures to see whether those things they say are so. Acts 17. 11. The officers CHRIST has commissioned in his church, as pastors or bishops, are to teach his laws, to explain as they are able the mind & will of CHRIST laid down in the scriptures; but they have no warrant to make any laws for them, nor are their sentiments the rule to any Christian, who are *all commanded to prove all Things, to try the Spirits whether they be of* GOD. 1 Thes. 5. 21. 1 Joh. 4. 1. *I speak as to wise Men*, says Paul, *judge ye what I say*, 1 Cor. 10. 15. These and many other texts I might have alledg'd, entirely answer the objection, and establish the point before us.

The evidence of the point before us arises out of the nature of a *rule of faith and practice*. For a rule of faith and practice is certainly that from which we must take and rectify all our conceptions, and by which we ought to regulate all our actions, concerning all those matters to which this rule relates. As it is the rule of our faith, we must receive no doctrines but what that contains: otherwise our faith is not directed by that rule; but other things in that case are taken up and believed for truths which that rule takes no notice of; and therefore it is done on some other authority, which in reality therefore becomes our rule, instead of that which of right ought to be so. A rule, considered as such, is a measure or director with which a thing is to be compared and made to agree: And therefore a rule of faith and practice is that which being applied to our minds directs and regulates them, by informing the understanding and guiding the will, and so influencing all our actions. That which is the rule of our faith must point out to us and teach us the several doctrines and inform us of the several facts which we are to believe: And if we have entertained any wrong notions or erroneous opinions, they are to be corrected and regulated, by being compared and made to agree with this rule. So also the rule of our practice is that from which we are to learn the several duties we are to perform, and how all our actions are to be regulated. 'Tis the nature of a rule of faith and practice to include all this. That whereby men examine into the truth of any thing, is to them the rule of truth; that from whence they learn what they ought to believe, is to them the rule of faith; and that to which they conform their actions, is their rule of practice. If men receive the doctrines prescribed to them by the pope, by a council, by a convocation or a parliament, from the writings of fathers, or any doctors of learning and reputation, and conform their actions to the dictates and commands of any of these or such like authorities; the authority to which they give this honour, is undoubtedly the rule of their faith and practice. And so if we submit our selves truly and impartially to the authority of CHRIST, and search for the truths we are to believe, and the duties we are to perform in his written word; then only do we make him our director and guide, and the scriptures the rule of our faith and practice. And it is the sacred scriptures alone which have this right to our intire submission, as now described: and no other authority which has yet been or ever shall be set up, has any manner of right at all to govern and direct our consciences in religious matters.

This is a truth of too great importance for a Christian ever in any measure to give up; and is so clear and obvious a truth, as may well pass for a self-evident maxim, *That a Christian is to receive his Christianity from CHRIST alone*. For what is it which is necessarily implied and supposed in the very notion of a Christian but this, that he is a follower and disciple of CHRIST, one who receives and professes to believe his doctrines as true, and submits to his commands? And so far only as any does this, is he a Christian: and so far therefore as he receives or admits any other doctrines or laws, is he to be denominated from that person or sect, from whose authority or instruction he receives them.

Every society ought to be subject only to its own proper legislature. The truth of this is evident at the first view; and civil societies readily adhere to this as an inviolable principle. And this holds equally true with respect to religious or civil societies; and therefore as in the church of CHRIST no other power or authority may be admitted but that of CHRIST alone; so no laws may be made for, or any doctrines be taught and enjoined upon the church of CHRIST besides those he has made and taught and enjoined. The laws of England are what the legislature of England has passed into laws; not what any other power or authority institute or teach under that name. And what these are, cannot be known from any other but the law makers, by the publications they have made and authorized. The doctrines of the church of Rome (if that by a figure may be called so) are such as that church and its legislature assert and own. So the doctrines or religion of CHRIST, is only that which he has appointed and taught, and all that is contained in scripture: every thing else is of men only, and no part of the Christian religion. What is taught by any established church, and not contained in scripture, is indeed the doctrine of that church, but not of CHRIST: For none can make laws to oblige the church of CHRIST but CHRIST himself. The church of CHRIST as such, must receive its laws from CHRIST only; *i.e.*, from the scriptures: for they are to be found no where else. The Christian religion is that which CHRIST has taught; and therefore what he has not taught, but some other person, is not the Christian religion. So also the church of CHRIST is that which is founded according to the directions and model by him laid down. That therefore which is not so founded, but upon principles and regulations laid down by men, is so far not a church of CHRIST, but of men: And in all these things the scriptures only can be our rule. For we cannot know what CHRIST teaches and commands, from what he does not say, and what is said only by some other person, but it must be from what he does teach and command; and all that is contained in his word.

Again, if CHRIST be the Lord of the conscience, the sole King in his own kingdom; then it will follow, that all such as in any manner or degree assume the power of directing and governing the consciences of men, are justly chargeable with invading his rightful dominion; He alone having the right they claim. Should the king of France take it into his head to prescribe laws to the subjects of the king of Great Britain; who would not say, it was an invasion of and insult offer'd to the British legislature.

I might also add, that for any to assume the power of directing the consciences of men, not leaving them to the scriptures alone, is evidently a declaring them to be defective and insufficient to that purpose; and therefore that our LORD who has left us the scriptures for that purpose, did not know what was necessary and sufficient for us, and has given us a law, the defects of which were to be supplied by the wisdom of some of his own wiser disciples. How high an impeachment this is of his infinite wisdom, such would do well to consider, who impose their own doctrines, interpretations or decisions upon any men by punishments, legal incapacities, or any other methods besides those used and directed to in the sacred scriptures.

And as all imposers on men's consciences are guilty of rebellion against GOD and CHRIST, of manifest disobedience to and contempt of their authority and commands; so all they who submit their consciences to any such unjust usurp'd authority, besides the share which such persons necessarily have in the guilt of the usurpers, as countenancing and giving in to their illegal claim and supporting their wicked pretensions, they do likewise renounce subjection to the authority and laws of CHRIST. To submit our consciences to the guidance of any man or order of men, is not to reason and act according to our own understanding; but to take every thing for true, that our spiritual guide affirms to be so, and that meerly upon his authority, without examining into, or seeing the truth and reasonableness of it: And in every instance wherein we thus submit our selves to the direction of any humane authority, so far we set aside and renounce all other authority, our own light and reason, and even the word of GOD and CHRIST: And the authority of the guide we subject our selves unto is substituted in the stead of all these. If we must be directed and governed by any humane power, it concerns us not what any other may teach and command; this the being subject to a power necessarily supposes and includes. An Englishman is subject to the crown and laws of England, and has nothing to do with the laws and courts of judicature in France or Spain, or any other state, but disowns and renounces all obedience thereto. This is a universal rule: And therefore if our consciences are under the direction of any humane authority as to religious matters; they cease to be under the direction of CHRIST. What CHRIST himself has told us is infallibly true, that *no Man can serve two Masters, but he must unavoidably prefer the one and neglect the other:* And consequently whoever looks upon himself to be under the direction and government of any humane power in matters of religion, does thereby renounce the authority of CHRIST, and withdraw obedience from him.

From these principles, we have here laid down, which can't but be held as indubitably true by every consistent Protestant, these corollaries may be deduced.

I. That the civil authority hath no power to make or ordain articles of faith, creeds, forms of worship or church government. This I think evidently follows from what has been said, that they can have no power to decree any articles of faith. For these are already established by CHRIST himself; and for mortals to pretend any right of determination what others shall believe, is really to usurp that authority which belongs to CHRIST the supream king and head of his church; who only hath and can have a right to prescribe to the consciences of men, as is evident from the last foregoing head. So it also follows, that they have no power to decree rites and ceremonies in religion, or forms of divine worship: And this not only because these things have no relation to the ends of civil society; it no ways concerns the common-wealth or any member of it, whether men pray kneeling or standing, whether the sign of the cross be used or omitted in baptism, that this or the other ceremony be made use of in the church; but also because this is already sufficiently done by CHRIST in the sacred scriptures. These contain every thing needful to be known or done by Christians. It is CHRIST'S sole prerogative to institute the whole and every part of religious worship. Who can tell what homage will be pleasing to GOD but he himself? Or in what way the creature shall attend upon him for the obtainment of any spiritual blessing but he himself? Can a creature connect a divine blessing with any of its own invented methods of worship? Or oblige him to be pleased or displeased in any other way, or upon any other terms, but those himself has made and proposed, and which are all manifestly contained in the scriptures?

Objection, if it should be here objected, "That although CHRIST has instituted every part of religious worship; yet the particular mode or manner wherein some of those acts are to be attended he has not specially pointed out, which therefore must be determined in order to perform the instituted act of worship: And why therefore may not the civil Authority determine such modes of worship as well as ecclesiastical rulers?"

I know very well, some are fond of that notion, that the church (by which they mean the church officers or ecclesiastical rulers in some form or other consider'd and acting) has power to decree rites and ceremonies in religion: and I am as willing for the present to allow the civil authority has as much power to do it, as those ecclesiastical rulers; because for any thing I can tell at present, my neck might be as easy under the usurpation of a civil ruler, as an ecclesiastical one: But neither of 'em have any power of determining in the case supposed.

As to ecclesiastical rulers, CHRIST has precisely bounded their authority. They are to do what he has bid them, they are to open and explain their Lord's will to others, or in a word to teach men CHRIST'S laws. For this I appeal to their commission, Math. 28. 20. And as this bounds their authority on the one side, so it draws the line or bound of submission on the other. When they teach us the mind and will of CHRIST our common lord and master; we are to hearken with deference to them: but if they get out of that line, and teach (or decree, I care not what you call it) some thing that is not his will, something to be necessary for me to do in religion which CHRIST has not made so; no regard is due to them therein. And I suppose I may venture to say, no one ceremony in religion or modality of any act of instituted worship, that has been devised and decreed by any since the apostles days as necessary, exclusive of any other, either was or is really necessary for a Christian to do in attending these acts of religion or parts of instituted worship: At least I know of no one: to be sure such as have been the subjects of debate between the Church of England on the one side and the dissenters from that establishment on the other; are unnecessary. The decreeing such unnecessary modalities of religion therefore is without any warrant from CHRIST: They teach therein what he has not commanded them, and no Christian is bound to regard them therein.

But that the objection may have a full and clear answer, I offer a few words farther. The objection supposes, that the mode of performing some acts of instituted worship is not determined by

CHRIST, which must therefore be determined by man in order to perform such acts of worship.

To which I say,

1. If there be several modes wherein such act or acts of instituted worship may be performed, man may not determine the one exclusive of the other; and if there be but one mode wherein it can be attended, there is indeed no occasion for a determination upon it, all must of necessity agree in such a mode of performing it. But in the former case, no determination may be made that it shall be performed only after such a particular mode, when it may be performed after another manner as well. As for instance, public prayer may be performed either standing or kneeling: it being supposed that CHRIST has not determined the one mode or the other; in such case man may not determine that it shall be performed only standing, or only kneeling; the worshippers must be left to their liberty as CHRIST has left it: For it being the only reason why man may determine any thing relating to an act of religion or divine worship, *viz.* the necessity of such a determination in order to the obeying a law of CHRIST; then it is certain, where that necessity is not found (as in the present case) there no such exclusive determination may be made. In these matters of divine worship, CHRIST'S officers have nothing to do but to teach CHRIST'S laws; and Christians nothing else but to obey CHRIST'S laws. It is therefore certain, that if all CHRIST'S laws relating thereto may be observed, without the determination of this or the other ceremony or mode of attending them; then the determination of this or the other ceremony as a rule of action for Christians, falls not within the compass of the power of man or any order of men. And I think the keeping to this rule alone, that man's power in these matters extends no farther than to a determination of those things necessary to be determined in order to the performing of CHRIST'S commands, is the only way to preserve CHRIST'S worship in its purity. Certain it is, that the going beyond it has sadly polluted it, and occasioned divisions and abundance of sinful strife.

2. In such cases where any thing is necessary to be determined in order to any worshipping assembly's obeying CHRIST'S laws, the power of such determination lies with such worshipping assembly. It is a law of CHRIST, that he be worshipped in publick assembly on the first day of the week; which can't be done unless some place & hour

of the day be fixed upon for that purpose. If CHRIST had determined where and when the worshipping assembly should meet, man could not determine any thing in the matter: But since CHRIST has not; time & place must be determined by man; else CHRIST'S law in that case could not be obeyed. And because that law must be obeyed, and can't be obeyed without such a determination of time & place; therefore it is, that man may determine them, and is warranted to do it. And every worshipping assembly best knowing their own particular circumstances, and being best able to judge what may be convenient or inconvenient in the case, are won't to fix time and place for the purpose: And who has right to intermeddle in the matter without their desire or consent, I can't imagine. This is a right our worshipping assemblies claim, and I know not that any call it in question. Now altho' in this instance, wherein something falls necessarily under the determination of man in order to Christians obeying a law of CHRIST, no ceremony or mode of worship is concerned; yet as I apprehend there is greater reason why every worshipping assembly should be left free in an uninterrupted enjoyment of this right to determine the mode of any act of worship (undetermined by Christ) where there is a necessity of such a determination in order to obey his laws: and that because conscience is immediately concerned therein. As I have said before, I know not of such a case. Yet if Christians do apprehend there is any necessity, every worshipping assembly must in that case determine for themselves. They may be under a great mistake in determining that to be necessary which may not be so: but herein I think no others have a power to determine for them. Not the civil authority: for the reason before given, *viz.* That the ceremony or particular mode of performing an act of divine worship, has no relation to the ends of a civil society: The preservation of person or property, no ways requires the giving up this liberty into the hand of the civil magistrate. This therefore must remain in the individuals. The civil interest of a state is no more affected, by kneeling or standing in prayer, than by praying with the eyes shut or open; or by making the figure of a triangle or a cross upon a person in baptism, than by making no figure at all. They have indeed none of them any relation to the ends of a civil institution. The civil authority therefore have no business with it. Nor have the ecclesiastical officers authority to determine in these cases for particular Christians; because it is not within their commission. We have seen before how their authority is limited, and what is the bound of submission from particular Christians. As they are CHRIST'S officers, they have authority to teach men his mind in things pertaining to his kingdom. So they have no authority to teach men any thing but the mind and will of CHRIST. It is a truth that shines with a meridian brightness, that whatever is not contained in a commission is out of it and excluded by it; and the teaching his laws only being contained in the commission, what is not his law is out of it and by that commission they are excluded from teaching it, or forbid by it. The power then of determining in these cases before us, must lie with *every distinct worshipping assembly*; I don't mean exclusive of their pastor but with him. And this I think is evident from the right of private judgment that every Christian has in matters of religion. We have seen evidently that the sacred scriptures are the rule of faith and practice to every Christian; from thence each one is bound to learn what that worship is which Christ requires from him, and in what manner he is to perform it: And therein is every one to be perswaded in his own mind. In all the worship he pays to GOD he is bound to act understandingly; which he can't be said to do if he does not understand for himself, and perform it in such a manner as he judges most agreeable to the mind of Christ, and so most acceptable to him. If another person sees for him, it will be but a blind service that he will yield. *Every one must give account of himself to GOD*, to whom alone as his only master he is to stand or fall: And it will be but a poor account the papist will have to give of all his ceremonious worship, that the pope or priest directed him so. How much farther will it go in that day to say, the king, or parliament, or convocation directed me to pay such or such a kind of worship.

But the last thing included in this corollary is, that civil rulers have no authority to determine for Christians the *form of church government:* and that for the reasons before given, *viz.* Because this would be going beside the end of civil government, and because this is already done by Christ. If his Word be a compleat rule of faith and practice to the Christian; it surely contains sufficient instruction in the nature of a church; what kinds of officers Christ has instituted, what their work and business is; what the rights and priviledges of the church are, and on what terms to be enjoyed; what the discipline thereof is, and how it is to be administred. For that which is the rule of faith and practice to a Christian (as he is a subject of Christ) must certainly be the measure of his faith and practice: For that certainly cannot be the measure of his faith and practice which contains any thing more or less than he ought to believe and practice. Christ is the head of his church, a king in his own kingdom; a part of whose royalty it is to give laws to his subjects; these are contained in the sacred scriptures, which are open to all for the learning and understanding of them. And so far are men from having any power of instituting or forming a church for Christ, that it is their greatest honour to be servants in the house of GOD. Heb. 3. 5. This being truth, that Christ has shown us what his will is touching the ordering of his house in the sacred scriptures; it then follows, that none either pope or Cæsar, can have any authority to prescribe to Christians how it shall be order'd, to form the model or any part of it.

II. The next corollary I shall deduce from the principles before laid down, is, That the civil authority have no power to establish any religion (*i.e.* any professions of faith, modes of worship, or church government) of a human form and composition, as a rule binding to Christians; much less may they do this on any penalties whatsoever. Religion must remain on that foot where Christ has placed it. He has fully declared his mind as to what Christians are to believe and do in all religious matters: And that right of private judgment belonging to every Christian evidenced in the preceeding pages, necessarily supposes it is every one's duty, priviledge and right to *search the sacred writings* as Christ has bid him, and know and judge for himself what the mind and will of his only Lord and master is in these matters. It does, I think, from hence follow, that no order of men have any right to establish any mode of worship, &c. as a rule binding to particular Christians. For if they may, then Christians are abridg'd or rather striped of their right, which is to involve our selves in a contradiction. For if *A* has a right to judge for himself what his master's will is, then *B* can have no right to impose his own sentiments concerning that master's will as a rule for *A*. For to suppose *A* has a right, which *B* has a right to take from him, is to suppose *A* has no right at all; which is a direct inconsistency. And to suppose *B* in such case has a right to punish *A* for not receiving his establishment, is but to increase the absurdity.

But here you will say, "Tho' they have no authority to establish a religion of their own devising, yet have they not authority *to establish a pure religion* drawn out of the sacred scriptures, either by themselves or some synodical assemblies, and oblige their subjects upon (at least) negative penalties to receive the same[?]" This I shall endeavour fairly to consider when I have observed, that if by the word *establish* be meant only an approbation of certain articles of faith and modes of worship, of government, or recommendation of them to their subjects; I am not arguing against it. But to carry the notion of a religious establishment so far as to make it a rule binding to the subjects, or on any penalties whatsoever, seems to me to be oppressive of Christianity, to break in upon the sacred rights of conscience, and the common rights and priviledges of all good subjects. For let it be supposed as now pleaded, that the clergy or a synodical assembly draw up the articles and form of religion, agreeable in their judgment to the sacred scriptures, and the reception of the same be made binding by the civil authority on their subjects; It will then follow, *That all such establishments are certainly right and agreeable to the sacred scriptures.* For it is impossible to be true that any can have right or authority to oblige Christians to believe or practice any thing in religion not true or not agreeable to the word of GOD: Because that would destroy the sacred scriptures from being the only rule of faith and practice in religion to a Christian. If the sacred scriptures are his rule of faith and practice, he is oblig'd and that by GOD himself, to believe and practice accordingly. No man therefore, or order of men can have any right or power to oblige the Christian to believe or do any thing in religion contrary to, or different from, what GOD has obliged him: The position of the one is the removal of the other. This then is certain, that if this proposition be true, that a humane religious establishment is a rule binding to Christians, or that the civil authority have power to oblige their subjects to receive them; then *they are always right and agreeable to GOD'S word*; but the latter is not true; therefore the proposition is false. Humane establishments in matters of religion, carry in them no force or evidence of truth. They who make them are no ways exempt from humane frailties and imperfections: They are as liable to error and mistake, to prejudice and passion, as any others. And that they have erred in their determinations, and decreed and established light to be darkness, & darkness to be light, that they have perplexed the consciences of men, and corrupted the simplicity of the faith in CHRIST, many councils and synods and assemblies of state are a notorious proof. King Henry the 8th's Parliament and convocation, who established the famous six bloody Articles of Religion in the year 1540, had as much right or power to make a religious establishment binding to the subjects, as any king and parliament since. If therefore the civil authority has a power to make a religious establishment binding to the subjects; those six articles were true, tho' they contained abominable absurdities, and amazing falshoods; and the people were obliged to believe them, and those who suffered for disbelieving them suffered justly.

Perhaps you will here say; "Altho' they have no authority to make an establishment contrary to scripture; yet why may they not have authority to make an establishment agreable to the scriptures, that shall be a binding rule to Christians, without the supposition of that proposition's being liable to such an inference from it (which I have made) *viz.* That then their establishments are certainly right and agreeable to scripture, or in other words that they who make them must be supposed to be vested with infallibility[?]" I will give then a reason, if what already said does not satisfy. Let us then have but a clear and determinate idea of the subject we are speaking of; and I think you will find the conclusion certain. This religious establishment that has this binding force in it, is either in the very words of the scriptures themselves; or in *propositions formed by this body of men* we are speaking of, which in their judgment contain the true sense and meaning of the scripture. There can be no other sense put upon it. The former of these can't be meant; for that is the scripture it self which I am pleading is the alone rule in the case before us: Besides 'tis a vanity to talk of mortals making the constitutions of GOD Almighty to become a binding rule to Christians. So that the point before us comes to this proposition, *viz.* That the civil authority have power to make such a religious establishment which they think is agreeable to scripture, a binding rule to Christians. Then it follows, that what they think to be the sense of the scriptures, is the rule for the Christian: for that what they so lay down for the sense of the scriptures should be a rule binding to Christians, and that yet what they think is the sense and meaning of the scripture, is not the rule for a Christian, is a contradiction. It follows also, that what they think to be the true sense of scripture, is certainly the true sense of it: For to suppose, that what they lay down for the sense and meaning of the sacred scriptures, is a binding rule to Christians, and that yet the same is *not the true sense* of scripture, is a contradiction; unless that proposition be false, that the sacred scriptures are the alone rule of faith and practice to a Christian, which is a sacred maxim with every true Protestant. So that if a religious establishment which they think to be agreeable to scripture is a binding rule to a Christian; it is the true sense of scripture, and the supposal that they are vested with authority to make their religious establishments a binding rule to a Christian, does necessarily infer their being invested with infallibility too. Again—to suppose any thing not agreeable to the sacred scriptures can be a binding rule in matters of religion to a Christian is what no Christian will assert; because it destroys the Christian's only rule in matters of religion. The sacred scriptures alone (or what is agreeable thereto) are a rule in matters of religion to a Christian: A religious establishment (say you) made by the civil authority which they think to be agreeable to the scriptures, is a rule binding to a Christian: Therefore (say I) such a religious establishment made by the civil authority which they think to be agreable to the scriptures, is certainly agreable to them. Until these contradictions can be reconciled—*viz.* That which is not agreable to the sacred scriptures cannot be a rule binding to a Christian in matters of religion—and this, That which is not agreable to the scriptures is (or may be) a rule binding to a Christian in matters of religion; or the scriptures are the alone rule of faith and practice to a Christian, and this—That something which the pope or Cæsar thinks to be agreable to the scripture, is a rule of the Christian's faith and practice; or the scriptures are the alone rule, and not the alone rule of faith and practice to a Christian; or that which is a binding rule to a Christian in these matters, is not a binding rule to him: Until these contradictions can be reconciled, it will stand for a truth, that if the civil authority have power to make a religious establishment which they think agreable to the scriptures, a rule binding to Christians; then such their establishments are certainly agreable to the scriptures, and so they invested with infallibility. So that instead of finding one infallible man upon earth (at Rome) we may find a body of them in every civil state at least throughout Christendom, and why not throughout the earth: For the civil authority, considered as such, must have equal right and power of determining in these matters in every state.

But you will say; "the question is concerning an establishment that is agreable to scripture and therefore whether such an one is not a rule binding to the subjects." I answer—It is no rule at all; and so has no binding force in it, as it is an human establishment: it's binding force is derived from another quarter. The only reason why it is a rule binding to a Christian is, because it is the scripture, or the will of GOD contained in the scripture. What binds the Christian in religion are the words of our Lord JESUS CHRIST, and the doctrine which is according to godliness. This true Christians receive out of a regard to a much higher authority than belongs to any set of mortals.

If it be still demanded; "But have not these synods who draw up these establishments out of the scriptures, or the civil authority with them, a right to judge of the sense and meaning of the scripture in those matters, and so determine what shall or shall not pass for true, and be received by the members of the community[?]" I know some plead for such a power: And I think if a human religious establishment can be a binding rule to Christians; they must, either a synod, or civil authority, or both together, have power to determine the sense of scripture as now pleaded for: and if they have no such power, it is most evident their establishments can be no binding rule to Christians. But this is certain, they have no such power: The pretence to it is a spice of that Antichristianism that ought to be banished out of the world. For that this very supposition removes the sacred scriptures from being a rule of faith and practice to private Christians, and sets up humane determinations instead of them; inasmuch as that from which the Christian receives his information what he is to believe & do, is evidently the rule of faith & practice in those particular cases at least; and in the present supposed case, he is to receive his information from a human determination. The scriptures therefore are struck out from being a rule of faith and practice to private Christians; and human determinations substituted in their room. However the scriptures may be supposed or pretended to be the rule to those bodies of men who make those determinations; yet it is evident in this case, the scriptures are so entirely reduced into the power of man, that in truth these bodies of men, or their determinations are render'd the only and compleat rule to others. A tenet that suits very well at Rome. But to show the absurdity and wickedness of this principle, that synods or the civil authority may determine the sense of scripture for private Christians as above supposed; let me add, That all, whether popes, councils, synods or civil states, that have made their religious establishments, have always pretended they took the sacred scriptures for their rule in making them, and that they are agreable to the scripture. Upon this principle, all these must be received in their turns, and in the several civil states where they are made. For those synods (or in a word) the civil authority in those several ages, or states, have had all equal claim to this right of determining the sense of scripture, and so of making these religious establishments. How very different and contrary these have been, one to another; who, at all acquainted with history does not know? That is falsehood in England, which is truth at Rome and France. And that was truth in England yesterday, which is false there to day. And so a man (I don't say a Christian; for as that means a disciple of CHRIST, and it can't consistently mean any thing else, it is by this principle banished out of the world both name and thing) might yesterday walk to heaven in a path, which if walked in this day wou'd lead him down to hell. Alas what is the Christian bid to search the scriptures for, to repair *to the law and testimony*, as being the only light to direct us in these religious and important concerns; if it comes to this at last, that he must receive his information and direction herein, from some poor fallible creatures. This principle, that a humane religious establishment is a rule binding to Christians, does eternally militate with those plain commands of the supream Lawgiver; is big with the absurdities I have just hinted at, and numberless more; has proved the grand engine of oppressing truth, Christianity, and murdering the best men the world has had in it; promoting and securing heresy, superstition and idolatry; and ought to be abhorred by all Christians.

But if you demand again; "Is it not evident GOD has vested them with such a power, since he has bid us, *obey them that have the Rule over us*, Heb. 13. 17. and *that we be subject to the higher Powers; for that the Powers that be, are of GOD*, Rom. 13. 1. Will it not follow, that if GOD requires our subjection to them, they must needs be *vested with such authority* as is now pleaded for." It has been already shewn that a supposal that they are vested with such authority, necessarily supposes they are vested with infallibility too; otherwise the Christian lies exposed to have a rule of practice in religion different from the word of GOD; which no Christian may admit of. If the sacred scriptures are the standing invariable rule in these matters to every Christian (which is an incontestible truth), then he can't possibly lie exposed to have any thing else made a binding rule to him in matters of religion; GOD has not subjected him in this case to any other: and he may properly be said to rebel against GOD, when he puts himself in subjection to any other; And the thing now pleaded for, that an order of men are vested with authority from GOD to make any religious establishment which they think agreable to the scriptures, a rule binding to Christians, does necessarily suppose one of these two things; that a Christian may have something different from the sacred scriptures for his rule (i.e. that it is GOD'S will he shall be in a state liable to be bound by a rule different from his word) which is impossible; or else, that these men vested with this authority, are also vested with infallibility. Now since it is most evident, they are not vested with this infallibility, it is equally evident they are not vested with this authority now pleaded for: and therefore no such thing is implied in those texts now adduced for the proof thereof. A great dust I know has been raised by the sophistical reasonings of some men from these texts, who would erect a spiritual tyranny over the consciences of men. I will therefore distinctly consider them, and show that they no ways suppose such an authority (as now pleaded for) is vested in any order of men.

The text in Heb. 13. 17. evidently relates to church-officers; because they are said to *watch for their souls*, which is not the business of civil rulers: and their being called in the text, rulers, will no ways infer they have this legislative authority over a church or particular Christians; any more than Jairus being called a ruler of a synagogue, will infer he had a legislative authority over that synagogue: Or that any subordinate judges who are strictly tied to the laws in their administration, being called rulers, must needs also infer a power of legislation. Nor can it be infer'd from our being commanded to obey them; any more than our obedience to judges in their just application of the laws to particular cases, infers a power of legislation also in those judges. In a word, these officers in the text have so much authority, and no more than what CHRIST has given them. They have no more authority in their commission, than what is to be found in

Math. 28. 19, 20. where they are expressly enjoined *to teach people to observe* CHRIST'S *laws*; which necessarily excludes them from a power of making laws of their own for CHRIST'S subjects. And the reason given for our obedience in the text, does also suppose it; viz. *for they watch for your souls*. By their adhering strictly to the will of CHRIST in their teaching Christians, do they truly watch for the salvation of their souls; and therein are they to be attended to as the faithful ministers of ambassadors of CHRIST, in hearing of whom (when they do so) we hear him that sends, as he elsewhere tells us. But if they *go out of this line* in teaching Christians, they then don't watch for their souls, but for themselves: and therein therefore no obedience is due to them, even according to this very text, which determines the measure of our regard to them, by their watching or not watching for the salvation of our souls.

The other text Rom. 13. 1. no doubt relates to civil powers: A text often wrecked and tortured by such wits as were disposed to serve the designs of arbitrary power, of erecting a civil tyranny over a free people, and as often wrested out of their hands by the force of truth. Tho' my business does not lie with civil tyranny now, yet the observation I shall make upon the text will show that neither civil, nor spiritual tyranny is at all favoured by it. Here then let me distinguish between two things, which as they are really different, must be kept so in our minds, if we would understand the Apostle; *viz*. between the powers which are, and the powers which are not. This is a plain and undeniable distinction; since it is well known there may be a pretended power where there is really none. Now the higher powers in the text are the powers which are. Since then it is express and certain, that the powers that be, are the powers in the text, the powers which be of GOD, the ordinance of GOD; it is only of such powers he speaks of subjection to. On the other hand—the powers that are not, are not the powers that be; and so not the powers in the text, not the powers that are of GOD, not his ordinance, and so no subjection to them required in this text. For instance: The powers that be in Great Britain are the government therein according to its own constitution: If then the higher powers for the administration rule not according to that constitution, or if any king thereof shall rule so, as to change the government from legal to arbitrary; the power from GOD fails them, it is then a power not in this text, and so no subjection due to it by the text. To apply this then to the present case; we have seen before that civil authority relates to the civil interests of a people (their persons and properties), and is bounded by the same; that they can have no power to make any religious establishment of their own devising, a rule binding to Christians: When therefore they attempt to do so, they get out of their line, with respect to which they are not the powers that be, in this text. A power that is no better than a pretended one, can't challenge any obedience by virtue of this text. As this text does not shew they have such a power, the pretence of obedience being due to them by this text, if they should be so vain as to fancy they have it, is a meer vanity. The truth of the case is plainly this; that this text shews obedience is due to civil rulers in those cases wherein they have power to command, and does not call for it any farther: And when rightly understood affords not a shadow of an argument, of obedience being due to them when they claim a power in matters of religion which does not belong to them. It appears indeed plainly (tho' I need not spend time upon it, in order to show no argument can be drawn from this text in favour of what it is now brought for, unless it be first proved from some other text or topick, that the civil magistrate's power does extend to the making any religious or ecclesiastical establishment a rule binding to a Christian, which never can be done, the contrary thereof being already demonstrated), I say it appears from what the Apostle says in the 3d and 4th verses, that their power is a limited one: and therefore the obedience due is a limited obedience. *Salus populi est lex suprema*, is the Apostle's maxim; for he is express that the end of all humane authority is the good of the publick. That therefore sets the bounds to civil authority, as such, on the one side, and fixes the bounds of obedience on the other. The ground of obedience cannot be extended beyond the ground of that authority to which obedience is required.

Besides, no obedience is here required to be given but to such power as is from GOD: Until therefore it be shown that the civil magistrate has power from GOD to make any such religious establishment (of which we are speaking) a rule binding to Christians; this text is in vain pressed into the service of such as plead for any obedience due to such an establishment. It must lie on them who plead this obedience is due from Christians, to prove that GOD has vested them with this power. To pretend this text for it, is begging the question, a taking the point for granted which must be first proved; which I scruple not to say will never be done 'till we have a new Bible. For by this which CHRIST has given us, he allows us not to be reduced under any yoke of bondage, or to become *the servants of men*, not only allows but requires us to stand fast in our Christian liberty, which subjects us in our faith and practice to CHRIST alone; and by that very thing exempts us from every other yoke, and from all other laws not given us by CHRIST. 1 Cor. 7. 23. Gal. 5. 1. CHRIST perfectly knew the weakness of humane nature, and how apt men are to assume power over one another, even in matters of a religious nature, and how unfit they are to have any dominion therein: He therefore charges and warns all his disciples and followers against this great and dangerous vice, which he knew would be very destructive to that religion which he taught in Mat. 23. 8, 9, 10. *Be not ye called Rabbi; For one is your Master even CHRIST, and all ye are Brethren: And call no Man your Father upon Earth; for one is your Father which is in Heaven: Neither be ye called Masters; for one is your Master even CHRIST.* Here all Christians are charg'd upon the duty and obedience they owe to CHRIST, that they should none of them set themselves up for authoritative masters, judges, or directors of men in religious matters (as the Pharisees did); and likewise that they should not submit to any who should set themselves up as such. CHRIST'S prohibition here is so strong, of this dangerous practice of setting up or admitting of any other rule or judge in religious matters besides the scripture, and of all attempts to strip Christians of the most valuable of all rights, even the right of judging for themselves in matters of religion (directly inconsistent with which, is the authority you have been now pleading for in the civil powers in the case we have been considering), that Christians here (I think) may safely take up their rest, and be resolved to give place by subjection, no, not for an hour to any humane authority on earth in any matters of religion, lest they cast dishonour on CHRIST their only lawgiver.

By what has been said you may see the falshood of another supposition or argument you bring to support the civil magistrate's authority in the case before us, *viz. That every law not contrary to a superior law, is to be obeyed;* which you seem to take for an allowed maxim, and so think you may fairly conclude, that any legal injunctions of the civil magistrate in matters of religion which are not contrary to some express law of GOD; are to be obeyed. If that proposition be limited to those things which are the objects of the civil magistrate's power, *viz.* the civil interests of the people; if it stands for a maxim it affects not the case before us at all. But if it be extended to things out or beyond the line of their power, as matters of religion are; it is then a falshood. In the latter extensive sense it seems you take it for a truth, or you would not argue from it as you do. The rule (then say you) to know whether a particular law is to be obeyed or not is to consider that law in relation to a superior law; and if it prohibits nothing which a superior law requires, or enjoins nothing which a superior law prohibits the doing of, then it is to be obeyed. This (I take it) is a principle invented for the support of tyranny, and industriously defended for the support of tyranny of the worst kind, i. e. spiritual: And if such as are so mean as to flatter civil rulers with notions of exorbitant power, and they only felt the effects thereof in fetters of slavery, the Christian church, and the world too, had been happier than now it is. Rulers have their infirmities as well as their subjects, and are too often carried away by the stream of temptation to play the tyrant: And still as heretofore, the world affords many in it that love to have it so, and too many assistants in forging the hateful chains of slavery and rivetting them on too if possible unseen, whilst they are industriously scattering false notions of power and obedience, such stupifying potions as this (you have now thrown in my way) that they may effectually lock up the senses of those whom they would enslave. But to return whence I have digressed. This pretended rule, as it holds not at all in matters of religion; so it does not hold true in all other cases, even in those that have no relation to the end of civil society, agreable to what has been already observed, page [61]. If civil rulers should take it into their heads to make a law, that no man shall have Luther's *Table-Talk* in his house, that every man shall *turn round upon his right heel at twelve of the clock every day* (Sundays excepted), or any such like wise laws (thousands of which might be invented by a wise tyrant); By this rule these laws are to be strictly obeyed, a higher law to the contrary not being found. And yet I think it may be presumed, a free-born people can never become so servile as to regard them, while they have eyes to see that such rulers have gone out of the line of their power. There is no reason they should be fools because their rulers are so. Whenever the power that is put in any hands for the government of any people is applied to any other end than the preservation of their persons and properties, the securing and promoting their civil interests (the end for which power was put into their hands), I say when it is applied to any other end, then (according to the great Mr. Lock) it becomes tyranny. And since their power would be as truly applied to another end, in making such laws as I have above hinted at, as in making those that are notoriously unjust and oppressive (tho' the latter is worse); then it as truly becomes tyranny. How long people are to bear with such tyranny, or what they may do to free themselves from it (I should refer you to that author in his *Treatise of Government*), were it at all needful to come into consideration in the present case, as it is not; since the only thing I had here to do, was to show obedience was not due to such laws, as I think I have done by shewing they had no rightful authority to make them.

Let me add a word farther for your serious consideration; do you think that when the edict went forth in Germany for the burning of all the above mention'd books of Martin Luther (when eighty thousand volumes of them were destroyed) did that good man, who hid one of them under the foundation of his house whereby it was perserved, sin in not delivering up the book? Or when the proclamation went forth in England in King Henry the Eight's time, that Wickliff's, Tindall's, and many other books, should on certain penalties be deliver'd up to be burned; did those good people sin, who refus'd to deliver them up? By the rule you are pleading for, I see not but that you must charge sin upon them for not obeying; when yet I believe you cannot but in conscience acquit them; and if you do, it must then be upon the principles I have laid down.

But I will no longer dwell here, it being somewhat foreign to the point in hand. I proceed to consider this rule as it respects religious matters; to which it is so confidently applied by the lovers of spiritual tyranny. And here, if this be the rule, that we ought to obey human laws in religious matters in every instance where we can't find a divine law enjoining what they forbid, or forbidding what they enjoin; then it is evident, religion is in danger of being made a very burdensome thing. To baptism you may add the sign of the cross, the salt, and cream, and spitting in the mouth, with a hundred other things, that a fruitful imagination could furnish out. The popish wardrobe will yield some furniture to dress up religion with. But the inventions of men may still go beyond. And if they do but take care not to enjoin any action or modality in religion not prohibited by some command in the Bible; by this rule Christians are bound to obey. It is a necessary consequence of this principle, that Christians are subjected to a heavier yoke than the Jews were under the Mosaick Dispensation. If you say, "not; because if the civil rulers should proceed so far (for I know not what else you can devise to say), it would be contrary to a general law we have from CHRIST; Gal. 5. 1. *Be not intangled again with the Yoke of Bondage*; which not only shows Christians are not subjected to that particular yoke, but also that their yoke is not to be so heavy as that was; so that if they should increase their injunctions to make religion now so burdensome, as the Jewish was, it would be contrary to this superior law." Be it so, but then remember this is true upon their principles, that if they stop but one hair short, they will tell you, their injunctions are not contrary to this general law. If the burden they lay upon you be at all less, by your principle you confess yourself under the obligation of obedience; and how miserable Christians would be if human lawgivers might go near such a length, I need not spend any time to show, it is so very obvious. But farther, suppose civil rulers should go still beyond; who are the judges whether they go contrary to this law or not? Are the rulers the judges, or have private Christians a right of judgment in this case? If the rulers only are to judge, we may be sure thay will judge in favour of their own laws: if they exceed this bound you suppose set to them by this general law; they will never judge that law of CHRIST to be contrary to their laws: and if so, more miserable yet is the Christian's condition. But if you say, private Christians have a right of judgment for themselves in this case; I then ask, if they judge the rulers in their injunctions exceed the bounds allowed by this law of CHRIST, whether they are to be tollerated by the rulers in their not conforming to those injuctions they judge contrary to this law? They have gone as far (it is to be supposed) in conforming, as their consciences will suffer them: Are they then to be indulged to stop there according to their own judgments, or must they still conform farther, or else be subjected to a penalty for not going farther? If they must be subjected to penalties for not conforming in this case; how deplorable is the condition of Christians? Obey the inventions of men or dye! You will doubtless answer; they must be tollerated, since it is supposed they have a right of judging for themselves, when a human injunction in religion is contrary to a divine law. This is undoubtedly true: for to suppose they have a right of judgment for themselves, is to suppose they have a right to act according to their judgment: and therefore none (not the civil magistrate) can have any right to hinder them. A right that in this case is dependent on the will of another, is no right at all. Suppose then, private Christians should judge that it is contrary to the will of CHRIST express'd in that text, Gal. 5. 1. that the civil magistrate should make *any legal injunction at all* in religion (which is the truth of the case); I then ask, whether these who so judge are not to be allowed to act according to their judgment, as well as the former? This surely can't be denied them; since the right of private judgment belongs to the latter as well as the former. If then Christians have a right to adhere strictly to the will of CHRIST delivered in the sacred scriptures in every thing relating to their faith and practice in religion, exclusive of all human legal injunctions; then no power on earth can have any right to make a law to restrain them therefrom, or to add the least thing thereto. For to have a right to adhere to the sacred scriptures alone as a rule in this case, and not to have such a right is a contradiction: and to suppose the civil magistrate has a right to restrain them, or to add any one law to CHRIST'S in this case, is to suppose Christians have not a right to adhere to the sacred scriptures as their alone rule. The supposition therefore of any rightful power in the civil ruler to make any one law in matters of religion, involves in it as plain a contradiction to truth, as a right to a thing and no right to it does. The rule therefore which you would set up, by which to try what humane laws in matters of religion are to be obeyed, is justly to be rejected; not only because it subjects Christians to an intollerable yoke (if admitted), but because it can in no instance be admitted, but at the expence of a Christian's *natural and unalienable right of private judgment* in matters of religion. It may do well enough to amuse men with a pretence they have found out a rule how far Christians ought to obey the laws of civil rulers in matters of religion, and where they may safely stop; where they can find persons so weak as to think that civil rulers have some power to make laws in these matters: But if that be the truth that they have no power at all to make any law in these cases, then the setting up such a rule is a grand absurdity. Now I have shown evidently before, that the civil magistrate can have no such power, that his power relates to the civil interests of a people, and is bounded thereby—that the sacred scriptures are the alone rule of faith and practice in religion to a Christian; that the right of private judgment, what the Christian is to believe and do in religion according to that rule, is his natural and unalienable right; so that he neither really may nor can give up his soul, his conscience in these matters to the controul of human laws. And the truth is, the civil magistrate is so far from having a rightful power in these cases, to make laws for CHRIST'S subjects; that in doing so, he violates the fundamental priviledge of the gospel, the birthright of believers, Christian liberty. 2 Cor. 3. 17. *Where the Spirit of the Lord is, there is Liberty.* Gal. 4. 31. *We are not Children of the Bondwoman, but of the Free.* It is impossible to suppose that GOD by his special grace in the gospel should free us from the bondage of ceremonies, his own commandments, in these things, and subject us to a more grievous yoke, the commandments of men. Nor has he given us his gift only as a special priviledge and excellence of the free gospel above the servile law; but has strictly commanded us to keep and enjoy it. *You are called to Liberty*, Gal. 5. 13. 1 Cor. 7. 23. *Be not ye the Servants of Men.* Gal. 5. 1. *Stand fast in the Liberty wherewith Christ has made us free.* A command accompany'd with the weightiest reasons. Rom. 14. 9, 10. *For to this End CHRIST both died and rose and revived; that he might be Lord, both of the Dead and Living: But why dost thou judge thy Brother*, &c. How presumest thou *to be his Lord?* To be whose only Lord, at least in these things, CHRIST both died and rose and lived again—*We shall all stand before the Judgment Seat of CHRIST.* Why pretend you then to be a Lord, a Judge, in these things, for which we are to be accountable to the tribunal of CHRIST only, our Lord and lawgiver? Who in so many express words, has told us we shall have himself only our Master in religion, Math. 23. 8, 9, 10. *One is your Master, even CHRIST.* By all which I think it is evident; that for men to exercise such a power in religious matters as you have been pleading for, is not only a violation of the rights of Christians, whose souls in matters of religion are subject to none but Christ and his laws; but an invasion of the royal power of CHRIST, who is the sole legislator in his own kingdom.

To illustrate and clear this point, let me bring it down to a plain and familiar instance. Let it be supposed a humane law is made, that the sign of a cross shall be made upon a person's forehead, after the use of water *&c.* in baptism, so that none shall be admitted to baptism but who submit to this manner of administration of it: or a law requiring all who attend the ordinance of the Lord's supper to do it in a kneeling posture: and let it be supposed, that there is no particular law to the contrary in the gospel forbidding those actions. Now according to the rule you plead for (on the supposition now made), Christians are bound to obey these laws. But the contrary is evident. For it has been already demonstrated, that every Christian has a right to adhere to the sacred scriptures as the only rule of his faith and practice in religion; and that the right of private judgment, what he is to believe and do in religion according to that rule, is really unalienable: he can't therefore be bound to yield any obedience to such laws of man, unless he be obliged to yield up an unalienable right, which is a contradiction. Besides—if the making such laws are an invasion of CHRIST'S authority; how is it possible the proposition should be true, that a Christian is obliged to obey them, unless the Christian has two masters in religion, contrary to Mat. 23. 8, 9, 10. Where there is no authority to command in matters of religion, there a Christian is under no obligation from such laws to obey: But in the case before us, such laws are not only enjoined without authority, but they interfere with CHRIST'S authority: So that a Christian is indeed very far from being bound to obey them.

Unto what has been already said that will shew this, I shall add but a few words. CHRIST has in the gospel charter made a grant of certain privileges to those who would be, and do approve themselves his subjects. To them he has granted the privilege of attending on him in the ordinances he has instituted, for the conveying the sanctifying graces of his spirit to their souls, to prepare them for the inheritance he has purchased and secured by promise to such as believe in and obey him. As this is clear and certain in the nature of the thing itself, that the grantor of a privilege has the sole right of fixing the condition on which the privilege shall be enjoyed by the grantee; so it is equally certain, that if any other attempts in the least measure to alter the condition on which such privilege is to be enjoyed by the grant, he does therein invade the indisputable right of the grantor. Now in the case before us there can't be a clearer truth, than that this is Christ's sole prerogative to make the grant and fix the conditions on which the privileges are to be enjoyed, and that this is done in the gospel charter. The privileges are granted on the conditions that are written in the charter. The privileges are not granted on certain conditions to be invented by men after the making of the charter: For that would suppose that infinite wisdom has granted certain privileges to Christians on such conditions as humane weakness establishes; and that Christ strips himself of his royalty to cloath a mere creature with it, and makes the creature the director of his bequests: To suppose which of Christ is to dishonour him with a witness. It is indeed the greatest absurdity imaginable, to suppose this matter could be settled by any other than Christ himself, who makes the grant: And the conditions lie as plainly in the grant as the privileges conveyed by it; That he who believes and obeys the gospel, has the right to the enjoyment of the privileges belonging to a subject of Christ. This then being certain, that Christ has fixed the conditions of Christians enjoying the privileges, the ordinances of the gospel; it is equally certain, that man and every order of men are excluded by Christ himself from any authority in this matter: So that if any man or order of men make any alteration in those conditions, or make any new ones; they do it not only without authority, but against it, and therein controul Christ's authority. To apply this then to the case before us: Since the making the above-mentioned figure on the person to be baptized, or such a particular bodily posture at the reception of the Lord's supper, are not fixed by Christ as the conditions of Christians enjoying these ordinances, or by any law of Christ made necessary in order to the observance of these institutions of his; for man to make them conditions, without a compliance with which Christians may not have the enjoyment of those ordinances, is not only to act without authority, but is assuming an authority which only belongs to Christ: it being a practical declaration that Christ's subjects shall not enjoy the privileges of the gospel upon the conditions fixed in Christ's grant: Which is therefore evidently an invasion of Christ's kingly office, and an evident violation of the rights of Christians. So that it is certain, Christians are not only, not bound to submit to such human laws, but do truly profess their adherence to CHRIST'S authority, when they refuse to do so.

But if you say here; "altho' the rule you have been pleading for will not hold; yet if every thing relating to decency and order in divine worship be not particularly determined by CHRIST, why may not what is referrible thereto fall under the determination of the laws of the civil authority, and be warranted by that apostolical precept, 1 Cor. 14. 40. *Let all Things be done decently and in Order*; and so those particular instances I have mentioned be justly warranted by that precept? If some body must determine in such cases, why may not the civil rulers do it?" I answer

1. If Christians keep from indecency and disorder in their worship, they come up to the rule given by the Apostle in the now mentioned text; and this they may certainly do without the civil magistrate's determining any thing about it. Christians observed this apostolick precept as well before there was any such thing as a Christian magistrate to be found, as they have done since: And may do it as well to the second coming of CHRIST, without the civil magistrate's intermeddling in this matter (not to say with more honour to Christ and greater peace in the church, if he forbears his injunctions). So that it is impossible to get an inference from this text in favour of the civil authority's determining any thing by their laws in these cases.

2. If by what you would call decency or order in worship be meant, either any act or mode of worship, or any ceremony that has any religion at all placed in it; then I say, no man or order of men has the least authority to invent or injoin any such thing: This would fall under our Saviour's condemnation in Mark 7. 7.

3. Any such modes or circumstances of divine worship which are supposed in this objection left undetermined by Christ, may not be determined by any legal injunctions of the civil authority. And that—

(1.) Because so to do, would be going out of their line; these things don't lie within the compass of the end of their institution: The civil interests of the people being no ways concerned therein, as has been shewn in the preceeding pages.

(2.) The supposition that such modes or circumstances of divine worship may be determined by human laws, does also suppose that the civil authority may fix terms of communion for Christians: What is thus supposed enacted by a legislature, is made a rule of action to the subject by the very supposition of its being made a law; so that in this case the subject is to attend divine worship, but according to a human law; and is therefore excluded from the benefit of divine worship and ordinances, in case of a non-compliance with that human injunction. This is the true state of the matter with respect to those instances I have just mentioned: And any the like modes of worship enjoined on Christians by the laws of men, they are made the terms of communion to Christians, the conditions of their enjoying the external privileges of Christians: And for men to fix any terms of communion for Christians in this manner, to make that necessary to their enjoyment of the privileges CHRIST has purchased for them which he has not made necessary, has been already demonstrated an invasion of Christ's kingly authority.

(3.) The civil authority may not determine such modes and circumstances of worship by legal injunctions; because this would interfere with the right of private judgment that belongs to Christians. The sacred scriptures are sufficient to furnish the Christian unto every good work; they hold forth sufficient light about the modes and circumstances of divine worship, which in this objection are supposed to be left undetermined by CHRIST. And it is the duty and right of Christians to learn from thence, and judge concerning their duty in these as well as more important matters of religion; and such determinations of them are lawful and warrantable as are according to the general rules of scripture given to direct us herein. And therefore there may be various modes of performing the same religious duties that are each allowable and lawful: tho' some particular circumstances may make one more expedient to some persons than the other, and these also may be varied by the providence of GOD. It is the right therefore of Christians, of every worshipping assembly, to determine for themselves these modes and circumstances of worship, as I have before observed. And for the civil authority here to step in and determine by a law, what modes or circumstances of worship shall be observed; for instance, what posture we shall use in prayer, when there are several equally expressive of our religious reverence; interferes with the Christian's unalienable right of private judgment. And when I say, every worshipping assembly has this right of determining or agreeing for themselves about the modes or circumstances of worship; it no way supposes they have a right to (or do by such agreements) exclude from their communion any of their Christian brethren who may prefer the use of a different allowable mode of worship. Whom

CHRIST receives they are also to receive. CHRIST has fixed the terms of Christian communion, and none may alter them.

But say you once more; "That the civil authority must have power to make such religious establishment which I have been impleading, in order to have unity of faith and uniformity of practice in religion. These you suppose necessary to peace and good order in the state; and that this unity &c. is effected by such a religious establishment, of which we are speaking; and consequently we must suppose them vested with power to make such a one." Much weight I know has been laid upon this argument by the lovers of spiritual tyranny, and many ignorant unthinking people have been amused and deceived by it: But if we will look closely into it, it will appear lighter than vanity. For

1. Unity of faith and uniformity of practice in religion, never was nor can be effected in a Christian state by any such legal establishment of religion pleaded for in the above-mentioned argument. By a Christian state, I mean at least such a one, where the sacred scriptures lie open to the people: and therefore I don't intend, to consider this proposition relative to a popish state, where people's eyes being put out, they are more easily induced to follow their leaders; tho' it be also true that this unity of faith is not found among them that are bound in the strongest chains of human establishments. This has been tried in Protestant states, to make all think and practice alike in religion by legal establishments and annexed penalties: but it never produced this effect. It were easy if needful to multiply instances: but it is sufficient to our purpose to instance in our own nation; where this method has been tried ever since the reformation, and as constantly found ineffectual for the accomplishing this uniformity, for the sake of which these legal establishments have been pretended to be made. So far is this method from bringing about an unity of faith, that this is not found even with them that submit to a legal establishment. It is notoriously known, that the clergy of the Church of England are bound to subscribe to the thirty nine articles, i.e. to the truth of Calvinistick principles: But has this subscription answer'd its end? Is it not known, that they subscribe those articles in as widely distant and contradictory senses as were ever put on the most dubious passage in the Bible. And the truth is, if we consider the almost

infinite variety with respect to the understandings, tempers and advantages of men for improvement in knowledge; it must be evident, that this uniformity of opinion and practice in religion (as it has not), so it never can be produced by the art and policy of man. A scheme for an artificial conformity in aspect, shape and stature of body, is not a whit more ridiculous, than an attempt to depress and contract the understandings of some, to stretch the capacities of others, to distort and torture all, 'till they are brought to one size, and *one way of thinking and practice.* So that if this unity of faith and uniformity of practice in religion is necessary to the peace of the state; then it follows, that the civil authority have a rightful power to put to death or banish all that cannot in conscience conform to their religious establishment. It will be to no purpose for the avoiding this consequence, to say; "the civil magistrate may not rise so high, or may affix some lower penalties for non-compliance with his establishment": For if this conformity to his establishment be necessary to the peace of the state, then the civil magistrate has a right to prevent a non-compliance with such establishment; and if lesser penalties will not do it (as experience has perpetually shown they will not), then they must rise so high as death, or banishment: For a right to prevent such non-compliance, that does not amount to a right to prevent it effectually, is no right to prevent it at all. So that on this hypothesis, all non-conformists to the religious establishment of any state, are to be rooted out by death, or banishment as fast as they appear: Which both experience and the nature of things evidence will be continual; the cutting off all that appear to day will no ways hinder others from appearing so to-morrow. Whence it is but a genuine consequence, that civil government is one of the greatest plagues that can be sent upon the world; since it must, in order to keep peace in it, be perpetually destroying men for no other crime but judging for themselves and acting according to their consciences in matters of religion (and so perhaps very often the best men in the state); and all this in vain too, as to the proposed end, *viz.* uniformity of practice in religion, that being for ever out of their reach.

2. Such unity, or uniformity in religion is not necessary to the peace of a civil state. Since God has formed the understandings of men so different, with respect to clearness, strength, and compass, and placed them in such very different circumstances; a difference of

sentiments in some things in religion, seems natural and unavoidable: and to suppose this does in its own nature tend to the public mischief of the state, seems little less than arraigning infinite wisdom. From thence will arise greater reason and scope for mutual forbearance and Christian charity. But it will certainly be found on reflection, that it has no ill aspect on the civil state. Have we not known persons of different sentiments and practices in religious matters, as Presbyterians, Congregationalists, Church-Men (as commonly called) Baptists and Quakers, all living in the same community in quiet and peace with one another? I mention not papists; because tho' the principles of a consistent Protestant, naturally tend to make him a good subject in any civil state, even in a popish one, and therefore ought to be allowed in every state; yet that is not the case with the papist: for by his very principles he is an enemy or traytor to a Protestant state: and strictly speaking popery is so far from deserving the name of religion, that it is rather a conspiracy against it, against the reason, liberties, and peace of mankind; the visible head thereof the pope being in truth the vice-gerent of the Devil, Rev. 13. 2. To pretend that such as own the sacred scriptures to be the alone rule of faith and practice in religion, can't live in peace and love as good neighbours and good subjects, tho' their opinions and practices in religious matters be different, is both false in fact, and a vile reproach cast upon the gospel, which breaths nothing but benevolence and love among men: and while it plainly teaches the right of private judgment in every one, it most forcibly enjoins the duties of mutual forbearance and charity. That golden precept of our blessed LORD; *Whatsoever ye would that Men should do unto you, do ye even so to them*, Math. 7. 12, well taught and enforced by the teachers of the gospel, would (if I may use the word) infinitely more tend to make Christians of the several denominations in the state, good neighbours and good subjects, than this whimsical notion of uniformity. Which if it had always had its due force on the minds of men, we should never have heard of the necessity of uniformity in religion to the peace of the state, nor any such legal establishment of religion I have been impleading. That precept being a sacred guard to the unalienable rights of conscience, which are always invaded by such establishments.

But if you say, "that different sects in religion aiming at superiority, and endeavouring to suppress each other, form contrary factions in the state; which tends to distress and thwart the civil administration." I answer; The civil authority's protecting all in their just rights, and particularly this inestimable and unalienable one, *the right of private judgment* in matters of religion, is the best guard against the evil supposed in the objection. Besides, this is no more a natural consequence of men's thinking differently in religion, than of different judgments about wit, or poetry, trade, or husbandry.

Or if you farther suppose, "that religion is a matter of much greater importance than these things, and demands therefore a more warm and active zeal." Be it so; nothing farther follows from thence, than that we should endeavour to support its honour in a way suited to its excellency; to instruct one another in its grand principles and duties, and recommend it by calm and strong perswasion. It is by truth CHRIST'S kingdom is set up, as he himself has taught us, Luke 18. 37. And it is a most unnatural excess of zeal, for the pretended defence of religion, to renounce humanity, and that equitable regard and kind affection, which are unalterably due from one man to another.

If it be again said, "that tho' these above-mentioned evils are directly contrary to the true genius and spirit of the Christian religion; yet they are the actual consequence of a variety of sects, exceeding fond of their particular schemes." I answer; they are only accidental abuses to which the best things are liable: The same argument may be urged against reason, and every branch of natural and civil liberty. It is equally conclusive as the papists have used it against the laity's having the Bible; *viz.* the consequence of people's having the Bible in their hands to read, has been the rising up of a variety of sects in the Christian world, and therefore they ought not to be permitted the use of it. As no such conclusion can be drawn against every body's having the Bible from such premises; so in the case before us, no conclusion against the *right of private judgment* for our selves in matters of religion, can be drawn from these inconveniencies; which do not spring directly from it, but arise entirely from different causes; from pride, or foolish bigotry, that either does not understand, or pays no regard to the unalienable rights of conscience.

3. Such legal establishments have a direct contrary tendency to the peace of a Christian state. As the *exercise of private reason*, and free enquiry in a strict and constant adherence to the sacred scriptures as

the only rule of faith and practice, is the most likely means to produce uniformity in the essential principles of Christianity as well as practice; so this is certainly the most sure method of procuring peace in the state. No man having any reason to repine at his neighbour's enjoyment of that right, which he is not willing to be without himself; and on the same grounds he challenges it for himself, he must be forced to own, that it is as reasonable his neighbour should enjoy it. But then on the other hand, *every claim of power* inconsistent with this right (as the making such a human establishment of religion of which we are speaking), is an encroachment on the Christian's liberty; and so far therefore he is in a state of slavery: And so far as a man feels himself in a state of slavery, so far he feels himself unhappy, and has reason to complain of that administration which puts the chain upon him. So that if slavery be for the peace of the civil state; then such establishments as we are speaking of, tend to promote the peace of the state: *i.e.* what makes the subjects miserable, really makes them happy. And as it necessarily tends to the misery of some, so it also promotes bigotry, pride, and ambition in such as are fond of such establishments: which have from time to time broken out in extravagancies and severities (upon good subjects) in men of authority and influence, and into rage and fury, hatred and obloquy, and such like wickednesses, in the impotent and commoner sort. This has been the case in all places, more or less, as well as in our own nation. Thus when K. Henry threw off the popish tyranny, he would not destroy and put an end to the exercise of that unjust power, but only transferred it to himself, and exercised it with great severity. The same unjust dominion over the consciences of men was again exercised in the reign of Elizabeth; who (tho' otherwise a wise princess) yet being of an high and arbitrary temper, pressed uniformity with violence; and found bishops enough, Parker, Aylmer, Whitgift and others, to cherish that temper, and promote such measures. Silencings, deprivations, imprisonments, fines &c. upon the account of religion, were some of the powerful reasonings of those times. The cries of innocent prisoners, widowed wives, and starving children, made no impression on their hearts: piety and learning with them were void of merit: Refusal of subscriptions, and Non-conformity, were crimes never to be forgiven. At the instigation of that persecuting prelate Whitgift, Archbishop of Canterbury, the High Commission Court was established; which had a near resemblance to the Court of Inquisition (a fine invention to promote uniformity): Which by the cruelties practiced in it in the two following reigns, was render'd the abhorrence of the nation; so that it was dissolved by parliament, with a clause, that *no such court should be erected for the future.* A creature framed to promote the wretched designs of such persecutors, was her weak successor James the First, who gave the Puritans to understand *that if they did not conform, he would either hurry them out of the kingdom, or else do worse.* The bishops supported by such an inspired king, according to Whitgift's impious and sordid flattery, pursued the maxim to accomplish uniformity by persecution. The grievous severities and numerous violences exercised on Non-conformists in that and the next reign, under that tyrannical prelate Laud (said in parliament by Sir Harbottle Grimstone, to be *the great and common enemy of all goodness and good men*), are well known by all truly acquainted with the history of those times: As well as the cruel injustice exercised after the Restoration on great numbers of as good subjects as any in the nation; meerly because they could not come up to this uniformity pleaded for, and enquired according to their measure of knowledge after the truth, and desired to worship GOD according to their consciences: until the late great deliverer (William the IIId. of happy memory) of the British nation from popery and slavery, freed those miserable sufferers (noble confessors for the truth) from a yoke of bondage laid upon them, and gave them a law for the security of their Christian liberty; this *right of private judgment* I have been pleading for. And that this has promoted peace in the state, experience since has proved; as well as former experience made it most evident, that the incroachments upon this right of private judgment, by such legal establishments, have been exceeding prejudicial to the peace of the state: It being impossible but that such methods should cause and perpetuate schisms and divisions of the church, and disturb and disquiet the state; since *the wrath of man cannot work the righteousness of GOD;* and since civil punishments have no tendency to convince the conscience, but only to inflame the passions against the advisers and inflicters of them. And as history gives us so dreadful an account of the melancholy and tragical effects of this practice, one would think, that no people who have any regard for the peace of the flock of CHRIST, who know the worth of liberty, would be fond of such legal establishments, or any such methods as encroach upon Christian liberty, the most valuable of all our rights.

Thus I think I have fully answered all your objections against my second corollary. I therefore proceed to a third.

III. That the civil authority ought to *protect all their subjects* in the enjoyment of *this right of private judgment in matters of religion*, and the liberty of worshipping GOD according to their consciences. That being the end of civil government (as we have seen) *viz.* the greater security of enjoyment of what belongs to every one, and *this right of private judgment*, and worshipping GOD according to their consciences, being the *natural and unalienable right of every man*, what men by entering into civil society neither did, nor could give up into the hands of the community; it is but a just consequence, that they are to be protected in the enjoyment of this right as well as any other. A worshipping assembly of Christians have surely as much right to be protected from molestation in their worship, as the inhabitants of a town assembled to consult their civil interests from disturbance *&c.* This right I am speaking of, is the most valuable right, of which every one ought to be most tender, of universal and equal concernment to all; and security and protection in the enjoyment of it the just expectation of every individual. And the civil magistrate in endeavouring and doing this, most truly comes up to the character of a nursing father to the church of CHRIST. If this had been protected as it ought to have been, what infinite mischief to the Christian church had been prevented? From the want of a due care of this, the clergy through pride and ambition assumed the power of prescribing to, imposing on and domineering over the consciences of men; civil rulers for their own private ends helping it forward; which went on 'till it produced the most detestable monster the earth ever had upon it, the pope, who has deluged the earth with the blood of Christians. This being the true spirit of popery, to impose their determinations on all within their power by any methods which may appear most effectual: and those civil magistrates that suffered and helped that beast to invade this right, did therein *commit fornication with her, and give her their strength and power;* and so instead of proving fathers to their people, proved the cursed butchers of them. It has been by asserting and using this right, that any of the *nations who have been drunk with the Wine of her Fornication, have come out from her Abominations:* and would the civil magistrates of those nations, who at this day worship the beast, but protect their subjects in *this natural right of every one's judging for himself in matters of religion*, according to that alone rule the Bible; that settled darkness of ignorance, error & idolatry, which now involves them, would vanish as the darkness of the night does by the rising of the sun. How unspeakable would the advantages be, arising from the protection of this right, did they reach no further than to the estates, bodies, and lives of men?

All reformations are built on this single principle I have been pleading for, from which we should never depart: yet it must be owned and deserves to be lamented, that the reformed have too much departed from this principle upon which they at first set up; whence it has come to pass that reformations in one place and another have not been more perfect. For the Prince of Darkness has always found means this way to make a stand against the most vigorous efforts; and if any advantages have been gained in any point, to secure a safe retreat, by infatuating men with that strange sort of pride, whereby they assume to themselves only, but allow to none else, a power of domineering over the consciences of others. Religion will certainly lie under oppression if this unjust authority be transferred, to *decrees of councils, convocations, injunctions of civil magistrates*, or from one man or any order of men to another; as it is if we have any other rule of faith and practice in religion, besides the Bible. It were easy to enlarge on the vast advantages and happiness of admitting no other rule or guide but the sacred scriptures only: thence would flow the greatest blessings to mankind, peace and happiness to the world: so that if there be any rights and liberties of men that challenge protection and security therein from the civil magistrate, it is *this natural right of private judgment in matters of religion*, that the sacred *scriptures only may become the rule to all men in all religious matters*, as they ought to be. In a word, this is the surest way for the ease and quiet of rulers, as well as peace of the state, the surest way to engage the love and obedience of all the subjects. And if there be divers religious sects in the state, and the one attempts to offend the other, and the magistrate interposes only to keep the peace; it is but a natural consequence to suppose that in such case they all finding themselves equally safe, and protected in their rights by the civil power, they will all be equally obedient. It is the power given to one, to oppress the other, that has occasioned all the disturbances about religion. And should the clergy closely adhere to these principles, instead of their being reproached for pride and ambition, as the sowers of strife and contention and disturbance of the peace of the church of God; they would be honoured for their work's sake, esteemed for their character, loved as blessings to the world, heard with pleasure, and become successful in their endeavours to recommend the knowledge and practice of Christianity.

IV. It also follows from the preceeding principles, that *every Christian has right to determine for himself what church to join himself to*; and every church has right to judge in what manner GOD is to be worshipped by them, and *what form of discipline* ought to be observed by them, and the right also of *electing their own officers*. (For brevity sake I put them all together.) From this right of private judgment in matters of religion, sufficiently demonstrated in the foregoing pages, it follows, that no Christian is obliged to join himself to this or the other church, because any man or order of men command him to do so, or because they tell him the worship and discipline thereof is most consonant to the sacred scriptures; For no man has right to judge for him, whether the worship and discipline of this or the other church be most agreeable to the sacred scriptures; and therefore no other can have right to determine for him to which he ought to join himself: This right therefore must lie with every Christian. As this is the right of each individual; so also of a number of them agreeing in their sentiments in these things, to agree to observe the ordinances of Christ together, for their mutual edification according to the rules of the gospel, which makes a particular Christian church. And having voluntarily agreed together for such an end, no man or order of men has any authority to prescribe to them, the manner of their worshipping GOD, or enjoin any form of church discipline upon them. So a *number of such churches* (who are all endowed with equality of power) have right to judge for themselves, whether it be most agreeable to the mind of CHRIST, to consociate together in any particular form; as for instance, of presbyteries, or synods, or the like. And if they should do so, such agreements of their's cannot be made a binding rule to them, by any law of man; as has been demonstrated in the preceeding pages. These churches are all of them as free to think and judge for themselves, as they were before such agreement; their right of private judgment not being given up, but reserved entire for themselves, when they entered into any such supposed agreement. And if on experience of such a method of regimen as they have agreed to, and farther light, they judge any of them, there is good reason for them to forbear practicing farther in that form; they are not held to continue therein, but have right to act according to their present light; they having no other rule but the sacred scripture, they have always a right to act their judgment according to that rule. So also if a greater or lesser number of Christians in any particular church, shall judge another way of worship, or method of discipline, more agreeable to the mind of CHRIST, than what is practised in that church; they have right to withdraw, and to be embodied by themselves. As they ought to signify this desire to their brethren, so they ought to consent; for they can have no right to hold them to themselves: and this without any breach of charity on either side; or of after communion, so long as they hold to CHRIST the head, and are agreed in the great essentials of Christianity. So also from the same premisses it follows, that every church or worshipping assembly has the *right of choosing its own officers:* Tho' it may ordinarily be a point of prudence for a church destitute of a pastor, to consult pastors of other churches where they may be supplied with a person suitable for that office; yet that no way supposes, the full power of election does not lie with the church. It is for the better improving their power of election, that such a method is ever to be taken, and not because they have not the power of election in themselves. Nor can they be bound to this, if they see good reason to act otherwise (as the case has sometimes happened and often may). *Nor can they be at all bound to elect the person recommended:* They are to prove him themselves, and be fully satisfied in his ministerial gifts and qualifications, and may herein be controuled by no power whatever. It is their own good, their everlasting interest that is concerned, and if they judge his doctrine not agreeable to the sacred scriptures, that he is not qualified as he ought to be for a gospel minister they have right to reject him. As they have a right of judging the doctrines taught them, by the sacred scriptures, and of rejecting the same if not agreeable thereto, so it necessarily follows they have equal right to refuse such a one for their teacher, who does not teach according to the scriptures.

But if it be demanded how this power can be exercised, must every individual be agreed in the person, or no election made?

I answer,

1. Such a universal agreement is not necessary, the election may be made by a majority. Experience has shewn where the candidate has had the gospel qualifications for the office, the concurrence in the choice has been universal, at least so general as to bring no difficulty in the exercise of this right. So when there has been any considerable number who judged they had any weighty reason against the election made by a majority, experience has also shewn the majority's denying themselves of that choice, and trying farther, has issued happily for the whole. In such cases, 'tis certain, *wisdom is profitable to direct.* And that rule of our Saviour's, Math. 7. 12. will go a great way in keeping churches in the peaceable exercise of this right.

2. Where a minor part cannot in judgment acquiesce in the choice made by the major part of the worshipping assembly, they have a right to withdraw and choose a minister for themselves, or if not able to support one may attend divine worship in a neighbouring church, where they find they may do it to greater edification. They are all equally vested in the same right, and hold it independent one of another, and each one independent of the whole, or of all the rest. So that the greater number can have no right to impose a minister on the lesser. It is not here as in civil societies where the right of each individual is subjected to the body, or so transferred to the society, as that the act of the majority is legally to be considered as the act of the whole, and binding to each individual. As to what concerns men's civil interests, there is nothing in the nature of things to hinder or prevent its being lawful or best, so to transfer their power to the community. But it is not so in religious matters, where conscience and men's eternal interests are concerned. If the power of acting be transferred in this case, as in that of civil societies (now mentioned)[,] thus, if for instance, the majority should elect an Arminian teacher, the minor part must be so concluded by that choice, as to submit to such a one as their teacher, when at the same time it may be directly against their consciences to receive such doctrines or such a teacher. But since the rights of conscience may not be touched, the right of electing a teacher is not transfer'd to the body by the individuals, as

civil rights may be in civil societies. That principle or supposition, which any ways infers an infringement upon the rights of conscience, cannot be true; as that does, which supposes a majority may impose a minister on a lesser part.

If to avoid what I have asserted, that in such case a minor part may withdraw and choose a minister for themselves, it be here said that they may remove their habitations—

I answer, Since this right of electing a teacher for themselves does truly remain with them, after the choice made by the majority, that right may be exercised by them, and why not in one part of the civil state as well as another? They are guilty of no crime for which they should be banished by the state, nor of any thing whereby they have forfeited a right of possessing their present freeholds: their right to their freeholds remains, and consequently their right to exercise their Christian rights where they be, and have a right to remain. It is to no purpose here to say, perhaps the legislature has fixed the bounds of the parish. For the legislature can make civil societies, and may fix the bounds of towns and parishes for civil purposes; yet they can't make churches, nor may they make any laws that interfere with the rights of Christians. Nor is it to any purpose to say, This would open a door to a great multiplication of churches: For how many populous places, as well as Boston have tried it, and found religion and peace best promoted on these principles; nor is there a probability that churches will by this means be increased beyond their ability to support their ministers.

By what I have said you will find some other of your queries answer'd, without my making particular application, and therefore I leave that for you to do at your own leisure: And should here finish my letter, but that you insist on my giving you my sentiments on a law made in your colony May 1742, intitled *An Act for regulating Abuses, and correcting Disorders in Ecclesiastical Affairs:* Which it seems, thro' the fond opinion some persons among you had of it, was thrust into one of our publick news papers, soon after it was passed; under which every wise by-stander, that was a hearty friend to your civil and religious interests, was ready to write, *Tell it not in Gath &c.*

I shall not descend into every particular that might be offered upon it—some few remarks may suffice.

I. The law is founded on this false principle, *viz.* that the civil authority hath power to establish a form of church-government by penal laws. The act relates wholly to matters of an ecclesiastical nature: and as it supposes, the civil magistrate has authority by penal laws to regulate ecclesiastical matters, so consequently to establish an ecclesiastical constitution by penal laws. It appears from the preamble to the act, that the declared design of it is to keep persons from deviating from the ecclesiastical discipline established by law, in the year 1708 and that under the penalties by this law enacted. But that they have no such authority, has been fully demonstrated in the foregoing pages, which I need not repeat. Whence it must follow, that the act is fundamentally wrong, being made without any authority. Be pleas'd to reflect one minute on this power challenged by this law, to correct, and that by penal laws, such disorders as are purely of an ecclesiastical nature, and see the consequence of it. One disorder to be corrected is, a minister's preaching out of his own parish undesired by the minister and major part of the church where he shall so preach. If the civil magistrate has this power the act supposes, if he judges it to be a disorder for the minister to preach in his own parish on a week day, he may then restrain him: or if he thinks it a disorder that there should be any public prayers but by a set printed form, he may then restrain all to such a form. It is plain, if the civil magistrate has authority to correct ecclesiastical disorders, he has a right to judge what is a disorder in the church, and restrain the same. If he may execute this in one instance, he may in another: and every thing is on this principle liable to be disallowed in the worship of God, which does not suit with the civil magistrate's opinion. Whatever he judges to be a disorder, is so by this principle, and may be restrained accordingly. And so farewell all Christian liberty. It signifies nothing to say, your civil magistrates are so sound in the faith, there's no danger they will go so far. I hope so indeed with you; tho' you can't tell what those or others in succeeding times may do. It is no new thing for civil authority to make dreadful havock of the liberties and religion of Christians; but the argument, you see, proceeds upon the nature of things. The principle, that law stands upon, you may plainly see, is directly inconsistent in its own nature, with the unalienable rights of Christians. What sad effects have been felt in our own nation, in some former reigns, from this very principle's being put in practice; who at all acquainted with history can be ignorant? While they were executing what they were pleased to call wholsome severities on dissenters, they were only in their judgment correcting disorders in ecclesiastical affairs. If this power belongs to the civil authority, as such, it must belong to those in one state as well as another; and is as justly challenged by the civil authority in France, as in New-England. Let it be but once supposed the civil magistrate has this authority, where can you stop? what is there in religion not subjected to his judgment? All must be disorder in religion, which he is pleased to call so; you can have no more of the external part of religion than he is pleased to leave you, and may have so much of superstition as he is pleased to enjoin under the head of order. So that this law stands on no better a foundation, than what infers the destruction of Christian liberty.

Having made this general observation, I go on, to consider the first paragraph, which runs thus—

> That if any ordained minister or other person licensed as aforesaid to preach, shall enter into any parish not immediately under his charge, and shall there preach or exhort the people, he shall be denied and secluded the benefit of any law of this colony made for the support and encouragement of the gospel ministry; except such ordained minister or licensed person shall be expresly invited and desired so to enter into such other parish, and there to preach and exhort the people, either by the settled minister, and the major part of the church of said parish; or in case there be no settled minister, then by the church or society in said parish.

The minister's heretofore supposed right to have assistance and help from his brethren in the ministry by preaching, is hereby cut off. None may preach unless the major part of the church desire it; tho' the minister and one half of the church and all the rest of the congregation, which make up much the greater part of the number, who have right to hear the word preached, are ever so desirous of hearing the word from another, and apprehensive (as the case may be) of the great necessity of it. Before this law was passed, I should have presumed, there was not one minister on the continent, but what thought he had good right to invite any orthodox minister to preach in his pulpit: not only ministers, but churches in every part of the world, have so supposed and practised. But it seems by this law this supposition is a mistake, and the practice a disorder in the church. Yet if the minister has no such right, how comes it to pass, that the greater part of his hearers are cut off from any right to hear such as may be ever so well qualified to instruct. The non-communicants, which perhaps make three quarters of the parish, are in one part of this paragraph consider'd as a cypher, and in another part as having full right to hear whom they desire, viz. *in a parish where they have no settled minister*. In such case, it is supposed by this law, they have right to hear any minister they desire tho' not one church-member join with them in the desire; for they may make up a majority of the society without one communicant with them. Yet the day before, while the minister of such a parish was living, it seems, if the same persons had been desirous of hearing the same man, they are by this law cut off the privilege; if the minister's desire too had been joined with them, it would have helped nothing: or rather (in short) as this law stands, this very circumstance of their having a minister extinguishes their right of hearing such preachers as they desire. Such now being the plain sense of this paragraph; I say then,

II. That it is apparently inconsistent with itself, deprives ministers and particular Christians of their rights and liberties, and invests a lordly power in a small part of a parish-society, viz. a major part or one half of a church, over a worshipping assembly, since they never had nor can have any rightful power to hinder other Christians in the parish from hearing such ministers as they judge may promote their spiritual good, as by this law they are enabled to do.

III. It invests an exorbitant power in ministers over a church and congregation. This may look very strange, especially when you reflect, that by the preamble to this law the ministers are represented as having departed from the established ecclesiastical discipline, and been guilty of disorderly and irregular practices; and therefore are such persons as are not fit to be left to conduct themselves, in their ministerial office, nor to be governed by their own ecclesiastical constitution, but must of necessity be laid under some extraordinary legal restraints. I say, they are thus plainly represented (whether truly, or not, is not the question) by the preamble; yet, nothwithstanding all this, they are by this law vested with an exorbitant power over the churches. Christians, it seems, must be strip'd of an invaluable branch of liberty Christ has vested them with, & the same must be lodged in that order of men, who are represented as unfaithful in the execution of their trust. For by this law every minister has not only power given him, to prevent any other minister's preaching in his parish, not only if a small number desire it, but if the whole worshipping assembly desire it; not only in the pulpit, but in any private house, which is directly inconsistent with the rights of Christians: but also in case a parish be under a necessity of settling another minister thro' the incumbent's disability to discharge his pastoral office, it is put into his power to negative any choice they shall make of a minister, and so churches are really stript of their right of electing their own ministers. It is plain by the words of the law, none can preach in the parish without the settled minister's consent: & if one preaches to day by his leave, and the whole worshipping assembly desire his continued preaching, he has it in his power by this law to prevent his preaching to-morrow. And therefore if a church can call and settle none (in such a case) but whom their present pastor pleases (as is certainly the case by this law), the right of electing their minister is taken from them. A supposed right in *A*, dependent on the will of *B*, is no right at all. And this, as I have heard, is the case of one church on Connecticut River, now groaning under this oppression: which may also prove the case of any, or of all other churches in that colony, if they remain under the misery of such a law.

IV. The persons supposed to be criminal by this law, are subjected to an unreasonable punishment, and this too without any trial in the law, in any form whatever. The supposed crime is a minister or licensed candidate's preaching in a parish where the incumbent and major part of the church have not invited: *i.e.* If the incumbent has invited with one half of the church and three quarters of the whole parish, or if the whole church and parish invite, and not the incumbent, or if there is not more than half of the church, or more than half of the society, where there is no incumbent; each of these is such a crime for which the punishment is, *the denial and seclusion from the benefit of any law of the colony made for the support and encouragement of the gospel ministry*. Now I find by looking into your colony law-book, the laws made for the aforesaid purpose may be sum'd up in these few words, *viz.*

> That all agreements made by the inhabitants of a society or the major part of them assembled in a society-meeting, respecting the settlement and maintenance of the minister they have chosen, shall be binding to all the inhabitants of such society, and to their successors; which sums or pay-

> ments so agreed to shall be levied and assessed on the several inhabitants in such society, according to their respective estates from time to time, as they shall be set in the general list; which sums or payments shall be gathered by such person said society shall appoint to be the collector of them, who is to repair to an assistant or justice of the peace for a warrant to enable him to collect the rate.

Now then, as by the preceeding laws, such agreements are made binding to the inhabitants of a society and their successors &c. hence to be denied and secluded the benefit of any law made for the support and encouragement of the gospel ministry, includes in it the being denied and secluded the benefit of holding the society to such agreements; and so this law plainly intends, by prohibiting any assistant or justice of the peace, to sign any warrant for collecting a rate where a minister has been certified against, as having acted contrary to this law. So that, in short, the punishment is the deprivation of his livelihood; and thence forward he may beg his bread. This appears unreasonable, to inflict so heavy a punishment for preaching in such cases as abovementioned, when (as it may happen) it might be evidently duty so to do. But let the preaching be at the desire of more or fewer, still it is no immorality: it is but an ecclesiastical disorder, even in the account of this law, which surely can't deserve so severe a penalty. Many gross immoralities have a much less punishment assigned for them, than this heretofore supposed innocent action of preaching the gospel. If the civil peace was broken by it, I can't see how so severe a punishment for it can be justified. But it is evident, the civil peace is not broken by this supposed crime, which is nothing but preaching the gospel; which is so far from breaking the peace, or tending thereto, that it intirely tends to make men better, and so better subjects. The preaching out of his own parish does not alter the nature of the action, nor is the natural tendency of the word changed thereby; no man's civil property or interest is at all invaded by it; and how such an action can be punished at all, appears mysterious to me! It is not for preaching sedition or treason, but even the gospel of peace, that CHRIST'S ministers are render'd liable to be deprived of their daily bread.

If it should be here said, That these laws made for the support of the gospel ministry, are to be looked upon as acts of favour, relative to such as comply with the ecclesiastical constitution of the government; and so if any ministers will not keep within the bounds of that constitution, they justly forfeit such favour; and so the punishment here is to be understood, a declaration that their right to such favour now ceases. I answer,

1. That action, which by this law is made thus criminal, is not contrary to, but well consistent with the ecclesiastical constitution, under which these ministers are supposed to settle. It is not inconsistent with that ecclesiastical constitution, for any minister to preach in any other parish than his own to any number of Christians on their desire at any of their private religious exercises. But I will only instance in one particular made thus criminal by this act, which is warranted by that ecclesiastical constitution, and the constant practice of the churches. The right hand of fellowship is given at every ordination, in which the ministers and churches concerned, do solemnly promise to esteem and treat the person ordained as a duly authorized minister of CHRIST, and to be ready on all occasions to own him as such, and to assist him in his work: In consequence of these solemn promises, ministers & churches have looked upon themselves under such obligations to each other, that if one of these ministers' judges he has real need of assistance in preaching, from another (where these mutual obligations take place) he has right to ask it, tho' the church does not join with him in it, and the church's so hearing him preach they have always judged (and therein they have judged truly) is acting but agreable to those previous obligations they have laid themselves under to him, to treat him as an authorized minister of CHRIST, and to hold communion with him as such; one way of doing which, is certainly hearing the word from him. So that it is plain, one minister's preaching for another upon his desire, tho' the church joins not in it, is at least well consistent with the ecclesiastical constitution (and I need say no more of it in this argument) under which these ministers are supposed to settle, according to the objection: and therefore no forfeiture is made, by such an action, of the benefit of the laws made in favour of the ecclesiastical constitution. They have right to this benefit so long (at least) as they act consistently with that ecclesiastical constitution under which they settled. The act, disallow'd by this law, and for which they are deprived of this benefit, is consistent with that constitution. In this manner therefore to deprive them of it, is to take it away while their right to it in equity remains

good. This, you see, I have said on the supposition, those laws are to be considered only as acts of grace, as laid in the objection. But then I say in the next place—

2. The laws here referred to, made for the support of the gospel ministry, are not acts of grace; they are no other than what the legislature tho't themselves obliged to make. If the civil authority of a state are obliged to take care for the support of religion, or in other words, of schools and the gospel ministry, in order to their approving themselves nursing fathers (as, I suppose, every body will own, and therefore I shall not spend any time in proving it), then the law especially referred to is *not an act of grace*. It was what the legislature judged most just, easy, and equal for the people, safe and easy for the minister, who is to give himself wholly to his work; or in a word, best for the people and the minister, that contracts should be so made, so binding and so performed; for both people and minister are concerned in the act. I don't say, the legislature could not have provided as well in some other way: this is no ways necessary to be supposed in the case. But as they were obliged to make some good provision in the case, both with respect to the people who are to pay, and the minister who is to receive, so in their wisdom they fixed on that method, as what was good for the whole. 'Tis therefore no more an act of grace, than any act of the legislature respecting any civil interests or contracts of the subject. What the public good calls for therein, they are obliged to do: And the acts they make in pursuance thereof are no acts of grace, but (strictly speaking) of debt to the people. And as the act, referred to, is not an act of grace, so this law brings a punishment, not only on the minister, as before observed, but on the people too, by letting them loose from their agreement with their minister, the now supposed offender. For the minister remaining with the people, they have a new contract to make, and must take some other method for performing it, than what the law in the former case had provided: And from the known straithanded disposition in too many towards the support of the gospel, it must needs follow, that the burden of the support of it must lie much more unequally upon the people, and perhaps on but a very few. As this is the certain consequence, so is it a certainty, that an innocent people are punished, with their minister, by this law. Besides, how the letting a people loose from their solemn agreements with their minister,

for an action never supposed criminal before this law was made, and is certainly no violation of the contract he made with them, can consist with justice and equity, is beyond the ken of ordinary understandings: which I might have argued from as a distinct head; but it is sufficient to observe it as I pass, it lying now in my way. To return, As the punishment is extraordinary, so is the *manner of inflicting it extraordinary too*, viz. *the minister of the parish where he shall so offend, or the civil authority or any two of the committee of such parish, sending an information thereof in writing under their hands to the clerk of the parish where such offending minister does belong*, this does the business at once, as appears by the third paragraph in the act. So that meerly from the information of one person (as it may be) of a different persuasion in religion, and inclined from a party-spirit to oppress, or one that has a personal prejudice against a minister, given to the clerk of a parish (whether true or false) the minister is deprived of his livelihood. Thus the business is effected without any formality of a legal trial, or the shadow of it. This, as I take it, is directly contrary to the priviledges of an Englishman contained in Magna Charta, which has cost our predecessors rivers of blood to defend, and transmit down as sacred to their descendants. If such a law as condemns a man without hearing him, deserves to be expunged the records of a free people (I might say, any; such a law being a scandal to human nature) I leave you to say, what fate such a law as this before us deserves.

V. I observe, by the second paragraph of this law, any association of ministers are subjected to the before-mentioned penalty,

> That shall undertake to examine or license any candidate for the ministry, or assume to themselves the decision of any controversy, or to counsel and advise in any affair that by the Say-Brook Platform is within the province and jurisdiction of any other association: Then and in such case every member that shall be present in such association so licensing, deciding or counselling, shall be each and every of them denied and secluded the benefit of any law of this colony made for the support and encouragement of the gospel-ministry.

Now this is subjecting men to a heavy punishment, for no crime against the civil state, nay for deeds in themselves good, and such as may be very serviceable to the interests of religion, as well as what may happen to be otherwise; for so the acts of any association sometimes may be, that are allowed of by this law.

As they who drew up the platform, tho't it would be best for the candidates of the ministry to be examined, so they no doubt tho't every association had men of learning and fidelity to do it: and if it were done by any of them, the great end proposed in such examination would be answered. And suppose the association of New-London county should examine and license a candidate, that belonged to the New-Haven association, may it not be supposed it would be as well done, and as well answer the end, as if done in New-Haven. Or if a parish within the district of New-Haven association, destitute of a minister, should after they had tried one candidate and another, which they had been advised to by the association, and not suited by any of them, ask advice of New-London association, and they advise them to one within their limits, who they judge well qualified for the ministry, whom upon trial they judge so too, and so are well suited in a minister, what harm comes of this? or what iniquity was there in the act of New-London association advising in that case? How often have churches found it needful to do so, and religion been served by it? How often have they gone out of the colony for such advice, and the ministers of the Massachusetts advised churches in Connecticut in such a case, on their application for it; and so on the contrary, ministers in Connecticut, advised churches in the Massachusetts? Where lies the difference! or was this always criminal in its own nature! or if not, why should a whole association of ministers, for doing what I have above instanced in, be stripped of their livings, as it seems by this law they must! And what is more extraordinary still, *a minister's meerly being present when it is done, renders him liable to this punishment*, whether he has any hand in it or no; nay, for ought appears, if he should protest against it, yet he escapes no part of the penalty. The crime, it seems, is of such a nature, that if a man be in the same room, tho' he protests against the action, he is still equally faulty with the actors: for since he is equally punished, he must be supposed equally faulty. I don't imagine, you will envy any set of men the glory of such a rare invention. But to finish on this head; nothing is more evident, than that such an examination or advice, now instanced in, does not touch the civil peace; and certainly therefore, the civil authority go out of their line to make this penal law. And how near this comes to *turning judgment into wormwood*, may deserve the serious consideration of some.

VI. The fourth paragraph respects a licensed candidate's or any layman's *publickly preaching and exhorting in any parish, not desired* in such manner as expressed in the first paragraph. On which I shall but briefly observe, that the words expressive of the offence, are of so loose or general signification, as that a person merely for religious discourse, or the most savoury advice, seasonably and prudently given at any private religious meeting of Christians, is liable to be treated as an offender; and if I have not been misinformed, there have been instances of this: However that be, there is danger of it. Or if a man going into any publick house, should hear a company talking profanely and wickedly, and thereupon seriously lay open their sin, and gravely advise them thereupon, he would be liable to be treated as an offender; and as the hands may be, into which he might happen to fall, he would not escape it. But further, if it be supposed such preaching and exhorting there referred to, be a disorder sometimes, yet it is not always so: but whenever it is so (unless you suppose it done to the interruption of some lawful assembly) it is no breach of the peace, and comes not under civil cognizance. Such disorderly persons ought to be proceeded against in an ecclesiastical manner, agreable to the laws of CHRIST.

VII. I come now to the last paragraph, which runs thus:

> That if any foreigner or stranger that is not an inhabitant within this colony, including as well such persons, that have no ecclesiastical character, or license to preach, as such as have received ordination or license to preach by any association or presbytery, shall presume to preach, teach or publickly to exhort in any town or society within this colony, without the desire and license of the settled minister and the major part of the church of such town or society; or at the call and desire of the church and inhabitants of such town or society, provided that it so happen that there is no settled minister there; that every such teacher or exhorter shall be sent (as a vagrant person) by warrant from any one assistant or justice of the peace from constable to constable, out of the bounds of this colony.

Since which, you tell me, there has been last October an addition made, *viz.*

> That whoso thus offends shall pay the costs of his transportation; and if he returns again and offends in such sort, it is made the duty of any assistant or justice of the peace that shall be informed thereof, to cause such person to be apprehended and brought before him, and if found guilty, to

> give judgment that such person shall become bound in the penal sum of an hundred pounds lawful money, to his peaceable and good behaviour until the next county court, in the county where the offence shall be committed, and that such person will not offend again in like manner; and the county court may (if they see cause) further bind &c. during their pleasure.

Occasioned, as I am informed, by that good gentleman Mr. Finl[e]y's coming at the direction of a presbytery in the New-Jersey government, who had been applied to for a minister, and preaching to a Presbyterian church at Milford, who had join'd themselves to that presbytery and put themselves under their care; for which being transported out of the government, he returned and preached to a congregational church at New-Haven, who had been allowed, as well as the former at Milford, to be a society for the worshipping of God, by the county court at New-Haven, by virtue of a law formerly made for the ease of such as soberly dissent from the way of worship and ministry established by the laws of Connecticut; and for this he was adjudged by the civil authority to be transported again, which was but in part effected thro' the negligence of some officer; and, I'm told, he returned and preached again. This his preaching and exhorting, it seems, *greatly disquieted and disturbed the people;* as the preamble to this act expresses it. Is it not strange, the preaching of that peaceable and humble Christian (as you confess his behaviour bespoke him to be while in the colony) unto a number of people, who had right to hear the gospel preached from him, should *greatly disquiet* and *disturb* such as had their choice in hearing others! Or could it disquiet and disturb any minds except such as can't bear their Christian neighbours should enjoy their unalienable rights! But to return to the before mentioned last paragraph, I observe, that *any stranger, not an inhabitant in the colony, who has received ordination or license to preach from any association or presbytery, that shall presume to preach undesired,* as expressed in the paragraph, is liable to be treated as a vagrant, unworthy to tread on that spot of earth: But if he should happen to be licensed by the patriarch of Greece, a super-intendant of Denmark, or any bishop, he may escape the lash of this law. If the coming in of a stranger and preaching in such a manner be such a breach of the peace, as is punishable by the state, why should there be such partiality? Why should Dr. Watt's preaching in such manner in Connecticut be a greater crime, because ordained by a presbytery, than any other stranger's doing so that was licensed by a patriarch or bishop, *&c.* However, that is much less to be wondered at, than such treatment as this law subjects orthodox ministers to, even the best ministers of Christ upon earth, for a mere non-conformity to a certain point of order, that never took place (I suppose) in any church upon earth.

But to be as brief as may be in the consideration of this paragraph; let the question be, if you please, exactly according to the words, *viz.* Whether a civil state has rightful authority to banish or thrust out a confessedly orthodox minister of Jesus Christ, tho' a foreigner or stranger, for only preaching the gospel to a number, without the desire of the incumbent, and major part of the church in the parish wherein he shall so preach; the said minister being supposed to have a right to protection, and a right to remain in that state, until he does something to forfeit it? I have truly stated it, because I have mentioned the very supposed crime for which such foreigners or strangers are to be thrust out of the government; and I must necessarily suppose them true or orthodox ministers of Christ, because this law supposes them so, since it speaks of such as are ordained or *licensed by any association or presbytery* not within that government; which includes all such as are on this continent, as well as Great-Britain (at least) all of which are esteemed orthodox. I put in the last words, because they really relate to the subjects of the king of Great Britain, from whom the government holds it charter, and so to any persons in the plantations, as well as on the isle of Great Britain, who have a right therefore to be treated as Englishmen, or fellow-subjects under King George, and so may be truly said to have a right to remain in the colony, in such a sense as you will not allow to any belonging to another kingdom. I don't mention this because I would go into the consideration of what particular powers may be in your charter, different from others; tho' I confess, I can't find any words in your charter, that express or imply a power to do any thing that is pretended to be done by this law, to establish or regulate by law any matters of an ecclesiastical nature, to impose any civil pains or penalties in matters of conscience, relating to the worship of God. But neither your colony, nor any other in the king's dominions, have any rightful authority to do as is here supposed, according to the question, as I have truly stated it. Let me here take a plain case to illustrate the point.

Wickliff arose a light in England, while popery prevailed: be it supposed, he instructed a few in the truth, but neither bishop nor incumbent of the parish would give leave for his preaching. However, he goes on preaching the gospel, and the people will hear him. In this case, the king and parliament had no rightful authority to banish Wickliff, or turn him out from the island, for his so preaching. For, as has been already shewn in the preceeding pages, *the end of civil government being the preservation of person and property, it would be a plain departing from the end of civil government, to inflict any punishment on Wickliff for his so preaching.* What the civil authority is obliged to defend and secure, is not hurt at all by the supposed action of Wickliff; and it is really acting against the design of the civil magistrate's trust, to hurt an innocent subject. Besides, the right of private judgment in matters of religion being unalienable, and what the civil magistrate is rather oblig'd to protect his subjects equally in, both Wickliff, and they who desired to hear him, had a just right to remain where they were, in the enjoyment of that right, free from all molestation from any persons whatsoever; agreeable to what has been sufficiently evidenced in the foregoing pages. On the other hand, see the absurdity of supposing that the civil magistrate had rightful authority to have sent away Wickliff. If the magistrate had right to send him away because the standing clergy were unwilling he should preach (that being one of the cases supposed in this law) then the civil authority must have had equal right to send any other such person away, as fast as they appeared; and consequently they must be supposed to have had rightful authority to hold their subjects in the worst slavery, i.e. to keep them from the exercise of their private judgment in matters of religion; a power to do which never was nor could be vested in the civil magistrate, by the people, by any original compact, which is truly supposed the foundation of all civil government. It alters not the nature of civil government, whether the magistrate be Protestant or papist, Christian or pagan. What of right appertains to the civil magistrate by virtue of his office, must also necessarily belong to him, tho' popish, or heathen. The supposal therefore that the civil magistrate in England at that day had rightful authority to have sent away Wickliff, for preaching the gospel without leave of the clergy, is big with too great an absurdity, for a consistent Protestant to swallow. Suppose then these colonies to have existed at that time, or Great

Britain and these colonies popish now, as Great-Britain was then, and Wickliff to come into any of them and preach in some parish without the consent of the incumbent, at the desire of a number of people, it is certain, in this case none of these colonies could have any rightful authority to thrust him out of their borders, or do any thing like it. The same reasons must conclude against these colonies authority to transport him, for coming and preaching now without an incumbent's leave at the desire of a number, as in the former case; the same principles and reasoning will hold equally true, applied to any such instance as now before us, any time since the reformation from popery. The civil peace is no ways broken by this action of preaching, of which we are speaking: But indeed if any should take occasion from it, to contend and quarrel with their neighbours, as papists and heathens have sometimes done, the Apostle (James 4. 1.) has shown us the true spring thereof, the lusts in men's hearts the outbreakings of which in injuries to their neighbours, fall under the civil magistrate's cognizance. And the rights of *conscience and private judgment* in matters of religion are unalterably the same: And 'tis a scandal to Christians, to contend and quarrel with their neighbours for enjoying them, and inexcusable in a Protestant state to make any infringement upon them. And it was on these very principles, which here advance (and by which this law must fall) that our first reformers acted, and on which all reformations must be built. And tho' our nation in times past under the influence of a bigotted clergy, and arbitrary weak or popish princes, have made laws founded on principle contrary to these I have been pleading for; yet they seem in great measure rooted out of the nation: and these principle[s] of truth have taken root, and been growing ever since the happy Revolution, and Act of Toleration; and 'tis to be hoped will prevail & spread more and more, until all spiritual tyranny and lording it over the consciences of men, be banished out of the world.

But I shall finish with observing, That by virtue of the Act of Toleration, all his majesty's subjects are so freed from the force of all coercive laws in matters of religion, relating to worship and discipline, that they act their own private judgment, without restraint: That any number of Christians greater or less, hear any Protestant minister they desire, without controul from the will of others, or authority of the civil state: Since this is the case, and withal as plain as the sun in the meridian, that where such a law as this I have been considering, takes place, there people are abridged of that Christian liberty, which the same persons would enjoy under the present constitution, if they were in England. And how far therefore it falls short of denying and secluding them from the benefit of the Act of Toleration, I leave you to say, who well know, that it is expressly provided by the terms of your charter, that *the laws to be made in virtue of it, shall not be contrary to the Laws of England.* This right of private judgment and liberty now mentioned, is confessed and secured to you by that law which was the glory of the reign of William and Mary; but by your law now before me, it is denied to you. How you will clear it from a contrariety to the former, I know not. Nor is this about a trivial matter, or what is dependent upon the will of your legislature. The rights of Magna Charta depend not on the will of the prince, or the will of the legislature; but they are the inherent natural rights of Englishmen: secured and confirmed they may be by the legislature, but not derived from nor dependent on their will. And if there be any rights, any priviledges, that we may call natural and unalienable, this is one, *viz.* the right of private judgment, and liberty of worshipping God according to our consciences, without controul from human laws. A priviledge more valuable than the civil rights of Magna Charta. This we hold, not from man, but from God: which therefore no man can touch and be innocent. And all the invaders of it will certainly find, when they shall stand at his bar, from whom we hold this, *that CHRIST will be king in his own kingdom.* In the mean time, it stands Christians in hand to hold fast this priviledge, and to be on their guard against all attempts made upon it. And I doubt not, those ministers who were apprehensive of this, and freely addressed the legislative body of Connecticut (as I hear was done October 1742) for a repeal of this law, did therein what was pleasing to their great Lord & Master which is in heaven. They acted becoming such as durst not themselves, and were willing to do what lay in their power that others might not, *lord it over God's heritage.* Not that I would insinuate, that there were no others like-minded with them—but that therein they set an excellent example for others to copy after, and what was proper to awaken the attention of Christians. It has commonly been the case, that Christian liberty, as well as civil, has been lost by little and little; and experience has taught, that it is not easy to recover it, when once lost. So precious a jewel is always to be watched with a careful eye: for no people are likely to enjoy liberty long, that are not zealous to preserve it. As a real friend to it, I have given you my thoughts with freedom and plainness, as you desired. If they prove satisfying to you, and you judge that they may be any ways serviceable to the cause of truth and Christian liberty, you may use them for that purpose as you shall think best.

I am &c.
Philalethes

Eleutheropolis,
March 30, 1744.

4

BRITAIN'S MERCIES, AND BRITAIN'S DUTIES

George Whitefield

BOSTON

1746

GEORGE WHITEFIELD (1714–1770). Although the Great Awakening was already in progress when Whitefield made his first journey to America in 1738, it owed more to him than to any other individual. He was truly the Great Awakener. Whitefield was born in Gloucester, England, and grew up in poverty. Two years after graduation from Oxford in 1736, he was ordained an Anglican priest. He made seven trips to America and preached in virtually every important town on the Atlantic seaboard during 1738, 1739–41, 1744–48, 1751–52, 1754–55, 1763–65, and 1769–70. He had begun his work with Charles and John Wesley in the Holy Club at Oxford, where Charles was a tutor at Christ Church, and he participated in their mission in Georgia, which remained his base over the decades. He shared the Wesleys' conviction that a "new birth" and a converted ministry were needed, but by 1740 he had become more strictly Calvinist, while John Wesley had turned to Arminianism.

Undoubtedly, Whitefield was the greatest evangelist of the century, preaching an average of forty hours each week, four times in a day that began at four in the morning and ended punctually at ten in the evening. It is estimated that he preached about 18,000 sermons in his lifetime. His histrionic gifts were the envy of David Garrick. Doubters, like Benjamin Franklin, who joined an audience of perhaps 30,000 Philadelphians in 1740, emptied their pockets, mesmerized, for Whitefield's Savannah orphanage, Bethesda.

After the Seven Years' (French and Indian) War ended in 1763, Whitefield arrived in America for his sixth tour. On April 2, 1764, he held a private conversation in Portsmouth, New Hampshire, with Samuel Langdon and other established ministers that alarmed Americans already worried about their liberty. Whitefield was quoted as saying: "I can't in conscience leave the town without acquainting you with a secret. My heart bleeds for America. O poor New England! There is a deep laid plot against your civil and religious liberties, and they will be lost. Your golden days are at an end. You have nothing but trouble before you. . . . Your liberties will be lost." Whitefield outlined the secret plans (as he said) of the British Ministry to end colonial self-government and to establish the Anglican Church (William Gordon, *The History of the Rise, Progress and Establishment of the United States* . . . [2d ed., 3 vols. New York: Samuel Campbell, 1794],

BRITAIN's *Mercies, and* BRITAIN's *Duty*;

Represented in a

SERMON

Preach'd at the NEW-BUILDING in

PHILADELPHIA,

On SUNDAY *August* 24, 1746.

Occasioned by the Suppression of the late

Unnatural Rebellion.

By *George Whitefield*, A. B.
Late of *Pembroke-College*, OXON.

The Second Edition.

BOSTON:

Printed and Sold by *S. Kneeland* and *T. Green* in Queen-Street. 1746.

1:102). This episode galvanized the clergy in their opposition to British policy, especially when the intelligence proved true and the 1765 Stamp Act was adopted.

Whitefield made one more trip to America, arriving in the fall of 1769. On September 30, 1770, the evangelist suddenly died of an apparent asthma attack in Newburyport, Massachusetts, at the home of the Reverend Jonathan Parsons, in whose church, the First (South) Presbyterian Church, he was scheduled to preach that morning.

The sermon reprinted here communicates little of the power of the spoken words of the great evangelist, a notorious characteristic of Whitefield's published works. Still, it gives the flavor of his political theology. The events he refers to are those of the War of the Austrian Succession (called King George's War in North America), in which the French forces' stronghold at Louisbourg had been captured by a ragtag collection of New England frontiersmen and militia under the command of William Pepperel in June 1745. While this victory is celebrated as pivotal, the specific reason for the day of thanksgiving being observed by Whitefield and his auditors was the recent destruction by a storm at sea of a French fleet sent to recapture Cape Breton and Nova Scotia, an event in which the hand of Providence could be seen. The vigorous Indian warfare along the Pennsylvania and New York frontier also influences the discourse.

The sermon was preached at the New Building in Philadelphia on Sunday, August 24, 1746. Whitefield, writes Michael A. Lofaro, "is central to the understanding of eighteenth century America. . . . The success of his itinerant ministry in the colonies indirectly hastened the break with England by increasing the number of dissenters and, by forming them into loosely affiliated, intercolonial, interdenominational 'congregations,' perceptibly encouraged American independence" (*American Writers Before 1800*, p. 1581).

That they might observe His Statutes, and keep his Laws.

Psalm CV. 45.

Men, brethren and fathers, and all ye to whom I am about to preach the kingdom of GOD, I suppose you need not be informed, that being indispensably obliged to be absent on your late thanksgiving-day, I could not shew my obedience to the Governor's proclamation, as my own inclination led me, or as might justly be expected from, and demanded of me. But as the occasion of that day's thanksgiving is yet, and I trust ever will be, fresh in our memory, I cannot think that a discourse on the subject can even now be altogether unseasonable. I take it for granted further, that you need not be informed, that among the various motives which are generally urged to enforce obedience to the divine commands, that of love is the most powerful and cogent. The terrors of the law may afright and awe, but love dissolves and melts the heart. The love of CHRIST, says the great Apostle of the gentiles, constraineth us. Nay, love is so absolutely necessary for those that name the name of CHRIST, that without it, their obedience cannot truly be stiled evangelical, or be acceptable in the sight of GOD. *Although*, says the same Apostle, *I bestow all my Goods to feed the Poor, and though I give my Body to be burnt, and have not Charity* (*i.e.* unless unfeigned love to GOD, and to mankind for his great name's sake, be the principle of such actions), howsoever it may benefit others, *it profiteth* me *nothing*. This is the constant language of the lively oracles of GOD. And, from them it is equally plain, that nothing has a greater tendency to beget and excite such an obediential love in us than a serious and frequent consideration of the manifold mercies we receive time after time from the hands of our heavenly Father. The royal Psalmist, who had the honour of being stiled *the man after GOD's own heart*, had an abundant experience of this. Hence it is, that whilst he is musing on the divine goodness, the fire of divine love kindles in his soul; and, *out of the abundance of his heart, his mouth speaketh* such grateful and extatic language as this—"*What shall I render unto the Lord for all His Mercies? Bless the Lord, O my Soul, and all that is within me bless his holy Name.*" And why? "*Who forgiveth all thine Iniquities, who healeth all thy Diseases, who redeemeth thy Life from Destruction, who crowneth thee with loving Kindness and tender Mercies.*" And when the same holy man of GOD had a mind to stir up the people of the Jews to set about a national reformation, as the most weighty and prevailing argument he could make use of for that purpose, he lays before them, as it were, in a draught, many national mercies, and distinguishing deliverances, which had been conferred upon, and wrought out for them, by the most high GOD. The psalm to which the words of our text belong, is a pregnant proof of this; it being a kind of epitome or compendium of the whole Jewish history: At least it contains an enumeration of many signal and extraordinary blessings the Israelites had received from GOD, and also the improvement they were in duty bound to make of them, viz. *to observe his statutes and keep his laws.*

To run through all the particulars of the psalm, or draw a parallel (which might with great ease and justice be done) between GOD's dealings with us and the Israelites of old—to enumerate all the national mercies bestow'd upon, and remarkable deliverances wrought out for the kingdom of Great Britain, from the infant state of William the Conqueror, to her present manhood, and more than Augustan maturity, under the auspicious reign of our dread and rightful sovereign King George the Second; howsoever pleasing and profitable it might be at any other time, would, at this juncture, prove, if not an irksome, yet an unseasonable undertaking.

The occasion of the late solemnity, I mean the suppression of a most horrid and unnatural rebellion will afford more than sufficient matter for a discourse of this nature, and furnish us with abundant motives to love and obey that glorious *Jehovah, who giveth Salvation unto Kings, and delivers His People from the hurtful Sword.*

Need I make an apology before this auditory, if, in order to see the greatness of our late deliverance, I should remind you of the many unspeakable blessings which we have for a course of years enjoy'd, during the reign of his present majesty, and the gentle mild administration under which we live? Without justly incurring the censure of giving flattering titles, I believe all who have eyes to see, and ears to hear, and are but a little acquainted with our publick affairs, must acknowledge, that we have one of the best of kings. It is now above nineteen years since he began to reign over us. And yet, was he to be seated on a royal throne, and were all his subjects placed before him;

was he to address them as Samuel once addressed the Israelites, "*Behold here I am, Old and Greyheaded, witness against me before the Lord, whose Ox have I taken? Or whose Ass have I taken? Or whom have I defrauded? Whom have I oppressed?* They must, if they would do him justice, make the same answer as was given to Samuel, "*Thou hast not defrauded us, nor oppressed us.*" What Tertullus, by way of flattery, said to Felix, may with the strictest justice be applied to our sovereign, "*By thee we enjoy great quietness, and very worthy deeds have been done unto our nation by thy providence.*" He has been indeed *pater patriæ*, a father to our country, and, tho' old and greyheaded, has jeoparded his precious life for us in the high places of the field. Nor has he less deserved that great and glorious title which the Lord promises kings should sustain in the latter days, I mean, *a nursing Father of the Church*. For not only the Church of England, as by law established, but Christians of every denomination whatsoever have enjoyed their religious, as well as civil liberties. As there has been no authorized oppression in the state, so there has been no publickly allowed persecution in the church. We breathe indeed in a free air; as free (if not freer) both as to temporals and spirituals, as any nation under heaven. Nor is the prospect likely to terminate in his majesty's death, which I pray GOD long to defer. Our princesses are disposed of to Protestant powers. And we have great reason to be assured that the present heir apparent, and his consort, are like minded with their royal father. And I cannot help thinking, that it is a peculiar blessing vouchsafed us by the King of Kings, that his present majesty has been continued so long among us. For now his immediate successor (though his present situation obliges him, as it were, to lie dormant) has great and glorious opportunities, which we have reason to think he daily improves, of observing and weighing the national affairs, considering the various steps and turns of government, and consequently of laying in a large fund of experience to make him a wise and great prince, if ever GOD should call him to sway the British sceptre. Happy art thou, O England! Happy art thou, O America, who on every side are thus highly favoured!

But, alas! How soon would this happy scene have shifted, and a melancholy gloomy prospect have succeeded in its room, had the rebels gained their point, and a popish abjured pretender been forced upon the British throne! For, supposing his birth not to be spurious (as we have great reason to think it really was), what could we expect from one, descended from a father, who, when duke of York, put all Scotland into confusion, and afterwards, when crowned king of England, for his arbitrary and tyrannical government both in church and state, was justly obliged to abdicate the throne, by the assertors of British liberty? Or, supposing the horrid plot, first hatched in hell, and afterwards nursed at Rome, had taken place; supposing, I say, the old pretender should have exchanged his cardinal's cap for a triple crown, and have transferred his pretended title (as it is reported he has done) to his eldest son, what was all this for, but that, by being advanced to the popedom, he might rule both son and subjects with less controul, and, by their united interest, keep the three kingdoms of England, Scotland and Ireland, in greater vassalage to the see of Rome? Ever since this unnatural rebellion broke out, I have looked upon the young pretender as the Phaeton of the present age. He is ambitiously and presumptuously aiming to seat himself in the throne of our rightful sovereign King George, which he is no more capable of maintaining than Phaeton was to guide the *chariot of the sun*; and had he succeeded in his attempt, like him, would only have set the world on fire. It is true, to do him justice, he has deserved well of the church of Rome, and, in all probability, will hereafter be canonized amongst the noble order of their fictitious saints. But, with what an iron rod we might expect to have been bruized, had his troops been victorious, may easily be imagin'd from those cruel orders, found in the pockets of some of his officers, "*Give no quarter to the elector's troops.*" Add to this, that there was great reason to suspect, that, upon the first news of the success of the rebels, a general massacre was intended. So that if the Lord had not been on our side, Great Britain, not to say America, would, in a few weeks, or months, have been an Aceldama, a field of blood. Besides, was a popish pretender to rule over us, instead of being represented by a free parliament, and governed by laws made by their consent, as we now are, we should shortly have had only the shadow of one, and, it may be, no parliament at all. This is the native product of a popish government, and what the unhappy family, from which this young adventurer pretends to be descended, has always aimed at. Arbitrary principles he has sucked in with his mother's milk; and if he had been so honest, instead of that immature motto upon his standard, *Tandem triumphans*, only to have put, *Stet pro ratione voluntas*, he had given us a short, but true, portraiture of the nature of his intended, but, blessed be God, now defeated reign. And, why should I mention, that the loss of the national debt, and the dissolution of the present happy union between the two kingdoms, would have been the immediate consequences of his success, as he himself declares in his second manifesto, dated from Holyrood House? These are evils, and great ones too; but then they are only evils of a temporary nature. They chiefly concern the body, and must necessarily terminate in the grave. But, alas! what an inundation of spiritual mischiefs would soon have overflowed the church, and what unspeakable danger should we and our posterity have been reduced to in respect to our better parts, our precious and immortal souls? How soon would whole swarms of monks, Dominicans and friars, like so many locusts, have overspread and plagued the nation? With what winged speed would foreign titular bishops have posted over in order to take possession of their respective sees? How quickly would our universities have been filled with youths who have been sent abroad by their popish parents, in order to drink in all the superstitions of the church of Rome? What a speedy period would have been put to societies of all kinds, for *promoting Christian knowledge, and propagating the gospel in foreign parts*? How soon would our pulpits have every where been filled with those old antichristian doctrines, freewill, meriting by works, transubstantiation, purgatory, works of supererogation, passive obedience, non-resistance, and all the other abominations of the Whore of Babylon? How soon would our Protestant charity schools in England, Scotland and Ireland, have been pulled down, our Bibles forcibly taken from us, and ignorance every where set up as the mother of devotion? How soon should we have been depriv'd of that invaluable blessing, liberty of conscience, and been obliged to commence (what they falsely call) Catholicks, or submit to all the tortures which a bigotted zeal, guided by the most cruel principles, could possibly invent? How soon would that mother of harlots have made herself once more drunk with the blood of the saints, and the whole tribe even of free-thinkers themselves, been brought to this dilemma, either to die martyrs for (tho' I never yet heard of one that did so), or, contrary to all their most avow'd principles, renounce their great Diana, unassisted, unenlightned reason? But I must have done, lest while I am speaking against Antichrist, I should unawares fall myself, and lead my hearers into an antichristian spirit. True and undefiled religion will regulate our zeal, and teach us to treat even the man of sin, with no harsher language than that which the angel gave his grand employer Satan, *The Lord rebuke thee.*

Glory be to his great name, the LORD has rebuked him, and that too at a time when we had little reason to expect such a blessing at GOD's hands. My dear hearers, neither the present frame of my heart, nor the occasion of your late solemn meeting, lead me to give you a detail of our publick vices tho' alas! they are so many, so notorious, and withal of such a crimson-dye, that a gospel minister would not be altogether inexcusable, was he, even on such a joyful occasion, *to lift up his voice like a trumpet, to shew the British nation their transgression, and the people of America their sin.* However, tho' I would not cast a dismal shade upon the pleasing picture the cause of our late rejoicings set before us; yet thus much may, and ought to be said, *viz.* that, as GOD has not dealt so bountifully with any people as with us, so no nation under heaven have dealt more ungratefully with him. We have been, like Capernaum, lifted up to heaven in priviledges, and, for the abuse of them, like her, have deserved to be thrust down into hell. How well soever it may be with us, in respect to our civil and ecclesiastic constitution, yet in regard to our morals, Isaiah's description of the Jewish polity is too too applicable, *The whole Head is sick, the whole Heart is faint, from the Crown of the Head to the Sole of our Feet, we are full of Wounds and Bruises, and putrifying Sores.* We have, Jeshurun-like, *waxed fat and kicked.* We have played the harlot against GOD, both in regard to principles and practice. *Our Gold is become dim, and our fine Gold changed.* We have crucified the Son of GOD afresh, and put him to an open shame. Nay, CHRIST has been wounded in the house of his friends. And every thing long ago seemed to threaten an immediate storm. But, Oh the long-suffering and goodness of GOD to-us-ward! When all things seemed ripe for destruction, and matters were come to such a crisis, that GOD's praying people began to think, that tho' Noah, Daniel and Job were living, they would only deliver their own souls; yet then, *in the midst of judgment, the most High remembred mercy*, and when a popish enemy was breaking in upon us like a flood, the Lord himself graciously lifted up a standard.

This to me does not seem to be one of the most unfavourable circumstances, which have attended this mighty deliverance; nor do I think you will look upon it as altogether unworthy your observation. Had this cockatrice indeed been crushed in the egg, and the young pretender driven back upon his first arrival, it would undoubtedly have been a great blessing. But not so great as that for which you lately assembled to give GOD thanks. For then his majesty would not have had so good an opportunity of knowing his enemies, or trying his friends. The British subjects would, in a manner, have lost the fairest occasion that ever offered to express their loyalty and gratitude to their rightful sovereign. France would not have been so greatly humbled; nor such an effectual stop have been put, as we trust there now is, to any such further popish plot, to rob us of all that is near and dear to us. *Out of the Eater therefore hath come forth Meat, and out of the Strong hath come forth Sweetness.* The pretender's eldest son is suffered not only to land in the north-west highlands in Scotland, but in a little while to become a great band. This for a time is not believed, but treated as a thing altogether incredible. The friends of the government in those parts, not for want of loyalty, but of sufficient authority to take up arms, could not resist him. He is permitted to pass on with his terrible banditti, and, like the comet that was lately seen (a presage it may be of this very thing) spreads his baleful influences all around him. He is likewise permitted to gain a short liv'd triumph by a victory over a body of our troops at Preston Pans, and to take a temporary possession of the metropolis of Scotland. Of this he makes his boast, and informs the publick (they are his own words) that "*Providence had hitherto favoured him with* wonderful success, *led him in the way to victory, and to the capital of the ancient kingdom, tho' he came without foreign aid.*" Nay he is further permitted to press into the very heart of England. But now the Almighty interposes, *Hitherto he was to go, and no further.* Here were his malicious designs to be staid. His troops of a sudden are driven back. Away they post to the Highlands, and there they are suffered not only to increase, but also to collect themselves into a large body, that having, as it were, what Caligula once wish'd Rome had, *but one neck, they might be cut off with one blow.*

The time, nature, and instrument of this victory deserve our notice. It was on a general fast-day, when the clergy and good people of Scotland were lamenting the disloyalty of their perfidious countrymen, and like Moses lifting up their hands, that Amalek might not prevail. The victory was total and decisive. Little blood was spilt on the side of the royalists. And to crown all, Duke William, his majesty's youngest son, has the honour of first driving back, and then defeating the rebel army—a prince, who in his infancy and nonage, gave early proofs of an uncommon bravery, and nobleness of mind—a prince, whose courage has increased with his years; who returned wounded from the battle of Dettingen, behav'd with surprizing bravery at Fontenoy, and now, by a conduct and magnanimity becoming the high office he sustains, like his glorious predecessor the prince of Orange, has once more delivered three kingdoms from the dread of popish cruelty and arbitrary power. What renders it still more remarkable is this—the day on which his highness gained this victory was the day after his birth-day, when he was entring on the twenty sixth year of his age; and when Sullivan, one of the pretender's privy council, like another Ahitophel, advised the rebels to give our soldiers battle, presuming they were surfeited and overcharged with their yesterday's rejoicings, and consequently unfit to make any great stand against them. But glory be to GOD, who catches the wise in their own craftiness! His counsel, like Ahitophel's, proves abortive. Both general and soldiers were prepared to meet them. GOD *taught their hands to war, and their fingers to fight*, and brought the duke, after a bloody and deserved slaughter of some thousands of the rebels, with most of his brave soldiers, victorious from the field.

Were we to take a distinct view of this notable transaction, and trace it in all the particular circumstances that have attended it, I believe we must with one heart and voice confess, that if it be a mercy for a state to be delivered from a worse than a Catiline's conspiracy; or a church to be rescued from a hotter than a Dioclesian persecution—if it be a mercy to be delivered from a religion that turns plowshares into swords, and pruning-hooks into spears, and makes it meritorious to shed Protestant blood—if it be a mercy to have all our present invaluable priviledges, both in church and state, secured to us more than ever—if it be a mercy to have these great things done for us at a season when, for our crying sins both church and state justly deserved to be overturned—and if it be a mercy to have all this brought about for us, under GOD, by one of the blood royal, a prince acting with an experience far above his years—if any or all of these are mercies, then have you lately commemorated one of the greatest mercies that ever the glorious GOD vouchsafed the British nation.

And shall we not rejoice and give thanks? Should we refuse, would not the stones cry out against us? Rejoice then we may and ought: But, Oh! let our rejoicing be in the Lord, and run in a religious channel. This we find has been the practice of GOD's people in all ages. When he was pleased, with a mighty hand and outstretched arm to lead the Israelites through the Red Sea as on dry ground, "*Then sang Moses and the Children of Israel; and Miriam the Prophetess, the Sister of Aaron, took a Timbrel in her Hand, and all the Women went out after her. And Miriam answered them, Sing ye to the Lord; for he hath triumphed gloriously.*" When GOD subdued Jabin the king of Canaan before the children of Israel, "*Then sang Deborah and Barak on that Day, saying, Praise ye the Lord for the avenging of Israel.*" When the ark was brought back out of the hands of the Philistines, David, tho' a king, danced before it. And, to mention but one instance more, which may serve as a general directory to us on this and such like occasions; When the great head of the church had rescued his people from the general massacre intended to be executed upon them by a cruel and ambitious Haman,

> *Mordecai sent Letters unto all the Jews that were in all the Provinces of the King Ahasuerus, both nigh and far, to establish among them that they should keep the Fourteenth Day of the Month Adar, and the Fifteenth Day of the same yearly, as the Days wherein the Jews rested from their Enemies, and the Month which was turned unto them from Sorrow unto Joy, and from Mourning into a good Day: That they should make them Days of Feasting and Joy, and of sending Portions one to another, and Gifts to the Poor.*

And why should not we go and do likewise?

And shall we forget, on such an occasion, to express our gratitude to, and make honourable mention of those worthies, who have signalized themselves, and been ready to sacrifice both lives and fortunes at this critical juncture? This would be to act the part of those ungrateful Israelites, who are branded in the book of GOD, for not shewing kindness "*to the House of Jerubbaal, namely Gideon, according to all the Goodness which he shewed unto Israel.*" Even a Pharoah could prefer a deserving Joseph, Ahasuerus a Mordecai, and Nebuchadnezar a Daniel, when made instruments of signal service to themselves and people. "*My Heart*, says Deborah, *is towards* (*i.e.* I have a particular veneration and regard for) *the Governors of Israel, that offered themselves willingly. And blessed*, adds she, *above Women shall Jael the Wife of Heber the Kenite be: For she put her Hand to the Nail, and her right Hand to the Workman's Hammer, and with the Hammer she smote Sisera, she smote off his Head, when she had pierced and stricken through his Temples.*" And shall not we say, "Blessed above men, let his royal highness the duke of Cumberland be: For, thro' his instrumentality, the great and glorious Jehovah hath brought mighty things to pass? " Should not our hearts be towards the worthy archbishop of York, the royal hunters, and those other English heroes, who *offered themselves so willingly?* Let the names of Blakeney, Bland and Rea, and all those who waxed valiant in fight, on this important occasion, live for ever in the British annals. Let that worthy clergyman who endured five hundred lashes from the cruel enemy (every one of which the generous duke said, he felt himself) be never forgotten by the ministers of Christ in particular. And let the name of that great that incomparably brave soldier of the king, and good soldier of JESUS CHRIST, Colonel Gardiner (excuse me if I here vent a sigh—he was my intimate friend), let his name, I say, be had in everlasting remembrance. His majesty has led us an example of gratitude. Acting like himself, upon the first news of this brave man's death, he sent immediate orders that his family should be taken care of. The noble duke gave a commission immediately to his eldest son. And the sympathizing prince of Hesse paid a visit of condolance to his sorrowful elect and worthy lady. The British parliament have made a publick acknowledgment of the obligation the nation lies under to his royal highness. And surely the least we can do, is to make a publick and grateful mention of their names, to whom under GOD, we owe so much gratitude and thanks.

But, after all, is there not an infinitely greater debt of gratitude and praise due from us, on this occasion, to him that is higher than the highest, even the King of Kings and Lord of Lords, the blessed and only Potentate? Is it not his arm, his strong & mighty arm (what instruments soever may have been made use of) that hath brought us this salvation? And may I not therefore address you in the exulting language of the beginning of this psalm from which we have taken our text,

> *O give Thanks unto the Lord; call upon his Name, make known his Deeds among the People. Sing unto him, sing Psalms unto him: Talk ye of all his wondrous Works. Glory ye in his holy Name. Remember this marvellous Work which he hath done.*

But shall we put off our good and gracious benefactor with a mere lip service? GOD forbid. Your worthy governour has honoured GOD in his late excellent proclamation, and GOD will honour him. But shall our thanks terminate with the day? No, in no wise. Our text reminds us of a more noble sacrifice, and points out to us the great end the almighty Jehovah proposes in bestowing such signal favours upon a people, viz. *That they should observe his Statutes, and keep his Laws.*

This is the return we are all taught to pray that we may make to the most high GOD, the father of mercies, in the daily office of our church, viz.

> *That our Hearts may be unfeignedly thankful, and that we may shew forth his Praise, not only with our Lips, but in our Lives, by giving up our selves to his Service, and by walking before him in Holiness and Righteousness all our Days.*

Oh that these words were the real language of all that use them! Oh that there was in us such a mind! How soon would our enemies then flee before us, and GOD, even our own GOD, yet give us more abundant blessings!

And, why should we not *observe GOD's Statutes and keep his Laws?* Dare any say that any of his commands are grievous? Is not CHRIST's yoke, to a renewed soul, as far as renewed, easy; and his burden comparatively light? May I not appeal to the most refined reasoner, whether the religion of JESUS CHRIST be not a social religion? Whether the moral law, as explained by the Lord JESUS in the gospel, has not a natural tendency to promote the present good and happiness of a whole commonwealth, supposing they were obedient to it, as well as the happiness of every individual? From whence come wars and fightings amongst us? From what fountain do all those evils which the present and past ages have groaned under, flow, but from a neglect of the laws and statutes of our great and all-wise lawgiver JESUS of Nazareth? Tell me, ye men of letters, whether Lycurgus or

Solon, Pythagoras or Plato, Aristotle, Seneca, Cicero, or all the ancient lawgivers and heathen moralists, put them all together, ever published a system of ethicks, any way worthy to be compared with the glorious system laid down in that much despised book (to use Sir Richard Steele's expression), emphatically called the scriptures? Is not the divine image and superscription written upon every precept of the gospel? Do they not shine with a native intrinsick lustre? And, tho' many things in them are above, yet, is there any thing contrary to the strictest laws of right reason? Is not JESUS CHRIST, in scripture, stiled the Word, the Λόγος the Reason? And is not his service justly stiled Λογικὴ Λατρεία a reasonable service? What if there be mysteries in his religion? Are they not without all controversy great and glorious? Are they not mysteries of godliness, and worthy that GOD who reveals them? Nay, is it not the greatest mystery that men who pretend to reason, and call themselves philosophers, who search into the *arcana naturæ*, and consequently find a mystery in every blade of grass, should yet be so irrational as to decry all mysteries in religion? Where is the scribe? Where is the wise? Where is the disputer against the Christian revelation? Does not every thing without and within us conspire to prove its divine original? And would not self-interest, if there was no other motive, excite us to *observe* GOD'*s Statutes, and keep his Laws*?

Besides, considered as a Protestant people, do we not lie under the greatest obligations of any nation under heaven, to pay a chearful, unanimous, universal, persevering obedience to the divine commands?

The wonderful and surprizing manner of GOD's bringing about a reformation in the reign of King Henry the Eighth—his carrying it on in the blessed reign of King Edward the Sixth—his delivering us out of the bloody hands of Queen Mary, and destroying the Spanish invincible Armada, under her immediate Protestant successor Queen Elizabeth—his discovery of the popish plot under King James—the glorious revolution by King William—and, to come nearer to our own times, his driving away *four thousand five hundred Spaniards*, from a weak (tho' important) frontier colony, when they had, in a manner, actually taken possession of it—his giving us Louisbourg, one of the strongest fortresses of our enemies, contrary to all human probability, but the other day, into our hands (which may encourage our hopes of success, supposing it carried on in a like spirit, in our intended Canada expedition)—These, I say, with the victory which you have lately been commemorating, are such national mercies, not to mention any more, as will render us utterly inexcusable, if they do not produce a national reformation, and incite us all, with one heart, *to observe GOD's Statutes, and keep his Laws.*

Need I remind you further, in order to excite in you a greater diligence to comply with the intent of the text, that tho' the storm, in a great measure is abated by his royal highness's late success, yet we dare not say, *it is altogether blown over?*

The clouds may again return after the rain; and the few surviving rebels (which I pray GOD avert) may yet be suffered to make head against us. We are still engaged in a bloody, and in all probability, a tedious war, with two of the most inveterate enemies to the interests of Great Britain. And, tho' I cannot help thinking, that their present intentions are so iniquitous, their conduct so perfidious, and their schemes so directly derogatory to the honour of the most high GOD, that he will certainly humble them in the end; yet, as all things, in this life, *happen alike to all*, they may for a time be dreadful instruments of scourging us. If not, GOD has other arrows in his quiver to smite us with, besides the French king, his Catholick majesty, or an abjured pretender. Not only the sword, but plague, pestilence and famine are under the divine command. Who knows but he may say to them all, *Pass through these lands?* A fatal murrain has lately swept away abundance of cattle at home and abroad. A like epidemical disease may have a commission to seize our persons as well as our beasts. Thus GOD dealt with the Egyptians. Who dare say, He will not deal in the same manner with us? Has he not already given some symptoms of it? What great numbers upon the Continent have been lately taken off by the bloody-flux, small-pox, and yellow-fever? Who can tell what further judgments are yet in store? However, this is certain, the rod is yet hanging over us; and, I believe it will be granted, on all sides, that if such various dispensations of mercy and judgment, do not *teach the inhabitants of any land to learn righteousness*, they will only ripen them for a greater ruin. Give me leave therefore, to dismiss you at this time with that solemn awful warning and exhortation with which the prophet Samuel, on a publick occasion, took leave of the people of Israel, "*Only fear the Lord and serve Him, in*

Truth, with all your Heart: For consider, how great Things He hath done for you. But if ye shall still do wickedly (I will not say as he did, *you shall be consumed;* but), *ye know not but you may provoke Him to consume both you and your King.*" Which GOD of his infinite mercy prevent, for the sake of JESUS CHRIST: *To whom with the Father and the Holy Ghost, three Persons but one GOD, be all Honour and Glory, now and for evermore.* Amen, Amen.

FINIS

5

CIVIL MAGISTRATES MUST BE JUST, RULING IN THE FEAR OF GOD

Charles Chauncy

BOSTON

1747

Charles Chauncy (1705–1787). The most influential clergyman in the Boston of his time and—apart from Jonathan Edwards the elder—in all New England, Chauncy was graduated from Harvard and served as pastor of the First Church in Boston for sixty years. A thoroughly prosaic character who opposed enthusiasm and the revivalism espoused by Whitefield and Edwards, he prayed he would never become an orator; those who knew him well concluded that this was one prayer that undoubtedly had been answered. He was nonetheless a vigorous controversialist and prolific pamphleteer, devoting the decade of 1762 to 1771 to combating the British threat to send an Anglican bishop to America. It was an issue that rallied Congregationalists across New England in the period leading up to the Revolution.

The election sermon reprinted here was preached to Governor William Shirley, the council, and the house of representatives of Massachusetts on May 27, 1747. The bracketed passages in the printed text of this sermon were omitted during the oral delivery.

Civil Magiſtrates *muſt be juſt, ruling in the Fear of God.*

A

SERMON

Preached before His EXCELLENCY

William Shirley, Eſq;

The Honourable

His Majeſty's COUNCIL,

AND

Houſe of Repreſentatives,

Of the Province of the

Maſſachuſetts-Bay in *N.England*;

May 27. 1747.

Being the ANNIVERSARY for the ELECTION of His Majeſty's Council for ſaid Province.

By *Charles Chauncy*, D. D.

One of the Paſtors of the firſt Church in BOSTON.

Deut. XVI. 20. *That which is altogether juſt ſhalt thou follow*---.

N. B. The ſeveral Paragraphs which, for want of Time, were omitted in Preaching, are inſerted in their proper Places, and, for Diſtinction's ſake, comprehended in Crotchets.

BOSTON:

Printed by Order of the Honourable Houſe of REPRESENTATIVES. 1747.

The God of Israel said, the Rock of Israel spake to me; he that ruleth over Men must be just, ruling in the Fear of God.

II Sam. xxiii. 3.

If we may judge by the manner in which these words are introduced, there are none in all the bible, applicable to civil rulers, in their publick capacity, of more solemn importance.

The last words of good men are commonly tho't worthy of particular notice; especially, if they are great as well as good, of an elevated station as well as character in life. This is a consideration that adds weight to my text. For it is enrolled among the last words of one of the best and greatest men that ever lived. Such was David, "the man after God's own heart," who was raised up from low life to the regal dignity, and stiled, on that account, "the anointed of the God of Jacob."

And was my text nothing more than his own private sentiments, formed with due care, upon long observation and experience, it might well deserve the particular attention of all in civil power; especially, as he was a man of extraordinary knowledge, penetration and wisdom, as well as piety; and, at the same time, singularly qualified to make a judgment in an affair of this nature, as he was called into publick service from a youth, and had for many years reigned king in Israel.

But it is not only David that here speaks. The words are rather God's than his. For they are thus prefaced, *The God of Israel said, the rock of Israel spake to me.* "That God who had selected the Jews to be his people, and was their God so as he was not the God of other nations; the rock on whom their political state was built, and on whom it depended for support and protection": This God spake unto David, either by Samuel, or Nathan, or some other inspired prophet, or himself immediately from heaven, saying, as in the words I have read to you, *He that ruleth over men must be just, ruling in the fear of God.* It is certainly some momentous truth, highly worthy of the most serious consideration of civil rulers, that is here delivered, or it would not have been ushered in with so much solemnity.

Some read the words, (agreable eno' to the original, as criticks observe) *there shall be a ruler over men that shall be just, ruling in the fear of God*; and refer them to Christ, as agreeing with other prophecies, which describe him as a "king that shall reign in righteousness," and be of "quick understanding in the fear of the Lord": But if they be allowed to look forward to him that has since "come forth out of Zion," they were also designed for the instruction and benefit of Solomon, David's son and appointed successor to the throne of Israel. And by analogy they are applicable to civil rulers, in their various stations, in all ages of the world.

In this view I shall now consider them, under the two following heads obviously contained in them.

I. There is a certain order among mankind, according to which some are entrusted with power to rule over others.

II. Those who rule over others must be just, ruling in the fear of God.

The whole will then be applied to the occasions of the day.

I. I am to say, in the first place, there is a certain order among men, according to which some are entrusted with power to rule over others. This is evidently supposed in the text; and 'tis supposed, not as a bare fact, but a fact that has taken place conformably to the will of God, and the reason of things.

This, to be sure, is the truth of the case, in it self considered. Order and rule in society, or, what means the same thing, civil government, is not a contrivance of arbitrary and tyrannical men, but a regular state of things, naturally resulting from the make of man, and his circumstances in the world. Had man abode in innocency, his nature as a sociable creature, and his condition as a dependent one, would probably have led to some sort of civil superiority: As, among the inhabitants of the upper world, there seems to be a difference of order, as well as species; which the scripture intimates, by speaking of them in the various stile of *thrones, dominions, principalities, powers, archangels and angels*. But however it would have been, had man continued in obedience to his maker, government is rendered a matter of necessity by the introduction of sin into the world. Was there no civil rule among men, but every one might do that which was right in his own eyes, without restraint from humane laws, there would not be safety any where on the earth. No man would be secure in the enjoyment, either of his liberty, or property, or life: But every man's hand would be against his fellow; and mankind must live in perpetual danger, from that oppression, rapine and violence, which would make this world rather a hell, than a fit place to dwell happily in.

The present circumstances of the human race are therefore such, by means of sin, that 'tis necessary they should, for their mutual defence and safety, combine together in distinct societies, lodging as much power in the hands of a few, as may be sufficient to restrain the irregularities of the rest, and keep them within the bounds of a just decorum. Such a superiority in some, and inferiority in others, is perfectly adjusted to the present state of mankind. Their circumstances require it. They could not live, either comfortably or safely without it.

And from hence, strictly and properly speaking, does that civil order there is among men take rise. Nor will it from hence follow, that government is a mere humane constitution. For as it originates in the reason of things, 'tis, at the same time, essentially founded on the will of God. For the voice of reason is the voice of God: And he as truly speaks to men by the reason of things, their mutual relations to and dependencies on each other, as if he uttered his voice from the excellent glory. And in this way, primarily, he declares his will respecting a civil subordination among men. The sutableness of order and superiority, both to the nature of man, and his circumstances in the world, together with its necessary connection, in the nature of things, with his safety and happiness, is such an indication of the divine pleasure, that there should be government, as cannot be gainsay'd nor resisted.

Only it must be remembred here, a distinction ought always to be made between government in its general notion, and particular form and manner of administration. As to the latter, it cannot be affirmed, that this or that particular form of government is made necessary by the will of God and reason of things. The mode of civil rule may in consistency with the public good, admit of variety: And it has, in fact, been various in different nations: Nor has it always continued the same, in the same nation. And one model of government may be best for this community, and another for that; nay, that model which may be best for the same community at one time, may not be so at another. So that it seems left to the wisdom of particular communities to determine what form of government shall take place among them; and, so long as the general ends of society are provided for and secured, the determination may be various, according to the various circumstances, policies, tempers and interests of different communities.

And the same may be said of the manner of vesting particular persons with civil power, whether supreme or subordinate. This is not so fix'd by the divine will, as that all nations are obliged to one and the same way of devolving the administration of rule. The supreme authority in Israel, 'tis true, from which, of course, all subordinate power in that state was derived, was settled by God himself on David, and entail'd on his family to descend in a lineal succession. But it does not appear, that this was ever intended to be a rule obligatory on all nations of the earth: Nor have they kept to it; but have varied in their manner of designing persons for, and introducing them into, the several places of civil trust. And this seems to be a matter alterable in its nature, and proper to be variously determined according to the different circumstances of particular nations.

But 'tis quite otherwise in respect of government itself, in its general notion. This is not a matter of meer humane prudence, but of moral necessity. It does not lie with men to determine at pleasure, whether it shall or shall not take place; but, considering their present weak, exposed and dependent condition, 'tis unalterably right and just there should be rule and superiority in some, and subjection and inferiority in others: And this therefore is invariably the will of God; his will manifested by the moral fitness and reason of things.

And the will of God, as discovered in the revelations of scripture, touching government among men, perfectly coincides with his will primarily made known, upon the same head, by the constitution of things: Or rather, 'tis more clearly and fully opened. For kings, and princes, and nobles, and *all the judges of the earth*, are here represented* as *reigning and ruling by God*: Yea, they are stiled, *the ministers of God*†; and *the powers that be* are declared to be *ordained of God*‡: And, upon this consideration, *subjection to them* is demanded, *for conscience*

* Prov. 8. 15, 16.
† Rom. 13. 4.
‡ Verse 1.

*sake**; and *whosoever resisteth,* is looked upon as *resisting the ordinance of God.*† From all which it is apparent, there is no more room to dispute the divinity of civil rule upon the foot of revelation, than of reason.

And thus we have seen, not only that some among men have rule over others, but that it is reasonable in itself, and agreable to the will of God, it should be so.

And 'tis easy to collect from the whole, the true design of that power some are entrusted with over others. It is not merely that they might be distinguished from, and set above vulgar people; much less that they might live in greater pomp, and be revered as gods on earth; much less still that they might be in circumstances to oppress their fellow-creatures, and trample them under their feet: But it is for the general good of mankind; to keep confusion and disorder out of the world; to guard men's lives; to secure their rights; to defend their properties and liberties; to make their way to justice easy, and yet effectual, for their protection when innocent, and their relief when injuriously treated; and, in a word, to maintain peace and good order, and, in general, to promote the public welfare, in all instances, so far as they are able. But this leads me to the next head of discourse, which is what I have principally in view; *viz.*

II. Those who rule over others must be *just, ruling in the fear of God.* Here I shall distinctly say,

1. They must be just. They ought to be so in their private capacity; maintaining a care to exhibit in their conduct towards all they are concerned with, a fair transcript of that fundamental law of the religion of Jesus, as well as eternal rule of natural justice, "all things whatsoever ye would that men should do to you, do ye even so to them." But private justice, tho' necessary in all, yet is not the virtue here especially intended. The injunction respects those who rule over men; and 'tis as magistrates, not private members of society, that they are required to be just.

And this duty includes in it more than a negation of unrighteousness. 'Tis not enough that rulers are not unjust; that they don't betray the trusts reposed in them; that they don't defraud the public;

* Verse 5.
† Verse 2.

that they don't oppress the subject, whether in a barefac'd manner, or in a more covert way; by downright violence, or under the cloak of law: 'Tis not enough, I say, that rulers don't, in these and such like ways, pervert judgment and justice; but, besides all this, they must be positively righteous. Being possess'd of an inward, steady, uniform principle of justice, setting them, in a good measure, above the influence of private interest, or party views, they must do that which is equal and right, in their various stations, from the king in supreme, to the lowest in authority under him.

It would carry me too far beyond the hour assigned me, should I make a distribution of rulers into their several ranks, and mention the more special acts of justice respectively required of them. I shall therefore content my self with speaking of them chiefly in the collective sense; pointing out, under a few general heads, some of the more important articles wherein they should approve themselves just. And they are such as these.

1. They must be just in the *use of their power*; confining it within the limits prescribed in the constitution they are under. Whatever power any are vested with, 'tis delegated to them according to some civil constitution. And this, so long as it remains the constitution, they are bound in justice to conform themselves to: To be sure, they ought not to act in violation of any of its main and essential rights. Especially, is this an important point of justice, where the constitution is branched into several parts, and the power originally lodged in it, is divided, in certain measures, to each part, in order to preserve a ballance in the whole. Rulers, in this case, in either branch of the government, are bounded by the constitution, and obliged to keep within the proper limits assigned them; never clashing in the exercise of their power, never encroaching upon the rights of each other, in any shape, or under any pretence whatever. They have severally and equally a right to that power which is granted to them in the constitution, and to wrest it out of each other's hands, or to obstruct one another in the regular legal exercise of it, is evidently unjust. As in the British constitution, which devolves the power of the state, in certain proportions, on *King*, *Lords* and *Commons*, they have neither of them a right to invade the province of the other, but are required, by the rule of righteousness, to keep severally within their own boundaries, acting in union among themselves, and consistency with the con-

stitution. If the prerogatives of the King are sacred, so also are the rights of Lords and Commons: And if it would be unjust in Lords or Commons, to touch, in any instance, the prerogative of the crown; so would it be in the crown, to invade the rights, which are legally settled in Lords and Commons: In either of these cases, the law of righteousness is violated: Nor does the manner in which it is done make any essential difference; for, if one part of the government is really kept from exerting it self, according to the true meaning of the constitution, whether it be done openly, or by secret craft; by compulsion or corruption, the designed ballance is no longer preserved; and which way soever the scale turns, whether on the side of sovereignty, or popularity, 'tis forced down by a false weight, which, by degrees, will overturn the government, at least, according to this particular model.

And the case is just the same in all dependent governments, as in those whose power originates in themselves: Especially, where the derived constitution, like that of Great-Britain, is divided into several ruling parts, and distributes the granted powers and priviledges severally among these ruling parts, to each their limited portion. The constitution is here evidently the grand rule to all cloathed with power, or claiming priviledge, in either branch of the government. And 'tis indeed a fundamental point of justice, that they keep respectively within the bounds marked out to them in the constitution. Rulers in one branch of the state should not assume the power delegated to those in another: Nay, so far should they be from this, that they should not, in any degree, lessen their just weight in the government; much less may they contrive, by an undue application to their hopes or fears, or by working on their ambition, or covetousness, or any other corrupt principle; much less, I say, may they contrive to influence them to give up their power, or, what is as bad, to use it unfaithfully, beside the intention for which it was committed to them. These are certainly methods of injustice; and, if put in practice, will, by a natural causality, weaken, and, by degrees, destroy those checks which rulers are mutually designed to have one upon another; the effect whereof must be tyranny, or anarchy, either of which will be of fatal consequence.

2. Another general instance wherein rulers should be just, relates to the *laws by which they govern*. [They have an undoubted right to

make and execute laws, for the publick good. This is essentially included in the very idea of government: Insomuch, that government, without a right to enact and enforce proper laws, is nothing more than an empty name.

And this right, in whomsoever it is vested, must be exercised under the direction of justice. For as there cannot be government without a right of legislation, so neither can there be this right but in conjunction with righteousness. 'Tis the just exercise of power that distinguishes right from might; authority that is to be revered and obeyed, from violence and tyranny, which are to be dreaded and deprecated.

Those therefore to whom it belongs to make, or execute the laws of a government ought, in these exercises of their power, to square their conduct by that strict justice, which will be to them a sure rule of right action.]

To be sure, if they would be just, they must make no laws but what bear this character. They should not, when upon the business of framing and passing acts, suffer themselves to be swayed by any wrong biass, either from self-will, or self-interest; the smiles or frowns of men greater than themselves; or the humour of the populace: But should bring the proposed laws to a fair and impartial examination, not only in their reference to the temper, genius and circumstances of the community, but to that justice also which is founded in the nature of things, and the will of the supreme legislator: And if they should appear to be inconsistent with this eternal rule of equity, they ought not to countenance them, but should do what they can to prevent their establishment. And the rather, because should they enact that into a statute, which is unrighteous; especially, if it be plainly and grosly so, they would be chargeable with "framing mischief by a law": The guilt whereof would be the more aggravated, as power, in this case, would be on the side of oppression; and, what is as bad, as unrighteousness, by this means, would take a dreadful spread thro' the community. For as the laws are the rule for the executive powers in the government, if these are unjust, all that is done consequent upon a regard to them, must be unjust too. That would be the state of things which Solomon describes, when he says, "I saw under the sun the place of judgment, that wickedness was there; and the place of righteousness, that iniquity was there:" Than which, there cannot be given a more terrible representation of the unhappy effect of a disregard to justice in the making of laws.

But rulers, in order to their answering the character of just, must not satisfy themselves with making none but righteous laws; but must provide also, so far as may be, a sufficiency of such to restrain the sons of wickedness, men of avaricious minds, and no consciences, from that rapine and violence, those frauds and oppressions, in their various kinds and degrees, which their lusts would prompt them to perpetrate, to the damage of society, and in violation of all that is right and just.

Besides which, they should be particular in their care to guard the important and extensive article of commerce; calculating laws so as that they may have a tendency to oblige every member of the community, to use the methods of fairness and honesty in their dealings with one another: In order whereto, one of the main things necessary is, to fix the precise weight and measure, according to which these and those commodities shall be bought and sold; hereby rendring the practice of honesty easy and familiar, while, at the same time, it is made a matter of difficulty, as well as hazard, for this member of the community to defraud that, by palming on him a less quantity than he bargain'd, for, and expected to receive.

[A noble example of this expedient to promote justice, the scripture presents us with, in the history it gives of the laws by which the Jews of old were governed. It was not thought sufficient to prohibit their "doing unrighteousness in mete-yard, or weight, or measure;" and to command their having "just ballances and just weights, a just ephah and a just hin:" But the standard was fixt by law, according to which all weights and measures must be regulated; and it was kept in the sanctuary of God. And so exact was the government in its care to prevent all fraud, that it allowed no "weights, ballances or measures to be made of any metal, as of iron, lead, tin, (which were obnoxious to rust, or might be bent or easily impaired) but of marble, stone or glass, which were less liable to be abused."* And officers also "were appointed in every city to go about into shops, and see that the ballances and measures were just, and determine the stated measure of

* Vid. Bp. Patrick on Levit. 19. 36.

them: And with whomsoever they found any weight or measure too light or short, or ballance that went awry, they were to be punished by the judges."* This pattern of justice has been copied after by all governments acquainted with it; and the more particular their laws have been for the regulation of weights and measures, the better calculated have they been to promote honesty in private dealing.]

And if justice in rulers should shew itself by reducing the things that are bought and sold to weight and measure, much more ought it to be seen in ascertaining the medium of trade, as nearly as may be, to some determinate value. For this, whether it be money, or something substituted to pass in lieu of it, is that for which all things are exchanged in commerce. And if this, which is of such universal use in the affair of traffick, be a thing variable and uncertain, of one value this week, and another the next, 'tis difficult to conceive, how justice should take place between man and man, in their dealings with one another. If the measure we call a foot might gradually, in the space of a few months or years, lengthen into a yard, or shorten into an inch; every one sees, it would, if used as a measure in trade, tend to spread unrighteousness in a community, rather than justice. So, if the weight we call a pound might gradually, in the like space, increase or diminish one half; 'tis past dispute, it would be an occasion of general iniquity, rather than a means to promote honesty. And the case is really the same (however insensible we may be of it) with respect to the passing medium in a government. If what we call a shilling, may, in a gradual way, in the course of a few months or years, rise in value so as to be equal to two or three, or sink in proportion; 'tis impossible, in the nature of things, but a wide door should be opened for oppression and injustice. An upright man, in this case, would find it extreamly difficult to do himself justice, or others he might be concerned with in business. And for those of dishonest minds, and no principles of honour or religion, if men of craft and foresight, they would have it very much in their power to enrich themselves by being unjust to their neighbour.

I am sensible, the case may be so circumstanced in a government, especially if it be a dependent one, as that it may be extreamly difficult, if not impossible, while they have no money, to keep that which

* So speaks Maimonides, as quoted by Ainswerth on the above text.

passes, in the room of it, from varying in it's real worth. But it is not very difficult; to be sure, it is not impossible, to pitch upon some certain standard, to which the current medium may be so related, as that it's true value, at different times, may be nearly ascertained: And if this was established as the rule in all public payments, as well as private contracts and bargains, it would be no other than what is right. It would certainly tend, not only to do every one justice, but to put it very much out of the power of men of no probity "to go beyond and defraud their brother:" Whereas, while the medium is connected with no established certain standard, but continually varies in it's real worth, it must be, in the natural course of things, an occasion of great injustice. [Some, on the one hand, under the fair pretence of a reasonable care to secure themselves, will injure those who lie at their mercy, by extorting from them more that is meet. And others, on the other hand, will take the advantage, to pay a just debt with one half the true value it was originally contracted for: Nor will the practice of unrighteousness be confined to these and such like instances, but unavoidably mingle itself with men's transactions in the whole business of trade, so as to put them upon making a prey of one another; as is too much the case among ourselves at this day.]

There is yet another thing, belonging to this head, wherein rulers should approve themselves just; and that is, the *execution of the laws.* [The power of executing as well as making laws (as has been hinted) is inseparable from government. And the demands of justice are to be comply'd with, in the one as well as the other. If 'tis just that rulers should make righteous laws, 'tis equally so, when they are made, that they should take effectual care to enforce a proper regard to them. Of what service would laws be, though ever so wisely calculated to promote the public good, if offenders against them should be connived at, or suffered, by one means or another, to go unpunished? And what might reasonably be expected in consequence of such a breach of trust, but that the best laws, together with the authority that enacted them, should be held in contempt? There is no such thing as supporting the honour of government, or securing the good ends proposed by the laws it establishes, but by unsheathing the sword, in a faithful and impartial execution of justice.

But here, that we may speak clearly, it may be proper to distinguish between those rulers to whom it belongs to *appoint and authorise persons to execute the laws*, and those who are *vested with authority for this purpose*. For the duty which justice requires is different, according to the nature of that power, wherewith these different rulers are betrusted.

It is certainly a point of justice, in those whose business it is to *empower others to execute the laws*, to select out of the community such as are well qualified for so important a trust. Every man is not fit to have the sword of justice put into his hands. And the main thing to be lookt at, in the choice of persons for this service, is their suitableness to it. Meerly their being men of birth and fortune, is not a sufficient recommendation: Nor, if they are eagerly forward in seeking for a post of honour or profit, is it a certain indication, that they are fit to be put into it: Neither, if they should offer money to purchase it, ought they, on this account, to be preferred to men of greater merit: Much less ought it to be looked upon as a turning argument in their favour, that they are fit instruments to serve the secret designs of those in superior station. These are considerations beside the true merit of the case: And those only ought to bear sway, which enter into the real characters of men, determining their qualifications for the trust that is to be reposed in them.

The advice which Jethro gave Moses is here proper, "Thou shalt provide out of all the people able men, such as fear God, men of truth, hating covetousness."* These are the men, men of understanding, courage and resolution; men of integrity, fidelity and honesty; men of piety and substantial religion; men of a noble generosity, setting them above the temptations, which those of narrow minds and selfish views, are easily drawn away by and enticed: These, I say, are the proper men to fill the various posts in the state. And it would be injustice to the public, for the persons concerned in the disposal of them, to neglect these, and bestow them on those of a contrary character. Men of low natural capacities, and small acquired accomplishments, are unmeet to be exalted to places of important trust. And should this be done, it would be acting over the evil, which Solomon complained of in his day, *Folly is set in great dignity*. And those are as unfit to be constituted guardians of the laws, who are indolent, inactive and irresolute; much more, if, together herewith, they are known

* Exod. 18. 21.

to be of a vicious turn of mind. It can't be supposed, men of this character should be faithful in the execution of justice; and to devolve this care on them, would be to wrong the community, and expose authority.

Not that those, with whom it lies to appoint officers, are always to blame, when unqualified persons are put into places of trust; for they are liable, after all prudent caution, to be mistaken in their own judgment, and to be imposed on by misinformation from others. But then, they should take due care, when such persons are found, upon trial, to be unequal to the trust committed to them, to remedy the inconvenience: Nor otherwise will they continue innocent, however faultless they might be at first. 'Tis evidently the demand of justice, that such unmeet persons should be displaced, and others better qualified put in their room.

And 'tis equally just, that those who are capable of behaving well, but behave ill in their respective stations, should be testified against. And should they be so unadvised, as grosly to abuse their power; applying it to the purposes of tyranny and oppression, rather than to serve the good ends of government, it ought to be taken out of their hands, that they might no longer be under advantages to injure their brethren of the same community.

These are the demands of justice from those, who are to *put others into the executive trust.*

And justice is likewise required of *this sort of rulers*, according to the respective trust that is committed to them.

If 'tis their business to sit in the place of judgment, they must judge uprightly in all cases, whether civil or criminal, and not under a wrong influence from favour to the rich, or pity to the poor, or fear of the great, or affection or disaffection to any man's person whatsoever; having that precept in the divine law ever in their eye, "Ye shall do no unrighteousness in judgment: Thou shalt not respect the person of the poor, nor honour the person of the mighty: But in righteousness shalt thou judge thy brother."* And that also, "Thou shalt not wrest judgment, thou shalt not respect persons, neither take a gift; for a gift doth blind the eyes of the wise, and pervert the words of the righteous."†

* Levit. 19. 15.
† Deut. 19. 16.

If 'tis their business to enquire who have been offenders against the laws, and to exhibit complaints against them as such; they must be courageous and impartial, complying with their duty equally in respect of all, be their character what it will.

If 'tis their business to act as executioners of justice, they must faithfully inflict the adjudged sentence: In doing of which, tho' there may be room for the exercise of compassion, especially in the case of some sort of debtors; yet the righteousness of the law may not be eluded by needless, much less fraudulent delays, to the injury of the creditor.

In fine, whatever their trust is, whether of less or greater importance, they must exercise it with care, fidelity, resolution, steadiness, diligence, and an entire freedom from a corrupt respect to men's persons, as those who are concerned for the honour of government, and that it's laws may take effect for the general good of the community.]

To go on,

3. Another instance wherein rulers should be just, respects the debts that may be due from the public. A government may be in debt, as well as private men. Their circumstances may be such, as to render it adviseable for them to borrow money, either of other governments, or within themselves: Or, they may have occasion to make purchases, or to enter into contracts, upon special emergencies, which may bring them in debt. In which cases, the rule of justice is the same to magistrates, as to men in a private life. They must pay that which they owe, according to the true meaning of their engagements, without fraud or delay.

[They may also be in debt for services done by labourers, in this and the other secular employment. And here the rule of justice is that, "withhold not good from them to whom it is due, when it is in the power of thine hand to do it. Say not unto thy neighbour, go, and come again, and to-morrow I will give, when thou hast it by thee."* Or if the labourers are such as have nothing beforehand, but their day-labour is what they depend on for the support of themselves and families, the rule is yet more particular, "Thou shalt not oppress an hired servant that is poor and needy; at his day thou shalt give him his hire, neither shall the sun go down upon it; for he is poor, and setteth his heart on it: Lest he cry against thee unto the

* Prov. 3. 27, 28.

Lord, and it be sin unto thee."* And again, "Thou shalt not defraud thy neighbour, nor rob him: The wages of him that is hired, shall not abide with thee all night until the morning."†]

In fine, they may be in debt to their own officers, whether in higher or lower station, the proper business of whose office calls off their attention from other affairs. And as their time, and care, and tho't, are employed in the service of the public, a public maintenance is their just due. "Who goeth a warfare any time at his own charge? Who planteth a vineyard, and eateth not of the fruit thereof? Or, who feedeth a flock, and eateth not of the milk of the flock? Say I these things as a man? Or saith not the law the same also?"‡ For it is written, "For this cause pay you tribute; for they are God's ministers, attending continually upon this very thing.§ Render unto Cæsar the things that are Cæsar's."¶

Nor is it sufficient that they be supported according to the condition of men in low life. This may be tho't enough, if not too much, by those who imagine, that the more strait-handed they are upon the head of allowances, the more serviceable they shall be to the public. But there is such a thing in the state, as a "withholding more than is meet." And it really tends to the damage of a government. Too scant an allowance may unhappily prove a temptation to officers, to be hard upon those dependent on them; and what they may injuriously squeeze out of them, by one artful contrivance or another, may turn out more to the hurt of the community, than if twice that sum had been paid out of the public treasury, and this evil, by means hereof, had been prevented. Besides, 'tis no ways fitting, that men cloathed with honour and power should be brought down to a level with vulgar people, in the support that is granted them. Their outward circumstances should be elevated in proportion to their civil character, that they may be better able to support the visible dignity of their station, and command that respect which is due to men of their figure. He that is *governour should eat the bread of a governour*; and subordinate officers should be maintained, according to the rank they bear in the state: Nor ought their honourable maintenance to be tho't

* Deut. 24. 14, 15.
† Lev. 17. 13.
‡ 1 Cor. 5. 7, 8.
§ Rom. 13. 6.
¶ Matth. 22. 21.

a matter of *meer* bounty; 'tis rather a debt, which can't be withheld without injustice.

[To be sure, where their stipends have been established, or, at least, they have had reasonable encouragement to expect such a certain acknowledgment for their service, righteousness requires that it be paid them: Nor may it be tho't that the same nominal sum, falling vastly below the real worth of the debt, will be sufficient to discharge it. It certainly is not sufficient, in the eye of justice, either natural or revealed; which respects no man's person, but will do that which is right to the lowest, as well as to the highest officer in the state.

And the case, in point of equity, is really the same, where a government has come into no special agreement; but the ascertaining the quantum proper for the support of it's officers, is left to it's own wisdom and probity. For an allowance is due to them by the law of righteousness: And it ought to be granted, both in proper season, and full proportion, that there may be no reason for complaint, either of penurious or unjust dealing.

I may add here, the distribution of rewards, in case of extraordinary service done for a government, falls properly under this head of justice. For tho' there may be bounty in it, there is also a mixture of righteousness. But however this be, it has been the practice of all nations to shew singular marks of respect to those who have distinguished themselves by their eminent labours for the public. And it is to be hoped, this government will never be backward, according to their ability, suitably to reward those who have signalized themselves, in doing service for their king and country.]

4. Another general instance wherein rulers should be just, concerns the liberties and priviledges of the subject. In all governments there is a reserve of certain rights in favour of the people: In some, they are few in kind, and small in degree: In others, they are both great and numerous; rendring the people signally happy whose lot it is to be favoured with the undisturbed enjoyment of them. And it would be no wonder, if they should keep a jealous eye over them, and think no cost too much to be expended, for the defence and security of them: Especially, if they were the purchase of wise and pious ancestors, who submitted to difficulties, endured hardships, spent their estates, and ventured their lives, that they might transmit them as an inheritance to their posterity.

And shall such valuable, dear-bought rights be neglected, or invaded by the rulers of a people? 'Tis a principal part of that justice which is eternally expected of them, as they would not grosly pervert one of the main ends of their office, to preserve and perpetuate to every member of the community, so far as may be, the full enjoyment of their liberties and priviledges, whether of a civil or religious nature.

Here I may say distinctly,

As rulers would be just, they must take all proper care to preserve entire the civil rights of a people. And the ways in which they should express this care are such as these.

They should do it by appearing in defence of their liberties, if called in question, and making use of all wise and sutable methods to prevent the loss of them: Nor can they be too active, diligent or laborious in their endeavours upon this head: Provided always, the priviledges in danger are worth contending for, and such as the people have a just right and legal claim to. Otherwise, there may be hazard of losing real liberties, in the strife for those that are imaginary; or valuable ones, for such as are of trifling consideration.

They should also express this care, by seasonably and faithfully placing a proper guard against the designs of those, who would rule in a dispotic manner, to the subversion of the rights naturally or legally vested in the people. And here 'tis a great mistake to suppose, there can be danger only from those in the highest station. There may, 'tis true, be danger from this quarter: And it has sometimes proved so in fact: An unhappy instance whereof was seen in the arbitrary reign of King James the second, in person at home, and by his representative here; as a check to which, those entrusted with the guardianship of the nation's rights were spirited to take such measures, as issued in that revolution, and *establishment of the succession*, on which his present majesty's claim to the British throne is dependent. May the succession be continued in his royal house forever! And may the same spirit, which settled it there, prevail in the rulers of the English nation, so long as the sun and moon shall endure!

But, as I said, a people's liberties may be in danger from others, besides those in the highest rank of government. The men who strike in with the popular cry of liberty and priviledge, working themselves, by an artful application to the fears and jealousies of the people, into their good opinion of them as lovers of their country, if not the only stanch friends to it's interests, may, all the while, be only aiming at power to carry every thing according to their own sovereign pleasure: And they are, in this case, most dangerous enemies to the community; and may, by degrees, if not narrowly watched, arrive to such an height, as to be able to serve their own ends, by touching even the people in their most valuable rights. And these commonly are the men, thro' whose influence, either as primary managers, or tools to others, they suffer most in their real liberties.

In fine, they should express this care in a constant readiness to bear due testimony against even the smaller encroachments upon the liberty of the subject, whether by private men's invading one another's rights, or by the tyranny of inferiour officers, who may treat those under their power, as tho' they had no natural rights, not to say a just claim to the invaluable priviledges of *Englishmen.*

The ancient Romans have set an illustrious example in this kind. Such was the provision they made to secure the people's priviledges, that it was dangerous for any man, tho' in office, to act towards the meanest freeman of Rome in violation of the meanest of them. Hence the magistrates who ordered Paul and Silas to be *beaten uncondemned, feared when they heard they were Romans.* And Lysias, the chief captain, was filled with the like fear for commanding, that Paul should be examined with scourging; when he understood, that he was born a freeman of Rome. And it would have a good tendency to secure to the people the enjoyment of their liberties, if these smaller instances of illegal power were carefully and severely chastised.

But justice in rulers should be seen likewise in their care of the religious rights and liberties of a people. Not that they are to exert their authority in *settling articles of faith*, or *imposing modes of worship*, so as that all must frame their belief, and order their practice, according to their decisions, or lie exposed to penalties of one kind or another. This would be to put men under restraint, as to the exercise of their religious rights: Nor are penal laws at all adjusted in their nature, to enlighten men's minds, or convince their judgment. This can be done only by good reason: And this therefore is the only proper way of applying to reasonable creatures.

Justice in rulers should therefore put them upon leaving every member of the community, without respect of persons, freely to choose his own religion, and profess and practice it according to that external form, which he apprehends will be most acceptable to his maker: Provided, his religion is such as may consist with the public safety: Otherwise, it would be neither wisdom nor justice in the government to tolerate it.

Nor is this all; but they should guard every man from all insult and abuse on account of his religious sentiments, and from all molestation and disturbance, while he endeavours the propagation of them, so far as he keeps within the bounds of decency, and approves himself a peaceable member of society.

Besides which, it would be no more than reasonable, if, as christian magistrates, they distinguished those in their regards, who professed the religion of JESUS, and in that way, which, to them, was most agreable to scripture rule. They should be guardians to such christian societies, by defending their constitution; by countenancing their manner of worship; by maintaining the liberties granted to them in the gospel-charter, in all their regular exercises, whether in church assemblies for the performance of the services of piety, or the choice of officers, or the administration of discipline; or in councils, greater or less, for the help and preservation of each other: And, in fine, by owning those who minister to them in sacred things, and providing for their support, according to that rule in scripture, as well as common equity, "They that preach the gospel should live of the gospel": Or if they are generally and wrongfully kept out of a great part of that support, which has been engaged, and is justly due to them, by taking their case into consideration, and doing what may be effectual for their relief.

This last instance of the care of rulers, I the rather mention, because it falls in so exactly with the circumstances of the pastors of the churches in this province. There is not, I believe, an order of men, in the land, more universally, or to a greater degree, injured and oppressed in regard of their just dues. While others have it, in some measure, in their power to right themselves, by rising in their demands, in proportion to the sinking of the current medium, they are confined to a nominal quantum, which every day varies in its real worth, and has been gradually doing so, 'till it is come to that pass, that many of them don't receive more than one half, or two thirds of the original value they contracted for. And to this it is owing, that they are diverted from their studies, discouraged in their work, and too frequently treated with contempt. And what is an aggravation of their difficulty, their only desiring that justice may be done them, often makes an uneasiness among their people: And if they urge it; to be sure, if they demand it, 'tis great odds but there ensues thereupon contention and strife, and, at last, such a general alienation of affection, as puts an entire end to their usefulness.

Suffer me, my fathers in the government, as I have this opportunity of speaking in your presence, to beseech the exercise of your authority, on the behalf, (may I not say) of so valuable and useful a part of the community: And the rather, because some special provision for their relief seems to be a matter of justice, and not meer favour; as it is by means of the public bills, tho' contrary to the design of the government, that they are injured. And might not this be made, without any great expence either of time or pains, and so as to be effectual too, to put it out of the power of people to turn off their ministers with any thing short of the true value of what they agreed with them for, when they settled among them? This is all they desire: And as it is nothing more than common equity, would it not be hard, if they should be still left to groan under their oppressions, and to have no helper?

The great and general court, it must be acknowledged, more than twenty years since, "upon serious consideration of the great distresses, that many of the ministers within this province laboured under, with respect to their support, resolved, that it was the indispensible duty of the several towns and parishes, to make additions to the maintenance of their respective ministers; and therein to have regard to the *growing difference in the value of the bills of credit*, from what they had sometimes been." And thereupon "earnestly recommended the speedy and chearful practice of this duty to the several congregations within this province." And that the recommendation might be universally known and comply'd with, "Ordered, that their resolve should be publickly read on the next Lord's day after the receipt thereof, and at the anniversary meeting of the several towns in the month of March next" following.*

* The resolve refer'd to above, and in part quoted, it's tho't proper to insert at large; and is in these words.

At a great and general court or assembly for his majesty's province of the Massachusetts-Bay in New-England, begun and held at Boston, upon Wednesday May 26, 1725.

And it is with thankfulness that we take notice of this instance of the care of our civil fathers; tho' we are sorry, we must, at the same time, say, it was generally treated with neglect by our congregations, as being void of power.

It will not be pretended, but that the distresses of the ministers, and from the same cause too, the sinking of the medium, are vastly greater now, than they were twenty years ago: And if it was then reasonable, in the great and general court, to recommend it to the several congregations, throughout the province, as their indispensable duty, to make additions to the maintenance of their ministers, and therein to have regard to the lower value of the bills of credit, from what they formerly were; it is certainly now high time to oblige them to this: Especially, as the grievances of the ministers have often, since that day, upon these occasions, been opened to their civil fathers, whose interposition has been humbly and earnestly intreated. But I would not be too pressing: Neither have I said thus much on my own account, who am not, thro' the goodness of God, in suffering circumstances myself, but in very pity to many of my poor brethren who are; because there may be danger lest guilt should lie on the government, if they take no notice of the sighing of so considerable a body of men; and because, I verily believe, the offerings of the Lord are

The following resolve pass'd both houses, and was consented to by his honour the lieutenant governour. *Viz.*

Upon serious consideration of the great distresses that many of the ministers of the gospel within this province labour under, with respect to their support or maintenance, their salaries being generally paid in the public bills of credit of this province, altho' many of the ministers contracted with their people in the time when silver money passed in payment; and the necessaries of life, such as cloathing, provisions, together with labour and other things, now demand so much more of the bills of credit than heretofore;

Resolved, that it is the indispensable duty of the several towns precincts and parishes of this province, to make such additions to the salaries or maintenance of their respective ministers, as may honourably support and encourage them in their work; and therein to have regard as well to the time of the contract between the minister and people, and the specie therein mentioned, as to the great and growing difference in the value of the bills of credit, from what they have sometimes been. And this court do therefore most earnestly recommend the speedy and chearful practice of this duty, to the several congregations and religious assemblies within this province: And that this resolve be publickly read on the next Lord's day after the receipt hereof, in the afternoon before the congregation be dismiss'd; and at the anniversary meeting of the several towns or precincts in the province in the month of March next.

By order of the great and general court or assembly,

Josiah Willard, Secr.

too often despised, by reason of that poverty those are unrighteously reduced to, by whom they are presented.

But to return,

5. Another instance of justice in rulers relates to the defence of the state, and it's preservation in peace and safety. [The happiness of a people lies very much in their living peaceably among themselves, and at quiet with their neighbours. For which reason, rulers are bound in justice to use all prudent endeavours, that they may "sit every man under his own vine, and under his fig-tree, and have none to make them afraid." In order whereunto,

They should take care to prevent intestine jarrs and commotions in the government, by giving no occasion for murmurings and complaints; or if any should unhappily arise, by speedily removing the causes of them: By testifying a just displeasure against the fomentors of animosities, fewds and factions: By watching the motions of uneasy, turbulent and mobbish spirits, and checking the first out-breakings of them; or if, thro' the lusts of men, insurrection or rebellion should happen, by seasonably putting a stop thereto, lest afterwards the whole force of the government should be scarce sufficient for this purpose.

It may be, the late unnatural rebellion, which began in Scotland, was too much despised at first. It would not otherwise, 'tis probable, have risen to such a formidable height: Tho' the alwise holy God, by permitting this, and then remarkably succeeding the king's arms, under the command of his royal highness the duke of Cumberland, to put an end to this traiterous attempt against the throne of Great-Britain, took occasion, not only to lay the nation and it's dependencies, under more sensible bonds to give glory to him, in language like that of the 18th Psalm, "Great deliverance hath he given to his king, and shewed mercy to his anointed: Therefore will we give thanks unto thee, O Lord, and sing praises to thy name": But to do that also, which was proper to engage their more fervent prayers of faith, that he would go on to *clothe the king's enemies with shame, and cause the crown to flourish on his head*, and the head of his posterity forever.

Rulers also should endeavour to keep the state from being embroiled in foreign war, by contriving, in all prudent ways, to engage and continue the friendship of neighbouring nations; by bearing with lesser injuries from them, and not hastily resenting greater ones, so far as may be consistent with the public safety; by sacredly adhering to the treaties and contracts, they may have entred into with them; by expressing a due caution not to invade their rights or properties, or in any instance whatever to give them just cause of provocation: Or if this shou'd at any time happen, by appearing ready to make them all reasonable satisfaction.

Or if, after all, war should arise, by means of the pride, or avarice, or self-will and tyranny of unreasonable men, their concern should now be to look to the preservation of the state at home, by providing a sufficiency of warlike stores, in their various kinds; by guarding the exposed frontiers and coasts; and, in a word, by putting and keeping things in such a posture of defence, that neither their people, nor their interests, may easily fall a prey in their enemy's hands.

Besides which, it would be both wisdom and justice to carry the war into their enemies territories; doing every thing in their power to humble their pride, curb their malice, and weaken their strength; especially, where there may be most danger of being annoyed by them.]

6thly, and finally, rulers should be just to promote the general welfare and prosperity of a people, by discouraging, on the one hand, idleness, prodigality, prophaneness, uncleanness, drunkenness, and the like immoralities, which tend, in the natural course of things, to their impoverishment and ruin: And by encouraging, on the other hand, industry, frugality, temperance, chastity, and the like moral virtues, the general practice whereof are naturally connected with the flourishing of a people in every thing that tends to make them great and happy. As also, by rendring the support of government as easy as is consistent with it's honour and safety; by calculating laws to set forward those manufactures which may be of public benefit; by freeing trade, as much as possible, from all unnecessary burdens; and, above all, by a wise and sutable provision for the instruction of children and youth: In order whereunto effectual care should be taken for the encouragement and support, not only of private schools, but of the public means of education. Colleges ought to be the special care of the government, as it is from hence, principally, that it has it's dependence for initiating the youth in those arts and sciences, which may furnish them, as they grow up in the world, to be blessings both in church and state. It would certainly be unrighteous, not to protect these societies in the full and quiet enjoyment of such rights as have been freely and generously granted to them: And if they should not have within themselves a sufficiency for the support of their officers, it would be a wrong to the community, not to do what was further wanting towards their comfortable and honourable support.

And having thus, in a general and imperfect manner, gone over the more important instances, wherein rulers should be just, it might now be proper to enlarge on the obligations they are under to be so: But the time will allow me only to suggest as follows.

[They are obliged to be thus just, from the fitness and reasonableness of the thing in itself considered. 'Tis a duty that naturally and necessarily results from the relation they stand in to society, and the power they are vested with, in all righteous ways, to promote it's welfare. And it would, in the nature of things, be incongruous and absurd for men so scituated and betrusted, and for such good ends, to injure those over whom they are exalted, by abusing their power to the purposes of tyranny and oppression. Such a conduct would evidently and grosly break in upon that propriety and fitness of action, which is immutably and eternally required, in such a constitution of things, as rulers and ruled, and the relative obligations respectively arising therefrom.

They are also obliged to be thus just, in virtue of the will of the supreme legislator, made known in the revelations of scripture; which enjoins such precepts as those, "Judges and officers shalt thou make thee;—and they shall judge the people with just judgment. Thou shalt not wrest judgment;—that which is altogether just shalt thou follow."* And again, "Thus saith the Lord, Execute ye judgment and righteousness, and deliver the spoiled out of the hand of the oppressor: And do no wrong, do no violence to the stranger, the fatherless, nor the widow":† To which laws of the great king of the world they owe an indisputed obedience, as they are, in common with the rest of mankind, the subjects of his government: Nor can they be freed from the charge of reflecting contempt on the divine majesty, and that sovereign authority by which he governs his creatures, if, in their administrations, they should express a disregard to them.

* Deut. 16. 18, 19, 20.
† Jer. 22. 3.

They are likewise obliged to be just, out of regard to the community, to which they are related; whose welfare is so dependent hereon, that if they act, in their respective stations, not from a principle of justice, but under the influence of worldly views and selfish designs, it may reasonably be expected, that "judgment should be turned away backward, and justice stand afar off"; that "truth should fall in the street, and equity not be able to enter": The natural effect whereof must be the ruin of a people. Whereas, if they "put on righteousness, and it clothes them; and their judgment is as a robe and a diadem: If they deliver the poor that cry, and the fatherless, and him that hath none to help him; and break to pieces the wicked, and pluck the spoil of his teeth"; they will approve themselves those "righteous ones in authority, who cause the people to rejoice": And the righteousness wherewith they rule them will be their exaltation.

In fine, it should be a constraining argument with rulers to be just, that they are accountable to that JESUS, whom God hath ordained to be the judge of the world, for the use of that power he has put into their hands. And if, by their unjust behaviour in their places, they have not only injured the people, but unhappily led them, by their example, into practices that are fraudulent and dishonest; I say, if they have thus misused their power, sad will be their account another day; such as must expose them to the resentments of their judge, which they will not be able to escape. It will not be any security then, that they were once ranked among the great men of the earth. This may now be a protection to them, and it often indeed screens them from that human vengeance, which overtakes those of less influence, tho' guilty of less crimes: But the "kings of the earth, and the great men, and the chief captains, and the mighty men," will in the day of the appearing of the son of God, be upon a level with the meanest of mankind, and as ready, if conscious to themselves that they have been unjust in their stations, to "say to the mountains and rocks, fall on us, and hide us from the face of him that sitteth on the throne, and from the wrath of the lamb: For the great day of his wrath is come, and who shall be able to stand?" A most affecting consideration, and should powerfully excite those who rule over others, to a righteous exercise of their power; especially, as they will by this means, if in other respects also they have behaved well, obtain the approbation of their judge; who will, as they have been "faithful over a few things, make them ruler over many"; placing them at his own right hand, in his kingdom.

II. I now proceed to say, in the second place, Those who rule over men, must *rule in the fear of God.*

The fear of God, being not only in itself a considerable part of religion, but also a grace that has a special influence on all the other parts of it, is commonly, and not unfitly, used in scripture to signify the whole of it. This seems to be the meaning of the phrase here: And the thing intended is, not only that rulers should be endowed with an inward principle of religion, but that they should exercise their authority, in their whole administration, under the influence of so good and powerful a disposition.

He that ruleth over men, must rule in the fear of God. As if the royal prophet had said, "It is necessary, civil rulers should have upon their minds a becoming sense of God and religion: And it should govern their public conduct. Whatever they do, in their several stations, should be done under the guidance of an habitual awe of God, a serious regard to his governing will, and their accountableness to him. This is the principle that should have a predominating sway in all exertments of themselves in their public capacity." This I take to be the true sense of the words.

To be sure, 'tis the truth of the thing. Civil rulers ought to be possessed of a principle of religion, and to act under the direction of it in their respective stations. This is a matter of necessity. I don't mean that it is necessary in order to their having a right to rule over men. *Dominion is not founded in grace*: Nor is every pious good man fit to be entrusted with civil power. 'Tis easy to distinguish between government in it's abstracted notion, and the faithful advantageous administration of it. And religion in rulers is necessary to the latter, tho' not to the former.

Not but that they may be considerably useful in their places, if the religious fear of God does not reign in their hearts. From a natural benevolence of temper, accompanied with an active honest turn of mind, they may be instrumental in doing good service to the public: Nay, they may be prompted, even from a view to themselves, their own honour and interest, to behave well in the posts they sustain, at least, in many instances. But if destitute of religion, they are possessed of no principle that will stimulate a care in them to act up to their character steadily and universally, and so as fully to answer the ends of their institution.

'Tis a principle of religion, and this only, that can set them free from the unhappy influence of those passions and lusts, which they are subject to, in common with other men, and by means whereof they may be betrayed into that tyranny and oppression, that violence and injustice, which will destroy the peace and good order of society. These, 'tis true, may be under some tolerable check from other principles, at least, for a while, and in respect of those actings that are plainly enormous. But no restraints are like those, which the true fear of God lays upon men's lusts. This habitually prevailing in the hearts of rulers, will happily prevent the out-breaking of their pride, and envy, and avarice, and self-love, and other lusts, to the damage of society; and not only so, but it will weaken, and gradually destroy, the very inward propensities themselves to the various acts of vice. It naturally, and powerfully, tends to this: And this is the effect it will produce, in a less or greater degree, according to the strength of the religious principle, in those who are the subjects of it.

And a principle of religion also, and this only, will be effectual to excite rulers to a uniform, constant and universal regard to truth and justice, in their public conduct. Inferiour principles may influence them in particular cases, and at certain seasons: But the fear of God only will prompt them to every instance of right action, and at all times. This will possess them of such sentiments, give such a direction to their views, and fix such a happy biass on their minds, as that their chief concern and care will be, to behave in their offices so as to answer the good ends for which they were put into them. In one word, they will now be the subjects of that divine and universal principle of good conduct, which may, under God, be depended on, to carry them thro' the whole of their duty, upon all occasions, under all difficulties, and in opposition to all temptations, to the rendring the people, over whom they bear rule, as happy as 'tis in their power to make them.

To be sure, without a principle of religion, none of their services for the public will meet with the divine approbation. 'Tis therefore, in respect of themselves, a matter of absolute necessity that they be possess'd of the true fear of God. It won't suffice, should they behave well in their places, if they have no higher view herein than their own private interest; if they are influenced, not from a due regard to God, his honour and authority, but from love to themselves. This will spoil their best services, in point of the divine acceptance: Whereas, if they act from a principle of religion, what they do in a way of serving their generation will be kindly taken at the hands of a merciful God, and he will, thro' Jesus Christ, amply reward them for it, in the great day of retribution.]

APPLICATION

It now remains to apply what has been said to rulers and people.

And 'tis fit I should first turn the discourse into an address to your Excellency, as it has pleased God and the king to advance you to the first seat of government, among those who bear rule in this province.

The administration, sir, is devolved on you in the darkest day, it may be, New-England ever saw; when there was never more occasion for distinguishing talents in a governour, to direct the public counsels, and minister to the relief and comfort of a poor people, groaning under the calamities of war and debt, and, what is worse than both, an unhappy medium, that fills the land with oppression and distress. We would hope, it was because the Lord loved this people, that he has set you over us; and that he intends to honour you as the instrument in delivering us from the perplexing difficulties wherewith our affairs are embarrass'd.

We have had experience of your Excellency's superiour wisdom, knowledge, steadiness, resolution, and unwearied application in serving the province: And would herefrom encourage our selves to depend on you for every thing, that may reasonably be expected of a chief ruler, furnished with capacities fitted to promote the public happiness.

We rejoice to see so many posts in the government, at the disposal of your Excellency, either alone, or in conjunction with your council, filled with men of capacity, justice and religion: And as the public good is so much dependent on the nomination and appointment of well qualified persons to sustain the various offices in the province, we promise our selves your eye will be upon the faithful of the land, and that, while you contemn every vile person, you will honour them that fear the Lord. And should any attempt by indirect means to obtain places of trust which others better deserve, we assure ourselves your Excellency will resent such an affront, and testify a just displeasure against the persons who shall dare to offer it.

The opinion we have of your Excellency's integrity and justice, forbids the least suspicion of a design in you to invade the civil charter-rights of this people. And tho' you differ in your sentiments from us, as to the model of our church-state, and the external manner of our worship; yet we can securely rely on the generosity of your principles to protect us in the full enjoyment of those ecclesiastical rights we have been so long in possession of: And the rather, because your Excellency knows, that our progenitors enterprized the settlement of this country principally on a religious account; leaving their native land, and transporting themselves and their families, at a vast expence, and at the peril of their lives, into this distant, and then desolate wilderness, that they might themselves freely enjoy, and transmit to us their posterity, *that manner of worship and discipline*, which we look upon, as they did, most agreable to the purity of God's word.

Your Excellency knows too well the worth of learning, and the advantage of a liberal education, not to be strongly dispos'd to cherish the college, which has, from the days of our fathers, been so much the glory of New-England: And we doubt not, you will be always tender of its rights, and exert your self, as there may be occasion, for its defence and welfare.

And as your Excellency is our common father, we repair to you as the friend and patron of all that is dear and valuable to us; depending that you will employ your time, your thought, your authority, your influence and best endeavours, to ease our burdens, to lead us out of the labyrinths we have run into, and to make us a happy and prosperous people.

We can wish nothing better for your Excellency than the divine presence enabling you to act, in your whole administration, under the influence of a steady principle of justice, and an habitual awe and reverence of that God, for whom ultimately you derived your authority, and to whom you are accountable for the use of it. This will recommend you to the love, and entitle you to the praise of an obliged happy people; this will yield you undisturbed ease of mind under the cares and burdens of government; this will brighten to you the shades of death, embalm your memory after you are dead, and, what is infinitely more desireable, give you boldness when great and small shall stand before the Son of man, and procure for you that blessed euge, from the mouth of your divine Saviour and Master, "Well done, good and faithful servant: Enter thou into the joy of thy Lord."

Permit me, in the next place, with a becoming respect, to apply myself to the honourable his majesty's council, and the honourable house of representatives; whose desire has ordered me into this desk.

Through the goodness of God, we see the return of this anniversary for the exercise of one of those charter-rights, granted to our fathers, and continued to us, on the wise and faithful management whereof, the public happiness is very much dependent.

His majesty's council, this afternoon to be elected, is an happy medium between the king and the people, and wisely designed to preserve a due ballance between the prerogatives of the one, and the privileges of the other. And as they constitute one branch of the legislature, they have a share in framing and passing all acts and orders. To them it appertains to assist the chief ruler with their advice upon all emergent occasions, especially in the court's recess. And without their consent, none of the civil posts in the government can be filled; in consequence whereof, no judges can be appointed, no courts erected, no causes tried, no sentences executed, but by persons who have had their approbation: All which, by shewing the weight of this order of men in the state, bespeaks the importance of this day's business, and, at the same time, demands a proportionable care and faithfulness in the discharge of it.

It is not, gentlemen, a trifling concern you have before you; an affair wherein you may act with carelessness or inattention; with a party or partial spirit; out of affection to friends, or complaisance to superiors; much less upon the corrupt design of making instruments to be imployed and managed to serve your own private schemes. It is not for yourselves only that you are empowered and called to vote in the elections of this day, but for your God, your king and your country: And you will be unjust to them all, if you give your voice as moved by any considerations, but those which are taken from the real characters of men, qualifying them to sit at the council-board.

You all know, from the oracles of God, how men must be furnished, in order to their being fit to be chosen into places of such important trust; that they must be wise and understanding, and known to be so among their tribes; that they must be *able men, and men of truth, men that fear God, and hate covetousness.* And 'tis to be hoped, we have a sufficiency of such, in the land, to constitute his majesty's council. It would be lamentable indeed, if we had not. 'Tis your business, gentlemen, to seek them out. And with you will the fault principally lie, if we have not the best men in the country for councillors; men of capacity and knowledge, who are well acquainted with the nature of government in general, and the constitution, laws, priviledges and interests of this people in particular: Men of known piety towards God, and fidelity to their king and country: Men of a generous spirit, who are above acting under the influence of narrow and selfish principles: Men of unquestionable integrity, inflexible justice, and undaunted resolution, who will dare not to give their consent to unrighteous acts, or mistaken nominations; who will disdain, on the one hand, meanly to withdraw, when speaking their minds with freedom and openness may expose them to those who set them up, and may have it in their power to pull them down, or, on the other, to accommodate their conduct, in a servile manner, to their sentiments and designs; in fine, who will steadily act up to their character, support the honour of their station, and approve themselves invariably faithful in their endeavours to advance the public weal.

These are the men, 'tis in your power, my honourable fathers, to choose into the council; and these are the men for whom, in the name of God, and this whole people, I would earnestly beg every vote this day: And suffer me to say, these are the men you will all send in your votes for, if you are yourselves men of integrity and justice, and exercise your elective-power, not as having concerted the matter beforehand, in some party-juncto, but under the influence of a becoming awe of that omnipresent righteous God, whose eye will be upon you, to observe how you vote, and for whom you vote, and to whom you must finally render an account, before the general assembly of angels and men, for this day's transaction.

We bow our knees to the alwise sovereign Being, who presides over the affairs of the children of men, in humble and fervent supplications, that he would govern your views, direct your tho'ts, and lead you into a choice that he shall own and succeed, to promote the best interests of this people.

And when the elections of this day are over, and the several branches of the legislature shall proceed upon the affairs of the public, we promise ourselves you will act as those, who have upon their minds a just sense of the vast importance of the trust that is reposed in you.

To you is committed the defence of the province, the guardianship of it's liberties and priviledges, the protection of it's trade, and the care of it's most valuable interests: And never was there a time, wherein it's circumstances more urgently called upon you to exert yourselves, in seeking it's welfare.

Religion is not in such a flourishing state, at this day, but that it needs the countenance of your example, and the interposition of your authority, to keep it from insult and contempt. We thankfully acknowledge the pious care, the legislature has lately taken to restrain the horrid practice of cursing and swearing, which so generally prevailed, especially in this, and our other sea-port towns, to the dishonour of God, and our reproach as wearing the name of christians. And if laws still more severe are necessary, to guard the day and worship of God from prophanation, we can leave it with your wisdom to enact such, as may tend to serve so good a design. And tho' we would be far from desiring, that our rulers should espouse a party in religion; yet we cannot but hope, they will never do any thing to encourage those, who may have arrived at such an height in spiritual pride, as to say, in their practice, to their brethren as good as themselves, "stand by thy self, come not near me; for I am holier than thou": Concerning whom the blessed God declares, "These are a smoke in my nose, a fire that burneth all the day." And as for those, be their character, persuasion, or party, what it will, who, under the notion of appearing zealous for God, his truths or ways, shall insult their betters, vilify their neighbours, and spirit people to strife and faction, we earnestly wish the civil arm may be stretched forth to chastise them: And if they suffer, 'twill be for disturbing the peace of society; the evil whereof is rather aggravated than lessened, by pretences to advance the glory of God and the interest of religion.

We are thankful for the good and wholesome laws which have been made, from time to time, for the suppression of vice, in it's various kinds; and, in particular, for the restraint that has been laid upon those, who may be inclined to excessive drinking. Alas! that such multitudes, notwithstanding, are overtaken with this fault. Hard drinking is indeed become common all over the land. And 'tis astonishing to think what quantities of strong drink are consumed among us! Unless some, well capable of forming a judgment, are very much mistaken, more a great deal is needlessly and viciously consumed than would suffice to answer the whole charge, both of church and state. A reproach this, to any people! And if something further is not done by the government, to prevent the use that is made of strong drink, it will, in a little time, prove the destruction of the country, in the natural course of things; if God should not positively testify his displeasure against such horrid intemperance. It may deserve your consideration, my fathers, whether one occasion of this scandalous consumption of strong drink, has not been the needless multiplication of taverns, as well as more private licensed houses, that are too commonly used for tipling, and serve to little purpose, but to tempt people, in low life sinfully to waste their time, and spend their substance.

[It would also redound much to the advantage of the province, if our civil fathers could contrive, some way or other that might be effectual, to prevent people's laying out so much of the fruit of their labour, in that which is needless and extravagant. It will not be denied, by any capable of making observation, that the excesses, all ranks of persons have unhappily run into, need correction. 'Tis owing, in a great measure, to our pride, discovering it self in the extravagance of our garb, as well as manner of living, that we are brought low. And, if some restraint is not laid upon this vicious disposition, so generally prevalent in the land, we may complain of our difficulties, but 'tis not likely, without a miracle, they should be redressed.]

But there is nothing more needs your awaken'd attention, my honoured fathers in the government, than the unhappy state of this people by means of the current medium. Whatever wise and good ends might be proposed at first, and from time to time, in the *emission of bills of credit*, they have proved, in the event, a cruel engine of oppression. It may be, there was scarce ever a province under more melancholly circumstances, by reason of injustice, which is become almost unavoidable. Sad is the case of your men of nominal salaries: And much to be pitied also are those widows and orphans, who depend on the loan of their money for a subsistance: While yet, these last, of all persons in the community, should be most carefully guarded against every thing that looks like oppression. This sin, when widows and fatherless children are the persons wronged by it, is heinously aggravated in the sight of a righteous God; as may easily be collected from that emphatical prohibition, so often repeated in all parts of the bible, "Thou shalt not oppress the widow, nor the fatherless." But the oppression reigning in the land, is not confined to this order or that condition of persons, but touches all without exception. None escape its pernicious influence, neither high nor low, rich nor poor. Like an over-bearing flood, it makes its way thro' the province; and all are sufferers by it, in a less or greater degree, and feel and own themselves to be so.

And will you, our honoured rulers, by any positive acts, or faulty neglects, suffer your selves to be instrumental in the continuance of such a state of things? God forbid! We don't think you would designedly do any thing to countenance oppression, or neglect any thing that might have a tendency to remove it out of the land.

Neither can we think, that any former assemblies have knowingly acted, in the *emission of public bills*, upon dishonest principles: Tho' it may be feared, whether the righteous God, in holy displeasure at the sins both of rulers and people, may not have witheld counsel from our wise men, and scattered darkness in their paths: And if, in consequence hereof, there has been disunion in the sentiments of our civil fathers, concerning the public medium, and unsteadiness in their conduct, 'tis no matter of wonder: Nor, upon this supposition, is it hard to be accounted for, that injustice, by means of the paper currency, should have taken such a general and dreadful spread, thro' the land.

But, by what means soever we became involved in these perplexities, 'tis certainly high time to make a pause, and consider what may be done that will be effectual towards the recovering and maintaining justice and honesty, that we may be called the *city of righteousness*, *the faithful city*.

It would be culpable vanity in me, to attempt to prescribe to our honourable legislature; yet may I, without going beyond my line, after the example of the great apostle of the gentiles, reason with you of public righteousness, and its connection with a judgment to come.

You are, my fathers, accountable to that God whose throne is in the heavens, in common with other men. And his eyes behold your conduct in your public capacity, and he sees and observes it, not merely as a spectator, but an almighty righteous judge, one who enters all upon record in order to a reckoning another day. And a day is coming, it lingers not, when you shall all stand upon a level, with the meanest subjects, before the tremendous bar of the righteous judge of all the earth, and be called upon to render an account, not only of your private life, but of your whole management as entrusted with the concerns of this people.

Under the realising apprehension of this, suffer me, in the name of God, (tho' the most unworthy of his servants) to advise you to review the public conduct, respecting the passing bills, and to do whatever may lay in your power to prevent their being the occasion of that injustice, which, if continued much longer, will destroy the small remains of common honesty that are still left in the land, and make us an abhorrence to the people that delight in righteousness.

Let me beseech you, sirs, for the sake of this poor people, and for the sake of your own souls, when you shall stand before the dreadful bar of the eternal judgment, to lay aside all party designs and private considerations, and to deliberate upon this great affair, with a single view to the public good, and under the uniform influence of a steady principle of righteousness; for, as the wise man observes, "transgressors shall be taken in their own naughtiness," while "the righteousness of the upright shall deliver them, and their integrity shall guide them"; and again, "as for the upright, the Lord directeth their way."

If there needs any excuse for my wonted plainness of speech, I can only say; my conscience beareth me witness, that what I have said has proceeded, not from want of a decent respect for those who are my civil fathers, but from faithfulness to God, whose I am, and whom I desire to serve, as well as from an ardent love to my dear country, which I am grieved to behold in tears, by reason of "the oppressions that are done under the sun."

Custom might now demand an address to my fathers and brethren in the ministry; but as a sermon will be preached to the clergy tomorrow, by one who is every way my superior, and from whom I expect myself to receive instruction, I shall no otherwise apply to them than as they may be concerned in the exhortation to the people, which, agreably to the preceeding discourse, speaketh in the words of the inspired Solomon, "Fear God, and honour the king."

Be, first of all, concerned to become truly religious; men of piety towards God, faith in our Lord Jesus Christ, and the subjects of that regenerating change, which shall renew your whole inner man, and form you to a resemblance of the blessed Jesus, in the moral temper of his mind.

And let your religion now discover itself in all proper ways; particularly, in doing your duty to those, whom it hath pleased God to entrust with power to rule over you.

Be exhorted to "make supplications, prayers and intercessions, with giving of thanks, for the king in supreme, and for all in authority" under him, that by means of their wise, and gentle, and just administrations in government, we may "lead quiet and peaceable lives in all godliness and honesty."

And as subjection to civil rulers is so peremptorily demanded of you, by the laws of our holy religion, that you can't be good christians without it, let me caution you, on the one hand, not to "despise dominion," nor "speak evil of dignities": And, on the other, let me "put you in mind to be subject to principalities and powers, and to obey magistrates; submitting to every ordinance of man for the Lord's sake: Whether it be to the king, as supreme; or unto governours, as unto them that are sent by him, for the punishment of evil doers, and for the praise of them that do well: For so is the will of God."

And as rulers are the ministers of God, his authoris'd deputies, for the people's good, and continually, so far as they answer the ends of their institution, attend on this very thing: "For this cause pay you tribute also": And do it, not grudgingly, but with a chearful mind, in obedience to that glorious sovereign Being, who has said, "render unto Cæsar the things that are Cæsar's."

In fine, let me call upon you to "render unto all their dues." Abhor the little arts of fraud and deceit that are become so common, in this day of growing dishonesty. Make use of conscience in your dealings with your neighbour; and be fair and equitable, wherein you may have to do with him in a way of commerce. In conformity to the righteous God, love righteousness, and discover that you do so, by constantly living in the practice of it: Always bearing it in mind, that he, "whose eyes behold, and whose eyelids try the children of men," will hereafter descend from heaven, "to give to every man according as his work shall be." Behold! He cometh with clouds, and we shall, every one of us, see him. We are hastening to another world; and it will not be long, before we shall all be together again, in a much more numerous assembly, and upon a far greater occasion, even that of being tried for our future existence, at the dreadful tribunal of the impartial judge of the quick and dead. The good Lord so impress the thought upon the hearts of us all, whether rulers, or ministers, or people, as that it may have an abiding influence on us, engaging us to be faithful and just in our respective places: And now may we hope, of the mercy of God, thro' the merits of our saviour Jesus Christ, to be acquitted at the bar of judgment, pronounced blessed, and bid to inherit the kingdom prepared from the foundation of the world.

A M E N

— 6 —

THE MEDIATORIAL KINGDOM AND GLORIES OF JESUS CHRIST

Samuel Davies

LONDON

1756

Samuel Davies (1724–1761). Fourth president of the College of New Jersey (now Princeton University), Delaware-born Samuel Davies was a Presbyterian and great pulpit orator whose published sermons remained popular for half a century after his death. Never physically robust, he nonetheless worked prodigiously in the Virginia back-country as a circuit-riding parson, regularly preaching in seven churches scattered over five counties. He settled in Hanover County, where dissenters were frowned upon, and soon became the leader in the campaign for civil and religious liberties in Virginia and North Carolina.

He accompanied the Great Awakening preacher Gilbert Tennent (1703–1764) to Great Britain in 1753, under commission of the Synod of New York, to raise funds for the College of New Jersey. He succeeded handsomely in this enterprise and also achieved fame in preaching some sixty sermons in England and Scotland, many of which were published and widely read. After Davies returned to America, the Presbytery of Hanover, the first in Virginia, was established largely by his efforts late in 1755. Jonathan Edwards the elder and Aaron Burr, Sr., sponsored Davies in all his endeavors, and upon the death of Burr, Davies was offered the college presidency in Princeton as his successor. He eventually accepted the offer in 1759, but died of pneumonia less than two years later. He still managed to achieve important reforms at the college by raising the standards for admission and graduation and by planning a new library.

This sermon was preached in Hanover County, Virginia, on May 9, 1756, at the beginning of the French and Indian War; it was published posthumously in London.

SERMON X.

The Mediatorial Kingdom and Glories of Jesus Christ.

John xviii. 37. *Pilate therefore said unto him, Art thou a King then? Jesus answered, Thou sayest that I am a King. To this end was I born, and for this cause came I into the world, that I should bear witness unto the truth.*

KINGS and kingdoms are the most majestic sounds in the language of mortals, and have filled the world with noise, confusions, and blood, since mankind first left the state of nature, and formed themselves into societies. The disputes of kingdoms for superiority have set the world in arms from age to age, and destroyed or enslaved a considerable part of the human race; and the contest is not yet decided. Our country has been a region of peace and tranquillity for a long time, but it has not been because the lust of power and riches is extinct in the world, but because we had no near neighbours, whose interest might clash with ours, or who were able to disturb us. The absence of an enemy was our sole defence. But now, when the colonies of the sundry European nations on this continent begin to enlarge, and approach towards each other, the scene is changed: now encroachments, depredations, barbarities, and all the terrors of war begin to surround and alarm us. Now our country is invaded and ravaged, and bleeds in a thousand veins. We have already,* so early in the year, received alarm upon alarm: and we may expect the alarms to grow louder and louder as the season advances.

These

* This sermon was preached in Hanover, Virginia, May 9, 1756.

Pilate therefore said unto him, Art thou a King then? Jesus answered, Thou sayest that I am a King. To this end was I born, and for this cause came I into the world, that I should bear witness unto the truth.

John xviii. 37.

Kings and kingdoms are the most majestic sounds in the language of mortals, and have filled the world with noise, confusions, and blood, since mankind first left the state of nature, and formed themselves into societies. The disputes of kingdoms for superiority have set the world in arms from age to age, and destroyed or enslaved a considerable part of the human race; and the contest is not yet decided. Our country has been a region of peace and tranquillity for a long time, but it has not been because the lust of power and riches is extinct in the world, but because we had no near neighbours, whose interest might clash with ours, or who were able to disturb us. The absence of an enemy was our sole defence. But now, when the colonies of the sundry European nations on this continent begin to enlarge, and approach towards each other, the scene is changed: now encroachments, depredations, barbarities, and all the terrors of war begin to surround and alarm us. Now our country is invaded and ravaged, and bleeds in a thousand veins. We have already,* so early in the year, received alarm upon alarm: and we may expect the alarms to grow louder and louder as the season advances.

These commotions and perturbations have had one good effect upon me, and that is, they have carried away my thoughts of late into a serene and peaceful region, a region beyond the reach of confusion and violence; I mean the kingdom of the Prince of Peace. And thither, my brethren, I would also transport your minds this day, as the best refuge from this boisterous world, and the most agreeable mansion for the lovers of peace and tranquillity. I find it advantageous both to you and myself, to entertain you with those subjects that have made the deepest impression upon my own mind: and this is the reason why I choose the present subject. In my text you hear one entering a claim to a kingdom, whom you would conclude, if you

* This sermon was preached in Hanover, Virginia, May 9, 1756.

regarded only his outward appearance, to be the meanest and vilest of mankind. To hear a powerful prince, at the head of a victorious army, attended with all the royalties of his character, to hear such an one claim the kingdom he had acquired by force of arms, would not be strange. But here the despised Nazarene, rejected by his nation, forsaken by his followers, accused as the worst of criminals, standing defenceless at Pilate's bar, just about to be condemned and hung on a cross, like a malefactor and a slave, here he speaks in a royal stile, even to his judge, *I am a King: for this purpose was I born; and for this cause came I into the world.* Strange language indeed to proceed from his lips in these circumstances! But the truth is, a great, a divine personage is concealed under this disguise; and his kingdom is of such a nature, that his abasement and crucifixion were so far from being a hindrance to it, that they were the only way to acquire it. These sufferings were meritorious; and by these he purchased his subjects, and a right to rule them.

The occasion of these words was this: the unbelieving Jews were determined to put Jesus to death as an imposter. The true reason of their opposition to him was, that he had severely exposed their hypocrisy, claimed the character of the Messiah, without answering their expectations as a temporal prince and a mighty conqueror; and introduced a new religion, which superseded the law of Moses, in which they had been educated. But this reason they knew would have but little weight with Pilate the Roman governor, who was an heathen, and had no regard to their religion. They therefore bring a charge of another kind, which they knew would touch the governor very sensibly, and that was, that Christ had set himself up as the King of the Jews; which was treason against Cæsar the Roman emperor, under whose yoke they then were. This was all pretence and artifice. They would now seem to be very loyal to the emperor, and unable to bear with any claims inconsistent with his authority; whereas, in truth, they were impatient of a foreign government, and were watching for any opportunity to shake it off. And had Christ been really guilty of the charge they alledged against him, he would have been the more acceptable to them. Had he set himself up as King of the Jews, in opposition to Cæsar, and employed his miraculous powers to make good his claim, the whole nation would have welcomed him as their deliverer, and flocked round his standard. But

Jesus came not to work a deliverance of this kind, nor to erect such a kingdom as they desired, and therefore they rejected him as an impostor. This charge, however, they bring against him, in order to carry their point with the heathen governor. They knew he was zealous for the honour and interest of Cæsar his master; and Tiberius, the then Roman emperor, was so jealous a prince, and kept so many spies over his governors in all the provinces, that they were obliged to be very circumspect, and shew the strictest regard for his rights, in order to escape degradation, or a severer punishment. It was this that determined Pilate, in the struggle with his conscience, to condemn the innocent Jesus. He was afraid the Jews would inform against him, as dismissing one that set up as the rival of Cæsar; and the consequence of this he well knew. The Jews were sensible of this, and therefore they insist upon this charge, and at length plainly tell him, *If thou let this man go, thou art not Cæsar's friend.* Pilate therefore, who cared but little what innovations Christ should introduce into the Jewish religion, thought proper to inquire into this matter, and asks him, "Art thou the King of the Jews?" dost thou indeed claim such a character, which may interfere with Cæsar's government? Jesus replies, *My kingdom is not of this world*; as much as to say, "I do not deny that I claim a kingdom, but it is of such a nature, that it need give no alarm to the kings of the earth. Their kingdoms are of this world, but mine is spiritual and divine,* and therefore cannot interfere with theirs. If my kingdom were of this world, like theirs, I would take the same methods with them to obtain and secure it; my servants would fight for me, that I should not be delivered to the Jews; but now, you see, I use no such means for my defence, or to raise me to my kingdom: and therefore you may be assured, my kingdom is not from hence, and can give the Roman emperor no umbrage for suspicion or uneasiness." Pilate answers to this purpose: Thou dost, however, speak of a kingdom; and *art thou a king then?* dost thou in any sense claim that character? The poor prisoner boldly replies, *Thou*

* Domitian, the Roman emperor, being apprehensive that Christ's earthly relations might claim a kingdom in his right, inquired of them concerning the nature of his kingdom, and when and where it should be set up. They replied, "It was not earthly, but heavenly and angelical, and to be set up at the end of the world." Οὐ κοσμικὴ μὲν οὐϐ᾽ ἐπίγειος, ἐπονϱάνιος ϐὲ καὶ ἀγγελικὴ τυγχάνει, ἐπὶ συντελείᾳ τοῦ αιῶνος γενησομένη. Euseb. Eccl. Hist. lib. iii. chap. 20.

sayest that I am a king; that is, "Thou hast struck upon the truth: I am indeed a king in a certain sense, and nothing shall constrain me to renounce the title." *To this end was I born, and for this cause came I into the world, that I should bear witness to the truth;* "particularly to this truth, which now looks so unlikely, namely, that I am really a king. I was born to a kingdom and a crown, and came into the world to take possession of my right." This is that great confession which St. Paul tells us, 2 Tim. vi. 13. our Lord witnessed before Pontius Pilate. Neither the hopes of deliverance, nor the terrors of death, could cause him to retract it, or renounce his claim.

In prosecuting this subject I intend only to inquire into the nature and properties of the kingdom of Christ. And in order to render my discourse the more familiar, and to adapt it to the present state of our country, I shall consider this kingdom in contrast with the kingdoms of the earth, with which we are better acquainted.

The scriptures represent the Lord Jesus under a great variety of characters, which, though insufficient fully to represent him, yet in conjunction assist us to form such exalted ideas of this great personage, as mortals can reach. He is a surety, that undertook and paid the dreadful debt of obedience and suffering, which sinners owed to the divine justice and law: He is a priest, a great high priest, that once offered himself as a sacrifice for sin; and now dwells in his native heaven, at his Father's right hand, as the advocate and intercessor of his people: He is a prophet, who teaches his church in all ages by his word and spirit: He is the supreme and universal Judge, to whom men and angels are accountable; and his name is Jesus, a saviour, because he saves his people from their sins. Under these august and endearing characters he is often represented. But there is one character under which he is uniformly represented, both in the Old and New Testament, and that is, that of a king, a great king, invested with universal authority. And upon his appearance in the flesh, all nature, and especially the gospel-church, is represented as placed under him, as his kingdom. Under this idea the Jews were taught by their prophets to look for him; and it was their understanding these predictions of some illustrious king that should rise from the house of David, in a literal and carnal sense, that occasioned their unhappy prejudices concerning the Messiah as a secular prince and conqueror. Under this idea the Lord Jesus represented himself while upon earth, and under this idea he was published to the world by his apostles. The greatest kings of the Jewish nation, particularly David and Solomon, were types of him; and many things are primarily applied to them, which have their complete and final accomplishment in him alone. It is to him ultimately we are to apply the second psalm: *I have set my king*, says Jehovah, *upon my holy hill of Zion. Ask of me, and I will give thee the heathen for thy inheritance, and the utmost parts of the earth for thy possession.* Psalm ii. 6, 8. If we read the seventy-second psalm we shall easily perceive that one greater than Solomon is there. *In his days shall the righteous flourish; and abundance of peace so long as the moon endureth. All kings shall fall down before him; all nations shall serve him. His name shall continue for ever; his name shall endure as long as the sun: and men shall be blessed in him; and all nations shall call him blessed.* Psalm lxxii. 7, 11, 17. The hundred and tenth psalm is throughout a celebration of the kingly and priestly office of Christ united. *The Lord*, says David, *said unto my Lord*, unto that divine person who is my Lord, and will also be my Son, *sit thou at my right hand*, in the highest honour and authority, *until I make thine enemies thy footstool.* Rule thou in the midst of thine enemies. *Thy people shall be willing in the day of thy power*, and submit to thee in crowds as numerous as the drops of morning dew. Psalm cx. 1–3. The evangelical prophet Isaiah is often transported with the foresight of this illustrious king, and the glorious kingdom of his grace: *Unto us a child is born, unto us a son is given; and the government shall be upon his shoulder; and he shall be called—the Prince of Peace. Of the increase of his government and peace there shall be no end, upon the throne of David and upon his kingdom, to order and to establish it with judgment and with justice, from henceforth even for ever.* Isa. ix. 6, 7. This is he who is described as another David in Ezekiel's prophecy, *Thus saith the Lord, I will take the children of Israel from among the heathen. And I will make them one nation—and one king shall be king to them all—even David my servant shall be king over them.* Ezek. xxxvii. 21, 22, 24. This is the kingdom represented to Nebuchadnezzar in his dream, as *a stone cut out without hands, which became a great mountain, and filled the whole earth.* And Daniel, in expounding the dream, having described the Babylonian, the Persian, the Grecian, and Roman empires, subjoins, *In the days of these kings*, that is, of the Roman emperors, *shall the God of heaven set up a kingdom, which shall never be destroyed: and the kingdom shall not*, like the former, *be left to other people; but it shall break in pieces and consume all these kingdoms, and it shall stand for ever.* Dan. ii. 34, 35, 44. There is no character which our Lord so often assumed in the days of his flesh as that of the Son of Man; and he no doubt alludes to a majestic vision in Daniel, the only place where this character is given him in the Old Testament: *I saw in the night visions,* says Daniel, *and behold, one like the Son of Man came to the Ancient of Days, and there was given to him dominion, and glory, and a kingdom, that all people, nations, and languages, should serve him: his dominion is an everlasting dominion, which shall not pass away, and his kingdom that which shall not be destroyed,* Dan. vii. 13, 14. like the tottering kingdoms of the earth, which are perpetually rising and falling. This is the king that Zechariah refers to when, in prospect of his triumphant entrance into Jerusalem, he calls the inhabitants to give a proper reception to so great a prince. *Rejoice greatly, O daughter of Zion; shout, O daughter of Jerusalem: behold thy King coming unto thee,* &c. Zech. ix. 9. Thus the prophets conspire to ascribe royal titles and a glorious kingdom to the Messiah. And these early and plain notices of him raised a general expectation of him under this royal character. It was from these prophecies concerning him as a king, that the Jews took occasion, as I observed, to look for the Messiah as a temporal prince; and it was a long time before the apostles themselves were delivered from these carnal prejudices. They were solicitous about posts of honour in that temporal kingdom which they expected he would set up: and even after his resurrection they cannot forbear asking him, *Lord, wilt thou at this time restore again the kingdom to Israel?* Acts i. 6. that is, "Wilt thou now restore the Jews to their former liberty and independency, and deliver them from their present subjection to the Romans?" It was under this view that Herod was alarmed at his birth, and shed the blood of so many innocents, that he might not escape. He was afraid of him as the heir of David's family and crown, who might dispossess him of the government; nay, he was expected by other nations under the character of a mighty king; and they no doubt learned this notion of him from the Jewish prophecies, as well as their conversation with that people. Hence the Magi, or eastern wisemen, when they came to pay homage to him upon his birth, inquired after him in this language, "Where is he that is born King of the Jews?" Matt. ii. 2. And what is still more remarkable, we are told by two heathen historians, that about the time of his appearance a general expectation of him under this character prevailed through the world. "Many," says Tacitus, "had a persuasion that it was contained in the ancient writings of the priests, that at that very time the east should prevail, and that some descendant from Judah should obtain the universal government."* Suetonius speaks to the same purpose: "An old and constant opinion," says he, "commonly prevailed through all the east, that it was in the fates, that some should rise out of Judea who should obtain the government of the world."† This royal character Christ himself assumed, even when he conversed among mortals in the humble form of a servant. *The Father*, says he, *has given me power over all flesh.* John xvii. 2. Yea, *all power in heaven and earth is given to me.* Matt. xxviii. 16. The gospel-church which he erected is most commonly called the kingdom of heaven or of God, in the evangelists: and when he was about to introduce it, this was the proclamation: *The kingdom of heaven is at hand.* Under this character also his servants and disciples celebrated and preached him. Gabriel led the song in foretelling his birth to his mother. *He shall be great, and the Lord shall give unto him the throne of his father David; and he shall reign over the house of Jacob for ever: and of his kingdom there shall be no end.* Luke i. 32, 33. St. Peter boldly tells the murderers of Christ, *God hath made that same Jesus whom you crucified, both Lord and Christ*, Acts ii. 36. *and exalted him, with his own right hand, to be a Prince and a Saviour.* Acts v. 31. And St. Paul repeatedly represents him as advanced *far above principality, and power, and might, and dominion, and every name that is named, not only in this world, but also in that which is to come: and that God hath put all things under his feet, and given him to be head over all things to his church.* Eph. i. 21, 22. Phil. ii. 9–11. Yea, to him all the hosts of heaven, and even the whole creation in concert, ascribe *power and strength, and honour and glory.* Rev. v. 12. Pilate the heathen was over-ruled to give a kind of accidental testimony to this truth, and to publish it to different nations, by the inscription upon the cross in the three languages then most in use, the Latin, Greek, and Hebrew: *This*

* Fluribus persuasio inerat, antiquis sacerdotum literis contineri, eo ipso tempore fore, ut valesceret oriens, profectique Judeâ rerum potirentur. Tacit. Hist. l. 5. p. 621.

† Percrebuerat oriente toto vetus & constans opinio, effe in satis, ut eo tempore Judeâ profecti rerum potirentur. Suet, in Vesp. c. 4.

The sameness of the expectation is remarkably evident, from the sameness of the words in which these two historians express it. *Judeâ profecti rerum potirentur.* It was not only a common expectation, but it was commonly expressed in the same language.

is Jesus of Nazareth, the King of the Jews; and all the remonstrances of the Jews could not prevail upon him to alter it. Finally, it is he that wears *upon his vesture, and upon his thigh, this name written, King of kings, and Lord of lords*, Rev. xix. 16. and as his name is, so is he.

Thus you see, my brethren, by these instances, selected out of many, that the kingly character and dominion of our Lord Jesus runs through the whole Bible. That of a king is his favourite character in which he glories, and which is the most expressive of his office. And this consideration alone may convince you that this character is of the greatest importance, and worthy of your most attentive regard.

It is the mediatorial kingdom of Christ that is here intended, not that which as God he exercises over all the works of his hands: it is that kingdom which is an empire of grace, an administration of mercy over our guilty world. It is the dispensation intended for the salvation of fallen sinners of our race by the gospel; and on this account the gospel is often called the kingdom of heaven; because its happy consequences are not confined to this earth, but appear in heaven in the highest perfection, and last through all eternity. Hence, not only the church of Christ on earth, and the dispensation of the gospel, but all the saints in heaven, and that more finished œconomy under which they are placed, are all included in the kingdom of Christ. Here his kingdom is in its infancy, but in heaven is arrived to perfection; but it is substantially the same. Though the immediate design of this kingdom is the salvation of believers of the guilty race of man, and such are its subjects in a peculiar sense; yet it extends to all worlds, to heaven, and earth, and hell. The whole universe is put under a mediatorial head; but then, as the apostle observes, *he is made head over all things to his church*, Eph. i. 22. that is, for the benefit and salvation of his church. As Mediator he is carrying on a glorious scheme for the recovery of man, and all parts of the universe are interested or concern themselves in this grand event; and therefore they are all subjected to him, that he may so manage them as to promote this end, and baffle and overwhelm all opposition. The elect angels rejoice in so benevolent a design for peopling their mansions, left vacant by the fall of so many of their fellow-angels, with colonies transplanted from our world, from a race of creatures that they had given up for lost. And therefore Christ, as a Mediator, is made the head of all the heavenly armies, and he employs them as *his ministering spirits, to min-*

ister to them that are heirs of salvation. Heb. i. 14. These glorious creatures are always on the wing ready to discharge his orders in any part of his vast empire, and delight to be employed in the services of his mediatorial kingdom. This is also an event in which the fallen angels deeply interest themselves; they have united all their force and art for near six thousand years to disturb and subvert his kingdom, and blast the designs of redeeming love; they therefore are all subjected to the controul of Christ, and he shortens and lengthens their chains as he pleases, and they cannot go an hair's breadth beyond his permission. The scriptures represent our world in its state of guilt and misery as the kingdom of Satan; sinners, while slaves to sin, are his subjects; and every act of disobedience against God is an act of homage to this infernal prince. Hence Satan is called *the God of this world,* 2 Cor. iv. 4. *the prince of this world,* John xii. 31. *the power of darkness,* Luke xxii. 53. *the prince of the power of the air, the Spirit that now worketh in the children of disobedience.* Eph. ii. 3. And sinners are said to be *taken captive by him at his will.* 2 Tim. ii. 26. Hence also the ministers of Christ, who are employed to recover sinners to a state of holiness and happiness, are represented as soldiers armed for war; not indeed with carnal weapons, but with those which are spiritual, plain truth arguments, and miracles; and *these are made mighty through God to the pulling down of strong holds, casting down imaginations, and every high thing that exalteth itself against the knowledge of God, and bringing into captivity every thought to the obedience of Christ.* 2 Cor. x. 3, 4, 5. And christians in general are represented as *wrestling, not with flesh and blood, but against principalities, against powers, against the rulers of the darkness of this world, against spiritual wickednesses in high places.* Eph. vi. 12. Hence also in particular it is that the death of Christ is represented not as a defeat, but as an illustrious conquest gained over the powers of hell; because, by this means a way was opened for the deliverance of sinners from under their power, and restoring them into liberty and the favour of God. By that strange contemptible weapon, the cross, and by the glorious resurrection of Jesus, he *spoiled principalities and powers, and made a shew of them openly, triumphing over them.* Col. ii. 15. *Through death,* says the apostle, *he destroyed him that had the power of death; that is, the devil.* Heb. ii. 14. Had not Christ by his death offered a propitiatory sacrifice for the sins of men, they would have continued for ever under the tyranny of Satan; but he has purchased liberty, life, and salvation for them; and thus he hath destroyed the kingdom of darkness, and translated multitudes from it into his own gracious and glorious kingdom.

Hence, upon the right of redemption, his mediatorial authority extends to the infernal regions, and he controuls and restrains those malignant, mighty, and turbulent potentates, according to his pleasure. Farther, the inanimate world is connected with our Lord's design to save sinners, and therefore is subjected to him as Mediator. He causes the sun to rise, the rain to fall, and the earth to yield her increase, to furnish provision for the subjects of his grace, and to raise, support and accommodate heirs for his heavenly kingdom. As for the sons of men, who are more immediately concerned in this kingdom, and for whose sake it was erected, they are all its subjects; but then they are of different sorts, according to their characters. Multitudes are rebels against his government; that is, they do not voluntarily submit to his authority, nor chuse they to do his service: they will not obey his laws. But they are his subjects notwithstanding; that is, he rules and manages them as he pleases, whether they will or not. This power is necessary to carry on successfully his gracious design towards his people; for unless he had the management of his enemies, they might baffle his undertaking, and successfully counteract the purposes of his love. The kings of the earth, as well as vulgar rebels of a private character, have often set themselves against his kingdom, and sometimes they have flattered themselves they had entirely demolished it.* But Jesus reigns absolute and supreme over the kings of the earth, and over-rules and controuls them as he thinks proper; and he disposes all the revolutions, the rises and falls of kingdoms and empires, so as to be subservient to the great designs of his mediation; and their united policies and powers cannot frustrate the work which he has undertaken. But besides these rebellious involuntary subjects, he has (blessed be his name!) gained the consent of thousands, and they have become his willing subjects by their own choice. They regard his authority, they love his government, they make it their study to please him, and to do his will. Over these he exercises a government of special grace here, and he will make them

* In the 10th and last Roman persecution, Dioclesian had a medal struct with this inscription, "The christian name demolished, and the worship of the gods restored."

the happy subjects of the kingdom of his glory hereafter. And it is his government over these that I intend more particularly to consider. Once more, the kingdom of Jesus is not confined to this world, but all the millions of mankind in the invisible world are under his dominion, and will continue so to everlasting ages. *He is the Lord of the dead and the living*, Rom. xiv. 9. and has the keys of Hades, the vast invisible world (including heaven as well as hell) and of death. Rev. i. 18. It is he that turns the key, and opens the door of death for mortals to pass from world to world: it is he that opens the gates of heaven, and welcomes and admits the nations that keep the commandments of God: and it is he that opens the prison of hell, and locks it fast upon the prisoners of divine justice. He will for ever exercise authority over the vast regions of the unseen world, and the unnumbered multitudes of spirits with which they are peopled. You hence see, my brethren, the universal extent of the Redeemer's kingdom; and in this respect how much does it differ from all the kingdoms of the earth? The kingdoms of Great-Britain, France, China, Persia, are but little spots of the globe. Our world has indeed been oppressed in former times with what mortals call universal monarchies; such were the Babylonian, the Persian, the Grecian, and especially the Roman. But in truth, these were so far from being strictly universal, that a considerable part of the habitable earth was not so much as known to them. But this is an empire strictly universal. It extends over land and sea; it reaches beyond the planetary worlds, and all the luminaries of heaven; nay, beyond the throne of the most exalted archangels, and downward to the lowest abyss in hell. An universal empire in the hands of a mortal is an huge, unwieldy thing; an heap of confusion; a burthen to mankind; and it has always rushed headlong from its glory, and fallen to pieces by its own weight. But Jesus is equal to the immense province of an empire strictly universal: his hand is able to hold the reins; and it is the blessing of our world to be under his administration. He will turn what appears to us scenes of confusion into perfect order, and convince all worlds that he has not taken one wrong step in the whole plan of his infinite government.

The kingdoms of the world have their laws and ordinances, and so has the kingdom of Christ. Look into your Bibles, and there you will find the laws of this kingdom, from its first foundation immediately upon the fall of man. The laws of human governments are often defective or unrighteous; but these are perfect, holy, just, and good. Human laws are enforced with sanctions; but the rewards and punishments can only affect our mortal bodies, and cannot reach beyond the present life: but the sanctions of these divine laws are eternal, and there never shall be an end to their execution. Everlasting happiness and everlasting misery, of the most exquisite kind and the highest degree, are the rewards and punishments which the immortal King distributes among his immortal subjects; and they become his character, and are adapted to their nature.

Human laws extend only to outward actions, but these laws reach the heart, and the principle of action within. Not a secret thought, not a motion of the soul, is exempted from them. If the subjects of earthly kings observe a decorum in their outward conduct, and give no visible evidence of disloyalty, they are treated as good subjects, though they should be enemies in their hearts. "But Jesus is the Lord of souls"; he makes his subjects bow their hearts as well as the knee to him. He sweetly commands their thoughts and affections as well as their external practice, and makes himself inwardly beloved as well as outwardly obeyed. His subjects are such on whom he may depend: they are all ready to lay down their lives for him. Love, cordial, unfeigned, ardent love, is the principle of all their obedience; and hence it is that his commandments are not grievous, but delightful to them.

Other kings have their ministers and officers of state. In like manner Jesus employs the armies of heaven as ministering spirits in his mediatorial kingdom: besides these he has ministers, of an humbler form, who negociate more immediately in his name with mankind. These are intrusted with the ministry of reconciliation, to beseech men, in his stead, to be reconciled to God. These are appointed to preach his word, to administer his ordinances, and to manage the affairs of his kingdom. This view gives a peculiar dignity and importance to this office. These should be adorned, not like the ministers of earthly courts, with the trappings of gold and silver, but with the beauties of holiness, the ornament of a meek and quiet, zealous and faithful spirit, and a life becoming the gospel of Christ.

Other kings have their soldiers; so all the legions of the elect angels, the armies of heaven, are the soldiers of Jesus Christ, and under his command. This he asserted when he was in such defenceless circumstances, that he seemed to be abandoned by heaven and earth. "I could pray to my Father, says he, and he would send *me more than twelve legions of angels.*["] Matt. xxvi. 53. I cannot forbear reading to you one of the most majestic descriptions of this all-conquering hero and his army, which the language of mortality is capable of. Rev. xix. 11, 16. *I saw heaven open*, says St. John, *and behold a white horse*, an emblem of victory and triumph, *and he that sat upon him was called Faithful and True*. How different a character from that of mortal conquerors! "And in righteousness he doth judge and make war." War is generally a scene of injustice and lawless violence; and those plagues of mankind we call heroes and warriors, use their arms to gratify their own avarice or ambition, and make encroachments upon others. Jesus, the Prince of Peace, makes war too, but it is in righteousness; it is in the cause of righteousness he takes up arms. The divine description proceeds: *His eyes were as a flame of fire; and on his head were many crowns*, emblems of his manifold authority over the various kingdoms of the world, and the various regions of the universe. *And he was clothed with a vesture dipt in blood*, in the blood of his enemies; *and his name was called, The Word of God: and the armies which were in heaven, followed him upon white horses, clothed in fine linen, white and clean:* the whitest innocence and purity, and the beauties of holiness are, as it were, the uniform, the regimentals of these celestial armies. *And out of his mouth goeth a sharp sword, that with it he should smite the nations: and he shall rule them with a rod of iron; and he treadeth the wine press of the fierceness and wrath of Almighty God; and he hath on his vesture and on his thigh a name written, King of kings, and Lord of lords.* In what manner the war is carried on between the armies of heaven and the powers of hell, we know not; but that there is really something of this kind, we may infer from Rev. xii. 7, 9. *There was war in heaven: Michael and his angels fought against the dragon; and the dragon fought and his angels, and prevailed not, neither was there place found any more in heaven. And the great dragon was cast out, that old serpant called the Devil and Satan.*

Thus you see all the host of heaven are volunteers under the Captain of our salvation. Nay, he marshals the stars, and calls them by their names. *The stars in their courses*, says the sublime Deborah, *fought against Sisera*, the enemy of God's people. Judges v. 20. Every part of the creation serves under him, and he can commission a gnat, or a fly, or the meanest insect, to be the executioner of his enemies. Fire and water, hurricanes and earthquakes; earthquakes which have so lately shattered so great a part of our globe, now tottering with age, and ready to fall to pieces, and bury the guilty inhabitants in its ruins, all these fight under him, and conspire to avenge his quarrel with the guilty sons of men. The subjects of his grace in particular are all so many soldiers; their life is a constant warfare; and they are incessantly engaged in hard conflict with temptations from without, and the insurrections of sin from within. Sometimes, alas! they fall; but their General lifts them up again, and inspires them with strength to renew the fight. They fight most successfully upon their knees. This is the most advantageous posture for the soldiers of Jesus Christ; for prayer brings down recruits from heaven in the hour of difficulty. They are indeed but poor weaklings and invalids; and yet they overcome, through the blood of the Lamb; and he makes them conquerors, yea more than conquerors. It is the military character of christians that gives the apostle occasion to address them in the military stile, like a general at the head of his army. Eph. vi. 10–18. *Be strong in the Lord, and in the power of his might. Put on the whole armour of God, that ye may be able to stand against the wiles of the devil. Stand therefore, having your loins girt about with truth, and having on the breast-plate of righteousness, and your feet shod with the preparation of the gospel of peace; above all, taking the shield of faith, wherewith ye shall be able to quench all the fiery darts of the wicked. And take the helmet of salvation, and the sword of the spirit, which is the word of God, praying always with all prayer and supplication.* The ministers of the gospel in particular, and especially the apostles, are soldiers, or officers, in the spiritual army. Hence St. Paul speaks of his office, in the military stile; *I have*, says he, *fought the good fight*. 2 Tim. iv. 7. *We war*, says he, *though it be not after the flesh*. The humble doctrines of the cross are our weapons, and these are mighty through God, *to demolish the strong holds of the prince of darkness, and to bring every thought into a joyful captivity to the obedience of faith*. 2 Cor. x. 3–5. *Fight the good fight*, says he to Timothy. 1 Tim. vi. 12. And again, *thou therefore endure hardness, as a good soldier of Jesus Christ*. 2 Tim. ii. 3. The great design of the gospel-ministry is to rescue enslaved souls from the tyranny of sin and Satan, and to recover them into a state of liberty and loyalty to Jesus Christ; or, in the words of the apostle, *to turn them from darkness to light, and from the power of Satan unto God.* Acts xxvi. 18. Mortals indeed are very unequal for the conflict; but their success more conspicuously shews that the *excellency of the power is of God:* and many have they subdued, through his strength, to the obedience of faith, and made the willing captives of the cross of our divine Immanuel. Other kingdoms are often founded in blood, and many lives are lost on both sides in acquiring them. The kingdom of Christ, too, was founded in blood; but it was the blood of his own heart: life was lost in the conflict; but it was his own; his own life lost, to purchase life for his people. Others have waded to empire through the blood of mankind, and even of their own subjects, but Christ shed only his own blood to spare that of his soldiers. The general devotes his life as a sacrifice to save his army. The Fabii and Decii of Rome, who devoted themselves for their country, were but faint shadows of this divine bravery. O! the generous patriotism, the ardent love of the Captain of our salvation! How amiable does his character appear, in contrast with that of the kings of the earth! They often sacrifice the lives of their subjects, while they keep themselves out of danger, or perhaps are rioting at ease in the pleasures and luxuries of a court; but Jesus engaged in the conflict with death and hell alone. He stood a single champion in a field of blood. He conquered for his people by falling himself: he subdued his and their enemies by resigning himself to their power. Worthy is such a general to be commander in chief of the hosts of God, and to lead the armies of heaven and earth! Indeed much blood has been shed in carrying on this kingdom. The earth has been soaked with the blood of the saints; and millions have resisted even unto blood, striving against sin, and nobly laid down their lives for the sake of Christ and a good conscience. Rome has been remarkably the seat of persecution; both formerly under the heathen emperors, and in latter times, under a succession of popes, still more bloody and tyrannical. There were no less than ten general persecutions under the heathen emperors, through the vast Roman empire, in a little more than two hundred years, which followed one another in a close succession; in which innumerable multitudes of christians lost their lives by an endless variety of tortures. And since the church of Rome has usurped her authority, the blood of the saints has hardly ever ceased running in some country or other; though, blessed be God, many kingdoms shook off the yoke at the ever-memorable period of the Reformation, above two hundred years ago; which has greatly weakened that persecuting power. This is that mystical Babylon which was represented to St. John as *drunken with the blood of the saints, and with the blood of the martyrs of Jesus.* Rev. xvii. 6. In her was found the blood of the prophets, and of the saints, and of all that were slain upon the earth. ch. xviii. 24. And these scenes of blood are still perpetrated in France, that plague of Europe, that has of late stretched her murderous arm across the wide ocean to disturb us in these regions of peace. There the Protestants are still plundered, chained to the gallies, broken alive upon the torturing wheel, denied the poor favour of abandoning their country and their all, and flying naked to beg their bread in other nations. Thus the harmless subjects of the Prince of Peace have ever been slaughtered from age to age, and yet they are represented as triumphant conquerors. Hear a poor persecuted Paul on this head: *In tribulation, in distress, in persecution, in nakedness, in peril and sword, we are conquerors, we are more than conquerors, through him that loved us.* Rom. viii. 36, 37. *Thanks be to God who always causeth us to triumph in Christ.* 2 Cor. ii. 14. *Whatsoever is born of God,* says the Evangelist, *overcometh the world.* 1 John v. 4. Whence came that glorious army which we so often see in the Revelation? We are told, *they came out of great tribulation.* ch. vii. 14. *And they overcame by the blood of the Lamb, and by the word of their testimony; and they loved not their lives unto the death.* ch. xii. 11. They that suffered tortures and death under the beast, are said *to have gotten the victory over him.* ch. xv. 2. Victory and triumph sound strange when thus ascribed; but the gospel helps us to understand this mystery. By these sufferings they obtained the illustrious crown of martyrdom, and peculiar degrees of glory and happiness through an endless duration. Their death was but a short transition from the lowest and more remote regions of their Redeemer's kingdom into his immediate presence and glorious court in heaven. A temporal death is rewarded with an immortal life; and *their light afflictions, which were but for a moment, wrought out for them a far more exceeding and eternal weight of glory.* 2 Cor. iv. 17. Even in the agonies of torture their souls were often filled with such delightful sensations of the love of God, as swallowed up the sensations of bodily pain; and a bed of flames was sweeter to them than a bed of roses. Their souls were beyond the reach of all the instruments of torment; and as to their bodies they shall yet have a glorious resurrection to a blessed immortality. And now I leave you to judge, whether they or their enemies got the victory in this conflict; and which had most cause to triumph. Like their Master, they rose by falling; they triumphed over their enemies by submitting, like lambs, to their power. If the soldiers of other generals die in the field, it is not in the power of their commanders to reward them. But the soldiers of Jesus Christ, by dying, are, as it were, carried in triumph from the field of blood into the presence of their Master, to receive his approbation, and a glorious crown. Death puts them into a capacity of receiving and enjoying greater rewards than they are capable of in the present state. And thus it appears, that his soldiers always win the day; or, as the apostle expresses it, *he causes them always to triumph;* and not one of them has ever been or ever shall be defeated, however weak and helpless in himself, and however terrible the power of his enemies. And O! when all these warriors meet at length from every corner of the earth, and, as it were, pass in review before their General in the fields of heaven, with their robes washed in his blood, with palms of victory in their hands, and crowns of glory on their heads, all dressed in uniform with garments of salvation, what a glorious army will they make! and how will they cause heaven to ring with shouts of joy and triumph!

The founders of earthly kingdoms are famous for their heroic actions. They have braved the dangers of sea and land, routed powerful armies, and subjected nations to their will. They have shed rivers of blood, laid cities in ruins, and countries in desolation. These are the exploits which have rendered the Alexanders, the Cæsars, and other conquerors of this world, famous through all nations and ages. Jesus had his exploits too; but they were all of the gracious and beneficent kind. His conquests were so many deliverances, and his victories salvations. He subdued, in order to set free; and made captives to deliver them from slavery. He conquered the legions of hell, that seemed let loose at that time, that he might have opportunity of displaying his power over them, and that mankind might be sensible how much they needed a deliverer from their tyranny. He triumphed over the temptations of Satan in the wilderness, by a quotation from his own word. He rescued wretched creatures from his power by an almighty command. He conquered the most inveterate and stubborn diseases, and restored health and vigour with a word of his mouth. He vanquished stubborn souls with the power of his love, and made them his willing people. He triumphed over death, the king of terrors, and delivered Lazarus from the prison of the grave, as an earnest and first-fruits of a general resurrection. Nay, by his own inherent powers he broke the bonds of death, and forced his way to his native heaven. He destroyed him that had the power of death, *i.e.*, the devil, by his own death, and laid the foundation in his own blood for destroying his usurped kingdom, and forming a glorious kingdom of willing subjects redeemed from his tyranny.

The death of some great conquerors, particularly of Julius Cæsar, is said to be prognosticated or attended with prodigies: but none equal to those which solemnized the death of Jesus. The earth trembled, the rocks were burst to pieces, the vail of the temple was rent, the heavens were clothed in mourning, and the dead started into life. And no wonder, when the Lord of nature was expiring upon a cross. He subdued and calmed the stormy wind, and the boisterous waves of the sea. In short, he shewed an absolute sovereignty over universal nature, and managed the most unruly elements with a single word. Other conquerors have gone from country to country, carrying desolation along with them; Jesus went about doing good. His miraculous powers were but powers of miraculous mercy and beneficence. He could easily have advanced himself to a temporal kingdom, and routed all the forces of the earth, but he had no ambition of this kind. He that raised Lazarus from the grave could easily restore his soldiers to vigour and life, after they had been wounded or killed. He that fed five thousand with five loaves and two fishes, could have supported his army with plenty of provision in the greatest scarcity. He that walked upon the boisterous ocean, and enabled Peter to do the same, could easily have transported his forces from country to country, without the conveyance of ships. Nay, he was capable by his own single power to have gained universal conquest. What could all the armies of the earth have done against him, who struck an armed company down to the earth with only a word of his mouth? But these were not the victories he affected: Victories of grace, deliverances for the oppressed, salvation for the lost; these were his heroic actions. He glories in his being mighty to save. Isaiah lxiii. 1. When his warm disciples made a motion that he should employ his miraculous powers to punish the Samaritans who ungratefully refused him entertainment, he rebuked them, and answered like the Prince of Peace, *The Son of man is not come to destroy mens lives, but to save.* Luke ix. 56. *He came to seek and to save that which was lost.* Luke xix. 10. O how amiable a character this! How much more lovely the Saviour of sinners, the Deliverer of souls, than the enslavers and destroyers of mankind; which is the general character of the renowned heroes of our world? Who has ever performed such truly heroic and brave actions as this almighty conqueror? He has pardoned the most aggravated crimes, in a consistency with the honours of the divine government: he has delivered an innumerable multitude of immortal souls from the tyranny of sin and powers of hell, set the prisoners free, and brought them into the liberty of the Son of God; he has peopled heaven with redeemed slaves, and advanced them to royal dignity. *All his subjects are kings.* Rev. i. 6. *To him that overcometh,* says he, *will I grant to sit with me in my throne, even as I also overcame, and am set down with my father in his throne.* Rev. iii. 21. They shall all be adorned with royal robes and crowns of unfading glory. They are advanced to empire over their lusts and passions, and all their enemies. Who ever gave such encouragement to his soldiers as this, *If we suffer with him, we know we shall also reign with him?* 2 Tim. ii. 12. What mortal general could bestow immortality and perfect happiness upon his favourites? But these boundless blessings Jesus has to bestow. In human governments merit is often neglected, and those who serve their country best are often rewarded with degradation. But none have ever served the King of kings in vain. The least good action, even the giving a cup of water to one of his necessitous saints, shall not pass unrewarded in his government.

Other kings have their arms, their swords, their cannon, and other instruments of destruction; and with these they acquire and defend their dominions. Jesus, our king, has his arms too, but O! of how different a kind! The force of evidence and conviction in his doctrine, attested with miracles, the energy of his dying love, the gentle, and yet efficacious influence of his holy spirit; these are the weapons with which he conquered the world. His gospel is the great magazine from whence his apostles, the first founders of his kingdom, drew their arms; and with these they subdued the nations to the obedience of faith. *The gospel,* says St. Paul, *is the power of God unto salvation.* Rom. i. 16. The humble doctrines of the cross became almighty, and bore down all before them, and after a time subdued the vast Roman empire which had subdued the world. The holy spirit gave edge and force to these weapons; and, blessed be God, though they are quite impotent without his assistance, yet when he concurs they are still successful. Many stubborn sinners have been unable to resist the preaching of Christ crucified: they have found him indeed the power of God. And is it not astonishing that any one should be able to stand it out against his dying love, and continue the enemy of his cross? *I*, says he, *if I be lifted up from the earth*, i.e., if I be suspended on the cross, *will draw all men unto me*. John xii. 32. You see he expected his cross would be an irresistible weapon. And O! blessed Jesus, who can see thee expiring there in agonies of torture and love; who can see thy blood gushing in streams from every vein, who can hear thee there, and not melt into submission at thy feet! Is there one heart in this assembly proof against the energy of this bleeding, agonizing, dying love? Methinks such a sight must kindle a correspondent affection in your hearts towards him; and it is an exploit of wickedness, it is the last desperate effort of an impenetrable heart, to be able to resist.

Other conquerors march at the head of their troops, with all the ensigns of power and grandeur, and their forces numerous, inured to war, and well armed: and from such appearances and preparations who is there but what expects victory? But see the despised Nazarene, without riches, without arms, without forces, conflicting with the united powers of earth and hell; or see a company of poor fishermen and a tent-maker, with no other powers but those of doing good, with no other arms but those of reason, and the strange unpopular doctrines of a crucified Christ! see the professed followers of a master that was hung like a malefactor and a slave, see these men marching out to encounter the powers of darkness, the whole strength of the Roman empire, the lusts, prejudices, and interests of all nations, and travelling from country to country, without guards, without friends, exposed to insult and contempt, to the rage of persecution, to all manner of tormented deaths which earth or hell could invent: see this little army marching into the wide world, in these circumstances, and can you expect they will have any success? Does this appear a promising expedition? No; human reason would forebode they will soon be cut in pieces, and the christian cause buried with them. But these unpromising champions, with the aid of the Holy Spirit, conquered the world, and spread the religion of the crucified Jesus among all nations. It is true they lost their lives in the cause, like brave soldiers; but the cause did not die with them. Their blood proved the seed of the church. Their cause is immortal and invincible. Let devils in hell, let heathens, Jews, and Mahometans, let atheists, free-thinkers, papists, and persecutors of every character, do their worst; still this cause will live in spite of them. All the enemies of Christ will be obliged to confess at last, with Julian the apostate Roman emperor, who exerted all his art to abolish christianity; but, when mortally wounded in battle, outrageously sprinkled his blood towards heaven, and cried out, *Vicisti, O Galilæe!* "Thou hast conquered, O Galilean!" Yes, my brethren, Jesus, the Prophet of Galilee, will push his conquests from country to country, until all nations submit to him. And, blessed be his name, his victorious arm has reached to us in these ends of the earth: here he has subdued some obstinate rebels, and made their reluctant souls willingly bow in affectionate homage to him. And may I not produce some of you as the trophies of his victory? Has he not rooted out the enmity of your carnal minds, and sweetly constrained you to the most affectionate obedience? Thus, blessed Jesus! thus go on conquering, and to conquer. *Gird thy sword upon thy thigh, O most mighty!* and in thy glory and majesty ride prosperously through our land, and make this country a dutiful province of the dominion of thy grace. My brethren, should we all become his willing subjects, he would no longer suffer the perfidious slaves of France, and their savage allies, to chastise and punish us for our rebellion against him; but *peace should again run down like a river, and righteousness like a mighty stream.*

The kingdoms of the world have their rise, their progress, perfection, declension, and ruin. And in these things, the kingdom of Christ bears some resemblance to them, excepting that it shall never have an end.

Its rise was small at first, and it has passed through many revolutions in various ages. It was first founded in the family of Adam, but in about 1600 years, the space between the creation and the flood, it was almost demolished by the wickedness of the world; and at length confined to the little family of Noah. After the flood, the world soon fell into idolatry, but, that this kingdom of Christ might not be destroyed quite, it was erected in the family of Abraham; and among the Jews it continued until the coming of Christ in the flesh. This was indeed but the infancy of his kingdom, and indeed is seldom called by that name. It is the gospel constitution that is represented as the kingdom of Christ, in a special sense. This was but very small and unpromising at first. When its founder was dying upon Calvary, and all his followers had forsaken him and fled, who would have thought it would ever have come to any thing, ever have recovered? But it revived with him; and, when he furnished his apostles with gifts and graces for their mission, and sent them forth to increase his kingdom, it made its progress through the world with amazing rapidity, notwithstanding it met with very early and powerful opposition. The Jews set themselves against it, and raised persecutions against its ministers, wherever they went. And presently the tyrant Nero employed all the power of the Roman empire to crush them. Peter, Paul, and thousands of the christians fell a prey to his rage, like sheep for the slaughter. This persecution was continued under his successors, with but little interruption, for about two hundred years.

But, under all these pressures, the church bore up her head; yea, the more she was trodden, the more she spread and flourished; and at length she was delivered from oppression by Constantine the Great, about the year 320. But now she had a more dangerous enemy to encounter, I mean prosperity: and this did her much more injury than all the persecutions of her enemies. Now the kingdom of Christ began to be corrupted with heresies: the ministry of the gospel, formerly the most dangerous posts in the world, now became a place of honour and profit, and men began to thrust themselves into it from principles of avarice and ambition; superstition and corruption of morals increased; and at length the bishop of Rome set up for universal head of the church in the year 606, and gradually the whole monstrous system of popery was formed and established, and continued in force for near a thousand years. The kingdom of Christ was now at a low ebb; and tyranny and superstition reigned under that name over the greatest part of the christian world. Nevertheless our Lord still had his witnesses. The Waldenses and Albigenses, John Hus, and Jerome of Prague, and Wickliffe in England, opposed the torrent of corruption; until at length, Luther, Calvin, Zuinglius, and several others, were made the honoured instruments of introducing the Reformation from popery; when sundry whole kingdoms, which had given their power to the beast, and particularly our mother-country, shook off the papal authority, and admitted the pure light of the gospel. Since that time the kingdom of Christ has struggled hard, and it has lost ground in several countries; particularly in France, Poland, Bohemia, &c. where there once were many Protestant churches; but they are now in ruins. And, alas! those countries that still retain the reformed religion, have too generally reduced it into a mere formality; and it has but little influence upon the hearts and lives even of its professors. Thus we find the case remarkably among us. This gracious kingdom makes but little way in Virginia. The calamities of war and famine cannot, alas! draw subjects to it; but we seem generally determined to perish in our rebellion rather than submit. Thus it has been in this country from its first settlement; and how long it will continue in this situation is unknown to mortals: however, this we may know, it will not be so always. We have the strongest assurances that Jesus will yet take to him his great power, and reign in a more extensive and illustrious manner than he has ever yet done; and that the kingdoms of the earth shall yet become *the kingdoms of our Lord and of his Christ*. There are various parts of the heathen world where the gospel has never yet been; and the Jews have never yet been converted as a nation; but both the calling of the Jews and the fulness of the gentiles, you will find plainly foretold in the 11th chapter to the Romans; and it is, no doubt, to render the accomplishment of this event the more conspicuous, that the Jews, who are dispersed all over the world, have, by a strange, unprecedented, and singular providence, been kept a distinct people to this day, for 1700 years; though all other nations have been so mixt and blended together, who were not half so much dispersed into different countries, that their distinct original cannot be traced. Posterity shall see this glorious event in some happy future period. How far it is from us, I will not determine: though, upon some grounds, I apprehend it is not very remote. I shall live and die in the unshaken belief that our guilty world shall yet see glorious days. Yes, my brethren, this despised gospel, that has so little effect in our age and country, shall yet shine like lightning, or like the sun, through all the dark regions of the earth. It shall triumph over heathenism, Mahometism, Judaism, popery, and all those dangerous errors that have infected the christian church. This gospel, poor negroes, shall yet reach your countrymen, whom you left behind you in Africa, in darkness and the shadow of death, and bless your eyes with the light of salvation: and the Indian savages, that are now ravaging our country, shall yet be transformed into lambs and doves by the gospel of peace. The scheme of Providence is not yet completed, and much remains to be accomplished of what God has spoken by his prophets, to ripen the world for the universal judgment; but when all these things are finished, then proclamation shall be made through all nature, "That Time shall be no more": then the Supreme Judge, the same Jesus that ascended the cross, will ascend the throne, and review the affairs of time: then will he put an end to the present course of nature, and the present form of administration. Then shall heaven and hell be filled with their respective inhabitants: then will time close, and eternity run on in one uniform tenor, without end. But the kingdom of Christ, though altered in its situation and form of government, will not then come to a conclusion. His kingdom is strictly the kingdom of heaven; and at the end of this world, his subjects will only be removed from these lower regions into a more glorious country, where they and their King shall live together for ever in the most endearing intimacy; where the noise and commotions of this restless world, the revolutions and perturbations of kingdoms, the terrors of war and persecution, shall no more reach them, but all will be perfect peace, love, and happiness, through immeasurable duration. This is the last and most illustrious state of the kingdom of Christ, now so small and weak in appearance: this is the final grand result of his administration; and it will appear to admiring worlds wisely planned, gloriously executed, and perfectly finished.

What conqueror ever erected such a kingdom! What subjects so completely, so lastingly happy, as those of the blessed Jesus!

7

THE PRESENCE OF GOD WITH HIS PEOPLE

Samuel Dunbar

BOSTON

1760

SAMUEL DUNBAR (1704–1783). After obtaining two degrees from Harvard College, in 1727 Dunbar settled, and was to remain, at the First Church in Stoughton, Massachusetts. An animated and forceful preacher, Dunbar was at odds with the revivalism of the Great Awakening and maintained the Calvinist orthodoxy of his mentor, Cotton Mather. "Inasmuch as he believed there was one, and only one, redeeming way to worship God, he preached outspokenly against Jewish dogma, Catholic grace, Antinomian morality, Arminian ecumenical salvation, and Deistic rationalism. In general, he preached against any organization that upheld free will and ignored or downplayed the concepts of original sin and the doctrine of the elect" (Bryan R. Brown in *American Writers Before 1800*, p. 491). He wrote over 8,000 sermons in his long career but published only nine of them, including an artillery sermon in 1748, the election sermon of 1760 reprinted here, and the convention sermon of 1769.

In 1755 Dunbar served as chaplain with the troops at Crown Point in the British victory over the French at Lake George. He was called the Son of Thunder by his funeral eulogist, the Reverend Jason Haven, because he had powerfully supported the patriot cause in the Revolution.

This election sermon was preached before Governor Thomas Pownall, the lieutenant governor, the council, and the house of representatives of Massachusetts on May 28, 1760. The brackets in this sermon indicate text that was omitted in delivery.

The Presence of GOD with his People, their only Safety and Happiness.

A

DISCOURSE

Delivered at BOSTON,

In the Presence of

His EXCELLENCY the GOVERNOUR,

THOMAS POWNALL, Esq;

His Honour the Lieutenant Governour,

The Honourable

His Majesty's COUNCIL,

AND

House of REPRESENTATIVES,

Of the Province of the

Massachusetts-Bay in NEW-ENGLAND;

May 28. 1760.

The Day for the Election of His Majesty's COUNCIL, for the Province.

The Paragraph and Addresses within such Marks [ ] were for Brevity omitted in Preaching.

By SAMUEL DUNBAR, A.M.

Pastor of the first Church in *Stoughton*.

BOSTON: Printed by S. KNEELAND, by Order of the Honourable House of REPRESENTATIVES. 1760.

And the Spirit of God came upon Azariah, the son of Oded. And he went out to meet Asa, and said unto him, Hear ye me, Asa, and all Judah and Benjamin, The Lord is with you, while ye be with him; and if ye seek him, he will be found of you; but if ye forsake him, he will forsake you.

2 Chron. XV. 1, 2.

The occasion of this divine message to King Asa, and his army, was the compleat victory, which, thro' help of God, and in answer to humble, believing prayer, they had very lately obtained over the huge and formidable army of Aethiopians, who had invaded their territories. Asa, as a wise and martial prince, led forth his army to put a stop to their progress, and set the battle in array: and, as a godly and religious prince, sought to God for help and success. He led them into the field of battle to fight; before the battle, he led them to the throne of grace to pray, to obtain mercy, and find grace to help them, in this time of need and danger. He lift up a cry to God, e're he gave the shout for the battle: That battle, that work is begun well, and like to succeed well, which is prefaced with holy, humble prayer. *Asa cried unto the Lord his God:* It was a cry of faith, rather than of fear. His prayer was short, but fervent; a prayer of faith, effectual and prevalent: it entred into the ears of the Lord of Sabaoth, found a gracious acceptance, and obtained divine help. God fought for them; and by them; gave their enemies a total overthrow. Thro' faith and prayer, out of weakness, they were made strong, waxed valiant in fight, and put to flight this vast army of aliens.

Something similar have been the exercise, the practice, and the experience of the people of God in these *British American provinces and colonies.* Envious and ambitious enemies made encroachments upon our king's territories, and erected several strong forts in them, to enable them to keep what they had got, and to win more. To oppose their further progress, and to drive them off from their unjust possessions, we mustered, and sent forth our forces; and our gracious sovereign, pitying us, sent brave troops to assist us; but we, not trusting to an arm of flesh, not to our numbers nor strength, not to our sword nor bow, like godly Asa, cried to the Lord our God; we fasted and wept, and made supplication to him; and, blessed be God, he turned not away our prayer nor his mercy from us; but has maintained our right, and given us a series of signal successes.

King Asa, and his victorious army were now returning in triumph, from the field of battle, to Jerusalem, laden and enrich'd with the spoils of their enemies: doubtless greatly affected with the goodness of God, for the victory they had won: their tho'ts might be much employed as to the advantages, they should make of it, to the kingdom. Perhaps they might also be too much disposed to applaud themselves and one another, for their skill, and bravery, and success, and so take to themselves that glory, which was due to God: however these things were, God sent a prophet to meet them, and to deliver them a message from him.

The manner of the prophet's address was plain, and earnest, and authoritative: he used no pompous titles of honour, no fulsome compliments, no ceremonious congratulations, nor flattering applauses. He came upon a more important errand, and with a holy zeal and vehemency delivered it: nor did he in a mean servile manner, beg leave to speak, or savour to be heard: but, coming in the name of God, and with a message from him, he demanded their reverent attention: *Hear ye me, Asa, and all Judah and Benjamin.* When God speaks by the mouth of a prophet, it becomes the greatest men, the highest in dignity and power, to attend with the deepest humility and reverence, to hear what God the Lord has to say unto them: considering that, how high soever they are above other men, they are infinitely more beneath the most high God: nor should they take it in disdain, if God's prophet, at such a time, give them not those honorary titles, which other men do.

The message was partly monitory to them of their duty and interest: *The Lord is with you, while ye are with him, and if ye seek him, he will be found of you:* and partly minatory; *but if ye forsake him, he will forsake you:* and partly memorative, to call afresh to their minds, that, before the battle, they were with God, in humble fervent prayer, and in the battle God was with them by his providence and power: before the battle they sought God, in the battle God was a present help: they prayed, God heard; they believed, and were established, were prospered: the victory they had gained, was owing more to God's presence and blessing, than to their prowess and swords. From the experience they had had of God's being with them, in the way of mercy and help, while they were with him, in the way of duty and trust, he shewed them what their duty and interest still were, even still to be with God, and he will still be with them. Their enemies were worsted, either fled or destroyed: *there was no more war in the land:* yet still they needed the divine presence and blessing, to direct their national affairs, and to prosper their public concerns: he let them know, that the continuance of God's gracious presence with them, depended upon their dutiful presence with him: and assured them from God, that so long as they should be with God, God would be with them; but withal assured them, that if they forsook God, God would in like manner, forsake them. As they behaved towards God, in respect of duty and obedience, God would deal with them, in respect of the ways of providence.

This divine message, I humbly conceive, is seasonable, and instructive to us, in our circumstances, as it was to them, in their's.

The experience, which we, the Lord's people, in this land, have had, of the happiness of engaging and enjoying the presence of God with our armies, should make us careful not to forfeit it by any sinful departure from God; and conscientious in our abiding with God, that he may still abide with us. Still we have need of the divine presence and help: we have not yet put off the harness, nor has our land rest from war. Again our troops are gone forth, and we may expect to hear of garments roll'd in blood. The presence of God is as necessary for the success of our arms this year, as it was the last: and if God go forth with our armies, they will be prospered.

As to the expert, the indefatigable, the magnanimous general, who led on his valiant army to battle last year; and that under the greatest disadvantages, and with the utmost difficulty and hazzard, but with an invincible resolution and courage, and a superior conduct, against the vastly greater number of his enemies; and who quickly scattered destruction among them, put them to the rout, and chased them before him: this super-eminent general, the glorious Wolfe, can be with us no more; he greatly fell in the last and conquering battle, and died in the bed of honour, fighting like an hero, in the service of his king, and in the defence of his subjects. But tho' Wolfe, the dear, the brave, the bold, leader of his troops, can no more stand in the front of the battle, nor give his orders, nor by his words and example, fire their spirits, and make them undaunted, amidst the terrors and tumults of the fight; yet God lives, and still we may have his favourable presence; this is infinitely more, infinitely better: this made our slain general, such an every way accomplished one: this can raise up, and give us other generals, of equal skill and conduct, of equal zeal and fidelity, of equal fortitude and success. And if God be with our troops, we may hope he will: yea, blessed be God, he has: tho' one is taken, another is left: a general who enjoyed the presence of God with him, in the reduction of Louisbourg, the pride and trust of our enemies, a general, whose very name struck such terror into them, the last year, that they quickly abandoned their strong forts, at his approach, and betook themselves to inglorious flight—Amherst, the wary, the valiant, the victorious, is still left unto us.

The presence of God is equally necessary and beneficial, for the governour, as the general; for the court, as the camp; for the field of husbandry, as the field of battle; in peace, as in war; and for the wise and successful management of affairs at home, as abroad: and our enjoyment of it turns upon our being with God.

There are two heads of discourse before me; viz. 1. *That the presence of God with his people, is their only safety and happiness.* 2. *That their enjoying the presence of God with them, depends upon their being with God.*

I. *The presence of God with his People, is their only safety and happiness.*

The presence of God may be considered, as his natural and essential presence: this is general and universal, absolutely necessary for upholding in being, all creatures, in all worlds. In respect of this, God is the God of all the earth, and has the absolute ordering and disposing of all things, in the kingdoms of men, according to his own will, with sovereign dominion, and irresistible power. Or, as his glorious, and majestick presence, which is peculiar to the heavenly world: there God dwells in the habitation of his holiness, and sits upon the throne of his glory: angels standing in his presence, & doing homage: or, as his judicial, vindictive presence, by which the damned in hell are punished with everlasting destruction, from the glory of his power—or, as his spiritual, gracious presence: which is peculiar to his church and saints in this world: this accomplishes for them, the everlasting purposes of his grace and mercy in Jesus Christ, and blesses them with all spiritual blessings, in heavenly things in him —or, as his special providential presence, which also is peculiar to his professing people: in respect of this, he is with them, sometimes in judicial dispensations, correcting them for, and recovering them from their degeneracies from him, and the ways of holiness: and sometimes in merciful dispensations, prospering them in their public concerns, and giving them all outward blessings richly to enjoy: health in their habitations, plenty in their substance, peace in their borders; and in case of war, success to their arms.

This *favourable providential presence* of God with his people, considered as a people, is that presence of God, which the text more especially, if not only, relates to. This God vouchsafes to them, for the sake of Christ, the great mediator, thro' whom he comes nigh to them, and they are made nigh to him.

The safety and peace, the prosperity and happiness of God's people, depends wholly upon this presence of God with them. This performs many great and distinguishing acts of kindness and mercy for them: for where God is thus with his people, he is for them, espouses their cause, consults their welfare, and promotes their happiness. His right hand, and his arm, and the light of his countenance, do great things for them, because he has a favour to them.

This presence of God with his people preserves them in their greatest sufferings & dangers: when like a bush on fire, flames threaten them with immediate destruction, they are not consumed: but according to the greatness of God's power and pity, he preserves them, when to themselves they seem appointed to perish. By this, the three Jewish worthies were preserved, in the midst of the burning fiery furnace; and Daniel in the lions den; in the mount the Lord is seen.

This delivers them, in their lowest and most desperate circumstances. When they are surrounded with difficulties and dangers, and reduced to the greatest streights: when they have neither wisdom to contrive, nor power to effect, any way of escape, but, as to any visible means, all hope of being saved is gone; now is God's times to work: *Now will I arise*, saith the Lord, *and set them in safety*. Providence wonderfully steps in, and opens a door of hope and help to them. So it did for Israel in delivering them from Egyptian bondage: then God went forth for the salvation of his people: yea, he rode upon his horses and chariots of salvation, made speed to help and save them. Miraculous appearances and operations of providence, for the deliverance of God's oppressed, endangered people, may not now be expected; yet God has very strange and unthought of ways, to accomplish deliverance for them: as we see, in the deliverance of God's people, from their Babylonish captivity, and also in the days of Esther.

This lays restraint upon their envious and malicious enemies: sometimes upon their spirits; tho' they envy them their enjoyments, and would fain deprive them of them, they cannot find an heart to do it. Thus tho' the enemies of Israel coveted the good land, God had given them, yet when all the males went up to the feast of the Lord, to Jerusalem, and left their borders exposed to their incursions and depredations, God put such a restraint upon their spirits, that no man then desired their land. *When a man's*, when a people's, *ways please the Lord, he maketh even their enemies to be at peace with them.* Sometimes upon their tongues; that not so much as a dog shall move his tongue against them: as Balaam, who loved the wages of unrighteousness, tho' hired with great rewards, could not curse Israel—and sometimes upon their hands; tho' they seemingly have them in their power, and are provoked enough to destroy them, and have resolved to do it, yet their hands are, as it were, bound; they cannot execute their bloody purposes. So, when the sons of Jacob, treacherously and cruelly murdered the Shechemites, the terror of God was upon the cities round about, that they should not pursue after them, nor avenge themselves upon them.

This defeats the mischievous plots and devices of their enemies against them. When their enemies conspire their ruin, and dig deep to hide their counsels; and when they imagine, they have brought their matters to bear, and are confident of their success, providence lays rubs in their way, and frustrates their machinations: their deep-lay'd plots, and long laboured schemes prove abortive: and God's people escape, as a bird out of the snare of the fowler. Thus Haman's plot for the destruction of God's people, ended in disappointment: and so did the horrible, the hellish powder-plot in the English nation, intended to blow up at once, and in a moment, the king and Parliament: when it was ripened, and just upon the point of execution, it was strangely discovered, and timously prevented. Yea, Providence often brings that mischief, upon the enemies of God's people, which they devised and intended against them: they are snared in the work of their own hands, and their designed mischief returns upon their own heads. So Haman handfell'd the gallows, he had prepared for Mordecai.

This supplies them, with the comforts of life, so that they want no good thing. This gives them rain in due season and measure: makes their fields, such as the Lord has blessed, to yield their fruits in plenty; so that their barns are filled with substance, their presses burst out with new wine, and their garners are full, affording all manner of store; they have plenty, variety, dainties. If at any time they seem to be cut short, and fear want of bread, and cleanness of teeth, the good providence of God finds out ways for their supply, and prevents them with the blessings of goodness. It was a wonderful work of God, for Israel in the wilderness, a land not sown, that for forty years together, they had supplies brought them, from day to day.

This directs them in all their darkness, and points out to them, the path of duty, the way of safety. When in some critical conjunctures, they are wholly at a loss, and, like Jehoshaphat, *know not what to do*; when they are perplexed in their minds, and hem'd in on every side with difficulties and perils, and can see no way to surmount, or escape them, providence, by some unexpected turns, opens a new scene, and shews them plainly the way, wherein they should go. God often gives his people direction, as to their present duty and safety, by an uncommon coincidence of things in providence; so that whoso is wise, and observes them, may understand the loving-kindness of the Lord. So God guided his people in the wilderness, and led them in a right way, in all their removes.

This protects them, from all enemies and dangers, and is as a wall of fire, round about them, to keep them from harm. When their enemies confederate against them, unite their counsels to deceive them, and their forces to destroy them, and thunder out their boasts and threats to terrify them; and when they themselves are sensible of their own inability to withstand, or defeat them, and, according to human view, must fall sacrifices to their rage and cruelty; *then God repents him for his servants when he sees they have no power:* then providence undertakes for them, interposes, and powerfully protects them: their enemies are scattered in the imagination of their hearts, and their hands are not able to execute their purposes and threats: So God defended Jerusalem from the numerous army, and proud threatnings of the Assyrian monarch. So God saved England in former days from the formidable Armada of the Spaniards, and the last year from the threatned, and perhaps really intended, invasion of the French: and but a few years ago, he saved New-England from the powerful armament of their French enemies, who came into these American seas. The ancient famous cloud, the symbol of God's presence, served to Israel, for protection, as well as direction. God's presence is to his people, a sun and a shield; a shield to defend them, as well as a sun to comfort and direct them.

This gives them success, in all their affairs. Success doth not constantly follow the probability of second causes. *The Race is not always to the swift, nor the battle to the strong*. Oft-times the best human counsels are turned into foolishness, the wisest measures are disconcerted, the greatest preparations brought to nothing, and the cunningest politicians befooled; while on the other hand, weak and contemptible means are prospered, and the most improbable, meet with the greatest success. This is entirely owing to the divine governing providence. But when God is present with his people, he orders all things well for them, and prospers all their lawful undertakings. The smiles of God upon them, make every thing flourishing—God's presence makes their land healthful, their fields fruitful, their merchandize gainful, and their armies successful: as in this last instance, we see by the great victory Asa obtained over his enemies—and may see in the repeated victories of our English fleets and armies, over our French enemies—and in the admirable success of our arms, in this quarter of the world, by the reduction of so many of the strong and important fortresses of our enemies, and even of their capital city.

This repairs the ruins, brought upon them, by the judgments of providence. When God's professing people forsake him, apostatize from his worship, and live in a presumptuous disobedience to his laws, it is necessary, for the vindication of the righteousness and holiness and honour of the divine government, that God testify his displeasure against them, and punish them, with judicial dispensations. And when he doth this, he often breaks them with breach upon breach, till he brings them very low. But he means not to make a full end of them, but to renew them to repentance, and to recover them from their declensions. When therefore they repent, and turn to him that smites them, he becomes to them a repairer of the breaches, and a restorer of paths to dwell in: and builds them up, as he had pluckt them down. Thus did he to his ancient people: he *raised up the tabernacle of David, that was fallen, and closed up the breaches thereof, and raised up the ruins thereof, and built them as in the days of old.* So did he by the great city, London, when, an hundred years ago, great part of it was laid in rubbish by devouring flames—so did he by this great town, Boston, when, near forty nine years since, this part of it, and the meeting-house, which stood in this place, and the town-house, and many other buildings along this street, on both sides of it, were laid in ashes. God being graciously present with his people, the ruins in a few years were repaired, and that with great advantage and splendor —and so will he again the dreadful desolations, made in it by the late fire, if he be graciously present with them.

This turns all the evils they meet with into real kindnesses to them. Providence has a vast reach, and by seemingly contrary methods, promotes the good of God's people: and when they are ready to say, *all these things are against us*, they are meant for good, tend to it, and terminate in it. So the Lord being with Joseph, all the hard things he met with, were the direct way to his future preferment and greatness. So God sent some of his people into captivity, in the land of the Chaldeans, for their good. So the repeated disasters we met with, in the beginning of this war, have been over-ruled for our advantage. God brings his people low, in order to exalt them the higher.

Finally, *This favourable providential presence of God with his people, builds his house, and appoints the ordinances of his worship, among them.* Where God is with his people, and walks among them, he sets his tabernacle among them, as he did among his people Israel. He institutes symbols of his gracious spiritual presence with them, to be means of keeping up a spiritual communion with him, and of conveying spiritual blessings to them; that so the common blessings of providence may be sanctified to them, by the special blessings of grace.

These are some of the special providential favours, which God bestows upon his people, according to their varied circumstances, when he is graciously present with them. Upon a review of them, who will not say with the renowned Jewish lawgiver, *What nation is there so great, who has God so nigh unto them in all things that we call upon him for? Happy art thou, O Israel, who is like unto thee, O people saved by the Lord, the shield of thy help, and the sword of thine excellency?* And with the devout king of Israel, *Happy is that people, that is in such a case; yea happy is that people, whose God is the Lord.* What wise people would not desire to be, and to continue, such a happy people? to know the means, and use them, to be such?

This brings me to the second head of discourse, viz.

[II.] That *God's people's enjoyment of this favourable providential presence of God with them, depends upon their being with God.*

The text assures us, that this is the only way to this felicity: *The Lord is with you, while ye are with him,* and no longer; *for if ye forsake him, he will forsake you.* Their obediential presence with God is the only condition, the only qualification of God's gracious providential presence with them.

All men, even they, who know not God, and are without God in the world, are yet with God, i.e. in his presence, under his inspection, and the government of his providence. They are encompassed with the divine immensity, and *in God they live, and move, and have their being.* But as God's presence with his people signifies something more, than his essential presence, and universal providence, even his voluntary, chosen, and gracious presence, so their presence with God, signifies something else, and something more, than this natural and necessary presence with him, even their voluntary, chosen, and dutiful presence. Their presence with God must correspond to his presence with them, be as a kind of counterpart to it; and answer to it, as the wax to the seal.

As God's being with his people is his being for them, taking care of them, and dispensing favours to them; so their being with God, is their being for God, owning his cause, pursuing his interest, doing his will, and advancing his glory. God's gracious providential presence with them performs great acts of favour for them, and their obediential presence with God, lies in performing religious duties to him. It implies in it, *their keeping covenant with God.* Their covenant relation to God constitutes them his peculiar people: and brings them into a state of nearness to him; for they, that are strangers from the covenant, are afar off from God: and their keeping covenant with God, being stedfast in it, abstaining from all sins forbidden, and doing all required duties, believing all revealed truths, and walking in all the commandments & ordinances of the Lord; and in all designing his glory, is their being with God. So also is *their eying God in all providential dispensations.* When they look thro' second causes, and above visible instruments, and see the sovereign providence of God in all events, and adore the divine wisdom & goodness, power and righteousness, truth and faithfulness, in them, and compose themselves to a behaviour, comporting with them, they are with God. When they express a dutiful submission to, and a fiducial dependance upon God in all their wants, and fears, & dangers: when they maintain a prayerful frame of spirit, seeking of God the supply of their wants, direction in their streights, deliverance from their dangers, protection from their enemies, and other judgments, success in their enterprizes, and a blessing upon their labours: when they excite themselves to a thankful praising God for all his benefits: when they endeavour a wise and good improvement of all God's dealings towards them: and when they conscienciously walk in obedience to his commands: then may they be said to be with God, and not to forsake him.

God's people being thus with him, God will be with them. Not as if their being with God merited his being with them. By no means: for after all, they are unprofitable servants: and there are so many sinful imperfections attending them, in their abiding with God, such as, distrust and impatience, carnal confidence and undue dependance upon themselves or others, or means, neglect of humble believing prayer, or of holy thankful praises, that God might justly withdraw from them, and deny them his gracious presence. But, these infirmities notwithstanding, his people may humbly hope for his presence & blessing; for God is not strict to mark iniquity, where he sees sincerity.

This hope they may build upon the *gracious promise of God:* the text carries the emphasis of a promise in it: and God expresly promised his people, *that if they would walk in his statutes, and keep his commandments, and do them*, i.e. if they would be with him, *he would walk among them, and be their God:* i.e. would be graciously with them. This promise God has ever made good to his people: they ever found that, when they were with God in the way of duty, God was with them in the way of providential mercy: and God will not now suffer his faithfulness to fail.

Besides, *the great concernment of God's glory secures his favourable pres-*

ence with them, while they are with him. Should God forsake his people, while they keep near to him; should he deny them the blessings, and load them with the judgments, of providence, while they are faithful in his covenant, and stedfast, and unmoveable, and always abounding in works of obedience to him; the wicked world would take occasion to blaspheme his name, as well as insult his people. They would say, *Where is now your God?* and upbraid them with his want of love to them, or care of them, or power to help them. Therefore, for the glory of his great name, he will not forsake them, while they abide with him. God's glory is his supreme end; and the advancement of this is the great design, he is carrying on in the world.

What remains is an application; which I shall attempt, by way of address to several orders of men amongst us. My incapacity for, as well as my unacquaintedness with, polite, courtly address, and its unsuitableness to my function, and the sacred desk, will, I trust, obtain an easy pardon, for my plainness of speech; and the example of our prophet, I conceive, will justify me in it.

As your Excellency is, as yet, in the first and chief seat of government over us, justice and decency require me, in the first place, to direct an address to you: an address of a *minister of Jesus Christ,* reminding of duty, and exciting to it.

Sir,

It was the providence of God, which advanced you to the exalted station, you are now in. God is the judge; he putteth down one, and setteth up another; he removes one, and replaces another. You are indeed greatly indebted to the king, for his royal favour and commission, but more to GOD, for *the king's heart was in the hand of the Lord.* God, by his special providence, was with you in your exaltation: and from the addresses of both houses of the last assembly, and from the addresses of the freeholders and merchants of this metropolis, in which they bear public, and most honourable, testimonies to your Excellency's administration, in respect of the wisdom and integrity, the clemency and tenderness of it, and of your constant views to the public good, and the spirited and successful measures you have taken to promote it; and of your tender care of our trade; we gather, that God has been with you in your administration, as he was with young King Solomon, *to give you a wise and understanding heart,* to rule and judge his people: and from the favour you have found in the sight of the king, in your preferment to a more advantageous command, we see, that God is still with you. Oh, doth not this favourable providential presence of God, which you have so evidently enjoyed, lay you under the strongest obligations to be, and to abide with God, in all the duties of religion, and in all the important affairs of your government?

Duty and gratitude to the king's majesty, for his repeated royal favours to you, worldly policy, and self-interest, oblige you to be often with him, by your letters, to his great ministers, to know his royal pleasure, to receive his instructions and orders, and to acquaint him with the state and affairs of his subjects. Do not duty and gratitude to the most high God, for providential favours to you; and do not spiritual wisdom, & your best interest, equally, at least, oblige you to be with him, for the continuance, and increase of political and divine wisdom, for the right management in your high office, & great trust, and for procuring his blessing to your self, and your administration? Sir, you are equally God's minister, as the king's governour.

Our gracious sovereign, like godly King Asa, is with God, as we gather from his royal pious proclamations: with God, in humble supplications, to implore his blessing & help: with God, in thankful praises, to give him the glory of his favours: and we see that God is with him, as he was with Asa, in the remarkable success, he hath given to his fleets and armies, and the great victories, which by them he has obtained over his proud enemies, in one part of the world and another. This pious example of the king, is worthy the closest imitation of his representative.

Your relation to us, as our governour, will soon cease: but you will need the divine presence, for a worthy and successful conduct, in the government you are appointed to; especially as it is embarrass'd with peculiar difficulties and dangers from perfidious and bloody Indians. Would you have the gracious presence of God go along with you, and abide with you; you must then be with God.

If you are with God, acknowledge your dependence upon him, put your trust in him, supplicate his direction and blessing, and design his glory: God will be with you, to support you under the public burdens, to guide you by his counsel, to make you faithful in your trust, to defend you from enemies, if any you have, to prosper your administration, to make you acceptable to the king, and to your people; to think upon you for good, and to reward you for your faithful services to his people. God's presence with you will add lustre to your dignity; this will command reverence to your person, and obedience to your government. And what is infinitely more and better, than even this gracious providential presence of God with you, if by faith and prayer, and a holy life, you are with God, God will vouchsafe to you, *his gracious spiritual presence*, and bless you with spiritual blessings: and when you die out of this world (for tho' you are an earthly God, you must die like a man), he will, thro' the merits of Christ, receive you into his immediate glorious presence in heaven, and bestow inconceivably higher honours on you there, than ever he did in this world: he will set you upon a more glorious throne, & crown you with a richer crown, than even your royal master himself is now possessed of.

[But it is fit, and safe to be told the worst, as well as best: therefore permit me, sir, in patience, and without offence, to add, what our prophet said to a great king, his own king, and a godly king; *if you forsake God*, which God forbid, *he will forsake you:* if you neglect and reject him, he will do so by you; and make as light account of you, as you can of him. Yea, and as was threatned to a great prince, *tho' you were the signet upon his right hand, he would pluck you thence*, and cast you off for ever; for the mouth of the Lord has spoken it, and spake it to the chief ruler of his people; *Them that honour me, I will honour: and they, that despise me, shall be lightly esteemed.* Wherefore, let king David's advice, or rather charge, to his royal son and successor, be acceptable to you, and his arguments, have their due weight: *And thou, Solomon, my son, know thou the God of thy father, and serve him with a perfect heart, and a willing mind; if thou seek him, he will be found of thee, but if thou forsake him, he will cast thee off for ever.*]

Your removal, excellent sir, from this seat of government, will be in a short time: The ancient form of blessing was, *The Lord be with thee.* A greater blessing we cannot wish you, *than that God's presence may go with you, when he carries you hence.* This blessing we wish you, this day, *out of the house of the Lord.*

In the next place, I shall offer an address, to the honourable, his majesty's council, and the House of Representatives; and that with a like plainness of speech.

Sirs,

God, in his providence, has devolved upon you a great share, as of the honours, so of the cares and burdens of the government: you are as the eyes and hands of this people, to see and to act for them. You are entrusted with our most valuable priviledges, civil and religious: and, according to your management of them, we are like to be a happy or miserable people. Very important therefore, is your trust and your work; and requires superior intellectual and moral endowments for the faithful discharge and performance of the same. Will you not then be with God, who saith, *counsel is mine, and sound wisdom: with God, who giveth wisdom to the wise, and knowledge to them that know understanding*. It was the wisdom, honour and safety of Judah, *that Judah yet ruleth with God, and is faithful with the saints*. It will be no less your's, to be and to do so to.

You are piously beginning the great affairs of the year with God, in the religious exercises of his house, into which you have called us. Your care must be to be with God in the court-house too; or your being with him here will be but base hypocritical flattery, and an affront to that God, who will not be mocked.

Would you be with God in the elections of the present day, you must, according to your best judgment, choose such as God will approve. As to us your subjects, you are at liberty to choose into the king's council whom you please: not so as to God. He has given you the character of those, that shall rule his people, and a charge to make choice of such: you are therefore bound in conscience to God, as well as honour to the king, and fidelity to this people, to do your best to elect such; *and to provide out of all the people, able men*, men of sense and substance; *such as fear God*; men of virtue and piety; *men of truth, hating coveteousness;* men of fidelity, generosity, and a public spirit: *for the God of Israel has said, and the rock of Israel spake; he that ruleth over men must be just, ruling in the fear of God.*

If, in the elections of this day, you have no regard to the intellectual powers, moral characters and qualifications of men: if from fear or favour, from party spirit or any sinister views, you knowingly make choice of those who want them; you will forsake God, and act without, or rather against, him; and give him just occasion to complain of you, as of his people of old; *they have set up kings, but not by me*, not by my direction and order, nor according to my will: *they have made princes, and I knew it not:* I approved it not. In this case, can you expect God's gracious presence with you? and if you forsake God the first day, and in the chief business of the day; and which has such an interesting influence upon all the succeeding businesses of the year, will it not bode ill to you, and to your people? But we hope better things; and that, as you are, now, and here, beginning with God, you will abide with him thro' the important elections of the day; and also thro' all the future sessions of the year; and that in the great & weighty affairs, that come before you, you will seek to God for that knowledge, that will make you understanding in the times, and enable you to know the true interests of your people, and the best methods to promote them; and for that fidelity and resolution, that will embolden you to pursue them, and for the divine blessing to prosper them.

Should you, from a vain conceit of your own wisdom and sufficiency, forsake God, and ask neither his counsel nor blessing; or do it only in a formal, customary, complimental manner; you may justly fear, that God will forsake you, turn you over into the hands of your own counsels, leave you to the darkness & lusts of your own minds, mingle a perverse spirit in the midst of you, suffer parties to be formed, dissentions to prevail, and passion, self-interest, and a party spirit, rather than reason, justice, and a public spirit, to influence and govern you. In this case, your counsels will be carried headlong; and, in all probability, be extreamly prejudicial, if not fatal, to the common-wealth.

Sirs,

God will be with you, in your assemblies, whether you be with him or no: judicially, if not graciously. He will be an inspecter, an observer, a judge. However unaccountable you may be to your people, you must give account to him. Bear it in mind then, and act under the solemn realizing thought of it, that *God standeth in the congregation of the mighty: He judgeth among the Gods.*

Would it not be tho't, without the limits of my present call, I would, in a few words, address the honourable the judges in our courts of judicature, and the honoured the justices in our towns and counties.

Sirs,

The names, the estates, the liberties, and even the lives of the subjects, are deeply interested in your judgments: high is your office, awful is your work: and in some cases, attended with peculiar difficulties, perhaps temptations. You need not only the laws of the land for your directory, but wisdom, fidelity and courage, to make a right and just application of them. You are to hear the cause of your brethren, and to judge righteously, between every man and his brother; not to respect persons in judgment, but to hear the small as well as the great; and not be afraid of the faces of men; for the judgment is the Lord's. You must take heed, therefore, what you do; for you judge not for man, but for the Lord, who is with you in the judgment. Wherefore be you with God, and let the fear of the Lord be upon you. Put on righteousness, and let it cloath you, and your judgment will be as a robe, and a diadem: your greatest comfort, your brightest ornament. God will own and honour you; men will fear and reverence you. But if you forsake God in the judgment, and judge after the sight of your eyes, respect persons and not causes, receive bribes, use partiality, justify the wicked, and condemn the righteous, you will be an abomination to the Lord, and the abhorrence of his people.

Remember, sirs, that tho' now you sit upon the bench, you must one day stand at the bar. If you have been with God in the judgment, and studied to do justice, to discountenance vice, and to encourage vertue, you will be acquitted in the great audit day; and Christ, the judge, will confer inexpressible honour upon you; will take you to be assessors with him, and you shall *judge the world, yea angels*. But, if you have forsaken God, and been unjust judges, wo unto you, a more severe & tremendous sentence will be past upon you, than you ever past upon the most flagitious criminal. *Now therefore, be instructed, ye judges of the earth, and serve the Lord with fear.*

The text leads me particularly to address the *gentlemen of the military order and life*: but, as they have willingly, and generously offered themselves, to the service, and defence of their country, and are gone to the help of the Lord, to the help of the Lord, against the mighty, and to jeopard their lives in the high places of the field, I forbear —only let our hearts be towards them, our good wishes follow them, and our fervent prayers be to God for them.

My reverend fathers and brethren, will not, I trust, take it amiss, if, upon this occasion, one of the least, and most unworthy, of their order, presumes, by a word of address, *to stir up their pure minds by way of remembrance;* notwithstanding we expect a sermon to morrow: for even we have need of line upon line.

My fathers and brethren,

God, in his providence, has seperated us, from the congregation of his people, to come near to him, to stand before him, and to minister in the holy things of his house. To us are committed the oracles of God, the ministry of the word, the administration of the sacraments, and the charge of precious souls: *And who is sufficient for these things?* Of all men in the world, we have need to be with God, and to *give our selves to prayer*, imploring his spirit, to give us a spiritual understanding in the mysteries of the gospel, & to lead us into all truth: his presence, to animate us in our holy work, and to carry us above all the discouragements we meet with, from the carnality and unbelief of our own hearts, from the temptations of satan, from the little visible success of our labours, from the unkindness of our people, and from the oppositions of an ungodly world: his help, to support us under our burdens, and to strengthen us to make full proof of our ministry: and his blessing upon our labours, that we may preach so, as to save our selves, and them that hear us. We had need be with God in our preaching, that we deliver to our people none other things than what we have received from the Lord, and plainly taught in his word; that we keep back nothing that is profitable, nor shun to declare the whole counsel of God: and that we do not offer to the Lord that which cost us nothing, nor utter rashly before him, the sudden, undigested conceptions of our minds. We should be with God in our lives, and like Noah that antediluvian preacher of righteousness, walk with God, and be exemplary in faith and purity, and all the vertues of a holy life; that all may take knowledge of us, that we have been, and are with God. If we are thus with God, we may hope, he will be graciously present with us, to assist, instruct, encourage, and succeed us, in our ministerial work. We have that gracious promise of our divine Master to rely upon, and plead, *Lo, I am with you always:* and when we have served our generation, according to his will, and are not suffered to continue by reason of death, he will take us into his immediate presence in glory; for he has said, *Where I am, there also shall my servant be:* and having, thro' grace, been instrumental of turning many to righteousness, we shall shine as the brightness of the firmament, and as the stars for ever and ever.

But, if we forsake God, become strangers to prayer, and ashamed of the gospel of Christ, and the religion of the Bible: if we trust to the strength of our own reason, and the imaginary greatness of our learning; and preach for doctrines, the unscriptural conceits of our own brains, or the erroneous notions of others; if we corrupt the word of God, and preach another gospel; if we neglect or mislead the souls committed to our charge; and, by the badness of our lives, contradict and frustrate the end of our ministry, we have reason to fear, that God will forsake us utterly; and abandon us to the giddiness and wildness of our own fancies, to the blindness and pride of our own natural reason, to a reprobate mind, and to the delusions of satan: and that, having been wandring stars, the blackness of darkness for ever will be reserved for us; and that, in that outer darkness, we shall have our miserable portion, but just punishment, and be the subjects of a greater damnation.

Finally, I would address a word to this whole people: *Hear ye me, all Judah and Benjamin:* hear this all ye people, and give ear all ye inhabitants of the land: and, if I might do it without presumption and offence, I would use the pathetic words of Moses; *and set your hearts to all the words, which,* from God's word, *I testify among you this day; for it is not a vain thing for you, because it is your life.* Your peace & safety, your prosperity and happiness, your life, your all turns upon it: *The Lord is with you, while ye be with him; if ye seek him, he will be found of you, but if ye forsake him, he will forsake you.*

If ye be with God, become a praying and religious people, acting up to your covenant relation and engagements to him, walking in all holy obedience to his laws, and attendance upon his worship and ordinances; God will be with you, and give you the tokens of his gracious presence, in providential mercies. The name of your land will be Jehovah Shammah, the Lord is there. God's presence with you, will be your surest defence, your highest glory, your truest felicity. This will derive a blessing upon all your labours, husbandry, merchandize, fishery, & whatever you set your hands unto—and upon all your enjoyments. This will make your governour a Nehemiah, seeking your prosperity; this will give you wise & faithful rulers, skilful and upright judges, zealous and godly magistrates; and will make your officers peace, and your exactors righteousness: this will give you holy & orthodox ministers, pure and peaceable churches, learned & flourishing academies; and, in time of war, valiant soldiers and victorious armies. Yea, if you are indeed religiously with God, he will afford his gracious spiritual presence with his word and ordinances; this will make you a holy, as his providential presence will make you, a happy people. *Then your righteousness will go forth as brightness, and your salvation, as a lamp that burneth:* they'll be conspicuous and comfortable.

But if you forsake God, cast off your dependance upon him, and refuse subjection to him: if you apostatize from his truths and ways and worship; if you disregard his interest & glory, God will forsake you; you will become the people of his wrath, and may fear, he will write *Lo-ammi* upon you, disown you, reject you, break down the hedge he has set about you; and open a gap for ruinous judgments to rush in upon you; that as he has loaded you with benefits, he will heap mischiefs upon you. Wo unto you, if God depart from you; with him goes all good. Sinning Judah and Benjamin at length found it so; and so may you too.

To prevent then the misery of a departed God, and to enjoy the blessedness of a graciously present God, Oh be ye with God! And, because this people have backslidden from God, with a grievous backsliding, are become loose in their principles, and vicious in their lives; a people laden with iniquity; Oh return to God, by a hearty repentance, and thorow reformation, and abide with him, in the ways of obedience, that God may abide with you, in the ways of mercy. *Then his salvation will be nigh unto you, and glory will dwell in your land.*

To conclude. Let us all, let persons of every order and condition, realize it, that the gracious presence of God with us, is the one thing needful, the all-comprehending blessing: and, by a conscientious walking with God, let us engage it with us. The presence of God makes heaven itself such a holy and blessed place: the more of God's presence we have with us, the more like heaven will it make our land, in point of true holiness and true happiness—let us then, with Israel, deprecate, *God forbid, we should forsake the Lord:* and with them deliberately resolve, *Nay, but we will serve the Lord;* and with Solomon, earnestly pray, *The Lord our God be with us, as he was with our fathers; let him not leave us, nor forsake us. Amen: And let all the people say, Amen.*

FINIS

8

THE SNARE BROKEN

Jonathan Mayhew

BOSTON

1766

JONATHAN MAYHEW (1720–1766). One of the celebrated names associated with early American opposition to British tyranny, Mayhew graduated from Harvard College in 1744 and received an S.T.D. from the University of Aberdeen, Scotland, in 1749. He was pastor of Boston's West Church from 1747, a position he retained for the remainder of his short life. According to Frederick L. Wcis, Mayhew was regarded by some as the best preacher in the New England of his day (*The Colonial Clergy and the Colonial Churches of New England* [1936]).

A Unitarian, Mayhew rejected Trinitarian views as early as 1755 and based his beliefs on his own reading of the Bible, not on Calvin's. He combatted Anglican evangelism in America through the Society for the Propagation of the Gospel in Foreign Parts and the looming installation of an Anglican bishop in America, which early on epitomized the tyranny threatened by London and Canterbury. His political views were imbued with the thoughts of Milton, Locke, and Sidney. He preached against "popish idolatry" in his Dudleian lecture at Harvard in 1765.

The Snare Broken, a "thanksgiving discourse," was preached by Mayhew in his own pulpit on May 23, 1766, less than two months before he died at the age of forty-six. Occasioned by Parliament's repeal of the Stamp Act, the sermon conveys a warning to William Pitt and other English readers that taking self-government into private hands in some circumstances must surely proceed from "self-preservation, being a great and primary law of nature."

The Snare broken.

A

Thanksgiving-Discourse,

PREACHED

At the Desire of the West Church

IN

BOSTON, *N. E.* Friday *May* 23, 1766.

OCCASIONED BY THE

REPEAL

OF THE

Stamp-Act.

BY

JONATHAN MAYHEW, D. D.

Pastor of said Church.

——*Brethren, ye have been called unto* LIBERTY *; only use not* LIBERTY *for an occasion to the flesh, but by love serve one another.* Ap. PAUL.

BOSTON

Printed and Sold by R. & S. DRAPER, in New-bury-Street; EDES & GILL, in Queen-Street; and T. & J. Fleet, in Cornhill. 1766.

THE DEDICATION

To the Right Honorable William Pitt, Esq.
One of His Majesty's Most Honorable Privy Council,
and an Illustrious Patron of America

Sir,

Did not a wide ocean intervene, the author of the ensuing discourse would not presume to prefix so great a name to a little performance of his, without first humbly requesting the indulgence, and obtaining it. Nor would he trust to the sufficiency of that apology for taking this liberty, did not some persons perswade him to hope, it will be kindly and condescendingly taken as a testimony of that sincere gratitude and high veneration, which not only he but his country has for one, who hath twice at least been a principal instrument in the hand of GOD, of saving Great Britain and her colonies from impending ruin: Once, by magnanimously conducting a just and glorious war against foreign nations; and once, by preserving peace in his own; by exerting himself to prevent a fatal rupture between Britain and her colonies, and to re-establish such an harmony as essentially concerns the welfare of both.

At the late most important crisis, you, sir, whom no rewards could ever tempt, no frowns of the great ever dismay, no dangers disconcert; and to whom, so good and great in yourself, no titles, however high, could possibly add any new dignity or lustre; you, great sir, was not "ashamed of our chain," or reluctant at standing forth to plead the cause of poor America; and to stem the mighty torrent that was against her, which threatened to end in a deluge of blood! When it was accounted criminal by many, even to lisp but a broken word or two in her favor, you, sir, was not ashamed or afraid to pour forth all your unrivall'd eloquence in a strenuous vindication of her infringed rights. And, indeed, her cause being supposed good, the more friendless she was, the more she needed, and in some sort deserved, so powerful a patronage. For, surely, great talents were given for great occasions; to be employed in defence of the innocent and feeble. GOD made some men strong, on purpose to "bear the infirmities of the weak"; that they might be able to assist and support them in their dangers and extremities; as you, sir, have ever done, since you adorned the British senate; and particularly in a late ever-memorable instance.

To you, great sir, under GOD and the king, grateful America chiefly attributes it, that she is now happily re-instated in the enjoyment of her former liberties and privileges; tho' she has, at the same time, a very deep sense of her obligations to other great and illustrious personages.

If, sir, you could, at this distance, have an adequate conception of the universal joy of America, preceeded by the most alarming apprehensions for her liberties: If you could be fully sensible how much we ascribe it to you, that they are not lost; how, next to the king, we bless you as our common father, and send up ardent vows to heaven for you; this would, it must give you a sublime, and truly godlike pleasure. It might even suspend, for a while, the severest pangs of that excruciating disorder, which has so often detain'd you from the British senate, to the great detriment of the public; particularly when the late dreadful Stamp-Act was passed. Nay, it might, perhaps, without any other miracle, give you such spirits and vigor, as to "take up your bed and walk," like those sick and lame persons instantly cured by the word of him, who came from heaven to make us "free indeed."

So universal, so great is our joy; and so much, sir, are we indebted for it to your good offices! But, alas! what can poor America do in return? Nothing but acknowledge the obligation with as much sincerity as a grateful country ever acknowledged one: Nothing but call you, over and over again, her father, her father; and endeavour to make good your generous engagements for her prudent, dutiful behaviour towards her mother-country: Nothing but erect a few marble, brass or copper statues in honor to you (for America has but little silver or gold); statues that will be of no service to you, since they will go to decay long before your name and memory will need any such poor helps to preserve them.

Alas! America can do no more! Yes, sir, there is one thing more: She will pray that you may long live in health, happiness and honor, that if there should be any occasion hereafter, as in time past, you may step in and prevent her's and Britain's ruin, when no other man could; and that, when you must, according to the common lot of men, however great and good (O may it be late!) cease to plead the cause of liberty on earth, you may in heaven, as your reward, enjoy "the glorious liberty of the sons of God"!

I am, with the warmest gratitude, and highest veneration, right honorable and most worthy

sir,
your most obedient,
most dutiful
and most humble servant,

Jonathan Mayhew

Our soul is escaped as a bird from the snare of the fowlers; the snare is broken, and we are escaped.

Our help is in the name of the Lord, who made heaven and earth.

Psalm CXXIV. 7, 8.

The late gracious appearance of divine providence for us, in the day of our trouble, seemed so seasonable, so signal, so important; in a word, so interesting to the present and future generations, that we of this society thought it expedient to agree among ourselves upon a day, in order to take a particular, religious notice of it; and to praise the name of the Lord, in whom is our help. If there had been any probability of our being called together for this end by proclamation, as upon some less memorable occasions, we should not have been desirous to anticipate the day; which might have had the appearance of ostentation. But of that, so far as I have heard, there was very little, if any, prospect. By this perfectly voluntary, and free-will offering, I hope we shall render to God, in some poor measure, the glory due to his name; and that he will graciously accept it, thro' our Lord Jesus Christ the righteous, our mediator and advocate with the Father. At the same time it is supposed that, in proceeding thus, we give no just ground of offence to Jew or gentile, or to the church of God; which we would by no means do. We only exercise that liberty, wherewith Christ hath made us free, being desirous that all other persons and churches should do the same; and not chusing that either they or we should be "entangled with any yoke of bondage."

Having rendered our devout thanks to God, whose kingdom ruleth over all, and sung his high praises; permit me now, my friends and brethren, with unfeigned love to my country, to congratulate you on that interesting event, which is the special occasion of this solemnity: An event, as I humbly conceive, of the utmost importance to the whole British empire, whose peace and prosperity we ought ardently to desire; and one, very peculiarly affecting the welfare of these colonies. Believe me, I lately took no inconsiderable part with you in your grief, and gloomy apprehensions, on account of a certain parliamentary act, which you supposed ruinous in its tendency to the

American plantations, and, eventually, to Great-Britain. I now partake no less in your common joy, on account of the repeal of that act; whereby these colonies are emancipated from a slavish, inglorious bondage; are re-instated in the enjoyment of their ancient rights and privileges, and a foundation is laid for lasting harmony between Great-Britain and them, to their mutual advantage.

But when you requested me to preach a sermon on this joyful occasion, I conclude it was neither your expectation nor desire, that I should enter very particularly into a political consideration of the affair. Had I conceived this to have been your intention, I must, tho' with reluctance, have given you a refusal; partly from a conviction of the impropriety of minutely discussing points of this nature in the pulpit, and partly from a sense of my own inability to do it as it ought to be done. I suppose I shall best answer your expectation, as well as most gratify my own inclination, by waving political controversy, and giving you such counsels and exhortations respecting your duty to God and man, as are agreeable to the sacred oracles, to the dictates of sober reason, and adapted to the occasion. This is, therefore, what I chiefly propose to do in the ensuing discourse, as God shall enable me: And may the Father of lights teach me to speak, and you to hear in such a manner, that our assembling together at this time, out of the ordinary course, may be to his honor, and to christian edification.

However, if my discourse is to be particularly adapted to this great occasion, instead of being so general, as to be almost as suitable to any other, you are sensible it is necessary that the occasion itself should be kept in view. I shall therefore briefly premise a few things relative thereto, by way of introduction to the main design; such things, I mean, as shall now be taken for granted. In mentioning which, my aim will be to express, in brief, what I take to be the general sense of these colonies, rather than to explain my own. For it is on such commonly-received opinions, that my exhortations and cautions will be grounded; leaving the particular discussion of them to others, who are better qualified for it, and to whom it more properly belongs. And if I should be mistaken in any of these particulars, it is hoped candor will excuse it; seeing these are matters out of the way of my profession.

In pursuance of this plan, it shall now be taken for granted, that as we were free-born, never made slaves by the right of conquest in war, if there be indeed any such right, nor sold as slaves in any open lawful market, for money, so we have a natural right to our own, till we have freely consented to part with it, either in person, or by those whom *we* have appointed to represent, and to act for us.

It shall be taken for granted, that this natural right is declared, affirmed and secured to us, as we are British subjects, by Magna Charta; all acts contrary to which, are said to be *ipso facto* null and void: And, that this natural, constitutional right has been further confirmed to most of the plantations by particular subsequent royal charters, taken in their obvious sense; the legality and authority of which charters was never once denied by either house of Parliament; but implicitly at least acknowledged, ever since they were respectively granted, till very lately.

It is taken for granted also, that the right of trial by juries, is a constitutional one with respect to all British subjects in general, particularly to the colonists; and that the plantations in which civil government has been established, have all along, till of late, been in the uninterrupted enjoyment of both the rights aforesaid, which are of the utmost importance, being essential to liberty.

It shall, therefore, be taken for granted, that the colonies had great reason to petition and remonstrate against a late act of Parliament, as being an infraction of these rights, and tending directly to reduce us to a state of slavery.

It is, moreover, taken for granted, whatever becomes of this question about rights, that an act of that sort was very hard, and justly grievous, not to say oppressive; as the colonies are poor, as most of them were originally settled at the sole and great expence of the adventurers; the expence of their money, their toil, their blood; as they have expended a great deal from time to time in their wars with their French and savage neighbours, and in the support of his majesty's government here; as they have, moreover, been ever ready to grant such aids of men and money to the crown, for the common cause, as they were able to give; by which means a great load of debt still lies on several of them; and as Great Britain has drawn vast emolument from them in the way of commerce, over and above all that she has ever expended for them, either in peace or war: So that she is, beyond all comparison, richer, more powerful and respectable now, than she would have been, if our fathers had never emigrated: And both they and their posterity have, in effect, been labouring, from first to last, for the aggrandizement of the mother-country. In this light, that share of common sense, which the colonists have, be it more or less, leads them to consider things.

It is taken for granted, that as the surprising, unexampled growth of these colonies, to the extension of his majesty's dominion, and prodigious advantage of Britain in many respects, has been chiefly owing, under God, to the liberty enjoyed here; so the infraction thereof in two such capital points as those before referred to, would undoubtedly discourage the trade, industry and population of the colonies, by rendering property insecure and precarious; would soon drain them of all their little circulating money; would put it absolutely out of their power to purchase British commodities, force them into manufactures of their own, and terminate, if not in the ruin, yet in the very essential detriment of the mother-country.

It shall, therefore, also be taken for granted, that altho' the colonies could not justly claim an exclusive right of taxing themselves, and the right of being tried by juries; yet they had great reason to remonstrate against the act aforesaid on the footing of inexpedience, the great hardship, and destructive tendency of it; as a measure big with mischief to Britain, as well as to themselves; and promoted at first, perhaps, only by persons who were real friends to neither.

But as to any methods of opposition to that measure, on the part of the colonies, besides those of humble petitioning, and other strictly legal ones, it will not, I conclude, be supposed, that I appear in this place as an advocate for them, whatever the general sense of the colonists may be concerning this point. And I take for granted, that we are all perfectly agreed in condemning the riotous and fellonious proceedings of certain men of Belial*, as they have been justly called, who had the effrontery to cloke their rapacious violences with the pretext of zeal for liberty; which is so far from being a new thing under the sun, that even Great Britain can furnish us with many, and much more flagrant examples of it.

But, my brethren, however unconstitutional, oppressive, grievous or ruinous the aforesaid act was in its nature, and fatal in its tenden-

* The Book of America, chap. II. v. 13.

cy, his majesty and the Parliament have been pleased to hearken to the just complaints of the colonies, seconded and enforced by the prudent, spirited conduct of our merchants; by certain noble and ever-honored patriots in Great Britain, espousing our cause with all the force of reason and eloquence, and by the general voice of the nation: So that a total repeal of that dreadful act is now obtained. His majesty and the Parliament were far too wise, just and good to persist in a measure, after they were convinced it was wrong; or to consider it as any point of honor, to enforce an act so grievous to three million good subjects, so contrary to the interest of the British merchants and manufacturers, and to the general sense of the nation. They have been pleased, in the act of repeal itself, greatly to their honor, implicitly to acknowledge their fallibility and erroneous judgment in the other act, by saying, that "the continuance of the said act would be attended with many inconveniences, and might be productive of consequences greatly detrimental to the commercial interests of those kingdoms." These being the reasons assigned for the repeal, we may justly conclude, that if those *many inconveniences and detrimental consequences* could have been foreseen, the act complained of would never have been passed. And as the same reasons will doubtless operate at least as strongly, probably much more strongly hereafter, in proportion to the growth of the colonies, than they do at present, we may naturally conclude also, that an act of the like nature will never again be heard of.

Thus "our soul is escaped as a bird from the snare of the fowlers; the snare is broken, and we are escaped"; tho' not without much struggling in the snare, before it gave way, and set us at liberty again. But when I speak of that pernicious act as a snare, and those who prepared it for us as fowlers, greedy of their prey, let it be particularly observed, that I intend not the least reflexion on our gracious sovereign or the Parliament; who must not be supposed to have any evil designs against the colonies, which are so necessary to Great Britain, and by which so many thousands of her manufacturers are supported, who, but for them, must actually starve, emigrate, or do what I chuse to forbear mentioning. No! I apply this, as I conclude you will, only to some evil-minded individuals in Britain, who are true friends neither to her nor us; and who accordingly spared no wicked arts, no deceitful, no dishonorable, no dishonest means, to push on and obtain, as it were by surprise, an act so prejudicial to both; and, in some sort, to the ensnaring of his majesty and the Parliament, as well as the good people of America: Being, not improbably, in the interests of the houses of Bourbon and the pretender, whose cause they meant to serve, by bringing about an open rupture between Great Britain and her colonies! These, these men, my brethren, are the cunning fowlers, these the ensnarers, from whose teeth "our soul is escaped as a bird": And such traitors will, doubtless, e'er long be caught in another snare, suitable for them, to the satisfaction of the king's good subjects on both sides the Atlantic, if his majesty and the Parliament should judge it necessary for the vindication of their own honor, or for the public good, to bring them to condign punishment.

Let me just add here, that according to our latest and best advices, the king, his truly patriotic ministry and the Parliament have the interest, particularly the commercial interest of the colonies much at heart; being now disposed even to enlarge, instead of curtailing their privileges, and to grant us every indulgence, consistent with the common good of the British empire: More than which we cannot reasonably, and, I am persuaded, do not desire.

These things being premised, let me now proceed to those reflections, exhortations and cautions relative to them, which were the chief design of this discourse. And the present occasion being a very peculiar one, such as never before occurred in America, and, I hope in God, never will again; I shall crave your indulgence if I am considerably longer than is customary on other occasions, which are less out of the ordinary course.

In the first place then, it is evident from the preceding view of things, that we have the greatest cause for thankfulness to Almighty God, who doeth his will among the inhabitants of the earth, as well as in the armies of heaven. He, in whose hands are the hearts of all men, not excepting those of kings, so that he turneth them whithersoever he will, as the rivers of water, hath inspired the people of America with a noble spirit of liberty, and remarkably united them in standing up for that invaluable blessing. He hath raised us up friends of the greatest eminence in Britain, in our perilous circumstances. He hath united the hearts of almost all wise and good men there, to plead our cause and their own successfully. He hath blessed the king with an upright ministry, zealous for the public good, and knowing wherein it consists. He hath given the king wisdom to discern, and integrity to pursue, the interests of his people, at the late alarming crisis, when so much depended on the measures that were then speedily to be taken! He hath changed his royal purpose, and that of his Parliament, in a matter which nearly and essentially concerned, at least our temporal happiness; disposing them to take off from our necks that grievous and heavy burden, which, to be sure, was not put upon us but with reluctance, and thro' the dishonest artifices of certain wicked men who, perhaps, intended, if possible, entirely to alienate the affections of the colonists from their common father the king, and from their mother-country. O execrable design! to the accomplishment of which, the pernicious measure aforesaid apparently tended. But blessed be he, who governeth among the nations, that he hath confounded the devices of such treacherous men. To allude to the psalm, a part of which I mentioned as my text; "If it had not been the Lord who was on our side, when men rose up against us," and if they could have had their wicked will, "then they had swallowed us up quick"; "then the waters had overwhelmed us, the stream had gone over our soul; then the proud waters had gone over our soul. Blessed be the Lord, who hath not given us as a prey to their teeth"; the ravening teeth of those cunning fowlers, from whose treacherous snare we have just escaped; "our help being in the name of the Lord, who made heaven and earth." To him, therefore, we justly owe the undissembled gratitude of our hearts, as well as the joyful praises of our lips: For I take it for granted, that you all firmly believe, that he who made the world, exercises a providential government over it; so that the very hairs of our head "are all numbered by," and that "a sparrow doth not fall to the ground without" him. How much more then, is his providence to be acknowledged in the rise, in the preservation, in the great events, the revolutions, or the fall of mighty states and kingdoms?

To excite our gratitude to God the more effectually, let us consider the greatness of our late danger and of our deliverance: Let us take a brief retrospective view of the perplexed, wretched state, in which these colonies were, a few months ago, compared with the joyful and happy condition, in which they are at present, by the removal of their chief grievances.

We have never known so quick and general a transition from the depth of sorrow to the height of joy, as on this occasion; nor, indeed, so great and universal a flow of either, on any other occasion whatever. It is very true, we have heretofore seen times of great adversity. We have known seasons of drought, dearth, and spreading mortal diseases; the pestilence walking in darkness, and the destruction wasting at noon day. We have seen wide devastations, made by fire; and amazing tempests, the heavens on flame, the winds and the waves roaring. We have known repeated earthquakes, threatning us with speedy destruction. We have been under great apprehensions by reason of formidable fleets of an enemy on our coasts, menacing fire and sword to all our maritime towns. We have known times when the French and savage armies made terrible havock on our frontiers, carrying all before them for a while; when we were not without fear, that some capital towns in the colonies would fall into their merciless hands. Such times as these we have known; at some of which almost every "face gathered paleness," and the knees of all but the good and brave, waxed feeble. But never have we known a season of such universal consternation and anxiety among people of all ranks and ages, in these colonies, as was occasioned by that parliamentary procedure, which threatned us and our posterity with perpetual bondage and slavery. For they, as we generally suppose, are really slaves to all intents and purposes, who are obliged to labor and toil only for the benefit of others; or, which comes to the same thing, the fruit of whose labour and industry may be lawfully taken from them without their consent, and they justly punished if they refuse to surrender it on demand, or apply it to other purposes than those, which their masters, of their mere grace and pleasure, see fit to allow. Nor are there many American understandings accute enough to distinguish any material difference between this being done by a single person, under the title of an absolute monarch, and done by a far-distant legislature consisting of many persons, in which they are not represented; and the members whereof, instead of feeling, and sharing equally with them in the burden thus imposed, are eased of their own in proportion to the greatness and weight of it. It may be questioned, whether the ancient Greeks or Romans, or any other nation in which slavery was allowed, carried their idea of it much further than this. So that our late apprehensions, and universal consternation, on account of ourselves and posterity, were far, very far indeed, from being groundless. For what is there in this world more wretched, than for those who were born free, and have a right to continue so, to be made slaves themselves, and to think of leaving a race of slaves behind them; even though it be to masters, confessedly the most humane and generous in the world? Or what wonder is it, if after groaning with a low voice for a while, to no purpose, we at length groaned so loudly, as to be heard more than three thousand miles; and to be pitied throughout Europe, wherever it is not hazardous to mention even the name of liberty, unless it be to reproach it, as only another name for sedition, faction or rebellion.

On the other hand, never did the tide of joy swell so high, or roll so rapidly thro' the bosoms and veins of the people in general, on any public occasion, as on the news of the repeal. "Then was our mouth filled with laughter, and our tongue with singing," *when the Lord turned our captivity*; this was received as an emancipation indeed from unmerited slavery. Nor were there ever before so great external demonstrations of joy among the people of America; not even when all Canada was reduced, or when it was secured to the crown of England by treaty, and our apprehensions of coming under the yoke of France were vanished away. And some there are, who suppose, that France would not have hesitated at allowing such a number of flourishing colonies the exclusive right of taxing themselves, for the sake of a free trade with them, could they have been prevailed on, by violating their allegiance, to put themselves under her protection; as I am fully persuaded these colonies would not do, for all that France has to give. In my poor opinion, we never had so much real occasion for joy, on any temporal account, as when we were thus emancipated, and our soul escaped as a bird from the dreadful snare. And I am perswaded it would rejoice the generous and royal heart of his majesty, if he knew that by a single turn of the scepter, when he assented to the repeal, he had given more pleasure to three million good subjects, than ever he and his royal grandfather gave them by all the triumphs of their arms, from Lake Superior eastward to the Isles of Manilla; tho' so numerous, so great, so illustrious; and though we partook so largely in the national joy on those occasions. *A pepper-corn* a year added to his majesty's exchequer*, would not surely—! But I forbear.

* See a certain ever-memorable speech in an august assembly.

If you please, we will now descend to some farther particulars, relative to our late unhappy and present joyful circumstances, in order to excite our thankfulness to God, for so memorable a deliverance.

This continent, from Canada to Florida, and the West-India Islands, most of them at least, have exhibited a dismal mixed scene of murmuring, despondence, tumult and outrage; courts of justice shut up, with custom-houses and ports; private jealousies and animosities, evil furnishings, whisperings and back-bitings, mutual reproaches, open railing, and many other evils, since the time in which the grievous act aforesaid was to have taken place. Almost every British American, as was before observed, considered it as an infraction of their rights, or their dearly purchased privileges, call them which you will; and the sad earnest of such a galling yoke to be laid on our necks, already somewhat sore by preceding grievances, as neither we nor our fathers were able to bear; or rather, as being itself such a yoke, and likely to grow heavier by length of time, without any increase, either of ability or patience to endure it. The uneasiness was, therefore, justly great and universal, except, perhaps, among a few individuals, who either did not attend to consequences, or who expected to find their private account in the public calamity, by exercising the gainful, tho' invidious, and not very reputable office of task-masters over their groaning countrymen and brethren. Even our bought Negro slaves apparently shared in the common distress: For which one cannot easily account, except by supposing that even some of them saw, that if the act took place, their masters might soon be too poor to provide them suitable food and raiment; and thought it would be more ignominious and wretched to be the servants of servants, than of free-men.

But to return. The general discontent operated very differently upon the minds of different people, according to the diversity of their natural tempers and constitutions, their education, religious principles, or the prudential maxims which they had espoused. Some at once grew melancholy, sitting down in a kind of lethargic, dull desparation of relief, by any means whatever. Others were thrown into a sort of consternation, not unlike to a phrenzy occasioned by a raging fever; being ready to do any thing or every thing, to obtain relief; but yet, unhappily, not knowing what, when, where, how; nor having any two rational and consistent ideas about the matter; scarce more than a person in a delirium has of the nature of, or proper method of curing the fever, which is the cause of his madness. Some few were, I believe, upon the principles of Sibthorp, Manwaring, Filmer, and that goodly tribe, determined to go no farther in order to obtain redress, than in the way of petition and remonstrance; and this, even tho' they had been sure of success in some hardy enterprize. Others, who had no religious scruples of this kind, yet thought it extremely imprudent and hazardous to oppose a superior power in such a manner as might, perhaps, draw the whole weight of its resentment on the colonies, to their destruction. But the greater part, as I conceive, tho' I may be mistaken in this, were firmly united in a consistent, however imprudent or desperate a plan, to run all risques, to tempt all hazards, to go all lengths, if things were driven to extremity, rather than to submit; preferring death itself to what they esteemed so wretched and inglorious a servitude. And even "of devout women not a few" were, I imagine, so far metamorphosed into men on this sad occasion, that they would have declined hardly any kind of manly exertions, rather than live to propagate a race of slaves, or to be so themselves. In short, such was the danger, and in their opinion, so great and glorious the cause, that the spirit of the Roman matrons in the time of the commonwealth, seemed to be now equalled by the fairer daughters of America. The uneasiness of some persons was much encreased by an imagination, that the money to be raised by the duty on stamps, would partly be applied to pay certain civil officers salaries; whereby they would become more entirely and absolutely dependent on the crown, less on the people, and consequently, as was supposed, more arbitrary and insolent. Others were anxious, because they imagined, with how much, or how little reason you will best judge, that the money was to be chiefly applied towards maintaining a standing army in America; not so much to defend and secure the colonies from enemies, of whom they had none, except the aforesaid fowlers, as to awe the colonies themselves into an implicit obedience to ministerial measures, however unjust or execrable in their nature. There is no end, you know, to peoples fears and jealousies, when once they are thoroughly alarmed. And so some suspected that this money was partly intended to maintain a standing army of bishops, and other ecclesiastics, to propagate the importance of certain rites and ceremonies, to which they had an aversion; the divine right of diocesan episcopacy and tythes, with many *et cætara's* of the like sacred and interesting importance. These strange notions and fears prevailed very much among certain odd people, who liked their old religion, and were not able to see the reasonableness of their paying for the support of any other. I am not accountable for other people's whimsical apprehensions: I am here only representing the perplexity, into which peoples minds were thrown by the novel taxation, according to their different views of it; a taxation, which was probably never thought of till a few years ago, when it was proposed to a great and good secretary of state, who was far too friendly to the colonies, as well as too wise, *to burn his fingers with an American Stamp-Act*.

This diversity of humours, sentiments and opinions among the colonists, of which I have been speaking, naturally occasioned great animosities, mutual censures and reproaches: Insomuch that it was hardly safe for any man to speak his thoughts on the times, unless he could patiently bear to lie under the imputation of being a coward, an incendiary, rebel, or enemy to his country; or to have some other odium cast upon him. In the mean time most of the courts were shut up, and almost all business brought to a stand; and, in some colonies, wide breaches were made between their several governors and houses of assembly; those governors thinking it their duty to push the execution of the stamp-act; and some of them trying to prevent the assemblies petitioning, in the joint manner proposed. In this state of general disorder, approaching so near to anarchy, some profligate people, in different parts of the continent, took an opportunity to gratify their private resentments, and to get money in an easier and more expeditious way than that of labor; committing abominable excesses and outrages on the persons or property of others.

What a dreadful scene was this! Who can take a cursory review of it even now, without horror, unless he is lost to all sense of religion, virtue and good order? These were some of the bitter, and in a good measure, the natural fruits of that unhappy measure which preceeded them. Nor were we wholly unapprehensive of something still worse; of having a more dreadful scene, even a scene of blood and slaughter opened! I will not be particular here; but ask you what you think of British subjects making war upon British subjects on this continent! What might this have terminated in? Perhaps in nothing less than the ruin of the colonies and the downfall of a certain great kingdom, which has long been the support of other states, the terror of her enemies, and the envy and glory of Europe! If I had myself, once, some apprehensions of this kind, as I confess I had, I was very far from being singular therein. One of the best judges of such matters, that any nation or age ever afforded, as well as one of the best men, and most accomplished orators, speaking on this point in a certain august assembly, is reported to have expressed himself thus.

> On a good, on a sound bottom, the force of this country can crush America to atoms. I know the valor of your troops; I know the skill of your officers. But on this ground, on the Stamp-Act, when so many here will think it a crying injustice, I am one that will lift up my hand against it. In such a cause your success may be hazardous. America, if she fell, would fall like a strong man, would embrace the pillars of state, and *pull down the constitution along with her*.

Thus the great patron of America.* Even the remotest apprehensions of this kind, must give a very sensible pain to any American, who at once sincerely loves his own country, and wishes that the happy civil constitution, the strength and glory of Great Britain may be as lasting as the world, and still increasing; as God is my witness, I both wish and pray. If Britain, which has long been the principal support of liberty in Europe, and is, at least was, the chief bulwark against that most execrable of all tyrannies, popery, should in destroying her colonies destroy herself (Heaven forbid it!); what would become of those few states which are now free? what, of the protestant religion? The former might, not improbably, fall before the grand monarch on this side the Alps; the latter before the successor of the apostle Judas, and grand vicar of Satan, beyond them; and so, at length, one universal despotism swallow up all! Some of us had, lately, painful apprehensions of this kind, when there was talk of a great military force coming to stamp America into a particular kind of subjection, to which most people here have an invincible aversion.

It would, doubtless, have been a noble effort of genius and human-

* The Right Hon. William Pitt, Esq. But the author thinks it a piece of justice due to so great and respectable a name, to acknowledge that he has no better authority for mentioning it on this particular occasion, than that of the public prints, lately spread over America; giving an account of some debates in the honorable House of Commons. He also acknowledges, that this is all the authority he has for citing some other passages afterwards, as from the same illustrious patriot.

ity in the—what shall I call them? fowlers or financiers?—to extort a little money from the poor colonies by force of arms, at the risque of so much mischief to America, to Britain, to Europe, to the world. And the golden temptation, it is said, took with too many, for while. A Pandora's box, or Trojan horse, indeed!

—O miseri, quæ tanta insania, cives!
Creditis avectos hostes? aut ulla putatis
Dona carere dolis Danaûm? sic notus—?*

But not to digress. I have now briefly reminded you of our late sad, perplexed, alarming circumstances; not for the sake of reproaching those who brought us into them, but to excite your gratitude to God, for our deliverance out of them, and for our present happy condition.

The repeal, the repeal has at once, in a good measure, restored things to order, and composed our minds, by removing the chief ground of our fears. The course of justice between man and man is no longer obstructed; commerce lifts up her head, adorned with golden tresses, pearls and precious stones. All things that went on right before, are returning gradually to their former course; those that did not, we have reason to hope, will go on better now; almost every person you meet, wears the smiles of contentment and joy; and even our slaves rejoice, as tho' they had received their manumission. Indeed, all the lovers of liberty in Europe, in the world, have reason to rejoice; the cause is in some measure common to them and us. Blessed revolution! glorious change! How great are our obligations for it to the supreme Governor of the world! He hath given us *beauty for ashes, and the oil of gladness for the spirit of heaviness*: He hath turned our groans into songs, *our mourning into dancing:* He hath *put off our sackcloth, and girded us with gladness*, to the end that our tongues, *our glory may sing praises to him*. Let us all then rejoice in the Lord, and give honor to him; not forgetting to add the obedience of our lives, as the best sacrifice that we can offer to heaven; and which, if neglected, will prove all our other sacrifices have been but ostentation and hypocrisy, which are an abomination to the Lord.

The apostle Peter makes a natural transition from fearing God to

* Aen. II.

honoring the king. Let me, accordingly, in the next place, exhort you, my friends and brethren, to a respectful, loyal and dutiful manner of speech and conduct, respecting his majesty and his government; thereby making a suitable return to him for the redress of our late grievances. I am, indeed, well apprised of the firm attachment of these colonies in general, and of our own province in particular, to the king's person, and to the protestant succession in his illustrious house; for the preservation of which, there is hardly a native of New-England, who would not, upon constitutional principles, which are those of liberty, chearfully hazard his life; or even more lives than one, if he had them to lay down in so good a cause. I have not the least suspicion of any disaffection in you to his majesty: But yet the duty of subjects to kings, and to all that are in authority, is frequently to be inculcated by the ministers of the gospel, if they will follow the example of the apostles in this respect. And the present occasion seems particularly proper to remind you of that important duty; since we have now before us a recent and memorable proof of his majesty's moderation, his attention to the welfare of his people, and readiness, so far as in him lies according to the constitution, to redress their grievances, on reasonable and humble complaint. If any persons among us have taken it unkindly, that his majesty should have given his royal assent to an act, which they think was an infraction of those liberties and privileges, to which they were justly intitled; and if the usual tide and fervor of their loyal affection is in any degree abated on that account; yet, surely, the readiness which his majesty has shewn to hear and redress his people's wrongs, ought to give a new spring, an additional vigor to their loyalty and obedience. Natural parents, thro' human frailty, and mistakes about facts and circumstances, sometimes *provoke their children to wrath*, tho' they tenderly love them, and sincerely desire their good. But what affectionate and dutiful child ever harboured resentment on any such account, if the grievance was removed, on a dutiful representation of it? Hardly any thing operates so strongly on ingenuous minds, tho' perhaps of quick resentment, as the mild condescension of a superior to the force of reason and right on the part of the inferior. I shall make no application of this, any farther than to remind you, that British kings are the political fathers of their people, and the people their children; the former are not tyrants, or even masters; the latter are not slaves, or even servants.

Let me farther exhort you to pay due respect in all things to the British Parliament; the Lords and Commons being two branches of the supreme legislative over all his majesty's dominions. The right of parliament to superintend the general affairs of the colonies, to direct, check or controul them, seems to be supposed in their charters; all which, I think, while they grant the power of legislation, limit the exercise of it to the enacting such laws as are not contrary to the laws of England, or Great-Britain; so that our several legislatures are subordinate to that of the mother-country, which extends to and over all the king's dominions: At least, so far as to prevent any parts of them from doing what would be either destructive to each other, or manifestly to the ruin of Britain. It might be of the most dangerous consequence to the mother-country, to relinquish this supposed authority or right, which, certainly, has all along been recognized by the colonies; or to leave them dependent on the crown only, since, probably, within a century, the subjects in them will be more than thrice as numerous as those of Great-Britain and Ireland. And, indeed, if the colonies are properly parts of the British empire, as it is both their interest and honor to be, it seems absurd to deny, that they are subject to the highest authority therein, or not bound to yield obedience to it. I hope there are very few people, if any, in the colonies, who have the least inclination to renounce the general jurisdiction of Parliament over them, whatever we may think of the particular right of taxation. If, in any particular cases, we should think our selves hardly treated, laid under needless and unreasonable restrictions, or curtailed of any liberties or privileges, which other our fellow subjects in common enjoy; we have an undoubted right to complain, and, by humble and respectful, tho' not abject and servile petitions, to seek the redress of such supposed grievances. The colonists are men, and need not be afraid to assert the natural rights of men; they are British subjects, and may justly claim the common rights, and all the privileges of such, with plainness and freedom. And from what has lately occurred, there is reason to hope, that the Parliament will ever hereafter be willing to hear and grant our just requests; especially if any grievances should take place, so great, so general and alarming, as to unite all the colonies in petitioning for redress, as with one voice. The humble united prayers of three or four million loyal subjects, so connected with Great Britain, will not be thought unworthy of a serious attention; especially when seconded by such spirited resolutions and conduct of the American merchants, as they have lately given an example of. Humble petitions, so enforced, always carry great weight with them; and, if just and reasonable, will doubtless meet with a suitable return, as in the late instance; since Great Britain can scarce subsist without the trade of her colonies, which will be still increasing. And an equitable, kind treatment of them, on her part, will firmly bind them to her by the threefold cord of duty, interest and filial affection; such an one as the wise man says, is not easily broken: This would do more, far more to retain the colonies in due subjection, than all the fleets or troops she would think proper to send for that purpose.

But to return; we ought, in honor to ourselves, as well as duty to the king and parliament, to frustrate the malicious prophecies, if not the hopes of some persons in Britain, who have predicted the most ungrateful and indecent returns from us to our mother-country, for deliverance from the late grievances. It has been foretold that, in consequence thereof, the colonies would grow insolent and assuming; that they would affect a kind of triumph over the authority of parliament; that they would little or nothing regard it hereafter, in other cases; that they would give some broad intimations of their opinion, that it was not for want of inclination, but of power, that the late grievous act was not enforced; that they would treat their brethren in Britain in an unworthy, disrespectful manner; and the like. Such things as these have been predicted, and, probably, by those very fowlers who contrived the snare, from which, to their great mortification, our soul is now escaped as a bird. Let us, my brethren (for it is in our power, and it is our duty), make such men false prophets, by a contrary behaviour; "prophets of the deceit of their own hearts." This might, probably, vex them sorely; since it is likely, their chief aim is, to bring about a fixed, confirmed disaffection on our part, and a severe resentment on the other, while the jealous enemies of the growing power of Britain, wagg their ever-plotting and enterprising heads, saying, "Aha! so we would have it." Let us highly reverence the supreme authority of the British empire, which to us is the highest, under that of heaven. Let us, as much as in us lies, cultivate harmony and brotherly love between our fellow subjects in Britain and ourselves. We shall doubtless find our account in this at last, much more than in a contrary way of proceeding. There are no other people on earth, that so "naturally care for us." We are connected with them by the strongest ties; in some measure by blood; for look but a century or two back, and you will find their ancestors and ours, in a great measure the same persons, tho' their posterity is now so divided. We are strongly connected with them by a great commercial intercourse, by our common language, by our common religion as protestants, and by being subjects of the same king, whom God long preserve and prosper, while his enemies are cloathed with shame.

If we consider things properly, it is indeed our great felicity, our best security, and highest glory in this world, to stand in such a relation as we do, to so powerful an empire; one which rules the ocean, and wherein the principles of liberty are in general predominant. It would be our misery, if not our ruin, to be cast off by Great-Britain, as unworthy her farther regards. What then would it be, in any supposeable way, to draw upon ourselves the whole weight of her just resentment! What are we in the hands of that nation, which so lately triumphed over the united powers of France and Spain? Though it must, indeed, be acknowledged, that she did this, in a great measure, by means of her commercial intercourse with, and aids from the colonies: Without which she must probably have made a more inglorious figure at the end, than she did at the beginning of the last war; even tho' Mr. Pitt himself had had the sole direction of it under his majesty. Consider how many millions of people there are in other countries, groaning in vain under the iron sceptre of merciless despotism, who, if they were but imperfectly apprised of the happiness we enjoy, would most ardently desire to be in our situation, and to stand in the like relation to Great Britain. Let us not be insensible of our own felicity in this respect; let us not entertain a thought of novelties or innovations, or be "given to change." Let us not indulge to any groundless jealousies of ill intentions towards us in our mother-country, whatever there may be in some designing individuals, who do the devil's work, by sowing discord. It is for the interest of Britain, *as she well knows*, to retain the affection of these growing colonies, and to treat them kindly to that end: And this bond of interest on her part, is the strongest security to us, which we can have in any political relation whatever. We are bound, in honor to the king and Parliament, to suppose, that it was not for want of ability to enforce a late act, and to crush us, that it was repealed; but from a conviction of the inexpediency, the dangerous consequences, and many inconveniencies of continuing it. And the like reasons will probably operate forever against any act of the same nature, and grow stronger and stronger.

It can answer no valuable end, for us to harbour grudges or secret resentment on account of redressed and past grievances; no good end wantonly and grossly to insult, and thereby to incense any particular powerful persons on the other side of the water, as the supposed enemies of the colonies. To me this seems impolitic at least; as it may perhaps make such persons our enemies, if they were not so before; or, if they were, fix their enmity; and make them more industrious than ever in seeking opportunities to do us mischief. Much less can it answer any good end, to affect to triumph over the power of Parliament: This would, in short, appear equally insolent, disloyal and ridiculous, in the eyes of all sober, unprejudiced men. May God give us the wisdom to behave ourselves with humility and moderation, on the happy success of our late remonstrances and struggles! We are bound in honor so to behave, not only that we may frustrate the malignant predictions before referred to, but that we may answer the just expectation of our friends in Britain, who so nobly espoused our cause, and, as it were, pawned their own honor (how great and sacred a pledge!), for our good conduct, if our grievances were removed. By such an engagement they did us honor, as it manifested their candid and kind sentiments concerning us. This lays us under an additional obligation, in point of gratitude, to that good behaviour, which would have been our duty without it. I cannot but here remind you particularly of the words of that immortal patriot in Parliament, who has now a second time, been the principal means of saving Britain and her colonies from impending ruin.* "Say," said he,

> the Americans have not in all things acted with prudence and temper: They have been wrong'd; they have been driven to madness by injustice.

* The Rt. Hon. Mr. Pitt.

> Will you now punish them for the madness you have occasioned? Rather let prudence and temper come first from this side; *I will undertake for America* that she will follow the example.

What son, either of America or of liberty is there, that has the least spark of ingenuity, who can help being touched and penetrated to the inmost recesses of the heart, by such magnanimous and generous expressions in behalf of the colonies? Who is there, that would not almost as willingly die, as that that illustrious patron of America should ever have occasion to be ashamed of espousing its cause, and making himself answerable for us? We had other advocates of distinguished eminence and worth, who generously came under similar engagements for us. God forbid, my brethren, that any one of them should ever have the least reason to blush for his ill placed confidence in us; as all of them will, if we shew any unworthy behaviour towards the king, the Parliament or our mother-country, after this proof of their moderation, and regard for us. And if they, our friends, should have cause to blush for us in this respect, what must we do for ourselves! Where shall we find caverns far enough removed from the light of day, in which to hide our heads! Or what reason shall we have to expect friends, advocates and sponsors again, how much soever we may need them, if we have no more regard for the honor of those who appeared for us at the late alarming crisis; when it was accounted almost criminal to say any thing in our behalf?

Let me subjoin, that as the good people of this province had the honor to lead in a spirited, tho' decent and respectful application for the redress of our late grievances; methinks they should now be ambitious to have the honor of leading in a prudent, temperate, wise behaviour, in consequence of the success; and, if need be, as I hope there is not, ambitious of setting an example of moderation and discretion to other colonies. This honor would be equal to the first mentioned; and would probably recommend us greatly to those, whom it will always be our interest and duty to please; so long, at least, as we can do it without renouncing our birth-right. It will contribute to remove any impressions that may have been made of late, to our disadvantage. It will at once gratify our best friends, and falsify the slanders of our enemies, who delight in representing us as a seditious, factious and turbulent sort of people, who cannot endure the wholesome and necessary restraints of government. May God rebuke them for, and forgive them this wrong!

Let none suspect that, because I thus urge the duty of cultivating a close harmony with our mother-country, and a dutiful submission to the king and Parliament, our chief grievances being redressed, I mean to disswade people from having a just concern for their own rights, or legal, constitutional privileges. History, one may presume to say, affords no example of any nation, country or people long free, who did not take some care of themselves; and endeavour to guard and secure their own liberties. Power is of a grasping, encroaching nature, in all beings, except in him, to whom it emphatically "belongeth"; and who is the only King that, in a religious or moral sense, "can do no wrong." Power aims at extending itself, and operating according to mere will, where-ever it meets with no ballance, check, controul or opposition of any kind. For which reason it will always be necessary, as was said before, for those who would preserve and perpetuate their liberties, to guard them with a wakeful attention; and in all righteous, just and prudent ways, to oppose the first encroachments on them. "Obsta principiis." After a while it will be too late. For in the states and kingdoms of this world, it happens as it does in the field or church, according to the well-known parable, to this purpose; That while men *sleep, then the enemy cometh and soweth tares*, which cannot be rooted out again till the *end of the world*, without rooting out the wheat with them.

If I may be indulged here in saying a few words more, respecting my notions of liberty in general, such as they are, it shall be as follows.

Having been initiated, in youth, in the doctrines of civil liberty, as they were taught by such men as Plato, Demosthenes, Cicero and other renowned persons among the ancients; and such as Sidney and Milton, Locke and Hoadley, among the moderns; I liked them; they seemed rational. Having, earlier still learnt from the holy scriptures, that wise, brave and vertuous men were always friends to liberty; that God gave the Israelites a king [or absolute monarch] in his anger, because they had not sense and virtue enough to like a free commonwealth, and to have himself for their king; that the Son of God came down from heaven, to make us "free indeed"; and that "where the Spirit of the Lord is, there is liberty"; this made me conclude, that freedom was a great blessing. Having, also, from my childhood up, by the kind providence of my God, and the tender care of a good parent now at rest with him, been educated to the love of liberty, tho' not of licentiousness; which chaste and virtuous passion was still increased in me, as I advanced towards, and into, manhood; I would not, I cannot now, tho' past middle age, relinquish the fair object of my youthful affections, liberty; whose charms, instead of decaying with time in my eyes, have daily captivated me more and more. I was, accordingly, penetrated with the most sensible grief, when, about the *first of November last*, the day of darkness, a day hardly to be numbered with the other days of the year, she seemed about to take her final departure from America, and to leave that ugly hag slavery, the deformed child of Satan, in her room. I am now filled with a proportionable degree of joy in God, on occasion of her speedy return, with new smiles on her face, with augmented beauty and splendor. Once more then, Hail! celestial maid, the daughter of God, and, excepting his Son, the first-born of heaven! Welcome to these shores again; welcome to every expanding heart! Long mayest thou reside among us, the delight of the wise, good and brave; the protectress of innocence from wrongs and oppression, the patroness of learning, arts, eloquence, virtue, rational loyalty, religion! And if any miserable people on the continent or isles of Europe, after being weakened by luxury, debauchery, venality, intestine quarrels, or other vices, should, in the rude collisions, or now-uncertain revolutions of kingdoms, be driven, in their extremity, to seek a safe retreat from slavery in some far-distant climate; let them find, O let them find one in America under thy brooding, sacred wings; where our oppressed fathers once found it, and we now enjoy it, by the favor of him, whose service is the most glorious freedom! Never, O never may he permit thee to forsake us, for our unworthiness to enjoy thy enlivening presence! By his high permission, attend us thro' life and death to the regions of the blessed, thy original abode, there to enjoy forever the "glorious liberty of the sons of God!" But I forget myself; whither have I been hurried by this enthusiasm, or whatever else you will please to call it? I hope your candor will forgive this odd excursion, for which I hardly know how to account myself. There were two or three things more which I intended to say relative to this joyful occasion.

To go on then, these colonies are better than ever apprised of their own weight and consequence, when united in a legal opposition to any unconstitutional, hard and grievous treatment; which may be an advantage to them. God often bringeth good out of evil; or what is intended for evil by men, is by him meant for good. So it was particularly in the memorable case of Joseph, whom his hard-hearted, envious brethren sold as a slave into Egypt. There he became great, and his father and brethren were at length obliged to have recourse to him, to keep them and their's from perishing. And thus, not improbably, may good come out of our late troubles, as well as out of those oppressions, which occasioned the flight of our forefathers into the desarts of America. The great shock which was lately given to our liberties, may end in the confirmation and enlargement of them: As it is said, the stately oaks of the forest take the deeper root, extend their arms the farther, and exalt their venerable heads the higher for being agitated by storms and tempests, provided they are not actually torn up, rent in pieces, or quite blasted by the lightning of heaven. And who knows, our liberties being thus established, but that on some future occasion, when the kingdoms of the earth are moved, and roughly dashed one against another, by him that "taketh up the isles as a very little thing," we, or our posterity may even have the great felicity and honor to "save much people alive," and keep Britain herself from ruin. I hope she will never put it out of our power, by destroying us; or out of the inclination of any, by attempting it.

It is to be hoped, the colonies will never abuse or misapply any influence which they may have, when united as aforesaid; or discover a spirit of murmuring, discontent or impatience under the government of Great Britain, so long as they are justly and kindly treated. On the other hand, it is to be hoped, they will never lose a just sense of liberty, or what they may reasonably expect from the mother-country. These things they will keep in mind, if they are wise; and cultivate a firm friendship and union with each other upon equal terms, as far as distance and other circumstances will allow. And if ever there should be occasion, as I sincerely hope and pray there may not, their late experience and success will teach them how to act, in order to obtain the redress of grievances; I mean, by joint, manly and spirited, but yet respectful and loyal petitioning. Setting aside some excesses and outrages which all sober men join in condemning, I believe history affords few examples of a more general, generous and just sense of liberty in any country, than has appeared in America within the year past: In which time the mercantile part in particular have done themselves much honor, and had a great share in preserving the liberties of the plantations, when in the most imminent danger: Tho' this is not said with the least thought of reflecting on any other body or order of men, as wanting in their endeavours to the same noble end. Had we patiently received the yoke, no one can tell when, or whether ever it would have been taken off. And if there be some animals, adapted by nature to bear heavy burdens submissively, one of which, however, is said, on a certain occasion, to have had the gift of speech, and expostulated with his master for unjustly smiting him; I hope the Americans will never be reckoned as belonging to that spiritless, slavish kind, tho' their "powers of speech"† should not, in the opinion of some nameless, heroic pamphleteer-scoffers in Britain, exceed those of the other. However defective they may be in point of "eloqence,"* I thank God they can at least feel, and complain so as to be tolerably understood.

If your patience will hold out, I will add a few words further, by way of advice, and so conclude. While we endeavour to cultivate harmony and union with our mother-country and our sister-colonies, in all generous and manly ways, we should not, surely, neglect to cultivate the same among ourselves.

There have, I am sorry to say it, but really there have lately been many unwarrantable jealousies, and bitter mutual reproaches among the people of this town and province, occasioned by that unhappy measure, which has been so often referred to. Even wise and good men, tho' all equally against that measure, could not, however, agree what was to be done, upon the maxims of prudence, tho' alike concerned for the public welfare. Accordingly some were blamed as too warm and sanguine, others as too phlegmatic and indifferent, in the common and noble cause of liberty. Many were censured, and some, I am well assured, very unjustly, as being friends to, and encouragers of, the fatal measure aforesaid. But how far these accusations were just or unjust, on either side, I will not take upon me particularly to determine. Be that as it may, is it not best, my brethren, to let these

* An abusive, superficial pamphlet in favor of the measures of the late ministry.

contentions subside, now the end is obtained, and we have so fair a prospect before us? Are there any valuable ends to be answered by perpetuating these disputes? I cannot readily conceive any: Perhaps it is, because I have less penetration than most others. Be it as it will, I know one, and one whom we all profess to reverence, who hath said, "Blessed are the peacemakers, for they shall be called the children of God." And, "Let us study the things that make for peace," said he that was not behind the chief of the apostles, "and the things wherewith one may edify another." These sayings may apologize for me, if I am wrong in "preaching peace" at this time. And if none will be offended with me for speaking plainly as to this matter, To me it really seems most prudent, most christian, to bury in oblivion what is past; to begin our civil, political life anew as it were, from this joyful and glorious æra of restored and confirmed liberty; to be at union among ourselves; to abstain from all party names and national reflections, respecting any of our fellow subjects; and to exert ourselves, in our several stations, to promote the common good, "by love serving one another." Let us make allowances mutually for human frailty, for our different views and conceptions of things, which may be in a great measure unavoidable; for difference of natural constitution, an unequal flow of animal spirits, or strength of nerves: Let no one censure another more hardly, if at all, than the necessity of the case plainly requires. I hope these counsels of peace will not be disrelished by any "son of peace," or any wise and good man, that does me the honor to be my auditor on this occasion; for I mean not to give offence, but only to do good. Such counsels as they are, I humbly commend them to the God of love and peace, to whose holy will I believe them agreeable, for his blessing; that they may have their just influence on all that hear them. And you will not forget, that we must all one day give an account to him; so that it nearly concerns us to have our ways, motives, and all our doings approved by him. In fine,

Let us all apply ourselves with diligence, and in the fear of God, to the duties of our respective stations. There has been a general dissipation among us for a long time; a great neglect and stagnation of business. Even the poor, and labouring part of the community, whom I am very far from despising, have had so much to say about government and politics, in the late times of danger, tumult and confusion, that many of them seemed to forget, they had any thing to do. Methinks, it would now be expedient for them, and perhaps for most of us, to do something more, and talk something less; every one "studying to be quiet, and to do his own business"; letting things return peaceably into their old channels, and natural courses, after so long an interruption. My immediate aim in what I now say, being only to recommend industry, good order and harmony, I will not meddle with the thorny question, whether, or how far, it may be justifiable for private men, at certain extraordinary conjunctures, to take the administration of government in some respects into their own hands. Self-preservation being a great and primary law of nature, and to be considered as antecedent to all civil laws and institutions, which are subordinate and subservient to the other; the right of so doing, in some circumstances, cannot well be denied. But certainly, there is no plausible pretence for such a conduct among us now. That which may be excuseable, and perhaps laudable, on some very singular emergencies, would at other times be pragmatical, seditious, and high-handed presumption. Let all therefore now join with heart and hand in supporting the lawful, constitutional government over us in its just dignity and vigor; in supporting his majesty's representative, the civil magistrates, and all persons in authority, in the lawful exercise of their several offices. No true friend of liberty can reasonably object against this; and if any persons should, it would shew that, while they speak great swelling words of vanity, making liberty the pretext, they themselves are the servants of corruption, the ignoble slaves of sin. Without this due regard to government and laws, we shall still be miserable, my friends, notwithstanding all that God and the king have done to make us happy. If one had wings like a dove, it were better to fly far away, and remain alone in the wilderness, where he might be at rest, than to live in a society where there is no order, no subordination; but anarchy and confusion reign. Of these we have surely had enough already; tho' at the same time I bless God, that there has not been much more, considering the great danger in which we have been, with the general alarm and consternation, by reason of that which is said to make "even a wise man mad," and much more the rash and indiscrete, of whom there is a great proportion in all communities; considering also the absolute necessity there was, or at least seemed to be, of some very uncommon struggles and exertions, in order to break the snare, and the natural impetuosity of many people's tempers. So important a change in the situation of public affairs, so great a deliverance, has, perhaps, seldom been brought about in any country, with so little criminal excess, unless it were done by God alone, without the instrumentality or agency of men, by nature liable to so many errors and infirmities. But whatever there has been of this kind, ought to bc, and I hope is, lamented by all good men. May that God, in whom our help has been, continue to protect us, our rights and privileges! May he direct our paths thro' this uncertain life, and all the changes of it; and, of his infinite mercy in Jesus Christ, finally bring us all to those peaceful and glorious regions, where no evil spirits, no wicked fowlers will come; where no snares will be spread for us; no *proud waters to go over our soul!* And if we hope for admission into those eternal mansions of joy, let every one of us, as the apostle Peter exhorts, "honor all men, love the brotherhood, fear GOD, honor the king.

AMEN

9

AN HUMBLE ENQUIRY

John Joachim Zubly

SAVANNAH[?]

1769

John Joachim Zubly (1724–1781). Born and educated in St. Gall, Switzerland, Zubly was ordained at the German Church in London in 1744 and went to South Carolina the same year to join his father. After preaching in various churches in South Carolina and Georgia, he became pastor in 1760 of the Independent Presbyterian Church in Savannah. Fluent in six languages, Zubly was widely read; John Adams called him a "learned man." The College of New Jersey gave him an honorary A.M. in 1770 and a D.D. four years later. He took an early lead in representing the dissenting denominations against the threat of Anglican tyranny. During the Stamp Act crisis he was a powerful voice for American rights. A delegate to the Georgia Provincial Congress in 1775, he was soon thereafter elected one of the colony's five representatives to the Continental Congress, where he took a prominent role. Although, by fall of that year, it had become clear that independence was in the air, Zubly did not favor that course. After being denounced by Samuel Chase (perhaps for asserting in Congress that republics are "little better than government of devils"), Zubly abruptly departed Philadelphia on November 10, 1775. In 1777 he was banished from Georgia as a Tory, and half his property was confiscated. He found shelter for a time with friends in South Carolina. When royal government was reestablished in Georgia, he was able to return and partially resume his pastoral duties in Savannah.

The leading spokesman for Georgia in the dispute with Great Britain, Zubly is regarded as an impressive literary figure of the time. His *An Humble Enquiry*, published pseudonymously (1769), presents a powerful constitutional argument against the 1766 Declaratory Act in response to Parliament's Townshend Acts.

A N

HUMBLE ENQUIRY

I N T O

The NATURE of the DEPENDENCY of the *AMERICAN* COLONIES upon the PARLIAMENT of *GREAT-BRITAIN*,

A N D

The RIGHT of PARLIAMENT to lay TAXES on the said COLONIES.

By a FREEHOLDER of *SOUTH-CAROLINA*.

A House divided against itself cannot stand.

When people heard ship money demanded *as a right*, and found it by sworn judges of the law adjudged so, upon such grounds and reasons as every stander-by was able to swear was not law, and so had lost the pleasure and delight of being kind and dutiful to the King, and, instead of GIVING, were required to PAY, and by a logick that left no man any thing that he might call his own, they no more looked upon it as the case of one man, but the case of the kingdom, nor as an imposition laid upon them by the King, but by the judges, which they thought themselves bound in publick justice not to submit to. It was an observation long ago of *Thucydides*, "That men are much more passionate for injustice "than for violence, because (saith he) the one proceeding as from an equal seems "rapine, when the other proceeding from a stranger is but the effect of necessity." —When they saw reason of state urged as elements of law, judges as sharp-sighted as secretaries of state, judgment of law grounded upon matter of fact of which there was neither enquiry, nor proof, and no reason given for the payment but what included all the estates of the standers-by, they had no reason to hope that doctrine, or the promoters of it, would be contained within any bounds; and it is no wonder that they who had so little reason to be pleased with their own condition were no less solicitous for, or apprehensive of the inconveniences that might attend any alteration.—*History of the long Rebellion, vol.* 1. *p.* 70, 71.

PRINTED in the YEAR M,DCC,LXIX.

[Price Twelve Shillings and Sixpence.]

Though few or none claim infallibility in express terms, yet it is very difficult ever to persuade some men they are mistaken. We generally have so good an opinion of our own understanding, that insensibly we take it for granted those that do not think as we do must needs be in the wrong. When disputes are once heightened by personal prejudice, or the bitterness of party, it becomes so much the more difficult to the disputants themselves to see their mistakes, and even to bystanders the truth appears wrapped up in a cloud, and through the fog and dust of argument becomes almost imperceptible.

These remarks I believe will particularly hold good in the subject now in agitation between Great-Britain and her colonies, a subject however of too serious a nature to be given up to prejudice, or to be decided by the rage of party. Every argument *pro* or *con* deserves to be most carefully weighed, and he that sets the whole in the clearest light does the publick no inconsiderable service, and that whether it be by pointing out the justice of the American claims to Great-Britain, or setting such constitutional arguments before the Americans as must either leave obstinacy inexcusable, or will dispose loyal and reasonable men to a chearful acquiescence.

The argument on which the Americans seem to lay the greatest stress is, they say that it is a principle of the British constitution, that no Englishman ought to be taxed but by his own consent, given either by himself or his representative. I find it admitted by such as disapprove the American claims, that no man is bound by any law to which he hath not given his consent either in person or by a representative. Perhaps these two propositions are not perfectly equivalent; however it seems clear, that he that holds that no man is bound by any law to which he has not personally or by a representative consented, must also admit, that no man is bound by any law that lays a tax on him without his consent given by himself or representative. What is true of all laws in general must also hold true of every law in particular. If no law can operate upon any man that hath not in the above manner given his assent to it, certainly no such law can be binding upon whole communities, or any considerable part of the whole nation. In the spirit of the above principle, it seems essential to law, that it be assented to by such on whom it is afterwards to operate. To suppose, therefore, that a law is binding upon such as have not given their assent, is to suppose (I argue upon that principle) a law may be valid and binding at the same time it is confessedly destitute of the very essential point to make it so; and if the assent of those that are to be governed by the law is not necessary or essential to the making of it, then representation is a mere superfluous thing, no better than an excrescence in the legislative power, which therefore at any convenient time may be lopped off at pleasure, and without the least danger to the constitution; the governed then have no part in the legislation at all, the will of those in power, whoever they be, is the supreme and sole law, and what hath been above asserted to be a constitutional principle seems to me to fall to the ground without remedy to all intents and purposes.

Supposing, on the other hand, that principle, as is asserted to be constitutional, then to me, as is further asserted, it seems to be of the very nature of it, that it be general and hold in all cases. This it does not only clearly imply, but also fully and strongly express; but yet if so, it would also seem that no man, or no people, in no case, or by no power whatever, can be bound to pay a tax to which they have not consented either personally or by their representatives. Every constitutional principle must be general and hold in all cases, and I may add in all places too, for it is usually said that the liberties of an Englishman follow him to the end of the world, much more then must they follow him over all the British dominions; this is so true, that by an express law, the children of British parents, though born in a foreign dominion, are just as much entitled to all British liberties as those who have been born within the realm.

An inference may possibly hence be drawn, that if so, the British colonies are subject to none of the acts of the British Parliament (*scil.* because they never assented to them neither in person nor by representative), and therefore must be considered as independent of the legal or parliamentary power of Great-Britain. I confess I should be sorry to see America independent of Great-Britain, and if any of the arguments the Americans make use of imply an independency on the mother state, I should shrewdly suspect there must be some fallacy couched under an otherwise specious appearance. The sum and strength of this inference I conceive lies thus: The British legislature must be the supreme power in all the British dominions, and if so, all the British dominions ought to pay obedience in all cases to all the laws in which they are mentioned that may be enacted by the British Parliament, and to refuse obedience in any such case is to declare themselves an independent people.

I freely own I have not heard any thing stronger said in favour of taxation by the British Parliament, and I think this argument is highly deserving the most serious consideration. Every good man would wish to hear the voice of dispassionate reason before he forms his judgment in any debate. Vulgar prejudices may sway vulgar minds, but a wise man is neither carried away by the torrent of power, nor the blast of popularity. I would endeavour therefore to consider this argument with all the candour and impartiality I am capable of; I would do it with a mind open to conviction, and with steadiness sufficient to follow truth wherever she may lead me.

To have a clear view how far this argument may affect the present question between Great-Britain and her colonies, it will be necessary carefully to state the relation which they bear to one another; without this we shall never have a precise and determinate idea of the matter. The argument I think is made up of two propositions, *viz.*

The Parliament of Great-Britain is the supreme legislature in all the British empire.

All the British dominions therefore ought to pay obedience thereto in all cases and to all the laws in which they are mentioned, and to refuse obedience to any such is to declare themselves an independent people.

Before I proceed to take a distinct view of each of these propositions, I repeat, that they are said to be built upon a constitutional principle, and that this principle must be general and hold in all cases; this must undoubtedly be admitted, for what enters into the very essence of the constitution must doubtless operate as far as the constitution itself. Let us now proceed to consider every part of these two propositions distinctly, and this must infallibly lead us to form a sound judgment of the whole.

The kingdom of Great-Britain consists of two parts, north and south, or England and Scotland, united since 1707 into one kingdom, under the name of Great-Britain. This union hath not been so full and absolute, as to put both kingdoms in all respects upon a perfect equality; but tho' the legislature is the same, yet the laws and the administration of justice are not the same in every instance. The same legislature making laws that affect only the one or the other of these kingdoms, and even laws made to be binding upon both, do not affect both alike, of which the difference in raising the supplies by land tax is a very full and striking proof, this could not be the case if the union between the two kingdoms was so entire and absolute, as for instance between England and the principality of Wales.

The British Empire is a more extensive word, and should not be confounded with the kingdom of Great-Britain; it consists of England, Scotland, Ireland, the Islands of Man, Jersey, Guernsey, Gibraltar, and Minorca, *&c.* in the Mediterranean; Senegal, *&c.* in Africa; Bombay, *&c.* in the East-Indies; and the Islands and Colonies in North-America, *&c.* As England, strictly so called, is at the head of this great body, it is called the mother country; all the settled inhabitants of this vast empire are called Englishmen, but individuals, from the place of their nativity or residence, are called English, Scotch, Irish, Welch, Americans, *&c.*

Scotland and Ireland were originally distinct kingdoms and nations, but the colonies in America, being settled upon lands discovered by the English, under charters from the crown of England, were always considered as a part of the English nation, and of the British empire, and looked upon as dependent upon England; I mean, that before the union of the two kingdoms (and very few colonies have been settled since), they depended on England only, and even now I suppose are rather considered as a dependance upon England than of the two kingdoms united under the name of Great-Britain. Were it not for the union, which incorporates the two kingdoms, the colonies never would have depended on that part of Britain called Scotland, and by the terms of the union I apprehend England has not given up or brought her colonies under the dominion of Scotland, but tho' dependent on Great-Britain, they still remain what they always were, English colonies.

All the inhabitants of the British empire together form the British nation, and that the British Parliament is the supreme power and legislature in the British nation I never heard doubted.

By the English constitution, which is that which prevails over the whole empire, all Englishmen, or all that make up the British empire, are entitled to certain privileges indefeasible, unalienable, and of which they can never be deprived, but by the taking away of that constitution which gives them these privileges. I have observed that the British empire is made up of different kingdoms and nations, but it is not the original constitution of Scotland or Ireland, but of England, which extends and communicates its privileges to the whole empire. This is an undeniable principle, and ought never to be lost out of sight, if we would form a sound judgment on the question now to be considered.

From the consideration above admitted, that the British Parliament is the supreme legislative power in the whole British empire, the following conclusion has been drawn; the colonies (and the same I suppose is meant of all the British empire, of which the colonies are a part) are bound by and subject to all the laws of the British Parliament in which they are mentioned, or are subject to none of any kind whatsoever.

Before this can be properly discussed, it must be observed, that Great-Britain has not only a Parliament, which is the supreme legislature, but also a constitution, and that the now Parliament derives its authority and power from the constitution, and not the constitution from the Parliament. It may also be very fairly inferred hence, that the liberties of Englishmen arise from and depend on the English constitution, which is permanent and ever the same, whereas the individuals which compose the Parliament are changed at least once every seven years, and always at the demise of a king.

The Parliament of Great-Britain is the supreme legislature in the British empire. It must be so either absolutely or agreeable to the constitution; if absolutely, it can alter the constitution whenever it sees fit; if absolutely, it is not bound by the constitution, nor any thing else; if agreeable to the constitution, then it can no more make laws, which are against the constitution, or the unalterable privileges of British subjects, than it can alter the constitution itself. Supposing a Parliament, under some of the arbitrary reigns of the last century, should have made a law, that for the future the king's warrant should be sufficient to lay a tax on the subject, or to oblige him to pay ship money, it would have been an act of the supreme legislature, but it may safely be doubted, whether the nation would have thought it constitutional. I conclude therefore, that the power of Parliament, and of every branch of it, has its bounds assigned by the constitution.

If the power of the Parliament is limited by the constitution, it may not be improper next to enquire, whether the power of the British Parliament affects all the subjects of the British empire in the same manner.

If the power of the British Parliament affects all the subjects of the British empire in the same manner, it follows, that all the laws made by the British Parliament are binding alike upon all those over whom this power extends, or in other words, that all the subjects of the British empire are bound not only by those laws in which they are expressly mentioned, but every law by the Parliament made, for what need is there to mention every individual of those for whom the law is made in general, every subject therefore of the British empire, upon this supposition, must be bound by every law of the British Parliament, unless expressly excepted.

Those that hold the subjects of Great-Britain, living without England or Scotland, are bound by every law in which they are mentioned, seem also clearly to hold, that the same persons are not bound by such laws in which they are not mentioned. Thus the alternative, that the subjects of the British empire must be subject to all or none of the laws of the British Parliament, is limited even by those who plead for an universal submission. He that is only bound to obey some laws, cannot be said to be bound by all laws, as, on the contrary, he that is bound to obey all laws, is excused in none.

I suppose, before the union with Scotland, none would have scrupled to call the English Parliament the supreme legislature of all the British empire, though Scotland was still an independent kingdom, and by the union Scotland and its Parliament was not swallowed up and absorbed by England and its Parliament, but united with the kingdom, and the Parliaments also of the two kingdoms united in one general legislature. The ecclesiastical laws and constitution also of each kingdom remains as it was before, *i.e.* entirely different from each other.

Perhaps it may not be amiss to conceive, that the authority of the

British Parliament extends over the whole British nation, though the different respective subjects are not altogether alike affected by its laws: That, with regard to national trade, the power of making it most beneficial to the head and every branch of the empire is vested in the British Parliament, as the supreme power in the nation, and that all the British subjects every where have a right to be ruled by the known principles of their common constitution.

Next, it may be proper to take a nearer view how far, and in what manner, the acts of Parliament operate upon the different subjects of the British empire.

England doubtless is the first and primary object of the British Parliament, and therefore all laws immediately affect every resident in England; and of the king himself it has been said, *Rex Angliæ in regno suo non habet superiorem nisi Deum & legem*. Proceedings at law I take to be the same in England and England's dependencies.

Scotland is united with England, and therefore there is a different operation of the laws that subsisted before and those that have been made since the union, and even these do not affect Scotland as of themselves; but in consequence of and in the terms of the union between the two nations, the union makes no alteration in proceedings at law, nor does it take away any private property.

Ireland is a distinct kingdom, and hath been conquered from the native Irish two or three times by the English; it hath nevertheless a Parliament of its own, and is a part of the British empire. It will best appear how far the British Parliament think Ireland dependent upon Great-Britain, by inserting, *A Bill for the better securing of the Dependency of Ireland*. The act was as follows:

> Whereas attempts have lately been made to shake off the subjection of Ireland unto, and dependence upon the imperial crown of this realm, which will be of dangerous consequence to Great-Britain and Ireland. And whereas the House of Lords in Ireland, in order thereto, have, of late, against law, assumed to themselves a power and jurisdiction to examine, correct and amend, the judgment and decrees of the courts of justice in the kingdom of Ireland; therefore, for the better securing of the dependency of Ireland upon the crown of Great-Britain, may it please your Majesty, that it may be enacted, and it is hereby declared and enacted, by the King's most excellent Majesty, by and with the advice and consent of the Lords Spiritual and Temporal, and Commons, in this present Parliament assem-

> bled, and by the authority of the same, That the said kingdom of Ireland hath been, is, and of right ought to be, subordinate unto, and dependent upon the imperial crown of Great-Britain, as being inseparably united and annexed thereunto, and that the King's Majesty, by and with the advice and consent of the Lords Spiritual and Temporal, and Commons of Great-Britain, in Parliament assembled, had, hath, and of right ought to have, full power and authority to make laws and statutes of sufficient force and validity to bind the people and kingdom of Ireland.
>
> And be it farther enacted, by the authority aforesaid, That the House of Lords of Ireland have not, nor of right ought to have, any jurisdiction to judge of, affirm, or reverse any judgment, sentence, or decree, given or made in any court within the said kingdom, and that all proceedings before the House of Lords upon any such judgment, sentence, or decree, are, and are hereby declared to be utterly null and void to all intents and purposes whatsoever.

The occasion of this bill was an appeal brought 1719 from the House of Peers in Ireland to the House of Peers in England. A Pitt was the first that spoke against it in the House of Commons, because, as he said, in his opinion it seemed calculated for no other purpose than to encrease the power of the British House of Peers, which in his opinion was already but too great. The duke of Leeds protested against it in the House of Lords, and gave fifteen reasons to support the claim of the House of Peers in Ireland. The bill however passed, though Mr. Hungerford, Lord Molesworth, Lord Tyrconel, and other members, endeavoured to shew, that Ireland was ever independent with respect to courts of judicature. Some proposals have several years ago been made to incorporate Ireland with Great-Britain, but without any effect.

The Islands of Guernsey and Jersey, though in ecclesiastical matters considered as a part of Hampshire, are under the direction of an assembly called the Convention of the States of Jersey, *&c.* The Isle of Man hath lately been annexed to the crown, but their own Manks laws still obtain in the island.

The British colonies and islands in America are not the least important part of the British empire; that these owe a constitutional dependence to the British Parliament I never heard they denied; though of late they have frequently been charged with it, these charges have not been grounded upon any declaration of theirs of the kind, their very petitioning, petitions and resolutions, manifestly speaking the very reverse; but their aversion to certain new duties, laid upon them for the sole purpose of raising a revenue, have been made a handle of against them, and they have as good as been charged, that they declare themselves an independent people. These insinuations the Americans are apt to look upon as being neither very fair nor very friendly; however at present I would only consider what kind of dependence is expected from the American colonies. An act of Parliament has fixed that of Ireland; a later act of the same power hath also fixed that of America, though, as will appear from the comparison, not altogether on the same footing. The act is entitled, *An Act for the better securing the Dependency of his Majesty's Dominions in America upon the Crown and Parliament of Great-Britain*, and runs thus:

> Whereas several of the Houses of Representatives in his Majesty's colonies and plantations in America have of late, against law, claimed to themselves, or to the General Assemblies of the same, the sole and exclusive right of imposing duties and taxes upon his Majesty's subjects in the said colonies and plantations, and, in pursuance of such claim, passed certain votes, resolutions and orders, derogatory to the legislative authority of Parliament, and inconsistent with the dependency of the said colonies and plantations upon the crown of Great-Britain, may it therefore please your most excellent Majesty, that it may be declared, and be it declared, by the King's most excellent Majesty, by and with the advice and consent of the Lords Spiritual and Temporal, and Commons, in the present Parliament assembled, and by the authority of the same, That the said colonies and plantations in America have been, are, and of right ought to be, subordinate unto and dependent upon the imperial crown and Parliament of Great-Britain, and that the King's Majesty, by and with the advice and consent of the Lords Spiritual and Temporal, and Commons, of Great-Britain, in Parliament assembled, had, hath, and of right ought to have, full power and authority to make laws and statutes of sufficient force and validity to bind the colonies and people of America, subjects of the crown of Great-Britain, in all cases whatsoever.
>
> And be it further declared and enacted, by the authority aforesaid, That all resolutions, votes, orders and proceedings, in any of the said colonies or plantations, whereby the power and authority of the Parliament of Great-Britain to make laws and statutes as aforesaid is denied, or drawn into question, are, and are hereby declared to be utterly null and void to all intents and purposes whatsoever.

This is the standard of dependence which the Parliament of Great-Britain hath fixed for the British colonies on the 18th of March, 1766. The Stamp Act was repealed the same day, and the opinion of several noblemen who protested against that repeal was,

> that this declaratory bill cannot possibly obviate the growing mischiefs in America, where it may seem calculated only to deceive the people of Great-Britain, by holding forth a delusive and nugatory affirmance of the legislative right of Great-Britain, whilst the enacting part of it does no more than abrogate the resolutions of the House of Representatives in the North-American colonies, which have not in themselves the least colour of authority, and declares that which is apparently and certainly criminal only null and void.

I presume I may venture to affirm, that in and by this act, the Parliament did not mean to set aside the constitution, infringe the liberties of British subjects, or to vindicate unto themselves an authority which it had not before, was known to have, and would always have had, though this act had never been made. I also find, that, in order to overset any act, law, resolution, or proceeding, of the colony assemblies, nothing seems necessary, but that the Parliament should declare it null and void to all intents and purposes whatsoever. And it seems pretty clear, that the same power that can disannul any act by a simple declaration, with one single stroke more, can also annihilate the body that made it.

The remark already made, that though all the different parts of the British empire are in a state of dependence upon the Parliament of Great-Britain, yet that the nature and degree of dependence is not exactly alike in the respective different parts of the same, will receive new strength and light, if we compare the act for better securing the dependency of Ireland with that for better securing the dependency of the colonies. Both acts, though at different times, have been made by the same authority, and for a similar purpose, and none can better tell us what kind and degree of dependency the Parliament expects and requires of its dependents than the Parliament itself.

The Irish is entitled in very general words, for the better securing the dependency of Ireland.

The title of the American law is more explicit; Ireland's dependency is mentioned, but the dependency of the Americans is more clearly expressed, and said to be upon the crown and Parliament of Great-Britain. America seems to owe two dependencies, one to the crown, and one to the Parliament.

The preamble of the Irish bill brings no less a charge than an attempt to shake off subjection unto and dependence upon the imperial crown of Great-Britain.

The preamble of the American bill brings no such accusation, but only, that the Americans have claimed an exclusive right to lay on taxes on his majesty's subjects within the colonies, and passed votes and resolutions derogatory to the legislative power of Parliament, and inconsistent with the dependency of the said colonies and plantations upon the crown (the word and Parliament is not made use of in this place) of Great-Britain. The principal differences between these bills seems to me to lie in this, that Ireland is said to be subject to and dependent only on the crown of Great-Britain, whereas America throughout is declared subject, at least dependent and subordinate, not only to the crown, but also to the Parliament of Great-Britain, and then Ireland is only declared dependent upon, and subordinate to, in very gentle terms, whereas the right of making laws to bind the Americans is expressed in these very strong, most extensive terms, *in all cases whatsoever*.

Time was when the dependency of the colonies upon England was spoke of exactly in the terms made use of for Ireland; the charter of this province saith, "our pleasure is, that the tenants and inhabitants of the said province be subject *immediately* to the crown of England, as depending thereof forever"; but by the late law all America is said to be dependent on crown and Parliament. This alteration seems to me by no means immaterial, but to imply a change both in the subjection expected from the colony and in the authority to which the colony owes dependency and subordination. In Parliament, king, lords, and commons, constitute the supreme power; but as each of these has its own distinct unalienable right, and incommunicable prerogatives, rights, or privileges, so I cannot but conceive dependency upon the crown and dependency upon crown and Parliament are things not exactly alike. If (as asserted in the charter) the colonies at some time or other were only dependent on the crown, and now are subordinate unto and dependent upon crown and Parliament, it should seem both the authority on which they depend, and the nature of their dependency, hath undergone some alteration; neither doth this appear to me a trifling alteration, and it seems to me at least if so it must needs make some alteration in the system of government and obedience.

Hitherto all appeals from the colonies, after passing thro' chancery in America, have been made to the king in council; this I conceive must have been in consequence of the dependency of the colonies immediately upon the crown; but perhaps for the future appeals will not be carried to the king in council, but to the king and Parliament.

The crown has hitherto had a right of a negative upon all American laws, and they were obliged to be passed in America with a saving clause; but if, as is asserted in the declaratory bill, the king has a right and power to make laws to bind the Americans, *by and with the advice and consent of the lords spiritual and temporal, and commons of Great-Britain, assembled in Parliament*, then probably the same authority must also concur to repeal the laws made in America, whereas the crown hitherto repealed any law made in America without asking or waiting for the consent of Lords and Commons.

It appears also, by a late act suspending the assembly of New-York, that the parliamentary authority also extends to suspend, which is but another word for proroguing or dissolving (or annihilating) assemblies; all which has hitherto been done by the crown without the interfering of Parliament: But that the crown hath a right of proroguing or dissolving the Parliament itself by its own authority I suppose will not be denied. I cannot dismiss this subject without observing, that even the declaratory bill speaks of the assemblies in America as Houses of Representatives. If it is allowed that they are represented in America, unless they are represented doubly, they cannot be represented any where else; this strikes at the root of virtual representation, and if representation is the basis of taxation, they cannot be taxed but where they are represented, unless they are doubly taxed, as well as doubly represented.

It is evident upon the whole, that a much greater degree of dependency and subordination is expected of America than of Ireland, though, by the way, Ireland, in the preamble of their bill, is charged with much greater guilt than America; nay, the words *in all cases whatsoever* are so exceeding extensive, that, in process of time, even hewing of wood, and drawing of water, might be argued to be included in them.

It was necessary to state the authority claimed by Parliament over America as clear and full as possible; with regard to the Americans it must be owned, when they profess to owe dependency and subordination to the British Parliament, they do not mean so extensive and absolute a dependency as here seems to be claimed, but that they think themselves in a constitutional manner dependent upon and in subordination to the crown and Parliament of Great-Britain, even those votes, resolutions, and proceedings, which are disannulled by the House of Commons and the declaratory bill, most fully and chearfully declare.

It has indeed been said, that unless they are subject to all the British acts in which they are mentioned, they are subject to none of any kind whatsoever, and consequently to be considered as independent of the legal and parliamentary power of Great-Britain; but I should think it might be as fairly and safely concluded, that while the Americans declare themselves subject to any one law of the British legislature, it cannot be said they declare themselves independent, or not subject to any law whatever.

In so delicate and important a matter, may I be permitted to observe, that the measure of power and of obedience in every country must be determined by the standard of its constitution. The dispute seems to lie between the Parliament and colonies; the Parliament will certainly be the sitting judges; I will not take upon me to say that the Americans may not look upon Parliament as judge and party; however, it is very possible for a judge to give a most righteous sentence, even where he himself is deeply interested, but they that are sufferers by the sentence will ever be apt to wish that he had not been party as well as judge.

From what hath been said hitherto, the due and constitutional authority of the British Parliament appears clear, and it does not less so I hope, that the subordination to and dependency on the British Parliament is not exactly the same in all the respective parts of that extensive empire; perhaps this will appear with still greater evidence by taking a particular view of the subject of taxation.

Any unlimited power and authority may lay on the subjects any tax it pleaseth; the subjects in that case themselves are mere property, and doubtless their substance and labour must be at their disposal who have the disposal of their persons. This is the case in arbitrary governments; but the British empire is an empire of freemen, no power is absolute but that of the laws, and, as hath been asserted, of such laws to which they that are bound by them have themselves consented.

Did the power and authority of the British Parliament in point of taxation extend in the same manner over all its dependencies, *e.g.* the same over Scotland as over England, over Ireland in the same manner as over Scotland, over Guernsey and Jersey as over Ireland, *&c.* then the very same act which lays a general tax would lay it also at the same time upon all over whom that authority extends. The laws of every legislature are supposed to extend to and be made over all within their jurisdiction, unless they are expressly excepted. Thus an excise law extends to all the British kingdom, because it is a publick law, but acts have frequently been made to lay on a penny Scots on beer, which, being for a local purpose, cannot operate on the whole kingdom. The same I believe may be said with regard to the method of recovering small debts; it seems absurd to say, that any supreme legislature makes an unlimited law which at the same time is designed not to be binding upon the greatest part of the subjects within that empire. Was it ever known that the land tax being laid on the whole united kingdom, the bishoprick of Durham, and the manor of East-Greenwich, were not also supposed to be included? and if any part within the immediate jurisdiction, and equally dependent on the same legislature, should be designed to be excused from, or not liable to pay a general tax, would it not be absolutely necessary that such a place should be expressly excepted? If, because America is a part of the British empire, it is as much so, or in the same manner is a part of it, as is the bishoprick of Durham, or the manor of East-Greenwich, nothing can be plainer than that it must be affected by every tax that is laid just in the same manner and proportion as is the bishoprick of Durham, or manor of East-Greenwich. This hath not been the case, nor thought to be the case hitherto. Ireland and America have not been called upon to pay the British land tax, malt tax, nor indeed any tax in which they have not been expressly mentioned; the reason of which I presume must be, either that the British

Parliament did not look upon them as any part of the kingdom of Great-Britain, or else did not think them liable to any tax in which they were not expressly mentioned. If any subjects of the British empire are not liable to any or every tax laid on by the British Parliament, it must be either because they are not liable by the constitution (as not being represented), or because they are excused by the favour of Parliament; if they are not liable by the privileges of the constitution, their not being compelled to pay is no favour, the contrary would be oppression and an anticonstitutional act; if they have been hitherto excused by the lenity of the British Parliament, it must be owned the Parliament bore harder on those who were made to pay those taxes than on those who by their lenity only were excused.

The noble lords who protested against the repeal of the Stamp Act observe,

> it appears to us, that a most essential part of that authority (*sc.* the whole legislative authority of Great-Britain, without any distinction or reserve whatsoever), the power of legislation, cannot be properly, equitably, or impartially exercised, if it does not extend itself to all the members of the state in proportion to their respective abilities, but suffers a part to be exempt from a due share of those burdens which the publick exigencies require to be imposed upon the whole: A partiality which is directly and manifestly repugnant to the trust reposed by the people in every legislature, and destructive of that confidence on which all government is founded.

If in the opinion of these noblemen, therefore, it is partiality to suffer any part of the state to be exempt from a due share of those burdens which the publick exigencies require should be imposed upon the whole, it would also seem to be a species of partiality, to lay a burden on any part of the state which the other parts of the same state are not equally bound to bear. Partial burdens, or partial exemptions, would doubtless affect those that are burdened or exempted in a very different manner; but if not extending alike to the whole, must still be looked upon as partial. And if this partiality is inconsistent with the trust *reposed by the people in every legislature*, it would also seem that the legislature could not lay any burdens but as entrusted by the people who chose them to be their representatives and a part of the legislature. We may hence also learn what is to be expected, if every other part of the British empire, England and Scotland only excepted, have hitherto been exempted from the taxes paid in England, which it must be owned are very heavy, by mere favour; or, as some seem to express it, "*flagrant partiality and injustice*"; their being indulged time immemorial will not be deemed a sufficient plea to excuse them always, but with an impartial hand the very same taxes that now obtain in Great-Britain will be laid upon Ireland, America, Jersey, Guernsey, the Mediterranean, African and East-India settlements, and, in short, on every individual part of the British empire. Whether a design to do this be not ripening apace I will not take upon me to say, but whenever it does, it must make some alteration in the policy of the mother and infant state, nay in the system of the whole British empire.

There are several parts of the British empire that pay no tax at all; this I take to be the case of Gibraltar, Minorca, Newfoundland, East-Florida, and all the African and East-India settlements, *&c.* The reason is, that all these places have no legislature of their own, and consequently none to give or dispose of their property; had these places been taxed by Parliament, there might however this reason been given, that having no representatives within themselves, and having never contributed any thing to the publick burdens, though they all receive protection, perhaps greater than the American colonies, the Parliament supplied that defect; but this cannot be urged against the colonies, who both have legislatures, and also contributed to the publick burdens, and that so liberally, that even the crown and Parliament thought they had exerted themselves beyond their abilities, and for several years gave them some compensation. I may mention those parts of the British empire as striking instances, that where there is no representation, taxation hath not been thought of, and yet Newfoundland, which is not taxed at all, is certainly as much represented in Parliament as all the colonies, which are designed to be doubly taxed.

By the constitution taxes are in the nature of a free gift of the subjects to the crown; regulations of trade are measures to secure and improve the trade of the whole nation. There is no doubt but regulations may be made to ruin as well as to improve trade; yet without regulations trade cannot subsist, but must suffer and sink; and it seems no where more proper to lodge the power of making these regulations than in the highest court of the empire; yet a man may trade or not, he may buy or let it alone; if merchandizes are rated so high that they will not suit him to purchase, though it may be an inconvenience, yet there is no law to compel him to buy; to rate the necessaries of life, without which a man cannot well do, beyond their real value, and hinder him at the same time from purchasing them reasonably of others, is scarce consistent with freedom; but when duties are laid on merchandizes not to regulate trade, but for the express and sole purpose of raising a revenue, they are to all intents and purposes equal to any tax, but they can by no means be called the free gift of those who never helped to make the law, but, as far as in them lay, ever looked upon it as an unconstitutional grievance.

If taxes are a free *gift* of the people to the crown, then the crown hath no right to them but what is derived from the givers. It may be absolutely necessary that the subject should give, but still he that is to give must be supposed the judge both of that necessity, and how much he may be able and ought to give upon every necessary occasion. No man can give what is not his own, and therefore the constitution hath placed this right to judge of the necessity, and of what is to be given, in the Commons as the representatives of all those who are to give, in vesting a right in them to give publick supplies to the crown; it did not, could not mean to invest them with any power to give what neither belongs to them, nor those whom they represent; and therefore, as no man constitutionally "owes obedience to any law to which he has not assented either in person or by his representative"; much less doth the constitution oblige any man to part with his property, but freely and by his own consent; what those who are representatives are not willing to give, no power in Great-Britain hath any right violently to take, and for a man to have his property took from him under pretence of a law that is not constitutional, would not be much better than to have it took from him against the express consent of those whom he constitutionally made his representatives.

It is held a maxim, that in government a proportion ought to be observed between the share in the legislature and the burden to be borne. The Americans pretend to no share in the legislature of Great-Britain at all, but they hope they have never forfeited their share in the constitution.

Every government supposes rule and protection from the governors, support and obedience from those that are governed; from these duly tempered arises the prerogative of the crown and the liberty of the subject; but he that has not a right to his own hath no property, and he that must part with his property by laws against his consent, or the consent of the majority of the people, has no liberty. The British constitution is made to secure liberty and property; whatever takes away these takes away the constitution itself, and cannot be constitutional.

To form a clear judgment on the power of taxation, it must be enquired on what right that power is grounded. It is a fundamental maxim of English law, that there is a contract between the crown and subjects; if so, the crown cannot lay on any tax, or any other burden, on the subject, but agreeable to the original contract by authority of Parliament; neither can the Lords properly concur, or the Commons frame a tax bill for any other purpose but the support of the crown and government, consistent with the original contract between that and the people.

All subjects are dependent on and subordinate to the government under which they live. An Englishman in France must observe the laws of France; but it cannot be said that the dependency and subordination in England is the same as dependency and subordination in France. In governments where the will of the sovereign is the supreme law, the subjects have nothing to give, their all is in the disposal of the government; there subjects pay, but having nothing of their own cannot give; but in England the Commons *give* and *grant*. This implies both a free and voluntary act, and that they give nothing but their own property.

Though every part of the British empire is bound to support and promote the advantage of the whole, it is by no means necessary that this should be done by a tax indiscriminately laid on the whole; it seems sufficient that every part should contribute to the support of the whole as it may be best able, and as may best suit with the common constitution.

I have before observed the different degree of dependency on the mother state; I shall now review the same again, with a particular regard to imposing or paying taxes, and if a material difference hath always obtained in this respect, it will confirm my assertion, that every branch of the British empire is not affected by the tax laws of Great-Britain in the self same manner.

The Parliament has a right to tax, but this right is not inherent to the members of it as men; I mean, the members of Parliament are not (like the Senate of Venice) so many rulers who have each of them a native and inherent right to be the rulers of the people of England, or even their representatives; they do not meet together as a court of proprietors to consider their common interest, and agree with one another what tax they will lay on those over whom they bear rule, or whom they represent, but they only exercise that right which nature hath placed in the people in general, and which, as it cannot conveniently be exercised by the whole people, these have lodged in some of their body chosen from among themselves, and they themselves, for that purpose, and empowered for a time only to transact the affairs of the whole, and to agree in their behalf on such supplies as it may be necessary to furnish unto the crown for the support of its dignity, and the necessities and protection of the people.

It would be absurd to say, that the crown hath a right to lay on a tax, for as taxes are granted to the crown, so in this case the crown should make a grant to itself, and hence the bill of rights expressly asserts, that *the levying of money for or to the use of the crown, by pretence of prerogative, without grant of Parliament, for a longer time or in any other manner than the same is or shall be granted, is illegal*; hence also there is a material difference between money bills and all other laws. The king and lords cannot make any amendment in money bills, as the House of Lords frequently doth in all others, but must accept or refuse them such as they are offered by the Commons, the constitutional reason of which is very obvious, it is the people only that give, and therefore giving must be the sole act of those by whom the givers are represented. The crown cannot take till it is given, and they that give cannot give but on their own behalf, and of those whom they represent; nay even then they cannot give but in a constitutional manner; they cannot give the property of those they represent without giving their own also exactly in the same proportion; every bill must be equally binding upon all whom they represent, and upon every one that is a representative.

Every representative in Parliament is not a representative for the whole nation, but only for the particular place for which he hath been chosen. If any are chosen for a plurality of places, they can make their election only for one of them. The electors of Middlesex cannot chuse a representative but for Middlesex, and as the right of sitting depends entirely upon the election, it seems clear to demonstration, that no member can represent any but those by whom he hath been elected; if not elected he cannot represent them, and of course not consent to any thing in their behalf. While Great-Britain's representatives do not sit assembled in Parliament, no tax whatever can be laid by any power on Great-Britain's inhabitants; it is plain therefore, that without representation there can be no taxation. If representation arises entirely from the free election of the people, it is plain that the elected are not representatives in their own right, but by virtue of their election; and it is not less so, that the electors cannot confer any right on those whom they elect but what is inherent in themselves; the electors of London cannot confer or give any right to their members to lay a tax on Westminster, but the election made of them doubtless empowers them to agree to or differ from any measures they think agreeable or disagreeable to their constituents, or the kingdom in general. If the representatives have no right but what they derive from their electors and election, and if the electors have no right to elect any representatives but for themselves, and if the right of sitting in the House of Commons arises only from the election of those designed to be representatives, it is undeniable, that the power of taxation in the House of Commons cannot extend any further than to those who have delegated them for that purpose; and if none of the electors in England could give a power to those whom they elected to represent or tax any other part of his majesty's dominions except themselves, it must follow, that when the Commons are met, they represent no other place or part of his majesty's dominions, and cannot give away the property but of those who have given them a power so to do by choosing them their representatives.

The Parliament hath the sole right to lay on taxes, and, as hath been observed in Parliament, 'tis not the king and lords that *give* and *grant*, but this is the sole act of the Commons. The Commons have the right to do so either from the crown or people, or it is a right inherent in themselves. It cannot be inherent in themselves, for they are not born representatives, but are so by election, and that not for life, but only for a certain time; neither can they derive it from the crown, else the liberty and property of the subject must be entirely in the disposal and possession of the crown; but if they hold it entirely from the people, they cannot hold it from any other people but those who have chosen them to be their representatives, and it should seem they cannot extend their power of taxing beyond the limits of time and place, nor indeed for any other purpose but that for which they have been chosen. As the Commons in Parliament cannot lay any tax but what they must pay themselves, and falls equally on the whole kingdom of England, so, by a fundamental law, they cannot lay out such a part of the general tax on some part of the united kingdom. The principality of Wales was never taxed by Parliament till it was incorporated and represented, and, poor as it is, it pays now considerably larger than Scotland, which is as big again. When England is taxed two millions in the land tax, no more is paid in Scotland than 48,000*l.* and yet to lay a higher land tax on North-Britain the British Parliament cannot, it cannot without breaking the union, that is, a fundamental law of the kingdom. All the right it hath to tax Scotland arises from and must be executed in the terms of the union.*

The Islands of Guernsey, *&c.* are not taxed by the British Parliament at all, they still have their own States, and I never heard that the British Parliament ever offered to hinder them to lay on their own taxes, or to lay on additional ones, where they are not represented.

Ireland is a conquered kingdom, the greater part of its inhabitants Papists, who in England pay double tax. The Romans always made a difference between their colonies and their conquests, and as reasonable, allowed greater and indeed all common liberties to the former. Ireland hath been conquered twice again upon the natives since its first conquest, nevertheless it hitherto had its own legislature; if the Parliament of Great-Britain claims a right to tax them, they never yet

* While Scotland was yet a separate kingdom, it was once debated in Parliament, whether a subsidy should first be granted, or overtures for liberty first be considered; when the queen's ministry insisted on the former, a member urged, that it was now plain the nation was to expect no return for their expence and toil, but to be put to the charge of a subsidy, and to lay down their necks under the yoke of slavery, *&c.* Another member said, that he insisted for having a vote upon the question which had been put: That he found as the liberties of the nation were suppressed, so the privileges of Parliament were like to be torn from them, but that he would rather venture his life than that it should be so, and should chuse rather *to die a freeman than live a slave*. Some pressed for the vote, adding, that if there was no other way of obtaining so natural and undeniable a privilege of the Parliament, *they would demand it with their swords in their hands*.

See Annals of Queen Anne for 1703, page 76. There were no American speakers.

have made use of that right, and seeing for ages past they enjoyed the privilege of having their own property disposed of by representatives in a Parliament of their own, it is very natural to suppose, that they think themselves entitled to these things, and the more so, because, in the very bill that determines their dependency, they are not said to be dependent on the British Parliament, nor yet on crown and Parliament, but only on the crown of Great-Britain.

I would now proceed to take a distinct view of the point in debate between Great-Britain and her colonies.

It seems to be a prevailing opinion in Great-Britain, that the Parliament hath a right to tax the Americans, and that, unless they have so, America would be independent of Great-Britain.

And it seems to be a prevailing opinion in America, that to be taxed without their consent, and where they are not and cannot be represented, would deprive them of the rights of Englishmen, nay, in time, with the loss of the constitution, would deprive them of liberty and property altogether.

It is easily seen, that this is a very interesting subject, the consequences in each case very important, though in neither so alarming and dangerous to Britain as to America. With regard to Great-Britain, if it should not prove so as is claimed, the consequence can only be this, that then no tax can be laid, or revenue be raised, on the Americans, but where they are represented, and in a manner which they think consistent with their natural rights as men, and with their civil and constitutional liberties as Britons. The dependency of America upon Great-Britain will be as full and firm as ever, and they will chearfully comply with the requisitions of the crown in a constitutional manner. The question is not, whether the Americans will withdraw their subordination, or refuse their assistance, but, whether they themselves shall give their own property, where they are legally represented, or, whether the Parliament of Great-Britain, which does not represent them, shall take their property, and dispose of it in the same manner as they do theirs whom in Parliament they actually represent. The Americans do not plead for a right to withhold, but freely and chearfully to give. If 100,000*l.* are to be raised, the question is not, shall they be raised or no? but shall the Parliament levy so much upon the Americans, and order them to pay it, as a gift and grant of the Commons of Great-Britain to the king? or, shall the Americans also have an opportunity to shew their loyalty and readiness to serve the king by freely granting it to the king themselves? It is not to be denied the Americans apprehend, that if any power, no matter what the name, where they are not represented, hath a right to lay a tax on them at pleasure, all their liberty and property is at an end, and they are upon a level with the meanest slaves.

England will not lose a shilling in point of property; the rights and privileges of the good people of Britain will not be in the least affected, supposing the claim of the Americans just and to take place; whereas every thing dreadful appears in view to the Americans if it should turn out otherwise. The crown cannot lose; the Americans are as willing to comply with every constitutional requisition as the British Parliament itself can possibly be. The Parliament cannot lose, it will still have all the power and authority it hitherto had, and ought to have had, and when every branch of the legislature, and every member of the British empire, has a true regard to reciprocal duty, prerogative and privilege, the happiness of the whole is best likely to be secured and promoted.

The Americans most solemnly disclaim every thought, and the very idea of independency; they are sometimes afraid they are charged with a desire of it, not because this appears to be the real cause, but to set their arguments in an invidious light, and to make them appear odious in the sight of their mother country. This is not a dispute about a punctilio, the difference in the consequence is amazingly great; supposing America is not taxed where not represented, and supposing things are left upon the same footing in which with manifest advantage to Britain and America they have been ever since Britain had colonies, neither the trade nor authority of Britain suffers the least diminution, but the mischief to the colonies is beyond all expression, if the contrary should take place. If they are not to raise their own taxes, all their assemblies become useless in a moment, all their respective legislatures are annihilated at a stroke; an act passed by persons, most of whom probably never saw, nor cared much for America, may destroy all the acts they ever passed, may lay every burden upon them under which they are not expected immediately to sink, and all their civil and religious liberties, for which their forefathers went into this wilderness, and, under the smiles of heaven, turned it into a garden, and of immense consequence to the mother country, will, or may be at an end at once. Probably the present Parliament or generation would never carry matters to this length, but who knows what might be done in the next? The first settlers of the American wilds never expected that would come to pass what we have seen already. It seems as if some evil genius had prevailed of late; had these new duties been laid on payable in England, at least the expence of a board of commissioners, and of the swarms of new officers, might have been prevented; but it looks as though some men wished that America might not only be borne hard upon, but also be made to know and feel that their liberty and property lay at the mercy of others, and that they must not flatter themselves to enjoy them any longer than the good pleasure of some who would willingly take away what they never did give. I have endeavoured candidly to state the question, let us now endeavour to view the claim made on each side as calmly and impartially as possible.

'Tis said the British Parliament hath a right to tax the Americans. If this proposition is incontrovertible, it must certainly be built on such a basis and such clear principles as will be sufficient to dispose loyal and reasonable men chearfully to acquiesce in it. There are some points in government which perhaps are best never touched upon, but when any question once becomes the subject of publick debate, strength of reason is the sole authority that with men of reason can determine the matter.

If the Parliament of Great-Britain have a right to tax the Americans, it must either be the same right in virtue of which they have a right to tax Great-Britain, and be vested in them by the same power, or it must be a distinct right either inherent in themselves, or vested in them by some other power.

The right of the Commons of Great-Britain to lay on taxes arises, as I conceive, from their having been chosen by the people who are to pay these taxes to act in their behalf and as their representatives. There may be other qualifications necessary, that a man be a Briton born, subject of the king, possessed of a certain estate, *&c.* but none is so absolutely necessary as election. He that hath been a representative had a right to refuse or concur in any tax bill whilst a member, but if he is not chosen again in a following Parliament, he hath no right whatever to meddle in the matter; this proves that the power is originally in the people, and the legislative capacity of the whole house, and of every member, depends upon their free election, and is of force no longer than for the time for which they have been elected; this being elapsed, the trust reposed in them entirely ceases, it absolutely returns to the body of the people; in that interval during which the people are unrepresented, any power their representatives might have is entirely and solely in the people themselves, no tax can be laid on, nor any law to bind the people be formed, for this plain reason, because there are no persons qualified for that purpose. The people have not representatives assigned, but chuse them, and being so chosen, the rights of the people reside now in them, and they may, but not before, act in their behalf. Now, when the crown issues writs of election, it is not to empower the electors to chuse representatives for America, nor yet for all Great-Britain, but only for some certain place specified in the writ; and when the electors of Great-Britain chuse representatives, their meaning also is not to chuse representatives for their fellow subjects in America, or any where else, but for themselves. In Great-Britain English electors cannot elect in behalf of Scotland, and Scotch electors cannot in behalf of England; and for the same reason neither Scotch nor English can elect any for America. These electors do not represent the Americans, nor are they their proxies to vote in members in their behalf; neither can British electors give any instructions to British representatives, or invest them with any power to dispose of the rights and property of any of their fellow subjects without the kingdom of Great-Britain. It seems not unreasonable then to conclude, that the right which the elected acquire by their election to pass tax laws binding upon their electors does not at the same time give them a right to represent and lay on taxes on those who never invested them with any such power, and by whom they neither were nor could be elected. If the Americans themselves are not received as voters in the bishoprick of Durham, manor of East-Greenwich, or any place mentioned in their charters, and the same liberty and privileges with those places therein secured unto them, if they are not allowed to chuse any representatives for themselves in the House of Commons, it seems natural, that what they have no right to do themselves, none can have a right to do for them, and so no body can chuse or send a representative for them to any place where they are not allowed to sit or be represented. If so, the electors of Great-Britain never in fact elected representatives for

America, nor could these electors possibly convey any power to give away property where they have no property themselves. The electors do not represent America, neither their representatives by them elected; the electors cannot dispose of the property of America, therefore they cannot give a power so to do unto others. In England there can be no taxation without representation, and no representation without election; but it is undeniable that the representatives of Great-Britain are not elected by nor for the Americans, and therefore cannot represent them; and so, if the Parliament of Great-Britain has a right to tax America, that right cannot possibly be grounded on the consideration that the people of Great-Britain have chosen them their representatives, without which choice they would be no Parliament at all.

If the Parliament of Great-Britain has a right to tax the Americans distinct from the right which they derive from their electors, and which they exercise as the representatives of the people of Great-Britain, then this right they must hold either from the crown, or from the Americans, or else it must be a native inherent right in themselves, at least a consequence of their being representatives of the people of Great-Britain.

It is plain that the colonies have been settled by authority and under the sanction of the crown, but as the crown did not reserve unto itself a right to rule over them without their own assemblies, but on the contrary established legislatures among them, as it did not reserve a right to lay taxes on them in a manner which, were the experiment made in England, might be thought unconstitutional, so neither do I find that a reserve of that kind was made by the crown in favour of the Parliament, on the contrary, by the charters all the inhabitants were promised the enjoyment of the same and all privileges of his majesty's liege subjects in England, of which doubtless not to be taxed where they are not represented is one of the principal. As to any right that might accrue to Parliament from any act or surrender of the Americans, I believe it hath never been thought of; they have a profound veneration for the British Parliament, they look upon it as the great palladium of the British liberties, but still they are not there represented, they have had their own legislatures and representatives for ages past, and as a body cannot be more than in one place at once, they think they cannot be legally represented in more than one legislative body, but also think, that by the laws of England Protestants ought not to be doubly taxed, or, what they think worse, taxed in two places.

If therefore this right of taxing the Americans resides in the Commons of Great-Britain at all, it must be an inherent right in themselves, or at least in consequence of their being representatives of the people of Great-Britain. The act for better securing the dependency of the colonies, which I have inserted at large, evidently seems to tend this way. That the colonies were thought at the disposal of Parliament one might be led to think, because by that act, from the simple authority of the crown, which they were till then subject to by their charters, they were now declared to be subordinate to and dependent (on the joint authority) of crown and Parliament. Yet, concerning this act, I would only observe, that however it may determine the case from that day, it cannot be the ground on which the subordination of the colonies originally was or now can be built; for it declares not only, that the colonies *are and ought to be*, but also that they *always have been*, subject to crown and Parliament. A law binds after it is made, it cannot bind before it exists, and so surely it cannot be said, that the colonies have always been bound by a law which is above a hundred years posterior to them in point of existence. It is also a little difficult to reconcile this law with prior charters; our Carolina charter makes our province subject immediately to the crown, and near a hundred years after a law is made to declare, that this was not and must not be the case, but that the Americans always were and ought to be subject to crown and Parliament. Perhaps this hath not been so seriously considered as it may hereafter, but neither this nor any law can be supposed to be binding *ex post facto*, or contrary to our fundamental constitution. Montesquieu observes, that the British constitution (which God preserves) will be lost, whenever the legislative power shall be more corrupted than the executive part of the legislature.

And after all, in this very law, the Americans are allowed to be represented in their own assemblies, and to lay on duties and taxes, though not exclusively; but whether America, or any part of the British empire, should be liable to have taxes imposed on them by different legislatures, and whether these would not frequently clash with one another to the detriment of crown and subjects, I leave others duly to consider.

It is said, if America cannot be taxed by the British Parliament, then it would be independent of Great-Britain. This is now a very popular cry, and it is well if many join in it only because they know no better. This is not, will not, cannot be the case. America confessedly hath not been thus taxed since it was settled; but no body in Britain or America ever dreamed that America was independent. In England the people cannot be taxed when the Parliament does not sit, or when it is dissolved; are they then therefore independent[?] Scotland cannot be taxed in the same degree as England; is it therefore independent? Ireland and Jersey have their own legislatures, and so tax themselves; will you call them independent? All those parts of the British empire that have no assemblies pay no taxes at all, neither among themselves, nor to Great-Britain; but it will not therefore be said, that they are independent. The Parliament itself claims a right to refuse supplies till their grievances are heard and redressed, this is looked upon as a constitutional remedy against any encroachments by the crown, and hath very often been made use of in for her reigns, and yet the Parliament neither claimed nor were charged with a desire of independency. Those who so freely charge with a desire of independency, and even treason and rebellion, would do well to consider, that this charge, heinous as it is, reflects greater disgrace on those who unjustly make it, than on those on whom it is unjustly made. A man of honour would not easily forgive himself whenever he should discover that he made so rash a charge against two millions of people, as innocent, loyal, and well affected to their King and country, as any of his fellow subjects or himself possibly can be. There never was an American Jacobite, the very air of America is death to such monsters, never any grew there, and if any are transported, or import themselves, loss of speech always attends them. The loyalty of the Americans to their king hath not only been ever untainted, it hath never been as much as suspected. There is a difference between independency and uneasiness. In the late reign, the people in England were uneasy at the Jew bill, and it was rapidly repealed; in the present, the Cyder Act was an odious measure, and immediately altered, and that without any disgrace or diminution of parliamentary authority. If there hath been any appearance of riot in America, perhaps it may hereafter appear at whose instigation, the law was ever open, and even overbearing odious custom-house officers might have been redressed, if they had thought fit to apply for a legal rather than a military remedy. In England it is possible majesty itself hath met with indignities which have not been shewn in America even to those men to whom the nation in general is indebted for the present uneasiness, and it is not improbable, that, after all that hath been said and done, the Americans will be found an exception to the general rule, that oppression makes even a wise man mad: An ancient rule, the truth of which hath been experienced in England oftener than in America. The opinion of the Americans is, that to be taxed where they are not represented would deprive them of the rights of Englishmen, nay, in time, with the loss of the constitution, might and must deprive them of liberty and property altogether. These it must be owned are gloomy apprehensions; two millions of people are so thoroughly prepossessed with them, that even their children unborn may feel the parents impressions; should there be any real ground for them, the Americans can hardly be blamed; they sit uneasy under them; they can no more help their uneasiness, than deny the blood which flows in their veins, or be angry with the milk that was their first nourishment. This is not a dark abstruse point, but seems plain and essential to the very being of liberty. The sole question is, Is it, or is it not, the right of an Englishman not to be taxed where he is not represented? Can you be tired of being represented, O Britons! Is it consistent with the constitution you so justly boast of to be thus taxed? Then representation is not essential to your constitution, and sooner or later you will either give it up or be deprived of it. A borough that does not exist shall send two representatives, a single county, neither the largest nor richest, shall send forty-four members, and two millions of souls, and an extent of land of eighteen hundred miles in length, shall have taxes laid on them by such as never were nearer to them than one thousand leagues, and whose interest it may be to lay heavy burdens on them in order to lighten their own. And are these, who are thus taxed, unrepresented, unheard and unknown, Englishmen, and taxed by Englishmen? Do these enjoy what the charters most solemnly ensure them, the same and all the privileges of the subjects born and resident within the realm? I must doubt it.

Let those who make light of American grievances give a plain answer to this plain question, Are the colonies to be taxed by Parliament represented in Parliament? if they are, by whom, or since when? if not, once more, Is it, or is it not, the right of Britons not to be taxed where not represented? Here the whole matter hinges, and surely the question is not so impertinent but a civil answer might be given before a mother sends fire and sword into her own bowels. When constitutional liberty is once lost, the transit is very short to the loss of property; the same power that may deprive of the one may also deprive of the other, and with equal justice; those that have not liberty enough to keep their property in reality have no property to keep. Some that look no further build right upon power, and insist the Parliament can do so. If power is all that is meant very like it may, so it may alter the constitution. If a stately tree should take umbrage at some diminutive shrubs, it can fall upon and crush them, but it cannot fall upon them without tearing up its own roots; it can crush those within reach, but its own branches will take off the weight of the impression, permit the shrubs to send forth new shoots, while there is no great probability that the envious oak will return to its former stand and vigour. *C'est une chose a bien considerer* (this ought to be well considered first), said Moliere's *Malade imaginaire*, when his quack proposed to him to have one of his arms cut off, because it took some of the nourishment which in that case would center in the other, and make it so much the stronger. If every assembly in America is suspended, the consequence must be, that the people are without their usual legislature, and in that case nothing short of a miracle seems capable to prevent an anarchy and general confusion. No power can alter the nature of things, that which is wrong cannot be right, and oppression will never be productive of the love and smiles of those that feel it.

The Parliament can crush the Americans, but it can also, and with infinitely greater certainty and ease, conciliate their affections, have the ultimate gain of all their labours, and by only continuing them the privileges of Britons, that is, by only doing as they would be done by, diffuse the blessings of love and concord throughout the whole empire, and to the latest posterity; and which of these two is the most eligible, is it now for you, O Britons! to consider, and in considering it, *majores vestros cogitate & posteres*, think on your ancestors and your posterity.

Those whom God hath joined together (Great-Britain and America, *Liberty and Loyalty*), *let no man put asunder: And may peace and prosperity ever attend this happy union.*

Feb. 1, 1769.

10

AN ORATION UPON THE BEAUTIES OF LIBERTY

John Allen

NEW-LONDON

1773

John Allen (*fl.* 1764–1774). For a time attributed to Isaac Skillman, but later identified by scholars as the work of Allen, *An Oration* went through seven printings and five editions within two years and became very popular in the four cities where it was reprinted. Its fiery author, called "that strange itinerant Baptist" by Bernard Bailyn and "New England's Tom Paine" by scholars John M. Bumsted and Charles E. Clark (*William and Mary Quarterly*, vol. 21) is little known.

He first appears in 1764 as pastor of the Particular Baptist Church in Petticoat Lane, near Spitalfields, London. He lost this post around 1767 and was tried for and acquitted of forgery in 1769 (events that followed him to America). He then published *The Spirit of Liberty* (1770), pleading the case of John Wilkes, urging that he be restored to his seat in Parliament or that the unconstitutional house be dissolved for abridging English liberties. This work, published in England under the pseudonym Junius, Junior, had as its chief purpose to expound "upon the rights of the people, and more particularly upon the perfect law of liberty of those ancient people called Christians," most especially of Baptists, to Allen the source of true religion's historical tradition.

Allen next appears in America, where he delivers this thanksgiving sermon on December 3, 1772, in the pulpit of the Second Baptist Church in Boston. The *Gaspee* affair (a schooner burned in June 1772) was the political occasion. A strong admixture of political theory and theology had by then become customary for Boston congregations, but it was less usual in Baptist churches; by any standard Allen was radical for the time. *An Oration*—published along with another pamphlet by Allen (*The American Alarm*) that was also aimed at arbitrary power—urged readers to "Engrave the motto!—May it be thus: *Liberty, Life, or Death*!" Allen's final appearance before lapsing back into obscurity came in 1774 with publication of *The Watchman's Alarm* in Salem. He may have died in 1789.

AN

ORATION,

Upon the Beauties of LIBERTY,

Or the Essential RIGHTS of the AMERICANS.

DELIVERED

At the Second Baptist Church in BOSTON,

Upon the last Annual THANKSGIVING.

Humbly dedicated to the Right-Honourable the Earl of DARTMOUTH.

PUBLISHED by the Request of many.

[The THIRD EDITION corrected.]

NEW-LONDON:

Printed by T. GREEN, for JOSEPH KNIGHT, Post-Rider.

MDCCLXXIII.

To the Right-Honourable
the Earl of Dartmouth

My Lord,

When I view the original right, power and charter, confirm'd, sealed, and ratified to the province, or inhabitants of Rhode-Island, and its standing in full force, and unrepealed for more than an hundred years, which is as follows: "Be it enacted, that no freeman, shall be taken, or imprisoned, or deprived of his freehold, or liberty, or free custom, or be out-law'd, or exil'd, or otherwise destroy'd, nor shall be oppressed, judged or condemned, but by the law of this colony. And that no man of what state or condition soever, shall be put out of his lands or tenements, nor taken, nor imprisoned, nor disinherited, nor banished (observe this my Lord), nor any ways destroy'd, or molested, without being, for it, brought to answer, by a due course of law of this colony": Methinks, that even your Lordship, will not blame them if they stand fast in the liberty wherein they were made free.

As a fly, or a worm, by the law of nature has as great a right to liberty, and freedom (according to their little sphere in life), as the most potent monarch upon the earth: And as there can be no other difference between your Lordship, and myself, but what is political, I therefore without any further apology, take leave to ask your Lordship, whether any one that fears GOD, loves his neighbour as himself (which is the true scripture-mark of a christian), will oppress his fellow-creatures? If they will, where are the beauties of Christianity? Not to be seen in this life, however they may be seen in the next.

I have seen what is said to be an authenticated copy of your Lordship's letter to the governor of Rhode-Island, in which there are such dictations, directions, and possitive commands, to oppress, with tyranny, a free people, which is inconsistent with a good man, or a Christian to have any concern or agency therein. The law of GOD directs us to do unto others, as we would they should do unto us. And knowing that your Lordship is well acquainted with the divine oracles, having had the honour to dine at your Lordship's seat, in Staffordshire, and was, when in England, personally acquainted with

Mr. Wright, your Lordship's steward, and with the good and pious character your Lordship bears, I therefore take this leave (as a fellow-christian, as one that loves, as the highest happiness of his existence, the beauties, spirit, and life of Christianity), to ask your Lordship, how your Lordship would like to have his birth-right, liberty and freedom, as an Englishman, taken away by his king, or by the ministry, or both? Would not your Lordship immediately say, it was tyranny, oppression and distruction, by a dispotic power? Would not your Lordship be ready to alarm the nation, and point out the state upon the brink of distruction?

My Lord,

Are not the liberties of the Americans as dear to them as those of Britons? Suppose your Lordship had broke the laws of his king, and country; would not your Lordship be willing to be try'd by a jury of your peers, according to the laws of the land? How would your Lordship like to be fetter'd with irons, and drag'd three thousand miles, in a hell upon earth? No! but in a hell upon water,* to take your trial? is not this contrary to the spirit of the law, and the rights of an Englishman? Yet thus you have given direction, as the king's agent or the agent of the ministry to destroy the rights and laws of the Americans. How your Lordship can answer for this agency of injustice before GOD, and man, will be very difficult: However, if great men, and good men, and Christians can dare to do such things as these (when in power), heaven grant that I may have an acquaintance with them in this world; or if they have any power in heaven, not in the world to come; for I think, my Lord, that such men, who will take away the rights of any people, are neither fit for heaven; nor earth, neither fit for the land or the dunghil.

Your Lordship lets us know that the case of burning the Gaspee schooner has been laid before the law servants of the crown, and that they make the crime of a deeper die than piracy, namely, an act of high treason, and levying a war against the king.

Well my Lord, and supposing this to be the case, are not the Rhode-Islanders subjects to the king of Great-Britain? Has not the king his attorney, his courts of judicatory to decide matters between

* Through a man of war's crew.

the king and the subjects? Why then must there be new courts of admiralty erected to appoint and order the inhabitants to be confin'd, and drag'd away three thousand miles, from their families, laws, rights and liberties, to be tried by their enemies? Do you think my Lord, this is right in the sight of God and man? I think if the Rhode-Islanders suffer this infringement of their liberties, granted them by their charter, from the king of England, any place out of hell is good enough for them, for was there ever such cruelty, injustice and barbarity ever united against free people before, and my Lord Dartmouth to have an hand in it, from whom we might rather have expected mildness, mercy, and the rights of the people supported.

Your Lordship's letter frequently reminds us that this destructive authority (to destroy the lives and liberties of the people), is his majesty's will and pleasure. How far his majesty may be influenc'd and dictated by his ministry I will not take upon me to say, but that it is his majesty's will and pleasure of his own mind and consent, I will not believe a word of it, for his majesty is a person of more tenderness and understanding, than to attempt such tyranny, besides, his attempt to destroy the rights of the people—destroys his right as king to reign over them, for according to his coronation oath, he has no longer a right to the British crown or throne, than he maintains inviolable firm the laws and rights of the people. For violating the people's rights, Charles Stewart, king of England, lost his head, and if another king, who is more solemnly bound than ever Charles Stewart, was, should tread in the same steps, what can he expect? I reverence and love my king, but I revere the rights of an Englishman before the authority of any king upon the earth. I distinguish greatly between a king and a tyrant, a king is the guardian and trustee of the rights and laws of the people, but a tyrant destroys them.

Besides my Lord, the inhabitants of America know as well

> as the people of England, that the people are the right and foundation of power and authority, the original seat of majesty—the author of laws, and the creators of officers to execute them. And if at any time they shall find the power they have conferred abused by their trustees, their majesty violated by tyranny, or by usurpation, their authority prostituted to support violence, or skreen corruption, the laws grown pernicious through accidents unforeseen, or rendered ineffectual through the infidelity of the executors of them. Then it is their right, and what is their right is undoubtedly

> their priviledge and duty (as their essential power and majesty), to resume that delegated power and authority they intrusted them with, and call their trustees to an account; to resist the usurpation, and extirpate the tyranny; to restore their sullied majesty and their prostituted authority; to suspend, alter or abrogate those laws, and punish the unfaithful and corrupt officers. Nor is it the duty only of the united body, but every member of it ought, according to his respective rank, power and weight in the community, to *concur* in advancing those glorious designs . . . This is, my Lord, the happy constitution of England; the power, right and majesty of the people which has been frequently recognized and established. By which majesty, right and power, kings are made, and unmade by the choice of the people; and laws enacted, and annulled only by their own consent, in which none can be deprived of their property, abridged of their freedom, or forfeit their lives without an appeal to the laws, and the verdict of their peers or equals.

My Lord, as this is according to the laws of England, the liberty, priviledge and power of his majesty's subjects in Great-Britain, why not then the priviledge of his majesty's subjects in America? has his majesty (as it all seems to be laid upon him) two kind of laws, one for England and the other for America? a power to reign as king and guardian of his people's rights at home, and a power to destroy the rights of the colonies abroad? I really don't understand it my Lord, if he has no right to do it, why do you say he does? This is using his majesty cruel. However somebody does it, your Lordship says it is his majesty with his privy counsel, the latter I rather think. However, be it who it will, whether the king, ministry, or Parliament, they have no more right to do it, than they have to cut your Lordship's throat. Has not your Lordship a right to oppose any power that may assault your Lordship's person, right or priviledge, without its being deemed rebellion against the king and state? Yes, sure you have! Then surely my Lord an American has the same right to oppose every usurping power (let it be from whom it will), that assaults his person, or deprives him of his own law or liberty as an American. Has he offended? yes! Is he willing to be tried by his own laws? yes! Then, that man, that king, that minister of state, be who he will, is worse than a Nero tyrant that shall assume to drag him three thousand miles to be tried by his enemies.

Besides my Lord, what is rebellion? if I understand it right, they are persons rising up with an assumed authority and power to act, dictate and rule in direct violation to the laws of the land—I believe my Lord, I am right here, for this reason, your G-ne-al F——c, and your G——r T——n, when in North-Carolina, thought so, and like *cruel blood-thirsty savages*, murdered mankind for thinking that they had a right to oppose any power that attempted to destroy their liberties. This was my Lord a cruel barbarous slaughter of mankind. However, if it was deemed rebellion in them, and they were treated as rebels, because they (as the ministry said) broke the laws of the government of the province; then surely it follows, that the k—g's m——y, and P—t, must be rebels, to GOD, and mankind, in attempting to overthrow (by guns, by swords, and by the power of war), the laws, and government of Rhode-Island. Have not the Rhode-Islanders as much right to the privileges of their own laws, as the king of England has to his crown? sure they have! Then surely, that man must be a tyrant in his soul, that shall deem it rebellion in the Rhode-Islanders, supposing they should kill every man, that shall attempt to destroy their laws, rights and liberties.

It is true my Lord, the Gaspee schooner is destroyed, and thereby the laws of England are violated (as you apprehend), by Indians out of the woods, or by Rhode-Islanders, I cannot say who; but it is a query with me my Lord, whether there is any law broke in burning the Gaspee schooner; if it was done by the Indians (which is the current report) then there is no law broke; for the scripture says, "*where there is no Law, there is no transgression.*" And it is well known, that the Indians were never under any law to the English; did I say, they were never under any law to the English, heaven forgive me! I mean my Lord no other law than the sword and bayonet; the same law that some would fain bring the Americans under now. But suppose my Lord, that this deed was done by the Rhode-Islanders, the query is still with me—whether there is any transgression committed? the scripture says, *where there is no Law, there is no transgression:* Now, the question is, *Do the Rhode-Islanders receive their laws from England?* If so, there is a transgression committed against those laws, but if not, there is no transgression, says St. James. For my part, I cannot see how any man in America, can properly break the laws of England. The whole lies here, the laws of America only are broke, let the offender then be tried by the law he has broke, What can justice, I had almost said *tyranny* desire more: However my Lord, there is no other idea arises in my mind (and it is no wonder, for the Bostonians are very notional), which is, if there is any law broke, it is the king and the ministry who have broke it; for I would be glad to know my Lord, what right the king and ministry has to send an armed schooner to Rhode-Island, to take away the property of the people, any more than they have to send an armed schooner into Brest, and demand the property of France? Know this, that the king of England has no more right, according to the laws of God and nature, to claim the lands of America, than he has the lands of France—America, my Lord, in the native rights of the Americans, it is the blood-bought treasure of their forefathers; and they have the same essential right to their native laws, as they have to the air they breathe in, or to the light of the morning, when the sun rises; and therefore they who oppress the Americans must be as great enemies to the rights of the laws of nature, as they who would (if it were in their power) vail the light of the sun from the universe. Remember my Lord, the Americans have a priviledge to boast of above all the world. They never were in bondage to any man, and therefore it is more for them to give up their rights into the hands of the Turks; consider what English tyranny their forefathers fled from, what seas of distress they met with, what savages they fought with, what blood-bought treasures, as the dear inheritance of their lives, they have left to their children, and without any aid from the king of England; and yet after this, these free-born people must be counted rebels, if they will not loose every right of liberty, which their forefathers bought, with their blood, and submit again to English ministerial tyranny—O America! O America!

My Lord, I hope I need not remind your Lordship of the enquiry that the divine Messiah made to Peter, when they required a tax, or tribute, from him. Of whom, says CHRIST, to Peter, do they gather tax, or tribute, of the children, or of strangers? And Peter said of strangers. Then, says CHRIST, the children are free. Now, the Gaspee schooner, my Lord, was a stranger; and they should, if it was in their commission, have gathered tax from strangers: But instead of which, they would have gathered it from the children. They forgot that the children were free: Therefore, my Lord, must it certainly be, that the Gaspee schooner has committed the transgression, & broke the laws, of the freedom of this country. No doubt, my Lord, but they have a right to tax the strangers, that come to dwell in their country; but to tax the children, which are free in their own native country, this will not do! Nature forbids it; the law of GOD condemns it. And no law, but that of tyranny, can desire it.

And therefore it was, my Lord, that the children (who are by the law of GOD, and the law of nature free), looked upon the Gaspee-schooner as a stranger, as such they treated her; but when the stranger attempted to gather tax of the children who are free then they looked upon her, as a pirate, who took away their property without their consent, by violence, by arms, by guns, by oaths and damnations: This they thought looked so like piracy, that the children did not like it; and they thought their behavior as strangers, was very unpolite, that they could not so much as pass by these strangers, but the children must bow to them, and come to them; this, the children being free, did not like, and they thought it was best for the children, and the strangers, all to be free: And therefore, one night, my Lord, they went and set the strangers (who, by the way, were all prisoners), free—free upon the face of the whole earth; and then to preserve them free, they burnt their prison. Now, my Lord, would it not be hard to hang these poor men for it? However,

If there is any law broke, it is this, that the Gaspee schooner, by the power of the English ministry and admiralty, have broke the laws, and taken away the rights of the Americans. And yet the Americans must be punish'd for it, contrary to their own laws. O! Amazing! I would be glad to know my Lord, what right the king of England has to America? it cannot be an hereditary right, that lies in Hanover, it cannot be a parliamentary right that lies in Britain, not a victorious right, for the king of England never conquered America. Then he can have no more right to America, than what the people have, by compact, invested him with, which is only a power to protect them, and defend their rights civil and religious; and to sign, seal, and confirm, as their steward, such laws as the people of America shall consent to. If this be the case, my Lord, then judge whether the king of England and the ministry are not the trangressors in this affair, in sending armed schooners to America, to steal by power and sword the people's property. And if any are to be try'd for law-breakers, it surely ought, in justice, to be them. But the people of America act my Lord very honest in the affair, they are willing to give and take, to give the English offenders the liberty to be try'd by their own laws, and to take the same liberty wherein they have offended to be tried by their own laws, as the king of England has to his crown, or that the natives of Britain has to the rights of an Englishman—consider then, my Lord, how cruel, how unjust, how unanswerable before God and man it must be, by any violence and power to destroy the rights of the Americans.

My Lord, the close of your Lordship's letter, is such that it is enough to make the blood of every vein stand stagnated as a testimony against ministerial bloody power. It not only gives a right to every American to be angry, but to be incensed against your lordship, wherein you tell the governor of Rhode-Island, that it is his majesty's pleasure, that General Gage, hold the troops in readiness to assist this assumed court of admiralty, to destroy the rights of the people. What my Lord, is bloody Bonner's days so near America! O America! O America! What, the blood-power of the sword and death to aid civil magistrates to destroy the people's rights? Stop a little my Lord, give a little breathing time—for it is a solemn thing to die. I wonder your Lordship's knees did not smite together, when as the king's, or ministerial agent, you wrote this authority, how a good man, a christian, and one that fears God, can be an agent not only to destroy the rights of a people, but to oppress them; with the military power of blood and death, is enough to make the earth to reel, and all heaven to stand aghast! Be astonish'd O ye heavens at this! I hope, my Lord, you do not intend to renew that bloody, barbarous assassination in America which I saw the Scotch barbarian troops thro' the orders of Lord B——n and Lord W———h spread in St. George's fields, remember the blood of young Allen cries to heaven for vengeance in their face, and a louder voice than Abel's blood, which cry'd to heaven for vengeance, is still heard in Boston streets, against a bloody military power, and tho' the murderers escaped by a scene well known to some, but too dark to explain—yet the God of truth and justice stands at the door. Supposing my Lord, that the Rhode-Islanders, for the sake of blood bought liberties of their forefathers, for the sake of the birthrights of their children, should shew a spirit of resentment against a tyrannical arbitrary power that attempts to destroy their lives, liberties and property, would it not be unsufferable, cruel, for this (which the law of nature and nations teaches them to do) to be butchered, assassinated and slaughtered in their own streets by their king? Consider, my Lord, that we must all appear before the judgment seat of Christ, and that it would be a cold cordial for your Lordship, at the bar of God, to have thousands of Americans rise up in judgment against you. Yet I would rather this was the case, tho' I suffer'd death with them, than they should lose their essential rights as Americans.

But it may be meet to let your Lordship know, that if the Americans unite (as there seems a good prospect of it) to stand as a band of brethren for their liberties, they have a right, by the law of GOD, of nature, and of nations, to reluct at, and even to resist any military and marine force, surely they must be intended in readiness for the French, and not for Americans, for can it ever enter into the heart of a mother to murder her children? of a king to kill his subjects? of an agent to destroy the rights of the colonies he represents? But suppose my Lord, that this should be the bloody intent of the ministry, to make the Americans subject to their slavery, then let blood for blood, life for life, and death for death decide the contention. This bloody scene can never be executed but at the expence of the destruction of England, and you will find, my Lord, that the Americans will not submit to be slaves, they know the use of the gun, and the military art, as well as any of his majesty's troops at St. James's, and where his majesty has one soldier, who art in general the refuse of the earth, America can produce fifty, free men, and all volunteers, and raise a more potent army of men in three weeks, than England can in three years. But God forbid that I should be thought to aim at rouzing the Americans to arms, without their rights, liberties and oppression call for it. For they are unwilling to beat to arms, they are loyal subjects; they love their king; they love their mother-country; they call it their home; and with nothing more than the prosperity of Britain, and the glory of their king: But they will not give up their rights; they will not be slaves to any power upon earth. Therefore, my Lord, as a peace-maker; as their agent; as their friend; lay their grievances before their king. Let the Americans enjoy their birthright blessings, and Britain her prosperity, let there be a mutual union between the mother and her children, in all the blessings of life, trade and happiness; then, my Lord, both Britons, and Americans, will call you blessed.

Wishing, from my heart, the inviolable preservation of the rights and liberties of the Americans, and the growing happiness of England:

I am, my Lord
his Majesty's loyal subject,
and your Lordship's
dutiful servant,
A British Bostonian

That they may do evil with both hands, earnestly, the Prince asketh, and the Judge asketh for a Reward; and the great Man he uttereth his mischievous desire: So they wrap it up.

Micah VII 3.

The faithfulness of the prophet Micah; the fidelity of his heart, and the zeal of his soul for the liberties of the people, was remarkable. His faithfulness when tyranny reigned by authority; when the laws, rights and liberties of the people were at the dispose of the arbitrary power of the wicked king Ahaz, as it is written 2 Chron. 28. 1.

> *And Ahaz was twenty years old when he began to reign, and he reigned sixteen years in Jerusalem, but he did not that which was right in the sight of the Lord; like David his father,* Ver. 19. *For the Lord brought Judah low, because of Ahaz king of Israel, for he made Judah naked, and transgressed sore against the Lord,* ver. 22 *And in the time of this distress did he trespass yet more and more against the Lord—this is that king Ahaz.*

And therefore this faithful prophet lays the matter to heart, as one that rever'd the liberties and happiness of the people above the authority of the king, and the power of his senates. And therefore says, in the verse preceeding the text, "The good man is perished out of the earth, and there is none upright among men; they all lie in wait for blood, they hunt every man his brother with a net." And is not this the case at this day? for what is the ministry hunting after now? is not every one hunting for their brother, with the net of admiralty-courts and tyranny? if they can but once get their American brethren in this net, they may kick and flirt as long as they will, they'll never get out any more. It is indeed said, "In vain is the net spread in the sight of any bird" and that "he has made us wiser than the fowls of the air," but wherein will the Americans appear to be wiser than the fowls of the air, if they suffer themselves to be taken in this ministerial net?

Observe, that it was a dark time with the nation, a dark time with the church of the living God, and a very distressing time respecting the people, when Micah appeared cotemporary with Isaiah, as a prophet of the Lord, and a son of liberty, therefore he tells the oppressors of the people, "*The best of them is a brier, and the most upright of them sharper than a thorn hedge—the day of the watchmen, and thy visitation cometh, now shall be their perplexity.*" And is not this the case? Is not the day of the watchmen of America come, who watch for the rights of the people, as the centinels of the land, to defend them from every invasion of power and destruction? Now their visitation in Providence is come—try the watchmen whether they will stand for God, and the people, or not. Now shall be their perplexity of the ministry, who lie in wait for blood and hunt every man his brother with a net, who utter their mischievous desire, and so *they wrap it up.* For this faithfulness, in King Ahaz, and Hezekiah's days, the prophet Micah's name has a singular honor in the annals of heaven above the rest of the prophets in Israel—Jer. 17, 18, 19. because he said—"hear this I pray you, ye heads of the house of Jacob, and princes of the house of Israel, that abhor judgment and pervert all equity."

Therefore, these sayings of that pious prelate of the church of England, bishop Burnet, in his history of his own time, are noble, valuable and great; especially where he says, "there is not any thing more certain than this: That kings are made for the people, and not the people for them." Was not David made a king for the people? Was not Saul? Was not Solomon? Then let not kings think too highly of themselves; for the GOD of heaven never intended they should be any more than the servants of the people; therefore the bishop adds, "that, perhaps, there is no nation under heaven more sensible of this than the English nation; so that, if the prince does not govern, by this maxim, the people will soon grow very unkind to him." If this be the case, the king of England may immediately see the reason of all his people's hard speeches, and unkindness to him: It is because he has departed, either by inclination, or persuasion, from this royal standard. Therefore he adds, "the interest, and essential rule for a king is to study the interest of the nation; to be ever in it; to be always pursuing it:" This will lay such a degree of confidence in him, that he will ever be safe in the people, while they feel they are safe in him; and not a moment longer. So that if the king of England is not happy let him thank himself for it: It is not his people's fault—it is his own. For that king is not worthy to reign, that does not make the *rights* of his people the rule of his actions: Knowing this, that he receives all his power, and majesty, from them; and how can he think that he has any right to rule over them, unless he rules in their hearts by inviolable maintaining their *rights*? For as the ministers of the gospel (when in their proper place) are no otherwise than the people's servants; so the king is no more than the servant of the people: And when at any time, he is unfaithful, as the people's servant, they have a right to say to him, "give an account of thy stewardship, that thou mayest be no longer steward." For what can he judge, when a free and affectionate people, lay their grievances, with tears, at his feet, praying, for years past, for redress? and yet he will not hear them!!! Or if he does, he answers them like Rehoboam—roughly: What can he expect, but Rehoboam's revolution? "What part have we in David? Or what portion have we in the son of Jesse? Every man to thy tent, O Israel." And there, the pious bishop further observes, "that a prince that would command the affections, and praise of the nation, should not study to stretch his prerogative"; here I think the pious bishop missed it, for it is not his prerogative but the people's; and this is what makes it so unsufferable, and unbearable, that the king should make use of their power and prerogative, to destroy their rights: This Charles Stewart did, and he fell into the hands of wicked men, and they cut off his head for it.

But to proceed to the words of the text. "That they may do evil with both hands earnestly; the prince asketh, and the judge asketh for a reward, and the great man he uttereth his mischievous desire: So they wrap it up."

Observation the first.

It is then plain that a craving, absolute prince, is a great distress to a people.

The prince asketh! What does he ask for? Why the tall pine trees, for masts for his great ships; well, let him have them, not as his right, no, but as your gift to him. Well, but the prince asketh? Well, what does he ask now? Why, that the British streets may be paved with American gold; well do not make a word about that? let him have it, but let it be in the fair way of trade, and commerce, not by taxation, and oppression. The essence of money, lies, in what money buys. This England can furnish you with.

But the prince asketh? Well what is it? will he never have done asking? What does he ask now? Have patience, and you shall hear, well what is it? Why it is the favour of the government of Rhode Island, to hold a court of admiralty to authorize them to confine suspected persons (guilty or not guilty), and drag them away three thousand miles, to take their trial by a jury of strangers, if not enemies. But the granting of this, in some measure, depends upon the consent of the governor. But all governors (who are worthy the name) are such as the scripture describes Judges 5. 9. "My heart, says one, nay every American will say the same, is towards the governours who offer themselves willingly among the people," to rule by their laws, to defend the rights of the people, to protect their persons, to secure their liberties. And this is (we hear) the happiness, power and bulwark of Rhode Island government. For its safety lies in this, that the governor of the province, and the judges of the superior court, the representatives of the people, and general assembly, are solemnly bound by oath, to rule, govern and decide, and determine only by their own laws; if so, they have a right to tell the prince, that though he asketh yet he will ask in vain.

Once more,

But the prince asketh, what now does he ask? Will he never have done asking? Well, but what does he ask? Why he asketh, the women, the wives upon the government of Rhode Island, to spare their husbands from their beds, from their bosoms, from their arms, and from their children; to be confin'd in the horrid kingdom of a man of war's crew; to be transported back again to tyranny their forfathers fled from, to a land of snares, *and the shadow of death.* This may be thought to be harsh language, and by the ministry, a *hard saying who can bear it*? But it is not a hair's breadth more in meaning, than the intended power and tyranny of this new court of admiralty. And will you not submit to it? No! that is right; I am glad of it, but perhaps, it may be thought rather hard, when a prince asketh, not to grant so small a favour.

But the text likewise says—*The Judge asketh for a reward.* The judges have the key of the laws, the hearts of the lawyers, and the power of juries, too much in their own hands. The lives of the people, the rights of the subject, and the disposal of their property, was originally intended to be determined by juries only. But as the judges have assumed by custom, a power of dictating to lawyers even at the bar, and a direction to the jury; it highly becomes them more than ever, to be *men fearing God and hating covetousness.* Therefore it is an ill sound to hear that the *judge asketh for a reward*, what can it be for? sure it cannot be for freeing the King street murderers, or pleading that it was only manslaughter; if he k—w that it was wilful murder. No doubt but this act of kindness will be rewarded, if not at the judgment seat of Christ, which some despise; yet at the bar of God, when, he shall say, arise ye dead and come to judgment: Then there will be no setting aside a witness in Mr. P——ms case, nor no other.

Again the text saith,

The Judge asketh for a reward! Well, what reward is it, a reward from the crown of Britain? if so, not to let him have it, by no means: For if once the judges of the courts of judicatory of this province become dependent for their support, or salaries, upon the favour of the crown, or ministry at home, you become a nation of slaves to ministerial power; for thereby you submit the key of all your essential rights as Americans, to be in the hands of your enemies: For if you suffer the judges to become dependent for their pay upon the ministry of England, what are they but the ministry's servants. If so, you may naturally suppose, they must do as the ministry directs them; if not, they will be unfaithful servants; and if faithful to the ministry, where then are your rights? Where is the security of your lives, or your property. For a more bolder, daring innovation upon your right of power, decision and determination by your own laws, respecting your right and property between man and man, between the crown of England, and the rights of America, cannot possibly be made, or attempted to be made, than to make your judges dependent upon the British ministry; it is in effect, giving up your right to all you have, to all that you, or your children can ever possess. As the possession of a person's right, whether hereditary, or by purchase, depends much upon the determination of the judges. And if the judges are wholly to be dependent upon the crown of England, for nomination and support, then you may easily judge whose servants and slaves you are to be. For it is well known that the judges, or general courts, or some body, has for these hundred years, and more, distressed their brethren in their estates, and in their consciences, by imposing payment for ministers, and for a worship of GOD contrary to the people's consciences; and if they have done these things in the green tree, what may you not expect in the dry.

But as the text says, *The Judge asketh for a reward.* If it be for his fidelity in his high office, for his honourable support, according to the dignity of his character, you are bound in duty, in affection, and in obedience to let him have it. Shew your affection, readiness and gratitude, to reward your judges, as the guardians of your rights; as those who from their hearts, should protect and hand forth the liberties of their brethren to them. This is the way to become a band of brethren from the governor, to the meanest subject. Perhaps, the whole of your complaint in this respect, is owing for want of your taking an earlier opportunity, to settle such salaries, as their merit, labour and expence deserves.

Yet let not this lead us from the observation, which was, that, an asking, craving, absolute prince, is a great distress to a people. Was not this the case of the people in King Ahaz, and in King Ahab's day, when he crav'd Naboth's vineyard? Likewise in Jeroboam's days, who deprived the people of their religious liberties, in worshipping the God of Israel, in his temple at Jerusalem? who set up his golden calves at Dan and Bethel, of whom it is said, this is Jeroboam the son of Nebat, who *taught Israel to sin.* Was not this the case in Zedekiah's days, though he was warned by the word of the Lord, and by the prophet of the GOD of Israel? Yet he was, notwithstanding, absolute and craving, though he was told, it would end in the destruction of himself, and his people. Was not this the case of almost all the distress, deaths, and bloodshed, that have ever happened in England since the conquest of Julius Cæsar? their king's ruling and reigning, by a dispotic power, which they assumed, contrary to the laws and rights of the people. Were not the Britons obliged by the love of liberty, to obtain their royal *Magna Charta*, sword in hand, from King John? Was not this the case in the reign of Charles the first, when the people and parliament took up arms, to maintain the rights and laws of the people; and when it required either the head of the king, or the loss of their liberties? they soon decided the matter; they soon let the king know that they rever'd their rights and liberties, above his life, power, and prerogative. In Charles the second's reign, there was much the same absolute power over the rights of the people, both civil and religious: But he had a peculiar politeness of temper in pleasing even his very enemies. In James the second's reign, dispotic power was too evident, and distressing for the people to bear; therefore a revolution, both of king, and state, by the spirit, power, and arms, of the people, was soon accomplished.

The second observation is,

That when the king, judges, and senates, unite to destroy the rights of the people by a dispotic power, or as the text expresses it, *that they may do evil with both hands*, then the prosperity of the nation totters; the crown shakes; and the destruction of the people's rights is near at hand. For the rights of the people, which is the supreme glory of the crown and kingdom of Britain, is the *Magna Charta* of the king as well as of the people; it is as much his previledge, as it is his glory, to maintain their rights; and he is as much under a law (I mean the law of the rights of the people), as the people are under the oath of allegiance to him. And therefore whatever power destroys their rights, destroys at the same time, his right to reign, or any right to his kingdom, crown, or glory; nay, his right to the name of a king among the people. Was not this the case in Rehoboam's days, when the people were distressed with large and heavy taxations, and oppressions? they petitioned the king to relieve them from such oppressions, but would he hearken to them, according to the advice of his father's counsellors? No! but according to the advice of his young counsel, he answered them like an arbitrary prince, in the speech of his dispotic ministry, roughly, *My father chastised you with whips, but I will chastise you with scorpions*: But, would the people bear this oppression? No! *What part*, said they, *have we in David? Or what portion in the son of Jesse? To thy tents, Oh Israel.* Was not this the case in Zedekiah's reign? And was not this lately the case in Sweeden, when the king with a few of his senates, and ministry, about him, destroyed the rights of the people, by the power of the sword, and established his despotic will as the law of the land, by the tyranny of death?

Observation the third,

This shews, that an arbitrary dispotic power in a prince, is the ruin of a nation, of the king, of the crown, and of the subjects; therefore it is to be feared, abhorred, detested and destroyed, because the happiness of the king, and the prosperity of the people are hereby, not only in danger, but upon the brink of destruction. Every age and every history furnishes us with proofs, as clear as the light of the morning, of the truth of this.

But it is the singular happiness of the Americans, according to their own laws, not to be in bondage to any power upon the earth. The king of England, has no power to enact, or put in force any law that may oppress them, his very attempting to do it, at once destroys his right to reign over them. For the brightest gem which the king of England wears, in the british crown, is that majesty, trust, and confidence, which the Americans invest him with as the king and guardian of their rights, and liberties.

The Parliament of England cannot justly make any laws to oppress, or defend the Americans, for they are not the representatives of America, and therefore they have no legislative power either for them or against them.

The house of Lords cannot do it, for they are peers of England, not of America; and, if neither king, lords, nor commons, have any right to oppress, or destroy, the liberties of the Americans, why is it then, that the Americans, do not stand upon their own strength, and shew their power, and importance, when the life of life, and every liberty that is dear to them and their children is in danger?

Therefore, let me address you with all the power of affection, with all the pathos of soul, as one who esteems the full possession of the rights of the Americans, as the highest blessing of this life—to stand alarm'd! See your danger, death is near, destruction is at the door—need I speak? Are not your harbours blockaded from you? Your castle secured by captives—your lives destroyed—revenues imposed upon you—taxation laid—military power oppressing—your charter violated—your g——r's heart not right—your constitution is declining—your liberties departing, and not content with this, they now attack the life, the soul, and capitol of all your liberties—to chuse your judges, and make them independent upon you for office or support, and erect new courts of admiralty to take away by violence, the husband from his family, his wife, his home, his friends, and his all, through a scene, less joyful than Pluto's horrid kingdom. To be confin'd, and tried for his life by the accusation of a negro.

Has not the voice of your father's blood cry'd yet loud enough in your ears, in your hearts "ye sons of America scorn to be slaves"? Have you not heard the voice of blood in your own streets, louder than that which reached to heaven, that cry'd for vengeance, that was, saith the Lord to Cain, the voice of thy brother's blood, of only one, but this of many brethren. Therefore, if there be any vein, any nerve, any soul, any life or spirit of liberty in the sons of America, show your love for it; guard your freedom, prevent your chains; stand up as one man for your liberty; for none but those, who set a just value upon this blessing, are worthy the enjoyment of it.

Which leads me to the fifth [*sic*] observation, which is,

That it is not rebellion, I declare it before GOD, the congregation, and all the world, and I would be glad if it reached the ears of every Briton, and every American; That it is no rebellion to oppose any king, ministry, or governor, that destroys by any violence or authority whatever, the rights of the people. Shall a man be deem'd a rebel that supports his own rights? it is the first law of nature, and he must be a rebel to GOD, to the laws of nature, and his own conscience, who will not do it. A right to the blessing of freedom we do not receive from kings, but from heaven, as the breath of life, and essence of our existence; and shall we not preserve it, as the beauty of our being? Do not the birds of the air expand their wings? the fish of the sea their fins? and the worm of the earth turn again when it is trod upon? And shall it be deem'd rebellion? Heaven forbid it! Shall Naboth's disputing with King Ahab, respecting his vineyard, be deemed rebellion? Or the people sending home their governor in irons some years ago, be deemed rebellion? It is no more rebellion, than it is to breathe.

Sixthly, to observe,

That when the rights and liberties of the people are destroyed, it is commonly by the mischievous design of some great man. The text says, *the great man uttereth his mischievous desire*: But who this great man is, we do not certainly know, but may shrewdly guess; but whether Lord Bute, duke of Grafton; or Lord Hillsborough, is not material, but the mischievous design, is what we fear, is what we feel, if they instill in the king's mind a divine right of authority to command his subjects, this is mischievous. King Charles found it so, Rehoboam found it so, and so will our present king, if he hearkens to such advice.

If they make the name of the king sacred, I hope they mean a political sacredness: If so, he is no more sacred than the people have made him, by investing him with the sacred trust of their rights. If any great man, or the whole ministry makes use of the king's name, or his authority, to enforce their arbitrary will, as a law to the subjects, that the subjects must obey, and passively submit, because, say they, it is his majesty's will and pleasure: This is a mischievous design—mischievous to the dignity of the crown—to his majesty's person—to his security—to his family—and their safety. It is likewise mischievous to his majesty's subjects, as it spreads discord, disunion and disaffection to the king, to his authority, and power, which is a mournful consideration, and is the bane of all our national distress. The people in England, and the people in America, would fain love their king, and obey him with reverence, and affection, and make him the most happy prince upon the earth, if he would but prevent this mischievous design of the ruin of their essential rights and liberties.

But the text says, "*The great man uttereth his mischievous desire*"—and indeed we believe he does, in the closet, in the cabinet, and in the ears of the king. Oh! it is a mischievous design, too deep for us to fathom, or come to the bottom of, it carries in it the plain aspect of distress to the king, and distruction to the people. Oh! kind heaven, prevent what king and people have too much cause to fear; however, at best, it is a mischievous design to alienate (by any direction, or dictation) the affections of his majesty's good subjects; as it destroys the bonds, and ties, of national blessings; their rights, their liberties; their lives; their properties: And if this is not a mischievous design there can scarce be one found out of the deeps of the dark mansions.

But to return to you, my dear Americans, you think hard to pay duties for *teas, imports, clearances, entries, &c. &c.* But what will you farmers and landholders think, of paying a fixed tax for every acre of land you enjoy? for every apple tree you rear? for every barrel of cyder you make, for every pound of candles you burn? for every pound of soap you use, for every pair of shoes you wear, for the light of the morning, and the sun, that a kind heaven gives you; what do you think of paying a continual tax for all these? this is contain'd in the mischievous design. Stand alarm'd, O ye Americans. But I close with the last remark from the text. *So they wrap it up.* It will do, it will do say they. The king, say they, has a right to appoint judges, courts of admiralty, impose revenues, lay taxes, send military forces, block up their harbours, command them—compel them by arms—pay their judges—get the key of their laws, rights and liberties into our hands, this will do! *and so they wrap it up*, as fine and smooth as can be: But I think it is better to *unwrap* it again. What do you think, my dear Americans? But I add no more—but advise you, as it is a day of public thanksgiving, to bless GOD for the liberties and mercies we do enjoy; not for those you are deprived of. My second advice is, love your king, pray for him, pray for your governor, pray for your judges, that all their reign may be easy to themselves, and happy for the people.

A M E N

II

AN APPEAL TO THE PUBLIC FOR RELIGIOUS LIBERTY

Isaac Backus

BOSTON

1773

Isaac Backus (1724–1806). Born in the village of Yantic in Norwich township, Connecticut, Backus converted to Christianity in 1741 as a result of the Great Awakening preaching of the theologian Eleazar Wheelock. For the decade prior to 1756, when he settled in Middleborough, Massachusetts, Backus was a separatist Congregationalist. From 1756, he was pastor of the Middleborough First Baptist Church until his death. He is ranked with Roger Williams, John Leland, Thomas Jefferson, and James Madison as a preeminent figure in the establishing of freedom of conscience in America. In William G. McLoughlin's words, Backus "was the most forceful and effective writer America produced on behalf of the pietistic or evangelical theory of separation of church and state" (*Isaac Backus on Church, State, and Calvinism: Pamphlets, 1754–1789* [Cambridge, Mass., 1968], p. 1). Intellectually, the chief attainment of Backus was his idea that "religion is ever a matter between God and individuals" (as he stated in 1783). Institutionally, his major accomplishment was the cultivation of the role of the Baptist church, and the religious sphere generally, as outside the jurisdiction of civil magistracy. As an evangelist–statesman, Backus preached the gospel far and wide; he calculated that during the period 1748 to 1802 he had made 918 trips longer than ten miles each and traveled a total of 68,600 miles, mostly on horseback.

Backus was a trustee of Brown University from 1765 to 1799. He served as an "agent" for the Warren Association from 1771 onward, looking after all Baptist interests, somewhat like a modern lobbyist. In that capacity, he conferred with the delegates to the First Continental Congress in 1774 in Philadelphia, upholding religious liberty, for Baptists in his day had suffered imprisonment for their views and practices. A supporter of the Revolution, he afterwards continued his battle for liberty of conscience in the states of the new Union. He served as a delegate from Middleborough to the Massachusetts convention that ratified the federal Constitution in 1788. He rejoiced in the coming of the Second Awakening to the Kentucky and Tennessee frontier in the early 1800s, having participated personally in camp meetings a decade earlier in North Carolina and Virginia. He renewed his efforts in the last years of his life to stir the embers of religious revival in New England.

AN APPEAL TO THE PUBLIC FOR RELIGIOUS LIBERTY,

Against the Oppressions of the present Day.

By Isaac Backus.

Brethren, ye have been called unto Liberty; only use not Liberty for an occasion to the Flesh, but by love serve one another. GAL. V. 13.

BOSTON:

Printed by JOHN BOYLE in Marlborough-Street.

MDCCLXXIII.

An Appeal to the Public (1773) is prefaced with an essay on political theory that shows charter rights and divine or supernatural rights to be fundamental to Backus's argument at this stage of his thinking. Natural rights of a Lockean kind he had not yet reconciled with his view of human depravity derived from John Calvin. The body of the piece explores in some detail the problems of church–state relations that so vitally interested Backus and the Baptists. Backus's most famous work is his "Baptist History," or *A History of New-England with Particular Reference to the Denomination of Christians Known as Baptists* (3 vols.: Boston, 1777–96; 2-vol. rev. ed.: David Weston, 1871).

INTRODUCTION

nasmuch as there appears to us a real need of such an appeal, we would previously offer a few thoughts concerning the general nature of liberty and government, and then shew wherein it appears to us, that our religious rights are encroached upon in this land.

It is supposed by multitudes, that in submitting to government we give up some part of our liberty, because they imagine that there is something in their nature incompatible with each other. But the word of truth plainly shews, that man first lost his freedom by breaking over the rules of government; and that those who now speak great swelling words about liberty, while they despise government, are themselves servants of corruption. What a dangerous error, yea, what a root of all evil then must it be, for men to imagine that there is any thing in the nature of true government that interferes with true and full liberty! A grand cause of this evil is, ignorance of what we are, and where we are; for did we view things in their true light, it would appear to be as absurd and dangerous, for us to aspire after any thing beyond our capacity, or out of the rule of our duty, as it would for the frog to swell till he bursts himself in trying to get as big as the ox, or for a beast or fowl to dive into the fishes element till they drown themselves. *Godliness with contentment is great gain*: But they that *will* take a contrary course *fall into temptation, and a snare, and into many foolish and hurtful lusts, which drown men in destruction and perdition.* 1 Tim. 6. 6, 9.

The true liberty of man is, to know, obey and enjoy his Creator, and to do all the good unto, and enjoy all the happiness with and in his fellow-creatures that he is capable of; in order to which the law of love was written in his heart, which carries in it's nature union and benevolence to being in general, and to each being in particular, according to it's nature and excellency, and to it's relation and connexion to and with the supreme Being, and ourselves. Each rational soul, as he is a part of the whole system of rational beings, so it was and is, both his duty and his liberty to regard the good of the whole in all his actions. To love ourselves, and truly to seek our own welfare, is both our liberty and our indispensible duty; but the conceit that man could advance either his honor or happiness, by disobedience instead of obedience, was first injected by the father of lies, and all such conceits ever since are as false as he is.

Before man imagined that submission to government, and acting strictly by rule was confinement, and that breaking over those bounds would enlarge his knowledge and happiness, how clear were his ideas! (even so as to give proper names to every creature) and how great was his honor and pleasure! But no sooner did he transgress, than instead of enjoying the boldness of innocency, and the liberties of paradise, he sneaks away to hide himself; and instead of clear and just ideas, he adopted that master of all absurdities (which his children follow to this day) of thinking to hide from omniciency, and of trying to deceive him who knows every thing! Instead of good and happiness, he felt evil, guilt and misery; and in the room of concord was wrangling, both against his Creator and his fellow-creature, even so that she who was before loved as his own flesh, he now accuses to the great Judge. By which it appears, that the notion of man's gaining any dignity or liberty by refusing an intire submission to government, was so delusive, that instead of it's advancing him to be as gods, it sunk him down into a way of acting like the beasts and like the devil! the beasts are actuated by their senses and inclinations, and the devil pursues his designs by deceit and violence. With malicious reflections upon God, and flattering pretences to man, he drew him down to gratify his eyes and his taste with forbidden fruit: and he had no sooner revolted from the authority of heaven, than the beauty and order of his family was broken; he turns accuser against the wife of his bosom, his first son murders the next, and then lies to his Maker to conceal it; and that lying murderer's posterity were the first who broke over the order of marriage which God had instituted; and things proceeded from bad to worse, till all flesh had corrupted his way, and the earth was filled with violence, so that they could no longer be borne with, but by a just vengeance were all swept away, only one family.

Yet all this did not remove the dreadful distemper from man's nature, for the great Ruler of the universe directly after the flood, gave this as one reason why he would not bring such another while the earth remains, namely, *For the imagination of man's heart is evil from his youth*,* so that if he was to drown them as often as they deserved it, one deluge must follow another continually. Observe well where the distemper lies; evil imaginations have usurped the place of reason and a well informed judgment, and hold them in such bondage, that instead of being governed by those noble faculties, they are put to the horrid drugery of seeking out inventions, for the gratification of *fleshly lusts, which war against the soul*; and to guard against having these worst of all enemies detected and subdued; enemies which are so far from being God's creatures, that strictly speaking, they have no being at all in themselves, only are the privation of his creatures well-being; therefore sin, with it's offspring death, will, as to those who are saved, be *swallowed up in victory*. Sin is an enemy both to God and man, which was begotten by satan, and was conceived and brought forth by man; for lust when it is conceived bringeth forth sin, and sin when it is finished bringeth forth death.†

Now how often have we been told, that he is not a freeman but a slave, whose person and goods are not at his own but anothers disposal? And to have foreigners come and riot at our expence and in the fruit of our labours, has often been represented to be worse than death. And should the higher powers appear to deal with temporal oppressors according to their deserts, it would seem strange indeed, if those who have suffered intolerably by them, should employ all their art and power to conceal them, and so to prevent their being brought to justice! But how is our world filled with such madness concerning spiritual tyrants! How far have pride and infidelity, covetousness and luxury, yea deceit and cruelty, those foreigners which came from hell, carried their influence, and spread their baneful mischiefs in our world! Yet who is willing to own that he has been deceived and enslaved by them? Who is willing honestly to bring them forth to justice! All acknowledge that these enemies are among us, and many complain aloud of the mischiefs that they do; yet even those who lift their heads so high as to laugh at the atonement of Jesus, and the powerful influences of the Spirit, and slight public & private devotion, are at the same time very unwilling to own that they harbour pride, infidelity, or any other of those dreadful tyrants. And nothing

* Gen. 4. 19. and 6. 13, 15. and 8. 21.
† Eccl. 7. 29. 1 Pet. 2. 11. Jam. 1. 14, 15.

but the divine law refered to above, brought home with convincing light and power, can make them truly sensible of the soul-slavery that they are in: and 'tis only the power of the gospel that can set them free from sin, so as to become the servants of righteousness: can deliver them from these enemies, so as to *serve God in holiness* all their days. And those who do not thus know the truth, and have not been made free thereby,* yet have never been able in any country to subsist long without some sort of government; neither could any of them ever make out to establish any proper government without calling in the help of the Deity. However absurd their notions have been, yet they have found human sight and power to be so short and weak, and able to do so little toward watching over the conduct, and guarding the rights of individuals, that they have been forced to appeal to heaven by oaths, and to invoke assistance from thence to avenge the cause of the injured upon the guilty. Hence it is so far from being necessary for any man to give up any part of his real liberty in order to submit to government, that all nations have found it necessary to submit to some government in order to enjoy any liberty and security at all.

We are not insensible that the general notion of liberty, is for each one to act or conduct as he pleases; but that government obliges us to act toward others by law and rule, which in the imagination of many, interferes with such liberty; though when we come to the light of truth, what can possibly prevent it's being the highest pleasure, for every rational person, to love God with all his heart, and his neighbour as himself, but corruption and delusion? which, as was before noted, are foreigners and not originally belonging to man. Therefore the divine argument to prove, that those who promise liberty while they despise government are servants of corruption is this; *For of whom a man is overcome, of the same is he brought in bondage.* 2 Pet. 2. 18, 19. He is so far from being *free* to act the man, that he is a bond slave to the worst of tyrants. And not a little of this tyranny is carried on by such an abuse of language, as to call it liberty, for men to yield themselves up, to be so foolish, disobedient and deceived, as to *serve divers lusts and pleasures.* Tit. 3. 3.

Having offered these few thoughts upon the general nature of government and liberty, it is needful to observe, that God has appointed

* Rom. 6. 18. Luke 1. 74, 75. John 8. 32.

two kinds of government in the world, which are distinct in their nature, and ought never to be confounded together; one of which is called civil, the other ecclesiastical government. And tho' we shall not attempt a full explanation of them, yet some essential points of difference between them are necessary to be mentioned, in order truly to open our grievances.

SECTION I

Some essential points of difference between civil and ecclesiastical government.

1. The forming of the constitution, and appointment of the particular orders and offices of civil government is left to human discretion, and our submission thereto is required under the name of their being, the ordinances of men for the Lord's sake. 1 Pet. 2. 13, 14. Whereas in ecclesiastical affairs we are most solemnly warned not to be *subject to ordinances, after the doctrines and commandments of men.* Col. 2. 20, 22. And it is evident that he who is the only worthy object of worship, has always claimed it as his sole prerogative, to determine by express laws, what his worship shall be, who shall minister in it, and how they shall be supported. How express were his appointments concerning these things by Moses? And so wise and good a ruler as Solomon, was not intrusted with any legislative power upon either of these articles, but had the exact dimensions of the temple, the pattern and weight of every vessel, with the treasuries of the dedicate things, and the courses of the priests and Levites, all given to him in *writing by the Spirit*, through the hand of his father David. 1 Chron. 28. 11–19. And so strict were God's faithful servants about these matters, that Daniel who in a high office in the Persian court, behaved so well that his most envious and crafty foes, could find no occasion against him, nor fault in him concerning the kingdom, till they fell upon the device of moving the king to make a decree about worship, that should interfere with Daniel's obedience to his God; yet when that was done, he would not pay so much regard to it as to shut his windows. Dan. 6. 4–11. And when the Son of God, who is the great Law-giver and King of his church, came and blotted out the handwriting of the typical ordinances, and established a better covenant, or constitution of his church, upon better promises, we are assured

that he was *faithful in all his house, and counted worthy of more glory than Moses.* What vacancy has he then left for faliable men to supply, by making new laws to regulate and support his worship? especially if we consider,

2. That as the putting any men into civil office is of men, of the people of the world; so officers have truly no more authority than the people give them: And how came the people of the world by any ecclesiastical power? They arm the magistrate with the sword, that he may be a minister of God *to them for good,* and might execute wrath upon evil doers; and for this cause they pay them tribute: upon which the apostle proceeds to name those divine commandments which are comprehended in love to our neighbour, and which work *no ill to him.* Surely the inspired writer had not forgotten the first and great command of love to God; but as this chapter treats the most fully of the nature and end of civil government of any one in the new-testament, does it not clearly shew that the crimes which fall within the magistrates jurisdiction to punish, are only such as work ill to our neighbour? Rom. 13. 1–10. While church government respects our behaviour toward God as well as man.

3. All acts of executive power in the civil state, are to be performed in the name of the king or state they belong to; while all our religious acts are to be done in the *name of the Lord Jesus;* and so are to be performed *heartily as to the Lord, and not unto men.* And it is but lip service, and vain worship, if our *fear toward him is taught by the precepts of men.* Col. 3. 17, 23. Isa. 29. 13. Mat. 15. 9. It is often pleaded, that magistrates ought to do their duty in religious as well as civil affairs. That is readily granted; but what is their duty therein? Surely it is to *bow to the name of Jesus,* and to serve him with holy reverence; and if they do the contrary they may expect to *perish from the way.* Phil. 2. 10. Psa. 2. 10–12. But where is the officer that will dare to come in the name of the Lord to demand, and forcibly to take, a tax which was imposed by the civil state! And can any man in the light of truth, maintain his character as a minister of Christ, if he is not contented with all that Christ's name and influence will procure for him, but will have recourse to the *kings of the earth,* to force money from the people to support him under the name of an embassador of the God of heaven! Does not such conduct look more like the way of

those who made *merchandize of slaves and souls of men*, than it does like the servants who were content to be as their master, who said, *He that heareth you heareth me; and he that despiseth you despiseth me?* Rev. 18. 9, 13. Luke 10. 3–16.

4. In all civil governments some are appointed to judge for others, and have power to compel others to submit to their judgment: but our Lord has most plainly forbidden us, either to assume or submit to any such thing in religion. Mat. 23. 1–9. Luke 22. 25–27. He declares, that the cause of his coming into the world, was to bear *witness unto the truth;* and says he, *Every one that is of the truth heareth my voice.* This is the nature of his kingdom, which he says, *is not of this world:* and gives that as the reason why his servants should not fight, or defend him with the sword. John. 18. 36, 37. And it appears to us that the true difference and exact limits between ecclesiastical and civil government is this, That the church is armed with light and truth, to pull down the strong holds of iniquity, and to gain souls to Christ, and into his church, to be governed by his rules therein; and again to exclude such from their communion, who will not be so governed; while the state is armed with the sword to guard the peace, and the civil rights of all persons and societies, and to punish those who violate the same. And where these two kinds of government, and the weapons which belong to them, are well distinguished, and improved according to the true nature and end of their institution, the effects are happy, and they do not at all interfere with each other: but where they have been confounded together, no tongue nor pen can fully describe the mischiefs that have ensued; of which the Holy Ghost gave early and plain warnings. He gave notice to the church, that the main of those antichristian confusions and abominations, would be drawn by philosophy and deceit, from the *hand-writing of ordinances* that Christ has blotted out. And to avoid the same, directs the saints to walk in Christ Jesus *as they received him*, rooted and built up in him, and stablished in the faith *as they have been taught*; viewing that they are *complete in him, which is the head over all principality and power.* Therefore he charges them not to be beguiled into a voluntary humility, by such fleshly minds as do not hold this head, but would subject them to ordinances after the doctrines and commandments of men. Col. 2.

Now 'tis well known that this glorious head made no use of secular force in the first sitting up of the gospel church, when it might seem to be pecularly needful if ever; and it is also very evident, that ever since men came into the way of using force in such affairs, their main arguments to support it have been drawn from the old Jewish constitution and ordinances. And what work has it made about the head as well as members of the church?

First they moved Constantine, a secular prince, to draw his sword against heretics; but as all earthly states are changeable, the same sword that Constantine drew against heretics, Julian turned against the orthodox. However, as the high priest's sentence in the Jewish state, decided matters both for prince and people, the same deceitful pilosophy that had gone so far, never left plotting till they had set up an ecclesiastical head over kingdoms as well as churches, who with Peter's keys was to open and shut, bind and loose, both in spiritual and temporal affairs. But after many generations had groaned under this hellish tyranny, a time came when England renounced that head, and set up the king as their head in ecclesiastical as well as civil concernments; and though the free use of the scriptures which was then introduced, by a divine blessing, produced a great reformation, yet still the high places were not taken away, & the lord bishops made such work in them, as drove our fathers from thence into America. The first colony that came to this part of it carried the reformation so far, as not to make use of the civil force to save the people to support religious ministers (for which they have had many a lash from the tongues & pens of those who were fond of that way) but the second colony, who had not taken up the cross so as to separate from the national church before they came away, now determined to pick out all that they thought was of universal and moral equity in Moses's laws, and so to frame a christian common-wealth here.* And as the Jews were ordered not to set up any rulers over them who were not their brethren; so this colony resolved to have no rulers nor voters for rulers, but brethren in their churches. And as the Jews were required to inflict corporal punishments, even unto death, upon non-conformers to their worship, this common-wealth did the like to such as refused to conform to their way; and they strove very hard to have the

* Massachusetts history, vol. 3. p. 161.

church govern the world, till they lost their charter; since which, they have yielded to have the world govern the church, as we shall proceed to shew.

SECTION II

A brief view of how civil and ecclesiastical affairs are blended together among us, to the depriving of many of God's people of that liberty of conscience which he has given them.

We are not insensible than an open-appearance against any part of the conduct of men in power, is commonly attended with difficulty and danger; and could we have found any way wherein with clearness we could have avoided the present attempt, we would gladly have taken it. But our blessed Lord & only Redeemer, has commanded us, to *stand fast in the liberty wherewith he has made us free*; and things appear so to us at present that we cannot see how we can fully obey this command, without refusing any active compliance with some laws about religious affairs that are laid upon us. And as those who are interested against us, often accuse us of complaining unreasonably, we are brought under a necessity of laying open particular facts which otherwise we would gladly have concealed: and all must be sensible that there is a vast difference between exposing the faults, either of individuals or communities, when the cause of truth and equity would suffer without it, and the doing of it without any such occasion. We view it to be our incumbent duty, to render unto Caesar the things that are his, but that it is of as much importance not to render unto him any thing that belongs only to God, who is to be obeyed rather than man. And as it is evident to us, that God always claimed it as his sole prerogative to determine by his own laws, what his worship shall be, who shall minister in it, and how they shall be supported; so it is evident that this prerogative has been, and still is, encroached upon in our land. For,

1. Our legislature claim a power to compel every town and parish within their jurisdiction, to set up and maintain a pedobaptist worship among them; although it is well known, that infant baptism is never express'd in the Bible, only is upheld by men's reasonings, that

are chiefly drawn from Abraham's covenant which the Holy Ghost calls, *the covenant of circumcision*, Acts 7. 8. And as circumcision was one of the hand-writing of ordinances which Christ has blotted out, where did any state ever get any right to compel their subjects to set up a worship upon that covenant?

2. Our ascended Lord gives gifts unto men in a sovereign way as seems good unto him, and he requires *every man, as he has received the gift, even so to minister the same*; and he reproved his apostles when they forbid one who was improving his gift, because he followed not them. 1 Pet. 4. 10, 11. Luk. 9. 49. But the Massachusetts legislature, while they claim a power to compel each parish to settle a minister, have also determined that he must be one, who has either an accademical degree, or a testimonial in his favour from a majority of the ministers in the county where the parish lies. So that let Christ give a man ever so great gifts, yet hereby these ministers derive a noble power from the state, to forbid the improvement of the same, if he follows not their schemes.* And if the apostles assumed too much in this respect to themselves, even when their Lord was with them, can it be any breach of charity to conclude that ministers are not out of danger of doing the like now? especially if we consider how interest operates in the affair. For,

3. Though the Lord hath *ordained that they which preach the gospel shall live of the gospel;* or by the free communications to them, which his gospel will produce. 1 Cor 9. 13, 14. Gal. 6. 6, 7. Yet the ministers of our land have chosen to *live by the law;* and as a reason therefor, one of their most noted writers, instead of producing any truth of God, recites the tradition of a man, who said, "Ministers of the gospel would have a poor time of it, if they must rely on a *free contribution of the people* for their maintenance." And he says, "The laws of the province having had the royal approbation to ratify them, they are the king's laws. By these laws it is enacted, that there shall be a

* It has been the custom of minister's who are settled in this way, for these thirty years past, to apply the gainsaying of Cere to those who have dissented from them; as if they were as certainly in the right way, as Moses and Aaron were. And 16 ministers in the county of Windham, in a public letter to their people in 1744, stile theirs, "The instituted churches"; and those who had withdrawn from them, "uninstituted worship"; and then they go on to assert, that Deut. 13, prove that the people, "May not go after it, any more than—after a false god." p. 42, 43.

public worship of God in every plantation; that the person elected by the majority of the inhabitants to be so, shall be looked upon as the minister of the place; that the salary for him, which they shall agree upon, shall be levied by a rate upon all the inhabitants. In consequence of this, the minister thus chosen by the people, is (not only Christ's, but also) in reality, the king's minister; and the salary raised for him, is raised in the king's name, and is the king's allowance unto him."*

Now who can hear Christ declare, that his kingdom is, *not of this world*, and yet believe that this blending of church and state together can be pleasing to him? For though their laws call them "orthodox ministers," yet the grand test of their orthodoxy, is the major vote of the people, be they saints or sinners, believers or unbelievers. This appears plain in the foregoing quotation; and another of their learned writers lately says, "It is the congregation in it's parocal congregational capacity that the law considers; and this as such does not enough partake of an ecclesiastical nature to be subject to ecclesiastical jurisdiction.†

Hence their ministers and churches must become subject to the court, and to the majority of the parish in order to have their salary raised in the king's name: But how are either of them in the mean time subject to the authority of Christ in his church? How can any man reconcile such proceedings to the following commands of our Master which is in heaven? Mat. 23. 9, 10. What matter of grief and lamentation is it that men otherwise so knowing and justly esteemed, should by the traditions of men be carried into such a crooked way as this is! for, though there is a shew of equity in allowing every society to choose it's own minister; yet let them be ever so unanimous for one who is of a different mode from the court, their choice is not allowed. Indeed as to doctrine ministers who preach differently, yea directly contrary to each other, about Christ and his salvation, yet are supported by these laws which at the same time limit the people to one circumstantial mode.

It is true the learned author just now quoted says, "If the most of

* Dr. Cotton Mather's *Ratio Discipline* [offers a] faithful account of the discipline professed and practised in the churches of New-England, 1726. p. 20.

† Dr. Stiles on the christian union. p. 85.

the inhabitants in a plantation are episcopalians, they will have a minister of their own persuasion; and the dissenters, in the place, if there be any, must pay their proportion of the tax for the support of this legal minister."* But then his next words shew that they did not intend ever to have such a case here; for he says,

> In a few of the towns, a few of the people, in hope of being released from the tax for the legal minister, sometimes profess themselves episcopalians. But when they plead this for their exemption, their neighbours tell them, *They know in their conscience they do not as they would be done unto.* And if a governor go by his arbitrary power, to supersede the execution of the law, and require the justices and constables to leave the episcopalians out of the tax, they wonder he is not aware, that he is all this while, forbidding that the king should have his dues paid unto him; and forbidding the king's ministers to receive what the king has given him.†

How essentially and how greatly does this constitution differ from the institutions established in God's word, both in their nature and effects?

1. In their nature. Here you find that every religious minister in that constitution, is called the king's minister, because he is settled by direction of the king's laws, and the tax for such a minister's support is raised in the king's name, and is called the king's dues: whereas no man in the Jewish church might approach to minister at the holy altar, but such as were *called of God, as was Aaron:* and the means of their support, were such things as God required his people to *offer and consecrate to Him*; and when they withheld the same, he says, *ye*

* According to this rule, whoever gets the upper hand may tax the rest to their worship; but when will men learn the madness of such conduct?

Sir Henry Vane, who was governor of the Massachusetts in 1636, but whom governor Winthrop obliged the next year to leave the colony, he at a time when he had great influence in the British parliament wrote to governor Winthrop thus: "The exercise and troubles which God is pleased to lay upon these kingdoms and the inhabitants in them, teaches us patience and forbearance one with another in some measure, though there be difference in our opinions, which makes me hope that, from the experience here, it may also be derived to yourselves, least while the congregational way amongst you is in freedom, and is backed with power, it teaches it's oppugners here to extirpate it and root it out, from its own principles and practice.

Sir, I am your affectionate friend, and servant in Christ,

June 10, 1645. H. Vane."

Massachusets history, vol. 3. p. 137.

† *Ratio Discipline*, p. 20, 21.

have robbed me, even this whole nation; and it is represented as his peculiar work to reward obedience, and to punish disobedience in such affairs.* It is evident from sacred record that good men in every station, used their influence by word and example to stir up their fellow servants to do their duty toward God in these respects; and good rulers, in conjunction with church officers, took care to have what was offered to him secured and distributed according to God's commandments.† But what is there in all this that can give the least countenance to the late method, of mens making laws to determine who shall be Christ's ministers, and to raise money for them in their own name! Christ said to the Jews, *I am come in my Father's name, and ye receive me not; if another shall come in his own name, him ye will receive. How can ye believe, which receive honor one of another, and seek not the honor that cometh from God only?* John 5. 43, 44.

Even a heathen monarch, when he was moved to make a decree in favour of God's minister's and worship at Jerusalem, it was to restrain their enemies from injuring or interrupting of them, and to order that a portion of the king's goods should be *given unto the elders of the Jews* for the building of *the house of God*, and for the *burnt offerings of the God of heaven*. Ezra 6. 6–9. Nothing appears of his levying any new tax for worship, only that he gave the articles there specified out of his own goods; yet some professed christians have imposed new taxes upon people on purpose to compel them to support their way of worship, and have blended in with other rates, and then called it all a civil tax. But as the act itself is deceitful so 'tis likely that the worship supported by such means is hypocrisy. For,

2. The effects of the constitution of our country are such, that as it makes the majority of the people the test of orthodoxy, so it emboldens them to usurp God's judgment seat, and (according to Dr. Mather's own account, which we have often seen verified) they daringly give out their sentence, that for a few to profess a persuasion different from the majority, it must be from bad motives; and that, *they know in their conscience* that they do not act by the universal law of equity, if they plead to be exempted from paying the money which the majority demand of them! And though in our charter the king grants to all

* Exod. 23. 15, 16. Deut. 16. 16, 17. and chap. 26. Mal. 3. 7–12. Hag. 1. 6–11. and 2. 17–19. Luke 12. 21.

† 1 Chron. 29. 2 Chron. 31. Nehem. 13. 10–13.

protestants *equal liberty of conscience*: yet for above thirty years after it was received, the congregationalists made no laws to favour the consciences of any men, in this affair of taxes, but their own sect; and it is here called arbitrary power, and even a forbidding that the king should have his dues, if a governor shewed so much regard to the charter, as to oppose their extorting money from people of the king's denomination, for their congregational ministers. And perhaps the learned author now referred to, never delivered a plainer truth, than when he said, "The reforming churches flying from Rome, carried some of them more, some of them less, all of them something of Rome with them, especially in that spirit of imposition and persecution which too much cleaved to them."

These evils cleaved so close to the first fathers of the Massachusetts, as to move them to imprison, whip and banish men, only for denying infant baptism, and refusing to join in worship that was supported by violent methods: yet they were so much blinded as to declare, That there was this vast difference between these proceedings and the coercive measures which were taken against themselves in England, viz. We compel men to "God's institutions"; they in England compelled to "mens inventions." And they asserted that the baptists were guilty of "manifest contestations against the order and government of our churches, established (we know) by God's law."* Though they professed at the same time that,

> It is not lawful to censure any, no not for error in fundemental points of doctrine or worship, till the conscience of the offender, be first convinced (out of the word of God) of the dangerous error of his way, and then if he still persist, it is not out of conscience, but against his conscience (as the apostle saith, Tit. 3. 11.) and so he is not persecuted for cause of conscience, but punished for sinning against his conscience.†

In reply to which Mr. Williams says,

> The truth is, the carnal sword is commonly the judge of the conviction or obstinacy of all supposed hereticks. Hence the faithful witnesses of

* Massachusetts history, vol. 3. p. 404, 406.

† Mr. John Cotton's piece which he called, *The bloody tenet washed*. Printed 1647, p. 126. Mr. Roger Williams in his reply, observes that Tit. 3. 11. and other texts which speak of church discipline, are perverted to support state-oppression and violence. p. 131.

Christ, Cranmer, Ridley, Latimer, had not a word to say in the disputations at Oxford: Hence the non-conformists were cried out as obstinate men, abundantly convinced by the writings of Whitgift and others; and so in the conference before king James at Hampton court, &c.*

But says he,

Every lawful magistrate, whether succeeding or elected, is not only the minister of God, but the minister or servant of the people also (what people or nation soever they be all the world over) and that minister or magistrate goes beyond his commission, who intermeddles with that which cannot be given him in commission from the people.† If the civil magistrate must keep the church pure, then all the people of the cities, nations and kingdoms of the world must do the same much more, for primarily and fundementally they are the civil magistrate. Now the world saith John lieth in wickedness, and consequently according to it's disposition endures not the light of Christ, nor his golden candlestick the true church, nor easily chooseth a true christian to be her officer or magistrate. The practising civil force upon the consciences of men, is so far from preserving religion pure, it is a mighty bulwark or barricado, to keep out all true religion, yea and all godly magistrates for ever coming into the world."‡

How weighty are these arguments against confounding church and state together? yet this author's appearing against such confusion, was the chief cause for which he was banished out of the Massachusetts colony. And though few if any will now venture openly to justify those proceedings, and many will exclaim against them at a high rate; yet a fair examination may plainly shew, that those fathers had more appearance of a warrant for doing as they did, than their children now have, for the actings which we complain of. For those fathers were persuaded, that the judicial laws of Moses which required Israel to punish blasphemers, and apostates to idolatry with death, were of moral force, and binding upon all princes and states;§ especially on such as these plantations were.¶ And how much more countenance did this give for the use of force to make men conform to what they believed to be the right way, than men can now have for compelling

* Williams's reply to Cotton, 1652, p. 192.

† Page 96.

‡ Page 112.

§ Bloody tenet washed, p. 55.

¶ Massachusetts history, vol. 3. p. 161.

any to support a way which at the same time they are allowed to dissent from? For the Jews also were required to pull down houses, and to have persons away out of their camps or cities, if the priests pronounced them unclean; and they were not permitted to set up any king over them who was not a brother in their church. Did not these things afford arguments much more plausible, for their attempt to compel the world to submit to the church, than any can have for the modern way, of trying to subject the church in her religious affairs to rulers, and the major vote of inhabitants, a great part of whom are not brethren in any church at all! Though the state of Israel was obliged thus to inflict death or banishment upon non-conformers to their worship, yet we have not been able to find, that they were ever allowed to use any force to collect the priests or prophets maintenance. So far from it, that those who made any such attempts were sons of Beliel, and persons that *abhorred judgment, and perverted all equity*. 1 Sam. 2. 12–16. Mic. 3. 5, 9.

Many try to vindicate their way by that promise, that kings shall become nursing fathers, and queens nursing mothers to God's people. But as the character carries in it's very nature, *an impartial care and tenderness for all their children;* we appeal to every conscience, whether it does not condemn the way of setting up one party to the injury of another. Our Lord tells us plainly, that few find the narrow way, while many go in the broad way; yet the scheme we complain of, has given the many such power over the few, that if the few are fully convinced that the teacher set up by the many, is one that causeth people to err, and is so far from bringing the pure gospel doctrine, that they should break the divine command, and become *partakers of his evil deeds;* if they did not *cease to hear him*, or to receive him into their houses as a gospel minister;* yet only for refusing to put into such a minister's mouth, the many are prepared with such instruments of war against them, as to seize their goods, or cast their bodies into prison, where they may starve and die, for all what that constitution has provided for them. In cases of common debts the law has provided several ways of relief, as it has not in the case before us; for here the assessors plead, that they are obliged to tax all according to law, and the collector has the same plea for gathering of it, and the minister says, I agreed with the society for such a sum, and it is not

* Prov. 19. 27. 2 John 10. 11.

my business to release any. So that we have had instances of serious christians, who must have died in prison for ministers rates, if christianity and humanity had not moved people to provide them that relief, which neither those ministers nor the law that upholds them have done.

Another argument which these ministers often mention, is the apostolic direction to us, to pray for all that are in authority, that we may lead a quiet and peaceable life in all godliness and honesty. But do they pray and act according to that direction? One while they cry up the great advantages of having religion established by law; and some have caused near as loud a clamour about it as the craftsmen did at Ephesus; but when it comes to be calmly represented, that, religion is a *voluntary obedience unto God*, which therefore force cannot promote; how soon do they shift the scene, and tell us, that religious liberty is fully allowed to us, only the state have in their wisdom thought fit to tax all the inhabitants, to support an order of men for the good of civil society. A little while ago it was for religion, and many have declared, that without it we should soon have no religion left among us: but now tis to maintain civility. Though by the way it is well known, that no men in the land, have done more to promote uncivil treatment of dissenters from themselves, than some of these pretended ministers of civility have done. In 1644 the court at Boston passed an act to punish men with banishment, if they opposed infant baptism; or departed from any of their congregations when it was going to be administered.* And after they had acted upon this law, one of their chief magistrates observed, that such methods tended to make hypocrites. To which a noted minister replied, that if it did so, yet such were better than profane persons, because said he, "Hypocrites give God part of his due, the outward man, but the profane person giveth God neither outward nor inward man."† By which it seems that in that day, they were zealous to have the outward man if no more given to God; but now that conduct is condemned as persecution, by their children, who profess to allow us full liberty of conscience, because they do not hinder our giving our inward man to God, only claim a power to seize our outward man to get money for themselves. And though many of us have expended ten or twenty

* Mr. Clark's narrative, p. 35.

† Massachusetts history, vol. 3. p. 405.

times as much, in setting up and supporting that worship which we believe to be right, as it would have cost us to have continued in the fashionable way, yet we are often accused of being coveteous, for dissenting from that way, and refusing to pay more money out of our little incomes, to uphold men from whom we receive no benefit, but rather abuse. How far is this from leading a peaceable life, either of godliness or honesty!

SECTION III

A brief account of what the baptists have suffered under this constitution, and of their reasons for refusing any active compliance with it.

Many are ready to say, the baptists are exempted from ministerial taxes, therefore why do they complain? Answer, We would be far from forgetting or undervaluing of our privileges: but are willing thankfully to acknowledge, that our honored rulers do protect our societies, so as not to allow them to be interrupted in their worship; and as the taking cognizance of marriage belongs to them, we take it as a favour that they grant our ministers power to administer it, so that we may have marriage solemnized among ourselves. Many other liberties we also enjoy under the government that is set over us, for which we desire to be thankful, both to the author, and to the instruments of them. Yet if our opponents could once put themselves into our place, we doubt not but they would think it was high time, to seek for more full liberty than we have hitherto enjoyed, a short view of but a little part of what we have met with, may be sufficient to evince this.

Our charter, as before observed, gives us equal religious liberty with other christians: yet the pedobaptists being the greatest party, they soon made a perpetual law to support their own way, but did nothing of that nature to exempt our denomination from it, for 36 years; and since that time, what they have done in that respect has only been by temporary acts, which have been so often changed, that many times their own officers have hardly known what the law was, that was in force; and as an exact conformity to the letter of their laws is much insisted upon in their executive courts, while those acts have never been enforced with penalties upon their own people, they have often broken them, and we have had but little chance to get them punished for so doing. For in all their acts till the last, they have imposed a name upon us, that signifies re-baptizers; which we cannot understandingly own. In many acts the words "belonging thereto" were inserted so ambiguously, as to leave it disputable, whether a being church members or only a belonging to the congregation or worshipping assembly were intended; and in the case of Haverhill, where their certificate was otherways compleat, and the case had been determined in the baptists favor, in that which both parties had agreed should be the final trial, yet another hearing was obtained in which the want of them ambiguous words in the certificate, was made, the main plea by which an action was turned against us, of near three hundred dollars. All their latter acts have required a list or lists of our societies, to be given in annually, by a certain day, signed by three principal members, and the minister if there be any; and because one of our churches of above 50 members (and which is now a church in good credit) happened one year to have such a difficulty with their minister, as prevented the giving in of said list, they were taxed to pedobaptist ministers; and tho' some of the society were advised to apply to their county court for relief, yet instead of obtaining any, the court took away 20 dollars more from them. Another church gave in their list by the direction of a noted lawyer, yet they were all taxed to the pedobaptist worship, and one of the principal members of the baptist church, which the law directed to sign the list, was strained upon; and both the inferior and superior court turned the case against him, because he was a party concerned.

Here note, the inhabitants of our mother-country are not more of a party concerned, in imposing taxes upon us without our consent, than they have been in this land who have made and executed laws, to tax us to uphold their worship. This party influence has appeared in a much larger number of instances than we are willing to trouble the public with at this time but one instance more will set our case in such a striking light, that we must ask for a very serious attention to it; we mean that of Ashfield, formerly called Hunts-town in the county of Hampshire. One of the conditions on which that plantation was granted by our legislature, was their settling a learned orthodox minister, and building a meeting-house. Now in the year 1761, full two thirds of the inhabitants called and settled a minister, who they believed was taught of God and truly orthodox. But not being of the same mode with the court (for they were baptists) other people were prompted on, before this society could get up a meeting-house, to settle another minister, and to tax the first minister with all his people to support their way. This burden the baptists bore for a number of years, till in 1768, they presented a petition to our general court for relief; who ordered that they should serve the town and proprietors of Ashfield with a copy of the petition, that they might shew cause, if any they had, at the next session of the court why it should not be granted, and that a further collection of taxes from the petitioners should be suspended in the mean time. Yet in the same session of the court, a law was made which cut the baptists in that place, off from any exemption from ministerial taxes at all. In consequence of which several hundred acres of their lands were sold at public auction, for but a small part of their real value; of which ten acres belonged to the baptist minister. And after five or six journies of above an hundred miles to seek relief, and long waiting without success, their messenger was at last plainly told, by a number of our representatives, "That they had a right to make that law, and to keep the baptists under it as long as they saw fit." Hereupon notice was given in some Boston papers, of a design among our churches of joining to seek redress from another quarter.

Accordingly at an association or general meeting of our churches at Bellingham, in September, 1770, these things were considered, and it was unanimously agreed upon to apply to his majesty for help, if it could not speedily be obtained here; and a committee and agents were chosen for that purpose. When news hereof was spread, our committee were urged by leading men both in church and state, to apply again to our general court; which therefore they did in October following. In the mean time a piece dated from Cambridge, where the court was then sitting, was published in all the Boston news-papers, wherein it was represented that, "All possible care had been taken to prevent our suffering the least disadvantage from our religious sentiments"; and we were challenged to shew the contrary if we could.

Upon this the pious and learned Mr. John Davis, who from Pennsylvania had not long before been ordained pastor of the second baptist church in Boston, and who was clerk of our committee, called them together to consider of this matter. And though they were far from desiring to enter into a news-paper controversy, yet they advised him to make some reply to that challenge: He did so; and on Dec. 27, published a brief and plain view of the case of Ashfield: but instead of any fair and manly treatment upon it, he in the Evening-Post of Jan. 7, 1771, was not only insulted with the names of, "A little upstart gentleman; enthusiastical biggot; and, this stripling high-fliar"; but had it also insinuated that he was employed "by the enemies of America to defame and blacken the colonies, and this town in particular." And they had the impudence to pretend to the world, that all this was wrote by a *catholic baptist*. And they inflamed the populace so against Mr. Davis, that his most judicious friends were afraid of his being mobbed. But can it be in the power of others to blacken any people so much, as by this treatment of a worthy stranger (now at rest) they have blackened themselves! Instead of honestly *coming to the light* (which our Lord gives as the criterion to know him that doth truth, John 3. 21.) how do they hover in the works of darkness.

The first article in our committee's petition to the legislature, being for Ashfield, they were ordered to notify the proprietors thereof: They did so; and in the spring session of the assembly, they came with a long address against us, in which they begin, with saying more generally of the baptists in that part of the province,

> The proprietors conceive it to be a duty they owe to God and their country, not to be dispensed with, to lay open the characters, and real springs of action of some of these people.

Then they go on to say,

> The rule the petitioners have set up, and on which alone they seem to ground their claim of exemption, is falsly applied, and therefore all arguments bottomed on it must be inconclusive. Natural rights,* as the respon-

* Here note, the plea of our petition was for what we are "Intitled to as men, as christians, and subjects of a free government. Some of the laws of this province, we think deprive us of a charter privilege." These are what we grounded all our claims upon; yet they insinuate that our claim was in this affair to be, "restored to a state of nature"; like those who are under no civil government at all. Notwithstanding we expresly speak of our being subjects of a free government; and pleaded charter-privileges. Remember what is said of those who *turn aside to their crooked ways!*

> dents humbly conceive, are in this province wholly superceded in this case by civil obligation, and in matters of taxation individuals cannot with the least propriety plead them.

Having thus denied us any claim from natural rights, they resume what they call an indispensible duty, viz. an attempt to lay before our honored legislature the baptists' character, and the springs of their actions; and after a number of mean reflections without any proof at all, they sum up the springs of the actions of most of them to be "Pride, vanity, prejudice, impurity and uncharitableness." Very dreadful indeed if it could be proved! but that is referred to a hereafter, and they say, "At present we shall content ourselves with assuring your excellency and honors, that the foregoing account is not exaggerated."

From this they proceed to observe, that as it belongs to rulers to "protect and support all regular religious societies of protestants," so they say, "Whenever any religion or profession wears an *ill aspect to the state*, it is become a proper object of attention to the legislature. And this is the religion of the people whom we have been describing." How much does this resemble the language of him who said, *It is not for the king's profit to suffer them!** or theirs who cried, *If thou let this man go, thou art not Cæsar's friend!*†

After thus representing that the religion of the baptists that way, wears an *ill aspect to the state*, they go on to speak of the conditions upon which Ashfield was granted; and then try to prove that Mr. Ebenezer Smith, pastor of the baptist church there, "is not a minister in law," because he has neither an accademical degree, nor a testimonial in his favor from the majority of the ministers of that county. And to give an idea of the smallness of his ability for teaching, they say,

> Taking occasion in one of his discourses upon that passage of scripture, in which mention is made of the thick bosses of God's buckler; instead of *buckler*, he gave his hearers the word *butler*. Being interrogated by one occasionally present as to his meaning, he explained himself so as clearly shewed, he meant to connect the other part of the sentence with the word butler, in the commonly received sense of the word.

The clearest light we have gained in the matter is this. After Mr.

* Ester 3.8.
† John 19. 12.

Smith had been preaching in a neighbouring town some years ago, a minister who was present asked him what a butler was? he readily replied, Pharoah's cup-bearer. After a little more talk, said minister* asserted, that Mr. Smith used the word butler instead of buckler in his sermon. He did not remember that he had; but if he did so, how injurious is the above representation? is it not the evil which we read of in Isa. 29. 20, 21? Having made this reflection upon Mr. Smith, they say, "He has none of the qualifications of a minister according to the laws of Christ, or of this province, unless those of simplicity and orthodoxy." We wish his accusers were so well qualified. 2 Cor. 1. 12. and 4. 2.

In April, 1771, the address we have made a few remarks upon was referred to a committee of both houses of our general court, who reported that, "Your committee find, that in the sale of those lands there was no unfairness, but every thing was quite fair, quite neighbourly, and quite legal."† And as to our plea for exemption from ministerial taxes they say, "There is an essential difference between persons being taxed where they are not represented, therefore against their wills, and being taxed when represented." So they advised the court to dismiss our petition as unreasonable; and though the honorable house of representatives did not accept that advice, but voted to repeal the Ashfield law; yet the council refused to concur with them therein; so that if his gracious majesty in council had not disannuled said law for us, our brethren of Ashfield must, for ought that appeared to the contrary, have been entirely stripped of the inheritances, which they had purchased, and subdued at the peril of their lives, because of the sword of the wilderness.

It may be remembered that the pedobaptist proprietors of Ashfield,

* The minister who thus treated Mr. Smith is nearly related to a ruler who has had a principal hand in all their troubles at Ashfield, and likely they were confederates in forming this address against them. And it is generally believed that it was the same minister who published a piece against the baptists of Ashfield, in the Boston News-Letter of Feb. 7, 1771; to which Mr. Smith returned an answer in the same paper of March 21, following; wherein, from public records and other ways, he detected said writer in a number of gross violations of truth.

† Twenty acres of said land with a good orchard upon it, a man bid off in April, 1770, for 35 shillings, which he sued for the next August, and laid his damages at eight pounds; but upon trial the court found that the sale was not legal, and therefore turned the case against him. With what face then, said Mr. Davis, could the writer of that report say as he does!

represented that the baptists there were not worthy of the protection of our legislature. The following narrative may help to explain what they meant by it. The news of what our king had done for them, arrived and was published in Boston the latter end of October, 1771, at which their oppressors discovered great uneasiness; and on the 8th of November came two officers with numerous attendants, to the house of Mr. Smith, father of the baptist minister in Ashfield (and very much of a father to that society), with a warrant from the chief judge of that county, to seize his person, and to search his house and shop for bad money: and it was said they had a like warrant for the minister, but he happened to be then absent on a journey. His father was made a prisoner before he was out of his bed in the morning, and though he promised the use of his keys, and desired that no lock might be broken, yet while he was at prayer with his family, for which he obtained leave of one officer, the other broke open his shop, and did considerable damage there; and after searching both that and his house as much as they pleased, they carried him before the aforesaid judge and others; where it plainly appeared that the complaint was entered against Mr. Smith from a report, that he had put off a counterfeit dollar; which report was then proved to be a false one. Yet the old gentleman was not released, but was kept a prisoner through a cold night, in circumstances that greatly injured his health, and next day was bro't on further examination, when even his frequent retirement for secret devotion, which he had practised for above forty years; was catched hold of to raise a suspicion of his being guilty: and he was bound over with two sureties to the next superior court in that county. Hereupon the following men who had been called as witnesses against him, gave him their testimony in writing, declaring that they were ready to make oath to it, in the following terms, viz.

Ashfield, Nov. 11, 1771

We the subscribers, who have been summoned to prove an indictment against Chileab Smith, of his coining and putting off bad money, do testify and say, that we did not, nor cannot understandingly attest to one tittle of the indictment, nor of any circumstance tending to prove the same. And we never saw nor heard any thing in him that gave the least ground to mistrust, that he kept a shop of secrecy, or did any thing there that he was afraid should be known; and do believe the reports to the contrary are entirely false. As neither did we in our judgments hear any of the said indictment in any measure proved by any of the rest of the evidences; as witness our hands,

Ebenezer Sprague,
Nathaniel Harvey,
Jonathan Sprague,
Nathan Chapin,
Moses Smith, 2d.
Chileab Smith, jun.
Nehemiah Sprague.

Also Leonard Pike, to whom the report was that Mr. Smith had put off a bad dollar, gave from under his hand that said report had no truth in it. These are eight of the ten witnesses that were summoned against Mr. Smith; & tho' much pains was taken to procure evidence against him at the superior court, yet he was entirely acquitted; and the law was open for him to come back for damages, for a malicious prosecution; but they had contrived to have the complaint against him entered by a bankrupt, so that no recompence might be obtained by him. Are these the goodly fruits of having a particular mode of worship established by law, and their ministers supported by force!

Though we are often accused of complaining without reason, yet no longer ago than the 26th of last January, three men of good credit, belonging to a numerous and regular baptist society in Chelmsford, were seized for ministerial rates (notwithstanding they had given in a list according to law) and though one of them was above four score years old, another very infirm in body, while the third had no man at home, able to take care of the out-door affairs of his numerous family, yet they, in that cold season, were all carried prisoners to Concord gaol.

These accounts we have received from good authority, and have taken great pains to have them stated as exactly and truly as possible; and if any can point out the least mistake in what has been now related, we shall be glad to correct it. At the same time we are far from charging all the evils we complain of, upon the whole congregational denomination without distinction; for we believe there are many among them in various stations, who are sorely grieved at these oppressions. We are willing also to make all the allowance that is reasonable, for the influence of old customs, education and other prejudices, in those who have injured their neighbours in these affairs; but is it not high time now to awake, and seek for a more thorough reformation! We agree with the committee of our honored legislature in saying, there is an essential difference between persons being taxed *where they are represented*, and being taxed where they are not so; therefore the whole matter very much turns upon this point, viz. Whether our civil legislature are in truth our representatives in religious affairs, or not? As God has always claimed it as his prerogative, to appoint who shall be his ministers, and how they shall be supported, so under the gospel, the peoples communications to Christ's ministers and members, are called sacrifices with which *God is well-pleased*. Phil. 4. 18. Heb. 13, 16–18. And what government on earth ever had, or ever can have any power to make or execute any laws to appoint and enforce sacrifices to God!

In civil states the power of the whole collective body is vested in a few hands, that they may with better advantage defend themselves against injuries from abroad, and correct abuses at home, for which end a few have a right to judge for the whole society; but in religion each one has an equal right to judge for himself; for we must all appear before the judgment seat of Christ, that every one may receive the things *done in his body*, according to that he hath done (not what any earthly representative hath done for him) 2 Cor. 5. 10. And we freely confess that we can find no more warrant from divine truth, for any people on earth to constitute any men their representatives, to make laws to impose religious taxes, than they have to appoint Peter or the Virgin Mary to represent them before the throne above. We are therefore brought to a stop about paying so much regard to such laws, as to give in annual certificates to the other denomination, as we have formerly done.

1. Because the very nature of such a practice implies an acknowledgment, that the civil power has a right to set one religious sect up above another, else why need we give certificates to them any more than they to us? It is a tacit allowance that they have a right to make laws about such things, which we believe in our consciences they have not. For,

2. By the foregoing address to our legislature, and their committees report thereon, it is evident, that they claim a right to tax us from civil obligation, as being the representatives of the people. But how

came a civil community by any ecclesiastical power? how came the kingdoms of this world to have a right to govern in Christ's kingdom which is *not of this world!*

3. That constitution not only emboldens people to *judge the liberty of other mens consciences*, and has carried them so far as to tell our general assembly, that they conceived it to be a *duty they owed to God* and their country, not to be dispensed with, to lay before them the springs of their neighbours actions;* but it also requires something of the same nature from us. Their laws require us annually to certify to them, what our belief is concerning the conscience of every person that assembles with us, as the condition of their being exempted from taxes to other's worship. And only because our brethren in Bellingham, left that clause about the conscience out of their certificates last year, a number of their society who live at Mendon were taxed, and lately suffered the spoiling of their goods to uphold pedobaptist worship.

4. The scheme we oppose evidently tends to destroy the purity and life of religion; for the inspired apostle assures us, that the church is *espoused as a chaste virgin to Christ*, and is obliged to be *subject to him in every thing*, as a true wife is to her husband. Now the most chaste domestic obedience, does not at all interfere with any lawful subjection to civil authority; but for a woman to admit the highest ruler in a nation into her husband's place, would be adultery or whoredom; and how often are mens inventions about worship so called in the sacred oracles?† And does it not greatly concern us all, earnestly to search out and put away such evils, as we would desire to escape the awful judgments that such wickedness has brought on other nations! Espe-

* How are men deluded to think they do God service, when they violate his word! 1 Cor. 4. 5. Would not the same principle carry them to kill Christ's disciples under the same pretence? John 16. 2.

† Psalm 106. 39. We delight not in hard names, but every vice ought to be called by it's proper name; and the custom in this adulterous age of calling those, natural children, which God calls children of whoredom, has doubtless had a pernicious effect upon many to embolden them to go on in their filthy ways. God charged his ancient church with playing the harlot, because she said, *I will go after my lovers, that gave me my bread and my water;—For she did not know that I gave her corn*, &c. Hosea 2. 5, 8. By which it appears, that to fix our dependence upon any other beside the divine Being, and to pursue any method beside his directions, to obtain the necessaries and comforts of life, is whoredom; and does not the chief sin of the mother of harlots lie in her fixing this dependence upon the kings of the earth? Rev. 18. 3–13.

cially if we consider that not only the purity, but also the very life and being of religion among us is concerned therein; for 'tis evident that Christ has given as plain laws to determine what the duty of people is to his ministers, as he has the duty of ministers to his people; and most certainly he is as able to enforce the one as the other. The common plea of our opponents is, that people will not do their duty if rulers do not enforce it; but does not the whole book of God clearly shew, that ministers as often fail of doing their duty as the people do? And where is the care of rulers to punish ministers for their unfaithfulness? They often talk about equality in these affairs, but where does it appear! As Christ is the head of all principality and power; so the *not holding the head, from which all the body by joints and bands having nourishment ministred, and knit together, increaseth with the increase of God*, but bringing in an earthly power between Christ and his people, has been the grand source of anti-christian abominations, and of settling men down in *a form of godliness*, while they *deny the power thereof*. Has not this earthly scheme prevailed so far in our land, as to cause many ministers, instead of *taking heed to the ministry received from the Lord*; and instead of *watching for souls as those who must give an account*,* rather to act as if they were not accountable to any higher power, than that of the men who support them? and on the other hand, how do many people behave as if they were more afraid of the collector's warrant, and of an earthly prison, than of Him who sends his ministers to preach his gospel, and says, *He that receiveth whomsoever I send, receiveth me;* but declares, That it shall be more tolerable in the day of judgment for Sodom, than for those who receive them not?† Yea, as if they were more afraid of an earthly power than of our great King and Judge, who can this night require the soul of him that layeth up *treasure for himself, and is not rich towards God*; and will sentence all either to heaven or hell, according as they have treated Him well or ill, in his ministers and members.‡

5. The custom which they want us to countenance, is very hurtful to civil society: for by the law of Christ *every man*, is not only allowed, but also required, to judge for himself, concerning the circum-

* Col. 4. 17. Heb. 13. 17.
† Joh. 13.20. Luk. 10. 10–12.
‡ Luk. 12. 20, 21. Mat. 25. 31, &c.

stantials as well as the essentials, of religion, and to act according to the *full persuasion of his own mind*; and he contracts guilt to his soul if he does the contrary. Rom. 14. 5, 23. What a temptation then does it lay for men to contract such guilt, when temporal advantages are annexed to one persuasion, and disadvantages laid upon another? i.e. in plain terms, how does it tend to hypocrisy and lying? than which, what can be worse to human society! Not only so, but coercive measures about religion also tend to provoke to emulation, wrath and contention, and who can describe all the mischiefs of this nature, that such measures have produced in our land! But where each person, and each society, are equally protected from being injured by others, all enjoying equal liberty, to attend and support the worship which they believe is right, having no more striving for mastery or superiority than little children (which we must all come to, or not *enter into the kingdom of heaven*) how happy are it's effects in civil society? In the town of Boston they enjoy something of these blessings, and why may not the country have the same liberty? The ministers who have had the chief hand in stirring up rulers to treat us as they have done, yet have sometimes been forced to commend the liberty we plead for. When they wanted to get footing in the town of Providence, they wrote to governor Jencks and other rulers there, in the following words, viz.

Honorable gentlemen,

How pleasing to almighty God and our glorious Redeemer, and how conducible to the public tranquility and safety, an hearty union and good affection of all pious protestants whatsoever particular denomination of account of some differences in opinion would be, by the divine blessing, yourselves as well as we, are not insensible: and with what peace and love societies of different modes of worship have generally entertained one another in your government, we cannot think of it without admiration: and we suppose under God, 'tis owing to the choice liberty granted to protestants of all perswasions in the royal charter graciously given you; and to the wise and prudent conduct of gentlemen that have been improved as governors & justices in your colony.

And after more of this nature, they close with saying,

We hope and pray, that ancient matters (that had acrimony unhappily in them) may be buried in oblivion; and that grace and peace and holiness and glory may dwell in every part of New-England; and that the several provinces and colonies in it, may love one another with a pure heart fervently. We take leave to subscribe ourselves, your friends and servants,

Dated Oct. 27. 1721.

Peter Thatcher,
John Danforth,
Joseph Belcher,
Committee of the Association.*

The town of Providence wrote them an answer the next February, in which they say,

> We take notice how you praise the love and peace that dissenters of all ranks entertain one another with in this government. We answer, this happiness principally consists in their not allowing societies any superiority one over another; but each society support their own ministry of their own free will, and not by constraint or force upon any man's person or estate. But the contrary that takes any man's estate by force to maintain their own or any other ministry, it serves for nothing but to provoke to wrath, envy and strife, and *this wisdom cometh not from above, but is earthly, sensual and devilish*. And since you wrote this letter, the constable of Attleborough has been taking away the estates of our dear friends, and pious dissenters to maintain their minister; the like hath been done in the town of Mendon. Is this the way of peace? Is this the fruit of your love? Why do you hug the iniquity of Eli's sons, and walk in the steps of the false prophets, to *bite with the teeth*, and cry peace; but no longer than men put into your mouths than you prepare war against them. Since you admire our love and peace, we pray you to use the same methods, and write after our copy and for the future never let us hear of your pillaging conscientious dissenters to maintain your ministers. You desire that all former injury done by you to us may be buried in oblivion. We say, far be it from us to revenge ourselves; or to deal to you as you have dealt to us, but rather say, *Father forgive them, they know not what they do*. But if you mean that we should not speak of former actions, done hurtfully to any man's person, we say, God never called for that, nor suffered it to be hid, as witness Cain, Joab and Judas, are kept on record to deter other men from doing the like.†

Here the public may take notice, how desirous pedobaptists ministers are to have odious things on their side buried out of sight, but

* The first of these was minister in Boston, the second in Dorchester, and the third in Dedham.

† These extracts were carefully taken from an ancient printed copy of those letters.

how contrary has their practice ever been toward us? Even to this day they can hardly preach a sermon, or write a pamphlet for infant-baptism, without having something to say about the mad men of Munster, who they tell us rebelled against their civil rulers: Whereas in truth we never had the least concern with them, any more than our opponents have with the pope or Turk. Indeed they often assert, that those mad men were the first that ever renounced infant-baptism; but there is proof enough from their own historians, that this story which they have so often told from their pulpits, is as absolute a falshood as ever was uttered by man. And though one learned and pious president of Cambridge college, was brought to embrace our sentiments, and to bear his testimony in the pulpit there, "against the administration of baptism to any infant whatsoever"; for which he suffered considerable abuse with much of a christian temper:* While his successor, another "very learned and godly man" (who therefore must have been well acquainted with the original), held that "baptism ought only to be by dipping or plunging the whole body under water["]:† yet these and other honorable examples in our favor have been passed over, and every scandalous thing that could be pick'd up, has been spread, to prejudice people's minds against our profession in general. And let it be remembred, that when pedobaptist ministers wanted to be favored in Providence, they declared, that they could not think of the peace and love which societies of different modes of worship have generally entertained one another with in that government without admiration; and they experienced so much of this from the baptists in Providence, that when some others made a difficulty about admitting Mr. Josiah Cotton (the first minister of the pedobaptists there) as an inhabitant in the town, Col. Nicholas Powers (a leading member of the baptist church) became his bondsman to the town: therefore we hope that our honorable rulers and others, will be cautious about giving credit to stories of a contrary nature, when they are told to procure or to justify the use of force in supporting ministers; especially since ministers refuse to share in the reproach of such proceedings. For a minister who has exerted himself very much of

* Mr. Henry Dunster. Vide Mitchel's life. p. 67, 70.

† Mr. Charles Chauncy. See an account of Plymouth church, added to Mr. Robbins's Ordination-Sermon, 1760.

late, to support the cause of those called standing churches, yet says,

> It is wholly out of rule, and quite injurious, to charge the churches or their ministers with sending men to gaol for rates, for these proceedings are evidently the acts of the civil state, done for it's own utility. The doings of the civil authority, and of that alone.*

Where are the rulers that will stand alone in that practice, without either ministers or truth to support them!

CONCLUSION

And now our dear countrymen, we beseech you seriously to consider of these things. The great importance of a general union through this country, in order to the preservation of our liberties, has often been pleaded for with propriety; but how can such a union be expected so long as that dearest of all rights, equal liberty of conscience is not allowed? Yea, how can any reasonably expect that he who has the hearts of kings in his hand, will turn the heart of our earthly sovereign to hear the pleas for liberty, of those who will not hear the cries of their fellow-subjects, under their oppressions? Has it not been plainly proved, that so far as any man gratifies his own inclinations, without regard to the universal law of equity, so far he is in bondage? so that it is impossible for any one to tyranize over others, without thereby becoming a miserable slave himself: a slave to raging lusts, and a slave to guilty fears of what will be the consequence. We are told that the father of Cyrus, tho' a heathen,

> Had often taught him to consider, that the prudence of men is very short, and their views very limited; that they cannot penetrate into futurity; and that many times what they think must needs turn to their advantage proves their ruin; whereas the gods being eternal, know all things, future as well as past, and inspire those that love them to undertake what is most expedient for them; which is a favor and protection they owe to no man, and grant only to those that invoke and consult them.

* Mr. Joseph Fish's late piece called, *The Examiner examined.* p. 56, 59. A reply thereto, in which that constitution is more distinctly opened, may be had at Mr. Freeman's in Union-Street, Boston.

And we are told by the same author,* of another wise heathen, who said, " 'Tis observable, that those that fear the Deity most, are least afraid of man." And shall not christians awake to a most hearty reverence of him who has said (and will ever make good his word), *With what measure ye meet, it shall be measured to you again.*

Suffer us a little to expostulate with our fathers and brethren, who inhabit the land to which our ancestors fled for religious liberty. You have lately been accused with being disorderly and rebellious, by men in power, who profess a great regard for order and the public good; and why don't you believe them, and rest easy under their administrations? You tell us you cannot, because you are taxed where you are not represented; and is it not really so with us? You do not deny the right of the British parliament to impose taxes within her own realm; only complain that she extends her taxing power beyond her proper limits; and have we not as good right to say you do the same thing? and so that wherein you judge others you condemn your selves? Can three thousand miles possibly fix such limits to taxing power, as the difference between civil and sacred matters has already done? One is only a distance of space, the other is so great a difference in the nature of things, as there is between sacrifices to God, and the ordinances of men. This we trust has been fully proved.

If we ask why have you not been easy and thankful since the parliament has taken off so many of the taxes that they had laid upon us? you answer that they still claim a power to tax us, when, and as much as they please; and is not that the very difficulty before us? In the year 1747, our legislature passed an act to free the baptists in general from ministerial taxes for ten years: yet because they increased considerably, when that time was about half expired, they broke in upon the liberty they had granted, and made a new act, wherein no baptist church nor minister was allowed to have any such exemption, till they had first obtained certificates from three other churches. By which the late Mr. John Procter observed (in a remonstrance that he drew, and which was presented to our court) that they had as far as in them lay,

> disfranchised, unchurched and usurped an illegal power over all the reli-

* Rollin in his ancient history.

> gious societies of the people in said act called anabaptists throughout this province:—For where is it possible for the poor anabaptists to find the first three authenticated ministers and churches to authenticate the first three!

So we have now related a case, in which a number of our brethren were put to new cost for copies to notify others, with hope of relief to themselves, and yet in the same session of court, they had a worse burden laid upon them than before; and their repeated cries, and then the petition of our united churches, were all rejected.

A very great grievance which our country has justly complained of is, that by some late proceedings a man's house or locks cannot secure either his person or his property, from oppressive officers. Pray then consider what our brethren have suffered at Ashfield.

Many think it hard to be frowned upon only for pleading for their rights, and laying open particular acts of encroachment thereon; but what frowns have we met with for no other crime? and as the present contest between Great-Britain and America, is not so much about the greatness of the taxes already laid, as about a submission to their taxing power; so (though what we have already suffered is far from being a trifle, yet) our greatest difficulty at present concerns the submitting to a taxing power in ecclesiastical affairs. It is supposed by many that we are exempted from such taxes, but they are greatly mistaken, for all know that paper is a money article; and writing upon it is labour, and this tax we must pay every year, as a token of submission to their power, or else they will lay a heavier tax upon us. And we have one difficulty in submitting to this power, which our countrymen have not in the other case: that is, our case affects the conscience, as their's does not: and equal liberty of conscience is one essential article in our charter, which constitutes this government, and describes the extent of our rulers authority, and what are the rights and liberties of the people. And in the confession of faith which our rulers and their ministers have published to the world, they say,

> God alone is Lord of the conscience, and hath left it free from the doctrines and commandments of men, which are, in any thing contrary to his word; or *not contained in it*; so that to believe such doctrines, or to obey such commands, out of conscience, is to betray true liberty of conscience;

and the requiring of an implicit faith, and an absolute blind obedience, is to destroy liberty of conscience and reason also.

And a most famous historian of their's, after mentioning some former violations of that liberty, says,

> The great noise that hath been made in the world about the persecution made in New-England, I will now stop with only transcribing the words uttered in the sermon to the first great and general assembly of the Massachusetts-Bay, after the two colonies of Massachusetts and Plymouth were by royal charter united. (from 2 Chron. 12. 12.)
>
> Things will go well, when magistrates are great promoters of the thing that good is, and what the Lord requireth of them. I do not mean that it would be well for the civil magistrate, with civil penalty to compel men to this or that way of worship, which they are conscientiously indisposed unto. He is most properly the officer of human society, and a christian by non-conformity to this or that imposed way of worship, does not break the terms on which he is to enjoy the benefits of human society. A man has a right unto his life, his estate, his liberty, and his family, although he should not come up unto these and those blessed institutions of our Lord. Violences may bring the erroneous to be hypocrites, but they will never bring them to be believers; no, they naturally prejudice men's minds against the cause, which is therein pretended for, as being a weak, a wrong, an evil cause.*

These things were then delivered and were received with the thanks of the house of representatives, and ten years after were spread by the historian thro' the nation, with the express design of stoping any further complaints about New-England's persecutions. But if the constitution of this government, gives the magistrate no other authority than what belongs to civil society, we desire to know how he ever came to impose any particular way of worship, upon any town or precinct whatsoever? And if a man has a right to his estate, his liberty and his family, notwithstanding his non-conformity to the magistrates way of worship, by what authority has any man had his goods spoiled, his land sold, or his person imprisoned, and thereby deprived of the enjoyment both of his liberty and his family, for no crime at all against the peace or welfare of the state, but only because

* Magnalia, B. 7. p. 28, 29.

he refused to conform to, or to support an imposed way of worship, or an imposed minister.*

In a celebrated oration for liberty, published last spring in Boston, a maxim was recited which carries it's own evidence with it, which is this, *no man can give that which is another's.* Yet have not our legislature from time to time, made acts to empower the major part of the inhabitants in towns and precincts, to give away their neighbours estates to what ministers they please! And can we submit to such doctrines and commandments of men, and not betray true liberty of conscience! Every person is or ought to be, benefited by civil government, and therefore they owe rulers honor and a tribute on that account; but the like cannot be truly said of an imposed minister; for as the gospel ministry is an ordinance of God and not of man, so the obligation that any person or people are under to obey and support any man as a minister of Christ, arises from the consideration of his appearing to them to resemble his Master in doctrine and conversation, and from the benefit which people receive under their ministrations.† From whence the law of equity makes the free communications of our carnal things to Christ's ministers, to be a matter that as really concerns the exercise of a good conscience toward God, as prayer and praise do; for they are both called sacrifices to him in the same chapter. Heb. 13. 15, 16.

Thus we have laid before the public a brief view of our sentiments concerning liberty of conscience, and a little sketch of our sufferings on that account. If any can show us that we have made any mistakes, either about principles or facts, we would lie open to conviction: But we hope none will violate the forecited article of faith so much, as to require us to yield a blind obedience to them, or to expect that spoiling of goods or imprisonment can move us to betray the cause of true liberty.

* Many pretend that without a tax to support ministers, the public would suffer for want of due encouragment of useful learning. But human learning is surely as needful for physicians and lawyers, as for spiritual teachers; and dare any deny that the affairs of law and physick fall more directly under the notice of the state than divinity does? why then do our legislature leave every man, and woman too, at liberty to choose their own lawyer and physician, and not oblige them either to employ or pay any other, though the majority may prefer them? Can any better reason be rendered for this difference in conduct than this, viz. It has been found to be an easier matter to impose upon people about their souls, than about their bodies or their temporal estates!

† Heb. 12. 7, 17. Phil. 4. 9, 10. 1 Cor. 9. 11. Gal. 6. 6. 1 Tim. 5. 17. 18.

A late writer in the Boston papers, has taken much pains to prove, that some other colonies have imposed upon people in such affairs worse than New-England has; and to prove it he informs us, that an act for ministers maintenance, was passed in New-York near eighty years ago, which succeeding rulers have turned to support a denomination that had very few representatives in court when the act was made, while the denomination who made it, have been denied any benefit from it. If so, how loud is the call to every man that is a friend to liberty, and who regards the good of posterity, to rise and exert all his influence, to demolish the engine which has done so much mischief in all ages! We are far from trying to represent the fathers of New-England as the worst of the colonists; We believe the contrary. But our veneration for their memory, is so far from reconciling us to, that it fills us with greater detestation of, that mystery of iniquity, which carried them into such acts or imposition and persecution as have left a great blemish upon their character. And since these are tedious things to dwell upon, we shall close with this remark.

The Massachusetts ministers, in their letter to governor Jencks and other baptists in Providence, said, We hope and pray that ancient matters that had acrimony unhappily in them may be buried in oblivion. Now we are told that acrimony signifies that quality in one body whereby it corrodes, eats up or destroys another. This eating destroying quality is truly unhappy: but how can it be buried before it is dead? The worst of criminals are to be executed before they are buried. Therefore let this cruel man-eater be fairly executed, and we are ready to join heart and hand to bury him, and not to have a bone of him left for contention in all the land. If it be so hard to our opponents to hear of these matters, what has it been to those who have felt their eating and destroying influence for these hundred and forty years? And how can any person lift up his head before God or man, and say he hopes to have these things buried, if he at the same time holds fast, and tries hard to keep alive the procuring cause of them!

The foregoing appeal, having been examined and approved by many of his brethren, is presented to the public, by their humble servant,

Isaac Backus

POSTSCRIPT

Since the above was written, I have received direct accounts, that at Montague (whose case is mentioned p. [349].) they continue from time to time, to make distress upon the principal members of the baptist church there, whom the law directs to sign their certificates, while they let the rest of the society alone. Also that William White a regular member of the baptist church in Ashfield, who lives in Chesterfield, and has had his standing in said church certified according to law; yet had a cow taken from him on August 25, 1773, and sold the 30th, for the pedobaptist ministers rate; and that in both of these places, the civil charges of the town, and the ministers salary are all blended in one tax (contrary as I am informed to the law of our province) so that our brethren who would readily pay their civil tax, yet cannot do it, without paying the ministers also! Now the grand pretence that is made for the use of the secular arm to support ministers is, that thereby equality is established among the people; but what religion, equality or equity can there be in the above proceedings!

THE END

Chronology

1774–1781

1774 SCRIPTURAL INSTRUCTIONS TO CIVIL RULERS, Samuel Sherwood

Coercive Acts are passed by Parliament, which, among other things, closes Boston Harbor (Mar. 25). The colonists term these the "Intolerable Acts." The First Continental Congress adopts a "Statement of Rights and Grievances" (Oct. 14), which strongly foreshadows the Declaration of Independence (Oct. 14).

Jefferson's *A Summary View of the Rights of British America* is published in Williamsburg.

Other influential pamphlets appear, including James Wilson's *Considerations on the Nature & Extent of the Legislative Authority of the British Parliament* and John Adams's (as Novanglus) *New England Letters*. In November, Thomas Paine emigrates and settles in Philadelphia.

1775 A CALM ADDRESS TO OUR AMERICAN COLONIES, John Wesley

A CONSTITUTIONAL ANSWER TO WESLEY'S CALM ADDRESS, Anonymous

AMERICA'S APPEAL TO THE IMPARTIAL WORLD, Moses Mather

In London, Edmund Burke makes a last-ditch appeal to the House of Commons to avert revolution in his *Speech on . . . Conciliation with the Colonies* (Mar. 22).

Patrick Henry delivers a speech in Richmond, concluding with "give me liberty, or give me death" (Mar. 23).

The ride of Paul Revere and the battles of Lexington and Concord (Apr. 18–19) begin the Revolutionary War. Ministers, in sermons and reprinted sermons, are in the vanguard to justify independence, defend liberty as a fundamental good, and encourage their congregations to sacrifice. Over 80 percent of the politically relevant pamphlets published during the 1770s and 1780s are either reprinted sermons or essays written by ministers.

Fort Ticonderoga and Crown Point are captured by the Green Mountain Boys led by Ethan Allen and Seth Warner (May 10).

The Second Continental Congress assembles at Philadelphia (May 10). Congress appoints George Washington commander-in-chief.

The first pitched battle of the Revolution (June 15) is fought at Bunker's Hill, near Boston (June 15).

The first anti-slavery society in America is formed in Philadelphia.

Massachusetts adopts its 1692 Charter as a functioning state constitution.

1776 THE CHURCH'S FLIGHT INTO THE WILDERNESS, Samuel Sherwood

THE DOMINION OF PROVIDENCE OVER THE PASSIONS OF MEN, John Witherspoon

THE BIBLE AND THE SWORD, John Fletcher

The Declaration of Independence is passed (July 4), but New Hampshire, South Carolina, Virginia, and New Jersey have, at the suggestion of the Continental Congress, already written constitutions as independent states.

The city of New York is occupied by the British (Sept. 15).

The presidio of San Francisco is founded by colonists from Mexico under Captain Juan Bautista de Anza and Alfréz José Moraga (Sept. 17); Franciscan friars, led by Father Francisco Palóu, established a mission one month later.

Washington retreats to Harlem Heights with an army of mostly ill-trained militia. In the Battle of Trenton (Dec. 26), Washington crosses the Delaware River and captures 1,000 Hessians.

Adam Smith publishes *Inquiry into the Nature and Causes of the Wealth of Nations* in London, Thomas Paine publishes "Common Sense," and John Adams publishes "Thoughts on Government."

The era of state constitution-making in America begins: Eight states write new constitutions, and three adopt revised charters as constitutions. Three more states will write constitutions in 1777, followed by one in 1778, 1780, 1784, and 1786. Each state ratifies freedom of conscience, which includes religious belief, even though several states still have established churches. Prohibitions on Catholics holding office, common everywhere in 1775, now disappear.

1777 GOD ARISING AND PLEADING HIS PEOPLE'S CAUSE, Abraham Keteltas

The British are defeated at the Battle of Princeton (Jan. 3). Gen. Howe defeats Washington at Brandywine and then occupies Philadelphia (Sept. 11). Gen. Burgoyne is defeated at Saratoga and surrenders his entire army of 6,000 (Oct. 17).

Congress agrees to the Articles of Confederation and sends the document to the states for approval (Nov. 15). After a long approval process, the Articles take effect in 1781.

Washington winters in Valley Forge, Pennsylvania, amidst great suffering.

1778 DIVINE JUDGMENTS UPON TYRANTS, Jacob Cushing

The French become more active in supporting America against the British.

The British invade the South and capture Savannah (Dec. 29).

Massachusetts rejects a proposed state constitution, in part because it has no bill of rights.

1779 Spain enters the war against Britain (June).

Capt. John Paul Jones, in the *Bonhomme Richard*, defeats the British at sea (Sept. 23).

The Universalist Church is founded, a Congregationalist offshoot that rejects the doctrine of predestination.

1780 A SERMON ON THE DAY OF THE COMMENCEMENT OF THE CONSTITUTION, Samuel Cooper

Charleston surrenders to the British (May 12), who also overrun South Carolina (July).

Rochambeau lands in Newport, Rhode Island, with 6,000 French troops (July).

Benedict Arnold's plan to surrender West Point to the British is uncovered (Sept.).

Pennsylvania passes a law that begins the gradual freeing of slaves in the state.

The American Academy of Arts and Sciences is formed in Boston.

Massachusetts writes a new state constitution.

1781 A SERMON PREACHED AT LEXINGTON ON THE 19TH OF APRIL, Henry Cumings

In the Battle of Cowpens, South Carolina, the British cavalry under Col. Tarleton are defeated by Gen. Morgan (Jan.); at the Battle of Eutaw Springs, British forces impel the withdrawal of Gen. Greene, then retreat to Charleston (Sept.).

The Siege of Yorktown ends with the surrender of 7,000 British under Gen. Cornwallis, ending British hopes for victory (Sept.–Oct.).

12

SCRIPTURAL INSTRUCTIONS TO CIVIL RULERS

Samuel Sherwood

NEW-HAVEN

1774

SAMUEL SHERWOOD (1730–1783). A 1749 graduate of Yale, Sherwood took his second degree there also and was later awarded an A.M. by the College of New Jersey at Princeton, where he tutored and where his uncle, Aaron Burr, Sr., was president. In 1757 he settled in Weston, Connecticut, as the first pastor of a church consisting of twelve members. There he remained for the rest of his relatively short life.

Only two of Sherwood's sermons have survived, and they are accorded such importance that both are reprinted in the present volume. The first, entitled *Scriptural Instructions to Civil Rulers, and all Free-born Subjects* (1774), is one of the most famous of all Revolutionary War sermons. An "address to the Freemen of the Colony" of Connecticut, it takes as one of its title-page epigraphs Acts 22:28: "And the chief Captain answered, With a great sum obtained I this freedom; and Paul said, but I was born free." Ranging through biblical and classical sources, and appealing to the English constitution as well, Sherwood eloquently urges the necessity of just rule for free men. In a passage reminiscent of Patrick Henry's famous speech, he writes: "No free state was ever yet enslaved and brought into bondage, where the people were incessantly vigilant and watchful; and instantly took the alarm at the first addition made to the power exercised over them."

A long Appendix (some forty pages in the original) has been omitted here. Written by Ebenezer Baldwin, pastor of Danbury and a powerful voice in the move to revolution, details the transgressions of Britain against its American colonies. It sounds the persistent refrain: "When our lives and property are subject to the arbitrary disposal of others; what have we valuable to call our own?" Baldwin died in the field at New York in 1776 at age 32.

A SERMON,

CONTAINING,

Scriptural Instructions to Civil Rulers, and all Free-born Subjects.

In which the Principles of sound Policy and good Government are established and vindicated; and some Doctrines advanced and zealously propagated by NEW-ENGLAND TORIES, are considered and refuted.

Delivered on the public FAST,

AUGUST 31, 1774.

With an Address to the FREEMEN of the Colony.

By *Samuel Sherwood*, A. M.

Pastor of a Church of Christ in FAIRFIELD.

Also, An APPENDIX,

Stating the heavy Grievances the Colonies labour under from several late Acts of the British Parliament, and shewing what we have just Reason to expect the Consequences of these Measures will be.

By the Rev. EBENEZER BALDWIN, of Danbury.

And the chief Captain answered, With a great sum obtained I this freedom; and Paul said, but I was born free.

ACTS xxii, 28.

Sit Denique Inscriptum in fronte unius Cujusque Civis quid De Republica sentiat. CICERO.

Patria mihi mea vita multo est Cario. CICERO.

New-Haven, Printed by *T.* and *S. GREEN.*

TO THE RESPECTABLE FREEMEN, OF THE ENGLISH COLONY OF CONNECTICUT

My Dear Countrymen and Friends,

The ensuing discourse was delivered on a very solemn occasion, before an auditory apparently serious and devout in their attention; and is now made public at the desire of some of my public spirited friends. Such as it is, I cheerfully offer it as my poor mite, into the public treasury; while others are casting in of their abundance. And I hope and trust that your candor will be such, amidst all the inaccuracies and imperfections that attend such an hasty composition, as to accept it for a real token and proof of my undissembled love and heart-felt concern for my dear country, under the dark and threatning aspects of divine providence on our most invaluable liberties and privileges. While I observe with the most sensible grief, and anxious concern, some of my countrymen, sunk into a state of worse than brutal stupidity and insensibility, who secretly rejoice in the distressing miseries and calamities brought on our suffering brethren at Boston; and ardently wish and pray, *in the most profane manner*, if I may be allowed the expression, that our charter and birth-right privileges may be taken from us; that we may be ruled by the iron rod of oppression, and chained down to eternal slavery and bondage. Whose factious and rebellious leaders improve every opportunity in their power, to impeach a loyal people; and to send misrepresentations of us to their correspondents that have access to the British court, to hasten our intended ruin and destruction. I say, while these clandestine, mischievous operations are carrying on against us, as black and dark as the powder-treason plot; it revives my soul, and rejoices my heart to find that the main body of the people, or at least, the most sensible and judicious part of them, are in some degree, awakened by the loud thunders in Providence, and have their eyes opened to the danger and ruin we are threatened with; that they are so far raised above that infamous herd of vile miscreants, as to know that they are men, and have the spirits of men; and not an inferior species of animals, made to be beasts of burden to a lawless, corrupt administration. This manly, this heroic, and truly patriotic spirit, which is gradually kindling up in every free-man's breast, through the continent, is undoubtedly a token for good; and will, if duly regulated by Christian principles and rules, ensure success to American liberty and freedom. No free state was ever yet enslaved and brought into bondage, where the people were incessantly vigilant and watchful; and instantly took the alarm at the first addition made to the power exercised over them. They are those only of the tribes of Issachar, who keep in profound sleep; and like strong and stupid asses, couch down between heavy burdens; that insensibly sink into abject slavery and bondage. It is a duty incumbent upon us at all times, to keep a watchful attention to our interests (especially in seasons of peril and danger), to watch and pray that we fall not.

I do not mean to encourage evil jealousies and groundless suspicions of our civil rulers, the guardians of our liberties; nor to countenance seditious tumults in the state, so destructive to our civil happiness and peace. I am a firm friend to good order and regularity; that all ranks of men move in strait lines, and within their own proper spheres: That authority and government be supported and maintained so as to promote the good of society, the end for which it was instituted; perfectly consistent with which, a people may keep a watchful eye over their liberties, and cautiously guard against oppression and tyranny, which I detest and abhor, and solemnly abjure.

But you, gentlemen freemen, have been so well indoctrinated in the principles of loyalty and good policy, have been so constantly taught from your infancy, to fear God, and honor the king, that 'tis needless to add any particular instructions on this head. However, as my heart, at this threatning period, is so full of apprehension of danger, you will not, I trust, take it as any reflection on your understanding and integrity as a body, should I drop the hint, that there may possibly be some here and there in disguise, against whose plausible pretences, and artful insinuations, it might be well for you to guard.

> Men *(says the truly ingenious and patriotic Farmer, in Pennsylvania)*, who either hold or expect to hold certain advantages by setting examples of servility to their countrymen; men, who trained to the employment, or self-

taught by a natural versatility of genius; serve as decoys, for drawing the innocent and unwary, into snares; it is not to be doubted but that such men will diligently bestir themselves on this, and every like occasion, to spread the infection of their meanness as far as they can. On the plans they have adopted, this is their course; this is their method to recommend themselves to their patron: they act consistently in a bad cause. From them we shall learn how pleasant and profitable a thing it is, to be, for our submissive behaviour, well-spoken of at St. James's, or St. Stephen's, at Guildhall, or the Royal-exchange. Specious fallacies will then be drest up with all the arts of delusion, to persuade one colony to distinguish herself from another by unbecoming condescentions, which will serve the ambitious purposes of great men at home; the way to obtain considerable rewards. It will be insinuated to us with a plausible affectation of wisdom and concern, How prudent it is to please the powerful—How dangerous to provoke them. And then comes in the perpetual incantation that freezes up every generous purpose of the soul, in cold inactive expectation, that if there is any request to be made, compliance will obtain favourable attention. Our vigilance, and our union are success and safety. Our negligence and our division are distress and death; nay, worse, they are shame and slavery. The persons here meant *(says the abovesaid gentleman)*, are those base spirited wretches, who may endeavour to distinguish themselves by their sordid zeal in defending and promoting measures which they know, beyond all question, to be destructive to the just rights and true interests of their country. It is scarcely possible to speak of them with any degree of propriety; for no words can truly describe their guilt and meanness; but every honest bosom, on this being mentioned, will feel what cannot be exprest.

Some of a narrow contracted turn of mind may think that by this quotation, and some other expressions I have used, I aim to point out persons of a certain religious profession, as objects of public odium and contempt. To which I answer, no further than their temper and conduct render them worthy of it. I do not think that piety, public virtue, and a love to one's country, are entailed to, or inseperably connected with any one mode of professing christianity; however some may have the advantage of others, in their tendency to promote these christian and political virtues; yet I believe there may be mean, base and mercenary wretches in every profession, who for one sweet delicious morsel to themselves, might be tempted to sell their country with all its liberties and privileges, as profane Esau sold his birthright. On the other hand, I believe there are many good men, of sound integrity, of unblemished morals, and truly lovers of their country in every denomination of christians. On this subject, it matters not with me, whether a man be a stated member of this or that church, whether he be in communion with that established in Old England, or in New; provided he be a good man, actuated by evangelical principles and motives, and will stand fast in the liberty wherewith Christ has made him free. I disdain the low singularities of a party. I desire that every man may think and judge for himself in religion, and enjoy all the sacred rights and liberties of conscience in full. There is but one general distinction that is of essential importance in the cause now depending, and that is to be made by drawing the dividing line between the true friends to the rights of humanity, our dear country, and constitutional liberties and privileges, civil and religious: And the base, traitorous and perfidious enemies thereto. Let the first sort of such an amiable character be honoured and beloved, and promoted to all public offices and employments in the state: let the latter sort have a public brand of infamy put upon them, to mark them out as the worst of villains, the open and avowed enemies of mankind, and traitors of their country, who are secretly hoping for ministerial favours. If any under pretence of great moderation, or a pacific disposition, stand as neuters in this important cause, skulking as behind the door, and undetermined on which side they can serve themselves to best advantage, sometimes appearing friendly to this party, and sometimes to that; we can have no safe dependence on them in a day of extremity. He that will not stand forth firmly and boldly for this country, when exposed so as to need his help; is no true friend to it. And as there may possibly be some such secret dissembling enemies acting in disguise, among us; it might be well for you, gentlemen freemen, to be cautiously on your guard against them: they cannot safely be trusted with the lowest office in the state. As you have it in your power to choose your own rulers and officers, from a governor even down to a tythingman, the present state of these times makes it requisite and necessary that you be very vigilant and watchful, and get a thorough knowledge of men's political principles, before you advance them to any seat in government, or any office in the state. If the office oaths had an additional clause to them, in this critical day, it might possibly be a stronger safeguard and security to us, *viz.* That every person who comes into office, solemnly swear, not only allegiance to the king, and faithfulness in general; but that he will maintain and defend the constitutional rights, and charter privileges of his country. I add but my best wishes and hearty prayers to God for the continuation of these rights and privileges to us, and our children after us, to the latest posterity. I remain your most cordial friend, and devoted humble servant,

Norfield, in Fairfield, September 8, 1774 The Author

The God of Israel said, the Rock of Israel spake to me, He that ruleth over men must be just, ruling in the fear of God.

II Samuel, xxiii. 3.

God the sovereign Lord and supreme Ruler of all things, has made men in such a manner, and placed them in such circumstances, as plainly to discover his will, that they should unite and combine into societies for their mutual benefit and advantage. He has not, by the light of nature, nor by any positive declarations of his will, infallibly directed what form of society he would have to prevail, nor prescribed any one particular species of civil government, as more agreeable to him, than another. But has made mankind rational creatures; and left them to choose that which they apprehend to be most perfect in its nature and kind, and best suited to their state, situation and circumstances. The divine constitution, and government of God over his intelligent creatures, is fixed; and it does not become men to exercise their invention or wisdom in seeking any alteration or change in it: but to study the most ready and cheerful submission; as they may be assured, that whatever God requires, is fit and right for his subjects to comply with. His authority and power over us is unlimited and uncontrolable, and cannot be denied, or opposed without our being guilty of the highest crime of rebellion. But no created being is invested with such absolute, unlimited power, nor qualified for the exercise of it. Error and imperfection belongs to every individual of the human race. The brightest character that was ever justly drawn among mortal men, has this dark shade in it: So that the will of none, is infallibly right in all things, and cannot therefore be complied with in all instances, consistent with a good conscience, and the superior obligations we are under to the sovereign Ruler of the world; who still maintains this rightful authority over us, and has not given it by delegation, to any one among created beings: all of whom were originally made free-agents; and considered as in a state of nature, previous to their uniting as members of society, have their liberty and free choice to agree upon such a form of government, and mode of administration in their civil and temporal affairs, as they judge most conducive to their happiness and good: any one of which has no more claim than another to be, *jure divino*, or of divine right, on any other principle, than its being more conformable to right reason and equity, by the eternal rules of which, God has manifested it to be his will, that his rational creatures be governed.

As societies and communities have their beginning and origin in voluntary compact and agreement; when persons have entered by consent and free choice, into society, they must acknowledge themselves under strict and sacred obligations to act toward one another agreeable to the laws and constitution of that society whereof they are members. There are certain duties required of rulers, as well as of subjects; and their obligations faithfully and punctually to fulfil them, rise in proportion to the dignity and importance of their high and elevated stations; and the effect and influence which their conduct has on the rest of the body. A man's being raised to honour and promotion above others, is so far from releasing him from, or lessening his duty, that every step he takes in his advancement, proportionably enlarges it, and adds a new and powerful obligation to the performance of it. The most absolute of sovereign princes owe something to the meanest of their subjects; and may be very criminal in the neglect or refusal of it. Subjects have rights, privileges and properties; and are countenanced and supported by the law of nature, the laws of society, and the law of God; in demanding full protection in the enjoyment of these rights, and the impartial distribution of justice, from their rulers. And when rulers refuse these, and will not comply with such a reasonable and equitable demand from the subject; the society is dissolved; and its fundamental laws violated and broken; and the relation between the ruler and the subject ceases, with all the duties and obligations that arose from it. For it must be supposed, and every one of common sense will readily allow, that no man would ever have consented to place himself in the state of a subject, on any other consideration or footing than that of his having protection and justice from those to whom he submitted. The good of society in all its individual members, is the end for which it is formed; and for which government is instituted and appointed. And this cannot be obtained, unless rulers exert their power, influence and authority to protect their subjects in all their valuable rights and privileges; defend them against their enemies, both from without, and within; and administer impartial justice among them. David, who had, for many years, exercised an absolute sovereignty and dominion over the kingdom of Israel, had no notion of aggrandizing himself, and his nobility, by enslaving his subjects, and striping them of their property, at his own arbitrary will and pleasure, contrary to law and right: but considers himself as appointed to serve them, whose rights and privileges were esteemed by him, more sacred and inviolable than those of the royal scepter and diadem. The best and most illustrious part of his character consisted in this, that he approved himself the faithful servant of God, and his generation. His ambition and desire was to serve his generation; not to be served by them in the character of abject vassals and slaves. A king or prince of his noble and heroic spirit could have no pleasure or satisfaction in ruling over their fellow-mortals, degraded to such a low, infamous state, so far beneath humanity. But to rule over men that have the spirit of men, the spirit of loyalty and liberty; and who possess some property too; is an honour to the most dignified king or prince. And the more of this spirit of liberty, in conjunction with property among the subjects, the greater is the honour of him that sways the scepter in righteousness over them. This Jewish, or Israelitish prince was very sensible, that kings and rulers were liable to do wrong, unjust actions, as well as others; that the subjects had rights and properties that might be invaded or encroached upon by them. We therefore find among his last words, the excellent sentence now read, which he spake just as he was leaving his earthly throne and kingdom, and going to appear before a higher tribunal. *He that ruleth over men must be just, ruling in the fear of God.* David himself had been a ruler over men: he was the man who was raised up on high; the anointed of the God of Jacob, must therefore, from his own great experience and observation, be supposed to have a thorough knowledge and understanding of the subject on which he here speaks with so much seriousness and solemnity, as in the near view of eternity, which consideration adds weight and importance to his expressions; and might be sufficient to engage the attention of the most dignified rulers, and sovereign princes, to them; who must be inexcusable if they refuse to receive instruction from them, since a greater than David is here: *The God of Israel has said, the Rock of Israel has spoken.* That glorious Being by whom kings reign, and princes decree justice, is the author of this divine sentence here given forth: to whom sovereign rulers are as strictly accountable for all their conduct, as the meanest of their subjects—may therefore properly be called upon, and that, by the authority of the great Lord and governor of the world, to attend to, and conscientiously practice their duty in such plain, important instances of it. *Be wise now therefore O ye kings*, says God, *be instructed ye judges of the earth; serve the Lord with fear, rejoice with trembling*. Psal. ii. 10, 11.

In further discoursing from these words, I shall,

I. Consider the necessity and importance of justice in civil rulers.

II. Shew that the fear of the Lord is the proper, effectual principle, to influence such to the observation and practice of justice.

I. 'Tis highly necessary and important, that civil rulers should be just. Such are concerned in the rules of justice and righteousness, as well as other men; and indeed, more so, in proportion as they are raised above others; and have it in their power to do greater good or evil, according as they are inclined. Was the doctrine true, *That all property is vested in the king, or chief rulers; and that they can do no wrong to their subjects:* Such scripture precepts and directions from the sovereign Ruler of the world as that in my text, would be entirely needless and impertinent; and seem, on this supposition, to argue his want of wisdom and knowledge, on this important subject. But however bold some conceited, ambitious mortals may be, in censuring others, when advanced a little above them in wealth and power; yet, I would hope that few or none will dare openly to attack divine revelation, and censure the ruling wisdom of God. *Let God be true, tho' every man be found a liar. Let God be wise, tho' every man be found a fool.* If those that rule over men, must be just; there is certainly some rule of justice and righteousness for them to observe in this office and character: and it may be infered by just consequence, *That they are capable of doing wrong*; and as liable so to do as other men, that those who stand related to them as subjects, have really something to call their own, that they have rights and properties distinct from their sovereign, are capable of suffering injustice, oppression and wrong, even from them; and that, in a greater degree than from any of their fellow-subjects, in proportion to the greater degree of their strength and power. The aforesaid doctrine therefore, advanced by some, *That kings and sovereign rulers with their ministry, can do no wrong*, is so far from being true, that it is the most false, absurd doctrine that was ever preached in the world; and of most pernicious bad consequence both to ruler and ruled, directly tending not only to the temporal, but eternal destruction of both. As rulers are capable, when they rightly improve the superiour advantages of their high and elevated stations, of doing more towards promoting justice and righteousness among their fellow-men: so, when of a contrary temper and disposition, that i[s] to say, when they neglect, and refuse to attend to those good laws and rules of equity; and take it into their heads to act in an arbitrary, tyrannical manner, to oppress and enslave their subjects; they do the highest injustice and wrong, and the greatest mischief and evil of any men in the world; and are the biggest plagues, and heaviest judgments upon a society that can be sent upon them.

Corruptio optimi est pessima.

None therefore that are promoted to the office and character of civil rulers, ought to think themselves above the observation of the eternal rules of justice and righteousness, by which they themselves, as well as their subjects, will be tried hereafter, and justified or condemned by the righteous judge of the world.

But that I may, to better advantage, illustrate the great necessity and importance of justice in civil rulers, I shall briefly consider them in their several capacities, and shew the necessity of their being just, while acting in them.

Now, under the name of rulers, are comprehended; both those who enact laws, and those who execute them; those who are cloathed with legislative authority, and those who have that which is judicial and ministerial.

When men first joined in society, 'twas impossible for them to form at once, a complete, perfect system of laws, to suit all exigences, and particular cases that might happen: they could not foresee all future events, and make provision for them. The body politic, is like the natural body; subject to a variety of distempers and diseases, 'tis sometimes strong, healthy and vigorous, and every part performs its proper office and function, without impediment or obstruction: At other times, it declines, grows weak and relaxed in all its nervous parts; and to use the significant and beautiful language of inspiration, *The whole head is sick, and the whole heart faint; from the sole of the foot, even unto the head, there is no soundness in it.* And as it is liable to be thus sickly and distempered; so 'tis liable to be dissolved and die.

Now, as a man finds it necessary to regulate himself in regard to diet, exercise, physic, &c. and suit his way of living to the present condition of his body, as will best serve to promote the health and activity of all the members of it; so there is the necessity of the like wise, prudential methods of administration in government, suited to the different state and circumstances of the body politic. And as circumstances vary, and new and different scenes open to view; new laws become necessary for the health and benefit of the community. All governments have therefore a legislative authority lodged in some hand or other; not to be exercised at the arbitrary will and pleasure of one or more individuals; but in the exercise of it to be restrained and limited, at least by the eternal rules of justice and righteousness, as it is designed, not for the destruction, but for the health and preservation of the body. And as it is necessary for the well-being of society, that good laws be made; so 'tis likewise necessary that they be duly put in execution; and that, both in civil and criminal cases: this being the life of the law, without which it signifies nothing toward answering the end for which it was made. Now, in order to this, some persons must have authority to judge between a man and his neighbour, and to put their judgments in execution.

Thus rulers considered either in their legislative or executive capacity, are designed for the general and public good of the community they serve; they are the ministers of God, instituted and ordained to attend continually unto this very thing; and in both these capacities, they must be just. Particularly,

1. There is justice to be observed in making laws. The legislative authority is usually stiled supreme. The power of making laws is undoubtedly the highest in every society. The executive officers are obliged to observe the rule prescribed them by the legislators; and all the subjects of every order, to yield obedience to their laws; provided they are not prejudicial to, but salutary and for the good of society; and do not interfere with the duty they owe to the great Sovereign of all men; and do not contradict the end for which men unite, as members of society; nor run counter to the fundamental constitution on which they are settled. While a society subsists, no man, or number of men, have authority to call to account those who are vested with supreme authority: which makes it extremely difficult to correct disorders in a state, when the foundations are out of course. But tho'

sovereign rulers cannot, while they continue in their high office and character, be called to account, by any under them; yet 'tis possible for them, by acting contrary to the design and intention of their office, to dissolve the society over which they rule; and so, at once lose all their sovereign power and authority: after which, they can have no more than other men, to screen them from such punishment as their crimes deserve. And when such a melancholy event takes place, that a civil society is dissolved, and men return to a state of nature; they have the same liberty they at first had, to form themselves into society again, in what form, and on what terms they please.

But notwithstanding the sovereignty of legislators, they are under strict and sacred obligations to observe the rule of justice, in enacting laws. 'Tis a great and very dangerous mistake to suppose, that legislators have a power absolutely arbitrary; or that their authority is under no limitation or restraint at all. Right and wrong, are founded in the nature of things; and cannot be altered and changed, even by the voice of such kings and monarchs as are betrusted with the power of making laws. The Psalmist mentions, *A throne of iniquity which frameth mischief by a law.* And if he had not mentioned such a thing, any person of common sense and understanding, who considered things with the least degree of attention, would soon be convinced, that 'twas in the nature of things, possible to establish iniquity by a law. And any one who is acquainted with the history of former ages; or even with the present state of the world, cannot but know, that this has in fact, been often done. No intelligent friends to the christian institution doubts, but the laws made by the heathen emperors for extirpating Christianity, and destroying the professors of it, were unjust. All sound protestants, I suppose, will agree on passing the same sentence on the laws which establish an inquisition in some popish countries. And it must be a pleasure to all lovers of liberty and virtue, to observe, that the number of those who wish that no penal laws might be enacted in matters merely religious, that no person might be liable to any penalty, or lie under any incapacity, on account of any opinion or practice in religion, which does not at all affect the peace and happiness of human society, is daily increasing.

Now, if there be any such thing as acting unjustly in making a law, 'tis plain that rulers, considered in their legislative capacity, are obliged to observe some rule of justice. For where there is no duty or obligation of this sort, there can be no such thing as acting unjustly.

'Tis a part of justice in legislators to enact such laws as are suited to the circumstances of the society for the regulation of which they are intended: such as conduce to the public good: And such as, instead of destroying, will secure and protect the just rights and privileges of every individual member: such as will in an equitable manner, decide controversies between particular subjects; and defend the weak, and prevent their becoming an easy prey to the strong: such, finally, as may be a terror to evil doers, and an encouragement to those that do well.

There is further, justice to be observed between the community and particular persons; under which head, are to be reckoned the granting proper reward to those who faithfully serve the public in any capacity: paying public debts: and sacredly observing the public faith. Here likewise may be mentioned the penalties annexed to laws. Penal laws are intended for the public good: The great intention of punishing the transgressors of them is, that others may be kept in awe. And legislators have a right to annex such penalties to their just and equitable laws, as are sufficient to maintain their authority, and secure the observation of them. But yet, there is justice to be observed in proportioning punishments to crimes: and no doubt, it would be unjust, cruel and barbarous, to affix the most severe punishments that could be invented, to small and trifling offences.

2. Rulers considered in their executive capacity as putting laws in execution, must be just. Executive officers are obliged to proceed according to the received and established laws of their country. By these, they are to judge and determine all controversies, both of a civil and criminal nature, which come before them; doing strict, impartial justice to all men, without respect of persons. Their duty is not to oppress: but to deliver the poor that cry to them; the fatherless, and him that hath none to help. They ought to endeavour that the blessing, not the curse of him that is ready to perish, may come upon them: and to cause the widow's heart to sing for joy. It concerns them to put on righteousness, and to clothe themselves with judgment, as with a robe and diadem. They must be eyes to the blind, and feet to the lame, and fathers to the poor; and the cause which they know not, ought to be searched out. To them it belongs to break the jaws of the wicked; and to pluck the spoil out of his

teeth: to curb and restrain the violent; and let the oppressed go free. But it being so evident, and universally acknowledged, that those who put the laws in execution, ought to be just men, I shall not enlarge upon this head: but proceed briefly to show the necessity and importance of rulers being just; or to mention some of the obligations they are under to this great duty. And here,

1. This is necessary to their answering the design of their office, and promoting the welfare and good of human society. Public good is the end of government of every sort. 'Tis with a view of promoting and securing this, that men enter into society. 'Tis for obtaining this, that some are appointed to rule over others; and that those submit to, and obey them. Now, this important end cannot be obtained, unless rulers act uprightly and justly. When civil rulers, forgeting the end of their institution, and the proper duties of their station, neglect and trample upon the rules of justice; and consult only to gratify their own pride and ambitious humour and passion: when they consider their subjects as an inferior species of beings, made as beasts of burden, for their pleasure or profit; when, instead of observing the reason and nature of things, they make their own mere will and pleasure, the rule of acting; and govern in an arbitrary, tyrannical manner; 'tis impossible to describe the evils and mischiefs they bring on mankind. These have been so great and terrible, that some have been ready to question, Whether civil rulers have not done more hurt than good, in the world. When we see an haughty and ambitious monarch, or corrupt ministry spending the blood and treasure of their subjects, in carrying on an unrighteous quarrel and contention with them, or against their neighbours; from a mistaken notion of glory; distressing their towns and cities with their troops and armaments, depopulating their country, and seeming to aim at the universal destruction of mankind; we may well be shock'd at the sight, and look on such a lawless, arbitrary ruler, as the heaviest calamity and judgment, that a righteous God can send upon a sinful people. But notwithstanding the dark and dismal prospect which a scene of tyranny and oppression affords; 'tis undoubtedly true, that civil government is designed for the good of men; and when administered with justice and mercy, it does excellently well answer this design. As tyrants are the greatest of temporal judgments, as being the cause of all the most distressing evils that can be imagined; so good rulers are the

greatest blessings to the world, and the instruments in God's hand, of securing all our other good things. But then, to render them such, they must be just, considered both in a legislative and executive capacity.

2. Rulers are obliged to be just, on account of the great trust reposed in them. Sovereign authority is the greatest trust that can be reposed in any man. The power of making laws is very great, and extensive in its nature, and of the utmost importance in the exercise of it. And next to this, is that of putting laws in execution. The man that is appointed to judge another, with authority to decide all controversies among his fellow-subjects: to determine and pass sentence upon the lives and properties of such vast numbers of men; has a very great and important trust reposed in him. And the weight and importance of the trust reposed in any inferiour executive officer, is proportioned to the authority vested in him. Now, the receiving such a trust lays a man under very great obligations to faithfulness in the discharge of it. Men in such high places of trust and authority, instead of being released from the laws of God, and having their obligations to faithfulness in the discharge of duty, lessened and diminished; have them increased, in proportion to their advancement; and it is not beneath the dignity of their stations, to attend very seriously to the advice and exhortation of the Psalmist, *Be wise now therefore, O ye kings; be instructed ye judges of the earth. Serve the Lord with fear; kiss the son, lest he be angry, and ye perish from the way, when his wrath is kindled but a little.* 'Tis of importance, if men have but one talent, that they improve it: but if they have ten, and neglect and refuse so to do; the punishment will be tenfold greater. If a private man neglects his duty, he, and others connected with him, may suffer. But if a chief ruler is unjust and unfaithful, the whole community or body politic suffers. As much therefore as the welfare and happiness of such a community, or body, is to be valued above, and preferred to the happiness of an individual; so much higher and greater are his obligations to faithfulness, than the obligations of a private member of society; and if he refuses to discharge them uprightly and conscientiously, as in the fear of God; a proportionably heavy and aggravated punishment must he expect to receive, when judged by him.

3. The exercise of justice is necessary in civil rulers, to their own present comfort, and future happiness. 'Tis a common observation,

that the greatest tyrants are the greatest and most miserable slaves. Those rulers who invade the rights and liberties of their own subjects, in an arbitrary, tyrannical manner, and seek to oppress and enslave them; are always in fear of being themselves destroyed by them. They are obliged, at vast expence, to keep up large armies to distress and enslave their peaceable subjects; who, under such a grievous yoke of bondage, cannot be easy and satisfied; but will be naturally struggling after liberty; and be ready, when it galls their necks, to turn against and depose such oppressing tyrants; and sometimes, to imbrue their hands in their blood: of which, many instances are to be found in the histories of the Roman, and of the Turkish empire. Whereas, when princes rule in a just and constitutional way, with mildness and benignity; and seek the good and welfare of their subjects; they may always put full, unreserved confidence in them, and depend on being supported and defended by them, at the expence of all that is dear and valuable to them; yea, at the expence of their lives, which will not be thought too dear a sacrifice for the safety and honour of such a worthy prince.

Again. This justice and faithfulness in rulers is necessary to their having peace in their own minds and consciences. Such have consciences as well as other men, accusing or else excusing; who, upon the faithful discharge of the high trust reposed in them, will have inward peace, security and joy, and heart-felt satisfaction such as the world can neither give, nor take away. But on the other hand; if the rules of justice and righteousness be neglected and trampled upon by them, and they practise high handed tyranny and oppression: and seek to enslave and destroy their subjects; what dreadful horrors of conscience must they necessarily feel when awakened to any serious reflections on their wicked, guilty conduct, which has been so distressing and ruinous to thousands more innocent and righteous than themselves.

Lastly. This justice and faithfulness is necessary to their future happiness. Tho' civil rulers are stiled *gods*, yet must they die like men; and at last, give an account of themselves to the judge of the quick, and the dead.

[II.] I now proceed to the next thing proposed, which as in the second place, to shew, That the fear of the Lord is the proper, effectual principle to influence civil rulers to the exact observance of justice.

He that ruleth over men, must be just: And that he may be so, he must rule in the fear of the Lord. If we consider human nature, as vitiated by the apostacy; we shall find, that hardly any thing but the fear of punishment, is able to keep men in awe, and due subjection. That it is thus with subjects, is evident from the many severe laws, and terrible executions of them, which the wisest and most merciful rulers in all nations, have found necessary to preserve the peace, and promote the happiness of civil society. Now, 'tis certain that the essential principles of human nature are the same in all men, whatever external relations they sustain. There is therefore great danger, that rulers will degenerate into tyrants; and of blessings, become plagues and curses to mankind; unless there be some way to keep them in awe, some principle to excite their fears, and by that means, keep them within their proper sphere, and engage them to the observation of justice. Now, this is not always to be done by a fear of men. Sovereigns are exempted from the common power of human laws; there is no ordinary authority that may judge them; and this their security may prove a strong temptation to them, to neglect the proper duties of their exalted stations. They may trust in their forces and armies to defend them from the resentment of an injured and oppressed people; and so imagine themselves perfectly secure from punishment at present; and the nearer any subordinate ruler approaches to sovereignty, the less has he to fear from men, and consequently, the greater prospect has he, of indemnification in acting unjustly. There is therefore the utmost need and necessity, that those who rule over men, should rule in the fear of the Lord; that they should have a firm belief of the being, perfections and providence of God; that they should not only fear his vindictive punishing justice, but beyond this, as the text requires, maintain an holy awe and reverence of him upon their minds; and consider him as that righteous judge to whom they must at last, give an account of the discharge of the great trust reposed in them; and from whom they shall receive a righteous sentence of absolution or condemnation.

IMPROVEMENT

1. What we have heard on this subject, should serve to excite our thankful acknowledgments to the supreme Ruler of the world for his great favour to us in the happy constitution of government we have hitherto lived under. The providence of God which rules the world (tho' it does not neglect the lesser affairs of men), especially concerns itself in more important things, which respect more large societies and communities of men. Civil government is one of the principal of these. *God is the judge; he setteth up one, and putteth down another;* and orders all the changes and revolutions that come to pass in the kingdoms and empires of the world: whose providence has been very extraordinary, and in a manner, miraculous, in conducting our fathers into this, once howling wilderness in preserving them in their weak, infant-state, when exposed to destruction many ways; and leading them to settle on such an excellent constitution of government; which affords such full protection, and ample security to the subjects, of their lives, liberties and properties; and in providing for us in succession down to this day, such a wise, virtuous and upright set of rulers who we have reason to think, have, in the main, ruled in the fear of the Lord. Our privileges in this respect are very great, beyond what any other people enjoy in any part of the earth. The bigger part of the world have had their liberties wrested out of their hands; been opprest and enslaved by lawless and cruel tyrants: while we are yet in the possession of freedom. May God preserve it to us safe, and hand it down to the latest posterity! Our fathers went through the greatest perils and dangers to procure these privileges for us; and we ought to be willing to do our utmost to preserve them, and hand them down to our children and offspring. Our treasure, and our blood too, are not too dear and costly sacrifices for such valuable things.

2. Of what importance is it, that civil rulers be men of uprightness and integrity; men of real piety and religion; who fear the Lord, and keep up a proper awe and reverence of him upon their minds? This is necessary to their own comfort and happiness; to the peace of their consciences; and to their having a well-grounded hope of a future crown of glory in the coming world. It is likewise necessary to the good and happiness of the society, over which they are appointed to rule. If a sovereign prince or ruler be destitute of integrity and jus-

tice; and has not the fear of the great God before his eyes: all inferior motives which might have influence on men in lower stations, will be insufficient to restrain him from wicked nets of tyranny and oppression, and keep him to his duty. As such cannot well be arraigned before any human tribunal on earth, to account for their conduct; if they have no fear and dread on their minds, of appearing before, and accounting to their supreme Judge, the sovereign ruler of the world; they will be in the utmost danger, not only of ruining themselves both for time and eternity; but also, of ruining their subjects in all their dear and valuable interests; and of involving them in the greatest conceivable distresses and troubles. This is so far from being true, *That such can do no wrong*; that on the contrary, the experience of all ages testifies, that they are capable, when they loose the principles of justice and religion, of doing the greatest mischief and wrong, of any men in the world. *As a roaring lion, and a raging bear*, says Solomon, *So is a wicked ruler over a poor people.* He adds further, *The prince that wanteth understanding is also a great oppressor.*

3. What has been said on this subject, is perfectly agreeable to, and justifies the principles on which the British nation acted, as a body, in deposing king James the second, that tyrannical oppressive prince, when pursuing measures tending to their destruction; and in introducing king William of glorious memory, to the throne, to sway the scepter in righteousness. This grand revolution happened between eighty and ninety years ago. The kings who have reigned over us, since which period, in succession, can make out no just claim and title to the throne, on any other principles than those advanced in this discourse. If these are not well grounded and established; but fail; they must fail with them, and be deemed only usurpers; and the pretender on the other hand, the only rightful heir to the crown. If we embrace the abovesaid doctrine, *The kings with their council and ministry can do no wrong*, but must be obeyed in all their edicts and commands; we must of necessity, condemn the conduct of the nation in general, in rising up against, and deposing king James; and join with the rebels in the highlands of Scotland, in their endeavours to overthrow the present constitution of Great Britain; and to bring in one of the descendents of James, as our rightful king, and disown him that now sits on the throne; and look upon the aforesaid rebels, as the only loyal people in the kingdom; if the nation had no right to oppose the

measures of that ancient king, when they evidently tended to deprive the subjects of their dear liberties and their best rights and properties. If the constitution of England forbids them to resume, and take their things into their own power, when they could not have protection from their sovereign: if it was wrong and unjustifiable for the people to think and judge for themselves, and seek the best remedy in their power, when they found themselves grievously oppressed by the unrelenting hand of arbitrary power: when they found their chief ruler fail in all the essential points of his high office and character, and to act contrary to the very end and design of its institution; then it will follow, that the very foundation-principles of government have been subverted by the revolution, and all, excepting a few that have been deemed rebels, both kings and their subjects have been upon a wrong, wicked plan, for near a century past. And to get right, we must throw up the present constitution of England and the Hanover family, that is in present possession of the throne; and return back in our allegiance to the Stuart family; and to their popish plan of government. These are the genuine consequences of the doctrine of *passive obedience and non-resistance*, so zealously preached up by some artful and designing men, who act as creatures of the state, and probably expect high honours and promotions from a corrupt ministry, as a reward for their labours, to be gathered out of the spoils of their country. A doctrine as unfriendly and injurious to the king, as it is dangerous to the rights and liberties of his subjects. The crown and dignity of the king can be maintained and defended, only on these just and equitable principles, on which the rights and privileges of the people are secured and established. He that denies the right which the body of the people have, to take care of their liberties when in danger, does virtually dethrone our present king, and make him only a usurper; and acts the most friendly and favourable part towards a popish pretender. For it was certainly in consequence of the people's taking their rights and liberties into their own hands, that the illustrious house of Hanover was advanced to the throne of England.

4. If the rules of justice and righteousness ever allowed a people, a right to take care of their liberties and privileges, as all I trust, will readily grant; they are still possessed of this right, and may lawfully use and exert it for those salutary purposes, as they have occasion or

call in divine providence. On this sure ground and footing, the wise and judicious part of the reputable inhabitants of America, proceed to consult the best measures of safety and preservation in this critical and alarming situation of our public affairs.†

The conduct of the several provinces thro' the continent, in sending commissioners to meet in general congress, to secure the threatned liberties and properties of the people, may be justified on these principles. If the people in these American colonies, have really any property, any thing to call their own; which cannot be denied without the most injurious reflection and insult upon, and abuse of them, and their ancestors, who have been labouring and toiling for this purpose, so many years: if this, I say, be granted; then they have a right to secure and defend themselves in the possession of it; and none have a right to take it from them without their consent. But as we hold our properties and privileges by royal charter, has not the

† I am sensible that the present controversy between Great Britain and the American colonies stands upon a different footing from that between king James and his subjects, at the revolution. That was a controversy between the king and his subjects: This is a dispute between the parliament of Great Britain, and the colonies. We have no controversy with the king; nor in the least, dispute his regal authority over us. The king, when at home, presides in person, in the British parliament; but when he goes out of the kingdom (to Hanover for instance) he appoints a regent as his representative, to preside in his absence. In Ireland, the king presides not in person; but by his representative, the lord lieutenant. And in like manner, the king presides in the several colonies, by his representatives, the governors, which are authorised by his charters, or immediate commissions. We have therefore no controversy with our king, whose authority we cheerfully acknowledge, and most loyally obey. But the point disputed is, *Whether his majesty's legislative body in Great Britain, has a right to exercise sovereign authority over his majesty's legislative assemblies in the colonies, for taxation, or the regulation of their internal policy.* The kingdom of *Ireland* owes allegiance to the king of Great Britain: but their internal policy is constitutionally regulated only by their own parliament. And they have a right to deny the authority of the British parliament to tax them; or to regulate the internal policy of the kingdom. And it is a like case with the *American* colonies. We owe allegiance to the king of Great-Britain: but this will not oblige us to yield ourselves up to the arbitrary controul of the British parliament. The parliament of Great Britain has no constitutional right to tax, or regulate the internal policy of the colonies; any more than the legislative body of one colony has to tax or regulate the internal policy of another colony. And therefore the attempts of the British parliament to impose taxes on the colonies, may be resisted by the colonies, perfectly consistent with their allegiance to their king. Altho' therefore our present controversy with Great Britain is on quite another footing than the contest of the nation in the days of king James; yet revolution-principles in their general nature, will fully justify the present constitutional opposition of the colonists to the arbitrary proceedure of the British court.

king and ministry a right to take this charter from us, and to strip us of all? I answer. No more than you that have wives, have a right to break the marriage covenant; and turn them out naked and destitute, and set them adrift. Property is prior to all human laws, constitutions and charters. *God hath given the earth to the children of men.* Our fathers acquired property in this land, and were rightfully possessed of it, previous to their obtaining a royal charter; as can easily be demonstrated. The charter is the most solemn stipulation and compact between the parties, the sovereign and the subject, on certain terms. "And the breaking of charters,["] says a late excellent writer,

> is making the worst war upon mankind. It involves the innocent, and those yet unborn. Every thing depends, with men, on their constitution of government. Such a measure is therefore, wantonly laying waste the territories of the earth, confounding and destroying all private property, and endeavouring to prevent Providence itself to make mankind happy thereon; unless he shall, for the undoing the works of unreasonable, ill-judging men, perform immediate miracles, and suspend, or counteract the established laws of nature, which is surely, not to be supposed, or expected.

5. As all human counsels and endeavours may be insufficient for these important purposes of securing and defending the rights and liberties of a people, when in danger of being, wrested out of their hands, by the violent exertions of arbitrary power; we see the propriety, and the reasonableness of the duty of looking to God, in a way of solemn fasting and prayer, at such a time, for deliverance and safe protection. God, the sovereign ruler of the world, has the great affairs of the kingdoms and empires of the earth, in his own hands; and can dispose of them as seems good unto him. He has the hearts of kings and ministers in his hands, and can turn them, as he turns the rivers of water. In seasons of such danger and distress, our eyes and our hearts should be lifted up to him, for that help and relief that we need. And as we are now called to this important duty, by the pious rulers of the land; all that are so far above the beasts that perish, as to know the rights, the liberties and privileges that essentially belong to humanity; and withal, have any belief of the being of a God, and of his governing providence, will, I trust, heartily unite herein, with a very serious and devout frame of mind; while the ignorant, the profane, and stupid infidals, may probably make a scoff and ridicule of these sacred solemnities.

The great controversy that has for some years, subsisted between the chief rulers in the mother country and the English colonies in America, has arisen to a very great height: and let the fault be on which side it will, we have reason to tremble at the consequences, as we are threatened with most awful ruin and destruction in all that is dear and valuable to us. A neighbouring province begins to feel very sensibly, the distressing effects thereof; as great numbers of its industrious inhabitants are reduced to a suffering state, and become real objects of charity; being turned out of the means by which they procured their daily bread. The chief rulers neither feed nor guide them: but are using means that tend to devour and destroy them; and no other colony or province on the continent has the least security from having the same cruel, oppressive and tyrannical measures used towards them. All the most judicious and sensible part of the inhabitants thro' the whole continent of America, view themselves as interested and concerned in the consequences of this dispute; and expect to stand or fall by the issue of it. The port and harbour of Boston has, for some time been shut up; their trade and commerce stopped; their charter-rights invaded; the security of their lives, liberties and properties, taken away; with an armed force in the midst of them, to heighten their distress, and bring on their complete ruin. Which respectable province, and metropolis of New-England, being once enslaved by the cruel exertions of arbitrary power, and stript of their property for which they, and their ancestors have been, for so many years industriously labouring; some other colony or province will, no doubt, be taken in hand: and so the horrid and execrable scene of tyranny and oppression be vigorously prosecuted from place to place, until it spread over the whole continent. The aspect of our public affairs was never more dark and gloomy, than at the present day. The kingdom under such a load of debt, in such a distracted, divided and convulsed state, as forebodes its speedy ruin and destruction. The foundations of government seem awfully out of course; and the righteous in a state of utmost peril and danger, as they have no sure ground of safety to stand upon.

We are certainly threatened with the loss of our precious liberties and privileges, and of all our dear and valuable interests. Allowing that our conduct as a body, has been loyal, dutiful and obedient to our earthly sovereign; that we have given no just cause or provocation to resolve on such severe, unprecedented measures, as these in the late acts of parliament; yet, can we say, it has been strictly right and justifiable in the sight of the sovereign Ruler of the world? Whose hand is to be considered in these dark clouds that hang over, these distressing judgments that are coming on the land. Have we done nothing to provoke his divine displeasure against us? It becomes us very seriously to inquire, *What meaneth the heat of his anger!* Who, or what has procured the tokens of his wrath and indignation; which some, as instruments stand ready to execute upon us? And how shall we obtain his favour? Sins of any kind, when they become common; when they are openly practised, and that with impunity; bring public guilt; and it may be expected, that if men don't testify against them, God himself will do it; and that, by sending distressing judgments on a people. And God's judgments and threatnings of providence are sometimes of such a nature, as to point out the particular kinds of sin by which he is offended. Let us try this rule in our present circumstances.

The first disadvantage people in general feel and complain of, from the late judicial system of tyranny and oppression; and the severe, unexampled acts of parliament that have been published in consequence of it is, that trade and commerce, and the means of increasing our wealth and riches, are obstructed; and great loss and damages sustained; and at the same time, public charges increased, in supporting agents and commissioners to consult, and look out a way of safety and deliverance for us. Those who live at a distance in the country, from those populous cities and towns that are the chief seat of trade and commerce are not so immediately affected at first, by the operation of these cruel and inhuman acts. Yet must, in time, and in a very short time too, feel the destressing and impoverishing effects of them: which, if carried into execution in the full length and breadth of them will not only diminish our estates; but strip us of all our substance, and reduce us to the condition of slaves that have no possession or property to call their own.

And does not this point out our sins, as especially provoking to God, and procuring the present tokens of his displeasure? Is it not a plain indication that God is offended with that covetousness, or excessive love of the world which abounds? That inordinate love of money, which is the root of all evil? It is owing to this, that men murmur and complain under that public charge which the present state of things makes necessary; and which, after all our complaints, is nothing like what the generality of men are subject to, in their best times, when they have the greatest peace, and least public expence. It has been represented, that some uneasy, dissatisfied persons, who are disaffected to the privileges of their country, have gone so far as to say, They had rather that the king and his ministry might come, and take away our charter-privileges, and all that we have, than to pay such taxes for the support of government over them. To such, if there are any such among us, I would recommend a serious consideration of the awful sentence God pronounced against the murmuring Israelites in the wilderness. Numb. xiv. 28. *As truly as I live, saith the Lord, as ye have spoken in mine ears, so will I do to you.* I will here cite a passage from a sermon of the Rev. Mr. Trumbull, delivered at the freeman's-meeting, in the town of New-Haven, April 12th, 1773, with his note subjoined thereto. Speaking of the advantages of free states, arising from their choosing rulers from among themselves, he observes concerning rulers thus chosen, "Their government is mild and righteous. And as they do not govern *to get their bread*, and advance their fortunes, at the ruin of ours; and as they can lay no burdens on us, without bearing the same weight themselves, their government is as remarkable for the little expence of it, as it is for its gentleness, impartiality and righteousness. All our expences, by way of salary to civil officers, do not, I imagine, amount annually, by considerable, to the one half of the salary of a king's governor, in any of the neighbouring provinces."* On the other hand, the present judgment and threatning discover God's displeasure against us, for

* "The whole amount of the salaries paid annually by the government is only £. 580. The salary of the governor is £. 300, of the deputy governour £. 100, of the secretary £. 20, and of the treasurer £. 160. The judges of the Superior Court have no salary from the government. The Chief Judge is allowed 18 shillings per day, and the four side judges have 17 shillings each per day. This court is obliged by law, to set 14 weeks annually and commonly setteth, by adjournment, much longer, and the cost of it is about £. 600 per annum. The expence of it for three years and a half past, upon a careful examination, appeareth to be about £. 2100, just £. 600 per annum. The avails of it, together with the forfeitures, for the same term, with proper allowances for such as may not be recovered, amount to £. 2200. So that the Superior Court is of no cost, at present, to the colonies considered as a government. In short the whole expence of government in Connecticut is trifling. The cost of the General Assembly annually is about £. 1500. A rate of one penny on the pound, on the grand list, which raiseth

indulging pride and vanity, luxury and intemperance. The plain voice of providence is, that God is awfully offended with all that practise these ruinous and destructive vices.

We are further threatened with being deprived of all our civil privileges, and brought under a most cruel, arbitrary and tyrannical kind of government. The scheme of government planned out for Boston, is in its whole frame and constitution, completely despotic and arbitrary. The will of the chief ruler is law; and the subject holds his estate, and even life, only during his pleasure. This arbitrary government will, no doubt, be carried to its greatest extent through all the American colonies, and exercised in all its terrors and cruelties upon them, if the present ministry are permitted to carry the point they are contending for, in such a sanguine manner.

Now, does not this threatning point out some particular sins, as procuring it? We have been greatly favoured of God in respect to the constitution of the government more immediately over us; and the administration of our public affairs. We in this colony enjoy, not only the full liberties of Englishmen; but even some peculiar privileges, confirmed by royal charter, which distinguish us from the rest of our fellow subjects in the plantations. But how far have we been from being truly thankful for such privileges? And how ready to slight and abuse them? How earnestly have some wished themselves in the condition of the poor tenants and slaves in a neighbouring province, rather than pay a trifle to support their liberties, and freedom, and real estate, in this? How apt have we been to despise the persons, and slight the authority of the rulers of our people? To hearken to, and propagate reports prejudicial to their character? To countenance and join with the disaffected, and begrudge their reward; which is far less than magistrates in any other province have? And after all the murmuring about it, is very inadequate to the public services they perform, and the advantages we derive from their administration. There was something of this disposition in the Jews of old: *They refused the waters of Shiloah that run softly*—they were discontented and unthankful under a mild government, and gentle administration, that allowed

about £. 6000 per annum, near the one half of which is annually taken out of the treasury for schooling, hath of late years been sufficient to defray our public charges as a government."

Mr. Trumbull's Discourse. page 28.

them great privileges and liberties; therefore God threatens to bring upon them *the waters of the river, strong and many*, or to subject them to the tyrannical government of the king of Assyria.

Once more. We are awfully threatened with being deprived of the liberty of our consciences, the liberty of professing the important truths of the gospel; and attending those sacred ordinances which God has instituted with a view to advance the glory of the Redeemer, and promote the salvation of his people. This will most probably be the consequence of carrying those schemes and plans into execution, which the present ministry have projected. And does not this loudly declare, That our having neglected the worship and turned our backs upon the ordinances of God; our distrusting and despising the grace of the gospel, and trifling away the day of salvation; are to be numbered among those sins by which we have awfully provoked a righteous God to anger against us. That omissions and neglects of this kind, have abounded to an unusual, and indeed, to an astonishing degree, cannot be denied. That such sins are provoking to God, and that especially, in a country which, like this, was originally settled principally for the purposes of reformation and religion, cannot reasonably be doubted. And therefore we may justly conclude, that God is testifying against these kinds of sin in particular, and threatning us on account of them. Shame and sorrow, humiliation and abasement become us for these things. We ought, each one, to examine his own heart and life, and enquire what has been done by, or among us, to provoke the Lord to such an awful controversy; and speedily to return, by gospel-repentance, to his love and service; and to the steady conscientious practice of all religious duties he requires of us. Let us be deeply affected with the present critical and alarming situation of our public affairs; and unite in fervent prayers to that God who is higher than the kings of the earth, that he would graciously interpose for our relief; that he would avert the impending storms of vengeance, and favour us with peace and tranquility, and the full enjoyment of all our valuable liberties and privileges; that our rulers may feed us according to the integrity of their hearts, and guide us by the skilfulness of their hands.

And let us be at peace among ourselves. It is at all times contrary to the temper and spirit of the gospel; but especially unsuitable and improper in such a day as this, to be widening differences, laying unreasonable stress upon disputable points, and to set on foot controversies that tend to alienate people's love and affection from each other, and to increase a party separating spirit, to sow the seeds of discord, and foment animosities. It rather becomes us to fix our attention upon the common cause, the public good and general interest of the land. Our strength, our glory, and our security depend very much upon our friendly agreement and firm union together. If we get divided and broken to pieces among ourselves, what will become of us? What advantage will it give an enemy to our liberties, to bring distressing burdens upon us, and lay such a yoke upon our necks that neither we, nor our posterity can bear. That to which our special attention is at this day called, is not a private by-interest, that concerns the men of one denomination only: but of a general, public nature that concerns men of every persuasion, that are well-wishers to their country's welfare. Even those who have gone off from the scheme and plan of religion professed by the first fathers of this country, have great cause of thankfulness for their liberties and privileges which they enjoy equally with others that still retain it. They have the same advantages from that happy form of civil government; the same protection from it, of their persons and properties; have the same liberty of conscience, worship where they please without controul or oppression; or if they choose to stay at home on the Lord's-day, and join with no worshiping assembly, it is seldom they meet with any interruption or disturbance. What more can they desire? There does not appear the least probability that either they, or we, should gain any advantage on civil or religious accounts, by giving up our privileges; and submitting to a new and different form of government in church and state; with a great additional burden of taxes which would be unavoidably connected with it; under which, who would groan and complain loudest, we cannot tell before trial be made. I hope none of us wish for such a fatal experiment and proof of a public spirit. We all doubtless think, whatever be our peculiar sentiments in religion, that we are sufficiently burdened already. The poor of the people are groaning under poverty and distress: many have a load of debt upon them, and know not which way to turn for the common daily necessaries: are loudly complaining of difficulties, and looking out for relief, some in one way, and some in another; plausible schemes are projected for this purpose, and set on foot and encouraged, to serve a present turn, without looking to the consequences; and very impolitic and imprudent measures taken by many, as a remedy which proves worse than the disease, or will do so in the end, and constantly increase the difficulties complained of. If our taxes at present, are heavy; they do not grow lighter or easier by the people's breaking into parties and divisions among themselves, and pursuing schemes that are in opposition to the main, standing interest, and public good of the country; but are evidently increased thereby to the disadvantage and hurt of all. If some few individuals find their account herein, yet 'tis certainly distressing to the public; and must, sooner or later, be so to all concerned in it. If those who stand in the gap, on whose shoulders the interest of the country stands for its support and defence, should, in any future time, find the burden too heavy for them to bear; and be over-powered by those who direct them, to promote a contrary interest; and this building should fall; the ruin of it would be wide and great. It might fall like a mill-stone upon some who least expect any evil, and grind them to powder. Or if they survived this sad catastrophe, instead of finding easier times, might be caught under such a yoke of bondage that would be insupportably grievous to them and their children; from which, no release or deliverance could be obtained. We are at present (blessed be God), a free people in this land; and might be as happy as any in the known world, did we duly attend to our public interest and welfare; and unite in all suitable ways for the security and advancement of it. Had we union and good agreement among ourselves in the management of our civil and religious affairs; our burdens would grow lighter and easier; and the poor of the people find comfortable relief in most of their difficulties.

Considering our present critical situation, it would, no doubt, be our wisdom and prudence to make up, unite, and gather into one common interest, all the good protestants in this land; notwithstanding lesser differences among them; that we may stand or fall together: and not be devoured one of another; nor become an easy prey to foreign enemies who may seek our ruin. What are those things worth, that alienate people's affections, and cause divisions; in comparison to our dear liberties and privileges that are endangered hereby? It may be the policy of some in power, to encourage such a party-spirit, that we may be weakened and distressed among ourselves; that the way may be prepared without resistance or opposition, to bring us into bondage, and fasten the chains of slavery upon us. And shall we be so infatuated and blind to our own interest, and that of our children's, as to pursue measures that are destructive of it? Measures that will rejoice the hearts of our enemies, and forward their schemes, to be put into execution against us to complete our ruin? Let us lay by passion and prejudice, and seriously and soberly consider this important subject of our common welfare; meddle with nothing that is inconsistent therewith, any sooner than with the rankest poison. Let our country's interest, glory and prosperity be uppermost in our hearts, and use our best endeavours for the advancement of it. Let all our strength center and unite in this grand point. Let us remember, this is the common interest of all the colonies; and that each particular inhabitant is concerned herein; and must expect to share the fate, in some degree, of the body he is connected with. If the foundation of our public liberties and privileges be overturned, all will be affected, and must expect to suffer in the said ruin. Let the melancholy prospect hereof, serve to unite our hearts and hands with all lovers of the rights of humanity, in upholding and defending this more valuable and important interest. Let us love as brethren and dear countrymen, that have but one common interest to pursue. Let us act on principles of moderation, candor and charity; and endeavour in meekness of wisdom to instruct those that oppose themselves, and their country's good; and recover them to the paths of truth. Let us prize and well improve our privileges, and use our influence to promote the public good. We should be especially careful that we engage in no measures or counsels, that we attend to no reasonings or pretences, how plausible and specious soever, which are inconsistent with the common interest and public good. So far as any of us have influence on our public affairs, let us use it for the promotion and advancement of the true friends to their country. We want wise, steady, judicious rulers in such a day as this; men of sterling integrity and real religion. It is of importance that all orders of men be faithful in their several departments, for defending and promoting the public good. Let us keep stedfastly fixed in the good old principles of our fathers, and cheerfully take our lot and portion one with another; saying as Ruth to Naomi, Whither thou goest, I will go; thy people shall be my people, and thy God my God. The Lord's hand has been very conspicuous in the first settlement, and past preservation of these plantations: He will take care of the generation of the righteous; and break the yoke of their oppressors; and give them peace and happiness. Blessed are the people that are under his care and conduct; yea, blessed are the people whose God is the Lord. Amen.

13

A CALM ADDRESS TO OUR AMERICAN COLONIES

John Wesley

LONDON

1775

JOHN WESLEY (1703-1791). Like his younger brother Charles, the founder of Methodism John Wesley was born in Epworth, Lincolnshire, England. He was graduated at Christ Church, Oxford, in 1724 and ordained by the Church of England in 1728. Wesley returned to Oxford the following year as a fellow of Lincoln College and, with his brother, organized the Holy Club, devoted to intense spiritual life and social service among England's poor, aged, and delinquent. (George Whitefield joined the club in 1734.) The Wesleys conducted an American mission in Georgia from 1735 to 1737, and in Charleston, South Carolina, they published their pioneering *Collection of Psalms and Hymns* (1737)—largely the work of Charles, who was a poet and musician. In later years John Wesley called their mission the "second rise of Methodism" (despite the meager results at the time).

Justification by faith alone, a solace gained by John Wesley from the Moravians, became a hallmark of his ministry, which became largely itinerant as ordinary pulpits were closed against him. It is estimated that, over a period of fifty years, he traveled a quarter of a million miles in the British Isles, mostly on horseback, and preached between forty and fifty thousand sermons. He remained within the Anglican Church throughout this time, but in 1784 he first consecrated preachers to further the American mission. By 1791, the year of John Wesley's death in London, he was admired everywhere, and Methodist societies in Great Britain included 300 traveling ministers, 72,000 members, and 500,000 adherents; there were about two-thirds that number abroad, especially in the United States, where growth was rapid.

John Wesley's one direct venture into American politics came with the publication in Bristol of *A Calm Address to Our American Colonies* (1775). It reversed his position of a year earlier on British oppression of the colonies and brought him down squarely on the side of the ministry, much to their delight. The pamphlet went through at least seventeen (and perhaps nineteen) editions; about 100,000 copies circulated within a year. The British government was happy to foster its distribution, since it justified its policies and bore Wesley's signature. In America, Wesley was vilified, not least because the first eighteen pages of *A Calm Address* plagiarized Dr. Samuel Johnson's assault on the American position, published in 1775 as *Taxation No Tyranny: An Answer to the Resolutions and Address of the American Congress*. (As Frank

A CALM ADDRESS TO *OUR AMERICAN* COLONIES.

By *JOHN WESLEY*, M.A.

Ne, pueri, ne tanta animis assuescite bella,
Neu patriæ validas in viscera vertite vires.

VIRGIL.

LONDON:
Printed by R. HAWES, in *Dorset-Street*, Spitalfields,
MDCC LXXV,

Baker has commented, this was "a fairly normal practice with Wesley.") To fill out the publication to a full sheet of type, Wesley added a five-page response to a sermon by William Smith, provost of the College of Philadelphia, entitled *A Sermon on the Present Situation of American Affairs* (June 23, 1775).

The second (London) edition of *A Calm Address* is reprinted here, the only significant change from the first edition being the asterisk note that softens the statement "Our sovereign has a right to tax me . . . whether we have votes for Parliament-men or no" with "That is, in connexion with the Lords and Commons."

The flavor of the response to Wesley's piece can be seen in the comparatively mild, anonymous *A Constitutional Answer to the Rev. Mr. John Wesley's Calm Address* (1775) and John Fletcher's *The Bible and the Sword* (1776). As Donald H. Kirkham has summarized the invective aroused by *A Calm Address*: "Calumny, name calling, and scurrilous innuendo (bordering on libel), abounded. Wesley was denounced as a wolf in sheep's clothing, a madman, a chaplain in ordinary to the furies, a cunning fox, a Jesuit in disguise, and a Jacobite traitor." That the cause of Methodism was not more adversely affected in America thereafter than it actually was turns on the fact that American ports were closed on July 20, 1775, and such copies as had arrived were promptly destroyed by American Methodists.

rethren and Countrymen,

1. The grand question which is now debated (and with warmth enough on both sides), is this, Has the English Parliament power to tax the American colonies?

In order to determine this, let us consider the nature of our colonies. An English colony is, a number of persons to whom the king grants a charter, permitting them to settle in some far country as a corporation, enjoying such powers as the charter grants, to be administered in such a manner as the charter prescribes. As a corporation they make laws for themselves: but as a corporation subsisting by a grant from higher authority, to the control of that authority, they still continue subject.

Considering this, nothing can be more plain, than that the supreme power in England has a legal right of laying any tax upon them for any end beneficial to the whole empire.

2. But you object, "It is the privilege of a freeman and an Englishman to be taxed only by his own consent. And this consent is given for every man by his representative in Parliament. But we have no representation in Parliament. Therefore we ought not to be taxed thereby."

I answer, This argument proves too much. If the Parliament cannot tax you, because you have no representation therein, for the same reason it can make no laws to bind you. If a freeman cannot be taxed without his own consent, neither can he be punished without it: for whatever holds with regard to taxation, holds with regard to all other laws. Therefore he who denies the English Parliament the power of taxation, denies it the right of making any laws at all. But this power over the colonies you have never disputed: you have always admitted statutes, for the punishment of offences, and for the preventing or redressing of inconveniences. And the reception of any law draws after it by a chain which cannot be broken, the necessity of admitting taxation.

3. But I object to the very foundation of your plea. That "every freeman is governed by laws to which he has consented," as confi-

dently as it has been asserted, it is absolutely false. In wide-extended dominions, a very small part of the people are concerned in making laws. This, as all public business, must be done by delegation, the delegates are chosen by a select number. And those that are not electors, who are far the greater part, stand by, idle and helpless spectators.

The case of electors is little better. When they are near equally divided, almost half of them must be governed, not only without, but even against their own consent.

And how has any man consented to those laws, which were made before he was born? Our consent to these, nay and to the laws now made even in England, is purely passive. And in every place, as all men are born the subjects of some state or other, so they are born, passively, as it were consenting to the laws of that state. Any other than this kind of consent, the condition of civil life does not allow.

4. But you say, *You are intitled to life, liberty and property by nature: and that you have never ceded to any sovereign power, the right to dispose of those without your consent.*

While you speak as the naked sons of nature, this is certainly true. But you presently declare, *Our ancestors at the time they settled these colonies, were intitled to all the rights of natural-born subjects, within the realm of England.* This likewise is true: but when this is granted, the boast of original rights is at an end. You are no longer in a state of nature, but sink down to colonists, governed by a charter. If your ancestors were subjects, they acknowledged a sovereign: if they had a right to English privileges, they were accountable to English laws, and had ceded to the king and Parliament, *the power of disposing without their consent, of both their lives, liberties and properties.* And did the Parliament cede to them, a dispensation from the obedience, which they owe as natural subjects? Or any degree of independence, not enjoyed by other Englishmen?

5. *They did not indeed*, as you observe, *by emigration forfeit any of those privileges: but they were, and their descendents now are intitled to all such as their circumstances enable them to enjoy.*

That they who form a colony by a lawful charter, forfeit no privilege thereby, is certain. But what they do not forfeit by any judicial sentence, they may lose by natural effects. When a man voluntarily comes into America, he may lose what he had when in Europe. Perhaps he had a right to vote for a knight or burgess: by crossing the sea he did not forfeit this right. But it is plain, he has made the exercise of it no longer possible. He has reduced himself from a voter to one of the innumerable multitude that have no votes.

6. But you say, *As the colonies are not represented in the British Parliament, they are entitled to a free power of legislation. For they inherit all the right which their ancestors had of enjoying all the privileges of Englishmen.*

They do inherit all the privileges which their ancestors had: but they can inherit no more. Their ancestors left a country where the representatives of the people were elected by men particularly qualified, and where those who wanted that qualification were bound by the decisions of men whom they had not deputed. You are the descendants of men who either had no votes, or resigned them by emigration. You have therefore exactly what your ancestors left you: not a vote in making laws, nor in chusing legislators, but the happiness of being protected by laws, and the duty of obeying them.

What your ancestors did not bring with them, neither they nor their descendants have acquired. They have not, by abandoning their right in one legislature, acquired a right to constitute another: any more than the multitudes in England who have no vote, have a right to erect a Parliament for themselves.

7. *However the colonies have a right to all the privileges granted them by royal charters, or secured to them by provincial laws.*

The first clause is allowed: they have certainly a right to all the privileges granted them by the royal charters. But as to the second there is a doubt: provincial laws may grant privileges to individuals of the province. But surely no province can confer provincial privileges on itself! They have a right to all which the king has given them; but not to all which they have given themselves.

A corporation can no more assume to itself, privileges which it had not before, than a man can, by his own act and deed, assume titles or dignities. The legislature of a colony may be compared to the vestry of a large parish: which may lay a cess on its inhabitants, but still regulated by the law: and which (whatever be its internal expences) is still liable to taxes laid by superior authority.

The charter of Pennsylvania has a clause admitting, in express terms, taxation by Parliament. If such a clause be not inferred in other charters, it must be omitted as not necessary; because it is manifestly implied in the very nature of subordinate government: all countries which are subject to laws, being liable to taxes.

It is true, *The first settlers in Massachusetts-Bay were promised an exemption from taxes for seven years.* But does not this very exemption imply, that they were to pay them afterwards?

If there is in the charter of any colony a clause exempting them from taxes for ever, then undoubtedly they have a right to be so exempted. But if there is no such clause, then the English Parliament has the same right to tax them as to tax any other English subjects.

8. All that impartially consider what has been observed, must readily allow, that the English Parliament has undoubted right to tax all the English colonies.

But whence then is all this hurry and tumult? Why is America all in an uproar? If you can yet give yourselves time to think, you will see, the plain case is this.

A few years ago, you were assaulted by enemies, whom you were not well able to resist. You represented this to your mother-country, and desired her assistance. You was largely assisted, and by that means wholly delivered from all your enemies.

After a time, your mother-country desiring to be reimbursed for some part of the large expence she had been at, laid a small tax (which she had always a right to do) on one of her colonies.

But how is it possible, that the taking [of] this reasonable and legal step, should have set all America in a flame?

I will tell you my opinion freely; and perhaps you will not think it improbable. I speak the more freely, because I am unbiassed: I have nothing to hope or fear from either side. I gain nothing either by the government or by the Americans, and probably never shall. And I have no prejudice to any man in America: I love you as my brethren and countrymen.

9. My opinion is this. We have a few men in England, who are determined enemies to monarchy. Whether they hate his present majesty on any other ground, than because he is a king, I know not. But they cordially hate his office, and have for some years been undermining it with all diligence, in hopes of erecting their grand idol, their dear commonwealth upon its ruins. I believe they have let very few into their design (although many forward it, without knowing any thing of the matter): but they are steadily pursuing it, as by vari-

ous other means, so in particular by inflammatory papers, which are industriously and continually dispersed, throughout the town and country: by this method they have already wrought thousands of the people, even to the pitch of madness. By the same, only varied according to your circumstances, they have likewise inflamed America. I make no doubt, but these very men are the original cause of the present breach between England and her colonies. And they are still pouring oil into the flame, studiously incensing each against the other, and opposing under a variety of pretences, all measures of accommodation. So that although the Americans, in general, love the English, and the English in general, love the Americans (all, I mean that are not yet cheated and exasperated by these artful men), yet the rupture is growing wider every day, and none can tell where it will end.

These good men hope it will end, in the total defection of North America from England. If this were effected, they trust the English in general would be so irreconcileably disgusted, that they should be able, with or without foreign assistance, intirely to overturn the government: especially while the main of both the English and Irish forces, are at so convenient a distance.

10. But, my brethren, would this be any advantage to you? Can you hope for a more desirable form of government, either in England or America, than that which you now enjoy? After all the vehement cry for liberty, what more liberty can you have? What more religious liberty can you desire, than that which you enjoy already? May not every one among you worship God according to his own conscience? What civil liberty can you desire, which you are not already possessed of? Do not you sit without restraint, *every man under his own vine?* Do you not, every one, high or low, enjoy the fruit of your labour? This is real, rational liberty, such as is enjoyed by Englishmen alone; and not by any other people in the habitable world. Would the being independent of England make you more free? Far, very far from it. It would hardly be possible for you to steer clear, between anarchy and tyranny. But suppose, after numberless dangers and mischiefs, you should settle into one or more republics: would a republican government give you more liberty, either religious or civil? By no means. No governments under heaven are so despotic as the republican: no subjects are governed in so arbitrary a manner, as

those of a commonwealth. If any one doubt of this, let him look at the subjects of Venice, of Genoa, or even of Holland. Should any man talk or write of the Dutch government as every cobler does of the English, he would be laid in irons, before he knew where he was. And then wo be to him! Republics shew no mercy.

11. "But if we submit to one tax, more will follow." Perhaps so, and perhaps not. But if they did; if you were taxed (which is quite improbable) equal with Ireland or Scotland, still were you to prevent this by renouncing connection with England, the remedy would be worse than the disease. For O! what convulsions must poor America feel, before any other government was settled? Innumerable mischiefs must ensue, before any general form could be established. And the grand mischief would ensue, when it was established; when you had received a yoke, which you could not shake off.

12. Brethren, open your eyes! Come to yourselves! Be no longer the dupes of designing men. I do not mean any of your countrymen in America: I doubt whether any of these are in the secret. The designing men, the Ahithophels, are in England; those who have laid their scheme so deep and covered it so well, that thousands who are ripening it, suspect nothing at all of the matter. These well-meaning men, sincerely believing, that they are serving their country, exclaim against grievances, which either never existed, or are aggravated above measure, and thereby inflame the people more and more, to the wish of those who are behind the scene. But be not you duped any longer: do not ruin yourselves for them that owe you no good will, that now employ you only for their own purposes, and in the end will give you no thanks. They love neither England nor America, but play one against the other, in subserviency to their grand design, of overturning the English government. Be warned in time. Stand and consider before it is too late; before you have entailed confusion and misery on your latest posterity. Have pity upon your mother country! Have pity upon your own! Have pity upon yourselves, upon your children, and upon all that are near and dear to you! Let us not bite and devour one another, lest we be consumed one of another! O let us follow after peace! Let us put away our sins; the real ground of all our calamities! Which never will or can be thoroughly removed, till we fear God and honour the king.

A sermon preached by Dr. Smith, in Philadelphia, has been lately reprinted in England. It has been much admired, but proceeds all along upon wrong suppositions. These are confuted in the preceding tract: yet I would just touch upon them again.

Dr. Smith supposes, 1. They "have a right of granting their own money": that is, of being exempt from taxation by the supreme power. If they "contend for" this, they contend for neither more nor less than independency. Why then do they talk of their "rightful sovereign"? They acknowledge no sovereign at all.

That they contend for "the cause of liberty" is another mistaken supposition. What liberty do you want, either civil or religious? You had the very same liberty we have in England. I say, you had: but you have now thrown away the substance, and retain only the shadow. You have no liberty, civil or religious now, but what the Congress pleases to allow.

But you justly suppose, "We are by a plain original contract intitled to a community of privileges, with our brethren that reside in England, in every civil and religious respect," p. 19. Most true. And till you appointed your new sovereigns, you enjoyed all those privileges. Indeed you had no vote for members of Parliament, neither have I, because I have no freehold in England. Yet the being taxed by the Parliament is no infringement either of my civil or religious liberty.

But you say again, "No power on earth has a right to grant our property without our consent," p. 22.

Then you have no sovereign: for every sovereign under heaven has a right to tax his subjects: that is, "to grant their property, with or without their consent." Our* sovereign has a right to tax me, and all other Englishmen, whether we have votes for Parliament-men or no.

Vainly therefore do you complain of "unconstitutional exactions, violated rights, and mutilated charters," p. 24. Nothing is exacted, but according to the original constitution both of England, and her colonies. Your rights are no more violated than mine, when we are

*That is, in connexion with the Lords and Commons.

both taxt by the supreme power: and your charters are no more mutilated by this, than is the charter of the city of London.

Vainly do you complain of being "made slaves." Am I, or two millions of Englishmen made slaves because we are taxed without our own consent?

You may still "rejoice in the common rights of freemen." I rejoice in all the rights of my ancestors. And every right which I enjoy, is common to Englishmen and Americans.

But shall we "surrender any part of the privileges which we enjoy, by the express terms of our colonization?" that is, of our charter? By no means: and none requires it of you. None desires to withhold any thing that is granted by the express terms of your charters. But remember! One of your first charters, that of Massachusetts-Bay, says in express terms, you are exempt from paying taxes to the king, for seven years: plainly implying, that after those seven years you are to pay them like other subjects. And remember your last charter, that of Pennsylvania, says, in express terms, you are liable to taxation.

But "a people will resume, you say, the power, which they never surrendered, except["]—no need of any exception. They never surrendered it at all; they could not surrender it; for they never had it. I pray[,] did the people, unless you mean the Norman army, give William the Conqueror his power? And to which of his successors did the people of England (six or seven millions) give the sovereign power? This is mere political cant: words without meaning. I know but one instance in all history, wherein the people gave the sovereign power to any one; that was, to Massaniello of Naples. And I desire any man living to produce another instance in the history of all nations.

Ten times over, in different words, you "profess yourselves to be contending for liberty." But it is a vain, empty profession: unless you mean by that threadbare word, a liberty from obeying your rightful sovereign, and from keeping the fundamental laws of your country. And this undoubtedly it is, which the confederated colonies are now contending for.

THE END

14

A CONSTITUTIONAL ANSWER TO WESLEY'S CALM ADDRESS

Anonymous

LONDON

1775

Hard on the heels of John Wesley's *A Calm Address to Our American Colonies* (number 13 herein), there appeared this anonymous rebuttal and attack entitled *A Constitutional Answer to the Rev. Mr. John Wesley's Calm Address to the American Colonies*, which was also published in London in 1775, one of at least fourteen tracts published in the last three months of that year attacking Wesley.

The approach taken is a point-by-point refutation of Wesley's argument in terms of constitutional law and the political theory of British government. In this respect, the argument nicely complements the analysis contained in John Joachim Zubly's *An Humble Inquiry* of 1769 (number 9 herein), which is to say that the American understanding of the British constitution is set forth precisely and concisely. The principles of free government require that taxes not be *taken*; rather they are *given* or *granted* by representatives of the people: no representatives, then no taxes; no elections, then no representatives. This is why the Tory position of Wesley is wrong and the American and parliamentary opposition position is right. The Americans are not and cannot be represented in the House of Commons. And the author comes very close to saying, as Edmund Burke had told the House of Commons a few months earlier, that England had long prized liberty, but slavery the Americans could have anywhere.

While *A Calm Address* was only the first of some eight royalist pamphlets published by Wesley during the course of the American Revolution, none of the others evoked anything like the same reaction. The primary reason for this was Wesley's expressed fear in the 1775 tract that republican agitators and supporters of America in England intended to seize the opportunity of overturning the monarchy and setting up a republic while British troops were engaged across the Atlantic. This attack on the patriotism and loyalty of pro-American Englishmen was regarded as scandalous and libelous, and the most immoderate invective was heaped upon Wesley's head. Thus, *A Constitutional Answer*'s author derisively writes: "I cannot think that you believe your own assertion."

The writer does not fail to twist the knife of plagiarism in Wesley's ribs for his "retailing [Dr. Samuel] Johnson's book without acknowledgement," a matter discussed in the note on Wesley. We know that Dr. Johnson was not annoyed by this use of his text. In a letter dated February 6, 1776, Johnson wrote Wesley that the borrowings from

A
Conſtitutional Anſwer
TO THE
Rev. Mr. JOHN WESLEY's
CALM ADDRESS to the *American Colonies*.

Talibus inſidiis — Credita res! VIRGIL.

" No man, or ſociety of men, have power to deliver up their
" preſervation, or the means of it, to the abſolute will of any
" man; and what they have not power to part with, they will
" always have a right to preſerve."

Lord SOMERS.

" The government of *every Colony*, like that of the Colonies of
" old ROME, may be conſidered as the *effigies parva* of the
" MOTHER STATE."

Hutchinſon's Hiſtory of Maſſachuſett's Bay.

LONDON:

Printed for E. and C. DILLY, in the Poultry; and
J. ALMON, Piccadilly, 1775.

[Price 1s. 6d. a Dozen, or 10s. per Hundred.]

Taxation No Tyranny Johnson much valued as "your important suffrage to my argument on the American question. To have gained such a mind as yours, may justly confirm me in my own opinion." The ministry certainly agreed with that view, for it had purchased the whole first edition of the Wesley publication and had it delivered to the door of every church in London.

An air of contempt pervades the piece reprinted here, which concludes by deploring the spectacle of a Christian minister deserving of esteem having now transformed himself into a "court sycophant" who cannot distinguish between the free government provided by the English constitution and the arbitrary government of France and Spain. The author proclaims himself a partisan of the "original universal rights of man."

Who was the author of this powerful rebuttal of the *Calm Address*? If a guess is to be ventured—and I stress that it is only a guess—a reasonable candidate may be John Almon (1737–1805), the "J. Almon" of the title page. Almon overtly had a hand in publishing the piece, and he or one of his close associates may well have written it. He himself was a bookseller, journalist, and confidant of John Wilkes and Edmund Burke. Almon had been convicted in 1770 for selling a copy of the *London Museum* containing a reprint of the *Junius Letter*. He had long been associated with opposition politics and was bookseller to "The Coterie," an opposition club. Beginning in 1774 Almon published *The Parliamentary Record*, the first monthly record of parliamentary proceedings. The political and constitutional perspective of the author of *A Constitutional Answer* and the subtle command of the technical subject matter of the law suggest the possibility of Almon's authorship.

Sir,

A pamphlet, to which you have affixed your name, has been lately distributed with uncommon diligence. You call it *A Calm Address to our American Colonies.* This title is a deception; you know that the colonies are determined: your design is, to deceive undetermined Englishmen, into approbation of the measures of administration.

You present your book to the world, as your own; but the greatest part of it is taken, *verbatim*, from *Taxation No Tyranny*, written by the pensioned Dr. Johnson, a declared enemy of civil and religious liberty! This is another deception, equally mean and obvious.

Your first section contains Johnson's definition of an English colony. It gives the idea of

> a number of persons, who, by the king's permission, emigrated in search of supposed advantages, which, if obtained, were to be secured to them by charters.

But the colonists were a number of persons, who fled from tyranny at home, to conquer and cultivate new countries at their own expence. From the parent state, for above a century, they received little or no assistance: their monopolized commerce was, at last, thought worth protection; their increased property is, now, thought worth taxation.

You say,

> Considering English colonies are a kind of corporations subsisting by charters, nothing can be more plain than that the supreme power in England has a right to tax them.

Do you mean, by the supreme power, the collective body of king, lords, and commons? If you do, you must be ignorant, that the Commons *only* have the power of taxing the people; that money is not *taken*, but *given*; that the concurrence of the lords, in money bills, is only to tax themselves; and that the concurrence of the king, in such bills, is only to give them the force of law.

You say,

> That the English government has made laws for the colonies, which laws they have received and obeyed; therefore, the English government has a

> right to tax them: the reception of any law draws after it, by a chain which cannot be broken, the necessity of admitting taxation.

This is false: the acts of legislation, and taxation, are distinct operations; the first is exercised by the three estates of king, lords, and commons, the last by the commons only. If the reception of a law is an acknowledgment of sovereignty, it is not an acknowledgment that such sovereignty may be maintained in an unconstitutional manner. Penal and œconomical laws are received and obeyed in England; the reception of them may be deemed an acknowledgment of the sovereignty of government; but does not prove, that government has a right to abrogate Magna Charta, abolish trial by jury, or vest in the king an arbitrary power of levying money on the subject: such acts, though sanctified by consent of the three estates, would be violations of the constitution, and, consequently, void in themselves, and "*to be holden for nought*." 42 Ed. III. Lord Coke, Lord Somers, &c.

You next attempt to prove, that the colonies are as much represented in the English Parliament, as the majority of the people of England: "All public business," you say,

> must be done by delegation; the delegates are chosen by a select number; and those who are not electors, who are by far the greater part, stand by idle and helpless spectators.

That most publick business must be done by delegation, is true; but the choice of delegates, or representatives in England, was originally in the people at large; the vesting it, afterwards, in a select number, was a variation made by consent of the people for the sake of convenience. The non-electors, and electors of England, are so blended together, that the former must often influence the conduct of the latter; and having, thereby, a share in the power of election, cannot be said, "to stand by idle and helpless spectators."

"The case of electors," you say, "is little better; when they are near equally divided, almost half of them must be governed, not only with, but against their consent."

This is a fallacy. The minority of electors cannot be said to be governed without their consent: they, in common with others, have previously consented, that it should be law to issue the dispute by the voice of the majority; they have, therefore, consented to be governed by him, on whom the choice of that majority shall fall.

You endeavour, by general positions boldly asserted, to represent government and slavery as inseparable. "How has any man," you say,

> consented to those laws, which were made before he was born? Our consent to these, nay and to the laws now made in England, is purely passive. In every place, as all men are born the subjects of some state or other, so they are born, passively as it were, consenting to the laws of that state. Any other than this kind of consent, the condition of civil life does not allow.

This is false: The English constitution has better provided for the preservation of liberty. Our consent to the laws by which we are ruled, is so far active, that we may in a manner be said to make them: "*The commons may be said to make law*," says Johnson himself, in his *False Alarm;* it then suited his purpose to say so. The people at large may, indeed, be said to make law. They desire to have some penal or œconomical law for general benefit; they instruct their delegates; a bill is brought into the House of Commons; the king may refuse the royal assent, but then the House may refuse supplies. Suppose the opinions of the constituents, and the delegates, are opposite; the latter reject the bill: their office is not perpetual, nor irresponsible; at seven years end they may be discarded, and their places filled with more compliant or more faithfull successors. *Vice versa*: suppose a law, proposed by any of the three estates of government, is thought oppressive, or otherwise offensive, by the people: the measure is talked of; they petition, they remonstrate; perhaps they succeed; perhaps they do not: in the latter case, the grievance is not eternal; a new parliament may repeal what the old one enacted. If the measure be not a favourite court measure, and the royal assent, as before, be denied; then supplies, as before, may be withholden, till that assent is granted. If the people have less influence over the second estate, the House of Lords; still that house may be supposed to consist of men, guided by reason, and wishing to act in consonance with the rest of their countrymen.

Such are the advantages of our excellent constitution! Blush, if ye can, ye Johnsons and ye Wesleys, who are endeavouring to destroy the idea of them, in the minds of unwary readers; endeavouring to perswade men, that they are inevitably born slaves! If Englishmen are slaves, whose consent to the laws they are ruled by, is merely passive; it is not the fault of their political system, but of their own corruption of morals, and supineness of spirit.

It is the usual art of the court writers of the day, to aim at sinking all ideas of natural equity, and of general popular franchises founded thereon, in the idea of absolute unconditional government, pretending such government indispensible to the subsistence of civil society. You say,

> If the ancestors of the colonists were subjects, they acknowledged a sovereign; if they had a right to English privileges, they were accountable to English laws; and had ceded, to the king and Parliament, the power of disposing, without their consent, of their lives, liberties, and properties.

This is both false and absurd. No Englishman ever ceded, to any king, absolute power over his life or liberty. That precious remain of ancient freedom, *trial by jury*, ever stood and now stands an insuperable bar against the power of sovereign over subject.

> No freeman shall be taken, or imprisoned, nor disseized, nor out-lawed, nor exiled, nor destroyed in any manner; nor will we pass upon him, nor condemn him, but by the lawfull judgment of his peers, or by the law of the land. Magna Charta, §. 43.

No Englishman ever ceded, to any king, any power over his property: the right of taxation, as has been shewn, is exclusively vested in the people. No Englishman ever ceded, to the parliament, a power over his life, liberty, and property: he could not cede it to the lords, for the lords, without the commons, cannot make law; he could not cede it to the commons, for ceding it to the commons, would, properly speaking, be ceding it to himself. The force of truth is often too strong, for every effort that can be made to conceal it. You talk of "the people ceding power to the king and Parliament": if they ceded power, they must have possessed it. *Nemo dat quod non habet:* what a man has not, he cannot give to another; what is given, if abused, may surely be resumed. If the doctrine of resumable power is not admitted, the doctrine of divine hereditary right must be maintained. The first king of every country, must have reigned by divine appointment; and all his successors, be their conduct what it will, must reign by the same title; their subjects must be hereditary slaves, whose lives and properties may be sported with, as men shoot birds, and catch fish, for diversion. Englishmen! beware of these insidious reasoners; these Johnsons and Wesleys, who would persuade you that ye are born slaves!

You admit (as above), that there are original rights of humanity. You tell us, that when the colonists say they are intitled, by nature, to life, liberty and property, they speak true; that when they claim a title to the rights of natural born subjects within the realm of England, they speak true also—but you assert, that "they must resign either one or the other." This is no consequence.

The rights of nature, and of civil society, are not incompatible; the former are mostly guarantied by the latter. A man has a natural right to the possessions of his parents, or to those which he has obtained by his own labour; and the laws of society, which prohibit fraud and rapine, instead of destroying that right, contribute to secure it. A man has a natural right to life and liberty: on entering civil society, he does not cede this right, only in certain stipulated circumstances, for the good of that whole whereof he becomes a part; while he is innocent, he is safe and free.

A man has a natural right to his own property: this, on entering civil society, he does not cede at all: he, indeed, by a kind of tacit compact, agrees to subscribe his share to the expence of public security and public œconomy, as the necessity of times may require; but, as no rational being would lavish his wealth without equivalent, he has reserved to himself the sole determination of the existence or degree of that necessity.*

If he does not properly regard the publick welfare, it is at his own risque; he is more or less a gainer, as it is more or less consulted. Of this general principle, an English House of Commons, in its primarily intended incorrupt state, is a visible modification; money, there, is *granted*, not *taken*; granting, not taking, is the language of the constitution in all ages.

Such are the simple principles of free government, in contradistinction to tyranny! Principles, alas, too little known, too much obscured by the glare of adventitious pomp and purchased power!

* Iniquum est, ingenuis hominibus non esse liberam rerum suarum alienationem. Co. Lit. 223. "It is iniquitous, that freemen should not have the free disposal of their own effects."

You say, that "the colonists, by emigration, did not forfeit the right of voting for representatives in the English Parliament; but lost it by natural effects." But the privilege of voting for, or chusing a deputy or proxy, to execute the office of a taxer; can be considered as a personal advantage, only in counterpoise to the personal burden of taxation: now, if the good be lost by natural effects, the evil should not be retained by unnatural political ones. There are things called right reason, equity, and justice, though they may not happen to exist in the ideas of Dr. Johnson and Mr. Wesley.

When a man removes to a distance, from the part of civil society with which he was connected, he can no longer enjoy the benefits of its political system; and, therefore, cannot justly be assessed to its maintenance.

If the colonists have hitherto supported the administration of justice, and other branches of internal polity, among themselves; what rational plea can be made, for requiring them to support them among us? Can a person be expected to pay for the same thing, in two places?

You say,

> He who had a vote for a knight or burgess, did not forfeit that right by crossing the sea, but made the exercise of it no longer possible; he reduced himself from a voter to one of the innumerable multitude that have no votes.

But if such a man was still liable to be taxed by the English Parliament, he reduced himself to a much worse condition.

Non-electors (as has been hinted) have, in England, much influence in elections: persuasion and information, have their weight; the man of superior opulence or knowledge, without a vote himself, can direct the voices of a number.

But an American can have no possible influence in the choice of an English senator; and an English senator, when he taxes an American, *cannot tax himself also*, because he has no property in America to be taxed: yet self-taxation is the sole pledge of the taxer, for security of the taxed. He, who does not tax himself, taxes others without feeling: he may, therefore, tax without propriety, and without measure; may take, not only a fifth, or a fourth, but the half, or even the whole of property; and make the wealthy subject an impoverished slave. The wisest forms of government, adverting to the imperfection of human nature, have, as much as possible, avoided leaving one man at the mercy of another; they have ever contrived some rational restraint on action, some bond of reciprocal safety.

You allow, that "the colonists inherit all the privileges of Englishmen, all the privileges that their ancestors had." They then inherit the grand privilege of Englishmen, *free government;* but this privilege they do not enjoy, if they are taxed without being represented. It is an axiom which cannot be too forcibly impressed on the mind— "Government cannot be free, where property is *taken* not *given.*"

You say,

> what the ancestors of the colonists did not bring with them, neither they nor their descendants have acquired. They have not, by abandoning their right in one legislation, acquired a right to constitute another; any more than the multitudes in England, who have no vote, have a right to erect a parliament for themselves.

You before said, "they had lost their right in the English legislature, by natural effects." There is difference between abandoning, and losing by natural effects; one is a voluntary, one an involuntary matter: you have not proved that they either abandoned this right, or lost it; if they have either abandoned, or lost it, and have no right to constitute another system, they must be slaves, or revert to a state of anarchy. Were the body of electors, in England, to become so corrupt or servile, as constantly to rechuse men, who had betrayed the cause of liberty; and were such men to subvert the constitution; would not the non-electors have a right to chuse a number of honester delegates, to restore their abolished freedom, to save their country?

You say,

> the colonies have a right to all the privileges granted them by regal charters, to all which the king has given them; but not to all which they have given themselves.

The first part of your assertion is undoubtedly true; but it is couched in terms, that might better become the despot of some barbarous region, whose ignorant natives had imbibed.

"The enormous faith of many made for one," than the advocate of a government that calls itself *free.* What right has any king to any thing (saving his own private property) which is not given him by the people? If the king is the fountain of honours and riches, whence is that fountain supplied? Whence does he derive the prerogative of conferring honours, the ability of bestowing riches—but from the people?

If the colonists are the *naked sons of nature*, they have a right to independence, and the enaction of their own laws; if they are subjects of the free English state, they have a right to the grand privilege of other Englishmen, a privilege which no king could confer—legislation, and taxation by representation only. The assertion, that "they are virtually represented," has been proved an absurdity; a sophism, which even you could scarcely repeat, with a serious countenance.

Your comparison of "a colonial legislature to the vestry of an English parish," proves nothing to the great point in question, the legality of taxation without representation. The parish assesses itself, in its parochial capacity, for local private uses; in its national capacity, by its representatives, for general publick ones.

The colonies have no representatives; therefore, cannot be liable to parliamentary taxation.

You say, "the charter of Pensylvania has a clause admitting, in express terms, taxation by Parliament." Why did you not then produce this clause, that your readers might have judged of its meaning and import for themselves? You do not even tell us the nature of the taxation; whether it was internal or external; whether levied by themselves, or by others. You add, "the first settlers in Massachusett's were promised an exemption from taxes for seven years." But promised by whom? If the charter contains such a promise, it must be made by the king who granted the charter; but the king could not legally promise an exemption from that which he had not legally a right to impose. I have not time nor opportunity to examine fully the truth of your assertions: but though I give you credit for them so far, as to admit that there are some such clauses as you mention; yet your disengenuous conduct, in retailing Johnson's book without acknowledgment, makes me justly doubt the truth of your representations. Those clauses could relate, not to taxation, but to requisition only: the right of taxation did not subsist with the king; it did not subsist with the Parliament; it subsisted solely and exclusively with the representatives of the Massachusett's people; and all the exemption promised that people could amount to no more than this, that the king would not require any subsidies from them for seven years. To serve your own purpose, you say, indeed, afterwards, that "the seven years exemption granted to the Massachusett settlers, was from paying taxes to the king." Then it may be justly inferred, that they were subsidies demanded by the king in way of requisition, not taxes imposed by Parliament: had the case been otherwise, it would have been produced, before now, as a precedent for external taxation. What opinion the provincials had of external taxation above a hundred years ago, appears from an article in the agreement made by the Virginians with the commonwealth of England, before they would permit a governor sent by that commonwealth to land in their province: "Virginia shall be free from all taxes, customs, and impositions whatsoever; and none shall be imposed upon them, without consent of the general assembly."*

"All countries," you say, "which are subject to laws, are liable to taxes." Perhaps so; but, perhaps, they are only liable to taxes, raised in a constitutional manner; perhaps it has not been usual, for the government of one country to tax the inhabitants of another, many thousand miles distant. If such taxation were founded on reason, might not the German princes think of taxing the Germans settled in Pensylvania and New-York? If the tie of birth, between sovereign and subject, is indissoluble by distance and time, they have a pretence for doing it.

You say,

> if there is no clause in the charters of the colonies exempting them from taxes, the English Parliament has the same right to tax them as to tax any other English subject.

Your argument here has been answered; I only quote it to demur once more to your mode of expression: the Parliament, collectively considered, has no right to tax any Englishman; it is the Commons, and the Commons only, who possess the peculiar incommunicable power of granting taxes for the people. This is not quibbling about mere insignificant expressions: Taking and giving (I repeat it) are terms affixed to ideas, which constitute the important difference between tyranny and freedom.

* See An Appeal to the Justice and the Interests of the People of Great Britain. p. 29.

I have now gone through the sum total of your arguments, which are every one, without exception, borrowed from Johnson: the remainder of your book is assertion, and declamation; it merits little notice.

An argument, which operates more in favour of the colonists, than any that Johnson has advanced operates against them, is this: That the English government, under the wisest administrations, and in the most necessitous circumstances, never, till lately, attempted to tax them. If government had that right of taxation, why did they not exert it? Perhaps, we are wiser than our fathers; wiser than those great statesmen, who planned and perfected the glorious revolution, *and gave the crown to the Brunswick family.* Our fathers made England the dread of Europe; Heaven grant their sons may not make it the contempt of its meanest enemy! If we are wiser than our fathers, I wish we were honester: our fathers did not plunder the East; we have plundered the East; let us not attempt to plunder the West also! Let not Englishman be a word of disgrace among all nations, a word synonymous with robber!

It has been said, "The longer the colonists have been spared paying taxes, the better able they are, and the greater reason they have to pay." Till the justice of taxing them at all, is clearly demonstrated, this argument is futile; it is the morality of those, who deem it less criminal to plunder him who has not been plundered before, than to plunder again him who has suffered previous depredation. It were to be wished, that we were less interested; at least, that we did not suffer our interest to outrun our virtue. "If America is taxed," it is said, "England will be eased of taxes." Ease from taxes, is an alluring object to an Englishman—but, during a thirteen years profound peace, what ease from taxes have Englishmen experienced? What we have not had in the past, can we have reason to expect in the future? We have not been eased in peace, but we are to be eased in war; eased by the taxes of a conquered country, which, in the act of conquering, we have laid desolate! Can we be the dupes of such self-contradictory pretences? Supposing it possible we could obtain, by conquest, a small accession to our property; could we enjoy it with the reflection, that it was obtained by the miseries of our own species? Could we revel in luxuries, bought with the price of blood, the blood of our countrymen? It is said, "We have protected the colonists, and that they ought to pay for our protection." Have they not paid for it by the benefits of their commerce? Have not two of our own Parliaments acknowledged, that they paid more than their quota of the expence of last war? A war, not commenced, as has been pretended, out of disinterested regard for them; but to secure the profits of their trade; a trade, which, had they become subjects to France, must have been lost to England—to secure the balance of European power—to prevent the aggrandizement of our natural enemies.

In page [416], you have stated the case, perhaps you think, fairly. Give me leave to draw a parallel—parallels have, probably, been often of use to you, at the foundry. We feel best for another, when we put ourselves in his place; the transposition is, *argumentum ad hominem.*

Suppose popery established in England. Popery, you know, is intolerant—burn, or conform, are its alternatives. You, and your disciples, profess to approve of neither. A certain number of you embark for the coast of New Zealand—you find part of the country uninhabited; your fire arms give you advantage over the savages of the rest. You form a settlement; you cultivate the ground; establish manufactures, and grow rich: you might export some of your commodities to Batavia, on very advantageous terms. Capt. Cook, in the course of his voyage, happens to touch on this same coast of New Zealand: the English government, and, indeed, every Englishman (who had heard that there was such a place) take it, therefore, into their heads to think it their own: they send a ship, to inform you that they think so; and to tell you, that you must not traffick with Batavia, but only with them; and that they will accept the profits of the trade, as a ground rent, an acknow[ledge]ment of their sovereignty. The Dutch grow jealous of your rising state; they send a fleet, and army, to attack and dispossess you. War is maintained with various success: you apply to England for assistance; England assists you: you not only continue your exclusive commerce with her, but contribute to the expence she has sustained by assisting you. After all, when you expect no such matter, comes a peremptory mandate from England,

> *We have protected you; we will be paid for our protection—we will have half the fruits of your labour, half the income of your lands, and manufactures, for ever.*

Lay your hand upon your heart, Mr. Wesley, and say, would you then defend the measures of government, as lenient and equitable? Or would you hesitate (if able) to act the modern American?

You assert, that

> There are men in England, determined enemies to monarchy, who wish to change the government into a republick.

I cannot think that you believe your own assertion. It is well known, that the republican form does not suit the genius of the nation; still less would it suit the character of the age. Commonwealths are not prolifick in honours and emoluments, nor propitious to grandeur and profusion—commonwealths must be founded by men of severe virtue, and strict self-denial. A much more probable supposition is, that some of the opponents of administration wish only to fill the seats of those whom they oppose; but the number, even of these, it is to be hoped is but small.

I know of no Englishman, who hates either the kingly office, or the prince by whom it is now exercised. I believe there are some millions of honest Englishmen, who perceive, with inexpressible grief and terror, our excellent constitution, planned by the best and wisest of our ancestors, and maintained with their blood, gradually deviating from its primitive purity: they see the regal estate, like Aaron's serpent, swallowing up the democratical; they see the influence of the crown over the Commons becoming so unlimited, that the dictates of the human will are not more implicitly obeyed by the members of the human body, than the former is by the latter; they see part of the elective body become so corrupt, that the intent of one principal security of English liberty, the circumstance of a senator vacating his seat on acceptance of a place, is now entirely frustrated; they see this corruption is an evil, which nothing can prevent the effects of, but such an absolute incapacitation of placemen, that they cannot be rechosen—but those who perceive these, and many other flagrant perversions of our glorious constitution, far from wishing to subvert that constitution, wish only to restore it to its pristine integrity.

There are also, I believe, many thousand of honest Englishmen, who wish well to their country and its liberties, but are ignorant what its constitution is, and, consequently, cannot know when it is violated: these are the men, who cannot fear danger, till they feel evil;

these are the men, whom the Johnsons and the Wesleys seek to deceive out of their birthright, and persuade them they are slaves.

You boast of our present liberty, civil and religious: "Every man," you say, "sits under his own vine, and under his own fig-tree." It is not my business, nor desire, to point out every minute step, by which I think liberty is losing ground. Nobody denies, that we do enjoy a reasonable share of liberty, at present—but is no regard due to the future? There is, surely, some difference in the tenure, by which we hold a possession: the lessee in perpetuum, is, surely, in a better situation, than the tenant at will.

Some have said, arbitrary government, well administered, is the best mode of government; but how many chances are there against its good administration?

We have now a good prince upon the throne; but who can ensure the character of his successors? Should the crown obtain plenary possession of the Parliament, leaving it only a form without a spirit; where will be the difference between the inhabitants of France and Spain, and our posterity? where will be the difference between those who are ruled by the command of one man, issued immediately from his own mouth; and those, who are ruled by the command of one man, issued mediately *through the mouths of many*?

I shall now, sir, take my leave of you and your performance. I have no attachment to, or connection of any kind with the colonists; I have no concern in the matter. I may say, as you say, and perhaps with more sincerity, "I shall get nothing by either party."—But, I am a friend, on principle, to the *original universal rights of man*.

As I have formerly seen you, with pleasure, in the character of a Christian minister, doing some good in the moral world; so it is, with regret, I now see you in the character of a court sycophant, doing much more mischief in the political world, injuring, perhaps irreparably injuring your country.

POSTSCRIPT

You ask, "Did the people give William the Conqueror the power?"

An able writer and eminent statesman (Lord Somers) positively asserts, that the people did give William the power:

> William the first (who is unjustly stiled the Conqueror, having subdued none but Harold and those who abetted him) did obtain the crown, by a free choice and submission of the peers, and body of the people: and, before his coronation, he was made to swear, that he would govern the people justly, and keep and observe to them their old laws.

This is a striking instance of the high sense the people of England once had of their own importance.

You assert, "that the people never gave the supreme power to any, but Massaniello of Naples." If you mean the supreme executive power, the English history repeatedly contradicts your assertion. Give me leave to ask you—Who gave that power to Charles II. at the Restoration? to William III. at the Revolution? and, afterwards, to the house of Hanover?

FINIS

15

AMERICA'S APPEAL TO THE IMPARTIAL WORLD

Moses Mather

HARTFORD

1775

MOSES MATHER (1719–1806). Born in Lyme, Connecticut, into a famous New England family of divines, Mather was a graduate of Yale in the class of 1739. He began preaching in 1742 in what is now the town of Darien, where he remained, preaching for sixty-four years. He was ordained in 1744. As a champion of liberty, he became an especially obnoxious personality to Tories in his vicinity; he was even twice imprisoned for his views: In 1779 he was seized in his home and imprisoned in New York for five weeks, and in 1781 the British arrived at his church during services and confined him and around fifty of his congregation in New York for some months. He conducted a doctrinal debate over infant baptism and communion with the unconverted with New Divinity leaders Joseph Bellamy and Samuel Hopkins in the late 1760s and early 1770s, but late in life he seems to have swung over to their views. Thrice married, he was the father of eight children.

Mather published eight pieces, including the Connecticut election sermon for 1781. He was honored with a D.D. from the College of New Jersey and was a fellow of Yale College from 1777 to 1790. President Dwight of Yale described him as "a man distinguished for learning and piety, a strong understanding, and [for having led] a most exemplary life" (*Yale Biographies and Annals*, 1:627).

America's Appeal to the Impartial World was published anonymously in Hartford in 1775, but it is known to be Mather's work. It breathes the fire of righteous patriotism characteristic of the pulpit of the time, as can be seen from the three mighty Old Testament texts on the title page, and is a superb statement of American liberty.

AMERICA's APPEAL

TO

The Impartial WORLD.

Wherein the RIGHTS of the *AMERICANS*, as MEN, BRITISH SUBJECTS, and as COLONISTS; the *Equity* of the *Demand*, and of the *Manner* in which it is made upon them by *Great-Britain*, are ſtated and conſidered. And,

The *Oppoſition* made by the Colonies to Acts of Parliament, their reſorting to ARMS in their *neceſſary* DEFENCE, againſt the Military Armaments, employed to enforce them, VINDICATED.

Wo! to thee that ſpoileſt when thou waſt not ſpoiled; and dealeſt treacherouſly, and they dealt not treacherouſly with thee, &c.
Iſaiah xxxiii.

My bowels, my bowels! I am pained at my heart, my heart maketh noiſe in me; I cannot hold my peace becauſe thou haſt heard, Oh my ſoul! the ſound of the trumpet and the alarm of war.
Jer. iv.

And they anſwered the King, the man that conſumed us and deviſed againſt us, that we ſhould be deſtroyed from remaining in any of the coaſts of Iſrael, let, &c. 2 Sam. xxi.

HARTFORD:

Printed by EBENEZER WATSON, 1775.

t a time when we are called upon to surrender our liberties, our religion, and country; or defend them at the point of the sword, against those, that were our friends, our brethren, and allies (whose swords, and ours, till lately were never drawn but for mutual defence; and in joint battalions, cemented in love, affinity, and valour, have wrought wonders, vanquished armies, and triumphed over the power of mighty potentates), nothing will inspire our councils with unanimity, our resolves with firmness, and render the exertions, the noble struggles of a brave, free and injured people, bold, rapid and irresistable, like a right understanding of the necessity and rectitude of the defence, we are compelled to make, in this unnatural contention.

To write upon a subject that hath been so often and ably handled —a subject so important in its nature, so extensive in its consequences, in which the fate of America, the rights and liberties of millions, nay more, of mankind, are involved; and to trace those rights to their native original source, develope the fountain from whence derived; define their nature and immutability, and shew wherefore the arbitrary institutions of civil government (originally ordained to connect the strength of each, for the security of all) cannot destroy or alter them, requires a fund of abilities far beyond mine; yet, to attempt it, may serve to awaken and stimulate some masterly pen, to execute a task so arduous, and beneficial to the world. And should these imperfect considerations, on a subject so important, call forth the prolific fire of some great intuitive genius, to lighten upon the subject, on which I have only glimmered, and like a skilful physician, comprehending the disease and the remedy, point out the one, and prescribe the other, or some mighty deliverer, while others lop here and there a scattered branch, with unerring aim, to give a blow at the root, my end would be answered, my pains compensated, and my country rescued from the darkness that invelops, and from the misery and slavery that impend it. With these views, the following pages are humbly dedicated to the candour and patronage of the impartial world; to whom (under God), we make our appeal, with fervent desires, that he, who hath the hearts of king's in his hands suspends the fate of empires on his nod, and whom, even angry, conflicting elements instantly obey, would hush the civil tumults, still and dispel the thundering tempest, that darkens and disquiets our hemisphere.

I shall consider the subject under the following divisions.

I. The natural rights of the Americans, considered as men.

II. The rights of Americans antecedent to any charters, or colony constitutions under the crown.

III. Their rights subsequent to such charters, or colony constitutions.

IV. The equity of the demand made on the colonies, and of the manner in which it is made.

Free agency, or a rational existence, with its powers and faculties, and freedom of enjoying and exercising them, is the gift of God to man. The right of the donor, and the authenticity of the donation, are both incontestable; hence man hath an absolute property in, and right of dominion over himself, his powers and faculties; with self-love to stimulate, and reason to guide him, in the free use and exercise of them, independent of, and uncontrolable by any but him, who created and gave them. And whatever is acquired by the use, and application of a man's faculties, is equally the property of that man, as the faculties by which the acquisitions are made; and that which is absolutely the property of a man, he cannot be divested of, but by his own voluntary act, or consent, either expressed, or implied. Expressed, by actual gift, sale, or exchange, by himself, or his lawful substitute: implied, as where a man enters into, and takes the benefits of a government, he implicitly consents to be subject to it's laws; so, when he transgresses the laws, there is an implied consent to submit to it's penalties. And from this principle, all the civil* exousiai, or rightful authorities, that are ordained of God, and exist in the world, are derived as from their native source. From whence are authorities, dominions and powers? from God, the sovereign ruler, as the fountain, *through the voice and consent of the people*. For what purpose are

*Exousia, in the original, which is translated power, signifies a rightful authority or moral power, and stands opposed to *dunamis*, a natural power or might.

they erected? *for the good of the people.* Wherefore the sovereign ruler, condescends to cloath, with authority, the man who by the general voice, is exalted, from among the people, to bear rule; and to pronounce him his minister for their good. Hence, it is evident, that man hath the clearest right, by the most indefeasible title, to personal security, liberty, and private property. And whatever is a man's own, he hath, most clearly, a right to enjoy and defend; to repel force by force; to recover what is injuriously pillaged or plundered from him, and to make reasonable reprisals for the unjust vexation.* And, upon this principle, an offensive war may sometimes be justifiable, viz. when it is necessary for preservation and defence.

II. I am now to consider the rights of the Americans, antecedent to any charters or colony constitutions under the crown.

When our ancestors left the kingdom of England, they were subjects of that kingdom, and entitled to equal privileges with the rest of its subjects; when they came into America, where no civil constitutions were existing, they joined themselves to none: the lands which they entered and possessed, they acquired by purchase, or by conquest of the natives: they came over of themselves, viz. were not colonies sent out, to make settlements by government; not to mention the intolerable oppressions, by which they were driven out, crossed the Atlantick, and availed themselves of possessions, at their own risque and expence, and by their own sword and prowess. Now, in America, they were still subjects of the kingdom of England, or they were not; if the former, then they were entitled to enjoy, in America, the same or equal privileges, with those enjoyed by the subjects residing in England—if the latter, then that kingdom had no right of jurisdiction over them, and they were in a state of nature, at liberty to erect such a constitution of civil government as they should chuse. Upon the supposition that they were still subjects of that kingdom, let us consider what rights and privileges they were entitled to enjoy:

*I have not noticed the authority of parents over children, it not being to the argument, but remark, that the Creator, foreseeing the necessity of civil government, arising from the depravity of human nature, hath wisely formed our infancy, and childhood, feeble and dependent on the protection, and government of parents, thereby preparing us, in childhood, for dependence on, and subjection to civil government, in manhood.

1st. In regard to legislation.
2d. Taxation. And,
3d. The mode of trial.

By nature, every man (under God) is his own legislator, judge, and avenger, and absolute lord of his property. In civil government, rightly constituted, every one retains a share in the legislative, taxative, judicial, and the vindictive powers, by having a voice in the supreme legislature, which enacts the laws, and imposes the taxes, and by having a right, in all cases wherein he is injured, to resort to, and demand redress, in a course of law, from the tribunal of the public, and the sword of state. And the English nation, early impressed, with these first great principles of natures dictates, erected a system of civil government, correspondent thereto; invested the parliament, which consisted of all the estates, that composed the nation, in epitome, with the supreme sovereignty of the kingdom; and in which, each estate made a part, and had a share, either personally or by actual representation, to advise, resolve, consent, or dissent, and in which, the concurrence of all three, viz. the King, Lords and Commons, was necessary, to every act of legislation. Thus the English government was constituted upon the foundation of reason; and the natural rights of the subjects, instead of being given up, or impaired, were confirmed, improved and strengthened, although the mode of exercising them was altered: Wherefore it is a maxim in the English laws, that to an act of parliament, every man, in judgment of law is party. The English constitution, like other imitations of nature, was a system of consummate wisdom, and policy, the balance of power, being so judiciously placed, as to connect the force, and to preserve the rights of all; each estate, armed with a power of self defence, against the encroachments of the other two, by being enabled to put a negative upon any or all of their resolves, neither the King, Lords or Commons, could be deprived of their rights or properties but by their own consent in parliament, and no laws could be made, or taxes imposed, but such as were necessary, and in the judgment of the three estates in parliament, for the common good, and interest of the realm. Most justly then did a celebrated French writer, treating of the English, and the excellence of their constitution, say, that England could never lose its freedom, until parliament lost its virtue.

The English, animated with the spirit of freedom, to their immortal honor, anciently claimed these privileges, as their unalienable rights, and anxious to preserve and transmit them unimpaired to posterity; caused them to be reduced to writing, and in the most solemn manner to be recognized, ratified and confirmed, first by King John, then by his son Henry the IIId. in the 3d and 37th years of his reign, at Westminster-Hall, where Magna Charta was read in the presence of the nobility and bishops, with lighted candles in their hands; the king, all the while laying his hand on his breast, at last, solemnly swearing faithfully and inviolably to observe all things therein contained, as he was a man, a christian, a soldier and a king; then the bishops extinguished the candles and threw them on the ground, and every one said, thus let him be extinguished and stink in hell, who violates this charter: Upon which there was universal festivity and joy, ringing of bells, &c. and again by Edward the 1st. in the 25th year of his reign, by the statute called *Confirmatio Cartarum.* Afterwards by a multitude of corroborating acts, reckoned in all, by Lord Cook, to be thirty-two, from Edw. 1st. to Hen. 4th. and since, in a great variety of instances, by the bills of right and acts of settlement; whereby Magna Charta, that great charter of liberties, hath been established as the standard of right throughout the realm, and all judgments contrary thereto declared void; it was ordered to be read twice a year in all the cathedral churches, and sentence of excommunication to be denounced against all, who by word or deed, acted contrary to, or infringed it.

2d. With regard to taxation.

As the rights of private property are sacred, and no one can be divested thereof without his free consent: The English constitution, in this also religiously follows the dictates of reason: No subject of England can be constrained to pay any aids or taxes, even for the defence of the realm, or the support of government, but such as are imposed by his own consent, or that of his representative in parliament. By the stat. 25 Edw. 1st. c. 5 and 6, it is provided, that the king shall not take any aids or taxes, but by the common assent of the realm: And what that common assent is, is more fully explained, by the 34th of Edw. 1st. stat. 4, c. 1, which enacts, that no talliage or aid shall be taken, without assent of archbishops, bishops, earls, barons, knights, burgesses, and other freemen of the land; and by the 14th Edw. 3. stat. 2. it is provided, that the prelates, earls, barons, commons, and citizens, burgesses and merchants, shall not be charged to make any aid, if it be not by the common assent of the great men, and Commons in Parliament: And as this fundamental principle had been shamefully violated by succeeding princes, it was made an article in the petition of right, third of King Cha. I. that no man shall be compelled to yield any gift, loan, or benevolence tax, or any such charge, without common consent, by act of Parliament; and again by the 1st of William and Mary, stat. 2, it is declared, that levying money for, or to the use of the crown, by pretence of prerogative, without grant of parliament, or for longer time, or in other manner, then the same is or shall be granted, is illegal; and that the subjects do claim, demand, and insist upon all and singular the premises, as their antient undoubted rights and liberties. Lastly, these rights and liberties were asserted and confirmed, in the act of settlement which limited the crown, to the illustrious house of his present majesty, in the beginning of this century. Talliage from the French taille to cut, signifies a part cut or carved out of the whole estate, and in a law sense includes all subsidies, taxes, impositions, and duties whatsoever, none of which might be taken without common consent in parliament. Hence, it is the antient and unalienable right of the House of Commons, to originate all money bills, they being the free donations of the people, and not the exactions of the prince; upon the principle that civil government is constituted for the good of the people, and not the people for government: And there is no difference in the reason and nature of the thing, between the king's levying money in England without consent of parliament, and the parliament's levying money in America without the consent of the Americans.

3d. In regard to the mode of trial.

As it is not the laws merely, that are made, considered in themselves, but the construction and sense put upon them, by the judges and triers, that falls upon the subject and affects him in his person and property; it was necessary that the constitution should guard the rights of the subject, in the executive as well as the legislative part of government: And no mode of trial would so effectually do this, be so unexceptionable, by reason of their equality, and the impartial manner in which they are taken and impanelled; so advantageous, on account of their knowledge of the parties, the credibility of the witnesses, and what weight ought to be given to their testimony, as that by our peers, a jury of the vicinity: For very good and wholsome laws may be perniciously executed. Wherefore it is expresly provided and ordained, in the Great Charter, chap. 29, "That no freeman shall be taken or disseised of his freehold, or liberties, or free customs, or be outlawed, or exiled, or any otherwise destroyed; and we will not pass sentence upon him, nor condemn him, but by lawful judgment of his peers; or by the laws of the land." By this no freeman might be molested in his person, liberty or estate, but according to the laws of the land, by lawful warrant, granted by lawful authority, expressing the cause for which, the time when, and place where he is to answer or be imprisoned, with the terms of his enlargement; nor have sentence passed upon him in any case, but by lawful judgment of his peers; who, in the instance of giving their verdict, do unanimously declare and announce the law, with respect to themselves, in like circumstances. It is, says Dr. Blackstone, the most transcendant privilege which

> any subject can enjoy or wish for, that he cannot be affected in his property, his liberty or person, but by the unanimous consent of twelve of his neighbours and equals: And when a celebrated French writer concludes, that because Rome, Sparta, and Carthage, lost their liberties, therefore England must in time lose theirs, he should have recollected, that Rome, Sparta, and Carthage were strangers to trial by jury; and that it is a duty which every man owes to his country, his friends, his posterity and himself, to maintain, to the utmost of his power, this valuable constitution in all its parts, to restore it to its antient dignity, if at all impaired, or deviated from its first institution, &c. and above all, to guard with the most jealous circumspection, against the introduction of new and arbitrary methods of trial, which, under a variety of plausible pretences, may in time, imperceptably undermine this best preservative of English liberties.

English subjects, therefore, could be bound by no laws, be liable to no taxes, but what were made and imposed by their own consent; nor have any sentence passed upon them but by the judgment of their equals. Glorious constitution! worthy to be engraved in capitals of gold, on pillars of marble; to be perpetuated through all time, a barrier, to circumscribe and bound the restless ambition of aspiring monarchs, and the palladium of civil liberty; especially, when in addition to these, we consider the habeas corpus act, passed in 31 Car. II. that second Magna Charta and stable bulwark of the subjects liberties, which provides a remedy for the immediate relief of such as are unjustly imprisoned, under colour of law. And enacts, that no subject of this our realm, who is an inhabitant of England, Wales, or Berwick, shall be sent a prisoner to Scotland, Ireland, Jersey, Guernsey, or places beyond the seas, and all such imprisonments are declared illegal, the party causing them disabled to bear any office, incurs the penalty of a premunire, becomes incapable of the king's pardon, and also is to answer damages to the party aggrieved. "Of great importance, says the above cited author, to the public, is the preservation of personal liberty, for if once it was left in the power of any, the highest magistrate, to imprison arbitrarily, whomsoever he or his officers thought proper (as in France is daily practised by the crown) there would soon be an end to all other rights and immunities." How consistent with these principles, the present mode of administring government is, the impartial world may judge, by the late revenue and other acts of parliament, relative to America, directing its inhabitants to be imprisoned, and transported beyond sea for trial; erecting courts of admiralty, and other arbitrary tribunals, to decide in matters most interesting, without the intervention of a jury.

These privileges, important and inestimable as they are, every subject of the realm of England hath right to possess and enjoy. And the Americans, antecedent to their charters, &c. if they were still subjects of that realm, had right to have and enjoy in America. Now, if it was impossible for the Americans, in their situation, to enjoy the rights and privileges of the English government, it follows, that they were not amenable to its power, nor taxable for its support; *nam qui sentit onus, sentire debet commodum*, he that bears the burden ought to enjoy the blessing, and *vice versa*. Can any thing be more absurd, than that a man should be tied to a government, bound to yield subjection, and contribute support, wherever he is, on the face of the earth, without having any part or voice in its administration, or power to enjoy its immunities. And that it was impossible for the Americans to enjoy the privileges of the English government, is evident, there being no provision in the constitution for summoning members to parliament from the American world; and if there was, the local distance, the risk and uncertainty of crossing the atlantic, the disparity between the two countries, in respect of situation, numbers, age, abilities and other circumstances, would render any representation of America in the parliament of England, utterly impracticable and vain. So that our ancestors, in America, were unable to exercise and enjoy that capital right of all English subjects, viz. the having a voice in the supreme legislature, without which, as the *causa sine qua non*, the parliament of England could not bind them in any respect. Hence the right of subjectship, on the part of the Americans, and of jurisdiction over them by parliament, became dormant, ineffectual rights, incapable of being exercised; for the whole ground of the parliament's right to bind the Americans, consisted in their being subjects; and for that very reason, if they were subjects, the parliament could have no right to bind them, or exercise jurisdiction over them, without their consent.

[II.] I will now enquire, whether the Americans, antecedent to their charters, &c. are to be considered as being subjects of the kingdom of England, or not.

From what hath been already said, it is evident, that they either were not subjects of that kingdom, or as though they were not: But this will be further illustrated, by considering, in what subjectship consists: Compleat subjectship,* consists in being under allegiance to the king, inhabiting territories within the kingdom, in having, or at least in being capable of having a voice in the supreme legislature, and enjoying, or in being able to enjoy the benefits and immunities of the government.

Allegiance, from *lige*, to bind, is the bond that connects the subjects with their sovereign, and their sovereign with them: Hence the king is called their liege lord, and they his liege subjects; because he is bound to protect and they to obey. And there are three kinds of allegiance, natural, acquired, and local, every one born within the realm, is by birth, inheritable to the laws, intitled to the immunities of the government, and to the protection of the king; wherefore his allegiance, like St. Pauls, is natural: Every alien friend that comes into the realm, who by the king's letters patent is made a denizen, or

*By this is meant one that is a subject of the kingdom as well as of the king.

by act of parliament is naturalized, hath an acquired allegiance; every alien friend that comes into the realm to reside for a time, oweth a local temporary allegiance, during his residence there. And the obligation to obedience in all these cases, arises from the reason and fitness of things, and is comprehensively expressed in this short law maxim, *protectio trahit subjectionem, & subjectio protectionem*, protection mutually entitles to subjection, and subjection to protection. Hence it follows (as mankind by joining to society do not mean, nor doth allegiance intend to confine them perpetually to dwell in one country) that when a person, under a natural, acquired, or local allegiance removes out of the realm to some distant climate, goes out of the protection of the king, and loses all benefit of the laws and government of the kingdom; his allegiance, which is mutual or not at all, ceaseth, for *cessante causa cesset effectus*, the cause or reason ceasing, which in this case is protection and the benefits of government, the effect, viz. the obligation of obedience also ceaseth. There is also what is called a legal allegiance, *ex provisione legis*, that is by positive institution, as the oath of allegiance taken by the subjects, wherein they swear to bear all true and faithful allegiance to the king; which is a counter part to the king's coronation oath, whereby he swears to protect his subjects in all their just rights, to abjure popery, and maintain the protestant religion, to govern the kingdom and administer justice according to the laws of the realm. Both which are only confirmations of the mutual obligations resulting from the relation, that subsists between them as king and subjects, and do attend upon and follow it, in its extent and duration. I am not insensible that it is a doctrine of antiquity, patronized by many, that natural allegiance is universal and perpetual; cannot be lost or forfeited, but by the commission of crimes, &c. but notwithstanding, I beg leave to suggest a few considerations on this point. The place of a man's birth, in respect to himself, is a matter of accident and necessity, and not of choice; and is a man so bound by accident and necessity, as to the place of his birth, that when he arrives to the age of discretion, he cannot remove into another kingdom and country, and become the subject of another prince? Doth not the obligation of subjection and obedience to parents, cease with our childhood and state of dependance, although that of respect and reverence ever remains? Should the king of Great-Britain voluntarily resign his crown, or abdicate the government, remove and reside in Italy, or enter into religion, whereby he would be civilly dead, would he, notwithstanding, be king, *de jure & de facto*, and would the subjects be under obligation of allegiance to him, as their liege lord? incapable of placing another on the throne, without incurring the crime of treason, or being involved in the dilemma of owing subjection to two rightful sovereigns, at one time? If so, then he that is once king, can never be divested of royal authority, the principles of the revolution are false; and no new subjects can ever be acquired, for all are born under allegiance to some prince or state; where, upon these principles, they must ever remain, fixed as fate; and acquired allegiance, by act of parliament in England, is all a farce.

But be this as it may, yet should a number of the subjects of Great-Britain, under a natural allegiance to the king, by his licence remove voluntarily, or by accident be carried to some distant, uncivilized, or uninhabited country, where they should find it convenient and beneficial to settle; would they be incapable of erecting civil government, and making laws, for the well ordering of their affairs, independent of the king and kingdom? If so, they would be of all men most miserable, and their boasted subjectship would be their greatest calamity, because they have the rights of British subjects, they are rendered incapable of enjoying the rights of men. Upon this contracted principle, no new countries could be peopled, or new empires founded; but all things must remain as they were. And is the world and its empires so fixed and concluded by an unalterable fate? Are men, who were created in the image of their maker, to contemplate the heavens and soar above the stars, whose first great law was to increase, multiply and replenish the earth, and by experiencing the boundless profusion of divine goodness, learn to be profusely bounteous and good, to be so restrained? Is this becoming the dignity of their rational nature, and suited to the selfish* social passions, implanted in the human soul? Whose motives are our own good and the good of mankind: To attempt to eradicate or alter these, by the arbitrary restraints of civil government, is to impeach the wisdom of the Creator, for not suiting man's passions and faculties, to his station

*By selfish here is meant virtuous passions that prompt us to seek our own preservation &c. as self-love, &c.

here, and offering violence to human nature. Let civil government then be suited to man's nature and passions (I mean not the depraved, ungodly desires and cravings of tyranny, which grasps for universal despotic sway; or of licentiousness, that is ever impatient of all legal restraints, how ever reasonable and righteous), for if it is not, there will be a perpetual conflict between the regulations and restraints of government, and the reasonable desires and passions of the subjects.

It may be said, that the reason why natural allegiance is perpetual, is not merely on account of our being born, &c. but the protection and support of the government, afforded us where born; this is an obligation of debt. Much, most undoubtedly, we owe to our parents and to the government that supported and protected our infantile state: But is it true, that because we were once dependant, we must ever be so? Because we were once obliged, we can never be disengaged from the obligation? If it is, then all mankind are insolvents, servants of servants, the curse of Canaan is the portion of all: And every alien born is utterly incapable of ever becoming a subject of the kingdom of Great-Britain.

But to return, allegiance is due to the king in his natural and political capacity; and doth not necessarily superinduce an obligation of obedience to the power of parliament; for a person may be a subject of the king of England and not of the realm; be under allegiance to the king, yet owe no obedience to parliament; as was the case of Scotland, upon the accession of King James the 1st. to the throne of England, before the act of union; and as the case is at present with Hanover; and as was the case of Normandy, when William the Conqueror wore the crown of England.

The rights of a subject may be suspended for a time, with respect to the enjoyment and exercise of them, by some temporary impediment, which when removed they revive: But when the obstacle that suspends and impedes the exercise and enjoyment of them, is universal, permanent and perpetual, it is an extinguishment of those rights. Thus much I thought necessary to observe, before I gave a relation of the cause and manner of our ancestors first coming and settling in America.

North-America was first discovered by Sebastian Cabot, in the reign of Henry the 7th, A.D. 1498, and was at that time inhabited by the Indian natives, who lived principally by hunting: In A.D. 1606

King James, by letters patent, erected two companies called the Virginia Companies, with power to make settlements in America. Though none were made in New-England by virtue of that authority. About the close of the sixteenth century, several attempts were made for settling Virginia, before any proved successful: The three first companies that came all perished, by hunger, diseases or Indian cruelty: The fourth was reduced to almost the same situation, when Lord Delaware came to their relief. Thus Virginia, being the first province that was settled in America, to her honour be it remembered, hath likewise been foremost in maintaining and vindicating the rights of the Americans.

In A.D. 1620, England, torn with religious dissentions, the friends of the reformation, persecuted with unrelenting cruelty, by the intolerant spirit that influenced government, were forced to renounce their religion and liberties, or assert them with their lives. The protestants, to the number of one hundred and fifty, who before had fled to Holland for safety, having made a purchase under the Plymouth Company, and obtained the royal licence, quitted their native country, preferring the enjoyment of their religion and liberty, in a howling desert, to the pomp and pleasures of luxury and sin in England; crossed the Atlantic and arrived at Plymouth in America in A.D. 1620, and by their own valour, industry, risk and expence (under the smiles of heaven) acquired plantations, subdued savage enemies, built cities, turned the wilderness into fruitful fields, and rendered it vocal with the praises of their Saviour, and from small beginnings, in process of time, became great in number, and in extent of territory; great numbers, not long after, from religious considerations, emigrating from England, came and settled the other colonies in America; for, says an English historian, "it seems that all the provinces of North-America were planted from motives of religion." Thus was gradually unfolded the rudiments of a future empire, before in embryo.

Upon what principles then, could England have jurisdiction over the persons and properties of those brave and free adventurers who settled the colonies? Because England was most powerful? This would be founding right in might, an argument too absurd to need refutation, applied to any but the supreme Being; who, though almighty, yet can do no wrong. Or because they were once subjects of that kingdom? This, if it proves any thing, proves too much, as hath been shown. Or was it because the country was discovered by the king of England? Whatever rights accrue by first discovering a vacant country, accrue to the prince, under whom it is made; and they are *jura coronæ*, rights of the crown, belonging to the king and not to the kingdom. But America, had long before been discovered and inhabited by numerous tribes of Indians, the original proprietors of the country; subjects capable of property, and who made a part of the human species, when the Almighty gave the earth to the children of men; and why black squalid hair, a tawny complexion, a particular manner of living, and ignorance of divine revelation, should be absolute disqualifications, to have and hold property, any more than a black skin, curled head, flat nose and bandy legs, should be the infallible criterion of slavery, I cant devise.

III. *Let us consider the rights of the Americans subsequent to their charters and colony constitutions.*

As there are certain rights of men, which are unalienable even by themselves; and others which they do not mean to alienate, when they enter into civil society. And as power is naturally restless, aspiring and insatiable; it therefore becomes necessary in all civil communities (either at their first formation or by degrees) that certain great first principles be settled and established, determining and bounding the power and prerogative of the ruler, ascertaining and securing the rights and liberties of the subjects, as the foundation stamina of the government; which in all civil states is called the constitution, on the certainty and permanency of which, the rights of both the ruler and the subjects depend; nor may they be altered or changed by ruler or people, but by the whole collective body, or a major part at least, nor may they be touched by the legislator; for the moment that alters essentially the constitution, it annihilates its own existence, its constitutional authority. Not only so, but on supposition the legislator might alter it; such a stretch of power would be dangerous beyond conception; for could the British parliament alter the original principles of the constitution, the people might be deprived of their liberties and properties, and the parliament become absolute and perpetual; and for redress in such case, should it ever happen, they must resort to their native rights, and be justified in making insurrection. For when the constitution is violated, they have no other remedy; but for all other wrongs and abuses that may possibly happen, the constitution remaining inviolate, the people have a remedy thereby.

The Americans antecedent to their colony constitutions, must be considered either as the subjects of the kingdom of England, or as subjects of the king and not of the kingdom, or as subjects of neither; and their territory as belonging either to that kingdom, the king, or to neither. In which of these lights they should be considered, I leave the impartial world to judge. If the first, then the grants and patents from the crown conveyed nothing, *nam ex nihilo nihil gignitur*, for what the king had not he could not grant, and the colonies, besides their rights as English subjects, have acquired an indefeasable title by prescription, to the lands they have possessed, to the privileges, immunities and exemptions they have enjoyed, and to all the powers of government, rights of jurisdiction, regalities, &c. which they have had and exercised, beyond which, the memory of man runneth not to the contrary. If the second, then by the royal grants, patents, &c. all the powers of government, rights of jurisdiction, liberties and privileges, with the property of the lands in fee, are passed from the crown, and vested in the colonies, absolutely and indefeasably, according to the tenor of their several grants and constitutions. If the last, then all these rights of jurisdiction, of property and liberty, were underived and self-originated. If, therefore, they were to be considered as English subjects, by the constitution of that kingdom, they had right to enjoy all these privileges; if not as English subjects, then they were theirs without being beholden therefor. In either view, therefore, they were entitled to have and enjoy all the rights, liberties and privileges, which, by their several constitutions, were granted and confirmed to them, antecedent thereto. And their constitutions are the original compacts, containing the first great principles, or stamina of their governments; combining the members, connecting and subordinating them to the king as their supreme head and liege lord; also prescribing the forms of their several governments, determining and bounding the power of the crown over them, within proper limits, and ascertaining and securing their rights, jurisdictions and liberties; and are not to be compared to the charters of corporations in England (although they are to be deemed sacred) which are royal favours granted to particular corporations, beyond what are enjoyed by the subjects in common; if they should be forfeited and taken away the members will still retain the great essential rights of British subjects, and these original compacts were made and entered into by the king, not only for himself, but expressly for his heirs and successors on the one part, and the colonies, their successors and assigns on the other; whereby the connection was formed, not only between the parties then in being, but between the crown and the colonies, through all successions of each; and those compacts are permanent and perpetual, as unalterable as Magna Charta, or the primary principles of the English constitution: nor can they be vacated or changed by the king, any more than by the colonies, nor be forfeited by one more than the other; for they are mutually obligatory on both, and are the ligaments and bonds that connect the colonies with the king of Great-Britain, and the king with them: cut, therefore, and dissolve them, and the colonies will become immediately disunited from the crown, and the crown from them. Should the original parties to these constitutions awake in their tombs, and come forth (on a controversy that would awake the dead, could the dead be waked) and with united voice testify, that this was their original, true intent and meaning, would it not be awfully striking and convincing? But we have greater evidence; we have their original declaration, made in that day, deliberately reduced to writing, and solemnly ratified and confirmed, which is as follows:

> We do, for us, our heirs and successors, grant to, &c. and their successors, by these presents, that these our letters patent, shall be firm, good, and effectual in the law, to all intents, constructions and purposes whatever, according to our true intent and meaning herein before declared, as shall be construed, reputed and adjudged most favourable on the behalf, and for the best benefit and behoof of the grantees, &c. notwithstanding any omissions therein, or any statute, act, ordinance, provision, proclamation or restriction heretofore made, had, enacted, ordained or provided, or any other matter, cause or thing whatsoever, to the contrary thereof, in any wise notwithstanding.

And the reasons for erecting these constitutions, are recited in the preamble of some of them, as follows, viz.

> Whereas by the several navigations, discoveries, and successful plantations of divers of our loving subjects of this our realm of England, several lands, islands, places, colonies and plantations have been obtained and settled, &c. and thereby the trade and commerce there, greatly increased, &c.

> and that the same, or the greatest part thereof, was purchased and obtained, for great and valuable considerations, and some other parts thereof gained by conquest, with much difficulty, and at the only endeavours, expence and charge of them and their associates and those under whom they claim, subdued and improved, and thereby become a considerable addition of our dominions and interest there. Now, know ye, that in consideration thereof, and in regard the said colony is remote from other the English plantations in the place aforesaid, and to the end the affairs and business which shall from time to time happen, or arise concerning the same, may be duly ordered and managed, we have therefore thought fit, &c.

Through this portal, majesty itself, like the meridian sun, lightens upon the subject, and makes plain and clear a matter, which the wits and disputers of a venal age, would envelope in midnight obscurity. In consideration that these discoveries, settlements, &c. were obtained for great and valuable considerations, &c. and at their, viz. the colonist's only endeavours and expence of blood and treasure, and in regard that they are remote, so that they cannot otherwise enjoy the benefits of civil government, &c. therefore, it is most reasonable and necessary, that they should have a government of their own. These constitutions are in some respects various in different colonies; all have their assemblies, or parliaments, consisting of the governor, council, and the representatives of the people; invested with the supreme power of legislation and taxation; though in some, their laws are subject to be negativ'd by the royal dissent, within a limited time: in some, the governor and council are chosen by the people, in others, the council; and in some, both governor and council are appointed by the crown. All have their courts of judicature, to take cognizance of all causes, arising within their territorial limits, and the power of judging in the last resort, though this right hath been infringed in sundry instances, by appeals to the king and council. But how a judgment in England can be executed in America, according to the course of law, is to me a paradox.

Further, it is ordained and declared,

> That all and every of the subjects of us, our heirs, &c. which shall go to inhabit in said colony, and every of their children that shall happen to be born there, or on the sea in going to or returning from thence, shall have and enjoy all liberties and immunities of free and natural subjects, within any the dominions of us, our heirs or successors, to all intents, construc-

> tions and purposes whatever, as if they and every of them were born within the realm of England.

This doth not bring the Americans within the realm of England; but it proves them to be out of it: For were it not so, the granting to them and to their children privileges equal to natural subjects, born within the realm, would have been idle and unnecessary, being no more than they would have been entitled to without it, after setling the foundation principles, and enumerating a variety of capital articles in the constitution of their governments; to avoid prolixity and all mistake and omissions in a recital of their rights and priviledges; they are in short, summed up and declared to be similar and as ample in every respect, as those of the natural born subjects of the realm, to which the colonists are referred, to learn the full extent of their own; which demonstrates the similarity and likeness that subsists between the civil constitutions of the two countries; although several and distinct; and the lands are granted to be holden, not in capite, or by knight service, but in free and common soccage, as of the manor of East-Greenwich; paying there for a certain proportion of the gold and silver ore, that should from time to time be found, &c. in lieu of all services, duties and demands whatsoever. Thus, whether the Americans, antecedent to their constitutions, were subjects of the kingdom of England or not, they have now the clearest right to enjoy the liberties and privileges of English subjects: and to hold their lands discharged of all duties and demands of every kind, except as above. And nothing is plainer, than that the colonists cannot enjoy such privileges, unless they have parliaments and assemblies of their own, invested with the supreme power of legislation and taxation, in which they may be represented, and for this I have a very great and antient authority, viz. the case of the Virginians, determined by one of the kings of England, near a century and a half ago, which, to use the words of the English historian, is as follows:

> The government of this province was not at first adapted to the principles of the English constitution, and to the enjoyment of that liberty, to which a subject of Great-Britain thinks himself entitled, in every part of the globe. It was governed by a governor and council appointed by the king of Great-Britain. As the inhabitants increased, the inconveniency of this form became more grievous; and a new branch was added to their constitution, by which the people, who had formerly no consideration,

> were allowed to elect their representatives from each county, with privileges resembling those of the representatives of the commons of England; thus two houses, the upper and lower house of assembly were formed; the upper house appointed by the crown are stiled honourable, and answer in some measure to the house of peers in the British constitution. The lower house is the guardian of the people's liberties. And thus, with a governor representing the king, and an upper and lower house of assembly, this government bears a striking resemblance to our own.

Now, if the parliament hath right to bind the colonists in any instance of legislation and taxation, it hath in all: Wherein, then, will consist the similarity of the colony constitutions to that of Great-Britain? Wherein the power of their assemblies to guard the rights of the people? In fine, where is the boasted English liberties of the subjects? All laid in the dust, and the colonies subjected to be governed and taxed by the parliament, who are, and their constituents both, interested in augmenting their taxes and burdens.

Realm signifies kingdom; and kingdom signifies the country or countries, that are subject to one sovereign prince. And should a school boy be asked, whether America, which is three thousand miles distant, was within the kingdom of Great-Britain, both being subject to one prince, he must answer that it was not; but that it was within the kingdom of the king of Great-Britain and America. Nor are the following questions more difficult, viz. whether the House of Commons, who have only a representative authority, have right to bind those whom they do not represent? Or whether, in virtue of their being the representatives of the people in Great-Britain, they are the representatives of the people in America? viz. whether the Britons and the Americans are identically the same persons, or whether the Britons are, have, or ought to have, every thing, and the Americans nothing? If the colonies, when they were first constituted, were not subject to the jurisdiction of parliament, they are not become so, by any thing since: and that they were not is evident, not only from the declaration of the king in the constitutions, but by the royal conduct towards them from time to time, treating them as though they were not.

Upon the remonstrance of the Virginians against the imposition of duties on their trade, King Charles the second issued a declaration under his privy seal, dated 19th of April, A.D. 1676, "affirming, that taxes ought not to be laid upon the proprietors and inhabitants of the colony, but by the common consent of the General Assembly." And when a revenue was wanted for the support of civil government in Virginia, in A.D. 1679, an act was framed and sent over to be passed by their assembly in these words, "Enacted by the king's most excellent majesty, by and with the consent of the General Assembly of the colony of Virginia, that a duty of, &c." which was accordingly passed into a law.

And it was declared by James the first and Charles first, when a bill was proposed in the House of Commons, and repeatedly and strenuously urged, to give liberty to the subjects of England to fish on the coast of America; "that it was unnecessary, that the colonies were without the realm and jurisdiction of parliament, and that the privy council would take orders in matters relating to them." And liberty of fishing in America, is reserved in some of the charters that were afterwards made; which shews that without such reservation, they would not have had right to fish on the coast of the colonies. And upon complaint of piracies, &c. committed off the coast of Connecticut, King Charles the second, in A.D. 1683–4, instead of causing an act of Parliament to be made to restrain and punish them, writes this letter to the General Assembly in Connecticut, which letter, is now extant in the hands of the secretary.

> Charles Rex, trusty and well-beloved, we greet you well: Whereas we are informed of great disorders and depredations daily committed, to the prejudice of our allies; contrary to treaties between us and a good correspondence that ought to be maintained between christian princes and states; and we having already given strict order in our island of Jamaica, against such illegal proceedings, by passing a law for restraining and punishing privateers and pirates, &c. our will and pleasure is, that you take care that such a law (a copy whereof is herewith sent you) be passed within our colony, under your government, which you are to certify unto us by the first opportunity, so we bid you heartily farewell: Given at our court at New-Market, the 8th day of March, A.D. 1683–4, in the 36th year of our reign. By his majesty's command, L. Jenkins.

And accordingly the bill was passed into a law by the general assembly of Connecticut. Can it be supposed, that this bill would have been sent to Connecticut to be passed into a law, if the parliament had had jurisdiction thereof? Further, Great-Britain sending their culprits into banishment in America, demonstrates, that America is out of the jurisdiction of that kingdom, for banishment consists in putting a subject out of the limits and jurisdiction of the government. It is in the memory of every one, that the king sent his requisitions to the colonies to raise men and money in the last war, which were readily complied with, by his most dutiful and loyal subjects, in the provinces: Wherefore was this, if the Parliament hath supreme legislative and taxative jurisdiction over them? And to put this matter beyond all doubt, and to shew that the colonies have right, not only to enjoy, but to defend themselves, and their liberties, against any and all (the parliament not excepted) that should be so stupid, or vile, as to invade them; hear the solemn declaration and warrant of their king, in their original constitutions:

> And we do for us, our heirs and successors, give and grant unto, &c. and their successors, by these presents, that it shall and may be lawful to and for the chief commanders, governors and officers of the said company for the time being, who shall be resident in the parts, &c. hereafter mentioned, and others inhabiting there, by their leave, admittance, &c. from time to time, and at all times hereafter, for their special defence and safety, to assemble, martial array, and put in warlike posture, the inhabitants of the said colony, and commissionate, impower and authorise such person or persons as they shall think fit to lead and conduct the said inhabitants; and to encounter, expulse, repel and resist, by force of arms, as well by sea as by land; and also to kill, slay and destroy, by all fitting ways, enterprises and means whatsoever, all and every such person or persons, as shall at any time hereafter, attempt or enterprise the destruction, invasion, detriment or annoyance of the said inhabitants or plantation; and to use and exercise the law martial, &c. and to take or surprize, by all ways and means whatsoever, all and every such person or persons, with their ships, armour, ammunition, and other goods of such as shall in such hostile manner, invade, or attempt the defeating of the said plantation, or the hurt of the said company and inhabitants.

Thus, these liberties and priviledges are not only granted and confirmed, but a power is expressly given to the colonies to defend them to the utmost, against those who should invade or attempt to destroy them. And are the Americans chargeable with treason and rebellion, for yielding to the irresistable impulses of self-preservation and acting under and in pursuance of the royal licence and authority of their king? It is certain that the colonies, in all their constitutions, were considered as being out of the jurisdiction of parliament, from the provisions made in every one, to supply the want of such jurisdiction, by investing their several assemblies with supreme power of legislation; and that their kings ever considered and treated them as being so, until that fatal period when George Grenville, that monster of ministers, came into administration; and that the colonies so understood themselves to be.

From all which I think we may infer, with great clearness and certainty, that he that is king of Great-Britain, is, by the constitutions of the colonies, also king of the American colonies, bound to protect and govern them according to their several constitutions, and not to destroy them: and that the parliament hath no jurisdiction or power with respect to them; for the parliament consists of the three estates, the king, lords and commons, and was constituted for the government of that realm; and the king sustains a three-fold capacity, as king of Great-Britain, the first of the three estates in parliament, and as king of the American colonies, and according to the maxim of the English laws, *Quando duo jura concurrent in una & eadem persona, idem est, ac si essent in diversis*; when several rights or capacities meet and are vested in one and the same person, they remain entire, and as distinct as though they were vested in different persons. This right of sovereignty over the Americans, is derived from a different source from that of Great-Britain, viz. the constitutions of the colonies, extends to different objects, viz. the colonies; and is exercisable in a different manner, viz. according to their several constitutions. And what the king doth as king of Great-Britain, or as one of the estates in parliament, he doth not as king of the colonies; for if so, then all the judges and officers appointed in the realm of England, would be judges and officers in America; all the laws and taxes that receive the royal assent in parliament, would immediately be binding upon the Americans, unless expresly excepted; contrary to the united voice of all their princes, politicians and lawyers, which is, that even Ireland, which they hold as a conquered country, is not bound by acts of parliament, unless specially named. The lords being the noble peers of that realm, set in parliament in right of their estates and dignity, their authority cannot extend beyond the limits of the kingdom of which they are peers. The House of Commons, act by a delegated authority, and can have no greater power than their constituents can give, and their constituents can give no greater than they have; and from whence, in the name of common sense, have the people of Great-Britain right of dominion over the persons, properties and liberties of the good people in America?

But some may object, that upon these principles, the colonies have an unlimited power of legislation, &c. within themselves, contrary to an express clause in their constitutions, which restrains them from making laws, &c. contrary to the laws of the realm of England.

These constitutions are to be considered, not only as the stipulations of the sovereign and the particular colonies with whom they are made, but also of the colonists among themselves; although they are conceived wholly in the style and language of grants from the crown. And the language of the clause referred to in the objection, is after this manner, "and we do further of, &c. give and grant unto the said governor and company, &c. that it shall and may be lawful for them, &c. to erect and make all necessary and proper judicatories; to hear and decide all matters and causes, &c. and to make, ordain and establish all manner of wholsome and reasonable laws, statutes, ordinances, directions and instructions, not contrary to the laws of this our realm of England."

This restraint to colony legislation, cannot be construed to extend the jurisdiction of parliament; for if it could, it would be repugnant to the grant, & void; for parliament might make laws contrary to all the laws the colonies have or could make; in this sense, it would be reserving a power that would devour and destroy all the powers constituted and granted in the patents, &c.

Nor is it to be understood, that the colonies may not make laws respecting their own people, which are contrary to laws in England, concerning a similar matter; for instance, in England the laws permit persons of certain rank and estate to play at games; in the colonies all persons without distinction are prohibited playing at games. By the laws of this our realm, then is not meant, any particular rules and regulations of law; but the grounds, principles and spirit of the laws and constitution, then existing in the realm of England, on which the whole system of their laws were founded, by which dictated, and to which they were conformed. As the constitutions of the colonies were founded on the same principles with that of England, and the colonists entitled to like privileges with the natural subjects of that realm, and referred to the great charter of English liberties, to learn the full extent and nature of their own: Therefore it is stipulated and granted, that they may make all reasonable laws, &c. not contrary, to what? To the genius of the laws and civil constitution of this our realm of England; for such would likewise be contrary to the genius of their own governments. Between which and the English constitution there is such a similarity, that you cannot thwart the principles of one, without contradicting the spirit of the other; and the sword that pierces the sides of one, penetrates the bowels of the other. This restriction is limited to the laws or system of government then in being in and over that realm: and doth not extend to any civil constitutions that might afterwards be made; nor to any laws made, or that should be made there, to extend to the colonies, out of that realm; for this would, as hath been shewn, be repugnant to the grant; and further, such would not be the laws of that realm, but of the colonies. This clause therefore, instead of restraining the colonies under the power of parliament, doth demonstrate them to be distinct states, without and independent of the jurisdiction of parliament.

I am not insensible, that by act of parliament 7 and 8 Will. III. cap. 22. it is declared, that all laws, by laws, usages and customs which shall be in practice in any of the plantations, repugnant to any law made, or to be made in England relative to the said plantations, shall be utterly void and of none effect. And by stat. 6 of Geo. III. cap. 12. It is further declared, that all his majesties colonies and plantations in America, have been, are, and of right ought to be, subordinate to and dependant on the imperial crown and parliament of Great-Britain, who have full power and authority to make laws and statutes of sufficient validity, to bind the colonies and people of America, subjects of the crown of Great-Britain, in all cases whatsoever, with a number of other statutes of the present reign, founded on the same principles and of the same fatal tendency. By these statutes, the Americans are deprived of all authority, even to make a by-law; and of all their liberties and properties; by subjecting both to the arbitrary power and disposal of parliament, in all cases whatsoever. Let these statutes be executed upon the Americans; and what, in the name of wonder, I ask, what will they have left, that has even the shadow of power or privilege, natural, civil, or religious; that they will be able to exercise and enjoy? But let us examine the ground and authority of these acts that sound such a peal, the knell of American freedom.

It is not the parliament's declaring a thing to be so, that makes it so, nor their enjoining a thing to be done, that makes it a duty to do it. Should the parliament, in the plenitude of their power, pass an act, that the four elements have been, are, and ought to be subordinate to, and dependant on the jurisdiction of parliament; and that they have full power, &c. to make laws of sufficient validity to bind them, in all cases whatsoever. And that there should be neither rain nor sunshine, seed time nor harvest, in all the continent of America, for three years and seven months; would the elements and the heavens be guilty of treason and rebellion, if they pursued their antient course: And are not the liberties of men, who are appointed lords of this lower creation, of more importance than those of the elements, and are they not equally sacred and inviolable?

The obligation of obedience to a law, arises wholly from the authority of the makers, over those on whom it is enjoined; so that if the Americans are naturally independant of the power of parliament, and by no concessions and civil constitutions of their own have submitted thereto, and put themselves under it; no acts of parliament can make them dependant. And if the parliament hath no right of dominion over the Americans; it follows that the Americans are under no obligation of obedience to its laws.

I cannot but remark upon the singular phraseology of this declaratory act of parliament, viz. that all his majesty's colonies (not our colonies) have been, are, and of right ought to be subordinate to, and dependant on the imperial crown and parliament of Great-Britain, who have full power and authority to make laws and statutes of sufficient validity to bind the colonies and people in America, subjects of the crown of Great-Britain, in all cases whatsoever. What strange circumlocution of law language is used to express what they meant to conceal! What is the amount of this declaratory act? That the parliament has full power and authority to make laws, &c. to bind the colonies and people of America in all cases whatsoever? No, but to bind the colonies and people of America subjects of the crown of Great-Britain, viz. they have power to bind the subjects of the crown of Great Britain in America. Now if the colonies are not subjects of the crown of Great-Britain, viz. are not subjects of the king in virtue of his crown of that kingdom, then by their own declaration the parliament hath no right to bind them. And it is very evident from what has been said, that the king's right of sovereignty over the colonies is not derived from, or holden in virtue of his crown, as king of Great-Britain; but from the particular stipulations entered into with the colonies by their several constitutions; otherwise their constitutions would have been idle and unnecessary. Nor will it help the matter, should we for argument's sake, yield to them that the colonies were subjects of the crown of Great-Britain; then they would be entitled to the privileges of subjects, which is an exemption from legislation or taxation without their voice or consent. So that whether the colonies are or are not subjects of the crown of Great-Britain, the act is altogether unfounded.

But it may be objected to the colonies claim of exemption from the jurisdiction of parliament on account of their not being represented; that there are many persons of property, and large towns in England who do not vote in the election of representatives to parliament, yet are bound by its laws, &c. There is no borough, city, town, or shire in England, nor any man of competent estate and a subject of the kingdom, but what may have a voice in the election of representatives to parliament; if, therefore, some do wave a privilege which they might enjoy, their stupidity ought to be a warning, and not an example for the Americans to imitate: Nor doth it by any means follow, that because some are bound, who might and will not send representatives; that therefore, the parliament hath right to bind all, even those who cannot, if they would, be represented. Besides, every member of parliament, though chosen by one particular district, when elected and returned, serves for the whole realm; and no laws or taxes are made and imposed on such, but what equally affect those that make them, and their constituents. The case of the unrepresented Americans is directly the reverse; they cannot be represented, and the burthens laid on them proportionably alleviate the burthens of those that impose them, and their constituents.

Again, it may be objected, that several acts of parliament respecting America, have been acquiesced in, &c. Neither the parliament's making laws, nor the American's acquiescing therein, can create an authority to make them on one hand, nor an obligation to obey them on the other, though they may be considered as some evidence thereof. From the first settlement of the colonies, to the conclusion of the last war, no taxes, or duties have been claimed, or imposed by act of parliament in America, for the purpose of raising a revenue, unless the act respecting the post-office is considered as such. The first act that was made to extend to America, equally extended to Asia and Africa; and was made in the 12th of Charles II merely for the regulation of trade; requiring all English goods to be shipped in English vessels, and navigated by English mariners. The 25th of the same reign produced the first act that imposed duties for any purpose in America, and the preamble declares it to be for the regulation of trade only; nor are the avails appropriated to any part of the revenue: Yet this produced an insurrection in Virginia, agents were sent to England on the account; and a declaration obtained from the king under his privy seal, dated April 19th, A.D. 1676 "That taxes ought not to be laid upon the proprietors and inhabitants of the colony, but by the common consent of the general assembly." The other acts that respected the colonies, except the 7 and 8 of Will. III. antea, were for the regulation of trade only, until of late; the duties were never acquiesced in, were always murmered at, protested against, as being oppressive and unjust, and eluded as far as possible. And as the trade of the colonies was, of choice, principally with Great-Britain and the British Islands, many of those acts did not much affect them in their interest or inclination. If such an acquiescence may be construed a submission to acts of parliament; the nonuser of such power by parliament, for so long a time, may, with greater reason, be construed a relinquishment thereof. For the non user of a power, by those that are able to exercise such power, is greater evidence against the existence of it, than the non-resistence of thousands is for it, who are incapable of making resistance.

But it will be said that the post-office in America was by act of parliament and is for the express purpose of raising a revenue.

The post-office is a convenient and useful institution, and on that account, it hath been received and used in America, and not on account of the act of parliament; and derives all its authority, in America, from its being received and adopted there: As many of the rules of the Roman civil law, are received and adopted by universal consent in England, and are obligatory upon the people, not from the authority of the Roman emperors that ordained them, but from their own act in receiving and adopting them. Further, the act of parliament forbids all persons to carry or transport any letters, &c. by land or water, on pain of severe penalties, except the post-master or his deputies: And it is well known, that this part of the act was daily violated; yet no person was ever prosecuted: Which shews that the post-office in America was not such, as the parliament had enacted; but such as the universal consent and practice of the people there had made it; and also, how little deference is paid to acts of parliament in America.

From all the cases of pretended acquiescence to acts of parliament, nothing can be inferred favourable to the jurisdiction of parliament, for either it was for the interest of the Americans to comply with them, or it was not; if the former, then they complied, not from a principle of obedience to them; but from motives of interest and inclination; if the latter, then they demonstrate the incompetency of parliament to make laws for the Americans; who thro' ignorance, or some other principle, hath enjoined what is prejudicial. And no wise constitution would vest a power in any body of men, who, from their situation and circumstances, are and must be, necessarily incompetent for the proper exercise of it.

It may be objected, that all these charters and colony constitutions were made by and with the king, in his political capacity, as the supreme head of the kingdom; and that whatever he doth as such, is in virtue of authority derived from the kingdom; and for the use and benefit thereof, and not with and for the king only.

These constitutions, are either the compacts of both the king and kingdom of Great-Britain with the colonies; entered into by the king for himself, and in behalf of his kingdom, or they are the compacts of the king only.

If the former, then the kingdom of Great-Britain, as well as the king, is a party to them, bound and concluded by them; and can have no greater authority over the colonies, than is therein expressly stipulated, and in no other manner than is therein provided. For if the kingdom will take the benefit of the king's acts, it must in those respects, be likewise bound by them. And there is not the least colour of legislative authority in the colony constitutions, stipulated or reserved to the parliament, over the persons or properties of the Americans, except in one or two instances, which are altogether singular, and as absurd as singular, but full and compleat power of legislation is vested in the general assemblies of the several colonies—subject only in some, to the royal dissent within a limited time; and to have the colony assemblies, subject at the same time to the legislative power of Parliament, would be constituting an *imperium in imperio*, one supreme power within another, the height of political absurdity.

But if these constitutions, are the compacts of the king, only with the colonies, then the kingdom and parliament of Great-Britain have no power over them, more than they and their assemblies have over the kingdom and parliament, for they are distinct sister states, neither having any power or authority over the other. And that these constitutions, were entered into and granted by the king for himself only, is evident, in that, no mention is made in them of the parliament, except as above, and in them the reservation is void, being against Magna Charta: Or of their being made by the king, in behalf of himself and kingdom; and this most certainly the king is capable of doing; for the king considered in his natural capacity as a man, is subject to all the frailties of human nature, hath sensations of pleasure and pain, which are his own, and may make contracts and be bound by them, although in his political capacity he is by way of eminence stiled perfect, &c.

In his political capacity he also hath certain prerogatives, royal rights and interests, which are his own, and not the kingdom's; and these he may alienate by gift or sale, &c.

Should France offer the king of Great-Britain the crown of that kingdom, and he accept it; could not France be subject to the king, without being subject to the kingdom of Great-Britain, and subordinate to the power of parliament? Upon these principles, should the king of England be elected emperor of Germany, the British parliament, would legislate for the whole Germanic body. And the case would not be otherwise, with a people in a state of nature, that should make choice of the king of Great-Britain for their king, and he accept thereof, they would not thereby, elect the kingdom for their masters nor be subjected to its parliament. Thus, whether these constitutions are considered as the compacts of the king and kingdom of Great Britain, or only of the king, the colonies are clearly out of the reach of the jurisdiction of parliament, and it is evident that they were originally intended so to be, and all the advantages expected from them by Great-Britain, were their trade, which has far exceeded their most sanguine expectations. For these constitutions were not entered into and granted by the king in virtue of his being the king of Great-Britain; the king of France or Prussia might have done the same; or any individual, the Americans should have elected for their king. The force and authority of these constitutions, is not derived from any antecedent right in the crown of Great-Britain to grant them; but from the mutual agreements and stipulations contained in them, between the crown of Great-Britain and the colonies.

Further, it is objected, that the settlement of the crown is by act of parliament; and the colonies do acknowledge him to be their king, on whom the crown is thus settled, consequently in this they do recognize the power of parliament.

The colonies do and ever did acknowledge the power of parliament to settle and determine who hath right, and who shall wear the crown of Great-Britain; but it is by force of the constitutions of the colonies only, that he, who is thus crowned king of Great-Britain, becomes king of the colonies. One designates the king of the colonies, and the other makes him so.

Lastly it is objected, that in all civil states it is necessary, there should some where be lodged a supreme power over the whole.

The truth of this objection will not be contested; but its application in the present argument is to be considered. If Great-Britain and America both constitute but one civil state, then it is necessary that there should be one supreme power, lodged either in Great-Britain or America, in such manner as is consistent with the liberties of the subjects. But if they are distinct states, then it is necessary, that there should be a supreme power lodged in each. The only thing then to be done is to prove, that Great-Britain and America are distinct states. And this point hath been already considered; so that little new can be said upon it. However it may be observed, that a civil state, is a country or body of people that are connected and united under one and the same constitution of civil government; by this the kingdoms and states in Germany and other parts of Europe are distinguished and known. Now there is no such civil constitution existing, as that of Great-Britain and America.

Great-Britain hath its civil constitution; the colonies have their's;

and though, the spirit and principles of them are similar, yet the constitutions of the two countries are entirely distinct and several: The constitution of Great-Britain is not the constitution of the colonies, nor *vice versa.* They are two countries, three thousand miles distant from each other, inhabited by different people, under distinct constitutions of government, with different customs, laws and interests, both having one king. Now, if any can believe that Great-Britain and America are but one civil state, they must overthrow the doctrine of identity and diversity, confound all distinctions in nature, and believe that two is one and one is two. Further, they are and must be distinct states from the nature of their situation, and in order to their enjoying the privileges of their respective governments. And the constitutions of civil government ought to be erected on the foundation of reason and be conformable to the nature of things; nor is it difficult to conceive of two distinct countries, independent of each other, each having its own civil constitutions, laws, parliaments, courts, commerce and interest, united under one sovereign prince. And would it be necessary that there should be in one of these states, a supreme power over the persons and properties of the other? If it would, then it follows, that it would be necessary in such case that the subjects of one should be slaves to the other, incapable of liberty or property. Are not Hanover and Saxony distinct states, both within the empire, and subordinate to the imperial crown of Germany? They are. And is not this the case of Great-Britain and America? Two distinct states, or countries under one sovereign prince, both equally his subjects and incapable of being slaves? Each invested with plenary powers of government, in their several countries? This is really the situation of the colonies; and not to admit of a system of civil government, adapted to their situation, or to insist on the exercise of such powers over them, as are inconsistent with, and subversive of their natural and constitutional rights and liberties, is really pointing the controversy, not merely at the Americans, but at the great former and ruler of the universe, for making and situating them as they are. From all which it follows that the colonies are distinct states from that of Great-Britain; have and ought to have a supreme power of government lodged in them.

Thus, the question is reduced to a single point, either the parliament hath no such power over the persons and properties of the

Americans as is claimed, or the Americans are all slaves. Slavery consists in being wholly under the power and controul of another, as to our actions and properties: And he that hath authority to restrain and controul my conduct in any instance, without my consent, hath in all. And he that hath right to take one penny of my property, without my consent, hath right to take all. For, deprive us of this barrier of our liberties and properties, our own consent; and there remains no security against tyranny and absolute despotism on one hand, and total abject, miserable slavery on the other. For power is entire and indivisible; and property is single and pointed as an atom. All is our's, and nothing can be taken from us, but by our consent; or nothing is our's, and all may be taken, without our consent. The right of dominion over the persons and properties of others, is not natural, but derived; and there are but two sources from whence it can be derived; from the almighty, who is the absolute proprietor of all, and from our own free consent. Why then wrangle we so long about a question so short and easy of decision? Why this mighty din of war, and garments roll'd in blood; the seas covered with fleets, the land with armies, and the nation rushing on swift destruction? Let the parliament shew their warrant, the diploma and patent of their power to rule over America, derived from either of the above fountains, and we will not contend; but if they cannot, wherefore do they contend with us? For even a culprit has right to challenge of the executioner, the warrant of his power, or refuse submission.

The question is not whether the king is to be obeyed or not; for the Americans, have ever recognized his authority as their rightful sovereign, and liege lord; have ever been ready, with their lives and fortunes, to support his crown and government, according to the constitutions of the nation, and now call upon him as their liege lord (whom he is bound to protect) for protection, on pain of their allegiance, against the army, levied by the British parliament, against his loyal and dutiful subjects in America.

Nor is the question Whether the Americans would be independent or not, unless the state they have ever enjoyed hath been such; for they ever have acknowledged themselves to be subjects of the king, subordinate to, and dependent on the crown, but not on the parliament of Great-Britain, unless any should think there is no medium between submission to parliament, and perfect independance. But the question is, Whether the parliament of Great-Britain hath power over the persons and properties of the Americans, to bind the one, and dispose of the other at their pleasure? Hear the language of parliament in their acts disposing of the property of the Americans: "*We, your majesty's dutiful subjects, the Commons of Great-Britain, in parliament assembled, have therefore resolved to give and grant unto your majesty, the several rates and duties hereinafter mentioned, &c. in America.*" Here the Commons in England are pluming themselves on their great liberality to their sovereign, with the property of the Americans, as though it was all their own. If the parliament have no such power as is claimed, their invading our rights, and in them the rights of the constitution, under pretence of authority; besieging and desolating our sea ports, employing dirty tools, whose sordid souls, like vermin, delight to riot on filth; to practice every artifice to seduce, that they may the easier destroy; with money tempting, with arms terrifying the inhabitants, to induce and compel a servile submission; is treason against the kingdom, of the deepest die, and blackest complexion: whereby the constitution, that firm foundation of the nation's peace, and pillar of government that supports the throne, is shaken to its very basis; the kingdom rent, and devided against itself; and those sons of thunder that should be the protectors of its rights, are become its destroyers. Nor will American freedom fall alone; Great-Britain's shakes, totters, and must tumble likewise, nor long survive the catastrophe: And the Americans resisting the measures, and defending against the force used to accomplish these dreadful events, and precipitate the nation into total, irreparable ruin and destruction, are deeds of the greatest loyalty to their king, and the constitution that supports him on the throne, and of fidelity to his government. For subjects to levy war against their king, is treason, but the king's levying war against his subjects, is a crime of royal magnitude, and wants a name. Should the king of France join with the enemies of his kingdom, and levy war against his subjects, would he notwithstanding, retain his royal authority over them, and they be incapable of defence against such an unnatural attack, without incurring the crime of treason and rebellion? If so, wo! to the inhabitants of kingdoms, for, by reason of their kings, the earth would be made desolate.

Let none be dismayed at the strength and power of our oppressors; nor at the horrors of war into which we are compelled, for the necessary defence of our rights. Can we expect the laurels, without entering the list? To be crowned without being tried? The fairest fruits are always most obnoxious to the birds of prey: English liberties, the boast and glory of the nation, the admiration of its friends, and envy of its foes; were obtained, sword in hand, from king John, by his free and spirited barons; and what rivers of blood have been shed, to maintain and defend them, against the encroachments of succeeding kings, to the time of the glorious revolution, is well known to all, acquainted with the English history. Such is the state of the world, that the way to freedom and glory, is a way of danger and conflict. The road to Canaan was through the desert and the deep; and the grave is the subterranean path to celestial bliss. And let it not be forgotten that those of Israel whose hearts failed them through fear of being destroyed by their enemies, and discouraged their brethren, were destroyed of their maker. Nor ought any to think, by joining themselves to the enemies of their country, they shall escape, however fair the promises, or great the reward; and though they should not meet with their deserts, from the hands of their injured countrymen: for the minister, wants your assistance to destroy your fellows, only, that yourselves may be the easier destroyed; and when you have done his drudgery, you will become his prey. *Divide & impera, divide & distrue, divide & command, divide and destroy*, are maxims of deep policy, fabricated in a very old cabinet.

IV. I shall now proceed in the last place to consider this question in another light, viz. the equity of the demand made upon the colonies, and of the manner in which it is made. The ill policy of such measures, having in a most inimitable manner, been considered and exposed by those illustrious patriots, the earl of Chatham, Burke, Barre, the bishop of Asaph, &c. (whose names and memories no distance of place or time, will be able to obliterate from the grateful minds of the Americans) with such dignity of sentiment, energy and perspecuity of reason, such rectitude of intention, uncorruptness and candor of disposition, and with such force of elocution, as must have rendered them irresistable, only by the omnipotence of parliament.

Great-Britain can have no demands upon the old colonies, except for assistance afforded them against their enemies in war, and protection to their trade at sea; for the lands were neither acquired or settled at the expence of the crown. New-York, indeed, was obtained by conquest from the Dutch, without much risk or loss; and was afterwards in the treaty at Breda, A.D. 1667, confirmed to the English in exchange for Surinam. Nor have those colonies since, been any expence to the crown, either for support of their governments, or inhabitants: And the Americans have had no enemies but what were equally the enemies of Great-Britain; nor been engaged in any wars, but what the nation was equally engaged in, except the wars with the Indians; which they carried on and maintained themselves. It will be necessary to state the advantages the Americans have been to Great-Britain, as well as those they have derived from thence, by assistance afforded in the wars, and by comparing, strike the ballance.

From the first settlement of the colonies, they have been almost continually engaged in a bloody and expensive, tho' successful war with the French and Indians, on their frontiers, until the reduction of Canada; whereby their settlements were extended; and by a rapid population, the number of inhabitants have been greatly encreased; and the trade to England proportionably augmented. In A.D. 1690, Sir William Phips raised an army in New-England, took Port Royal, or Annapolis, in Nova-Scotia, from the French; and reduced another settlement of considerable consequence, at the mouth of the river St. John's, on the Bay of Fundy, both which, king William ceded to the French at the peace of Riswick, A.D. 1697; and received an equivalent for them. In A.D. 1703, the beginning of Queen Ann's war, Annapolis was retaken, by the New-England people. Afterwards Sir William Phips, with the New-England people, attempted the reduction of Canada, and was obliged to return, not by the arms of the enemy, but by the severity of the season coming on earlier than usual: However, he built a fort on the mouth of Pemaquid on the frontiers of the country, which reduced all the Indians, north west of Merimac river, under the crown of England. By these successes, Great-Britain was induced to engage in an expedition against Quebec. In A.D. 1711, Admiral Walker was sent to Boston, with a fleet, and some land forces; New-England furnished their quota of troops for the expedition; but by reason of the great fogs, and some mistake of the pilot's, part of the fleet was stove upon the rocks; eight hundred of the men lost, and the expedition rendered abortive. Annapolis, and all Nova-Scotia was confirmed to Great-Britain, at the peace of Utrecht, A.D. 1713; whereby all that country, its valuable fisheries, and trade, were added to the crown of Great-Britain. Not to mention the ineffectual, but costly expedition, formed by the New-England people against Canada, in A.D. 1740; and that against the island of Cuba, at another time. On the 16th of June, A.D. 1745, the important fortress of Louisbourgh surrendered to Commodore Warren, and Mr. Pepperel; reduced by a long and perilous siege of forty-nine days (through the smiles of heaven) by the valour and intrepidity of American troops, assisted by Commodore Warren, with a small squadron in the harbour; by which, the command of the Newfoundland fishery, the gulph of St. Lawrence, the only pass by sea to Quebec, the capital of the French settlements in America, fell into the hands of the English, and which afterwards purchased the peace of Europe, and procured to the crown of England, in the peace of Aix Chappelle, sundry important places that had been taken. Thus, the Americans laboured, fought and toiled; and the Britons reaped the advantage. The noble exertions of the Americans, and the part they took in the last war; their laudable emulation to be foremost, in complying with the requisitions of their sovereign; their troops contending for stations of danger, as posts of distinction; esteeming their lives and their properties, an inconsiderable sacrifice, for the glory of their king, and the renown of his arms; and the large levies of men and money made by them, are fresh in every one's memory. The amazing advantages derived from the war in America, to the crown and kingdom of Great-Britain, is also well known. The whole eastern and northern country, the New-foundland fishery, trade, and navigation, a source of boundless wealth; the island of Cape-Breton, the extensive country of Canada and Louisiana, from the arctic pole, to the tropic of Cancer, with their train of fortresses, lakes, &c. the peltry and furr trade of that whole country, with the almost inexhaustable treasures of the Havanna; a harvest in which the Americans, with the Britons, bore the heat and burthen of the day; yet the Americans shared little or none of the fruit, except being delivered from troublesome neighbours, on their frontiers, and some individuals drawing a share in the plunder, at the Havanna. And what a mighty accession of weight and importance was this, to the crown of Great-Britain, in the scale of power, among the European states and princes! But why need I dwell upon these? At the conclusion of the last war, justice swayed the sceptre; and a righteous minister had the royal ear; the Americans were considered as creditors to the nation; and thousands of pounds were sent over to reimburse them. But Oh! the sad reverse of times, ministers and of measures!

In the next place, let me enquire, in respect to the protection afforded our trade at sea. Our trade, from inclination and choice, hath been principally with Great-Britain and the British isles, and like the trade in all cases, carried on between an infant country, in want of all kinds of manufactures, and an old, wealthy, manufacturing kingdom. Our's was of necessity and for consumption; their's for profit and advantage. They purchased of us our raw materials, and sold to us their wrought manufactures; both at their own price, and at their own ports. In this view of the matter, must it not be supposed, that the advantages of this trade to that kingdom, amply paid for its protection; and their motives to protect it were their own emolument and profit? But this will be more fully illustrated, when we consider, that the amount of the trade between Great-Britain, and the colonies, at a medium for three years, before it was interrupted by these unhappy disputes, is computed at about three millions, three hundred and eighty-five thousand pounds per annum: From which deduct a certain proportion, for raw materials, that are imported into England, which is comparatively inconsiderable; the remainder is a clear profit and gain to Great-Britain; and is divided between the public exchequer, and private coffers—for the whole cost of the raw materials, the duties on the importation of them, the manufacturer's labour, his living and his family's, his taxes upon his house, windows, salt, soap, candles, coal, &c. &c. &c. upon his eatables, his drinkables, and cloathing; those of his family, his apprentices and journeymen; and not only so, but also the taxes his shoemaker, weaver, and taylor paid, when working for him; the merchants profits, the charges of bailage, truckage, freight, insurance; and the duties upon the articles themselves, all go in to make up the price, and are paid by the American consumer. In this view of the matter, I believe I am within bounds to suppose, that the direct trade (leaving out of the question the cercuitous trade by way of the West-Indies and other parts), neats a profit of three millions to Great-Britain: And near one half of that sum, is made up of taxes and duties, which are paid in England; whereby the public revenue is so much increased & eventually is actually paid by the Americans.

Can any suppose, that this is not an ample compensation, for all the protection afforded our trade at sea? What nation in Europe would not rejoice to receive our trade on these terms, and give us thousands for its purchase? But, upon supposition it is not sufficient, and that the colonies are indebted to them; ought they not to state the account, that the balance might be seen; and to make a demand of payment? And not without doing either, thrust their hands into our pockets; and rend from thence, not only what we owe them, but what they please: Not only what we ought to pay, but our whole property; nor that only, but our liberties too. And if asked wherefore this? the answer is, that the nation is in debt, and that we owe them. If we owe them, let them make it appear, and the colonies will pay them; that the nation is in debt, needs no proof; but for what? For expence in war, and for charges of government in time of peace? Could these have accumulated—the enormous sum of 145,000,000, the national debt in A.D. 1766? Bribery and corruption, luxury and exorbitant pensions multiplied, might.

But it is time to close these enquiries; and what may we not expect, from what is threatened and already done, that is in the power of parliament to do?

Is not the king of Great-Britain, the visible head of the christian church in England? and by the Quebec bill, is he not, as amply constituted the head of the romish church in Canada? Have not the Americans, by the constitution of nature, as men, by the constitution of England, as Englishmen, and by the constitutions in America, as colonists, a right of exemption from all laws, that are made, and taxes that are imposed, without their voice and consent? and from other mode[s] of trial, than by their peers of the vicinity?

And by the late acts of parliament, are not taxes and duties imposed, and laws enacted to bind them, not only without, but in which, they neither had nor could have any voice? And is not the whole government, of that ancient province of the Massachusetts, demolished at a blow, by an engine of tyranny, without being summoned, heard or tried? Are not strange and unusual methods for imprisonment, transportation and trial, introduced? arbitrary tribunals erected, to decide in matters most interesting, without the intervention of a jury? In a word, are not all our rights and liberties, natural, religious and civil, made a mark for their arrows, and threatened to be laid in the dust? And to compleat our ruin, are not our harbours blocked up? our coasts lined with fleets? our country filled with armed troops? our towns sacked? inhabitants plundered? friends slaughtered? our pleasant places desolated with fire and sword? all announced rebels? our estates declared forfeit, and our blood eagerly panted for? When I think of Boston, that unhappy capital; what she once was, and the miserable captive state, to which she is now reduced, I am almost ready to adopt the plaintive strains of captive Israel concerning her:

> By the rivers of Babylon there we set down, yea, we wept when we remembered Zion; we hanged our harps upon the willows, in the midst thereof, for there they that carried us captive and wasted us, required of us a song and mirth, saying, sing us one of the songs of Zion. How shall we sing the Lord's song in a strange land? if I forget thee Oh Jerusalem! let my right hand forget her cunning, if I do not remember thee, let my tongue cleave to the roof of my mouth; if I prefer not Jerusalem, above my chief joy. Remember O Lord! the children of Edom, in the day of Jerusalem, who said rase it, rase it, even to the foundation thereof.

What shall we say, is there any force in sacred compacts and national constitutions? any honour in crowned heads? any faith to be put in ministers, the nobles and great men of the nation? In a word, is there any such thing as truth and justice? Is there not a power above us? and that there is all nature declares; the vindicator of right and avenger of wrong. To him therefore we make our last appeal; and to the impartial world, to judge between Great-Britain and America.

These unheard of intolerable calamities, spring not of the dust, come not causeless, nor will they end fruitless. They call on the Americans for repentance towards their maker, and vengeance on their adversaries. And can it be a crime to resist? Is it not a duty we owe to our maker, to our country, to ourselves and to posterity? Does not the principle of self-preservation, which is implanted by the author of nature in the human breast (to operate instantaneous as the lightning, resistless as the shafts of war, to ward off impending danger), urge us to the conflict; add wings to our feet, firmness and unanimity to our hearts, impenatrability to our battalions, and under the influence of its mighty author, will it not render successful and glorious American arms? But it may be said that the Americans have destroyed the tea of the East-India company, at Boston, which was a violation of private property, & ought to be paid for. That tea was sent on the same errand that Gage and his troops are; to effect by artifice what they are now attempting by force. I mention not Thomas Hutchinson, for his crimes here, and condign punishment hereafter, without repentance, must exceed all conception or description. Should the British parliament cause cargoes of wine, impregnated with poison, to be sent to America, with orders to have them dispersed amongst the inhabitants: and their servants, the miscreants of their power, should obstinately insist on doing it, the Americans must destroy the wines, which, by their baneful mixture would be justly obnoxious to destruction, or be destroyed by their poison.

My countrymen, we have every thing to fear, from the malignity, power and cunning of our adversaries. Yet, from the justness of our cause, the greatness of our numbers and resources, the unanimity of our hearts, cemented by interest and by perils; the bravery, and what's more, the desperateness of our spirits; who think not life worth saving, when all that is dear in life is gone, we have reason to be afraid of nothing. For your animation, hear the advice and lamentation of a French gentleman, Monsieur Mezeray, over the lost liberties of his country, to an English subject:

> We had once in France, the same happiness and the same privileges, which you now have. Our laws were made by representatives of our own choosing; therefore our money was not taken from us, but granted by us. Our kings, were then subject to the rules of law and reason. Now alas! we are miserable and all is lost. Think nothing sir, too dear to maintain these precious advantages, if ever there should be occasion; venture your life and estate, rather than basely submit to that abject condition to which you see us reduced.

And for your encouragement, turn your eyes to the free states of Holland and Switzerland; and in them, as in a glass, see America struggling under intolerable oppressions; and with an intrepid, unconquerable spirit, overlooking all danger, bursting the bonds, and demolishing the engines of tyranny, emerging from a sea of calamities, rising superior to every obstacle; and overlooking in time the power and towering heights of their haughty oppressors.

Since then we are compelled to take up the sword, in the necessary defence of our country, our liberties and properties, ourselves and posterity: Let us gird on the harness, having our bosoms mailed, with firm defiance of every danger; and with fixed determined purpose, to part with our liberty only with our lives, engage in the conflict; and nobly play the man for our country, the cities and churches of him that transplanted and hitherto sustained them; thereby prove the truth of our descent, and demonstrate to the world, that the free irrepressable spirit, that inspired the breasts and animated the conduct of our brave fore-fathers; is not degenerated in us, their offspring. With fair pretences, they invite us to submit our necks to their yoke; but with unheard of cruelties and oppressions, they determine us, to prefer death to submission. Let none be disheartened from a prospect of the expence; though it should be to the half, or even the whole of our estates. Compared with the prize at stake, our liberty, the liberty of our country, of mankind, and of millions yet unborn, it would be lighter than the dust on the balance: For if we submit, adieu for ever; adieu to property, for liberty will be lost, our only capacity of acquiring and holding property.

And what shall I say, of the officers and soldiers of the British army, who are the appointed ministers of this vengeance on the Americans? against whom are they come forth, in hostile array? Strangers and foes to them and their nation? No, it is against their brethren, their fellows and companions, of their flesh and of their bone; members of the same nation, subjects of the same king; and entitled to the same or equal privileges; with kindred blood in their veins, and a pulse beating high for English liberties. And can their hearts be courageous, and their hands strong, when they level the shaft, or lift up the spear against those, with whom of late, side by side and shoulder to shoulder, in compacted battalions, they fought, bled, and conquered, in defence of the country, and the liberties, they are now sent to lay waste and destroy. I appeal to their sense of honour, their sentiments of justice, to their bowels of humanity, those tender feelings of sympathy, these social passions, that possess and warm the human heart, and are the spring of all social and public virtues, and let their tongues utter the sentiments of their souls, and America will be justified, they being the judges.

Methinks I hear the king, retired with his hand upon his breast, in pensive solliloquy, saying to himself, who, and what am I? A king, that wears the crown, and sways the scepter of Great-Britain and America; and though a king, robed in royalty, yet I am a man, my power finite, my body mortal, and myself accountable to him, who raised me to this dignity, that I might be his minister for the people's good. But Oh! what tragic scenes do I behold? One part of my dominions aiming destruction against the other, plunging their swords in the bosoms, and imbruing their hands in the blood of their fellows and brethren. Is it possible, that Britons should become the foes and assassins of Britons, or their descendants? My throne totters, my loins tremble, my kingdom is divided and torn, my heart ready to fail, for the glory of my reign is departing. What can be the cause of these tremenduous convulsions, that threaten the dissolution of my kingdom? Do my subjects in America, refuse to resign their liberties and properties, to the disposal of my subjects in Great-Britain? And insist on holding and enjoying them as their unalienable rights? Well, what will be the mighty injury to my crown, or to the nation, in its wealth, strength, or honour, if America should enjoy its former freedom? What will be gained by reducing them to submission and slavery? lifeless carcases, a desolated country, millions in wealth, and millions in strength dashed at a blow. Mighty acquisition of loss. Should the attempt be pursued and fail, America will be lost, nay more, she will become Great-Britain's determined enemy. Have not my subjects in Great-Britain rights that are sacred and inviolable, and which they would not resign but with their lives? They have. Have not my subjects in America rights equally sacred, and of which they are and ought to be equally tenacious? They have. And are not those rights, for which they now so earnestly contend, of that kind? Certainly there is much in favour of their claim. What if they are mistaken? Ought they to atone for their mistake by rivers of blood, and the sacrifice of themselves, their country and their posterity? but what, my mind shudders and recoils at the thought, what, if the Americans are right? Oh heaven forgive! And all this ghastly ruin, is owing to the blunder of a minister, and the fatal errors adopted by parliament.

Of whom will these rivers of blood be required? What can expiate such accumulated wrongs? and atone for such amazing devastations? I am sorely distressed, civil war rages within, foreign enemies threaten without, the commerce of my kingdom languisheth, manufacturers famish and fail, and discontentment is almost universal. What shall I do for the dignity of my crown, the peace of my dominions, and the safety of the nation? All is at risk. I have been deceived by my informers, misguided by my ministers, and by my own inattention to the sufferings, and dutiful petitions of my subjects, reduced all to the most dreadful hazard. For British troops cease to be glorious, in so inglorious a cause. Should their sea-ports, from Georgia to Nova-Scotia, be desolated with fire and sword, it would only consolidate their union, and render more impregnable their resistance in the interior country. Could we dry up their harbours, and bar every out-let to the sea, unless we had power to restrain the showers and the shines of heaven; and the fertility of the earth, they will possess inexhaustable resources. America must and will be free, their ancestors acquired it for them, my royal predecessors guaranteed it to them; it is theirs by purchase, it is theirs by the plighted faith of kings; they are deserving of it; and with them it flourisheth, like a plant of generous kind, in its native soil, and the heavens are propitious to liberty. My legions must be recalled, the sword must be sheathed, the olive branch, the symbol of peace be held out; for it was never designed that Britons, invinsible by others, should contend with Britons or their descendants, in battle; and royal munificence be exerted, to alleviate the distresses, console the miseries, and repair the injuries, caused by the unhappy error, which let eternal darkness veil. Oh! may the future make reparation for the past, my crown flourish in the prosperity, liberty, and the happiness of all my dominions. Thus will my reign become glorious, my demise tranquil. But alas! where am I transported on the wings of groundless fancy? Repentance I fear is too late, for crimes so enormous; the injuries are irreparable, and America is irretrievably lost: the thunders I prepared, to lay her breathless at my feet, have discharged her of her allegiance, and driven her forever from my power.

The preceeding pamphlet was wrote some time past, and not published sooner for want of paper: The author hath subjoined an appendix, containing some thoughts on government, and American independance.

To consider things rightly, is to consider them truly as they are, with all their relations and attending circumstances; to investigate truth, is the highest atchievement of reason; and to follow nature, the perfection of art. That which is conformable to axioms of immutable truth, founded in reason, and productive of general security and happiness to mankind, must in every sense, be denominated good.

Civil society, is allowed by all to be the greatest temporal blessing; and civil government is absolutely necessary to its subsistence; it is a temporary remedy, against the ill effects of general depravity; and because the introduction of moral evil has made it necessary; it is not therefore a necessary evil.

Liberty consists in a power of acting under the guidance and controul of reason: Licentiousness in acting under the influence of sensual passions, contrary to the dictates of reason; whilst we contend for the former, we ought to bear testimony against the latter: And whilst we point out arguments against the errors and abuses of government, we ought cautiously to distinguish between government and its abuses; to amputate the latter, without injuring the former, and not indifferently charge both; lest we raise an army of rebel spirits more dangerous and difficult to reduce, than all the legions of Britain.

Government originates (under God) from the people; as from its native source; centers in them, their good is its ultimate object; and operates by securing to them, the enjoyment of their natural rights and civil privileges; and as the mode of doing this, hath no prescribed form in nature, or revelation; mankind, at their option, have endeavoured it variously; and thereby given rise to the various forms of government subsisting in the world, as monarchy, aristocracy, democracy, &c. each of these have failed in their turns, through want of integrity, or discernment, or both in the administration; and have been alternately preferred or discarded by writers, not so much on account of their own excellence or defects, as of those who administered them. That form of goverment that is adapted to the genius and circumstances of the governed, affords them the greatest security, and places the authority of the governing most out of the reach of the former, to violate and contemn, their corruptions and abuses most within, to prevent and redress, is the best. A perfect model of civil government perfectly administered and obeyed, cannot be expected, but in a state of perfection, where it would be perfectly unnecessary. That government in ordinary is the best that is best administered.

Some begin their government with their political existence; it grows up with them; the great first principles thereof, are never altered while they continue a people, & become so incorporated with their being, that they have the force of natural, rather than political institutions. Others, after a century or two have occasion to alter and new model their old governments, or frame new ones: This is usually attended with much difficulty and great danger, requires an extensive knowledge of the genius, tempers, circumstances, situation, ancient customs, habits, laws and manners of the people; and great judgment and skill, to adapt new regulations to old usuages, so as to form a happy coalition. The British nation, at the time of forming their great charter (no matter how they became so) consisted of a king, nobility and commons: To connect the strength and wisdom of these, for the public weal, without infringing or endangering the rights of either, was their great object: And this was done in the constitution of parliament, so far as it concerned legislation and taxation. Its object therefore, was directly, political and civil liberty. All offices were in the gift of the crown; and the payment of them in the option of the people; the powers of government were so balanced, as to render all mutual restraints upon, and mutually restrained by each other. If the people have lost their liberties, suffered themselves to be bought and sold, like beasts of burden, the fault is theirs and their corrupters, and not the constitution's, which put in their power to have preserved them.

Thus, the principles were excellent, altho' the practice hath been most perverse. Amongst all the forms of civil government, none can be pronounced absolutely best, and only relatively so: For that which best suits one people would badly suit another, or the same, at a different period.

The strength and spring of every free government, is the virtue of the people; virtue grows on knowledge, and knowledge on education.

Most nations have established a falshood for their first principle, viz. that their kings are perfect; and the consequence of this, is a second, that gives them a licence to serve the devil with impunity, viz. that they can do no wrong: Then follows the most impious ascriptions of divine qualities and titles to him; and to compleat the image, the riches of the nation are lavished in the magnificence, costly equipage and dazzling splendors of their prince; thereby to build power on show; and like the *formido avium*, or scare crow, derive respect and obedience only from the passion of fear: A multitude of criminal laws, with severe penalties are necessary to support the authority of the rulers, and secure the obedience of the subjects; whilst the sovereign himself, is wholly insecure in the midst of his subjects, without a life guard. This is inverting the order of nature and civil government; and leaving the necessary means of rendering mankind wise, virtuous and good. Rulers ought to know, and be known to their subjects, to be but men; and the punishment of their crimes, to be in proportion to their elevation in power. Half the sum, employed to diffuse general knowledge; by erecting public seminaries, with masters well furnished to teach children, not only common learning, but to instruct and impress on their young and tender minds, the principles of virtue and the rudiments of government, which would grow up with their growth, and derive strength from age; would be more effectual than all the brilliancy of a crown, or tortures of a rack; this is the only permanent foundation of a free government; this is laying the foundation in a constitution, not without or over, but within the subjects; love and not fear will become the spring of their obedience: the ruler be distinguished, only by his distinguished virtues, and know no good, separate from that of his subjects; and his authority be supported, more by the virtue of the people, than by the terror of his power. The only way to make men good subjects of a rational and free government, is to make them wise and virtuous; but such a government as this is utterly incompatible with the idea of slavery, because incompatible with a state of ignorance.

OF INDEPENDANCE

It is with states as it is with men, they have their infancy, their manhood and their decline: Nature hath its course in all, and never works in vain; when a people are ripe for any mighty change, means wont be wanting to effect it. From what providence hath done and is doing for us, we must learn, what is our duty to do; for we may only follow, where nature leads, and in this is infinite safety; from small, we are become great, from a few, many, from feeble, powerful, from poor, rich; nature has stored our country with all necessaries for subsistence in peace, and for defence in war; it has united our hearts, our interests, and our councils, in the common cause.

Independance consists in being under obligation to acknowledge no superior power on earth: The king by withdrawing his protection and levying war upon us, has discharged us of our allegiance, and of all obligations to obedience: For protection and subjection are mutual, and cannot subsist apart: He having violated the compact on his part, we of course are released from ours; and on the same principles, if we owed any obedience to parliament (which we did not) we are wholly discharged of it. We are compelled to provide, not only for our own subsistence, but for defence against a powerful enemy: Our affections are weaned from Great-Britain, by similar means and almost as miraculously as the Israelites were from Egypt: These are facts, a surprising concurrence of incidents, equally out of our knowledge to have foreseen, or our power to have prevented, point us to some great event. Providence has furnished us with the means; the king, contrary to his design, hath discharged us of our allegiance and forced us from our dependance, and we are become necessarily independant, in order to preservation and subsistence, and this without our act or choice. And is it a crime to be, what we cant help but be? It is not from a rebellious spirit in the Americans, but unavoidable necessity, that we are become so: Like a timorous child that is able to walk but disinclined to attempt it, placed in the middle of a floor, must use his legs or fall; while the tender parent that placed him there, stands ready to save him, if likely to fall, *nam qui transtulit sustinet*, He that transplanted, upholds and sustains. All Europe, must gaze with wonder, approbation and applause; Great-Britain join in acquitting us; while the tyrant minister (Lord North) in his own bosom reads the sentence of his condemnation, for condemning us: to be where nature and providence hath placed us, is to be right, and to do what such a state points out and requires to be done, is duty. In this situation two objects of the greatest importance demand our attention, viz. defence and government; these we ought diligently to attend to and leave the event; and let those who begun the war, be first in the proposals of peace; those who have refused to hear others, when they prayed, pray without being heard. And since parliament will have our trade, only on terms incompatible with our liberty, permit them to have neither; welcome all nations to our ports and to a participation of our trade, and enter into alliance with none; thus, we may enjoy the commerce of all, without being concerned in the quarrels of any. Providence has furnished us with resources for defence; numbers to constitute armies, materials for constructing a navy, for making of powder, ball, cannon, mortars, arms, &c. and all kinds of ordnance and military stores. Our threatened situation demands, that we immediately take every precaution, and use all the means in our power for our preservation & defence, and with noble and valiant exertions, withstand and repel the attacks of tyranny. Nature hath placed the island of Great-Britain, and the continent of America so distant from each other, that it is impossible for them to be represented in one legislative body: The consequence is, that their distant situations are incompatible with their being subjects to one supreme legislature. Representation is the feet on which a free government stands, it ought therefore to be equal and full; maim and render partial the former, and it will infallibly mutilate the latter. The measures of government necessary to be adopted, at present, are the same, either for a temporary or a perpetual expedient.

The colonies have so long subsisted separate and independant of each other, enjoyed their particular forms of government, laws, customs and manners and particular rules for the regulation and distribution of property; that it will, doubtless, be thought expedient for each to retain its antient form of government, laws, &c. as far as possible; to have supreme legislative and executive powers of government over all causes, matters and things within its territorial limits, and to regulate its own internal police. Those whose governors, or other officers, are taken off by the crown, to have them elected by the freemen, or appointed by their several assemblies; for which purpose particular constitutions to be framed, as they shall elect. That a certain number of delegates be annually elected by the freemen in each colony, to form a general council or congress, whose power to extend over all matters of common and general concernment: Such as making war and peace, sending and receiving ambassadors, general regulations respecting trade and maritime affairs; to decide all matters of controversy between colony and colony, relative to bounds and limits, &c. &c. of whom one to be chosen president, and to continue in office until another be chosen and sworn. And in matters so interesting, as that of making war and peace, to be a majority of at least two thirds, computed by colonies; and for carrying on a war to have power to levy troops and provide for their subsistence, &c. to have an explicit constitution, ascertaining the number of members the congress shall consist of, and that each colony shall send; containing regulations for convening, proroguing and adjourning; also granting, defining, and limiting the powers they are to have, exercise, &c. which constitution to be laid before the several assemblies, and by them acceded to and confirmed. By some such method the colonies may retain their independance of each other; and all their former usuages, laws, &c. and the wisdom and strength of each, be connected in general congress, for the security and defence of the whole.

To be reconciled to Great-Britain upon unjust terms, is to be reconciled to injustice, ruin and slavery; until they shall have condemned the measures that have been pursued against America, recalled their fleets and armies, exposed to the public eye, and condign punishment, the authors and advisers of the present unjust and cruel war; and have repaired the damage and expence caused thereby in America, and given up the claim of power in parliament, to dominion over us, they cannot expect that we will treat with them, about future connections. They have endeavoured, by all the arts of seduction, and of power, to destroy and enslave us; and now they have sent commissioners, under pretence of treating with the Americans. Accomodation is their ostensible, but we have reason to fear that to divide, corrupt and destroy is their real object: For with whom are they to treat? With the general Congress? No; it is said, with the several governors; all of whom, except one or two, live, and breath, and have their being, in the minister, and are mov'd by him like the puppets in the show, by the hand that pulls the wire, to which they are hung. They might as well have stayed at home, and treated with the minister. But it is said they are to treat with the several colonies. But how is this? unless they acknowledge their independence of parliament? The supreme legislature of a country only, hath power to treat and be treated with respecting war and peace. The act, 6th Geo. III. declares that the parliament of Great-Britain hath supreme power of legislation over the colonies; and to establish such power, the parliament is in war with America: The commissioners therefore, cannot, consistent with their ideas of power, treat with any but the British parliament. By sending commissioners to treat with us, they would acknowledge our power to make a treaty; which is predicable only of independence. Query then whether those commissioners are coming to treat for peace, with a mighty armament for war? In fine, that government, in which the people are subject to no laws, or taxes, but by their voice or consent; condemned by no sentence but by the verdict of their equals; where property is near equally distributed; crimes clearly defined and distinguished; & punishments duly proportioned to their nature and magnitude; and where the rising generation are universally instructed in the principles of virtue, and the rudiments of government, there civil liberty & general public felicity, will flourish in the greatest perfection.

FINIS

16

THE CHURCH'S FLIGHT INTO THE WILDERNESS: AN ADDRESS ON THE TIMES

Samuel Sherwood

NEW YORK
1776

SAMUEL SHERWOOD (1730-1783). Perhaps the most frequently cited sermon of the revolutionary era on the millennialist theme in politics, *The Church's Flight into the Wilderness* of 1776 is the second of the two Sherwood sermons that survive. The first, *Scriptural Instructions to Civil Rulers* (1774), is reprinted earlier in this volume. Both are regarded as being of the first importance—a tribute to Sherwood's intellect and to the ardor of his patriotism.

Preached on the text of Revelation 12:14-17, Sherwood's discourse relates the American cause to the Apocalypse and does not shrink from concluding that "we have incontestible evidence, that God Almighty, with all the powers of heaven, are on our side. Great numbers of angels, no doubt, are encamping round our coast, for our defence and protection. Michael stands ready, with all the artillery of heaven, to encounter the [British] dragon, and to vanquish this black host." This powerful sermon was preached in January 1776 to an audience that included John Hancock. Publication came some months later. The Introduction is dated April 1, around the time the British were besieging Boston, German mercenaries were entering the conflict, Thomas Paine's *Common Sense* appeared, and American resolve for independence was crystallizing in the face of Britain's unyielding policy.

The "Appendix by Another Hand" that follows Sherwood's message is by an author unknown. It concludes the sermon with a speculative note on Revelation 13, whose prophecy of the last days was much in the minds of Americans about to plunge into the turmoil of the Revolution.

THE CHURCH's FLIGHT INTO THE WILDERNESS: AN ADDRESS ON THE TIMES.

CONTAINING

Some very interesting and important OBSERVATIONS on SCRIPTURE PROPHECIES:

Shewing, that sundry of them plainly relate to GREAT-BRITAIN, and the AMERICAN COLONIES; and are fulfilling in the present day.

Delivered on a PUBLIC OCCASION, January 17, 1776.

By SAMUEL SHERWOOD, A. M.

Come out of her, my people, that ye be not partakers of her sins; and that ye receive not of her plagues. Reward her, even as she rewarded you; and double unto her double, according to her works. In the cup which she hath filled, fill to her double.

Glorious things are spoken of Zion.
He that hath an ear to hear, let him hear.

NEW-YORK: Printed by S. LOUDON.
M.DCC.LXXVI.

INTRODUCTION

The author declares his abhorrence of a bigotted attachment to the low singularities of a party, and professes to act on the benevolent and catholic principles of the gospel; therefore hopes his readers will not conceive any obnoxious idea from the word *church*, as he uses it in this discourse, nor indulge or give way to jealousy and prejudice so far, as once to suspect, that he means by this term, to point out any one denomination of Christians, exclusive of all others—as distinguished by their location and other peculiarities. The church, in his sense of it, includes all the worthy professors of christianity, who conduct themselves on their probation here, as those that expect to be judged hereafter, by the great evangelical law of liberty. He fully believes the Apostle, when he says, "where the spirit of the Lord is, there is liberty"; and doubts not, but this spirit has been plentifully poured out, not only in the New-England colonies, but likewise on his Episcopalian brethren in the Southern provinces, for whom he has the highest esteem and affection, and would not for his right hand, speak or write any thing that might give umbrage or just cause of offence to such worthy patriots, so ardently engaged in the common cause, and using such vigorous, spirited exertions for the defence and preservation of American liberty. He is fully convinced of the absolute importance of uniting in the most cordial friendship, as christian brethren and fellow-countrymen, in this glorious contest and struggle, and fully sensible, that to give the ark a wrong touch in this critical moment, might be of unspeakably dangerous consequence. But, however, apprehends no hazard or danger of being misguided by the scriptures of truth, which consideration, amidst all his diffidence, has prevailed with him to comply with the importunity of some of his friends, in consenting to this publication. His earnest wish and daily prayer is, that all differences and disputes may terminate in the firmest union and harmony of those colonies, and that liberty inviolate, may be secured to every individual of every denomination, so long as sun and moon shall endure.

April 1, 1776

And to the woman were given two wings of a great eagle, that she might fly into the wilderness, into her place; where she is nourished for a time, and times, and half a time, from the face of the serpent. And the serpent cast out of his mouth water as a flood, after the woman; that he might cause her to be carried away of the flood. And the earth helped the woman, and the earth opened her mouth, and swallowed up the flood which the dragon cast out of his mouth. And the dragon was wroth with the woman, and went to make war with the remnant of her seed, which keep the commandments of God, and have the testimony of Jesus Christ.

Revelation xii. 14, 15, 16, 17

This prophetic book is entitled, The Revelation of Jesus Christ, which he sent and signified to his servant John, by his angel; and which he received when in a state of banishment, in the isle called Patmos, for the word of God, and the testimony of Jesus Christ. It pleased the all-wise and omniscient God, to give to this his faithful servant, a very full and glorious vision of the things which then were, or of the state of the church at that time; and of the things which should be hereafter, or the then future state and condition of the church, the seasons of its flourishing and prosperity, and of its declension; its trials and sufferings to the end of the world. Which vision he was ordered to write, for the instruction, support, and consolation of God's saints, in the wars and conflicts they might have with their enemies, in every age and period of time, till the old serpent, the great dragon should be entirely overcome, and his kingdom compleatly destroyed. "And blessed is he that readeth, and they that hear the words of this prophecy, and keep those things which are written therein; for the time," that is, of their accomplishment, "is at hand." The diligent and serious study of this sacred book ought not to be neglected and despised, nor the things it contains be viewed as idle speculations, and vain empty amusements; but every man is bound in duty, to attend to the things contained herein, as to matters of great importance, with all the wisdom, sobriety and reverence he is capable of. It may with propriety be stiled, "The sure word of prophecy." The apostle John was so highly favoured, as to behold a door opened in heaven; so near to which he was brought as to look in, and see the glorious things transacted there, to confirm his faith as to the truth of these wonderful predictions and prophecies to be accomplished on earth. Chap. iv. 1[:] and the first voice which he heard, was as of a trumpet talking with him, which said, "Come up hither, and I will shew thee things which must be hereafter." Accordingly God discovered to him all the most remarkable events that should befal his church, and the nations and kingdoms of the world, even to the closing period when the angel should stand up and swear, that time should be no more: Which things he was ordered to pen down in dark, emblematical, and figurative language, the meaning of which, tho' it cannot be fully comprehended in the present dark state of the church; yet may be so far understood as to afford much support and encouragement to God's people in times of their greatest distress and suffering, and tend to establish their belief of the truth of this part of divine revelation, and of the ruling providence of God which is constantly at work to fulfil and accomplish the events herein predicted and foretold.

With a view to assist us in forming just conceptions of the nature and design of these prophecies and predictions, and to lead us to a right improvement of such providences of God by which they are fulfilled, I shall make two or three observations, before I proceed directly to explain the passages that have been read.

1. I would observe with all judicious commentators and expositors that have wrote on the subject, that popery, or the reign and kingdom of the man of sin, the old serpent, the dragon, its rise and progress, and its downfal and overthrow, is the greatest, the most essential, and the most striking part of this revelation of St. John. There has been a mortal enmity between the seed of the woman, and the seed of the serpent, ever since the fall of man, and the promise of a saviour for his recovery. The old serpent, who seduced man by his temptations, to fall, has ever been using his subtility and malice to defeat the purposes of divine grace, and to destroy Christ's kingdom on earth; and has, in all ages of the world, been successful in stirring up agents and instruments to accomplish this diabolical and hellish design. Among all his crafty and subtle inventions, popery, which exalts the principal leaders and abettors of it, high in the honours and emoluments of this world, seems most cunningly devised, and best adapted to answer his purpose; and has proved the most formidable

engine of terror and cruelty to the true members of Christ's church. And this has been the chief subject of prophecy since the coming of Christ; and was foretold by some of the prophets under the Jewish dispensation. And whatever difficulty and perplexity there may be in many of these dark, mysterious passages, yet in this view, the application of most of them is rendered easy and obvious. As popery has been the greatest enemy, and the greatest corrupter of christianity, we may rationally conclude that more prophecies relate to that, than to any other distant event.

By carefully reading and studying the prophecies given forth by Daniel, by St. Paul, and more fully by St. John, it will appear to be clearly and evidently foretold, that such a power as that of the pope of Rome should be exercised in the Christian church, and should authorize and establish such doctrines and practices as are publicly taught and embraced by the wicked, corrupt members of that mother of harlots and abomination. The time also is signified when, and how long it should prevail; and that at last, upon the expiration of this term, it should be destroyed forevermore.

2. This popish mysterious leaven of iniquity and absurdity, by which the Christian religion has been so awfully adulterated and corrupted, has not been confined to the boundaries of the Roman empire, nor strictly to the territory of the pope's usurped authority and jurisdiction; but has spread in a greater or less degree, among almost all the nations of the earth; especially amongst the chief rulers, the princes and noblemen thereof. When this great whore of Babylon, or papal Rome is described, Rev. xvii. 1[:] her bewitching, infatuating enchantments are said to be such, that the kings of the earth have been enticed, and inflamed in their wicked lusts, to that degree as to have committed fornication with her; and the inhabitants of the earth have been made drunk with the wine of her fornication or whoredom. They have been so far corrupted and debauched by this mother of harlots, as to sacrifice every dictate of religion and reason, and even common sense, to those alluring arts with which she has been tempting them. The prophet Isaiah had long before this, foretold, "That she should turn to her hire, and commit fornication with all the kingdoms of the world, upon the face of the earth." Isaiah xxiii. 17.

When the great red dragon, described, Revel. xii. having seven heads, and ten horns, and seven crowns upon his heads, made his first public appearance, his tail drew a third part of the stars of heaven, and did cast them to the earth. The apostle, under these symbolical characters and attributes of the great red dragon, undoubtedly meant to point out Satan or the Devil with his agents and instruments, who are acting the part of avowed enemies to the church of Christ; and his drawing the stars of heaven with his tail, must mean his subjecting the princes and potentates of the earth, with great numbers of the clergy, to his tyrannical influence and oppressive scheme of government. The prophets often describe the persecuting enemies of the church, under this emblem and figure. Psalm lxxiv. 13[:] "Thou breakest the heads of the dragons in the waters, &c." And when God comes to destroy these enemies, he is said "to cut Rahab, and to wound the dragon," Isaiah li. 9[;] see also Ezekiel xxix. 3[:] "Thus saith the Lord God, behold, I am against thee Pharaoh, king of Egypt, the great dragon that lieth in the midst of his rivers, which hath said, my river is mine own, and I have made it for myself." When the frightful monster of a beast, in such terrible array, is described, Rev. xiii. the dragon is said to give him his power, and his seat, and great authority; and all the world wondered after the beast; and said, "Who is like unto the beast? Who is able to make war with the beast?" Which expressions denote the great extent of his power and dominion, as well as the blind infatuation of his deluded subjects who made their boast of it. It is added, "And power was given him over all kindreds, and tongues, and nations, and all that dwell upon the earth, shall worship him, whose names are not written in the book of life, of the Lamb slain from the foundation of the world." Now, it can admit of no doubt, but that there are multitudes of this character in other nations and kingdoms, besides papal Rome. This is further evident from chap. xiv. 8. when the angel comes to proclaim the fall of Babylon, the reason given why God thus proceeded in righteous vengeance and wrath, is this, viz. "Because she made all nations drink of the wine of the wrath of her fornication." Her's was a kind of Circean cup, as one observes, with poisoned liquor, to intoxicate and inflame mankind to spiritual fornication. The prophet Jeremiah hath assigned much the same reason for her destruction, chap. li. 7[:] "Babylon hath been a golden cup in the Lord's hand, that made all the earth drunk; the nations hath drunken of her wine, therefore the nations are mad." When the sixth angel poured out his vial, Rev. xvi. Three unclean spirits like frogs, are said to come out of the mouth of the dragon, and out of the mouth of the beast, and out of the mouth of the false prophet, which are said to be spirits of devils, working miracles, which go forth unto the kings of the earth, and of the whole world, to gather them to the battle of the great day of God Almighty. These unclean spirits here compared to frogs, a very low-lived, inferior kind of animals, who are peeping and croaking in the dark holes and corners of the earth, most probably represent popish, jesuitical missioners, or the tools and emissaries in general, of anti-christian, tyrannical power, who are the spirits of devils, and have free access to the kings of the earth, and are said to be gone forth through the whole world, and are industriously using all their most artful stratagems, and diabolical craft and subtility, to impose upon mankind, and to engage them in the support and defence of the kingdom of Satan, in opposition to the mighty host marshalled up by the Lord Almighty, for the overthrow and destruction thereof. These scripture prophecies and predictions that have now been cited, to which more might be added, were it necessary, make it abundantly evident and manifest that the anti-christian, tyrannical scheme of popery, in one shape and form, and another, was to have a very extensive spread and influence, not only thro' the territories of papal Rome, but thro' all the nations and kingdoms of the world in general, and that the kings and princes of the earth, as well as their subjects, were to be much intoxicated and infatuated therewith; to the great distress and perplexity of the true church of Christ, which, so far as I have been able to observe, has not been suitably noticed and attended to by expositors and divines that have wrote on the subject; the want of which has occasioned much perplexity and obscurity in their comments on some passages, which, in the right view of them, are full of significance and importance. For instance, that passage in the xiii. chap[ter] of this mysterious book, where the image of the beast is spoken of, "I confess," says a great expositor, "I know not what the image of the beast is, distinct from the beast itself." The reason of which was, no doubt, his limiting and confining these prophecies to so narrow a circle, as papal Rome. Every man of common sense, knows that the image of a thing is something different from the thing itself. Therefore, to make sense of the language here used, we must suppose that the apostle intended to describe another persecuting tyrannical power, in some nation or kingdom of the world, which was a lively figure and resemblance of that exercised at Rome, the head-quarters of tyranny and persecution.* Whether that persecuting power be intended, that has in years past, been so cruelly and barbarously exercised in France, and other popish countries, against the humble followers of Christ, to the massacre and destruction of so many thousands of protestants;† or whether there be a reference to the corrupt system of tyranny and oppression, that has of late been fabricated and adopted by the ministry and parliament of Great-Britain, which appears so favourable to popery and the Roman catholic interest, aiming at the extension and establishment of it, and so awfully threatens the civil and religious liberties of all sound protestants; I cannot positively determine. But since the prophecies represent this wicked scheme of anti-christian tyranny, as having such an extensive and universal spread over the earth, like Nebuchadnezzar's tree which reached unto heaven, and the light thereof to all the ends of the earth, it need not appear strange or shocking to us, to find that our own nation has been, in some degree, infected and corrupted therewith, and that some of our princes and chief rulers have had a criminal converse and familiarity with the old mother of harlots; and been sipping of the golden cup of her fornication, so as to be intoxicated, if not wholly drunk with her poisonous liquors. "Before what is called the reformation, the man of sin reigned triumphant in our mother-country, without much check or controul; which reformation was not set on foot on the purest principles of genuine christianity, nor carried to perfection by King Hen-

* See the appendix.

† In the war with the Albigenses and Waldenses, there were destroyed of them, in France alone, one million.

From the first institution of the Jesuits, to the year 1450, that is, in little more than thirty years, nine hundred thousand orthodox christians, were slain. In the Netherlands alone, the duke of Alva boasted, that within a few years, he had dispatched to the amount of thirty six thousand souls; and those all by the hand of the common executioner. In the space of scarce thirty years, the Inquistion destroyed, by various kinds of torments, a hundred and fifty thousand christians. Besides these, an innumerable multitude have been persecuted to death, throughout all Europe, by the cruel hand of tyranny and persecution. As to the number that have been, and may yet be slain in America, in the war and conflict with the beast, and the image of the beast, it cannot yet be ascertained.

ry the Eighth, who is so celebrated as the author of it. In the reign of Queen Mary, the doctrine and ceremonies of the catholic religion were re-established, and the pope's authority and jurisdiction acknowledged in full; and a very cruel, severe persecution rigorously carried on against the innocent, conscientious professors of the protestant religion; and a most tragical scene of bloodshed and slaughter exhibited, as ever England beheld.

If we pass from this dark and bloody period of English history, and come down to the reign of the Stuart family, we shall find three or four of our kings successively, seduced and infatuated by the enticing and bewitching inchantments of the old whore of Babylon, to that degree, as to drink deep of the intoxicating wine of her fornication, to the entire destruction of two of them; and to the great distress of the nation in general. How far the present ministry have walked in this enchanting road, and how fond they are of the kind embraces of this old filthy harlot, the world will judge from their open attempts to propagate and establish popery, that exotic plant, in these northern regions; which is not a native of our benign soil, nor of our heavenly Father's planting; and their gathering up of armies professedly Roman catholics to dragoon us into slavery and bondage, or massacre and butcher us and our families, and lay our pleasant country in desolation and ruin.

3. Since these prophecies and predictions, relating to the trials and sufferings, the wars and conflicts of the church with her anti-christian enemies and adversaries, may be justly taken in such a large, extensive sense and latitude; we may rationally conclude that many of them have reference to the state of Christ's church, in this American quarter of the globe; and will sooner or later, have their fulfilment and accomplishment among us. The providences of God in first planting his church in this, then howling wilderness, and in delivering and preserving of it to this day, are in a manner unequalled, and marvelous; and are reckoned among the most glorious events that are to be found in history, in these latter ages of the world. And there are doubtless yet more glorious events in the womb of providence, which the present commotion thro' the nation and land may (however unlikely in the view of some) be the means of bringing to pass. There is no part of this terraqueous globe better fitted and furnished in all essential articles and advantages, to make a great and flourishing em-

pire; no part of the earth, where learning, religion, and liberty have flourished more for the time. And as to the rapid increase of its inhabitants, and swift population, it cannot be paralleled in all history. There is no part of the world where its inhabitants, through such a large extent of territory, are under such bonds and obligations, from self-interest, to keep in the strictest union and harmony together. They have every motive and inducement to this, that can well be conceived of. And this union, by the blessing of heaven, is become as general, perfect and complete, as could well be expected in such a corrupt disordered world as this in which we live.

These united colonies have arisen to such a height as to become the object of public attention thro' all Europe, and of envy to the mother from whence they derived; whose unprovoked attack upon them in such a furious hostile manner, threatening their entire ruin, is an event that will make such a black and dark period in history, and does so deeply affect, not only the liberty of the church here in the wilderness, but the protestant cause in general, thro' the christian world, and is big with such consequences of glory or terror, that we may conjecture at least, without a spirit of vanity and enthusiasm, that some of those prophecies of St. John may, not unaptly, be applied to our case, and receive their fulfilment in such providences as are passing over us.

I do not mean to undertake a nice, exact calculation of the periods pointed out in this prophetic book; nor to range thro' the history of the world for events to find their accomplishment. I am of opinion, that the church of Christ in every age, may find something in this book applicable to her case and circumstances; and all such passages that are so, may lawfully be applied and improved by us accordingly. There are many cases which happen, that bear a near likeness and resemblance to each other, and which the same prophecy may well suit, in the most material parts of it. It has pleased that God who exercises a universal providence over all things, so to dispose and order events, that the calamities and afflictions of the church, in some measure, run parallel one to another; and all the former efforts of that tyrannical persecuting power, called the beast, may be the types and figures, as it were, of his last and general effort against the faithful witnesses of Christ, and the true members of his church.

These preliminary observations may assist us in explaining and improving these prophecies of St. John; particularly the passages that have been read, to the consideration of which I now proceed.

Verse 14. "And to the woman were given two wings of a great eagle, that she might fly into the wilderness, into her place, where she is nourished for a time, and times, and half a time, from the face of the serpent."

The woman in this passage, is represented in verse 2. as in a pregnant state, travailing in birth, and in violent pangs to be delivered, which is doubtless designed as an emblem of the true church of Christ. She is elsewhere spoken of as the spouse of Christ, who owns himself to be her head and husband. A woman, we know, is the weaker sex, and looks to her husband for support and protection. So the church has always been the weakest part of the world, in herself considered, and had her dependence on Christ her head, for preservation and safety in times of peril and danger. This woman, the church, being in such a near relation to Christ, the brightness of the Father's glory, and express image of his person, amidst all her own natural weakness and infirmity, has never appeared contemptible; but the most glorious society that ever existed in our world. She is the king's daughter, all glorious within. She is spoken of, verse 1. as being cloathed with the sun, and having the moon under her feet, and upon her head a crown of twelve stars; which is a magnificent description of her comeliness, beauty and lustre. She is enlightened, invested and adorned with the rays of Jesus Christ, the great sun of righteousness, which makes her form illustriously bright and majestic. She is in such a state of dignity and triumph, as to have the moon, with all sublunary enjoyments and terrors, under her feet. And on her head, to compleat her glory, a crown of twelve stars, an emblem of her being under the light and guidance of the twelve inspired apostles, who had been improved as master-builders under Christ, in laying the foundation of this honourable society, and were such useful and distinguishing ornaments to it. One would think that such a society as this, would have nothing to fear from all the combined powers of earth and hell; and indeed, they have not in reality, since stronger is he that is for them, than those that are against them. However, they are not exempted from trials and sufferings in this world. We find, when the great red dragon appeared with his seven heads and ten horns, that frightful monster the devil instigated the tyrannical persecuting powers of the earth, against this harmless and innocent woman, the amiable spouse of Christ. He had impudence and boldness enough to make an unprovoked attack upon her, which occasioned her to leave the imperial and wealthy abodes of earthly grandeur and magnificence, the courts and palaces of emperors and princes, and retired to some obscure, solitary condition, for the sweets of liberty and peace. This furious attack of the great dragon on the woman, was an event of such importance, as to produce war in heaven between the angels of light, and the angels of darkness. See verse 7. "Michael and his angels fought against the dragon; and the dragon fought, and his angels." This Michael was the tutelar angel and protector of the Jewish church. Daniel x. 12. And he performs here the same office of champion for the Christian church.

He, and the good angels who are sent forth to minister to the heirs of salvation, were the invisible agents on one side, as the devil and his evil angels were on the other. The visible actors in the cause of christianity, were believers, whether in a civil or ecclesiastical character, with the glorious martyrs and confessors. And in support of the opposite side, were the persecuting powers of the world, with the whole dark train of the artillery of hell. In this great conflict and war, let it relate to what period of the church it will, which I am not anxious to determine with mathematical certainty; we find that those on the side of God and true religion, overcame their formidable enemy, with all his confederate powers, by the blood of the Lamb, and by the word of their testimony; and they loved not their lives unto the death. They were of such a brave, heroic spirit, as to chearfully expose themselves to the greatest dangers in this glorious cause; and many of them actually met death in the terrible conflict. But they fell, as one observes, to rise, and triumph, and reign. The dragon being thus defeated and vanquished at his head-quarters, pagan or papal Rome: He takes a wider scope and range, thro' the other nations and kingdoms of the earth. He was doubtless greatly enraged at the ill success of his first encounter, and marshals up all his forces abroad, and proceeds with violence, to persecute the woman which brought forth the man-child. Upon this the woman has a second flight into a more distant and solitary wilderness, "unto her place"; to prepare her for which, two wings of a great eagle were given her, which is not mentioned in her first flight; and probably she did not then need them. There seems an evident allusion here, to what God said to the children of Israel, Exod. xix. 4. after their deliverance from cruel oppressive slavery in Egypt, when encamp'd before Sinai, and on their way to the good land of Canaan, "Ye have seen what I did unto the Egyptians, and how I bore you on eagles wings, and brought you unto myself." He was not conducting them from a land of liberty, peace, and tranquility, into a state of bondage, persecution and distress; but on the contrary, had wrought out a very glorious deliverance for them, and set them free from the cruel hand of tyranny and oppression, by executing his judgments in a most terrible and awful manner, on the Egyptians, their enemies; and was now, by his kind providence, leading them to the good land of Canaan, which he gave them by promise, for an everlasting inheritance. Hence, as the trials and sufferings of the Christian church were parallel in some measure, with those of the Jewish, and there is a great similarity and likeness in the manner of God's dealings with the one to the other; it must be evident, that expositors have been mistaken, when they represent this flight of the woman into and the wilderness, as denoting the church's going into greater peril, danger and affliction, where she was to be more violently distressed and persecuted, for a long time. The word *wilderness* might possibly suggest to their delicate, but inattentive minds, this frightful and shocking idea. It is true, our fathers had the difficulties of an uncultivated wilderness to encounter; but it soon, by the blessing of heaven on their labour and industry, became a pleasant field or garden, and has been made to blossom like the rose. The passage, in its most natural, genuine construction, contains as full and absolute a promise of this land, to the Christian church, as ever was made to the Jewish, of the land of Canaan. It is, in an appropriated sense, "her place"; where she is nourished, from the face of the serpent. And the dealings of God in his providence, in bringing his church from a state of oppression and persecution, into this good land, are very parallel and similar to his dealings with the Israelites, in delivering them from the tyrannical power of the haughty, cruel monarch of Egypt, and conducting them to the good land of promise in Canaan. Thus, they that wait on the Lord, shall renew their strength; they shall mount up with wings, as eagles; they shall run, and not be weary, they shall walk and not faint.

Thus the church, in this difficult, distressed season, whenever it happened, was supported and carried, as it were, on eagles wings, to a distant remote wilderness, for safety and protection. And what period or event is there in all the history of her trials and persecutions, which these expressions more exactly describe, and to which they can be applied with more truth and propriety, than to the flight of our fore-fathers into this then howling wilderness, which was a land not sown nor occupied by any ruling power on earth, except by savages and wild beasts? It is an indisputable fact, that the cruel hand of oppression, tyranny and persecution drove them out from their pleasant seats and habitations, in the land of their nativity; and that the purest principles of religion and liberty, led them to make the bold adventure across the wide Atlantic ocean; for which they surely needed the two wings of the great eagle, to speed their flight, and to shelter and cover them from danger, while seeking a safe retreat from the relentless fury and shocking cruelty of the persecuting dragon; and a secure abode for unadulterated christianity, liberty and peace. It is remarked by the inspired penman of this prophecy, and is worthy of notice, that when the woman fled into the wilderness, she came into her place. This American quarter of the globe seemed to be reserved in providence, as a fixed and settled habitation for God's church, where she might have property of her own, and the right of rule and government, so as not to be controul'd and oppress'd in her civil and religious liberties, by the tyrannical and persecuting powers of the earth, represented by the great red dragon. The church never before this, had prime occupancy, or first possession of any part of this terraqueous globe, in any great extent of territory. In all countries and kingdoms wherever Christianity had been planted, before its introduction into this American wilderness, the ruling powers in possession of the property, and right of jurisdiction and dominion, were in opposition to this benevolent institution; and the church had to make her way through the greatest possible difficulties and dangers. While thus in an enemy's land, her persecutions and oppressions, her bloody trials and sufferings furnish out the chief subject of her history from her beginning to the present day, in other parts of the world, from which she is not wholly exempted in this. However, her degree of peace and quiet rest has been greater than she has ever known since she has had existance and being. When that God, to whom the earth belongs, and the fulness thereof, brought his church into this wilderness, as on eagles wings, by his kind, protecting providence, he gave this good land to her, to be her own lot and inheritance for ever. He planted her as a pleasant and choice vine; and drove out the heathen before her. He has tenderly nourished and cherished her in her infant state, and protected and preserved her amidst innumerable dangers. He has done wonders in his providence for our fathers, and for us their sinful posterity: "They, and we have many a time, stood still, and seen the salvation of the Lord.["] The woman, the church of Christ, has such a gift and grant from heaven, of this part of God's world, for the quiet enjoyment of her liberties and privileges, civil and religious, that no power on earth can have any right to invade, much less to dispossess her of them. And every attempt of this kind to oppress and enslave her, must be absolutely unrighteous, and a gross violation of justice and truth. He that has all power in heaven and on earth, who will soon destroy the man of sin, and all his confederate powers, by the spirit of his mouth, and brightness of his coming, declares in this prophecy, that the "woman" shall be nourished and preserved in her place here described, "from the face of the serpent." The serpent spoken of, is the great dragon, called the Devil and Satan; the chief directing agent in all the dark plots of tyranny, persecution and oppression; from whose malignant rage, the church has a promise of future protection. This old serpent shall never be permitted to shew his deformed face, much less to lift up his monstrous head, and frightful horns in this place here given to the woman for a safe retreat and secure abode, "for a time, and times, and half a time"; which probably means, "to the end of the world," or till all the times and periods spoken of in this prophetic book are fulfilled and accomplished. I know that expositors take these expressions, "for a time, and times, and half a time," to include only the period of one thousand two hundred and sixty days, mentioned verse 6, and so understood the phrase "for a time," to mean one prophetical year, and "times," to mean two years, and "half a time," an half year; in the whole, three years and a half: But it seems more natural, and more agreeable to the phraseology of scripture, as well as the connection of these prophecies, in the events foretold, to interpret this passage as signifying all future time indefinitely. Or, if we apply it to distinct periods, the first expression, "for a time," I should think, might, with great propriety, be taken for the time or period, that hath already been mentioned. This construction appears natural, and not in the least forced or strained. Then the "times" will mean such times or periods as follow after the fulfilment of the above; and the "half time," must signify the closing period, when time is near run out, and just come to an end. Taking the passage in its proper connection, and plainest and most obvious sense, we may well understand it as containing a prophetic promise to the church, of safety and preservation, during the period that had been described above, and thro' all succeeding times, even to the end of the world. Not but what the old dragon, with his black train of tyrannical persecuting powers, might greatly afflict and distress her. Yet, with all his cunning, art, policy and power, shall never be able to establish his enslaving doctrines, nor to erect his head and horns, to exercise his usurped authority and uncontrouled dominion, as in papal Rome. We may expect, however, that he will be putting forth most violent struggles and efforts for this base, malignant purpose.

One objection of weight, I have against the current opinion of expositors, who interpret the passage, "a time, and times, and half a time," to signify the same period as the thousand two hundred and three-score days, is, that this is dishonourable to the sacred writer, and shews that he rather meant to puzzle and perplex his readers, than to enlighten and instruct them. I believe that all will allow, that the language used in the 6th verse, is more plain and intelligible, and has a more fixed and determinate meaning, than that in the 14th verse. Now, to suppose the same period of time, is described in the one, as in the other, is to suppose, that the apostle, after he had described a thing in a plain, easy way to be understood, proceeds on to involve the same subject in a cloud of mysticism, darkness and obscurity, which could not tend, very much, to the improvement and edification of Christ's church. It is usual with all good writers, as they advance on their subject, to elucidate and illustrate their meaning more and more, to set it in a plainer and more intelligible point of light. And this is, especially, the tone of all inspired writers, and of St. John in particular. The light of revelation is like the path of the just, shining brighter and brighter in every page, till we come to the close of it.

But, should my explanation of this passage, after all, be disputed, and the time, times, and half time, allowed to include no more, altogether, than the period of twelve hundred and sixty years, which I have taken to be included in that expression only, "a time," yet it will not materially affect my scheme. For, on the old plan of exposition, it is supposed, that after the expiration of these twelve hundred and sixty years, the trials and sufferings of the church will be chiefly over; and that a scene of great peace, prosperity and happiness will open and commence. Hence, if the prophetic promise in the text, extends no further than to that happy and blessed period, the church will safely get through the long storm and tempest, raised by the dragon; and so, be ready for a share in the blessings of that glorious and happy period to succeed; during which, we need not be very anxious about her safety, considering other precious promises that are made in her favour.

The serpent is said, verse 15, "to cast out of his mouth, water, as a flood, after the woman, that he might cause her to be carried away of the flood." This, perhaps, is one of the artifices, says a learned expositor, which these enormous creatures make use of, "to beat down their prey," when flying from them. The common signification of a flood is an inundation of water, &c. The psalmist sets forth extreme dangers, under the notion of a flood. Psalm lxix. 15[:] "Let not the water-flood overflow me." And the violent assaults, and subtle temptations, and sudden incursions of the Devil and his instruments against the church, are compared to a flood, Isaiah lix. 19[:] "When the enemy shall come in like a flood, the spirit of the Lord shall lift up a standard against him." Which prophecy may refer to, and have its accomplishments in the present state of the church, about which we are treating. The oppressive and persecuting power here figuratively described, under the emblem of the serpent, which occasioned the flight of the woman, the church, into this wilderness, whenever it has prevailed, has been full of the most inveterate malice and envy against her; and used every art and stratagem to extirpate and destroy her from the earth. Hence, the flood which the serpent cast out of his mouth after the woman, may very naturally and properly be interpreted to signify all the subtle temptations, artful schemes, and machinations of our enemies and adversaries, to ensnare and corrupt us, and to destroy our liberties and privileges, that we might be embarrassed again under the old tyrant, the dragon, and patiently submit to the iron yoke, and galling chains of cruel oppression and bondage; which machinations and contrivances have been too many to be enumerated in a short, concise discourse. Every one acquainted with the history of our country, of the New-England colonies in particular, must know, that there have been floods issued from the mouth of the old serpent, after the woman, to effect her destruction and overthrow. Whenever a spirit of despotism has run high, and a lusting ambition after arbitrary power and lawless dominion has prevailed; when the dragon dare venture to put on and wear his long horns; the woman in the wilderness has felt the grievous distressing effects. At such seasons, jesuitical emissaries, the tools of tyrannical power, have been employed to corrupt her doctrines, and lead her into the belief of the darling doctrines of arbitrary *power, passive obedience and nonresistance;* who, like the frogs that issued out of the mouth of the false prophet, who are said to have the spirit of devils, have been slyly creeping into all the holes and corners of the land, and using their enchanting art and bewitching policy, to lead aside, the simple and unwary, from the truth, to prepare them for the shackles of slavery and bondage. Thousands and millions of money, have, at one time and another, been expended for the purposes of bribery and corruption, to accomplish this malignant design. Evil, wicked men have been entrusted with the chief command in one province and another, where the door has been open, to act as tools of a corrupt administration and tyrannical power, in forwarding and ripening their deep-laid schemes, for the destruction of the woman. The colonies in America will not soon forget the cruel and tyrannical administration of Sir Edmond Andross, at Boston, and his evil designs against them in general; and Lord Cornbury, at New-York; the late insidious and traiterous conduct of Bernard and Hutchinson, is still more fresh in every one's mind; and like-wise of Gage, Carlton, and Dunmore, who, by their base, perfidious and cruel behaviour, have rendered themselves universally odious and detestable to the American colonies. In these and such like ways, not to mention the unrighteous statutes restricting and interdicting our trade and commerce, the stamp-act, &c. we have had floods poured forth from the mouth of the serpent, which at length, have brought on a civil war. The dragon finding his artful temptations on the one hand, and his cruel menaces and threatenings on the other, ineffectual to gain the woman to a compliance with his terms, has at length become wroth with her, and brought over his troops and armies to make war with the remnant of her seed. But, blessed be God! all his efforts and struggles have hitherto been unsuccessful; for the earth helped the woman. Verse 16[:] "And the earth opened her mouth, and swallowed up the flood which the dragon cast out of his mouth."

If this is taken in the literal sense, to signify that gross terrestrial element which sustains and nourishes us, it is strictly true; in which sense some of the prophecies have been, and yet will, no doubt, be accomplished. The earth has ever helped the woman since her arrival to these shores, with every article necessary to her comfortable support. She has never wanted for nourishing food, and good raiment; has never known the distresses arising from scarcity of bread, pinching hunger and famine; has always, from the first settlement and cultivation of the country, had things convenient for her, and, as I trust, been contented with her lot and condition. The earth has, in a very remarkable manner, thro' the blessing of heaven, been profuse and liberal in her precious fruits and productions, the year past, when the dragon has been wroth with the woman, and using all possible schemes and contrivances to distress her, and starve her into a compliance to his despotic and arbitrary rule, by shutting up her ports and harbours, and interdicting her trade and commerce, and cutting her off from all supplies from her fishery, a very useful and necessary branch of her trade and livelihood, by which thousands were maintained. I say, when the woman has, in these, and in such like ways, been distressed, she has been helped in a very extraordinary way, by the earth. Our crops of all kinds have been plentiful. Our fruit-trees loaded with fruit, and pressed down with their burdens. Our granaries are full. There is such an uncommon plenty of all kinds of good provisions for man and beast, that some inconsiderate persons are ready to esteem it rather a curse, than a blessing; as we know not how to dispense with, or dispose of it. But not to enlarge here.

Should we take the expression in a figurative sense, to mean the men of the earth, and earthly powers, it may still, with truth and propriety be applied to our present case. For as the oppressive measures pursued by the British parliament, strike at our temporal interest and property, as well as our civil and religious privileges, it will engage those of an earthly temper to exert themselves in the present struggles; by which means the earth helpeth the woman. And besides, the vast advantage of these American plantations, in point of traffic and merchandise, to all such as trade in ships, will doubtless, if the present system is pursued, engage the kingdoms of the world, and the merchants of the earth, to espouse the cause of the colonies, to such purposes as will, in their operation, greatly help the woman against the flood cast out of the dragon's mouth.

And not only the earth, but the God that made it, nourisheth the woman in the wilderness, amidst the most violent and cruel attempts of a tyrannical and persecuting power, and has raised up persons of a martial, heroic spirit, and endowed them with skill, courage and fortitude, to defend and protect his church. The flood of the dragon that has been poured forth to the northward, in the Quebec bill, for the establishment of popery, and other engines and instruments that have been set to work, to bring the savages down upon us, to our utter destruction, have been chiefly swallowed up by our late successful enterprizes against them; and the woman has received a great addition of strength from this quarter, as a door is opened for breaking up the seat of the dragon in Canada; and for bringing in the heathen tribes, perhaps, the fulness of the gentiles, into firm league and friendship with her, for her future defence and protection. So that instead of being carried away with this flood, she stands on more firm ground, and is better established than ever. Should we extend the meaning of the phrase, so as to take in other neighbouring powers of the earth, they have likewise helped the woman in her distresses and troubles, by affording a competent supply of military instruments and warlike stores for her defence and protection; when all possible precaution had been used by her enemies, to deprive her of these useful articles, so necessary for self-preservation; and these other powers seem so friendly disposed, that it is highly probable, should the serpent continue to persecute and distress the woman, that they will soon open their mouth, and swallow up the whole flood, even all the fleets and armies which the dragon may cast out of his mouth.

The probability or conjecture of neighbouring nations continuing to help the woman, the church, to that degree, as to swallow up all the floods, the serpent may cast out of his mouth after her, is founded, not only on their present friendly appearance, and the part which their interested views may lead them to take in the present controversy, but on the sure word of prophecy. See Rev. xvii. 16, 17[:] "And the ten horns which thou sawest upon the beast, these shall hate the whore; and shall make her desolate and naked; and shall eat her flesh, and burn her with fire. For God hath put in their hearts to fulfil his will." These ten horns, doubtless mean some of the kingdoms and princes of the earth, that have, for a long time, been under the influence of the beast, the great whore of Babylon, and had a great share with her, in the cruel and bloody work of tyranny, persecution and oppression. But the time is coming, and perhaps near at hand, when their league and friendship with her, will be dissolved and broken; and their love turned into hatred and a spirit of revenge. They will turn with warm zeal and violence against her; and use all their strength and power for her destruction and overthrow. These shall hate the whore to a degree beyond what they ever loved her, and shall make her desolate and naked. They shall strip her of all her costly ornaments which they have lavished away upon her, and effectually humble her insolence and pride, and expose her to public shame and disgrace; in the heat of their indignation and zeal, shall eat her very flesh, and burn her with fire. They will do the most thorough execution upon this old harlot, by whom they had been so long infatuated and deceived; and wholly break up the stupid schemes of idolatry, with all the monuments of it, and bring the abettors and instruments of tyranny and persecution to their condign punishment. This God will put into their hearts, by a strong and powerful impression, to fulfil his will; and they shall agree in it, to perform his purpose and design. This prediction or prophecy, it is thought by judicious expositors, refers to the destruction of papal Rome, or to the demolishing of the popish hierarchy in general; and that the kings of France are pointed out, as the principal instruments to effect it. They have, in years past, contributed greatly to her growth and advancement; and done much at the cruel work of persecution. It is not impossible, nor improbable, that the time is coming, when their hearts will be turned against her, and be improved by heaven, as the principal authors of her overthrow and ruin. France has been satiated with the blood of Protestants, and 'tis to be hoped, will never thirst after it any more. She has already shewn some tendency towards a reformation; and therefore may be judged very likely to effect such a revolution. It appears from verse 17, that the infatuation of popish princes will be permitted by divine providence, only for a certain limited period, till the words of God be fulfilled. And then their minds shall be turned and their eyes opened; and they shall ruin and destroy all oppressive, tyrannical combinations, more eagerly than they established them. Should our honourable Continental Congress, see fit, in their great wisdom, at this difficult juncture, to open a free trade, and correspond with that nation, in a way in which our threatened rights and liberties might have such security and indemnification, as to be in no hazard or danger of any future encroachment on them, the spirit of liberty might spread and circulate with commerce; and from small sparks, kindle up into a bright and inextinguishable flame, in that, and in other kingdoms of the earth; and so hasten the fulfilment of this prophecy, in the entire destruction of the beast, or man of sin, and in the complete and glorious salvation of God's afflicted church.

The dragon, in this situation, is represented as much embarrassed in his black system of politics, in a state of great perplexity, and high paroxism of passion. Verse 17[:] "He was wroth with the woman, and went to make war with the remnant of her seed, which keep the commandments of God, and have the testimony of Jesus Christ." Which may refer to the present war that is carrying on with such heat and fury against us; which seems chiefly levelled against those who most strictly and conscientiously adhere to the pure, uncorrupted doctrine and worship of our pious forefathers; and have not been seduced nor perverted from the right ways of the Lord, but still keep God's commandments, and have the testimony of Jesus Christ, in his pure gospel. Amidst all our declensions and back-slidings, our divisions and heresies, our contentions and separations, there remain yet in the land a godly remnant of the true seed of the woman, who have not been enticed away to worship the beast, nor prevailed upon to receive his mark; who have never apostatised nor departed from the faith and practice of the church, as first planted in the wilderness; but have continued stedfast and immoveable amidst all the storms of temptation, and violent assaults of the adversary. And these seem the principal objects which excite the wrath and resentment of the dragon, and against which, the whole artillery of his indignation and vengeance has been pointed and aimed. Who, tho' few in number, yet with such other helps and advantages as they are furnished with, will overcome by the blood of the Lamb, and by the word of their testimony. Their fidelity, courage and zeal is such, that should it come to a case of extremity, they will not love their lives unto the death. But this part of the prophecy will admit of a different interpretation, and as well suit the present times.

By the "remnant of her seed," we may understand those worthy, true members of the church, staunch friends to liberty and the protestant religion, who remained still in the mother-country, and did not come over with her when she took her flight into this wilderness. There has, ever since the settlement of these colonies, been numbers of pious, godly persons, on the other side of the water, who have been friendly and well-disposed towards us, and have used all their power and influence to promote our growth, our wealth and prosperity. This remnant of the seed of the woman, since our troubles have begun in America, have exerted themselves to their utmost in our favour, to divert the impending storm of vengeance from lighting on us; have made most moving and affecting speeches in parliament, on the subject; have published many useful pieces in vindication of the colonies; and have been, to the last degree, faithful in corresponding with their friends on this side of the Atlantic, to inform of the intrigues and dark plots that were contriving against us. These things, together with the disappointment, shame and disgrace that have attended the enterprizes of the dragon against us, have roused his wrath against them likewise, which appears by a very severe and extraordinary proclamation, published to forbid this correspondence between them and us, on the highest penalty. And from the commotions that began to be raised among them therefor, should this civil war continue, it is highly probable, that within the term of another year, it may flame forth from the very bowels of the kingdom, where it seems to be already kindling up, and where our brethren, which keep the commandments of God, will unavoidably be distressed. But in the issue hereof, it is to be hoped, that the dragon will be wholly consumed and destroyed; that the seat and foundation of all tyranny, persecution and oppression, may be for ever demolished; that the horns, whether civil or ecclesiastical, may be knocked off from the beast, and his head receive a deadly wound, and his jaws be effectually broken; that peace, liberty and righteousness might universally prevail; that salvation and strength might come to Zion; and the kingdom of our God, and the power of his Christ might be established to all the ends of the earth.

IMPROVEMENT

1. We learn from what has been said, the true cause, as well as the deplorable efffects of all dissentions and violent commotions amidst the Christian states and kingdoms of the world; which, like terrible earthquakes, to which they are compared, often shake them from the centre, and convulse them to death and ruin. If we trace them up to their time, source, and origin, we shall presently find, by the help of scripture-light, they all proceed from the inveterate envy and malice which the dragon has against the woman, and the war and contest he is carrying on against her, and her seed. This is plainly held forth in these prophecies of St. John, and is the grand subject of them. It has, from the beginning, been the constant aim and design of the dragon, sometimes called the beast, and the serpent, satan, and the devil, to erect a scheme of absolute despotism and tyranny on earth, and involve all mankind in slavery and bondage; and so prevent their having that liberty and freedom which the Son of God came from heaven to procure for, and bestow on them; that he might keep them in a state of servile subjection to himself. He has been, and still is the chief counsellor and directing agent in all the dark plots of oppression and persecution against God's church, to effect her destruction; that his own wicked scheme of tyranny might have a full establishment on earth, and bear down all before it. And it is truly marvellous what success he has been permitted to have in accomplishing this malignant design: How, not only men of lower abilities and less discernment have been deluded and infatuated by him; but many kings and chief rulers in church and state, of whom better things might have been expected. Such, after they have been made drunk with the intoxicating wine of his fornication and whoredom, have been his chief instruments in this cruel and bloody work. They are of such dark complexion in their counsels, and pursuing such black designs, that they are represented as "ascending out of the bottomless pit, to make war against the faithful witnesses and servants of Jesus Christ, and to kill them." And who can count up the numbers that have been

slain by them? Rivers of blood have been shed, at one time and another, in this terrible war and conflict which the tyrannical, persecuting powers of the earth have been instigated by Satan, to carry on against the church of Christ. In the first beginning of the Christian dispensation, ten persecutions followed successively one after another, while the government of Rome was in the hands of pagan emperors.

In this struggle between paganism and Christianity, thousands of martyrs and confessors were most cruelly and barbarously tormented, and put to death. These horrid massacres of the saints may be emblematically, or figuratively represented in the 6th chapter of this prophetic book, in the 9th verse of which, the apostle is said to have seen under the altar, the souls of them that were slain for the word of God, and for the testimony which they held. And after Rome became Christian, or rather papal, and the man of sin made his public appearance, the woman and her seed, the humble followers of Christ, fared yet worse, and were more hardly and cruelly dealt with than ever, by their persecuting enemies, who are inwardly galled in their consciences, and said to be tormented at their pure doctrines, plain faithful remonstrances, and exemplary lives. See chap. xi. 10. When this great red dragon was mounted on high, with his seven heads and ten horns, the first object on which he exercised his tyrannical and persecuting power, was the church, represented in these prophecies by the woman and her seed. Hence, when she appeared pregnant, ready to bring forth children, when the gospel began to have success, and new converts were born, and added to the church, this dragon stood ready to seize and devour them, like a hungry lion, eagerly waiting for his prey; and has persecuted her with rage and fierceness, not only thro' the imperial populous cities of Italy and Bohemia, France, Spain, and England, and thro' their colonies and plantations, even to the uttermost ends of the earth. When she took the wings of the great eagle, and, under the protecting providence of God fled into the wilderness, he continued wroth with her, and poured forth floods of his indignation and vengeance against her. "Wo to the inhabitants of the earth, and of the sea," says the apostle, "for the devil is come down to them, having great wrath, because he knoweth that he hath but a short time." This dragon, the great enemy of God, and of his church, whatever shape or form he has assumed, whether that of the spotted leopard, with the feet of a bear, and the mouth of a lion; whether his horns have been ten, or only two, like a lamb or goat, giving life unto the image of the beast; yet he has in every appearance, when he had opportunity, discovered the like fierceness and cruelty of temper, thirsting for the blood of the saints. When his shape and form has wore a milder aspect, he has yet spoke as a dragon; and when times would allow of it, exercised all the power of the first beast, causing the earth, and them that dwell therein, to worship him; giving forth tyrannical mandates and decrees, that as many as would not worship the image of the beast, should be killed: Gathering all into his service, both small and great, rich and poor, free and bond, slaves and savages, catholics and barbarians, to accomplish at any rate, his black and dark designs; passing the most vigorous acts, and severe edicts against those who refused compliance; enacting by his omnipotent power, that they should not buy nor sell, nor carry on any trade or commerce by land or sea. Now, the administration seems here described, that has for a number of years, been so grievous and distressing to these colonies in America, claiming an absolute power and authority to make laws, binding in all cases whatever, without check or controul from any; which has proceeded in the exercise of this despotic, arbitrary power, to deprive one of them, of their most essential and chartered privileges; sent over fleets and armies to enforce their cruel, tyrannical edicts, which have involved us in all the calamities and horrors of a civil war; which have destroyed many useful lives, burnt two of our flourishing towns, captured many of our vessels that fell in their way, prohibited and destroyed our fishery and trade, forbidding us to buy or sell, and taken in a hostile manner, in a way of piracy and robbery, our interest and property, and threaten us with general destruction, for no other reason than that we will not surrender our liberties, properties and privileges, and become abject vassals and slaves to despotic and arbitrary power. I say, the administration seems described, and appears to have many of the features, and much of the temper and character of the image of the beast which the apostle represents, which had two horns like a lamb, and spoke as a dragon. And the language of our pusillanimous foes, and even their adherents amongst us, seems plainly predicted, Rev. xiii. 4[:] "Who is like unto the beast? Who is able to make war with him[?]"

2. From what has been said, we see reason gratefully to acknowledge and adore the kind, watchful providence of God, in preserving his church, the woman and her seed, amidst the storms and tempests, the commotions and convulsions that have been occasioned by the oppressive tyrannical powers of the earth. The great dragon, her formidable enemy, notwithstanding his mighty strength and power, cruelty and rage, has always been overcome by the blood of the Lamb, and by the word of their testimony, in all her wars and conflicts with him; which, instead of answering his design to crush and destroy her, have ever been over-ruled by her all-wise benevolent king, to promote her growth and advancement in the world. The church, though often surrounded by the flames of persecution, like the burning bush which Moses beheld as a type and emblem of it, yet has never been consumed. The gates of death and hell have never prevailed against her. Christ has been with her from the beginning, agreeable to his divine promise; and will so continue to the end of the world. The blood of the saints and martyrs that has been shed, and flowed down like rivers and seas, has been like seed planted for the church, and made it spread thro' a wider compass, and grow faster in the world. All the combined policy of earth and hell has not been able to overthrow and demolish this building of God, who has established it, and will preserve it by his almighty power, till all the purposes of his redeeming love and grace are accomplished in the complete salvation of his chosen ones. It must be confessed, that the trials, afflictions and distresses of the church have been very great; but these have been as a purifying furnace, to cleanse her from dross and corruption, and to make her shine brighter in all the graces and virtues of Christianity. Her enemies and adversaries, in all their furious attacks and malicious encounters, have never gained any considerable and lasting advantage to themselves; but generally have come off with loss, disappointment and shame; and had their own weapons, and the blows they have struck, retorted back on them, with redoubled force and vengeance. God promises to give power to his faithful witnesses and servants, "And if any man will hurt them, fire proceedeth out of their mouth, and devoureth their enemies. And if any man will hurt them, he must in this manner be killed." Rev. xi. 3, 5. If the enemies of the church, in the wars they set on foot, take any of her members captive, they themselves shall go into captivity; and he that killeth them

with the sword, must be killed with the sword. Agreeable to the great law of retaliation, which is wisely adopted at this day, by the honourable Continental Congress; and the execution of it in full, is warranted and justified by this, and other passages of sacred writ. Those that have undertaken to distress and persecute the woman and her seed, the faithful servants of Christ, have ever found the interprize dangerous and ruinous to themselves. When the wicked persecuting tyrants of the earth, appear to have great power and strength, some of a selfish and timerous turn of mind, may inadvertantly think it safest to pay worship and allegiance to them, and receive their mark, and seek shelter and protection under their wings, from the impending storm: But they are most artfully deluded and mistaken. "The same," says the apostle, Rev. xiv. 10. "shall drink of the wine of the wrath of God, which is poured out without mixture, into the cup of his indignation. And he shall be tormented with fire and brimstone, in the presence of the holy angels, and in the presence of the Lamb; and the smoke of their torment ascendeth up for ever and ever, and they have no rest day nor night."

3. We may, in a peculiar manner, notice the kind dealings of God in his providence towards this branch of his church, that he has planted as a choice vine, in this once howling wilderness. He brought her as on eagles wings from the seat of oppression and persecution, "to her own place," has, of his unmerited grace, bestowed liberties and privileges upon her, beyond what are enjoyed in any other part of the world: He has nourished and protected her from the face of the serpent, and preserved her from being carried away to destruction, when great floods of his wrath and vengeance have been poured forth after her. God has, in this American quarter of the globe, provided for the woman and her seed, a fixed and lasting settlement and habitation, and bestowed it upon her, to be her own property forever.* In this just view of the distinguished favours of heaven toward

*As the church has such a gift and grant of this good land, from that God to whom the earth belongs, and the fulness thereof; the present war set on foot by the British ministry and parliament, against her true and worthy members, the American sons of liberty, to dispossess them hereof, is not only felonious and murderous, as stiled by the noble lord mayor of London, in his excellent speech on this subject; but seems likewise a very bold and daring attack upon the sovereign prerogative of that Being, who is the Great Lord Proprietor of all, to whom vengeance belongeth; who has already inter-

our fathers, and, as their sinful posterity, while on the one hand, we see abundant cause for thanksgiving and praise to our almighty preserver, and most gracious benefactor; we may on the other hand see the greatest reason for the deepest humiliation, repentance, and contrition of heart, for our vile abuse and misimprovement of these privileges and favours. What an amazing low sense have we had, of the worth of the uncommon gifts and bounties of heaven? How awfully have they been slighted and undervalued by us? What astonishing stupidity, ingratitude and unthankfulness has reigned in our hearts? How lukewarm and indifferent have we been, in the most important concerns of religion? How careless and unconcerned about the interest and welfare of the church of Christ? How backward to come into fellowship and communion with her, and to attend the rites and ordinances which distinguish (at least outwardly) God's children from the profane wicked world? How does iniquity abound among us, and the love of many wax cold? How has the gold become dim, the most fine gold changed? What awful backslidings and declensions in this land, once dedicated to the Lord as a mountain of holiness, and an habitation of righteousness, liberty and peace? Surely the great head of the church, who knows our works, must have not a few, but many things against us. We have, in a great measure, lost that lively faith, zeal and brotherly love, so conspicuous in the temper and conduct of our pious fore-fathers, and added such a beauty and lustre to their characters. The true and noble spirit of primitive christianity is scarce to be found among us; have lost our first love, the love of our espousals, and kindness of our youth. Our churches decline in doctrine, worship and discipline; and have had awful schisms and rents made in them. A spirit of contention, division and separation has prevailed to the great wounding of the church, and to the dishonour and shame of

posed in a very signal manner, to display his awful vengeance against this wicked nefarious undertaking, by plunging four thousand of these our malignant foes in the ocean, with an hundred and fifty thousand pounds sterling of their property; by setting fire to two of their ships with lightening from heaven; and by a late very sweeping storm on the coasts of Great-Britain, to an immense destruction of both men and shipping; by which, and other remarkable providences in our favour, we have incontestible evidence, that God Almighty, with all the powers of heaven, are on our side. Great numbers of angels, no doubt, are encamping round our coast, for our defence and protection. Michael stands ready; with all the artillery of heaven, to encounter the dragon, and to vanquish this black host.

all the promoters and abettors thereof. How have the prophets, the faithful witnesses of Christ, been despised and treated with contempt; while prophesying in sackcloth; and the woman, the true church, in her plain dress of gospel purity and simplicity, been ridiculed, and thought to have no beauty or comeliness in her? How eager have many been, in their attention to lying deceivers, the frogs that have issued out of the mouth of the false prophet; and charmed and captivated with their croaking noise, full of discord and confusion? How has the beauty of this pleasant land of Immanuel been defaced, and its glory spoiled by the little foxes treading down our tender vines; and by the inroads of the wild boar of the wilderness? These things are justly matter of deep and serious lamentation, as they are doubtless the causes of the present calamities and judgments with which we are visited.

4. As there still remains among us, a godly remnant that have not apostatized from God, nor departed from the faith of the gospel; and as these prophecies on which we have been treating, will, many of them, most probably have their fulfilment in this land; there are yet solid grounds of hope and encouragement for us, in this dark and gloomy day. Tho' we may, in God's righteous providence, be sorely rebuked and chastised for our woful apostacies, declensions and backslidings; yet we have, I think, good reason to believe, from the prophecies, so far as we are able to understand them, and from the general plan of God's providence, so far as opened to view, in past and present dispensations of it, that we shall not be wholly given up to desolation and ruin. It is not likely nor probable, that God will revoke the grant he has made of this land to his church. His gifts as well as calling are without repentance. It does not appear probable, that a persecuting, oppressive and tyrannical power, will ever be permitted to rear up its head and horns in it, notwithstanding its present violent assaults and struggles. Liberty has been planted here; and the more it is attacked, the more it grows and flourishes. The time is coming and hastening on, when Babylon the great shall fall to rise no more; when all wicked tyrants and oppressors shall be destroyed for ever. These violent attacks upon the woman in the wilderness, may possibly be some of the last efforts, and dying struggles of the man of sin. These commotions and convulsions in the British empire, may be leading to the fulfilment of such prophecies as relate to his downfal

and overthrow, and to the future glory and prosperity of Christ's church. It will soon be said and acknowledged, that the kingdoms of this world, are become the kingdoms of our Lord, and of his Christ. The vials of God's wrath begin to be poured out on his enemies and adversaries; and there is falling on them a noisome and grievous sore. And to such as have shed the blood of saints and prophets, to them, blood will be given to drink; for they are worthy. And they will gnaw their tongues of falsehood and deceit, for pain; and have the cup of the wine of the fierceness of her wrath; and be rewarded double. The Lamb shall overcome them, for he is Lord of Lords, and King of Kings; and they that are with him, are called, and chosen, and faithful. May the Lord shorten the days of tribulation, and appear in his glory, to build up Zion; that his knowledge might cover the earth, as the waters do the seas; that wars and tumults may cease thro' the world, and the wolf and the lamb lie down together, and nothing hurt or destroy throughout his holy mountain.

AMEN

APPENDIX

BY ANOTHER HAND

In the thirteenth chapter of Revelation, the apostle saw in vision, two beasts coming up; which, as far as I am acquainted, expositors have generally explained as a two-fold figurative representation of the same event. But to me it appears, that as the beasts were very diverse, the one from the other; so very different events were figured out by them. It is said, verse 1[:] "And I stood upon the sand of the sea, and saw a beast rise up out of the sea," i.e. out of the church, "having seven heads, and ten horns," &c. And in the 11th verse, it is said, "And I beheld another beast coming up out of the earth," i.e. of an earthly extract, springing up from very terrene, sensual motives, "and he had two horns like a lamb, and he spake as a dragon." This first beast here described, has been well explained by expositors, and applied to the man of sin, to the rise and establishment of popery. But this second beast, with equal justice and propriety, may be considered as figurative of, and fulfilled in what is called, King Henry's reformation. Every one that is acquainted with the personal character of that prince, cannot but be sensible, that the motives by which he was influenced to separate from the church of Rome, were of a very terrene, sensual, earthly nature; fitly described by the beast's coming up out of the earth. "And he had two horns," civil and ecclesiastical power, "like a lamb," with a more mild, benign and favourable aspect on the church, than the first beast. King Henry, when he broke with the pope, assumed the chief and supreme authority in the British church, as well as nation; here decyphered by the "two horns." And "he spake as a dragon." Witness, the many hot and cruel persecutions that have been carried on in the kingdom, since the reformation, to the destruction of multitudes of the faithful servants of Jesus Christ. Altho' Henry assumed headship in the church as well as state; yet it was a work of time to get himself acknowledged and established in that character; in the accomplishment of which, he may be said, "To do great wonders," &c. Verse 13, 14. "Saying to them that dwell on the earth, that they should make an image to the beast, which had the wound by a sword, and did live," i.e. the first beast, the pope.

The apostle Paul, prophesied of the man of sin, 2 Thess. ii. 4. and describes him as one, "Who opposeth and exalteth himself above all that is called God, or is worshipped; so that he as God sitteth in the temple of God, shewing himself that he is God." Claiming to be the head of the church, and assuming supreme, sovereign, absolute authority in it, is here pointed out as the grand, peculiar, and distinguishing mark and character of the man of sin; most clearly and plainly fulfilled in the pope. Consequently, headship and supremacy in the church, must be the peculiar and distinguishing features of this image of the first beast, which the second beast required to be made. And what can be a more clear, plain and express fulfilment of this prophecy, than that supremacy in the church, given to our kings, ever since the reformation, by the British ecclesiastical constitution? Where can we find any thing in all history, that bids so fair for an accomplishment of this emblematical prediction, in the rising of the second beast? Nothing but a fond partiality, of applying every thing that is bad, to the pope, can, I conceive, prevent our embracing this application of the prophecy.

"Let not those who are friends to the episcopal form of church government, look upon themselves pointed at, by any thing I have here said. For real episcopacy does not imply an alliance between church and state; nor necessarily require an earthly head to the church; much less to invest the king with that character, as every one must acknowledge who will plead for episcopacy as the primitive form of the church, set up by the apostles. Because all the kings of the earth, in their day, and for many years after, were so far from being esteemed heads to the church, that they were not so much as members in it."

The time prefixed for the continuance of the first beast, is "forty and two months." See verse 5. But the number of the second beast is mentioned in the 18th verse. "Here is wisdom. Let him that hath understanding count the number of the beast: For it is the number of a man, and his number is six hundred threescore and six." Expositors have, many of them, supposed that this number intended the period from the time the apostle's receiving this vision, to the rising of the first beast. But as this is the number of the second beast, if it be applied in such a manner, it must be taken for that period between the rise of the first, and of the second beast. But as the continuance of the first beast was limited to forty two prophetic months, or a thousand two hundred and seventy seven years; so this number six hundred sixty six, may denote the duration of the second beast.

THE END

17

THE DOMINION OF PROVIDENCE OVER THE PASSIONS OF MEN

John Witherspoon

PRINCETON

1776

JOHN WITHERSPOON (1723–1794). Born in Scotland and educated at Edinburgh, Witherspoon came to America in 1768 to be president of the College of New Jersey (Princeton), a position he held until 1792, when blindness forced his retirement. He had led the Popular Party among Scottish Presbyterians before his emigration, and he was prominent among ecclesiastical leaders in America. In the pre-Revolutionary years, the college at Princeton prospered under Witherspoon; with the Scotch-Irish influx into America, the Presbyterian church enjoyed great popularity and prosperity in the country, especially in the middle Atlantic colonies and on the frontier, where by 1776 there were many ministers who had been Witherspoon's students. He closed the schism among the Presbyterians, and he made alliance with Ezra Stiles (president of Yale) to forge strong ties with the Congregationalists of New England as the Revolution bore down on the country. With Stiles he shared a distaste for the New Divinity and revivalism generally. He introduced into American thought the Scottish Common Sense philosophy of Thomas Reid and Dugald Stewart, which dominated the young nation's thought for a century.

Because Witherspoon had been captured and imprisoned in Scotland during the Highlander uprising in 1745–46, his critics called him a Jacobite. Witherspoon eschewed politics in America until 1774, but after that he steadily participated, directly and indirectly, in the leading events of the day. In 1776 he was elected to the Continental Congress in time to urge adoption of the Declaration of Independence and to be the only clergyman to sign it. To the assertion that America was not ripe for independence he retorted: "In my judgment, sir, we are not only ripe, but rotting."

Witherspoon served intermittently in Congress until 1782 and was a member of over a hundred legislative committees, including two vital standing committees, the Board of War and the Committee on Foreign Affairs. In the latter role, he took a leading part in drawing up the instructions for the American peace commissioners who concluded the Treaty of Paris, which ended the war in September 1783. He later served in the New Jersey legislature and was a member of that state's ratifying convention for the Constitution in 1787.

Witherspoon has been called the most influential professor in American history, not only because of his powerful writing and speaking style—and he was carefully attended to on all subjects, both

The Dominion of Providence over the Passions of Men.

A

SERMON

PREACHED

AT PRINCETON,

On the 17th of MAY, 1776.

BEING

The GENERAL FAST appointed by the CONGRESS through the UNITED COLONIES.

TO WHICH IS ADDED,

An ADDRESS to the NATIVES of SCOTLAND residing in AMERICA.

BY *JOHN WITHERSPOON*, D. D.

PRESIDENT OF THE COLLEGE OF NEW-JERSEY.

PHILADELPHIA:

PRINTED AND SOLD BY R. AITKEN, PRINTER AND BOOKSELLER, OPPOSITE THE LONDON COFFEE-HOUSE, FRONT-STREET.

M.DCC.LXXVI.

here and abroad—but also because of his long tenure at Princeton. His teaching and the reforms he made there radiated his influence across the country. He trained not only a substantial segment of the leadership among Presbyterians but a number of political leaders as well. Nine of the fifty-five participants in the Federal Convention in 1787 were Princeton graduates, chief among them James Madison (who, among other things, spent an extra year studying Hebrew and philosophy with Witherspoon after his graduation in 1771). Moreover, his pupils included a president and a vice-president of the United States, twenty-one senators, twenty-nine representatives, fifty-six state legislators, and thirty-three judges, three of whom were appointed to the Supreme Court. During the Revolution, his pupils were everywhere in positions of command in the American forces.

Witherspoon's *The Dominion of Providence Over the Passions of Men* caused a great stir when it was first preached in Princeton and published in Philadelphia in 1776, about a month before he was elected to the Continental Congress on June 22. He reminds his auditors that the sermon is his first address on political matters from the pulpit: ministers of the Gospel have more important business to attend to than secular crises, but, of course, liberty is more than a merely secular matter.

Surely the Wrath of Man shall praise thee; the remainder of Wrath shalt thou restrain.

Psalm LXXVI. 10.

here is not a greater evidence either of the reality or the power of religion, than a firm belief of God's universal presence, and a constant attention to the influence and operation of his providence. It is by this means that the Christian may be said, in the emphatical scripture language, "to walk with God, and to endure as seeing him who is invisible."

The doctrine of divine providence is very full and complete in the sacred oracles. It extends not only to things which we may think of great moment, and therefore worthy of notice, but to things the most indifferent and inconsiderable; "Are not two sparrows sold for a farthing," says our Lord, "and one of them falleth not to the ground without your heavenly Father"; nay, "the very hairs of your head are all numbered.[''] It extends not only to things beneficial and salutary, or to the direction and assistance of those who are the servants of the living God; but to things seemingly most hurtful and destructive, and to persons the most refractory and disobedient. He overrules all his creatures, and all their actions. Thus we are told, that "fire, hail, snow, vapour, and stormy wind, fulfil his word," in the course of nature; and even so the most impetuous and disorderly passions of men, that are under no restraint from themselves, are yet perfectly subject to the dominion of Jehovah. They carry his commission, they obey his orders, they are limited and restrained by his authority, and they conspire with every thing else in promoting his glory. There is the greater need to take notice of this, that men are not generally sufficiently aware of the distinction between the law of God and his purpose; they are apt to suppose, that as the temper of the sinner is contrary to the one, so the outrages of the sinner are able to defeat the other; than which nothing can be more false. The truth is plainly asserted, and nobly expressed by the psalmist in the text, "Surely the wrath of man shall praise thee; the remainder of wrath shalt thou restrain."

This psalm was evidently composed as a song of praise for some signal victory obtained, which was at the same time a remarkable deliverance from threatening danger. The author was one or other of the later prophets, and the occasion probably the unsuccessful assault of Jerusalem, by the army of Sennacherib king of Assyria, in the days of Hezekiah. Great was the insolence and boasting of his generals and servants against the city of the living God, as may be seen in the thirty-sixth chapter of Isaiah. Yet it pleased God to destroy their enemies, and, by his own immediate interposition, to grant them deliverance. Therefore the Psalmist says in the fifth and sixth verses of this psalm, "The stout-hearted are spoiled, they have slept their sleep. None of the men of might have found their hands. At thy rebuke, O God of Jacob! both the chariot and the horse are cast into a deep sleep." After a few more remarks to the same purpose, he draws the inference, or makes the reflection in the text, "Surely the wrath of man shall praise thee; the remainder of wrath shalt thou restrain["]: which may be paraphrased thus, The fury and injustice of oppressors shall bring in a tribute of praise to thee; the influence of thy righteous providence shall be clearly discerned; the countenance and support thou wilt give to thine own people shall be gloriously illustrated; thou shalt set the bounds which the boldest cannot pass.

I am sensible, my brethren, that the time and occasion of this psalm, may seem to be in one respect ill suited to the interesting circumstances of this country at present. It was composed after the victory was obtained; whereas we are now but putting on the harness and entering upon an important contest, the length of which it is impossible to foresee, and the issue of which it will perhaps be thought presumption to foretell. But as the truth, with respect to God's moral government, is the same and unchangeable; as the issue, in the case of Sennacherib's invasion, did but lead the prophet to acknowledge it; our duty and interest conspire in calling upon us to improve it. And I have chosen to insist upon it on this day of solemn humiliation, as it will probably help us to a clear and explicit view of what should be the chief subject of our prayers and endeavors, as well as the great object of our hope and trust, in our present situation.

The truth, then, asserted in this text, which I propose to illustrate and improve, is, That all the disorderly passions of men, whether exposing the innocent to private injury, or whether they are the arrows of divine judgment in public calamity, shall, in the end, be to the praise of God: Or, to apply it more particularly to the present state of the American colonies, and the plague of war, The ambition of mistaken princes, the cunning and cruelty of oppressive and corrupt ministers, and even the inhumanity of brutal soldiers, however dreadful, shall finally promote the glory of God, and in the mean time, while the storm continues, his mercy and kindness shall appear in prescribing bounds to their rage and fury.

In discoursing on this subject, it is my intention, through the assistance of divine grace,

I. To point out to you in some particulars, how the wrath of man praises God.

II. To apply these principles to our present situation, by inferences of truth for your instruction and comfort, and by suitable exhortations to duty in the important crisis.

In the first place, I am to point out to you in some particulars, how the wrath of man praises God. I say in some instances, because it is far from being in my power, either to mention or explain the whole. There is an unsearchable depth in the divine counsels, which it is impossible for us to penetrate. It is the duty of every good man to place the most unlimited confidence in divine wisdom, and to believe that those measures of providence that are most unintelligible to him, are yet planned with the same skill, and directed to the same great purposes as others, the reason and tendency of which he can explain in the clearest manner. But where revelation and experience enables us to discover the wisdom, equity, or mercy of divine providence, nothing can be more delightful or profitable to a serious mind, and therefore I beg your attention to the following remarks.

In the first place, the wrath of man praises God, as it is an example and illustration of divine truth, and clearly points out the corruption of our nature, which is the foundation stone of the doctrine of redemption. Nothing can be more absolutely necessary to true religion, than a clear and full conviction of the sinfulness of our nature and state. Without this there can be neither repentance in the sinner, nor humility in the believer. Without this all that is said in scripture of the wisdom and mercy of God in providing a Saviour, is without force and without meaning. Justly does our Saviour say, "The whole have no need of a physician, but those that are sick. I came not to call the righteous, but sinners to repentance." Those who are not sensible that they are sinners, will treat every exhortation to repentance, and every offer of mercy, with disdain or defiance.

But where can we have a more affecting view of the corruption of our nature, than in the wrath of man, when exerting itself in oppression, cruelty and blood? It must be owned, indeed, that this truth is abundantly manifest in times of the greatest tranquility. Others may, if they please, treat the corruption of our nature as a chimera: for my part, I see it every where, and I feel it every day. All the disorders in human society, and the greatest part even of the unhappiness we are exposed to, arises from the envy, malice, covetousness, and other lusts of man. If we and all about us were just what we ought to be in all respects, we should not need to go any further for heaven, for it would be upon earth. But war and violence present a spectacle still more awful. How affecting is it to think, that the lust of domination should be so violent and universal? That men should so rarely be satisfied with their own possessions and acquisitions, or even with the benefit that would arise from mutual service, but should look upon the happiness and tranquility of others, as an obstruction to their own? That, as if the great law of nature, were not enough, "Dust thou art, and to dust thou shalt return," they should be so furiously set for the destruction of each other? It is shocking to think, since the first murder of Abel by his brother Cain, what havock has been made of man by man in every age. What is it that fills the pages of history, but the wars and contentions of princes and empires? What vast numbers has lawless ambition brought into the field, and delivered as a prey to the destructive sword?

If we dwell a little upon the circumstances, they become deeply affecting. The mother bears a child with pain, rears him by the laborious attendance of many years; yet in the prime of life, in the vigor of health, and bloom of beauty, in a moment he is cut down by the dreadful instruments of death. "Every battle of the warrior is with confused noise, and garments rolled in blood"; but the horror of the scene is not confined to the field of slaughter. Few go there unrelated, or fall unlamented; in every hostile encounter, what must be the impression upon the relations of the deceased? The bodies of the dead can only be seen, or the cries of the dying heard for a single day, but many days shall not put an end to the mourning of a parent for a beloved son, the joy and support of his age, or of the widow and helpless offspring, for a father taken away in the fullness of health and vigor.

But if this may be justly said of all wars between man and man, what shall we be able to say that is suitable to the abhorred scene of civil war between citizen and citizen? How deeply affecting is it, that those who are the same in complexion, the same in blood, in language, and in religion, should, notwithstanding, butcher one another with unrelenting rage, and glory in the deed? That men should lay waste the fields of their fellow subjects, with whose provision they themselves had been often fed, and consume with devouring fire those houses in which they had often found a hospitable shelter.

These things are apt to overcome a weak mind with fear, or overwhelm it with sorrow, and in the greatest number are apt to excite the highest indignation, and kindle up a spirit of revenge. If this last has no other tendency than to direct and invigorate the measures of self-defence, I do not take upon me to blame it, on the contrary, I call it necessary and laudable.

But what I mean at this time to prove by the preceding reflections, and wish to impress on your minds, is the depravity of our nature. James iv. I. "From whence come wars and fighting among you? come they not hence even from your lusts that war in your members?" Men of lax and corrupt principles, take great delight in speaking to the praise of human nature, and extolling its dignity, without distinguishing what it was, at its first creation, from what it is in its present fallen state. These fine speculations are very grateful to a worldly mind. They are also much more pernicious to uncautious and unthinking youth, than even the temptations to a dissolute and sensual life, against which they are fortified by the dictates of natural conscience, and a sense of public shame. But I appeal from these visionary reasonings to the history of all ages, and the inflexible testimony of daily experience. These will tell us what men have been in their practice, and from thence you may judge what they are by nature, while unrenewed. If I am not mistaken, a cool and candid attention, either to the past history, or present state of the world, but above all, to the ravages of lawless power, ought to humble us in the dust. It should at once lead us to acknowlege the just view given us in scripture of our lost state; to desire the happy influence of renewing grace each for ourselves; and to long for the dominion of righteousness and peace, when "men shall beat their swords into plow-shares, and their spears into pruning hooks; when nation shall not lift up sword against nation, neither shall they learn war any more."* Mic iv. 3.

2. The wrath of man praiseth God, as it is the instrument in his hand for bringing sinners to repentance, and for the correction and improvement of his own children. Whatever be the nature of the affliction with which he visits either persons, families, or nations; whatever be the disposition or intention of those whose malice he employs as a scourge; the design on his part is, to rebuke men for iniquity, to bring them to repentance, and to promote their holiness and peace. The salutary nature and sanctifying influence of affliction in general, is often taken notice of in scripture, both as making a part of the purpose of God, and the experience of his saints. Heb. xii. 11. "Now, no affliction for the present seemeth to be joyous, but grievous: Nevertheless, afterwards it yieldeth the peaceable fruit of righteousness unto them which are exercised thereby." But what we are particularly led to observe by the subject of this discourse is, that the wrath of man, or the violence of the oppressor that praiseth God in

* I cannot help embracing this opportunity of making a remark or two upon a virulent reflection thrown out against this doctrine, in a well known pamphlet, *Common Sense*. The author of that work expresses himself thus: "If the first king of any country was by election, that likewise establishes a precedent for the next; for to say, that the right of all future generations is taken away, by the act of the first electors, in their choice not only of a king, but of a family of kings forever, hath no parallel in or out of scripture, but the doctrine of original sin, which supposes the free will of all men lost in Adam; and from such comparison, and it will admit of no other, hereditary succession can derive no glory. For as in Adam all sinned, and as in the first electors all men obeyed: as in the one all mankind were subjected to Satan, and in the other to sovereignty; as our innocence was lost in the first, and our authority in the last; and as both disable us from re-assuming some former state and privilege, it unanswerably follows that original sin and hereditary succession are parallels. Dishonorable rank! Inglorious connexion! Yet the most subtle sophist cannot produce a juster simile."† Without the shadow of reasoning, he is pleased to represent the doctrine of original sin as an object of contempt or abhorrence. I beg leave to demur a little to the candor, the prudence, and the justice of this proceeding.

1. Was it modest or candid for a person without name or character, to talk in this supercilious manner of a doctrine that has been espoused and defended by many of the greatest and best men that the world ever saw, and makes an essential part of the established creeds and confessions of all the Protestant churches without exception? I

† *Common Sense, page 11. Bradford's Edition.*

this respect, it has a peculiar tendency to alarm the secure conscience, to convince and humble the obstinate sinner. This is plain from the nature of the thing, and from the testimony of experience. Public calamities, particularly the destroying sword, is so awful that it cannot but have a powerful influence in leading men to consider the presence and the power of God. It threatens them not only in themselves, but touches them in all that is dear to them, whether relations or possessions. The prophet Isaiah says, Is. xxvi. 8, 9. "Yea, in the way of thy judgments, O Lord, have we waited for thee,—for when thy judgments are in the earth, the inhabitants of the world will learn righteousness." He considers it as the most powerful mean of alarming the secure and subduing the obstinate. Is. xxvi. 11. "Lord when thy hand is lifted up, they will not see, but they shall see and be ashamed for their envy at the people, yea the fire of thine enemies shall devour them." It is also sometimes represented as a symptom of a hopeless and irrecoverable state, when public judgments have no effect. Thus says the prophet Jeremiah, Jer. v. 3. "O Lord, are not thine eyes upon the truth? thou hast stricken them, but they have not grieved; thou hast consumed them, but they have refused to receive correction: they have made their faces harder than a rock, they have refused

thought the grand modern plea had been freedom of sentiment, and charitable thoughts of one another. Are so many of us, then, beyond the reach of this gentleman's charity? I do assure him that such presumption and self-confidence are no recommendation to me, either of his character or sentiments.

2. Was it prudent, when he was pleading a public cause, to speak in such approbious terms of a doctrine, which he knew, or ought to have known, was believed and professed by, I suppose, a great majority of very different denominations. Is this gentleman ignorant of human nature, as well as an enemy to the Christian faith? Are men so little tenacious of their religious sentiments, whether true or false? The prophet thought otherwise, who said, *Hath a nation changed their gods which yet are no gods?* Was it the way to obtain the favor of the public, to despise what they hold sacred? Or shall we suppose this author so astonishingly ignorant, as to think that all men now, whose favor is worth asking, have given up the doctrine of the New Testament? If he does, he is greatly mistaken.

3. In fine, I ask, where was the justice of this proceeding? Is there so little to be said for the doctrine of original sin, that it is not to be refuted, but despised? Is the state of the world such, as to render this doctrine not only false, but incredible? Has the fruit been of such a quality as to exclude all doubts of the goodness of the tree? On the contrary, I cannot help being of opinion, that such has been the visible state of the world in every age, as cannot be accounted for on any other principles than what we learn from the word of God, that *the imagination of the heart of man is only evil from his youth, and that continually*. Gen. vi. 5.–viii. 21.

to return." We can easily see in the history of the children of Israel, how severe strokes brought them to submission and penitence, Ps. lxxviii. 34, 35. "When he slew them, then they sought him, and they returned and inquired early after God, and they remembered that God was their rock, and the high God their redeemer."

Both nations in general, and private persons, are apt to grow remiss and lax in a time of prosperity and seeming security; but when their earthly comforts are endangered or withdrawn, it lays them under a kind of necessity to seek for something better in their place. Men must have comfort from one quarter or another. When earthly things are in a pleasing and promising condition, too many are apt to find their rest, and be satisfied with them as their only portion. But when the vanity and passing nature of all created comfort is discovered, they are compelled to look for something more durable as well as valuable. What therefore, can be more to the praise of God, than that when a whole people have forgotten their resting place, when they have abused their privileges, and despised their mercies, they should by distress and suffering be made to hearken to the rod, and return to their duty?

There is an inexpressible depth and variety in the judgments of God, as in all his other works; but we may lay down this as a certain principle, that if there were no sin, there could be no suffering. Therefore they are certainly for the correction of sin, or for the trial, illustration, and perfecting of the grace and virtue of his own people. We are not to suppose, that those who suffer most, or who suffer soonest, are therefore more criminal than others. Our Saviour himself thought it necessary to give a caution against this rash conclusion, as we are informed by the evangelist Luke, Luke xiii. 1. "There were present at that season some that told him of the Galileans, whose blood Pilate had mingled with their sacrifices. And Jesus answering said unto them, Suppose ye that these Galileans were sinners above all the Galileans, because they suffered such things? I tell you nay, but except ye repent, ye shall all likewise perish." I suppose we may say with sufficient warrant, that it often happens, that those for whom God hath designs of the greatest mercy, are first brought to the trial, that they may enjoy in due time the salutary effect of the unpalatable medicine.

I must also take leave to observe, and I hope no pious humble sufferer will be unwilling to make the application, that there is often a discernible mixture of sovereignty and righteousness in providential dispensations. It is the prerogative of God to do what he will with his own, but he often displays his justice itself, by throwing into the furnace those, who though they may not be visibly worse than others, may yet have more to answer for, as having been favored with more distinguished privileges, both civil and sacred. It is impossible for us to make a just and full comparison of the character either of persons or nations, and it would be extremely foolish for any to attempt it, either for increasing their own security, or impeaching the justice of the Supreme Ruler. Let us therefore neither forget the truth, nor go beyond it. "His mercy fills the earth." He is also "known by the judgment which he executeth." The wrath of man in its most tempestuous rage, fulfills his will, and finally promotes the good of his chosen.

3. The wrath of man praiseth God, as he sets bounds to it, or restrains it by his providence, and sometimes makes it evidently a mean of promoting and illustrating his glory.

There is no part of divine providence in which a greater beauty and majesty appears, than when the Almighty Ruler turns the counsels of wicked men into confusion, and makes them militate against themselves. If the psalmist may be thought to have had a view in this text to the truths illustrated in the two former observations, there is no doubt at all that he had a particular view to this, as he says in the latter part of the verse, "the remainder of wrath shalt thou restrain." The scripture abounds with instances, in which the designs of oppressors were either wholly disappointed, or in execution fell far short of the malice of their intention, and in some they turned out to the honor and happiness of the persons or the people, whom they were intended to destroy. We have an instance of the first of these in the history to which my text relates.* We have also an instance in Esther, in which the most mischievous designs of Haman, the son of Hammedatha the Agagite against Mordecai the Jew, and the nation from which he sprung, turned out at last to his own destruction, the honor of Mordecai, and the salvation and peace of his people.

* The matter is fully stated and reasoned upon by the prophet Isaiah ch. x. from the 5th to the 19th verse.

From the New Testament I will make choice of that memorable event on which the salvation of believers in every age rests as its foundation, the death and sufferings of the Son of God. This the great adversary and all his agents and instruments prosecuted with unrelenting rage. When they had blackened him with slander, when they scourged him with shame, when they had condemned him in judgment, and nailed him to the cross, how could they help esteeming their victory complete? But oh the unsearchable wisdom of God! they were but perfecting the great design laid for the salvation of sinners. Our blessed Redeemer by his death finished his work, overcame principalities and powers, and made a shew of them openly, triumphing over them in his cross. With how much justice do the apostles and their company offer this doxology to God, "They lift up their voice with one accord, and said, Lord thou art God which hast made heaven and earth, and the sea, and all that in them is; Who by the mouth of thy servant David hast said, Why did the Heathen rage, and the people imagine vain things? The kings of the earth stood up, and the rulers were gathered together against the Lord, and against his Christ. For of a truth, against thy holy child Jesus, whom thou hast anointed, both Herod and Pontius Pilate, with the Gentiles, and the people of Israel were gathered together, for to do whatsoever thy hand and thy counsel determined before to be done." Acts iv. 24. 28.

In all after ages, in conformity to this, the deepest laid contrivances of the prince of darkness, have turned out to the confusion of their author; and I know not, but considering his malice and pride, this perpetual disappointment, and the superiority of divine wisdom, may be one great source of his suffering and torment. The cross hath still been the banner of truth, under which it hath been carried through the world. Persecution has been but as the furnace to the gold, to purge it of its dross, to manifest its purity, and increase its lustre. It was taken notice of very early, that the blood of the martyrs was the seed of christianity; the more abundantly it was shed, the more plentifully did the harvest grow.

So certain has this appeared, that the most violent infidels, both of early and later ages, have endeavored to account for it, and have observed that there is a spirit of obstinacy in man which inclines him to resist violence, and that severity doth but increase opposition, be the cause what it will. They suppose that persecution is equally proper to propagate truth and error. This though in part true, will by no means generally hold. Such an apprehension, however, gave occasion to a glorious triumph of divine providence of an opposite kind, which I must shortly relate to you. One of the Roman emperors, Julian, surnamed the apostate, perceiving how impossible it was to suppress the gospel by violence, endeavored to extinguish it by neglect and scorn. He left the Christians unmolested for sometime, but gave all manner of encouragement to those of opposite principles, and particularly to the Jews, out of hatred to the Christians; and that he might bring public disgrace upon the Galileans, as he affected to stile them, he encouraged the Jews to rebuild the temple of Jerusalem, and visibly refute the prophecy of Christ, that it should lie under perpetual desolation. But this profane attempt was so signally frustrated, that it served, as much as any one circumstance, to spread the glory of our Redeemer, and establish the faith of his saints. It is affirmed by some ancient authors, particularly by Ammianus Marcellinus, a heathen historian, that fire came out of the earth and consumed the workmen when laying the foundation. But in whatever way it was prevented, it is beyond all controversy, from the concurring testimony of heathens and Christians, that little or no progress was ever made in it, and that in a short time, it was entirely defeated.

It is proper here to observe, that at the time of the reformation, when religion began to revive, nothing contributed more to facilitate its reception and increase its progress than the violence of its persecutors. Their cruelty and the patience of the sufferers, naturally disposed men to examine and weigh the cause to which they adhered with so much constancy and resolution. At the same time also, when they were persecuted in one city, they fled to another, and carried the discoveries of popish fraud to every part of the world. It was by some of those who were persecuted in Germany, that the light of the reformation was brought so early into Britain.

The power of divine providence appears with the most distinguished lustre, when small and inconsiderable circumstances, and sometimes, the weather and seasons, have defeated the most formidable armaments, and frustrated the best concerted expeditions. Near two hundred years ago, the monarchy of Spain was in the height of its power and glory, and determined to crush the interest of the reformation. They sent out a powerful armament against Britain, giving it ostentatiously, and in my opinion profanely, the name of the Invincible Armada. But it pleased God so entirely to discomfit it by tempests, that a small part of it returned home, though no British force had been opposed to it at all.

We have a remarkable instance of the influence of small circumstances in providence in the English history. The two most remarkable persons in the civil wars, had earnestly desired to withdraw themselves from the contentions of the times, Mr. Hampden and Oliver Cromwell. They had actually taken their passage in a ship for New England, when by an arbitrary order of council they were compelled to remain at home. The consequence of this was, that one of them was the soul of the republican opposition to monarchical usurpation during the civil wars, and the other in the course of that contest, was the great instrument in bringing the tyrant to the block.

The only other historical remark I am to make, is, that the violent persecution which many eminent Christians met with in England from their brethren, who called themselves Protestants, drove them in great numbers to a distant part of the world, where the light of the gospel and true religion were unknown. Some of the American settlements, particularly those in New-England, were chiefly made by them; and as they carried the knowledge of Christ to the dark places of the earth, so they continue themselves in as great a degree of purity, of faith, and strictness of practice, or rather a greater, than is to be found in any protestant church now in the world. Does not the wrath of man in this instance praise God? Was not the accuser of the brethren, who stirs up their enemies, thus taken in his own craftiness, and his kingdom shaken by the very means which he employed to establish it.*

II. Proceed now to the second general head, which was to apply the principles illustrated above to our present situation, by inferences of truth for your instruction and comfort, and by suitable exhortations to duty in this important crisis. And,

* Lest this should be thought a temporising compliment to the people of New-England, who have been the first sufferers in the present contest, and have set so noble an example of invincible fortitude, in withstanding the violence of oppression, I think it proper to observe that the whole paragraph is copied from a sermon on Psal. lxxiv. 22. prepared and preached in Scotland, in the month of August, 1758.

In the first place, I would take the opportunity on this occasion, and from this subject, to press every hearer to a sincere concern for his own soul's salvation. There are times when the mind may be expected to be more awake to divine truth, and the conscience more open to the arrows of conviction, than at others. A season of public judgment is of this kind, as appears from what has been already said. That curiosity and attention at least are raised in some degree, is plain from the unusual throng of this assembly. Can you have a clearer view of the sinfulness of your nature, than when the rod of the oppressor is lifted up, and when you see men putting on the habit of the warrior, and collecting on every hand the weapons of hostility and instruments of death? I do not blame your ardor in preparing for the resolute defence of your temporal rights. But consider I beseech you, the truly infinite importance of the salvation of your souls. Is it of much moment whether you and your children shall be rich or poor, at liberty or in bonds? Is it of much moment whether this beautiful country shall increase in fruitfulness from year to year, being cultivated by active industry, and possessed by independent freemen, or the scanty produce of the neglected fields shall be eaten up by hungry publicans, while the timid owner trembles at the tax gatherers approach? And is it of less moment my brethren, whether you shall be the heirs of glory or the heirs of hell? Is your state on earth for a few fleeting years of so much moment? And is it of less moment, what shall be your state through endless ages? Have you assembled together willingly to hear what shall be said on public affairs, and to join in imploring the blessing of God on the counsels and arms of the united colonies, and can you be unconcerned, what shall become of you for ever, when all the monuments of human greatness shall be laid in ashes, for "the earth *itself* and all the works that are therein shall be burnt up."

Wherefore my beloved hearers, as the ministry of reconciliation is committed to me, I beseech you in the most earnest manner, to attend to "the things that belong to your peace, before they are hid from your eyes." How soon and in what manner a seal shall be set upon the character and state of every person here present, it is impossible to know; for he who only can know does not think proper to reveal it. But you may rest assured that there is no time more suitable, and there is none so safe, as that which is present, since it is wholly uncertain whether any other shall be your's. Those who shall first fall in battle, have not many more warnings to receive. There are some few daring and hardened sinners who despise eternity itself, and set their Maker at defiance, but the far greater number by staving off their convictions to a more convenient season, have been taken unprepared, and thus eternally lost. I would therefore earnestly press the apostles exhortation, 2 Cor. vi. 1, 2. "We then, as workers together with him, beseech you also, that ye receive not the grace of God in vain: For he saith, I have heard thee in a time accepted, and in the day of salvation have I succoured thee: Behold, now is the accepted time; behold, now is the day of salvation."

Suffer me to beseech you, or rather to give you warning, not to rest satisfied with a form of godliness, denying the power thereof. There can be no true religion, till there be a discovery of your lost state by nature and practice, and an unfeigned acceptance of Christ Jesus, as he is offered in the gospel. Unhappy they who either despise his mercy, or are ashamed of his cross! Believe it, "there is no salvation in any other. There is no other name under heaven given amongst men by which we must be saved." Unless you are united to him by a lively faith, not the resentment of a haughty monarch, but the sword of divine justice hangs over you, and the fulness of divine vengeance shall speedily overtake you. I do not speak this only to the heaven, daring profligate, or grovelling sensualist, but to every insensible secure sinner; to all those, however decent and orderly in their civil deportment, who live to themselves and have their part and portion in this life; in fine to all who are yet in a state of nature, for "except a man be born again, he cannot see the kingdom of God." The fear of man may make you hide your profanity: prudence and experience may make you abhor intemperance and riot; as you advance in life, one vice may supplant another and hold its place; but nothing less than the sovereign grace of God can produce a saving change of heart and temper, or fit you for his immediate presence.

2. From what has been said upon this subject, you may see what ground there is to give praise to God for his favors already bestowed on us, respecting the public cause. It would be a criminal inattention not to observe the singular interposition of Providence hitherto, in behalf of the American colonies. It is however impossible for me, in a single discourse, as well as improper at this time, to go through every

step of our past transactions, I must therefore content myself with a few remarks. How many discoveries have been made of the designs of enemies in Britain and among ourselves, in a manner as unexpected to us as to them, and in such season as to prevent their effect? What surprising success has attended our encounters in almost every instance? Has not the boasted discipline of regular and veteran soldiers been turned into confusion and dismay, before the new and maiden courage of freemen, in defence of their property and right? In what great mercy has blood been spared on the side of this injured country? Some important victories in the south have been gained with so little loss, that enemies will probably think it has been dissembled; as many, even of ourselves thought, till time rendered it undeniable. But these were comparatively of small moment. The signal advantage we have gained by the evacuation of Boston, and the shameful flight of the army and navy of Britain, was brought about without the loss of a man. To all this we may add, that the counsels of our enemies have been visibly confounded, so that I believe that I may say with truth, that there is hardly any step which they have taken, but it has operated strongly against themselves, and been more in our favor, than if they had followed a contrary course.

While we give praise to God the supreme disposer of all events, for his interposition in our behalf, let us guard against the dangerous error of trusting in, or boasting of an arm of flesh. I could earnestly wish, that while our arms are crowned with success, we might content ourselves with a modest ascription of it to the power of the Highest. It has given me great uneasiness to read some ostentatious, vaunting expressions in our news-papers, though happily I think, much restrained of late. Let us not return to them again. If I am not mistaken, not only the holy scriptures in general, and the truths of the glorious gospel in particular, but the whole course of providence, seem intended to abase the pride of man, and lay the vain-glorious in the dust. How many instances does history furnish us with, of those who after exulting over, and despising their enemies, were signally and shamefully defeated.* The truth is, I believe, the remark may be applied universally, and we may say, that through the whole frame of

* There is no story better known in British history, than that the officers of the French army the night preceding the battle of Agincourt, played at dice for English prisoners before they took them, and the next day were taken by them.

nature, and the whole system of human life, that which promises most, performs the least. The flowers of finest colour seldom have the sweetest fragrance. The trees of quickest groweth or fairest form, are seldom of the greatest value or duration. Deep waters move with least noise. Men who think most are seldom talkative. And I think it holds as much in war as in any thing, that every boaster is a coward.

Pardon me, my brethren, for insisting so much upon this, which may seem but an immaterial circumstance. It is in my opinion of very great moment. I look upon ostentation and confidence to be a sort of outrage upon Providence, and when it becomes general, and infuses itself into the spirit of a people, it is a forerunner of destruction. How does Goliath the champion armed in a most formidable manner, express his disdain of David the stripling with his sling and his stone, 1 Sam. xvii. 42, 43, 44, 45. "And when the Philistine looked about and saw David, he disdained him: for he was but a youth, and ruddy, and of a fair countenance. And the Philistine said unto David, Am I a dog, that thou comest to me with staves? And the Philistine cursed David by his gods, and the Philistine said to David, come to me, and I will give thy flesh unto the fowls of the air, and to the beasts of the field." But how just and modest the reply? ["]Then said David to the Philistine, thou comest to me with a sword and with a spear, and with a shield, but I come unto thee in the name of the Lord of hosts, the God of the armies of Israel, whom thou hast defied." I was well pleased with a remark of this kind thirty years ago in a pamphlet,* in which it was observed, that there was a great deal of profane ostentation in the names given to ships of war, as the Victory, the Valient, the Thunderer, the Dreadnought, the Terrible, the Firebrand, the Furnace, the Lightning, the Infernal, and many more of the same kind. This the author considered as a symptom of the national character and manners very unfavorable, and not likely to obtain the blessing of the God of heaven.†

* Britain's Remembrancer.

† I am sensible that one or two of these were ships taken from the French, which brought their names with them. But the greatest number had their names imposed in England, and I cannot help observing, that the Victory, often celebrated as the finest ship ever built in Britain, was lost in the night without a storm, by some unknown accident, and about twelve hundred persons, many of them of the first families in the nation, were buried with it in the deep. I do not mean to infer any thing from this, but, that we ought to live under the practical persuasion of what no man will doctrinal-

3. From what has been said you may learn what encouragement you have to put your trust in God, and hope for his assistance in the present important conflict. He is the Lord of hosts, great in might, and strong in battle. Whoever hath his countenance and approbation, shall have the best at last. I do not mean to speak prophetically, but agreeably to the analogy of faith, and the principles of God's moral government. Some have observed that true religion, and in her train, dominion, riches, literature, and arts, have taken their course in a slow and gradual manner, from east to west, since the earth was settled after the flood, and from thence forebode the future glory of America. I leave this as a matter rather of conjecture than certainty, but observe, that if your cause is just, if your principles are pure, and if your conduct is prudent, you need not fear the multitude of opposing hosts.

If your cause is just—you may look with confidence to the Lord and intreat him to plead it as his own. You are all my witnesses, that this is the first time of my introducing any political subject into the pulpit. At this season however, it is not only lawful but necessary, and I willingly embrace the opportunity of declaring my opinion without any hesitation, that the cause in which America is now in arms, is the cause of justice, of liberty, and of human nature. So far as we have hitherto proceeded, I am satisfied that the confederacy of the colonies, has not been the effect of pride, resentment, or sedition, but of a deep and general conviction, that our civil and religious liberties, and consequently in a great measure the temporal and eternal happiness of us and our posterity, depended on the issue. The knowledge of God and his truths have from the beginning of the world been chiefly, if not entirely, confined to those parts of the earth, where some degree of liberty and political justice were to be seen, and great were the difficulties with which they had to struggle from the imperfection of human society, and the unjust decisions of usurped authority. There is not a single instance in history in which civil liberty was lost, and religious liberty preserved entire. If therefore we yield up our temporal property, we at the same time deliver the conscience into bondage.

ly deny, that there is no warring with the elements, or him who directs their force; that he is able to write disappointment on the wisest human schemes, and by the word of his power to frustrate the efforts of the greatest monarch upon earth.

You shall not, my brethren, hear from me in the pulpit, what you have never heard from me in conversation, I mean railing at the king personally, or even his ministers and the parliament, and people of Britain, as so many barbarous savages. Many of their actions have probably been worse than their intentions. That they should desire unlimited dominion, if they can obtain or preserve it, is neither new nor wonderful. I do not refuse submission to their unjust claims, because they are corrupt or profligate, although probably many of them are so, but because they are men, and therefore liable to all the selfish bias inseparable from human nature. I call this claim unjust, of making laws to bind us in all cases whatsoever, because they are separated from us, independent of us, and have an interest in opposing us. Would any man who could prevent it, give up his estate, person, and family, to the disposal of his neighbour, although he had liberty to chuse the wisest and the best master? Surely not. This is the true and proper hinge of the controversy between Great-Britain and America. It is however to be added, that such is their distance from us, that a wise and prudent administration of our affairs is as impossible as the claim of authority is unjust. Such is and must be their ignorance of the state of things here, so much time must elapse before an error can be seen and remedied, and so much injustice and partiality must be expected from the arts and misrepresentation of interested persons, that for these colonies to depend wholly upon the legislature of Great-Britain, would be like many other oppressive connexions, injury to the master, and ruin to the slave.

The management of the war itself on their part, would furnish new proof of this, if any were needful. Is it not manifest with what absurdity and impropriety they have conducted their own designs? We had nothing so much to fear as dissension, and they have by wanton and unnecessary cruelty forced us into union. At the same time to let us see what we have to expect, and what would be the fatal consequence of unlimited submission, they have uniformly called those acts *lenity*, which filled this whole continent with resentment and horror. The ineffable disdain expressed by our fellow subject, in saying, "That he would not harken to America, till she was at his feet," has armed more men, and inspired more deadly rage, than could have been done by laying waste a whole province with fire and sword. Again we wanted not numbers, but time, and they sent over handful after handful till we were ready to oppose a multitude greater than they have to send. In fine, if there was one place stronger than the rest, and more able and willing to resist, there they made the attack, and left the others till they were duly informed, completely incensed, and fully furnished with every instrument of war.

I mention these things, my brethren, not only as grounds of confidence in God, who can easily overthrow the wisdom of the wise, but as decisive proofs of the impossibility of these great and growing states, being safe and happy when every part of their internal polity is dependant on Great Britain. If, on account of their distance, and ignorance of our situation, they could not conduct their own quarrel with propriety for one year, how can they give direction and vigor to every department of our civil constitutions from age to age? There are fixed bounds to every human thing. When the branches of a tree grow very large and weighty, they fall off from the trunk. The sharpest sword will not pierce when it cannot reach. And there is a certain distance from the seat of government, where an attempt to rule will either produce tyranny and helpless subjection, or provoke resistance and effect a separation.

I have said, if your principles are pure—the meaning of this is, if your present opposition to the claims of the British ministry does not arise from a seditious and turbulent spirit, or a wanton contempt of legal authority; from a blind and factious attachment to particular persons or parties; or from a selfish rapacious disposition, and a desire to turn public confusion to private profit—but from a concern for the interest of your country, and the safety of yourselves and your posterity. On this subject I cannot help observing, that though it would be a miracle if there were not many selfish persons among us, and discoveries now and then made of mean and interested transactions, yet they have been comparatively inconsiderable both in number and effect. In general, there has been so great a degree of public spirit, that we have much more reason to be thankful for its vigor and prevalence, than to wonder at the few appearances of dishonesty or disaffection. It would be very uncandid to ascribe the universal ardor that has prevailed among all ranks of men, and the spirited exertions in the most distant colonies, to any thing else than public spirit. Nor was there ever perhaps in history so general a commotion from which religious differences have been so entirely excluded. Nothing of this kind has as yet been heard, except of late in the absurd, but malicious and detestable attempts of our few remaining enemies to introduce them. At the same time I must also, for the honor of this country observe, that though government in the ancient forms has been so long unhinged, and in some colonies not sufficient care taken to substitute another in its place; yet has there been, by common consent, a much greater degree of order and public peace, than men of reflection and experience foretold or expected. From all these circumstances I conclude favorably of the principles of the friends of liberty, and do earnestly exhort you to adopt and act upon those which have been described, and resist the influence of every other.

Once more, if to the justice of your cause, and the purity of your principles, you add prudence in your conduct, there will be the greatest reason to hope, by the blessing of God, for prosperity and success. By prudence in conducting this important struggle, I have chiefly in view union, firmness, and patience. Every body must perceive the absolute necessity of union. It is indeed in every body's mouth, and therefore instead of attempting to convince you of its importance, I will only caution you against the usual causes of division. If persons of every rank, instead of implicitly complying with the orders of those whom they themselves have chosen to direct, will needs judge every measure over again, when it comes to be put in execution; if different classes of men intermix their little private views, or clashing interest with public affairs, and marshal into parties, the merchant against the landholder, and the landholder against the merchant; if local provincial pride and jealousy arise, and you allow yourselves to speak with contempt of the courage, character, manners, or even language of particular places, you are doing a greater injury to the common cause, than you are aware of. If such practices are admitted among us, I shall look upon it as one of the most dangerous symptoms, and if they become general, a presage of approaching ruin.

By firmness and patience, I mean a resolute adherence to your duty, and laying your account with many difficulties, as well as occasional disappointments. In a former part of this discourse, I have cautioned you against ostentation and vain glory. Be pleased farther to observe that extremes often beget one another, the same persons who exult extravagantly on success, are generally most liable to despondent timidity on every little inconsiderable defeat. Men of this character are the bane and corruption of every society or party to which they belong, but they are especially the ruin of an army, if suffered to continue in it. Remember the vicissitude of human things, and the usual course of providence. How often has a just cause been reduced to the lowest ebb, and yet when firmly adhered to, has become finally triumphant. I speak this now while the affairs of the colonies are in so prosperous a state, lest this propriety itself should render you less able to bear unexpected misfortunes—the sum of the whole is, that the blessing of God is only to be looked for by those who are not wanting in the discharge of their own duty. I would neither have you to trust in an arm of flesh, nor sit with folded hands and expect that miracles should be wrought in your defence—this is a sin which is in scripture stiled tempting God. In opposition to it, I would exhort you as Joab did the host of Israel, who, though he does not appear to have had a spotless character throughout, certainly in this instance spoke like a prudent general and a pious man. 2 Sam. x. 12. "Be of good courage, and let us behave ourselves valiantly for our people and for the cities of our God, and let the Lord do that which is good in his sight."

I shall now conclude this discourse by some exhortations to duty, founded upon the truths which have been illustrated above, and suited to the interesting state of this country at the present time; and,

1. Suffer me to recommend to you an attention to the public interest of religion, or in other words, zeal for the glory of God and the good of others. I have already endeavored to exhort sinners to repentance; what I have here in view is to point out to you the concern which every good man ought to take in the national character and manners, and the means which he ought to use for promoting public virtue, and bearing down impiety and vice. This is a matter of the utmost moment, and which ought to be well understood, both in its nature and principles. Nothing is more certain than that a general profligacy and corruption of manners make a people ripe for destruction. A good form of government may hold the rotten materials together for some time, but beyond a certain pitch, even the best constitution will be ineffectual, and slavery must ensue. On the other hand, when the manners of a nation are pure, when true religion and internal principles maintain their vigour, the attempts of the most

powerful enemies to oppress them are commonly baffled and disappointed. This will be found equally certain, whether we consider the great principles of God's moral government, or the operation and influence of natural causes.

What follows from this? That he is the best friend to American liberty, who is most sincere and active in promoting true and undefiled religion, and who sets himself with the greatest firmness to bear down profanity and immorality of every kind. Whoever is an avowed enemy to God, I scruple not to call him an enemy to his country. Do not suppose, my brethren, that I mean to recommend a furious and angry zeal for the circumstantials of religion, or the contentions of one sect with another about their peculiar distinctions. I do not wish you to oppose any body's religion, but every body's wickedness. Perhaps there are few surer marks of the reality of religion, than when a man feels himself more joined in spirit to a true holy person of a different denomination, than to an irregular liver of his own. It is therefore your duty in this important and critical season to exert yourselves, every one in his proper sphere, to stem the tide of prevailing vice, to promote the knowledge of God, the reverence of his name and worship, and obedience to his laws.

Perhaps you will ask, what it is that you are called to do for this purpose farther than your own personal duty? I answer this itself when taken in its proper extent is not a little. The nature and obligation of visible religion is, I am afraid, little understood and less attended to.

Many from a real or pretended fear of the imputation of hypocrisy, banish from their conversation and carriage every appearance of respect and submission to the living God. What a weakness and meanness of spirit does it discover, for a man to be ashamed in the presence of his fellow sinners, to profess that reverence to almighty God which he inwardly feels: The truth is, he makes himself truly liable to the accusation which he means to avoid. It is as genuine and perhaps a more culpable hypocrisy to appear to have less religion than you really have, than to appear to have more. This false shame is a more extensive evil than is commonly apprehended. We contribute constantly, though insensibly, to form each others character and manners; and therefore, the usefulness of a strictly holy and conscientious deportment is not confined to the possessor, but spreads its happy influence to all that are within its reach. I need scarcely add, that in proportion as men are distinguished by understanding, literature, age, rank, office, wealth, or any other circumstance, their example will be useful on the one hand, or pernicious on the other.

But I cannot content myself with barely recommending a silent example. There is a dignity in virtue which is entitled to authority, and ought to claim it. In many cases it is the duty of a good man, by open reproof and opposition, to wage war with profaneness. There is a scripture precept delivered in very singular terms, to which I beg your attention; "Thou shalt not hate thy brother in thy heart, but shalt in any wise rebuke him, and not suffer sin upon him." How prone are many to represent reproof as flowing from ill nature and surliness of temper? The spirit of God, on the contrary, considers it as the effect of inward hatred, or want of genuine love, to forbear reproof, when it is necessary or may be useful. I am sensible there may in some cases be a restraint from prudence, agreeably to that caution of our Saviour, "Cast not your pearls before swine, lest they trample them under their feet, and turn again and rent you." Of this every man must judge as well as he can for himself; but certainly, either by open reproof, or expressive silence, or speedy departure from such society, we ought to guard against being partakers of other men's sins.

To this let me add, that if all men are bound in some degree, certain classes of men are under peculiar obligations, to the discharge of this duty. Magistrates, ministers, parents, heads of families, and those whom age has rendered venerable, are called to use their authority and influence for the glory of God and the good of others. Bad men themselves discover an inward conviction of this, for they are often liberal in their reproaches of persons of grave characters or religious profession, if they bear with patience the profanity of others. Instead of enlarging on the duty of men in authority in general, I must particularly recommend this matter to those who have the command of soldiers inlisted for the defence of their country. The cause is sacred, and the champions for it ought to be holy. Nothing is more grieving to the heart of a good man, than to hear from those who are going to the field, the horrid sound of cursing and blasphemy; it cools the ardor of his prayers, as well as abates his confidence and hope in God. Many more circumstances affect me in such a case, than I can enlarge upon, or indeed easily enumerate at present; the glory of God, the interest of the deluded sinner, going like a devoted victim, and imprecating vengeance on his own head, as well as the cause itself committed to his care. We have sometimes taken the liberty to forebode the downfall of the British empire, from the corruption and degeneracy of the people. Unhappily the British soldiers have been distinguished among all the nations in Europe, for the most shocking profanity. Shall we then pretend to emulate them in this internal distinction, or rob them of the horrid privilege? God forbid. Let the officers of the army in every degree remember, that as military subjection, while it lasts, is the most complete of any, it is in their power greatly to restrain, if not wholly to banish, this flagrant enormity.

2. I exhort all who are not called to go into the field, to apply themselves with the utmost diligence to works of industry. It is in your power by this mean not only to supply the necessities, but to add to the strength of your country. Habits of industry prevailing in a society, not only increase its wealth, as their immediate effect, but they prevent the introduction of many vices, and are intimately connected with sobriety and good morals. Idleness is the mother or nurse of almost every vice; and want, which is its inseparable companion, urges men on to the most abandoned and destructive courses. Industry, therefore is a moral duty of the greatest moment, absolutely necessary to national prosperity, and the sure way of obtaining the blessing of God. I would also observe, that in this, as in every other part of God's government, obedience to his will is as much a natural mean, as a meritorious cause, of the advantage we wish to reap from it. Industry brings up a firm and hardy race. He who is inured to the labor of the field, is prepared for the fatigues of a campaign. The active farmer who rises with the dawn and follows his team or plow, must in the end be an overmatch for those effeminate and delicate soldiers, who are nursed in the lap of self-indulgence, and whose greatest exertion is in the important preparation for, and tedious attendance on, a masquerade, or midnight ball.

3. In the last place, suffer me to recommend to you frugality in your families, and every other article of expence. This the state of things among us renders absolutely necessary, and it stands in the most immediate connexion both with virtuous industry, and active

public spirit. Temperance in meals, moderation and decency in dress, furniture and equipage, have, I think, generally been characteristics of a distinguished patriot. And when the same spirit pervades a people in general, they are fit for every duty, and able to encounter the most formidable enemy. The general subject of the preceding discourse has been the wrath of man praising God. If the unjust oppression of your enemies, which withholds from you many of the usual articles of luxury and magnificence, shall contribute to make you clothe yourselves and your children with the works of your own hands, and cover your tables with the salutary productions of your own soil, it will be a new illustration of the same truth, and a real happiness to yourselves and your country.

I could wish to have every good thing done from the purest principles and the noblest views. Consider, therefore, that the Christian character, particularly the self-denial of the gospel, should extend to your whole deportment. In the early times of Christianity, when adult converts were admitted to baptism, they were asked among other questions, Do you renounce the world, its shews, its pomp, and its vanities? I do. The form of this is still preserved in the administration of baptism, where we renounce the devil, the world, and the flesh. This certainly implies not only abstaining from acts of gross intemperance and excess, but a humility of carriage, a restraint and moderation in all your desires. The same thing, as it is suitable to your Christian profession, is also necessary to make you truly independent in yourselves, and to feed the source of liberality and charity to others, or to the public. The riotous and wasteful liver, whose craving appetites make him constantly needy, is and must be subject to many masters, according to the saying of Solomon, "The borrower is servant to the lender." But the frugal and moderate person, who guides his affairs with discretion, is able to assist in public counsels by a free and unbiassed judgment, to supply the wants of his poor brethren, and sometimes, by his estate and substance to give important aid to a sinking country.

Upon the whole, I beseech you to make a wise improvement of the present threatening aspect of public affairs, and to remember that your duty to God, to your country, to your families, and to yourselves, is the same. True religion is nothing else but an inward temper and outward conduct suited to your state and circumstances in providence at any time. And as peace with God and conformity to him, adds to the sweetness of created comforts while we possess them, so in times of difficulty and trial, it is in the man of piety and inward principle, that we may expect to find the uncorrupted patriot, the useful citizen, and the invincible soldier. God grant that in America true religion and civil liberty may be inseparable, and that the unjust attempts to destroy the one, may in the issue tend to the support and establishment of both.

18

THE BIBLE AND THE SWORD

John Fletcher

LONDON

1776

JOHN FLETCHER (1729–1785). Born John de la Flechere in Nyon, Switzerland, Fletcher studied at the University of Geneva, where he excelled in classical literature, and became a commissioned officer in the Portuguese army. He emigrated to England in 1752 and became an intimate of John and Charles Wesley, with whom he avidly corresponded. Embracing Methodism, he was ordained a priest in 1757 at London's Whitehall; he assisted John Wesley in the Lord's Supper the same day.

An outstanding writer, Fletcher became a leading Methodist theologian. And although he did not follow the itinerant pattern of the Wesleys, Fletcher was one of the founders of the Wesleyan movement. He became Vicar of Madeley, Salop (Shropshire) in 1760 and spent his life in that hard region. He was for a time superintendent of Selina, the Countess of Huntingdon's College of Trevecca in Wales (1768–71). He resigned when his Arminian views clashed with Lady Huntingdon's strict Calvinism.

Comparing him with George Whitefield, John Wesley declared Fletcher to be superior "in holy tempers and holiness of conversation"; indeed, Wesley claimed that he had "never met so holy a man and never expected to do so this side of eternity" (*A Short Account of the Life and Death of the Reverend John Fletcher*, 1795). Other contemporaries seem to have shared this assessment of Fletcher's saintliness.

The Bible and the Sword (1776) reflects the Wesleyan view of the righteousness of the British in suppressing the American rebellion. God was on England's side. Fletcher also wrote *A Vindication of the Rev. Mr. Wesley's "Calm Address . . ."* (1776).

The BIBLE *and the* SWORD:

OR,

THE APPOINTMENT OF THE *GENERAL FAST* VINDICATED:

In an Addreſs to the Common People,

CONCERNING

THE PROPRIETY OF REPRESSING OBSTINATE LICENTIOUSNESS WITH THE SWORD, AND OF FASTING WHEN THE SWORD IS DRAWN FOR THAT PURPOSE.

"From all Sedition, privy Conſpiracy, and Rebellion, Good "Lord deliver us." [*And, in order to this we pray*] "That it "may pleaſe Thee to give the Magiſtrates grace to EXECUTE Juſtice." *Litany.*

He [*the ſupreme Magiſtrate*] beareth not the SWORD in vain: for he is the Miniſter of God, a Revenger to EXECUTE wrath upon him that doeth evil. Rom. xiii. 4.

LONDON: Printed by R. HAWES,
And ſold at the FOUNDRY, in Moorfields, and at the Rev. Mr. WESLEY's Preaching-Houſes in Town and Country. 1776.

My dear fellow-subjects

In a late publication,* too large and too dear for common readers, we find the following observations.

"Dr. Price, the champion of the American patriots, has advanced an argument, which deserves the attention of all, who wish well to church and state: Take it in his own words.

> In this hour of tremendous danger, it would become us to turn our thoughts to heaven. This is what our brethren in the colonies are doing. From one end of North America to the other, they are fasting and praying. But what are we doing? Shocking thought! we are ridiculing them as fanatics, and scoffing at religion. We are running wild after pleasure, and forgetting every thing serious and decent at masquerades. We are gambling in gaming houses; trafficking for boroughs; perjuring ourselves at elections; and selling ourselves for places. Which side then is Providence likely to favour? In America we see a number of rising states in the vigour of youth, and animated by piety. Here we see an old state, inflated and irreligious, enervated by luxury, and hanging by a thread. Can we look without pain on the issue?

"There is more solidity in this argument, than in all that Dr. Price has advanced. If the colonists throng the houses of God, while we throng play-houses, or houses of ill fame; if they croud their communion-tables, while we croud the gaming table or the festal board; if they pray, while we curse; if they fast, while we get drunk; and keep the sabbath, while we pollute it; if they shelter under the protection of heaven, while our chief attention is turned to our troops; we are in danger—in great danger. Be our cause ever so good, and our force ever so formidable; our case is bad, and our success doubtful. Nay, *the Lord of hosts*, who, of old, sold his disobedient people into the hands of their unrighteous enemies, to chastise and humble them, this righteous Lord, may give success to the arms of the colonies, to punish them for their revolt, and us for our prophaneness. A youth that believes and prays as David, is a match for a giant that swaggers

* "American Patriotism confronted with Reason, Scripture and the Constitution." Price nine-pence.

and curses as Goliath. And they that, in the name of the Lord, enthusiastically encounter their enemies in a bad cause, bid fairer for success than they that, in a good cause, prophanely go into the field; trusting only in the apparent strength of an arm of flesh. To disregard the king's righteous commands, as the colonists do, is bad: But to despise the first-table commandments of the King of kings, as we do, is still worse. Nor do I see how we can answer it, either to reason or our own consciences, to be so intent on forcing British laws, and so remiss in yielding obedience to the laws of God.

"Is it not surprizing, that amidst all the preparations, which have been made to subdue the revolted colonies, none should have been made to check our open rebellion against the King of kings; and that in all our national applications to foreign princes for help, we should have forgotten a public application to *the Prince of the kings of the earth?* Many well-wishers to their country flattered themselves, that at a time, when the British empire stands, as Dr. Price justly observes, "on an edge so perilous," our superiors would have appointed a day of humiliation and prayer; a day to confess the national sins, which have provoked God to let loose a spirit of political enthusiasm and revolt upon us; a day to implore pardon for our past transgressions, and to resolve upon a more religious and loyal course of life; a day to beseech the Father of lights and mercies to teach at this important juncture, our senators wisdom in a peculiar manner; and to inspire them with such steadiness and mildness, that by their prudence, courage, and condescension, the war may be ended with little effusion of blood; and, if possible, without shedding any more blood at all. Thousands expected to see such a day; thinking that it becomes us, as reformed christians, nationally to address the throne of grace, and intreat God to turn the hearts of the colonists towards us, and ours towards them, that we may speedily bury our mutual animosities in the grave of our common Saviour. And not a few supposed, that humanity bids us feel for the myriads of our fellow-creatures, who are going to offer up their lives in the field of battle; and that charity and piety require us to pray that they may penitently part with their sins, and solemnly prepare themselves for a safe passage, I shall not say from Britain to America; but, if they are called to it, from time into eternity. Such, I say were the expectations of thousands, but hitherto their hopes and wishes have been disappointed.

"Dr. Price knows how to avail himself of our omission or delay in this respect, to strengthen the hands of the American patriots, by insinuating, that heaven will not be propitious to us; and that '*our cause is such, as gives us* [no] *reason to ask God to bless it*.' None can tell what fewel this plausible observation of his, will add to the wild fire of political enthusiasm, which burns already too fiercely in the breasts of thousands of injudicious religionists. I therefore humbly hope, that our governors will consider Dr. Price's objection taken from our immorality and prophaneness; and that they will let the world see, we are neither ashamed nor afraid to spread the justice of our cause before the Lord of hosts, and to implore his blessing upon the army going to America, to enforce gracious offers of mercy, and reasonable terms of reconciliation.

"And why, after all, should we be ashamed of asking help of God, as well as of German princes? Have we never read such awful scriptures as these?

> Save us, O king of heaven, when we call upon thee. Some put their trust in chariots, and some in horses: But we will remember the name of the Lord our God. Blessed be my strong helper, who subdueth the people unto me, and setteth me above mine adversaries. Thro' thee will we overthrow our enemies, and in thy name will we tread them under that rise against us. For I will not trust in my bow: It is not my sword that shall [comparatively] help me. Be not afraid of this* great multitude; for the battle is not yours, but God's—all the assembly shall know, that the Lord saveth not with sword and spear: For the battle is the Lord's.

"Our own history, as well as the scripture, confirms Dr. Price's objection taken from our neglect of the religious means of success in the present contest. It is well known to many, that in the civil wars of the last age, a national disregard of the Lord's day, and the avowed contempt of God's name, which prevailed in the king's party, did

* Dr. Price, speaking of the numbers of the Americans, says, "To think of conquering that whole continent with 30,000 or 40,000 men, to be transported across the Atlantic, and fed from hence, and incapable of being recruited after any defeat—This is folly so great, that language does not afford a name for it."

him unspeakable injury. For multitudes of men who feared God, seeing prophaneness reign in the army of the royalists, while religious duty was solemnly performed by the forces of the parliament; and being unable to enter into the political questions, whence the quarrel arose, judged of the cause according to religious appearances; and sided against the king, merely because they fancied that he sided against God. Nor were there wanting men of the greatest candour and penetration, who thought, that this was one of the principle causes of the overthrow of our church and state; Cromwell then availing himself of this appearance, as Dr. Price does now, to persuade religious people, that he was fighting the Lord's battles, and that opposing the king and the bishops, was only opposing tyranny and a prophane hierarchy."

The author, after supporting this assertion by divers quotations from the works of a judicious and pious historian of the last century, adds what follows:

"From this extract it appears, that Cromwell, like Dr. Price, rode the great horse religion, as well as the great horse liberty; and that the best way to counter-work the enthusiasm of patriotic religionists, is to do constitutional liberty and scriptural religion full justice; by defending the former against the attacks of despotic monarchs on the right hand, and despotic mobs on the left; and by preserving the latter from the opposite onsets of prophane infidels on the left hand, and enthusiastical religionists on the right. I humbly hope, that our governors will always so avoid one extreme, as not to run into the other; and that, at this time, they will so guard against the very appearances of irreligion and immorality, as to leave Dr. Price, so far as in them lies, no room to injure our cause by arguments taken from our want of devotion and of a strict regard to sound morals. What we owe to God, to ourselves, and to the colonists, calls upon us to remove whatever may give any just offence to those who seek occasion to reflect upon us. The colonists narrowly watch us: Let their keen inspection make us look to ourselves. &c.

"Should we have given them any just ground of complaint, it becomes us to remove it with all speed: setting our seal to the noble maxim, which Dr. Price advances after Lord Chatham; *Rectitude is dignity. Oppression only is meanness; and justice, honour.*

"*Righteousness exalteth a nation*, says the wise man, *but sin is a reproach to any people*, and may prove the ruin of the most powerful empire. Violence brought on the deluge. Luxury overthrew Sodom. Cruel usage of the Israelites destroyed Egypt. Complete wickedness caused the extirpation of the Canaanites. Imperiousness, and an abuse of the power of taxation, rent ten tribes from the kingdom of Judah. Pride sunk Babylon. Nineveh and Jerusalem, by timely repentance, once reversed their awful doom; but returning to their former sins, they shared at last the fate of all the states, which have *filled up the measure of their iniquities*. And have we taken so few strides towards that awful period, as to render national repentance needless in this day of trouble? By fomenting contentions and wars among the natives of Africa, in order to buy the prisoners whom they take from each other; have not some of our countrymen turned Africa into a field of blood? Do not the sighs of myriads of innocent negroes unjustly transported from their native country to the British dominions, call night and day for vengeance upon us; whilst their groans upbraid the hypocritical friends of liberty, who buy, and sell, and whip their fellow men as if they were brutes; and absurdly complain that *they* are enslaved, when it is they themselves, who deal in the liberties and bodies of men, as graziers do in the liberties and bodies of oxen?

"And is what I beg leave to call our Nabob-trade in the East, more consistent with humanity, than our slave-trade in the South and West? Who can tell how many myriads of men have been cut off in the East Indies by famine or wars, which had their rise from the ambition, covetousness, and cruelty of some of our countrymen? And if no vindictive notice has been taken of these barbarous and bloody scenes, has not the nation made them in some degree her own? And does not that innocent blood, the price of which has been imported with impunity, and now circulates through the kingdom to feed our luxury—does not all that blood, I say, speak louder for vengeance against us, than the blood of Abel did against his murderous brother?—'The justice of the nation, says Dr. Price, has slept over these enormities: Will the justice of heaven sleep?'—No: but it still patiently waits for our reformation; nor will it, I hope, wait in vain; but if it does, the suspended blow will in the end descend with redoubled force, and strike us with aggravated ruin. For God will be avenged on all impenitent nations: He has one rule for them and for individuals: *Except they repent*, says Christ himself, *they shall all likewise perish.*

"Let our devotion be improved by the American controversy, as well as our morals. Instead of 'scoffing at religion,' as Dr. Price says we do, let us honour the piety of the colonists. So far at least, as their religious professions are consistent, sincere, and scriptural, let them provoke us to a rational concern for the glory of God, and our eternal interests. Were we to contend with our American colonies for *supremacy in virtue and devotion*, how noble would be the strife! How worthy of a protestant kingdom, and a mother-country! And does not political wisdom, as well as brotherly love, require us to do something in order to root up their inveterate prejudices against us and our church? Have we forgotten that many of the first colonists crossed the Atlantic for conscience' sake; seeking in the woods of America, some, a shelter against our once persecuting hierarchy; and others, a refuge from our epidemical prophaneness? And does not their offspring look upon us in the same odious light, in which Dr. Price places us? Do they not abhor or despise us, as impious, immoral men, 'enervated by luxury;'—men, with whom it is dangerous to be connected, and who '*may expect calamities, that shall recover to reflection*' [*perhaps to devotion*] '*libertines and atheists*' themselves?

"And is it only for God's sake, for the sake of our own souls, and for the sake of the colonists, that we should look to our conduct and christian profession? Are there not multitudes of rash religionists in the kingdom, who suppose that all the praying people in England are for the Americans, and who warmly espouse their part, merely because they are told, that the colonists '*fast and pray*,' while '*we forget every thing serious and decent*,' and because prejudiced teachers confidently ask, with Dr. Price, '*Which side is providence likely to favour?*'— Would to God all our legislators felt the weight of this objection, which can as easily mislead moral and religious people in the present age, as it did in the last! Would to God they exerted themselves in such a manner, that all unprejudiced men might see, the king and parliament have 'the better men,' as well as 'the better cause!' Would to God, that by timely reformation, and solemn addresses to the throne of grace, we might convince Dr. Price and all the Americans, that in submitting to the British legislature, they will not submit to libertinism and atheism; but to a venerable body of virtuous and godly senators, who know that the first care of God's representatives on earth—the principal study of political gods, should be to promote God's fear, by setting a good example before the people committed to their charge, and by steadily enforcing the observance of the moral law!

"These are some of the reflections, which Dr. Price's religious argument has drawn from my pen, and which I doubt not but some of our governors have already made by the help of that wisdom, which prompts them to improve our former calamities, and to study what may promote our happiness in church and state."

The royal proclamation, which has been lately issued out, shews that the hopes expressed in the preceding lines were well-grounded. The heart of every good, unprejudiced man, must rejoice at reading this truly christian decree:

> We, *&c.* command that a public fast and humiliation be observed throughout England upon Friday Dec. 13. that so both we and our people may humble ourselves before almighty God, in order to obtain pardon of our sins; and may in the most devout and solemn manner send up our prayers and supplications to the divine Majesty for averting those heavy judgments, which our manifold sins and provocations have justly deserved; and for imploring his intervention and blessing speedily to deliver our loyal subjects. *&c.* . . .

The sovereign acts herein the part of a Christian prince and of a wise politician. As a Christian prince, he enforces the capital duty of national repentance; and as a wise politician, he averts the most formidable stroke which Doctor Price has aimed at his government. May we second his laudable designs by acting the part of penitent sinners and loyal subjects; tho' mistaken patriots should pour floods of contempt upon us on the occasion.

It would be strange, if an appointment, which has a direct tendency to promote piety, to increase loyalty, and to baffle the endeavours of a disappointed party, met with no opposition. If we solemnly keep the fast, we must expect to be ridiculed by the men, who imagine that liberty consists in the neglect of God's law, and the contempt of the king's authority. The warm men who have publickly asserted, that his last speech from the throne is full of insincerity, daily insinuate that his proclamation is full of hypocrisy, and that it will be as wrong in you to ask a blessing upon his arms, as to desire the Almighty to bless the arms of robbers and murderers. Nor are there few good men among us, who think that it is absolutely inconsistent with christianity to draw the sword and proclaim a fast.

Lest the insinuations of such patriots and professors should cast a damp upon your devotion, and make you leave the field of national prayer to our revolted colonies, I beg leave to remind you of a similar case, in which God testified his approbation of a fast connected with a fight; yea, with a bloody civil-war.

We read in the book of Judges, that *certain sons of Belial*, belonging to the city of Gibeah in the land of Benjamin, beset a house; obliged a Levite who lodged there, to *bring forth his concubine to them; and they knew her, and abused her all night*, in such a manner that she died in the morning. The Levite complained of this cruel usage to the eleven tribes. *All the men of Israel were gathered* on this occasion, against the inhospitable *city of Gibeah, and sent men thro' all the tribe of Benjamin saying, What wickedness is this that is done among you? Now therefore deliver us the sons of Belial, who are in Gibeah, that we may put them to death, and put away evil from Israel. But the children of Benjamin* [instead of condescending to this just request] *gathered themselves together unto Gibeah, to go out to battle against the children of Israel.* Judg. xix. 20.

Let us apply this first part of the story to the immediate cause of the bloodshed, which stains the fields of British America, and we shall have the following state of the case. *Certain sons of Belial*, belonging to the city of Boston, beset a ship in the night, overpowered the crew, and feloniously destroyed her rich cargo. The government was informed, that this felonious deed had been concerted by some of the principal inhabitants of Boston, and executed by their emissaries; and being justly incensed against the numerous rioters, it requested the unjust city to make up the loss sustained by the owners of the plundered ship, or to deliver up the sons of Belial who had so audaciously broken the laws of the land; and a military force was sent to block up the port of Boston, till the sovereign's just request should be granted. The other colonists, instead of using their interest with the obstinate inhabitants of Boston to make them do this act of loyalty and justice, *gathered themselves together unto Boston to go out to battle against the* sons of Great-Britain, and by taking up arms against the king to protect felons, made themselves guilty both of felony and high treason.

Return we now to the children of Israel, and let us see if God forbad them to bring their obstinate brethren to reason by the force of arms, and considered the prayers made to him, on this occasion, as improper and hypocritical. *The children of Israel* (says the historian) *arose and went up to the house of God, and asked counsel of God, and said, Which of us shall go up first to battle against the children of Benjamin? And the Lord* [instead of blaming their design] *said, Judah shall go up first.* In consequence of this direction, Judah marched up to the enemy. But alas! the righteousness of a cause, and the divine approbation, do not always ensure success to those who fight in the cause of virtue. Judah lost the day and 22000 men. *The children of Israel,* greatly affected with this misfortune, *went up and wept before the Lord until even, and asked counsel of the Lord, saying, Shall I go up* [a second time] *to battle against the children of Benjamin my brother? And the Lord said, Go up against him.* Judges xx. 23. However they were as unsuccessful in the second engagement, as they had been in the first. *Then all the children of Israel, and all the people went up, and came unto the house of God, and wept, and sat before the Lord, and fasted that day until even. And the children of Israel enquired of the Lord, saying, Shall I yet again go out to battle against the children of Benjamin my brother, or shall I cease? And the Lord said, Go up; for to-morrow I will deliver them into thine hand.* And accordingly *the Lord smote Benjamin before Israel.* Judges xx. 26, &c. And the few Benjamites that escaped the edge of the vindictive sword, lamented the obstinacy, with which their infatuated tribe had taken up arms for *the sons of Belial,* who had beset the house, in the inhospitable city of Gibeah. And so will the revolted colonies one day bemoan the perverseness, with which their infatuated leaders have made them fight for the sons of Belial, who beset the ship in the inhospitable harbour of Boston.

To return; From the preceding scriptural account, it evidently appears: (1) That God allows, yea commands the sword to be drawn for the punishment of daring felons, and of the infatuated people who bear arms in their defence, as the Benjamites formerly did, and as the revolted colonies actually do. (2) That, in this case, a sister-tribe may conscientiously draw the sword against an obstinate sister-tribe; much more a parent-state against an obstinate colony, and a king against rebellious subjects: (3) That Providence, to try the patience of those who are in the right, may permit that they should suffer great losses: (4) That whilst the maintainers of order and justice draw the sword to check daring licentiousness, it is their duty to *go up unto the house of God*, and to *weep and fast before the Lord:* (5) That God makes a difference between the enthusiastical abettors of felonious practices, who fast to smite their brethren and rulers *with the fist of wickedness;* and the steady governors, who, together with their people, fast to smite the wicked *with the sceptre of righteousness:* And that, whilst God testifies his abhorrence of the former fast, he shews that the latter ranks among the *fasts which he has chosen;* the end of true fasting being to repress evil without us, as well as within us: And lastly, that, although no war is so dreadful as a civil war, yet when God is consulted three times following, all his answers shew, that the most bloody civil war is preferable to the horrible consequences of daring anarchy; and that it is better to maintain order and execute justice with the loss of thousands of soldiers, than to let the mobbing sons of Belial break into ships or houses, to commit with impunity all the crimes which their lust, rapaciousness, and ferocity prompt them to.

Now if fasting and drawing the sword of justice, are duties consistent with scriptural religion; it follows, that praying and using that sword are compatible ordinances. To be convinced of it, you need only consider the following scripture.

> Moses said to Joshua, Chuse us out men, and go out, fight with Amalek. Joshua did as Moses had said to him, and fought with Amalek. And Moses, Aaron, and Hur went up to the top of the hill. And it came to pass when Moses held up his hand [in earnest prayer] that Israel prevailed: and when he let down his hand, Amalek prevailed. But Moses's hands were heavy, and Aaron and Hur stayed up his hands, and his hands were steady till the going down of the sun. And Joshua discomfited Amalek and his people, with the edge of the sword. And the Lord said to Moses, Write this for a memorial in a book. Exod. xvii. 9, &c.

"But supposing war and blood-shed were allowed under the Jewish dispensation, are they not absolutely forbidden under the gospel? Is not Christ *the Prince of peace*, and his gospel *the gospel of peace?* And is it not said, that men *shall neither hurt nor destroy in God's holy mountain?* How then can we suppose that drawing the sword, and fasting on that occasion, can be evangelical duties?"

This objection is specious, and deserves a full answer.

(1) Our Lord, who said to his apostles, that a kind of raging spirit *goeth not out but by fasting and prayer*, said also to them, *He that hath no sword, let him sell his garment, and buy one. And they said, Lord, behold, here are two swords. And he said, It is enough.* Luke xxii. 36, 38. I grant, that when *Peter drew his sword, and* [rashly] *struck a servant of the high-priest, Jesus said unto him, Put up again thy sword into its place: for all they that take the sword* [to use it rashly as thou dost, without any order, and without the least probability of success] *shall perish with the sword.* Matt. xxvi. 52. From the whole of this evangelical account it appears, that our Lord allows his followers the use of the sword; and that he only blames it when it is precipitate, and likely to answer no other end than that of throwing the triumphant friends of vice into a greater rage.

(2) If indeed all men were Christians, and every nominal Christian was *led by the spirit of Christ*, there would be absolutely no need of the sword; for there would be nothing but justice, truth, and love in the world. But reason dictates, that, so long as the wicked shall use the sword in support of vice, the righteous, who are in power, must use it in defence of virtue. *The Lord of hosts*, and *Captain of our salvation*, who *girds his two-edged sword upon his thigh*, or causes it to *proceed out of his mouth*, to devour the wicked—this righteous *lion of the tribe of Judah*, will never suffer Satan and his servants so to bear the sword, as to engross the use of it. This would be letting them have *the kingdom, the power, and the glory*, without controul.

(3) The Psalms and Revelation are full of prophecies concerning the righteous wars, which the godly will wage against the wicked, before iniquity is rooted out of the earth. When the place of the ungodly shall know them no more, and *righteousness shall cover the earth, as the waters do the sea*, Isaiah's prophecy shall be fulfilled. *It shall come to pass in the last days, that the mountain of the Lord's house shall be established in the top of the mountains, and all nations shall flow into it. The Lord shall then judge among the nations, &c. and they shall beat their swords into plow-shares, and their spears into pruning hooks: Nation shall not lift up sword against nation, neither shall they learn war any more.* Is. ii. 2, 4. But till this happy time come, when one nation, or one part of a nation unjustly rises up against another, as the men of Boston did against our merchants, it will be needful to oppose righteous force to unrighteous

violence. It is absurd therefore to measure the duty of the christians who live among lawless men, by the duty of the christians, who shall live when all lawless men shall have been destroyed.

(4) If Michael and his angels could fight in heaven against the dragon and his angels, I do not see why general Howe could not fight on earth against general Lee. And if the Congress unsheathes the sword to protect felons, to redress the imaginary grievance of an insignificant tax, and to load thousands of the king's loyal subjects with grievances too heavy to be borne; it is hard to say, why he and his parliament should not use the sword to redress these real grievances, and to assert the liberty of our American fellow-subjects, who groan under the tyranny of republican despotism.

(5) St. Paul, who knew the gospel better than English mystics and American patriots, asserts the lawfulness of using the sword in order to maintain good government and execute justice. Hear his doctrine. "*The Ruler is the minister of God to thee for good. But if thou do that which is evil, be afraid; for he beareth not the sword in vain: for he is the minister of God,*" [of that God who says, *If ye be obedient, ye shall eat the good of the land: but if ye rebel, ye shall be devoured by the sword,* Is. i. 19, 20. And, of consequence, he is] "*a revenger to execute wrath upon him that doeth evil.*["] Rom. xiii. 4. Hence it appears, that the king is entrusted with the sword, and that if he does not use it, *to execute wrath upon* criminals, *he bears the sword in vain*, and defeats one of the capital ends of his coronation: for *Governors are sent by God for the punishment of evil doers,* 1 Pet. ii. 14.

(6) Some people rejoice, that we have watch-men to guard our streets, constables to apprehend house-breakers, jailors to confine high-way-men, and executioners to put them to death. And yet they blame the use of an army. Is not their conduct, in this respect, highly unreasonable? For, after all, what are soldiers but royal watch-men, royal constables, royal jailors; and, if need be, royal executioners? If it be lawful to place watch-men, in long white coats, at the corners of our streets, for public security; why should it be unlawful to place there watch-men in red coats, for the same good purpose? If it be right to send an unarmed constable, with a justice's warrant, against an unarmed outlaw, or a defenceless debtor; can it be wrong to send thirty thousand armed constables, with the sovereign's warrant, to disarm a countless multitude of lawless men, who assume the

supreme power of the sword, with as much propriety as the pope does the power of the keys of heaven and hell? Again, if it be not contrary to christianity, to put under a jailor's care a number of dangerous men, who have already disturbed the public peace, and who seem bent upon doing it again; why should it be deemed contrary to Christ's religion, to check, by a military guard, a dangerous city, or province, which has forfeited its former liberty, by adding the guilt of felonious and treasonable practices, to that of daring licenciousness? Once more: if the king, by signing a death-warrant, can justly commission a sheriff, and an executioner, to take away the life of an house-breaker, or of a man who has presented a pistol to you, on the high way; why can he not, by the advice of his council and parliament, give to his generals and soldiers a commission to shoot lawless men, who have broken into a ship, to destroy the property of his loyal subjects, or have taken up arms in defence of the men, that committed this crime; and who, instead of presenting a pistol to an individual, to rob him of a few shillings, have brought large trains of artillery into the field, to kill the embodied officers of justice, who bear the ruler's sword, and to rob the king himself of some of the brightest jewels of his crown? If you attend to these hints, you will not find fault with our sovereign for shewing, that *he does not bear the sword in vain:* and you will praise him, if you consider, that the first commission, which he has given to the commanders of his forces, is a commission to offer gracious terms of peace to those very men, who, by wantonly shedding the blood of his loyal subjects, and by repeatedly pouring floods of contempt upon his sacred person, have forfeited all just pretensions to his royal favour.

(7) Soldiers, like watch-men, jailors, and executioners, are a needful burden upon the public. I heartily wish, we were virtuous enough to do without them: but as this is not the case, they are a strong, bitter, and costly remedy, which is absolutely necessary to prevent or cure our licentiousness. So long as human bodies shall want to be preserved by the amputation of painful, mortifying limbs, we shall want surgeons: And so long as political bodies shall be in danger of being destroyed by the moral corruption of their members, we shall want soldiers to do bloody operations. May the Lord grant us a constant succession of wise, conscientious, mild, and yet steady rulers, who may never *bear the sword in vain;* and who may never use it but

with the same tenderness, with which a surgeon uses his knife, when he cuts a mortified limb from the body of a beloved child. His heart bleeds, while the dreadful operation is performed; and yet his judicious, parental affection makes him consent to sacrifice a part of his son's body, in order to prevent the destruction of the whole. As punishing is God's strange work, so should it be that of governors, who are his political representatives. Wo to the man, who, to shew that he has power to use a knife, wantonly cuts his own flesh! And wo to the ruler, who, to make appear, that he bears the sword, butchers his loyal subjects, and wantonly cuts off the sound limbs of the political body, of which he is the head! A crime, which no candid person can lay to the charge of our mild sovereign.

To conclude: If Christianity prohibited fighting for the execution of justice, the continuance of peace, and the support of good government; when penitent soldiers asked John the Baptist, *What shall* we *do?* he would undoubtedly have intimated, that they should renounce their bloody profession, as soon as they could. But, instead of doing it, he charged them to *do violence* [or injustice] *to no man, and to be content with their wages;* a direction which amounted to bidding them continue to serve their country, by helping the ruler not to *bear the sword in vain.* Nor was our Lord of a different mind from his forerunner: for he praised a centurion, or captain in the Roman army, declaring he *had not found such faith in Israel,* as he discovered in that gentile: and he parted from him, as Peter afterwards did from Cornelius and his devout soldiers, without giving him the least hint, that his profession was unlawful. From the whole I infer, that if Christianity allow a man to be a soldier, it allows him to fight for the maintenance of order. And, if it be lawful to fight for this purpose, it must be lawful, nay, it is highly necessary, to fast and pray before an engagement. For the greater is the temptation of soldiers to indulge uncharitable tempers, the more earnestly ought they to pray, that they may fight in the same spirit of love, in which Christ was, when he uttered his last woe against rebellious Jerusalem. He beheld the obstinate city, wept over it, and pronounced its awful doom: *Thine enemies shall lay thee even with the ground, and shall not leave in thee one stone upon another.*

Nor should soldiers fast and pray alone. We ought to bear a part in the solemn duty; because our sins have helped to fill up the measure of the national guilt, which has provoked God to permit the colonists to rise against us. We owe much to the gentlemen of the fleet and army. Whilst they lift up the sword, which lingering justice has reluctantly drawn; whilst they stand between us and the desperate men, who break into our ships, set fire to their own houses, tar, feather, goog,* and scalp their captives; whip, cut, and torture their slaves: and whilst they expose their lives, by sea and land, for our protection, or [which comes to the same thing] for the defence of the government that protects us; it is our bounden duty to feel for them, and to bear them on our hearts. Nay, we shall be guilty of inconsideration, uncharitableness, and base ingratitude, if we do not hold up their hands, by lifting up our own to the Lord of hosts in their behalf, and by asking, that neither prophaneness, lewdness, intemperance, nor cruelty, may stain their laurels; and that they may all be endued with every virtue, which can draw the love of their enemies, and fit them to live or die as faithful soldiers of our Lord Jesus Christ.

Nor should we fast only with an eye to ourselves, and those who fight our battles. We ought also to do it out of regard to our American brethren. If they act at this time the part of enemies, does not our Lord say, *Love your enemies, and pray for them that despitefully use you?* Should we not remember, that British blood flows in their veins—that they are not all guilty—that many of them have been deceived by the plausible and lying speeches of some of their leaders—that the epidemical fever of wild patriotism seized multitudes before they were aware of its dreadful consequences—and that numbers of them already repent of their rashness; earnestly wishing for an opportunity of returning with safety to their former allegiance?

If you consider these favourable circumstances, you will be glad to have an opportunity of solemnly approaching the throne of grace in behalf of your unhappy brethren: You will intercede for them with an heart full of forgiving love, and christian sympathy. You will ardently pray, that God would open the eyes and turn the hearts of the Congress-men, and their military adherents; that he would fill the breast of the king, and of all who are in authority under him, with every virtue, which can render his steady and mild government acceptable to the most discontented of his subjects; and that, on both

* A kind of American torture, which consists in wrenching a man's eyes out of their sockets.

sides of the Atlantic, all persons in power may chearfully use all their influence to promote the speedy reconciliation, and lasting union we wish for.

Should piety, loyalty, and charity, thus animate your prayers; our day of fasting and humiliation will infallibly usher in a day of praise and general thanksgiving; and the eloquent senator, who, in the house of commons lately condemned the religious appointment which I vindicate, will himself partake of the universal joy, and be sorry to have declaimed against a royal proclamation, which so justly deserves his assent, concurrence, and praises.

I am,
My dear fellow-subjects
Your obedient servant,
John Fletcher

London, Dec. 6, 1776.

19

GOD ARISING AND PLEADING HIS PEOPLE'S CAUSE

Abraham Keteltas

NEWBURY-PORT

1777

Abraham Keteltas (1732–1798). Born in New York City of Dutch ancestry and educated at Yale, Keteltas resided for a period in a Huguenot settlement near New Rochelle, New York. He was licensed to preach in 1756. He became pastor of the First Presbyterian Church in Elizabethtown, New Jersey, the following year, only to withdraw in 1760 and subsequently be dismissed. Although the censure was later lifted, Keteltas was not reinstated, and he withdrew from the Presbyterian body in 1765. He held no regular pastorate thereafter, but he preached frequently in Dutch and French Reformed churches because of his fluency in those languages.

Keteltas was a patriot deeply interested in politics. He served as a delegate for Queens County to the Provincial Congress that adopted New York's first state constitution (1776–77). He then fled to Connecticut from his home in Jamaica (Long Island) when the British occupied it after 1776. He supplied the pulpit of the Newburyport, Massachusetts, First Presbyterian Church during this period, later returning to Jamaica to live out his life.

The sermon reprinted here, preached at the evening Lecture in Newburyport in 1777, is a rather remarkable example of the portrayal of the Revolution as a holy war, as "the cause of God."

GOD ARISING AND PLEADING HIS PEOPLE'S CAUSE; OR THE AMERICAN WAR IN FAVOR OF LIBERTY, AGAINST THE MEASURES AND ARMS OF GREAT BRITAIN, SHEWN TO BE THE CAUSE OF GOD:

IN A

SERMON

PREACHED OCTOBER 5TH, 1777

AT AN EVENING LECTURE,

IN THE

PRESBYTERIAN CHURCH

IN

NEWBURY-PORT:

By ABRAHAM KETELTAS, A. M.

Publiſhed by particular deſire.

NEWBURY-PORT:

PRINTED BY *JOHN MYCALL*, FOR EDMUND SAWYER, AND TO BE SOLD AT HIS SHOP IN NEWBURY.

MDCCLXXVII.

Arise O God*! Plead thine own Cause.*

Psalm 74, Verse 22.

When David, the inspired penman of this psalm, was greatly distressed, unjustly blam'd on account of the Amalekites invading, spoiling, and burning Ziklag; and carrying away captive the women that were therein, and when the people talked of stoning him on that account, we read, that under these afflicting circumstances, *he encouraged himself in the Lord his God.* I Sam. 30:6. In this respect, the royal Psalmist exemplified in his conduct, the exercise of every believer. They all fly to God for refuge in time of trouble, and expect comfort and relief from his power and grace, from his glorious perfections and precious promises. The language of their hearts, in any deep distress, is that of Asaph,

> *Whom have I in heaven but thee, and there is none upon earth that I desire besides thee; my flesh and my heart faileth, but God is the strength of my heart and my portion for ever; although the Fig tree should not blossom, though there should be no fruit on the Vine, though the labor of the Olive should fail, though the field should yield no meat, though the flock should be cut off from the fold, and though there should be no herd in the stall, the believer will rejoice in the Lord, and joy in the God of his salvation.*

If prospects should look dark, earth should shudder on her basis, and no light nor relief should appear to the eye of sense, yet the believing heart will trust in the name of the Lord, and stay itself upon its God. Should all the powers of earth and hell combine, for the destruction of God's people, should evil tidings assault the ear from every quarter, and human understanding be at a loss for means of deliverance and safety, yet the believer's heart is fix'd, trusting in the Lord. He expects every thing from the divine power and all sufficiency; he looks up to his God in time of trouble for relief, he cries out with the royal Psalmist in my text, *Arise, O God, and plead thine own cause.*

In discoursing on these words I shall endeavor by divine assistance,

I. To shew you what we are to understand by the cause of God.

II. What is meant by his arising and pleading this cause; and what encouragement his people have that he will effectually do it.

1st then I am to shew you what we are to understand by the cause of God.

By the cause of God we are to understand the whole system of divine truth. Our blessed Lord, when he was arraigned before Pilate, declar'd, *for this end was I born, and for this end came I into the world, that I might bear witness to the truth.* This also was thc grand design of all the dispensations of God to men. The old and new Testament were both of them written, and have been hitherto preserv'd, that they might exhibit to men a scheme of truth. God has display'd to our view the volume of nature, that we may therein read his sublime glories and perfections, *for the heavens declare his glory, and the firmament sheweth forth his handy work, and from the things that are made, are clearly seen his eternal power and Godhead.* The invisible things of him are discovered, by a survey of the creation.

All the doctrines contained in the old and new Testament, from that system of truth, of which we are speaking, amongst these doctrines, those most essential to man, are his fall in Adam, and redemption by the Lord Jesus Christ, the necessity of being regenerated and sanctified by the spirit of God, and being justified by the righteousness of his son imputed to them, and received by faith, the necessity of holiness in order to happiness, and of conformity in heart and life to the nature and will of God: These, and all the other doctrines of his word, are the cause of God. For this cause he sent prophets and apostles to preach and reach mankind, by their discourses and writings: For this cause he sent his son and spirit in the world. These doctrines have been maintained by the saints in all ages, at the peril of their lives and all they held dear: This cause, Christ, his apostles, martyrs, and confessors, have held so dear, that they have seal'd them with their blood. This is a cause that God loves and upholds, he has styl'd himself *the God of truth,* Deut. 32, 4. David declares, that *the Lord keepeth truth for ever,* Ps. 146, 6. Jeremiah cries out, *O Lord, are not thine eyes upon the truth,* Jer. 5, 3.

But 2dly. By the cause of God, we are to understand, the cause of universal righteousness: The moral law, or the ten commandments is the rule of this righteousness, and besides the moral law, all those duties which are incumbent upon us, as fallen creatures; such as the great duties of faith, repentance and conversion, which imply the forsaking of every sin, and the practice of every virtue. This righteousness includes whatsoever things are true, whatsoever things are pure, whatsoever things are honest, lovely, and of good report. It includes a temper and conduct, entirely conformable to the truth revealed in the holy scriptures. This righteousness includes our duty to God, our fellow creatures and ourselves; it implies that we love God supremely, that we worship him in spirit and in truth, with reverence and godly fear, that we submit with patience and resignation to all the strokes of his rod, that we trust in his providence, rely on his mercy, goodness, truth, and other glorious perfections, that we fear to offend him, and strive to please him, always endeavoring to obey his will and commandments; it implies benevolence, justice, charity, integrity, truth, and kindness in our conduct to our fellow creatures, that we love our neighbor as ourselves, and do to others as we would they should do unto us, that we forgive our enemies, and do good to all as we have opportunity. That we be meek, sober, humble, heavenly minded, patient under injuries, contented with our condition, temperate, as to the use of earthly enjoyments, zealous for God's glory, and advancement of truth and religion in the world—the above particulars constitute that righteousness which is God's cause, a great part of which is the image of his own nature and perfections: This is what he delighteth in, for he loveth righteousness, and hateth iniquity; he gave his laws to mankind that they might be holy, as he is holy; he gave his word and spirit to sanctify the souls of men; he gave his only begotten and dearly beloved son, to redeem us from all iniquity, and to purify us unto himself, a peculiar people, zealous of good works. All the dispensations of divine providence, prove God's love of holiness. All the favors of his goodness to the righteous, and the awful judgments executed on the ungodly, prove how much righteousness is the cause of God. The incarnation, agonies and sufferings of Immanuel, were to magnify the law, and make it honorable, and demonstrate how much the righteous God loveth righteousness.

3dly. I add the welfare of the people, who believe and profess the above mentioned system of divine truths, and practice the righteousness just now describ'd, is the cause of God. They are a society of holy and regenerate souls; trusting in the mercy of God through Christ, conforming the temper of their minds and the tenor of their lives, to the nature, will, and perfections of God; they are represented in Scripture, as a kingdom, of which Jesus Christ is the monarch, as a body, of which the son of God is the head: They are described by St. Peter, as a chosen generation, a royal priesthood, an holy nation, a peculiar people, destined to shew forth the praises of him who called them from darkness to his marvellous light: They are in scripture styl'd Zion, Jerusalem, the kingdom of God, and the church of Christ: This society are called elect, as being chosen out of the world, saints as being sanctified and made holy by the spirit, and beloved of God, as being the favorites of the most high. He loves them with a distinguishing love; as a father pitieth his children, so the lord pitieth those his servants that fear him. God loves his people, infinitely more than all the rest of the world: He loves the gates of Zion, more than all the dwellings of Jacob. Zion is represented by the prophet Isaiah, under a melancholy gloom, complaining, the Lord hath forsaken me; and my GOD hath forgotten me: to which complaint, the Father of mercies most graciously replies, *Can a woman forget her sucking child, so as to have no compassion for the son of her womb, yea they may forget, yet will I not forget thee: I have graven thee on the palms of my hands, and thy walls are continually before me.* Thus you see the tender and inexpressible love that God bears to Zion; no affectionate parent ever loved the most amiable child; no fond enraptured bridegroom ever loved the most charming bride, as God loves his people: Listen a little longer to the voice of inspiration to be convinced of this comforting, reviving truth. God's portion is his people, and Israel the lot of his inheritance—he led him about, he instructed him, he kept him as the apple of his eye, as an eagle stirreth up her nest, fluttereth over her young, spreadeth abroad her wings, taketh them, beareth them on her wings, so the Lord alone did lead them. God so loved the church, that he redeemed it by his own blood, he spared not his own Son, but gave him for his chosen people; Christ loved the church, and gave himself for it, gave himself to a life of sorrows, to inexpressible agonies, and to the accursed death of the cross. Immanuel regards the injuries and favors done the church, as if done to himself: When Saul persecuted the church, he said unto him, *Saul, Saul, why persecutest thou me*, and at the last day he will say to those who have fed the hungry saint, given drink to the thirsty believer, cloathed his naked disciples, visited the sick and imprisoned members of his invisible body, inasmuch as ye have done it to the least of these my brethren, ye have done it unto me. When the true believer is injured, oppressed, persecuted, plundered, imprisoned, tormented, and murdered, he looks upon their cause as his own, *precious in his sight is the death of his saints:* he is the father of their fatherless children, the God and protector of their widows, the friend of their friends, and the enemy of their enemies. The enraptured psalmist thus celebrates the kindness of God to his people:

> *The Lord upholdeth all that fall, and raiseth up all that be bowed down, the Lord is righteous in all his ways, and holy in all his works; the Lord is nigh unto all them that call upon him, to all that call upon him in truth,* Ps. 140, 146. *He will fulfil the desire of them that fear him, he will also hear their cry and will save them. The Lord preserveth all them that love him, but all the wicked will he destroy. Happy is he that hath the God of Jacob for his help, whose hope is in the Lord his God, which made heaven and earth, the sea and all that in them is; who keepeth truth for ever; who executeth judgment for the oppressed, who giveth food to the hungry; The Lord looseth the prisoners: the Lord openeth the eyes of the blind: the Lord loveth the righteous: the Lord preserveth the strangers, he relieveth the fatherless and the widow, but the way of the wicked he turneth upside down: the Lord doth build up Jerusalem, he gathereth together the outcasts of Israel; he delighteth not in the strength of the horse; he taketh not pleasure in the legs of a man: the Lord taketh pleasure in them that fear him, in those that hope in his mercy.*

Thus you see my brethren, that the cause of truth, the cause of religion, the cause of righteousness, the cause of his church and people, is the cause of God. It is, as the psalmist expresses it, his own cause.

Thus my brethren, I have shewn you what is meant by the cause of God.

I now proceed to explain what we are to understand by God's pleading this cause, which was the second point proposed.

The Hebrew word here translated plead, may be rendered litigate, strove, contend, fight, but being here connected with cause, it is best translated, by the English word plead, a term very familiar to most of us, which signifies an advocate, lawyer, or patron's arguing, supplicating, interceeding, contending for his client, and representing his case to the best advantage, espousing or patronizing it, or taking it in his own hands and managing it. The phrase of God's pleading his people's cause, frequently occurs in scripture. Thus David, Psalm 35, 1, invokes the divine help saying, *plead my cause O Lord with them that strive with me, fight against them that fight against me:* and when Saul unjustly persecuted him and sought his life, he thus accosts the cruel tyrant, 1 Sam. 24, 15. *the Lord therefore be Judge, and judge between me and thee, and see and plead my cause, and deliver me out of thine hand:* and in the 143d Psalm he saith, *Judge me O God and plead my cause against an ungodly nation: O deliver me from the deceitful and unjust man.* Solomon exhorts, Proverbs 22, 23. *Rob not the poor because he is poor; neither oppress the afflicted in the gate; for the Lord will plead their cause, and spoil the soul of those that spoiled them:* And again he says in the next chapter: *Remove not the old land marks, and enter not into the field of the fatherless, for their Redeemer is mighty; he shall plead their cause with thee:* See also Jeremiah 50, 33–34.

> *Thus saith the Lord of Hosts, the children of Israel and the children of Judah were oppressed together, and all that took them captives, held them fast, they refused to let them go. Their Redeemer is strong, the Lord of Hosts is his name, he shall strongly plead their cause, that he may give rest to the land and disquiet the inhabitants of Babylon.*

There is a remarkable passage in the ensuing chapter, in which God speaks of the injuries done to his people, as if done to himself; he makes their cause his own, and declares that he will plead it. See Jeremiah 51, 33 &c.

> *Thus saith the Lord of Hosts, Nebuchadnezzar, king of Babylon hath devoured me, he hath crushed me, he hath made me an empty vessel, he hath swallowed me up like a dragon, he hath filled his belly with his delicates, he hath cast me out. The violence done to me and to my flesh, be upon Babylon, shall the inhabitant of Zion say; and my blood upon the inhabitants of Chaldea, shall Jerusalem say, therefore thus saith the Lord, behold I will plead thy cause, and take vengeance for thee:*

and this was by punishing Nebuchadnezzar in a most signal manner, and by destroying the inhabitants of Babylon. See the declaration of God's injured Church, Micah 7, 8 &c.

> *Rejoice not against me, O mine enemy: when I fall I shall arise: when I sit in darkness, the Lord shall be a light unto me. I will bear the indignation of the Lord, because I have sinned against him, untill he plead my cause, and execute judgment for me: he will bring me forth to the light, and I shall behold his righteousness: Then she that is mine enemy shall see it, and shame shall cover her which said unto me, where is the Lord thy God? mine eyes shall behold her: now shall she be trodden down as the mire in the streets.*

Thus you see that God will plead his own and his people's cause, against their common enemies. But how doth God plead for his people, how doth he plead his own cause? I answer, he pleads it by his word, his spirit, and his providence.

I. He pleads his own and his people's cause by his word, both in a general and particular manner. He forbids all injustice, oppression, tyranny, murder, theft, plunder, adultery, slander, false witness, unjustly coveting our neighbour's property: he inculcates universal love, benevolence, compassion, humanity, peace, and righteousness: he commands all christians to love their neighbour as themselves, and to do to others as they would that others should do unto them: he commands brethren to dwell together in unity, concord, and mutual forbearance; he declares that to subvert a man in his cause, is not right; he forbids the injuring our neighbour's name, life, or property; he pronounces a woe against them that decree unrighteous decrees, and that write grievousness which they have prescribed, to turn the needy from judgment, and to take away the right of the poor of his people; he commands that he who ruleth over men, must be just, ruling in the fear of the Lord; he commands magistrates to be a terror to evil doers, and a praise to them that do well.

God pled the cause of liberty with the Israelites, when they foolishly desired a king to reign over them: he told them the prejudice it would be to their freedom and happiness, in order to discourage them from it: he said,

> *this will be the manner of the king that shall reign over you; he will take your sons and appoint them for himself, for his chariots and to be his horsemen, and some shall run before his chariots, and he will appoint him captains over hundreds, and over fifties, and will set them to ear his ground, and to reap his harvest; and he will take your fields and your vineyards, and your olive yards, even the best of them, and he will take your men and maid servants, and your goodliest young men, and your asses, and put them to his work, and ye shall be his servants.*

God commanded the Israelites, saying, *ye shall not oppress one another.* Leviticus 25, 14–17. When the ten tribes had revolted from Rehoboam, because of oppression, and when Rehoboam and Judah went out to fight against them to bring them back to subjection, God sent his prophet to Rehoboam and Judah, saying, *ye shall not go up, nor fight against your brethren!* 1 Kings 12, 24. God declared to Abraham, *I will bless them that bless thee, and curse them that curse thee.* See also 1. Chron. 16, 22, compared with Psalm 105, 15, where Jehovah is represented, saying, *touch not mine anointed, and do my prophets no harm*: i.e. God's anointed people, and not kings, because it is said in the preceeding verse, *he suffered no man to do them wrong, yea, he reproved kings for their sake.* I need not multiply arguments, to prove that God by his word, pleads his own and his people's cause, what has been said is sufficient —I shall now point out some particular instances, in which God has by his word, pled his people's cause. He pled the cause of pious Abel, against cruel Cain, Gen. 4, 10,

> *And he said, what hast thou done? the voice of thy brother's blood crieth unto me from the ground. And now thou art cursed from the earth, which hath opened her mouth to receive thy brother's blood from thy hand. When thou tillest the ground, it shall not henceforth yield unto thee her strength. A fugitive and a vagabond shalt thou be in the earth.*

God pled the cause of righteous Lot, to save him as a brand out of the burning of Sodom; see Gen. 19, 17. *He said, escape for thy life; look not behind thee, neither stay thou in all the plain; escape to the mountain, lest thou be consumed.* When Laban pursued Jacob with persecuting rage, God came to Laban the Syrian in a dream by night, and said unto him, *take heed that thou speak not to Jacob either good or bad*, Gen. 31, 24. Thus he pled his cause. He pled for the life of Joseph by the mouth of Reuben, and he pled the cause of Israel by the mouth of Moses, to Pharaoh, saying, *thus saith the Lord God of Israel, let my people go*, Exodus 5, 1. God pleads his people's cause by the mouth of all his faithful ministers, admonishing mankind to do their duty to each other, and perpetually praying and interceeding for the peace, prosperity, and enlargement of the church of Christ; their cry is, spare thy people, bless thine inheritance. He frequently raises up faithful counsellors, and able advocates, to plead his people's cause. Thus he raised up Esther and Mordecai in the court of Ahasuerus, to intercede for the people of the Jews, who were devoted to destruction. God pled for his distressed people, by the mouths of Ezra, Nehemiah, Daniel, Shadrach, Meshac, and Abed-nego, at the courts of the kings of Babylon and Persia. See the affecting prayers made by the above eminent servants of the most High, and by the mouths of the prophets and apostles, in behalf of his people. Now as they were moved to these prayers, by the inspiration and influence of the Holy Ghost, those prayers may be regarded as God's wrestlings for his people.

In all ages of the world, God has raised up men who have by their writings and public speeches, pled his people's cause. How many able advocates in both houses of parliament, have warmly pled and espoused the cause of this much injured country. How many learned, sensible, and excellent pamphlets have been written, both in England and America, to vindicate our rights and liberties, and prevent our destruction; and blessed be God, that all true christians, in every part of the world, who plead the cause of truth, liberty, and virtue, are in effect interceeding for us. How many fervent prayers are continually ascending from millions of sanctified and benevolent hearts in our behalf, to the throne of grace; and what is more important than all these, we are deeply interested in the all-powerful and all-prevailing intercession of Jesus our merciful High Priest. We have an infinitely important friend at the court of heaven, a friend who so loved us, as to die for us; a friend who has all power in heaven and upon earth, and who is omnipotent to quell the rage, and subdue all the efforts of earth and hell. See the intercession of this glorious advocate:

> *I pray for them, I pray not for the world, but for them which thou hast given me, for they are thine, and all thine are mine, and I am glorified in them. And now I am no more in the world, but these are in the world, and I come to thee. Holy Father, keep through thine own name, those whom thou hast given me, that they may be one as we are. I have given them thy word; and the world hath hated them, because they are not of the world, even as I am not of the world. I pray not that thou shouldest take them out of the world, but that thou shouldest keep them from the evil. They are not of the world, even as I am not of the world. Sanctify them through thy truth: thy word is truth. As thou hast sent me into the world, even so have I also sent them into the world. And for their sakes I sanctify myself, that they also might be sanctified through the truth. Neither pray I for these alone, but for them also which shall believe on me, through their word. That they all may be one, as thou Father are in me, and I in thee; that they also may be one in us; that the world may believe that thou hast sent me.*

Thus we are interested in the all prevailing intercession of Jesus Christ. But

II. God pleads his own and his people's cause, by his omnipotent, omniscient, and omnipresent spirit; He sets home his divine word upon the hearts of men; he removes their enmity against God and his people; he convinces and converts the unconverted; he sheds abroad the love of God and man on the human soul; he melts the obdurate heart, and fills it with pity and compassion towards God's suffering servants; he opens the blind eyes, and convinces misguided souls of their errors; he makes the enemies of the righteous their friends; he alarms the guilty mind with a consciousness of its sins, and makes their knees smite together. Of stones he raises up children to Abraham—he excites in the breasts of men, a glowing zeal for Christ, his kingdom and subjects—he is continually making intercession for them, in the hearts of the faithful, with groanings that cannot be uttered—he turns wolves into lambs, softens the savage disposition, promotes truth and righteousness, and thus pleads the cause of God and his people. This glorious and divine spirit, has all hearts (even of kings) in his hand, and turns them as the rivers of waters, whithersoever he pleases; he fills the souls of God's people with faith and courage, and those of their enemies with terror and dismay; he causes the wicked to fly when no man pursueth, but maketh the righteous bold as a lyon—he can cause the wrath of men, their most turbulent and headstrong passions to praise God, and promote the interests of his people, and the remainder of that wrath he can restrain. How happy for the church that she has so irresistable, and omnipotent a spirit to plead her cause: No mortal upon earth can resist his all conquering energy. It was this spirit that pled the cause of Abraham, and of Isaac, with Pharaoh and Abimelech, and prevented them from dishonoring the wives of those illustrious patriarchs. He pled powerfully in the heart of Reuben for the life of Joseph: he even melted the hard hearted Esau into pity and love towards his brother Jacob, against whom he had entertained the most deadly hatred. He prevail'd over the obdurate heart, stubborn disposition and otherwise inflexible resolution of Pharaoh, and constrained him to let Israel go: He was a powerful advocate in the breast of Pharaoh's daughter, in behalf of the infant Moses: He disquieted Ahasuerus on his royal couch, and rendered him favorable to the devoted Jews: He influenced Nebuchadnezzar, Belshazzar, Cyrus, Darius, Artaxerxes, and other monarchs to be kind to them, and pled powerfully in their behalf, in the hearts of kings. This glorious spirit is continually convincing the world of sin, of righteousness, and of judgment to come, and pleads the cause of universal truth and holiness in the souls of men.

Lastly: God pleads his own, and his people's cause by his providence. The whole history of it, from the creation of the world, is a series of wonderful interpositions in behalf of his elect. The sacred writers scarce mention the affairs of any other nations, save those that were connected with the church, as tho' God regarded nothing in the world, save the church, and when all the elect shall be gathered in; the present earth, and all the works that are thereon, shall be burnt up. For them the sun stood still in Gibeah, and the moon in the valley of Ajalon; and the stars in their courses fought against Sisera: For them, he dried up the red sea, to make them a passage, and drowned Pharaoh and his host in a watery grave: he went before them with a pillar of cloud by day, and a pillar of fire by night: he fed them with manna and quails in the wilderness, and brought them water out of the flinty rock: to promote the cause of truth and righteousness, he has perform'd the most surprising prodigies, and shaken heaven and earth. God has pled for his people, by confering the most signal favors upon their friends, and by executing the most awful judgments upon their enemies. For them he stopped the mouths of lions, quenched the violence of fire, turned aside the edge of the sword, of weak made them strong and valiant in battle, and put to flight and destroyed whole armies of their enemies. The angel of the Lord encampeth round about them that fear him, and delivereth them: the Lord forsaketh not his saints, they are preserved forever. God shewed favor to Potipher, Pharaoh, and the Egyptians, for the sake of Abraham, Isaac, Jacob, and their posterity, and he severely punished the kings and people of Egypt, Assyria, Canaan, Philistia, Babylon, and Syria, for the injuries they offered to his chosen. He saved Noah and his family from the flood that drowned the old world —he preserved righteous Lot from the destruction of Sodom and Gomorrha. David from Saul's fury, Daniel in the lion's den, and the three children in the burning fiery furnace—he enabled Abraham with his own servants (amounting to little more than three hundred) to defeat the combin'd army of the four kings. When Israel repented of their sins, and cried to him for deliverance, he enabled them and their judges, with inferior numbers, to conquer and rout large armies of their foes—he pled the cause of Israel, when by the hand of Gideon, with only 300 men, he defeated an host of Midianites as numerous as the grasshoppers in the fields. He pled the cause of his people against Pharaoh, by ten successive plagues, and by the death of all the first-born of the land of Egypt—he pled in favor of Asa and the children of Judah, when he enabled them (although only a handful) to defeat a vast army of the Ethiopians, almost inumerable; and he sent his destroying angel in the camp of the Assyrians, who in one night slew [1]85,000 of the adversaries of Jerusalem and her pious king.

I might easily shew from prophane, as well as sacred history, that God has pled his own and his people's cause; the cause of religion, liberty, and virtue. I will only mention two instances of modern history.

The first I shall relate, is the revolt of the seven united provinces of the Netherlands.

Philip the 2d, king of Spain, was on the throne of the most powerful kingdom in the world; he had not only great dominions in Europe, Spain, and Portugal, under his command: but he had the East and West Indies, and the mines of Mexico and Peru. He oppressed the Dutch, and began to abridge their civil and religious liberties; they petitioned for a redress of their grievances; but they were ignominiously styled *Geux*, that is beggars, and their petitions with the greatest scorn and contempt: whereupon, relying on God, they, although but a handful of men, against a mighty monarchy, rebelled against Spain, under the conduct of the prince of Orange, and at length, after a long, and arduous struggle, were acknowledged by their tyrants, to be free and independent states!

The Swiss cantons, long oppressed by the mighty house of Austria, at last formed the glorious and magnanimous resolution of throwing off the abhor'd yoke of slavery and vile subjection; they fought against multitudes, a most unequal match; but what they wanted in numbers, was supplied in bravery and resolution. The goodness of their cause, and the blessing of God was in the stead of armies—they fought with unparaleled intrepidity against the slaves and instruments of arbitrary power, and they gloriously triumphed, and established their liberties upon a strong foundation, which remains unshaken to the present day—they are now the freest people upon earth; nay, they are supposed to be the only free people in three quarters of the terraqueous globe.

Thus I have shewn you how God has pled his own, and his people's cause. I shall now just touch upon the Psalmist's petition, that God would arise and plead this cause. This word seems to allude to the ark of the covenant, on which the cloud of glory, the symbol of God's presence, rested. This ark was carried by the Levites on their shoulders, when the Israelites marched to attack their enemies. When the march began, and the Levites were about to take up the ark, they sang, *Let God arise; let his enemies be scattered: let those that hate him, flee before him.* So that this custom teaches us, that the Israelites looked to, and depended entirely upon God for the success of their military enterprizes—they sought his aid, they invoked his blessing, presence, and protection; they did as it were, cry out with Moses, *Lord if thy presence go not along with us, suffer us not to go up hence.* Arise O God, like an almighty conqueror; exert thine almighty power, make bare thine everlasting arm in our behalf: go before us, direct our way, and succeed our operations. O Lord, make speed to save us; O God make hast to help us.

Thus my brethren, I have explained the text: Let us proceed to the application of it.

From the preceeding discourse, I think we have reason to conclude, that the cause of this American continent, against the measures of a cruel, bloody, and vindictive ministry, is the cause of God. We are contending for the rights of mankind, for the welfare of millions now living, and for the happiness of millions yet unborn. If it is the indisputed duty of mankind, to do good to all as they have opportunity, especially to those who are of the houshold of faith, if they are bound by the commandment of the supreme law-giver, to love their neighbor as themselves, and do to others as they would that others should do unto them; then the war carried on against us, is unjust and unwarrantable, and our cause is not only righteous, but most important: It is God's own cause: It is the grand cause of the whole human race, and what can be more interesting and glorious. If the principles on which the present civil war is carried on by the American colonies, against the British arms, were universally adopted and practiced upon by mankind, they would turn a vale of tears, into a paradise of God: whereas opposite principles, and a conduct, founded upon them, has filled the world with blood and slaughter, with rapine and violence, with cruelty and injustice, with wretchedness, poverty, horror, desolation, and despair: We cannot therefore doubt, that the cause of liberty, united with that of truth & righteousness, is the cause of God. This is the glorious cause in which Great-Britain herself, has frequently and strenuously contended against tyrants and oppressors, not to mention preceeding struggles for liberty, when Charles the first invaded the rights of his people, the Lords and Commons, aided by their adherents, rose up in arms, and waged a war against him, which terminated in the loss of his crown and life: and when his infatuated son, James the second; imitating his father's fatal example, endeavoured to introduce popery and arbitrary power into his kingdom; the people of England, invited the prince of Orange to vindicate their liberties, who expel'd the tyrant from his throne, and was placed on it himself, by the votes of a free parliament. For the sake of liberty and the protestant religion, during the reign of this glorious and auspicious king, the pretender was excluded from the throne, and the succession to it, was settled in the royal house of Hanover. Great-Britain cannot in justice blame us, for imitating her in those noble struggles for liberty, which have been her greatest glory—she cannot condemn us, without condemning the conduct of her greatest patriots and heroes, virtually denying her king's right to his crown, and acting in manifest opposition to the spirit and interest of her even excellent constitution. I am bold to affirm, that all the surpassing glory, by which she has eclipsed other nations, has been owing to this admirable form of government, so favorable to the rights of mankind. She never has been more illustrious at home or abroad, never more remarkable for her internal glory or external splendor, her peace, plenty and prosperity at home, or her victories, atchievments, & conquests abroad, than when her liberties flourished, and a patriot king sway'd the sceptre; as she never has been poorer, more miserable and inglorious, never been more impotent in herself, or made a meaner figure in the eyes of her neighbors, than when her liberties were violated, and a tyrant sat upon the throne. The attentive reader of English history, who compares the auspicious reigns of William, George the first and second, and part of Queen Ann's, with the fatal administrations of the former and latter James and Charles, will see the striking contrast, & be fully convinced of the truth of this remark. England, during the last war, happy in a king that lov'd his people, and favored their rights, happy in a people that lov'd their king, and were zealous for his honor, triumph'd, gloriously triumph'd over the united fleets of France and Spain, and the confederate powers of tyranny. England I am bold to say, has prospered, as her liberty prospered, and declined, as despotism has prevailed. When principles of liberty, and a ministry and parliament under their influence have governed Great-Britain, how happy have her subjects been? how formidable to her enemies? but when opposite principles, and rulers have been predominant. What misery has overwhelmed her inhabitants? and what a contemptible appearance did she make in the sight of other nations? How has she been torn to pieces by civil broils, and been covered with her own blood? How evident is this from the present unnatural war waged against her own children, to establish arbitrary power? How have her once victorious troops fled ignominiously, before an army of undisciplined peasants, commanded by officers, most of them utterly inexperienced in war! How have her sturdy veterans been led captive by country boys, and her transports, merchantmen and military stores, been taken by our privateers? What insults doth she not continually meet with from her enemies, without daring to resent them? And unhappily divided against herself, doth she not totter on the brink of destruction, and owe her present precarious respite from ruin, to the policy and forbearance of her foes? O England! thou once beloved, happy, and glorious country! Thou land of freedom and delight! How is thy gold become dim, and thy fine gold changed! It was full of judgment; righteousness lodged in it, but now murderers. Thy rulers are companions of thieves, every one loveth gifts, and followeth after rewards: they judge not the fatherless, neither doth the cause of the widow come unto them.

You see my brethren, from the preceeding observations, the unspeakable advantages of liberty, to Great-Britain, and how fatal to her have been the invasion and decline of this inestimable blessing. How absurd then! how inglorious! how cruel and unjust is her conduct, in carrying on this bloody war, to ruin and enslave us—Liberty is the grand fountain, under God, of every temporal blessing, and what is infinitely more important, it is favorable to the propagation of unadulterated christianity. Liberty is the parent of truth, justice, virtue, patriotism, benevolence, and every generous and noble purpose of the soul. Under the influence of liberty, the arts and sciences, trade, commerce, and husbandry flourish and the wilderness blossoms like the rose.

O Liberty, thou Object heav'nly bright
Profuse of bliss, and pregnant with delight,
Eternal pleasures in thy presence reign,
And smiling Plenty leads thy joyful Train.
Eas'd of her load, subjection grows more light,
And Poverty looks chearful in thy sight.
Thou mak'st the gloomy Face of Nature gay,
Giv'st Beauty to the Sun, and Pleasure to the Day.

Addison

Under the auspicious smiles of Liberty, riches increase, industry strains every nerve, secure of property, and joy and plenty smile on every side. How inestimable a blessing then must liberty be, and how inconceivably great its loss!

But if liberty is thus friendly to the happiness of mankind, and is the cause of the kind parent of the universe; certainly tyranny & oppression are the cause of the devil, the cause which God's soul hates. The holy scriptures abound with instances and prophecies of his judgments against tyrants and oppressors; and not only sacred, but prophane history, prove the fulfilment of those prophesies.

You have seen the truth of this observation, from the preceeding discourse, how extremely odious and detestable tyranny and oppression are in his sight. How signal was the divine vengeance against king Ahab and his queen, for falsly accusing Naboth, murdering him upon groundless pretences, and unjustly seizing upon his property? Hear the tremendous judgments denounced by the Lord against those vile oppressors; and O that it might ring in the ears and consciences, of all the authors, abettors, and voluntary executioners of this unnatural, unprovoked, iniquitous, fellonious war. *Arise*, said the Lord, to Elijah the Tishbite,

Go down to meet Ahab king of Israel, who is in Samaria: behold he is in the vineyard of Naboth, whither he is gone down to possess it, and thus shalt thou speak unto him saying: Thus saith the Lord, in the place where the dogs licked the blood of Naboth, shall dogs lick thy blood, even thine. Behold I will bring evil upon thee, and will take away thy posterity, and will cut off from Ahab

> *his male children. And of Jezebel (by whose advice Ahab slew Naboth, and took possession of his vineyard) spake the Lord also, saying, the dogs shall eat Jezebel, by the wall of Jezreel. Him that dieth of Ahab in the city, shall the dogs eat, and him that dieth in the fields, shall the birds of the air eat.*

This curse was awfully and punctually executed, and stands recorded on the Bible, as a tremendous warning against tyranny and oppression. God has shewn his vehement abhorrence of these attrocious crimes, by smiting the perpetrators of them with loathsome diseases, and has commissioned lice, worms, and vermine to crawl within and upon them, to devour them alive, to render them a living carrion, spectacles of horror and deformity, and insufferable stench and abomination to all about them. Thus has God, in the most lively characters, written his hatred and detestation of tyranny and oppression, upon the bodies of those who have been guilty of those heaven daring offences—thus hath he shewn how much he detests, and how severely he will punish cruelty and injustice, the murder of the innocent, and the invasion of their rights and property. And now are there any who call themselves christians, who dare avow, espouse and support, the invasion of liberty, and the murder of those who rise up in its vindication? Yes, to the disgrace of human nature be it spoken, there are such inveterate foes to mankind: and who are they? They are the ministry and parliament of Great-Britain, with their adherents and abettors. The ground work of their present destructive measures, is this most iniquitous decree—that the parliament of Great-Britain, hath power, and of right ought to have power, to make laws and statutes to bind these colonies in all cases whatsoever. This decree is contrary to the laws of God and man, to the British constitution, Magna-Charta, the bill of rights, the charters of the colonies, and the express stipulations of preceeding kings and their representatives; and as the cause is iniquitous in itself, so the war to support it, has been carried on, in the most inhuman, cruel, and injurious manner. The houses and possessions of the friends to their country, have been seiz'd and plundered, rich and valuable furniture has been wantonly destroyed, or meanly seized and carried away: Our negroes, who have been nourished and brought up by us, and the savages of the wilderness, for whose temporal and eternal welfare we have labored, have been instigated to mangle, scalp, and murder us. Every engine has been employed to ruin our commerce, trade, husbandry and religion: Every method has been contrived and executed, to deprive us of the necessaries of life, and cause us to perish for the want of food, cloathing, and the means of defence. Our ships have been seized and confiscated, our poor brethren, taken in them, compelled to fight against us: our prisoners starved to death; our wives and daughters have been ravished: numerous families of little ones compelled to leave their own habitations and provisions, wander about in a strange land, beg their bread, and expose themselves to all the severity of the season.

Ye cruel and bloody authors of this unjust, unnatural war! what desolation, what misery have ye not brought on this once happy land? How many old men's sighs, and widows moans! how many orphans water standing eyes; men for their sons, wives for their husbands fate, and children for their parents timeless death, shall rue the hour that ever ye were born, how many tents of affliction? how many weeping Rachels have ye made? how many disconsolate mothers, bewailing the death of their children, and refusing to be comforted, because they are not? how many bleeding bosoms reproach you with the murder of their beloved? what distressed multitudes upbraid you with the loss of their dwellings, their comforts, and the means of their subsistence? Go to Charlestown my brethren, go to Norfolk, go to New-York, go to Danbury, and to other places, and let the smoaking ruins of well finished and valuable houses, by their speechless, but flaming oratory, melt you into tears, over your country's ruin, and enkindle your indignation against her barbarous, unrelenting foes. Behold your ministers mocked, insulted, buffeted, mark'd out for destruction, for their attachment to religion and liberty, and their zeal against illegal and oppressive measures. Behold numbers of the most pious and respectable characters and families, compelled to fly from their habitations and churches, and seek for refuge in the uninvaded parts of the land. Behold those houses of God, where the great Father of the universe, was worshipped without superstition, in spirit and in truth, where the glad tidings of great joy were published to the adoring throng—where Jesus Christ was held forth crucified, and the whole counsel of God was faithfully declared—behold those sacred, magnificent, and costly structures, destroyed by fire, and levelled with the ground, or converted into magazines for warlike stores, receptacles for rapine and plunder, riding schools, for the exercise of horsemanship, theatres, for prophane and wanton plays, or prisons, for starving, groaning, expiring captives. See our unnatural foes, exulting over the ruins they have made, soliciting foreign aid, and hiring at an expensive rate, German mercenaries, to butcher their own best friends, and 'till cruelly and unjustly invaded and slain, their most affectionate children. Hear the shrieks of ravished women, the cries of helpless orphans, and the groans of murdered patriots. Are these things right? is a cause, that stands in need of, and encourages such measures, the cause of God? is it not glaringly the cause of the devil? can God give a privilege to any man, or number of men, to violate his own sacred and immutable laws? Reason, conscience, humanity, recoil at the horrid thought!

Can any man yet think, that the measures of the British ministry, in invading the lives, liberties, and properties of the inhabitants of these colonies, are right; let him then read the protests of Lords and Commons, the petitions, addresses, and remonstrances of whole islands, and the most respectable corporations in England, against those measures—let him read and attentively reflect upon the excellent pamphlets and speeches, made in England itself in our behalf; hear the worthy bishop of St. Asaph; "My lords" (says he) "we seem not to be sensible of the high, & important trust, which providence has committed to our charge. The most precious remains of civil liberty the world can now boast of, are lodged in our hands; and God forbid that we should violate so sacred a deposit! By enslaving your colonies, you ruin, not only the peace, the commerce, and the fortunes of both countries; but you extinguish the fairest hopes, shut up the last asylum of mankind. I think my lords, without being weakly superstitious, that a good man may hope, that heaven will take part, against the execution of a plan, which seems big, not only with mischief, but impiety."

The time would fail me, if I should produce extracts from the speeches, and addresses, of some of the wisest and best men in England, and in both houses of parliament, who have, with indignation, reprobated the measures of the ministry, and warmly espous'd the cause of America.

The right honorable the earl of Chatham, the ablest and best friend of Great-Britain now living: a man, to whose great endowments, vast attainments, wise, faithful, and glorious administration, she was, under God, indebted, for all the great and important conquests she made the last war. This illustrious statesman, distinguished patriot, and unrivall'd benefactor of his country, has been, from the begining, a warm advocate for America. Lord Camden, that celebrated chancellor, that great oracle of the law, that unshaken patron of the rights of mankind, that counsellor of unsullied honor, and incorruptible integrity, who sacrificed a most lucrative, and highly dignified office, to the love of truth and justice: this excellent man has, with the irresistable force of demonstration, pled and justified our cause. Many noble lords, and distinguished gentlemen, whose eloquence, virtue, genius, and learning, are the greatest ornaments of their country, have been zealous in our behalf, and approved our resistance to the infringement of our rights. Is not then the cause good, which is applauded, patronized, and defended, by such consummate politicians, and exalted worthies.

The iniquity of our enemies, in striving to crush this cause, will appear highly aggravated, if we consider the ingratitude with which their military operations in this country, are attended. Against whom doth Great-Britain wage war? Against those who were once her most affectionate children, her most faithful and hearty friends, and who still, notwithstanding the unparallelled injuries, suffered from her, earnestly deprecate her ruin, and pray for her peace and prosperity.

But once more. Whom doth Great-Britain destroy, whose blood doth she shed, whose houses doth she burn, whose temples doth she demolish, whose lands doth she desolate, whose ruin doth she seek? Why of those who have rejoyced in her happiness, bewailed her calamities, earnestly prayed for her welfare, implored the greatest earthly blessings, and the unspeakable joys of immortality, in behalf of her sovereign, and his royal house—who have rendered her the most signal, and important services, enabled her to make the most glorious, and extensive conquests; caressed, and honored her officers and soldiers, treated them with distinguished hospitality, kindness, and respect; fought, and bled at her side, and assisted her in the last war, with so liberal a generosity, that she frankly aknowleged, we had gone vastly beyond the bare line of duty, and our exact proportion of service.

Besides all this, the principles of liberty, upon which we act, are the same, which expell'd James the second, from the British throne, and seated his present majesty, and his royal ancestors upon it; and if those principles and measures, according to which the present ministry conduct themselves, had prevailed, at the time of the revolution, they would effectually have prevented their accession to it. How hard! how cruel! how painful the thought; that the best friends to the principles upon which this throne was erected and established, should suffer from it, all the horrors of war, at the instigation of its worst enemies!

We have this further consolation to support us under our present affliction; that all our assemblies on the continent, and the Congress at two several times, have endeavored, by the most humble and earnest petitions to the throne, to prevent the fatal war, which now rages and desolates our land. Every expedient, that human sagacity could dictate, to divert the gathering storm, has been tried; both houses of parliament, and the people of England and Ireland, have been most affectionately addressed and supplicated, to pity and relieve us, and suffer us to enjoy our ancient privileges; and it was not until every pacific measure failed, and our petitions were scornfully treated, and rejected, and a powerful fleet and army had actually invaded us and shed our blood; that we took up arms, in behalf of our lives and liberties. Our cause therefore, my dear brethren, is not only good, but it has been prudently conducted: Be therefore of good courage; it is a glorious cause: It is the cause of truth, against error and falshood; the cause of righteousness against iniquity; the cause of the oppressed against the oppressor; the cause of pure and undefiled religion, against bigotry, superstition, & human inventions. It is the cause of the reformation, against popery; of liberty, against arbitrary power; of benevolence, against barbarity, and of virtue against vice. It is the cause of justice and integrity, against bribery, venality, and corruption. In short, it is the cause of heaven against hell—of the kind Parent of the universe, against the prince of darkness, and the destroyer of the human race. It is the cause, for which heroes have fought, patriots bled, prophets, apostles, martyrs, confessors, and righteous men have died: Nay, it is a cause, for which the Son of God came down from his celestial throne, and expired on a cross—it is a cause, for the sake of which, your pious ancestors forsook all the delights and enjoyments of England, that land of wealth and plenty, and came to this once howling wilderness, destitute of houses, cultivated fields, the comforts and conveniencies of life. This is a cause, for the prosperity of which, millions of saints are praying, and our gracious High Priest is interceeding: it is a cause, which thousands, and ten thousands of our friends in England and Ireland, are patronizing, and for which, even the consciences of our very enemies are pleading: therefore do not despond, my dear brethren, at the present gloomy prospects.

The cause of God—his own cause, must prosper, in spite of earth and hell—God will effectually plead it; he will plead it by his almighty word, his all conquering spirit, and his over ruling providence. No weapon formed against Zion, shall prosper: every tongue that riseth up against her, shall be condemned: God is in the midst of her, she shall not be moved: God will help her, and that right early: Trust ye therefore in the Lord Jehovah, for in the Lord Jehovah there is everlasting strength. Cast all your burdens and cares upon the Lord, and he will sustain you—he will never suffer the righteous to be moved. Eminent divines, celebrated poets, have given it as their opinion, that America will be a glorious land of freedom, knowledge, and religion, an asylum for distressed, oppressed, and persecuted virtue. Let this exhilerating thought, fire your souls, and give new ardor and encouragement to your hopes—you contend not only for your own happiness, for your dear relations; for the happiness of the present inhabitants of America; but you contend for the happiness of millions yet unborn. Exert therefore, your utmost efforts, strain every nerve, do all you can to promote this cause—plead earnestly with God, in its behalf, by continual prayer and supplication, by repentance and reformation, by forsaking every vice, & the practice of universal virtue. Be ready to fight for it, and maintain it to the last drop of your blood. *Herein was the love of God manifested, that he laid down his life for us, and we ought to lay down our lives for the brethren.* Pray for the happy period when tyranny, oppression, and wretchedness shall be banished from the earth; when universal love and liberty, peace & righteousness, shall prevail; when angry contentions shall be no more, and wars shall cease, even unto the ends of the earth. When the Jews shall be brought into the christian church, with the fulness of the gentiles, and all Israel shall be saved. When the celestial court and the heaven of heavens shall resound with joyful acclamations, because the kingdoms of this world, are become the kingdoms of our Lord and of his Christ. *Hasten this blessed, this long wish'd for period, O Father of mercies, for thy dear Son's sake.* Amen, and Amen.

20

DIVINE JUDGMENTS UPON TYRANTS

Jacob Cushing

BOSTON

1778

Jacob Cushing (1730–1809). A Harvard graduate (1748) and the minister at Waltham, Massachusetts, from 1752 onward, Cushing was a lively personality and an effective minister. He stayed close to the Bible in his preaching and so managed to satisfy conservatives as well as liberals. He was modest, reasonable, and methodical. He kept a voluminous diary in which all of the minutiae of his long life were carefully recorded. He was on good terms with the eminent of Massachusetts politics, including John Hancock, James Bowdoin, and Thomas Cushing. He delivered the convention sermon in 1789, and the Dudleian lecture at Harvard in 1792 (not printed). Harvard conferred a doctor of divinity degree upon him in 1807.

Of Cushing's fifteen published sermons, this one of April 20, 1778, is the sole political sermon, a fiery denunciation of inhumane acts of two brigades of British soldiers in Lexington, Massachusetts, on April 19, 1775.

Divine judgments upon tyrants: And compassion to the oppressed.

A

SERMON,

PREACHED AT LEXINGTON,

APRIL 20th, 1778.

In *commemoration* of the *MURDEROUS WAR* and *RAPINE*, inhumanly perpetrated, by two brigades of *British troops*, in that town and neighbourhood, on the NINETEENTH of APRIL, 1775.

BY JACOB CUSHING, A.M.

PASTOR *of the* CHURCH *in* WALTHAM.

According to their deeds, accordingly he will repay, fury to his adversaries, recompence to his enemies. ISAIAH lix. 18.

Say to them that are of a fearful heart, be strong, fear not; behold! your God will come with vengeance, even with a recompence he will come and save you. IBID. XXXV. 4.

MASSACHUSETTS-STATE; BOSTON:
PRINTED BY POWARS AND WILLIS.
M,DCC,LXXVIII.

Rejoice, O ye nations, with his people, for he wilt avenge the blood of his servants, and will render vengeance to his adversaries; and will be merciful unto his land, and to his people.

Deuteronomy, XXXII. 43.

That there is a GOD, "is the prime foundation of all religion." We should therefore employ our utmost diligence to establish our minds in the stedfast belief of it. For when once we have firmly settled in our minds the belief of GOD's being, it will mightily influence all our powers of action; it will invite our hope, alarm our fear, and address to every passion within us, that is capable of persuasion, and be in us a never-failing source of devotion and religion.

A GOD without a providence, is a solitary kind of being, and affords but gloomy apprehensions. For 'tis by his providence that all intercourse between GOD and his rational creatures is maintained, therein he exercises and displays his perfections, therein his power executes the contrivances of his wisdom, and his wisdom plans the methods of his goodness and grace, which open to the view and admiration of the wise and good, through successive ages and generations.

But that branch of providence, which, in a peculiar manner, demands our attention on this occasion, and should excite our gratitude, is GOD's uninterrupted government of the rational part of his creation, mankind in particular. For as all government, so the divine, supposes laws, and laws suppose rewards and punishments, of which intelligences only are capable.

Since, therefore, GOD interests himself in the affairs of mankind, and the universal administration of his providence extends to all his works, a large field opens for the employment of our contemplative minds. And we are naturally led to consider this divine government, as respecting communities; the affairs whereof are important, and upon which the order and felicity of the world greatly depend.

GOD is the sovereign of the world, and disposes all things in the best manner. All blessings and calamities, of a public nature, and the revolutions of kingdoms and states, are to be viewed as under the special direction of heaven. Hence the scripture saith, that GOD "increaseth the nations, and destroyeth them, he enlargeth the nations, and straitneth them again—sometimes he blesseth them, so that they are multiplied greatly; again, they are minished, and brought low, through oppression, affliction and sorrow."

These truths being necessarily interwoven with religion, and extensively useful under the varying scenes of life, and misteries in providence—the main design of the present discourse, is to awaken our attention to the passages of divine providence—and lead us to a religious improvement of GOD's hand, in the tragical events that took place on the nineteenth of April, 1775. I mean the *murderous war, rapine and devastation of that day*, which we are now met to commemorate.

Under this visitation, or the greatest trials imaginable, we have abundant consolation, that GOD rules in the armies of heaven, and among the inhabitants of this earth.

The words but now read, may be, perhaps, not unfitly applied to us, for comfort and encouragement under GOD's chastisements, and his usual conduct towards the enemies of his church and people: "Rejoice, O ye nations, with his people, for he will avenge the blood of his servants, and will render vengeance to his adversaries, and will be merciful unto his land, and to his people." These are the concluding words of Moses his song, which setteth forth GOD's works of mercy and judgment towards the children of Israel, his covenant people. And though, in their primary meaning, they respect that nation only, yet they may be accommodated and fairly applied to GOD's faithful and obedient people, at all times, and in all ages; inasmuch as the latter part of the prophecy reaches unto the latter days, and is not yet wholly fulfilled.

Some interpret the former part of the verse thus, "Rejoice ye nations, who are his people," supposing it to be a prophecy of the gentiles becoming one body with the people of Israel; because Moses had supposed in this song, great enmity between them, and that sometimes they had sorely plagued Israel; as at others, GOD rendered to them according to what they had done unto his people: but now breaks out in a rapture of joy, to think that they should one day be reconciled, and made one people of GOD.

The prophecy then before us, is not limited to the Israelites; but may be understood as extending to all GOD's chosen, though oppressed and injured people, in all generations, that he will recompense their wrongs—plead their cause—and do justice upon their enemies. And taking it in this latitude, we may collect several things from it, as worthy our notice, and pertinent to this occasion. Accordingly I observe,

First, that GOD, in the righteous administrations of his providence, permits the sons of violence to oppress his saints and people; and, in their malice and rage, to attempt their ruin, by waging war with them.

GOD is a being of infinite power and inflexible justice, as well as consumate wisdom; and doth according to his sovereign pleasure, in the natural and moral world. He over-rules all things for his own glory, and in subordination to that, has a particular regard to the happiness of his covenant people: His church and chosen are not without mistakes and errors, in this imperfect state—hence they are prone to degenerate and transgress—to be too regardless of GOD, and deficient in their obedience—nay, to be guilty of great wickedness. And it becomes necessary, to punish such revolters from the ways of GOD, and purity of manners. Hence, when the all-wise GOD designs the chastisement and reformation of his backsliding people, he "visits their transgressions with the rod, and their iniquity with stripes," and uses those methods, that shall best promote his moral government; inflicting this or that judgment, as pleases him. The divine providence then is to be devoutly acknowledged in all events, in all public evils and calamities.

Sometimes there are visible marks of GOD's anger and displeasure against his people. Their counsels are divided, and their strength impaired—their enemies are permitted to distress and injure them—or they have been harrassed by the will and conduct of ambitious, designing men, who have contributed to the ruin of their country, even at the same time they pretend a mighty zeal for its interest: Or, they are scourged by haughty tyrants and cruel oppressors: Yet the hand of GOD, and his over-ruling providence is to be acknowledged in these things, as much as when a people suffer by famine, pestilence, earthquakes, storms and tempests, &c. which are commonly regarded as the more immediate tokens of GOD's anger, and works of his providence.

In all public evils, calamities and distresses of GOD's people, he, in his providence, proceeds according to equal rules, and for wise and salutary purposes. Hence the promises of temporal blessings made to the Israelites, in case of their obedience to the divine commandments, and the threatnings of temporal evils and plagues denounced against them, in case of their disobedience, recited in Levit. XXVI, and Deut. XXVIII chapters; related chiefly to them as a body politic, because with regard to the public, they always took place. When religion and virtue flourished among them, and they walked in obedience to the divine laws, they prospered, were successful in their wars, had great plenty, and all things conducive to their welfare and happiness.

But when they revolted from GOD, and were generally corrupt and dissolute, they were despised, miserable, and a prey to their jealous and envious neighbours. And it may be noted, in general, that when public calamities were inflicted upon them, whether by the more immediate hand of heaven, as drought, pestilence, famine, and the like; or, by instruments in providence, as the hands of their enemies and oppressors; it was always as a just punishment for their national iniquities; their idolatry, irreligion and abounding wickedness. And upon their repentance and reformation, these calamities were removed, and their prosperity restored.

Nor was this course of providence peculiar to the Jews. The established rule of the divine proceedure towards nations is ascertained in Jer. XVIII, 7, &c. "At what instant I shall speak concerning a nation, and concerning a kingdom, to pluck up, and to pull down, and to destroy it: If that nation against whom I have pronounced, turn from their evil, I will repent of the evil that I thought to do unto them. And at what instant I shall speak concerning a nation, and concerning a kingdom, to build, and to plant it; if it do evil in my sight, that it obey not my voice, then I will repent of the good wherewith I said I would benefit them."

We are assured, in the oracles of truth, that "Righteousness exalteth a nation; but sin," i.e. abounding vice and wickedness, "is a reproach to any people." And with regard to mankind in all ages, may it not be said, that when a people have been remarkable for justice, temperance, industry, and zeal for the public good, they have prospered in all their affairs, and been high in reputation? And, perhaps, no instance can be produced of a nation's being given up to exterminating judgments and calamities, so long as virtue, probity and religion flourished among them. But when falshood and perfidy, injustice and general corruption, with a contempt of religion, have generally prevailed among them, they have fallen into many calamities, and been deprived of those advantages they so much abused.

Thus GOD, in a variety of ways, may correct and punish his degenerate people; and, among others, permit enemies to oppress them, shed blood in their land, and lay them waste.

It by no means reflects upon the righteousness of GOD, that those whom he employs as instruments in the execution of his judgments upon a revolting, sinful people, are themselves chargeable with injustice and cruelty; and have nothing in view but the gratifying their own ambition, avarice and lust of power. And commonly they who are the authors, or perpetrators of such violence and severity upon a people, are afterwards, in GOD's time, justly punished in their turn, for their vices, their pride, wantonness and barbarity.

Wherefore, if we make a religious improvement of such dispensations, we shall resolve all into the good pleasure of him, who is "higher than the highest," and has the absolute disposal of all in his hands. And however undeserving we may be of such unrighteous treatment from men, our fellow-mortals; yet we are to adore the great —the wise—the powerful GOD, humble ourselves under his mighty hand, accept the punishment of our sins, learn righteousness, patiently bear the indignation of the Lord, and quietly submit to his providences; and, while his judgments are upon us, repent and reform, confide in his almighty power, hope in his mercy, and plead his compassion and the riches of his grace, that in his own way and time, which is the fittest, we may see his salvation. Pass we, therefore,

Secondly, to observe, the dispensations of heaven towards oppressors and tyrants, the enemies of GOD's people. "For he will avenge the blood of his servants, and will render vengeance to his adversaries," none shall hinder his proceedings, to be fully avenged of them.

He is the supreme Lord, governor and judge of the world, therefore will he chastise offenders; to him belongeth vengeance, therefore the wicked shall not go unpunished.

The enemies of GOD's church and people, are GOD's adversaries.

"The Lord's portion is his people, he keeps them as the apple of his eye" verses 9, 10, of the context. Whoever grieves or afflicts them, provokes GOD, for they are "his peculiar treasure." And having a singular concern for them, he will be their shield and their defence, however they may be persecuted by their enemies. "For the Lord shall judge his people"; verse 36. i.e. plead their cause, and deliver them from the oppression of their enemies; as this phrase is frequently used in the book of Psalms. He will have mercy upon his servants, and turn his hand, which punishes them, upon their adversaries.

Thus utter destruction is denounced upon Edom, for their unnatural enmity against the Jews, and cruelty towards their brethren, in Obad. ver. 10, "For thy violence against thy brother Jacob, shame shall cover thee, and thou shalt be cut off forever."

To confirm our faith and hope in GOD, in troublous times, in days of darkness and misery, it may be proper to look back, and devoutly contemplate that most signal act of divine providence, that when the primitive religion which had been derived from the beginning, was in danger of being lost among men, and the world became generally involved in gross superstition and idolatry, it pleased GOD to single out a nation from the rest of mankind, and to erect them into a sacred polity, set apart by their fundamental constitution for the profession and worship, the faith and obedience of the one true GOD, in opposition to the worshipping idols or false deities, and to the worshipping the true GOD by images. The more effectually to awaken the attention of mankind, and to give the more illustrious confirmation to that church constitution, it was wisely ordered, that in the founding and establishing of it, there were repeated and amazing exertions of the power of GOD.

And the whole of that dispensation was admirably so contrived, as to prepare the way for a more spiritual and perfect state of the church, which was to succeed it, and was to be more universally diffused; in the founding of which, providence interposed in a yet more remarkable manner, by a series of most astonishing events.

Through the powerful influence of a wise providence, events that were designed for the destruction of the church, have been made subservient to its greater stability. Thus Haman's malicious, revengeful plot, which threatned utter ruin to the Jewish nation and religion, was most marvellously over-ruled to contribute to the confirmation thereof.

Likewise the christian church, though the world ever was an enemy to it, has been firmly established: It has been maintained against cruel persecution, and the greatest violence. And though continually burning, it has not been consumed, though tossed with tempests, and worried by its oppressors and adversaries, frequently passing through the furnace of affliction; yet it retains a form more bright and beautiful, as of the spouse of Christ, and the joyful mother of children, which no man can number.

Indeed churches are not perfect or compleat; they are apt to decline and transgress; nothing therefore can be more equal and fit, than that GOD should, in his holy providence, manifest his righteous displeasure against backsliding churches that have fallen from the power and purity of religion, into a state of corruption.

Should it happen that, in times of persecution, bloodshed and war, the church may be reduced in its members, still the remnant may become more refined, holy and heavenly. The faith and patience of the saints be more exercised, their zeal and piety more eminent, and practical godliness more gloriously appear. And then, in due season, GOD raiseth his church and people from their afflicted and oppressed state, and rendereth vengeance to their adversaries and persecutors. Thus Babylon of old was punished for her cruelty and oppression of the Jewish church. And thus shall it likewise be in the case of mystical Babylon; which, after having been long suffered to prevail, and to "make war with the saints of the most High," shall have a mighty downfall, wherein the vengeance and justice of almighty GOD, shall be illustriously displayed; of which we have a striking description in XVIII. chap. of the Revelation.

And that we may be established in the faith of the prophecy before us, that GOD "will avenge the blood of his servants," and execute "vengeance upon their adversaries," we may advert to the animating promise of our blessed Saviour, in the parable of the unjust judge, who, neither fearing GOD nor regarding man, was nevertheless prevailed on by the continual cries of the widow, to do her justice against her adversary; our Lord adds, *And shall not GOD avenge his own elect?* "Will he not much more be moved to vindicate his chosen and dearly beloved people, that cry to him day and night, under the cruel oppression of their insulting enemies, even though he may seem to *bear long with them*, to give them space for repentance? I tell you, he will certainly vindicate them, and when once he undertakes it, he will do it speedily too." Herein, "our condescending Lord only intended to intimate, that if the repeated, importunate cries of the afflicted, may at length prevail even upon an inhuman heart, they will be much more regarded by a righteous and merciful GOD, who is always ready to bestow his favours, when he sees we are prepared to receive them. We may rely upon it, that GOD will vindicate his saints. Let this encourage them, though the rod of the wicked may for a while rest on them—and let it intimidate the proud oppressors of the earth, who, in the midst of all their pomp and power, are so wretched, as to have the prayers of GOD's people against them."

We have encouragement then, to hope in GOD; that he will build up Zion—that he will appear still for us, under all our distresses and oppression—that he will *avenge the innocent blood* of our brethren, inhumanly shed in the beginning of the present unjust war—that he will *render vengeance to his and our adversaries*—and one day restore tranquility to our country—that he will make our land "a quiet habitation," when we may view it in perfect peace, and free from all fears of hostile invasions. For, to use the words of the prophet Isaiah, "The Lord is our judge, the Lord is our lawgiver, the Lord is our King, he will save us." Hence we are naturally led, in the last place, to observe from the concluding words of my text.

Thirdly, the kindness and compassion of GOD, to his penitent, praying and obedient people: "And will be merciful unto his land, and to his people."

Though GOD chastise his people with the rod of his hand, or permit enemies to oppose and oppress them, yet he will remember his holy covenant, and shew compassion to them, upon their humiliation and repentance. This is illustrated in Neh. ix chap. wherein the Levites make a religious confession of GOD's goodness, and the Israelites wickedness—greatly provoking GOD by their disobedience and rebellion against him, and contempt of his law; therefore, as in verse 27, "Thou deliveredst them into the hands of their enemies, who vexed them, and in the time of their trouble, when they cried unto thee, thou heardest them from heaven; and according to thy manifold mercies thou gavest them saviours, who saved them out of the hand of their enemies."

GOD will not "cast off his people, neither will he forsake his inheritance: The Lord will not cast off forever—but though he cause grief, yet will he have compassion, according to the multitude of his mercies." He will arise, and have mercy upon Sion, when the set time to favor her, is come.

To represent the perpetual love of GOD to his church and people, the prophet Isaiah utters himself in this rapturous strain, "Sing, O heaven, and be joyful, O earth, and break forth into singing, O mountains, for GOD hath comforted his people, and will have mercy upon his afflicted"—chap. XLIX. 13. And speaking of their deliverance at last, saith, ver. 26. "And I will feed them that oppress thee, with their own flesh, and they shall be drunken with their own blood, as with sweet wine, and all flesh shall know that I the Lord, am thy Saviour, and thy redeemer, the mighty one of Jacob."

The intention of GOD's severe dispensations being not the destruction of his people, but their amendment, it becomes them to acknowledge his hand, confess and forsake their sins, and importunately seek to him for needed salvation. Hence, we are frequently exhorted in scripture to repentance, as the surest way to obtain mercy from GOD; Job v. 17. "Behold, happy is the man whom GOD correcteth; therefore despise not thou the chastening of the Almighty—for he maketh sore and bindeth up, he woundeth, and his hands make whole. He shall deliver thee in six troubles, yea, in seven, there shall no evil touch thee. In famine he shall redeem thee from death, and in war from the power of the sword."

The corrections of his hand are the scourges of a faithful GOD, who retaineth not his anger forever, because he delighteth in mercy. To this purpose we have a more general exhortation to repentance, in Hos. VI. 1. "Come, and let us return unto the Lord, for he hath torn, and he will heal us; he hath smitten, and he will bind us up." The same GOD that punisheth us, can only remove his judgments, and shew us mercy. GOD will "speak peace to his people, and to his saints, if they return not again to folly—surely his salvation is nigh them that fear him."

And the church of Christ, notwithstanding all oppression and persecution, shall one day break forth as the morning, clear as the sun, fair as the moon, and triumph over all its potent, cruel adversaries; even when the glorious things spoken of her, in the latter days, shall be accomplished; corresponding to the prophecy of Isaiah, chap. lx. wherein describing the Jews restoration from captivity, takes occasion therefrom to represent the glories of Christ's kingdom, which began upon the first publication of the gospel, but will not be compleated 'till the fullness of Jews and gentiles are come into the church; and saith, "Violence shall no more be heard in thy land, wasting nor destruction within thy borders: Thy sun shall no more go down, neither shall thy moon withdraw itself; for the Lord shall be thine everlasting light, and the days of thy mourning shall be ended: Thy people also shall all be righteous; they shall inherit the land forever, the branch of my planting, the work of my hands, that I may be glorified. A little one shall become a thousand, and a small one a strong nation: I the Lord will hasten it in his time."

From the preceeding discourse, in connexion with our context, arise the following truths, for instruction and improvement of the dispensations of heaven; and therefore proper for our meditation, on the present occasion. As,

That we should extol the Lord of heaven and earth, who is possessed of glorious perfections, which render him the only fit object of our religious worship.

That we should acknowledge the infinite power of our GOD, and his sovereign dominion over all; and give honour and service to none other.

That his works of providence, no less than of creation, are most perfect; since he doth nothing without the greatest reason, and according to the rules of exact justice.

That we are ignorant of the methods and reasons of GOD's judgments, that take place in the world.

That all the evil, and all the good, that befalls any man, or the whole church, proceeds from the just and equal administrations of divine providence.

That in GOD we may find a sure refuge, at all times, for he is in one mind, and changeth not.

That he will *render vengeance to his adversaries*, and do justice to the enemies of his church.

That he will be merciful to his people, his humble, penitent, praying people, and will, in his own way and time, *avenge the blood of his servants.*

That therefore we have abundant cause to *rejoice with his people;* and to yield chearful and constant obedience to him.

These hints might be profitably enlarged upon; but I must leave the more particular improvement of them, to your own private meditations; and fall in closer with the design of this anniversary, which is to keep in mind a solemn remembrance of the origin of the present murderous war, and more especially of the innocent blood wantonly shed around this sacred temple; and the subsequent slaughter and desolation by British troops, on that memorable day, April nineteenth, one thousand, seven hundred, seventy-five: A day religiously to be regarded by all professed christians.

The distress and anxiety of the inhabitants of this town, and the adjacent, arising from the singular and horrid scenes of that dismal and dark day, tho' diminished by time, can never be effaced in the human breast.

With compassion and tender sympathy, we renew the sorrow and lamentation of the bereaved, for their deceased friends and relatives, who then fell a sacrifice, bled and died, in the cause of GOD and their country, by the sons of violence, and hands of murderers, as multitudes have fallen since in our land, whose blood we hope in GOD, he will speedily and righteously avenge, and restore peace and tranquility.

The all-interesting events of that day, that distressing day, have been painted in lively colours, by my worthy brother:* and the leading steps, or rather stretches of parliamentary power, and hasty strides of British ministerial vengeance, to reduce Americans to submission and abject slavery (as introductory to this unjust and ruinous war) have been set in a striking point of light, by my rev. father,† who have gone before me in this lecture.

* The Rev. Mr. Clark, in his printed sermon, preached April 19, 1776, and his annexed impartial narrative.

† The Rev. Mr. Cooke, in his printed sermon, preached April 19, 1777.

Nothing new therefore, can be suggested by me on this occasion. I have only to stir up your pure minds, by way of remembrance, of the transactions of that awful day; to excite your devotion, and to recommend a religious improvement of GOD's righteous dispensations then, and through three revolving years now compleated.

In pursuance of their oppressive measures (if not intentionally to begin the barbarous and bloody scene) the enemy came upon us like a flood, stealing a march from Boston, through by-ways, under the darkness and silence of the night; and, like cowards and robbers, attacked us altogether defenceless; and cruelly murdered the innocent, the aged and helpless. Accordingly they are described by the prophet, as persons whose *hands are defiled with blood*; adding, "their works are works of iniquity, and the act of violence is in their hands. Their feet run to evil, and they make haste to shed innocent blood; their thoughts are thoughts of iniquity, wasting and destruction are in their paths."

With astonishment and gratitude we recollect the kindness of our almighty Preserver, that no more were slain by the hand of violence; and that the people willingly offered themselves to *the help of the Lord against the mighty*, who manfully opposed the efforts of British pride, power and barbarity. The hand of GOD was visible in these things; and the power and goodness of GOD manifested in our deliverance, from the enraged, disappointed enemy, is to be devoutly retained in memory, and thankfully acknowledged. When we consider, how weak and unprepared we were at that time, for such a sudden assault (though the behaviour of the British troops might have led us to expect hostile measures would ensue*), we may, not unfitly, adopt the words of the psalmist, concerning the church of old; in Ps. 124, wherein she blesseth GOD for a miraculous deliverance from a formidable enemy; I say, we may apply the words in the beginning of the psalm, to ourselves and circumstances, with a little variation; "If it had not been the Lord, who was on our side, now may New-England say: If it had not been the Lord, who was on our side, when men rose up against us; then they had swallowed us up quick, when their wrath was kindled against us," and began to break out in fierceness:

* Witness their numerous insults to the inhabitants of town and country: And their warlike preparations, and formidable fortifications on Boston-Neck, and at the entrance of the town, erected *in terrerum*.

In their furious rage they would have suddenly devoured us, and laid waste the country.

But blessed be GOD, to whose infinite mercy we ascribe our deliverance, who was then a present help. These barbarous savage enemies were put into fear; they were made to flee before us, and hastily to retreat (as wild beasts to their dens) before a few scattered, undisciplined freemen:* Not to our courage or conduct, but to GOD's name be all the praise and glory.

A close attention to the occurrences in this unnatural war, from its rise to the present time, affords us great occasion to sing of GOD's mercy, and to rejoice with his people; and likewise to fear and tremble before the Lord, that his anger is not yet turned away, but his hand is stretched out still.

If this war be just and necessary on our part, as past all doubt it is, then we are engaged in the work of the Lord, which obliges us (under GOD mighty in battle) to use our "swords as instruments of righteousness, and calls us to the shocking, but necessary, important duty of shedding human blood"; not only in defence of our property, life and religion, but in obedience to him who hath said, "Cursed be he that keepeth back his sword from blood."

Here I shall take occasion, to address the companies of militia in this town;† our brethren, now under arms. My friends, having early distinguished yourselves in a readiness to promote the common good, and safety of your country; by opposing, with others, its invaders, and the murderers of your brethren in this town and neighbourhood, on that day we are now commemorating: You escaped the arrows of death, when perhaps equally exposed, as those that were cut off by the hand of violence: To the GOD of your life, and who was then, in a peculiar sense, your preserver, defence and shield, you owe everlasting love and obedience.

You were spared, it may be, further to signalize yourselves, and to do yet greater service for GOD and your bleeding country, which

* From the best accounts it appeared, that not more than 300 of these, were, at any time properly engaged with the two British brigades (in their flight from Concord to Charlestown), near 2000 strong.

† Under the command of Capt. John Briggs and Capt. Francis Brown, which by their military parade on this and similar occasions, and military appearance, while attending the religious exercise, add to the solemnity of the day.

calls aloud to you, and all its hearty friends, to rouse and exert themselves, for the destruction of the common enemy and oppressor; and to wipe away the blood wherewith this land has been stained. To arms! To action, and the battle of the warrior! is the language of divine providence; and you have every motive imaginable to awaken, and excite you to be up and doing the work of the Lord faithfully. The honor and glory of GOD, and the salvation of your country under GOD, call aloud upon all. Duty, interest, liberty, religion and life, every thing worth enjoyment, demand speedy and the utmost exertions.

Cultivate, my friends, a martial spirit, strive to excel in the art of war, that you may be qualified to act the part of soldiers well; and, under providence, be helpful in vanquishing and subduing the enemies of GOD and this people; and be numbered among those who shall be worthy to wear the laurels of victory and triumph.

Above all, let me recommend and urge it upon you, to strive for a more honorable and shining character; I mean, that of true christians, good soldiers of JESUS CHRIST; and to fight manfully under his banner, as the high priest of your profession, and great captain of your salvation. Then whatever service he shall call you to, or sufferings allot you; wherever he shall lead, you will chearfully follow, be ready to face the enemy and every danger, and meet death with calmness and intrepidity, whenever arrested, and be conquerors through him.

We wish you, and all our friends and brethren, called to bear arms, and jeopard their lives in defence of their country, and support of the common rights of mankind, the presence of GOD, and a blessing this day, from the house of the Lord, all grace and good in time, and glory everlasting.

Finally, let us all devoutly worship and honor, fear and serve the Lord of hosts, and GOD of armies; hearken to his word, and seriously attend to every providence. Let us continue our fervent cries to GOD, and offer up importunate, unceasing supplications to the most High, to "avenge the blood of his servants," and be "merciful to" this "his land, and to his people." We are encouraged to this from the providence and promises of a powerful and faithful GOD. The repeated successes during this calamitous war, from its beginning to the present day, have been great and wonderful; and give us confidence in GOD, and hope of a happy conclusion, if we amend our ways and doings. Our enemies, indeed, have been permitted to make great destruction in divers parts of our land (in their rage and cruelty unequall'd) who have attempted, with fire and sword, to spread desolation far and wide.* For as they began the war with a mean, dastardly spirit, so they have prosecuted it, in all their measures, with a rigour and barbarity, exceeding the savages of the wilderness; yet, through the interposition of heaven, they have been frustrated in their grand design, defeated and disgraced.

In various instances, particularly in the last campaign, a merciful GOD hath crowned our arms, with singular success and victory;† enabling us to destroy and break up a whole army, under one of the greatest generals, perhaps, that Britain can boast of. This is the Lord's doing, and 'tis marvelous in our eyes.

The Lord's hand is not shortened, that it cannot save. We may then confidently put our trust in the living GOD, and refer our cause to him that judgeth righteously, the cause of our oppressed and bleeding country—inasmuch as "he will be merciful to his land." We are assured, "The Lord loveth the gates of Sion"; that he "will bless his own inheritance"; and that when "the Lord shall build up Zion, he shall appear in his glory. He will regard the prayer of the destitute —the children of his servants shall continue, and their seed shall be established before" him; and enjoy the tokens of the divine presence among them.

These assurances of our covenant-GOD and Father, may well animate our spirits, invigorate our faith, confirm our hope, and establish

* Among many instances, may be mentioned the burning of Charlestown, Falmouth, Norfolk, Kingston. The rapine and devastation in New York and the Jersies; and their unparalleled treatment of the inhabitants there, both for inhumanity and debauchery. To which may be added, their murdering our friends, whom the fortune of war put into their hands; I mean their starving them to death: *inhumanity more than savage!* And to compleat their accursed plan, they have hired and let loose upon us the Indians, to scalp and butcher of every age and sex, to plunder and lay waste wherever they came: All this has been acted by Britons, who glory in their valor and humanity.

† Our army in the northern department, was remarkably successful in divers actions; particularly on the 7th October, in which they attacked the lines of the enemy, and drove them from their works, killing and captivating several of their principal officers, and many privates; gaining great advantages. On the 17th October, 1777, Lieut. Gen. Burgoyne surrendered himself, and his whole army into the hands of the brave Major-General Gates, at the head of well-disciplined continental troops, and intrepid militia of New-England.

our confidence in him, under the severest trials and miseries that befall us, in this day of calamity and war.

Whether the prophecy and promise in our text, shall be accomplished, while we of the present generation, are upon the stage of action; is known only to him, who is the Lord of life and death. However, we may piously and chearfully leave the event to GOD, whose righteousness remaineth, and his faithfulness to all generations.

I cannot conclude, without just hinting, that though we must necessarily concern ourselves, in some degree, with the things of this present evil world, so long as GOD shall protract our lives; yet our highest interest lies in another region, far beyond this state of noise and war, danger and misery. And whoever faithfully serves GOD and their generation here, in a wise improvement of their talents, shall in the end, receive a crown of life, unfading and eternal.

Here is nothing, my hearers, nothing worthy your highest affection and unceasing pursuit. "All that cometh is vanity." All things are liable to change, and in perpetual uncertainty. Every thing tends to dissolution, and GOD alone is invariable.

We are all children of mortality—and must die out of this world. Blessed be GOD, honor and immortality beyond the grave is ascertained by divine revelation. Being called to glory by virtue, let us diligently and conscientiously perform all the duties of our holy religion; labor to secure our peace with GOD, through Jesus Christ our only Savior—that we may be perfect and compleat in him, as our head.

That so, when contending powers and jarring nations on earth shall be removed—all kingdoms and states dissolved—and all empire and dominion blotted out, excepting his, who is the first cause, and last end of all things: We may have a place in the highest heavens; be admitted to dwell in GOD's immediate presence—and join the heavenly host in the warmest ascriptions of blessing, and honor, and praise and glory to GOD and the lamb, for ever and ever.

AMEN

21

A SERMON ON THE DAY OF THE COMMENCEMENT OF THE CONSTITUTION

Samuel Cooper

BOSTON

1780

SAMUEL COOPER (1725-1783). A life-long Bostonian, Samuel Cooper was trained at Harvard and received a D.D. from the University of Edinburgh. In 1743 he followed his father, Reverend William Cooper, as the junior pastor of Boston's Fourth, or "Manifesto," Church, also known as the Brattle Street Church. In 1747 he became the successor to Benjamin Colman as senior pastor, and until his death he was the sole pastor of that church. Until 1767 he served as a member of the Harvard Corporation. In 1774 he declined the presidency of Harvard. Active in the cause of American freedom from 1754, when he published a pamphlet entitled *The Crisis*, he was a frequent contributor to newspapers and was much in demand as an orator. With other leaders, he was warned in time to flee on April 8, 1775, to avoid arrest by the British authorities. He died, in Boston, eight years later.

The 1780 sermon reprinted here is regarded as Cooper's best. He had preached the artillery election sermon at the age of twenty-six (1751) and had preached an earlier election sermon (1756). The 1780 sermon was regarded as the model of a patriotic sermon, and it had the distinction of being translated into Dutch and included in *Verzameling van stukken tot de dertien Vereenigde Staeten van Noord-America betrekkelijk* (Leyden, 1781).

A SERMON

PREACHED BEFORE HIS EXCELLENCY

JOHN HANCOCK, Esq;

GOVERNOUR,

THE HONOURABLE THE

SENATE,

AND

HOUSE OF REPRESENTATIVES

OF THE

COMMONWEALTH

OF

MASSACHUSETTS,

October 25, 1780.

BEING THE DAY OF THE

COMMENCEMENT OF THE CONSTITUTION

AND

INAUGURATION OF THE NEW GOVERNMENT.

By Samuel Cooper, D. D.

COMMONWEALTH of MASSACHUSETTS:
Printed by T. and J. FLEET, and J. GILL.

Their Congregation shall be established before me: and their Nobles shall be of themselves, and their Governor shall proceed from the midst of them.

XXXth Jeremiah, 20, 21 Ver.

Nothing can be more applicable to the solemnity in which we are engaged, than this passage of sacred writ. The prophecy seems to have been made for ourselves, it is so exactly descriptive of that important, that comprehensive, that essential civil blessing, which kindles the lustre, and diffuses the joy of the present day. Nor is this the only passage of holy scripture that holds up to our view a striking resemblance between our own circumstances and those of the antient Israelites; a nation chosen by God a theatre for the display of some of the most astonishing dispensations of his providence. Like that nation we rose from oppression, and emerged "from the House of Bondage": Like that nation we were led into a wilderness, as a refuge from tyranny, and a preparation for the enjoyment of our civil and religious rights: Like that nation we have been pursued through the sea, by the armed hand of power, which, but for the signal interpositions of heaven, must before now have totally defeated the noble purpose of our emigration: And, to omit many other instances of similarity, like that nation we have been ungrateful to the Supreme Ruler of the world, and too "lightly esteemed the Rock of our Salvation"; accordingly, we have been corrected by his justice, and at the same time remarkably supported and defended by his mercy: So that we may discern our own picture in the figure of the antient church divinely exhibited to Moses in vision, "a bush burning and not consumed." This day, this memorable day, is a witness, that the Lord, he whose "hand maketh great, and giveth strength unto all, hath not forsaken us, nor our God forgotten us." This day, which forms a new æra in our annals, exhibits a testimony to all the world, that contrary to our deserts, and amidst all our troubles, the blessing promised in our text to the afflicted seed of Abraham is come upon us; "Their Nobles shall be of themselves, and their Governor shall proceed from the midst of them."

This prophecy has an immediate respect to the deliverance of the Jews from the cruel oppressions of the king of Babylon. Their sufferings, when they fell under the power of this haughty tyrant, as they are represented to us in sacred history, must harrow a bosom softened with the least degree of humanity. They give us a frightful picture of the effects of despotic power, guided and inflamed by those lusts of the human heart with which it is seldom unaccompanied. Can we forbear weeping for human nature, or blushing for its degradation, when we view either the sufferer or the actor in such a scene; the relentless oppressor, or those who are "sore broken in the place of dragons"? What can be more pathetic than the description of it given by the same prophet who gave the consolation in our text[?]

> How doth the city sit solitary that was full of people? How is she become as a widow: she that was great among the nations, and princess among the provinces? She weepeth sore in the night, and her tears are on her cheeks; she hath none to comfort her; her friends have dealt treacherously with her. Judah is gone into captivity; because of affliction, and because of great servitude, she findeth no rest. Her mighty men are trodden under foot; her young men are crushed; the young and the old lie on the ground in the streets—Mine eyes do fail with tears; my bowels are troubled, my liver is poured on the earth, for the destruction of the daughter of my people.

Such are the fruits of lawless and despotic power in a mortal man intoxicated with it: Such desolations does it make in the earth—such havock in the family of God, merely for the sake of enlarging it's bounds and impressing its terror on the human bosom. It often, indeed, claims a divine original, and impudently supports itself not barely on the permission, but the express designation of him "whose tender mercies are over all his works"; though it exactly resembles the grand adversary of God and man, and is only a "roaring lion that seeketh whom he may devour." To plead a divine right for such a power is truly to teach "the doctrine of devils." It covets every thing without bounds: It grasps every thing without pity: It riots on the spoils of innocence and industry: It is proud to annihilate the rights of mankind; to destroy the fairest constitutions of wisdom, policy and justice, the broadest sources of human happiness: While it enslaves the bodies, it debases the minds of the offspring of God: In its progress it changes the very face of nature, it withers even the fruits of the earth, and frustrates the bounties of our common parent. "Before it is the garden of God, behind it is a desolate wilderness."

Looking upon the Jews when groaning under such a power; their armies vanquished; the flower of their country cut off by the sword; their fortresses reduced; their cities in ashes; their land ravaged; their temple and worship destroyed, and the remnant of the nation led in chains to a foreign land; who would have thought that in a few years, these cities and this temple should rise again from their ruins, and a people so totally enslaved and widely dispersed be restored to their rights and possessions, their laws and institutions; peace, liberty and plenty daily augmenting their numbers, and lighting up the face of joy through their whole land; while the haughty empire of Babylon, from which they had suffered so much, should set to rise no more! Such, however, were the decrees of heaven; such the predictions of the inspired prophets; and such the event.

> Thus saith the Lord of Hosts, I will break his yoke from off thy neck, and will burst thy bonds, and strangers shall no more serve themselves of thee; but thou shalt serve the Lord thy God: and the city shall be builded upon her own heap, and they shall come and sing in the height of Zion: And fields shall be bought in this land whereof ye say it is desolate, it is given into the hand of the Chaldeans—men shall buy fields for money. And they that devour thee shall be devoured; and they that spoil thee shall be a spoil. And out of Judah shall proceed thanksgiving and the voice of them that make merry: and I will multiply them and they shall not be few; I will also glorify them and they shall not be small. Their children also shall be as aforetime, and their congregation, their religious and civil assemblies, shall be established before me: and I will punish all that oppress them: and their Nobles shall be of themselves, and their Governor shall proceed from the midst of them, and I will cause him to draw near, and he shall approach unto me.

When Nebuchadnezzar invaded the land of Judea, and brought upon it such devastations and miseries, it was governed by a king, who shared in the captivity of his subjects, and was led with them by the conqueror in chains to Babylon. But in the happy restoration promised in our text, it is observable, that the royal part of their government was not to be renewed. No mention is made in this refreshing prediction of a king, but only of nobles, men of principal character and influence, who were to *be of themselves*, and such as they would chuse to conduct their affairs; and a governor, who should also *proceed from the midst of them*, and preside over all, cloathed with a tempered authority and dignity, not with arbitrary power, and the means of gratifying an unbounded avarice and ambition.

The form of government originally established in the Hebrew nation by a charter from heaven, was that of a free republic, over which God himself, in peculiar favour to that people, was pleased to preside. It consisted of three parts; a chief magistrate who was called judge or leader, such as Joshua and others, a council of seventy chosen men, and the general assemblies of the people. Of these the two last were the most essential and permanent, and the first more occasional, according to the particular circumstances of the nation. Their council or Sanhedrim, remained with but little suspension, through all the vicissitudes they experienced, till after the commencement of the christian æra. And as to the assemblies of the people, that they were frequently held by divine appointment, and considered as the fountain of civil power, which they exerted by their own decrees, or distributed into various channels as they judged most conducive to their own security, order, and happiness, is evident beyond contradiction from the sacred history. Even the law of Moses, though framed by God himself, was not imposed upon that people against their will; it was laid open before the whole congregation of Israel; they freely adopted it, and it became their law, not only by divine appointment, but by their own voluntary and express consent. Upon this account it is called in the sacred writings a covenant, compact, or mutual stipulation.

A solemn renewal of this covenant was the very last public act of Joshua their renowned leader. "He gathered all the tribes of Israel to Sechem, and called for the elders of Israel, and for the heads and for the judges, and for their officers, and they presented themselves before God." The occasion was great and important; being nothing less than to renew their acceptance of the constitution they had received from heaven, and solemnly to confirm the national compact. How august was this assembly of a great nation, it's representatives and magistrates of every order, with their brave and faithful leader at their head; he, who had been foremost to face the dangers of their cause, who had fought so many battles for their happy settlement, and rendered such various and important services to his country. In a short but nervous and pathetic address to the assembly, he reminded them of their small original; of the peculiar favors granted by heaven to their progenitors; of their remarkable deliverance from the slavery of Egypt; of the wonders wrought for them by a divine hand in their progress thro' the wilderness; in their conquests on the borders of Canaan, and their firm possession of that promised land. Deeply impressed with this interesting recollection, he warmly declares his own resolution to abide by that noble cause for which they had been led by heaven from an ignominious and servile dependence, and formed into a distinct and respectable nation. But as the memorable act of the day depended intirely on the consent of the people, he accordingly refers the matter to their own free determination. "Chuse you this day whom you will serve." It was impossible for the people not to be moved by such an address; not to discern the excellency of the mosaic constitutions; how well they were adapted to the particular circumstances of the nation, and the noble purposes they were designed to promote. The people replied, *the Lord our God we will serve*; we consent, and are determined to be governed by the laws and the statutes he has been so graciously pleased to afford us. "Then Joshua said unto the people, ye are witnesses against yourselves that ye have chosen the Lord to serve him; and they said, we are witnesses." If ever we renounce the constitution and happy settlement granted to us by heaven; if ever we break the sacred compact; this day, and all the public and voluntary transactions of it, must be a witness against us. "Thus Joshua made a covenant with the people at Sechem," which, we are afterwards told, he recorded in a book, and at the same time erected a monumental stone upon the spot, as a memorial of these sacred stipulations, and as a perpetual testimony, that the Supreme Ruler himself had not established their polity without their own free concurrence, and that the Hebrew nation, lately redeemed from tyranny, had now a civil and religious constitution of their own choice, and were governed by laws to which they had given their solemn consent.

To mention all the passages in sacred writ which prove that the Hebrew government, tho' a theocracy, was yet as to the outward part of it, a free republic, and that the sovereignty resided in the people, would be to recite a large part of it's history. I will therefore only add a single instance. When the tribes of Reuben and Gad, and the half tribe of Manassah had erected a separate altar, tho' it afterwards appeared with no bad intention, all the other tribes were extremely alarmed, and being met in general assembly, determined to make war on their offending brethren. But previous to the intended assault they agreed to send an embassy to expostulate with them on the occasion. Phinehaz and ten princes, or principal men, were appointed for this purpose. Here was an act of sovereignty, and an act of the highest importance to the interest of any nation, involving in it nothing less than the power of making peace or war. It was not done by Joshua, tho' he was then alive; it was an act of the congregation of Israel: The embassy upon this momentous matter was chosen, commissioned, and instructed by them. "As it was democratically sent,["] says a great author,* who wrote conclusively, who fought bravely, and died gloriously in the cause of liberty, ["]it was democratically received: It was not directed to one man, but to all the children of Reuben, Gad and Manassah, and the answer was sent by them all." The report was made to the congregation, who finally determined the grand question, and decided for peace.

Such was the civil constitution of the Hebrew nation, till growing weary of the gift of heaven, they demanded a king. After being admonished by the prophet Samuel of the ingratitude and folly of their request, they were punished in the grant of it. Impiety, corruption and disorder of every kind afterwards increasing among them, they grew ripe for the judgments of heaven in their desolation and captivity. Taught by these judgments the value of those blessings they had before despised, and groaning under the hand of tyranny more heavy than that of death, they felt the worth of their former civil and religious privileges, and were prepared to receive with gratitude and joy a restoration not barely to the land flowing with milk and honey, but to the most precious advantage they ever enjoyed in that land, their original constitution of government: They were prepared to welcome with the voice of mirth and thanksgiving the re-establishment of their congregations; nobles chosen from among themselves, and a governor proceeding from the midst of them.

Such a constitution, twice established by the hand of heaven in that nation, so far as it respects civil and religious liberty in general, ought to be regarded as a solemn recognition from the Supreme Ruler himself of the rights of human nature. Abstracted from those append-

*See Algernon Sidney upon government.

ages and formalities which were peculiar to the Jews, and designed to answer some particular purposes of divine Providence, it points out in general what kind of government infinite wisdom and goodness would establish among mankind.

We want not, indeed, a special revelation from heaven to teach us that men are born equal and free; that no man has a natural claim of dominion over his neighbours, nor one nation any such claim upon another; and that as government is only the administration of the affairs of a number of men combined for their own security and happiness, such a society have a right freely to determine by whom and in what manner their own affairs shall be administered. These are the plain dictates of that reason and common sense with which the common parent of men has informed the human bosom. It is, however, a satisfaction to observe such everlasting maxims of equity confirmed, and impressed upon the consciences of men, by the instructions, precepts, and examples given us in the sacred oracles; one internal mark of their divine original, and that they come from him "who hath made of one blood all nations to dwell upon the face of the earth," whose authority sanctifies only those governments that instead of oppressing any part of his family, vindicate the oppressed, and restrain and punish the oppressor.

Unhappy the people who are destitute of the blessing promised in our text; who have not the ulterior powers of government within themselves; who depend upon the will of another state, with which they are not incorporated as a vital part, the interest of which must in many respects be opposite to their own; and who at the same time have no fixed constitutional barrier to restrain this reigning power: There is no meanness or misery to which such a people is not liable: There is not a single blessing, tho' perhaps indulged to them for a while, that they can call their own; there is nothing they have not to dread. Whether the governing power be itself free or despotic, it matters not to the poor dependent. Nations who are jealous of their own liberties often sport with those of others; nay, it has been remarked, that the dependent provinces of free states have enjoyed less freedom than those belonging to despotic powers. Such was our late dismal situation, from which heaven hath redeemed us by a signal and glorious revolution. We thought, indeed, we had a charter to support our rights: but we found a written charter, a thin barrier against all-prevailing power, that could construe it to its own purpose, or rescind it by the sword at its own pleasure.

Upon our present independence, sweet and valuable as the blessing is, we may read the inscription, *I am found of them that sought me not.* Be it to our praise or blame, we cannot deny, that when we were not searching for it, it happily found us. It certainly must have been not only innocent but laudable and manly, to have desired it even before we felt the absolute necessity of it. It was our birth right; we ought to have valued it highly, and never to have received a mess of pottage, a small temporary supply, as an equivalent for it. Going upon the trite metaphor of a mother country, which has so often been weakly urged against us, like a child grown to maturity, we had a right to a distinct settlement in the world, and to the fruits of our own industry; and it would have been but justice, and no great generosity, in her who so much boasted her maternal tenderness to us, had she not only readily acquiesced, but even aided us in this settlement. It is certain, however, that we did not seek an independence; and it is equally certain that Britain, though she meant to oppose it with all her power, has by a strange infatuation, taken the most direct, and perhaps the only methods that could have established it. Her oppressions, her unrelenting cruelty, have driven us out from the family of which we were once a part: This has opened our eyes to discern the inestimable blessing of a separation from her; while, like children that have been inhumanly treated and cast out by their parents, and at the same time are capable of taking care of themselves, we have found friendship and respect from the world, and have formed new, advantageous, and honorable connections.

Independence gives us a rank among the nations of the earth, which no precept of our religion forbids us to understand and feel, and which we should be ambitious to support in the most reputable manner. It opens to us a free communication with all the world, not only for the improvement of commerce, and the acquisition of wealth, but also for the cultivation of the most useful knowledge. It naturally unfetters and expands the human mind, and prepares it for the impression of the most exalted virtues, as well as the reception of the most important science. If we look into the history and character of nations, we shall find those that have been for a long time, and to any considerable degree dependent upon others, limited and cramped in their improvements; corrupted by the court, and stained with the vices of the ruling state; and debased by an air of servility and depression marking their productions and manners. Servility is not only dishonorable to human nature, but commonly accompanied with the meanest vices, such as adulation, deceit, falshood, treachery, cruelty, and the basest methods of supporting and procuring the favour of the power upon which it depends.

Neither does the time allow, nor circumstances require, that I should enter into a detail of all the principles and arguments upon which the right of our present establishment is grounded. They are known to all the world; they are to be found in the immortal writings of Sidney and Locke, and other glorious defenders of the liberties of human nature; they are also to be found, not dishonored, in the acts and publications of America on this great occasion, which have the approbation and applause of the wise and impartial among mankind, and even in Britain itself: They are the principles upon which her own government and her own revolution under William the third were founded; principles which brutal force may oppose, but which reason and scripture will forever sanctify. The citizens of these states have had sense enough to comprehend the full force of these principles, and virtue enough, in the face of uncommon dangers, to act upon so just, so broad, and stable a foundation.

It has been said, that every nation is free that deserves to be so. This may not be always true: But had a people so illuminated as the inhabitants of these states, so nurtured by their ancestors in the love of freedom; a people to whom divine Providence was pleased to present so fair an opportunity of asserting their natural right as an independent nation, and who were even compelled by the arms of their enemies to take sanctuary in the temple of liberty; had such a people been disobedient to the heavenly call, and refused to enter, who could have asserted their title to the glorious wreaths and peculiar blessings that are no where bestowed but in that hallowed place?

It is to the dishonor of human nature, that liberty, wherever it has been planted and flourished, has commonly required to be watered with blood. Britain, in her conduct towards these states, hath given a fresh proof of the truth of this observation. She has attempted to destroy by her arms in America, what she professes to defend by these very arms on her own soil. Such is the nature of man, such the tendency of power in a nation as well as a single person. It makes a perpetual effort to enlarge itself, and presses against the bounds that confine it. It loses by degrees all idea of right but its own; and therefore that people must be unhappy indeed, who have nothing but humble petitions and remonstrances, and the feeble voice of a charter to oppose to the arms of another nation, that claims *a right to bind them in all cases whatsoever*.

Poor Genoa! says an author* who exposes with great energy and spirit the idea of receiving as the gift of a despot, by a written charter, a title to the rights of human nature, and to which all men are born;

> Poor Genoa! wherefore shouldest thou be vain of exhibiting a charter of privileges given thee by one Berenger: Concessions of privileges are but titles of servitude: The true charter of liberty is *independency supported by force*. It is with the point of the sword the diplomas that ratify this natural right must be signed. Happy Switzerland! To what placart owest thou thy liberty? To thy courage, thy firmness, thy mountains. But hold—I am your emperor. "We do not chuse you should be any longer so." But your fathers were my father's slaves. "It is for that reason their children will not be your's." But I have a right by dignity. "And we have a right by nature.["] When did the seven united provinces become possessed of this incontestable right? ["]From the moment they united; and from that moment Philip II became the rebel."

Heaven and earth can bear witness that these states are innocent of the blood that hath been shed, and the miseries diffused by this unrighteous war. We have stood upon the ground of justice, honor, and liberty, and acted meerly a defensive part. Not unreasonable in our demands, not violent in our councils, not precipitate in our conduct, our "moderation has been known to all men"; and without refusing a single claim that Britain could in equity make upon us, our persons, our property, our rights have been invaded, in every step that led to this revolution. I do not wish that this should be taken for granted barely upon our own declaration. Without appealing to foreign nations, whose conduct towards us demonstrates what opinion they form of our principles and measures; we have an acknowledgment of the truth of this assertion from Britain itself; from men of approved

*Voltaire.

wisdom, integrity and candor; from some of the first characters, and brightest ornaments in her own government; from innumerable speeches in her Parliaments, and from solemn protests in her House of Lords.

Allow me particularly to mention on this occasion the letters of Mr. Hartley, member of the British House of Commons for Hull, to his constituents; in which he gives a detail of the measures of that government respecting America, and upon which he says; "Thinking, as I have always thought, that the foundation and prosecution of the war against America has been unjust, I have taken some pains to lay open those insidious arts which ministers have practised, that I may contribute my feeble efforts to vindicate my country at large from so grievous a charge as that of supporting an unjust cause, knowing it to be unjust." In another place, he says, "When all those transactions shall come hereafter to be revised in some cooler hour, I am confident there is not a man with a British heart who will not say, that in the same circumstances he would have acted as the Americans have done." He goes on,

> What had the Americans to look to after the refusal of their last petition, but to seek for shelter in their own strength and independence? They were cut off from all possible communication with their sovereign and their mother country; and the first act of the second session of parliament was to cast them out of all national and parliamentary protection; to send 20,000 German mercenaries against them; to incite an insurrection of negroes against their masters, and to let loose the Indian savages upon their innocent and unarmed back settlers, and upon defenceless women and children. They had petitioned and addressed; they had disclaimed every idea of independence; in return for which administration sends against them an army of 50,000 men. Now let ministers answer to God and their country for the blood which they have shed. The blood of thousands of their fellow creatures, wilfully and premeditatedly shed in an unjust cause, will be required at their hands; who have taken their full stretch of vengeance, in their attempts to destroy and to lay waste to the utmost of their malignant power the lives, liberty, property, and all the rights of mankind.

Nothing can be more full to the point than this acknowledgment from a gentleman of such distinguished character: He imputes indeed the whole to the ministers, but as it was all adopted and authorised by the whole British government, it became an act of the nation in general; though many worthy individuals, with himself, abhorred the injustice and cruelty.

In the protest of the Lords, against the prohibitory bill, the dissentient Peers say, "We are preparing the minds of the Americans for that independence we charge them with affecting, whilst we drive them to the necessity of it by repeated injuries." "I rejoice that the Americans have resisted," said Lord Chatham in parliament; a short but full testimony from that great man to the justice of our cause.

Thus are we acquitted from the guilt of all this blood that "crieth from the ground," by the public declarations of many of the wisest and best men in Britain; men who perfectly knew all the measures of her government, and all that could be offered to justify them, being themselves a part of this government: Men deeply versed in natural and political law, capable of forming the truest judgment upon so important a point, and who cannot be suspected of partiality in our favour. With all this justice on our side, we still put our cause to great hazard by delaying to declare ourselves a seperate nation, even after Britain had with her own hands violently broken every bond of union.

By this conduct of our enemies, heaven hath granted us an inestimable opportunity, and such as has been rarely if ever indulged to so great a people: An opportunity to avail ourselves of the wisdom and experience of all past ages united with that of the present; of comparing what we have seen and felt ourselves, with what we have known and read of others; and of chusing for ourselves, unencumbered with the pretensions of royal heirs, or lordly peers, of feudal rights, or ecclesiastical authority, that form of civil government which we judge most conducive to our own security and order, liberty and happiness: An opportunity, though surrounded with the flames of war, of deliberating and deciding upon this most interesting of all human affairs with calmness and freedom. This, in all it's circumstances, is a singular event; it is hard to tell where another such scene was ever beheld. The origin of most nations is covered with obscurity, and veiled by fiction; the rise of our own is open as it is honorable; and the new-born state, may I not be allowed to say, is a "spectacle to men and angels." For as piety, virtue, and morals are not a little interested in government, such a transaction has an aspect upon both worlds; and concerns us not only as members of civil society upon earth, but as candidates for "the city of the living God, the Jerusalem on high."

Happy people! who not awed by the voice of a master; not chained by slavish customs, superstitions, and prejudices, have deliberately framed the constitution under which you chuse to live; and are to be subject to no laws, by which you do not consent to bind yourselves. In such an attitude human nature appears with it's proper dignity: On such a basis, life, and all that sweetens and adorns it, may rest with as much security as human imperfection can possibly admit: In such a constitution we find a country deserving to be loved, and worthy to be defended. For what is our country? Is it a foil of which, tho' we may be the present possessors, we can call no part our own? or the air in which we first drew our breath, from which we may be confined in a dungeon, or of which we may be deprived by the ax or the halter at the pleasure of a tyrant? Is not a country a constitution —an established frame of laws; of which a man may say, "we are here united in society for our common security and happiness. These fields and these fruits are my own: The regulations under which I live are my own; I am not only a proprietor in the soil, but I am part of the sovereignty of my country." Such ought to be the community of men, and such, adored be the goodness of the supreme Ruler of the world, such, at present is our own country; of which this day affords a bright evidence, a glorious recognition.

To the disappointment of our enemies, and the joy of our friends, we have now attained a settled government with a degree of peace and unanimity, all circumstances considered, truly surprizing. The sagacity, the political knowledge, the patient deliberation, the constant attention to the grand principles of liberty, and the mutual condescention and candor under a diversity of apprehension respecting the modes of administration, exhibited by those who were appointed to form this constitution, and by the people who ratified it, must do immortal honor to our country. It is, we believe, "an happy foundation for many generations"; and the framers of it are indeed the fathers of their country; since nothing is so essential to the increase, and universal prosperity of a community, as a constitution of government founded in justice, and friendly to liberty. Such men have a monument of glory more durable than brass or marble.

I need not enlarge before such an audience upon the particular excellencies of this constitution: How effectually it makes the people the keepers of their own liberties, with whom they are certainly safest: How nicely it poizes the powers of government, in order to render them as far as human foresight can, what God ever designed they should be, powers only to do good: How happily it guards on the one hand against anarchy and confusion, and on the other against tyranny and oppression: How carefully it separates the legislative from the executive power, a point essential to liberty: How wisely it has provided for the impartial execution of the laws in the independent situation of the judges; a matter of capital moment, and without which the freedom of a constitution in other respects, might be often delusory, and not realized in the just security of the person and property of the subject.

In addition to all this, what a broad foundation for the exercise of the rights of conscience is laid in this constitution! which declares, that "no subject shall be hurt, molested, or restrained in his person, liberty or estate, for worshipping God in the manner and season most agreeable to the dictates of his own conscience, or for his religious profession or sentiments; and that every denomination of christians, demeaning themselves peaceably, and as good subjects of the commonwealth, shall be equally under the protection of the law, and no subordination of any one sect or denomination to another shall be established by law." It considers indeed morality and the public worship of God as important to the happiness of society: And surely it would be an affront to the people of this state, as the convention speak in their previous address, "to labor to convince them that the honor and happiness of a people depend upon morality; and that the public worship of God has a tendency to inculcate the principles thereof, as well as to preserve a people from forsaking civilization, and falling into a state of savage barbarity."

Of these, and other excellent properties of our present constitution, the citizens of this state are throughly sensible, or well informed, and jealous as they are of their rights, they never would have adopted and ratified it with so great a degree of unanimity. They know it is framed upon an extent of civil and religious liberty, unexampled perhaps in any country in the world, except America. This must highly endear it to them; and while it is written upon their own hearts, they have the satisfaction to find that it has already received the elogiums of others, whose capacity and distinction render their testimony truly honorable. But left thro' the imperfection of human nature, and after all the deliberation and caution with which it has been formed and approved, some inconveniences should be found lurking in it, of which experience can best inform us, a right is expressly reserved to the people of removing them in a revision of the whole, after a fair experiment of fifteen years.

When a people have the rare felicity of chusing their own government, every part of it should first be weighed in the balance of reason, and nicely adjusted to the claims of liberty, equity and order; but when this is done, a warm and passionate patriotism should be added to the result of cool deliberation, to put in motion and animate the whole machine. The citizens of a free republic should reverence their constitution: They should not only calmly approve, and readily submit to it, but regard it also with veneration and affection rising even to an enthusiasm, like that which prevailed at Sparta and at Rome. Nothing can render a commonwealth more illustrious, nothing more powerful, than such a manly, such a sacred fire. Every thing will then be subordinated to the public welfare; every labour necessary to this will be chearfully endured, every expence readily submitted to, every danger boldly confronted.

May this heavenly flame animate all orders of men in the state! May it catch from bosom to bosom, and the glow be universal! May a double portion of it inhabit the breasts of our civil rulers, and impart a lustre to them like that which sat upon the face of Moses, when he came down from the holy mountain with the tables of the Hebrew constitution in his hand! Thus will they sustain with true dignity the first honours, the first marks of esteem and confidence, the first public employments bestowed by this new commonwealth, and in which they this day appear. Such men must naturally care for our state; men whose abilities and virtues have obtained a sanction from the free suffrages of their enlightned and virtuous fellow citizens. Are not these suffrages, a public and solemn testimony that in the opinion of their constituents, they are men who have steadily acted upon the noble principles on which the frame of our government now rests? Men who have generously neglected their private interest in an ardent pursuit of that of the public—men who have intrepidly opposed one of the greatest powers on earth, and put their fortunes and their lives to no small hazard in fixing the basis of our freedom and honour. Who can forbear congratulating our rising state, and casting up a thankful eye to heaven, upon this great and singular occasion, the establishment of our congregation; our nobles freely chosen by ourselves; and our governour coming forth, at the call of his country, from the midst of us?

Behold the man, whose name as president of Congress, authenticates that immortal act, which, in form, constitutes the independence of these United States, and by which a nation was literally born in a day! See him, who had taken too early and decided a part, and done too much for the liberties of America, to be forgiven by it's enemies! See him, whose name, with that of another distinguished patriot,* was expressly excepted from a British act of grace, and upon whose head a price was virtually bid by those who meant to enslave us: Behold this very man, declared by the voice of his country, "the head of the corner" in our political building; the first magistrate of this free commonwealth. It was not in the power of his fellow-citizens to give an higher testimony how well they remember the generous and important services he has already rendered to his country, and how much they confide in his disposition and abilities still to serve it.

May God Almighty take his Excellency and the other honourable branches of the government, the lieutenant-governour, the council, the Senate, and House of Representatives into his holy protection, and unite them in measures glorious to themselves, and happy to their country! Vested as they are with particular honours, they have a painful prehеminence: Their distinctions call them to the most weighty and important cares, at a time when the administration of public affairs is attended with peculiar difficulties. They need therefore the gracious direction and assistance of the "blessed and only potentate," which, in this solemn assembly of rulers and people, we jointly and devoutly implore.

The people of a free state have a right to expect from those whom they have honoured with the direction of their public concerns, a faithful and unremitting attention to these concerns. He who accepts a public trust, pledges himself, his sacred honour, and by his official

*The Honorable Samuel Adams, Esq.

oath appeals to his God, that with all good fidelity, and to the utmost of his capacity he will discharge this trust. And that commonwealth which doth not keep an eye of care upon those who govern, and observe how they behave in their several departments, in order to regulate its suffrages upon this standard, will soon find itself in perplexity, and cannot expect long to preserve either its dignity or happiness.

Dignity of conduct is ever connected with the happiness of a state; particularly at its rise, and the first appearance it makes in the world. Then all eyes are turned upon it; they view it with attention; and the first impressions it makes are commonly lasting. This circumstance must render the conduct of our present rulers peculiarly important, and fall with particular weight upon their minds. We hope from their wisdom and abilities, their untainted integrity and unshaken firmness, this new-formed commonwealth will rise with honour and applause, and attract that respect, which the number and quality of its inhabitants, the extent of its territory and commerce, and the natural advantages with which it is blest, cannot fail, under a good government, to command.

From our present happy establishment we may reasonably hope for a new energy in government; an energy that shall be felt in all parts of the state: We hope that the sinews of civil authority through its whole frame will be well braced, and the public interest in all its extended branches be well attended to; that no officer will be permitted to neglect the duties, or transgress the bounds of his department; that peculations, frauds, and even the smaller oppressions in any office, will be watchfully prevented, or exemplarily punished; and that no corruption will be allowed to rest in any part of the political body, no not in the extremest, which may spread by degrees, and finally reach the very vitals of the community.

Righteousness, says one of the greatest politicians and wisest princes that ever lived, "Righteousness exalteth a nation." This maxim doth not barely rest upon his own but also on a divine authority; and the truth of it hath been verified by the experience of all ages.

Our civil rulers will remember, that as piety and virtue support the honour and happiness of every community, they are peculiarly requisite in a free government. Virtue is the spirit of a republic; for where all power is derived from the people, all depends on their good disposition. If they are impious, factious and selfish; if they are abandoned to idleness, dissipation, luxury, and extravagance; if they are lost to the fear of God, and the love of their country, all is lost. Having got beyond the restraints of a divine authority, they will not brook the control of laws enacted by rulers of their own creating. We may therefore rely that the present government will do all it fairly can, by authority and example, to answer the end of its institution, that the members of this commonwealth may *lead a quiet and peaceable life in all godliness as well as honesty*, and our liberty never be justly reproached as licentiousness.

I know there is a diversity of sentiment respecting the extent of civil power in religious matters. Instead of entering into the dispute, may I be allowed from the warmth of my heart, to recommend, where conscience is pleaded on both sides, mutual candour and love, and an happy union of all denominations in support of a government, which though human, and therefore not absolutely perfect, is yet certainly founded on the broadest basis of liberty, and affords equal protection to all. Warm parties upon civil or religious matters, or from personal considerations, are greatly injurious to a free state, and particularly so to one newly formed. We have indeed less of this than might be expected: We shall be happy to have none at all; happy indeed, when every man shall love and serve his country, and have that share of public influence and respect, without distinction of parties, which his virtues and services may justly demand. This is the true spirit of a commonwealth, centring all hearts, and all hands in the common interest.

Neither piety, virtue, or liberty can long flourish in a community, where the education of youth is neglected. How much do we owe to the care of our venerable ancestors upon this important object? Had not they laid such foundations for training up their children in knowledge and religion, in science, and arts, should we have been so respectable a community as we this day appear? Should we have understood our rights so clearly? or valued them so highly? or defended them with such advantage? Or should we have been prepared to lay that basis of liberty, that happy constitution, on which we raise such large hopes, and from which we derive such uncommon joy? We may therefore be confident that the schools, and particularly the university, founded and cherished by our wise and pious fathers, will be patronized and nursed by a government which is so much indebted to them for its honour and efficacy, and the very principles of its existence. The present circumstances of those institutions call for the kindest attention of our rulers; and their close connection with every public interest, civil and religious, strongly enforces the call.

The sciences and arts, for the encouragement of which a new foundation* hath lately been laid in this commonwealth, deserve the countenance and particular favour of every government. They are not only ornamental but useful: They not only polish, but support, enrich, and defend a community. As they delight in liberty, they are particularly friendly to free states. Barbarians are fierce and ungovernable, and having the grossest ideas of order, and the benefits resulting from it, they require the hand of a stern master; but a people enlightened and civilized by the sciences and liberal arts, have sentiments that support liberty and good laws: They may be guided by a silken thread; and the mild punishments proper to a free state are sufficient to guard the public peace.

An established honour and fidelity in all public engagements and promises, form a branch of righteousness that is wealth, is power, and security to a state: It prevents innumerable perplexities: It creates confidence in the government from subjects and from strangers: It facilitates the most advantageous connections: It extends credit; and easily obtains supplies in the most pressing public emergencies, and when nothing else can obtain them: While the want of it, whatever benefits some shortsighted politicians may have promised from delusive expedients, and deceitful arts, renders a state weak and contemptible; strips it of its defence; grieves and provoke[s] its friends, and delivers it up to the will of its enemies. Upon what does the power of the British nation chiefly rest at this moment? That power that has been so unrighteously employed against America? Upon the long and nice preservation of her faith in all monied matters. With all her injustice in other instances, meer policy hath obliged her to maintain a fair character with her creditors. The support this hath given her in frequent and expensive wars, by the supplies it has enabled her to raise upon loan, is astonishing. By this her government hath availed itself of the whole immense capital of the national debt, which

*The American Academy of Arts and Sciences.

hath been expended in the public service, while the creditors content themselves with the bare payment of the interest. It may be demonstrated that the growing resources of these states, under the conduct of prudence and justice, are sufficient to form a fund of credit for prosecuting the present war, so ruinous to Britain, much longer than that nation, loaded as she now is, can possibly support it.

But need I urge, in a christian audience, and before christian rulers, the importance of preserving inviolate the public faith? If this is allowed to be important at all times, and to all states, it must be peculiarly so to those whose foundations are newly laid, and who are but just numbered among the nations of the earth. They have a national character to establish, upon which their very existence may depend. Shall we not then rely that the present government will employ every measure in their power, to maintain in this commonwealth a clear justice, an untainted honour in all public engagements; in all laws respecting property; in all regulations of taxes; in all our conduct towards our sister states, and towards our allies abroad.

The treaty of alliance and friendship between *his most christian majesty* and these states, is engraved on every bosom friendly to the rights and independence of America. If fidelity dwells in such bosoms, it will be conspicuous on every occasion of performing our own part of these sacred stipulations. The interest is indeed mutual, as was openly confessed: The treaty is therefore natural, and likely to be lasting. But mutual interest doth not always banish generosity; a proof of which our illustrious ally hath given in this compact; a proof not unapplauded in Europe, tho' particularly felt and acknowledged in America. I will not affront either the understanding or the feelings of this respectable audience, by attempting formally to demonstrate that we have received great advantages and support from this friendship. It is impossible we should forget the first pledge of it, in the squadron sent to our aid under the orders of that vigilant, active and intrepid commander the Count d'Estaing; who greatly disconcerted the designs of the enemy, and did everything for us that wisdom and valour, in his situation, could perform. Nor need I call your attention to that important armament lately arrived to our assistance, under leaders of distinguished abilities, and the most established military reputation. France, tho' a monarchy, has been the nurse and protectress of free republics. Switzerland among others can attest to this:

Her free states can attest, that during an alliance with France of more than three hundred years, their liberties have been constantly befriended by that nation, and every part of the treaty for their support punctually performed. This they have acknowledged in a late solemn renewal of the alliance. An happy omen to these states, whose circumstances are in many respects similar to those of the united cantons of Switzerland.

The personal and royal accomplishments of Louis the Sixteenth are known and admired far beyond his own extended dominions, and afford the brightest prospect to his subjects and allies. The reign of this monarch diffuses new spirit through his kingdom, and gives freshness to the glory of France. A British author, in his account of the regulations which took place after this prince had ascended the throne, calls him "a paternal and patriotic sovereign, who wherever he appears is loaded with the blessings of his subjects." The celebrated Mr. Burke, in his speech before the British House of Commons on February last, adds his own testimony to this, when speaking of some reforms in the finances and the court of France, he says, "The minister who does these things is a great man, but the prince who desires they should be done, is a far greater: We must do justice to our enemies; these are the acts of a patriot king." The friendship of such a monarch must be valuable indeed!

The other great and powerful branch of the house of Bourbon, the king of Spain, tho' not at present formally allied to us, is yet evidently engaged in our cause, by the union of his arms with those of France. We cannot be wanting in the sentiments due to the amity and aid of so respectable a potentate. May God Almighty bless these princes, and their dominions; and crown their arms, and those of America, with such success as may soon restore to a bleeding world the blessings of peace!

Peace, peace, we ardently wish; but not upon terms dishonourable to ourselves, or dangerous to our liberties; and our enemies seem not yet prepared to allow it upon any other. At present the voice of providence, the call of our still invaded country, and the cry of every thing dear to us, all unite to rouze us to prosecute the war with redoubled vigour; upon the success of which all our free constitutions, all our hopes depend. I need not enumerate the former or more recent events of the war, and the favours or chastisements of heaven sent to us in these events: They are known to you; they cannot be forgotten: God grant they may be properly improved! Thro' his aid, amidst all our mistakes and errors, we have already done great things; but our warfare is not yet accomplished: And our rulers, we hope, like the Roman general, will think nothing done, while any thing remains undone.

We have depended too much upon partial measures, temporary expedients, short and interrupted efforts made only upon the spur of the occasion. An army established in proper numbers, for the whole duration of the war and seasonably furnished with all necessary supplies, is now universally acknowledged of the utmost consequence to the liberties of America. Particular attention will certainly be paid to the recommendations of this great object from the commander in chief—that illustrious man, formed by heaven for the important trust he sustains, and to draw to a point the confidence of these free states, and a patriotic army. Part of the gladness of this day rises from the general expectation, that our new government will give new vigour to the measures necessary to this momentous purpose; that these measures will be instantly pursued, and without that delay we have too much experienced in times past; and which, at this season, must prove greatly distressing, if not fatal to our country.

Can we hesitate a moment at the burden and expence? It is impossible. Why have the citizens of America been framing such wise and excellent constitutions, if they meant not to maintain, but leave them to become the sport of their enemies? If after all the memorable things we have done to repel lawless power, and establish our rights; if after all we have endured in a war savagely conducted by our enemies; if after the rank we have taken, and the reputation we have acquired as an independent nation, we should now relax in our efforts, and suffer tyranny finally to prevail, who can bear to think of the consequences or to look upon the picture imagination presents? In such a reverse, we may "write" upon this fair region the inscription given to an antient dungeon—"You who enter here, leave behind you every hope." What would not this people do; what exertions would they not make, rather than submit to such debasement and misery? It is with you, our civil fathers, to direct such a spirit, and such exertions, in a manner the most effectual to the salvation of our country.

What heroes have bled, what invaluable lives have been offered up to redeem us from slavery, and place us on a free constitution? Their names will never die: Their honours will never wither. Among these we see a Warren, and a Montgomery: Liberty wept over their tombs; and there would have remained inconsolate, had she not beheld a succession of patriots and warriors rising in the same spirit. Rights retrieved with such blood as hath flowed from the veins of America in our great cause, must certainly be held by us at an inestimable price, and improved to the greatest advantage; nor can any thing shew their value in a clearer light, than a good administration of our free governments.

Our present rulers, as principal founders of the constitution, cannot but regard it with parental tenderness. They cannot but love their own offspring, especially when it has features and charms to attract the love and admiration of the world: And hoping that their names and their glory may long live in such an offspring, they have an irresistible motive to guard against every thing that may weaken or deform it; every thing that may render its existence short, precarious, or dishonourable.

The same kind of motive must excite the body of the people to the same care. It is with you also my fellow-citizens, by whose appointment this constitution was framed, and who have solemnly acknowledged it to be your own; it is with you to give life and vigour to all its limbs[,] freshness and beauty to its whole complexion; to guard it from dangers; to preserve it "from the corruption that is in the world"; and to produce it upon the great theatre of nations with advantage and glory. We have now a government free indeed; but after all, it remains with the people, under God, to make it an honourable and happy one: This must ultimately depend upon the prudence of their elections, and the virtue of their conduct. A government framed by ourselves for our own benefit, and according to the fairest models of our own minds, and administred by men of our own choice, ought to be more deeply respected, and more religiously supported by us than any kind of imposed authority. Having defined and adjusted its powers by our own decisions, and made those who are vested with such as are improper to be long continued in the same hands, amenable, at short intervals, to the judgment of the people, we never can allow it too much weight and energy; we only support ourselves in supporting such authority: While to oppose or weaken it, or bring it under an undue influence, is with the hand of a parricide to destroy order, liberty, and happiness. Upon this general principle, and to establish a dignity and independence, where they must forever operate to the benefit of the community; the citizens of this state have by their present constitution, most freely and wisely secured to their chief magistrate, and the justices of the supreme judicial court, permanent and honourable salaries; an article which, we cannot doubt, will be sacredly observed in the true spirit of the constitution.

In a word, if the rulers and the people act throughout in this spirit; if they mutually watch over and sustain each other; and those virtues are cultivated among us which support and are supported by a free republic, our new government will then open with the most happy omens, and the commencement of it will be the æra of our rising felicity and glory.

While we receive in the settlement of our commonwealth a reward of our atchievements and sufferings, we have the further consolation to reflect, that they have tended to the general welfare, and the support of the rights of mankind. The struggle of America hath afforded to oppressed Ireland a favourable opportunity of insisting upon her own privileges: Nor do any of the powers in Europe oppose our cause, or seem to wish it may be unsuccessful. Britain has maintained her naval superiority with such marks of haughtiness and oppression as have justly given umbrage to the nations around her: They cannot therefore but wish to see her power confined within reasonable bounds, and such as may be consistent with the safety of their own commercial rights. This, they know would at least be exceeding difficult, should the rapidly increasing force of these states be reunited with Britain, and wielded by her, as it hath been in time past, against every nation upon whom she is pleased to make war. So favourable, through the divine superintendence, is the present situation of the powers in Europe, to the liberties and independence for which we are contending. But as individuals must part with some natural liberties for the sake of the security and advantages of society; the same kind of commutation must take place in the great republic of nations. The rights of kingdoms and states have their bounds; and as in our own establishment we are not likely to find reason, I trust we shall never have an inclination to exceed these bounds, and justly to excite the jealousy and opposition of other nations. It is thus wisdom, moderation and sound policy would connect kingdoms and states for their mutual advantage, and preserve the order and harmony of the world. In all this these free states will find their own security, and rise by natural and unenvied degrees to that eminence, for which, I would fain perswade myself, we are designed.

It is laudable to lay the foundations of our republicks with extended views. Rome rose to empire because she early thought herself destined for it. The great object was continually before the eyes of her sons: It enlarged and invigorated their minds; it excited their vigilance; it elated their courage, and prepared them to embrace toils and dangers, and submit to every regulation friendly to the freedom and prosperity of Rome. They did great things because they believed themselves capable, and born to do them. They reverenced themselves and their country; and animated with unbounded respect for it, they every day added to its strength and glory. Conquest is not indeed the aim of these rising states; sound policy must ever forbid it: We have before us an object more truly great and honourable. We seem called by heaven to make a large portion of this globe a seat of knowledge and liberty, of agriculture, commerce, and arts, and what is more important than all, of christian piety and virtue. A celebrated British historian observes, if I well remember, that the natural features of America are peculiarly striking. Our mountains, our rivers and lakes have a singular air of dignity and grandeur. May our conduct correspond to the face of our country! At present an immense part of it lies as nature hath left it, and human labour and art have done but little, and brightened only some small specks of a continent that can afford ample means of subsistence to many, many millions of the human race. It remains with us and our posterity, to "make the wilderness become a fruitful field, and the desert blossom as the rose"; to establish the honour and happiness of this new world, as far as it may be justly our own, and to invite the injured and oppressed, the worthy and the good to these shores, by the most liberal governments, by wise political institutions, by cultivating the confidence and friendship of other nations, and by a sacred attention to that gospel that breaths "peace on earth, and good will towards men." Thus will our country resemble the new city which St. John saw "coming down from God out of heaven, adorned as a bride for her husband." Is there a benevolent spirit on earth, or on high, whom such a prospect would not delight?

But what are those illustrious forms that seem to hover over us on the present great occasion, and to look down with pleasure on the memorable transactions of this day? Are they not the founders and lawgivers, the skilful pilots and brave defenders of free states, whose fame "flows down through all ages, enlarging as it flows"? They, who thought no toils or vigilance too great to establish and protect the rights of human nature; no riches too large to be exchanged for them; no blood too precious to be shed for their redemption? But who are they who seem to approach nearer to us, and in whose countenances we discern a peculiar mixture of gravity and joy upon this solemnity? Are they not the venerable fathers of the Massachusetts; who though not perfect while they dwelt in flesh, were yet greatly distinguished by an ardent piety, by all the manly virtues, and by an unquenchable love of liberty—they, who to form a retreat for it, crossed the ocean, through innumerable difficulties, to a savage land: They, who brought with them a broad charter of liberty, over which they wept when it was wrested from them by the hand of power, and an insidious one placed in its room. With what pleasure do they seem to behold their children, like the antient seed of Abraham, this day restored to their original foundations of freedom! their Governor "as at the first, and their Councellors as at the beginning"? Do they not call upon us to defend these foundations at every hazard, and to perpetuate their honour in the liberty and virtue of the state they planted?

O thou supreme Governor of the world, whose arm hath done great things for us, establish the foundations of this commonwealth, and evermore defend it with the saving strength of thy right hand! Grant that here the divine constitutions of Jesus thy Son may ever be honoured and maintained! Grant that it may be the residence of all private and patriotic virtues, of all that enlightens and supports, all that sweetens and adorns human society, till the states and kingdoms of this world shall be swallowed up in thine own kingdom: In that, which alone is immortal, may we obtain a perfect citizenship, and enjoy in its completion, "the glorious Liberty of the Sons of God![''] And let all the people say, *Amen!*

22

A SERMON PREACHED AT LEXINGTON ON THE 19TH OF APRIL

Henry Cumings

BOSTON
1781

HENRY CUMINGS (1739–1823). One of the ablest men of his time, Cumings was graduated with the 1760 class at Harvard, awarded an S.T.D. by Harvard in 1800, and spent his career as pastor of the First Congregational Parish of Billerica, Massachusetts. From the early 1770s Cumings was a zealous patriot who decried the tyranny of Great Britain in its dealings with the colonies; to him, Americans were "the chosen people of God, raised up and sustained by his Providence" (*Sibley's Harvard Graduates*, 14:580). Favoring the revivalism of the Great Awakening and of Edwards and Whitefield, he placed reason and biblical revelation at the center of his religion so as to be regarded as an Arminian and, later, as a Unitarian, despite his insistence that he was an evangelical. "God is love" stood at the center of his faith, and he defined Christianity as "a religion calculated to exalt and elevate human nature, and array it with the glorious ornaments of moral beauty and grace divine . . . which irradiates the understanding, with the brightest lights, and fires the passions, with an inestimable prize" (in Joseph Sumner, *A Sermon Delivered at Chelmsford* [Cambridge, Mass., 1804], p. 18). He argued against deism and Jacobinism in later life with the same verve he had brought to the patriot cause earlier. He was a delegate to the Massachusetts constitutional convention in 1780 and made important contributions there.

Cumings published seventeen works, many having considerable value and demonstrating his incisive and distinguished mind. The sermon reprinted here is from the middle of his life, preached at Lexington on April 19, 1781, on the sixth anniversary of the beginning of the Revolution.

A
SERMON

PREACHED AT

LEXINGTON.

ON THE 19th OF *April*, 1781.

Being the Anniversary of the Commencement of Hostilities between *Great Britain* and *America*, which took Place in that Town, on the 19th of *April*, 1775.

By *HENRY CUMINGS*, A. M.

Pastor of the Church in *Billerica*,

Hitherto hath the LORD helped us.

SAMUEL.

There are many devices in a man's heart; nevertheless the council of the LORD, that shall stand.

SOLOMON.

BOSTON:

Printed by BENJAMIN EDES & SONS,

IN STATE-STREET.

M,DCC,LXXXI.

Surely the wrath of man shall praise thee: the remainder of wrath shalt thou restrain.

Psalm LXXVI. 10.

Though God, (for wise reasons, best known to himself) has permitted sin to enter into the world; yet, we may be sure, he will not suffer the purposes of his goodness to be frustrated by it; but will, in some way or other, over-rule this worst of evils, for good; and make sinners themselves (contrary to their design and intention), the instruments of promoting the great ends of his moral government, and the occasional causes of benefit to others, at the same time, that they expose themselves to misery and ruin, which will inevitably come upon them, either in this world or in that to come, or in both, as a just punishment for their wickedness, unless prevented by repentance.

It cannot be doubted, but the infinitely wise God knows how to promote his own glory, by those ungoverned lusts of envious, discontented and proud mortals, which are a prolific source of continual mischief and misery, both to particular persons and societies, and whereby thousands and ten thousands are involved in great troubles and grievous distresses, all the days of their lives. And as God knows how to promote his own glory, by the lusts of men, so we have reason to believe that he will do it (as he has done it already, in innumerable obvious instances, from the beginning of the world), either by laying restraints upon those lusts, or over-ruling their operations in such a manner, as to make them contribute (in direct contrariety to their natural aim) to the execution of his own gracious purposes; or, by taking occasion from them, to exhibit such remarkable displays of his power, wisdom and goodness, as shall be admirably adapted to beget and cherish adoring thoughts of his being, perfections, and providence, and to produce all those external honorary acts of worship and homage which he requires of us.

We live in an angry and provoking world. Ever since the fatal apostacy of our first parents, *the wrath of man* has been at work to spread misery and wretchedness over the face of the earth. *Hateful and hating one another*, is too much the character of by far the greater part of the human race. It seems indeed, that it must be evident to every one, that the happiness of social life depends essentially upon the exercise of mutual benevolence and the constant reciprocal interchange of kind and friendly offices; but yet, as if men were entirely ignorant of the vast advantages of love and harmony, peace and friendship, it may, with truth, be affirmed of the generality, that they

> Live in hatred, enmity and strife
> Among themselves, and levy cruel wars,
> Wasting the earth, each other to destroy.

Through the prevalence of pride, envy, ambition, avarice, and other corrupt lusts, the earth is full of the habitations of violence, cruelty and war. These passions are the grand source of mutual jealousies, animosities, enmities, reproaches, insults and injuries; they lead directly to a violation of every moral obligation, and of every principle of social virtue; their natural fruits are injustice, unrighteousness & oppression, from whence come strife and contention, discord, tumult and disorder; and when they are inflamed with wrath and armed with power, they generally drive matters to extremity, pushing men into such arbitrary and cruel actions and pursuits, as enkindle the flames of war, which it often requires a vast effusion of human blood to extinguish.

But when we see or feel the sad effects of the disorderly passions and baneful distempers of human nature, our comfort is, *that the Lord God omnipotent reigneth*, who can and will answer his own most wise purposes thereby, or set bounds thereto, as to his infinite wisdom shall seem best. This comfortable doctrine is clearly contained in the text. We may rest assured, that the supreme governor of the world, will not suffer *the wrath of man*, of a weak and impotent mortal, (how much soever advanced above his fellow mortals) to overthrow his government, or defeat the counsels of his wisdom; but will cause it to praise him; that is, (as was just now suggested) he will either so check and restrain it, or so manage and over-rule the operations of it, as to make it subservient to the ends and designs of his providence, and the occasional cause of such events, as shall shew forth his perfections, and induce every attentive and pious observer, to praise and glorify him.

I doubt not, my hearers, but you can recollect instances that have fallen under your own observation, wherein the lusts of particular persons have been either remarkably restrained, or remarkably overruled, as occasions of good, where evil was designed and intended. Every instance of this kind, that comes within our view, should lead us to admire and adore the wisdom and goodness of God, who disappointeth the evil designs of sinners, and causeth even the operation of their lusts to be productive of events, in favour of those, whom they meant to injure.

Sacred history furnishes us with many instances, to this purpose. I will mention a few of them, which will serve, at once, to illustrate the meaning of the text, and to suggest some thoughts and reflections, suitable to the present occasion.

The story of Joseph, in the book of Genesis, affords one instance, to this purpose. Instigated by pride, envy, anger and unreasonable resentment, his brethren sold him into Egypt. They had nothing in view, in this base and unnatural action, but the gratification of their own unruly passions and corrupt lusts; but the wisdom of GOD overruled it for good, contrary to their expectation and design. They thought evil against their innocent brother, when they sold him for a slave; but this heinously wicked action of theirs, was the occasion of his promotion to high honor and authority in the Egyptian court, whereby he was enabled to *save his father's house, and much people alive* in a time of famine.

Another pertinent instance, we may find in the history of Pharaoh, in the beginning of the book of Exodus. The wrath and madness of Pharaoh, and the cruelties which his haughty and savage temper prompted him to exercise upon the children of Israel, in order to check their growth, and secure them in a state of dependance and base servitude, prepared the way, under the government of Providence, for their remarkable deliverance; and afforded occasions for a series of such wonderful displays of the power of GOD, as could not but excite all pious observers, to pay him their devout honors and adorations. And the destruction, which Pharaoh's pride and obstinacy plunged him into, was no less remarkable, than was the deliverance of Israel. From whence it is natural to observe, that proud aspiring mortals are often *ensnared in the work of their own hands*, and defeated by the very measures which they take to carry their iniquitous schemes into execution. *There are many devices in a man's heart*, says the wise man, *but the counsel of the Lord, that shall stand.*

The great men, the princes and potentates of the earth, who are entrusted with the management of the affairs of states and kingdoms, are as much subject to the controul of an higher power, as any of the lower ranks and classes of people. They are all at the disposal of the supreme Governor of the world, whose providence, as it is concerned in all occurrences and events, and in all the vicissitudes of human affairs, so does more especially interpose in the rise and fall of empires, and in all the great revolutions that take place among the nations of the earth. In ways and by means unthought of and unforeseen, the profoundest policies and most promising schemes of restless ambition, are often disconcerted, and the measures adopted by it, made to terminate in its own confusion. When this is the case, we have always reason to adore the providence of that almighty Being, who presides over the world, and as the disposer of all events.

Those men, who are actuated by a lust of power and domination, seem, sometimes, to be judicially left of God, to use such methods, for the promotion of their ambitious schemes, as have a direct tendency to defeat their enterprizes, and to preserve to others those important rights and liberties, of which they endeavour to rob them, for the sake of aggrandizing themselves. The conduct of Rehoboam, after the death of his father Solomon (as it is recorded in the twelfth chapter of the first book of Kings) affords a very striking example of this kind. As soon as Rehoboam came to the throne of his father, the people applied to him, with their petitions, for a redress of grievances: But Rehoboam, despising the moderate counsels of the aged and wise, and following the imprudent advice of young and unskilful courtiers, as being more agreeable to his own aspiring and ambitious views, answered the people roughly, and rejected their petitions with insult. In consequence of such ill-treatment, ten tribes revolted, and set up another king over them: Of this revolt and revolution, Rehoboam himself was the immediate occasional or procuring cause. His pride and haughtiness, alienated from him the hearts of the greatest part of his subjects, and divided his father's dominion into two kingdoms. But it is very observable, that it is expressly said, *The cause was from the Lord;* and this is assigned as the reason why Rehoboam, adhering to the imprudent counsels of raw and rash politicians, rejected, with affrontive insolence, the reasonable petitions of the people. This revolution being agreeable to the will of GOD, Rehoboam was left to his own folly, which kept the things of his peace out of sight, and influenced him to take a step, which provoked the most of the tribes to throw off their allegiance, and reject him from being king over them. Thus GOD often *taketh the wise in their own craftiness;* causing the measures which they principally depend upon, for accomplishing their ambitious designs, to produce events directly contrary to their views and expectations.

By their wrath, by their vindictive resentments, the haughty and ambitious, are sometimes precipitated into actions, for the gratification of their pride and revenge, which not only issue in their own ruin, but in the advancement of those whom they meant to destroy. Haman (of whom we have a particular account in the book of Esther) is an instance, in proof of this. In the fierceness of his wrath (the occasion of which, it may be presumed you are not ignorant of) Haman plotted the destruction of Mordecai, and all the Jews in the kingdom of Ahasuerus; and had the address to obtain a decree from the king, for that purpose. But this infernal plot terminated in his own utter ruin, and led the way to Mordecai's promotion, affording, at the same time, an occasion for a signal display of the wisdom and goodness of Providence, in the deliverance of the Jews from the destruction that was just ready to fall upon them. This instance, with that of Pharaoh before mentioned, will sufficiently justify the following observation, viz. that,

Great and important revolutions, in favour of the cause of righteousness and liberty, are sometimes brought about, by means of the cruel and vindictive measures, which powerful oppressors take, to promote their ambitious views, and to keep others in awe and servile dependence. Wrath and cruelty are generally rash and precipitate, and calculated to raise a spirit of indignation and desperate opposition, in those who feel the sad effects of them. The haughty tyrant, who endeavours to advance his oppressive schemes, and to set himself up above all law and justice, by severities and cruelties, dictated by wrath, does thereby frequently work out his own disappointment, and is forced eventually to acknowledge his impotence, and to own a power above himself.

But when the power of oppressors is so great, as to bear down all opposition, and compel people to a servile submission, it is to be considered as a just judgment of GOD, who sometimes causes *the wrath of man to praise him*, by employing it to punish a people for their sins. And herein we may observe the unsearchable wisdom of GOD, who, while man (unnecessitated by any foreign impulse) is impiously and wickedly gratifying his lusts, makes those very lusts subservient to his providence, for the punishment of others. This is admirably set forth in the conduct of the Assyrian monarch (as the same is recorded in the tenth chapter of the prophecy of Isaiah.) GOD was pleased to make use of this haughty tyrant, as a rod, for the correction and chastisement of his people; wisely managing the distempers of his proud and ambitious mind, for the punishment of the Jews, for their sinful defections from him. But as the Assyrian acted freely, being under no constraint, it was no excuse for him, that GOD made his pride and ambition, instrumental in bringing his righteous judgments on the Jewish nation; but his conduct was highly affrontive to heaven, and exposed him to the righteous resentments of the supreme Governor. *Wherefore*, says GOD, *when I have performed my whole will on Zion and Jerusalem, I will punish the fruit of the stout heart of the king of Assyria, and the glory of his high looks.*

In the instances that have been mentioned above, we see, that so far as GOD permits *the wrath of man* to exert itself, he will over-rule the operations of it, for advancing the important purposes of his government; and we are fully assured that he will, in no cases, suffer it to break out farther, than shall redound to his praise and honor. *The remainder of wrath he will restrain;* that is, he will set bounds to it, and render it unable to accomplish what it aims at. Thus (as we are informed in the 37th chapter of the prophecy of Isaiah) he restrained Sennacherib's wrath, and forced him to quit his enterprize against Jerusalem. Sennacherib carried his boasts and menaces to such an height, as implied a defiance of the great Lord of heaven and earth; but the GOD whom he defied interposed, and prevented his attempting what he designed, by the miraculous destruction of one hundred and eighty-five thousand of his army in one night; *thus putting an hook in his nose, and a bridle in his jaws*, and obliging him to return home ashamed. Such miraculous interpositions of providence for *restraining the wrath of man*, cannot indeed be rationally expected, in common cases; but GOD can do this as effectually, without a miracle, as with, as will appear from what will presently be offered.

Should GOD permit the wrath of man to do all that it designs, what havock and devastation, what mischief and wretchedness, would it spread through the world? This world, at best, is a very turbulent scene; but it would be much more so, did not providence lay restraints upon the lusts and passions of ill-designing men, and prevent their going to such lengths in mischief, as they wish. It is happy for the world, that man's power is not equal to his wrath; and that those, who, instigated by an evil temper, form mischievous projects, are often hindered from executing them; at least, to that extent, which they desire.

There are many ways, wherein GOD checks and restrains *the wrath of man*, and defeats its pernicious devices, when, and so far as he pleases.

Sometimes he does this by raising a spirit of fear, whereby men are discouraged from undertaking or prosecuting those mischievous enterprizes, which their wrath and corrupt lusts would otherwise prompt them to undertake and pursue. As GOD has the *hearts of all men in his hands, and turneth them whithersoever he will, as the rivers of water*, so there is reason to believe that, by secret influences, he does sometimes raise and sometimes depress the natural spirits of men, for the promotion of his purposes of judgment or of mercy. Every one who is acquainted with, and firmly believes the divine philosophy of the scriptures, must be clear in this, that GOD can, and frequently does, by immediate impressions on the mind, so effectually dishearten and intimidate those, whose vindictive passions would lead them into all manner of mischief and cruelty, as either to confine the operations of their wrath to themselves, or to render it weak and impotent, faint and irresolute, in its attempts against others. The tyrants of the earth are, no doubt, often thus restrained. *Faintness is sent into their hearts*, and fear takes hold on them, which serves as a barrier against that torrent of wrath, which would otherwise spread destruction and desolation all around them. Again,

Sometimes GOD restrains men's wrath by interposing unthought-of accidents, obstacles and difficulties, which entirely disconcert their measures and overthrow their mischievous schemes and devices. *The race is not to the swift*, says the royal preacher, *nor the battle to the strong, neither yet bread to the wise, nor yet riches to men of understanding, nor yet favour to men of skill; but time and chance happeneth to them all:* by which he doubtless means to teach us, "that there is a secret providence concerned in all human affairs, which sometimes presents men with unexpected opportunities, or interposeth accidents, which no human wisdom could foresee; which sometimes produceth events contrary to human probabilities, giving success to very unlikely means, and defeating the swift, the strong, the learned, the industrious, and those that are best versed in men and business, of their several ends, and designs." All nature is at the beck of the great Creator, who, when he pleases, can employ any part thereof, to *disappoint the devices of the crafty, and carry the counsels of the froward headlong.* What we call second causes, are entirely dependent upon the great first cause, to whom they owe all their force and energy; and who can, and, no doubt, often does (either immediately by himself, or mediately by subordinate agents) occasionally suspend, retard or quicken their influence, to frustrate the most promising schemes of men, and thereby to humble their pride, to teach them their dependence, and to promote his own most wise purposes. Secret and hidden causes he often sets to work, whereby unforeseen and unexpected events are produced, which overthrow the schemes of human pride, ambition and revenge. By storms and pestilences, by disasters and misfortunes, which no human skill could foresee, or power obviate, he frequently cohibits the wrath of the mightiest potentates, and crushes the mischievous machinations of his people's enemies into abortion.

Further, GOD sometimes checks and *restrains the wrath of men*, by leaving them to judicial infatuation, whereby they are led to adopt counsels and measures, tending, in the natural course of things, to defeat their designs, and overthrow their enterprizes. When men are pushing forward their iniquitous schemes with the greatest zeal and vehemence, and have the most flattering prospects of success, they are sometimes, by an unaccountable imprudence, led to reject the counsels most favourable to their designs, and to embrace those that lead directly to disappointment. The story of Absolom, in the second book of Samuel (not to mention again the case of Rehoboam) furnishes an instance of this kind. Absolom raised a rebellion against his father David; but in prosecuting his ambitious views, he was remarkably influenced to adopt measures, calculated to defeat and disappoint him. The sage advice of Ahithophel, a judicious and skilful counsellor, though most favourable to his designs, was turned into foolishness in his sight, and he was left to comply with counsels of a different nature, which issued in the ruin both of his wicked projects, and himself. This was the Lord's doing. And thus GOD sometimes judicially *hides wisdom from the wise*, and leaves them to pursue such imprudent methods, as directly tend to disappoint their hopes, and frustrate their most promising schemes.

Once more, another way wherein GOD *restrains the wrath of man*, is, by rousing those who suffer, or are likely to suffer by it, to stand in their own defence; and inspiring them with courage and resolution, to oppose and resist, to the utmost, all the mischievous efforts of the ambition, wrath and anger of those proud aspiring mortals, who would, if possible, rob them of their natural rights, and plunge them into a state of servility. And this is the most usual method of Providence, for restraining and curbing the disorderly passions and corrupt lusts of ambitious and revengeful men. Sometimes indeed GOD is pleased to interpose in an extraordinary way, for the deliverance of his people from the rage and wrath of their enemies; to take their controversy, as it were, into his own hands; and to work salvation for them, by means, in which their own agency is not at all concerned: but most commonly, it is by the right use, of those means of preservation and safety, which he has put into their power, that he defends & saves them. There is nothing more irrational than to neglect such means, and depend upon miraculous protections. When GOD purposes to restrain the wrath of his people's enemies, he usually rouses a spirit of opposition, stirs them up to make a resolute resistance, and animates and excites them to the most vigorous efforts for the maintenance of their rights. And whenever a people are enabled to baffle and disappoint their enemies, and defeat their attempts to gratify their ambition or revenge, they ought to ascribe the glory to GOD, whose interposing providence has prospered their endeavours, and crowned their enterprizes with success.

And now, my hearers, as the subject does naturally suggest such reflections as are suitable to this anniversary, you may very reasonably expect an application of what has been said, adapted to the present occasion. This therefore will now be attempted.

In the rise and progress of the present war, we have seen both parts of our text verified, in innumerable instances. *The wrath of man* has been made to praise GOD, by producing events contrary to those, which it aimed at. *The wrath of man* has also been restrained, defeated and confounded, and after all its vaunting boasts, been obliged to own its impotence and weakness. And, in short, though GOD has permitted *the wrath of man* to plunge us into great troubles and distresses, as a just punishment for our manifold impieties and vices, yet he has hitherto so managed and over-ruled it, so curbed and checked it, as to afford the clearest evidence of his powerful providence, which presides over the world, and governs all things.

The pride, avarice and ambition of Great Britain, gave rise to the present hostile contests. From this source originated those oppressive acts, which first alarmed the freemen of America; and provoked them, after petitioning in vain for redress, to form plans of opposition and resistance. This conduct of America exasperated the British administration, and roused all their wrath. Transported with angry resentments, they proceeded from oppression to open war, in order to frighten and compel us into a submission to those arbitrary and despotic schemes, which they were determined, at all hazards, to carry into execution. But those vindictive and sanguinary counsels and measures, which, in the vehemence of their passions, they adopted, for this purpose, have, by the providence of GOD, contrary to their expectations, involved them in the most perplexing difficulties, by uniting thirteen provinces of America, in that declaration of independence, which they now wish us to rescind.

I believe it will be obvious to every one, who will take a survey of the violent and hostile proceedings of Great-Britain, and of the measures she took to intimidate these states, and awe them into unconditional submission, prior to their declaration of independence, that every part of her conduct, was calculated to produce this great event; having a direct tendency to plunge the people of America, into a state of desperation, by cutting them off from every chance of maintaining their liberties, in any other way, than by erecting themselves into an independent nation, and opposing force with force. Now, when we consider, that, before our breaking our connection with Great-Britain, the methods and measures used and pursued by her, in order to accomplish her unrighteous designs against us, and promote her ambitious views, did all uniformly tend to reduce us to the necessity of taking that step, does it not seem, as if she had been left to judicial infatuation, and that her conduct can best be accounted for, by saying, as in the case of the revolt of the ten tribes from Rehoboam, *The cause was from the Lord*? This (as has been observed) is expressly assigned, as the reason why Rehoboam *hearkened not to the people*, but *answered them roughly*. And may we not, with equal propriety, assign this as the reason, why the British king, instead of hearkening to the cries and prayers of his loyal subjects in America, should either treat their complaints and petitions with neglect, or answer them only with insult and additional injuries, and send forth his fleets and armies, to awe them into silence, and force them into servile submission? May we not reason thus; *The cause was from the Lord*, therefore the king of Great-Britain, judicially blinded to his own interest, hearkened not to the prayers and petitions of the oppressed and aggrieved people of America; but took such violent methods, in order to compel them into slavish passive obedience, as reduced them to the disagreeable necessity of a revolt and final separation? Had our petitions and prayers been properly regarded, and moderate pacific measures pursued, we should have entertained no thoughts of a revolt; for even after hostilities had commenced, we were ardently desirous of continuing united with our mother country, if such an union could have been preserved, without making a sacrifice of our liberties. I am persuaded, we may safely appeal to that Being, who searches all hearts, to justify us, when we declare, that it was far from our intention or inclination to separate ourselves from Great-Britain; and that we had it not even in contemplation to set up for independency; but on the contrary, earnestly wished to remain connected with her, until she had deprived us of all hopes of preserving such a connection, upon any better terms than unconditional submission. It was her refusing to grant us better terms, that united these states, and formed the confederation, which has connected them together like a band of brethren, and, of many members, made them one compacted and well-cemented body. And that she should insist upon this, and, depending upon her power to crush us, should reject and trample under foot all our petitions, and come against us with hostile force, in order to establish an absolute despotic dominion over us, argues that she was left to her own folly (as Rehoboam was) to pursue measures contrary to her peace, and which, in the natural course of things, tended to produce that revolution, which has dismembered the British empire, and raised so great a part of it to a state of independence.

And as the wrath of Great-Britain, under the over-ruling providence of GOD, first occasioned this great revolution, so her wrath has hitherto been defeated in all its powerful efforts to reduce us back to a state of dependence; which can be ascribed to nothing but the interposition of a powerful Providence, laying restraints upon her, and weakening her hands, so that she could not perform her enterprizes. For if we look back, and consider the strength of our enemies, and our own weak condition, when the awful scenes of war first opened upon us, we cannot but acknowledge it to be owing to the special interposing power of the supreme Disposer of all things, that we were not soon overcome, but have been enabled to maintain our cause hitherto, in many severe conflicts, through several bloody campaigns.

When we consider how unprepared and unprovided we were for the contest, when hostilities first commenced; that we were without money, without ammunition, without magazines, without cloathing for soldiers; that we had neither military discipline nor any regular settled civil government; that we were destitute of that assistance from foreign powers, which we have had since; and, in short, that under the greatest disadvantages, being deficient in all military preparations, we were forced into a war, with an enemy, well prepared and well provided with all essentials for the conflict, having a numerous and well-disciplined army, commanded by skillful and experienced officers, who had been bred to arms; and a navy superior to any in Europe, which gave them the empire of the seas, and rendered their resources almost inexhaustible; when we consider these things, what reason have we to adopt the language of the psalmist, and say, *If it had not been the Lord, who was on our side, our enemies would have swallowed us up quick*? Especially, when we consider further, the peculiar hazards and difficulties we were subjected to, from internal enemies, who under the pretext of neutrality, or the disguise of friendship, were constantly plotting mischief against us, and doing all that they could, with safety, to weaken our hands; to discourage and dishearten us; to obstruct our operations; to perplex and entangle our affairs; and to aid and assist the British forces. The principal advantages gained, at one time or another, by our professed enemies, who have openly waged war against us, have been greatly owing to assistances afforded them, by secret enemies among ourselves, who, had not the mercy of GOD prevented, would, before now, have ruined their country. We have therefore abundant reason to be thankful to the sovereign Ruler of the world, not only that he hath hitherto protected us against the open violence of our avowed foes; but also that he hath guarded us against the treacheries and treasonable conspiracies, of false and disaffected persons, whom we have harboured in our own bosoms; and defeated those hidden and mischievous artifices, which they have used to work our destruction.

The scene of war, in which we have been involved, has been chequered with an alternate succession of favourable and unfavourable events. Sometimes we have met with disappointments and defeats, when we had raised expectations of success. At other times we have been prospered, even beyond our most sanguine expectations. In several instances our enterprizes have been crowned with wonderful success, exceeding our most flattering hopes. And, on the whole, we have great reason to adore the providence of GOD, who has hitherto remarkably restrained the wrath of our enemies; mercifully defended and protected us; and supported our righteous cause, by many signal interpositions.

To every attentive observer, it must be obvious, that the wrath of Great-Britain, so far as it has been permitted to exert itself, has contributed to bring about and establish our independency. It has evidently been the occasion of events, which have raised us to an honorable consideration among the European powers, and induced some of them openly to espouse our cause, and aid us by a friendly alliance. It is also worthy of observation, that the wrath, which has been enkindled in American breasts, has been over-ruled for the promotion of the same great ends. Great-Britain first prepared fewel, and then put fire to the combustibles, which she had prepared, for setting the passions of America into a flame. And the wrath, which she has thus roused in America, has been wisely managed by Providence, for checking and restraining her rage and vengeance. Her conduct has not only been the occasion of stirring up a noble spirit of liberty throughout America, and kindling into a blaze every spark of virtuous patriotism, and true courage; but of firing the mind with honest indignation and resentment; yea, of transporting the passions, in some instances, among individuals, into criminal excesses. But even these excesses of the passions, have, by Providence, been made to conspire with better principles, and more laudable springs of action, to strengthen the opposition to British tyranny, and check the career of British rage and cruelty.

Far be it from me to justify any excesses of wrath and anger. I am no advocate for outrages, even on the most provoking occasions. But I cannot but observe, that, as on the one hand, it will not be denied, that the human passions have, in some instances, among particular persons broken forth into a criminal excess of riot; so, on the other, it cannot but be acknowledged, that there have been many instances of a very culpable indifference and tameness of temper, which, without any emotion, could behold the impending ruin of the country, or have quietly submitted to concessions fatal to liberty.

We are not to suppose, that either reason or religion requires the total suppression of the passions. It is both rational, and a duty, to stir them up into exercise, when suitable objects are presented to view. None of our original passions, are in themselves vicious. They become vicious only by their exorbitancy. It is the excess of them that is criminal. While they are tempered with prudence and discretion, and kept within due bounds, they may be indulged to advantage upon many occasions.

Though rage, and inflamed wrath, are no essential properties of patriotism; yet patriotism without feeling or sensibility, is a meer name. The passionate appearance of the same love of one's country, and of the same determined zeal for promoting the honor and interest of it, will indeed be different, in different constitutions. A patriot of a calm and dispassionate temper, tho' he cannot but feel just resentment at the wrongs, and injuries done to his country, and shew a steady resolution to do all, that in him lies, to maintain his country's cause, against all its enemies, will yet not shew the same vehement warmth, that will discover itself in a patriot, of a more sanguine and fiery temper, nor be so liable to be betrayed, by a fierce zeal, into imprudent and rash measures.

And here let me observe, that to me it seems an argument of the wisdom of GOD, that (as there are few comparatively possessed of virtuous principles; and as even the best principles, without a stimulus from the passions, would remain dormant and inactive; and as the generality are influenced by their passions only, which need something to restrain and direct them, or to rouse them up, when the public good calls for great and general exertions) Providence has so ordered it, that there should be a diversity of tempers and constitutions among men, to be both a spur and a check to one another; that the more warm and vehement might give an active spring to the more cool and sluggish, and, on the contrary, the more calm and moderate be a curb to the more sanguine and hasty; and that the two extremes, meeting with those, who are more equally tempered with due proportions of zeal and prudence, all might happily unite; and, by the mutual collision of their different tempers and passions, be enabled to collect their several powers, into one combined and vigorous effort, for carrying into execution, every necessary enterprize, against a common enemy, and for the promotion of the welfare and prosperity of society.

But whatever we may think of the ends of Providence, in ordering such a diversity of tempers among men, this is certain, that GOD will so manage the most disorderly, turbulent and boisterous passions, as to make them promotive of the designs of his government, or lay such restraints upon them, that instead of frustrating, they shall really subserve the purposes of his wisdom. Of this we have had the clearest evidence, in a variety of instances in the course of the present war; which affords substantial ground for a rational hope and trust in GOD, for the future.

Had the power of Great-Britain been equal to her wrath, what a miserable and wretched situation should we have been in, before now! From the rage and vindictiveness, which she has discovered; from the threats which she has thrown out; and from the barbarous cruelties which have marked her steps in the prosecution of the present war (especially when she gained any advantages over us) we may easily infer what would be our unhappy fate, should her wrath prevail, at last, and force us to surrender at discretion. In this case, all would be seizure and process, confiscation and imprisonment, blood and horror, insolence and arbitrary punishment. For so it always has been, and always will be, when what is called a rebellion is suppressed, and the supposed rebels obliged to throw themselves unconditionally upon the mercy of their incensed prince.

Great-Britain indeed, since our alliance with France, has made a shew of offering a redress of grievances, and of granting us even more than we asked for, before our declaration of independence; on condition of our re-uniting ourselves with her, in violation of our national faith and honor, which we have solemnly plighted to our generous ally; but should we comply with this condition, what security could we have of her lasting friendship? Philip, of Spain, when he found that his arbitrary proceedings had thrown his subjects, in the low countries, into a ferment and flame, and raised such an opposition to his government, as he was unable immediately to suppress, was once prevailed upon by the representations of the governess, the duchess of Parma, to hearken to their complaints and petitions, and grant a redress of grievances; in consequence of which, things in general, soon returned to a tollerably quiet and peaceable state. But notwithstanding this seeming compliance with the desires of his subjects, Philip only meant to gain time, being determined, as soon as circumstances should be more favourable, to prosecute his ambitious and tyrannical schemes. Accordingly, in a little while, he commissioned the duke of Alva, at the head of a large army of veteran troops, to carry the same into the most rigorous execution: This conduct of his, rekindled the flame, and revived those commotions, which, eventually cost Spain a great part of her low country provinces. Should we, in contradiction to our solemn engagements to others, return to our connection with Great-Britain, upon the plan proposed by her commissioners (who, by the way, are not empowered to ratify any thing) we might soon, after the example of the low countries, be again obliged to separate from her, and to fly to arms for our defence. And in this case she would have a fairer chance of subjugating us, and we should be in the utmost danger of falling a prey to her power and wrath, because, having violated our faith with foreign powers, they would hardly be persuaded to trust us again, or to afford us those supplies and succours, that we might stand in need of.

It is doubtless the ardent desire of every one, now present, to see a speedy and happy end to the war. But can any suppose, that a separate composition with Great-Britain, upon her terms, would restore public peace and tranquility, and close the scenes of war? Have we not rather reason to believe, that it would oblige us immediately to engage in her quarrel with those, who have befriended us in our distress, and assist her in avenging herself upon them, for the aid which they afforded us? A separate peace with Great-Britain, upon any other plan, than that of equality and mutual independence, would plunge us directly into a war with France and Spain, who would have reason to resent such a flagrant violation of our national faith and honor. And probably it would also arm many other European powers against us. We can therefore have no hopeful prospect, of enjoying the blessings of peace, or of enjoying them long, but upon the plan of independency.

The appeal has been made to heaven, and heaven has hitherto supported us, and restrained the wrath of our enemies. Trusting in GOD therefore, we should take courage still to *stand fast in the liberties, wherewith he has made us free*, without fondly desiring any dishonorable and dangerous compositions.

But though from the great things which GOD has done for us, we are encouraged to hope, that his providence will, in due time, work compleat salvation for us, if we continue to exert ourselves, as becometh free men; yet no one can certainly tell what will be the issue of the present contest, or how it will terminate. The volumes of futurity are locked against human inspection; nor is it possible to ascertain the event of any human enterprize or undertaking. Our concern should be, to make the great Governor of futurity our friend, as we desire the kind assistances of his propitious providence, to bring our enemies to make peace with us, upon terms of honor, justice and equality.

And here, let me observe, that nothing darkens our prospects more, or gives us more reason to be fearful, as to the event of the present contest, than the great and general prevalence of unrighteousness among us. He must have been very unobserving, who does not know, that by means of unrighteousness, the body-politic has been, and still is, labouring under a dangerous disease, *the whole head being sick and the whole heart faint*, and there being but little *soundness, from the crown of the head to the sole of the foot.*

The goodness of our cause does not make success certain. A good cause often suffers, and is sometimes lost, by means of the sin and folly of those, who are engaged in it. This is a consideration, which ought to lie with weight on our minds, at the present day, and engage us to *put away the evil of our doings*, and *keep ourselves from every wicked thing.*

When Solomon says, *righteousness exalteth a nation*, he asserts no more, than what the experience of all ages has found to be true. For righteousness not only procures the smiles of a propitious Providence upon a people; but also tends, in the natural course of things, to promote their prosperity; being adapted to prevent dissentions and discords among them, to cement them together in the firmest union, and, by preserving public and private credit, to enable them to collect their force and strength, when the case requires, for repelling an invading enemy, and defending themselves against all the hostile attempts of aspiring ambition. The effects of unrighteousness are very different; for unrighteousness not only provokes GOD to withhold his blessings from a people; but it also tends, in its own nature, to entangle and perplex their affairs, and to render them weak, and unable to oppose any violent assaults of arbitrary power, by creating among them internal strife and contention; by dividing them into angry parties; by destroying mutual trust and confidence; and so rendering it extremely difficult, and next to impossible, to unite them in measures, necessary for their safety and defence against a common enemy, or the despotic views of designing ambition.

We have therefore reason to fear, if unrighteousness should continue to abound, that the righteous Judge of the world, will cease to restrain the wrath of our enemies, and, leaving us in the hands of our own folly, permit them to execute the dreadful purposes of their furious resentments, as a just punishment for our obstinate perseverance in our evil ways. But if we will put away our unrighteousness, *cease to do evil, and learn to do well*, we shall have grounds to hope, that *the righteous Lord, who loveth righteousness*, will still be our friend and patron, and enable us to maintain our cause, against the utmost force of our enraged enemies, until they are brought to reason or ruin. For,

> To the righteous, GOD is near,
> And never will their cause forsake.

Though GOD is pleased to employ the wrath of our enemies, as a rod of correction, to punish us, for our sins; and may permit them to proceed to great lengths, in the prosecution of their arbitrary and unrighteous schemes, in order to teach us righteousness, and make us pious and virtuous; yet their conduct is nevertheless odious and abominable in his sight, and will not (as we have reason to believe) pass unpunished. We may therefore assure ourselves, that when we leave our sins, and become an obedient people, GOD will bring to nought all their mischievous designs, either by disposing them to peace, or by leaving them to follow the lead of their own haughty temper, until they plunge themselves into destruction. For GOD often turns the oppression of the oppressor upon his own head and causes him, in the end, to fall into the pit which he digged for others. And a people, who have smarted under the cruel rod of oppression, may rationally expect this, when they are suitably prepared for salvation by repentance and reformation. For the most powerful and successful oppressors, are only rods of GOD's school (like the proud Assyrian beforementioned) and when he has answered the designs of his providence by them, he usually lets loose his wrath upon them, and punishes them for their arrogance, pride and mischievous ambition. The destruction which sometimes falls upon such men, is finely described in the fifteenth chapter of the book of Job, from the 31st verse to the end, which I will give you in the words of an elegant modern version:

Woe to the man, who by oppression climbs,
Drunk with successes, and secure in crimes;
For bitter change shall come; untimely blast
His boughs shall wither, and his fruit shall cast.
As when the vine her half-grown berries showers,
Or poison'd olive, her unfolding flowers.
Know, all ye wicked, all ye venal crew,
Your splendid tents the shulking bribe shall rue;
A fire it kindles, and the flame supplies,
'Till the gay scene a dismal desart lies.
See how oppression (and its boasted gain)
Conceiv'd, and usher'd into birth in vain;
The flattering crime, which so much anguish bred,
Turns all its plagues on its own parent's head.

Before I conclude, let me apply myself, in a few words to the militia of the town, who appear under arms, on this memorable occasion.

Sirs,

The manner of your observing this day, in commemoration of the commencement of the present war, the scene whereof, was first opened in this place, does you honor, as it gives an evidence, at once, of your piety, and of your patriotism and firm attachment to the cause of your country. With honest indignation we recollect the day, when the storm of British vengeance, which had been long gathering, first burst upon your heads, in the wanton massacre of several of your brave fellow citizens and soldiers. The memory of those, who have magnanimously jeoparded their lives, and shed their blood in the country's cause, will ever be dear to us. We particularly retain an honorable remembrance of those, who first fell a sacrifice to British wrath; and feel emotions of sympathy toward their surviving relatives, who cannot but be sensibly affected on this occasion. We would also join with you, in grateful acknowledgments to God, who mercifully checked the wrath of our enemies in its first eruptions, and caused it to recoil back on their own heads. We doubt not, but from the warmth of honest resentment; from a love of liberty and of your country, you will persevere to oppose and resist those insolent and haughty enemies, of whose wanton cruelty, you have had too melancholy a specimen, to permit you to expect much mercy at their hands, should they gain their point.

Let me now observe, that your appearing equipt in military armour, as soldiers prepared for war, naturally leads to reflections on the pernicious influence of those corrupt lusts of human nature, *from whence come wars.* They who would be glad to *live peaceably with all men*, are often unhappily forced into contention, and obliged to take arms, and engage in hazardous contests, in order to defend their lives and liberties, against the evil designs of unreasonable men, who when they suppose they have power and strength to accomplish their purposes, scruple not to give unbounded scope to their pride, covetousness and ambition; which passions are mortal enemies to the rights of mankind, and the source of that slavery and cruel bondage, under which so many of the nations of the earth groan at this day.

A consideration of the pernicious influence and effects of these corrupt lusts and passions should engage you and should engage us all to mortify them in ourselves. For where they prevail, they not only lead to a conduct prejudicial to the peace and welfare of human society, but make men slaves in the worst sense, how much soever they may hate the name.

While therefore, you are engaged with a laudable zeal in the cause of civil liberty, you will permit me to remind you, that there is another kind of liberty of an higher and nobler nature, which it is of infinite importance to every one to be possessed of; I mean that glorious internal liberty, which consists in a freedom from the dominion of sin, and in the habit and practice of all the virtues of a good life. This is that noble and exalted liberty of the *sons of God*, of which our saviour speaks, when he says, *If the Son of God shall make you free, then shall ye be free indeed.* And this, once gained, will inspire you with the greatest magnanimity and fortitude, in the cause of outward liberty. *For the righteous are bold as a lion.*

To conclude. Let us all, with that ardor and earnestness which the importance of the thing requires, labour after this *glorious liberty of the sons of God*, that when we shall quit this tumultuous warring world (having acted our parts well in it), we may be admitted to those peaceful mansions, where, free from strife and contention, and all the pernicious effects of ungoverned wrath and ambition, we shall enjoy a blessed immortality, in the tranquil uninterrupted possession of every felicity that our natures are capable of.

A M E N

Chronology

1782–1788

1782 A DIALOGUE BETWEEN THE DEVIL, AND GEORGE III, TYRANT OF BRITAIN, Anonymous

Congress officially adopts the Great Seal of the United States. The war continues on the frontier and in the South. The British evacuate Savannah (July 11) and Charleston (Dec. 14).

In the last engagement of the Revolutionary War, George Rogers Clark retaliates against loyalists and Indians by attacking the Shawnee village of Chillicothe in the Ohio Territory (Nov. 10).

The Unitarian Church is founded in Boston.

1783 DEFENSIVE ARMS VINDICATED, A Moderate Whig [Stephen Case?]

Some 7,000 loyalists depart New York for Canada (Apr. 23) as the British army's return home becomes imminent, bringing to about 100,000 the number of loyalists to leave for Europe or Canada since the Revolution began.

The Society of Cincinnatus is formed during a meeting at the headquarters of Baron von Steuben in Fishkill, New York, at the instigation of Gen. Henry Knox; George Washington is chosen to be the first president of this fraternity of 2,000 Continental Army officers (May 13).

The Treaty of Paris is signed (Sept. 3), which recognizes American independence; on the same day, Britain signs a peace pact at Versailles, ceding Florida to France.

The last British troops leave Manhattan, as George Washington and Governor George Clinton enter the city (Nov. 25).

Washington ends a triumphant journey to appear before Congress (then meeting in Annapolis) and formally resigns his commission as Commander-in-Chief of the Continental Army (Dec. 23).

The Massachusetts supreme court holds that the state's constitution prohibits slavery; its slaves are accordingly freed.

1784 A SERMON PREACHED ON A DAY OF THANKSGIVING, George Duffield

A SERMON ON OCCASION OF THE COMMENCEMENT OF THE NEW-HAMPSHIRE CONSTITUTION, Samuel McClintock
A SERMON PREACHED BEFORE A CONVENTION OF THE EPISCOPAL CHURCH, William Smith

Congress ratifies the Treaty of Paris (Jan. 14).

Spain closes the lower Mississippi River to navigators of the new Union (June 26).

John ("Nolichucky Jack") Sevier leads the formation of the independent State of Franklin in the western lands of North Carolina (Aug.). He fails to gain admission to the Union, despite repeated efforts, until 1796, when the territory is admitted as Tennessee.

Russians make the first permanent settlement in Alaska, on Kodiak Island (Sept. 22).

James Madison publishes *Remonstrance Against Religious Assessments*, arguing for separation of church and state (Dec. 24).

Jedidiah Morse publishes *Geography Made Easy* to provide an American textbook that will not be infected with the monarchical and aristocratical ideas of England.

Francis Asbury calls a meeting of Methodist preachers at Baltimore and launches the Methodist Protestant Church.

The American ship *Empress of China* sails from New York to Canton (Guangzhou) to open regular trade with the Orient.

1785 THE DANGERS OF OUR NATIONAL PROSPERITY; AND THE WAY TO AVOID THEM, Samuel Wales

Congress relocates to New York City (Jan. 11).

John Adams is appointed minister to England, a post he retains for three years (Feb. 24).

Thomas Jefferson is appointed minister to France, replacing Benjamin Franklin (Mar. 10).

Congress enacts the Ordinance of 1785, pertaining to immense public-domain lands in the west. Pre-purchase surveying and purchases in minimum tracts of 640 acres, for not less than $1 per acre, are stipulated (May 20).

Bourbon County, in present-day Alabama and Mississippi, is ordered to be surrendered by Spain (Oct. 10).

John Adams formally demands that the British leave military posts along the Great Lakes and in Ohio, as agreed in the Treaty of Paris (Nov. 30).

Abraham Baldwin charters the University of Georgia, the first state university; it will admit students in 1801, by which time the

University of North Carolina has also begun classes at Chapel Hill (in 1795).

1786 Virginia's House of Burgesses adopts Jefferson's "Statute of Religious Liberty," introduced by James Madison in the Virginia legislature and enacted Jan. 16. A portion of the First Amendment to the U. S. Constitution would later be modeled on it.

Led by Daniel Shays and other Revolutionary War veterans, Shays' Rebellion erupts in western Massachusetts. Moves to secure a more powerful national government, leading to the Philadelphia Convention, are one result.

1787 A SERMON ON A DAY APPOINTED FOR PUBLICK THANKSGIVING, Joseph Lathrop
THE DIGNITY OF MAN, Nathanael Emmons
THE PRINCIPLES OF CIVIL UNION AND HAPPINESS CONSIDERED AND RECOMMENDED, Elizur Goodrich

Congress endorses a resolution from the Annapolis Convention to call a federal constitutional convention in Philadelphia (Feb. 21). Only Rhode Island abstains from the convention, which convenes with a working quorum on May 25.

The Northwest Ordinance is passed by the Congress of the Confederation (July 13); among other things, slavery is prohibited in the territories.

The Constitution is signed on Sept. 17 and sent to the states for ratification.

The first of the 85 essays urging ratification, to be entitled *The Federalist*, is published on Oct. 27 in New York City by *The Independent Journal*. Under the pseudonym *Publius*, the authors are Alexander Hamilton, James Madison, and John Jay (their identities remain largely unknown until the 1792 publication of the French edition).

In Delaware, Oliver Evans opens a flour mill he designed to use continuous conveyor belts and machines driven by the same water wheel; only two men are needed to do the work of twenty.

John Adams publishes *Defense of the Constitutions of Government of the United States of America*.

Joel Barlow publishes *Vision of Columbus*, which sees America as the "last and best hope for the improvement of mankind."

1788 THE REPUBLIC OF THE ISRAELITES AN EXAMPLE TO THE AMERICAN STATES, Samuel Langdon
A CENTURY SERMON ON THE GLORIOUS REVOLUTION, Elhanan Winchester

Richard Henry Lee publishes *Letters of the Federal Farmer*, opposing ratification of the Constitution unless it is amended to include a Bill of Rights (June 2).

Ratification on June 21 by New Hampshire, the ninth state, puts the new Constitution into effect. Several states ratify on the basis of the Federalists' promise to attach a Bill of Rights.

Virginia ratifies (voting 89 to 79) on June 25.

New York ratifies (voting 30 to 27) on July 8. Over 200 amendments are proposed by the several state ratifying conventions.

A former Revolutionary War general, Arthur St. Clair, is made first governor of the Ohio area (July 15).

Cincinnati is founded as Losantiville (its present name dates to 1790) and is the first seat of the legislature for the Northwest Territories.

Congress, under the Articles of Confederation, adjourns (Nov. 1), leaving the United States with no central government until the following April, when the Congress under the new Constitution finally achieves a quorum.

Philip Freneau, America's leading poet and Madison's roommate at the College of New Jersey (Princeton), publishes *The Miscellaneous Works of Freneau*, including "To the Memory of the Brave Americans" and "The Wild Honeysuckle."

The complete edition of *The Federalist*, by Hamilton, Madison, and Jay, is published.

23

A DIALOGUE BETWEEN THE DEVIL, AND GEORGE III, TYRANT OF BRITAIN

Anonymous

BOSTON

1782

Not a sermon and by an author anonymous and unknown, this satirical dialogue first appeared in 1782 in Boston, was reprinted in the Frederick-Town, Maryland, *Chronicle* on June 27, 1787, and appeared yet a third time in Augusta, Maine, in 1797. Much in the spirit in which we have rediscovered it, the Maryland publisher said of the piece, it "just come to hand." The dialogue covers the reign of George III from his ascent to the throne in 1760 to the defeat of Cornwallis at Yorktown and the overthrow of his and the Devil's scheme to establish the greatest tyranny in the history of the world by first enslaving the Americans and then the native Englishmen. A sprightly exercise in political theology, the dialogue gives a special play to the role of the Scots in the diabolical plot and to John Adams as the quintessential American champion of liberty and Providence. As for George III, his early aspiration to become the greatest tyrant since Nero and Caligula gives way as the tide of revolution turns to hopes of lesser magnitude. "I had rather be a little tyrant than a great king," George says. His inability to swear proficiently proves particularly embarrassing for the Devil, who places great stock in fluent profanity, such as Charles II commanded. He gives the king lessons but finally despairs of his inept pupil. "George you swear poorly, not fit for company," the Devil moans.

A ringing affirmation of the patriot cause by an "American plenipotentiary" who addresses George III and his privy council concludes the dialogue—perhaps emblematic of John Adams, John Jay, and Benjamin Franklin, who concluded peace negotiations with Britain on November 30, 1782.

A

DIALOGUE

BETWEEN THE

DEVIL,

AND

GEORGE III.

TYRANT OF *BRITAIN*,

&c. &c. &c. &c.

BOSTON,
Printed and sold by BENJAMIN EDES and SONS, at their Office, in State-Street. M,DCC,LXXXII.

1760

evil. George hearken to my council.

George. Thy servant attends.

D. My trusty servants Bute and Mansfield, have educated thee for my service, and taught thee the way wherein thou shouldst go, obey them and I will make thee a king indeed; make yourself absolute, or die in the attempt: a king dependent on the people, is no monarch; he is a mere puppy.

G. Your words I have a heart to obey; 'tis the bent of my soul, and the world shall soon know that I am a king in reality, and my people shall feel that my wrath is like the roaring of a lion.

D. I doubt not you will equal my ancient servants Nero, Caligula, Borgia, Charles, and others; but you must use great art lest a spirit of liberty should rise among the people and blast your great designs, as happened to my faithful servant Charles.

G. I will begin with my colonies; the idea of enslaving them to the power of parliament, and make them tributary to the old dominion, suits the pride and avarice of Britons: when this [is] done, the way will be open and easy to complete the work in Britain: with places pensions titles and bribes, I can soon make myself as absolute as any tyrant that ever stept.

D. Go on my beloved servant, and cut the work short; thou art the darling of my heart; I hope you will yet shed a sea of human blood, sufficient for the British navy to ride in.

1774

G. See how things ripen. I'll soon kindle rebellion in America, and then with a few troops subdue the rebels, confiscate the country, and establish my will as law.

D. Pox take ye, what have ye been about these fourteen years? The work ought to have been done; 'ere now you should have been as terrible to your people as the lion to the tame beast of the field; but you are yet a beggar to parliaments.

1775

G. See the field of Lexington and Bunker-Hill. Now the wheels begin to move—the torrent of blood is rapid: I trust you will never again have cause to lash my delays. In time past my counsels have been divided; & that timid goose of a Gage has been dilatory: But I have sent Howe, Burgoyne and Clinton to assist him, and push things: Howe is a true blood-hound; Burgoyne is ambitious as Lucifer, and would kill his father for promotion; and Clinton is obedient to his master as a shepherd's dog.

1776

D. You now begin to do something: But you in your speeches, and your generals in their proclamations, tell too many lies, and commit too many horrid acts of barbarity, for the success of your cause; in these you run too fast; they strike mankind with horror, and unite them against you—there is not a character in Tophet stinks (above ground) worse than yours.

G. You told me to make short work, and I said I had a heart for it: accordingly by perjury and lies, fire and sword, by the gallows & dungeons, freezing and starving, I have been subduing the rebels, and hope to finish the work in America soon; for I want to begin with my subjects at home.

1777

D. Where is Burgoyne? Howe has taken Philadelphia, and is shut up in it. Clinton has, with great loss, taken a small fort and burnt a town up Hudson's river, and run back to New York. Damn'd work, you'll stink in hell George!

G. We are all in tears, but what can I do more; I sent fleets and armies, which all my ministers swore were more than sufficient to lay America prostrate at my feet.

D. Instead of showing the spirit of a lion, you have the head of a goat and the heart of a sheep; and if you don't pursue your plan until the work is complete, by the ghost of Nero, I hope the English will play Charles with you. If you fail, what a deform'd mongrel puppy you will appear to all the world; neither generosity and benevolence to gratify your people, nor art and spirit enough to make yourself a tyrant—poor dog! you'll be the scorn of the world, and the derision hell.

G. I wish I had not begun, but there is no retreat. I'll move every wheel to increase my force by sea and land; I will send commissioners with great promises (which I can easily break when the business is done) and large bribes, and partly by art and partly by force, I may yet succeed. I know my crown will sit uneasy and my life be wretched after this, unless I gain my point.

D. Do you see what the French are doing?

G. Yes, my liege; do help me curse them; O for a flood of anathemas that would sweep them to the centre.

D. Words are but wind, a million oaths won't sink a French ship, nor will ten thousand curses kill one rebel. You stupid dog, if you would reign you must fight. It is now or never with you, not only the French but all the nations in Europe secretly aid America, and wish her success. You ought to have done the work at once, and not have allowed time for the rebels to form alliance.

G. My liege, don't use me ill, you never had a servant more devoted to thy service, and very few have ever done so much to promote thy kingdom. In my early youth I debauch'd the fair quaker, and had three bastards by her, besides innumerable other instances of wickedness, of which you are witness. I have deceived my people with a show of religion (this proves that I am no fool in hypocrisy); and at the same time have practiced every iniquity, have employed such men in public office as were thy faithful servants—and my head is full of schemes and my heart full of malice for every evil work. And—

D. You have a good heart, George, and I'll make something of you yet.

G. I have the heart of a tyrant. I never felt one tender emotion for all the sufferings of mankind, and I hope to prove that my head is equal to my heart. Permit me, my liege, to say that I have some merit for past services, and for my future designs. I have, at a moderate computation, by my attempts to enslave America, destroyed at least fifty thousand people—and have destroyed the happiness of fifty thousand more—and should I succeed, I'll surpass in barbarity any tyrant that ever lived. I mean to be a demi-devil. I have in my imagination new tortures for mankind; I mean that my furnace of torture should be seventy seven times hotter than Nebuchadnezzar's; for a novelty, and to show my genius, I will have a saw mill carried by a stream of virgin blood to saw off rebels heads!—think of this, my liege, and allow me the credit of it. Did ever Nero, or Caligula, perform any thing equal to this?

D. Your heart is good, George, and you may yet make a figure if you persevere.

G. As to perseverance, never fear my failing in that, I am of the blood hound breed, never leave the track, and my best friends have for this reason call'd me obstinate. I have said, and I swear to it, and stand to it, that I'll lose my crown before I'll give up America.

D. In case America should prove unconquerable, what then?

G. Why, even in that desperate extremity, I shall still have great designs left; I mean to perfect my tyranny in Britain if I fail in America; this I can easily do by bribing parliaments; and the immense increase of public burdens will facilitate my design; the spirits of the people are more and more depressed and broken, and the avarice of the great is likewise increased; the work is easy, and I had rather be a little tyrant than a great king. To be a despot over the rest of my dominions, would be a compensation even for the loss of America: tyranny has been the plan and pursuit of my life, it is sweet to my soul, and a tyrant I will be, or be nothing.

1778

D. Things don't go well in America, George, the rebels gain ground, and they exult in the most insulting stile since your General Clinton and his army got a flogging at Monmouth, and performed their moon-light retreat.

G. I am vexed to the soul and with burning indignation I curse all around me—let firebrands, arrows and death seize all that oppose my will. I will be a tyrant, and a tyrant I will be; I'll set the world on fire and spill the blood of all Adam's race but I'll have my will—my wrath kindles, my blood boils, and vengeance burns; North and Germaine where are you, ye scoundrels! I am mocked and deceived by you—ye swore by Hercules that I should hear of nothing but victory and triumph, and now what a tale do I hear of the rout and retreat of my army. North you are a purblind puppy, and that Minden bastard is no better—curse all your politics, if the Devil had taken you two, with old Bute and Mansfield, to himself, twenty years ago, I might have spent all my days as I spent my youth, in debauching fair quakers, without interruption—curse ye.

1779

D. You must use other weapons besides curses, or you'll never correct the blunders of your wooden headed ministers. You seem fond of swearing, but you blunder out your oaths wrong end foremost; your tongue is too big to swear off hand; and like many other boobies, by your aukward curses you scandalize swearing, and injure the Satannic cause. My servant, Charles 2d, did eminent service by swearing; his example made a whole nation swearers, and greatly advanced my kingdom; but you, George, are formed for a hypocrite; your solemn phiz and sullen air, serve as a mask to cover your vices and devices, from the view of the people. Under this cloak, you have practiced debauchery, and numerous vices, and still had a tolerable character: your bishops and their underlings puff'd you off for a saint in folio—'tis necessary to avoid some vices, in order to practice others with more success.

G. I want sometimes to give vent to my wrath by royal execrations —and I hate restraint in any vice: however, if your highness forbids, I'll try to hold in for the present.

D. When your tyranny is compleated, you will need no disguise; then the more you swear, the better for my cause. And remember, that swearing is a genuine criterion by which you may know my children—for altho' all my children don't swear yet all swearers are my sons and daughters—and morally your brethren and sisters. If you swear it ought to be done with royal dignity, and not lisp & mutter out your oaths like thousands, who ought to have their throats cut for the disgrace they bring on this sin, by slabbering out "curse damn ye" like damn'd boobies.

G. Will your royal highness please to give me a rule by which I may swear in a stile becoming my royal dignity?

D. Observe the following. First begin with *faith*, this is the *a b* in swearing; when you can make this run off your tongue glib, then proceed to *curse it* and *damn it*, and so on until you can real off as the saying is, fifteen double damns in a second, and make St. James's ring with royal swearing. But mind what I say George, be sure you never swear in company, until you can damn with an air of royal grandeur. The best place for you to learn is in a horse stable, shut out all company, excepting a few of your menial lords, (and they p–x take 'em, your lords I mean[,] have yet to learn, altho' some of them have swore sixty years they yet murder their oaths: but, poor fellows, this excusc is made for them, that their tongues are half eat off with the p–x) and exercise your lungs in the following manner. Take a horse by the tail, count the hairs, and damn each hair as you count it; thus proceed, until you have gone thro' a stable of forty-nine horses; and if you cannot then swear fit for company you must swear thro' the stable again; and conclude by damning each horse, his sire who begat him, his dam who bore him, his grand sire and grand dam, and trace his genealogy to his Adam; damn every generation up hill and down—and then, if you can't swear fit for company, set yourself down for a puppy—and try no more.

G. I bow with reverence to your sublimity, and will observe your directions.

D. At present your attention should be more fixed on the rebels, and the means to subdue them.

G. I have now a grand plan in agitation, that will do the business soon, I'll warrant: I began at the wrong end of America.

D. You have generally been at the wrong end of every thing, and when will you be at the right end?

G. I am now forming a plan to subdue the southern provinces, and out of them I'll gather wealth and strength to conquer the northern rebels: I am now on the right track, and e'er two years run round I'll have all America prostrate at my sovereign royal feet! and then nothing but blood and royal thunder, and George the Third, shall be heard through the regions of rebellion.

D. Evil tidings from America: the rebels have taken a strong fort by storm, and six hundred men! May the curse of Scotland catch you George, if you don't look out better. You blind whoresbird, why don't you send officers who know how to command?

G. My liege, I have done every thing a king can do. I can't stand centinel over my generals: I did not think Harry Clinton, after knighting the scoundrel, would have let my wheels run backward. I can't depend on no body; curse damn 'em in these Scotch-days.

1780

G. O now, my royal master, now, now! see how my arms triumph! Georgia taken! Charlestown humbled to the dust! Tories increasing—rebellion dying—the rebel army starving—mutinying—huzza! I'll complete my glorious plan, and have the necks of five hundred rebel chiefs in my noose e'er the sun has measured nine months on the reel of time.

1781

D. Rebellion breaks out with new kindled rage in the southern provinces like the flames of Aetna. French and rebels, combined by links of adamant against you, and inspired by all the lion passions; bestir yourself, George, or perdition will catch you!

G. The rebels have no forces to make any figure in the field this year: Lord Cornwallis will sweep all before him, and the southern provinces will fall like leaves in autumn. And then for a trip and twitch at Old Massachusetts, that ancient seat of rebellion—I have fire and brimstone, and wrath and vengeance, laid up for those venomous cockatrice sons of rebellion. I'll make the smoke of their torment rise seven hundred and seventy cubits high. My soul burns to be at 'em. Adamses and Hancocks will be sweet fuel for my furnace! I'll fill the Old South in Boston full of the chief rebels, with five hundred barrels of tar and brimstone: this conflagration will serve to illuminate the town on the glorious restoration of my royal government; and all the tories will say Amen. Old Time make haste and bring the blazing day.

D. You have a satannic heart; I wish your head was equal to it. I warn you again to look out for the French and rebels, or they'll give you an Irish hoist e're long.

G. As to the French fleet, my lions of the ocean will crack their bones: I expect this campaign will nearly swallow up rebellion; for all my ministers have sworn by the Stuart race, that I've nothing more to fear from the Gallic and rebel forces, than from a snow storm in the centre of Vesuvius.

D. What avail your puffs; the French fleet is now triumphant, and has shut up Cornwallis with the flour of your army, as a prey for the rebels! Volcanoes and whirlwinds blast them! George ye whoremonger, where are you? your kingdom totters while you are wenching.

G. May it please your majesty of the air, I am, as at all other times, at thy service; and I am firm and composed as mount Atlas. When an east wind shall drive Albion upon the American shore, then will I believe a French fleet may drive the British, and not 'till then.

Germaine to George. I am sorry to inform your majesty, that—

G. Curse your buttons, Germaine, are you come with bad news; but yesterday you swore by Minden, the first tidings you brought me would produce another discharge of the park guns. Well, what would you say?

Germaine. To the astonishment of every body, and every thing, Greaves has suffered the French fleet to beat him, and—

G. I won't hear any more; thunder and lightening blast him to the centre, and burn him to a cinder at the bottom of the ocean. What was you going to add to your Scotch "and" if I would hear it?

Germaine. I was going to inform your majesty, that Greaves has returned to New York with the loss of one ship of the line, and the rest in a ragged plight—and—

G. No more of your Scotch "ands," I won't hear it nor bear it —what! a British fleet turn tail to Frenchmen and run: If Greaves has run, I hope he won't stop 'till he gets to Tophet—I'll Bing the dog. If I would suffer you to speak what more would you subjoin to your last "and" (pox take you)?

Germaine. It makes my heart bleed and tremble, but duty and loyalty to the best of kings, obliges me to acquaint your majesty, that in consequence of Greaves' returning to New York, my lord Cornwallis is—

G. Stop, stop, stop, ye Minden scoundrel, I see it now, I see what is to follow, but I won't hear it from your coward lips—Lord Cornwallis is left to defend both land and ocean; and he'll do it! his noble blood, his titled name, his martial frame, will conspire to kindle the British peer into heroic fire: he'll fight and conquer until his laurels reach the skies: and that son of Neptune, Digby, has spread his canvas wings to join him—then Gallic ships and rebel troops will fly before the British thunder like feathers in a whirlwind!

D. All Europe bends a willing ear to this rebellion: Behold the rebel plenipoes receiv'd with royal smiles in every court! To them your realms, your trade and wealth are become a prey. Behold the rebel Adams, he lifts his head above the clouds, turns Europe pale, and governs kings with a nod; with more than sovereign voice he tells the monarchs (with whom he deigns to speak), "he represents the New World, and came to give them commerce round the globe—and to establish eternal peace." And he lets astonished nations know he came from Congress (compar'd with whom the asssembled Greek and Roman gods, sink in human view), who claim kindred with the stars, and call the sun their elder-brother; and whose puissant arm makes the Caesars tremble; hushes the warring realms to peace, and binds the omnipotence of Britain—he even aims a stroke at my domains; not confin'd to earth, he talks that providence divine has pointed out to every land to form a *union with his world*—and that heaven hath set its seal to independence—and said, Amen!

Did sun, or moon, or stars, or earth, or sky, from creation's early dawn, ever behold an equal to this rebel[?] But remember George, such is human kind, men will gaze at, wonder, and adore the man, who adores himself—and this rebel will shake Europe.

G. If I had gone through one lesson in the horse stable—I'd damn him.

Can't we, my royal master, with our united powers of earth and hell, overset such a being as this Adams, who says he came from the New World—I fear he'll drive bad spokes in my wheel of fortune, unless we demolish him soon; can't I hire a fellow for a few guineas, to poison him? I have just thought of an easy & expeditious way to extirpate rebellion, by poisoning all the leaders; and I'll give Louis a dose, if he has any more to do with my rebel subjects—this will do it quick. What a curse ail'd my Scotch ministers, that they could not see this short cure for rebellion in the beginning.

D. You are a Scotch damn'd goat—who begat ye, or bore ye—you've no more political eye sight than a blind curst puppy, three days old. A Dutch bull frog would learn navigation, sooner than you'll learn the first lesson in politicks—for you to talk of poison, why you mongrel booby, the subtle French and hawk ey'd rebels penetrate all your councils and designs; and before you could form such a plan, they'd fill your maw with arsenic! You and all your ministers would be dead as Nimrod in three days!

G. It won't do then; but I must take off Adams, for he appears in such a pompous stile, that all Europe is fascinated with his fine stories about the New World; he has a serpentine head & heart—he's all treason—and nothing of the dove in him, except the wings, to fly from one mischief to another—his soul contains the quintessence of all rebellion—O master, double your curses upon him—I have try'd to buy some of the rebel chiefs, but I can purchase none, excepting a few scoundrels, who are only a curse to me. That perjured thief of an Arnold cost me upwards of five thousand sterling (with a less sum I can purchase nineteen lords and sixty commoners) and I've only a piece of the scoundrel, for he lost one leg before I bought him—a dear bargain, you'll say, dear indeed; for I would sell him for ten yards of Scotch plaid. I've poor bargains of all the tories, these slaves don't pay for the salt they eat; take them one with another and altogether, they are not worth a curse; they are of no more use to me, than a wooden leg to a man that has no body.

D. In fact, the tories are a nuisance in creation, every one curses 'em; but *I must take them.*

G. If you must take 'em, pray take 'em soon, for I want to be quit of all such lumber—I've been curst with them long enough. They pretend great loyalty, but I find 'em hollow hearted fellows, who fawn round, for the same reason a dog does his master, to get a crust. Besides, their fulsome adulation is enough to turn my guts inside out. They perfectly stink in my nostrils, and scent the world.

D. Your best way, George, will be to sell the tories at vendue; they are form'd for slaves, and altho' the meanest, yet the Dutch will buy them for the Guinea trade.

G. I'll sell them, knock them off for something or nothing, any how, so that I am rid of them. But I must not waste time about these rascalls, I must attend to the war, for I will prosecute it with rigour, until I obtain an honorable peace. I'll humble the Dons, until they'll acknowledge my sovereignty, whereby I'll add to my royal titles, "King of Spain," &c.[—]this will be a new jewel to my crown.

D. It will be well if you can at the next peace, retain your former titles—the French will contend, that you shall relinquish your empty title, "King of France." And, indeed, you may with equal propriety, call yourself king of Jupiter. You must exert every nerve, or your dominions will become a prey to the hawks and ravens of Europe;

they are all gasping like so many vultures to devour you. They mean not only to get the new world, but to knock you out of the old.

G. When I've subdued America, I'll "knock" the dogs till they'll lick the dust under my royal feet. Although the French king is not to be compared with any king like me for royal greatness; yet I cannot but wonder that he could disgrace royalty by a connection with the rebels. I'll be curst through Billingsgate, by all the whores in Drury-Lane, before I'd stoop so low.

D. George, you lie like hell, for you've employ'd Indians, Negroes, Tories, thieves, robbers, counterfeiters of money, and the off-scouring, scum, and sweepings of the world; formed treaties with the little nabobs of Hesse and Brunswick, who, compared with America, are no more than a hen roost to a kingdom. George, when you address me, do it in a language of truth; I allow you to lie to every one else; but don't tell foolish lies that no body will believe, as you and your ministers often do. George, I tell you, between me and you, this rebellion is alarming to my dominions, and threatens your's with ruin. The vast continent of America, pregnant with the richest stores of nature, inhabited with a brave and enterprising people; enthusiastic in religion and liberty; and have laid foundations to perpetuate both; penetrating and daring in all their views; inflamed by your attempts to enslave them, have written your crimes in marble, with a "cursed be he that forgets or forgives the tyrant"—"and blessed be their memory, and only theirs who preserve independence." With whom magnanimity and virtue recommend to office (and rulers stamp the manners of the people) in whose creed I and you, are equally opposed and execrated. This people, I say, have excited and will command the admiration and imitation of mankind. In their public writings, speeches and transactions, they stamp glory on religion and liberty, and aim to make them both eternal: and if they succeed, I and you are eternally excluded from their favor: and that they will succeed we have every reason to fear; for all the old world is now gazing with admiration on the new. Kings hope to derive glory from an early friendship with the rising nations; and their subjects expect to gain infinite wealth by this union. Every Dutchman has his golden dreams about the New World; they would not have listened with half the attention to the prophet Daniel they did to Adams; and this frenzy spreads like a pestilence through the nations and fascinates the world. If America is independent, universal ruin follows; therefore, George, hold out to the last and be as obstinate as hell.

G. Let me alone for obstinacy, I've an heart of adamant, there's no turn to me; my will never was broke, nor ever can be, there's no break nor bend to it if once I say no—neither soothing nor praying, nor freezing nor burning, will ever move me; there's no move to me, I tell you, I'll be curst if there is. They tell me of Nero's firmness in fiddling while the city of Rome was burning: damn his buttons, why I could fiddle and wench too, if half the world was in flames. As to the terrors of the new world they tell too much about, I fear not any world, new or old—let the worlds go which way they will, I'll go to mine; and may all the scoundrels in the universe buffet me through creation, if ever I submit to independence; may annihilation catch me, and I never more darken any point of space if I do.

D. Well said my son, I admire your royal spirit, I wish for a diffusion of it, 'tis this alone can save ye now.

G. I have many cards yet to play: the world doesn't know me; they've not measur'd the length and breadth, and heighth and depth of my genius: the time of calamity is the hour of genius to shine. I've had no trials severe enough to rouse my energy, and to turn the bright side of my abilities to the day. Genius, like the richest mines, lies deep.

D. True, George, but I should have thought your genius had been called for some years ago. How can you bear the insolence and pomposity of the rebels—hear their titles of "Excellency," which royalty alone has a right to give.

G. It kindles my ire, and goes cross my soul like a lion teeth harrow; but I'll soon bring down their Excellency's, and turn them to axletrees for my waggons, with a cursation after them, to transport chains for rebels. Let Hancock, Trumbull, Clinton, Livingston, and other rebel governors look not for me, I'll pulverize them in the jaws of my vengeance. As for the rebel general, I'll pause and study to fix him in the focus of my burning wrath—in the crucible of my royal indignation—I'll warrant the sky of my reign will never be clouded with another rebellion.

D. Should you reduce the rebels, it will be necessary to extirpate great part of the breed, otherwise they may in future revolt again.

G. I know them root and branch; they're the old cursed Oliverian breed of king killers, whose ancestors fled from the axe and halter of my good progenitors the Stuarts (of blessed memory), but I'll never leave one on this side the stygian lake, I'll leave none of these cursation white weed to seed the land again. My weapons of death shall drink the last drop of their rebel blood—and then I'll plant the provinces with loyal Scotchmen, and a due mixture of my royal breed among them for rulers. I shall have enough for my own for every office of consequence; my German rib (known by the name of Pug) has brought me upwards of a dozen. I've five, by a Quaker girl—three by a Drury Lane bunter—four by Billingsgate Dab—several by Blue Moll, &c. &c.—I've enough I'll swear, and more coming.

D. There's a report that Cornwallis is a prisoner!

G. It's nothing but one of the rebel curst lies; they're eternally blowing about the victories, which ever turn out a royal triumph. Cornwallis surrender to the rebel Washington, no! he'd fight through the stygian sea first, and then he wouldn't. Mars and Jupiter would sooner surrender to the moon, and bow to a foot ball. Curse damn the rebels, to think my heroes will ever yield to them! no damn curse 'em—earthquakes, inundations and whirlwinds swallow 'em up, and blast 'em for their stygian impudence, and tumble 'em headlong through creation to the centre.

D. George, you swear poorly, not fit for company, you'll disgrace swearing; you havn't observ'd my rules, for learning the art.

G. I beg your pardon, my liege, but I have, I've swore through the stable, and damn'd every hair upon the tail of every horse, and curst every generation, up to the horse Caligula made one of his council; and faith I thought I swore with an air.

D. Then you're a numskull booby, and fit only to be a king of horses; and many of your counsellors are no better than Caligula's horse—he was much such another horse-king as yourself. But let me never hear you attempt to swear again; you'll cause swearing to go out of fashion; no gentleman will swear after you. This is one of the great supports of my kingdom, and it costs me nothing; swearers are all volunteers in my service, and go to hell without fee or reward.

G. That's poor wages.

D. What news from America, George?

G. I have none; but expect every hour to hear something glorious from the brave Cornwallis—O there's North and Germaine coming upon the trot, they've good news I know by their speed—well, North, what tidings?

North. I have nothing authentic; but there are evil reports respecting Lord Cornwallis.

G. I am not to be hum bugg'd by the rebel lies—its only the forerunner of victory. Well, Germaine, what news have you?

Germaine. I have this moment received a packet from Sir Henry Clinton, which confirms all the melancholy reports from America.

G. What! is it possible that Lord Cornwallis, with the flower of all my veterans, is fallen a prey to rebels?

Mansfield. I come to condole with your Majesty, upon one of the most melancholy events that ever wrung tears from royal eyes—and I could mingle my hearts blood with my tears if it might lessen the affliction which now fills your royal bosom with anguish—

Sandwich. No one can feel more on this occasion than myself; but I have done every thing for the good of the service; and I feel every thing which loyalty to the best of king's can inspire.

Bute. I beg leave with duty and gratitude, to mingle my tears with your majesty's, on this dreadful occasion.

(North to *Germaine*, aside. The king is sullen as the devil—look at his eyes, they roll like two fire balls; he'll break out like thunder presently; he grates his teeth like the devil biting steel bars to let tories out of prison.)

G. Oh—Oh—Oh—Vengeance! Vengeance!

D. George, and be damn'd to ye, where are ye? Cornwallis is a prisoner—his whole army—an immensity of stores and ships, are all in the hands of the French and rebels—O ye mongrel bastard, George, you'll turn out another bull-headed cur like Charles the First. I have been trying one hundred and fifty years to raise a tyrant out of the breed, but ye are a sap headed generation, fit only for backlogs in Tophet, and for mud boars in the stygian lake.

G. May curses in whirlwinds blast my ministers and commanders. Attend here, North and Germaine, what! Is the nation all going to the devil in a French wheelbarrow, and the rebels to reign triumphant?

North. It is not in human wisdom always to foresee or guard against misfortunes. Every thing has been done by your majesty and by your ministers, that wisdom could dictate; and your commanders must answer for their conduct.

G. Aye, you'll all excuse yourselves; but I'll be curst if I don't make a button of some of your heads and scaffold the rest of ye, unless ye retrieve my affairs. Summon a privy council instantly; call all the lords and bishops who have advised to prosecute the war against America.

Bute. I beg leave to inform your majesty the privy council is assembled, and waits your royal pleasure.

G. Let them attend me immediately. I am betrayed by your council; by your council I am now suffering the greatest calamity that can wound the heart of a king.

Bute. Your majesty will remember that the plan for enslaving America, was ever dear to your royal breast, and the offspring of your own heart.

G. Remember it is one of the wise maxims in English politics, "a king can do no wrong." The plan was good, ye have murdered it by your blunders in the execution—the fault lies with ye, and ye shall bear it—and I'll give ye all up a sacrifice to appease the rage of the people.

Mansfield. I hope your majesty will recollect my long and faithful services; I have twisted the law into all shapes and forms to answer royal purposes. And—

G. Tell me no more of your services. I have been deceived and ruined by the advice of my ministers and council—pox take them all—it makes my blood curdle in my veins to think of it! America is lost forever! and all owing to my scoundrel ministers—if I had rak'd hell, and skin'd the devil, I could not have found a worse set.

D. Sirrah! Sirrah—I don't allow you to use my name by way of reproach to your rascally ministers.

G. Your highness will excuse what is said in the heights of passion, I am all rage and vengeance—I could spit fire—my very vitals burn like tinder—I could swear fast enough to carry a wind mill—attend me this moment all my ministers and council: Now what do you say to the American war, ye wrong headed Scotch bastards.

D. Hold! Hold! George, come I'll be moderate, and see that every one has fair play; ye are all my servants, and every one shall speak freely in his own cause.

Bute. I thank your highness for this liberty, as we have much to offer in our justification—our king has never been entirely governed by our advices; his mulish temper was such while a boy, that I had rather borne the misfortunes of Job, than to have been his tutor; and as he grew in years he grew in obstinacy; and—

G. You lie! ye old plain stocking'd whoresbird—I'll—

D. Silence! George, don't you interrupt my old servant.

Bute. And when we gave him the best counsel, he'd often follow the worst; I often told him—

G. I won't bear an insult from that Highlander, I'll—

D. Silence! Tom Firetongs, take George by the nose and give the scoundrel a twist.

Bute. I told him his measures were inadequate to the purpose: but when once he gets wrong, no one can right him.

Germaine. I can witness to the truth of what my Lord Bute hath declared. Had our council been always duly regarded—

G. What! dares the Minden coward to rise?

D. Here! Triphammer, make a tongue cuff for George instantly; rivet it on red hot: I'll see if we can't keep that fellow's tongue still.

North. I beg leave to speak one word; it is notorious where the fault lies; but it is vain to waste time in criminations, we must now consult our safety. I beg the ministers of the crown would withdraw with me a few minutes.

(Aside. *North.* Ye all know the maxim, "a king can do no wrong"; and although it is the quintessence of nonsense, yet the wise people of Britain hold it as sacred; and whenever the king will give up his ministers to the rage of the people, they will absolve the criminal, and cry him up for the best of kings; therefore we must take him off before he makes a sacrifice of us. Let us give the mule a dose of arsenic, and let him go off with the dry belly ache, and be pox'd to him.

Sandwich. This plan will do, and nothing else, for the sullen dog can never be brought to good humour, and if he lives he'll play fury with us.

Bishop. 'Tis the only plan, and I'll read the funeral service, and give thanks heartily that he is taken out of this evil world.

Germaine. I like it much: for the joy which a new king will diffuse, will allay the present tumult about America; every one will be paying his addresses to the new king, and no one will care who has got the old one; we will retire from the helm and live in domestic peace. I beg that this motion may be put to vote—all hands are up, it passes *nem. con.* Let one of the family physicians prepare the dose.)

North. Ever animated with the most ardent affection to the best of kings, I feel the sighs of loyalty whenever his majesty meets with any misfortune. I wish not to criminate any one: but, as I said before, it is notorious where the fault lies: his majesty's commanders, by sea, and land, have trifled away the opportunities that offered for defeating the French, and subduing the rebels. I should be happy to hear his majesty express his royal sentiments on this great occasion.

G. North, you are an honest fellow, and your remarks are just; but in our infernal situation, how can we make peace? A peace we must have, for destruction gapes to receive us!

(*North* to *Germaine*, aside. I'll flatter the king 'till the poison is ready, and then we'll jirk him out of the world.)

North. If your majesty will be graciously pleased to signify the terms on which you would treat for peace, your majesty's ministers will lose no time in pursuing your royal wishes.

G. What is the first step we ought to take, North, in your opinion, to obtain an honorable peace?

North. May it please your majesty, I conceive that we must now endeavour to gain the favor of America, and as there is an American plenipotentiary not far distant, I humbly conceive it might be proper to consult him, and feel his pulse.

G. Invite the American to meet us in council to morrow.

The dialogue concluded by the speech of an *American.*

A. By the providence of the Almighty, the time is come which compels the reluctant wish for peace—since your sword can no longer devour, and is ready to be plung'd in the guilty bosom that kindled the war, you think of peace. Peace is the desire of humanity, the constant object of the wise and good; it hath ever been the ardent wish of America, and all her views have centered in this; but your hostile heart hath hitherto shut the door against it. I will express the views of America, in a few words. She means not only to be independent, sovereign and free, but to communicate as far as may be in her power, the superlative blessings herself enjoys, to all mankind. As she means that all the treaties she forms should be lasting as time, and thereby to establish perpetual peace, in her treaty with Britain she will not measure her terms by the injuries she hath received, but looking forward to distant ages, and measuring things on the great scale of the world, with benevolent views to humanity, she will give to [the] British such terms of peace and commerce, as shall be for the general good of mankind: and leave it to providence, to punish the enormities of the present rulers of Britain and their abettors, who have shed the innocent blood of Americans. In a word, America will be in every view as completely an independent sovereign nation, as any power that now exists in the world; and she will give to every nation with whom she forms a treaty, the same privileges she receives, and nothing more.

By the favor and protection of GOD, who hath given her the best quarter of the world, and exalted her to the rank of empire, she means by sacred honour, and justice, and humanity, to hold the balance of the nations, and to be a friend to the oppressed, and an enemy to none but the enemies of peace. From these general principles, the concessions you must make, in order to obtain peace, are obvious, and I need not name them. But before I conclude, let me remind you "*there is no peace to the wicked*"—and your crimes are numberless, and their enormity is equal to their number. You were exalted to reign over a grateful people, who loved you with parental tenderness and brotherly affection; they expected a return of love, and in the careless confidence which love inspires, exposed their liberties to the grasp of a tyrant. You conceived their security afforded the wished for moment to enslave them, and equally regardless of your duty to GOD and to man, you formed the horrid design, and have pursued it by means too infernal to be named; you have violated all the sacred laws of heaven and earth, and sported with human misery. When America asked only for liberty, peace and safety—only for the enjoyment of what GOD had given, you sent fire and sword; and while they begged for mercy, you added torture and death in the most horrid forms. Thousands who once sent up ardent prayers for you, changed them into petitions that GOD would stay your murdering hands. For many long years every breeze hath wafted the groans of dying prisoners to heaven against you, while every hour hath witnessed the big tears and swelling bosoms of their surviving friends! What myriads have you sent down to the chambers of death; and in the bosom of surviving thousands, you have planted the sharp thorn of affliction! The aged parents cry with anguish, "O my son! my son! my only son is murdered by the tyrant George." The bereaved widow and weeping children, with bleeding hearts, cry out, "O my husband! my father! we shall never never see him again! he is murdered by the tyrant." The virgin, whose dearer second self, was gloriously contending in the field to save his country, became a captive and suffered complicated death by cold and hunger; she cannot speak for grief—in silent sorrow sinks down, and in her languid eye, she looks a prayer to heaven! Her anguish is too great to find a voice, but heaven can hear her wishes, and will avenge her wrongs! Well may you turn pale at your picture, and faint at the prospect of wrath divine, and triple vengeance arm'd with almighty thunder! You have slighted the commands of your GOD and Saviour, and despised the precepts of the Prince of Peace; therefore you may justly fear that he will "laugh at your calamity, and mock when your fear cometh"; that as you refused mercy it shall be refused to you, and when "destruction and desolation cometh upon you like a whirlwind," no arm shall relieve you, no eye shall pity you; but wrapt in final ruin, sink down, down, down to the regions of horror and death eternal!

(*The physicians in waiting, observing the king to swoon, apply strong drops, and prepare to let blood.*)

And you his guilty ministers, who have shared in his crimes, shall be partakers of his plagues—your infidel hearts have laughed at the judgment to come, and said, "to whom shall we give account?" but the time is near, when, like "the father of lies", ye shall "believe and tremble." While your master faints with conscious guilt, can ye lift an eye to the sun, or look on the face of man, while nature, scarred with your cruelties, and weeping, cries for vengeance, and the slighted mercy of heaven is just signing your doom.

(*The physicians cry out, "the king is dead, and all their lordships are fainting, and have the symptoms of death."*)

The American then turned from them, as the angel from Satan, and went his way.

(P. S. *The reader will observe that the prophane language in the dialogue, is only between the vilest being in the other world, and the worst in this, and is inserted with a view to render the odious practice of swearing perfectly infamous. Surely no one will imitate the Devil, or the tyrant, unless he is dead to virtue, and lost to all the noble sentiments and feelings of the soul.*

Tories may perhaps think the tyrant is ill used: but his crimes are so black and numerous, that it is perhaps impossible to represent him worse on the whole, than he really is, or even so bad: and the Tories may as well undertake to vindicate the conduct of the Devil, as that of the tyrant.)

FINIS

24

DEFENSIVE ARMS VINDICATED

A Moderate Whig

[Stephen Case?]

[NEW-MARLBOROUGH]

1783

STEPHEN CASE (1746–1794). Neither the author nor the place of publication of *Defensive Arms Vindicated* (1783) has been determined with certainty. It is signed "A Moderate Whig," dated June 17, 1782 at New-Marlborough, and dedicated to George Washington. In the text the author indicates that the piece was actually written in 1779. Scholars believe that a Stephen Case was the author because his name is written in manuscript on some extant copies of the pamphlet. This may be the Captain Stephen Case born in Orange County, New York, in 1746, who served in Colonel Jonathan Hasbrouck's regiment of the Ulster County militia during the Revolution, and who died in Marlborough, Ulster County, New York, in 1794. In the Preface to the Reader the author addresses "my dear brother soldiers," which bears out the identification to some extent.

Defensive Arms Vindicated is a learned and brilliant, if unpolished, discourse intended to prove that resistance against the abuse of a lawful power is not only justified but is a positive duty of the people. In the manner of a sermon, this condemnation of tyranny ranges through biblical texts and historical examples, and it draws from the writings of learned authors as well, including Jean Bodin and Hugo Grotius. It ends with a homely postscript on the war debt and other economic disorders that the Golden Rule would solve, if rightly applied.

Concerning the identification of Stephen Case, see the letters of R.W.G. Vail to Willard O. Waters, July 4 and 5, 1950; and the letter of Ruth A. (Mrs. L.G.) Duncan to Leslie E. Bliss, April 10, 1954, in the Henry E. Huntington Library, pamphlet folder 121761.

DEFENSIVE ARMS VINDICATED

AND THE

LAWFULNESS

OF THE

AMERICAN WAR

MADE MANIFEST.

TO WHICH IS ADDED,

A ſhort Receipt for a Continental Diſeaſe, &c.

DEDICATED TO HIS EXCELLENCY

GENERAL WASHINGTON.

By A MODERATE WHIG.

PRINTED FOR THE AUTHOR, 1783.

To His Excellency George Washington, Esq. Generalissimo of the army of the United States in America, Lieutenant General in the army of France, and Commander in Chief of all the French forces by sea and land in America.

Sir,

Much might be said, were it necessary, for the dedication of books unto persons of worth, interest, service, and honour, by reason it has been the almost constant practice of the best and wisest men, in all the ages of the world. Besides, sir, a performance of this nature could not possibly be dedicated to any person more suitable than yourself, as being the great patron of the American cause; and one who has shewn to the world that he was sent into it to perform wonders, under God. It is needless to relate your great talents in bearing both with prosperity and adversity, therefore I need not make no other apology for my present practice. What is written is permanent *litera scripta manet*, and spreads itself farther by far, for time, place, and persons, than the voice can reach. Augustine writing to Volusian saith, "That which is written is always at hand to be read when the reader is at leisure." Great sir, pray let it be the top of your ambition, and the heighth of all your designs, to glorify God, to secure your interest in Christ, to serve your generation, to provide for eternity, to walk with God, to be tender of all that have, *aliquid Christi*, any thing of Christ shining in them, and so to steer your course in this world as that you may give up your account at last with joy. Matt. XXX. 21. For, dear sir, all other ambition is base and low ambition (saith one), a gilded misery, a secret poison, a hidden plague, the engineer of deceit, the mother of hypocrisy, the parent of envy, the original of vices, the moth of holiness, the blinder of hearts. It is said that it so blinded Cardinal Bourbon, that he said he would not lose his part in Paris for his part in paradise. But, alas! what is all the glory of this world but a mere blaze. It is said that at the enthronization of the pope before he is set in his chair, and puts on his tripple crown, a piece of tow, or a wad of straw, is set on fire before him, and one appointed to say, *sic transit gloria mundi*, the glory of this world is but a blaze. High seats are always uneasy, and crowns themselves are always stuffed with thorns, which made one say of his crown[:] O crown! More noble than happy! May the spirit of God, the grace of God, the power of God, the presence of God, arm you against all other sins, evils, snares, and temptations, as you are by a good hand of heaven armed against worldly ambition and worldly glory.

Sir, you know he was a Saul that said honour me before the people, and he was a Jehu that said come see my zeal for the Lord of hosts. Sir, men of great honour and worldly glory stand but in slippery places. Adonibezek, a mighty prince, was made fellow commoner with the dogs. Judges i. 7. Henry IV emperor, in sixty-two battles for the most part became victorious, yet he was deposed and driven to that misery that he desired only a clerk's place in a house at Spire, of his own building, which the bishop of that place denied him, whereupon he broke forth into that speech of Job, chap. xix. 21. *miseremini mei amica quia manus dei tetigit me*, have pity upon me, O my friends, for the hand of God hath touched me. He at last died of grief and want. By which instances, and many more that might be brought, it is most evident that worldly glory is but a breath, a vapour, a froth, a phantom, a shadow, a reflection, an apparition, a very nothing.

Sir, if there be any thing glorious in the world, 'tis a mind that wisely contemns that glory; and such a mind I judge and hope God hath given unto you. I have given this small hint of worldly glory, and the vanity thereof, because happily this little piece passing up and down this continent, may chance to fall into the hands of such as may in fact be troubled with that itch; and if so, who can tell but what that little which I have said may prove a sovereign salve to cure that Egyptian botch; and if so, I have my end. And now, sir, to conclude, I pray the day may shortly commence, when you can, with honour and safety, withdraw from the noise of war and clashing of arms to your seat, from which you have been so long absent, in the service of your country, and in the cause of religion and virtue; and may your lady live to be an honour to God, to be truly wise for eternity, to be a pattern of piety, humility, modesty, &c to others.

O may you both be blessed, with all spiritual blessings in heavenly places in Christ Jesus! And may you all around be crowned with the highest glory, happiness, and blessedness in the world to come; may you long live in the sense of divine love; and, at last, die in the sense of divine favour. Now, to the everlasting arms of divine protection, and to the constant influences of free, rich, and sovereign grace and mercy he commends you and your's, who is, sir, your unknown friend and most obedient humble servant,

A Moderate Whig

New-Marlborough, June 17, 1782

PREFACE TO THE READER

It is now going on three years since I first wrote this piece. Great and glorious events have since taken place in our political affairs; and, I hope, the day is not far distant when peace, on the most honourable and advantageous terms, for America, shall be proclaimed throughout these United States. However, not knowing how much longer the war, by reason of our sins, might be continued, I concluded it might not be amiss to cast my mite into the treasury, in order to vindicate the conduct of all those brave officers and men who have already and may yet fall in the American war, in defence of our rights and liberties, civil and religious; and also to clear up the doubts and scruples of tender consciences, as to the lawfulness of taking up arms in any case whatsoever. I acknowledge that there have already been many able pens employed in stating the justice of our cause, and none, in my opinion, merits more our thanks than the author of Common Sense; but none, that I have seen, has, to my satisfaction, cleared up the lawfulness of the use of defensive arms against tyrants and tyranny, whenever they shall endeavour to deprive a people of their liberty and property. It is, surely, a pity that some abler hand had not undertaken the task, who might have done greater justice to the cause. All that I have, or chuse, to say, in praise of the performance, is, that the author means honestly, and shall ever pray for the success of the American arms, and those of her allies, in the present just defensive war; and that he never has, nor never means to spare himself, whenever he may be called upon to face the enemies of his country, if even it should as it may, cost him his life; for where could he offer it better than on the altar of religion and liberty, fighting in defence of both?

And now for a word of advice to the brave officers and soldiers composing the American army. Gentlemen officers, let me entreat you to desist from all vice, and practice virtue; fear God and obey your superiors; set good examples before your men; be tender and careful of their lives and health; discountenance vice and encourage virtue in them; do not correct nor abuse them but according to martial law. I once read of a good old general that was walking through his army, when, at length, he saw a young prodigal officer beating an old soldier unmercifully: O! says the general, *lay on, for you know that he dare not strike you again!* Which reproof, though very modest, covered the officer with blushes, and caused him to desist—and, in fact, it is a sure sign of a coward, to be beating a man that we know dare not, for his life, resist.

Some time past I was at West-Point, and saw an officer, with an unmerciful club, beating a poor drunken soldier; and, after he was tired, ordered some underling to continue the chastisement, which he did in a most horrid manner, knocking him down, and beating him over head and face, until the blood gushed out of almost every part of his body; many officers gathering round, said *lay on*, and damning him that dare say otherways, until I thought he would have been killed right out; but at length one humane, good officer spoke, and said, stop! if he has done amiss, confine him; and if, upon trial, he is found guilty, let him be punished accordingly. He was confined, and, I suppose, punished again for the same offence; which is contrary to all justice, to punish a man twice for the same crime.

And you, my dear brother soldiers, let me beg of you to consider you have souls to be saved or lost; therefore cease from the practise of sin, and practise holiness in the fear of God; honour and obey your officers; and see that you become the true soldiers of Jesus Christ; and not only be fighting soldiers, but praying ones also. But to conclude I would inform both gentlemen officers and soldiers, that you shall have my prayers for your present and eternal welfare, &c. . . .

A Moderate Whig

New Marlborough, June 17, 1782

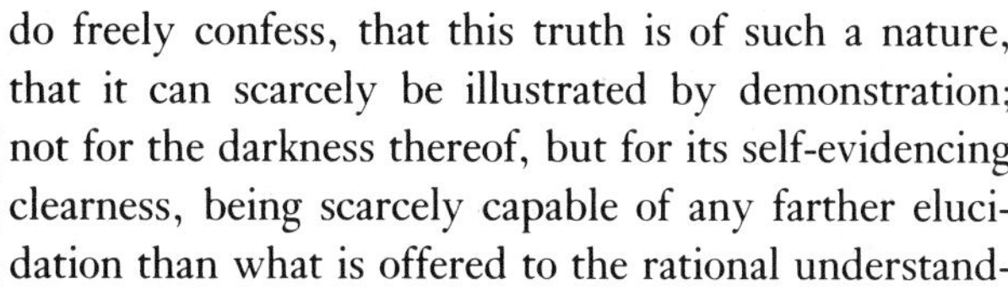

I do freely confess, that this truth is of such a nature, that it can scarcely be illustrated by demonstration; not for the darkness thereof, but for its self-evidencing clearness, being scarcely capable of any farther elucidation than what is offered to the rational understanding by its simple proposition, as first principles can hardly be proven, because they need no probation, and cannot be made any clearer than they really are; and such persons as cannot, or will not, consent to them, are, in my opinion, incapable of conceiving any probation. And I do affirm, that self preservation and defence is right and lawful, because it is congenite with, and irradicated in every nature that hath a self which it can preserve, can scarcely be more illustrated that it may do so, than that it can do so; and therefore, all that have a true respect to their own, as well as a due concern in the interest of mankind, and their country's rights and liberties; I say, to such worthy characters it might seem superfluous to make a doubt or a debate of this self-evident truth. And was it not that there have been, and still are, a generation of mortals (shall I call them men) in our land that are as great monsters in nature as they are malignant in religion; and as great perverters of the law of nature as they are subverters of municipal laws, and everters of the laws of God, I have reason to believe this present war would not have been spun out to such a length. I have not undertaken to write this small piece with any great prospect of convincing such characters; but my chief view was to comfort the minds of such persons whose near and dear connections have fallen, or may yet fall, in the glorious cause of liberty and virtue; and to clear up the doubts that tender consciences may entertain, as to the lawfulness of a defensive war. It does appear clear, that it has been the practice of all nations in the world, and the greatest and best of men have, in all ages, maintained this principle; and many, for adhering to it, have suffered death, and sealed the truth thereof with their blood. Read Woodrow's and Cruckshank's history of the two brothers bloody reign, from 1660, to the glorious revolution in 1688, containing twenty-eight years; which, by the godly, was justly called the killing time. Also let us read our own history of the American war from April 19, 1775, to June 17, 1779, and we shall not be wanting of instances of many suffering by the hands of British tyranny, for maintaining this principle of self defence, in defence of our lives and liberties. It is well known that the Americans did not hastily, nor violently, rush in to the present war. They did petition, remonstrate, and restrained trade; nay, took every reasonable method that reasonable creatures could invent, in order to prevent the effusion of human blood. But when they found all their humble petitions rejected, and treated with the greatest scorn and contempt; and that nothing would go down with proud, haughty North and his silly tool George the III, and their associates in wickedness, but a total surrender of all our rights and liberties, and an unconditional submission, they did take up arms to defend themselves from the unjust and wicked encroachments of haughty Britain; and, if we may judge from the success of our arms, we may rationally conclude that heaven approves of our undertaking, and that the God of battle has gone forth with our armies. But not to enlarge upon a subject so manifest, I now proceed to prove the lawfulness of taking up arms to oppose all tyranny, oppression, and those who abuse and misuse their authority. This great truth is sufficiently made manifest by the most famous and learned patrons and champions for this excellent privilege of mankind, the unanswerable authors of *Lex Rex,* the apologetical relation Naphtali and *Jus Populi Vindicatum.* But because it is easy to add to what is found, I shall subjoin my mite; and their arguments being various and scattered at large through their books, I shall endeavour to collect a compend of them in some order.

The two first of these authors do treat of a defensive war, under the direction of a parliament, like that in England about the year 1645; and the two last of resistance against the abuse of a lawful power, when there is no access to maintain our rights and liberties in any other way; which seems to come the nearest to our case, for we had no British parliament to be conducted by; but, in the lieu thereof, had recourse to a congress; nor did we ever dispute the lawfulness of the king of England's right to the crown, and to govern according to the laws and constitution thereof; but when he and his creatures undertook to govern us contrary to law, then did we most justly undertake to defend ourselves from the unjust encroachments of a tyrant. But, says the enemies of our country, it is no ways lawful, in any case, or upon any pretence whatsoever, to resist kingly authority, in whomsoever it be resident, or which way soever it be erected or conducted. O! poor passive slaves!

I shall now endeavour to consider it more complexly and extensively, and plead both for resistance against the abuse of a lawful power, and against the use and usurpation of a tyrannical power, and infer not only the lawfulness of resisting kings, when they abuse their power, as is made manifest by the above named authors, but also the expediency and necessity of the duty of resisting this tyrannical power, whenever we are, by a good providence of God, called thereunto; and this we must do, if we would not be found betrayers of the liberties of our country and brethren, together with the ruin of our poor posterity, which, if we should neglect to do, we shall be instruments of delivering up these inestimable blessings into the devouring jaws of tyranny; which if we should be tame enough to do, shall we not bring on us the curse of Meroz and the curse of our brethren's blood, crying for vengeance on the heads of the shedders thereof, and upon all who being in a capacity came not to their rescue; and the curse of posterity would have been upon us for not transmiting that liberty whereof we were, by the valour of our worthy forefathers, put and left in possession of. I shall not, therefore, restrict myself to the question propounded ordinarily, to wit, whether or not, when a limited king doth really injure, oppress, and invade his subjects civil rights and liberties, and sends out his bloody emissaries, with armed violence against them; and when all redress, or hope, by any address or petition, is rendered void; then, and in that case, may a community of such subjects defend themselves and their liberties by arms, in resisting his bloody emissaries. But to bring it home to our present case, and answer the laxness of the adversaries position of the uncontroulableness of every one that wears a crown, I shall state it thus, whether or not it is a duty for a community to endeavour, in the defence of their lives, laws, and liberties, to resist the tyranny of prevailing dominators, using and abusing their power, to the subverting and invading the liberties and overturning the fundamental laws of the country? I hold to the affirmative, and shall attempt to prove it; and, in prosecuting this subject, I shall first permit some concessory considerations to clear it, and then bring reasons to prove it.

In the first place for clearing of this truth, and taking of mistakes, then concessions may be considered.

First. I do allow that the ordinance of majestracy, which is of God, is not to be resisted; no, not so much as by disobedience or non-obedience; nay, not so much as mentally, by cursing in the heart, Eccles. x. 20. But a person clothed therewith, abusing his power, may be so far resisted; but tyrants, or magistrates turning tyrants, are not God's ordinances; and there is no hazard of damnation for refusing to obey their unjust commands; but rather, the hazard of that is in walking willingly after the commandment, when the statutes of Omri are kept; so that what is objected from Eccles. viii. 2. 4. *I counsel thee to keep the king's commandments, &c.* Is to be understood only of the lawful commands of lawful things.

Second. I do allow that rebellion is a damnable sin, except where the word is taken in a lax sense, as Israel of old is said to have rebelled against Rehoboam, and good Hezekiah against Senacherib, which was a good rebellion and a clear duty. Being taken there for resistance and revolt, in this sense, the Americans rising in arms may be called rebellion, for it is right and lawful, to all intents and purposes, to rebel against tyrants, as all are who offer, or attempt, to govern contrary to the laws of the land; for where law ceases, tyranny begins. But because the word is generally taken in an evil sense, many do not make the proper distinction between a lawful rebellion against tyrants, and an unlawful one against lawful authority. As I said before, I do allow that rebellion against lawful magistrates is a most damnable sin, which was of old most exemplarily punished in Korah and his company, who rebelled against Moses; and in Sheba and Absalom, who rebelled against David. *For to punish the just is not good, nor to strike princes for equity.* Prov. xvii. 26. *And they that resist shall receive to themselves damnation.* Rom. xiii. 2. So that this objection, brought from this place, as if the apostle was commanding their subjection, without resistance, to Nero and such like tyrants as he, is very impertinent; and to explain this a little, I shall shew that the apostle was here vindicating christianity from that reproach of casting off, or refusing subjection to all magistrates, as if christian liberty had destroyed that relation, or that they were not to be subject to heathen magistrates; whereupon, to undeceive them in this point, he binds this duty of subjection to magistrates for conscience sake in general; and it is very considerable what Buchanan says in his book *(De Jure regai:)* that Paul did not write to the kings themselves, because they were not christians, and therefore the more might be borne with from them, though they should not understand the duty of magistrates. But upon supposition there had been some christian king who had turned tyrant, and a limited one also who, by his tyrannical proceedings, was endeavouring to overturn the laws, charters, and liberties of his subjects, what would he have written then? Surely if he had been like himself he would have denied that he should be owned for a king; and would have interdicted all christian communion with him; and that they should account him no king, but such as they were to have no fellowship with according to the law of the gospel.

Second. The apostle here was, no doubt, speaking of lawful rulers, not tyrants; but of all such as are defined and qualified here, being powers ordained of God, terrors to evil works, ministers of God for good. Yea, but say tories and their adherents, these are only motives of subjection to all powers, not qualifications of the powers. To which I answer, they are indeed motives, but such as can be extended to none but to those powers that are so qualified.

Third. He speaks of lawful powers indefinitely in the plural number, not specifying any kind or degree of them, as if only kings and emperors were here meant. It cannot be proved that the power of the sword is only in them, neither was there, at that time, at Rome a plurality of kings and emperors to be subject to. It is clear to me, that if he had meant the Roman emperor, he would have designed him in the singular number; for all the reasons of the text agree to inferior judges. Also, for they are ordained of God; they are called rulers in scripture, and God's ministers, revengers by office, who judge not for man but for the Lord. And inferior magistrates also are not to be resisted when doing their duty, 1 Peter, ii. 13. Yet all will allow, when they go beyond their bounds, and turn little tyrants, they may be withstood.

Fourth. He does not speak of Nero, concerning whom it cannot be proved, that at this time he had the sovereign power, as the famous and learned Mr. Prin shews; or if he had, that he was a tyrant at this time; and if he meant him at all, it was only as he was obliged to be by right, not as he was indeed: all men know, and none condemns the fact of the senate that resisted Nero at length, without transgressing this precept. Yea, I should rather think the senate is the power that the apostle applies this text to, if he applied it to any in particular.

Fifth. The subjection here required is the same with the honour in the fifth command, whereof this is an exposition, and is opposite to the contraordinateness here condemned. Now subjection takes in all the duties we owe to magistrates, and resistance all the contraries forbidden; but unlimited obedience is not here required, so neither unlimited subjection.

Third. I do allow passive subjection, in some cases, even to tyrants, when the Lord lays on that yoke; and, in effect, says he will have us lie under it awhile, as he of old commanded the Jews to be subject to Nebuchadnezzar. Of which passage, adduced to prove subjection to tyrants universally, Buchanan as above infers, that if all tyrants are to be subjected to because God by his prophet commanded his people to be subject to one tyrant, then it must be likewise concluded that all tyrants ought to be killed, because Ahab's house was commanded to be destroyed by Jehu. But passive subjection, when people are not in a capacity to resist, is necessary; but I do not say passive obedience, which is a mere chimera, invented in the brains of such sycophants and jack asses as would make the world slaves to tyrants. Whosoever suffereth, if he can shun it, is an enemy to his own being, and is a first cousin to a self-murderer; for every natural thing must strive to preserve itself against what annoyeth it; and also, he sins against the order of God who, in vain, hath ordained so many lawful means for the preservation of our being, if we suffer it to be destroyed, having power to help it.

Fourth. I do abhor all war of subjects, professedly declared against a lawful king, who governs and rules according to law; as also all war against lawful authority, founded upon, or designed for maintaining principles inconsistent with government, or against policy and piety; yea all war without authority; yet when all authority of magistrates supreme and subordinate is perverted and abused, contrary to the ends thereof, to the oppressing of the people and overturning their laws and liberties, people must not, in such cases which was exactly ours, suspend or delay their resistance, waiting for the concurrence of men of authority, and neglect the duty in case of necessity, because they have not men of authority to lead them; for if the ground be lawful, the call clear, the necessity cogent, the capacity probable, they that have the law of nature, the law of God, and the fundamental laws of the land on their side, cannot want authority, although they may be destitute of a king to lead them. Also, it is proper here to observe, that people have this privilege of nature to defend themselves, and their rights and liberties, as well as kings; and had it before they erected and constituted kings; for I affirm, that there is no distinction of quality in interests of nature, though there be in civil order; but self defence is not an act of civil order, in such interest people must not depend upon the priority of their superiors, nor suspend the duties they owe to themselves and their neighbours, upon the manuduction of other mens greatness, the law of nature allowing self defence, and the defence of our brethren, against all unjust violence, which fully justifies the conduct of the different states appearing in and flying to arms in defence of our distressed and injured brethren of the Massachusetts Bay state, in the year 1775, when Britain laid her iron hand of tyranny and oppression upon them. It is a great and incumbent duty on all people to defend their religion and liberties, and those of their countrymen, against king or parliament who shall attempt to destroy the rights and liberties of the subjects; for all the power of a king or ruler is surely cumulative, not privative, for the worse condition of a ruler ought not to be by procuring. Why then shall the king, betraying his trust, wrong the cause of the people whose trustee he is? Nay if it were not lawful for people to defend their religion, lives, and liberties against the unjust encroachments of a tyrannical king, then I say the people would be in a worse situation with a king than without him, for they have done it before they had them, and so had better be without them still. But it is as clear as the sun at noon day in the firmament, that it is lawful to resist kings when they, by their mal administration, forfeit their subjects allegiance, as the king of England, by his has surely done. Poor soul, I believe he repents, but it is like poor Esau's all too late.

Fifth. I do disallow all war, without real necessity and great wrongs sustained; and that it ought not to be declared or undertaken upon supposed grounds, or pretended causes; and so the question is impertinently stated by the tories, whether or not it be lawful for subjects, or a party of them, when they think themselves injured, or to be in a capacity, to resist or oppose the supreme power of a nation? For the question is not if, when they think themselves injured, they may resist; but when the injuries are real. Neither is it every reality of injuries will justify a people's resistance; but when their dearest and nearest liberties are invaded, especially when such an invasion is made as threatens the total subversion of them. Nor do I say that a people, esteeming themselves in a capacity, or their being really in a capacity, doth make resistance a duty, except all alike they have a call, as well as a capacity, which requires real necessity, and a right to the action; and the things contended for to be real and legal. Rights really and illegally encroached upon their capacity, gives them only a conveniency to go about the duty that is previously lawful upon a moral ground. No man need to say who shall be judge the king or people.

For first. All who have eyes in their head may, I think, judge whether the sun shines or not; and all who have common sense may judge in this case; for when it comes to a necessity of resistance, it is to be supposed that the grievances complained of, and sought to be redressed by arms, are not hid, but manifest. Now it cannot be so with a people only pretending their suffering wrong. As to the grievances of the good people of America, it is so manifest to the world, that some of the nations thereof have espoused our righteous cause, and the rest seems to be silent.

Second. There is no need of the formality of a judge in things evident to nature's eye, a grass is not tyranny. Undermining and overturning religion and liberty, must be nature in the acts of necessitated resistance. In such a case is judge, party, accuser, witness, and all. Neither is it an act of judgment for people to defend their own. Defence is no act of jurisdiction, but a privilege of nature. Hence arises these common sayings, all laws permits force to be repelled by force; and the great and first law of nature allows self-defence. I say, that the defence of life is necessary, and flows from the law of nature.

Third. Be judge who will, the tyrant cannot be judge in the case; for in those tyrannical acts that forces people to resistance, he cannot be acknowledged as king, and of course no judge; for it is always supposed that the judge is absent when he is the party that does the wrong; as such, is inferior to the innocent.

Fourth and lastly. Let God be judge, and all the world take cognizance of the justness of our cause.

Sixth. I condemn all rising to revenge private injuries, whereby a country may be covered with blood, for some petty wrongs done to some persons great or small. I also abhor all revengeful usurping of the magistrates sword, to avenge ourselves for personal injuries, as David's killing of Saul would have been. 1 Sam. xxiv. 10, 12, 13. Ibid xxvi 9, 10. To object this, in this case, were very impertinent; for it would have been an act of offence, in a remote defence, if Saul had been immediately assaulting of him, it could, by no means, be deemed to have been lawful; and it would have been an act of private revenge, for a personal injury, and a sinful preventing of God's promise of David's succession, by a scandalous assassination; but it is clear then, David was resisting him and that is enough for my argument; and he supposes he might descend into battle and perish. 1 Sam. xxvi. 10. Not excluding but that he might perish in battle against himself resisting. I do allow, indeed, that we are commanded, in scripture, not to resist evil, but whosoever shall smite us on the one cheek, to turn to him the other also. Mat. v. 39. And to recompence to no man evil for evil. Rom. xii. 17. But this doth not condemn self-defence, and resisting of tyrants, violently endangering our lives, laws, religion, and liberties; but only resistance by way of private revenge and retaliation; and enjoins patience, when the clear call and dispensation do inevitably call unto suffering, but not to give way to all violence, to the subverting of religion and liberty. These texts do no more condemn private persons retaliating the magistrates than magistrates retaliating private persons; unless magistrates be exempted from this precept, and consequently be not among Christ's followers; yea, they do no more forbid private persons to resist the unjust violence of a king than to resist the unjust violence of any private person. That objection from our Lord's reproving Peter[—]Matt. xxvi. 3, 2. Put up thy sword, for all they that take the sword shall perish by the sword[—]hath no weight here, for this condemns only making use of the sword either by way of private revenge, or usurping the use of it without authority, and so condemns all tyrants, which private subjects do not want to defend themselves, their religion, and liberty, or using it without necessity, which was not Peter's case, both because Christ was able to defend himself, and because he was willing to deliver up himself. *Pool's synops critic in locum.* Christ could easily have defended himself, but he would not, and, therefore, in course there was not the least necessity for Peter's rashness. It condemns, also, a rash precipitating, and preventing the call of God, to acts of resistance. But otherwise it is plain it was not Peter's fault to defend his master, but a necessary duty. The reason our blessed Lord gives for that inhibition at that time was twofold, one expressed Matt. xxvi. 52. For they that take the sword, &c. Which do not belong to Peter, as if he was hereby threatened, but to those that were coming to take Christ. They it were that, indeed, usurped the sword of tyrannical violence, and therefore are threatened with destruction by the bloody sword of the Romans. So is that commination to be understood of antichrist and the tyrants that serve him. Rev. xiii. 10. He that killeth with the sword must be killed with the sword. Which really is a most terrible word against persecutors and tyrants. The reason is, John xviii. 11. The cup which my father hath given me shall I not drink [it?] Which clearly repels that objection of Christ's non-resistance. To which it is answered, that suffering was the end of his voluntary suscepted humiliation, and his grand errand to the world, appointed by the father, and freely undertaken by himself, which is not the rule of our practice; though it be true that, even in his suffering, he left us an example, that we should follow his steps. 1 Pet. ii. 21. In many things, as he was a martyr, his sufferings were the purest rule and example for us to follow, both for the matter and frame of spirit, submission, patience, constancy, meekness, &c. But not as he was our sponsor, and after the same manner, for then it would be unlawful for us to flee, as well as to resist, because he would not flee at that time.

Seven. I do also disclaim all rising in arms for trifles of our own things, or small injuries done to ourselves, but in a case of pure necessity, for the preservation of our lives, religion, laws, and liberties, when all that is dear to us as men and christians, are in hazard. So I am not for rising in arms to force any people to be of any particular religion, but to defend my own, and my country's religion and liberties, from unjust force and violence, against kings and tyrants, that may encroach thereon. I do not believe that it is the way that Christ hath appointed to propagate religion by arms. Let persecutors and limbs of antichrist take that to them. But I am convinced that it is a privilege that Christ hath allowed to mankind, to defend and preserve their religion and liberties by arms, especially when they have been established by solemn charters, and the laws and constitution of the land, and thereby become a land right, and the dearest and most precious of all rights and interest we have to contend for. It is true, saith

Christ, John xviii. 36. My kingdom is not of this world; if it was of this world, then would my servants fight, that I should not be delivered to the Jews. But this objection, which is so much relied on by Quakers, and those who disown all use of war and arms, in any case whatsoever, will not conclude that Christ's kingdom is not to be defended and preserved by resistance of all such who would impiously and sacrilegiously spoil us of it in this world, because it is not of this world, for then all would be obliged to suffer it to be run down by slaves of hell and satan, and antichrists vassals; yea, kings themselves, in such a case, must not fight for it, for they are among his servants. But the good confession he witnesses here before Pilate, is, that he hath a kingdom which, as it is not in opposition to any Cesarean majesty, must not be usurped by any king of clay; but is specially distinct from all the kingdoms of the world, and subordinate to no earthly power, being of a spiritual nature, whereof this is a demonstration, and sufficient security for earthly kingdoms, that his servants, as such, that is as christians and as ministers, were not appointed by him to propagate it by arms, nor to deliver him their king, at that time, because he would not suffer his glorious design of redemption to be any longer retarded. But this doth not say that though they are not to propagate it as christians and as ministers, by carnal weapons, yet they may preserve it with such weapons as men. Hence that old saying may be vindicated, prayers and tears are the arms of the church. I grant they are so, the only best prevailing arms, and without which all others would be ineffectual, and that they, together with preaching and church discipline, are the only ecclesiastical or spiritual arms of a church as a church; but the members thereof are also men, and as men they may use the same weapons as others do. And ye my flock, the flock of my pasture, are men, saith the Lord, Ezek. xxxiii. 31. And from this I shall take an argument, that if it be lawful for private subjects to resist a tyrant by prayers and tears, than it is lawful also to resist them by violence; but the former is true, therefore the latter. This personal resistance by violence is as consistent with that command, Rom. xiii. 1, 2. Let every soul be subject unto the higher powers. Whosoever, therefore, resisteth the power, resisteth the ordinance of God; as resistance by prayer is with that 1 Tim. ii. 1, 2 I exhort that supplication be made for kings and for all that are in authority. If the king be good, the one resistance is as unlawful as the other; and is a sinful resistance of the ordinance of God, to pray against him no less than the other to fight against him. Therefore, when a king turns a tyrant, and a destroyer of the religion and liberties of the people, I may not pray for him, except conditionally, but against him as an enemy, so I may also fight against him. As such the tyrant of Britain, I mean George the III, and his burning bloody emissaries, who do, at least, by their actions, acknowledge that the resistance made against them, by the prayers and tears of the faithful, is more powerful and effectual than that made by arms. Witness the spite and enmity they have shewn in all their tours of plunder and burnings, against the houses dedicated and set apart for prayers and praises to Almighty God. What has become of one or two near Springfield, in the state of New-Jersey, when they murdered the minister's wife there? How have they destroyed two at Somerset, in said state? Also, at Crumpond, and Bedford, in the state of New-York? And no doubt many more that at present does not occur to my mind. And farther, the law used to make the one resistance as treasonable as the other, and that very deservedly too, when the king was doing his duty. But when he turns tyrant, neither of those methods of resistance can justly be condemned.

These things being admitted, I shall now come to the thing in hand, and endeavour to prove this truth, that it is a necessary duty for a people to endeavour, in the defence of their religion, lives, laws, and liberties; to resist and repress the tyranny of a king, using and abusing his power for subverting religion, invading the liberties, and overturning the fundamental laws of the country. I propose to be as short as possible, because I think this truth is sufficiently confirmed already, to convince any but those who are determined not to be convinced; yet I propose to hint at some others, and prosecute them in the following order. First, I shall produce some arguments from the law of nature and nations. Secondly, From the common practices of all christian people. Thirdly, From express scriptures.

First, The arguments of the first class are very multifarious. I shall endeavour to reduce them to a few as compendiously as may be, and only give the strength of them in a syllogistical form, without expatiating, save where the matter requires.

First, The great antagonists of this truth, through the clearness thereof, are forced to assert and grant such particulars as will, by consequence, justify this plea. First, Barclay, *contra monarchum*, is cited by the *Apal Relat*, and *Jus Populi*, asserting, "That if a king will alienate, and subject his kingdom, without his subjects consent, or be carried with a hostile mind to the destruction of his people, his kingdom is actually lost, and the people may not only lawfully resist, but also depose him." *Grotius de jure Belli*, *lib.* 1, cap. 4, asserts the same, and adds, "If he but attempt to do so, he may be resisted." The Surveyor of Naphtali grants the same, p. 23, 24. Yea, this has been granted in many of the councils and open courts of christian nations, that in case of the king's alienating his kingdom, he may be resisted; which will fully justify the American resistance; for surely Britain, by her conduct, was about to sell or destroy her liberties and property; and has effectually estranged and drawn off our affections from her, even to the world's wonder. I need say no more than this, that a king's carrying a hostile mind, to the destruction of his people and kingdom, does give the people a right to resist him. Doctor Ferne acknowledgeth, "That personal defence is lawful against the sudden, illegal, and inevitable assaults of the kings messengers, or of himself, so far as to ward off his blows, or hold his hands; as also he alloweth private persons liberty to deny subsidies and tribute to the prince, when he employeth it to the destruction of the commonwealth." From hence I argue, if one may defend himself against the sudden, illegal, and inevitable assaults of the king or his messenger, then may many men, in defence of their lives and liberties, defend themselves against the surprizing massacres, and sudden assaults of the king of England and his bloody emissaries, which were all illegal; but the former is true, therefore the latter.

Thirdly, *Bodin de Repub. lib.* 2. chap. 5, granteth, "If a king turn tyrant, he may lawfully, at his subjects request, be invaded, resisted, condemned, or slain by a foreign prince"—hence, if a foreign prince may lawfully help a people, oppressed by their own sovereign, then people may resist themselves, if they be able; but the former is true, therefore the latter. The consequence cannot be denied, for foreigners have no more power or authority over another sovereign, than the people have themselves.

Fourth, *Arnisaeus de author Prici.* chap. 2. 10, granteth, "That if the king proceed extrajudically, without order of law, by violence, every private man hath power to resist." So the Surveyor of Naphtali, as above, grants, "So much of a womans violently resisting attempts against the honour of her chastity, and tending to ensnare her in sin, whereof her non-resistance makes her guilty." Hence, if every extrajudical violence of a prince may be resisted, then also all contrajudical violence against law or reason, must be opposed, for that is more grievous, and all their violences, wherein they do not act as judges, must be resisted and that is altogether, for in none of them they can act as judges; but the former is true, therefore the latter. If a woman may defend her chastity against the king, lest her non-resistance make her guilty, then may a nation, or any part of it, resist a king's attempt upon their religion and liberties, enticing them to fornication, lest their non-resistance make them guilty; but the former is true, therefore the latter.

Five, That same *Arnisaeus*, cap. 4, saith of the former, to wit,

> He who is called a tyrant in title, it is determined by all, without any difficulty, that he may be lawfully repulsed, or if by force he be gotten into the throne, he may warrantably be thence removed, because he hath not any jot of power which is not illegitimate, and unto which resistance is forbidden, for the fear of God and for conscience sake; and therefore he is no further to be looked at than as an enemy.

Sixth. *Grotious de jure belli*, lib. i, cap. 4, granteth, "the law of not resisting does not bind, when the danger is most weighty and certain"; and I do not plead for it in any other case. And further, he saith,

> the law of non-resistance seemeth to have flowed from them who first combined together into society, and from whom such as did command, did derive their power. Now if it had been asked of such whether they would chuse to die, rather than in any case to resist the superior with arms, I know not if they would have yielded thereto, unless with this addition, if they could not be resisted but with the greatest perturbation of the common wealth, and destruction of many innocents.

And afterwards he hath the words, "Nevertheless I scarce dare condemn every one, or the lesser part, which may only be done, at utmost extremity; notwithstanding respect is to be had to the common good." From all which I need not make the least inference, the concession is so large, that it does to all intents and purposes confirm my arguments.

Seventh. The surveyor of Naphtali, in the place above cited, "grants legal self-defence, against the sovereign, by way of plea in court, for safety of a man's person or estate; as also is the case of most habited, not our and compleat tyranny, against law to the destruction of the body of a people; and of all known legal liberties, and the being of religion, according to law, and in case of his not being in his right wits."

Hence I argue, that if it be lawful to resist the king by a plea in law, for an estate, yea the law will allow, by actual force, if he come to take possession of it illegally; then it must be law for their lives and estates, liberties and religion, to resist him by force, when the legal resistance is not admitted; but the former is true, therefore the latter. The reason of the connexion is, the municipal law permits the one, and the law of nature and nations, which no municipal law can infringe, will warrant the other. He hath no more right to be both judge and party, in this case, than in the other. Second. If it be lawful to resist tyranny against law, to the destruction of the rights of the people, their religion and liberties, then I want no more to prove the lawfulness of the American resistance against the tyranny of Britain, exercised for years past against us, which has proven the desolation and ruin of many hundreds of families, besides all the rivers of blood that have been drawn from the veins of our dear countrymen; and all this perpetrated for the profest purpose of subverting our religion and liberties, and to establish an arbitrary government. And here I think it proper to answer an objection that some may make, viz. That I have blended religious liberty with civil, as a cause of the American resistance, when the former was not in the least invaded by any British act of parliament that was complained of; but all freedom left to the conscience in that respect, and therefore I ought not to have made use of the word in this piece. In answer whereof, I offer the following as my reason for so doing: I do freely acknowledge that I have not seen or heard of any British act of parliament that did, in direct terms, and in so many words, declare that the people of America should all be of one uniform religion, upon pain of death and confiscation of goods; but I have seen and read one that carried all that in it's bowels, to wit. The declaratory act, wherein they declare they had a right to bind the Americans in all cases whatsoever; which if once they could have put into full execution, what would there be left we could call our own any longer than at the will and pleasure of a tyrannical king and parliament, for there is no exception in the word whatsoever? Besides, whoever knew or heard of a people's enjoying their religious liberties when their civil was taken from them? They were born twins, knit together, therefore if one of them dies, the other cannot live; at least this is my opinion, and every one has a right to judge for themselves. Now under the full conviction of this, and that had our civil liberties been taken from us, our religious ones would not long survived. I was led to blend them together, and shall throughout this piece.

Third. Suppose the king should run mad, and out of his wits, and then should run upon an innocent man to kill him, or make an attempt to cut his own throat, would it then, and in that case, be lawful to resist him? Yea, it would be a great sin not to do it. Then surely, when in a mad rage, he is seeking to destroy many hundred of the good people of America, he may and ought to be resisted. But the former is true therefore the latter. It is easily to be seen by the above concessions of adversaries to my principles, that the absolute subjection they talk of will not hold good, nor the prerogative be so uncontroulable in every case as they would pretend; and that in many cases the safety of the people hath the supremacy above it, and that also in these cases the people must be judges whether they may resist or not.

Second. From the law of nature I may argue. First. If God the fountain of all power, and author of all right, hath given unto man both the power, and the right of, and reason to manage self-defence, and hath no ways interdicted it in his word, to be put forth against tyrants, then it is duty to use it against him upon occasion; but the former is true, therefore the latter. Second. If this power and right were restrained in man against the unjust violence of any, it would either be by policy or grace, or some express prohibition in the word of God; but none of these can be said, therefore policy cannot destroy nature, but is rather cumulative to it. A man entering into a politic incorporation, does not lose the privilege of nature. If one particular nature may defend itself against destroying violence out of society, then must many of these natures, combined in society, have the same right; and so much the more that their relative duties superadd an obligation of mutual assistance. Grace does not restrain the right of sinless nature, though it restrains corruption. But self-defence is no corruption. Grace makes a man more a man than he was, and nothing can be more dishonourable to the gospel than that, by the law of nature, it is lawful to resist tyrants. But we are bound by religion from withstanding their cruelty. The laws of God do not interfere one with another. Third. That law which alloweth comparative re-offending, so as to kill rather than be killed, teacheth resistance. But so the law of nature alloweth, except we be guilty of murder, in the culpable omission of self defence. The reason is because the love of self is nearer and greater, as to temporal life, than the love of our neighbour; that being the measure of this, therefore it obliges rather to kill than be killed, the exigence of necessity so requiring. Fourth. If nature put no other difference between the violence of a tyrant than of another man, then it teaches to resist both alike; but it putteth no difference, but rather aggravates that of a tyrant, being the violence of a man, the injustice of a member of the common wealth, and the cruelty of a tyrant; and it is most absurd to say, that we might defend ourselves from the lesser violence, and not from the greater. Fifth. If particular nature must yield to the good of universal nature, then must one man, though in greatest power, be resisted rather than the universal common wealth suffer hurt. But the former is true therefore the latter; for that dictates the necessity of the distracted father to be bound by his own sons, lest all the family be hurt; therefore the greatest of men, or kings, when destructive to the common wealth, must be resisted, for he is but one man, and so but particular nature. Sixth. That which is irrational, and reflects upon providence, as putting men in a worse condition than brutes, is absurd and contrary to the law of nature; but to say that the brutes have power to defend themselves, by resisting what annoys them, and deny this power to men, is irrational, and reflects upon providence as putting men in a worse condition than brutes; therefore it is absurd and contrary to the law of nature.

Third. From the institution of government, I may argue thus, that power and government, which is not of God, may be resisted. The tyrant's power and government in breaking charters, overturning laws, subverting religion, oppressing subjects, is not of God, therefore it may be resisted. This is clear, because that is only the reason why he is not to be resisted, because the ordinance of God is not to be resisted. Rom. xiii. 2. But they resisting a man, destroying all the interests of mankind, do not in this resist the ordinance of God. And if it were not so, this would tend irremediablessly to overthrow all politics, and open a gap to all disorder. Injustice and cruelty would give as great encouragement to tyrants to do what they list, as thieves would be encouraged, if they knew that nobody would resist them, or bring them to punishment.

Fourth. From the original constitution of government by men, it may be argued thus, if people, at the first erection of government, acted rationally and did not put themselves in a worse case than before wherein it was lawful to defend themselves against all injuries, but devolved their rights upon the fiduciary tutory of such as should remain still in the rank of men, that can do wrong, who had no power but by their gift, consent, and choice, with whom they associated, not to their detriment, but for their advantage; and determined the form of their government, and time of its continuance, and in what cases they might recur to their primeval liberty, and settled a succession to have course, not by hereditary right, but by right and force of law for good ends; then they did not give away their birth right of self defence and power of resistance, which they had before, to withstand the violence, injuries, and oppressions of men they set over them, when they pervert the form, and convert it to tyranny; but did retain a power and privilege to resist and revolt from them, and repel their violence when they should do violence to the constitution, and pervert the ends thereof. But the former is true, ergo, the connexion is confirmed from this. If the estates of a kingdom give the power to a king, it is their own power in the fountain; and if they give it for their own good, they have power to judge when it is used against themselves and for their evil; and so power to limit and to resist the power that they gave.

Fifth. From the way and manner of erecting governors, by compact, the necessity whereof is clear, many arguments might be deduced. I shall reduce them to this form, if people must propose conditions unto kings to be by them acquiesced in, and submitted unto, at their admission to the government, which thereupon becomes the fundamental laws of the government, and security for the peoples rights and liberties, giving a law claim to the people to pursue the king, in case of failing in the main and principle thing covenanted, as their own covenanted mandatarius, who hath no right or authority of his own, but what he hath from them, and no more power but what is contained in the conditions upon which he undertaketh the government. Then whenever a tyrant doth break all these conditions, which he once accepted, and so become, in strict law, no king and the people be, in strict law, liberated from subjection to him, they may and must defend themselves, and their fundamental rights and privileges, religion and laws, and resist the tyranny overturning them. But the former is true, therefore, &c.

Sixth. From the nature of magistracy, it may be argued thus: That power which is properly neither parental nor marital, nor masterly and despotick over the subjects and goods, but only fiduciary, and by way of trust, is more to be resisted than that which is properly so. But that power which is properly so, that is parental power and marital and masterly, may be resisted in many cases. Therefore that power which is not so properly, but only fiduciary, is more to be resisted than a king's power over his subjects, is neither parental nor marital, &c. is most clear. The minor is clear, by instances. First. If children may, in case of necessity, resist the fury and mad rage of their father, seeking to destroy them, then must private subjects resist the rage and tyranny of kings, seeking to destroy them, and what is dearest to them; for there is no stricter obligation moral between king and people, than between parents and children, nor so strict; and between tyrants and people there is none at all, therefore the former cannot be denied. Second. If wives may lawfully defend themselves against the unjust violence of enraged husbands, then must private subjects have power to resist the furious assaults of enraged tyrants, for there is not so great a tie betwixt them and people as between man and wife; yea there is none at all; but the former is true. Ergo, Three. If servants may defend themselves against their masters, then must private subjects against a tyrant or his emissaries; but the former is true. Ergo, Four. If the king's power is only fiduciary, and by way of pawn, which he hath got to keep, then when that power is manifestly abused, to the hurt of them that entrusted him with it, he ought, by all means, to be resisted by all those which he undertook to protect; but the former is true, therefore the latter.

Seventh. From the limited power of kings it may be thus argued: If kings be limited by laws and contracts, and may be resisted by pleas in law, and have no absolute power to do and command what they will, but must be limited both by the laws of God and man, and cannot make what laws they will, in prejudice of the people's rights, nor execute the laws made according to their pleasure, nor confer on others a lawless license to oppress whom they please; then when they turn tyrants, and arrogate a lawless absoluteness, and cross the rules and transgress the bounds prescribed by God's laws and man's laws, and made their own lusts a law, and execute the same arbitrarily, they must be resisted by force when a legal resistance cannot be had, in defence of religion and liberty. But all kings are limited, &c and the connexion may be thus confirmed in short: That power which is not the ordinance of God, may be resisted; but an absolute illimited power, crossing the rules and transgressing the bounds prescribed by God's law and man's, is not the ordinance of God, therefore it may be resisted.

Eighth. Further from the rules of government it may be argued several ways. First. That power which is contrary to law, evil and tyrannical, can tie none to subjection; but if it oblige to any thing, it ties to resistance. But the power of a king against law, religion, and liberty, is a power contrary to law, evil and tyrannical, therefore, &c.

The major is plain, for wickedness can tie no man but to resist it. That power which is contrary to law, evil and tyrannical is wickedness. Second. That power and those acts, which neither king can exercise nor command, nor others execute, nor any obey, must certainly be resisted; but such is the power and acts that oppress the subjects, and overturn religion and liberty, therefore, &c.

The minor is evident from scripture, condemning oppression and violence, both in them that command and in them that execute the same, and also them that obey such wicked commands. The major is very clear from reason, both because such power and such acts as cannot be commanded cannot be executed, cannot be obeyed lawfully, are sinful and wicked; and because it cannot be a magistratical power, for that may always be exercised and executed lawfully; and what a man cannot command, the resisting of that he cannot punish; but acts of oppression against law, religion, and liberty, a man cannot command, ergo the resisting of these he cannot punish. Third. That government and administration which is not subordinate to the law and will of God, who hath appointed it, must be resisted. But that government, or administration, which undermines or overturns religion and liberty, is not subordinate to the law and will of God, therefore, &c. The major is clear, for nothing but what is the ordinance of God, subordinate to his law and will, is irresistable. Rom. xiii. 2. The assumption is undeniable.

Ninth. From the very end and true design of government, which must be acknowleged by all to be the glory of God and the good of mankind; yea all that have been either wise or honest have always held that the safety of the people is the supreme law. The argument may run thus in short. First. That doctrine which makes the holy one to cross his own ends, in giving governors, must be absurd and unchristian, as well as irrational; but such is the doctrine that makes all kings, and tyrants irresistable upon any pretence whatever; which, by the bye, is the ancient and modern tory doctrine, ergo the minor. I prove that doctrine which makes God, intending his own glory, and the peoples good, to give governors both as fathers to preserve and as murderers to destroy them, must make the holy one to cross his own ends, for these are contradictory; but the doctrine that makes all kings and tyrants irresistable, &c. is such, for by office they are fathers to preserve, and by office also they must be murderers, vested with such a power from God by the first act. If they be irresistable when they do so, seeing every power that is irresistable is the ordinance of God. Hence also when a blessing turns a curse it is no more the ordinance of God, but to be resisted with all our might and strength; but when a king turns a tyrant, overturning religion and liberty, then a blessing turns a curse, therefore, &c.

Second. Means are to be resisted when they are not useful for, but destructive to the ends for which they were appointed; but kings overturning religion and liberty, are means not useful for, but destructive to the ends for which they were appointed. Seeing then they are neither for the glory of God nor the good of mankind, therefore, &c.

Third. If all powers and prerogatives of men are only means appointed for, and should vail unto the supreme law of the peoples safety, and all laws be subordinate to and corroborative of this law; and when cross to it, are in so far null, and no laws; and all law formalities in competition with it are to be laid aside, and all parliamentary priviledges must yield to this, and king and parliament, both conspiring, have no power against it; and no sovereign power, by virtue of any resignation from the people can comprize any authority to act against it; then it is duty to obey the supreme law, in resisting all powers and prerogatives, all laws and law formalities, and all conspiracies whatsoever against this supreme law, the safety of the people; but the former is true, therefore, &c.

Fourth. That power which is obliged and appointed to command and rule justly and religiously, for the good of the people, and is only set over them on these conditions, and for that end, cannot tie them to subjection, without resistance, when the power is abused to the destruction of laws, religion, liberty, and people; but all power is so appointed and obliged, therefore whensoever it is so abused it cannot tie people to subjection, but rather oblige them to the rejection of it.

Tenth. From the obedience required to government it may be argued thus: First. If we may flee from tyrants then we may resist them; but we may flee from tyrants therefore we may resist them. The connexion I prove, First. If all grounds of justice will warrant the one as well as the other, then, if the one be duty so is the other; but the former is true; for the same justice and equity that warrants declining a tyrants unjust violence by flight, will warrant resistance when flight will not do it; the same principle of self defence that makes flight duty, when resistance is not possible, will also make resistance duty when flight is not possible: the same principle of charity to wives and children, that makes flight lawful when, by resistance, they cannot avoid tyranny, will make resistance duty when by flight they cannot evitate it; the same principle of conscience to keep religion free, that prompts to flight when resistance will not save it, will also prompt to resist it when flight is not practicable. Second. If to flee from a just power when, in justice we are obnoxious to its sword, be to resist the ordinance of God, and so sin, then to flee from an unjust power must be also a resisting of the abusing of it, and so duty, for the one is resistance as well as the other; but the difference of the power resisted makes the one lawful, the other not. Again, if kingly power may be resisted, by interposing seas, and miles, why not by the same rule by interposing walls and arms? Both is resistance, for against a lawful king or magistrate that would be resistance. Third. If a tyrant hath irresistable power to kill and destroy the people, he hath also irresistable power to cite and summon them before him; and if it be unlawful to resist his murders, it must be as unlawful to resist his summons. Fourth. For a community of people to flee with wives and children, strong and weak, young and old, to escape tyrannical violence, and leave the land, were more unlawful than to resist, Alas! where should or could we of America have fled to have escaped the power of tyranny? Therefore it was our duty to resist, for what is not possible as a natural means of preservation, is not a lawful mean; but this was not a possible mean, neither is it warranted in nature's law, or God's word, for a people that have God's right, and man's law, to the land, and the rights and liberties thereof, to leave the country and its liberties all into the hands of a tyrant, and his crew. And farther, if it is duty to disobey, 'tis also duty to resist tyrants in defence of religion and liberty. But it is duty to disobey them, therefore, &c. The connection only will be stuck at, which is thus strengthened, if subjection be no more pressed in scripture than obedience. Then, if non-obedience be duty, non subjection must be so also, and consequently resistance; but subjection is no more pressed in scripture than obedience, for all commands of subjection, to the higher powers, as God's ministers, under pain of damnation, do only respect lawful magistrates, and in lawful things, and do include obedience; and non-obedience to the power so qualified is a resisting of the ordinance of God, as well as non subjection. If then obedience to magistrates be duty, and non-obedience sin, and obedience to tyrants sin, and non-obedience duty, then, by parity of reason, subjection to magistrates is duty, and non-subjection is sin; and also subjection to tyrants is sin, and non-subjection duty.

Eleventh. From the resistance allowed in all governments, it may be argued thus: If it be duty to defend our religion, lives and liberties, against an invading army of cut throats, Turks, Tartars, &c. without or against the king's warrant, then of course, it is and must be duty to defend the same against home bred tyrants, except we would subscribe ourselves home born slaves; but the former is true, therefore, &c. The minor cannot be doubted, because the king's power cannot be privative and destructive to defence of our religion, lives, and liberties; nor neither can it take away nature's birth right, to defend these or make it fare the worse than if we had no king at all. Now if we had no king at all, we might defend these against invaders; and whether we have king's or not, we are under moral obligations of the law of God to endeavour the defence of these. But this need not be insisted on; the connexion of the proposition is clear, if king's be more tyrannical, in invading religion and liberty themselves, than in suffering others to do it, or hindering them to be opposed; and if their invasion be more tyrannical, hurtful, and dangerous, than the invasion of strangers, then, if it be duty to resist strangers, invading these interests, it is more duty to resist home bred tyrants invading the same; but the former is true, therefore the latter. Resistance in the one case is no more resisting the ordinance of God than in the other.

Twelfth. From the motives of resistance we may draw this argument, which might indeed be branched out into several; but for brevities sake, I propose to reduce it to this complex one: If when we are in a capacity we cannot acquit ourselves in the duty that we do owe to our country, ourselves, and posterity, and absolve ourselves from the sin and judgment of tyrants, who overturn religion and liberty, oppress our countrymen, impose slavery on ourselves, and intail it upon posterity, by a passive subjection, submission to, and not opposing these mischiefs, then this instance is necessary; but the former is true, therefore, &c. The connexion is clear, for there cannot be a medium, if we cannot discharge these duties by subjection, submission, and not opposing; then, we must do them by non-subjection, non submission and opposing, since they must be done some way. The assumption is thus confirmed. Second. The duties we owe to religion, when it is like to be overturned, which no doubt would have been the case had our civil liberties been taken from us, it is, I say, in this case, our duty to resist tyranny, by making use of defensive arms. This must surely be as necessary as that of our civil liberties, which is an interest of our bodies, which is, indeed far inferior, and as necessary a duty as to defend our civil liberties from perpetual slavery, and as preferable thereunto as Christ's interests is to man's; and as the true end of all self preservation is to the means of it, the preservation of religion being the end of all self preservation. But this duty cannot be discharged without resistance in a mere passive subjection and submission, otherwise the same might be discharged in our universal submission to Turks or Indians, coming to destroy our religion. Surely this passive way of conducting ourselves cannot answer the duty of pleading for truth. Isa. ix. 4. Seeking the truth. Jer.

v. 1. Being valliant for it. Jer. lix. 3. Making up the hedge, standing in the gap, &c. Ezek. xxii. 30. Which yet are really necessary and incumbent duties according to our capacity; therefore we cannot answer the duties we owe to religion, in a mere passive way. I say farther, the duty we owe to our countrymen, and to those of each state, is to assist and defend them, and relieve them when oppressed, which fully and compleatly justifies the conduct of all those brave officers and men who so chearfully flew from their ploughs to the sword, to the relief of our brave, but oppressed brethren at Boston, in the year 1775, as truly we were bound, by all laws of humanity, and of God, to do; and by the royal law of Christ, the foundation of all righteousness among men, towards each other. Matt. vii. 12. All things whatsoever ye would that men should do to you, do ye even so to them. Reader, never let this direction slip your memory, for surely as we would wish to have others help us, when we are oppressed, so should we do to them when it is in the power of our hands to do it, and not forbear to deliver them, for the Lord will require their blood at our hand. Prov. xxiv, 11, 12. But this cannot, by any means, be done by a mere subjection without resistance. Third. There is no way to free ourselves of the sin and judgment of tyrants, by mere passive subjection. We find in the sacred scriptures, how that the people of old have been involved and punished for the sins of tyrants, as the people of Judah for Manasseh. 2 Kings xxi. 11, &c. Jer. xv. 4. Whose sins, if they had not been committed, the judgment for them had been prevented; and if the people had hindred them, they had not smarted, but being jointly included with their rulers in the same bond of fidelity to God, and made accountable as joint principles with their kings for that debt, by their mutual as well as several engagements, to walk in his ways, they were liable to be punished for their rebellion and apostacy, because they did not hinder it. Hence I say, resistance against tyrants and tyranny is right and lawful, &c.

Secondly. This truth is confirmed from the common practice of the people of God, even under persecution, from whence I propose to draw an argument from some notable examples which, to condemn, were impious, and to deny were most impudent; and, for forms sake, it may run thus: What the people of God under both testaments have frequently done, in time of persecution, for defending, vindicating, or recovering their religion and liberties, may and ought to be done again in the like circumstances, when these are in the like hazard; but under both testaments, the people of God frequently, in times of persecution, have defended, vindicated, and recovered their religion and liberties by defensive arms, resisting the sovereign powers that sought to destroy them; therefore this may, and ought to be done again when these religious, civil and natural privileges are in the like hazard to be destroyed by the violent encroachments of the sovereign powers. The proposition cannot be denied, except by all such as are open professed enemies to the people of God, as I take all the enemies to their country really to be. And I am ready to believe that, by an impartial and strict scrutiny, it will be found that the examples of their endeavoured resistance will be little inferior, if not superior, in number and importance to the examples of their submissive sufferings in all ages of the world, which will appear in the probation of the assumption by adduction of many instances which I shall only cursorily glean out of that plentiful harvest that histories do afford us, both of ancient and modern date.

First. I need only just touch on that most well known and famous history of the Maccabees, of undoubted verity, though not of cannonical authority, in which, according to scripture predictions, we have a most notable account of many heroick enterprises, atchievements, and exploits performed by them that knew their God, and tendered his glory and their religion and country's liberties, above the common catechrestick notions of uncontroulable, irresistable royalty and absolute, implicit, loyalty, that have abused the world in all ages. There we have an account of the noble and successful resistance of a party of a few godly and zealous patriots, without the concurrence of civil authority, or countenance of the ephori or nobles of the kingdom, against a king universally acknowledged and subjected unto, that came in peaceably and obtained the kingdom by flatteries, with whom the greatest part, and those of the greatest note, took part and did wickedly against the covenant and nation's interest, and were corrupted by flatteries; yet a few priests, with the assistance of some common countrymen, did fly to arms against him and them, and the Lord did wonderfully assist them for a considerable time, as was foretold by Daniel xi. And all this did fall out under the persecution of Antiochus Epiphanes, and was happily begun by Matthias, a godly priest and his five sons, who being commanded, under severe certifications, to worship according to the law then and at that time in force, and according to the king's wicked lusts. However they refused, and did most valiantly resist that most horrible abomination, and flew to defensive arms, which, while living, he patronized, and when dying did encourage his sons to it by a notable oration, shewing them what a deplorable case his country was in, and what a duty and dignity it was to redeem and deliver it; and this was vigorously prosecuted by Judas Maccabeus, expressly for the quarrel of religion and liberty, against the mighty tyrant and all his emissaries. A great undertaking indeed. And have not we of America great reason to bless God, and to stand amazed at the great goodness and providence of God, that when the king of Great-Britain, and his venal parliament, was about to destroy our civil, and of course, our religious liberties, that he raised us up a second Matthias, even the great Washington, as an instrument in his hands to save this land from ruin and slavery; who has, by his great generalship, rendered himself a world's wonder and a wonder to the world. But nothing is too hard or impossible with God, who always fits and furnishes instruments suitable to the work he has to do.

Second. To come down to the history of the gospel dispensation, I allow indeed that in the time of the primitive persecutions, under the heathen emperors, this great and well approved privilege of self defence was not much improved or made use of by christians, who studied more to play the martyrs than to play the men as christian soldiers; because, at that time, the Lord was pleased, in his good providence, to spirit them up, and call them unto, and accept of their hands passive testimonies, while they were incorporate under a civil relation with the heathens, in subjection to governors, who did not, by open tyranny overturn their civil liberties; but did only endeavour to eradicate religion, which, at that time, had never become their right by law, while they were scattered, and out of capacity, and never could come to a separate, formed community, by joint concurrence and correspondence, to undertake a declared resistance, while religion was only propagating through the nations, and the Lord did providentially preclude the least appearance that might be of propagating of it by any armed and formed force, being the gospel of peace, designed to save and not to destroy; yet even then, and in that case, there were instances of christians resisting their enemies, and rescuing of their ministers, &c. as they are found on record. First. How some inhabiting Marcota with force rescued Dionysius of Alexandria out of the hands of such as were carrying him away, about the year of our Lord 255. Second. How about the year 310 the Armenians waged war against Maximus, who was come against them with an army, because of their religion. Third. About the year 342 the citizens of Athanasius their minister, against Gugorious, and Syrianus the emperor's captain, who came with strong force to put him in. Fourth. How about the year 356 the people of Constantinople did, in like manner, stand to the defence of Paulus against Constantius the emperor, and killed his Captain Hermogenes; and afterwards, in great multitudes, they opposed the intrusion of the heretick Macedonius. Fifth. How when a wicked edict was sent forth to pull down the churches of such as were for the clause of one substance, the christians that maintained that testimony resisted the bands of soldiers that were procured at the emperors command, by Macedonius, to force the Mantinians to embrace the Arian heresy, but the christians at Mantinium kindled with an earnest zeal towards the christian religion, went against the soldiers with chearful minds, and valliant courage, and made a great slaughter of them. Sixth. How about the year 387 the people of Cesarea did defend Basil their minister. Seventh. How for fear of the people, the lieutenant of the emperor Vallens durst not execute those eighty priests who had come to supplicate the emperor, and was commanded to be all killed by him. Eighth. How the inhabitants of Mount Nitria espoused Byril's quarrel, and assaulted the lieutenant, and forced his guards to flee. Ninth. How about the year 404, when the emperor had banished Chrysostom, the people flocked together, so that the emperor was necessitated to call him back again from his exile. Tenth. How the people resisted also the transportation of Ambrose by the command of Valentinian the emperor, and chused rather to lose their lives than to suffer their pastor to be taken away by the soldiers. Eleventh. How the christians, oppressed by Baratanes king of Persia, did flee to the Romans to seek their help, and Theodosius the emperor is much praised for the war; (which, by the bye, fully justifies the Americans seeking relief from France, from the cruel tyranny of Britain, and of Louis XVI for granting of it, by which conduct of his he has endeared himself to every good whig, and to all who has a true regard for the rights of mankind; and to add still more to his greatness and goodness, if I am rightly informed, he tolerates the free exercise of the protestant religion throughout his dominion. Who can say but what God, in his providence, is about by this great revolution to pull down one of the ten horns which has long supported the beast?). But not to add here, pardon the digression, I now return; which he had commenced against Chrasroes king of Persia upon this inducement that the king sought to ruin and extirpate those christians in his dominions that would not renounce the gospel.

Third. But when religion was once embraced in imbodied corporations, and established by law, and became a people's common interest and liberty, in a capacity to defend it with their lives and other liberties, and when it was propagated thro' the nations, then the Lord did call for other more active testimonies in the preservation and defence of it, of which we have many instances in histories. About the year 894 the Bohemian christians resisted Drahomica their queen, who thought to have destroyed them, and to have re-introduced paganism. About the year 1420 they maintained a long defensive war against the government, and the popes legates, under the management of their brave Captain Zizca, which was further prosecuted after him by the remaining Thaborites; and again in the year 1618, they maintained a defensive war against the emperor Ferdinand. Eleventh. Electing and erecting a new king in opposition to him Frederick Palitine of the Rhine in which cause many received a crown of martyrdom; and this was also espoused by king James the First of England, who aided his son in law against the emperor; but it is generally allowed not so effectually as he ought, and might have done, for indeed he was a poor weak prince, and the father of tyrants.

Fourth. If we look into the history of the Waldenses, alias, Walloons, these constant opposers of antichrist, we will find many instances of their resistance about the year 1194. Very early, while Waldo, from whom they had their name, was alive, they began to defend themselves by arms, after the bloody edict of Alphonsus, king of Arragon; and in the year 1488, they resist by arms Albert de Capitaneis, sent by Pope Innocent VIII, in Pragola and Frassaniere, and throughout Pied Mont, wherefor the most part the offspring of the old Waldenses had their residence, where, very evidently, through many successions of ages, they shewed themselves to be the true successors of their worthy progenitors, valliant for the truth; that is a most famous instance of their resistance in opposing vigorously the Lord of Trinity, in that same Pied Mont, at which time they so solemnly asked their ministers whether it was lawful or not to defend themselves against his violence, who did answer them in the affirmative, and accordingly they did it with wonderful success at that time, and many times afterwards; especially it is most remarkable how, in the year 1655, a most vigorous defensive war was prosecuted against the duke of Savoy, by their captains Ginavel, Jahiers, &c. which was espoused by many protestant princes.

Fifth. If we take a survey of the histories of the Albigenses, we find many instances of their defensive resisting their oppressing superiors. About the year 1200 they defended themselves against the popes legate, and his crossed soldiers, under the conduct first of the Earl of Beziers, and then of the Earl of Foise, and Earl of Remand, of Thoulouse, and where helped by the English, who then possessed Guienne, bordering upon Thoulouse, which resistance continued many years.

Sixth. In Spain we find the people of Arragon contesting with Alphonsus III, and associating themselves together against him; and they tell Pedro III, their king, that if he would not govern by, and according to law, they would pursue him by arms, about the year 1283, as also other Spaniards who rose in arms several times against Pedro, the first king of Castile.

Seventh. It was this that brought the cantons of Helvetia into this state of freedom, wherein they have continued many years; for about the year 1260, they levied war against their oppressing nobles; and in the year 1308, they joined in covenant to defend themselves against the house of Austria; and in the year 1315, they renewed it at Brenna, in which, at length, the rest of the cantons joined and formed themselves into a common wealth.

Eighth. If we take a view of the Germans, we will find, at the very commencement of the reformation, as soon as they got the name of protestants, they resisted the emperor Charles V, the Duke of Saxon[y], the Landgrave of Hesse, and the city of Magdeburgh, with the advice of lawyers concluded, "that the laws of empire permitted resistance of the emperor, in some cases; that the times were then, so dangerous, that the very force of conscience did leave them to arms, and to make a league to defend themselves, though Cæsar, or any in his name, should make war against them; for since he attempteth to root out religion, and subvert our liberties, he giveth us cause enough to resist him with a good conscience." The matter standing as it doth, we may say they resist, as may be shewed, both by sacred and profane histories, and so on, the whole they undertook, and stated the war upon the account of religion and liberty.

Ninth. If we but cast an eye over the history of Holland, we will find how much they are indebted to this practice of defensive arms, having thereby recovered both religion and liberty, and established themselves into a most flourishing state; we find even in the time of D. de Alvas's persecution, they began to defend Haerlem, and Valenciennes in Hainault, and went on till under the conduct of William of Nassau, Prince of Orange, they declared the king of Spain to have fallen from the government of those countries, and so effectually shook off the yoke of tyranny.

Tenth. If we turn to the French Hugenots, we will find many instances among them, and many brave heroes raised up to maintain the principles, and prosecute the practices thereof, of older and later date. The history of the civil wars of France is stored with their trophies, and the memories of Conde and Coligni will ever be fragrant. There were many instances of resistance in those times, &c.

Eleventh. The many practices of the Hungarians, resisting the encroachments of the house of Austria, prove the same; and when Matthias denied the free exercise of religion unto the protestants of Austria, they took up arms in their own defence, and sent a protestation unto the states of Hungary, requiring their assistance agreeable to their league.

Twelfth. The Polonians have oftentimes levied war against their kings, and we are furnished by Clark in his Martyrol. with a late instance of their resistance against the sovereign powers at Lesna, in Poland, as late as the year 1655.

Thirteenth. The Deans and Swedes have not been slack on their parts, in taking course with their Christierns, kings of that name, whom they resisted and punished, and generally, wherever the reformation was received, we find this principle espoused, and the practice of it prosecuted; nay there hath been no nation in the world but it will be found they have either resisted or killed tyrants.

Fourteenth. The most deserving and celebrated monarchs in the world, have espoused the quarrel of oppressed subjects not only such as Tamerlane, whose observable saying is noted when he advanced against Bajazet, I go (says he), to chastise his tyranny, and to deliver the afflicted people; and Philip and Lewis of France, who assisted the barons of England, against king John; and Charles the great, who upon this ground undertook a war against the Lombards, in Italy. But even Constantine the Great hath it recorded, to his great honour, that he employed his power and force against Licinius, upon no other motive but because he banished, tortured, and destroyed those christians in his dominions that would not renounce their religion. And queen Elizabeth, of glorious memory, is to be highly commended for assisting the Dutch to maintain their religion by force, when they could not enjoy it by favour. And king James First did give public aid to the Protestants in Germany and Bohemia, against the emperor; against whom also Gustavas Adolphus marched, that he might deliver the oppressed cities from the bondage that Ferdinand had brought them into. Yea poor silly Charles First pretended, at least, to assist the protestants in France at Ree and Rochel; and though he himself was resisted by the parliaments of both kingdoms, yet he did declare in his acts of oblivion and pacification, the Scots taking up arms against him, in defence of their religion and liberties, to be no treason or rebellion. See Apol. Relat. Sect. II. page 149; and although the late tyrant Charles Second condemned all the risings of the people of Scotland for defence of religion and liberty, which his own tyranny forced them into; yet he justified the revolt of heathen and Mahometan subjects, as in the instance of the young king of Bantam, when by reason of his tyranny his subjects revolting and resisting of him, he the said Charles Second, furnished the revolters with ammunition, &c. Indeed many instances might be adduced which shews the righteousness of such resistances, when the greatest of kings and queens have undertaken the patronising of them.

Third. From scripture proofs, the best of all proofs, I shall endeavour briefly to gather some of the many that might be pressed, which being put together to me, seem impregnable. I shall reduce them to these heads. First. I shall adduce some practices of the Lord's people, frequently reiterated, never condemned, always approved, confirming this point. Second. Some severe reprehensions for their omission of this duty in the season thereof. Third. Some promises both of spiriting for the duty and of countenancing of it when undertaken. Fourth. Some precepts commanding such atchievements. Fifth. Some prayers, supplicating for them, all which, put together, I think will make a strong argument, for practices of this kind is common in scripture history.

First. I shall begin at the first war, which we find recorded in the world, wherein it seems the godly at first suffered some, but afterwards, by the virtue and valour of their brethren, they were vindicated, and the victory recovered with great honour. Lot and his family, living in Sodom, were taken prisoner by Chedarlaomer and his confederates. Gen. xiv. 12. But Abraham soon hearing of it armed his trained servants, and pursued them hot foot to Dan, and rescued him. Verse 14, 19. Thereby justifying that rebellion of the cities of the plain by taking part and vindicating the rebels. Hence he that may rescue subjects from the arms of tyrants, by arms, may also rise with these subjects to oppose that violence; but here is a clear example of that in Abraham, therefore, &c.

Second. When the Lord's people were possessed of Canaan, and forgetting the Lord, did enter into affinity with these interdicted nations, some of them were left to prove Israel, that the generations of the children of Israel might know to teach them war. Judges iii. 1. 2. And when they did evil in the sight of the Lord, he sold them into the hand of Cushan-rishathaim king of Mesopotamia, whom they served and were subject to full eight years. Verse 8. But when they humbled themselves, and cried unto the Lord, their rebellion, in shaking off that yoke, was successful under the conduct of Othniel. Verse 10. And after a relapse, unto the like defection, they became subject to Eglon, king of Moab, whom they served eighteen years. Verse 14. But attempting the same remedy by arms, under the conduct of Ehud, they recovered their liberty; and after his death, falling into that sin again, which procured the like misery, they became subject to Jabin king of Canaan, who twenty years mightily oppressed them. Judg. iv. 1, 3. But by the Lord's commandment, under the conduct of Deborah and Barak, they rebelled and prevailed. Whence I infer, if the Lord's people, serving a haughty tyrant, may shake off the yoke of their subjection, then it is duty to defend themselves, and resist them, for there is no other way of shaking it off; but these examples prove the former, therefore, &c. Obj. if any should reply, and cavil, and declare these were not their own kings, to whom they owed allegiance, but only invading conquerors, whom they might resist, I answer, First, Yet they were the sovereign powers, for the time being, and therefore if the doctrines and principles of both antient and modern torics be true and good, they ought, upon no pretence whatsoever, to be resisted (O! poor slaves, that believes such doctrines!) and perhaps by compact, they were not their kings, yet by conquest they were, as much as that would make them, and by their own consent, when they paid them kings due, (viz) tribute. Second, No more are they our kings who attempts to destroy charters, overturn religion, liberty, and law, as the king of Britain and his venal parliament lately did. Witness the Boston charter, &c. I say to such we owe no allegiance, no more than Israel of old did to those tyrants, for tyranny is the same in all ages. Third, I retort that old colewort, twice boiled, who should be judge whether they were their own lawful kings or not, for they acted as kings, and thought themselves their absolute lords, and gave themselves out to be such; and yet we find an approved rebellion against them. Mr. Gee, in his magistrates original, Chap. 8. Sect. 4. Page 268, improves these instances to the same purpose, and adds, "Neither as far as my observation goes, can any immediate or extraordinary command of word, for what they so did, be pretended to or pleaded from the text, for many of them, or for any, save Barak or Gideon."

Third. Yet Gideon's example, though he had an extraordinary call, cannot be pretended as unimotable on the matter, for that was ordinary, though the call and manner was extraordinary; he, with the aid of a few men, did break the yoke of subjection to Midian. Judg. vi. 7. And having called his brethren out of all Mount Ephraim, into a conjunction with him, in the pursuit of his victory, when he demanded supply of the princes of Succoth, and of the men of Penuel, and they denied it, he served them as enemies. Whence I conclude, if a small party may, with God's approbation, deliver themselves and the whole of their community from the bondage of their oppressing masters, whom they had served several years, and may punish their kings that do not turn out to their assistance, and encourage them in that attempt, then must it be duty to defend themselves against their oppressors, that rule over them, and all ought to concur in it, or else there would not be justice in punishing them that were defective in this work; but we see the former by this example, therefore, &c. Obj. If it be said that Gideon, and the rest of the extraordinary raised judges, were magistrates, therefore they might defend and deliver their country, which a private people, that are only subjects, may not do. I answer, First, They were subject to those tyrants that oppressed them, who were then the sovereign powers of that time; and yet they shook off that yoke by defensive arms. Second, They were not then magistrates when they first appeared for their countries defence, and deliverance; neither in that did they act as such, but only as captains of rebels in the esteem of them that had power over them. Just so has our modern oppressors and tories looked upon all our generals and officers in this grand struggle for American liberty. It is clear, Gideon was no ruler, until that authority was conferred on him after the deliverance. See Judg. viii. 22, &c. Yet he did all this before.

Fourth. When his bastard Abimelech usurped the government, and was made king by the men of Shechem, at length, God sending an evil spirit between him and his complices, that set him up not only was he resisted by the treacherous Shechemites, which was their brand and bane, in the righteous judgment of God, for their aiding at first in killing his brethren. Judg. ix. 23, 24. &c. But also he was opposed by others of the men of Israel, as at Thebez, where he was slain by a woman. Verse 50, at the end. Whence, if an usurping tyrant acknowleged as king by the generality, may be disowned by the godly and threatened with God's vengeance to consume both him and his complices, that comply with him; and if he may be opposed and resisted, not only by those that set him up, but also by others that were in subjection to him, and at length be killed by them, without resentment of the rest of the nation, then must it certainly be duty for a people who had no hand in the setting up such a tyrant to defend themselves against his force; but the former is true by this example, therefore, &c.

Fifth. When Israel of old, fell under the tyranny of a Ammon, oppressing them eighteen years, they did, by resisting these supreme powers, shake off their yoke, under the conduct of Jephthah; and being challenged sharply by the men of Ephraim, who, it seems, claimed the prerogative of making war, and therefore came to revenge and reduce Jephthah and his company to order, just like tories, who are very tenacious of this plea of the Ephraimites, that at least, without the nobles of the kingdom, no war is to be made; yet we find Jephthah did not much regard it, but stoutly defended himself, and slew of them 42,000 men, by their Shibboleth. Judg. xii. If people then, when questioned for defending themselves by them that claim a superiority over them, and should deliver them, may defend themselves both without them, and against them, then I say, it is a people's duty and privilege; but the former is true by this example, therefore, &c.

Sixth. They were then made subject to the Philistines forty years, whom the men of Judah acknowledged for their rulers, yet Samson, that rough-handed saint, never ceased from pelting them upon all occasions; and when challenged for it by the men of Judah saying, knowest thou not that the Philistines are rulers over us, what is that thou hast done? Samson objects nothing against their being rulers, but notwithstanding prosecutes his purpose of vindicating himself in defence of his country. As they did unto me says he, so have I done unto them. Judg. xv. 11. Hence, if saints may avenge themselves upon them whom the country calls rulers, and when enabled by God, may do to them as they did to them, then must it be a duty for them to defend themselves against them; but the antecedent is true by this example, therefore, &c.

Seventh. When Saul, in the pursuit of the Philistines, had charged the people with a foolish oath not to eat any food until the evening, Jonathan his own son tasted but a little honey, and so he must die! which Saul confirmed with another peremptory oath, God do so to him, and more also, if he should not die. Whereupon the people, as resolute on the other hand to save him, resisted the rage of Saul, and swore as peremptorily that not one hair of his head should fall to the ground, so the people rescued Jonathan that he died not. 1 Sam. xiv. 44, 45. Hence if people may covenant, by oath, to resist the commands and rescue a man from a tyrant's cruelty, then it is duty to defend themselves against him. The antecedent is true here.

Eighth. Afterwards, when the manner of the king presaged by Samuel, was verified in Saul's degeneration, into many abuses of government, this privilege of resistance was not wholly mancipated, but maintained by David's defensive appearance; with his little army, he took Goliath's sword, not for ornament or only to fright Saul, but to defend himself with it, and was captain first to 400 men. 1 Sam. xxii. 2. Had a mind to keep out Keilah against him with 600 men. 1 Sam. xxiii. 13. And afterwards a great host came to him to Ziklag, while he kept himself close because of Saul, the son of Kish. 1 Chron. xii. 1. Throughout where they left Saul, and came and helped David against him. This is proved at large by Lex Rex, Quest. 22. page 340.

Ninth. The city Abel, whether Sheba the traitor had fled, did well to resist Joel the king's general coming to destroy a whole city for one traitor's sake, and not offering peace to it according to law. Deut. xx. 10. And defended themselves by gates and walls, notwithstanding he had a commission, from the king. 2 Sam. xx. And after the capitulating, they are never challenged for rebellion.

Tenth. The ten tribes revolted from the house of David, when Rehoboam claimed an absolute power and would not acquiesce to the people's just conditions. 1 King's xii. 2 Chron. x. Hence if it be lawful for a part of the people to shake off the king, refuse subjection to him, and set up a new one, when he but resolves to play the tyrant, then it must be duty to resist his violence when he is tyrannizing; but the antecedent is clear, by this example, and is fully vindicated by Jus. Pop. Ch. 3. p. 52.

Eleventh. The example of Elisha the prophet is considerable. 2 Kings vi. 32. Elisha sat in his house, and the elders sat with him, and the king sent a man before him, but ere the messenger came to him, he said to the elders see how this son of a murderer hath sent to take away mine head. Look when the messenger cometh, shut the door: is not the sound of his masters feet behind him? Here is a violent resistance resolved both against the man and his master, though the king of the land for the time; and this calling him the son of a murderer, and resisting of him is no more extraordinary, though it was an extraordinary man's act, than it is for a plaintiff to libel a true crime against a wicked person, and for an oppressed man to close the door upon a murderer. Lex Rex, Quest. 32 p. 346. Hence I argue, if a king or his messenger coming to use unjust violence, against an innocent subject, be no more to be regarded than a murderer's emissary, but may be resisted by that innocent subject, then must a community of such innocent subjects defend themselves against a tyrant, or his bloody emissaries, coming against them on such a wicked errand. The antecedent is here clear, which to all intents and purposes, justifies the justness of the American defence, as Gage, George's tool and bloody emissary, was sent for the express purpose to murder the Bostonians, if they should not tamely surrender up all their rights and privileges without resistance.

Twelfth. The city Libnah revolted from under Jehoram's tyranny. 2 Chron. xxi. 10. P. Martyr on the place saith, they revolted because he endeavoured to compel them to idolatry. Hence if it be lawful for a part of the people to revolt from a tyrant, then it is duty to defend themselves against his force. The former is true therefore, &c.

Thirteenth. When Athaliah usurped the monarchy, Jehoiada the priest strengthened himself and made a covenant with the captains, &c to put her down and set up Joash, 2 Kings xi. 2. 2 Chron. xxiii. and when she came and cried out treason! treason! they regarded it not, but commanded to kill her and all that help her. Whence I argue, if those that are not kings, may lawfully kill an usurpress, and all that help her, then may a people resist them. But Jehoiada, though no magistrate, did it; therefore, &c.

Fourteenth. The repressing and punishing Amaziah, the son of Joash, is an undeniable instance, vindicated by the great and learned Mr. Knox. After the time that he turned away from following the Lord, the people made a conspiracy against him in Jerusalem, and he fled to Lachish; but they sent and slew him there. 2 Kings xiv. 19. 2 Chron. xxv. 27. Hence a fortiori if people may conspire and concur in executing judgment upon their king, turning tyrant, then much more must they defend themselves against his violence.

Fifteenth. The same power of people's resisting kings was exemplified in Uzzah, or Azariah, when he would needs be supreme in things sacred as well as civil. 2 Kings xv. 2 Chronicles xxvi. Fourscore priests that were valliant men withstood him and thrust him out of the temple; they troubled him, saith Natablus; they expelled him saith Armon. Vid. Pool Synopsis &c. See this vindicated by Mr. Knox, page 48, 49. Hence if private subjects may by force resist and hinder the king from transgressing the law, then must they resist him when forcing them to transgress the law.

Sixteenth. After the return from the Babylonish captivity, when the Jews set about building the Temple, which they chose to do themselves, and not admit of any association with enemies upon their misinformation and false accusation, that they were building the rebellious and bad city, and would refuse to pay the king his custom, they were straightly discharged by Artaxerxes to proceed in their work, and the inhibition was executed by force and power. Ezra iv. But by the encouragement of the prophets Haggai and Zechariah, countermanding the king's decree they should not be hindred, the eye of their God being upon them, though Tatnai the governor of those parts Shetharboznnai and their companions would have boasted them from it, with the usual arguments of tories. Who hath commanded you to do so and so? Ezra v. 3, 5. And yet all this was before the decree of Darius was obtained in their favour. Ezra vi. Hence I argue if a people may prosecute without and against a king's command and before all allowance by law can be obtained, then may a people resist these commands, and force used to execute them.

Seventeenth. When Nehemiah came to Jerusalem, and invited the Jews to build up the walls of the city, they strengthened their hands for that very good work against great opposition; and when challenged by Sanballat the Horonite, Tobiah the servant, the Ammonite, and Geshem the Arabian, great king's men all of them, who despised and boasted them, what is this that you do? Will ye rebel against the king? Say they he would not plead authority, though in the general he had the king's authority for it; yet he would not give them any other satisfaction than to intimate whether they had that or not, having the call of God to the work, they would go on in their duty, and God would prosper them against their opposition. Nehemiah ii 19, 20. And they went on, and were directed to remember the Lord and fight for their brethren, &c. and to build, with weapons in their hands. Neh. iv. And brought it to an end, notwithstanding of all their practices to fright them from it. Chap. vi. Hence I argue, if neither challenges of rebellion, nor practices of enemies, who pretend authority, nor any discouragements whatsoever, should deter people from a duty which they have a call and capacity from God to prosecute, and if they may remove it against all opposition, by defensive arms, then when a people are oppressed and treated as rebels for a necessary duty, they can and must defend themselves and maintain their duty, notwithstanding of all pretentions of authority against them.

Eighteenth. I shall now conclude with one instance more, which is vindicated by Jus. Populi, from the history of Esther, because Mordecai refused to do homage to a hangman, Haman I would say, at that day, now a proud North, a cruel edict was secured from Ahasuerus to destroy all the Jews at that time; now from George III. to destroy all the Bostonians by starving them &c. which was written and sealed with the king's ring, according to the laws of the Medes and Persians, becoming a [decree] irrevocable and irreversable. Esther iii. 12, 13. Yet the Lord's providence, always propitious to his people, brought it about so that Haman being hanged, and Mordecai advanced, the Jews were called and capacitated as well as necessitated to re[ject] that armed authority that decreed to massacre them, and that [by] the king's own allowance. Esther ix. When his former decree drew near to be put in execution, in the day that the enemies of the Jews hoped to have power over them, it was turned to the contrary, that no man could withstand them. Here they had the allowance of authority to resist authority, and this was not a [gift] of a new right by that grant, which they had not before, [merely] it was corroborative of the irradical right to defend themselves; which is not the donative of kings, and which they had power to exercise and use without this, though may be not the same capacity, for the king's warrant could not make it lawful in point of conscience, if it had not been so before. Hence I argue, if people may have the allowance of well advised authority to resist the decree and force of unlawful authority, then may people maintain right authority; but by the very instance we plainly see, that the Jews had Ahasuerus's allowance to fulfill the decree and force of his own ill-advised authority, though irreversable, and hence we learn that distinction in this point is not groundless between resisting the authority of supreme power and the abuses of the same.

Secondly. We have in scripture both tacit and express reproofs for neglecting this duty in the right season thereof.

First. In Jacob's swan song, or prophetical testament, wherein he foretels what should be the fate and future condition of each of the tribes, and what should be remarked in their carriage influencing their after lot in their generations, for which they should be commended or discommended, approved or reproved: coming to Issachar he prophetically exprobates his future ass-like stupidity, and that indulging himself in his lazy ease and lukewarm security, he should emancipate himself and his interests into a servile subjection unto his oppressors impositions; even when he should be in a capacity to shake them off, and free himself by resistance. Gen. xlix. 14,15. Issachar is a strong ass, couching down between two burthens. A true picture this of toryism. This is set down by the Holy Ghost as the brand and bane, not of the person of Issachar, Jacob's son, but of the tribe to be innured upon them, when they should be in such a condition, by their own silliness. Hence I argue, if the Holy Ghost exprobate a people for their stupid subjection to prevailing tyranny, when they do not approve their ability, capacity, and right to maintain and defend their liberties and privileges, then this implies a commanded duty to defend them according to their capacity from all unjust invasion. But the former is true here, also the latter.

Second. In Deborah's song, after their victorious resistance, the people are severely upbraided for not assisting in that expedition. Judges v. 16, 17, 23. And Meroz is particularly cursed for not coming to the help of the Lord, against the mighty. This is recorded as a resting reproof against all that will withdraw their helping hand from the Lord's people, when necessitated to appear in defensive arms for the preservation of their lives and liberties. On the other hand, Zebulun and Naphtali are commended for jeoparding their lives in the high places of the fields, and are approved for that practice of fighting against the king of Canaan, that then ruled over them. Verse 18, 19. Hence I argue, if people be reproved and cursed for staying at home to look to their own interests, when others jeopard their lives for their country's defence and freedom, then this implies it is duty to concur in so venturing. But here Reuben, Dan, Asher, and Meroz, are reproved and cursed for staying at home, when Zebulun and Naphtali jeoparded their lives. Ergo.

Third. We have in scripture many promises of the Lord's approving and countenancing the duty of defensive arms, even against their oppressing rulers.

First. In that foresighted testament of the patriarch Jacob, in that part of it which concerns God, he prophecies that tribe shall have a lot in the world, answering his name, and be engaged in many conflicts with oppressing dominators, who at first should prevail over him, but at length God should so bless his endeavours to free himself from their oppressions, that he should overcome. There is an excellent elegancy in the original, answering to the etymology of the name of Gad, which signifies a troop, reading thus in the Hebrew: Gad a troop, shall over-troop him, but he shall over-troop them at the last. Gen. xlix. 19. And Moses, homologating the same testimony in his blessing the tribes before his death, shews that he should make a very forcible and successful resistance, and should execute the justice of the Lord over his oppressors. Deut. xxxiii. 20, 21. Wherein is implied a promise of resistance to be made against oppressing tyrants, who should acquire the supreme rule over them for a time, and the success of that resistance for overcoming necessarily supposes resistance to be made against oppressing conquerors and tyrants. Hence I argue, where there is a promise of success at last, to a people's conflicts against tyranny, there is implied an approbation of the duty, and, also a promise of its performance wrapped up in that promise. But here is a promise, &c.

Second. In that threatening against tyrants, shewing how they shall be thrust away and burnt up with fire, there is couched a promise, and also an implied precept of resisting them. 2. Sam. xxiii. 6. The sons of Belial shall be all of them as thorns thrust away with hands fenced with iron, &c. Which clearly implies resistance, and even more than that, rejection and repression. Hence I farther argue, if it be threatened as a curse against rulers of Belial, and promised as a blessing that they shall be so roughly handled, then this implies a duty to resist them, who cannot be otherwise taken; but here this is threatened, therefore, &c.

Third. When the Lord shall have mercy on Jacob and chuse Israel, it is promised, Isaiah xiv. 2, 3. That they shall take them captives whose captives they were, and they shall rule over their oppressors. This necessarily implies and infers a promise of resistance against these oppressing rulers, in the time of their domineering, as well as revenge, after their yoke should be broken, and something of men's actions, as well as God's judgment, in breaking that yoke for they could not take them captives, nor rule over them, except first they had resisted them whose captives they were. There is resisting the supreme power, subjection whereunto was the bondage wherein they were made to serve. Hence I argue, that if it be promised that a captivated, subjugated people, shall break the yoke, and free themselves of the bondage of them that had them in subjection, then it is promised, in that case, they must resist the supreme powers for such were they whose captives they were. The antecedent is here express.

Fourth. There are promises that the Lord's people, when those that rule over them are incensed against them on account of their holy lives, and when many shall be frighted from their duty by fear, or corrupted with flattery, shall be made strong to exploits, though in such enterprizes they may want success for some time, and fall by the sword and flame and by captivity and spoil many days. Dan. xi. 30, 34. This was very eminently fulfilled in the history of the Maccabees before rehearsed. Hence I argue, if it be promised that a people shall be strong to do exploits in resisting the arms of their rulers opposing their religion and liberties, then it is clear such resistance is lawful even though it should fail of success for a time. But this is here promised to the same purpose. It is promised that after the Lord's people have been long kept as prisoners under the bondage of tyrants they shall, by a vigorous resistance, be saved from their tyranny. Zech. ix. 13, 17. When the Lord shall bend Judah for him, and raise up Zion's sons against the sons of Greece.

So it was in their resistances and victories against the successors of Alexander, who had the rule over them for a time. And so it may be again, when the Lord shall so bend his people for him. Hence I argue, that if the Lord promises to fit and spirit his people for action against their oppressing rulers, and to crown their attempts, when so fitted and spirited, with glorious success, then it is their duty, and also their honour, to resist them; but here that is plainly promised, therefore, &c.

Fifth. There are promises of the Lord's making use of his people, and strengthening them to break in pieces the power of his and their enemies, and his defending and maintaining them against all their power and projects when they think most to prevail over them, as is promised in the threatened catastrophe of the Babylonian usurpation. Jer. ii. 20, 25. Thou art, says he to Israel (of whom he speaks), as the rod of his inheritance. In the preceding verse. My battle-axe and weapons of war, and with thee will I break in pieces powers that were supreme over them. Hence I argue, that if the Lord will make use of his people's vindictive arms against Babylon, ruling over them, then he will justify their defensive arms against Babylon oppressing them. Here it is promised therefore, &c. So Micah, iv. 11. To the end many nations shall be gathered to defile and look upon Zion, and then the Lord shall give allowance and commission to his people to arise and thresh, &c. What time the full accomplishment is refered to is not my concern at present to enquire into. It seems to look towards the New Testament times, wherein the Lord's people shall be first in great straits and then enlarged. But to restrict it to the spiritual conquest over the nations, by the ministry of the word (though I will not deny but that may be included) seems too great a straitning of the scope, and not so opposite to the expressions, which certainly seem to import some forcible action of men, and more than the peaceable propogation of the gospel. It is usually referred to the latter days of that dispensation, when both the Jewish and gentile Zion shall be totally and finally delivered from Babylonian or anti-christian tyranny, before or about which period the enemies of Christ and of his people shall attempt their utmost power to destroy the church, groaning under their bondage. But when they are all well mustered in a general rendezvous, the Lord's people shall have a gallant game at the chase. But whensoever the time be of fulfilling the promise it ensures to the people of God, the success of their defensive arms against them that pretended a domination over them. And it looks to a time when they should have no rulers of their own, but them under whose subjection they had been long groaning, and now brought to a very low pass; yet here they should not only resist but thresh them. Hence I argue, that if in the latter days the people of God are to be honoured and acted forth with such a spirit and capacity to thresh and beat down these powers under which they have been long groaning, then, when the Lord puts them in such capacity to attempt it, they should be ambitious of such an honour. But here it is promised, therefore, &c.

The same may be infered from the prophets vision. Zach. i. 19, 20. He sees four carpenters resisting the four horns; the horns scattered Judah, so that no man did lift up his head; but the carpenters came to pray them to cast out the horns of the gentiles which lifted up their horn over the land of Judah. These horns had the supreme power over Judah for a time, while they were in no capacity to resist them; but as soon as the Lord furnishes them with capacity and instruments, impowered to resist them, they do it effectually. The carpenters are certainly the Lord's people themselves, for here they are opposite to the gentiles, which all were except the Lord's people. Hence I argue, that if the Lord promises, when reconciled to his people, to furnish them with instruments to fray and scatter the power of tyrants, who have long bore down their head, then, when they are so furnished, they may resist them; but the Lord here promises that; therefore, &c. This is more plainly promised, also. Zech. x. 5. &c. Then they shall be as mighty men, which shall tread down their enemies and the pride of Assyria shall be brought down. Hence I further argue, that if the Lord shall have mercy on his people, will bless their resistance against their enemies, then defensive arms is lawful and duty to use, when the call is clear, &c.

Fourth. We have also precepts from whence we may consequently conclude the approven duty of defensive arms against oppressing rulers.

First. The children of Israel are commanded to vex the Midianites and smite them, for, saith the Lord, they vex you with their wiles. Numb. xxv. 17, 18. And to avenge themselves. Numb. xxx. 2. Which did not only oblige the people when they had Moses for their magistrate to lead them forth, but, in the days of Gideon, when they were under their rule, whom they were to avenge themselves upon. Hence I argue, if people must vex their enemies, and avenge themselves of them by a war offensive, much more may they resist them by a war defensive, when invaded by their cruelty.

Second. There is a command to punish every city or party, making apostacy unto idolatry. Deut. xiii. 12, 15. upon this moral ground was Israel's war against Benjamin. Judges xx. and their bringing Amaziah unto condign punishment, which is vindicated by Mr. Knox. Hence I argue, if people are to bring to condign punishment idolatrous apostates, much more ought they to resist all tyrants, seeking to destroy all religion and liberty, for they are twins. Where the spirit of the Lord is, there is liberty. As I said before, destroy the one and the other cannot live.

Third. There is a precept not only to defend, but also, to rescue and deliver our brethren when in hazard. Prov. xxiv. 11, 12. we must not forbear to deliver them when drawn to death; which will at least infer the duty of assisting them when forced to defend themselves; for if it be a duty to rescue them from any prevailing power that would take their lives and liberties unjustly much more is it duty to rescue them by defensive arms, and ourselves both from and against their murdering violence. But it is duty to rescue them, therefore, &c.

Fourth. All those that would learn to do well are commanded, Isa. i. 17. to relieve the oppressed; which is not spoken to kings only, many of whom were the oppressors. The princes were rebellious and companions of thieves. Verse 23. So also, Isa. lviii. 6. It is required of a people that would be accepted of God in their humiliations, to let the oppressed go free, and to break every yoke. Hence I argue, if it be duty to relieve the oppressed, by breaking the yoke of them that oppress them, then it is duty to defend them and ourselves, both against them that would oppress us more. But the former is here commanded, therefore, &c.

Fifth. There is a command for a spoiled oppressed people, when the Lord is reconciled to them, and sympathizes with them, to deliver themselves from their rulers servitude. Zech. ii. 7. Deliver thy self O Zion, which dwelleth with the daughter of Babylon. Which comprehends all the ordinary active means of people's delivering themselves from oppressing powers that rule over them; and consequently defensive resistance, for it cannot only be restricted to flight, included verse 6, the promise annexed verse 9, imports more, when they that spoiled them, shall be a spoil to their servants. Whereby it is insinuated they were so to deliver themselves as not only to free themselves from their servitude, but to bring their masters under subjection. Hence I argue, if the Lord's people being subject to tyrants ruling over them for the time, may deliver themselves from their oppressing masters, then may they resist them, and defend themselves, therefore, &c.

Sixth. There is a command given by the blessed Jesus to his disciples, to provide themselves with weapons for their defence against them that should attempt their lives, as well as with other things necessary for their sustenance. Luke xxii. 36. Now he that hath a purse, let him take it, and likewise his scrip; and he that hath no sword, let him sell his garment and buy one. Before, when he had sent them out upon an extraordinary commission, as it were to serve their apprenticeship in the work of the gospel, he did not allow them such solicitous care to provide themselves, because he would give them a proof of his sufficiency to sustain and protect them without the ordinary means of their own diligence; but now, when he was about to withdraw his bodily presence from them, and would warn them of the many discouragements they were to look for in the prosecution of their more continued work, which they had a commission for, not to be retracted, he would not have them expect provision and protection by a course of miracles, but to provide themselves with means for their sustenance, and also for their defence against the violence of men, which chiefly was to be expected from their rulers, who would persecute them under the notion of transgressors of the laws of the kingdoms and countries. He was not, indeed, to make much use of them at that time for himself, who was then to finish the work of redemption by suffering, only that what was written might be accomplished in him, he would make so much use of them as voluntarily to be involved under the censure and reproach of rebellion, being taken among men in arms, that he might be reckoned among transgressors. Verse 37. Therefore when they told him they had two swords, he said it is enough. Verse 38. I think I need not stand long here to confute that impertinency of a conceit that these were spiritual swords, which indeed deserves no confutation, being fitter to be put among the many delirious destractions, and other errors of Quakers, than to be numbered among the notions of men of common understanding. Indeed I could hardly be brought to believe they did hold such an error, if I had not been informed by a person of credit, who assured me he had it from the mouth of one of their speakers or teachers. O horrid blasphemy! Purchase the spirit of God, or the sword of the spirit, or a spiritual sword, with the price of an old garment. Surely if this was true, then the purse and scrip must be spiritual too, and these bought by selling of old garments; and yet they would be such spiritual swords as would cut off carnal ears, and such as would be both visible and sensible, and two of them would be enough. But it does not admit of a doubt, but what they were ordinary and material swords, which the Lord did command his followers to provide themselves with for their defence as men, in cases of necessity, and when they should be in a capacity to improve them against their murdering persecutors, against whom he gives his royal grant of resistance, that the world may know his subjects, though they have more privileges spiritual, yet they have no less human privileges than other men, although at that period of his determined suffering, he would not allow the present use of them. From hence I argue, that if the Lord's people should provide themselves with arms of defence, though they should, by a wicked world, be reputed sinners and the greatest of transgressors for so doing, then surely they may use these arms of defence against them that persecute them; therefore, &c.

Fifth. We may infer the same truth from some of the prayers of the saints, wherein they glory in the constant expectation of the Lord's strengthening them, and favouring and approving their helpers, and in the experience of the Lord's assisting them, while in the mean time constitute in a formed appearance of resistance. I shall only hint these.

First. In that prayer, Psal. xliv. 5. They glory in hope, that through the Lord they will push down their enemies, &c. Yet then at that time they were under the power of tyrants, which they were resisting, for Verse 9. They complain they were put to shame, because the Lord went not forth with their armies, and they which hated them spoiled them; and for his sake were killed all day long. Hence they plead, that the Lord would awake and not forget their affliction and oppression; whereby it is evident, they were under the yoke of tyrants, and resisting according to their mights which, by whomsoever or upon what occasion soever, the psalm was compiled, shews that no want of success in resisting tyrants can mar the saints faith in pleading for the Lord's assistance and approbation of the duty. Hence I argue, that if they that in faith may pray for and boast of their treading down their enemies, that rise like tyrants up against them, they may also in faith attempt the resisting them in their own defence. But here the Lord's people did the former; therefore, &c.

Second. We find David, under Saul's persecution, while he had a party of 600 men to defend himself against his rage, in the psalms which he composed upon that occasion, not only complaining of oppressors, but encouraging himself in the faith that God would be with them that assisted him in his attempt to defend himself, and imprecating destruction to Saul and his complices. That the Lord would cut them off in his truth and let him see his desire upon them. Psal. liv. 4, 5. last verse, and Psal. lvii. 4. and Psal. lvii throughout, and Psal. cxl. 7, 9. He imprecates against the head of them that compassed him about, and of course against Saul. Whence I argue, First.

If the Lord's people, conflicting with and encompassed with oppressing rulers, as so many lions and dogs, may pray and praise for the help of those that assist them in their endeavours of self-preservation from them, then may they make use of their help for their defence for which they pray and praise. But here we see the Lord's people did the former; therefore they may and ought to do the latter.

Second. If we may pray against kings, and for preservation from them, then may we defend ourselves against them, and endeavour the means of that preservation for which we pray? The connection is before cleared, yet here I add, that which will give a dispensation from our duty of praying for them, will also dispense from the duty of being passively subject to their will, and consequently will allow the defending ourselves from their violence. And here we see tyranny and treachery, and designed mischief, will give a dispensation from our duty of praying for them, altho' that be duty as indispensible as subjection. Again if any thing deter us from resisting of kings, it must be respect to their majesty and the character of the Lord's anointing upon them. But we see no respect to that will deter a believer from praying in faith against them, therefore no such respect will hinder, but that he may defend himself against his violence; and indeed, if we do but consider it right, if the impression of any majesty God hath put upon kings, should tie up our hands from any resistance, it will also restrain from prayer resistance; for if that impression have any force at any time, it must be when a man is most solemnly stated before God, and speaking to God as a christian, rather than when he is acting as a man with a man like himself; and as prayer resistance is the most formidable and forceable resistance of any in the world, as this Saul, and our late George, and many other tyrants have found, by their woful experience, so it is more restricted than other resistance, for we may defend ourselves against many whom we must not pray against, to wit, our private enemies, for whom we are commanded to pray; yet no body will deny but we may resist their violence; and likewise, we are commanded to pray for kings, when invested with God's authority; but when, by their degeneration, we are loosed from that obligation to pray for them, and allows us to pray against them, when they turn enemies to God, and oppressors of his people, as we see in the prayer of the psalmist, then may we most warrantably resist them by defensive arms.

Third and lastly. Among the hallelujahs in the end of Psalms, there is one calculated for the prevailing time of the church, when the Lord shall take pleasure in his people. In that time of the saints being joyful in glory, when they may glory in the rest and security the Lord will vouchsafe upon them, they are prophetically, and very pathetically, excited to praise prayer wise. Psal. cxlix. 6. To the end let the high praises of God be in their mouth, and a two edged sword in their hand to bind their kings with chains, to execute upon them the judgment written. This honour have all the saints, hallelujah. This was their praise and honour when they were brought on to execute vengeance on their kings and nobles of Canaan; this also in David's time was the ambition and also the attainment of the saints in their triumphant victories over many of their oppressors round about them. But it looks to a further and more famous execution of vengeance upon the tyrants of the world, when they have long kept under the church of God, and at length, the Lord shall give his people a capacity to break their yoke, which, whenever it shall be, shall be their great honour. Hence I argue lastly, if it will be the honour of the saints, when the Lord puts them in capacity to execute vengeance upon their enemies, though they be kings, nobles, &c. that oppress them, then it may be their ambition to seek it; at least they may resist them. Thus I think I have fully shewn from the law of God, the law of nature, the custom of nations, the lawfulness of the use of defensive arms, in order to defend our rights, liberties civil and religious, when attacked by tyrants; at least I think it will convince all but such as are determined not to be convinced. Especially, I think it appears clear from scripture practices, reproofs, promises, precepts, and prayers, this truth has been proven; although I allow that other precious truths are more natively deduced, yet this great truth by unstrained and unconstrained consequence, may, and is also, clearly inferred.

A SHORT RECEIPT FOR A CONTINENTAL DISEASE

The name whereof is the love of Money.

The holy scriptures informs us, that the love of money is the root of all evil. And this our daily experience doth also make manifest. It drives people into the commission of all evil, to the ruin of themselves and others. How are people daily distressing each other in sueing and tearing each other limb from limb, in order to handle a little of this trash, a world of which will not purchase a spark of grace, nor one inch of time, when on a death bed. Paying no regard to the distress of the times, nor to the cries of the poor, the needy, widow, and fatherless children. Perhaps such whose fathers have fought, bled, and died by our sides, nobly fighting in our glorious cause. How doleful the thought, that we who have so nobly joined hand in hand to defeat British cruelty and oppression, should now devour one another? Which is daily practicing. I shall now give a word of advice to creditors and debtors, which I shall divide into two classes. First publick creditors and debtors. Secondly private ditto. Publick creditors is our rulers and governors, who have a right, for our good and safety, to demand taxes from us. Gentlemen, let me beg of you to be as sparing in your demands as possible. You are not unsensible that the times are hard, and cash scarce. Endeavour to give satisfaction to the commonalty, that what they pay in taxes is faithfully applied to the uses it were paid for. The money is the people's to pay and yours to apply, which ought to be done with the greatest œconomy. Let no one get rich that handles publick money. I think I have once read of a great general that had served his country long and faithfully, when he came to die all he could call his own was his dish and spoon, and was buried by charity. A rare instance indeed, but a noble one. He prefered the publick's interest to his own.

You, my countrymen, publick debtors. Gentlemen, please to consider that no war can be carried on, no government kept up, without taxes, and heavy ones too; and consider what a situation you would soon be in, if there was no government. Could you sleep one night in peace? Could you call any thing your own one day? Therefore if you are wise you will most chearfully part with some of your wealth to secure the rest; for I am confident he is an enemy to himself and country too, that is backward in paying his taxes. Consider that it is not for us common people to be led into all the secrets of government. Surely we must believe that those which we have trusted at the helm of affairs does know best what sums is necessary to be raised from us for our good and protection; and I think we may rest assured that our legislature will not lay any needless burthens upon us; for my own part, I have that confidence in them that I am determined to pay my taxes as long as I have a copper left, or can raise it; for I am sure if the enemy should overcome, or government fails, I am gone finally.

You gentlemen that may be called private creditors, let me intreat of you to make use of every method to come at your rights and money, besides law. If it is a matter of dispute submit it to reference. If it is clear debt, exercise patience, bear and forbear with your poor debtors. Let nothing but the utmost necessity, let me say extremity, drive you to distress mankind at this doleful day. Cause not the cries of the poor and needy widow, fatherless and orphan children, to ascend up to heaven against you for distressing them in order to obtain cash to lay out in toys, to adorn your and families bodies with. Remember, O remember, a judgment day to come.

And now to you gentlemen debtors. I would have you remember those scripture sayings owe no man any thing, pay to all their dues. See that you pay to all their just dues, as fast as possible. If you have not cash turn out any thing you can possibly spare; yea, offer all you have to your creditors; and surely, if they are christians, and endowed with humane hearts, if they see you thus willing to distress yourselves to pay them, they will nobly refuse it and grant you longer day. Use them well, give them good language, and if possible deceive them not. Practice industry and good œconomy, for a creditor has hawk's eyes; and do not love to see their debtors struting about in fine rigging at their expence. Above all, remember the golden rule, do to all men as you would have them do to you again.

June 17, 1782 A Moderate Whig

FINIS

25

A SERMON PREACHED ON A DAY OF THANKSGIVING

George Duffield

PHILADELPHIA
1784

George Duffield (1732-1790). A Presbyterian, Duffield studied at the Academy of Newark and graduated from the College of New Jersey (later Princeton) in 1752. His father—who was of French Huguenot extraction, his name anglicized from Du Fielde—and his mother had migrated from the north of Ireland to settle near Pequea, in Lancaster County, Pennsylvania. From 1757 until 1772 Duffield ministered in Big Spring, Carlisle, and Monaghan, frontier areas constantly subject to Indian attack. He himself led his parishioners in Carlisle on expeditions against the Indians. He then became pastor in Philadelphia of the Third, or Pine Street, Church, a post he kept (amid interruptions for chaplain service during the war, when the British put a price on his head) until his death.

Theologically, Duffield was a New Light Presbyterian, and politically, he identified himself with the boldest proponents of independence. His theological position, as a partisan of the views of George Whitefield and Jonathan Edwards, who favored a converted ministry and revivalism, had caused acrimonious conflict in Carlisle. Worse, in Philadelphia, Old Side religious views and Tory politics at first predominated, and his ministry at Pine Street Church had a stormy beginning when he found the building locked against him. He forced the door open and held service anyway. When a British magistrate appeared and demanded that the congregation disperse, he was physically ejected for disturbing divine worship. Duffield and some of his supporters were then jailed for causing a riot.

Duffield was popular with the members of the Continental Congress, who attended his services when in Philadelphia. Among them was John Adams, who wrote of "the genius and eloquence of Duffield." He served as chaplain (with Reverend William White) of the Congress, became a trustee of the College of New Jersey, and was appointed the first clerk of the General Assembly.

The sermon reprinted here was given at the Pine Street Church on December 11, 1783, in thanksgiving for the restoration of peace after the Revolution.

A
SERMON
PREACHED IN THE
THIRD PRESBYTERIAN CHURCH
IN THE
CITY OF PHILADELPHIA,

On Thurſday December 11, 1783.

The Day appointed by the United States in Congreſs aſſembled, to be obſerved as a Day of Thankſgiving, for the reſtoration of Peace, and eſtabliſhment of our Independence, in the Enjoyment of our Rights and Privileges.

By GEORGE DUFFIELD, A.M.
Paſtor of ſaid Church, and one of the Chaplains of CONGRESS.

And the LORD ſpake unto the Fiſh: and it vomited out Jonah upon the dry land. *Jonah* 2. 10.

I will praiſe thee, O LORD, with my whole heart. I will ſhew forth all thy marvellous works.—For thou haſt maintained my right and my cauſe. *Pſalm* 9. 1, 4.

PHILADELPHIA Printed:
BOSTON: Re-printed and Sold by T. & J. FLEET.
MDCCLXXXIV.

An event of such magnitude and importance, as that which has occasioned our convening to day, accomplished in so short a space of time, and with so small a share of difficulty in comparison of what might have been expected, is one of those occurrences in the kingdom of providence that command the admiration of every observer. And whilst it affords an irrefragable argument (to convince even an atheist) that the Most High ruleth over the affairs of men, and raiseth up, and casteth down, at his pleasure; demands also our warmest gratitude to that GOD, who has done great things for us, whereof we are glad.

With a view therefore to assist in this delightful service; permit me to invite your attention to those emphatical words of the Prophet.

"Who hath heard such a thing? who hath seen such things? shall the earth be made to bring forth in one day? shall a nation be born at once? for as soon as Zion travailed, she brought forth her children!"

Isaiah 66.8.

This passage, it must be confessed, has a manifest respect to that happy period, generally termed the latter day glory; when the various nations of the earth, formerly stiled gentiles, and yet in darkness, shall in a sudden and surprizing manner, be converted to the knowledge and obedience of Christ: And the Jews, so long rejected of God, shall by an admirable display of divine power and grace, be gathered home from their dispersion, as in one day; and being formed into a people in their own land, shall become the most remarkable and leading part of the christian church, in activity and zeal for their God, and for JESUS the Saviour, their then acknowledged Messiah. The former of these events appears designed, by the earth bringing forth in a day; and the latter, by a nation viz. the Jewish, being born to God at once. Both which, taken together, will constitute that joyous state of affairs, which the apostle terms life from the dead. *(a)* But as the prophet has evidently in view to awake our attention to the

(a) Rom. 11.15.

hand of God, in his works of wonder among the children of men: and it is not without example in sacred record, to accommodate passages to similar events *(b)*; the importance of that event we celebrate to day; and the remarkable interposition of the providence of God, so manifestly displayed therein, will I trust, sufficiently justify my applying the passage before us to the present occasion *(c)*. To which also, it appears with peculiar propriety adapted. For who indeed hath heard such a thing? who, but a few years back, would have believed the report, had a prophet himself declared it? his credentials, at least, and marks of authority, had first been carefully scann'd with a critical eye. Who since time began, hath seen such events take place so soon? The earth has indeed brought forth, as in a day. A nation has indeed been born, as at once. It has not been Israel's forty years of tedious wilderness journey; nor Rome's, or the United Belgic provinces, long continued scene of arduous, dubious struggle: But almost as soon as our American Zion began to travail; and without experiencing the pangs and pains which apprehensive fear expected; she brought forth her children, more numerous than the tribes of Jacob, to possess the land, from the north to the south, and from the east to the yet unexplored, far distant west: That with great propriety, may we hail every friend of liberty, on this auspicious day, in the language nearly following our text; rejoice ye, with America, and be glad with her, all ye that love her, rejoice for joy with her, all ye that mourned for her. For thus saith the Lord; behold, I will extend peace to her, like a river, and glory, like a flowing stream. Here then, as from one of those hills from whence the tents of Jacob were viewed of old, let us look back, on what God hath done; and contemplate the prospect he opens before us. And may he, in whose hand are the hearts of the children of men, inspire every breast with a grateful sense of his goodness, so liberally bestowed through the whole. The British monarch had formed a design (for actions speak louder than words) to reduce these states, then British colonies, into absolute vassalage. A venal Parliament had approved the unrighteous purpose; and passed a decree to bind us in all cases, both civil and religious, to the obedience of such laws as they might see meet to enact. Some have ascribed this extravagant conduct to the same spirit of jealousy,

(b) Jer. 31.15. *(c)* Matt. 2.18.

which once influenced the councils of Egypt against the house of Joseph; lest waxing too powerful, they might break off their connection, and pursue a separate interest of their own. Pharaoh, indeed, might have reason to fear, because Israel were an entirely different people; and in their religion and manners separated far from the people of the land. But in the present case, though the court of Britain appear carefully to have copied the Egyptian model; and their measures have produced a similar event; yet, as the people of these states were the same as the people of Britain, their religion and manners the same; and no disposition to separate from them had ever appeared: But an attachment, even to enthusiastic fondness, had always obtained; it must have required an exorbitant share of infatuation to have raised a suspicion so high, as to produce the spirit and zeal that directed the British cabinet. To raise a revenue, and bring America to bear her proportion of the national debt has been assigned as the motive. America, by centring her trade in Britain, contributed her liberal share, nor had she ever withheld her blood or her treasure when requisitions were made; that even malevolence itself had been nonplussed from thence to derive a plea, unless through a mad desire to take by compulsion, what would otherwise be cheerfully given. It seems therefore most probable, his Britannic majesty wished to increase the power of the crown, so as to wrest the very shadow of liberty out of the hands of all his subjects, and reign an absolute monarch; and for this end began where he hoped, by bribes and craft, to cloak his design under the cover of parliamentary sanction. It may be, he desired to urge America to arms; that being vanquished (which seems to have been taken as a granted point) and her principal men, and all who should dare to oppose his views, having either fallen in the field, or been executed as traitors, or constrained to fly to some foreign land; the whole of the country, with the subdued, dastardly inhabitants that remained, might revert to the crown. This, with it's native consequences of American lords and vassals, all at the monarch's pleasure, must soon have weighed down the liberty of Britain. Or, perhaps he expected to intimidate into submission, by the appearance of a determined military force. This charity would fondly persuade us to admit, as being the least wicked of the two. And in that case, an host of placemen and pensioners, with their influence among a people, destitute of spirit and subdued by threats;

though not so suddenly, would yet as certainly have produced the desired effect: And finally imposed the same humiliating terms on Britain herself. But whatever might be the motive, America was marked out, for servile submission, or severe subjugation: and the power of Britain employed to accomplish the end. A day now rose, lowering thick with dark and heavy clouds. A scene now opened, painful to the mind only to review. On the one hand, to resign every dearest birthright privilege; and bow down unconditional to foreign masters, from whom we had nothing to expect, but sovereign contempt, and heavy burdens imposed; who, by their remote situation, could neither see our calamity, nor partake in our sufferings. Or on the other hand, to wage war with the most formidable power on earth, that had been for ages a terror to the nations; and had lately risen into a state of grandeur and glory far surpassing all her former greatness. A nation long inured to war: Her fleets commanding the ocean: Her troops numerous and veteran; and in martial deeds, famed as inferior to none: Her wealth immense: Her resources many: And her pride and mistaken sense of honor prompting her to exert every nerve, to secure a compliance with her claims and demands. Hard alternative! to resign liberty, or wage this hazardous war. And yet none other remained. America had her numerous husbandmen, her merchants and mechanics; and her sons of the learned professions, and students in every science. Her inhabitants were many: But untaught in the policy of courts and cabinets; and strangers from the art of war: And divided into different colonies, under different forms of government, had scarce ever communicated sentiments on a single point. Armies she had none; nor a single ship of war to protect her coast. Arms and ammunition had never been her care; and her money scarce sufficient for common occasions. Resources 'tis true there were; but as the precious metal lies hid in the unsought-for oar, they remained unexplored and unknown. In this situation, shall she dare to provoke the vengeance of Britain? a stoical observer would have pronounced it madness. But *Liberty* was the prize. She chose "Freedom or Death" as her motto; and nobly resolved on war with all it's horrors; that at least, her last expiring groan might breathe forth freedom. Already had Britain planted her baleful banner on our coast; and her proud insulting flag had possessed our harbours. Her oppressive edicts had gone forth; and her naval and military strength were combined to enforce obedience. As the careful mariner watches the heavy gathering cloud, and dreads the approaching storm; America, with anxiety beheld, and waited the event. Prudence would have seemed to dictate an early resistance to manifest hostile designs; nor suffer an avowed enemy to every privilege to entrench in quiet, and strengthen themselves in a capital town *(a)*. Nor was America blind to the measure: but that God, who so early espoused her cause, that her innocence in the case, and her reluctance to arms, might be evident to all, withheld her from the deed; and left Britain, on Lexington's ever-memorable day, to open the scene of war. Quick as the flash of lightning glares from pole to pole, so sudden did a military spirit pervade these then united colonies; but now, blessed be God, confederated, established states. The peaceful husbandman forsook his farm; the merchant relinquished his trade; the learned in the law dismissed their clients; the compassionate physician forgot his daily round; the mariner laid aside his compass and quadrant; the mechanic resigned his implements of employment; the sons of science ceased their philosophic pursuits; and even the miser half neglected, for a time, his gold and his gain, and the griping landlord his rents. All prepared for war, and eagerly flew to the field. The delicate female herself forgot her timidity; and glowing with patriot zeal prompted the tardy to arms; and despised and reproached the lingerer that meanly loitered behind. Nor were those of the sacred order wanting to their country, when her civil and religious liberties were all at stake: But as became faithful watchmen, they blew the trumpet on the walls of our Zion; and sounded an alarm for defence. From then, standard was pitched against standard; and the battle was fought with various success, from the east to the west, and from the north to the south; and the field and the forest, the hills and the vallies, the shore and the inland parts, have all heard the shoutings of the warrior, and the clang of arms, and seen garments rolled in blood; and summer's scorching heat, and winter's parching cold, borne testimony to American perseverance and valour. Nor was military prowess only given. He that put of the spirit of Moses on the elders of Israel, raised up senators, and guided them in council, to conduct the affairs of his chosen American tribes *(b)*; and though like the Jewish congregation

(a) Boston. *(b)* The Congress.

of old, the language of murmur and complaint has been heard in our land; and we have had our Korahs and Dathans, whose endeavours have been to weaken the hands of our rulers; depreciate their merit, and lessen their esteem in the eyes of the people; yet (I hesitate not to pronounce it) generations yet unborn will look back with wonder; and venerate the memories, and long perpetuate the names of those who guided the helm through the storm; nor sunk dismayed, whilst so furious an Euroclydon of innumerable difficulties lashed so sore, and lay so long upon us; but have at length, by the good hand of our God upon them, brought the billow-beaten vessel of public affairs safe into harbour. These, posterity will admire and revere; and wish to have seen the day when those men lived on the earth. A day, which commanded the attention of states and kingdoms, far and wide. And as Joshua's day arrested the sun in his course, the nations stood still in silent surprize, to see the balance of war so nearly poized, between contending parties so unequal. Fondly, would the spark of humanity within have led them to aid the American cause. Their wish was all they durst give: For, they dreaded the omnipotent arm of Britain; nor dared to awake her resentment. The monarch of France alone was found, whose generous zeal for the rights of humanity inspired him, beyond the power of every meaner consideration. Solemn ties had bound him, to consult the good of the people over whom he was placed: Nor could he have answered to his God, his conscience, or his kingdom, to have involved the nation in the calamities of an arduous, hazardous war, had no prospect of advantage risen into view. God, who had early designed him for distinguished honor; and raised him to the throne, to establish his name and his glory, as lasting as the annals of time, as the *Protector of the rights of mankind*, had therefore, by a firm decree, united the interest of America and France; that his majesty might be just to his conscience, his people, and his God, whilst indulging the ardent glow of his magnanimous breast, in affording to the distressed a vigorous aid: And his fleets and his armies were embarked in our cause. Let detraction therefore be silent, nor object the influence of interest, to sully the generous deed. God has connected duty and interest, by indissoluble bonds; nor may either, of right, assume the name alone. Ancient prejudices, instilled by Britain, seemed to forbid connection with a nation, we had long been taught to consider faithless, pusillanimous, and cruel. The generosity of France recovered the mind to judge by a candid scale. And as a mutual intercourse increased our acquaintance, the scales of ignorance fell from our eyes; the mist of prejudice vanished: And America found herself united to the most enlightened civilized nation on earth; and rejoiced in an alliance, cemented, not by interest only, but the strong additional bonds of cordial affection. An alliance, which may that God whose watchful eye guards the affairs of men, perpetuate unimpaired, while sun and moon shall endure. The citizens and subjects of both nations embraced as brethren; and fought side by side, with united hearts and hands, in the then made common cause. Their only strife was, who should display the noblest deeds; and render themselves most worthy each other's esteem. America's day, the morning of which had lowred with heavy clouds, began to brighten a pace; and it's hurrying hours hastened their way to a noon tide glow. The justice of her cause; the influence of her great ally; and the insults and injuries experienced by other nations, from British arrogance, procured her still farther support; and narrowed the distance to the object of her wish. Britain saw, with indignation: And in firm alliance with every infernal power (for, from heaven she dared not expect; nor would any on earth, Hesse, Anspach, and savages excepted, afford her aid) she resolved on utmost vengeance: And as a tyger in the forest, taken in the toiles, exerted her every effort. Nor need I here recount Monmouth, Cowpens by Catawba, or Eutaw, with the many sore fought days on the land; or the briney ocean, repeatedly stained with the generous blood of war, or the ravages that desolated the south; or the devastation and ruin that ranged along our coast; whilst their ruthless savage allies, to the eternal infamy of those who employed them, drenched the wide frontier with the warless blood of helpless women and babes. These deeds of Britain are written with the pen of remembrance on the minds of all. They are engraved, as with the point of a diamond on a rock, on the pillars of time; and handed down in the faithful historic page, shall long be read by ages yet to come. Nor shall Carolina or Georgia, New-York or Virginia, Philadelphia, Rhode-Island, or Boston, be named, but grateful acknowledgments shall rise of the kind deliverance afforded. And oft shall the traveller turn aside to survey the seat of Glocester and York in Virginia, and view the spot, ever to be remembered, where the great decisive event took place; and read inscribed on the memorative marble *(a)*, the important victory there obtained. The inhabitant, instructed from father to son, shall bear him company, and recount the various parts of the scene.

> On this point, the blood-stained British general, Lord Cornwallis, held his garrison. Yonder the great Washington & illustrious Rochambeau made their first approach. Across that rivulet, and through that valley, ran their first parallel; and where now that range of buildings stands, they drew their second. There stood a redoubt, carried by cool, determined Gallic bravery: And there the Americans stormed and conquered. Here, encaved in the brow of the bank, the Britons met, to hold their dark and gloomy councils; in that part of the river the Charon was set on fire. And yonder, across the water, the generals Weedon and Choissey hemmed in the imprisoned British ranks. There the French and American troops formed a glittering lane: And on yonder plain the numerous garrison piled their arms.

The listening child, led forth in his father's hand, shall hear him relate; and repeat it over again to his little companions. And they also shall rejoice in that great event, which struck Britain with terror and despair; and led on to that happy restoration of peace, for which, to day, we give thanks to our God. For, according to this time shall it be said of these United States, what hath God wrought for them? Great indeed, is the salvation he hath shown! And great the obligations we are under to praise! For, had we failed in our just attempt to secure our invaluable rights, America's choicest blood had flowed in liberal streams: And her most valuable citizens, throughout the states, had expired by halters and in gibbets. The daring patriot, whose zeal for his country had led him, with his life in his hand, to take a seat in the great council of the states, or in legislation, or administering justice; or, who had led in the field, in his country's cause: These had been led forth the first, in haughty triumph, amidst ten thousand insulting scoffs, as the victims of insatiable vengeance. Nor only these; but all who had dared to follow their councils, and abett the cause for which they contended; nor a single character worth notice left remaining, that dared to breathe the language of freedom. And the paths of life had now been thin of the many virtuous citizens convened to day, throughout these states, to give thanks on this happy

(a) A marble pillar appointed by Congress to be erected there.

occasion. America had been enriched indeed; and her soil made fat with the blood of her children. Made fat, not for the rightful owners; but to pamper the lusts of tyrannical landlords, sharing the country among themselves: The surviving former possessors, only vassals at pleasure, and slaves to their lordly masters. This, my friends, is not a flight of fancy; or apprehensive imagination run wild: It is founded in just observation; and what bitter experience would have taught, but taught too late, had our enemy prevailed. But blessed be God, with Israel of old we may take up our song; "blessed be the Lord who gave us not as a prey to their teeth. Blessed be the Lord, the snare is broken, and we are escaped." We cried unto him in the day of our distress. He heard our intreaties; and hath brought us forth into a large place; and established our rights; and opened before us a glorious prospect. May wisdom be given, to esteem and improve the invaluable blessing. Here has our God erected a banner of civil and religious liberty *(a)*: And prepared an asylum for the poor and oppressed from every part of the earth. Here, if wisdom guide our affairs, shall a happy equality reign; and joyous freedom bless the inhabitants wide and far, from age to age. Here, far removed from the noise and tumult of contending kingdoms and empires; far from the wars of Europe and Asia, and the barbarous African coast; here shall the husbandman enjoy the fruits of his labour; the merchant trade, secure of his gain; the mechanic indulge his inventive genius; and the sons of science pursue their delightful employment, till the light of knowledge pervade yonder, yet uncultivated, western wilds; and form the savage inhabitants into men. Here also, shall our Jesus go forth conquering and to conquer; and the heathen be given him for an inheritance; and these uttermost parts of the earth, a possession. Zion shall here lengthen her cords, and strengthen her stakes; and the mountain of the house of the Lord be gloriously exalted on high. Here shall the religion of Jesus; not that, falsely so called, which consists in empty modes and forms; and spends it's unhallowed zeal in party names and distinctions, and traducing and reviling each other; but the pure and

(a) Religious liberty, is a foundation principle in the constitutions of the respective states, distinguishing America from every nation in Europe; and resting religion on its proper basis; as supported by it's own evidence, and the almighty care of it's divine author; without the aid of the feeble, angry arm of civil power; which serves only to disgrace the name and religion of Jesus, by violating the rights of conscience.

undefiled religion of our blessed Redeemer: here shall it reign in triumph, over all opposition. Vice and immorality shall yet here, become ashamed and banished; and love to God, and benevolence to man, rule the hearts and regulate the lives of men. Justice and truth shall here yet meet together, and righteousness and peace embrace each other: And the wilderness blossom as the rose, and the desart rejoice and sing. And here shall the various ancient promises of rich and glorious grace begin their compleat divine fulfilment; and the light of divine revelation diffuse it's beneficent rays, till the gospel of Jesus have accomplished it's day, from east to west, around our world. A day, whose evening shall not terminate in night; but introduce that joyful period, when the outcasts of Israel, and the dispersed of Judah, shall be restored; and with them, the fulness of the gentile world shall flow to the standard of redeeming love: And the nations of the earth, become the kingdom of our Lord and Saviour. Under whose auspicious reign holiness shall universally prevail; and the noise and alarm of war be heard no more. Nor shall there be any thing to hurt or destroy, or interrupt the tranquility of men, through all the wide dominions of this glorious prince of peace. How pleasing the scene! How transporting the prospect! And how thrice happy they, whom God has honored, as instruments in the great work now brought to pass, subservient to these important events! May the blessings of heaven surround them; and the honor and esteem of a grateful country attend them through life. May the names and memories of those, oh my country! who have planned your measures, and guided your councils through a wilderness of innumerable difficulties, and brought your affairs, by the blessing of God, to a happy conclusion, may they ever be had in kind remembrance. Errors and mistakes may have been: But it is [a] matter of wonder and praise, that whilst treading an unknown, a difficult and dangerous path, their mistakes and errors have been so few. Surely the hand of God was in it, to guide and guard their way. And let the illustrious Washington, the Joshua of the day, and admiration of the age; who, inspired from above with every military endowment, to command the American arms; and great in the field beyond example, retires still greater, to the humble character of a private citizen, among the citizens of the states; let him live perpetual in the minds and the praises of all. Aid here, ye his highly honored fellow citizens, aid feeble fame with her hundred wings and tongues, to proclaim his worth: And let time, on his full and ever rolling stream, convey down through every age, the unsullied remembrance of the patriot, the hero and citizen combined, and deliver his name and his praise to the unbounded ocean of immortal esteem. And from the commander in chief down to the faithful centinel, let the officer and soldier who have bravely offered their lives; and nobly dared death and danger in the bloody field, on the horrid edge of the ranks of war, be remembred with kindness. Let their services of hardship, toil and danger be never forgot: But may they ever experience a kind attention from their fellow-citizens; and a faithful reward from their country, whose rights they have so firmly defended. Let their military garb and character ever command esteem. Let their wounds and their fears plead their cause and extenuate their foibles; and the residue of their exhausted days be crowned with honor and ease. With these let also be joined in never dying remembrance, a Warren, a Montgomery, a Biddle embraced by the briney waves, a Macpherson and a Laurens, in the bloom of youth, fallen in the bloody field, in their country's cause; with the countless train of martyrs for American freedom, who, from the ocean and the land, from prison-ships and jails, have sealed with their lives, their attachment to her cause. These—these—number them not of the dead. They are enrolled in the list of glory and fame; and shall live immortal, beyond the power of death and the grave. Bind their brows, oh ye American daughters, haste ye, haste ye, bind their brows with never-fading laurel, and glittering crimson wreaths; and let the evening song and noon-day recital perpetuate their deeds and their fame; while the silent tear stealing from the eye, shall testify how dear their memory and how high their esteem. And whilst the curse of Meroz remains on lasting record, for those who withheld their aid, let the blessings of all rest on every friend of liberty, who willingly offered himself, when his country's necessity called him to the field: And on all who have cheerfully borne and suffered in it's cause. Nor let our great and generous ally, who afforded an early and vigorous aid, be forgot. But let every American lip pronounce a "*Vive le Roi*," and every heart conspire, "long may his most Christian majesty, Lewis the Sixteenth," long may he live, a blessing, and blessed, on earth; and late resign an earthly crown, to shine in brighter glory, and wear a crown immortal, among the blessed above. And may his subjects ever be embraced as brethren and dearest friends who have fought our battles, and bled in our cause; and partiality here held worthy of praise. Nor may a due esteem ever be wanting to the United Netherland States, whose heart and endeavours were with us; or to the court of Spain for assistance afforded; but be generously paid to all who have aided to secure our rights. And whilst, with a grateful sense of their services done, we pay deserved honours to those whom God has honored, to bear a part in the great work performed; let every heart adore the God of goodness in all: And every lip, and every life, proclaim his praise. 'Tis he, the sovereign disposer of all events, hath wrought for us: and brought the whole to pass. It was he, who led his Israel of old, by the pillar and the cloud, through their wilderness journey; wherein they also had their wandrings; 'twas he the same, presided over our affairs; directed our councils, and guided our senators by the way. 'Twas he, who raised a Joshua to lead the tribes of Israel in the field of battle, raised and formed a Washington, to lead on the troops of his chosen states, to final conquest, and endued him with all his military patience, perseverance, prowess and skill; and admirably preserved his life and his health, through all the danger and toil. 'Twas he, who in Barak's day spread the spirit of war in every breast, to shake off the Canaanitish yoke, inspired thine inhabitants, oh America, with an ardent glow through every rank, to assert the cause of freedom: And led forth the husbandman and mechanic; with those of every class, to offer themselves undaunted in the daring conflict. It was he hid fear from their eyes, of either the superior number or skill, of the powerful foe they rose to withstand. And from him came down that firmness and fortitude, that raised American officers and soldiers, beyond all former example, through hunger, nakedness and cold, to fight the battles of their country; and never forsake it's standard. It was he breathed from above, and fired their bosoms, in the hour of action, to crop the laurels of triumph; or, having dearly sold their precious lives, to embrace death, in all his glory, on the bloody field. And he only inspired our generous seamen with invincible firmness, to endure the horrors of prison-ships and jails; and expire by famine and British barbarity, rather than renounce the virtuous cause in which they embarked. It was he, who raised up Cyrus, to break the Assyrian force, and say, "let Israel be free," endued the monarch of France with an angel's mind, to assert and secure the freedom of his United American States. And, by him were the hearts of other nations disposed to our aid. And he, and he alone, who saith to the proud waves of the sea, "Hitherto shall ye come, but no farther," restrained the councils and arms of Britain from improving against us many opportunities and advantages, which evidently lay within the line of their power. Who can recollect the critical night of retreat from Long-Island; the scene of retiring from New-York; the day of Brandywine; or the endangered situation of the arms of America, on Trenton's ever memorable night; and not be constrained to say, "if it had not been the Lord, who was on our side, if it had not been the Lord, who was on our side, our enemy had swallowed us up: The waters had overwhelmed us: The proud stream had swept us away." But blessed be his name, our help was found in him, who made the heavens and the earth. It was God, who blasted the secret designs of enemies and traitors against us. And, by an admirable interposition, brought forth into light, the dark and deep-stained villainy of an Arnold, cursed and detested of God and men.* And converted our repeated misfortunes and even mistakes, into singular mercies, and peculiar advantage, that, not more manifest was his voice on Sinai; or his hand, in the affairs of his Israel of old; than we have seen the wisdom, the power, and the goodness of our God, displayed through the whole of our arduous contest, from it's earliest period down: And may, with emphatical propriety, say, it is he the Almighty GOD, has accomplished the whole, in every part; and by his kind care, and omnipotent arm, has wrought out our deliverance; cast forth our enemy; bestowed upon us a wide extended, fruitful country; and blessed us with a safe and honorable peace. And has brought the whole to pass, in so short a space of time; and with so few difficulties attending, in comparison of what we had reason to expect, that the establishment of these United States, in the peaceful possession of their rights and privileges, stands an instance of divine favour, unexampled in the records of time. Who does not remember the general language, when the war commenced? cheerfully to pay one half of our property, to secure our rights. But, far from even the half of this has been required. Individuals, 'tis true, and those amongst the most virtuous of

* Deut. xxvii. 25.

the community, have suffered—have sorely suffered, by speculative miscreants, and a depreciating currency: And their confidence in the public faith has proved the temporal ruin of many; and widows and helpless orphans been made a prey. Many of whose sufferings might yet still be greatly alleviated, by a due attention; and a sacred regard to justice, and good conscience directing affairs: Which must also, sooner or later, take place; or the righteous God, who hates injustice, oppression and fraud, be highly displeased; and his judgments be yet poured out on our land: As he afflicted Israel of old, for unredressed injuries to the Gibeonites among them. And his justice, and his power are still the same. But, the price of our peace, taken on a national scale; compared with the advantages gained, and the number, by whom to be paid, scarce deserves a name. That, in whatever point of light we view this great event, we are constrained to say, "it is the doing of the Lord; and marvellous in our eyes." And to him be rendered the thanks, and the praise—*not unto us; not unto us; but to thy name, O Lord, be the glory*. For thine is the power, and the victory, and the greatness. Both success and safety come of thee. And thou reignest over all: And hast wrought all our works, in us, and for us. *Praise, therefore, thy God, O America, praise the Lord, ye, his highly favoured United States*. Nor let it rest in the fleeting language of the lip; or the formal thanksgiving of a day. But, let every heart glow with gratitude: And every life, by a devout regard to his holy law, proclaim his praise. It is this, our God requires, as that wherein our personal, and national good, and the glory of his great name consist. And without which, all our professions will be but an empty name. It is, that we love the Lord our God, to walk in his ways, and keep his commandments, to observe his statutes and his judgments. That a sacred regard be maintained to righteousness and truth. That we do justice, love mercy, and walk humbly with our God *(a)*. Then shall God delight to dwell amongst us. And these United States shall long remain, a great, a glorious, and an happy people. Which may God, of his infinite mercy, grant. Amen.

FINIS

(a) Deuteronomy 30. 16. Amos. 5. 24. Micah 6. 8.

— 26 —

A SERMON ON OCCASION OF THE COMMENCEMENT OF THE NEW-HAMPSHIRE CONSTITUTION

Samuel McClintock

PORTSMOUTH

1784

Samuel McClintock (1732–1804). A graduate of the College of New Jersey in Princeton and pastor (ordained in 1756) of the Greenland, New Hampshire, Congregational Church, McClintock (also written "Mcclintock" and "MacClintock") spent his life in that post, except for periods as chaplain during the French and Indian War and with the New Hampshire troops during the Revolution. (He was present at the Battle of Bunker Hill in 1775.) McClintock was awarded an M.A. by Harvard in 1761 and a D.D. by Yale in 1791. He had a keen mind and was a fine preacher, a number of whose sermons were published.

The sermon reprinted here is of interest because it was preached on June 3, 1784, at the beginning of the new government under the recently adopted constitution of the state of New Hampshire.

McClintock and his first wife (Mary Montgomery of Portsmouth) had fifteen children in the first sixteen years of their marriage. Three of their sons died fighting in the Revolution. Although he pursued the deists and infidels with zeal during the 1790s, McClintock thereafter became a strong supporter of Thomas Jefferson (a novelty among New England Congregational ministers) because, he said, he saw the country being ruled by a "junto of little tyrants . . . a proud domineering aristocracy." In Jefferson he saw "a great man of great, and distinguished abilities . . . now placed in the chair of government, who all along has shewn himself the friend . . . of the natural rights of man" (James McLachlan, *Princetonians, 1748–1768* [1976]).

A SERMON

PREACHED BEFORE THE HONORABLE THE

COUNCIL,

AND THE HONORABLE THE

SENATE,

AND

HOUSE OF REPRESENTATIVES,

OF THE

STATE OF NEW-HAMPSHIRE,

JUNE 3, 1784.

ON OCCASION OF THE COMMENCEMENT

OF THE

NEW CONSTITUTION

AND

FORM OF GOVERNMENT.

BY SAMUEL McCLINTOCK, A. M.

NEW-HAMPSHIRE:

PORTSMOUTH, PRINTED BY ROBERT GERRISH.

M,DCC,LXXXIV.

Honored and respectable Audience,

It is with diffidence I appear in this place, on the present great occasion, before such an assembly. Nothing, besides the respect I owe to the supreme legislative of this state, could so far have overcome the sense of my own insufficiency, as to induce me to comply with their invitation. Your candor will make a favourable allowance for the imperfections which your discernment will perceive, while I attempt to offer some observations suitable to the occasion, from Jeremiah XVIIIth, 7–10th.

At what instant I shall speak concerning a nation, and concerning a kingdom, to pluck up, and to pull down and to destroy it: If that nation against whom I have pronounced, turn from their evil, I will repent of the evil that I thought to do unto them. And at what instant I shall speak concerning a nation and concerning a kingdom, to build and to plant it: If it do evil in my sight, that it obey not my voice, then I will repent of the good wherewith I said I would benefit them.

he being and providence of God are the great principles of religion, which as they are conformable to the light of nature and reason, have obtained the general consent of mankind in all ages. It is not more evident from the visible works of creation that there is a God, who made all these things, than it is from the course of events in this world that they are under the direction and government of a wise, good, holy and powerful providence. By this natural conviction of the superintendence of the Deity over the affairs of this world, the pagan nations were led to consult their gods, and seek to them for direction and assistance, when they were engaging in affairs of great and public concernment, and to offer to them public thanks when their enterprizes were successful. And do they seek to them that are no gods? shall not a people then who are enlightened with the beams of divine revelation, in which the character and perfections of the true God, the necessary dependence of all creatures on him, and the government of his providence over all events, are so clearly taught, acknowledge him in all their ways, if they would expect that he will direct their paths? How becoming is it that we should render unto him in a public manner, the most devout ascriptions of praise for the great things he hath done for us, in delivering us from the cruel hand of oppression, and the impending miseries of abject servitude, crowning our arduous struggle in defence of the rights of human nature, with triumphant success, in the acknowledgment of our independence and sovereignty, and giving us the singular advantage of framing a constitution of government for ourselves and our posterity? If we should neglect to render due praise to him on such a great occasion, the heathen would rise up in judgment and condemn us for our impiety and ingratitude: For, though they were ignorant of the true God, and by reason of this their natural blindness, became vain in their imaginations, and changed his glory into the likeness of corruptible man, and of four-footed beasts, and creeping things; and in consequence thereof, practiced a multitude of idle superstitious ceremonies, suitable enough indeed to the character of their gods—I say, tho' their worship was false and erroneous, yet it was founded in a right principle—a conviction of a supreme power upon whom they were dependent, and who they believed governs and directs all human affairs—a principle so deeply imprinted in their hearts, that the habits of vice were not able wholly to efface the impression.

To men whose practice says there is no God—who view the events of time merely as effects of natural causes, of blind chance, or fatal necessity; and in the pride of reason, conceit that their own wisdom is sufficient to manage the affairs of states and empires, religion must appear an idle superstition; but to those who are convinced of the important truth taught in the words now read, the sovereign dominion of God over the nations of the earth, and the necessary dependence of all things on him, nothing can appear more rational than to seek to him on whom they depend, and in whose hand is the disposal of their circumstances, for direction in all their undertakings; more especially in affairs of public and national concernment, such as the present occasion, when a constitution of government is to take place, which in its operation may essentially affect the interest and happiness of present and future generations.

The Jewish nation, in consequence of renouncing their dependance on God, disregarded the threatnings of those desolating judgments which were coming upon them, and confiding in their numbers, their wisdom, the strength of their walls and the sanctity of their temple, set at defiance the attempt of the king of Assyria; but their hopes were vain. They were ripe for ruin. God had determined to punish them for their sins by delivering them into the hands of that monarch, to suffer the miseries of a long captivity in Babylon; and no human wisdom or might could frustrate his design. He had sent his prophet to them with repeated messages, to warn them of their danger, and caution them against trusting in the vain words and assurances of the false prophets; but they refused to obey his voice, and persisted in their own ways. In opposition to their vain confidence, God teaches them in the context his sovereign power over them, to exalt or abase them, by a significant emblem—the power of the potter over the clay to make one vessel to honor, and another to dishonor. O house of Israel, cannot I do with you as this potter? saith the Lord: Behold, as the clay is in the potter's hand, so are ye in my hand, O house of Israel. The text contains a farther explication of this instructive emblem. When God is spoken of in this and other scriptures as repenting of the good or evil he thought to do to a people, upon a change in their character, it is not to be understood in the same sense as repentance in creatures, which always implies sorrow for what they have done, and a change in their thoughts and purposes. In this sense, God cannot repent. It is inconsistent with the perfection of his nature. He speaks of himself in these words, after the manner of men. And the meaning is, that he changes and varies the conduct of his providence toward nations, according to their moral character. When he threatens to pluck up and destroy a sinful nation, if they turn from their evil ways, he will avert the threatned destruction; and on the other hand, when he intimates, by events of providence, his intention to build and plant a nation or kingdom, if they forsake the paths of virtue, and do evil, he will withdraw from them the tokens of his favor, and withhold the blessings he was ready to bestow. This is entirely consistent with the plan of the divine government, and the unchangeable purposes of the infinite mind.

Two things are principally taught in the text[:]

I[st]. That GOD *exercises a sovereign dominion over the nations and kingdoms of this world, and determines their rise, growth, declension and duration* –*and*

II[d]. That *his sovereign power is invariably directed by perfect and infinite rectitude; in plucking up and destroying, and in building and planting them, he treats them according to their moral character.*

GOD is an absolute sovereign. He presides with an uncontrouled sway over all the nations of this earth, and orders all the events, changes and revolutions by which they are either exalted to power and dignity, or brought to dishonor and ruin. By a turn of the wheel of providence, he can form a people into a respectable and happy, or a mean and contemptible nation; more easily than the potter, of the same lump, can make one vessel to honor and another to dishonor.

Agreeable to which, his sovereign power is expressed by the prophet Isaiah, in this beautiful language—all nations, before God, are as the drop of the bucket, or the small dust of the ballance, as easily plucked up or destroyed, or built and planted, as the former is wiped by a touch of the finger; or the other blown away with a breath of air. That sovereign word which gave existence to all things at first, continually supports their being, and gives efficacy to all the secondary causes of the growth and prosperity, or the decline and ruin of nations and empires. When he speaks and intimates his design by favorable events of providence, to plant and build up a nation, things are so ordered that there is a concurrence of causes to promote this end. Their public counsels are directed by wisdom, and their enterprizes crowned with success; they are prospered in their agriculture, commerce, manufactures, and all their undertakings—happy in their union at home, and respectable among their neighbours, for their wisdom, virtue, and magnanimity. And when, on the contrary, he determines to destroy an impenitent nation for their sins, no human wisdom, counsel or might, can prevail to frustrate the execution of his threatnings; but they are so infatuated, that even the methods they take to support their tottering state, serve to precipitate their ruin. Thus he increaseth the nations and destroyeth them; he enlargeth the nations and straitneth them.

This sovereign power of God over the nations of the earth, was manifested in a convincing manner, in his dispensations toward that favorite people whom he chose for himself, to preserve the true religion amidst the false worship and superstitions that reigned in the world, and to be a figure of the nations of the redeemed. His almighty hand was signally displayed toward them in a series of unusual and miraculous events; in delivering them from the house of their bondage, preserving them in the wilderness for the space of forty years, giving them possession of, and planting them in the land of Canaan, oftentimes bringing them low for their iniquity, and then upon their repentance, delivering them from the hand of their enemies, and restoring them to their former prosperity, by means altogether inadequate to such effects, and which afforded the clearest evidence of the interposition of divine providence. The Almighty arm was made bare in his dispensations toward them.

But in the common method of his government over the nations of the earth, God brings to pass his designs by means and instruments, and as it were, conceals himself, in his immediate operations, behind the scene of nature; so that we are apt to overlook the power that actuates all the parts of the system, and to ascribe effects to their immediate causes, which in reality are nothing more than effects of the first cause, and produce their effects by his continual influence on them. What is called the course of nature is only the continual operation of God on this visible system of things, producing the events we behold in a uniform manner, according to certain laws which he hath established; so that these common and ordinary events by which nations are blessed or chastised, are in reality as much effects of his power as miracles are; and to this, we are constantly taught in the sacred pages to ascribe them. And even reason would lead us to the same conclusion; for what power is there in nature equal to such effects? What but an almighty hand could have kept this system of nature, these amazing bodies of matter, the sun, moon and stars, revolving in their appointed courses through so many thousands of years, with the most exact order and regularity and without the least interference of their spheres? and to what but this can we ascribe numberless events to which their visible and immediate causes are inadequate, or which come to pass contrary to all rational grounds of probability? In a human view, the voluntary actions of free agents, and the events which depend on them, seem to be wholly in their own power; yet we are taught that the hearts of men are in the hands of God, their thoughts, counsels and designs are so entirely under his controul, that they are often led by a secret influence on their minds to pursue a course of conduct quite different from that which they had chosen. A man's heart deviseth his way, but the Lord directeth his steps. Even the proudest and mightiest of mortals who are raised abovc all human restraints, and seem to have it in their power to act as they please, are as much under his controul as the horse we govern by the bit and bridle, or the fish in whose mouth the hook is fastened, is under our command. I, saith God, speaking of the proud king of Assyria, who boasted of his irresistable power, I will put my hook in thy nose and my bridle in thy lips, and I will turn thee back by the way by which thou camest. There was nothing in the wars and victories of Nebuchadnezzar and Cyrus, but what seemed to be the effects of natural causes. They were prompted by a lust of power and a love of vain glory, and seemed to gain their victories by superior skill and numbers, but at the same time they were instruments in the hand of God, to accomplish the designs of his providence; the former to punish the nations, and in particular his own people, for their wickedness, and the latter to deliver them from their long captivity, and restore them to their own land.

Thus the sacred scripture leads our views up to God as the first cause, the fountain of all life, power, and motion, and the author of all the events and revolutions which take place in the nations and empires of this world. It is God who does all these things by the influence of his providence, whatever means and instruments may be employed in their accomplishment.

The present glorious revolution in this land affords a striking proof of the truth we are considering. The divine hand hath been so signally displayed in the events and occurrences which have led to it, that those who are not convinced of the government of providence over the affairs of nations by what has passed before them in these late years, would not have been persuaded if they had been eye-witnesses of the mighty works which God wrought in the midst of his peculiar people. For though the events were not strictly miraculous, yet they were truly marvellous, and so circumstanced, that they never can be rationally accounted for without admitting the interposition of providence. The greater the disproportion between the means and the effect, the more evident is the divine power: And surely there has seldom, in any case, been a greater disproportion between the means and event, than in the present one. Hardly any people were ever less prepared to enter the lists with such a great and powerful nation. War was not our object or wish: on the contrary, we deprecated it as a dreadful calamity, and continued to hope, even against hope, that the gentler methods of petitioning and remonstrating might obtain a redress of grievances. The war, on our part, was not a war of ambition, but a justifiable self-defence against the claims of an arbitrary power, which was attempting to wrest from us the privileges we had all along enjoyed, and to subject us to a state of abject servitude. In this light it was viewed by the nations of Europe, and even by some of the most illustrious characters in both houses of the British parliament, who, in their public speeches, have justified our resistance, and acquitted us from the guilt of the blood that has been spilt.

It was after we had been treated with repeated insults and injuries—after our dutiful petitions had been rejected with contempt—after the British administration had held up the high claim of authority to make laws, binding us in all cases whatsoever; the plain language of which was, we have authority and power to do with you as we please; and if you will not quietly submit, and deliver up your earnings to support us in our luxury and extravagance, and be hewers of wood and drawers of water for us, we will lay waste your country with fire and sword, and destroy you from under heaven—it was after the sword had been drawn, and blood shed on the plains of Lexington, and on the fatal Bunker-hill, so that no alternative remained, but either absolute submission or open resistance—it was, I say, after all this, that the representatives of the people in Congress chose the latter, declared for independence, and relying on the justice of their cause, and the aid of the Almighty, resolved to support it by force of arms. At that time our contest with Britain appeared, from a consideration of the difference between their circumstances and our's, as unequal, as that between the stripling David and the giant of Gath; and the improbability of our success as great, as that he with a sling and stone should overcome that proud and mighty enemy, cloathed with armour from head to foot.

They were men of war from their youth. They had regular troops, used to service, who had signalized their valour on the plains of Minden, and the heights of Abraham, commanded by able, experienced generals, amply furnished with all the terrible apparatus of death and destruction, and aided by mercenary troops, who had been bred to arms, and were versed in all the stratagems of war—add to this, they had a navy that ruled the ocean, and regular resources to supply their demands—on the other hand, we were inexperienced in the art of war, and had neither disciplined troops, nor magazines of provision and ammunition, nor so much as one ship of war to oppose to their formidable fleets, nor any regular resources, nor even so much as the certain prospect of any foreign aid—besides, all the civil governments were dissolved, and the people reduced back to a state of nature, and in danger of falling into anarchy and confusion. From this comparative view of their strength and our weakness, to what can our success be ascribed but to that omnipotent hand which directed the stone from the sling? The several steps which led to this great event, cannot be rationally accounted for from any other cause. Among these the general union of the people throughout these states is not the least remarkable.

That people so widely seperated from one another by their situation, manners, customs, and forms of government, should all at once be willing to sacrifice their private interests to the public good, and unite like a band of brothers, to make the cause of one state, and even of one town, a common cause; and that they should continue firm and united amidst the greatest discouragements and the most trying reverses of fortune.

That an army of freemen, voluntarily assembling at the alarm of danger—men who had been nurtured in the bosom of liberty, and unused to slavish restraints, should be willing to submit to the severity of military government, for the safety of their country, and patiently endure hardships that would have overcome the fortitude of veterans, following their illustrious leader in the depths of winter, through cold and snow, in nakedness and perils, when every step they took was marked with the blood that issued from their swoln feet, and when they could not be animated to such patience and perseverance by any mercenary motives, was a rare spectacle, and for its solution must be traced to a higher source than mere natural causes —in a word, the hand of providence evidently appeared in the various incidents and secondary causes which concurred to secure to us success.

In raising up, at the beginning of the contest a group of noble patriots to counteract the political manœuvres of the British administration, and expose to view their dark designs to enslave this country, and who with peculiar strength of argument and power of persuasion, so ably defended the cause of their country, as to engage the attention and approbation of all Europe, and gain immortal honor to themselves—in bringing on the stage a great military character, the American Fabius, to take the command of our armies, endowed with those qualities which in a peculiar manner fitted him for such a command, at such a time and in such circumstances—in overruling things, so that the very instruments of war which had been prepared for our destruction, should fall into our hands when they were most wanted, and be turned against the enemy in our own defence—in disposing the heart of the illustrious monarch of France to aid and assist us in our virtuous struggle—in sending divisions into the councils of the enemy, disconcerting their measures, and discovering their secret plans, at the critical moment, by a concurrence of incidents which no human wisdom could have foreseen—in the repeated signal instances of success, particularly the capture of two of the best armies of the enemy, in which we had a convincing demonstration that the race is not to the swift, nor the battle to the strong; but that the victory was of the Lord; and finally, in disposing the enemy to acknowledge our independence and sovereignty, and to withdraw their fleets and armies.

By this revolution, we are not only delivered from the calamities of a long, expensive and bloody war, but may now sit quietly under our own vine and fig-tree, without any to make us afraid, and every man is left at full liberty to pursue the means of opulence and happiness, without the danger of being deprived of the fruits of his industry by the hand of rapine and violence, which is ever the case of those who are either the subjects of arbitrary power or exposed to the ravages of war. By this revolution, the rights and privileges of men in a state of civil society, are secured to us; and we have the precious opportunity, which few nations have ever enjoyed, to take up government on its first principles, and to chuse that form which we judge best adapted to our situation, and most promotive of our public interests and happiness. America seems like a young heir, arrived to mature age, who, being freed from the restraints of tutors and governors, takes the management of his estate into his own hands, and makes such laws for the regulation of his domestic affairs, as he judges will be most conducive to establish peace, order and happiness in his family.

The form now to take place, though the best that could be obtained, where so many were to be consulted, no doubt has its defects, which time and experience will discover better than any speculations, and for the amendment of which, express provision is made in the constitution itself—its excellencies are apparent, and justly entitle its worthy framers to the honorable appellation of *fathers of their country*. Were it necessary, I might shew with what precision the rights belonging to men in a state of society are defined in the Declaration of Rights, and the life, liberty and property of the subject guarded with a jealous care against oppressive power—how the sacred rights of conscience are secured from human impositions, and equal liberty allowed to all denominations of professing christians, and equal protection promised to them so long as they demean themselves good subjects, by which the many headed monster, persecution, is excluded from our state. I might show how the several powers of government are nicely adjusted, so as to have a mutual check on each other, and despotic power guarded against by keeping the *legislative*, *judicial and executive* powers, distinct and seperate, an essential arrangement in a free government; and how the impartial execution of the laws is provided for by the independent situation of the judges; but it is needless to be particular before such an assembly.

Hail the auspicious day that sees our inestimable privileges established on such a foundation!* It affords a peculiar satisfaction, on this occasion, to find the man chosen to fill the chair of government, who at the beginning of the late contest espoused the cause of his injured country, who nobly sacrificed his domestic ease and private interest to the public good; and with unshaken firmness and resolution persevered in his virtuous efforts till success has realized his hopes. His election to the office of chief magistrate by the free suffrages of the people, as it is a demonstration of their sense of superior merit, confers a much greater honor than that of an hereditary crown—may the Almighty take his excellency under his holy protection—may he still preside with wisdom and dignity in his exalted station, and after en-

* What respects his excellency President Weare, was omitted in the delivery of the sermon, his excellency being absent. It is now inserted in the publication, as a small tribute of gratitude to one, who has deserved so well of the public.

joying the deserved approbation of his country for meritorious services, be raised to immortal honors in the kingdom of God. It heightens the joy of the day to see the other important branches of government supplied with such a number of respectable characters. May the honorable the Senate and House of Representatives be directed by supreme wisdom to such measures as will most effectually promote the best interests of their constituents, and particularly in the choice of the most suitable persons to fill the vacant seats of government. It is to be presumed out of such a number of chosen men, there can be no difficulty in making the right choice.

Happy people! if you have wisdom and virtue to improve the advantages now presented to you, under a free government and the administration of wise and faithful rulers, you may go on for ages to come increasing in your numbers and improvements, so as to become the greatest and most powerful empire that ever rose on the face of this earth. There will be no occasion to make war upon your neighbours, to enlarge your boundaries, and it will ever be contrary, as we are situated, to the principles of true policy.

That vast extent of territory comprehended within the limits of the United States, situated under every climate, is capable of containing a countless number of inhabitants, and the rich soil, which wants only the hand of industry to subdue and cultivate it, of producing all the necessaries and comforts of life in the greatest abundance for their support. If the people in these states double their numbers every twenty-five years, supposing them to be three millions at present, according to this calculation, a century hence, they will be increased to forty-eight millions, even without the accession of any foreigners. Imagination already anticipates with pleasing wonder the future prosperity and grandeur of these rising republics. It sees the wilderness changed into a fruitful field, and the desert blossoming as the rose; populous towns and cities rising to view in those vast tracts of uncultivated soil, which hitherto have been the haunt of beasts of prey and savage men. It sees the commodities of every other country flowing into our harbours with every tide, while our store-houses are crowded with the various productions of our own. It sees science flourishing under the refreshing shade of the tree of liberty, and the encouragement of a wise and patriotic government, and Locks and Newtons making new discoveries in the laws of nature, and the latent powers of the human mind, rising to a degree of perfection hitherto unknown; and, which is the most joyful part of the scene, it sees the benevolent religion of the divine Saviour extended far and wide, and christian churches planted where satan's seat now is.

How charming the prospect! But it is to be considered, that its being realized, depends on the practice of that righteousness which alone exalteth a nation; for,

It is laid down in the text, as the rule of the divine government over the nations of the earth, to deal with them according to their moral character. Tho' God is an absolute, yet he is a holy and righteous sovereign. Such is the perfection of his nature, that he never can do any thing but what is fit and right. That the righteous should be as the wicked, that be far from him. Perfect justice is the invariable rule of his government over the nations. As to individuals, all things come alike to all, and there is one event to the righteous and to the wicked in this present world; the recompence of their doings is reserved for a future state, in which every one shall receive according to the deeds done in the body: But with regard to nations, God hath always made a distinction between the righteous and the wicked, and in plucking up and destroying, or building up and planting them, has ever treated them according to the rule of justice laid down in the text. This would appear with abundant evidence from a review of the history not only of the Jewish nation, but of all other nations that ever have existed. When God commissioned his people to exterminate the nations of Canaan, it was because they had filled up the measure of their iniquity, and it was the crying sins of Sodom and Gomorrah, that brought down upon them the exemplary vengeance of heaven. While virtue was the character of the citizens of Rome; while they practised temperance and sobriety, justice and honesty, and maintained a reverence of the laws and a sacred regard to their promises and treaties, they were prosperous and happy, and from small beginnings rose to be a mighty people. They were not more revered for their valor than for their wisdom and virtue, but as soon as venality and corruption crept in among them their decline was rapid. After the conquest of Asia, the luxuries of the east entered Rome in triumph, and the vices of the conquered soon effected that which their arms could not do—it produced an entire change in the public state and manners, so that a people who had been celebrated for their virtue and courage, became effeminate and luxurious, and sold their birth-right for a mess of pottage; and even the Roman senate, which had resembled an assembly of gods, became dupes to the tyrant, and the mere echo of his arbitrary edicts. It was the wisdom of their laws and the virtue of their citizens, that raised the free states of Greece to such importance, and made them superior to the whole force of Asia, and it was their departure from that virtue, and falling into the contrary vices, that proved their ruin. In a word, the history of all nations and ages, shews that public virtue makes a people great and happy, vice contemptible and miserable. This is the constitution of God—the immutable law of his kingdom, founded in the infinite perfection of his nature, so that unless God should change, that is, cease to be God, we cannot be a happy, unless we are a virtuous people. In absolute governments, the principle of honor may in some measure supply the place of virtue, and there may be the shew of public happiness and grandeur, while the people are really in a state of slavery; but as virtue is the basis of republics, their existence depends upon it, and the moment that the people in general lose their virtue, and become venal and corrupt, they cease to be free. This shews of what importance it is to preserve public virtue under such a constitution as our's, and how much it becomes all who have any regard to the good of their country, and of posterity, and who wish the scenes of future happiness and grandeur, which present themselves to the imagination, may be realized to do every thing in their power, to promote that virtue upon which this depends. This is more especially the duty of rulers, as the end for which they are cloathed with power is, that, that power may be employed for the good of the people—to protect their lives and interests—to make wise and salutary laws, for the regulation of their public affairs, to administer justice with impartiality, and to promote those virtuous sentiments and dispositions among the people, which are the surest foundation of their true happiness and glory. The benevolent design of the institution of civil government, the duty of rulers, and the benefits to be expected from their administration, are represented in Nebuchadnezzar's dream, under the beautiful and significant emblem of a tree, whose top reached to heaven, and its branches to the ends of the earth, and afforded both food and protection to the beasts of the field, and the fowls of the air. "Can there, as one says, be a more just and instructive idea of sovereign power? whose true grandeur and solid glory, does not consist in that splendor, pomp, and magnificence which surrounds it; nor in that reverence and exterior homage which are paid to it by subjects; but in the real services and solid advantages it procures to nations; whose support, defence, security and asylum it forms, both from its nature and institution, at the same time it is the fruitful source of terrestial blessings of every kind; especially to the poor and weak, who ought to find beneath its shade and protection, a sweet peace and tranquility not to be interrupted, or disturbed; whilst rulers sacrifice their ease, and experience alone those storms and tempests from which they shelter all others."

Rulers, by the very design of their institution, are ministers of God for good to the people; and their situation gives them a peculiar advantage to promote this benevolent design. They are placed on high, like a city set upon a hill: The people look up to them as their fathers, guides and guardians, and confide in their wisdom to devise the best means to alleviate their burdens, to promote their interests, and perpetuate their happiness; and when their authority is exercised with justice and moderation, their example has a leading influence in forming the public taste and manners: They are the head of the political body, which moves, animates and guides the members in their motions. From all these considerations, people have a right to expect that their rulers, to whom they have delegated their authority for this express purpose, will do all in their power to promote their interests and happiness. Before I conclude, I will take the liberty briefly to mention some things which it is in a more especial manner the duty of rulers to promote, as the surest means of establishing their own authority on a firm basis, lengthening the public tranquility, and realizing those future scenes of felicity and grandeur, the prospect of which lies before us.

1st. As religion has a manifest tendency to promote the temporal as well as eternal interests of mankind, it is the duty of rulers to give all that countenance and support to religion that is consistent with liberty of conscience. And it is perfectly consistent with that liberty and equal protection which are secured to all denominations of christians, by our excellent constitution, for rulers in the exercise of their authority to punish profane swearing, blasphemy, and open contempt of the institutions of religion, which have a fatal influence on the interests of society, and for which no man, in the exercise of reason, can plead conscience; and by their example, to encourage the practice of those things which all denominations allow to be essential in religion. Even on the supposition that the christian religion were, as its enemies would insinuate, a cunningly devised fable, yet as its genius and precepts are so friendly to civil government; as it contains a system of the most pure and sublime morality, and enjoins on its professors in the most express manner, and by the most powerful sanctions, subjection to the powers that are ordained of God, it would be sound policy in rulers to give all possible countenance and encouragement to this religion as the means of strengthening their own hands; and to treat it with neglect and contempt, and teach the people by their own example to do so likewise, would be undermining their own authority; cutting off the branch on which they themselves stand; for when men have cast off the fear of God, it is a natural consequence, that neither will they regard man. The religion of Christ, where it has its proper influence on the hearts and lives of men, will not fail to make the best rulers and the best subjects. It is unnecessary to enlarge before rulers, one requisite qualification in whom is, that they are of the protestant religion: They will surely encourage and promote their own religion.

2^d. However much men may differ in their religious sentiments, all, even the vicious themselves, are agreed in condemning vice, and approving of virtue; and universal experience shews that the certain tendency of the former is to bring ruin upon a people, and of the latter to make them great and happy. It may then justly be expected from those who are the fathers and the guardians of the people, and who according to the design of their institution, are to be a terror to evil doers, and a praise to them that do well, that they will do every thing in their power, both by their authority and example, to encourage and promote the practice of those public virtues among the people, industry, œconomy, frugality, obedience to the laws, a reverence of solemn oaths (the bond of civil society and security of life and property) public spirit and love of their country, with which our prosperity and happiness are closely connected: and that they will discountenance and suppress, by all possible ways and means, the opposite vices, luxury, dissipation, extravagance, gaming, idleness and intemperance, which lead to certain ruin, and have already made such an alarming progress as forebodes that this new empire will not be of long duration, at least in its present form, unless they are restrained by some effectual expedients. They are the diseases of the political body, which prey upon its very vitals, and by certain, tho' insensible degrees, bring on its dissolution. They call for speedy and efficacious remedies.

In absolute governments, where the power is lodged in the hands of one, or a few, the constitution may be maintained, tho' the people are grossly ignorant and corrupt, because they have no concern in the affairs of government. They are governed by brutal force, and are mere machines which move only as they are moved by an exterior power; but in free governments, where all supplies originate with the people, and the authority delegated by them to their rulers, is revocable at their pleasure, it is essential to existence and to the public welfare, that people should be virtuous, and entertain just ideas of the relation and mutual obligations between them and their rulers, and the common interest they have in the good of their country. It is of great importance they should be sensible that their country is not the land where they were born, or the soil they possess, but the great body of the people of which they are members, and the laws and constitution under which they live—that the people are their people—the laws their laws, which they have consented to be govern'd by, and the rulers their rulers, to whom they have solemnly promised obedience and subjection, in the exercise of lawful authority; and that as in the natural, so in the political body, its prosperity and happiness depend on the wisdom of the head, the soundness of the vitals, and the activity and regular exercise of the members in their several places—such sentiments generally diffused among a people, will engage them to obey from a principle of duty, and will make them ready and chearful in contributing their support to measures calculated to promote the public good—they will prefer the welfare of their country to their chief joy. It was this principle of public spirit and love of their country, which was cultivated with a religious care, from their earliest age, in the citizens of Sparta, Athens and Rome, that produced such astonishing efforts of heroic virtue. This leads me to add,

3^d^. The education of youth in useful knowledge and the principles of virtue, being essential to the preservation of a free government, and the public welfare, should be a main object of every wise government. The faculties of the human mind, in their natural state, are like precious metal in the ore, which must be refined and polished by the hand of education to make them useful. Knowledge is not only necessary in rulers to qualify them to fill public posts with dignity and reputation; but also in the people to make them good subjects. A wise and knowing people will think it no less their interest than duty to support government and yield obedience to the laws; whereas the ignorant being governed wholly by their passions, are dangerous subjects of any government, especially a free one. They are mere machines, and ever liable to be excited by an artful designing demagogue, to such acts of violence and outrage, as have sometimes brought the public to the brink of ruin. Witness the frequent revolutions in the Ottoman government, where sometimes a sultan is deposed and strangled by a sudden insurrection, while the grand seignior sits trembling in his palace. It would then render a most essential service to the public, and be a happy mean of securing to distant posterity the blessings of that free and wise government we are placed under, if rulers would take effectual measures for the instruction of the rising generation in useful knowledge—posterity will rise up and call them blessed.

But surely I need not dwell on this subject before such an assembly, as all wise men are sensible of the advantages of knowledge. The worthy framers of our constitution have expressed their sense of it, when they say, that "Knowledge and learning generally diffused through a community are essential to the preservation of a free government," and when they add, that "it shall be the duty of the legislators and magistrates, in all future periods of this government, to cherish the interest of literature and the sciences, and all seminaries and public schools."

4th. It is of the last importance to the honor of a nation, to maintain the public credit and the faith of solemn treaties inviolate. The credit of a nation as well as of individuals, depends on their punctuality in fulfilling their engagements. What but this enabled Britain, under such an enormous load of national debt, to raise supplies to carry on the late expensive war? No other nation, nor even their own citizens, will trust a people in their exigencies, who have often violated their promises, and defrauded their creditors. Public credit is of a delicate nature, easily destroyed, but with difficulty retrieved. Nothing fixes a deeper and more lasting mark of infamy on a nation than their breach of public faith. It was this made Carthage a by-word among their neighbours, so that Carthaginian faith became a term of reproach to signify a faithless perfidious people. It is devoutly to be wished that we may be saved from that infamy, by a punctual fulfilment of the promises of the public to individuals, and a sacred adherence to the faith of treaties and the articles of confederation, that our enemies may be disappointed of their hopes from our intestine divisions, and convinced that we have virtue to preserve, and wisdom to improve, the inestimable blessings we have defended by our valour. At the same time that the honor and credit of a nation depend on their preserving the public faith inviolate; it is to be remembered that treaties and alliances between nations, being founded on their mutual interests, are like a rope of sand, easily broken; and we are not to expect they will be regarded any longer than it is for the interest of the contracting powers to observe them: We must therefore, under providence, depend for defence against foreign invasion, and the security of our liberty and privileges, on the wisdom and firmness of our councils, the public virtue of citizens, the good order of our finances, and a well disciplined militia.

If rulers and people would unite in their endeavors to promote the things that have been mentioned, it would infallibly secure the future happiness and glory of this new empire.

The Almighty Ruler of nations and kingdoms sets before us this day, life and death, blessing and cursing, and leaves it to ourselves which we will chuse. Altho' true religion, the religion of the heart, consisting in faith and love unfeigned, and a real conformity to the divine character, is necessary in all who on good grounds would hope for eternal life; yet those who are wholly destitute of this religion, have it in their power to practice, on natural principles, that virtue, which according to the constitution of the divine government over nations, will ensure their temporal prosperity and glory.

While we are obedient and do that which is right, we have the highest assurance that our tranquility shall be lengthened, and the increase of our happiness and glory like the light of the morning; but if we do evil and fall into the vices and corruptions that have ever brought ruin on other nations, we may assuredly expect that we shall meet with their doom. Our situation, and the constitution of our government makes this warning peculiarly necessary.

Young states, like young men in the vigor of life, by their exertions attain to wealth; and exorbitant wealth begets luxury, dissipation, and those other vices which bring on their ruin. Republics, in their very constitution, are shorter lifed than other governments: their foundation being laid in virtue, when the body of the people become corrupt, the enemy takes advantage while they are lull'd into a fatal sleep on the soft lap of pleasure, to bind them with the cords of absolute power; so that when they awake, like Sampson, too late, they find themselves deprived of that in which their strength lay. This was formerly the fate of the Roman commonwealth, and is at present the case of Venice and the United Netherlands. All empires have had their period, and without doubt our's, like them, will also be lost in the lapse of time. We would fain place that event at a distant period. We cannot but hope that the Almighty has designed America as the stage on which he will make the most illustrious displays of his power and glory—let us unite our endeavors for its accomplishment. Let vice in every form be discountenanced, that, as ashamed, it may hide its head, and genius, merit and virtue, be encouraged and rewarded. Let wisdom guide our public councils, and equity and moderation mark our public measures. Let us guard against a spirit of discord, the bane of society; and laying aside those personal prejudices which have arisen from the opposition of sentiments and interests in the late contest, endeavor to cultivate peace and to strengthen the union among all the members of the state, that our moderation may be known to all men. Let us with a conscientious care preserve the spirit of the constitution, and guard against whatever would be an infraction of the social compact between the rulers and the people. It would be a glaring inconsistency, after people have chosen a form of government, and delegated authority to rulers to exercise the several powers of that government, to form combinations within the state in opposition to their own laws and government. It would be pulling down with one hand what they build up with the other, and setting up a government within a government, the greatest absurdity in politics. While on the one hand we reject the doctrine of passive obedience and nonresistance, and with a jealous eye watch the motions of those in power; let us on the other hand, equally guard against a spirit of faction, that from selfish motives would overturn the foundations of government, and throw all things into confusion.

The citizens of a free state should learn to think on a large scale. This would guard them against the designs of the selfish and interested. They should rise above that contracted spirit which centers all the views and pursuits of men in their own private seperate interest, or that of the little circle with which they are immediately connected. They should consider themselves as members one of another, and the particular state to which they belong, a member of the great national body, composed of the United States, and upon this principle, study to promote the general good of the whole; in which also their own safety and happiness are involved. Instead of weakening they should do every thing in their power to strengthen the hands of rulers, and to support them in the exercise of lawful authority.

Government is necessary, and must be supported; and it ought to be a humiliating consideration that the necessity and expences of this divine institution, is founded in the corruption and vices of human nature; for if mankind were in a state of rectitude there would be no need of the sanctions of human laws to restrain them from vice or to oblige them to do what is right. They would be detered from the former by a sense of its deformity, and led to practice the latter by a view of its intrinsic beauty. But in the present disordered state of our nature there would be no safety of life or property without the protection of law. A state of nature would be a state of continual war and carnage. The weak would be devoured by the strong, and every affront avenged with the death of the offender. Even under the best governments, we see the human passions often break through all the restraints of law in acts of violence and outrage! which shews what reason we have to be thankful to God for that excellent Constitution we live under, and how incumbent it is on every one who is a friend to the order, peace and happiness of society, or who even regards the safety of his own life and property, to support and maintain it.

To conclude—it is matter of solid consolation and exalted joy to the friends of God and religion, amidst the darkness and imperfection of this present state, that all human events are under the direction of an infinitely wise, good, holy and powerful providence, and are subservient to the peculiar kingdom of the Mediator, and uniformly working together to bring it to that state of perfection and glory for which it is designed. It is delightful to observe, how all things from the beginning of time, in the four great monarchies that rose in succession, that of the Babylonians, that of the Medes and Persians, that of the Macedonians, and that of the Romans, were disposed by divine providence to prepare the way for the coming of the Mediator, and the introduction of his kingdom; and how the kings and rulers of the earth in those enterprizes, in which they were actuated by pride and vain glory, were only instruments in his hand to accomplish the predictions of his holy word respecting his church and people, though they meant not so, neither came it into their heart. The design of God in all his dispensations and in all events that have come to pass in every age, has been to serve the interest of the Redeemer's kingdom. And this, doubtless, is his design in the present revolution. It may be to prepare the way for the accomplishment of glorious things spoken of Zion in the latter days which remain yet to be accomplished. All power in heaven and on earth is given to Christ as mediator for the church; and is invariably exercised by him to promote her interest.

Let Zion rejoice that her King reigneth and is governor among the nations, and sovereign of universal nature; so that no weapon formed against her shall prosper, but all the designs and attempts of her malicious foes shall be over-ruled to promote her interest, happiness and glory. This stone which was cut out of the mountain without hands, has already smote the feet of the image in Daniel's vision, which represented the four monarchies before-mentioned, and broken them in pieces; and this stone shall finally become a great mountain and fill the whole earth, when all the glory and magnificence of earthly kingdoms shall vanish away as the illusions of a dream when one awaketh. May we be built by faith on this tried precious corner stone which God hath laid in Zion for a foundation, and be found diligent and faithful in the duties of our several stations, that so through his mercy and the merits of the great Redeemer we may be approved when we shall appear before him in judgment, and be finally admitted to the joys and glories of that kingdom that cannot be moved, in which peace and righteousness reign forever, *Amen*.

27

A SERMON PREACHED BEFORE A CONVENTION OF THE EPISCOPAL CHURCH

William Smith

BALTIMORE
1784

WILLIAM SMITH (1727–1803). Born in Aberdeen, Scotland, Smith was educated at the University of Aberdeen and then emigrated to New York in 1751. A man of controversy and extremes, Smith immediately joined Samuel Seabury and other Anglicans in the struggle to define King's College as an Anglican rather than a nonsectarian institution. The controversy, and his *A General Idea of the College of Mirania* (1753), brought Smith to the public's attention and to the favor of Benjamin Franklin, who brought him to the College of Philadelphia, as it became in 1755. Smith was appointed a professor of logic, rhetoric, and natural and moral philosophy and was ordained an Anglican priest. He served as provost of the College until 1779 and again from 1789 to 1791, when the University of Pennsylvania was formed. He was awarded doctorates of divinity by the universities at Oxford, Dublin, and Aberdeen and became a member of the American Philosophical Society in 1768.

Along the way Smith had parted company with his more moderate sponsor, Franklin, taking the side of the colonial proprietors in favoring a vigorous policy against the French and Indians during the war that raged from 1755 to 1763, rather than the passivity and compromise favored by the Quakers, Germans, and colonial assembly. He made many enemies in the process, and even though he opposed the Stamp Act in 1765 and preached *A Sermon on the Present Situation* (1775) arguing the American case (responded to by John Wesley in *A Calm Address to Our American Colonies*), Smith could never warm to the cause of independence and was driven out of Pennsylvania in 1779. He moved to Maryland and spent a decade there, establishing the Kent School (later renamed Washington College), and becoming a founder of the Protestant Episcopal Church. He spent his last years in Philadelphia and died there.

A fine writer, gifted teacher, and powerful preacher, Smith held uncompromisingly to a view of religion and culture that he saw threatened by multiple dangers: the popery of the French, the barbarity of the Indians, the enthusiasm of the revivalists, the quietism of the Quakers, the alien culture of the Germans, and the dangers of republicanism bereft of virtue and the steadying hand of traditional authority.

AN ADDRESS TO THE MEMBERS OF THE PROTESTANT EPISCOPAL CHURCH OF MARYLAND,

CONTAINING,

An ACCOUNT of the *Proceedings* of ſome late CONVENTIONS both of CLERGY and LAITY, for the Purpoſe of organizing the ſaid *Church*, and providing a Succeſſion in her *Miniſtry*, agreeably to the Principles of the *American Revolution*.

Publiſhed by a COMMITTEE of Clerical and Lay-Members, appointed for that Purpoſe, by a *Convention* held at Annapolis, June 22*d*, 1784.

TO WHICH IS ADDED

A SERMON,

Preached at the Opening of the ſaid Convention,

BY WILLIAM SMITH, *D. D.* PRESIDENT OF THE SAME.

BALTIMORE:

PRINTED FOR WILLIAM GODDARD.

MDCCLXXXIV.

Hold fast the form of sound Words *which thou hast heard of me in Faith and Love which is in Christ Jesus—That good Thing which was committed unto thee, keep by the Holy Ghost which dwelleth in us.*

For the Time will come when they will not endure sound Doctrine, but after their own Lusts shall heap to themselves Teachers, *having itching Ears, and they shall turn away their Ears from the Truth, and shall be turned unto Fables.*

2 Tim. ch. i. ver. 13, 14,—and ch. iv. ver. 3, 4.

In this very adventurous and inquisitive day, when men spurning their kindred-earth, on which they were born to tread, will dare, on airy (or baloon) wing to soar into the regions of the sky; were it the pleasure of our Almighty Creator to purge any of us mortals of our terrestrial dross, and to place us, in good earnest, upon some distant orb, from which with clear and serene view, corporeal as well as intellectual, we could survey this world of ours—what a strange scene would it appear? Itself, in the rank of worlds, dwindled into a small mole-hill; and men, the little Emmets upon it, bustling and driving and crossing each other, as if there were no settled walk of life, no common tie, or *"Form of sound words to be held fast of all, in faith and love which is in Christ Jesus![")]*

In our intellectual view, from this eminence of station, we should behold one sett of men boasting of the all-sufficient and transcendent power of reason as their rule and guide, yet all wandering through different tracts in the same pursuits of happiness and peace! We should find another sett of men declaring themselves the special favorites of heaven, directed by a glorious inward light, communicated (or as they apprehend, communicated) immediately from the everlasting *fountain of all light*; yet neither should we perceive them to be travelling in the same common way! But, thirdly, we should find another sett of men, and those of truly respectable and venerable name, professing themselves guided only by a *sure and written form of sound words*, revealed and given to them for their instruction and salvation, by their Almighty Creator himself. Yet, alas! they would be seen, perhaps, almost as irregular and eccentric in all their motions as the rest!

This is a sad view of things—and as the poet says—

> In pride, in reasoning pride, the error lies,
> All quit their sphere and rush into the skies!

And would to God, therefore, that, in all religions and in all sciences, this accursed root of bitterness and contrariety could be wholly plucked out. For until humanity and divine charity can have their sway, until our faith is exercised in love, and the truths of GOD are held in righteousness of life, there will never be a total harmony among men!

However strong our reason, however enligtened our souls, however ardent our faith; unless that spirit of love and humanity be in us, which was in CHRIST JESUS, all besides will be of little value.

With good reason, therefore, does St. Paul admonish his beloved Timothy to let his faith be exercised in love, and "to hold fast the *form of sound words* which he had heard of him"; for even in those early days, some had begun to depart from the foundation laid by CHRIST and his apostles; following "vain babblings," being like withered leaves, sticking to the tree, only to be blown away by the first wind of doctrine; still desiring to hear some new thing; led by the ear and not by the heart, or as it is strongly expressed in my text, "heaping to themselves teachers, having itching ears, &c."

A venerable old luminary of our church, soon after the Reformation, preaching even before princes and nobles, has a most severe stroke of irony against this itching humour, according to the honest and indignant (altho perhaps blunt) satyr of the times. It is to the following* effect—

"All is hearing, now a-days—no fruits—the ear is all! and if it were not for our ear-mark, no man could tell we were Christians!"

* This Quotation is made from the strong impression which the sentiment made upon the author's memory, many years ago, on reading over the works of the old *Divines of the Church of England;* and he thinks the words are those of Bishop Andrews. But as the author never made any *Common-Place* of his reading, and composed this sermon, or rather threw it together, on a few hours notice, to suit the occasion on which he was to appear; he cannot be sure that he retains any thing more than the general sentiments of those respectable Divines, upon whose writings and sentiments of orthodoxy, he endeavoured to form himself in his youth, and which he hath never scrupled freely to make use of in his pulpit-compositions. In this sermon he hath fully delivered his sentiments, as to whatever may be pretended new in the divinity of the gospel.

But, if I may pursue the allusion, it is not the ear-mark but the heart-mark, by which at the great day of accounts, we shall be known and acknowledged as belonging to Christ's sheepfold in the other world; nor is it the despising sound doctrine, the following vain fables and still seeking something new, that can denominate us of his flock in this world.

This whole epistle of St. Paul to Timothy (in whose character as a preacher of the gospel he appears peculiarly interested) is intended to stir him up, and all preachers and friends of the gospel after him, to diligence and zeal in maintaining and enforcing its divine truths, against heresies and corruptions.

"I charge thee, before God and the Lord Jesus Christ who shall judge the world at his appearing, and kingdom." And what does he charge in this awful manner? It is a charge which, as it may be drawn from the whole of this epistle, it becomes all the preachers of the gospel of every age and denomination to hear, and (thro' grace) to follow with reverence and awe.

"I charge thee, preach the word"—even the eternal word of truth and salvation by Jesus Christ, or, as he has it a little above—"Stir up the gift of God which is in thee, by the putting on of my hands." Consider thyself as called and separated to this great work of the ministry, according to the true appointment of Christ, "by *the putting on of an apostle's hands.*" Wherefore, "be instant in season and out of season." Let no occasion escape you either in public or private, in times of ease or times of difficulty. Be not dismayed, nor fear the powers of this world; "for God hath not given us the spirit of fear, but of power, of love and of a sound mind"; and therefore, "Reprove, rebuke" —reprove transgression and sin, even tho' cloathed with terror and seated in high places. "Be not ashamed of the testimony of our Lord"; but hold it forth boldly against whatever is at enmity to his cross, and the truth and spirit of his holy religion. Be not weary nor faint in this great work; but, if thereunto called, "Be thou partaker of the afflictions of the gospel, according to the power of God, who hath saved us and called us with an holy calling."

Thus, in all trials and conditions, continue stedfast in the faith of Jesus, and "exhort with all long suffering and [soundness of] doctrine"; leaving the success and issue in the hands of our great Master and Judge—"For the time will come" (when the preaching of the gospel may not have any visible influence on the hearts of many, nay a time) "when they will [not] endure sound doctrine, but after their own lusts shall heap to themselves teachers, having itching ears, and shall turn away their ears from the truth, and shall be turned unto fables."

In these words are described with wonderful majesty and simplicity, the chief obstacles to the success of the preached gospel, and the establishment of the kingdom of JESUS in the hearts of men.

They will not endure sound doctrine. They will not, by faith resign their spirits to the holy influence and direction of the spirit of God. Whatever runs contrary to their carnal and unrenewed affections, they wish to reject; never considering that the gospel of Christ was not intended, by its divine author, to flatter our corrupt lusts, or gratify the irregularities of sense and unsubdued appetite; but to reform the heart and regulate the will; or, as it is more fully and beautifully expressed by our apostle, "to cast down imaginations and every high thing that exalteth itself against the knowledge of God, and to bring into captivity every thought to the obedience of Christ."

Thus it is that men turn away their eyes from the pure light of the gospel, because it would render their darkness visible. They seek to follow the shadow of truth and "cunningly devised fables," in order to stifle their own convictions, and gain a temporary quiet, rather than strive, through the grace offered them, to cast down all vain imaginations, and yield to their great Creator that pure *worship of the heart*, that *evangelical obedience and righteousness of life*, which Christ died to establish; and by which only we can derive true peace and everlasting joy; so true it is (what the scriptures tell us) that where "the gospel is hid, it is hid to them whom the God of this world hath blinded."

This perverseness of temper subsisted in the hearts of men, even before "the glorious gospel of Christ, who is the image of God, shone unto them." Men had then, at least, the light of conscience and natural reason (and one people had also the law and the prophets superadded) as their rule and guide. But these were disregarded by far too many; and when their lives became corrupted, they corrupted their reason, their conscience, their rules of wisdom and religion also; fashioning the whole to their own imaginations, and opening the way to all that ignorance and idolatry, which philosophers and patriarchs, holy men and prophets, patriots and lawgivers, strove in vain to eradicate or destroy. For, as our apostle tells us, God did not leave even the heathen world without a witness in their hearts; because "The invisible things of him from the creation of the world were clearly seen, being [to be] understood by the *things that are made;* namely his *eternal power and godhead*"—visible and speaking in the hearts of men, through his great and gracious *works of creation and Providence!*

But men revolted against the God within them, "and became vain in their imaginations, and their foolish hearts were darkened"; so that professing "themselves to be wise [in their own conceits] they became foolish, and changed the glory of the incorruptible God into an image made like unto corruptible man, and birds and four-footed beasts and creeping things."

The like corruptions (I need not mention it to a Christian audience) are recorded, for our instruction, to have taken place among the Jewish nation, under the law and the prophets. And, alas! how short a time was the gospel of CHRIST received (as we learn from our apostle and other sacred writers) before some who had been baptized into the name of Christ, fell from their faith; "denying the Lord that bought them and through covetousness, with feigned words, making merchandize of souls." From Simon Magus downwards they began to "heap to themselves teachers"; dividing the Christian world with endless disputes and speculations about the form and shadow of religion, neglecting the substance; till, at length, scarce any where could be found that purity of manners, that sanctity of life, that spirit of truth and love, that holy zeal and fortitude, that simplicity and beauty of holiness, which were the glory of primitive Christianity.

It became almost a vain doctrine, that Jesus Christ had come into the world to blot out the hand-writing of ordinances, or nail them to his cross. For in what was then considered as the universal Christian church, the inventions of men were more and more multiplied, and the pure light of the gospel obscured, until at length it was almost wholly overshadowed or hid under an enormous pile of rubbish, and superstition, and pageantry, and will-worship and bodily servitude, more monstrous and burdensome than all the idolatry of the Jews, or even the barbarous rites of the gentiles!

Yet God, of his infinite goodness, in those corrupt ages of the church, did not leave himself wholly without some chosen witnesses;

who contended for the *faith once delivered to the saints*, till at length, after the long night of darkness and error, the day dawned, and the glorious *sun of the gospel* again shone forth under the blessed Reformation; when our fathers, the founders, or rather the restorers, of the church whereof we profess ourselves the members, bore an illustrious part (many of them with the price of their blood) in throwing down the vast fabric of straw and stubble, and building again upon the pure and stable foundation, that *rock of ages which is* CHRIST! True religion again lifted up her radiant head in ours and other reformed churches, who "sought the good old way to walk therein, that so they might find rest to their souls." They turned their hearts to the truth as it is in JESUS, and did not seek to be turned unto fables. For truth is ancient, and whatever any reformers may propose that is altogether new, we may well suspect to be altogether false; the *religion of the gospel* being stamped with this great character of its adoreable author, that it is *the same to day*, *yesterday and for ever!*

But it is a misfortune incident to our imperfect condition in this world, that the best things may be abused. That liberty which is necessary for repelling temporal as well as spiritual bondage—that *freedom of debate and enquiry* which ought to be maintained for the further investigation and dissemination of truth in a liberal, enlightened and philosophic age—all these may be perverted and abused! Even with the broad day-light of the gospel shining round us, and while that church* which was once the great bar to Christian Reformation, is now giving most comfortable and edifying proofs of a contrary temper, and of an enlarged and tolerating spirit (except so far, Alas! as she yet finds it convenient to accommodate religion to worldly purposes)—I say, even amidst this abundance of light and liberty, this general reforming spirit, occasion hath been taken to reform too

* The Rev. Mr. Charles Henry Wharton of Maryland, but late chaplain to the Roman Catholic Society in the city of Worcester in England, has the following truly candid and liberal remark, in a most excellent letter "Stating the motives which induced him to relinquish their communion and become a member of the Protestant church.

"From my own observation I am happy to assure them, that the Roman church in this, as well as in many other particulars, is daily undergoing a silent reformation. The dark monsters of persecution and bigotry are retreating gradually before the light of genuine religion and philosophy. Mankind begins to blush that near fifteen centuries have been necessary to convince them, that humanity and toleration are essential branches of the religion of JESUS!"

much, to fill the world, as of old, with disputes and distinctions totally unessential to Christianity, and destructive of its true spirit, when set in opposition to the *weightier matters of the law*—vital piety and true evangelical obedience.

Thus, too many seem to run a constant round from error to truth, and from truth to error back again—

As if religion were intended
For nothing else—but to be mended;*

—there being scarce a folly of all the ancient corruptions of Christianity, which might not be shown to be now acting over again, by some novel-sect or another of the present day!

How long, alas! how long shall such things be! How long shall circumstantials prevail over essentials, embittering the followers of the lowly Jesus, and "enflaming their breasts with a madness even unto death"?

The first Christians were the admiration of the world for their love and union in their humble and suffering state. And will nothing less than suffering, will not the spirit of the gospel itself, prevail on us to remove this stone of stumbling, to wipe away this reproach of our profession, and to heal our unchristian breaches!

Why should those part on earth, who all wish to meet again in heaven? Although a perfect union in lesser matters may not be attainable, nor perhaps needful, in this world; yet the want of this could never lead to a breach of unity in affection, if men would not lay stress, where God has laid none. Unity of judgment is, indeed, a great ornament of Christianity and needful to its well-being; but unity of affection is essential to its very being and existence, and was the great badge by which Christ declared his disciples should be known. "By this shall all men know that ye are my disciples, if ye love one another." If, therefore, upon every slight notion or apprehension, we cast this badge away, we are none of his.

Those things which he hath declared necessary to our salvation, as might well be expected from so wise and merciful a lawgiver, are so clear as not to be easily mistaken by an honest mind; and they have all this plain mark, that they tend to make men wiser and better;

* Butler.

whereas those things that occasion so much unchristian noise and uncharitable censure in the world, are, for the most part but points of doubtful speculation; in which good men might suffer each other to be at rest, according to that measure of light which they have attained. For why should an agreement in some poor controversial point of faith or doctrine, be set in eminent place above all other virtues or graces, and made the badge of our Christianity? Surely, brethren—and I will repeat it again and again—there is a greater weight of religion in the evangelic grace of charity, in one sigh of *good-will to men*, than in all the doubtful questions about which the Protestant churches have been puzzling themselves, and biting and devouring each other since the days of their Reformation!

Thus to seek our religion in things without us, is to seek the living among the dead. The gospel of Christ teaches far different things. It teaches us to look for God and religion within us;—that we are to be renovated and strengthened by the intellectual touches of his divine spirit upon our spirits;—that we are to "taste and see that he is good," —see with our eyes, hear with our ears and handle with our hands the word of life. And the marks of this gracious state, this experimental knowledge and vital religion will be manifested, not in loud and lofty pretensions to superior knowledge and sanctity; but by the calm spirits of love and good works—in mildness, serenity and resignation of the whole soul to God.

But too many, letting go their hold of the form of sound words, and substituting or mistaking mere mechanical motions—the fervors of heated imagination—for the true and active signs of grace, those living impulses of God on the soul, are often carried into the wildest extravagances. Fetching the marks of their religion from the notions of visionary or mystical men, instead of looking for them in the life and gospel of Christ, they set their passions to work, and at length persuade or terrify themselves into all those experiences and feelings, which pass, in their creed, as the evidences of salvation.

Buoyed up by such strong delusions, they think "they have built their mansions among the stars, have ascended above the moon, and left the sun under their feet"; while they are still but like their kindred-meteors, which having scarce mounted to the middle regions are precipitated downwards again by their own gross and earthly particles! A devotion worked up by fervor, whatever proceeds from the mere force of animal spirits *is of the earth, earthy*; in no manner like to that true spirit of regeneration which is *of the Lord from heaven*, and begets the divine life in the souls of men. This true celestial warmth will never be extinguished, being of an immortal nature; and, when once vitally seated in the heart, it does not work by fits and starts, but expands itself more and more, regulating, purifying and exalting the whole inward man!

It is, indeed, of great importance that we should be grounded in our principles, and adhere to the *form of sound words*, as my text directs us—but we must not stand still at principles or doctrines, but "go on to perfection." Our faith must not be a mere empty assent to the truth, but the *holding the truth in love*. It is love that shews our faith to be genuine. By this it must work, and by this only can God be well pleased. For love flowing from faith is the hand-writing of God on the heart. Whatever proceeds from it will *bear his image and superscription*. He will know it as his own, and openly acknowledge as such, before men and angels, at the last day.

This fruit of love is what St. Paul every where holds up for the *trial of our faith and spirits*. "The fruits of the spirit are love, joy, peace, long-suffering, gentleness, goodness, meekness, temperance and the like!" All other marks of the soundness of our faith, except these gospel-marks, namely *the fruits of the spirit*, are only a dangerous ministration of fuel for inflammable tempers, or of despair to those of a contrary frame.

How think you, brethren, shall the branch of a tree most safely know whether it derives sap from the body and root? Is it by tracing minutely all the vessels and canals thro' which the moisture is ever silently flowing? This would be too intricate a labor—but to find itself covered with leaves, flowers and fruit, leads to a sure conclusion.

Far be it from me to question what may pass on the inner stage of a man's heart; or to deny that God, who pervades and actuates the whole material world with his goodness, should not also delight to influence the world of spirits, and to give *testimony to the souls of men* in every thing well-pleasing to him. This world were a most gloomy scene without the belief of God's active presence and applauding testimony.

My text is love. I would not do violence to my subject. My disposition forbids uncharitable censure—I would judge no man's heart, nor seek to weaken those comfortable workings or experiences which any may apprehend there—But I would warn and exhort all "who think they stand, to take heed lest they fall." And especially, if they think they have ascended high, and skip *like roes on the mountains*, let them remember that the greater their height, the more will it be necessary to have all their own eyes about them. Let them not look down in scorn upon those who walk humbly on through the vale below; lest thereby they miss their own tract, and be precipitated with the greater ruin. Whoever may think to climb up to God, and by immediate vision or illumination to read in his effulgent countenance their own special favor, will (it may be feared) find their wings scorched, their wax melted, and fall down from this towering height of ungrounded persuasion!

Safer far, most surely it is, to discover the conformity of our souls to God's will, through the reflected light of his *written word*. The Lamb's book of life is a great mystery, reserved for himself to open at the last day. Who, then, shall think to open it immediately and read its awful secrets, either concerning himself or others?

All ages have witnessed numerous delusions from this source. The heart of man is very deceitful, and evil will often pass upon us for good; even as Satan, for certain purposes, will sometimes transform himself into an angel of light.

Hence it is that, among men, spiritual pride will assume the guise of extraordinary sanctity; censoriousness will pass for a just reproof of sin; gloomy severity for strictness of conscience; backbiting and busy meddling with the affairs of others, as a zealous concern for their reformation; our own prejudices or hasty conceptions, as improvements in the modes of faith; vain phantasies for divine impulsies; and a fierceness for the particular shibboleths of party, as a zeal for the essentials of Christianity! But, be assured that none of these things have the stamp of JESUS on them. His wisdom begets and teaches far different things. It is the modest, humble, ingenuous, charitable spirit that denominates the true believer; and whenever we see any sect or party of men more closely linked to each other, by their peculiarities of thinking, than the great law of gospel charity can bind them to the *whole houshold of faith*, to all sincere Christians—we may well doubt whether such ties can be of God!

Love and good-will to our fellow-travellers, through this valley of tears to a better country, as it is above all speculative points of belief, so it is the true mark of our own belief. To multiply *matters of faith by human inventions*, and to let our zeal run out in things of this nature, is to weaken charity and to tempt God. It is to be for ever laying foundations, neglecting the superstructure, and forgetting St. Paul's judgment, that *concerning such things we trouble not the brethren*.

We should all be workers together in building up the *body of Christ's church*. But what sort of building must that be where the hearts and tongues of the builders are at variance with each other? Where there is no unity of design, but envyings, strifes and confusions among the workmen? Where some members will attach themselves immoderately to some particular points of faith or doctrine; where they will not bear the whole truth, nor fully ponder the *form of sound words;* where they are full of censure and bitterness; pronouncing even their instructors ignorant or carnal, who labor with all conscience to lay before them the *whole* counsel of God; and desert their stated ordinances, following after cunningly devised fables, and *heaping to themselves teachers having itching ears?*

Can this be the true fruits of the spirit, or tend to the edification, or building up the body of Christ's church? I would speak with great love, but with great plainness too—this may build up the walls of a Babel, but cannot rear up the walls of Jerusalem, which is to be a city of peace, at unity within itself.

Unbelievers, too, receive great triumph at this. In vain do we tell them that "our religion is divine and worthy of all acceptation." Their answer is at hand—"If you would be called the disciples of Christ, shew us that you have the *spirit of Christ dwelling in you*. Shew us the divinity of your religion by its influence on your lives. First be agreed among yourselves what your religion is, before you press it for our acceptance. Were it truly divine, it would be so clear and explicit as not to be easily mistaken by an honest enquirer, nor to admit of the least controversy in points of faith. Would a religion from God kindle the wild-fire of unhallowed zeal, or sanctify wrath, and railings, and persecutions, and frauds, and perjuries, and even murders, to do God service?"

These charges, brethren, have had their answers. For from the abuse against the use there is no conclusion. But the most powerful answer would be *in our own lives as Christians*; bringing our religion down from our heads to our hearts, and following that divine law of love, which is the very spirit of the gospel!

What need I spend more of your time in applying the doctrine of my text to the present occasion of our meeting? an occasion (I will only add) on which if you could be indulged to hear the voice of an apostle or angel from God, he would preach to you—love and unity!

Consider that you are members of a church, which is acknowledged by all the Christian world to teach the doctrine of the gospel, and to hold fast the *form of sound words*, the *faith once delivered to the saints*—a church which has given to the world a long and illustrious list of eminent divines, pious preachers and even glorious confessors and martyrs for the truth as it is in JESUS.

But in this country, at present such is her state, that she calls for the pious assistance and united support of all her true sons, and of the friends of Christianity in general. Besides a famine of the preached word, her sound doctrines are deserted by many, who "turn away their ears from the truth" as taught by her, and heap to themselves teachers as described in the text. But let us leave all such to God and their own consciences—if they have but weighed matters seriously, and have not suffered themselves to be imposed upon by cunningly devised fables—they have a right to follow St. Paul's advice and to be *persuaded in their own mind*. If the kingdom of JESUS be promoted, by whatsoever means and instruments, let us with the same Apostle have joy therein; Some, says he, preach Christ even of envy and strife, supposing to add afflictions to my bonds—notwithstanding this, every way, whether in pretence or truth, CHRIST is preached; and therein do I rejoice, yea, and will rejoice. As to those who profess not to oppose our church, but to be fellow-workers with us in the same great cause, nay, to go beyond us in all godly zeal and holiness—let us be roused by their example and pray them God-speed. A time will come when whatever is intemperate and new-fangled in religion will be done away, or lost and swallowed up in Christian charity; and those who have been tossed upon the ocean of doubt and uncertainty, will again seek for rest and comfort in the bosom of the true church of Christ.

It is not from such that our church receives her chief wounds. It is from the luke-warmness and growing indifference of her own professed members—who are supplied with the word and doctrine, but know not how to value the things that belong to our peace until they are now almost *hid from our eyes!* Any excuse of weather, any worldly avocation of pleasure or profit, any hasty grudge or prejudice against the ministers of religion, will induce many to neglect the worship of their great Creator. Too many more are spoiled or staggered in their faith by what is called the free and philosophic, but more truly, the loose and libertine principles of the present day. Many others, from a selfish and niggardly spirit, or from a dissipation of their substance in luxury and intemperance, will not, or cannot, yield the mite which is necessary for supporting the ordinances of religion. Thus they become ashamed to appear in the place of God's worship, leaving the burden of all upon a few, whose conscience and the awful dread of an account to be given hereafter, will not suffer them to desert their Master's gospel, to renounce their baptism, and trample under foot *the blood of the covenant wherewith they are sanctified.*

Hence religion mourns, and the houses and altars of God, erected by the piety of our forefathers, are deserted and running into ruin. The tempests beat and the winds howl thro' the shattered roofs and mouldering walls of our places of worship; while our burying-grounds and church-yards, the graves, the monuments, and the bones of our fathers, mothers, brothers, sisters, children, and friends, are left open and unprotected from the beasts of the field; as if all our care was only to succeed to the honors, the estates and places of emolument which belonged to our friends and ancestors, without any regard to their memories or venerable ashes!

In the late times of war, distress and confusion, there might be some plea for this reproach of our Christian name; but now, with the blessed prospects of peace, liberty, safety, and future prosperity before us, I trust this reproach will be speedily done away; to which nothing can so eminently contribute as love and union among ourselves joined to a rational and enlightened zeal and public spirit. For, in all our pursuits, we must rest at plain and practical points at last, which are few in number, and in religion come to little more than Solomon found, viz. that "the fear of God and keeping his commandments is the whole duty of man"; or, in all the sciences, what another wise man found as the sum of his enquiries—that

Temperance is the best physic,
Patience the best law,
Charity the best divinity!

O heaven-born charity! what excellent things are spoken of thee! What a transcendent rank was assigned thee, when the Saviour of the world gave thee as the badge of his holy religion; and his inspired apostles enthroned thee as the queen of all Christian virtues, declaring that neither the martyr's zeal, the self-denial of the saint, nor all languages, nor all knowledge, nor any virtue besides, would profit the man any thing who is unadorned with thy sweet cœlestial garb. Christ himself vouchsafed to wear thee as his own garb on earth, and if we expect to be benefited by his death, it must be by following that great law of love, which he enforced with his last words. All other virtues shall have their completion, and be of no service to us beyond our pilgrimage on this earth. But charity thou shalt endure for ever! —Even as some majestic river, when it comes to mix its streams with its parent ocean, needs no further supply from the scanty rills, and tributary fountains which flowed in its course from every mountain-side—so charity, which is now fed and nourished by the streams of faith and hope in this lower world, when it comes to its native heaven shall have no further need of their scanty supply, but shall mix and flow for ever undiminished in the unbounded ocean of the Father's love.

Wherefore then, brethren, put on this most excellent gift of charity. Try the faith that is in you by this great test—Hold fast the form of sound words, the holy scriptures, the pure doctrines, the excellent forms of prayer, praise and thanksgiving, drawn from scripture by our church—hold them fast in faith working by love. Take them for your perfect rule and guide—they will make you wise unto salvation —what ever is imagined more, or beyond scripture—all that is beside final perfection and salvation, count it vain and superfluous. Seek not to be *wise above what is written*, nor establish any vain imaginations of your own for the sure form of sound words. What you have received, hold fast with a fervent and enlightened, but with a holy and charitable, zeal. Add nothing; diminish nothing; but let this lamp of God shine among you till the day-dawn, till the morning of the resurrection, and walk ye in the light of it, not kindling any sparkles of your own to mix with its pure and hallowed lustre.

Let not your best state too much elevate, nor your worst too much depress, you. Whereunto you have attained, walk; yet sit not down with attainments, but forgetting what is behind press still forward, having perfect holiness in your eye and purpose.

"Remember that faith without works is dead. Remember that God commands works, grace establishes them, Christ died to confirm them, the spirit is given to influence them; and that without a holy, humble and peaceable life, we annul the law, abuse the gospel, trample upon grace, frustrate the end of Christ's death, grieve the spirit, dishonor God, and give the lie to our holy profession." If one coming as an apostle or as an angel from heaven were to preach to you any other gospel than you have received, I trust, you would say, let him not be believed.

Thus, with the truth in our heads and love in our hearts; with zeal and public spirit; with a concern for liberty, civil and religious; with industry and economy; with a strict care for the education of youth and their nurture and admonition in the fear of the Lord; this American land shall become a great and glorious empire!

Transported at the thought, I am born into future days! I see this new world rising in her glory, and behold period still brightening upon period. Where depths of gloomy wilderness now extend and shut out even beams of day, I behold polished villas and religious domes spreading around. In places now accustomed only to the yell of savage beasts, or men more savage than they, I hear the voice of happy labor, and behold towery cities growing into the skies. Even the native Indian forgets his wonted rudeness and is patient of the lore of dove-eyed wisdom. His bloody hatchet he buries deep under the ground, and his murderous knife he turns into a pruning hook to lop the tender vine, and teach the luxuriant shoot how to grow.

Hasten, O blessed God, hasten this glorious period of thy son's kingdom which we know shall yet come! And, O ye, who now enjoy the blessed opportunity, be ye the happy means of hastening it. Adorn by your lives the divine doctrines which you profess with your lips, that the heathen and unbeliever, seeing your good works may be the sooner led to glorify your Father who is in heaven!

For this cause, I now bow my knees unto the Father of our Lord Jesus Christ, of whom the whole family in heaven and earth is named, most earnestly beseeching him that he would grant you according to the riches of his glory to be strengthened with might by his spirit in the inner man; that Christ may dwell in your hearts by faith, that ye being rooted and grounded in love, may be able to comprehend with all saints what is the breadth and length and depth and height, and to know the love of Christ, which passeth knowledge, that ye may be filled with all the fullness of God.

Now unto him that is able to do exceeding abundantly above all that you can ask or think, according to the power that worketh in us, unto him be glory in the church, by Christ Jesus, world without end.

FINIS

— 28 —

THE DANGERS OF OUR NATIONAL PROSPERITY; AND THE WAY TO AVOID THEM

Samuel Wales

HARTFORD

1785

Samuel Wales (1748–1794). The son of Reverend John Wales and a classmate at Yale of Nathanael Emmons, Samuel Wales studied theology with Eleazar Wheelock, taught at Wheelock's Indian School at Lebanon Crank, and was licensed to preach by the Plympton, Massachusetts, ministerial association in 1769. He served as a tutor at Yale for a time before accepting the call of the First Congregational Church in Milford, Connecticut, where he remained for eleven years. He resigned this post to accept appointment in 1782 as Livingston Professor of Divinity at Yale, a chair created upon the death of Reverend David Daggett. He was subsequently honored with a D.D. from both Yale and Princeton. Shortly afterward Wales began to suffer from epilepsy, which, from 1786 onward, became steadily worse until he was all but incapacitated. He died at the age of forty-six of burns suffered when he fell into a fire during a seizure. Ezra Stiles described Wales as "eminent for superior abilities, strong mental power, perspicuity & solemnity in pulpit eloquence, for clear and just views of theology, and a most venerable piety." Young David Daggett wrote that "To a genius rarely surpassed for strength and penetration, the embellishments of literature gave peculiar lustre. . . . In the pulpit, his eloquence persuaded—his learning instructed—his reasoning convinced, and his fervour animated. He was the man of God thoroughly furnished unto every good work" (in Dexter, *Yale Biographies and Annals*, 3:260).

The Connecticut election sermon reprinted here, was preached before the General Assembly in Hartford on May 12, 1785, and shows a powerful mind at work.

The Dangers of our national Prosperity; and the Way to avoid them.

A SERMON,

PREACHED BEFORE THE

GENERAL ASSEMBLY

OF THE

STATE OF *CONNECTICUT,*

AT

HARTFORD,

MAY 12th, 1785.

BY SAMUEL WALES, D. D.
PROFESSOR of DIVINITY at YALE-COLLEGE.

Do ye thus requite the LORD, *O foolish people and unwise?* MOSES.

Justice standeth afar off; for truth is fallen in the street, and equity cannot enter. And he that departeth from evil, maketh himself a prey: and the LORD *saw it, and it displeased him.* ISAIAH.

Justum et tenacem propositi virum,
Non civium ardor prava jubentium,
Non vultus instantis tyranni
Mente quatit solida;——
Si fractus illabitur orbis,
Impavidum ferient ruinæ.' HOR.

HARTFORD:
PRINTED BY BARLOW & BABCOCK.
M,DCC,LXXXV.

Beware that thou forget not the Lord thy God, in not keeping his commandments and his judgements and his statutes which I command thee this day:—Lest when thou hast eaten and art full, and hast built goodly houses, and dwelt therein; And when thy herds and thy flocks multiply, and thy silver and thy gold is multiplied, and all that thou hast is multiplied;—Then thine heart be lifted up, and thou forget the Lord thy God which brought thee forth out of the land of Egypt, from the house of bondage.

Deuteronomy VIII. 11, 12, 13, and 14.

These words contain a divine instruction to the people of Israel, respecting their state of prosperity in the promised land. The instruction is not typical or merely local, but of a moral and universal nature. It may therefore with propriety, be applied to all people in every age, whenever they are in a prosperous state. With singular propriety may it be applied to the people of these United States, who, after the severe distresses of unnatural war and civil discord, are now happy in the blessings of peace and plenty. Let me then request the indulgence of this very respectable auditory, while, in order to apply to ourselves the divine caution of our text, I endeavour,

I. To point out some of those evils which, as a people we have reason to fear in our present national prosperity. And then,

II. To exhibit, in a very concise manner, that line of conduct which we ought to pursue, in order to secure through the divine favour the continuance of those blessings which we now enjoy.

A political discussion of these points, it is presumed will not be expected nor desired. It is proposed to consider them especially in a moral and religious view. Indeed never should it be forgotten that all the measures of civil policy ought to be founded on the great principles of religion; or, at the least, to be perfectly consistent with them: otherwise they will never be esteemed, because they will be contrary to that moral sense of right and wrong which God has implanted in the breast of every rational being. But to proceed,

I. Let us attend to some of those evils which, as a people, we have reason especially to fear in our present national prosperity. That we have been and still are greatly blessed with national prosperity, I conceive, will not be doubted. We have been often delivered in a most signal manner, both from the secret stratagems and the open assaults of our enemies. Great is the salvation which heaven hath wrought for us in the full restoration of the blessings of peace. *The Lord hath done great things for us; whereof we are glad.* He hath given us a very extensive country abounding with the richest gifts of nature. With sufficient ease do we procure all the necessaries, together with most of the conveniencies and delicacies of life. Could we procure them with more ease or in greater plenty, we should not be in so desirable a situation as we are now. A proper view of all our various blessings will lead us to conclude that we are indeed the most highly favoured people under heaven. *God hath not dealt so with any other nation.*

But security in happiness is not the lot of humanity. This is equally true of all mankind, whether we consider them as individuals or as united in society. In the midst of all our present publick happiness, dangers surround us and evils hang over our heads.

The greatest evil by which we are endangered, and which indeed is the source of all others, is the want of true religion. It is true, the superior blessings which we enjoy are well calculated to promote religion, to promote each of its essential branches, piety and charity. And such affects would those blessings naturally produce, did we improve them as we ought. But through the perverseness of our nature there is much danger that we shall use them for very different purposes. When we are favoured with a profusion of earthly good, we are exceedingly prone to set our hearts upon it with an immoderate affection, neglecting our bountiful Creator from whom alone all good is derived. We bathe and bury ourselves in the streams, forgetting the fountain whence they flow. This is indeed a very disingenuous behaviour towards the Father of mercies. It certainly discovers a very sordid disposition, a depraved and contracted mind. Such a disposition, however, is but too natural to man in his present degenerate state.

We are much more inclined to murmur at God's justice in adversity than to acknowledge his goodness in prosperity; more ready to view God as the author of evil than as the author of good. In the distresses of the late war, though they were most evidently brought upon us by the instrumentality of men, we were nevertheless much more ready to impute them to the hand of God, than we now are to acknowledge the same hand in the happiness of peace, and the other rich blessings of his providence and grace. When our wants are very pressing, we are willing, or pretend to be willing to apply to God for relief. But no sooner is the relief given than we set our hearts upon the gift, and neglect the giver; or rather make use of his own bounty in order to fight against him. The reason is, because we are more inclined to love the creature than the Creator, to be *lovers of pleasure rather than lovers of God.* On this account, Moses with peculiar emphasis warns the Israelites to stand on their guard against such impiety in the days of their prosperity: *Beware that thou forget not the Lord thy God.*

If we now attend to matters of fact we shall find no reason to think more lightly of the dangers before us. The history of the Israelites shews us that they greatly needed the caution which Moses gave them. Scarcely a prosperous period in their history can be pointed out which was not followed by a decay of piety, and a corruption of morals. This was the case soon after their happy settlement in the land of Canäan. This was the case very frequently in the times of their judges and kings. And this was eminently the case with respect to their highest state of wealth and power under the reign of Solomon. The very great prosperity of this happy reign produced very unhappy effects, even upon that wise king, as well as upon his court, and his subjects. The profligacy of his court may be seen in the history of his life: and that the moral state of his subjects was also exceedingly corrupt, appears from their conduct immediately after his death. Even in the good reign of the pious Hezekiah, ingratitude and irreligion were the consequences of success and prosperity. *Hezekiah rendered not according to the benefit done unto him, for his heart was lifted up; therefore there was wrath upon him, and upon Judah and Jerusalem.** The character of Israel, as drawn in the spirit of prophesy by Moses may, with the utmost propriety, be applied to them in every stage of their prosperity.

> *They have corrupted themselves, their spot is not the spot of his children: they are a perverse and crooked generation. Do ye thus requite the Lord, O foolish people and unwise? is he not thy father that hath bought thee? hath he not made thee and established thee? But Jeshurun waxed fat and kicked, thou art waxen fat, thou art grown thick, thou art covered with fatness; then he forsook God*

* 2 Chron. xxxii. 25.

*which made him, and lightly esteemed the rock of his salvation. They provoked him to jealousy with strange gods, with abominations provoked they him to anger.**

Nor was this pernicious effect of abused prosperity peculiar to the people of Israel. It has, in one degree or another, been common to all people in every age of the world. It has been the case even with the Christian church. The consequences of outward prosperity have been often more fatal to the Christian cause than those of adversity. Indeed the distresses and persecutions of the church have often produced a very happy effect in the advancement of true Christianity. Hence that observation in primitive times: "*The blood of the Martyrs is the seed of the Church.*" But the like happy effect has seldom if ever followed from a state of external peace and opulence. The first great instance of signal prosperity granted to the Christians in the beginning of the fourth century under Constantine the great, was soon followed by a great loss of fervent piety, and a sad corruption both of doctrines and morals. And the same sad effect has followed from many instances of their prosperity in succeeding ages; particularly from the flourishing state of many protestant churches since the grand emancipation from the papal See. Indeed wealth and power have been and still are the great supporters of that *man of sin who opposeth and exalteth himself above all that is called God, or that is worshipped.*

Wealth, with its common attendants, idleness and pleasure, were the ruin of Sodom and Gomorrah. "Behold, this was the iniquity of Sodom, pride, fulness of bread, and abundance of idleness was in her and in her daughters."† These same things were the ruin of mighty Babylon. "*Thou that art given to pleasures*, said the prophet, *that dwellest carelessly, that sayest in thine heart, I am, and none else besides me.*" ‡ In what a striking manner were these words verified in the day of her fall! The same things brought destruction upon each of the four great monarchies, and upon most of the other states and kingdoms which have fallen, one after another in the successive ages of time. And the very same things have proved ruinous to individuals without number. Surely we have no reason to *call the proud, happy*, or to look with a

* Deut. xxxii. 5, 6, 15, 16.

† Ezek. xvi. 49.

‡ Isaiah xlvii. 8.

covetous eye upon the glare of earthly greatness. Misery lies hid beneath it, and destruction is its usual attendant.

Since then a prosperous state has been so often followed with such an effect both on public communities, and on individuals, have we not reason to fear a similar effect from our national prosperity at the present day? Is it not a sad truth, that since the commencement of the late war, and especially since the restoration of peace, the holy religion of Jesus, that brightest ornament of our world, is, by many less regarded than it was before? And are not the sacred institutions of the gospel more neglected and despised? Are not the friends of Christianity treated with more disregard? Are not infidelity and profligacy of manners, viewed with less concern, and by many considered as matters of trivial consequence? Still, we ought with the highest gratitude to acknowledge the sovereign grace of Almighty God, which has, in some places, been manifested in the support of his own cause. In several of our states he has been pleased to excite in the minds of many individuals, here and there, an unusual attention to divine and eternal things. He saw us unpurified by the furnace of affliction: He saw us disregarding him while he spake to us in the whirlwind, the earthquake, and the fire. Yet has he been pleased to speak to us not only by the still voice of peace after war, but also by the omnipotent voice of his holy Spirit; inviting us to become the subjects of the Prince of peace, and making numbers in one place and another, as we trust, the actual possessors of that peace which the world can neither give nor take away. To his great name be all the glory ascribed.

But notwithstanding some pleasing appearances of true religion, in several places, we have too much reason to fear that "the unthinking many" are abusing our present prosperity in such a manner as to produce a very different effect. We have reason to fear that they are fast growing into that state of irreligion which has been noticed already. The symptoms and effects of this evil are already too manifest; and will probably continue and increase unto more ungodliness, unless vigorous measures be taken to prevent them. Some few of these evils which may be called symptoms and effects of irreligion I beg leave particularly to mention.

[1.] In the first place, one of them which we have much reason to lament and fear, is ingratitude, vile ingratitude both to God and to man. During the troubles of the late war, how ardently did we wish for peace? While our lives and liberties were endangered; while our very existence as a nation, was in doubt; while we were threatened with all the horrors of a crushed rebellion and all the vengeance of a very potent enemy peculiarly incensed against us; how eagerly did we long after that independence, that established liberty and national happiness which we now enjoy? We then saw and felt our need of help from God. While the horrid contest was long doubtful, we acknowledged that the issue must be determined by the sovereign disposer of events. At some periods victory and success were so greatly in favour of our enemies, and our own affairs were, in many respects, so exceedingly embarrassed, that the stoutest hearts were almost ready to fail. At some seasons there seemed to be no way left but *to stand still and see the salvation of the Lord.* This salvation we sought of him; nor did we seek in vain. His own arm brought salvation. By a series of the most visible interpositions of his providence, he has made wars to cease thro' the land, and blest us with all that our hearts desired.

But alas! what poor returns have we made to our great Deliverer! Witness our cold hearts and our irreligious lives. How much less inclined are we to return him sincere thanks for these favours now, than we were to ask them of him in the times of our distress? How small are the emotions of gratitude in our hearts, towards the God of all our salvations! And what little honour do we bring to his name by our lives and conversation! With too much propriety may we apply to ourselves these words of the psalmist:

> *When he slew them, they sought him: and they returned and enquired early after God. And they remembered that God was their rock, and the high God their Redeemer. Nevertheless they did flatter him with their mouth and they lied unto him with their tongues. For their heart was not right with him, neither were they stedfast in his covenant.**

Nor have we been guilty of ingratitude towards God only; we have been guilty of the same evil towards man. Although this be a less evil than the former, it is nevertheless an evil which we ought to condemn

* Psalm 78. 34–37.

and reform. We are certainly under great obligations to those who have voluntarily taken an hazardous or an expensive part, in effecting our late happy revolution. They have been, under God, the saviours of our country. They have been instrumental in effecting one of the most happy and interesting events which have taken place in the present age, or in any other. Their merit is certainly great. Yet after all, are they not too much in the situation of the poor wise man, mentioned in sacred writ, who by his wisdom delivered from impending danger, the city in which he dwelt, but was nevertheless soon universally forgotton? Do we give them that praise, that respect, that reward to which they have a just claim? That we have not yet afforded that reward which they justly claim, cannot be denied. This thought leads me to say,

2. That another particular evil into which we have fallen, and by which we are much endangered, is injustice, injustice to the best and most deserving friends of our country. Those are certainly to be esteemed some of the most deserving friends of the country, who have willingly lent her either their lives or their property in the late important struggle. To such persons we are under obligations not only of gratitude but of justice. Their voluntary sacrifices have, through the divine blessing, purchased for us our lives and fortunes, our liberties, our independence, our peace, and in a great measure, all our temporal happiness.

Whether all who thus served their country acted wholly from disinterested views, is a question which we ought not to ask them, and which, with honour, we cannot ask. That many of them acted from the most generous and patriotic motives, cannot be doubted by a candid mind. The least that we can do for them, according to strict justice, is to afford them a reward equal to the full import of our promises. This, however, with regret be it spoken, has not been done. But in lieu of this, many who have generously loaned their property to the country in the season of her most pressing want and danger, have for a long time been unable to obtain a single farthing either of the principle or of the interest, though both have been long justly due.* And whenever any payments of annuities have been

* Since the above was written, the author is happy to find that provision has been lately made for the payment of some part of the interest of our national debt, to which debt he here referred.

attempted, they have been generally, if not universally made in a depreciating medium which immediately annihilated in their hands a very considerable part of its nominal value. In a similar way have we effected most of the payments which have been made to our armies. Indeed as to most of our public securities, there has uniformly been a wide difference between their real and their nominal value. This is a difference which never ought to have existed: a difference manifestly contrary to the nature and claims of justice and truth. And after all, the faithful soldier who has in the face of the greatest discouragements and dangers persevered in the service of his country to the close of the war, receives a very considerable part of his pay in a paper medium which he is obliged to sell or barter for one eighth part of its nominal value, one half quarter only of the value of which he receives it.

Gladly would I draw a veil over this part of our national conduct, were it possible, and could it be done with propriety. But it cannot be done, it ought not to be attempted. The best and wisest thing which we can now do with regard to this matter, is, to reprobate our own conduct and reform it for the future. Let us not pretend any longer to excuse ourselves by promising and promising that we will do justice to our creditors at some distant period of time. Such promises are easily made and commonly of little worth. Nor do they by any means answer the demands of justice provided they should be hereafter fulfilled. For justice requires punctuality with respect to the time of payment as really as with respect to the sum which is due. A failure in the former of these points, is often more pernicious than in the latter. Let us no longer plead inability in our own vindication. I hope indeed this plea may be made in vindication of some of our past deficiences, but I fear it can by no means justify them all. It is, at best, but a very dishonourable plea because it is so often used merely as a mask for injustice, and always can be used in one shape or another by those who are unwilling to pay their debts. As a people, we are not poor, but rich, and have large resources of public revenue. If we are but willing to do justice, and do not needlessly embarrass the hands of government, we shall be under no necessity of defrauding or injuring our creditors. If we cannot immediately pay them the principle of our debt, we can, at least, pay the interest, and thereby at once place our credit on a more respectable footing.

Britain, loaded with a debt more than thirty times so large as ours, and carrying an annual interest larger than our whole debt, nevertheless pays the interest punctually, maintains her credit, and can borrow money from her subjects at pleasure. At the same time her civil list and other annual expences are far greater than ours even in proportion to her wealth, and perhaps greater almost in the same proportion with her national debt.* Whatever difference there may be between her source of revenue and ours, or what ever difference there may be between her and us in any other respect, still with regard to public justice to her creditors, she affords us an example which we ought not to behold without self-condemnation.

Our public injustice is attended with consequences most deplorable and alarming. It exposes us to the high displeasure of that God who from everlasting to everlasting, *loveth righteousness and hateth iniquity.* It tends to render public faith contemptible and is highly injurious to our national character. It gives too much countenance to the reproach of our enemies who have stigmatized us with the character of a knavish, faithless people; covering the most iniquitous designs under the garb of liberty and the cloak of religion. It is hurtful to many literary and religious institutions; while the monies which were charitably given for their support are detained and perverted to a very different purpose. It is attended with great cruelty towards widows and orphans, towards the poor and needy, and many other individuals who have suffered extremely for the want of those monies which are their just due, and to which they have an indisputable claim.

The cries of such persons *enter into the ears of the Lord of Sabaoth.* Is not this unjust detention of property, in a particular manner attended with cruelty to the generous soldier, who has nobly braved fatigues, and dangers, and deaths, for our sake, who has faithfully adhered to our cause while thousands deserted it, while thousands and ten thousands of his brethren perished around him by the horrors of sickness and the sword, and the far greater horrors of British prison-ships, and British jails? Who of us would be willing to endure the like fatigues and be exposed to the like dangers for the contemptible reward which we now afford the soldier? Who would not think him-

* The national debt of Britain is 280 millions sterling, carrying an interest of £9500000. The national debt of the United States is not far from 9 millions in the same money.

self affronted by the very proposal of so small a reward for so great a service [?]

This public injustice destroys some of the most important ends of civil society; such as an equal administration of justice, and the security of property. It involves us in some of the worst evils of tyranny and despotism, while we are flattering ourselves with the pleasing names of liberty and independence. It tends to destroy all confidence in the public, and to create a distrust of government. For if such a flagrant violation of justice may be practised in one instance, how do we know but the like may be practised in many instances; or what one right have we which is properly secured? If the public, as a body, will allow themselves, in any one instance, to injure an individual, every member of the public is in constant danger. For who can tell where the injury will fall next? If one part of our property may be detained from us for a long time, contrary to the plainest promises, without our consent and without any unavoidable necessity; how can we know but that another part may be soon as unjustly wrested from us in the very first instance? In either case the injustice is equally real and equally manifest: and which would be the greater evil of the two, can be determined only by concurrent circumstances. If our property must be taken or detained without our consent, what great choice is there as to the mode, whether it be taken by fraud or by force, whether we be robbed by an highwayman or cheated by a knave? In this latter case we have often the long pain of repeated disappointments, which does not take place in the former.

Further, is it certain that government will never again want the voluntary aid of individuals, aid which she cannot compel them to yield? Should she be again in such a situation what encouragement would individuals have to afford the needed aid? Will they not be ready to fear that all state-policy is founded merely on Machiavelian principles, and that public bodies will practise fraud in order to accomplish their own ends, whenever they can do it with impunity? Honest minds hope that such fears are groundless, and that some public communities at least, as well as some individuals, mean to make justice a rule of conduct. If this be the case, let us make it manifest by our own conduct; if it be not the case, let the truth be known, that faithful citizens and honest men may be no longer deceived and duped out of their property. *Heu pietas, heu publica fides!*

But the most pernicious consequence of our public injustice is still to be mentioned. It has a fatal influence upon the morals of the people at large. It is like the sin of Jereboam the son of Nebat; it makes Israel to sin, and thereby still further provokes the Lord God of Israel to anger. It is a trite observation and a very just one, that example has more influence than precept. And if our public conduct may be adduced by knaves and sharpers, as an example and pretext of injustice, will it not have a greater tendency to promote this evil than all our laws will have to prevent it? Too many are there of that smooth-speaking class of people, who mean to get their living out of others; who, whenever they can run into debt, consider it as so much clear gain; because, forsooth, they can make ample payment by fair promises and soft words, by complaints of the scarcity of money and the hardness of the times. Better payment than this they do not wish to make. *The words of their mouths are smoother than butter, but war is in their heart: Their words are softer than oil, yet are they drawn swords.* To our reproach and our shame, we are already too much inclined to dishonesty. It is already practised by too many to the detriment of the public, and to the ruin of their own true interest both temporal and eternal. Too many motives are there already to this accursed evil, too many are its friends and votaries. For Gods sake let it not have any more. Many even of our religious societies have long conducted as if they thought it no evil to violate the most explicit and solemn covenants with the ministers of religion by withholding from them the stipulated support. If the religious scarcely escape this evil, what may be expected from the ungodly and profane? *There is*, however, *a generation that are pure in their own eyes, and yet is not washed from their filthiness.* Let this wise maxim be remembered by us all, and particularly by those very religious people who make high professions of Christianity, and yet at the same time bid defiance to the plainest rules of justice, and trample under foot the most sacred obligations of truth and plighted faith.

3. Another particular evil by which we are endangered, is the want of true patriotism. By true patriotism I mean a real concern for the welfare of our whole country in general. This patriotism is a branch of that extensive benevolence which is highly recommended by our

holy religion, and is at the same time most evidently consentaneous to the dictates of sound reason. Genuine patriotism of the best kind, is peculiar to those only who are possessed of a principle of true virtue. Some semblances and imitations of this patriotism are nevertheless to be found in those who are not, on the whole, of a truly virtuous character. Yet even these imitations of pure patriotism have often proved very beneficial in civil society.

While the war lasted our patriotism was eminent and produced the most happy effects. Common danger was a common bond of union, cementing us together. But as this bond has now in some measure ceased, there is danger that our union will not be so great as will be necessary for the general good. There is danger not only that factions will arise in particular states, but that particular states will attempt to pursue their own particular interests without a due regard to the common good, and perhaps in direct opposition to it. But we should remember that these states are, by voluntary and solemn agreement united as one nation, one body, of which each particular state is a member. *And the eye cannot say unto the hand, I have no need of thee: nor again the head to the feet, I have no need of you: but the members should have the same care one for another.** It will doubtless be necessary not only that individual persons, but also particular states should often give up, in many cases, their own particular interest for the common benefit. To do thus is generous, is wise, is necessary for our existence as a free and independent people. Some generous examples of this kind have been given, and it is to be hoped they will be universally followed. If we are unwilling to act on this liberal scale we shall be in perpetual danger of that evil which our Saviour points out when he tells us, "*That every kingdom divided against itself cannot stand, but is brought to desolation.*"

It was the want of this extensive patriotism that ruined the states of Greece. A party spirit, a spirit of jealousy and discord prevailed among them, and divisions and wars exposed them for a long time to the invasions of the Persian empire, and finally subjugated them all to the Macedonian yoke.

If the same spirit prevail among us we have no reason to suppose but it will produce the most unhappy consequences. Human nature

* 1 Cor. 12. 21, and 25.

is the same in every age, and similar causes will produce similar effects. In this view we may see how much it concerns us to support our grand bond of union, or, in other words, to maintain the rights of our honourable Congress, and even to enlarge their powers, should this be proved necessary for the general good.

That want of patriotism, of which we speak, produces very different effects in persons who are in different situations of life. It is nearly the same thing with selfishness. It often leads the ambitious and aspiring to seek their own promotion by very improper means. It leads them into a mad pursuit of low popularity, to the violation of honour and honesty and to the neglect of the public good. For not these things, but popular applause and their own advancement in office are the objects of their first concern. And they sometimes have their reward: but a very contemptible one it is. True popularity or the real esteem of the virtuous and the wise, procured by a steady course of benevolent and virtuous conduct, is well worthy of pursuit and is indeed the greatest earthly good that we can enjoy. This popularity is not procured by time-serving, by flattery or any improper compliances. It is seldom if ever gained without a manly opposition, in some cases at least, to popular prejudice and vulgar error. The man who can make it appear that he conscienciously acts from a virtuous principle will command the veneration even of the most unprincipled, and of those who oppose him. But the fame of the popular drudge, that fame which is gained by low arts of deceiving the ignorant and abusing their prejudices, to the public detriment, is not only unworthy of a Christian, but beneath the character of an honest man.

This same selfish spirit, when it possesses the minds of the common people, has this bad consequence, among many others, that it subjects them to an undue influence in the choice of civil rulers. Possessed of this spirit, they will not regard the probity or abilities of the candidates for office; but will be very ready to give their voice for those to whom they happen to be particularly attached by any private and sinister motives; for those by whom they are most humoured in their prejudices and follies; and especially for those who most loudly exclaim against the payment of public debts and most vigorously oppose taxation however just or necessary. All such operations of selfishness; whether in popular demagogues or in the people at large, in whatever shape they appear, tend ultimately to the public detriment and to the encouragement of deceit and dishonesty.

4. A fourth evil by which we are threatened is a disregard of civil authority. Great is our privilege in choosing our own rulers, and, by them, of making and executing our own laws. But this privilege we are in great danger of abusing, for this strange reason, because it is the effect of our own voluntary act. While the people at large are too ready to yield to this temptation, even rulers themselves are in danger of relaxing too far the reigns of government, thro' fear of displeasing the people by whom they are chosen to office. But certain it is that no state can be long happy or even answer the most important ends of civil society, unless government be revered and the law obeyed. Tyranny and despotism are undoubtedly very great evils, but greater still are the dangers of anarchy.

Those persons who have the most power in their own hands are in the greatest danger of abusing it. No people on earth have so much power in their own hands as those of the United States. All the powers of government are at their disposal. We ought therefore to be much on our guard against the abuse of this power. The abuse of this power may perhaps produce tyranny or aristocracy; but the proper use of it will be the best way to prevent them both. Never let us forget that the dignity of government and the energy of the law, are essential to the continuance of our public happiness and prosperity. Reason and experience teach us this lesson, while the more special voice of God enforces the same, by commanding *every soul to be subject to the higher powers.**

5. I will only add once more, in the fifth place, that we are in much danger of the evils which arise from luxury and extravagance in our expences. After all that has been said in favour of foreign trade and foreign luxuries, it still remains a demonstration in politics, that when our imports exceed our exports, the course of trade is against us, and we are constantly growing poor. This, it is to be feared, is our state at the present, especially on account of those very extravagant importations which we have made since the peace. Our very great consumption of foreign luxuries not only impoverishes the

* Rom. 13.1.

country to an high degree, but at the same time, tends directly to enervate both our bodies and our minds, to produce indolence and pride, and to open the door to every temptation and every vice. In this case, as well as many others, experience is a faithful teacher. And if we consult the experience of mankind in every age, and in every part of the world, we shall not find a single instance wherein luxury and extravagance have subserved the true interest of a people. But instances in which they have proved hurtful and ruinous are to be found in abundance. And to republican governments they have proved more fatal than to others. By cultivating industry, frugality, and a patriotic spirit, Rome extended her conquests wherever she pleased, and was revered as the arbitress of kings and the mistress of the world. But by adopting the luxuries of Asia where her arms had proved victorious, she soon enfeebled her true republican spirit and prepared the way for her own ruin. Let not the same scene be again acted over in America. America has by her noble exertions repelled the force of Britain. But if America persists in her present rage after British gew-gaws and foreign luxuries, she must expect the fate of Rome, her ancient predecessor; or at least, that very unhappy consequences will ensue. To prevent these impending evils we need the exertions not only of the sons, but also of the daughters of America. Very great are your influence and importance, my fair hearers, in this respect, as well as in many others. Be assured that oeconomy and frugality with an elegance of dress, on the plan of that modest apparel recommended by St. Peter, would add more grace to your charms and more dignity to your characters than all the tinsel of British ornament, or the greatest extravagance of foreign dress.

II. It now remains that we exhibit, in a very concise manner that line of conduct which we ought to pursue in order to secure, through the divine favour, the continuence of those blessings which at the present we enjoy.

In the first place, it is, I conceive, sufficiently evident that we ought most earnestly to endeavour after a reformation of those particular evils aforementioned, and at the same time, to use the best means in order to prevent them for the future. We must first *cease to do evil* or we shall never *learn to do well.*

In the second place we must use our best endeavours to promote the practice of virtue and true religion.

I will not indeed presume to assert, that God's conduct towards nations under the gospel, is exactly parallel to his conduct towards the ancient Israelites. They were under a dispensation of grace different from ours, and, for a long time under that peculiar kind of civil government which has been called a theocracy. National blessings are not promised, and national judgements are not threatened under the gospel in like manner as they were under the law. The gospel being a more spiritual dispensation, its blessings and its curses are of a more spiritual nature, and less obvious to the view of the world. They are designed, in a special manner, to prepare persons for the more full retributions of eternity. This we know is the case with regard to the blessings conferred, and the chastisements inflicted on the children of God. And that this is also the case with regard to the judgements inflicted on the man of sin and his followers, we are expressly told: *God shall send them strong delusion, that they should believe a lie: that they all might be damned.** Still, this is certain, that by the constitution of nature which God has established, vice tends to the misery, and virtue to the happiness not only of individuals, but of public communities. The practice of religion must therefore be considered as absolutely essential to the best state of public prosperity, it must be so, unless we may expect happiness in direct opposition to the constitution of nature and of nature's God. "*Righteousness exalteth a nation: but sin is a reproach to any people.*"† This is the course of nature, this is the voice of heaven, this is the decree of God.

In the third place, we ought especially in the use of all proper means, to pray fervently for the effusions of the divine Spirit.

Without a divine and supernatural influence, true religion will never prevail. This is a doctrine clearly taught in divine revelation and perfectly consonant to the dictates of reason. It has been taught even by heathen philosophers, such as Socrates and Plato, Cicero and Seneca. It has been acknowledged, in one shape or another, in every nation and in every age. Indeed it may be considered as a doctrine of natural religion. Nor is there any thing enthusiastical or unreasonable in this doctrine, any more than there is in that other great doctrine of natural religion "*That in God we live and move and have our being.*" Di-

* 2 Thes. 2. 11, 12.

† Prov. [xiv. 34.]

vine influence is absolutely necessary both in the natural and in the moral world. All creatures of every kind, from the most exalted seraph before the eternal throne, to the smallest animal which escapes our sight, are wholly dependent on God. Our souls and all their powers are in his hand, and he can form and incline them at his pleasure, in full consistency with our most perfect freedom of action.

That divine influence which is necessary in order to a pious life we are taught to expect from the operations of the third person in the holy Trinity. We cannot therefore do a more faithful or important service for our country than to pray fervently and perseveringly to the Father of mercies, that he would by the energy of the Holy Ghost, form the hearts of this people to an holy life, and thus "*Purify unto himself a peculiar people, zealous of good works.*"*

In the review of our subject, I think we may justly make this reflection: Let us not flatter ourselves too much with an idea of the future prosperity and glory of these United States.

While we thus flatter ourselves, we are in danger of expecting the end without a proper attention to those means which are absolutely necessary in order to obtain it. Young states are like young men; exceedingly apt, in imagination, to anticipate and magnify future scenes of happiness and grandeur, which perhaps they will never enjoy. It has lately become very fashionable to prophesy about the future greatness of this country; its astonishing progress in science, in wealth, in population and grandeur: to tell of Lockes and Newtons, of poets, philosophers and divines greater than have ever yet lived; of towering spires, and spacious domes, of populous towns and cities rising thick throughout an empire greater than the world has ever seen. Such representations may perhaps be beautiful in poetry and declamation, but cannot with equal propriety be admitted, in an unqualified sense, into serious and didactic prose. And true indeed it is, Providence has here laid a foundation for a very flourishing and mighty empire. But although the foundation is laid, the superstructure is not yet finished, nor ever will be, unless we use the proper means. And whether we shall use such means or not, is a matter of very great uncertainty. Foundations for happiness have been often laid where happiness has never followed. This is no less true of states

* Tit. ii. 14.

and kingdoms than of individual persons. It is remarkable that many places which were in ancient times, the seats of mighty states and empires, and might perhaps have continued with increasing greatness to the present time, had proper means been used, are nevertheless now covered with ruin and desolation, or at best, in a very depressed and miserable condition. What is become of Nineveh and Babylon, and those mighty empires of which they were the capital cities? What is become of Persepolis, of Antioch, of Jerusalem, of Carthage, of Athens and Sparta? And how wide is the difference between ancient and modern Rome? Had the inhabitants of such places, from age to age, known the things of their peace and pursued them, their glory might have remained to the present day.

If we abuse the signal favours which God has granted us, we have no right to expect that he will favour us in the like manner for the future. Although it be possible we may be a flourishing and happy people, it is equally possible we may be far otherwise. When we have reached the pinnacle of our hopes, it is often connected with evils far greater than the loss of that envied height would have been. *The fashion of this world passeth away.* The greatest worldly good is often succeeded by the greatest evil; the greatest happiness by the greatest misery. Who would have thought, after the happy establishment of peace between France and Britain, twenty years ago, that the late war between Britain and America, with all its attending horrors, could possibly have taken place so soon?

When *God gave Israel their request, but sent leanness into their souls,** these two things, taken in their connexion, were the greatest curse that could have befallen them. When Jephthah had ended a successful war against the children of Ammon, and thereby become the saviour of his country, he seemed to have gained the whole desire of his heart, even all that happiness for which he had most ardently wished. But this same event which made him so happy a man was closely connected with two sore evils which came nearer to his heart and more sensibly affected him, than all his former concerns respecting the Ammonites. It was connected with the mournful affair respecting his only child, and it was the occasion of a very bloody civil war in which, beside others, forty and two thousand Ephraimites were slain

* Psalm cvi. 15.

with the sword. And thus, as in ten thousand similar instances, the occasion of his greatest happiness was turned into the occasion of his greatest misery.

So, although we have gained that for which we most ardently wished, an happy period to the late war, yet we can by no means be certain but that some far greater evils are now before us. We may be over-run and ruined both for time and eternity by a torrent of vice and licenciousness, with their never-failing attendants, infidelity and atheism. We may be left to destroy ourselves by intestine divisions and civil wars: or we may be visited with such sickness and pestilence as would soon produce a far greater destruction than any war of what kind soever. God has many ways, even in the present world, to punish the sins both of individuals and of nations. He has ten thousand arrows in his quiver, and can always direct any or all of them unerring, to the victims of his wrath. No possible concurrence of circumstances can screen us from the notice of his eye or the power of his hand. Never, never, can we be secure but in the practice of true virtue and in the favour of God.

From long and general custom, it will, I conceive, be expected that I do not close this discourse without some of those addresses which have been usual on the present occasion.

In the first place, I beg leave, with great veneration to address myself to his Excellency our governor and commander in chief.

May it please your Excellency,

It is with great pleasure we behold you at the helm of government in this sovereign and independent state. While we sympathize with you under the burdens and difficulties of your very important station, we cannot but congratulate you on a variety of circumstances which are peculiarly satisfactory. Highly honourable, in many respects, is the office which your Excellency fills with so much honour. Much dignity is derived to it from its high importance and extensive utility. It has been rendered honourable by a long succession of worthy and eminent characters, who have filled it from one time to another, and particularly by that very illustrious and immortal character, your immediate predecessor in office. Great is the honour of having a place in such a succession as this, and much greater still the honour of appearing in it, as your Excellency does, with a venerable dignity. Connecticut can boast of a number of her sons in the vigour of life, who are equal to the first offices in government. Yet, by the suffrages of a free and discerning people, your Excellency, though far advanced in life, has been raised to the first chair of government. A greater mark of esteem could not have been given; an equal one, probably never was given by this state or by any other.

Very great is the public esteem for those abilities with which the fountain of wisdom has endowed you, and for that large store of knowledge which you have acquired from a most extensive reading in the various branches both of civil and sacred science. And yet all good men rejoice that you are thus highly esteemed, not merely for your natural or acquired endowments, but more especially for the moral virtues and your sacred regard for the religion of Jesus. May your singular piety and wisdom, your extensive influence and most excellent example, contribute much to prevent those public evils by which we are endangered. This effect in some good measure they have already had, God grant they may have, in a still greater degree, the same happy effect for the future.

We cannot but view your Excellency as a Moses, a Joshua or a Samuel, giving the most important instructions at the close of a most useful life. With painful apprehension of our great loss, and yet with joy in the prospect of your far more exceeding gain, we view you as an Elijah ready to mount the fiery car and ascend to your native heaven, followed with the most eager exclamations of your country: "my father, my father, the chariot of Israel and the horsemen thereof."* Whenever that time shall come, mournful to us but joyful to you, may a double portion of your spirit descend and rest upon your successors in office and upon all our civil rulers. May your Excellency have, both while with us and when taken from us, all the peace and joy of that holy religion to which you have so devoutly adhered. May the God of all consolation be your support through life and your portion forever. Amen.

May I now be permitted to turn my address, with great respect, to the other branches of our honourable legislature; to his Honour the lieutenant governor, the honourable assistant counsellors, and the very respectable representatives of the people.

* 2 Kings ii. 12.

May it please your Honours and the gentlemen of the other house of assembly.

While prosperity is dangerous to a people in general, it is peculiarly so to those who are elevated above the common walks of life. Honour, power and wealth are attended with strong temptations, temptations which in most instances have proved too powerful for man. Indeed they have been and always will be too powerful for him, unless when he calls in foreign aid, even the aid of almighty grace. They who are possessed of these worldly goods, those envied distinctions, it is to be feared, often have their portion in this life only, and are therefore of all men the most miserable. Hence that ancient objection against the Saviour when here on earth, "Have any of the rulers, or of the Pharisees believed on him?"* Hence his own proverbial observation: "It is easier for a camel to go through the eye of a needle, than for a rich man to enter into the kingdom of God."† Hence his question to the Jews: "How can ye believe, which receive honour one of another, and seek not the honour that cometh from God only?"‡ Hence we read of those among the chief rulers who, in spite of conviction, refused to confess Christ, because "They loved the praise of men more than the praise of God."§ Hence the observation of St. Paul: "Not many wise men after the flesh, not many mighty, not many noble are called." (1) But although we thus speak in order *to stir up your pure minds by way of remembrance*, yet we hope better things of you, venerable fathers, things which accompany salvation, and things which have a favourable aspect, both on our civil and on our religious concerns.

Singularly happy has Connecticut been, even from the beginning, in a legislature friendly not only to civil liberty but also to true religion. And this most excellent character, we trust, may with propriety be applied to this present honourable assembly. May your public measures and your whole conduct, be a demonstrative proof that our hopes are well founded.

In a particular manner, may your vigourous exertions be directed

* John vii. 48.
† Mat. xix. 24.
‡ John v. 44.
§ John xii. 43.
(1) 1 Cor. i. 26.

against those evils by which we are threatened in our present prosperous situation. More especially, may such measures be adopted as shall be well calculated to restore public faith, and to free this state, so far as possible, from the crying guilt of public injustice, which will otherwise be our reproach and perhaps our ruin. In the name of all honest men, let me presume to entreat you, honoured fathers, that such measures be not neglected. *The God of Israel said, the Rock of Israel spake to me, He that ruleth over men must be just, ruling in the fear of God.** The measures necessary to the exercise of public justice will accord with the judgement of all wise politicians as well as with the judgement of God and of all good men. Such measures may possibly be burdensome, in some degree to the people. But weak or wicked we must have been if we ever hoped to gain the glorious prize of independence, without bearing burdens and particularly a very considerable burden of expence. The prize which we have gained, well improved, will infinitely more than counterbalance all the expences we have borne or ever need to bear. Every honest man will gladly bear his proportion of such burdens, rather than to transgress the eternal law of righteousness and truth. Every man who has the smallest pretensions to honour or spirit, will willingly bear his proportion, rather than to be guilty of the meanness, the baseness of cruelly defrauding the most faithful servants of the public, in order to save an inconsiderable expence to himself. Every man who is unwilling to forward those measures which are necessary in order to the exercise of public justice, ought to lie under the imputation of shameful ignorance or a more shameful dishonesty. After all, such measures may perhaps through the weakness of human nature, be unpopular with many and meet with opposition. But should they be opposed by multitudes numerous as the army of Xerxes or the more numerous future armies of Gog and Magog, still, while engaged in the cause of righteousness, we may say as the prophet did when he and his servant were surrounded by a mighty Syrian host: "*Fear not; for they that be with us are more than they that be with them.*" All the hosts of the Lord in heaven and on earth will support us, while the Lord of hosts himself will be on our side. "*For the righteous Lord loveth righteousness, his countenance doth behold the upright.*" He has given the strongest evidence

* 2 Sam. xxiii. 3.

in his word and in his works, particularly in the great work of redemption, given the strongest evidence of his unalterable determination to support the cause of righteousness and truth. Righteousness will finally prevail over iniquity, and truth over falsehood. Indeed were we designed only for the present world, even then the practice of justice and the other moral virtues, would undoubtedly be the safest and the happiest course not only for individuals but for states and kingdoms.

In the executive department of government, it is greatly to be wished not only that impartial justice may be administered, but that it be done with dispatch and with as little expence as may be consistent with the dignity of government. Unhappy indeed is the case when a legal process is attended with such expence, delay and other embarrassments that one had better lose his just dues than to recover them by a course of law. Not a few instances of this kind have taken place. Can no measures be adopted which may serve to remedy so great an evil?

The university of this state, the education of youth and the advancement of literature, are kindred objects of such immense importance, that it is presumed they will not pass unnoticed by this honourable assembly. May you, honoured fathers, in your great wisdom and benevolence, adopt such measures with regard to each of them as shall be worthy of yourselves and most conducive to the true interest of the public. And may all your measures be such as shall evince to the world that you are not only our worthy and faithful civil fathers, but also that you are, at the same time, acting in a far more amiable and honourable character, even that of *nursing fathers to the church of Christ.*

I now beg the patience of this auditory, while, with the most effectionate esteem and reverence, I address myself to my fathers and brethren in the sacred character.

Reverend and worthy sirs,

Although Christ's kingdom is not of this world, yet is it perfectly friendly to civil government. It requires us to obey and honour civil rulers, and to conduct ourselves as peaceable and useful subjects of the state. By serving God and your generation in this way, much good may be done, and much has been done by the members of your venerable order. Great was your influence and great your merit in producing the late glorious revolution. And although by the temporary losses which most of you have sustained during the arduous conflict and even to the present day, you have doubtless borne more than your equal proportion of the expences of the war, yet will this burden be considered as trifling when compared with the peace of a good conscience and the salvation of your country.

Your virtuous exertions are now again greatly needed in preventing those evils with which we are threatened in our present prosperous state. No order of men have equal advantages with you, to warn the people against the encroachments of power on the one hand, and the evils of anarchy on the other; and at the same time to instruct them in all those various duties which they owe to civil rulers and to their country.

Let us however, never forget that civil and secular affairs ought to be viewed by us as matters of no more than a secondary consideration. The weightier matters of the law and the gospel ought always to engage our chief attention, our highest concern.

We are ambassadors for God to a revolted world. In the guilt and wretchedness of this revolt, we ourselves are personally involved. Jesus in extremest agonies both of body and soul, has died for our salvation. He has gone into heaven to prepare mansions of glory for his faithful followers. Hell from beneath is moving to receive the despisers of his grace. Satan and the powers of darkness, in conjunction with the world and the flesh, are plotting the destruction of men. The people of our charge are daily passing the vale of death and receiving the retributions of eternity. The eye of omniscience is continually upon us. *He who walketh in the midst of the gold candlesticks and holdeth the stars in his right hand*, hath said, "*All the churches shall know that I am he which searcheth the reins and hearts: and I will give unto every one of you according to your works.*" *We watch for souls as those who must give an account:* If unfaithful, an aggravated doom will be our portion: if faithful, *we are unto God a sweet favour of Christ in them that are saved and in them that perish. And who is sufficient for these things? What manner of persons then, ought we to be in all holy conversation and godliness?* With what fervour and fidelity ought we to preach the pure doctrines of the gospel and the unsearchable riches of Christ? Death will soon put an end to our labours. Let us be animated by the promised presence of our great Lord and Master and by his voice which now speaks to each one of us in particular, saying "Be thou faithful unto death, and I will give thee a crown of life." Amen.

Let me now conclude with one word to this whole numerous and respectable auditory.

Fellow citizens and fellow Christians,

Great are the benefits of good government. But let us not imagine that these benefits are to be expected by us, unless, as a people and as individuals, we are willing to perform those duties which we owe to our civil rulers and to the public in general. Unspeakably great are the blessings of the gospel. But let us not imagine that ministers or churches or any power whatever can force these blessings upon us without our consent. They are not, they cannot be ours unless we live as the gospel directs.

We are happy in being now met together in this large assembly and on this great occasion. But before the next return of this anniversary, how many, who are now here, will belong to the great congregation of the dead, and be fixed unalterably in their eternal state! Who, where, now in this assembly are the persons thus destined so soon to another world? Perhaps none more likely than the person speaking, were we to form our judgement from apparent symptoms. But if this be the case with him, he is not alone. Others will also travel with him the same dark road of death. And what one individual here present can say that he is not one of this number? Are we all prepared for our eternal state? In that state we shall all soon be found, while other busy mortals, like our ourselves, will take our places on this stage of life. And never, never shall we all meet together again, till we meet with the assembled universe before the tribunal of our final Judge.

The God of all grace enable us so to live that we may, at that solemn period, be found on the right hand of our Judge, and, by the sentence of his mouth, have our portion assigned us with a far greater and more glorious assembly than the present; even with *the general assembly and church of the first born which are written in heaven; with the spirits of just men made perfect, with an innumerable company of angels, with Jesus the Mediator of the new covenant and with God the Judge of all. Blessing and honour and glory and power be unto him that sitteth on the throne and unto the Lamb, forever and ever.*

A M E N

29

A SERMON ON A DAY APPOINTED FOR PUBLICK THANKSGIVING

Joseph Lathrop

SPRINGFIELD
1787

Joseph Lathrop (1731–1820). Born in Norwich, Connecticut, and a graduate of Yale College (1754), Lathrop spent his life as pastor of the Congregational Church in West Springfield, Massachusetts, where he died at the age of eighty-nine. A liberal Calvinist and a fellow of the American Academy of Arts and Sciences, Lathrop was honored with S.T.D. degrees from Yale in 1791 and Harvard in 1811. He published more sermons than any Yale graduate before him (F.B. Dexter lists forty-nine published items in *Biographical Sketches of the Graduates of Yale College*, 2:335–43). Lathrop was one of the eminent preachers of his day. His secret, a contemporary said, lay in his "ability, beyond almost any man, of saying the best things, at the most fitting time, in the most graceful and effective manner. . . . His strength lay not in any one predominant quality, but in the harmonious blending of all" (Ibid., 335).

A

S E R M O N,

REACHED IN THE

FIRST PARISH *in* WEST-SPRINGFIELD,

DECEMBER 14, MDCCLXXXVI,

Being the DAY appointed by AUTHORITY [illegible]

PUBLICK THANKSGIVING.

By *JOSEPH LATHROP*, A. M.

Publiſhed at the general *deſire of the hearers.*

PRINTED *by* JOHN RUSSELL, AT HIS OFFICE,
IN SPRINGFIELD.
MDCCLXXXVII.

If ye be willing and obedient, ye shall eat the good of the land: But if ye refuse and rebel, ye shall be devoured with the sword; for the mouth of the Lord hath spoken it.

Isaiah I. 19,20.

What was spoken by the prophets to the ancient people of God, is written for our use, that we, through the warnings of scripture, might be moved with fear; and, through the comforts of scripture, might have hope.

Our relation to God, as a people redeemed by his hand and preserved by his care, as a people enjoying his oracles and professing obedience to his laws, is so similar to theirs, that we may justly apply to ourselves what was here spoken to them. I shall therefore consider my text in accommodation to our own case: and shall observe,

I. That the land, in which we are placed, is a good land: and,

II. That our enjoyment of the good of the land depends on our obedience to God.

I. It may as truly be said of us, as of ancient Israel, that God has given us a good land.

We lately thought it worth defending by our arms: it is still worth securing by our virtue.

It is an extensive land. Few empires on the globe are so large, as the territory claimed by these states. It will admit a vast increase of numbers; and probably distant generations will not find themselves straitened for room.

It is a pleasant and fruitful land. As it lies in the midst of the temperate regions, no part of it is afflicted with intolerable heat, or rendered uninhabitable by eternal frosts and snows. With proper culture it yields us, not only the necessaries, but the delicacies of life, in such plenty and variety, that we need to be but little indebted to foreign trade.

Greater industry may be necessary here, than in some other climes: but this is no unfavourable circumstance; for industry contributes to health, virtue, freedom and security.

With regard to commerce, nature has given us every advantage that can be wished. We have an extensive coast, convenient harbours, navigable bays and rivers, materials of all kinds for shipping, a rich and inexhaustible fishery, and a variety of exportable produce, which may be exchanged for the riches of other climes. Late experience shews, that we are in greater danger from the excess, than from the want of commerce. Moderate trade contributes to polish and enrich a people; but when it is carried beyond its proper limits, it produces contrary effects, dissipation, poverty and vice.

This is a healthful land. Those direful pestilences, which have ravaged other countries, are unknown here. A considerable proportion of the people live to old age; fewer die in infancy than in most European nations: Our natural increase is supposed to double our numbers as often as once in twenty five years.

It is a land of liberty, and has been so, with little interruption, from the days of our fathers.

The royal charters first granted to the American colonies, particularly to those of New-England, were of the most liberal kind, and fully agreeable to their views and wishes. No attempts hitherto made, to subvert our liberties, has been successful. They will probably be preserved, until the people themselves, sunk in vice and corruption, destroy them with their own hands. How near we are to this fatal period, heaven knows!

The freedom of these colonies was first invaded by James II, who, with a design to establish an absolute monarchy, seized their charters, together with those of the corporations in England. But by the revolution, which took place on the accession of the prince of Orange to the throne, the freedom both of Britain and America was restored and established.

The late encroachments of the British court on our charter-rights awakened a just and general concern. Though we were but an infant people, and our enemies were an ancient, rich and powerful nation, we ventured to resist their claims; and, by a series of wonderful interpositions, our resistance defeated their designs, and terminated in the establishment of our independence.

We are now under a government of our own framing and chusing. There is perhaps scarcely another instance of the kind on earth. It is a privilege, which few nations ever enjoy, and which the same nation probably can never enjoy more than once.

Many of the governments, now subsisting in the world, were established by the conquering arms of a powerful invader; some were introduced by the usurpation of princes; others have been fixed in consequence of a civil war, in which one part prevailing has by arms given law to the rest. Governments, which owe their existence to such a birth, must, you know, in their very nature, be tyrannies. The British constitution was settled in a more liberal manner, by an explicit compact between the king, the hereditary nobles and the representatives of the people; and it is undoubtedly more favourable to liberty, than most other forms of government in Europe. But the constitution of these states, and particularly of this, was framed and ratified in a manner still more liberal. It is not, in any sense whatever, a compact between the rulers and the people; but it is a solemn, explicit agreement of the people among themselves. It was constructed by a convention of wise men, whom the people deputed solely for that purpose, and who, at that time, could have no share, and no appearance of a future share in the government they were framing. It was then remitted to the people at large, and competent time allowed for their deliberate examination and discussion; and it was finally adopted and confirmed in consequence of their general approbation. So happily was it adjusted to the views of the people, at a time when the spirit of liberty was at the height, that not a single article was found in the whole, but what met the approbation of more than two thirds of the inhabitants assembled in the several towns to give their voices upon it. It is therefore, in the most absolute sense, *the constitution of the people;* and, in this view, it is more sacred than any form of government in Europe. Being framed by the people, it never ought to be changed or altered without their general consent fairly asked, and freely given. There may undoubtedly be defects in it: nothing human is perfect: but still it is our own; not imposed, but chosen. And whatever imperfections attend it, yet it is acknowledged by all, to be formed on the highest principles of liberty. The administration of it is committed to men appointed by, and from among ourselves; to men who are frequently to return to private life; to men who are subject to the same laws and burthens, which they impose on their fellow citizens. The people have it in their power always to influence the measures of government by petition and instructions, and often to change their rulers by new elections. Nations, whose government is absolute, may be under the sad necessity of submitting to oppression, or of repelling it by force. This is a dreadful alternative, and usually terminates in the increase of the evil. We are under no such necessity. Our government is so constituted, that publick oppressions may be soon removed without force, either by remonstrances against the measures of rulers, or by a change of the rulers themselves.

You will ask, "What if our new-chosen rulers pursue the measures of the former?" In this case candour will lead us to suspect, that possibly they may judge better than we. If their measures meet with general approbation, the few who are dissatisfied, must submit, until, by speaking and publishing their sentiments, they can given general conviction. If we should ever be so unhappy as to fall under a succession of wicked rulers, we must censure our ill choice. We have still wise and good men among us. If the time should come, when there is not a man to be found, who will execute judgment, and seek the truth, how will God pardon us for this! Nothing, but immediate reformation, can prevent the fatal consequences of such woful depravity. These follow by a divine establishment, and it is not in the power of human government to guard against them.

Perhaps it will be asked, "Is there no case in which a people may resist government?" Yes, there is one such case; and that is, when rulers usurp a power oppressive to the people, and continue to support it by military force in contempt of every respectful remonstrance. In this case the body of the people have a natural right to unite their strength for the restoration of their own constitutional government. And, for the same reason, if a part of the people attempt by arms to controul or subvert the government, the rulers, who are the guardians of the constitution, have a right to call in the aid of the people to protect it. If the people may use force to suppress an armed usurpation of unconstitutional authority, rulers may, on the same principle, use force to suppress an armed insurrection against constitutional authority.

Civil liberty is a very valuable blessing. It was the professed object of the late dangerous war. It is secured to us, as far as success in the prosecution of the war, wisdom in the settlement of the peace, and deliberation in framing our government, could secure it. Our own virtue and prudence, under providence, must do the rest.

This is a land, not only of civil, but religious liberty. The enjoyment of gospel-privileges was a grand motive with our ancestors to enterprise on emigration to this distant world. They brought with them the sacred scriptures, early formed churches for divine worship, diligently instructed their children in the knowledge of religion, erected private schools for their education, and, as soon as the abilities of the country would permit, they established larger seminaries, in which youth might be trained up for publick employments, especially for the ministry, that this important office might not become useless and contemptible by falling into the hands of illiterate men. Care was taken to secure to the churches the privilege of chusing their own teachers, and of worshipping God according to the dictates of their own consciences; a privilege which these churches now possess in the amplest manner, and which is happily confirmed by the civil government under which we are placed. In consequence of the pious zeal of our fathers, we still, through the divine goodness, enjoy the gospel of the Redeemer, and the offers and means of eternal salvation. The word of God is dispensed, his ordinances administered, his sabbaths continued, churches are maintained and religious worship preserved in them, and, we have reason to hope, that the gracious influences of the divine spirit, are not wholly withdrawn, but are still vouchsafed to render the gospel successful.

Is any thing now wanting to make this a good land? Nothing but our own virtue and wisdom in improvement of these advantages.

This thought naturally introduces our other observation,

II. That our enjoyment of the good of this land depends on our obedience to God.

External advantages, without wisdom and virtue to apply them, will make neither a people, nor a person happy. A man, surrounded with all the means of wealth, will be indigent, if he knows not how to use them. One possessed of the amplest fortune, without a capacity to enjoy it, will suffer all the miseries of real poverty. The best natural constitution of body will soon be ruined by excessive indulgence. So a people, blest with all imaginable circumstances of national felicity, may be enslaved, and even destroyed by their own vices and follies.

There is a connection between virtue and happiness; between vice and wretchedness, in social as well as private life. From the justice and goodness of the supreme Governour, we may naturally conclude, that he will protect and prosper a virtuous people, while he leaves corrupt and irreclaimable nations to suffer the fatal effects of their own perverseness. This natural conclusion from the divine character is confirmed by the declarations of scripture, and the usual course of providence. The threatning and the promise in our text are most explicit and peremptory; and to give them the greater solemnity, it is added, *The mouth of the Lord hath spoken them.*

It will be proper for us particularly to consider, what those virtues are, on which our national happiness principally depends.

1. The first thing that here meets our thoughts is internal peace and union.

Can a man be happy, whose breast is the seat of contending passions? Can a family prosper, whose members continually oppose and counteract each other? Can the harvests of your fields stand secure amidst a war of conflicting elements? No more can a nation flourish, while it is distracted with intestine broils. "Every kingdom divided against itself is bro't to desolation." A small people united will be strong and respectable: the largest community broken and disjointed becomes impotent and contemptible. It was our union in the late war, that gave us strength to bear up against the power of a superiour enemy. Had we been divided, we must have fallen. The union, which was necessary to an effectual defence, is still necessary to our enjoying the good of the land.

It is not uncommon, that when the burthens arising from a long war press hard on a people, and the terrour of the invading enemy, which for a while animated and united them, is intirely removed, they lose their patriotick zeal, and fall into dangerous contentions. This is an event which our enemies predicted for us; which our friends forewarned us of, and which, to our disgrace, we now begin to realize.

Whatever oppressions we suffer, or seem to suffer, our measures of redress must be only such, as may consist with our internal peace; for being divided against ourselves, we shall become an easy prey to foreign invaders; or rather, shall fall a contemptible prey to one another. Contentions, once begun, may proceed to, we know not what, dreadful lengths; and may terminate in, we know not what, direful events. While, with a watchful eye we guard against every real invasion of our rights, we must place a reasonable confidence in our rulers, and study and pursue the things which contribute to peace, both in our smaller societies, and in the community at large.

A general distrust is inconsistent with government and subversive of all security. Confidence joined with circumspection tends both to peace and liberty. Let not Ephraim envy Judah, nor Judah vex Ephraim, and their common adversaries will be removed.

2. In order to our enjoying the good of the land, there must be mutual justice and benevolence.

These are necessary to internal peace, and branches of the obedience recommended in the text. *Seek judgment, relieve the oppressed, plead for the widow.*

Our first obligation to mankind is justice. This is rendering to all their dues, in opposition to every kind of fraud, oppression and violence. The great law, which ought to govern our social conduct, is *to do to others, as we would, that they should do to us; to owe no man any thing, but to love one another.* This law, written in the heart, will prompt us to the voluntary exercise of equity, integrity and righteousness. It is the want of this, that makes the coercion of human government so absolutely necessary to the subsistence of society. "The law is made for the lawless." Every man can easily judge of himself what is right, by asking his own heart, what, in a similar case, he would expect from another.

Our next obligation is goodness. The poor we have always with us: and there are times when their number is increased. The late war, as might naturally be expected, has made a considerable change of property. It has reduced many to absolute poverty, and others to an incapacity of sustaining any great share of the common burthen without leaving their families to want. Government, at such a time, ought to adjust their demands to the common ability; and this, we hope, is their aim, for they bear a part of the burthen with others. But it should be considered, that the general rules, by which the measures of government must be directed, will often operate with some inequality. This is an unavoidable imperfection of human society. In such cases, instead of charging government with cruelty, it would be proper for the more strong to assist the weak. *Bear ye one another's burthens*, says the law of Christ. The law of reason says the same.

No community ought to leave her prudent and industrious members to struggle in vain under an insupportable load. By mutual succour in times of distress we increase the common strength. Reciprocal support and protection is one end of society. "Two are better than one, for if they fall, the one will lift up his fellow; but wo to him that is alone when he falleth, for he hath not another to help him up. And if one prevail against him, two shall withstand him, and a threefold cord is not quickly broken."

A community, in which an opposite spirit prevails, cannot be happy. Mutual fraud, injustice and oppression cause perpetual animosities, and frequent litigations, discourage industry and enterprize, destroy all confidence, and obstruct every measure proposed for the common good.

3. The happiness of a people farther depends on industry and frugality.

This, though a good land, will not support us in idleness and profuseness. If it would, it must soon cease to be a good land. In a country, where every man could grow rich with little labour, almost every man would in fact be poor; for there being no spur to industry and few examples of it, the body of the people would sink into idleness, luxury and wretchedness. All the wealth, and all the power would be engrossed by the provident and enterprizing few. The rest would be slaves, or little superiour.

At a time like this, when the expenses, incurred by the late contest for independence, are lying as a burthen on the country, diligence in our callings, and prudence in our manner of living, are of peculiar importance. While the object of the war appeared precarious, we thought no sacrifice too great to obtain it. Since we have obtained it, let us submit to some self-denial, that we may secure it. Tho' our burthens are heavy, yet we may hope, that by those smiles of heaven, which will always attend a virtuous people, we shall soon, in a way of prudence and industry, find relief: without these, miracles could not make us happy. Idleness and luxury brings on poverty; this multiplies the temptations to injustice; injustice breeds contention, and this makes confusion and every evil work.

4. Our enjoyment of the good of the land will depend on the regular administration of, and a peaceable submission to civil government.

Mankind cannot subsist without society, nor society without government. If there was no way to controul the selfishness, check the passions and restrain the vices of men, they would soon become intolerable to each other. Government is the combination of the whole community against the vices of each member. The design of it is not meerly to provide for general defence against foreign power, but to exercise a controul over every individual, to restrain him from wrong, and compel him to right, so far as the common safety requires. The best form of government will not make a people happy, without a just administration of it, and cheerful obedience to it; and both these very much depend on the virtue of the people. We must commit the administration of our government to our wisest and best men: not to those, whom we would not dare to trust in our private affairs; but to those, whose known ability and integrity intitle them to our confidence; for "he that is faithful in the least, is faithful also in much; and he that is unjust in the least, is unjust also in much."

Will you think a man capable of being a patriot whom you see to be dishonest, unfaithful, dissolute, and profane? You may as well judge him a saint. As well may your charity send him to heaven, as your prudence prefer him to be a leader in the affairs of state. We must also contribute our aid to carry into effect the good laws of the state, especially those which relate to virtue and morals. If we discover errours, we must endeavour to rectify them; but let us not, under pretence of redressing wrongs, destroy what is right; nor in our zeal to amend the state, forget to amend ourselves. The more virtue there is among the people, the more there will be among rulers, because better men will be elected to power; and they, who are elected, will be more strongly influenced to a right use of their power. If we indulge in ourselves the faults that we condemn in rulers; if, while we complain of publick oppression or profuseness, we are prodigal in our expenses, or unjust to our neighbours, we are grossly inconsistent. We shew, how government would be administred, if it was committed to our hands.

Zealous for a good government, let us be zealous of good works, maintain them ourselves, encourage them among others, and, as far as our influence extends, give efficacy to wholesome laws, that they may be a terrour to evil doers and a protection to them who do well.

5. Another thing necessary to our national happiness is a *diligent attendance on the instituted means of religion.*

The gospel inculcates those virtues, which immediately conduce to publick felicity, such as peace, justice, charity, industry and temperance; and therefore our attendance on its institutions, which are designed for the promotion of these virtues, is a principal mean of national prosperity. The observance of sabbaths and of social worship is, in this view, of vast importance to society, and of still higher importance to each individual in regard to his future salvation. It much concerns us therefore as members of civil society, and more as christians, to maintain the publick dispensation of God's word and ordinances, to attend on it ourselves and encourage the attendance of others, and to be likeminded one toward another, that we may with one mind and one mouth glorify God.

6. As we wish to transmit to our children the goodness of our land, we must train them up in such a manner, that they may be capable of enjoying it.

We have generally professed, that the happiness of posterity, rather than our own, was our object in the late war. This was our language, "The present generation will suffer much in the conflict; but we cannot be reconciled to the prospect of leaving our children slaves. *We* suffer to purchase freedom for *them*? The war has ended as successfully as we wished, and we have suffered no more than we professed to exert. If the good of posterity was our aim, let us not lose sight of it now. Let us educate them in knowledge and virtue, and teach them to be willing and obedient, that they may eat the good of the land. What benefit will all our labours and sufferings in the cause of liberty transmit to them, if we leave them to grow up slaves to their own lusts and to the evil manners of the world, and thus to bring down on themselves the fatal judgments of an angry Deity?["]

Political liberty depends on national virtue. Prevailing vice sooner or later introduces national slavery. Under almost any form of government a virtuous people will be free and happy. But a people sunk in corruption must be wretched. Their government, however liberal in its principles, will be severe in its administration, because they can subsist under no other. If we would convey to our children the greatest possible freedom, we must train them up in virtuous sentiments and manners.

Having illustrated the observations contained in the text, let us now seriously apply them.

We see what obligations we are under to God for his goodness to our nation; and how we may enjoy the continuance of his goodness.

He has placed us in a land of health, plenty, freedom and gospel light; defended us in the enjoyment of our privileges; prospered us in a dangerous war; granted the sweet return of peace; allowed us the independence which we sought; settled us under a government of our own chusing; given us abundance of health; made the seasons peculiarly favourable for several years, and especially in the year past, and smiled on all the labours of our hands.

It becomes us, under a thoughtful sense of his great goodness, to praise and exalt his name, and to resolve that our future conduct shall be correspondent with our present professions of gratitude. "They who offer praise glorify God,["] and to them who order their conversation aright, "he will shew his salvation."

Let us, as becomes a people professing their dependence on God, deeply humble ourselves for our sins. One principal design of his goodness is, to lead us to repentance.

Let the restoration of peace, after a bloody and distressing war, influence us to peace and union among ourselves. How provoking, in the sight of the God of peace, would be intestine divisions and animosities, after such recent experience of the calamities of war, and of the divine goodness in our deliverance! Would he not be angry with us, till he had consumed us?

Let the bounty of our divine Benefactor, in supplying our various wants, excite us to do good to the needy. The best expression of gratitude to God, is an imitation of his beneficence. We are to offer the sacrifice of praise continually, and especially to do good and communicate, for with such sacrifices he is best pleased.

Let us use the bounties of his providence with temperance and moderation. This is a moral duty at all times; it is a political duty at such a time as this. As christians we are required to be temperate in all things, and with quietness to work the thing that is good, that we may eat our own bread, and have to give to those who need. As members of society we are now under additional obligations to industry and sobriety, that we may relieve ourselves and our country from the peculiar burthens of the day, and may enjoy the good of the land.

Let us remember our obligations to God for continuing to us his glorious gospel, and pray for its general success, and for a divine power to accompany it in our own souls.

Let us attend on the instituted worship of God, cultivate peace in the religious societies of which we are members, and avoid all such divisions as tend to obstruct the influence of the gospel and to defeat the end for which churches are formed.

Let us bring up our children in the knowledge, and inculcate on them the duties of religion, teaching them to deny ungodliness and worldly lusts, and to live soberly, righteously and piously in the world, and thus to look for the blessed hope which the gospel sets before them.

Worldly prosperity, however desireable, is not an object of the first importance. We are soon to quit this mortal state; let us be chiefly solicitous to secure a title to a better country.

We have here no continuing city. In a few days we shall make our final remove, and another set of mortals will succeed in our places. Every year makes considerable changes; a few years produce vast alterations in the inhabitants of this dying world. Though the past year has been generally healthful, yet the number of deaths in this society has been greater than usual.

God's providence utters a warning voice to people of every age.

Children and youths are solemnly warned of their mortality, and urged to give an immediate attention to their everlasting concerns. Let this day, be with you, my children, not a day of thoughtless levity, wanton mirth and wild dissipation; but a day of serious recollection, fervent prayer, and humble dedication of yourselves to God. While you praise him for his goodness in preserving you another year, repent of the sins and follies of the year past, consecrate your spared lives to his service and enter on a speedy preparation for the changes, that may await you in the year to come.

Heads of families, and persons in the midst of life, are taught the uncertainty of their continuance here. While the death of a neighbour and friend awakens in our minds a grateful remembrance of God's sparing mercy to us and our families, let it also impress us with a sense of the changes to which we are exposed, and excite a serious concern to maintain religion in our hearts, and promote it in our houses.

The aged have been repeatedly warned. My fathers, a greater number of your contemporaries have been removed in the year past, than has been common in preceding years. God's voice to you is, *Be ye also ready*. You stand on the borders of the eternal world. Soon you must go the way, whence you will not return. Within the ensuing year, it is probable, some of your small number will make their last remove. You ought to examine your state, to be instant in prayer, to live in the daily exercise of faith and piety, and by a holy and blameless example recommend religion to those who are coming after you. May you, and may we all, when the time of our departure is come, be able to rejoice in the reflection, that we have finished our course well, and in the hope that there is laid up for us a crown of righteousness.

This, though on many accounts a day of rejoiceing, is, in other respects, a day of danger and darkness.

The general indifference to the instituted ordinances of the gospel, threatens the discontinuance of them; the prevalence of wickedness forbodes divine judgments; and our civil commotions and disturbances give cause to apprehend a troublous scene approaching. Should they spread and prevail so far as to involve the state in a civil war, what have we to expect as the consequences, but general poverty, bondage and wretchedness?

That the people are under great burthens, all are agreed. Whether there are grievances, I leave with others to determine. Admitting there are, undoubtedly there may be methods of redress more safe, and more effectual than arms. If any of you have thought this a necessary measure, I only ask, that you would calmly review what I have said on the nature of our government, and seriously consider what may be the consequences of drawing the sword; and possibly you will see reason to alter your sentiments.

I have spoken with freedom, because I am anxious for my country; and without fear of offending, because I know the candour of my audience.

Let us all be solicitous to prove what is acceptable with God. Let us study the wisdom which is pure and peaceable, full of mercy and good fruits. Let us humbly implore the interposition of that being, who has all events, and all hearts in his hand, to avert the evils that threaten us, to awaken our drowsy hearts to a sense of the importance of religion, to lead us to repentance and amendment of life, to prepare us for his mercies and make us a happy people.

30

THE DIGNITY OF MAN

Nathanael Emmons

PROVIDENCE

1787

Nathanael Emmons (1745–1840). The youngest of twelve children, Emmons lived nearly a century and spent fifty-five of those years as pastor of the Congregational Church in Franklin, Massachusetts, on the border of Rhode Island. He was a Yale graduate and studied theology with various ministers, including Nathan Strong and John Smalley. Given to tobacco-chewing, he was "a plump little man, with a squeaky voice, and a sharp tongue." But despite his unimposing appearance, he was a superb preacher and an educator of over one hundred other preachers. His sermons were marked by their intellectual pungency, and he summed up the art of preaching in the axiom: "Have something to say; say it." He was a deeply committed Calvinist, a fervent patriot during the Revolution, and a Federalist afterward. Sensing diabolical significance in the rise of the Jeffersonian Republicans to power, he preached his noted "Jeroboam" sermon, comparing the new President to the man "who made Israel sin."

A cardinal figure in the rise of a "New Divinity" following Jonathan Edwards the elder, Emmons ranks in this respect with Samuel Hopkins, Joseph Bellamy, and Jonathan Edwards the younger. Emmons's theories grappled with Edwards's doctrine of the will and came down to a single proposition: "the divine influence upon the heart, in producing volitions, does not imply compulsion on the part of God, nor destroy liberty on the part of man" (*Works* [1861], 6:712). Bruce Kuklick, in *Churchmen and Philosophers: From Jonathan Edwards to John Dewey* (Yale, 1985), observed: "The New Divinity and the [American Founders'] philosophy of the state shared the vocabulary of republicanism" (p. 60).

THE DIGNITY OF MAN.

A

DISCOURSE

Addreſſed to the Congregation in

FRANKLIN,

Upon the Occaſion of their receiving from

Dr. FRANKLIN,

The Mark of his Reſpect, in a rich

DONATION OF BOOKS,

Appropriated to the Uſe of a

PARISH-LIBRARY.

BY *NATHANAEL EMMONS,*
PASTOR OF THE CHURCH IN FRANKLIN.

PROVIDENCE:
PRINTED BY BENNETT WHEELER, IN
WESTMINSTER-STREET.

Shew thyself a Man.

1 Kings 2.2

David closed the scene of life, with that propriety of conduct, and that composure of mind, which at once displayed the beauty of religion, and the dignity of human nature. When the time of his departure drew nigh, he had nothing to do to prepare for death, but only, like other pious and illustrious patriarchs, to converse with his friends, and to give them his last and best advice. And, as he had, some time before, committed to Solomon the care of his family and government of his kingdom; so he felt a strong and ardent desire, that this beloved son, in whom he had reposed such important trusts, should appear with dignity, and act a noble and worthy part upon the stage of life. Accordingly he called him into his presence, and with equal solemnity and affection, addressed him in these memorable words, "I go the way of all the earth: be thou strong therefore, and shew thyself a man." This appellation sometimes signifies the dignity, and sometimes the meanness of our nature. Job makes use of it to express our meanness and turpitude in the sight of God. "How can man be justified with God? or how can he be clean that is born of a woman? Behold, even to the moon and it shineth not, yea the stars are not pure in his sight. How much less man that is a worm, and the Son of Man which is a worm." But Isaiah employs this same appellative to represent the dignity of human nature, when he calls upon stupid idolaters to "remember this, and shew themselves men." So here, David in his dying address to Solomon, "shew thyself a man," evidently means to use the term in the best sense, and to urge him to act up to the dignity of his nature, and the end of his being.

Agreeably therefore to the spirit and intention of the text, the subject which now properly lies before us, is the dignity of man. And, I hope, the observations which shall be made upon this subject, will do honour to our nature in one view, and pour contempt upon it in another, and so lead us all into a clear and just apprehension of ourselves, which is the most useful, as well as the most rare and high attainment in knowledge.

The dignity of man appears from his bearing the image of his Maker. After God had created the heavens and the earth, and furnished the world with a rich profusion of vegetive and sensitive natures, he was pleased to form a more noble and intelligent creature, to bear his image, and to be the lord of this lower creation. "And God said, Let us make man in our image, after our likeness. And the Lord God formed man of the dust of the ground, and breathed into his nostrils the breath of life; and man became a living soul." This allows us to say, that man is the offspring of God, a ray from the fountain of light, a drop from the ocean of intelligence. Though, man, since the fall, comes into the world destitute of the moral image of God, yet, in the very frame and constitution of his nature, he still bears the natural image of his Maker. His soul is a transcript of the natural perfections of the Deity. God is a spirit, and so is the soul of man; God is intelligence and activity, and so is the soul of man. In a word, man is the living image of the living God, in whom is displayed more of the divine nature and glory, than in all the works and creatures of God upon earth. Agreeably therefore to the dignity of his nature, God hath placed him at the head of the world, and given him the dominion over all his works. Hence says the Psalmist, "Thou hast made him a little lower than the angels, and hast crowned him with glory and honour. Thou madest him to have dominion over the works of thy hands; thou hast put all things under his feet: all sheep and oxen, yea the beasts of the field; the fowls of the air; and the fish of the sea." How wide is the kingdom of man! how numerous his subjects! how great his dignity!

God has, besides, instamped a dignity upon man by giving him not only a rational, but an immortal existence. The soul, which is properly the man, shall survive the body and live forever. This might be argued from the nature, the capacity, and the desires of the human mind, and from the authority of the wiser heathens, who have generally supposed the soul to be a spiritual and immortal principle in man. But, since the heathen moralists might derive their opinion from a higher source than the light of nature, and since every created object necessarily and solely depends, for continued existence, upon the will of the Creator; we choose to rest the evidence of this point upon the authority of the sacred oracles. Here indeed we find the immortality of the soul sufficiently established. Solomon saith, "Who knoweth the spirit of man that goeth upward, and the spirit of the beast that goeth downward to the earth?" And, in another place, after describing the frailty and mortality of the body, he adds, "Then shall the dust return to the earth as it was, and the spirit shall return unto God who gave it." Agreeably to this, our Lord declares that men are able to kill the body, but are not able to kill the soul. And God has told us that he will, at the last day, separate the righteous from the wicked, and fix the latter in a miserable, but the former in a blessed immortality. Hence immortality appears to be the common property and dignity of the human kind.

The creatures and objects, with which we are now surrounded, have but a short and momentary being. One species of insects, we are told, begin and end their existence in twenty-four hours. Others live and flutter a few hours longer, and then drop into their primitive dust. The larger animals, which people the air, the earth, and the sea do, day after day, in a thick and constant succession, die and dissolve in their own elements. And even the whole material system will, after a few ages, either by the immediate hand of God, or by the gradual operation of the laws of nature, be rolled together as a scroll, and tumbled into one vast and promiscuous ruin. But we shall survive all these ruins and ravages of time, and live the constant spectators of the successive scenes of eternity. And this renders us infinitely superior, in point of dignity and importance, to all the objects and creatures, whose existence expires with time.

The dignity of man also appears, from the great attention and regard, which God hath paid to him. God indeed takes care of all his creatures, and his tender mercies are over all his works: but man has always been the favorite child of Providence. God, before he brought him into being, provided a large and beautiful world for his habitation; and ever since the day of his creation, he has commanded all nature to contribute to his support and happiness. For his good, he has appointed the sun to rule the day, and the moon to rule the night. Into his bosom, he has ordered the earth and the sea to pour all their rich and copious blessings. And for his use and comfort, he has given the fowls of the mountains, the beasts of the forests, and the cattle upon a thousand hills. He has also given his angels charge over him, to keep him in all his ways. Accordingly they have appeared from time to time, to instruct him in duty, to deliver him from danger, to bring him good tidings, to attend his dissolution, and to convey his departing spirit to the mansions of rest. But, the most distinguishing and most astonishing display of the divine mercy, is the incarnation and death of the Son of God for the salvation of man. By the incarnation of Christ, our nature was united with the divine, and the dignity of man with the dignity of Christ. Hence all the sufferings, which Christ hath endured on earth, and all the honours, which he hath received in heaven, have displayed the dignity of man. And for the same reason, the dignity of man will be eternally rising, with the rising honour and dignity of Christ.

But, we must furthermore observe, that the large and noble capacities of the human mind, set the dignity of our nature in the clearest and strongest light. Let us therefore consider, in this place, several of these with particular attention.

First, man hath a capacity for constant and perpetual progression in knowledge. Animals, indeed, appear to have some small degree of knowledge. "The ox knoweth his owner, and the ass his master's crib." But, as all the lower species are destitute of the power of reasoning, or the faculty of arranging and comparing their ideas; so they are totally incapable of enlarging their views, by intellectual improvements. The bee cannot improve her skill, nor the ant her prudence, by observation or study. All their knowledge is the mere gift of God, which he bestows upon them without any application or exertion of theirs.

But, man is capable of improving in knowledge as long as he enjoys the means or materials of improvement. Indeed he has power to improve the smallest stock forever. The faculty of reason, with which he is endowed, enables him to proceed from one degree of knowledge to another, in a constant and endless progression. The grounds of this are obvious. As a certain chain, or connection runs through all branches of knowledge; so the acquisition of one degree of knowledge facilitates the acquisition of another, and the more a man knows, the more he is capable of knowing. And, as all the powers and faculties of the mind brighten and expand by exercise; so a man's capacity for improvement increases, as the means and thirst for improvements increase. Accordingly the path of knowledge, has resembled the path of the just, which shineth more and more unto the perfect day. One generation have been improving upon another, from age to age. And the improvements and discoveries of the last and present century are truly surprizing, and justify this grand and bold description,

Earth's disembowell'd, measured are the skies,
Stars are detected in their deep recess,
Creation widens, vanquish'd nature yields,
Her secrets are extorted, art prevails.
What monuments of genius, spirit, pow'r!

But to show that reality in this case surpasses description, let me here mention Solomon, that great man, who is addressed in our text, and whose astonishing improvements in knowledge are recorded by the pen of inspiration, for the encouragement, as well as the instruction of all future ages. "And Solomon's wisdom excelled the wisdom of the east country, and all the wisdom of Egypt. For he was wiser than all men: than Ethan the Ezrahite, and Heman, and Chalcol, and Darda, the sons of Mahol: and his fame was in all nations round about. And he spake three thousand proverbs, and his songs were a thousand and five. And he spake of trees, from the cedar-tree that is in Lebanon, even unto the hyssop that springeth out of the wall: he spake also of beasts, and of fowls, and of creeping things, and of fishes." The children of the east country were the Chaldeans, who, after the flood, made the first advances in astronomy, philosophy and other abstruse sciences. Next to them the Egyptians turned their attention to learning, and soon outrivalled all other nations in literary fame. Solomon therefore surpassed all the priests and poets, all the physicians and historians, and all the naturalists, philosophers, and astronomers of the two most antient, and most refined nations in the world. What an exalted idea does this exhibit of his wisdom and learning! And, as we must suppose that he made these improvements by reading, by observation, and study; so he stands a lasting ornament of human nature, and a perpetual monument of man's capacity for constant and endless advances in knowledge.

Secondly, man hath a capacity for holiness as well as knowledge. The horse and mule which have no understanding, and indeed all the lower animals, are utterly incapable of holiness; and even omnipotence himself, to speak with reverence, cannot make them holy, without essentially altering the frame and constitution of their natures. But man is capable of holiness. His rational and moral faculties both capacitate and oblige him to be holy. His perception and volition, in connection with his reason and conscience, enable him to discern and feel the right and wrong of actions, and the beauty and deformity of characters. This renders him capable of doing justly, loving mercy, and walking humbly with God. In a word, this renders him capable of every holy and virtuous affection. And, as he is capable of growing in knowledge, so he is capable of growing in grace, in a constant and endless progression. What a dignity does this give to man, and how near does it place him to principalities and powers above! This leads me to observe,

Thirdly, that man hath a capacity for happiness, equal to his capacity for holiness and knowledge. Knowledge and holiness are the grand pillars which support all true and substantial happiness; which invariably rises or falls, accordingly as these are either stronger or weaker. Knowledge and holiness in the Deity are the source of all his happiness. Angels rise in felicity as they rise in holiness and knowledge. And saints here below grow in happiness as they grow in grace, and in the knowledge of holy and divine objects. Of this, we have a beautiful and striking instance in Solomon. View him at the dedication of the Temple, when he fell upon his knees, and lifted up his hands and his heart to God, and poured into the ear of the divine Majesty the voice of prayer and supplication, the voice of joy, of gratitude and praise. How near did he approach to God! how high did he rise in felicity! how much did he anticipate the joys of the blessed! And, if we now follow him to the Temple above, where his views, his affections, and his joys are incessantly enlarging; we may form some faint conception of that amazing height, to which man is capable of rising in pure and divine enjoyments. What a vessel of honour and dignity will man appear, when all his capacities for knowledge, for holiness, and for happiness, shall be completely filled! And to all this we must add,

Fourthly, that man hath a capacity for great and noble actions. Of this, we might find numerous monuments, if we had time to survey the land of Shinar, where Babel, Babylon, and Ninevah stood; or the land of Egypt, where so many grand and costly pyramids, tombs, and temples were erected; or the famous cities of Greece and of Rome, where the nobler efforts of human power and genius, have been still more amply displayed. But, the bounds of this discourse will allow us only to mention a few individuals of our race, who, by their great and noble exertions, have done honour to human nature.

Noah, the second father of mankind, saved the world from total extinction. Joseph preserved two nations from temporal ruin. Moses delivered the people of God from the house of bondage, and led them through hosts of enemies and seas of blood to the land of promise. David settled the kingdom of Israel in peace; and Solomon raised it to the summit of national glory. Paul, in spite of pagan superstition, laws and learning, established Christianity in the heathen world. Luther, by the tongue and pen of controversy, brought about a great and glorious revolution in the christian church. Newton, by his discoveries in the material, and Locke, by his discoveries in the intellectual world, have enlarged the boundaries of human knowledge, and of human happiness. And, to name no more, Franklin in the cabinet, and Washington in the field, have given independence and peace to America. But greater things than these remain to be done. The kingdom of Antichrist is to be destroyed, the Mahomedans are to be subdued, the Jews are to be restored, the barbarous nations are to be civilized, the gospel is to be preached to all nations, and the whole face of things in this world, is to be beautifully and gloriously changed. These things are to be done by the instrumentality of man. And by these, his capacity for great and noble actions, will be still more illustriously displayed. Thus the image, which man bears of his Maker, the immortal spirit which resides with him, the distinguishing favours, which he has received from the Father of mercies, and all his noble powers and faculties, unite to stamp a dignity upon his nature, and raise him high in the scale of being.

It now remains to make a few deductions from the subject, and to apply it to the happy occasion of our present meeting.

First, we may justly infer from the nature and dignity of man, that we are under indispensible obligations to religion. Our moral obligations to religion are interwoven with the first principles of our nature. Our minds are so framed, that we are capable of knowing, of loving, and of serving our Creator; and this lays us under moral obligation to worship and obey him. Nor is there one of our race, who is incapable of feeling his moral obligations to religion. Only draw the character of the Supreme Being, and describe his power, wisdom, goodness, justice, and mercy, before the most ignorant and uncultivated savage; and, as soon as he understands the character of God, he will feel that he ought, that he is morally obliged to love and obey the great Parent of all. He will feel himself under the same moral obligation to pay religious homage to God, as to speak the truth, or to do justice to man. Every man in the world is capable of seeing that the worship of God is a reasonable service. Religion therefore takes its rise and obligation not from the laws of politicians, nor from the ignorance and superstition of priests; but from the immutable laws of nature, and the frame and constitution of the human mind. Hence it is utterly impossible for men wholly to eradicate from their minds all sense of moral obligation to religion, so long as they remain moral agents, and are possessed of common sense.

And, as man is formed for religion, so religion is the ornament and perfection of his nature. The man of religion is, in every supposable situation, the man of dignity. Pain, poverty, misfortune, sickness and death, may indeed veil, but they cannot destroy his dignity, which sometimes shines with more resplendent glory, under all these ills and clouds of life. While the soul is in health and prosperity; while the mind is warmed with holy and religious affections, the man appears with dignity, whether he is in pain, or in sickness, or even in the agonies of death. But, atheism and infidelity, with their evil offspring, serve more than all other causes put together, to defile the nature, and sink the dignity of man. This appears from the black description, which the great apostle Paul has drawn of those nations, who *liked not to retain God in their knowledge*. "They changed the glory of the uncorruptible God into an image made like to corruptible man, and to birds, and to four-footed beasts, and creeping things. They changed the truth of God into a lie, and worshipped and served the creature more than the Creator. They dishonoured their own bodies by the most mean and infamous vices. And they became of a reprobate mind, being filled with all unrighteousness, fornication, covetousness, maliciousness; full of envy, murder, debate, deceit, malignity; whisperers, backbiters, haters of God, despiteful, proud, boasters, inventors of evil things, disobedient to parents, without understanding, covenant-breakers, without natural affection, implacable, unmerciful." These are things which defile the nature, and degrade the dignity of man.

And these too are prejudicial to all learning and mental improvements. These debilitate the mind, cloud the imagination, and cramp all the noble powers and faculties of the soul. These degraded the

Alexanders, the Pompeys, and the Cæsars of the world, below the human kind. Had they been influenced by truly virtuous and religious motives, their great exertions would have done honour to human nature, but now they have stained the glory of all flesh. Nay, even a declension in religion hath left indelible stains upon the brightest characters recorded in sacred story; I mean Noah, David, and Solomon. Solomon was at the height of his glory, when at the height of religion; but when he declined into vice and idolatry, he fell into shame and disgrace, and lost that dignity, which had filled the world with his fame.

Now there is nothing that can wipe off from human nature these blemishes, and restore the dignity of man, but true religion. That charity which seeketh not her own, that love which is the fulfilling of the law, is the essence of religion and the bond of perfection. This cures the mind of atheism, infidelity and vice. This fills the soul with noble views and sentiments, and directs all its powers and faculties to their proper use and end. This exalts the dignity of human nature, and spreads the greatest glory around any human character. This rendered Noah superior to Nimrod, Moses superior to Pharaoh, David superior to Saul, Solomon superior to Socrates, Daniel superior to the wise men of Babylon, and Paul superior to Plato, and all the sages of the pagan world. "Happy is the man who findeth religion: For the merchandise of it is better than the merchandise of silver, and the gain thereof than fine gold. She is more precious than rubies; and all the things thou canst desire, are not to be compared to her. Length of days are in her right hand; and in her left hand riches and honour. Her ways are ways of pleasantness, and all her paths are peace. She is a tree of life to them that lay hold upon her; and happy is the man that retaineth her." Let us all then put on this rich and beautiful ornament, and shew ourselves men.

Secondly, this subject may help us to ascertain the only proper and immutable boundaries of human knowledge. I mean such boundaries of our knowledge, as arise from the frame and constitution of our nature, and not from any particular state or stage of our existence. Our rational powers, it is often said, are limited, and therefore all our intellectual pursuits and improvements must be equally limited. This is doubtless true in a certain sense, but not in the sense in which it is generally understood. It appears from what has been observed in this discourse, concerning the powers and faculties of the human mind, that men are capable of making constant and eternal progression in knowledge. The only bounds therefore that can be set to their intellectual improvements, must be such as have respect to the kinds, and not to the degrees of their knowledge. There are, indeed, certain kinds of knowledge, which men are totally incapable of understanding; but these are only such kinds of knowledge, as require more than created faculties to understand. For, whatever kinds of knowledge any created beings are capable of understanding, men are also capable of understanding, though with more difficulty, and less rapidity. As Newton knew nothing, which any man is now incapable of knowing, in a certain time, and under certain circumstances; so there is nothing, which any intelligent creatures now know, that men are incapable of knowing, in a given time, and under proper advantages. The truth is, rationality is the same in all intelligent beings. Reason is the same thing in God, in angels, and in men. As men therefore bear the image of God, in point of rationality; so they possess all the rational powers and faculties, which bear any analogy to the divine intelligence; or, which can be communicated to created beings. Accordingly angels are superior to men in the same sense, and perhaps nearly in the same degree, that Newton was superior to most of his own species. As Newton had no rational power or faculty peculiar to himself; so angels have no rational powers or faculties which are not common to all intelligent creatures. Every man therefore is capable of learning all that any man, or any intelligent creature has learned, or can learn. Hence the only natural and necessary distinction between angels and men, and between one man and another is this; that angels are capable of acquiring knowledge more easily, and more swiftly than men; and some men are capable of acquiring knowledge more easily, and more swiftly than others. And this difference between angels and men, and between man and man, to whatever cause it may be owing, will probably continue forever; and forever keep up a distinction in their knowledge and improvements for the time being.

Now this being a settled point, we may easily, perhaps, fix the proper boundaries of human knowledge, or determine the proper subjects of human enquiry. It is a caveat given to men, but especially to inquisitive men, not to pry into things above their measure. This caveat, undoubtedly, in some cases, may be very proper and necessary; but generally, I imagine, it is not only needless but absurd. For, unless men attempt to pry into things which surpass created powers and faculties, I do not know that they transgress the boundaries of human knowledge. There are some things, which, in a moment, we know cannot be understood by creatures. And there may be many others, which, by a little attention, we may perceive come under the same predicament. All therefore that divines and metaphysicians, as well as philosophers have to do, in order to know where to begin, and, where to end their researches, is only to determine whether or not, the proposed subjects require more than created abilities to investigate them. If they do require more than created abilities, it is vain and absurd to proceed: but if they do not, we have the same grounds to proceed, that men have ever had, to attempt new discoveries.

Thirdly, this subject gives us reason to suppose, that men, in the present state, may carry their researches into the works of nature, much further than they have ever yet carried them. The fields of science, though they have been long traversed by strong and inquisitive minds, are so spacious, that many parts remain yet undiscovered. There may be therefore room left in divinity and metaphysics, as well as in philosophy and other sciences, to make large improvements. The large and growing capacities of men, and the great discoveries and improvements of the last and present century, give us grounds to hope, that human learning and knowledge will increase from generation to generation, through all the remaining periods of time. Men have the same encouragements now, that Bacon, Newton and Franklin had, to push their researches further and further into the works of nature. It is, therefore, as groundless, as it is a discouraging sentiment, which has been often flung out, that all the subjects of divinity, all of human inquiry, are nearly exhausted, and that no great discoveries or improvements, at this time of day, are either to be expected or attempted. The present generation have superior advantages, which, with capacities no more than equal to their fathers, may enable them to surpass all who have gone before them in the paths of science. Let this thought rouse their attention, and awaken their exertions, to shew themselves men.

Fourthly, the observations, which have been made upon the noble powers and capacities of the human mind, may embolden the sons of science to aim to be originals. They are strong enough to go alone, if they only have sufficient courage and resolution. They have the same capacities and the same original sources of knowledge, that the antients enjoyed. All men are as capable of thinking, of reasoning, and of judging for themselves in matters of learning, as in the common affairs and concerns of life. And would men of letters enjoy the pleasures of knowledge, and render themselves the most serviceable to the world, let them determine to think and judge for themselves. Their progress may perhaps, in this way, not be so rapid; yet it will be much more entertaining and useful. When I say their progress may not be so rapid, I mean with respect to those only, who possess moderate abilities; for as to those of superior powers, they will make much swifter progress by going alone out of the common, beaten track. The way to outstrip those who have gone before us, is not to tread in their steps, but to take a nearer course. What philosopher can expect to overtake Newton, by going over all the ground, which he travelled? What divine can expect to come up with Mede, Baxter, or Edwards, while he pursues their path? Or, what poet can hope to transcend Homer and Milton, so long as he sets up these men as the standards of perfection? If the moderns would only employ nature's powers, and converse freely and familiarly with nature's objects, they might rise above the antients, and bear away the palm from all who have gone before them in the walks of science.

Fifthly, what has been said concerning the nature and dignity of man, shows us, that we are under indispensable obligations to cultivate and improve our minds in all the branches of human knowledge. All our natural powers are so many talents, which, in their own nature, lay us under moral obligation to improve them to the best advantage. Being men, we are obliged to act like men, and not like the horse or the mule which have no understanding. Besides, knowledge, next to religion, is the brightest ornament of human nature. Knowledge strengthens, enlarges, and softens the human soul, and sets its beauty and dignity in the fairest light. Learning hath made astonishing distinctions among the different nations of the earth. Those nations, who have lived under the warm and enlightening beams of science, have appeared like a superior order of beings, in comparison with those, who have dragged out their lives under the cold and dark shades of ignorance. The Chaldeans and Egyptians, as well as the

Greeks and Romans, while they cultivated the arts and sciences, far surpassed, in dignity and glory, all their ignorant and barbarous neighbours. Europe, since the resurrection of letters in the sixteenth century, appears to be peopled with a superior species. And the present inhabitants of North-America owe all their superiority to the aboriginals, in point of dignity, to the cultivation of their minds in the civil and polite arts. Learning has also preserved the names, characters, and mighty deeds of all antient nations from total oblivion. A few learned men in each nation, have done more to spread their national fame, than all their kings and heroes. The boasted glory of Britain is more to be ascribed to her Newtons, her Lockes, and her Addisons, than to all her kings, and fleets, and conquerors.

But the cultivation and improvement of the mind is more necessary for use, than for ornament. We were made for usefulness and not for amusement. We were made to be the servants of God, and of each other. We were made to live an active, diligent, and useful life. As men therefore we cannot reach the end of our being, without cultivating all our mental powers, in order to furnish ourselves for the most extensive service in our day and generation. Knowledge and learning are useful in every station; and in the higher and more important departments of life, they are absolutely and indispensibly necessary.

Permit me now, therefore, my hearers, to suggest several things, which may serve to excite you to improve your minds in every branch of useful knowledge, which, either your callings, or your circumstances require.

I am happy to congratulate you, my country-men, that we live in an age, which is favourable to mental and literary improvements. In the present age, our country is in a medium between barbarity and refinement. In such an age, the minds of men are strong and vigorous, being neither enfeebled by luxury, nor shackled by authority. At such an happy period, we have come upon the stage, with the fields of science before us opened but not explored. This should rouse our dormant faculties, and call up all our latent powers in the vigorous pursuit of knowledge. Those, who have gone before us in these pursuits, have only set us an example, and facilitated our progress, without damping our hopes, or forbidding our success.

Again, we live under that form of government, which has always been the friend of the muses, and parent and nurse of arts. It was while Greece and Rome were free, republican states, that learning there sprang up, flourished, and rose to its height; and enrolled their names in the annals of fame. Liberty, which is the birth-right of man, and congenial with his nature, ennobles and exalts the mind; inspires it with great and sublime sentiments; and, at the same time invites and encourages its highest exertions, with hopes of success and the promises of reward. For, in free republics, where liberty is equally enjoyed, every man has weight and influence in proportion to his abilities, and a fair opportunity of rising, by the dint of merit, to the first offices and honours of the state.

Another motive to improvement, you will allow me to say, may be taken from your past singular and laudable efforts to cultivate and diffuse useful knowledge in this place. It is now more than thirty years, since this single and then small congregation collected a very considerable parish-library, in order to improve their minds in useful and divine knowledge. This was such an effort to promote mental improvements as, I imagine, cannot be easily found in this country. The benefit of this library you have all perhaps more or less experienced; and, to its happy influence owe, in a measure, your general character as a religious and intelligent people. May this consideration have all its weight upon you, since our Lord hath said in the parable of the talents, "Whosoever hath, to him shall be given, and he shall have more abundance."

In this respect, how wonderful the smiles of Providence upon you! Whose heart doth not glow with gratitude for the auspicious occasion which hath now brought us together! How great our obligations to God for the unmerited and unexpected favour of a rich collection of books now received, as a mark of respect of the first literary character in America, his excellency President Franklin! This well chosen and very valuable library, while it sets the divine kindness in a high and engaging light, lays you under the strongest ties of gratitude to improve the means of cultivating your minds for the service of God and of your fellow-men. Should you second the views of that great man, and build upon the broad foundation which he has generously laid, you may enjoy ample advantages, in point of books, to improve your mental powers, and furnish yourselves for usefulness in all your various stations and employments of life. Nor can you neglect or abuse such advantages, without drawing upon yourselves the reproach of the world, and which is infinitely more, the reproach of your own consciences. Be entreated then to improve to the best advantage, every price put into your hands to get wisdom.

There are three grand sources of knowledge before you, nature, men, and books. Attentively read each of these great volumes.

Read nature, which is truly an original author. King David, studying this large and instructive volume, which filled his mind with the noblest views and sentiments, broke forth in a rapture of praise, "The heavens declare the glory of God; and the firmament sheweth his handy work. Day unto day uttereth speech, and night unto night sheweth knowledge."

Read men. "For as in water face answereth to face, so the heart of man to man." This volume David perused and digested in the court and camp of Saul, where human nature, with, and without a veil, was very visible to his critical and discerning eye.

But the design of this discourse more directly leads me to urge the reading of books in particular. These are a grand magazine of knowledge, and contain the learning and wisdom of ages. But, you must know, that books are a peculiar fountain, from whence may be drawn either sweet waters or bitter, the waters of life, or the waters of death. For this reason, you will allow me here to advise you, to take heed how you read.

And, in the first place, read with caution. A person may be undone by a single volume. Nothing contains such secret and fatal poison as books. Though they profess a kind and friendly intention, yet they often bite like a serpent and sting like an adder. Be careful what books you read. There are many, which the young and inexperienced at least, should totally avoid. In this particular, if you are wise, and faithful to yourselves, you will endeavour to obtain and follow good advice.

Read with judgment. This is, in every view, indispensibly necessary, in order to read to advantage. This will enable you to discover and ascertain the main object of your author, which will be a key to all he says in the various parts and branches of his subject. This will help you to distinguish truth from error, good sentiments from bad, and sound reasoning and strict demonstration, from mere conjectures and bold assertions. But if you read without judgment, you will be in danger of imbibing error as well as truth, of always believing the last author you read, and of never having any fixed and settled sentiments of your own.

Read for use and not for amusement. The time is worse than thrown away, which is spent in reading for amusement, without any particular end or object in view. We should be careful how we take up a book, especially if it be an entertaining one, with which we have no particular concern; for it will require a considerable effort of the mind to throw it aside, and if we do not throw it aside it will steal away our time, and prevent our being better employed. Almost any book, if read for use, may be of advantage. We may read amusing, and, even corrupting books to advantage, if we read them in order to make a good use of them. The bee can suck honey from the same flowers, from which other insects suck poison. But we may read all our lives to very little purpose, if we read every book which happens to fall in our way for amusement and not for use. We should always read with reference, either to our own particular profession, or to the particular state and situation of our own minds. When we read with either of these objects in view, we shall be apt both to understand and digest what we read. There is great and singular advantage in reading proper books at a proper time, when we really stand in need of them. This is of the same happy tendency, as eating and drinking at the proper seasons, when it serves to nourish and strengthen, instead of clogging and surfeiting the body.

Read with patience. Many authors are both prolix and obscure in conveying their ideas; and after all, have much more chaff than wheat in their writings. In reading such, we must go over a great deal of ground in order to reap a small harvest of ideas. It is difficult, however, for any man to treat any subject in a method entirely new. We must expect therefore to find many common and familiar thoughts in every author, which we must patiently read, if we would properly come at those which are more new, entertaining and instructive. And for this reason it is generally best perhaps, if authors are of any tolerable size, to read them through, with patience and attention. This is but justice to them, and prudence to ourselves.

Read with confidence. In our first essays after knowledge, we are obliged, by the laws of our nature, to depend upon the assistance and instruction of others, and in consequence of this, we are apt to feel, through life, too great a sense of our own weakness and imbecility, and to despair of going a step further than we are led. This, however is very unfriendly to all improvement by reading. We ought therefore to feel that we are men, and place a proper degree of confidence in our own strength and judgment. We ought to fix it in our minds that we are capable of improvement. Such a confidence in ourselves as this, will embolden us to read with a view not only of understanding, but of improving upon the authors we read. Very few authors have exhausted the subjects upon which they have treated, and therefore have generally left us ample room to improve upon what they have written. And by reading with this view, if we fail of improving upon those we read, we shall, however, more clearly and fully understand their meaning, and more thoroughly make their ideas and sentiments our own.

Yet, at the same time, every one should read with humility. Reading, more than any other method of improvement, is apt to puff up the mind with pride and self-conceit. For, persons of reading are very prone to estimate their knowledge more according to the number of books which they have read, than according to the number of ideas which they have collected and digested. And so are ready to imagine, that they have engrossed to themselves all knowledge; though, in reality, they have not read enough, to learn their own ignorance. This should teach us to take the poet's advice.

> A little learning is a dangerous thing:
> Drink deep, or taste not the Pierian spring.
> There shallow draughts intoxicate the brain;
> And drinking largely sobers us again.

Nor is pedantry peculiar to those only, who begin to read and study late in life; for it is too often found among those, who have enjoyed a regular and liberal education. Do not physicians and attorneys, by reading a few books in divinity, sometimes fancy themselves masters of that sacred and sublime science? And, on the other extreme, do not divines, by reading a few books in law and physic, sometimes fancy themselves masters of those two learned professions? But this is rank pedantry. It is an easy matter to gain a superficial acquaintance with the general objects of science; but it is a laborious task to acquire a deep and thorough acquaintance with any single branch of knowledge. It is easy to know something about every thing;

but it is difficult to know every thing about any thing. If men of reading would collect the whole stock of their knowledge, and the whole force of their genius more to a point, and aim to be complete masters of their own professions; they would become at once, much less pedantic, and much more useful to the world. Many men of real abilities and learning, have defeated their own usefulness, by attempting to know, and to do too much.

In the last place, read prayerfully. "If any of you lack wisdom, says the Apostle, let him ask of God, that giveth to all men liberally, and upbraideth not; and it shall be given him." This Solomon found to be true, by happy experience. "In Gibeon the Lord appeared to Solomon, in a dream by night; and God said, Ask what I shall give thee. And Solomon said, Thou hast shewed unto thy servant David my father great mercy, according as he walked before thee in truth, and in righteousness, and in uprightness of heart with thee; and thou hast kept for him this great kindness that thou hast given him a son to sit on his throne, as it is this day. And now, O Lord my God, thou hast made thy servant king instead of David my father; *and I am but a child; I know not how to go out or come in.* And thy servant is in the midst of thy people which thou hast chosen, a great people that cannot be numbered nor counted for multitude. *Give therefore thy servant an understanding heart;* to judge thy people, that I may discern between good and bad: for who is able to judge this thy so great a people? *And the speech pleased the Lord, that Solomon had asked this thing.* And God said unto him, Because thou hast asked this thing, and hast not asked for thyself long life; neither hast asked riches for thyself, nor hast asked the life of thine enemies, but hast asked for thyself understanding to discern judgment; behold, I have done according to thy words: lo, I have given thee *a wise and understanding heart.*" It was Dr. Doddridge, I think, who never used to take up a new book to read, without an ejaculatory prayer for divine influence and direction. This example is worthy of universal imitation. Let us therefore always accompany our essays after knowledge with a humble and prayerful spirit; and then we may hope to read and study with safety and success.

To all these directions, I might now add, diligence and perseverance, which always have had, and always will have, a mighty influence, in all the great things done by mankind. But I shall only add a few words to those, who are very immediately and deeply interested in the things which have been said in this discourse.

This subject calls upon parents in particular, to shew themselves men. You are, my respectable hearers, men in years, be men also in virtue, in religion, and in understanding. Let the dignity of man appear in all your conduct, and especially in your conduct towards your children. Let them see the dignity of human nature exemplified before their young and attentive minds. They are every day, and every hour, watching your conduct, and looking up to you for example and instruction. Take heed, that none of your words, none of your actions, none of your pursuits, be unworthy of men. But, let all your conversation and behaviour be such as your children may follow with propriety, with safety, and dignity. And while you are teaching them by example, teach them also by precept. Give them good instruction; and for this purpose, provide them good instructors. These are of great importance to your children, whose progress in knowledge, will generally bear a very exact proportion to the abilities and fidelity of their teachers. The education of children has always been an object of great attention among all wise nations, and especially among all wise and good parents. Let this then be the object of your attention. Consider the dignity of man. Consider the worth of the soul. Consider the rich and invaluable treasure put into your hands. Consider how much the dignity and happiness of your children both in time and in eternity, depend upon your care and fidelity. And let the ties of nature, the authority of God, and your own solemn vows, engage you to bring them up in the nurture and admonition of the Lord, and to cultivate and embellish their opening minds in every branch of useful and ornamental knowledge. Admit not the thought, that such little, such weak, and to appearance, such useless creatures, are of small importance; but remember that they are men in miniature, and may, one day, surprize the world with their dignity. When a young prince is born, all the kingdom feel the importance of his education, and are anxiously concerned to have the ablest instructors employed, to form him for great and noble actions. But you have more than princes, even young immortals, committed to your care, whose powers and capacities, whose dignity and importance, will astonish you, at the great day, if not before. How happy will that parent be, who shall then be found to have been faithful to his children! "He will then join, as a celebrated writer observes, his virtuous offspring in the habitations of the just, and there see them rise up and call him blessed. But if a parent neglects his duty to his children; if he sets before them an example of irreligion, and suffers them to grow up loose and unprincipled, he may expect that their blood will be required at his hands, and he should tremble to think of that period of retribution, when probably they will curse him for that negligence which has ruined them."

Finally, let this subject awaken the attention of the youth, to the dignity of their nature and the end of their being. My dear young friends, you will soon be called to act your various parts upon the stage of life. You are now the hope of your parents, of your pastors, and of your country. The eyes of the world are upon you. Be entreated then to cultivate all your noble powers, and to shew yourselves men, in whatever departments of life, divine Providence shall place you. Piety and knowledge will prepare you for a useful and honourable life, and for a peaceful and triumphant death. Let these then be the supreme objects of your pursuit. Early consecrate all your time and all your talents to the service of God, and of your fellow-men. Seek for knowledge, as for silver, and search for it, as for hid treasures; and sacrifice every object which obstructs your pursuit of it. "Through desire a man having separated himself, says Solomon, seeketh and intermeddleth with all wisdom." If you would make progress in learning, and rise to any distinguishing degrees of knowledge, you must separate yourselves from the vanities of youth, and devote those vacant hours to mental improvements, which, too many of your age trifle away in folly and vice. In particular, flee youthful lusts, which war against both the body and the mind. Shun that all-devouring monster, intemperance, by which so many strong minds have been cast down and destroyed. Avoid bad company and unmanly diversions, which are an inlet to every vice. Hold in steady contempt, beaus and fops, those butterflies which live upon the filth and dregs of the earth. Diogenes walking the streets of Athens at noonday with a lanthorn in his hand; and being asked, as he intended to be, what he was searching after, tartly replied, "I am looking for men." A severe satire upon the luxury and effeminacy of that once manly and virtuous people. The dignity of man appears in the ornaments of the mind, and not in those of the body. Seek therefore to adorn and embellish your minds both by reading and observation, and your gifts and abilities will make room for you, and bring you before great men. You have peculiar advantages and encouragements to animate you to great and noble exertions. *Therefore set your mark of intellectual attainments as high as you please, and, according to the common course of events, you will, by uniformity, diligence, and perseverance, infallibly reach it.* Your generous benefactor hath set you an example, as well as given you the means of intellectual improvements. That great man, in the morning of life, was surrounded with uncommon difficulties and embarrassments, but by the mere dint of genius and of application, he surmounted every obstacle thrown in his way, and by his rapid and astonishing progress in knowledge, he hath risen, step by step, to the first offices and honours of his country, hath appeared with dignity in the courts of Britain and of France, and now fills more than half the globe with his fame. Keep this illustrious example in your eye, and shew yourselves men.

31

THE PRINCIPLES OF CIVIL UNION AND HAPPINESS CONSIDERED AND RECOMMENDED

Elizur Goodrich

HARTFORD

1787

ELIZUR GOODRICH (1734-1797). One of the stalwarts of the established order, a fine scholar, and able preacher, Goodrich was pastor of the Durham, Connecticut, Congregational Church from his ordination in 1756 until his death. He was a Yale graduate, and when he and Ezra Stiles received the same number of votes for president of that institution in 1777, Goodrich exerted himself to ensurc Stiles's selection. He was an excellent biblical scholar and an accomplished astronomer and mathematician.

Goodrich was a leader in the fight for liberty from the Stamp Act crisis onward, writing on the subject of religious liberty in Connecticut and vigorously opposing a British threat to send an Anglican bishop to America. He argued that participation in the Revolution was a religious duty.

The election sermon reproduced here is regarded as one of his finest. It was preached to Governor Samuel Huntington and the legislature in Hartford on May 10, 1787, on the eve of the convening of the Philadelphia Convention.

The Principles of civil UNION *and* HAPPINESS *considered and recommended.*

A

SERMON,

PREACHED BEFORE HIS EXCELLENCY

SAMUEL HUNTINGTON, ESQ. L.L.D.

GOVERNOR AND COMMANDER IN CHIEF,

AND THE HONORABLE THE

GENERAL ASSEMBLY

OF THE

STATE OF CONNECTICUT.

CONVENED AT HARTFORD, ON THE DAY OF THE

ANNIVERSARY ELECTION,

MAY 10th, 1787.

BY ELIZUR GOODRICH, D. D.

Pastor of the CHURCH of CHRIST in DURHAM.

HARTFORD:

PRINTED BY HUDSON AND GOODWIN.

M.DCC,LXXXVII.

Jerusalem is builded, as a City that is compact together.

Psalm cxxii. 3.

Jerusalem was a city, defended with strong walls, the metropolis of the kingdom of Israel, and the capital seat of the Hebrew empire. It's inhabitants were not a loose, disconnected people, but most strictly united, not only among themselves, but with all the tribes of Israel, into a holy nation and commonwealth, under Jehovah their king and their God. And as Jerusalem was the place, which he was pleased to honour as the seat of his royal residence and government, it was most truly the city of the great King. Hence both by divine appointment, and the common consent of the nation, it was established as the local centre of communion in all the privileges of their civil and sacred constitution. There were the thrones of judgement, the thrones of the house of David, and the supreme courts of justice, and of the public administration: There were the Levites, waiting in their courses, and the priests, ministering in their offices, before the Lord: There was the testimony, the ark of the covenant, the temple, and the solemn services of religion: And there all the tribes and sceptres of the people, assembled three times in the year, to present national homage to Jehovah, their king and their God.

In all these respects, whether Jerusalem be considered in a natural, civil or religious view, its strength and beauty consisted, in being builded "as a city, that is compact together." Hence the psalmist's affection for Jerusalem expressed in this psalm was not a meer partial and local fondness; but had in view, and was excited by the most noble objects. These were the exaltation of Jehovah, the king and God of Zion—the honour and happiness of the nation—the preservation of the true religion, and the peace and best good of all the tribes of Israel. Religion therefore, and public spirit were united in the ardent affection of the pious Israelites, toward Jerusalem, which they preferred above their chief joy.

We have also a Jerusalem, adorned with brighter glories of divine grace, and with greater beauties of holiness, than were ever displayed, in the most august solemnities of the Hebrew-temple-worship; and presents, to our devout admiration, gratitude and praise, more excellent means of religion and virtue, peace and happiness, than ever called the attention of the assembled tribes of Israel. We enjoy all the privileges of a free government, the blessings of the gospel of peace, and the honours of the church of God. This is our Jerusalem.

The safety and preservation of it depend, under God, on the friendly agreement of its citizens in all those things, necessary for its honour and defence, happiness and glory. Without this agreement, it cannot be "builded as a city, that is compact together." There will be no peace within its walls, nor prosperity within its palaces: It can have neither strength or beauty, nor administer protection to its inhabitants; but it will be as a city broken down, and without walls.

The text therefore, and the great occasion, on which we are assembled in the house of God, justify a discourse on the great principles and maxims, of civil union—the importance of a good, public administration, to answer the great ends of government—and the necessity of the joint exertions of subjects, with their rulers, in promoting the public peace and happiness.

I am then, in the first place, to point out some of the great principles and maxims, which are the foundation and cement of civil union and society.

The principles of society are the laws, which Almighty God has established in the moral world, and made necessary to be observed by mankind; in order to promote their true happiness, in their transactions and intercourse. These laws may be considered as principles, in respect of their fixedness and operation; and as maxims, since by the knowledge of them, we discover those rules of conduct, which direct mankind to the highest perfection, and supreme happiness of their nature. They are as fixed and unchangeable as the laws which operate in the natural world.

Human art in order to produce certain effects, must conform to the principles and laws, which the Almighty Creator has established in the natural world. He who neglects the cultivation of his field, and the proper time of sowing, may not expect a harvest. He, who would assist mankind in raising weights, and overcoming obstacles, depends on certain rules, derived from the knowledge of mechanical principles applied to the construction of machines, in order to give the most useful effect to the smallest force: And every builder should well understand the best position of firmness and strength, when he is about to erect an edifice. For he, who attempts these things, on other principles, than those of nature, attempts to make a new world; and his aim will prove absurd and his labour lost. No more can mankind be conducted to happiness; or civil societies united, and enjoy peace and prosperity, without observing the moral principles and connections, which the same Almighty Creator has established for the government of the moral world.

Moral connections and causes in different circumstances produce harmony or discord, peace or war, happiness or woe among mankind, with the same certainty, as physical causes produce their effect. To institute these causes and connexions belongs not to men, to nations or to human laws, but to build upon them. It is no more in the power of the greatest earthly potentate to hinder their operation, than it is to govern the flowing and ebbing of the ocean.

The great and most universal principle and law of rational union and happiness, is the love of God and of our neighbour: This in the moral, is like the great law of gravitation and attraction in the natural world; and its tendency in human society, is to universal good. The first maxim derived from it, is that divine precept in the gospel, "whatsoever ye would that men should do unto you, do ye also the same unto them." Hence religion and virtue are the great principles on which the happiness of human societies must be built; and from these principles must be derived the knowledge of all laws, which determine the order of that benevolence, we owe to one another, and point out the means of attaining the greatest good.

If this were a state of so much innocence and perfection, that the law of reason and of love directed and influenced all the views and actions of mankind, there would be no necessity for the coercion of civil government. But in the present depraved state of human nature, the various dispositions and differing pursuits, the jarring interests, and unruly passions, the jealousies and misapprehensions of neighbours would spoil their harmony and good agreement; and, when disputes arose, there would be no common judge, to whom they might refer their differences; but every one would be an avenger of his own wrong: This would soon end in a state of hatred and war; and destroy all human peace and happiness. To prevent this mischief, and to secure the enjoyment of rational liberty, which summarily consists in the unmolested privilege and opportunity of "leading a quiet and peaceable life, in all godliness and honesty," is the great end of the institution of civil society and government.

The end therefore, and nature of civil government imply that it must have for its foundation, the principles and laws of truth, justice and righteousness, mercy and the fear of God; or it can never advance the happiness of mankind. For that mankind by uniting into society, and putting themselves under a common government, can promote their true interest, otherwise than by observing these laws, is as contrary to reason as, that a machine may be of great and beneficial use in human life, when its whole construction is contrary to all the principles, by which the world of nature is actuated and kept together.

There can be no beneficial union among the members of a community, where these great principles of righteousness and truth integrity and the fear of God, are not maintained, both among themselves, and towards all mankind. Any number of men, confederated together in wickedness and injustice, can have no strength, but what they derive from being faithful to one another. Such a combination may exist among robbers and pirates: but their agreement ought not to be dignified by the name of civil union: it ought rather to be esteemed a wicked conspiracy against the rights of mankind, which can never be justified by number, nor on any pretence of public good.

These moral principles and connections are moral laws, not only, as they point out a fixed order of events respecting moral ends, in which view the meer politician, who has no fear of God before his eyes, may consider them; but to the enlightened and religious mind, they are moral laws, in a higher sense—laws of our creator, for the conduct of our life and manners. They cannot therefore be transgressed, without offending against his will and authority—without incurring guilt in his sight, and rendering ourselves obnoxious to his wrath and displeasure, as the great and righteous governor of the world.

> The Lord is in his holy temple, the Lord's throne is in heaven; his eyes behold, his eye-lids try the children of men. The Lord trieth the righteous; but the wicked and him that loveth violence, his soul hateth. Upon the wicked he shall rain snares, fire and brimstone and an horrible tempest. This shall be the portion of their cup. For the righteous Lord loveth the righteous, his countenance doth behold the upright.

If we can find what are the laws and rules, which men, as rational creatures, must observe, that they may arrive at the greatest happiness and perfection of their nature, these are the laws which they must observe, when united in political bodies, in order to promote the common good of society. The same virtue and integrity, truth, justice and honour, which we venerate in a private character, must be found in the public administration, and generally prevailing among a people, or a state, cannot be united, peaceful and happy in itself, and respectable in the world.

Hence in all well regulated civil communities, laws of natural, universal and unchangeable obligation hold the first rank: They are such fixed means of union, peace and happiness, that no other can or ought to be substituted in their room. It may however be observed, that the force of civil society cannot extend to all laws of this kind; but only to such upon the observation of which the common quiet of mankind entirely depends. To do to our neighbour as we would that he should do to us is one of the plainest dictates of reason, and a law of universal equity and obligation. It comprehends the whole of social duty, and extends to kindness, humanity and mercy, as well as to truth and justice. But although it is the great rule of our conduct and the bond of society, it cannot in its whole extention have the force of a civil law in commonwealths. Controversies about the violation of it would be perplexed and intricate: Litigious suits would be infinitely multiplied: The good and virtuous would be deprived of the most valuable part of their character: and the state would be torn with intestine division and discord.

But, tho' all the laws of nature cannot be enforced with civil sanctions, yet every righteous state adopts those, which are necessary for the preservation of the public peace, and for an equal and impartial distribution of rewards and punishments. The good and virtuous, who are influenced to do well out of reverence to GOD, and sincere love to mankind, must be protected and encouraged; and the wicked and disorderly, restrained by the dread of punishment. The great laws of justice must be armed with a civil force, and never allowed to be transgressed with impunity. Such, for instance, is that statute of Jehovah, the GOD and king of Israel, "Ye shall do no unrighteousness; in judgement, in mete-yard, in weight or in measure. Just balances, just weights, a just ephah, and a just hin, shall ye have." This law must be admitted into every civil state; but, that it may have force in society, the public standard must be fixed; the most convenient weights and measures, determined; the manner of their being tried, ascertained; and an awful penalty annexed to transgression. These are circumstances, which are not determined by the law of nature; but must be adjusted by civil regulations suited to the condition of particular commonwealths.

The principles and laws of justice are fixed and unchangeable—they depend not on human authority; but the particular regulations, by which they have force in society, as civil laws, not being determined by the law of nature, may be changed, when they are found inconvenient and hurtful to the community. Hence the legislative authority of a state, extends to the repealing of old, as well as the making of new laws.

Nevertheless, great care should be taken in framing laws, that they may be suited to the peculiar state of a people, and have an equal and uniform operation for the public good. New and different circumstances require new and different regulations in society, fitted to the occasions which produce them: But the fundamental laws, by which a people are compacted together, like the laws of the natural world, must have a fixed consistence and duration. Such, in general, are laws relating to personal liberty, the privileges of the subject, and the powers of the magistrate—to private property and the execution of justice—to the punishment of evil-doers and the preservation of the public peace—to marriage, education, religion, and the rights of conscience—to the public forms, and order of government—and to the revenues and taxes, by which the state is supported. Frequent changes even in the external appendages, much more an unfixedness in the laws, and a want of stability in the public administration, diminish the energy and dignity of government, and will be attended with uneasiness and discord.

I shall only add, that as the best and most useful laws can be of no use, unless subjects be trained up and educated in a manner of living conformable to them, every wise state will pay great attention to the education of children, and to all such regulations, as are necessary for the instruction of the people in the principles of piety and virtue. The best security men can have, of living together in harmony and love, is from the prevalence of true religion, and a due regard to the will and authority of the supreme being. Religion and virtue, are the strongest bond of human society, and lay the best foundation of peace and happiness in the civil state.

I proceed, in the next place, to consider the importance of a good public administration of government, to the peace and happiness of a people.

All the qualifications of a good administration may be summed up in two heads, the ability and faithfulness of those, who are intrusted with the weighty concerns of the state: To one or the other of these two things may be referred, whatever can be desired or expected in a good ruler. These qualifications are of the highest importance, in every administration. A free people, under GOD, may justly put confidence in such an administration, and not find themselves disappointed, as they must unavoidably be if they commit themselves into the hands of weak or wicked men. The former, though they mean never so well, are unable to do good; the latter may improve their great talents, to do mischief: Neither of them are fit to be intrusted with the great affairs of state. Who, on the one hand, would willingly trust his whole interest to the power and disposal of a man of the greatest abilities, but destitute of honour and conscience; or on the other hand, who would undertake a dangerous voyage, on the boisterous ocean, under the command of the most upright and honest man, who had no knowledge of the art of navigation, nor any acquaintance with the seas. In common affairs no honest man will undertake any business for which he knows he is unfit, though he should be solicited to do it: The same should be observed by men, invited to serve the public. When a people have raised men of weak abilities to posts of honour, it may seem hard to neglect them; and it must, indeed, be ungrateful, if in any good degree, they maintain the dignity of their stations, and advance the public good; and especially, if the posts they hold, were unsought, and conferred without solicitation. Nevertheless it should be considered, that those, who undertake the affairs of the public, are as answerable for their abilities, as the soldier for his courage, when he inlists into the service of his country. The safety of the public is to be preferred to the honour of an individual.

Here I might delineate more fully the character of an able and faithful administration; but I will not enlarge, and shall say only in a few words, that the principal lines of it, are knowledge, wisdom, and prudence, courage and unshaken resolution, righteousness and justice, tempered with lenity, mercy, and compassion, and a steady firmness of public measures, when founded in wisdom and the public good, together with inflexible integrity, the fear of GOD, and a sacred regard to the moral and religious interests of the community. These are the great characteristics of an administration, which will procure respect and confidence; and has the best tendency to promote the happiness, union and strength of a people, and to render them as a "city, that is compact together."

If a virtuous people venerate rulers of this character, and unite their endeavours with them in advancing all the noble ends of society, they will have the fairest prospect of peace and prosperity; which was the last thing, I proposed to be considered.

Let the first object, exciting the attention of a free people, be the character of those, whom they introduce into public offices; and, the next, that they reverence the worthy magistrate, support him in his office and dignity, and shew a ready obedience to the laws of the state.

Not only may a people be delivered into the hands of tyrants, as the rod and scourge of heaven for their impiety and madness; but through their own folly, "children may be their princes, and babes rule over them." Such a "people shall be oppressed every one by another, and every one by his neighbour."

Happy the free and virtuous people, who pay strict attention to the natural aristocracy, which is the institution of heaven; and appears in every assembly of mankind, on whatever occasion, they are met together. Happy the people who have wisdom to discern the true patriot of superiour abilities, in all his counsels ever manifesting a sincere regard to the public good, and never with a selfish view attempting to deceive them, into hurtful measures; and happy the people who distinguish him from the designing demagogue, who, while he sooths them in their vices, and flatters them with high notions of liberty, and of easing their burdens, is plunging them into the depths of misery and bondage.

How idle are all disputes about a technical aristocracy, if people disregard that divine injunction, given by Moses, to the free electors of Israel, when he was about to appoint some assistants in government. "Take ye wise men and understanding and known among your tribes" for their great abilities and good deeds, "and I will make them rulers over you."

Such an aristocracy is founded in merit and designed by the God of government and order, to direct a free people in the choice of their judges and public magistrates. Riches are so far necessary as to raise the judge and counsellor above the temptation of transgressing for a piece of bread, nevertheless this aristocracy is derived from merit and that influence, which a character for superiour wisdom, and known services to the commonwealth, has to produce veneration, confidence and esteem, among a people, who have felt the benefits, and enjoy the advantage of being under so happy a direction.

This influence of character in the language of the Roman republic, was called *Auctoritas patrum*, and the veneration paid to it by the people, *Verecundia plebis*. It is essentially necessary in all good governments, but especially the life and spirit of a happy, free and republican state, which subsists on the virtues of its citizens, and can never, while any sound wisdom is left to direct the public choice, by design commit the civil administration into the hands of men destitute of political abilities, or who are the patrons of vice.

It is therefore, of the highest importance to the being, happiness and peace of free republics, to shew a fixed and unalterable regard to merit in the choice of their rulers: The next thing is to discover a deference and submission to authority, obedience to the laws, a spirit of righteousness and peace, and a disposition to promote the public good.

Honour and respect are due to rulers: The order and good of society require external marks of distinction, and titles of eminence to be given them. This is due to their office; an honour paid to the institution of government; but there is a further honour due to them, when they are faithful in executing the trust committed to them, and direct all their actions to advance the true interest of the state. In this view, good rulers alone can be honoured, because they alone deserve esteem and respect. We owe obedience and subjection to all rulers in the execution of their office, according to the laws of the land; but, as to cordial affection, veneration, esteem and gratitude, these are due only to the worthy magistrate; and the debt will be paid by all virtuous citizens, although he should be blasphemed, arraigned, and condemned by the factious and discontented; who wish that there should be no righteous government in the world.

If we wilfully transgress the laws of society and resist the just commands of civil authority, we do an injury not so much to the magistrate, as to the community, and expose ourselves to the high displeasure of Almighty GOD, whose authority is above all human constitutions, and can never be annulled by the decrees of kings and nobles, the consults of senates, or the joint consent of a people.

This is the sentiment of a great and good man, who well knew the rights of human nature, and the privileges of a subject, which he had the courage to plead before kings and magistrates; I mean the apostle Paul, who, illuminated with the knowledge of christianity, and inspired with the benevolence of the gospel, the slave of no party, in the greatest transports of zeal, spoke only the words of truth and soberness. The doctrine he delivered was not the effect of servile flattery and shameful cowardice: It proceeded not from the spirit of fear, but of love and a sound mind: It is so expressed as at once to declare the great end of civil government, the duty of the magistrate, and the reasonableness of the subjects obedience. It contains both an effectual guard against supporting tyranny and oppression, and a most serious and solemn warning against lawless rebellion, anarchy and confusion: It is delivered as a divine injunction upon christians, in a letter to the saints at Rome, and is profitable for all ages, and especially reasonable for the present.

Let every soul be subject to the higher powers. For there is no power but of GOD. The powers that be are ordained of GOD. Whosoever therefore resisteth the power, resisteth the ordinance of GOD, and they that resist shall receive judgment to themselves. For rulers are not a terror to good works, but to the evil. Wouldst thou then not be afraid of the power? Do that which is good, and thou shalt have praise of the same. For he is the minister of GOD to thee for good. But if thou dost evil, be afraid, for he beareth not the sword in vain: for he is the minister of GOD, a revenger to execute wrath, upon him that doeth evil. Wherefore ye must needs be subject, not only for wrath, but for conscience sake. For, for this cause pay ye tribute also: for they are GOD's ministers, attending continually upon this very thing. Render therefore to all their dues: tribute to whom tribute is due; custom, to whom custom; fear to whom fear; honour to whom honour.

When a constitutional government is converted into tyranny, and the laws, rights and properties of a free people are openly invaded, there ought not to be the least doubt but that a remedy consistent with this doctrine of the apostle, is provided in the laws of GOD and reason, for their preservation; nor ought resistance in such case to be called rebellion. But who will imagine, that GOD, whose first law, in the world of nature and reason, is order and love, has commissioned men of a private character, with a lawful power, on every pretence of some public mismanagement, to inflame and raise the multitude, embroil the state, and overturn the foundations of public peace.

Civil society can exist no longer, than while connected by its laws and constitution: These are of no force, otherwise than as they are maintained and defended by the members of the commonwealth. This regular support of authority is the only security, a people can have against violence and injustice, feuds and animosities, in the unmolested enjoyment of their honest acquisitions: Hence the very end of civil society demands, that the orders of government be enforced; the fountains of justice, kept open; the streams, preserved pure; and the state, defended against all internal and foreign violence. These ends can never be attained, under the most excellent constitution and laws, but by means of an able and faithful administration, and the concurring zeal and assistance of all good and virtuous citizens.

Although some exclude religion and the profession and worship of the gospel from having any concern in the happiness of civil society and in the choice of rulers among a free people, yet without religion, a people happily united in all other respects, want the bond, most essentially necessary to preserve the union, and to excite every one to faithfulness in his station.

The chief glory of the gospel is, that it opens the way of salvation to a fallen world, and contains the words of eternal life: And were not this its great and distinguishing excellence, it would be of so much less importance to mankind, as the concerns of eternity are greater than those of time. It does every thing for our happiness in this world, which can be effected by the most excellent precepts of morality, and by instructing us in all the duties, we owe to GOD, our neighbour and ourselves: At the same time, it binds us to the most unremitting diligence and perseverance in all good works, by the solemn account we must give to our righteous judge, for all the deeds done in the body.

The blessed gospel is therefore the best privilege which a people can enjoy; and were its precepts duly observed, the civil state would be in the best order, and in the most excellent condition. Persons of all ranks, according to their abilities, would be blessings to the community. The foundations of our Jerusalem would be laid with polished stones, and the city of our habitation be built up without the noise of saws and hammers. The stone would not cry out of the wall of public fraud and oppression, nor the beam out of the timber answer it; but our officers would be peace, and our exactors righteousness; our walls would be called salvation and our gates praise, and no wasting violence and destruction would be heard in our borders.

Having pointed out the principles and maxims, on which civil union and happiness depend, and considered both the character of a good administration of government, and what is required of the subjects and citizens of a free state, I proceed to address and exhort the several orders of men present, that in their several places they use their best and most faithful endeavours for promoting the public peace and prosperity, that this and the United States, may, after the model of Jerusalem, be "builded, as a city that is compact together."

In the first place, duty requires, that with the greatest respect and reverence the public exhortation be addressed to his Excellency, Governor Huntington, the chief magistrate of this free state.

May it please your Excellency,

While I congratulate my fellow-citizens, on the return of this joyful anniversary, I beg leave to address your Excellency, with the honours of the day, and the thanks of a grateful people for all the peaceful blessings of your administration.

The many faithful and important services rendered to your country, in the most difficult and interesting affairs of this and the United States have distinguished you with honour, among the patriots of America—enrolled your name, in the immortal list of those great and noble personages, who in the most heart-searching times, sealed the independence of America, adventured to sit at the head of the national council—and added you to the bright constellation of the illustrious statesmen and governors of this free commonwealth.

How different is the station of a chief magistrate in a free government, who lives in the hearts of the people, from that of the arbitrary despot, who has many slaves, but not a loyal subject? All seem to adore the tyrant, and tremble at the least motion of his eye, while they sigh for a change; and at the first blow, the idol is pulled down, and trampled under foot. The confidence and esteem of a virtuous and free people are derived from known and approved merit, and have a lasting foundation. The chair of state is marked with this motto, *for the best and the worthiest citizen.*

I sincerely wish your Excellency, the most pleasing satisfaction, in the esteem, veneration and gratitude of your citizens; but I persuade myself, you look to an higher source of joy, and to a greater witness of integrity, than the most unanimous approbation of a sensible and grateful people: I mean the witness of conscience, appealing to the great searcher of hearts, that in the whole of your public conduct, and in all the private walks of life, you have considered yourself, as the servant of the most high GOD, and devoted all your abilities, ultimately to the honour and service of the eternal king.

This is that rectitude of intention and endeavour, which is able to give calm peace through all the changing scenes of life, and all the uncertainties of earthly greatness; and even in the view of approaching death, and the prospect of the appearing and kingdom of our Lord JESUS CHRIST. It cannot therefore, fail of affording your Excellency serene joy, while with an unreproaching heart, you look round on the assembled commonwealth; and with an unruffled mind, meet the great event of this day.

Should the providence of GOD, and the voice of this free people continue your Excellency in the first seat of government, I would with the deepest humility and respect, honoured sir, beseech and even charge you, in the presence of the supreme judge and this great congregation, to look to the grace of the eternal Jehovah, that you may be furnished for, and be found faithful in the high employment. You will not think it beneath your exalted dignity, to be exhorted by one of the meanest of CHRIST's servants, to acknowledge the infinite source of wisdom, in all your ways, and to ask the direction of heaven, in all your paths, that truth and integrity may ever guide you; and righteousness and mercy be the girdle of your loins.

I am persuaded, that the peace and happiness of this, and the United States, cannot be built up and established, but upon the maxims I have pointed out and recommended. You, sir, are a master-builder on the walls of our Jerusalem: Let not these walls be daubed with the untempered mortar of injustice, jealousy and discord; but may they be cemented by the uniting principles of justice, benevolence and public spirit.

The post assigned your Excellency, in divine providence, is high and honourable, the employment, great and weighty, the objects in view, beautiful and glorious, and the motives, such as may well inspire a noble and generous breast, with the warmest zeal, the most unshaken fortitude, and the most unremitting perseverance, in the most faithful endeavours, to answer the great ends of the exalted station, you hold in this commonwealth. Some of these objects, motives and ends are the exaltation of Jehovah, the king and governor of the universe—the high importance and dignity of government, the great foundation of peace and quiet—your own honour in being furnished by GOD with great abilities of eminent usefulness—the loss or preservation of public liberty, and the rights of a free people, on which depends the happiness of thousands, or the misery of millions, the cause of religion and virtue, and the consequences of them on the present and eternal interests of mankind—the peace and best good of civil society, and the honour and safety of this, and the United States, and finally the joys or the sorrows of that great and glorious day, when dignity and power will be no defence; but the highest potentate, and the meanest slave, will stand without distinction before the supreme and eternal judge, and receive the solemn, and decisive sentence from his mouth.

These, sir, are weighty considerations, which I humbly address to your constant attention, that under the influence of them, you may be found faithful, and meet the final approbation of your Lord. In the weight of government, you will be encouraged and assisted by good men and virtuous citizens; whose continual and earnest prayer will be, that the blessing of Almighty GOD may attend and render your administration successful for the honour of GOD, the advancement of piety and virtue, the true interest of this and the United States of America, and the general good of mankind.

May your Excellency long live, the ornament of your country and the church of CHRIST. May you be happy in the consciousness of faithfully serving GOD and your people; and have the unspeakable joy of beholding them safe, virtuous and free. And, when the supreme Disposer of all events, shall dismiss you from the services of this world, whether you shall then be in public life, and the chief magistracy over this people, or free from public cares in the serene retirements of a peaceful old age, may you experience the solid supports of the christian hope, share in the rewards of grace, and shine with unfading glories, in the kingdom of the Redeemer.

Let the public exhortation in the next place be acceptable to his honour, Lieutenant-Governor Wolcott, the honourable councellors, and the respectable representatives of this state.

Honoured gentlemen,

How happy will it be if the magistrates and representatives of this state shall enter upon public business, with a noble spirit of true patriotism, having no narrow and private interests at heart; but seeking the good of our Jerusalem, build it up on the great foundations of truth and righteousness. Then peace will be within our walls, and prosperity within our palaces.

A selfish and contracted spirit in any member of society is a great blemish; but in a chief ruler—in a senator—in the representative of a free people, it is vile—it is odious, and unpardonable. Let this spirit be banished from public counsel; or it will destroy all harmony of sentiment, and lead into the narrow by-paths of private ambition and self-exaltation: The builders will not understand each other's language; scenes of confusion ensue, and the public resolutions shew more the complexion of party-attachment, than the public good.

If the leaders of a people are not united in the great maxims of government, and maintain not steadiness in the public administration, the people never will, nor can be easy. And when a community is rent by the animosities and different views of their principal leaders and citizens, a republic is verging towards an ochlocratical state, in which the prevalence of a party, is no sure token of truth. In this situation, justice may be overborne by the violence of misguided passion, blind to the true interest of the people and, the best means of safety. An Aristides through envy, was banished by his citizens; and Cicero, the friend of liberty, of the laws and constitution of his country, for his wise and vigorous measures, in defeating and crushing the Catalinarian conspiracy and rebellion, under the administration of a furious tribune was driven from Rome: But, when the fire of party had subsided, and the people were recovered to their senses, they recalled him, with every mark of public honour; and stiled him the father and preserver of his country; an honour never before conferred, on a Roman citizen.

Never was union in counsel and in public exertions, more necessary in America, than at the present day. If we improve the advantages, which Providence has put into our hands, we may be a great and flourishing people, happy and united among ourselves, and our name be respectable among the nations. But, if we forget the GOD of our salvation, and neglect the means of virtue and religion, with which we are favoured above any people on earth—if we are divided, and contend about every plan devised for strengthening the national union, and restoring the national honour and safety—if the several states, losing sight of the great end of the confederation, are influenced by meer local and partial motives, and if, in their respective and distinct jurisdictions, they forsake the paths of righteousness, we shall become the scorn and contempt of foreign nations, a prey to every bold invader; or fall by intestine divisions, till we sink into general ruin, and universal wretchedness.

If any one doubt this, let him consult the history of nations, and especially of Israel: Let him look into the book of the Lamentations of Jeremiah. There, the Hebrew prophet and mourner appears a man of sorrows, and compacted with griefs: He breathes in sighs, and speaks in groans: Complicated scenes of horror and distress strike all our senses, while we hear the lamentations of his broken heart, mourning the ruins of Jerusalem, the cruel slaughter, and captivity of the people, the desolation of the temple, and that "from the daughter of Zion, all her beauty" was "departed."

I therefore, persuade myself, gentlemen, that in full confidence of your zeal for the public good, I may with all deference and freedom, recommend to your attention, the honour and safety of the confederate republic, as being of the same importance to the happiness and defence of the several states, as the peace and prosperity of Jerusalem, were to the several tribes of Israel.

If the national union, by concentrating the wisdom and force of America, was the means of our salvation from conquest and slavery —if the existence, liberty and independence of these states, and their national character, importance and glory depend still upon their united firmness and strength—if this union be necessary for the decision of controversies, which might otherwise engender wars among themselves, and be the only probable means of their safety and defence against foreign nations—and if without it, the American commerce and intercourse can never be respectable, safe and extensive in the various parts of the world—If these things are true, which I leave, gentlemen, to your own consideration, certainly there are no objects of greater magnitude and importance, more loudly calling the attention of America, than the national union, the necessity of supporting the national honour, and to give the federal government energy at home, and respectability abroad.

I would, gentlemen, beg leave to ask, whether to neglect the great interest of the whole, and to imagine that each state can singly preserve and defend itself, be not as absurd, as if several men, at an amazing cost, should lay a costly foundation, and erect the mighty frame of a most magnificent palace; and then, before the expence be paid, from a fondness of finishing, each one, his own room, and of enjoying the pleasures of his separate apartment, they should fall into such contention and division, as not only to leave the frame neglected, uncovered and exposed to continual decay and ruin, but the whole undertaking liable to that curse, pronounced in the book of GOD. "Wo unto him, that buildeth his house by unrighteousness, and his chambers by wrong; that useth his neighbours service without wages, and giveth him not for his work."

I own, gentlemen, I am concerned for the national honour and happiness; and were I to consult only my own feelings, I might hold up to your view, the dying languors of the national union, as foreboding ruin, division, or some dreadful convulsion, to these states. But perhaps, my fears are grounded not in the state of the nation, but in the want of an extensive knowledge of public affairs. You will, however, give me leave to hope, that the greatest attention will be paid to all just and reasonable measures, for supporting and maintaining the liberty and glory of the American states, and republic.

I only add, gentlemen, on this subject, my most sincere prayer, that heaven would guide all your deliberations, and collect and unite the wisdom and patriotism of America, in the proposed convention of the states, in some just and equal system of federal subordination, effectually securing the internal liberty and sovereignty of the states, and giving such dignity and authority to the federal government, that it may be the means of securing the peace, and prosperity of the whole, and the benefit of it reach to the most distant ages, and increase from generation to generation to the latest posterity.

I persuade myself, gentlemen, you will have a watchful regard to the rights and privileges of this people; and in all reasonable ways, ease their burdens and relieve their sorrows. You are too well acquainted, to need any information of the uneasiness, discontent and complaints, which prevail in the state. I will not presume to say, how far, these complaints are without any just foundation—how far, they arise from the real distresses and burdens of the times—how far, they are founded in any real, or supposed mistakes, in the public administration—or how far they have been nursed and cherished, by men of power and influence; whose office required them, to quiet the voice of murmuring, instead of inflaming the public, in order to answer their own ends, and procure self exaltation, or to prevent that of others. But, from whatever different and opposite sources, these complaints arise, you cannot do your people more essential service, than to apply the most faithful counsels and prudent means, for the removing and healing [of] them.

If any of the evils the people suffer, have been occasioned by their own imprudent conduct, you will nevertheless pity them; and afford all the relief in your power. This is to act the part of a kind and tender father, who would not by unreasonable severity, push his children on to ruin and despair. But, though you pity and study to relieve them in trouble, you must not support them in vice and disorder. As a faithful physician will sometimes use palliatives, but will never gratify a sick patient to his distruction: So as far as may be consistent with the great rules of righteousness, you will suit the public conduct to the infirmities of the people, but you cannot consent to measures of iniquity, which will work ruin and misery to the state.

Hear all the equitable petitions of the people; but should they ask you to be unrighteous, stop your ears: Be merciful and compassionate; but maintain a conduct consistent with the dignity, faith and honour of government, and with those fixed rules and everlasting maxims, by which it is to be administered. It is a day, in which trimmers and time-servers are very unfit to direct the affairs of state. I wish, none such may be found among the honourable personages, whom I now address. If any of you, gentlemen, for acting the dictates of an upright conscience, should fall under the displeasure of the people, you will have infinitely greater support and consolation in the rectitude of your own minds, than the highest applause fellow-mortals can give. Superior dignity and virtue, in these circumstances of trial, appear to the best advantage, and shines with the brightest lustre; and will meet the approbation of the great judge in the presence of an assembled world. The frowns of a misguided, and the resentments of an ungrateful people, cannot bend the true patriot to meanness; nor the loss of honour and public station, tempt him to iniquity, and to consent to such measures, as in his fixed opinion and judgement, will end in public shame and ruin.

Remember, gentlemen, that while you are examining the rights of individuals, and their claims on one another, or on the public, you drop the character of legislators, and should act by the same fixed rules of law and equity, as the judge on the bench. In causes of a judicial kind, your high character of sovereignty will not excuse an arbitrary decision, or denial of justice, any more than the same may be excused in the lowest executive court. In granting favours, you have only to consider, whether they are equitable and consistent with the good of the community; but in doing justice, you have no sovereign discretion. No wise man thinks his life and estate safe in the hand of a tyrant, bound by no restraint of law: Excuse me, gentlemen, when I add, that the discretion of a popular assembly acting by no fixed and known rules of equity, is a different expression, but the same in effect, as the arbitrary will of a despot. Sovereign power should never be perverted to acts of unrighteousness: Let not therefore the notion of omnipotence, and of being above controul, insensibly insinuate itself into your deliberations, and lead to a different determination, from what you would give in a different character.

With deference to your high stations, I am warranted with all freedom to assure you, in the fear of God, the almighty and eternal Judge, that the consideration of not being accountable to an higher court on earth, should be one of the most forcible motives, to engage you to the greatest uprightness and impartiality, not only between subject and subject, but especially the subject and the public. Remember, that as in this world, there is an appeal from a lower to an higher court, so when the most sovereign and uncontroulable court on earth, gives an unrighteous sentence, and wickedly perverts judgment, there is immediately entered in the high court of heaven, an appeal, which, in the great day of general assise, will be called, and must be answered. Then you, my honourable auditors, and all the kings and judges of the earth shall appear, and give an account for your conduct, while you acted in the character of gods, on earth.

I have not pointed out, wherein the difficulties and embarrassments of the present day consist; nor what political measures are best to extricate the people from them: These things, gentlemen, belong to you, and demand the exercise of your superior wisdom and prudence; but I am confident of the real advantage of those principles and maxims, I have insisted on as the great foundation of the happiness and strength of civil society. In this, I think, I have kept within my own limits, and can therefore with an humble freedom, commend them to your attention and consideration. To you it belongs to build upon them, and to improve all your dexterity, zeal and authority to compact us together. To you we look to heal our wounds, to appease our disquiet, to rectify our disorders, and to apply those bands and ligaments, which shall hold us together, and prevent our dissolution and ruin. This is the righteous expectation of God, and the desire and hope of all good men. Be not like the ten spies, who brought up an evil report of the good land of Canaan, and discouraged the hearts of their brethren: but like Joshua and Caleb, who endeavoured to still the people with the assurances of good hope, that under God they were able to surmount the difficulties before them.

Notwithstanding the darkness of the present day, and the public difficulties we labour under, be of good courage, and the Lord be with you: Though the earth and it's inhabitants be dissolved, hold up the pillars thereof; and never let this state be removed from the foundations of righteousness and truth. If these foundations have by any means received a shock, and seem to be in a tottering condition, let your wisdom and courage give them stability. If the pillars of public faith and justice, judgment and equity have been bent and twisted, like the limber osier, give them that strength and firmness, that they may hereafter stand unshaken as the aged oak: and let this people, and all the world know, that you mean to be a righteous legislature; and wish to rule over a righteous people.

I shall add only in a few words, that while in all other ways, you endeavour the good of this people, and expect from them a reverential regard for magistracy, and a peaceable behaviour in the state, you will, gentlemen, appoint men of virtue and religion to all important offices of executive trust: And be yourselves the best examples of righteousness and the fear of GOD. Shew yourselves friends to religion and virtue—to the church of CHRIST, and the worship of GOD—to the ministers of the gospel—and to the great and important interests of education and learning in the state: By this you will do honour to yourselves, and essential service to your country, merit the esteem and gratitude of good men, and meet the approbation of GOD. If religion and good manners be legible, not only in your laws, but in your lives, rendering you conspicuous for piety and mercy, justice and sobriety, your authority will be strengthened, and your administration supported. The attractive force of your examples, will engage your people to that behaviour, which is necessary to the peace and prosperity of the state; and the endeavours of good citizens will be united in procuring and advancing the noble and beneficial ends of society. Thus you will be the lights of the world, the ornaments of mankind; and having with eminent usefulness served your generation according to the will of GOD, may you finally enjoy the rewards of faithful servants.

The public exhortation and address now turns itself to the ministers of the gospel.

My fathers and brethren,

We are members of civil society, equally interested in it's peace and prosperity, with the rest of our fellow-citizens; and especially "because of the house of the Lord our GOD," we are bound "to seek" it's "good." The immediate ends of the magistracy and ministry are different, but not opposite: They mutually assist each other, and ultimately center in the same point. The one has for its object the promotion of religion and the cause of CHRIST; the other immediately aims at the peace and order of mankind in this world: Without which, there could be no fixed means of religion; nor the church have a continuance on earth, but through the interposition of a miraculous providence, constantly displayed for its preservation. Hence the church of CHRIST will have no fixed residence, where there is no civil government, until he, whose right it is, shall take to himself his great power, and reign king of nations, even as he is king of saints.

How thankful then should we be for the ordinance of civil government, which is a token of divine forbearance to a guilty world; and will continue till the designs of the christian ministry, are accomplished. How many have no higher conception of the christian ministry, and the wisdom and goodness of GOD in appointing it, than as relating to this world? Hence, while they pride themselves in civil privileges, and perhaps, allow the morality of the gospel to have some good influence on the happiness of society, they have no idea of the glory of the christian scheme of salvation, and despise the gospel, the ministry and the church of GOD. And yet, were it not, that the gospel might be preached, and the church have a being on earth, civil government would cease among men.

To preach the gospel of the Redeemer, to open his salvation, to explain and urge his precepts, and to represent the motives of the religion taught by him, together with the administration of the ordinances, which he hath appointed, are the immediate end; and the peculiar work of the christian ministry. This is the part, my fathers and brethren, assigned to us, on the walls of our Jerusalem; and whoever is faithful in this divine employment, will at once advance the temporal and eternal interests of mankind.

To this work, therefore, let us attend with all diligence and faithfulness, and use our utmost endeavours to promote the designs of redeeming love, in recovering sinful, guilty and miserable men, to the image and favour of GOD, in bringing them to a life of holiness, and to the practice of all righteousness and virtue. In doing this, we shall be the happy instruments of advancing the best good of society, by leading them to the diligent practice of all the duties of the social and christian life; and render them, most useful in their respective places: But, more especially, we shall be happy, in being made instruments, under the sacred influence of our divine Lord, of plucking them from the jaws of destruction, and the power and tyranny of Satan, of raising them to the greatest dignity and perfection of their nature; and of preparing them for the new Jerusalem, the city of our GOD, "wherein dwelleth righteousness."

While we look to our civil fathers for their kind countenance and protection, it will be our constant care to strengthen and encourage them, in the great and weighty concerns of government, by our prayers, by our public instructions, and by our examples, not only of civil subjection and obedience, but of all virtues, which adorn the christian profession and ministry, and conduce to the peace and prosperity of the commonwealth.

In this let us strive to excite, and unite all our endeavours. What is more necessary, than union among the ministers of CHRIST? What gives the enemies of religion more advantage, than the discord, which has prevailed among christians? Or what stabs the cause of the Redeemer, with deeper wounds, than the contention of his ministers? Let us not look to the coercive power of the civil sword, to heal these wounds; but to our divine and almighty Saviour, to give us one heart and one way; and let us study his gospel, which contains not only the doctrines we are to teach, and the duties we are to inculcate; but the most forcible motives of mutual love, kindness and forbearance. If we drink at this pure fountain of benevolence, and imbibe the spirit of the meek and lowly JESUS, it will cleanse away our envy, pride and ambition, the great sources of ministerial contention. We shall love one another, and strive together in our endeavours, and in our prayers for the success of the gospel, and the peace of churches.

Brethren, our time is short: Our fathers many of them are gone: Every year makes breaches upon our order. May GOD sanctify the heavy strokes of the year past, upon the churches, and the ministry, that we may be quickened to greater zeal and diligence in our important work. He that is faithful to the death, shall receive the crown of everlasting life and love, in the kingdom of our heavenly Father.

An address to the numerous audience present, on this joyful occasion, shall conclude my discourse.

Friends and fellow citizens,

A constitution of government, which gives a people the liberty of choosing their own rulers, and of being governed by laws, established by common consent, while they make a wise use of it, is a privilege more valuable, than the gold of Ophir, and of greater importance to public happiness, than the rich mountains of Peru. What shall you do to render this privilege a blessing to the present age, and hand down the joys of it to future generations? Make it your constant aim to choose able and faithful men, who fear GOD and hate covetousness, to be your rulers; honour and encourage them in all their endeavours to make you a virtuous, prosperous and happy people, and apply yourselves with diligence to your own business, that in your several stations, you may contribute to the public good.

The burden of government at all times, and especially at the present, is very great. We may so behave as to render it far greater and more difficult, by our misconduct and disorderly practices; and prevent the best fruits of the most wise and righteous administration. We may discourage the hearts and slacken the hands of the most worthy magistrates, by an unruly and discontented spirit, and by an opposition to all their designs for the public good. How many endeavour to enervate and avoid the force of the most wholesome laws of society; and use every art to make the people discontented, and to promote factions in the state.

I think it my duty on this solemn occasion, to warn my fellow citizens, against all such vile and wicked practices, which tend to the ruin of magistracy, and the destruction of peace and order. I wish, my fellow-citizens, all had a due sense of the high importance of civil government, and the protection afforded us by the laws of our country. Whatever security and peace, we enjoy by day or night, at home or abroad, in the house, in the field, or by the way, are by means of civil union and society. Without this bond, and the restraint of civil institutions, no one would be safe in his person or property. The weak would be continually exposed to the oppression and injustice of a more powerful neighbour. Civil government therefore, well constituted, and impartially administered, is one of the most important blessings, a gracious GOD has bestowed upon a guilty world; and the laws and constitution of our country are our best inheritance, which we should defend at the hazard of our lives and fortunes.

If any real or supposed grievances should arise in a republic, they may be examined and redressed, without having recourse to arms, and opposing the government of the people, in the hands of the constitutional authority of the state. Good rulers will esteem it an honour that the public conduct should be examined, and the errors of administration rectified: And if rulers appointed by the people abuse their authority, they may be displaced. A republic has the means of redress within itself; and cannot be oppressed, but by its own fault and neglect.

But while in a free government, the public conduct is open to inspection and discussion, there is a great difference between the reproof of friendship, and the reproach of an enemy; much more between personal slander and abuse, and a candid examination of public mistakes and grievances, that they may be rectified and redressed. The latter is the right of the people and may be encouraged; the former is to be detested, nor can its venom be hidden or justified, under the cloak of public good. Its tendency is to introduce an imbittered party-spirit, and to promote factions and disturbances: It savours, not of that wisdom from above, pure, peaceable, gentle, easy to be intreated, full of mercy and good fruits, without partiality, and without hypocrisy, but of that which is earthly, sensual, devilish: It is not a cement, having the least tendency to add strength to the foundations, beauty to the walls, or peace and prosperity to the palaces of our Jerusalem.

I sincerely condole with my country, under the heavy burden lying on the people. If a considerable part of this burden has been brought upon ourselves by imprudent conduct, we ought not to complain to our rulers, and think ourselves hardly used, if the foundations of justice be not removed for our sakes. If any part of it be occasioned by unnecessary expences in government, and by salaries and rewards, too lavishly bestowed on those, who serve the public, we have right to complain, and to expect redress. And if the claims of any men on the public, or other burdens in the state, be unjust, we may boldly apply to our rulers for relief: For to execute judgement, to do justice, to loose the bands of wickedness, to undo the heavy burdens, to let the oppressed go free, and to break every yoke, is the great end of their institution and office: Surely then, a righteous legislature will hear all our reasonable complaints, and ease our sorrows.

But if these burdens are just, the price of our liberty, and of all the privileges which we enjoy, what can our rulers do, but encourage us to be a righteous and industrious people, and contrive the best, most easy and effectual measures for discharging the public debt? They cannot deny that we have had an army—hired soldiers, and carried on a long and expensive war, in which through the signal interposition of a wonder-working Providence, we have been gloriously successful —that we are indebted to France, Holland and Spain, in sums to a large amount—and that thousands of our citizens have lent their substance and treasure to this and the United States; many of whom are distressed by the public failure. They cannot create silver and gold: But supposing, it were in their power to furnish a full and rich store of these articles, for which we might sell and mortgage our estates, would not this be the ruin of the greater part of the debtors in the state, and of many other citizens, now in flourishing circumstances? But, it will be said, they can emit a bank of paper money, the benefit of which was experienced in former times. A mighty benefit; a blessed privilege, indeed, if it be on such a sinking foundation, that the dishonest taking advantage of its depreciation may defraud their creditors, and live and riot on the simplicity of their neighbours, and the spoils of public faith. Would it be right, my fellow-citizens, to force such a medium into the hands of the people, against their will and consent? A tyrant may compel his vassals for gold or silver promised, to take lead, tin, wood or stubble: But this would be esteemed in an eastern despot no better, than open and bare faced robbery. Such a thought ought not to be entertained of the righteous legislature of a free people, who enjoy the bible, in which we are taught, that whoever expects to be an inhabitant of the heavenly Jerusalem, though he sware to his hurt, changeth not. If this bank of paper-money be on a sure foundation, and have a currency, equal to gold and silver, the question returns, how shall we obtain it, unless we earn it, or pledge our estates for the redemption of it? In the first method, we might as well obtain silver and gold; the latter is big with ruin to thousands, and would tend to discourage the frugality, industry and economy, which begin to have so promising an appearance; and must be the means of freeing us from the great embarrassments we are under.

A sudden plenty of money, would not help us; nay it would do us hurt, unless it were obtained in that way, which would encourage those virtues in society, which are the strength, the happiness, and beauty of a people. These are industry, honesty, frugality, and the reciprocal acts of friendship, kindness, and mercy, which arise from the dependencies of one upon another. Had we a thousand tons of silver dispersed in this state, in such manner as should check the growth of those virtues, it would be truly the root of all evil, and dispose us to such a conduct, that in a few years, this mighty sum would vanish and the people become reduced to a more wretched state of indigence and want, than before: The years of plenty would soon be over, and there arise a louder cry for the suspension of public and private justice, than has ever been heard in America.

I cannot my fellow-citizens but flatter myself, that the necessity of the times has begun to work for its own relief, in a way conducive to the public good, and the virtue and peace of the people. Agriculture is more encouraged and attended to—the herds and flocks of large and small cattle are increasing—wool and flax are more prized—home-manufactures begin to be thought necessary—the distaff, the wheel and loom are becoming more fashionable—the shops of trifling baubles and gewgaws are less crouded—suits at law diminished—a general spirit of industry is more prevalent, and patience and perseverance seem only necessary to crown the work.

But to close this discourse and address; let us my friends and fellow-citizens, faithfully attend to our true interest and safety, in all those ways which are pointed out in wisdom and the circumstances we are under. Encourage your rulers in building up our Jerusalem, on the strong foundations of truth and righteousness—maintain in your hearts and conduct, those principles and maxims of love, benevolence and goodness, which will render you a united, happy and prosperous people. Let GOD be honoured, and the grace of the Redeemer exalted; the sabbath sanctified; the worship and ordinances of the Lord's house, maintained: The pious and virtuous education of the rising generation, religiously regarded; and a firm and inviolable adherence to the laws and institutions of CHRIST, manifested by all orders and ranks of men. Then virtue and peace, righteousness, mercy and the fear of GOD, will flourish; and every member of the community, will be found fixed in his proper place, and discharging the duties of it.

This is that peaceful and happy state, which King David so earnestly desired might be the portion of Jerusalem, and make it a joy and a praise in all the earth. Let his holy and pious wish be the language of all our hearts: "Pray for the peace of" our "Jerusalem: They shall prosper that love thee: Peace be within thy walls, and prosperity within thy palaces: For my brethren and companions sake, I will now say, peace be within thee; because of the house of the Lord our GOD, I will seek thy Good."

AMEN

32

THE REPUBLIC OF THE ISRAELITES AN EXAMPLE TO THE AMERICAN STATES

Samuel Langdon

EXETER
1788

Samuel Langdon (1723-1797). A native of Boston, Langdon was graduated from Harvard in the class of 1740 with Samuel Adams. The two young men shared the same political views during the revolutionary and early national periods—which is to say, Langdon was a Whig and a patriot in the sacred cause of liberty. Soon after graduation, Langdon, a Congregational minister, served as chaplain of the New Hampshire Regiment at the taking of Louisbourg (1745), then became pastor of the North Church in Portsmouth, where he served until becoming president of Harvard College in 1774. That tenure was difficult and unpleasant for Langdon, and he was glad to relinquish it in 1780 and return to the pulpit at Hampton Falls, New Hampshire, where he remained during the final seventeen years of his life.

As a confidant of the leading patriots of the region, Langdon well represented the mind of the revolutionary generation in his political sermons. His 1775 election sermon, *Government Corrupted by Vice, and Recovered by Righteousness*, preached in Watertown, Massachusetts, is a classic; it was reprinted in John W. Thornton, ed., *The Pulpit of the American Revolution* (1860). Langdon was prominent in securing the adoption of the federal Constitution as a delegate to the New Hampshire state convention in 1788.

The Republic of the Israelites an Example to the American States was the election sermon for New Hampshire preached in 1788.

The Republic of the ISRAELITES *an Example to the* AMERICAN STATES

A SERMON,

PREACHED AT

CONCORD,

IN THE STATE OF

NEW-HAMPSHIRE;

BEFORE THE HONORABLE

GENERAL COURT

AT THE ANNUAL

ELECTION.

JUNE 5, 1788.

By SAMUEL LANGDON, D. D.

PASTOR OF THE CHURCH IN HAMPTON-FALLS.

EXETER:
PRINTED BY LAMSON AND RANLET
M,DCC,LXXXVIII.

I think myself happy that, after reiterated invitations from this honourable court, I am at length permitted by divine providence, though under peculiar difficulties, and in the decline of life, to appear in this place, and speak on this public occasion, when the principal officers of government are to be appointed to their several departments, according to the suffrages of the people. I will endeavor to give due honor to the rulers of the people, while I declare, with simplicity of heart and honest freedom, the admonitions which the great Lord of the universe gives; and offer my best thoughts as to the general administration of public affairs, and the way to secure the prosperity and happiness of a nation.

There is a remarkable paragraph in the sacred writings, which may be very well accommodated to my present purpose, and merits particular attention. You have it in Deuteronomy, IV, 5–8.

> *Behold, I have taught you statutes and judgments, even as the Lord my God commanded me, that ye should do so in the land whither ye go to possess it. Keep therefore and do them; for this is your wisdom and your understanding in the sight of the nations, who shall hear all these statutes, and say, surely this great nation is a wise and understanding people: for what nation is there so great, which hath God so nigh unto them as the Lord our God is in all things that we call upon him for? and what nation is there so great, which hath statutes and judgments so righteous as all this law which I set before you this day.*

Here Moses recommends to Israel the strict observance of all the laws which he had delivered to them by God's command, relating both to their civil polity and religion, as the sure way to raise their reputation high among all nations as a wise and understanding people; because no other nation was blessed with such excellent national laws, or the advantage of applying to the oracle of the living God, and praying to him in all difficulties, with assurance that all their requests would be answered.

As to every thing excellent in their constitution of government, except what was peculiar to them as a nation separated to God from the rest of mankind, the Israelites may be considered as a pattern to the world in all ages; and from them we may learn what will exalt our character, and what will depress and bring us to ruin.

Let us therefore look over their constitution and laws, enquire into their practice, and observe how their prosperity and fame depended on their strict observance of the divine commands both as to their government and religion.

They had both a civil and military establishment under divine direction, and a complete body of judicial laws drawn up and delivered to them by Moses in God's name. They had also a form of religious worship, by the same authority, minutely prescribed, designed to preserve among them the knowledge of the great Creator of the Universe, and teach them to love and serve him; while idolatry prevailed through the rest of the world: and this religion contained not only a public ritual, but a perfect, though very concise, system of morals, comprehended in ten commands, which require the perfection of godliness, benevolence, and rectitude of conduct.

When first the Israelites came out from the bondage of Egypt, they were a multitude without any other order than what had been kept up, very feebly, under the ancient patriarchal authority. They were suddenly collected into a body under the conduct of Moses, without any proper national or military regulation. Yet in the short space of about three months after they had passed the red sea, they were reduced into such civil and military order, blended together by the advice of Jethro, as was well adapted to their circumstances in the wilderness while destitute of property. Able men were chosen out of all their tribes, and made captains and rulers of thousands, hundreds, fifties and tens: and these commanded them as military officers, and acted as judges in matters of common controversy.

But the great thing wanting was a permanent constitution, which might keep the people peaceable and obedient while in the desert, and after they had gained possession of the promised land. Therefore, upon the complaint of Moses that the burden of government was too heavy for him, God commanded him to bring seventy men, chosen from among the elders and officers, and present them at the tabernacle; and there he endued them with the same spirit which was in Moses, that they might bear the burden with him. Thus a senate was evidently constituted, as necessary for the future government of the nation, under a chief commander. And as to the choice of this senate, doubtless the people were consulted, who appear to have had a voice in all public affairs from time to time, the whole congregation being called together on all important occasions: the government therefore was a proper republic.

And beside this general establishment, every tribe had elders and a prince according to the patriarchal order, with which Moses did not interfere; and these had an acknowledged right to meet and consult together, and with the consent of the congregation do whatever was necessary to preserve good order, and promote the common interest of the tribe. So that the government of each tribe was very similar to the general government. There was a president and senate at the head of each, and the people assembled and gave their voice in all great matters: for in those ages the people in all republics were entirely unacquainted with the way of appointing delegates to act for them, which is a very excellent modern improvement in the management of republics.

Moreover, to compleat the establishment of civil government, courts were to be appointed in every walled city, after their settlement in Canaan, and elders most distinguished for wisdom and integrity were to be made judges, ready always to sit and decide the common controversies within their respective jurisdictions. The people had a right likewise to appoint such other officers as they might think necessary for the more effectual execution of justice, according to that order given in Deut. 16. 18, 19—

> *Judges and officers shalt thou make thee in all thy gates which the Lord thy God giveth thee throughout thy tribes; and they shall judge the people with just judgment: thou shalt not wrest judgment; thou shalt not respect persons, neither take a gift; for a gift doth blind the eyes of the wise, and pervert the words of the righteous.*

But from these courts an appeal was allowed in weighty causes to higher courts appointed over the whole tribe, and in very great and difficult cases to the supreme authority of the general senate and chief magistrate.

A government, thus settled on republican principles, required laws; without which it must have degenerated immediately into aristocracy, or absolute monarchy. But God did not leave a people, wholly unskilled in legislation, to make laws for themselves: he took this important matter wholly into his own hands, and beside the moral laws of the two tables, which directed their conduct as individuals, gave them by Moses a complete code of judicial laws. They were not numerous indeed, but concise and plain, and easily applicable to almost every controversy which might arise between man and man, and every criminal case which might require the judgment of the court. Of these some were peculiarly adapted to their national form, as divided into tribes and families always to be kept distinct; others were especially suited to the peculiar nature of the government as a theocrasy, God himself being eminently their king, and manifesting himself among them in a visible manner, by the cloud of glory in the tabernacle and temple. This was the reason why blasphemy, and all obstinate disobedience to his laws, were considered as high treason, and punished with death; especially idolatry, as being a crime against the fundamental principles of the constitution. But far the greater part of the judicial laws were founded on the plain immutable principles of reason, justice, and social virtue; such as are always necessary for civil society. Life and property were well guarded, and punishments were equitably adapted to the nature of every crime: in particular, murder stands foremost among capital crimes, and is defined with such precision, and so clearly distinguished from all cases of accidental and undesigned killing, that the innocent were in no danger of punishment, and the guilty could not escape. And if we still pay regard to this divine law, which is evidently founded on reason and justice, the modern distinction of manslaughter must be rejected as a popish invention, contrived and added in times when superstition reigned and claimed a power above all laws. These laws were sufficient for a nation which had but little commerce abroad; especially as the oracle of Jehovah might be consulted in all cases of a very extraordinary nature.

Let us now consider the national worship which God established among his people; on which their obedience to the moral law very much depended: for unless they paid constant reverence and homage to their God, agreeable to his nature and will, they would soon break loose from all other obligations to morality.

Now as to their ritual; however contemptible, and even ridiculous, it may seem to men whose ideas are all modern, and who proudly contemn divine revelation; and notwithstanding it is now abrogated by a far more glorious revelation of grace and truth by Jesus Christ;

no religious institution could be more perfectly accommodated to those early ages of the world, and the situation of the Israelites in the midst of idolaters, or better prepare the way for the truth and mercy of the gospel. In those ages the minds of men were not sufficiently cultivated to receive that religion which is spiritual and simple, detached from sensible objects, and destitute of worldly grandeur. Other nations worshipped their gods with an endless variety of superstitious rites, a multitude of costly sacrifices, and all kinds of external pomp, which they fancied would be acceptable to deities to whom they attributed the imperfections and even the worst vices of men. Their worship gratified all the senses, was accommodated to every passion and lust, and indulgent to gross immoralities; it not only captivated vulgar minds, but bound the greatest heroes, politicians, and philosophers, fast in the chains of superstition. Therefore it was necessary that the worship of the true God should not be destitute of that splendour which, in those ages, struck the minds of men with awe and reverence. Without some magnificence the best religion would have appeared contemptible in the view of the world; and the Israelites themselves, dazzled with the pageantry of idols, would almost inevitably have been captivated; as, notwithstanding every guard which could be placed about them, we find the fashion of the rest of the world had surprising power over them. But the ceremonies of worship which God commanded his people to observe, were not, like those of the heathen, inhuman, frantic, obscene, varied a thousand ways according to the different characters of their gods; no, but by infinite wisdom they were calculated to promote the knowledge of the divine perfections, and obedience to the laws of righteousness, and give the most encouraging hope in the goodness and mercy of God. The ritual of the Israelites was rational, sober, uniform, plainly intended to exhibit the majesty, purity, and mercy of the eternal king; to humble men before him under a continual sense of guilt; and to assure true penitents of free pardon by virtue of the appointed sacrifices, which were types of that one sacrifice which Christ has offered for the sins of the world. And to render their worship more striking in their own view; and in the eyes of the world, their tabernacle and temple, their priesthood with its ornaments, their solemn assemblies and great festivals, were decent and magnificent beyond every thing seen among the nations around.

How unexampled was this quick progress of the Israelites, from abject slavery, ignorance, and almost total want of order, to a national establishment perfected in all its parts far beyond all other kingdoms and states! from a mere mob, to a well regulated nation, under a government and laws far superior to what any other nation could boast!

It was a long time after the law of Moses was given before the rest of the world knew any thing of government by law. Where kings reigned their will was a law. Where popular governments were formed, the capricious humour of the multitude ordered every thing just according to present circumstances; or their senators and judges were left to act according to their best discretion. It was six hundred years after Moses before the Spartans, the most famous of the Grecian republics, received a very imperfect, and in some particulars very absurd code of laws from Lycurgus. After this feeble attempt of legislation, three hundred years more elapsed before Solon appeared and gave laws to Athens, though a city long famous for arms, arts, eloquence, and philosophy. And it was about five hundred years from the first founding of the celebrated Roman empire, and nearly three hundred years after Solon, before the first laws of that empire were imported from Greece in twelve tables, by ten embassadors sent there for that purpose. But even when that empire had attained the summit of glory, and legislation was carried to great perfection, however well adapted to a government so extensive and complicate their laws might be, they were far from being worthy to be compared with the laws of Israel, as to the security of life, liberty, property, and public morals: and as to their religion, which was from the beginning interwoven with the state, instead of receiving any greater perfection from the increase of knowledge, wealth and power, it only became a more abundant congeries of ridiculous and detestable superstitions. Moreover; when the Roman empire was overwhelmed and destroyed by an inundation of barbarous nations, and many kingdoms were erected in Europe out of its ruins by the conquerors, laws were extinct under the feudal system; the will of the barons was a law for their vassals; and but a few centuries have past since kings began to introduce law into their courts of justice. And now, though legislation has been carried to such perfection in Great Britain, that land of knowledge and liberty, yet in a political and judicial view the laws of that kingdom may be charged with many great faults, which ought not to be copied: particularly, the tediousness, voluminous bulk, intricacy, barbarous language, and uncertain operation of many of them as to equity, ought to be avoided by legislators who wish for an easy and speedy course of justice among a free people. And perhaps our own courts might be so reformed as to prevent cases of inconsiderable value, and easy decision, from rising through all the stages of the law. Against these imperfections good provision was made in the law of Moses, and it might be much for our advantage to pay greater attention to that example.

Upon a review of what has been said, must it not appear quite unaccountable, that the Israelites should so speedily attain to such an height of good policy and legislation, beyond all other nations? Are we not constrained to acknowlege an immediate interposition and direction of heaven? Had the unexperienced multitude been left to themselves to draw up a system of civil and military government for themselves, it would have been entirely beyond their abilities to comprehend so complicated a subject; they must have committed innumerable mistakes, in attempting to introduce and establish it; they would have been in danger of jarring opinions, tumults, and insurrections; and probably before the design could be effected, discouragement and confusion would have forced them to surrender into the hands of despotism. But their God provided every thing necessary for their happiness, and nothing more was left to their own wisdom than to submit to his authority, and adhere strictly to his commands: by this, their reputation among the nations would have been equal to the excellency of their laws.

But now you may say, Why then were they not universally celebrated? Why did not princes and politicians from all parts of the world visit them, to learn maxims of polity from so well regulated a nation? Why did not philosophers come, and enquire into that system of religion and morality which carried virtue to such an height of perfection? Surely a nation, of which all the parts were so firmly cemented, must be strong and formidable: a people, who enjoyed the most rational liberty, and yet were under the most voluntary and absolute subjection to authority, free from all the convulsions and revolutions which frequently arise from the raging folly of the populace, must become famous: a wise and impartial administration of justice, according to the most excellent laws, by which all were kept in perfect security and peace, could not but be admired: and the commerce of a people, whose morals were governed by the best precepts, whose word might be trusted, who practised no kind of fraud, and whose behaviour was always benevolent, sober, prudent, and sincere, must be highly valued by the world. Whereas on the contrary, the Israelites were often weak, distressed, and generally despised and hated by all their neighbours. The plain answer to this objection is—They never adhered in practice either to the principles of their civil polity or religion: but on their practice depended the prosperity and honor of the nation. They received their law from God, but they did not keep it. They neglected their government, corrupted their religion, and grew dissolute in their morals, and in such a situation no nation under heaven can prosper.

Let us view their state, in the first place, under the judges. Tho' the national senate was instituted for the assistance of Moses as captain-general and judge of the nation, and this was a plain intimation that in all succeeding times such a senate was necessary for the assistance of the supreme magistrate: yet after Joshua and the elders of his time were dead, it does not appear that they took the least care to fill their places. They left all the affairs of the nation to chance, or extraordinary providence, and had no chief commander, except when God in compassion to them in their troubles raised up judges for their deliverance. And as they suffered the general government to drop, we may well think them as careless of the government of the particular tribes. In each tribe, as we have observed, a government ought to have been kept up similar to the national authority, by the elders and prince of the tribe. But we find this remark repeatedly made in the book of Judges—"*In those days there was no king in Israel, but every man did that which was right in his own eyes*"—that is in plain terms, there was no authority any where, but every man was left to act as he pleased. No wonder therefore if they were weak in council and war, and exposed on every side to the insults of their neighbours, being unable to unite in their own defence. This neglect of government was wholly inexcusable: for however they might plead, that Moses, and Joshua, and the seventy elders, were of God's immediate appointment, and that they had no warrant to fill up their places; they could not but know they had an undoubted right to provide for their own welfare, especially when there was so plain an intimation that the same government was to be continued. If they were at a loss what to do, they had the greatest oracle in the world among them, and they ought to have enquired of God, their king, how to proceed and what persons to choose. Nay, they were some times sensible enough of their right to appoint a chief commander, and even to make the command hereditary, as appears by the address to Gideon —"*Rule thou over us; both thou, and thy son, and thy son's son also*"—by the choice which the Shechemites made of Abimelech to be their king; and by Jephtha's bargain with the Gileadites to be their head and captain, if he fought for them against the Ammonites. By all this we may plainly see that the general neglect of government is to be charged as the fault of the people.

And now we cannot wonder if courts of justice ceased, when the higher powers of government were wanting. These courts, which should have been continued in every walled city, dwindled way and came to nothing; crimes were unpunished, and the most abominable vices spread their infection through all ranks. No law was executed to deter men from murders, robberies, rapes, or any other kind of wickedness. This is evident by the case of the Levite whose concubine was abused to death by the mob of Benjamites at Gibeah: the city in general discovered no disposition to do justice upon the offenders; there were no judges near, to whom complaint might be made; nay, it seems the whole tribe were ready to abett the crime rather than punish it; nor was there any authority in the nation to take cognizance of the matter; and therefore the Levite was obliged to take a method, shocking to humanity, in order to excite the indignation of the other tribes, and bring their forces against the Benjamites to their destruction.

We have also good reason to think the military affairs of the nation were not in a much better state than the civil. They could not wholly omit the care of their militia, because they were continually exposed to wars in their own defence. It was necessary to provide officers, and keep up some degree of discipline; but they were very deficient in this respect, especially as to superior command. In almost every battle, against the most contemptible of their neighbours, they were unsuccessful; and were ravaged, plundered, and brought under tribute by all in their turns, and delivered only when God mercifully interposed by raising up a general in an extraordinary way. On an alarm, instead of forming a regular army, they seem to have ran together suddenly from all quarters, without order, as if to stop a conflagration. Such disunited undirected force was never able to sustain a heavy attack, but gave every invader an easy victory.

But that which was the main force of all their disorder and misery, was their neglecting and corrupting that religion which God commanded. As long as those elders lived, who were with Joshua, and had seen all the great works of the Lord which he did for Israel, the people adhered to the worship of the true God as prescribed in the law: but when they were dead, the impressions which had been made by miracles wore off, as is natural; and they grew regardless of the worship of the sanctuary, gave scope to their own imaginations, and soon made a mixture of all the superstitions and idolatries of the heathen with the worship of Jehovah. They kept up no method of religious instruction; and as they grew more and more ignorant, they thought it too inconvenient to travel so often from all parts of the country, to offer sacrifices at the tabernacle, though it was very centrally placed at Shiloh, not much more than eighty miles distant from the remotest towns; but every man chose to worship nearer home: and so they made groves, and built altars for themselves, and soon set up images of Baal, Ashteroth, and other genteel deities which their neighbours worshipped. By these idols, however, they pretended to worship the true God, and brought sacrifices after their own hearts; for they imagined that all kinds of religion came much to the same thing, and whether precisely agreeable to the command or not, would be acceptable, if they were sincere. Thus Micah made images, and procured a priest in his own house, which the children of Dan afterwards took away, and fixed in their new conquered city, in the northern bounds of Canaan, where this idolatry continued until the ten tribes were carried into captivity; and Joash, the father of Gideon, had a grove, and an altar of Baal, for his own family; likewise Gideon himself, though highly honoured of God in being the deliverer of Israel from the Midianites, made an ephod, which was soon the occasion of superstitious worship, and drew him and the people from attending at the tabernacle.

Now by the foregoing view of the general state of the nation during the time of the judges, we may plainly see the reason why, instead of rising to fame by the perfection of their polity, religion, and morals, their character sunk into contempt. But let us see whether they conducted better afterwards, under their kings.

It was their crime to demand such a king as was like the kings of other nations, *i.e.* a king with the same absolute power, to command all according to his own pleasure. In this view God only was their king, and the head of the nation was only to be his vicegerent. Therefore as they had implicitly rejected the divine government, God gave them a king in his anger; the consequence of which was, the total loss of their republican form of government, and sad experience of the effects of despotic power. Indeed their religious establishment, which had been very much impaired in the days of the judges, was restored, and brought to its greatest glory, by David the most pious, and Solomon the wisest of kings; and during their reigns, the nation gained the height of grandeur; but no national senate was appointed, and the power of the kings continued to be despotic, and so the days of their prosperity were soon over. As soon as Rehoboam ascended the throne he openly avowed the most despotic principles, so that ten tribes revolted, and made Jeroboam their king. Jeroboam, out of policy, to prevent a reunion with Judah by means of the temple worship, placed two calves at the extremities of his kingdom, and persuaded the people to worship God by them instead of going to Jerusalem: and this false worship, together with a multitude of other idolatries introduced by this means, was the religion of the ten tribes, until they were captivated by the king of Assyria, and dispersed and lost among the nations. Nor did Rehoboam pay greater regard to the law of Moses; for he built high-places, and made images and groves on every high hill and under every green tree, and did according to all the abominations of the heathen; and in consequence of this, every kind of vice, and even sodomy, prevailed in the land. From this time the propensity of the people to idolatry increased, so that they readily followed the examples of succeeding bad kings, and it became a very difficult task for the best to make an effectual reformation. Nor is it to be wondered at that false religion so easily gained ground; for the people grew very ignorant: no care was taken to instruct them, in their several cities, in the law of God; but, being without teachers, they were very little acquainted with their own religious institutions. For this reason when good king Jehoshaphat resolved upon a reformation in church and state, after having taken a circuit thro' his kingdom to

> *bring the people back to the Lord God of their fathers, he sent out some of his principal officers, with priests and levites, to teach the people in the cities of Judah; and these carried the book of the law with them, and went about throughout all the cities of Judah, and taught them that religion which God commanded by Moses.*

It likewise appears by what immediately follows this account of his proceedings, that there had been a long omission of the administration of justice in the cities; that no courts had been kept up by preceeding kings, or such as were corrupt, in which the judges paid little regard to law and equity: for the king

> *set judges in the land, throughout all the fenced cities of Judah, city by city, and said unto the judges, take heed what ye do, for ye judge not for man but for the Lord, who is with you in the judgment:—wherefore now let the fear of Lord be upon you, take heed and do it, for there is no iniquity with the Lord our God, nor respect of persons, nor taking of gifts.*

Repeated attempts were made by the few pious kings, to put a stop to the corruption of religion and morals; but all in vain; the people relapsed again and again into ignorance, idolatry, and wickedness: their vices had increased to the utmost degree of enormity in Jeremiah's time; and their complicated crimes at length brought upon them desolation and a long captivity.

And now let us just take a glance at their general state after the captivity in Babylon. When they returned to their own land they endeavored to conform their religion and government to the mosaic standard; idolatry was entirely purged out; they discovered great zeal for the law of their God and the instituted worship; they appointed a general senate of seventy elders, called by them the Sanhedrin, with a supreme magistrate at the head, for the government of the nation; and while their pious zeal continued they grew and prospered. But, according to the common course of things in the world, religion soon degenerated into mere formality, without proper regard to its principal intention, and became only a shadow of that delivered to their fathers; the affairs of state were badly administered, and the highest honors were gained by favor, bribery, or violence; hypocrisy was substituted in the room of the true fear of God, and the practice of righteousness; all the vices natural to mankind daily increased; and finally they filled up the measure of their sins by crucifying the Lord of Glory, and rejecting his gospel, for which they have been made monuments of the divine displeasure unto this day.

Therefore upon the whole view we see, that the Israelites never attained to that fame and dignity among the nations which their constitution encouraged them to expect, because they took little care to practice agreably to the good statutes and judgments given them by Moses. Their constitution both of government and religion was excellent in writing, but was never exemplified in fact.

APPLICATION

And now, my fellow citizens, and much honored fathers of the State, you may be ready to ask *"To what purpose is this long detail of antiquated history on this public occasion?"* I answer—Examples are better than precepts; and history is the best instructor both in polity and morals. I have presented you with the portrait of a nation, highly favoured by heaven with civil and religious institutions, who yet, by not improving their advantages, forfeited their blessings, and brought contempt and destruction on themselves. If I am not mistaken, instead of the twelve tribes of Israel, we may substitute the thirteen states of the American union, and see this application plainly offering itself, viz. —That as God in the course of his kind providence hath given you an excellent constitution of government, founded on the most rational, equitable, and liberal principles, by which all that liberty is secured which a people can reasonably claim, and you are impowered to make righteous laws for promoting public order and good morals; and as he has moreover given you by his son Jesus Christ, who is far superior to Moses, a complete revelation of his will, and a perfect system of true religion, plainly delivered in the sacred writings; it will be your wisdom in the eyes of the nations, and your true interest and happiness, to conform your practice in the strictest manner to the excellent principles of your government, adhere faithfully to the doctrines and commands of the gospel, and practice every public and private virtue. By this you will increase in numbers, wealth, and power, and obtain reputation and dignity among the nations: whereas, the contrary conduct will make you poor, distressed, and contemptible.

The God of heaven hath not indeed visibly displayed the glory of his majesty and power before our eyes, as he came down in the sight of Israel on the burning mount; nor has he written with his own finger the laws of our civil polity: but the signal interpositions of divine providence, in saving us from the vengeance of a powerful irritated nation, from which we were unavoidably separated by their inadmissible claim of absolute parliamentary power over us; in giving us a Washington to be captain-general of our armies, in carrying us through the various distressing scenes of war and desolation, and making us twice triumphant over numerous armies, surrounded and captivated in the midst of their career; and finally giving us peace, with a large territory, and acknowledged independence; all these laid together fall little short of real miracles, and an heavenly charter of liberty for these United-States. And when we reflect, how wonderfully the order of these states was preserved when government was dissolved, or supported only by feeble props; with how much sobriety, wisdom, and unanimity they formed and received the diversified yet similar constitutions in the different states; with what prudence, fidelity, patience, and success, the Congress have managed the general government, under the great disadvantages of a very imperfect and impotent confederation; we cannot but acknowledge that God hath graciously patronized our cause, and taken us under his special care, as he did his ancient covenant people.

Or we may consider the hand of God in another view. Wisdom is the gift of God, and social happiness depends on his providencial government; therefore, if these states have framed their constitutions with superior wisdom, and secured their natural rights, and all the advantages of society, with greater precaution than other nations, we may with good reason affirm that God hath given us our government; that he hath taught us good statutes and judgments, tending to make us great and respectable in the view of the world. Only one thing more remains to complete his favor toward us; which is, the establishment of a general government, as happily formed as our particular constitutions, for the perfect union of these states. Without this, all that we glory in is lost; but if this should be effected, we may say with the greatest joy, "*God hath done great things for us.*" The general form of such a constitution hath already been drawn up, and presented to the people, by a convention of the wisest and most celebrated patriots in the land: eight of the states have approved and accepted it, with full testimonies of joy: and if it passes the scrutiny of the whole, and recommends itself to be universally adopted, we shall have abundant reason to offer elevated thanksgivings to the supreme Ruler of the universe for a government completed under his direction.*

Now our part is to make a wise improvement of what God grants us, and not neglect or despise our distinguishing privileges: for the best constitution, badly managed, will soon fall, and be changed into anarchy or tyranny. Without constant care of your families, you will have bad servants, and your estates will be wasted. So we must pay constant attention to the great family, if we desire to be a free and happy people.

The power in all our republics is acknowleged to originate in the people: it is delegated by them to every magistrate and officer; and to the people all in authority are accountable, if they deviate from their duty, and abuse their power. Even the man, who may be advanced to the chief command of these United States, according to the proposed constitution; whose office resembles that of a king in other nations, which has always been thought so sacred that they have had no conception of bringing a king before the bar of justice; even he depends on the choice of the people for his temporary and limited power, and will be liable to impeachment, trial, and disgrace for any gross misconduct. On the people, therefore, of these United-States it depends whether wise men, or fools, good or bad men, shall govern them; whether they shall have righteous laws, a faithful administration of government, and permanent good order, peace, and liberty; or, on the contrary, feel insupportable burdens, and see all their affairs run to confusion and ruin.

* Soon after this sermon was delivered, the convention of the state of New-Hampshire, met according to adjournment, and on the twenty first day of June accepted the proposed general Constitution of government. This being the ninth state which has acceded to this form of national union, it will be carried into effect; and there is no reason to doubt of the speedy accession of all the other states, which are now debating on the important question. May all rejoice in the Lord, who has formed us into a nation, and honour him as our judge, lawgiver, and king, who hath saved us, and will save us from all enemies and fears, if we thankfully receive and rightly improve his great mercies.

Therefore, I will now lift up my voice, and cry aloud to the people; to the people of this state in particular, whom I will consider as present by their representatives and rulers, and the congregation here collected from various towns. Rise! Rise to fame among all nations, as a wise and understanding people! political life and death are set before you; be a free, numerous, well ordered, and happy people! The way has been plainly set before you; if you pursue it, your prosperity is sure; but if not, distress and ruin will overtake you.

Preserve your government with the utmost attention and solicitude, for it is the remarkable gift of heaven. From year to year be careful in the choice of your representatives, and all the higher powers of government. Fix your eyes upon men of good understanding, and known honesty; men of knowledge, improved by experience; men who fear God, and hate covetousness; who love truth and righteousness, and sincerely wish the public welfare. Beware of such as are cunning rather than wise; who prefer their own interest to every thing; whose judgment is partial, or fickle; and whom you would not willingly trust with your own private interests. When meetings are called for the choice of your rulers, do not carelessly neglect them, or give your votes with indifference, just as any party may persuade, or a sordid treat tempt you; but act with serious deliberation and judgment, as in a most important matter, and let the faithful of the land serve you. Let not men openly irreligious and immoral become your legislators; for how can you expect good laws to be made by men who have no fear of God before their eyes, and who boldly trample on the authority of his commands? And will not the example of their impiety and immorality defeat the efficacy of the best laws which can be made in favour of religion and virtue? If the legislative body are corrupt, you will soon have bad men for counsellors, corrupt judges, unqualified justices, and officers in every department who will dishonor their stations; the consequence of which will be murmurs and complaints from every quarter. Let a superior character point out the man who is to be your head; for much depends on his inspection and care of public affairs and the influence of his judgment, advice and conduct, although his power is circumscribed: in this choice therefore be always on your guard against parties, and the methods taken to make interest for unworthy men, and let distinguished merit always determine your vote. And when all places in government are filled with the best men you can find, behave yourselves as good subjects; obey the laws; cheerfully submit to such taxation as the necessities of the public call for; give tribute to whom tribute is due, custom to whom custom, fear to whom fear, and honor to whom honor, as the gospel commands you. Never give countenance to turbulent men, who wish to distinguish themselves, and rise to power, by forming combinations and exciting insurrections against government: for this can never be the right way to redress real grievances, since you may not only prefer complaints and petitions to the court, but have the very authority, which you think has been misused, in your own power, and may very shortly place it in other hands. How happy was it for this state, that the insurrection, attempted here two years ago, was so seasonably and with so little difficulty suppressed, when the neighbouring state was brought into such a difficult and critical situation by the distracted populace, and has now scarcely recovered from that violent political paroxism.

I call upon you also to support schools in all your towns, that the rising generation may not grow up in ignorance. Grudge not any expence proportionate to your abilities. It is a debt you owe to your children, and that God to whom they belong; a necessary evidence of your regard for their present and future happiness, and of your concern to transmit the blessings you yourselves enjoy to future generations. The human mind without early and continual cultivation grows wild and savage: knowledge must be instilled as its capacities gradually enlarge, or it cannot expand and extend its sphere of activity. Without instruction men can have no knowledge but what comes from their own observation and experience, and it will be a long time before they can be acquainted even with things most necessary for the support and comfort of the present life. Leave your children untaught to read, write, cypher, &c. teach them no trade, or husbandry; let them grow up wholly without care; and they will be more fit for a savage than civil life, and whatever inheritance you may think to leave them will be of no advantage. But, on the contrary, train them up in the fear of God, in an acquaintance with his word, and all such useful knowledge as your abilities will allow, and they will soon know how to provide for themselves, perhaps may take care of their aged parents, and fill the various stations in life with honor and advantage. Look round and see the growing youth. they are to succeed in your stead; government and religion must be continued by them; from among these will shortly rise up our legislators, judges, ministers of the gospel, and officers of every rank. Can you think of this, and not promote schools, academies, and colleges? Can you leave the youth uninstructed in any thing which may prepare them to act their part well in the world? Will you suffer ignorance to spread its horrid gloom over the land? An ignorant people will easily receive idolatry for their religion, and must bow their necks to the tyrant's yoke, because they are incapable of using rational liberty. Will you then consign over your posterity to foolish and abominable superstitions instead of religion, and to be the slaves of despotism, when a small proportion of the produce of your labours will make them wise, free, and happy?

Will you hear me patiently a little farther, while I say one thing more of very great importance, which I dare not suppress. I call upon you to preserve the knowledge of God in the land, and attend to the revelation written to us from heaven. If you neglect or renounce that religion taught and commanded in the holy scriptures, think no more of freedom, peace, and happiness; the judgments of heaven will persue you. Religion is not a vain thing for you because it is your life: it has been the glory and defence of New-England from the infancy of the settlements; let it be also our glory and protection. I mean no other religion than what is divinely prescribed, which God himself has delivered to us with equal evidence of his authority, and even superior to that given to Israel, and which he has as strictly commanded us to receive and observe. The holy scriptures are given as the only rule of our faith, worship and obedience, and if we are guided by this perfect rule, we shall keep the way of truth and righteousness, and obtain the heavenly glory. We are now no more at liberty to draw up schemes of religion for ourselves, according to our own deceitful reasonings and vain imaginations, or to comply with the traditions and commands of men, or fall in with the refinements of human wisdom and the fashionable sentiments of the world, than Israel was to substitute modes of serving God different from what he had expressly required. We must believe what the Son of God, who made the worlds, and was sent by the Father with a proclamation of mercy to mankind, has declared to us. He died to redeem men from the servitude of sin, and reconcile them to God that they may be raised to life eternal; and he is appointed to be like a second Moses, the captain of our salvation to conduct us to heaven: to him therefore we must hearken in all things. The principal doctrines of his gospel are quite simple, plain and important. He teaches us that the commands of God reach to the inward thoughts, principles, and affections of the heart, as well as the outward conduct, and are as pure and perfect as the divine nature; that according to the laws of his moral government all men universally are sinners, and must repent in order to obtain mercy; that remission of sins is obtained only by believing on his name, and through his blood shed for us on the cross; that his disciples must receive his word, and obey whatsoever he hath commanded, endeavoring to be holy in all manner of conversation and avoid all the vices and corruptions of the world; that there will be a resurrection from the dead both of the just and unjust; and a day of solemn judgment, when all mankind must give an account of their conduct in this world, and receive their sentence from him whom the Father hath constituted to be the judge; and that in consequence of their sentence mankind will depart into very opposite states; the wicked into everlasting punishment, and the righteous into life eternal, the present visible system of nature being then dissolved in flames. In the belief of these plain truths, and that worship and obedience connected with them, the religion of christians consists. As to worship, no multiplied forms, and punctilious ceremonies are prescribed, which only serve to throw a veil over the mind; no certain modes are made necessary; but we must worship God, who is a spirit, in spirit and in truth, by prayer and praise, with love and fear, hope and joy. For such worship christians are united into societies called churches; and are required to assemble every Lord's day, that they may glorify God with one heart and voice, and be instructed and edified by his word, and the two only ordinances of baptism and the Lord's supper; which are very simple, but well adapted to the nature and design of our religion.

The christian religion, therefore, is confined to no particular nation, sect, or denomination; but is designed to call all men to repentance and newness of life; to encourage their hope in the mercy of God, thro' the only mediator Jesus Christ; persuade them to the most cheerful, persevering obedience; and comfort them, under all the labours and sorrows of the world, and the natural dread of death, with the assurance of a glorious immortality. This religion may be believed and practised, so as to answer the main purposes of it, under the various forms in which christian churches now appear: just as the principal ends of civil government may be obtained under the various constitutions which have taken place in different nations, however one may be much more eligible than another.

Therefore, regard not men who are continually crying up their own sect, and employing their utmost zeal and art to proselyte men to their party: they aim to strengthen themselves by your numbers and purses, more than to save your souls. If any say, lo here is Christ! or lo there! go not after them: for wherever his word abides, there is Christ; in and by his word he is already with us, and dwells in the hearts of believers. Listen to no enthusiasts, who instead of enlightening confound your understandings; and substitute folly, nonsense, and hypocritical grimace, in the room of a clear manifestation of truth and conformity of heart and life to the gospel. Take heed of imbibing the licentious principles of men who affect to render all religion doubtful, by persuading you that every kind of religion is equally acceptable to God if a man is but sincere in it; for this renders revelation useless. Beware of receiving new opinions, which militate with the plain and obvious meaning of the word of Christ, however they may pretend to be clearer discoveries of truth, and more comfortable and beneficial to mankind: but adhere to the written word, taken in the most natural sense, without forced allegories, whimsical constructions, or torturing criticisms; especially hold fast those doctrines which meet your eye in almost every page of the new testament. Read and meditate in the word of God day and night, and diligently attend on the public ministrations which Christ hath appointed in his church; and consider that as a true church where the truth as it is in Jesus is preached, and his plain institutions observed, whatever the particular form or denomination may be, avoiding all contentions and uncharitable separations. Be earnest to procure ministers, who preach the uncorrupted doctrines of the gospel, in all your towns: let none of your parishes continue vacant thro' indifference, negligence, or covetousness; and never withhold from faithful ministers a comfortable support. When we look round and see so many churches destitute of teachers, contenting themselves in the total neglect of all divine institutions, have we not reason to fear that

God is departing from us? And if our religion is given up, all the liberty we boast of will soon be gone; a profane and wicked people cannot hope for divine blessings, but it may be easily foretold that *"evil will befall them in the latter days."*

While I thus earnestly exhort you to religion, it must be understood as equally an exhortation to every branch of morality; for without this all religion is vain. That excellent sentence of the wise king ought forever to be in our minds—*"Righteousness exalteth a nation, but sin is the reproach of any people."* Sobriety, good order, honesty, fidelity, industry, frugality, and the like virtues must prevail; public crimes against person or property must be restrained and punished; or a people cannot be happy. Therefore let all maintain rectitude of conduct, and practise every thing virtuous and praise-worthy among their neighbours, and be just and true in all their intercourse and commerce. Unite in assisting the government in the execution of all good laws: and let all the members of the body politic consider that their own happiness depends on the welfare of the whole.

My subject hath lead me into this long and earnest address to the people. But it suggests some things which may properly be addressed to this honorable court. Will you hear me patiently, while with the utmost respect, I say a few words to excite the wise reflections of your own minds.

You will consider that you assemble from time to time as fathers of the large family, which depends on you to take care of its general welfare, and that no local views ought to govern you, nor partial instructions of your constituents bind you to act contrary to the clear conviction or your own minds. You will be cautious of forming parties for any selfish purposes, and of being too hasty in determining important matters, or too slow in your proceedings when business is urgent. In order to form a wise judgment of every thing that comes before you, you are sensible of the propriety of examining things to the bottom, attending patiently to every argument on both sides, and asking conscience, rather than any friend, what ought to be done. Like frugal housholders you will save all unnecessary expences, and take good care of the treasury; but not suffer the faithful servants of the state to be so stinted in their reward as to discourage them from their duty. Lay no grievous burdens on the people beyond their abilities; but take the earliest, easiest, and most righteous methods to reduce and pay off the public debt, unhappily involved in all the perplexities occasioned by boundless emissions of depreciating paper notes. Be liberal, yet frugal in grants of money, according to the exigencies of the public. Let no laws be wanting which good order, and the proper administration of government and justice require; but make no law which establisheth iniquity. And may I propose it, as worthy of your consideration, whether some reformation may not be necessary as to processes in our courts of justice: whether appeals from court to court are not allowed beyond reason and equity, in the plainest cases, and of too trivial value: by which some of our courts are made mere vehicles, justice is delayed, and the law made unnecessarily expensive, tedious and vexatious; and whether some method may not be thought of to determine the judgment of causes in lower or higher courts in proportion to their value and importance. I beg leave to say one word as to religion. With respect to articles of faith or modes of worship, civil authority have no right to establish religion. The people ought to choose their own ministers, and their own denomination, as our laws now permit them; but as far as religion is connected with the morals of the people, and their improvement in knowledge, it becomes of great importance to the state; and legislators may well consider it as part of their concern for the public welfare, to make provision that all the towns may be furnished with good teachers, that they may be impowered to make valid contracts, and that the fulfilment of such contracts should be secured against the fickle humours of men, who are always ready to shift from sect to sect, or make divisions in parishes that they may get free from all legal obligations to their ministers. Perhaps a little addition to the law already in force in this state might sufficiently secure the continuance of religious instruction, enlarge rather than diminish liberty of conscience, and prevent envyings, contentions, and crumbling into parties. Will you permit me now to pray in behalf of the people, that all the departments of government may be constantly filled with the wisest and best men; that his excellency the president may have the assistance of an able and faithful council; that the administration of justice may be in the hands of judges and justices well qualified for their offices, who will not take bribes, or in any manner pervert judgment; in a word, that the constitution established may in every respect be well supported by your care, and that the people may know the blessings of good government by the union of your counsels, and the wisdom of your proceedings. May the Almighty King of kings always be in the midst of you, direct and assist you, impress your hearts with his fear, and grant present and future blessings in reward of your fidelity.

And now if I have delivered words of truth, agreeably to my text; and pointed out the sure way to be a prosperous and happy people; may these things sink deep into your hearts, and be accompanied with the divine blessing! May the general government of these United States, when established, appear to be the best which the nations have yet known, and be exalted by uncorrupted religion and morals! And may the everlasting gospel diffuse its heavenly light, and spread righteousness, liberty, and peace, thro' the whole world.

A M E N

33

A CENTURY SERMON ON THE GLORIOUS REVOLUTION

Elhanan Winchester

LONDON
1788

Elhanan Winchester (1751–1797). A native of Brookline, Massachusetts, Winchester was at first a Baptist and later a Universalist clergyman at churches in Massachusetts and South Carolina, in Philadelphia and London. A remarkable personality possessed of a photographic memory, he became learned in biblical languages and interpretation. During his longest pastorate, at the Baptist Church in Philadelphia (1780–87), he was friends with leading citizens, including Benjamin Rush and John Redman, and his brilliant preaching attracted large crowds. His acceptance of Universalism split the congregation, and he was driven out. He moved to London and remained there until 1794. Again he was successful and moved in the circles of such luminaries as Thomas Belsham, Joseph Priestley, and John Wesley.

Winchester's family life could be justly considered a darkly troubled one. He married four women, each of whom died within a year or two, and of his eight children seven were stillborn and the eighth lived only seventeen months. A fifth wife made violent attacks upon Winchester. He left her, and England, in 1794, but she followed him to Connecticut, where they lived together again. He died of tuberculosis soon after, at the age of forty-five.

Winchester was a prolific author and for two years in London edited *The Philadelphian Magazine*. The publications setting forth his theological views were widely read on both sides of the Atlantic. They include *The Universal Restoration* (1788); *A Course of Lectures on the Prophecies That Remain to Be Fulfilled* (3 vols., 1789–90); *The Process and Empire of Christ* (1793), a long poem of 384 printed pages; and *A Defence of Revelation in Ten Letters to Thomas Paine* (1796), a response to *The Age of Reason*. In 1796 Winchester published, for use in American schools, *A Plain Political Catechism*, "wherein the great principles of liberty, and of the federal government, are laid down and explained by way of question and answer. Made level to the lowest capacities."

The sermon reprinted here was preached in both Canterbury and London in November 1788 (one hundred years after the landing in England of William of Orange) as a century sermon celebrating the Glorious Revolution and the securing of English liberty. In the important political passages of the sermon, Winchester takes the occasion to trace the genealogy of liberty in Britain and America, from the defeat of the Spanish Armada in 1588 to the stirring crescendo

GOD THE GLORIOUS, HOLY, WONDER-WORKING GOD; WORTHY TO BE FEARED AND PRAISED!

A

CENTURY SERMON,

ON THE

GLORIOUS REVOLUTION;

Preached in LONDON, Nov. 16, 1788, (The Subſtance of which had been delivered, in CANTERBURY, Nov. 5,) being juſt an Hundred Years from the

LANDING OF

WILLIAM, PRINCE OF ORANGE,

AFTERWARDS

KING OF ENGLAND.

In which the Events of 1588, 1688, and 1788 are mentioned, and the Bleſſings of Civil and Religious Liberty conſidered.

BY ELHANAN WINCHESTER,
(FROM AMERICA.)

LONDON:

Printed for J. JOHNSON, No. 72, St. Paul's Church-yard; J. SCOLLICK, City-Road, Moorfields; J. GARNER, No. 57, Wych-ſtreet; Mr. BICKNEL, No. 8, Blackman-ſtreet, and the AUTHOR, No. 17, Holywell-ſtreet, Shoreditch.

MDCCLXXXVIII.

reached in the framing of the Constitution of the United States in 1787. He stresses that the American Revolution was a war between the Americans and the British *ministry*, not the British people themselves. He concludes with an apocalyptic sketch of the end of history, the Second Coming, and the dawn of the Millennium.

Who is like unto thee, O Lord, amongst the gods? Who is like thee, glorious in Holiness, fearful in Praises, doing Wonders?

Exodus XV. 11

This grand and noble song (the first we find in the sacred writings), celebrates a most astonishing event. The children of Israel went down into Egypt, and had there increased from about seventy persons, to near three millions, in two hundred and fifteen years; and though Egypt was greatly indebted to the children of Jacob, especially to Joseph, yet the king and people of the land, forgetting those obligations, and greatly envying the increase of the tribes of Israel, cruelly oppressed them, by causing them to labour without reward; and not content with this tyranny, the cruel Pharaoh ordered their males to be cast into the river, to prevent their increase.

In this time Moses was born and by the special providence of God was brought up in Pharaoh's court, till he was come to years; when he chose rather to suffer with his brethren, the children of Israel, than to enjoy the pleasures of the court, which the scriptures call *the pleasures of sin*. For avenging one of his brethren upon an Egyptian, who cruelly beat him, he was obliged to leave the country; and after dwelling forty years a stranger in Midian, God sent him as a special messenger, and leader, to bring forth Israel out of Egypt. He came invested with divine authority, and going to the king in the name of the Lord, demanded of him to let the people go, that they might serve God. Pharaoh refused, and said, "Who is the Lord, that I should obey his voice? I know not the Lord; neither will I let Israel go."

The land of Egypt was then visited with ten dreadful successive plagues. God "turned their waters into blood, and slew their fish. Their land brought forth frogs in abundance," even in the chambers of their monarch. The dust of the land became lice upon man and beast. Divers sorts of flies came at the command of the Lord; such as were intolerable to endure. A grievous murrain came upon their cattle, and the beasts suffered for the sins of their owners. Ashes of the furnace sprinkled in the air became a grievous sore upon man and beast throughout all the land of Egypt. "He gave them hail for rain;

and flaming fire in their land: He smote their vines also, and their fig-trees, and brake the trees of their coasts."

That storm must have been very terrible in a country where even rain itself is unusual; it was threatened to be such as had not been in Egypt, from the foundation of the kingdom till that time. So terrible as to slay whatever man or beast should be exposed to its fury. There was "thunder and hail, and the fire ran along upon the ground; and the Lord rained hail upon the land of Egypt. So there was hail, and fire mingled with the hail, very grievous, such as there was none like it in all the land of Egypt, since it became a nation." This dreadful hail smote all men, beasts, trees, and vegetables, throughout the land of Egypt, except such as were housed, and secured therefrom. The next plague that followed was that of the locusts; of which the Psalmist says, "He spake, and the locusts came; and caterpillers, and that without number, and did eat up all the herbs in their land; and devoured the fruit of their ground."

The next plague was that of a miraculous thick darkness, which for three days and nights covered the land of Egypt, so that "they saw not one another, neither rose any from his place for three days."

But the tenth and last plague, more terrible than all the rest, was that of the death of the first-born of Egypt, of which the Psalmist says, "He cast upon them the fierceness of his anger, wrath and indignation, and trouble, by sending evil angels among them. He made a way to his anger, he spared not their soul from death: but gave their life over to the pestilence. And smote all the first-born in Egypt; the chief of their strength in the tabernacles of Ham."

What a most awful dispensation was this! in the dead and silent hour of midnight, while the inhabitants of Egypt lay slumbering on their couches, little dreaming of such destruction being near them; the dreadful angel of death, whom the Jews call Samael, went through the land of Egypt, and slew the first-born in every family, from the first-born of the king on the throne, to the captive in the dungeon; no rank was spared; high and low, rich and poor, bond and free, were visited alike with affliction in that sad distressing night. It is no wonder that "Pharaoh rose up in the night, he and all his servants, and all the Egyptians; and (that) there was a great cry in Egypt: for there was not a house where there was not one dead." Pharaoh and the Egyptians were now as anxious to send the children of Israel away, as they had been before to keep them in subjection; they "were urgent upon the people, that they might send them out of the land in haste; for they said, We be all dead men."

So the children of Israel departed from Egypt, just four hundred and thirty years from the call of Abram to leave his native land; and "Egypt was glad when they departed"; for the fear of the Israelites fell upon the Egyptians.

But God, who knew that Pharaoh would repent of letting Israel go, and pursue after them, ordered the people to encamp near an arm of the Red-sea; so that no apparent possibility of escape might be seen; and that if deliverance came, it might be plainly manifest to be the Lord's doing, and appear marvellous in their eyes. For it may be observed, that when God is about to work a great deliverance for his people, he usually first brings them into a great strait, so that destruction seems inevitable; and this he doth for the glory of his name, that their salvation may appear to be wholly his work, and that all the praise may be given to him alone, and that men may learn to know and reverence him, and acknowledge his hand in all things.

Pharaoh with his six hundred chosen chariots, and all the chariots of Egypt, and captains over every one of them, with his horses, horsemen, and his army, overtook the children of Israel, just as they were encamping by the sea; in such a place, that it seemed absolutely impossible for them to escape the enraged and armed Egyptians, who advanced against them with all their force, in a most warlike and terrible manner. Nothing but death or slavery appeared before their eyes; they were equally unable to fight or to fly; they were unarmed, unused to war, and had they been ever so much exercised in warlike arts, and ever so well armed, the mixed multitude of women, old people and children, with the abundance of cattle and goats they had with them, would have rendered them unable to maintain a conflict with a large army of warlike men, prepared to the battle, with horses and chariots in abundance. Neither was it more practicable for them to fly, even upon a supposition that the country had been open; for women, little ones, and droves of cattle and sheep could never march so fast as to escape a pursuing army, mounted on the best horses in the world, and in chariots prepared for war.

But even this was not the case, they had not this chance of escaping; far from having an open country, they were entangled in the land, the wilderness had shut them in; difficulties on the right hand and on the left, rendered it impossible for them to turn off, so as to escape; the red sea before, and the pursuing army behind, overtaking them at the greatest disadvantage, when they were just encamping, increased their distresses, dangers, and fears to the highest possible pitch. Despair seized the host of Israel, the people lifted up their eyes, and saw the Egyptians marching after them,

> and they were sore afraid: and cried out unto the Lord. And they said unto Moses, Because there were no graves in Egypt, hast thou taken us away to die in this wilderness? Wherefore hast thou dealt thus with us, to carry us forth out of Egypt? Is not this the word that we did tell thee in Egypt, saying, Let us alone, that we may serve the Egyptians? For it had been better for us to serve the Egyptians, than that we should die in the wilderness.

This was the language of despair and madness; no hope or expectation of deliverance now remained; they gave up themselves for lost. But Moses, directed by God, said unto the people, "Fear ye not, stand still, and see the salvation of the Lord, which he will shew you to day: for the Egyptians whom ye have seen to day, ye shall see them again no more for ever," (in any capacity to hurt you). "The Lord shall fight for you, and ye shall hold your peace." And verily the Lord did fight for them indeed! for he commanded Moses to stretch out his wonderful rod over the sea, and he obeyed; and the Lord caused a strong east wind to blow, and divided the waters of the sea; and in the mean time, to prevent the Egyptians from coming near to distress the Israelites, or even to incommode them in their passage, the Lord removed the cloud of glory that went before the camp of the Israelites, as their light and guide, and placed it between them and the Egyptians; so that it was a cloud and darkness to their enemies, but on the contrary, a bright and glorious light to them: this kept the armies apart, and answered the double purpose of greatly incommoding the Egyptians, while it secured the Israelites; gave them light to pursue their journey, and forwarded them on their way. Is it not astonishing, that the Egyptians, seeing the waters of the sea divided, and this extraordinary cloud placed between them and the Israelites, should not have been deterred from their pursuit? for they must have perceived, that the God who had sent so many plagues upon Egypt, whereby his name and power had been abundantly made known, had taken the Israelites under his protection, and was determined to deliver them, and that he was manifestly fighting for them. But so were they blinded, and hardened, that they ventured to pursue Israel into the sea; and they did not appear to have taken up this plain and obvious consideration, viz. *The Lord fighteth for Israel against the Egyptians*, till it was too late for them to profit by it, not until the Lord looked through the pillar of fire and of the cloud upon their host, and troubled it; and took off their chariot wheels, that they drave them heavily. Then would they fain have fled, but the time was past; that which they seemed blind unto before, now appeared self-evident; but their knowledge was then unprofitable and tormenting. O, could men learn to be as wise and considerate in the proper season, as they are when it is past, how many difficulties would they escape?

God then ordered Moses to stretch out his hand over the sea, that the waters might return again upon the Egyptians; and he did so. "And the waters returned and covered the chariots, and the horsemen, and all the host of Pharaoh that came into the sea after them: there remained not so much as one of them."

This great overthrow of the Egyptians, and deliverance of Israel, are the wonders celebrated in this piece of sacred poetry, which is truly worthy of its excellent composer.

Moses, whether considered as a historian, poet, legislator, judge, general, prophet, or intercessor, whether viewed in his private character, or public life, is one of the greatest and best men that ever existed on earth. His meekness, courage, prudence, humility, benevolence, wisdom, and piety, may stand as an eternal example to all men in high stations, to teach them what they should be, and how they ought to conduct themselves.

This song is a most glorious and triumphant ode, which celebrates the victories of the God of Israel in the most strong and beautiful language. It needs only to be read even under all the disadvantages of a literal translation, to observe very uncommon beauties in it; What then must it have been to have heard it performed in the original language, accompanied with suitable musick, by the many thousands of glad hearts and voices, of those who had not only been spectators, but sharers in the glorious deliverance, which it celebrates in so sublime a manner? But it is time to attend a little particularly to the words which I first read.

Who is like unto thee, O Jehovah amongst the Gods? There is none like the great Supreme, his awful name Jehovah, contains the past, present and future tenses; He is the Being who is, who was, and shall be; He ordered Moses to proclaim his name, Ehejah; that is, *I will be what I will be*; this none but the most high alone could say, for he hath manifested himself as the Being who *is*, and the causer or creator of all other beings, who all owe their existence, and continuance to him alone, for as he created all things, so he preserveth all, and all nature adores him.

There is none like him in his self-existence; he only exists of and from, and by himself; all other beings owe their existence to him.

There is none like him, self sufficient, and independent; no created being possesses these perfections in a proper sense, not in the least degree; all are insufficient in themselves, and must be forever dependent upon him the great fountain of existence, both for their being, and well being; for as they could not exist of themselves, so neither can they sustain or support themselves, nor enjoy any felicity, but from him, on whom the whole creation is dependent.

None are like him in his eternity, *he is*, and none beside him, without beginning, all others had a commencement of existence: he only is without beginning, the first and the last, from eternity to eternity.

Who is like him in his immensity and infinity? not one: none can compare with him in these characters; all created beings are finite and circumscribed, bounded in all respects, both in knowledge, power, and goodness, but he is infinite and unbounded.

God is unchangeable; in this respect, who can compare with him? surely none in the earth or heaven.

"I am Jehovah; I change not." This God could say, and none but he.

Who is like Jehovah in his omniscience? even the consideration of this perfection, is too much for the highest wisdom of men.

David was astonished at this boundless subject, and cried out,

> O Lord, thou hast searched me, and known me; thou knowest my down-sitting, and mine up-rising; thou understandest my thought afar off.

> Thou compassest my path, and my lying-down, and art acquainted with all my ways. For there is not a word in my tongue, but lo, O Lord, thou knowest it altogether. Thou hast beset me behind and before, and laid thine hand upon me. Such knowledge is too wonderful for me: it is high, I cannot attain unto it.

He was overwhelmed at the thought of God's omniscience, which equally extends to things past, present, and to come: and includes the knowledge of all his creatures, and all their circumstances, thoughts, words, ways, &c and in a word, his knowledge is infinite, and there is none like him in this.

Omnipresence is another divine perfection, which none can claim in any degree but God; "Who among the sons of the mighty can be likened to him," who is in all places at once, not included in any one place, nor excluded from any: he fills heaven and earth; neither is there any thing hid from him.

David says,

> Whither shall I go from thy spirit? or whither shall I flee from thy presence? If I ascend up into heaven, thou art there: if I make my bed in hell, behold thou art there. If I take the wings of the morning and dwell in the uttermost parts of the sea: even there shall thy hand lead me, and thy right hand shall hold me. If I say, Surely, the darkness shall cover me: even the night shall be light about me: Yea, the darkness hideth not from thee; but the night shineth as the day: the darkness and the light are both alike to thee.

God is present every where, beholding all things, hell and destruction have no covering to hide them from his face; all things are naked to his eye. O, what a Being is this! and who is like unto him amongst the gods?

His omnipotence is another glorious perfection, in which none may dare to compare themselves with him. He can do whatsoever he pleases, without restriction or exception. The works of creation evidence this abundantly: the heavens, earth, and seas, with all their numberless hosts, proclaim the power of God to be infinite; the heaven of heavens with the innume[ra]ble multitude of angels, all join to proclaim the omnipotence of the Deity. Neither is it by creation alone that the knowledge of this perfection is revealed; the works of Providence declare it.

Who could provide for such a numerous family, as the wide creation contains, but a God all-powerful, as well as infinitely wise? The judgments which Jehovah executeth upon his enemies, and the deliverances which he gives to those who trust in him, have contributed to cause his power to be known, and declared, as much as any of his works. Thus God's mighty hand upon the land of Egypt, and upon Pharaoh and his host, hath made his power known, and caused his name to be declared through the earth.

And when the children of Israel saw these mighty works, they cried out in the words of my text, *Who is like unto thee, O Lord, amongst the gods?*

In all these perfections which I have mentioned, there is none like Jehovah. Amongst the gods there is none like him; amongst all the holy angels in heaven, who are called gods, there are none who can compare with him; still less can emperors, kings, princes, nobles, rulers, judges, and magistrates of the earth, those gods below, pretend to be likened unto the Majesty of heaven and earth. But most of all, it is absurd and ridiculous to compare God with the idols of the heathen; he challenges these, with all their adherents to enter the lists with him, either in telling events that are past, foretelling those to come, or bringing any thing to pass, whether good or evil, as may be seen in my Preparatory Lecture upon the Prophecies; and his challenges may be read at large in several prophecies, especially in Isaiah. If none amongst angels or men, the works of his hands, may be compared to Jehovah; how much less idols of gold, silver, brass, iron, wood and stone, the work of mens hands, which neither hear, nor speak, nor see, nor know? "But our God is in the heavens, he hath done whatsoever he pleased. Their idols are silver and gold, the work of men's hand. They have mouths, but they speak not; eyes have they, but they see not. They have ears, but they hear not; noses have they, but they smell not. They have hands, but they handle not; feet have they, but they walk not; neither speak they through their throat. They that make them are like unto them; so is every one that trusteth in them." These idols are not even shadows of divinity; they are vanity, wind, and confusion: they are meaner than the meanest of men, viler than the beasts, and therefore would not be worthy to be mentioned in such a discourse as this, had not the nations of the world been generally guilty of worshipping them: and therefore Jehovah deigns to reason with men, and to convince them of the vanity and folly of such conduct.

Well might Israel say, "Who is like unto thee, O Lord, amongst the gods? Who is like thee, glorious in holiness?" Not only the essential attributes of God, which I have mentioned, are such as neither angels nor men can claim, but also his moral character and perfections as holiness, justice, goodness, truth, and righteousness, are such as none can claim but God alone; "there is none good but one, that is, God." "There is none holy as the Lord; for there is none beside thee." "The Lord is righteous." "Justice and judgement are the habitation of thy throne: mercy and truth shall go before thy face." God is indeed glorious in holiness!

So pure is he, that "the heavens are not clean in his sight; he putteth no trust in his saints, and his angels he charged with folly: he is of purer eyes than to behold evil, and cannot look upon iniquity." The seraphim in his presence continually cry; "Holy, holy, holy, is Jehovah of hosts, the whole earth is full of his glory." He is indeed glorious in holiness; "Holy and reverend is his name." "Holiness becometh thy house, O God, for ever." "Exalt ye the Lord our God, and worship at his footstool, for he is holy." This is the universal language of God's word and providences; God is holy. Yea, he *is glorious in holiness*, he shines most superlatively in this part of his character: his judgements against sin and iniquity bespeak his holiness: as the destruction of Pharaoh and his host in the sea; which is celebrated in this song.

So holy is God, that no unclean thing, or person can dwell with him; and therefore we are exhorted, to follow holiness, without which no "man shall see the Lord."

God is also "fearful in praises; he is greatly to be feared in the assembly of the saints, and to be had in reverence of all them that are about him. For the Lord is great, and greatly to be praised; he is to be feared above all gods. For all the gods of the nations are idols, but the Lord made the heavens."

Though he is to be loved and praised, yet with holy fear and reverence; for he is most holy, wise, and powerful, just, righteous, true, pure, and good; he knows all things, is every where present; his eyes are as a flame of fire; he is jealous for his honour and glory; and will not suffer his holy name to be profaned by the highest personage on the earth with impunity. He will be sanctified by all that approach him. And he *is fearful in praises*, for the very things for which he deserves praise, are those things which cause his name to be feared and reverenced; as for instance, the judgements brought on the land of Egypt, and on Pharaoh and his host, are celebrated in this song of praise; and yet they were terrible things in righteousness. So that he is the great and terrible God, worthy to be praised, and yet to be feared.

He is farther described in my text as, *doing wonders*; and I have mentioned some of the wonders which he wrought before the eyes of those who sang this song of praise to his holy name; and if time would permit, I might speak of many more that they beheld; they had bread rained from heaven, during forty years, for their support; and all that time their clothes waxed not old, neither did their feet swell. The bitter waters of Marah were made sweet for them. They had living waters given them out of the flinty rock. They were miraculously provided with food, both bread, and meat; and water in the barren desert; not a few people only, but several millions; not for a few days, but for forty years. They saw many wonders which God wrought, both in judgements and mercies towards them; of which time would fail me to speak particularly. And indeed one of the principal designs of this discourse, is to celebrate some of the wonders which God hath done for this nation in times past; and which are worthy to be remembered, and celebrated with praise and thanksgiving.

In the year 1588, two centuries ago, Philip of Spain (a second Pharaoh for pride and cruelty), thought to have the glory of conquering this kingdom (that had then newly embraced the Protestant religion), and of annexing it to the See of Rome.

At that time Spain was at the zenith of its earthly glory, possessing an extent of empire, on which they boasted the sun never went down.

The rich mines of Mexico and Peru, poured in silver and gold in abundance, into the treasuries of the king of Spain. America had been discovered ninety-six years, and the Spaniards alone had derived any advantages from the discovery. The resources they drew from that country were amazing indeed. But besides plenty of money, which may be called, the sinews of war, Spain, at that time had the best army, and finest navy in Europe; and the greatest commanders of the age, both by land and sea.

Under all these advantages, they doubted not of success in their intended invasion of England; but to make the matter more sure, they kept the expedition as secret as possible; but in the mean time fitted out a most formidable armament, destined to destroy the lives, but especially the liberties of the inhabitants of these isles. The cruel bishop, or pope of Rome, willing to give the greatest possible encouragement to the undertaking, published a bull by which he excommunicated Queen Elizabeth over again, and absolved all her subjects from their allegiance to her: proclaimed a crusade against her, with the usual indulgences; promising the pardon of sins, and an inheritance in the kingdom of heaven, to those who should die in this war. And he gave the name of *the invincible armada*, to this armament; and moreover presented a consecrated banner to Philip, with his blessing; which in those days of superstition, was thought sufficient to ensure success. So confident were they of obtaining an easy victory, that about two thousand volunteers entered into the service; many of whom were noblemen, belonging to the first families in Spain and Italy. And indeed there was hardly a family of rank in those countries, that had not some one or more of its connections on board the fleet. England at that time was so weak, had so small a navy, and no regular army, that the Spaniards expected little or no resistance would be made; and therefore they had agreed how to divide the spoils among themselves; and this made such numbers ambitious to enjoy the triumph.

Thus prepared, the fleet was ready to sail; but just at that time one of their greatest admirals died, and the chief command was given to a nobleman of one of the first families in Italy, but who was entirely unacquainted with maritime affairs. This was the first check to their design, in which the hand of Providence plainly appeared. During this time the inhabitants of England were not idle, but considering their all at stake, property, liberty, and life, made the best preparation they were able, to meet their formidable enemies; and in truth, much better than was expected. The hand of the Lord seemed evident in giving courage, unanimity, and a fixed resolution to defend themselves against their cruel invaders. This preparation was what the Spaniards did not expect, and may be reckoned under the direction of Providence, one of the causes of their defeat.

The fleet set sail in the beginning of summer, but a storm, obliged it to return again into port, considerably damaged. When the news came to England, it was commonly thought that the expedition would be laid aside for that season; and the queen sent orders upon that supposition, to her admiral, to dismiss most of the sea-men, and lay up some of the largest of the ships; but he, more wary, begged leave to retain them all in the service; even though it should be at his own expence.

The Spanish fleet by this time was refitted, and ready to go to sea, and the English admiral sailed out to make discoveries, and by some means found out that the armada had sailed, and he fearing that they would pass by him, hasted and returned up the channel, and waited their arrival. The Spaniards had orders to coast near France, to form a junction with the army, that waited to join them. But at sea they took a fisherman, who informed them, that the English admiral had been out to sea; but hearing that the armada had been driven back by a storm, returned into port, and had laid up his ships. This mistake of a fisherman probably saved this nation; for hearing this intelligence, the commander ventured to disobey his orders, and determined to sail directly to England, and destroy the shipping in the harbours and docks. The English fleet met them, and falling upon their fear, and waiting the events of the night, had the good fortune to take some of their richest store ships, and send them into port. They now, perceiving their mistake, made to the coast of France, when they cast anchor. But the English admiral watched his opportunity, and filling a number of ships with combustibles, set them on fire, and sent them down among the thickest of the enemies battle ships. Terrified at this new appearance, they slipped their cables and would fain have gone out to sea, and returned home, but could not, for the wind was contrary; the English fleet falling upon them in this confusion, took twelve of their largest ships without losing more than one. The Spanish armada had no other way of returning home but going into the North sea, and sailing round the island; the English fleet followed and grievously harrassed their enemies, who were now in the utmost distress, and had thoughts of surrendering at discretion;

and it is said the commander in chief had once determined to do so, but was dissuaded by his confessor. However, the event was almost equally fatal to them; for a terrible storm compleated their overthrow, and shameful defeat; many of their ships foundered at sea, and others were wrecked upon the coast of Ireland, and the western isles of Scotland, and not more than half of them ever returned to Spain.

Thus was this formidable armada defeated, without having done the smallest injury to this kingdom, or even landing any troops upon the island. And thus England was miraculously saved from destruction, by the immediate hand of Providence; which was scarcely, ever more visibly manifested in any affair, than in that very great, and singular deliverance of this land, from tyranny, popery, and slavery.

From the year 1588, we pass to the year 1688 (a most important year to this kingdom). Then it was that the king who swayed the sceptre of these realms, a bigotted member of the church of Rome, plotted to overthrow and destroy the liberties of his subjects; and render England again dependent upon the See of Rome. How miserable would the situation of these lands have now been, had he succeeded in his designs! But he that doeth wonders, wrought for his name's sake, and raised up a glorious deliverer, in the person of William, prince of Orange, stadholder of Holland, and afterwards king of England.

As Cyrus was raised up by God, strengthened and preserved, to give liberty to the captive Jews; so by the same divine hand of Providence, this wonder of a man was called, chosen, strengthened, and encouraged to undertake the dangerous enterprize of making a descent upon this island, not to conquer and enslave the inhabitants, but to give them liberty and happiness.

This day, an hundred years ago, he landed on this island: he was marvellously helped and preserved by God, till he had established and secured the liberties of these kingdoms; which, in consequence of the glorious revolution, we at present enjoy. I need not take the time to follow the valiant hero through all his journies, voyages, fore battles, and remarkable deliverances; many of you no doubt are better acquainted with the history of those times and things, than I can pretend to be.

I will rather demand your attention, while I consider some of the inestimable liberties and privileges we possess, as a fair inheritance in consequence of that event, which we celebrate on this happy day. Among all the liberties with which the inhabitants of these kingdoms are favoured, I shall only mention the following.

I. The liberty of acquiring and peaceably possessing property. This, though by no means the greatest blessing we enjoy, is yet very great. In many parts of the world nothing is more dangerous than for a man to be known, or even thought to possess riches: in those countries none can enjoy the good things of life in peace; property is there precarious, and may be taken away at any time at the command of a tyrant, and it is well if life itself is not in danger. But in this country, property may be acquired, and possessed with safety; persons may have all the security for it here, that in the nature of things can be expected in this fleeting state.

II. Personal freedom and safety may be enjoyed in these kingdoms: we are but in little danger of assassinations and private murders here, while in many countries nothing is more common, than for these diabolical acts to be committed with impunity, and even without any enquiry. Life cannot be taken away here by the will and at the command of a lawless tyrant, as in most parts of the world. A man must be found guilty by his unbiassed peers before he can be put to death. The king may pardon some criminals, but cannot condemn any; he has it in his power in this, as in many other instances to do much good, but is happily restrained by the laws and constitution of this country, from doing any harm to the meanest of his subjects. And this is so far from abridging the rights, and felicity of the sovereign; that he is most happy in this god-like liberty of doing good, like the great Author of nature, but not of doing evil.

We may therefore justly reckon personal security, and trial by juries, among the great and invaluable liberties that we enjoy: as also that slavery or perpetual servitude, is not allowed in these kingdoms; every slave being free, the moment he treads on British ground. And it would be well if it were so in all the British dominions abroad.

III. The liberty and freedom of the press; this may be considered as the great palladium of liberty, and it cannot exist but in a free country: while this remains in a country, there can be no danger of tyranny. Tyrants always aim to abridge, weaken, restrain, or destroy this liberty. They cannot endure it; and hence it comes to pass that in no place where arbitrary government prevails, is this liberty allowed.

And I do not know that the press is wholly free and unrestrained in any part of the globe, save only in the dominions of the king of Great Britain, and the United States of America.

And it was not till after the glorious revolution, that this was wholly the case in these kingdoms; before that time the press was under many restraints; and books were obliged to be licensed, before they could be printed; and at some times nothing could be published but what was according to the views of corrupt statesmen, or arbitrary tyrants. This freedom is of infinitely more consequence than some imagine; for by this it comes to pass, that knowledge is more generally disseminated among all ranks of people, from the highest to the lowest; and thus they are rendered capable of knowing their native rights, of asserting, contending for, and maintaining their freedom: yea, by this knowledge they are rendered worthy of being free, and of enjoying so inestimable a blessing as liberty. If any attempts should be made against the unalienable rights of men, by those in power, they will be much checked, if not rendered wholly abortive, by the unrestrained liberty of the press. Besides all these advantages, the press communicates the means of pleasure and improvement: O, what sublime pleasure may be found in reading well-written productions, which, owing to the noble art of printing, and the freedom of the press, are so plenty and cheap, as to be within the reach of most who choose to employ part of their time in that delightful exercise. And how surprizingly have all kinds of inventions and improvements been propagated, and arts and useful sciences flourished, since the art of printing has been found out; and especially in those countries where the liberty of the press has been free and unrestrained. Add to all, that the very knowledge of salvation, and the means of present happiness, and future felicity, have been communicated to millions of the human race, by this noble art of printing, and glorious freedom of the press. When all these things are considered, it will easily be seen, that the liberty of the press is no small blessing.

IV. The liberty of conscience; this is such a blessing, that mountains of gold, and rocks of diamonds offered in exchange for it, ought to be esteemed as trifles unworthy of a name. Who can look back upon the history of this country, before the revolution, and not exult in the consideration of this privilege inestimable, that the inhabitants of these realms enjoy, in consequence of that memorable event, and the glorious accession of king William to the throne? for he was the illustrious person, that procured the act of toleration to be past, which has been the greatest national blessing that England ever enjoyed. And there is nothing that renders the illustrious house of Hanover so truly great, as the constant attention which the successive kings of that line have paid to the liberties of their subjects; and especially their continuing, enlarging, confirming, and establishing, this beneficent act, and by their influence discountenancing all persecution for conscience sake.

Here we may worship God, according to the dictates of our own consciences; and none to make us afraid. No inquisitions, no instruments of torture worse than death; no faggots, stakes, and flames; no axes, halters, wheels, or racks; no fines, imprisonments, whippings, banishments, or deaths await us, for daring to think for ourselves, in matters of religion. A man once lost his life in this kingdom for saying these words, "I believe my God is in heaven, and not in the Pix," the place where they kept the consecrated wafers. Another young man, an apprentice, about nineteen years of age, was burnt, because in a dispute with a cunning priest, who laid wait for him, he had inadvertently been drawn in to deny the real presence in the sacrament.

Another man lost his life, only because on Sundays, he used to accustom himself to read aloud in a great Bible that was chained in the church, and the people flocked around to hear him. This was his crime; for which he suffered death. And even since the days of Henry, and those of bloody Mary, though few have been burned for daring to think differently from the church, or dissenting from the religion established by law; yet thousands have been fined, have lost their all, have suffered great penalties, banishments, and imprisonments, have died in dungeons, &c. &c. for no other cause. More than six thousand worthy persons, whose only crime was a tender conscience perished in loathsome dungeons, only in the reign of King Charles the Second. But, blessed be God, the scene is changed; let us forget the past, except so far as the remembrance of the same may cause us to enjoy, and be thankful for the present.

There is but one country in the world where liberty, and especially religious liberty, is so much enjoyed as in these kingdoms, and that is the United States of America: there religious liberty is in the highest perfection. All stand there on equal ground. There are no religious establishments, no preference of one denomination of Christians above another. The constitution knows no difference between one good man, and another. A man may be chosen there to the highest civil offices, without being obliged to give any account of his faith, subscribe any religious test, or go to the communion-table of any church.

We that here are called dissenters, there stand upon a level with the highest dignitaries in the episcopal church. Our marriages are as valid in law as theirs; and we are as much respected as they, if we behave as well: and the members of our churches are as eligible to posts of honour and profit as theirs. And what is the consequence of this equality? Does the episcopal church suffer by it? far from it; she gains. She has in reality prospered more, since this has been the case, than before. She has good bishops, respectable clergy, and many worthy members. She is no longer envied and hated by her sister-churches; far from it; she is respected. Her worthy clergy are better supported now by free contributions, donations, subscriptions, &c than formerly they were by compulsion in those places, where episcopacy was established and supported by law. Unworthy, ignorant and vicious clergymen, of which there were formerly many, are now discarded, and obliged to cease exercising their functions; for none are obliged to hear or support them. And all the people of every denomination, through the United States, enjoy that highest perfection of religious liberty, viz. the choosing and supporting their spiritual guides, in that way which is most agreeable to them; and also the power of rejecting them for immoral conduct. There are no patrons there, none to present to vacant churches; all must be approved by the people to whom they are to minister.

The authority in many places does not even interfere at all, in matters of religion; and in no part of the states, are ministers, or houses, under the least necessity of being licensed by authority; each denomination licensing, calling, and setting apart their ministers to the sacred work, in that manner which they think most fit.

I am of opinion that religious establishments, have generally, if not always, defeated their own designs.

No doubt, Constantine the Great, who first established christianity, had a good intention in the same; but all the darkness that has since overspread the Christian church, the exorbitant power of the popes and church of Rome, all the oceans of blood that have been shed in the contests about religion, between different sects of Christians, the almost total cessation of the progress of christianity, the rise of Mahometanism, the rise and spread of deism, the general contempt into which christianity is fallen; all may fairly be laid at the door of that establishment.

Had the Christian religion been left to itself, armed with its proper weapons, truth and love; had the civil authority never interfered with it at all, but only protected all men in the enjoyment of their equal and unalienable rights, such as life, liberty, property, and the lawful pursuit of happiness; I am of mind, that long ago christianity would have triumphed over all its enemies, idolatry, superstition, ignorance, and cruelty; and would before now have covered the earth, banished paganism, prevented Mahometanism, and infidelity, healed all divisions, convinced the world at large of its divine original; popery and persecution would never have been heard of amongst Christians: the ministers of the gospel would have been burning and shining lights, the churches would have been united in essential things, and those professing christianity, would have been ornaments to their profession.

And I am of the opinion, that if there had never been an establishment in England, or any act of uniformity past, but every one had been left to enjoy full free and absolute liberty of conscience, and the state had made no difference between those who followed the religion of the court and others, but raised, and encouraged all according to their merit and abilities, I fully and firmly believe that if there had remained any different sentiments and modes of worship at all till this time, they would have been nothing in comparison of what they are now. For I argue in this, from the very nature of man, who is an imitative being and is apt to follow those about him, unless compelled so to do, and then behaving as contrary; for the very nature and dignity of man abhors compulsion and restraint.

As a proof of my hypothesis, I need only mention, that where the law does not interfere at all, people generally follow one another, and sometimes where even it is inconvenient, and expensive so to do.

As in learning and speaking the language, practising the manners of those about them, building their houses, having the same kind of windows, chimneys, furniture, &c. eating the same kinds of food, and the same number of meals in a day; as for instance; in places where the people commonly eat four, three times, twice, or but once a day, most follow the same general rule, and those also who come to sojourn amongst them, soon conform to the same way. In generally using the same drink, and in many other ways, men shew that they do not need force and law to cause them to follow one another. But nothing shews people's abhorrence of singularity more than copying after each other in the articles of dress and amusements, which are frequently very expensive and inconvenient, and what is worse, perpetually changing, yet where there is no compulsion, men of even the most independent spirits, will, through a desire to please, a fear of appearing singular, or from some other cause, clothe themselves like their neighbours; even though it may be inconvenient, expensive, and contrary to what they would choose or desire in their own secret opinions. But though men are so apt to imitate each other when left to themselves, yet where force and compulsion are used, the sense of freedom frequently gets the better of every other consideration, and men dare to appear singular, though pains and penalties await them, where otherwise they would conform to the same customs with their neighbours, without a thought of differing. I will therefore now mention the greatest maxim in politics that was ever delivered, and which deserves to be written in letters of gold, over the doors of all the state houses in the world. *The great secret of governing, consists in not governing too much.*

Religious establishments, in countries where persecution is allowed, cause people to become hypocrites; in other places they cause many to dissent. They raise envy, strife, contempt, hatred, wrath, and every evil work: give occasion to reproach christianity and its author; rob the church of its life, power, love, and purity; darken, debase, and obscure its doctrines; pervert, corrupt, and change its institutions.

It is true that religious establishments cause the church so established to be rich, grand, honourable, and powerful in the world's esteem; but at the same time she becomes poor, and wretched, and miserable, and blind, and naked, in her Lord's esteem; his presence, power, and protection depart from her; she in a sort ceases to be his spouse.

This was evident in the days of Constantine; before that time christianity flourished, conquered its foes, triumphed over all opposition, miracles, and the gifts of the spirit were common; but all this beauty faded like a moth, when once the church was established by law. It was soon filled with unworthy members, idle ministers, and vicious, proud, domineering ecclesiastics of all sorts: And thus its glory departed, and has never wholly returned since.

The genuine love of liberty is, next to benevolence, or the love of God and man, the noblest motive that ever influenced the human mind. And whatever faults, failings, or infirmities the true lovers of liberty, may have in common with their neighbours, there will be generally if not always the absence of the following vices in every breast where the love of liberty dwells.

I. *The love of money*. This sordid vice, which St. Paul stiles, *the root of all evil*, can never dwell with the love of liberty. They who love money, will sell their king, country, freedom, their souls and their God for gold. But stop: gold is their God. They, on the other hand, who are lovers of liberty, will part with wealth, and frequently life itself, for the good of their country. The lovers of liberty may be distinguished by their noble contempt of riches, honours, pleasures, &c. when put in competition with their rights and liberties, the freedom of their country, and of mankind.

II. The lust of power is entirely incompatible with the love of liberty; as is evident from the nature of things, as well as the experience of all past ages.

III. Cruelty and revenge, cannot abide in the same breast with that offspring of heaven, the true love of freedom.

The love of liberty makes men noble, brave, generous, kind; it arms them with patience, fortitude, and true valour. But as for those vices which I have named above, they are so contrary to the love of heaven born freedom, that we may set it down for a maxim, never to expect the friend of liberty in the man in whom these, or any of them, have the government of the soul.

As I never shall have a better opportunity, give me leave here to introduce a greater hero on the stage than William the Third; even Jesus Christ, the great deliverer of mankind.

If any should dispute the truth of the historical fact which we celebrate this day, namely, the landing of King William on this island, an hundred years ago, he would be justly laughed at for a very ignorant and incredulous man. But what shall we say of those who, favoured with the means of knowledge, deny the history of the gospel? Surely they are, or pretend to be, the most ignorant and conceited of mortals.

It is as certainly true that there was such a person as Jesus Christ, that he was born in Bethlehem, in the days of Augustus, emperor of Rome, that he wrought miracles, died on the cross, in the reign of Tiberius, Pontius Pilate being governor of Judea; that he was buried, and the third day rose again, and on the fortieth day from his resurrection, ascended up on high; I say these facts are as well authenticated, as any historical facts that ever happened in the world. It is no less certain that these things were so, than that William, prince of Orange did, on the 5th of November, 1688, land on this island. If any say that the time when Christ was said to be born, &c. was so long ago, that we cannot be so certain of it, as of things that happened lately. I answer, that what is true now, will be so a thousand years hence; time never can turn truth into falsehood. And it is pretty well worthy of observation, that they who cavil at the gospel history, never hesitate to believe, that there was such a person as Alexander the Great, and Julius Caesar, and that the latter made a descent upon this island; though these are more antient things, than the birth of Christ.

It is indeed impossible that any events should be better attested than the life and actions of our Saviour. The four marks that no falsehood ever had, or can have, and which even many true facts want, all meet to confirm christianity.

I. It is necessary that the things done, or said to be done, be such as the senses of men can judge of; such were the actions and sufferings of Christ. And the apostles could say, "That which we have heard and seen, and our hands have handled of the word of life, declare we unto you," &c.

II. The actions done, must be performed before a number of witnesses; and Christ wrought his miracles, &c. was crucified, and buried, before many evidences; he was seen after his resurrection, at one time by above five hundred; and eleven different appearances of his, after his resurrection, are recorded; numbers saw him ascend; so that all these wonderful things were done openly.

III. It is not only necessary that authentic records of these things should be kept, and histories written by eye and ear witnesses of the several facts, but that certain ordinances should be instituted, and observed in commemoration of them. This is the case with christianity; the history of our Lord's life, actions, death, &c. was written by those who saw, heard, and attended him through the whole course of his ministry on earth; and who therefore were as well prepared to write a genuine history of those things, as any historians could be to write of King William the Third. And besides, there are many institutions kept up in remembrance of some of these great events. As the observance of Sunday, weekly, in remembrance of Christ's resurrection, the holy communion of bread and wine, in remembrance of his death.

Good Friday, yearly, in remembrance of the time of his sufferings; Easter Sunday, as the time of his resurrection; Holy Thursday, as his ascension day; and Whit-sunday, as the day of the descent of the Holy Ghost. All these things testify the truth of christianity.

IV. These institutions in order to be standing evidences of the facts, must begin to be observed from the very time when the things were done. And this hath certainly been the case with respect to christianity; there has been an order of men set apart, from that time to this, to declare these great things; sacraments have been used, and days constantly observed in commemoration of these grand events, from the very time when they happened, down to this period. So that we may challenge all mankind to overthrow the external evidence of christianity.

Christ Jesus came into the world, for purposes infinitely more important than those for which William came to England. William came hither to deliver this nation from tyranny, arbitrary government, popery, and slavery; to give, confirm, and transmit down to the inhabitants of these kingdoms, the natural rights and privileges of freemen; which I have briefly considered. Jesus Christ came into the world to save us from the tyranny and bondage of Satan, the world, and our own evil lusts and passions; to give us eternal life, and liberty, with the privilege of being the adopted children and heirs of God; these are greater blessings than earth can bestow, and will not only be of use to us a few days, as the things of time are, but during our whole existence.

William came over here for the benefit of the people of this nation, who were his friends, invited him over, and joined his standard. But Jesus Christ came into the world for the benefit of all mankind, even those who were his enemies; he was hated, despised, opposed and rejected, by his own kindred, according to the flesh; yet still his love and kindness continued to the last towards them.

William did many things for the good of this land; suffered much, and ventured his life for the people of these kingdoms; for which his memory is precious, and ought to be regarded with sincere affection. But O, what love, gratitude and praises, are due to Jesus Christ, who came into the world, and wrought so many works of mercy for mankind? He healed the sick, opened the eyes of the blind, caused the deaf to hear, gave speech to the dumb, caused the lame to walk, restored the maimed, cast out demons, cleansed the lepers, and raised the dead.

He suffered hunger, thirst, weariness, cold, want, poverty, disgrace, reproach, contempt, slander, temptation, and distress of various kinds: and he not only ventured his life, but actually laid it down for mankind.

William was of a noble family, was a prince by birth, and allied by marriage to the royal family of Great Britain; but Jesus Christ was the Son of God, the brightness of his Father's glory, and the express image of his person; the prince of peace, head over all things, for he created all things, preferred all things, and hath redeemed all things; was in the form of God, yet he humbled himself so as to become obedient unto death, even the accursed death of the cross, the most painful and shameful of all kinds of deaths.

Thus is Jesus Christ infinitely superior to King William, and the blessings of the gospel as much surpass all earthly advantages, as the soul exceeds the body, or eternity time: the certainty of christianity is as much to be depended upon, and is in every respect as authentic as that grand event, the Revolution, and infinitely more important.

Therefore while we remember King William, and what we owe to him, let us not forget Jesus Christ, to whom we are infinitely more indebted.

And while we would wish to abide by revolution principles, maintaining our glorious liberties, so dearly purchased, and constantly abhorring popery and slavery, let us remember the most excellent maxims of christianity, delivered by the mouth of our blessed Saviour, whose morals exceed all others, as much as his character is superior, and his mission more important than other men's.

He commanded love to God and man, universal benevolence to all, even to our enemies, justice and righteousness towards all, to do to others as we would wish them to do to us; to avoid selfishness, envy, pride, wrath, the love of the world, the love and practice of every sin, to avoid rash judging, a bitter and censorious spirit, slander, reviling, and provoking speeches, and behaviour; to beware of hypocrisy, covetousness, &c. To be faithful, prudent, virtuous, innocent, humble, meek, kind, courteous, compassionate, merciful, sober, generous, patient, and resigned to the will of God.

These are brief abstracts of the morality taught by the Saviour of mankind, and which as Christians we should remember and practise.

What I have more to say at present, is just to notice the events of the present year, and mention some of those great things that may be expected shortly to come to pass.

We are now arrived almost at the close of the year 1788, a year in which great things have been long expected to manifest themselves. Many years have I waited, and I imagine many thousands more, with great expectation, to see what wonders would be wrought at this time; and if the events of 1788, have not been so extraordinary as were looked for, they have been such as deserve notice. Let us look around the world, and see if we can find nothing worth preserving, and transmitting down to future generations.

In England, this has been a remarkable year on many accounts. The nation has enjoyed the continuance of peace, while wars and rumours of wars have terrified many parts of Europe.

This has been a year of blessings to this nation; the season has been so remarkably mild, and plentiful, as the like has scarce ever been known; not only has there been a plentiful crop, but a most excellent season for gathering it in. We have not been visited this year with the wasting pestilence, devouring sword, black famine, horrid tempests, sweeping storms, dreadful fires, earthquakes, inundations, &c. but on the contrary, have enjoyed peace, health, plenty, and prosperity. One alarming event hath indeed taken place here; the present indisposition of his majesty. But, except this, I know of nothing that has happened this year in England, but one continued scene of blessings.

Great events may be expected to arise out of the present war between the Turks, and their powerful opponents, the Russians and the Austrians. Perhaps the return of the Jews to their own land may be one of the consequences.

If we turn our eyes to France, we see the spirit of liberty, which has been asleep, or crushed to death in that kingdom for more than two hundred years, beginning to revive; and what events will follow the general meeting of the states in that empire (a thing which has not been known since the days of Henry the Fourth, of France), time must discover. If the establishment of civil and religious liberty there should take its date from this year, it would be a great and glorious wonder of God, and would cause this season to be long remembered with pleasure.

In Italy we find the power of the pope greatly weakening, and the influence of the See of Rome every where diminishing. In Spain the horrid inquisition falling; arts and sciences flourishing; and such events are taking place through Europe, as will ere long astonish the world.

But one of the greatest and most important events of the year 1788, and which will cause it to be long remembered, has taken place in the United States of America. There a new constitution and settled form of government has been adopted, after being formed deliberately, and confirmed unanimously, in a general convention of the States; then recommended to the people at large, and by them examined, approved, and ratified.

This is such an astonishing event to those who know the situation of the United States of America, that nothing less than a very special Providence, and divine interference could have brought it about. Many instances of the visible protection and goodness of God towards the American states, have appeared from the beginning of the unhappy contest, between them and the *ministry* of this nation, to the present time; but in no instance has a divine hand so plainly appeared as in the present. God was gracious to them in raising them up friends in this land (and indeed, the people of England in general were far from approving the unnatural and horrid war), also in causing foreign powers to declare in their favour, in raising them up a noble and valiant general (whose name will be transmitted with immortal honour in the historic page, to the latest periods while histories shall be read); in supporting them during a long and expensive war, and in giving them such a glorious peace. But all these blessings and advantages would probably have been wholly lost, had not a solid and effective plan of government been formed and embraced. Their enemies both at home and abroad, waited to see their downfal and ruin; and even their best friends trembled for their situation, and feared their overthrow. Every appearance was truly alarming, and the dangers continued increasing, till at last the very existence of government seemed dubious.

In this distressing situation, recourse was had to a general convention, composed of the ablest persons in all the states, who were chosen by the people at large, to form a plan of government; but when met, they were not invested with power to declare such constitution binding, even after they had unanimously agreed upon it among themselves (which was difficult enough), it was to undergo another severe trial, by being examined by the people at large; and it was not to be in force till nine states agreed to adopt and ratify it. This appeared a very hazardous experiment; but, through the goodness of God, it succeeded well, and eleven states have acceeded to it, several of them unanimously. This new constitution is formed after the model of the British, without its defects; and bids fair to confirm and establish the liberties of the people in those states till the latest period; and I make no doubt, but the inhabitants of that empire in the year 1888, will (if the world continues in the same manner as at present) look back upon this year, with the same admiration, as the people here do upon the year 1688.

The states have certainly enjoyed advantages in framing their constitution, that no other people ever had; they have met in peace, and deliberated, and agreed upon a form of government, suitable to their situation; having the wisdom and experience of all nations and ages before them; as well as their own experience for twelve years; but considering their fallibility, and the possibility of defects, even in this constitution, they have left an opening that the inconveniences, if any are found, may be rectified every fifteen years, if it be judged necessary.

I have taken the liberty of mentioning the affairs of my dear native country, believing that you will rejoice with me in the prosperity of that land; for we have the satisfaction to say, that since we have been in England, we have scarce ever been in company with the natives of this island, but who in general seemed very friendly towards the United States of America. And I hope the affection between the two countries will continue and increase.

Thus far we are come, but who can tell what wonders are about to take place in the world? Those who may live in 1888, will be able to look back upon great events that will then have happened, that are now future. Though I cannot exactly tell you when the following great things will take place, yet they must all happen before the conflagration, according to the prophecies.

The Turkish empire is to be weakened, and by some means the way will be opened, and the Jews will return to their own land.

After they have been there settled some time, their enemies will gather together and ravage their country, come to Jerusalem and take it, will carry half of the people out into captivity; but before they have time to compleat their purpose, the Lord will appear in the air, he will bring the spirits of his faithful servants and martyrs with him, raise their bodies from the dead, change the living saints, who shall be caught up with the raised saints into the air to meet the Lord. Christ shall appear to all the inhabitants of the world, who shall tremble at his presence: the Jews shall look upon him whom they pierced, knowing him by the sears of his wounds, they shall mourn bitterly, and this event shall issue in their long promised conversion. The coming and appearance of Christ will destroy Antichrist, will overthrow and disconcert the enemies of the Jews, who shall fall slain upon the mountains of Israel. Christ will personally descend to the Mount of Olives, from whence he ascended; when his feet shall touch it, the mount shall cleave asunder, towards the east, and towards the west, and half of it shall remove towards the north, and half of it towards the south. The Lord will execute such judgments on the rebellious nations of the world, as shall cause the earth to disclose its blood, and the slain shall lie unburied; the nations who refuse to obey the command of the Lord, to come or send to Jerusalem yearly to worship him, shall have no rain upon their land.

The whole earth shall be as it were devoured with the fire of God's jealousy, and the wicked shall be destroyed root and branch; all nations that remain shall submit to the Lord; Satan shall be bound, and confined in the abyss; all the twelve tribes being returned and settled anew in their own land, shall become the people of God; the Lord shall reign over them in his holy mount. He will turn to all the people of the earth a pure language, and they shall all call upon the name of the Lord, and serve him with one consent. Then comes that glorious period of a thousand years, when peace, harmony, prosperity, love, and the knowledge and glory of God shall fill the earth as the waters cover the sea. To that period vast numbers of prophecies allude, as I have shewn in my Lectures upon those which remain to be fulfilled. I cannot enlarge upon these matters here, having already drawn out this discourse to a great length; which I trust you will excuse, in consideration of the vast variety and importance of the subjects upon which I have spoken.

When we consider the great things which God hath wrought already; and those greater things which he hath promised to perform in his own time, we may say in the words of my text, with which I shall conclude:

"Who is like unto thee, O Lord, amongst the gods? who is like thee glorious in holiness, fearful in praises, doing wonders?"

FINIS

Chronology

1789–1794

1789 The first Congress under the new Constitution meets at Federal Hall in New York (Mar. 4). George Washington is inaugurated as President (Apr. 30). The Judiciary Act creates the federal court system, and the departments of state, war, and treasury are created to compose the executive branch.

The Society of St. Tammany is organized in New York City by William Mooney as an Antifederalist political fraternity (May 12).

The French Revolution begins with the fall of the Bastille (July 14), an event witnessed by Thomas Jefferson, then minister to France.

President Washington transmits to the states the proposed amendments to the Constitution (Oct. 2). The states ratify ten of them as a Bill of Rights and reject two.

John Carroll, ordained the first Catholic bishop in America, founds Georgetown, the first Catholic university in America.

The University of North Carolina is founded.

William Hill Brown publishes the first American novel, *The Power of Sympathy*.

David Ramsay's *The History of the American Revolution*, the first national history, is published.

The first national Thanksgiving Day is established, by Congress's resolution and Washington's proclamation, to give thanks for the Constitution; the Antifederalists object, claiming that this violates states' rights (Nov. 26).

1790 A DISCOURSE ON THE LOVE OF OUR COUNTRY, Richard Price

A Quaker delegation petitions Congress to abolish slavery (Feb. 11).

The first census is completed (Mar. 1), showing a total U.S. population of 3,929,625, including 59,557 free blacks and 697,624 enslaved blacks. The largest cities are Philadelphia (42,000), New York (33,000), Boston (18,000), Charleston (16,000), and Baltimore

(13,000). The most populous state is Virginia (820,000). Only Massachusetts reports no slaves.

Jefferson returns from France to become Secretary of State (Mar. 22).

Universalists convene in Philadelphia, led by Dr. Benjamin Rush and Reverend Elhanan Winchester, and assert an anti-Trinitarian doctrine denying the divinity of Jesus (May 25).

Rhode Island finally ratifies the Constitution, the thirteenth state to do so (May 29).

At the urging of Noah Webster, the first Copyright Act is passed and signed into law by President Washington (May 31).

A ten-square-mile Potomac River site is authorized (July 10) for a new national capital (Washington is to select the precise tract), with Philadelphia to serve in the interim (the government moves there in Dec.).

Samuel Slater builds a spinning mill for the Quaker merchant Moses Brown at Pawtucket, Rhode Island, beginning factory production in America (Dec. 21).

1791 THE AFRICAN SLAVE TRADE, James Dana

A SERMON DELIVERED AT THE ANNUAL ELECTION, Israel Evans

THE RIGHTS OF CONSCIENCE INALIENABLE, John Leland

The Whiskey Act places an excise tax on distilled liquors and stills, despite the opposition of farmers who dispose of surplus grain by distilling it (Mar. 3).

Vermont becomes the fourteenth state (Mar. 4).

Jefferson and Madison organize Antifederalist factions in Middle Atlantic and New England states during a "botanizing excursion"; they oppose Washington's and Hamilton's Federalist policies, giving birth to the Democratic-Republican Party (May–June).

Benjamin Banneker, a black mathematician, scientist, and clockmaker, is appointed one of three commissioners to survey the site for the new federal capital on the Potomac River (July 16).

Partisan newspapers fuel the conflict between Hamilton and Jefferson; Philip Freneau's *National Gazette* of Philadelphia is a major voice for Jeffersonian views.

Hamilton presents to Congress a report of manufacturers that aims at developing American industry and agriculture (Dec. 5).

The main office of the Bank of the United States opens in Philadelphia (Dec. 12).

Thomas Paine publishes the first part of *Rights of Man*; from opposing viewpoints, Vice President John Adams publishes *Discourses of Davila* and his son John Quincy Adams publishes the *Publicola* papers.

The University of Vermont is founded.

1792 A SERMON FOR THE DAY OF GENERAL ELECTION, David Tappan

The second part of Paine's *Rights of Man* appears (Jan.).

Congress enacts the Militia Act in the face of growing Indian hostilities in the Northwest Territory; Gen. St. Clair, defeated by the Ohio Indians, is replaced as governor by Gen. Anthony Wayne.

Kentucky is admitted as the fifteenth state.

In a national election (Nov. 1), President George Washington and Vice President John Adams are re-elected by 132 and 77 electoral votes, respectively (results promulgated Dec. 5); the Antifederalist George Clinton, Governor of New York, receives 50 electoral votes.

The Second Congress convenes in Philadelphia (Nov. 5).

In England, Mary Wollstonecraft publishes *A Vindication of the Rights of Women*, a work widely read in America.

Denmark becomes the first nation to abolish the slave trade.

The first turnpike opens, running the 60 miles from Philadelphia to Lancaster on a hard-packed surface of crushed rock.

1793 A SERMON PREACHED BEFORE THE ARTILLERY COMPANY, Peter Thacher

A SERMON ON THE ANNIVERSARY OF THE INDEPENDENCE OF AMERICA, Samuel Miller

AN ORATION IN COMMEMORATION OF THE INDEPENDENCE OF THE UNITED STATES OF AMERICA, Enos Hitchcock

King Louis XVI and Queen Marie Antoinette are guillotined in Paris (Jan. 21), dampening the enthusiasm of Americans for the French Revolution.

France's revolutionary government declares war on Great Britain, Spain, and the Netherlands (Feb. 1), further chilling American sympathies and intensifying acrimony against Jeffersonian–Antifederalist sympathies for the French Revolution.

Washington inaugurated for a second term as president (Mar. 4).

Citizen Edmond Genêt, the French minister to the United States, lands in Charleston and commissions privateers to raid British shipping. During a 28-day journey to Philadelphia to present credentials to President Washington (Apr. 8–May 18), Genêt lobbies for American support for the French Republic. However, Washington issues a proclamation of neutrality (Apr. 22).

Jefferson submits his resignation as Secretary of State (July 31), to become effective at the end of the year.

The Genêt crisis intensifies, as he appeals over Washington's head to the American public, but the Jacobins come to power in Paris and issue a warrant for his arrest. Granted asylum (June–Aug.), Genêt later becomes an American citizen and marries New York Governor Clinton's daughter.

A slave revolt in Albany, New York, devastates the city with fires (Nov. 25).

Williams College is founded.

Eli Whitney invents the cotton gin.

1794 THE NECESSITY OF THE BELIEF OF CHRISTIANITY, Jonathan Edwards, Jr.

THE WONDERFUL WORKS OF GOD ARE TO BE REMEMBERED, David Osgood

THE REVOLUTION IN FRANCE, Noah Webster

Edmund Randolph succeeds Jefferson as Secretary of State (Jan. 2).

The Whiskey Rebellion is put down in Pennsylvania by a 12,900-man militia led by Gen. Henry ("Light Horse Harry") Lee (July–mid-Nov.).

Jay's Treaty with Britain is concluded (Nov. 19), settling matters left unresolved by the Treaty of Paris (the terms publicly disclosed Mar. 1795).

"Mad" Anthony Wayne defeats a large force of Indians at the Battle of Fallen Timbers, securing what will later become the state of Ohio.

34

A DISCOURSE ON THE LOVE OF OUR COUNTRY

Richard Price

LONDON

1790

RICHARD PRICE (1723–1791). Born at Tynton in Glamorganshire, Wales, Price gained fame as a supporter of the American and French revolutions. A friend of Benjamin Franklin, he was a liberal Presbyterian minister and a moral philosopher whose critique of the Scottish philosophy of Francis Hutcheson in *Review of the Principal Questions and Difficulties in Morals* (1758) came to be regarded as a significant anticipation of Kant's ethics in certain respects and of nineteenth-century intuitionism in others. With Joseph Priestly, Price also published *A Free Discussion of the Doctrines of Materialism and Philosophical Necessity* (1778), written in the form of a debate. As a result of his publication of a reply to David Hume's essay on miracles, Price had a D.D. degree conferred upon him by the University of Aberdeen.

As an expert on finance and insurance, Price was selected to become a member of the Royal Society in 1765 for work on the theory of probability as applied to actuarial questions. His recommendation of a sinking fund to cope with problems of national debt influenced both French and British policy.

Price's vehement support for American independence came primarily through publication of two pamphlets that circulated widely at home and in America: *Observations on the Nature of Civil Liberty, the Principles of Government, and the Justice and Policy of the War with America* (1776) and *Additional Observations* . . . (1777). Offered American citizenship, he declined, but he did address Congress when invited in 1778, was inducted into the American Philosophical Society, and was awarded (along with George Washington) an LL.D. by Yale in 1781. Price's *The Importance of the American Revolution* appeared in 1784.

The celebrated sermon that follows was preached in London on November 4, 1789, the 101st anniversary of the Glorious Revolution. It presents Price's apocalyptic view of the dawning of the millennium through the spread of liberty and happiness over the world, especially as evinced in French developments at the time. This point, according to A. J. Grieve, was for Edmund Burke the "grit around which he built up his pearl"—namely, *Reflections on the Revolution in France* (1790). The gentility of Price's encomium for the French revolutionaries contrasts drastically with Burke's savage ridicule:

> Is it because liberty in the abstract may be classed amongst the blessings of mankind, that I am seriously to felicitate a madman, who has escaped

A

DISCOURSE

ON THE

LOVE OF OUR COUNTRY,

DELIVERED ON NOV. 4, 1789,

AT THE

MEETING-HOUSE IN THE OLD JEWRY,

TO THE

SOCIETY

FOR

COMMEMORATING THE

REVOLUTION

IN

GREAT BRITAIN.

By RICHARD PRICE, D.D. LL.D. F.R.S.

AND FELLOW OF THE AMERICAN PHILOSOPHICAL SOCIETIES AT PHILADELPHIA AND BOSTON.

LONDON, PRINTED:
BOSTON, REPRINTED:
BY EDWARD E. POWARS, COURT STREET.
M.DCC.XC.

> from the protecting restraint and wholesome darkness of his cell, on his restoration to the enjoyment of light and liberty? Am I to congratulate a highwayman and murderer, who has broke prison, upon the recovery of his natural rights? This would be to act over again the scene of the criminals condemned to the galleys, and their heroic deliverer [Don Quixote], the metaphysic knight of the sorrowful countenance.

In rebuttal to Price's central proposition that the people of England have three fundamental rights that the French aspire to ("To choose our own governors; to cashier them for misconduct; and to frame a government for ourselves"), Burke scathingly retorted: "We have an inheritable crown; an inheritable peerage; and a House of Commons and a people inheriting privileges, franchises, and liberties, from a long line of ancestors." Burke was answered not only by the aged, ailing Price, but also by Thomas Paine in *The Rights of Man* (1792). Paine, a writer of comparable intellect but of far less gentility—being every bit Burke's equal in the fine old art of invective—vindicated Price's three fundamental rights. Indeed, Price's sermon was the starting point for what Thomas W. Copeland designated "the most crucial ideological debate ever carried on in English."

Our feet shall stand within thy gates, O Jerusalem, whither the tribes go up; the tribes of the Lord unto the testimony of Israel. To give thanks to the name of the Lord, for there sit the thrones of judgment; the throne of the House of David. Pray for the peace of Jerusalem. They shall prosper that love thee. Peace be within thy walls, and prosperity within thy palaces. For my brethren and companions sake I will now say, peace be within thee. Because of the House of the Lord our God, I will seek thy good.

Psalm cxxii, 2d, and following verses.

In these words the Psalmist expresses, in strong and beautiful language, his love of his country, and the reasons on which he founded it; and my present design is, to take occasion from them to explain the duty we owe to our country, and the nature, foundation, and proper expressions of that love to it which we ought to cultivate.

I reckon this a subject particularly suitable to the services of this day, and to the anniversary of our deliverance at the Revolution from the dangers of popery and arbitrary power; and should I, on such an occasion, be led to touch more on political subjects than would at any other time be proper in the pulpit, you will, I doubt not, excuse me.

The love of our country has, in all times, been a subject of warm commendations; and it is certainly a noble passion; but, like all other passions, it requires regulation and direction. There are mistakes and prejudices by which, in this instance, we are in particular danger of being misled. I will briefly mention some of these to you, and observe,

First, That by our country is meant, in this case, not the soil, or the spot of earth on which we happen to have been born; not the forests and fields, but that community of which we are members; or that body of companions and friends and kindred who are associated with us under the same constitution of government, protected by the same laws, and bound together by the same civil polity.

Secondly, It is proper to observe, that even in this sense of our country, that love of it which is our duty, does not imply any conviction of the superior value of it to other countries, or any particular preference of its laws and constitution of government. Were this implied, the love of their country would be the duty of only a very small part of mankind; for there are few countries that enjoy the advantage of laws and governments which deserve to be preferred. To found, therefore, this duty on such a preference, would be to found it on error and delusion. It is however a common delusion. There is the same partiality in countries, to themselves, that there is in individuals. All our attachments should be accompanied, as far as possible, with right opinions. We are too apt to confine wisdom and virtue within the circle of our own acquaintance and party. Our friends, our country, and, in short, every thing related to us, we are disposed to overvalue. A wise man will guard himself against this delusion. He will study to think of all things as they are, and not suffer any partial affections to blind his understanding. In other families there may be as much worth as in our own. In other circles of friends there may be as much wisdom; and in other countries as much of all that deserves esteem; but, notwithstanding this, our obligation to love our own families, friends, and country, and to seek, in the first place, their good, will remain the same.

Thirdly, It is proper I should desire you particularly to distinguish between the love of our country and that spirit of rivalship and ambition which has been common among nations. What has the love of their country hitherto been among mankind? What has it been but a love of domination; a desire of conquest, and a thirst for grandeur and glory, by extending territory, and enslaving surrounding countries? What has it been but a blind and narrow principle, producing in every country a contempt of other countries, and forming men into combinations and factions against their common rights and liberties? This is the principle that has been too often cried up as a virtue of the first rank: a principle of the same kind with that which governs clans of Indians, or tribes of Arabs, and leads them out to plunder and massacre. As most of the evils which have taken place in private life, and among individuals, have been occasioned by the desire of private interest overcoming the public affections; so most of the evils which have taken place among bodies of men have been occasioned by the desire of their own interest overcoming the principle of universal benevolence: and leading them to attack one another's territories, to encroach on one another's rights, and to endeavour to build their own advancement on the degradation of all within the reach of their power —what was the love of their country among the Jews, but a wretched partiality to themselves, and a proud contempt of all other nations? What was the love of their country among the old Romans? We have heard much of it; but I cannot hesitate in saying that, however great it appeared in some of its exertions, it was, in general, no better than a principle holding together a band of robbers in their attempts to crush all liberty but their own. What is now the love of his country in a Spaniard, a Turk, or a Russian? Can it be considered as any thing better than a passion for slavery, or a blind attachment to a spot where he enjoys no rights, and is disposed of as if he was a beast?

Let us learn by such reflections to correct and purify this passion, and to make it a just and rational principle of action.

It is very remarkable that the founder of our religion has not once mentioned this duty, or given us any recommendation of it; and this has, by unbelievers, been made an objection to Christianity. What I have said will entirely remove this objection. Certain it is, that, by inculcating on men an attachment to their country, Christianity would, at the time it was propagated, have done unspeakably more harm than good. Among the Jews, it would have been an excitement to war and insurrections; for they were then in eager expectation of becoming soon (as the favourite people of heaven) the lords and conquerors of the earth, under the triumphant reign of the Messiah. Among the Romans, likewise, this principle had, as I have just observed, exceeded its just bounds, and rendered them enemies to the peace and happiness of mankind. By inculcating it, therefore, Christianity would have confirmed both Jews and gentiles in one of the most pernicious faults. Our Lord and his apostles have done better. They have recommended that universal benevolence which is an unspeakably nobler principle than any partial affections. They have laid such stress on loving all men, even our enemies, and made an ardent and extensive charity so essential a part of virtue, that the religion they have preached may, by way of distinction from all other religions, be called the Religion of Benevolence. Nothing can be more friendly to the general rights of mankind; and were it duly regarded and practised, every man would consider every other man as his brother, and all the animosity that now takes place among contending nations would be abolished. If you want any proof of this, think of our Saviour's parable of the good Samaritan. The Jews and Samaritans were two rival nations that entertained a hatred of one another the most inveterate. The design of this parable was to shew to a Jew, that even a Samaritan, and consequently all men of all nations and religions, were included in the precept, *Thou shalt love thy neighbour as thyself.*

But I am digressing from what I had chiefly in view; which was, after noticing that love of our country which is false and spurious, to explain the nature and effects of that which is just and reasonable. With this view, I must desire you to recollect that we are so constituted that our affections are more drawn to some among mankind than to others, in proportion to their degrees of nearness to us, and our power of being useful to them. It is obvious, that this is a circumstance in the constitution of our natures which proves the wisdom and goodness of our Maker; for had our affections been determined alike to all our fellow-creatures, human life would have been a scene of embarrassment and distraction. Our regards, according to the order of nature, begin with ourselves; and every man is charged primarily with the care of himself. Next come our families, and benefactors, and friends; and after them, our country. We can do little for the interest of mankind at large. To this interest, however, all other interests are subordinate. The noblest principle in our nature is the regard to general justice, and that good-will which embraces all the world. I have already observed this; but it cannot be too often repeated. Though our immediate attention must be employed in promoting our own interest and that of our nearest connexions; yet we must remember, that a narrower interest ought always to give way to a more extensive interest. In pursuing particularly the interest of our country, we ought to carry our views beyond it. We should love it ardently, but not exclusively. We ought to seek its good, by all the means that our different circumstances and abilities will allow; but, at the same time, we ought to consider ourselves as citizens of the world, and take care to maintain a just regard to the rights of other countries.

The enquiry by what means (subject to this limitation) we may best promote the interest of our country, is very important; and all that remains of this discourse shall be employed in answering it, and in exhorting you to manifest your love to your country, by the means I shall mention.

The chief blessings of human nature are the three following: Truth

—Virtue—and Liberty. These are, therefore, the blessings in the possession of which the interest of our country lies, and to the attainment of which our love of it ought to direct our endeavours. By the diffusion of knowledge it must be distinguished from a country of barbarians: by the practice of religious virtue, it must be distinguished from a country of gamblers, atheists, and libertines: and by the possession of liberty, it must be distinguished from a country of slaves. I will dwell for a few moments on each of these heads:

Our first concern, as lovers of our country, must be to enlighten it. Why are the nations of the world so patient under despotism? Why do they crouch to tyrants, and submit to be treated as if they were a herd of cattle? Is it not because they are kept in darkness, and want knowledge? Enlighten them and you will elevate them. Shew them they are men, and they will act like men. Give them just ideas of civil government, and let them know that it is an expedient for gaining protection against injury and defending their rights, and it will be impossible for them to submit to governments which, like most of those now in the world, are usurpations on the rights of men, and little better than contrivances for enabling the few to oppress the many. Convince them that the Deity is a righteous and benevolent as well as omnipotent Being, who regards with equal eye all his creatures, and connects his favour with nothing but an honest desire to know and do his will; and that zeal for mystical doctrines which has led men to hate and harass one another, will be exterminated. Set religion before them as a rational service, consisting not in any rites and ceremonies, but in worshipping God with a pure heart, and practising righteousness from the fear of his displeasure and the apprehension of a future righteous judgment, and that gloomy and cruel superstition will be abolished, which has hitherto gone under the name of religion, and to the support of which civil government has been perverted. Ignorance is the parent of bigotry, intolerance, persecution and slavery. Inform and instruct mankind, and these evils will be excluded. Happy is the person who, himself raised above vulgar errors, is conscious of having aimed at giving mankind this instruction. Happy is the scholar or philosopher who at the close of life can reflect that he has made this use of his learning and abilities: but happier far must he be, if at the same time he has reason to believe he has been successful, and actually contributed, by his instructions, to disseminate among his fellow-creatures just notions of themselves, of their rights, of religion, and the nature and end of civil government. Such were Milton, Locke, Sidney, Hoadly, &c. in this country; such were Montesquieu, Fenelon, Turgot, &c. in France. They sowed a seed which has since taken root, and is now growing up to a glorious harvest. To the information they conveyed by their writings we owe those revolutions in which every friend to mankind is now exulting. What an encouragement is this to us all in our endeavours to enlighten the world? Every degree of illumination which we can communicate must do the greatest good. It helps to prepare the minds of men for the recovery of their rights, and hastens the overthrow of priestcraft and tyranny. In short, we may, in this instance, learn our duty from the conduct of the oppressors of the world. They know that light is hostile to them, and therefore they labour to keep men in the dark. With this intention they have appointed licensers of the press; and, in popish countries, prohibited the reading of the Bible. Remove the darkness in which they envelope the world, and their usurpations will be exposed, their power will be subverted, and the world emancipated.

The next great blessing of human nature which I have mentioned, is virtue. This ought to follow knowledge, and to be directed by it. Virtue without knowledge makes enthusiasts; and knowledge without virtue makes devils; but both united elevates to the top of human dignity and perfection. We must, therefore, if we would serve our country, make both these the objects of our zeal. We must discourage vice in all its forms; and our endeavours to enlighten must have ultimately in view a reformation of manners and virtuous practice.

I must add here, that in the practice of virtue I include the discharge of the public duties of religion. By neglecting these, we may injure our country essentially. But it is melancholy to observe that it is a common neglect among us; and in a great measure owing to a cause which is not likely to be soon removed: I mean, the defects (may I not say, the absurdities?) in our established codes of faith and worship. In foreign countries, the higher ranks of men, not distinguishing between the religion they see established and the Christian religion, are generally driven to irreligion and infidelity. The like evil is produced by the like cause in this country; and if no reformation of our established formularies can be brought about, it must be expected that religion will go on to lose its credit, and that little of it will be left except among the lower orders of people, many of whom, while their superiors give up all religion, are sinking into an enthusiasm in religion lately revived.

I hope you will not mistake what I am now saying, or consider it as the effect of my prejudices as a dissenter from the established church. The complaint I am making, is the complaint of many of the wisest and best men in the established church itself, who have been long urging the necessity of a revisal of its liturgy and articles. These were framed above two centuries ago, when Christendom was just emerging from the ignorance and barbarity of the dark ages. They remain now much the same they were then; and, therefore, cannot be properly adapted to the good sense and liberality of the present times. This imperfection, however, in our public forms of worship, affords no excuse to any person for neglecting public worship. All communities will have some religion; and it is of infinite consequence that they should be led to that which, by enforcing the obligations of virtue and putting men upon loving instead of damning one another, is most favourable to the interest of society.

If there is a Governor of the world, who directs all events, he ought to be invoked and worshipped; and those who dislike that mode of worship which is prescribed by public authority, ought (if they can find no worship out of the church which they approve) to set up a separate worship for themselves; and by doing this, and giving an example of a rational and manly worship, men of weight, from their rank or literature, may do the greatest service to society and the world. They may bear a testimony against that application of civil power to the support of particular modes of faith, which obstructs human improvement, and perpetuates error; and they may hold out an instruction which will discountenance superstition, and at the same time recommend religion, by making it appear to be (what it certainly is when rightly understood) the strongest incentive to all that is generous and worthy, and consequently the best friend to public order and happiness.

Liberty is the next great blessing which I have mentioned as the object of patriotic zeal. It is inseparable from knowledge and virtue, and together with them completes the glory of a community. An enlightened and virtuous country must be a free country. It cannot suffer invasions of its rights, or bend to tyrants. I need not, on this occasion, take any pains to shew you how great a blessing liberty is. The smallest attention to the history of past ages, and the present state of mankind, will make you sensible of its importance. Look round the world, and you will find almost every country, respectable or contemptible, happy or miserable, a fruitful field or a frightful waste, according as it possesses or wants this blessing. Think of Greece, formerly the seat of arts and science, and the most distinguished spot under heaven; but now, having lost liberty, a vile and wretched spot, a region of darkness, poverty, and barbarity. Such reflections must convince you that, if you love your country, you cannot be zealous enough in promoting the cause of liberty in it. But it will come in my way to say more to this purpose presently.

The observations I have made include our whole duty to our country; for by endeavouring to liberalize and enlighten it, to discourage vice and to promote virtue in it, and to assert and support its liberties, we shall endeavour to do all that is necessary to make it great and happy. But it is proper that, on this occasion, I should be more explicit, and exemplify our duty to our country by observing farther, that it requires us to obey its laws, and to respect its magistrates.

Civil government (as I have before observed) is an institution of human prudence for guarding our persons, our property, and our good name, against invasion; and for securing to the members of a community that liberty to which all have an equal right, as far as they do not, by any overt act, use it to injure the liberty of others. Civil laws are regulations agreed upon by the community for gaining these ends; and civil magistrates are officers appointed by the community for executing these laws. Obedience, therefore, to the laws and to magistrates, are necessary expressions of our regard to the community; and without this obedience the ends of government cannot be obtained, or a community avoid falling into a state of anarchy that will destroy those rights and subvert that liberty, which government is instituted to protect.

I wish it was in my power to give you a just account of the importance of this observation. It shews the ground on which the duty of obeying civil governors stands, and that there are two extremes in this case which ought to be avoided. These extremes are adulation and servility on one hand; and a proud and licentious contempt on the other. The former is the extreme to which mankind in general have been most prone; for it has oftener happened that men have been too passive than too unruly; and the rebellion of kings against their people has been more common, and done more mischief, than the rebellion of people against their kings.

Adulation is always odious, and when offered to men in power, it corrupts them, by giving them improper ideas of their situation; and it debases those who offer it, by manifesting an abjectness founded on improper ideas of themselves. I have lately observed in this kingdom too near approaches to this abjectness. In our late addresses to the king, on his recovery from the severe illness with which God has been pleased to afflict him, we have appeared more like a herd crawling at the feet of a master, than like enlightened and manly citizens rejoicing with a beloved sovereign, but at the same time conscious that he derives all his consequence from themselves. But, perhaps, these servilities in the language of our late addresses should be pardoned, as only forms of civility and expressions of an overflow of good-nature. They have, however, a dangerous tendency. The potentates of this world are sufficiently apt to consider themselves as possessed of an inherent superiority, which gives them a right to govern, and makes mankind their own; and this infatuation is almost every where fostered in them by the creeping sycophants about them, and the language of flattery which they are continually hearing.

Civil governors are properly the servants of the public; and a king is no more than the first servant of the public, created by it, maintained by it, and responsible to it: and all the homage paid him, is due to him on no other account than his relation to the public. His sacredness is the sacredness of the community. His authority is the authority of the community; and the term *majesty*, which it is usual to apply to him, is by no means his own majesty, but the *majesty of the people*. For this reason, whatever he may be in his private capacity; and though, in respect of personal qualities, not equal to, or even far below many among ourselves—for this reason, I say (that is, as representing the community and its first magistrate), he is entitled to our reverence and obedience. The words *most excellent majesty* are rightly applied to him; and there is a respect which it would be criminal to withhold from him.

You cannot be too attentive to this observation. The improvement of the world depends on the attention to it: nor will mankind be ever as virtuous and happy as they are capable of being, till the attention to it becomes universal and efficacious. If we forget it, we shall be in danger of an idolatry as gross and stupid as that of the ancient heathens, who, after fabricating blocks of wood or stone, fell down and worshipped them. The disposition in mankind to this kind of idolatry is indeed a very mortifying subject of reflection. In Turkey, millions of human beings adore a silly mortal, and are ready to throw themselves at his feet, and to submit their lives to his discretion. In Russia, the common people are only a stock on the lands of grandees, or appendages to their estates, which, like the fixtures in a house, are bought and sold with the estates. In Spain, in Germany, and under most of the governments of the world, mankind are in a similar state of humiliation. Who, that has a just sense of the dignity of his nature, can avoid execrating such a debasement of it?

Had I been to address the king on a late occasion, I should have been inclined to do it in a style very different from that of most of the addressers, and to use some such language as the following:

> I rejoice, sir, in your recovery. I thank God for his goodness to you. I honour you not only as my king, but as almost the only lawful king in the world, because the only one who owes his crown to the choice of his people. May you enjoy all possible happiness. May God shew you the folly of those effusions of adulation which you are now receiving, and guard you against their effects. May you be led to such a just sense of the nature of your situation, and endowed with such wisdom, as shall render your restoration to the government of these kingdoms a blessing to it, and engage you to consider yourself as more properly the servant than the sovereign of your people.

But I must not forget the opposite extreme to that now taken notice of; that is, a disdainful pride, derived from a consciousness of equality, or, perhaps, superiority, in respect of all that gives true dignity to men in power, and producing a contempt of them, and a disposition to treat them with rudeness and insult. It is a trite observation, that extremes generally beget one another. This is particularly true in the present case. Persons justly informed on the subject of government, when they see men dazzled by looking up to high stations, and observe loyalty carried to a length that implies ignorance and servility: such persons, in such circumstances, are in danger of spurning at all public authority, and throwing off that respectful demeanor to persons invested with it, which the order of society requires. There is undoubtedly a particular deference and homage due to civil magistrates, on account of their stations and offices; nor can that man be either truly wise or truly virtuous, who despises governments, and wantonly *speaks evil of his rulers*; or who does not, by all the means in his power, endeavour to strengthen their hands, and to give weight to their exertions in the discharge of their duty. *Fear God*, says St. Peter. *Love the brotherhood. Honour all men. Honour the King. You must needs*, says St. Paul, *be subject to rulers, not only for wrath* (that is, from the fear of suffering the penalties annexed to the breach of the laws) *but for conscience sake. For rulers are ministers of God, and revengers for executing wrath on all that do evil.*

Another expression of our love to our country is defending it against enemies. These enemies are of two sorts, internal and external; or domestic and foreign. The former are the most dangerous, and they have generally been the most successful. I have just observed, that there is a submission due to the executive officers of government, which is our duty; but you must not forget what I have also observed, that it must not be a blind and slavish submission. Men in power (unless better disposed than is common) are always endeavouring to extend their power. They hate the doctrine, that it is a trust derived from the people, and not a right vested in themselves. For this reason, the tendency of every government is to despotism; and in this the best constituted governments must end, if the people are not vigilant, ready to take alarms, and determined to resist abuses as soon as they begin. This vigilance, therefore, it is our duty to maintain. Whenever it is withdrawn, and a people cease to reason about their rights and to be awake to encroachments, they are in danger of being enslaved, and their servants will soon become their masters.

I need not say how much it is our duty to defend our country against foreign enemies. When a country is attacked in any of its rights by another country, or when any attempts are made by ambitious foreign powers to injure it, a war in its defence becomes necessary: and, in such circumstances, to die for our country is meritorious and noble. These defensive wars are, in my opinion, the only just wars. Offensive wars are always unlawful; and to seek the aggrandizement of our country by them, that is, by attacking other countries, in order to extend dominion, or to gratify avarice, is wicked and detestable. Such, however, have been most of the wars which have taken place in the world; but the time is, I hope, coming, when a conviction will prevail, of the folly as well as the iniquity of wars; and when the nations of the earth, happy under just governments, and no longer in danger from the passions of kings, will find out better ways of settling their disputes; and beat (as Isaiah prophesies) *their swords into plow-shares, and their spears into pruning-hooks.*

Among the particulars included in that duty to our country, by discharging which we should shew our love to it, I will only further mention praying for it, and offering up thanksgivings to God for every event favourable to it. At the present season we are called upon to express, in this way, our love to our country. It is the business of this day and of the present service; and, therefore, it is necessary that I should now direct your attention to it particularly.

We are met to thank God for that event in this country to which the name of the Revolution has been given; and which, for more than a century, it has been usual for the friends of freedom, and more especially Protestant Dissenters, under the title of the Revolution Society, to celebrate with expressions of joy and exultation. My highly valued and excellent friend, who addressed you on this occasion last year, has given you an interesting account of the principal circumstances that attended this event, and of the reasons we have for rejoicing in it. By a bloodless victory, the fetters which despotism had been long preparing for us were broken; the rights of the people were asserted, a tyrant expelled, and a sovereign of our own choice appointed in his room. Security was given to our property, and our consciences were emancipated. The bounds of free enquiry were enlarged; the volume in which are the words of eternal life, was laid more open to our examination; and that æra of light and liberty was introduced among us, by which we have been made an example to other kingdoms, and became the instructors of the world. Had it not been for this deliverance, the probability is, that, instead of being thus distinguished, we should now have been a base people, groaning under the infamy and misery of popery and slavery. Let us therefore, offer thanksgivings to God, the author of all our blessings. *Had he not been on our side, we should have been swallowed up quick, and the proud waters would have gone over our souls. But our souls are escaped, and the snare has been broken. Blessed then be the name of the Lord, who made heaven and earth.* CXXIVth Psalm.

It is well known that King James was not far from gaining his purpose; and that probably he would have succeeded, had he been less in a hurry. But he was a fool as well as a bigot. He wanted courage as well as prudence; and, therefore, fled, and left us to settle quietly for ourselves that constitution of government which is now our boast. We have particular reason, as Protestant Dissenters, to rejoice on this occasion. It was at this time we were rescued from persecution, and obtained the liberty of worshipping God in the manner we think most acceptable to him. It was then our meeting houses were opened, our worship was taken under the protection of the law, and the principles of toleration gained a triumph. We have, therefore, on this occasion, peculiar reasons for thanksgiving—But let us remember that we ought not to satisfy ourselves with thanksgivings. Our gratitude, if genuine, will be accompanied with endeavours to give stability to the deliverance our country has obtained, and to extend and improve the happiness with which the Revolution has blest us—let us, in particular, take care not to forget the principles of the Revolution. This society has, very properly, in its reports, held out these principles, as an instruction to the public. I will only take notice of the three following:

First; The right to liberty of conscience in religious matters.

Secondly; The right to resist power when abused. And,

Thirdly; The right to chuse our own governors; to cashier them for misconduct; and to frame a government for ourselves.

On these three principles, and more especially the last, was the Revolution founded. Were it not true that liberty of conscience is a sacred right; that power abused justifies resistance; and that civil authority is a delegation from the people—were not, I say, all this true, the Revolution would have been not an assertion, but an invasion of rights; not a revolution, but a rebellion. Cherish in your breasts this conviction, and act under its influence; detesting the odious doctrines of passive obedience, non-resistance, and the divine right of kings—doctrines which, had they been acted upon in this country, would have left us at this time wretched slaves—doctrines which imply, that God made mankind to be oppressed and plundered; and which are no less a blasphemy against him, than an insult on common sense.

I would farther direct you to remember, that though the Revolution was a great work, it was by no means a perfect work; and that all was not then gained which was necessary to put the kingdom in the secure and complete possession of the blessings of liberty. In particular, you should recollect, that the toleration then obtained was imperfect. It included only those who could declare their faith in the doctrinal articles of the church of England. It has, indeed, been since extended, but not sufficiently; for there still exist penal laws on account of religious opinions, which (were they carried into execution) would shut up many of our places of worship, and silence and imprison some of our ablest and best men. The Test Laws are also still in force; and deprive of eligibility to civil and military offices, all who cannot conform to the established worship. It is with great pleasure I find that the body of Protestant Dissenters, though defeated in two late attempts to deliver their country from this disgrace to it, have determined to persevere. Should they at last succeed, they will have the satisfaction, not only of removing from themselves a proscription they do not deserve, but of contributing to lessen the number of public iniquities. For I cannot call by a gentler name, laws which convert an ordinance appointed by our Saviour to commemorate his death, into an instrument of oppressive policy, and a qualification of rakes and atheists for civil posts. I have said, should they succeed—but perhaps I ought not to suggest a doubt about their success*. And, in-

* It has been unfortunate for the Dissenters that, in their late applications for a repeal of the Test Laws, they have been opposed by Mr. Pitt. He has contended that, on account of their not believing and worshipping as the Church of England does, they ought to be excluded from that eligibility to public offices which is the right of other citizens, and consequently denied a *complete* toleration; acknowledging, however, their integrity and respectability, but reckoning it only the more necessary on that account to defend the national church against them. Such sentiments in these times can do no honour to any man, much less to a son of the late Lord Chatham, whose opinion of toleration and Protestant Dissenters may be learnt from the following account.

In 1769 and 1772, the ministers among the Dissenters applied to Parliament for relief from the obligation they were then under to subscribe the doctrinal articles of the Church of England in order to be entitled to a toleration, and both times succeeded in the House of Commons, in consequence of Lord North's neutrality, but were defeated in the House of Lords, in consequence of an opposition from the Episcopal bench. They persevered, however; the bishops repented; and a third application proved successful in both houses. In the debate occasioned in the House of Lords by the second application, Dr. Drummond, the archbishop of York, having called the dissenting ministers "men of close ambition," Lord Chatham said, that this was judging uncharitably;

deed, when I consider that in Scotland the established church is defended by no such test—that in Ireland it has been abolished—that in a great neighbouring country it has been declared to be an indefeasible right of all citizens to be equally eligible to public offices—that in the same kingdom a professed dissenter from the established church holds the first office in the state—that in the emperor's dominions Jews have been lately admitted to the enjoyment of equal privileges with other citizens—and that in this very country, a Dissenter, though excluded from the power of executing the laws, yet is allowed to be employed in making them. When, I say, I consider such facts as these, I am disposed to think it impossible that the enemies of the repeal of the Test Laws should not soon become ashamed, and give up their opposition.

But the most important instance of the imperfect state in which the Revolution left our constitution, is the *inequality of our representation.* I think, indeed, this defect in our constitution so gross and so palpable, as to make it excellent chiefly in form and theory. You should remember that a representation in the legislature of a kingdom is the basis of constitutional liberty in it, and of all legitimate government; and that without it a government is nothing but an usurpation. When the representation is fair and equal, and at the same time vested with such powers as our House of Commons possesses, a kingdom may be

and that whoever brought such a charge against them, without proof, defamed. Here he paused; and then went on—

> The dissenting ministers are represented as men of close ambition. They are so, my lords; and their ambition is to keep close to the college of fishermen, not of cardinals, and to the doctrine of inspired apostles, not to the decrees of interested and aspiring bishops. They contend for a spiritual creed, and scriptural worship. We have a Calvinistic creed, a popish liturgy, and an Arminian clergy. The Reformation has laid open the scriptures to all. Let not the bishops shut them again. Laws in support of ecclesiastical power are pleaded for, which it would shock humanity to execute. It is said, that religious sects have done great mischief, when they were not kept under restraint: but history affords no proof that sects have ever been mischievous, when they were not oppressed and persecuted by the ruling church.

See the Parliamentary Debates, 1772.

In one of his letters to me, not long after this debate, dated Burton-Pynsent, January 16, 1773, he expresses himself in the following words:

> In writing to you, it is impossible the mind should not go of itself to that most interesting of all objects to fallible men—toleration. Be assured, that on this sacred and unalienable right of mankind, and bulwark of truth, my warm wishes will always keep pace with your own. Happy, if the times had allowed us to add hopes to our wishes.

said to govern itself, and consequently to possess true liberty. When the representation is partial, a kingdom possesses liberty only partially; and if extremely partial, it only gives a semblance of liberty; but if not only extremely partial, but corruptly chosen, and under corrupt influence after being chosen, it becomes a nuisance, and produces the worst of all forms of government—a government by corruption, a government carried on and supported by spreading venality and profligacy through a kingdom. May heaven preserve this kingdom from a calamity so dreadful! It is the point of depravity to which abuses under such a government as ours naturally tend, and the last stage of national unhappiness. We are, at present, I hope, at a great distance from it. But it cannot be pretended that there are no advances towards it, or that there is no reason for apprehension and alarm.

The inadequateness of our representation has been long a subject of complaint. This is, in truth, our fundamental grievance; and I do not think that any thing is much more our duty, as men who love their country, and are grateful for the Revolution, than to unite our zeal in endeavouring to get it redressed. At the time of the American war, associations were formed for this purpose in London, and other parts of the kingdom; and our present minister himself has, since that war, directed to it an effort which made him a favourite with many of us. But all attention to it seems now lost, and the probability is, that this inattention will continue, and that nothing will be done towards gaining for us this essential blessing, till some great calamity again alarms our fears, or till some great abuse of power again provokes our resentment; or, perhaps, till the acquisition of a pure and equal representation by other countries (while we are mocked with the shadow) kindles our shame.

Such is the conduct by which we ought to express our gratitude for the Revolution. We should always bear in mind the principles that justify it. We should contribute all we can towards supplying what it left deficient; and shew ourselves anxious about transmitting the blessings obtained by it to our posterity, unimpaired and improved. But, brethren, while we thus shew our patriotic zeal, let us take care not to disgrace the cause of patriotism, by any licentious, or immoral conduct. Oh! how earnestly do I wish that all who profess zeal in this cause, were as distinguished by the purity of their morals, as some of them are by their abilities; and that I could make them sensible of the advantages they would derive from a virtuous character, and of the suspicions they incur and the loss of consequence they suffer by wanting it. Oh! that I could see in men who oppose tyranny in the state, a disdain of the tyranny of low passions in themselves; or, at least, such a sense of shame, and regard to public order and decency as would induce them to bide their irregularities, and to avoid insulting the virtuous part of the community by an open exhibition of vice! I cannot reconcile myself to the idea of an immoral patriot, or to that separation of private from public virtue, which some think to be possible. Is it to be expected that—but I must forbear. I am afraid of applications, which many are too ready to make, and for which I should be sorry to give any just occasion.

I have been explaining to you the nature and expressions of a just regard to our country. Give me leave to exhort you to examine your conduct by what I have been saying. You love your country, and desire its happiness; and, without doubt, you have the greatest reason for loving it. It has been long a very distinguished and favoured country. Often has God appeared for it, and delivered it. Let us study to shew ourselves worthy of the favour shewn us. Do you practice virtue yourselves, and study to promote it in others? Do you obey the laws of your country, and aim at doing your part towards maintaining and perpetuating its privileges? Do you always give your vote on the side of public liberty; and are you ready to pour out your blood in its defence? Do you look up to God for the continuance of his favour to your country, and pray for its prosperity; preserving, at the same time, a strict regard to the rights of other countries, and always considering yourselves more as citizens of the world than as members of any particular community? If this is your temper and conduct you are blessings to your country, and were all like you, this world would soon be a heaven.

I am addressing myself to Christians. Let me, therefore, mention to you the example of our blessed Saviour. I have observed, at the beginning of this discourse, that he did not inculcate upon his hearers the love of their country, or take any notice of it as a part of our duty. Instead of doing this, I observed that he taught the obligation to love all mankind, and recommended universal benevolence, as (next to the love of God) our first duty; and, I think, I also proved to you, that this, in the circumstances of the world at that time, was an instance of incomparable wisdom and goodness in his instructions. But we must not infer from hence, that he did not include the love of our country in the number of our duties. He has shewn the contrary by his example. It appears that he possessed a particular affection for his country, though a very wicked country. We read in Luke x. 42, that when, upon approaching Jerusalem, in one of his last journies to it, he beheld it, he wept over it, and said, *Oh! that thou hadst known (even thou, at least in this thy day) the things that belong to thy peace.* What a tender solicitude about his country does the lamentation over Jerusalem imply, which is recorded in the same gospel, chap. xiii. and 34. *Oh! Jerusalem, Jerusalem, thou that killest the prophets, and stonest them who are sent to thee, how often would I have gathered thy children together, as a hen gathereth her brood under her wings, but ye would not.*

It may not be improper farther to mention the love St. Paul expressed for his country, when he declared, that, for the sake of his brethren and kinsmen, he could even wish himself *accursed from Christ.* (Rom. ix. 3.) The original words are an *anathema from Christ;* and his meaning is, that he could have been contented to suffer himself the calamities which were coming on the Jewish people, were it possible for him, by such a sacrifice of himself, to save them.

It is too evident that the state of this country is such as renders it an object of concern and anxiety. It wants (I have shewn you) the grand security of public liberty. Increasing luxury has multiplied abuses in it. A monstrous weight of debt is crippling it. Vice and venality are bringing down upon it God's displeasure. That spirit to which it owes its distinctions, is declining; and some late events seem to prove that it is becoming every day more reconcileable to encroachments on the securities of its liberties. It wants, therefore, your patriotic services; and, for the sake of the distinctions it has so long enjoyed; for the sake of our brethren and companions, and all that should be dear to a free people, we ought to do our utmost to save it from the dangers that threaten it; remembering, that by acting thus, we shall promote, in the best manner, our own private interest, as well as the interest of our country; for when the community prospers, the individuals that compose it must prosper with it. But, should that not happen, or should we even suffer in our secular interest by our endeavours to promote the interest of our country, we shall feel a satisfaction in our own breasts which is preferable to all this world can give; and we shall enjoy the transporting hope of soon becoming members of a perfect community in the heavens, and having *an entrance ministered to us, abundantly into the everlasting kingdom of our Lord and Saviour Jesus Christ.*

You may reasonably expect, that I should now close this address to you. But I cannot yet dismiss you. I must not conclude without recalling, particularly, to your recollection, a consideration to which I have more than once alluded, and which, probably, your thoughts have been all along anticipating: A consideration with which my mind is impressed more than I can express. I mean, the consideration of the favourableness of the present times to all exertions in the cause of public liberty.

What an eventful period is this! I am thankful that I have lived to it; and I could almost say, *Lord, now lettest thou thy servant depart in peace, for mine eyes have seen thy salvation.* I have lived to see a diffusion of knowledge, which has undermined superstition and error—I have lived to see the rights of men better understood than ever; and nations panting for liberty, which seemed to have lost the idea of it. I have lived to see thirty millions of people, indignant and resolute, spurning at slavery, and demanding liberty with an irresistible voice; their king led in triumph, and an arbitrary monarch surrendering himself to his subjects. After sharing in the benefits of one revolution, I have been spared to be a witness to two other revolutions, both glorious. And now, methinks, I see the ardour for liberty catching and spreading; a general amendment beginning in human affairs; the dominion of kings changed for the dominion of laws, and the dominion of priests giving way to the dominion of reason and conscience.

Be encouraged, all ye friends of freedom, and writers in its defence! The times are auspicious. Your labours have not been in vain. Behold kingdoms, admonished by you, starting from sleep, breaking their fetters, and claiming justice from their oppressors! Behold, the light you have struck out, after setting America free, reflected to France, and there kindled into a blaze that lays despotism in ashes, and warms and illuminates Europe!

Tremble all ye oppressors of the world! Take warning all ye supporters of slavish governments, and slavish hierarchies! Call no more (absurdly and wickedly) reformation, innovation. You cannot now hold the world in darkness. Struggle no longer against increasing light and liberality. Restore to mankind their rights; and consent to the correction of abuses, before they and you are destroyed together.

FINIS

— 35 —

THE AFRICAN SLAVE TRADE

James Dana

NEW-HAVEN

1791

JAMES DANA (1735–1812). A graduate of Harvard and an Old Light Congregationalist minister, Dana became pastor in Wallingford, Connecticut, in 1758, an event that precipitated a flurry of pamphlets between partisans of the Old and New Light factions that came to be called the Wallingford Controversy. (See Leonard Bacon, *Thirteen Historical Discourses*, [1839].) Though he overcame this inauspicious beginning to his career, gaining the admiration of his clerical colleagues generally, he continued through the years to argue the merits of the Old Divinity against the New and, hence, against the doctrines of both the elder and the younger Jonathan Edwards and their allies, Doctors Bellamy, Hopkins, and West. Early on, he strongly declared for American independence. Dana became pastor of the First Church of New Haven in 1789, a position he held until 1805, when he lost out to the brilliant preaching of Moses Stuart and was dismissed by the council. He received a D.D. from the University of Edinburgh, and he married three times. Senator and lawyer Samuel Whittelsey Dana was his son by his first wife, Cathrine Whittelsey. Dana continued to live in New Haven until his death.

The African Slave Trade (1791), delivered in New Haven before the Connecticut Society for the Promotion of Freedom, demonstrates Dana's abolitionist convictions. A truly remarkable document, it is one of the mere handful of his published sermons.

THE AFRICAN SLAVE TRADE.

A

DISCOURSE

DELIVERED IN THE CITY OF NEW-HAVEN,

SEPTEMBER 9, 1790,

BEFORE

THE CONNECTICUT' SOCIETY

FOR

THE PROMOTION OF FREEDOM.

BY JAMES DANA, D. D.

PASTOR OF THE FIRST CONGREGATIONAL CHURCH IN SAID CITY.

NEW-HAVEN:

PRINTED BY THOMAS AND SAMUEL GREEN.

M,DCC,XCI

So then, brethren, we are not children of the bond-woman, but of the free.

Epistle to the Galatians, IV. 31.

The churches of Galatia consisted principally of Jewish converts, who were engaged to incorporate the Mosaic ritual with the Christian profession. They boasted, at the same time, "We be Abraham's children, and were never in bondage." With great address and pertinency St. Paul reminds them, "Abraham had two sons; one by a bond-maid, the other by a free-woman." These were emblems of the two covenants. Ishmael, by Hagar the bond-woman, represented the Sinai covenant; Isaac, by Sarah the free-woman, represented the Abrahamic covenant. The former was local and temporary, founded in worldly promises, had burthensome appendages, and only a shadow of heavenly things. The latter was universal and permanent, a covenant of better hopes, and stripped of that ceremonial which was a yoke of bondage.

The apostle hath described the Christian church in distinction from the Jewish thus: The Jews under Moses were like an heir in his minority, who is under tutors and governors. The law was a schoolmaster to bring them to Christ. He came to redeem them that were under the law; that they might be no longer servants, but sons; heirs of full age, heirs of God through Christ. "Now we, brethren, are the children of promise, as was Isaac," with whom the covenant of better hopes was established. *We are not children of the bond-woman, but of the free.*

The apostle proceeds: "Stand fast therefore in the liberty wherewith Christ hath made us free, and be not entangled again with the yoke of bondage." The Sinai covenant was subservient to the Abrahamic, till the seed promised to Abraham came. When this seed came, that covenant had answered its purpose, and gave place to a more liberal one. The Jewish converts acknowledged that this seed was come: But they encroached on the liberty of their fellow-Christians, by attempting to compel their observance of the abrogated ordinances of Moses. This was falling from grace, cutting themselves off from the privileges of the children of the free-woman, and desiring again to be in bondage to weak and beggarly rudiments. It was returning to a state of minority, after the time appointed of the father for their majority and freedom.

The apostle further acquaints them, that "the blessing of Abraham was come on the gentiles through Jesus Christ." For the promise was thus expressed: "In thee shall all nations be blessed." There is therefore no difference, under the Christian institution, between Jews and other nations. The latter, though by nature in bondage, are made equally free of the family of Christ as the former. This is the fulfilment of the prediction, "I will call them my people, which were not my people; and her beloved, which was not beloved. Where it was said unto them, Ye are not my people, there shall they be called the children of the living God." The text, though immediately addressed to Jewish believers, is equally applicable to believing gentiles. These are not, any more than those, children of the bond-woman, but of the free. They are "all one in Christ Jesus—children of God, whether Jew or Greek, bond or free, male or female—If Christ's, then Abraham's seed, and heirs according to the promise."

Christian freedom, being alike the privilege of converts from Judaism and heathenism, primarily intends, on the part of the former, the abolition of the encumbered ritual of Moses; and, on the part of the latter, liberation from idolatrous superstition, to which they were in servile subjection: On the part of both it intends deliverance from the slavery of vicious passions.

When Christ appeared, the whole world were sunk in ignorance and wickedness. The gentiles, *professing themselves to be wise*, *knew not God*, and worshipped and served the creature more than the Creator. They were vassals to the prince of the power of the air. The Christian dispensation, accompanied with the holy Ghost sent down from heaven, called them out of darkness into marvelous light; they were turned from dumb idols, from the power of Satan, from worldly pollutions, to serve the living God. The Jewish church had corrupted and made void the law of God. Their guides taught for doctrines the commandments of men, perverted to a worldly sense the promises of spiritual redemption, and imposed a greater burthen of ceremonies than Moses had enjoined. Christ removed the vail of Moses, *consecrated a new and living way* to God, rescued the precepts of the decalogue from the glosses of blind and interested guides, and disburthened religion of that weight under which it had groaned. *His yoke is easy, and his burthen light. Where the spirit of the Lord is, there is liberty* in the highest sense. The spirit of life in Christ removes the dominion of sin. His disciples, made free from sin, *walk not after the flesh, but after the spirit. There is no condemnation to them.* Thus emancipated, they "wait for the hope of righteousness by faith—the redemption of the body." When made free of the kingdom promised them, sin and the curse, pain, sorrow, death shall be no more. How glorious this liberty!

Further: Christianity is a reasonable service, and founded in personal persuasion. It permits us to "call no man master; for one is our master, even Christ"; to whom alone every one must stand or fall. His religion is friendly to free enquiry: It directs us to "prove all things"—to claim the liberty of grounding our faith, not on the wisdom of man, but the power of God; and to allow others the same. Our liberty may not be judged of their consciences, nor their liberty of our conscience. They who are strong ought to bear the infirmities of the weak; and should take heed lest by any means their liberty, their improved knowledge in Christianity, should be a stumbling block to uninformed minds. "Use not liberty for an occasion to the flesh, but by love serve one another. There is one body, and one spirit, and we are called in one hope. One Lord, one faith, one baptism, one God and Father of all."

How then should different professors, and different denominations, endeavour to keep the unity of the spirit in the bond of peace, with all meekness, humility and charity? The body of Christ is one, and hath many members. The members then "should have the same care one for another. If one suffer, all the members should suffer with it; or if one be honoured, all the members should rejoice with it." Those are *carnal, and walk as men*, who contend for the system of this or that man, or body of men. The children of the bond-woman would exclude from the privileges of the Christian church, and doom to eternal chains, such as do not embrace the faith or opinions they hold: But the children of the free-woman *have not so learned Christ*. The simplicity and perspicuity of this heavenly institution, designed to guide men of common understanding in the paths of salvation, can derive no assistance from speculations too high for the generality of mankind—too high also for those who exercise themselves therein.

In going off from one extreme, let us shun the other. "We are called unto liberty": Should it be an occasion of infidelity and indifference to all religion, the guilt and shame must be aggravated. The real friends of liberty always distinguish between freedom and licentiousness. They know that the mind cannot be free, while blinded by sceptical pride, or immersed in sensuality. Liberty consists not in subverting the foundations of society, in being without law. Nor doth it consist in reasoning against God, and providence, and revelation. Nor in attempting to explain his nature, his government, and the secret things which belong to him.

Christian liberty supposeth that we receive the record which God hath given of his Son—that we be not the servants of sin, but have our fruit unto holiness—that we abide in our callings.

Lastly, The spirit of Christianity hath the best aspect on general liberty and the rights of mankind. Would we persuade men to *look, not on their own things, but on the things of others*, let us set before them the pattern of Christ. Was ever grace or liberality like his, "who though he was rich, for our sakes became poor, that we through his poverty might be rich?" He was "in the form of God,—but took upon him the form of a servant." He "came not to be ministred unto, but to minister, and gave his life" to purchase spiritual and eternal redemption for the slaves of Satan. Possibly for a friend, or a good man, some might dare to die. But he died for enemies, for the ungodly. Is it glorious to die for one's country? He died for all the world. Were the same mind in us, we should love all mankind, and do good to all as we have opportunity. They who hate and persecute us would be the objects of our good wishes and forgiveness. We should pray, "Father, forgive them." We should have compassion on them, as the good Samaritan had on the Jew whom he found helpless and ready to perish. Every natural and friendly, every private and public affection is cherished and improved by looking unto Jesus. And if we speak of universal philanthropy, how doth every example fade before his? He is not ashamed to call mankind his brethren. His love to them was stronger than death, when they had forfeited the privileges of children, and might have been consigned, with apostate spirits, to chains and blackness of darkness. They owe all the liberty they have or hope for to his friendship.

Where the spirit of Christ is, there is no envy, strife or confusion; no discord and war; no invasion of the rights of others, either those of individuals, or of societies and nations; but meekness, peace, and harmony, joy in the happiness, and commiseration of the distresses of others. This spirit doth no ill to others, but all possible good. Rulers, under its influence, are not oppressors, but benefactors. Subjects do not resist lawful authority; but render tribute, custom, fear, honour to whom they are due, leading a quiet life in godliness and honesty. When the spirit of Christianity shall universally prevail, as our hope is that it will, nations will "learn war no more; they shall not hurt nor destroy in all God's holy mountain."

Our Lord undertook not to say what men's personal and civil rights are—what the prerogatives of princes, or the sovereign power of a nation, and what the privileges of subjects. He left civil distinctions among men as he found them. He taught his disciples to "render to Cesar the things that are Cesar's, and to God the things that are God's.["]

Among other relative duties, his religion particularly requires of servants, that they *be subject to their masters with all fear; not only to the good and gentle, but also to the froward: Shewing all good fidelity, that they may adorn the doctrine of God our Savior in all things. Let every man wherein he is called, therein abide with God. Let as many servants as are under the yoke, account their own masters worthy of all honor, that the name of God and his doctrine be not blasphemed. And they that have believing masters, let them not despise them, because they are brethren.*

Revelation has not informed us, what form of government is best adapted to answer the ends of society. Every form must be some abridgment of natural liberty. Our being social creatures, our dependence on one another, shew that government is the will of the Creator. The original form was probably patriarchal. The theocracy of the Jews was appropriate to them. Monarchy was a subversion of their constitution. No other form than theirs can be pronounced divine. Nations have a right to institute such form as they chuse. The government of most nations, therefore, hath been mere usurpation. Far from being sanctioned by divine authority, we might rather consider the permission of such government as his greatest scourge on mankind.

Relying on the candor which I need from my present auditory, I address myself more particularly to the design of our coming together.

A manner of address calculated to inflame the passions would neither become my station, nor be respectful to an audience well acquainted with the rights of men and citizens, educated in principles of liberty.

The Africans belong to the families for whom heaven designed a participation in the blessing of Abraham. We need not discuss the question, what the state of those, whom the Europeans have enslaved, was antecedently to such their slavery. It is more proper to enquire when and how the African slave-trade commenced—what nations have engaged in it—in what manner they have carried it on—what the probable numbers they have reduced to slavery—in what condition these slaves are held—and what reasons are offered in vindication of the trade.

A zeal for the discovery of new territory marked the fifteenth century. The first navigations of the Europeans for this purpose were concerted and directed by prince Henry, fourth son of John I. king of Portugal. He was born 1394. His valor in the assault and capture of the city Ceuta in Africa, A.D. 1415, presaged the fame he afterwards acquired. From this period he devoted himself to naval expeditions for the discovery of unknown countries. The ships he sent out subjected divers parts of Africa, and the neighbouring islands, to the dominion of Portugal. After the success in doubling cape Bojador, he gave to his father and his successors all the lands he had discovered, or might discover, and applied to pope Martin V. to ratify the donation. He engaged, that in all their expeditions the Portuguese should have mainly in view the extension of the Roman church and authority of its pontif. Martin granted the prince's request. In his bull of ratification, which was about the year 1430, it is declared, that "whatever might be discovered from the said cape to the utmost India, should pertain to the Portuguese' dominion." Edward, brother to prince Henry, succeeded to the throne of Portugal 1433, on the death of John I. Pope Eugene IV, by his bull in 1438, ratified to Edward the grant made by Martin V. A bull of Nicholas V. dated January 8, 1454, refers to the aforesaid bulls of his predecessors, Martin and Eugene. It recites the declaration prince Henry had made of his achievements —"*that for 25 years he had not ceased to send annually almost an army*" of Portuguese, "with the greatest dangers, labors and charges, in most swift ships, to *search out the sea and maritime provinces towards the southern parts and antarctic pole*"—that these ships "came at length to the province of Guinea, and took possession of some islands, havens and sea adjoining"—that "sailing further, war was waged for some years with the people of those parts, and very many islands near thereunto were subdued and peaceably possessed, and still were possessed, with the adjacent sea"—that "many Guineans and other negroes were taken thence by force, and some by barter." The bull describes prince Henry as "a true soldier of Christ, a most courageous defender and intrepid champion of the faith, aspiring from his early youth with his utmost might to have the glorious name of Christ published, extolled and revered throughout the world." It recogniseth the exclusive right of Portugal to the acquisitions and possessions aforesaid, in virtue of the letters of Martin and Eugene, which granted to the king of Portugal and prince Henry "free and ample faculty to *invade, search out, expugn, vanquish and subdue* all pagans and enemies of Christ wheresoever placed, *and their persons to reduce to perpetual slavery*, and all their kingdoms, possessions and goods to apply and appropriate," &c. Pope Nicholas's letter then goes on to "decree and declare, the acquests already made, and what hereafter shall happen to be acquired, after that they shall be acquired, have pertained, and forever of right do belong and pertain, to the aforesaid king and his successors, and not to any others whatever." It forbids, on the severest penalties, all Christian powers from settling in the countries discovered by the Portuguese, or any way molesting them in their expeditions for the discovery and conquest of unknown countries. It speaks of prince Henry's plan and his prosecution of it as "a most pious work, and most worthy of perpetual remembrance, wherein the glory of God, with the interest of the commonwealth of the universal church are concerned."

Thus were prince Henry's views and operations sanctioned by the highest authority at that time acknowledged in Christendom. A right derived from a source so venerable was then undisputed. The Roman pontif bound princes at his pleasure; and, as vicar of Christ, was allowed to have at his disposal all the kingdoms of the earth. This grant of Nicholas was confirmed by his successor, Calixtus III. August 6, 1458.

On the death of Edward, his son Alphonsus, then in his minority, succeeded to the throne of Portugal 1438, and died 1481. Prince Henry died 1460, or 1463. At his death the spirit of discovery languished;

but revived with the accession of John II. son of Alphonsus. John, the year after his accession (1482), sent an embassy to Edward IV. of England, to acquaint him with the title acquired, by the pope's bull, to the conquest in Guinea; and requested him to dissolve a fleet which some English merchants were fitting for the Guinea trade. The king of England shewed great respect to the ambassadors, and granted all they required. The king of Portugal assumed, and the king of England gave him, this style, *Rex Portugaliæ et Algarbiorum citra at ultra mare in Africa*. Pope Sixtus IV. not long before his death, which was August 12, 1484, confirmed all the grants made by his predecessors to the kings of Portugal and their successors.*

"In 1481 John II. sent 100 artificers, 500 soldiers, and all necessaries, to build a fort in Guinea. The large kingdoms of Benin and Congo were discovered 1484, 1485"; and the cape of Good-Hope 1486. The Portuguese built forts and planted colonies in Africa; "established a commercial intercourse with the powerful kingdoms, and compelled the petty princes by force of arms to acknowledge themselves vassals."

At this period, and by these means, the power and commerce of the Portuguese in Africa were well established. The wholesome decrees of five successive Roman pontifs granted, conveyed and confirmed to the most faithful king a right to appropriate the kingdoms, goods and possessions of all infidels, wherever to be found, *to reduce their persons to perpetual slavery*, or destroy them from the earth, for the declared purpose of bringing the Lord's sheep into one dominical fold, under one universal pastor. Succeeding kings of Portugal have not forfeited the large grant by any undutifulness to their holy father. Portugal long enjoyed the trade to Africa and the East-Indies without the interference of any European power. For more than half a century before she exported any Negroes from Africa, she made and held many of them slaves in their native country.

The Portuguese first imported slaves into Hispaniola,† A.D. 1508, and into their Brazilian colonies 1517.‡ Their sugar works were first set up in these colonies 1580. Their union with Spain at that time

* Plantation of colonies, part I. sect. 26.

†It is observable, that the island which first received slaves from Africa, suffers at this time (October 1791) the most exemplary and threatning vengeance from them. How perilous such property!

‡ Brazil was discovered A.D. 1500, by Cabral's fleet, fitted out by John II. king of Portugal.

was most unfortunate for them. Hence the Dutch became their enemies, who took from them their East-India and Brazilian conquests, and part of their African colonies. They recovered Brazil, and their African establishments 1640; but have never recovered the riches of India.

After the Dutch quitted Brazil, and the gold mines were discovered, the trade of Portugal improved, and a great importation of slaves took place. "They carry yearly from Loango to the Brazils 25,000." At Goango "they get abundance." At cape Lopos they "get a great many." They themselves say, "that they carry over to Brazil 50,000 and more every year from Melinda" on the Mozambique coast. Such hath been the increase of their Brazilian and African colonies for about a century past, that they "have taken off since the year 1700 more English goods annually than Portugal and Spain had before done."* From their greater dominions, and greater extent of territory, in Africa, than any other European power, this quarter of the world "is not of less consideration to them, perhaps, than to all the other powers of Europe unitedly comprehended—It supplies them with Negroes in abundance, to carry on their sugar works, mines, and planting business in the Brazils.† They are said to bring annually from the Brazils £.5,000,000 sterling in gold, coined and uncoined."‡

"It is difficult to ascertain the number of slaves, which the Portu-

* Postlethwait, vol. I, tit. Brazil.

† Ibid. vol. II. p. 521–524.

‡ Beawes saith *(Lex mercatoria)*, that the trade for slaves at Senegal "amounts to 15,000 in a common year." (p. 726.) At Sierra Leona "the trade in slaves is not a little." (p. 728.) At Des Trois Pointes the Dutch trade for "many slaves." In the kingdom of Ardres, &c. between three and four thousand are annually purchased. (p. 729.) On the coast of the kingdom of Benin, at Sabe, the English, French, Dutch and Portuguese "export annually above 20,000." (p. 730.) "The number sent from Congo by the Portuguese is surprizingly great." (Ibid.) "Of all the African coasts, Angola furnisheth the Europeans with the best negroes, and commonly in the greatest quantities. Though the Portuguese are extremely powerful in the interior parts of this kingdom, yet the negro trade on the coast is free to other nations. The English, French and Dutch send yearly a great number of vessels, who carry off many thousands for their American settlements, and for sale in those of the Spaniards. There is hardly any year that the Portuguese do not ship off 15,000 for Brazil. The villages of Cambambe, Embaco and Missingomo furnish most slaves to the Portuguese merchants"—the negro trade at Longo, Malindo and Cabindo, on the Angolian coast, is not one of the least considerable that the English and Dutch are concerned in, whether for the number, strength or goodness of the slaves—the inhabitants of the American colonies always give for them an higher price, as more able to sustain the labours and fatigues of the culture and manufacturing of sugar, tobacco, indigo, and other painful works." (p. 731.)

guese residing in Africa have in possession. Those who are least rich have fifty, an hundred, or two hundred belonging to them, and many of the most considerable possess at least three thousand. A religious society at Loanda have of their own 12,000 of all nations." (Beawes, lex mercatoria, p. 790, 791.)

Spanish America hath successively received her slaves from the Genoese, Portuguese, French and English. A convention was made at London between England and Spain, A.D. 1689, for supplying the Spanish West-Indies with negro slaves from Jamaica.* The French Guinea company contracted, in 1702, to supply them with 38,000 negroes, in ten years; and if peace should be concluded, with 48,000. In 1713 there was a treaty between England and Spain for the importation of 144,000 negroes in thirty years, or 4,800 annually.† If we include those whom the Portuguese have held in slavery in Africa, with the importations into South-America, twelve millions may be a moderate estimate from the commencement of the traffic to the present time.

We shall now attend to the importations into the West-India islands and the United States.

The English fitted out three ships for the slave trade in 1562.‡ For a full century this trade hath been vigorously pursued, without intermission, by England, France and Holland; as it had been long before, and continued to be, by Portugal.

"The trade of Barbadoes, in 1661, maintained 400 sail of ships of 150 tons one with another, and 10,000 seamen. The running cash was computed at £.200,000 at least. In 1676 this island had 80,000 negroes. In one hundred years the inhabitants of Great-Britain have received £.12,000,000 in silver by means of this plantation. On a parliamentary enquiry into the African trade 1728, it appeared that in three years only, 42,000 slaves had been imported at Barbadoes, Jamaica and Antigua, besides what were carried to their other islands."§

In pursuance of an order from the king of France, a survey was made in 1777, of the slaves in the French islands, when the number

* Anderson's commerce, vol. V. p. 120.

† Postlethwait, *assiento.*

‡ Anderson's commerce, vol. II, p. 156:

§ Postlethwait, vol. II. p. 766.

returned was 386,500.* The council of Paris determined, that an annual importation of 20,000 was necessary to supply the annual decrease. (Anderson, vol. V. p. 276.)

The number of slaves in the several British West-India islands is stated by Anderson at 410,000, (vol. VI. p. 921, 922.) A later account makes them 461,669.†

"Since the peace of 1763," saith M. le Abbe Raynal,‡ "Great-Britain hath sent annually to the coast of Guinea 195 vessels, consisting, collectively, of 23,000 tons, and 7 or 8,000 seamen. Rather more than half this number have sailed from Liverpool, and the remainder from London, Bristol and Lancaster. They have traded for 40,000 slaves." An average for each vessel will be 205. Postlethwait informs us, that in 1752 eighty eight vessels from Liverpool to Africa brought away 25,940 slaves.§ If the Liverpool vessels brought away this number, we may suppose that those of London and Bristol made up the full number of 40,000.

M. le Abbe Raynal saith (probably without sufficient attention, vol. IV. p. 99.), "The trade of Africa hath never furnished the French colonies more than 13 or 14,000 slaves annually." This importation, he grants, was "insufficient" for her colonies. It doth not correspond to the number of slaves in them. If the trade had not furnished a sufficiency for themselves, would they have contracted to

* St. Domingo	240,000
Martinico	75,000
Guadaloupe	64,000
St. Lucia	4,000
Cayenne	3,500
Total	386,500

† The account published 1791 stands thus:

Jamaica	256,000	St. Vincent	14,353
Barbadoes	62,100	Montferrat	10,000
Antigua	37,808	Nevis	8,420
Grenada	23,926	Virgin Islands	6,500
St. Christophers	20,435	Bermuda	4,919
Dominico	14,967	Bahamas	2,241
		Total	461,669

‡ Vol. IV. p. 98.

§ Vol. I. p. 709, 710. The names of the masters, and number of slaves in each ship are inserted, 296 on an average.

supply Spain with 4,000 slaves annually for ten successive years? "Good judges," saith Postlethwait (vol. I. p. 726.), "reckon that 30,000 negroes are annually imported into the French sugar islands." But we will suppose they import 20,000 into these islands. This is the importation which their council supposed requisite to supply the decrease. The general computation is five per cent. decrease annually.

The present number of slaves in the West-Indies is 930,669.* There are in the United States 670,633.† To this number may be added about 12,000 manumitted Africans. In all 1,613,302. Were the mortality among them as great in the five states south of Delaware as in the West-Indies, the above number could not be kept up but by an annual importation of 80,000. The probability is, that 70,000 hath been the annual average for a century at least.

In seventy seven years there were imported into Jamaica 535,549.¶ By the census of the United States, taken 1791, they contain 3,925,247 souls.* Of these, in the states south of Delaware, more

* British islands	461,669
French islands	386,000
Other islands	83,000
Total	930,669

† In this estimate 80,000 slaves are set to South-Carolina, which hath made no return.

¶ Negroes imported from Africa into Jamaica, and exported from thence yearly, between the 2d September 1702, and the 31st December 1778.

Years	Ships	Imports	Exports	Years	Ships	Imports	Exports
1702	5	843	327	1741	19	4255	562
1703	14	2740	481	1742	22	5067	792
1704	16	4120	221	1743	38	8926	1368
1705	16	3503	1661	1744	38	8755	1331
1706	14	3804	1086	1745	18	3843	1344
1707	15	3358	897	1746	16	4703	1502
1708	23	6627	1379	1747	33	10898	3378
1709	10	2234	1275	1748	39	10430	2426
1710	15	3662	1191	1749	25	6858	2128
1711	26	6724	1532	1750	16	3587	721
1712	15	4128	1903	1751	21	4840	713
1713	19	4378	2712	1752	27	6117	1038
1714	24	5789	3507	1753	39	7661	902
1715	10	2372	1089	1754	47	9551	1592

Years	Ships	Imports	Exports	Years	Ships	Imports	Exports
1716	24	6361	2872	1755	64	12723	598
1717	29	7551	3153	1756	46	11166	1902
1718	27	6253	2247	1757	32	7935	943
1719	25	5120	3161	1758	11	3405	411
1720	23	5064	2815	1759	18	5212	681
1721	17	3715	1637	1760	23	7573	2368
1722	41	8469	3263	1761	29	6480	642
1723	30	6824	4674	1762	24	6279	232
1724	25	6852	3449	1763	33	10079	1582
1725	41	10297	3588	1764	41	10213	2639
1726	50	11703	4112	1765	41	8931	2006
1727	17	3876	1555	1766	43	10208	672
1728	20	5350	986	1767	19	3248	375
1729	40	10499	4820	1768	27	5950	485
1730	43	10104	5222	1769	19	3575	420
1731	45	10079	5708	1770	25	6824	836
1732	57	13552	5288	1771	17	4183	671
1733	37	7413	5176	1772	22	5278	923
1734	20	4570	1666	1773	49	9676	800
1735	20	4851	2260	1774		18448	2511
1736	15	3943	1647	1775		16945	5272
1737	35	8995	2240	1776	456	19231	1343
1738	32	7695	2070	1777		5255	492
1739	29	6787	598	1778		5674	734
1740	27	5362	495				
On an average 220 slaves in each ship					2436	535,549	132,115

* Districts	Free white males of 16 years and upwards, including heads of families	Free white males under 16 years	Free white females, including heads of families	All other free persons	Slaves	Total
Maine	24,384	24,748	46,870	538	None.	96,540
N. Hampshire	36,086	34,851	70,160	630	158	141,885
Massachusetts	95,453	87,289	190,582	5463	None.	378,787
Rhode-Island	16,019	15,799	32,652	3407	948	68,825
Connecticut	60,523	54,403	117,448	2808	2764	237,940
Vermont	22,435	22,328	40,505	252	16	85,539
New-York	83,700	78,122	152,320	4654	21,324	340,120
New-Jersey	45,251	41,416	82,287	2762	11,453	184,139
Pennsylvania	110,788	106,948	206,363	6537	3737	434,373
Delaware	11,783	12,143	22,384	3899	8887	59,094

than one quarter are negro slaves. In the four states next north of Maryland are 45,401 slaves. In New-England 3870. There may have been brought into all the West-India-Islands, and into the United States, from first to last, seven millions. One million more must be allowed for mortality on the passage. How many have been destroyed in the collection of them in Africa, we cannot justly conjecture. It is judged that Great-Britain sustain the loss of twice as many seamen in this, as in all their other extensive trade.

We suppose, then, that eight millions of slaves have been shipped in Africa for the West-India islands and the United States; ten millions for South-America; and, perhaps, two millions have been taken and held in slavery in Africa. Great-Britain and the United States have shipped about five millions, France two, Holland and other nations one; though we undertake not to state the proportion with exactness. The other twelve millions we set to Portugal. Twenty million slaves, at £.30 sterling each, amount to the commercial value of £.600,000,000. *Six hundred times ten hundred thousand pounds sterling traffic in the souls of men!!!*

By whom hath this commerce been opened, and so long and ardently pursued? The subjects of their *most faithful*, *most catholic*, *most Christian*, *most protestant majesties*, *defenders of the faith*; and by the citizens of the most republican States, with the sanction of St. Peter's

Districts	Free white males of 16 years and upwards, including heads of families	Free white males under 16 years	Free white females, including heads of families	All other free persons	Slaves	Total
Maryland	55,915	51,339	101,395	8043	103,036	319,728
Virginia	110,936	116,135	215,046	12,868	292,627	747,610
N. Carolina	69,988	77,506	140,710	4975	100,572	393,751
S. Carolina					80,000	240,000
Georgia	13,103	14,044	25,739	398	29,264	82,548
Kentucky	15,154	17,057	28,922	114	12,430	73,677
S.W. Territory	6,271	10,277	15,365	361	3417	35,691
N.W. Ditto,						5,000
Total	781,769	764,405	1,488,748	57,709	670,633	3,925,247

successor. Unprovoked, without any pretended injury, these have kindled and kept alive the flame of war through three quarters of the continent of Africa; that is, all the interior as well as maritime parts south of Senegal and Abyssinia. These have taught the Africans to steal, sell and murder one another. On any or no pretence the different tribes make prisoners of each other, or the chiefs seize their own people, and drive them, as herds of cattle, to market. The natives are trepanned by one another, and by the Europeans; forced from their flocks, and fields, and tenderest connexions. This vile commerce hath depopulated the sea-coast: It must now be carried on in the inland parts.

As though it were not sufficient to force the Africans from their country, and every thing dear to them, they are made to travel in irons hundreds of miles through their native soil, through sands and morasses, down to the sea shore; and there stowed, as lumber, for transportation. The cruelty of the captains of the Guinea ships, in many instances, is not inferior to that of Clive or Hastings.

The servitude of the greatest part of the slaves after their arrival, the scantiness of their provision and its bad quality, their tyrannical and merciless discipline, are well known, and too painful to recollect. It is a law in Barbadoes, "that if any slave, under punishment by his master or his order, suffer in life or limb, no person shall be liable to any fine for the same. But if any man shall wantonly or cruelly kill his own slave, he shall pay into the treasury £.15."

With what reason or truth is it urged, that the condition of the Africans is meliorated by their slavery? They, not their masters, are the proper judges in this matter. Wretched as you may suppose their condition was in Africa, the nefarious commerce of foreigners may have been the principal cause of that wretchedness. Should foreigners desist from this commerce, and the holders of slaves propose to transport them back to Africa, how would their *mouth be filled with laughter, and their tongue with singing?* Instead of thinking their condition meliorated by slavery, they most sincerely join in that execration on their oppressors: *Happy shall he be that taketh and dasheth thy little ones against the stones.* The imaginary expectation that death may transport them to their own country is their chief consolation. Under unlimited power, accustomed to the most inhuman usage, no example of mercy relenting for them being exhibited, no marvel that the language of insurgents is, *Death or conquest.* Their cries will sooner or later reach the ears of him to whom vengeance belongeth.

Will any one say, that their condition is meliorated by their being taught the knowledge of GOD and CHRIST? How many of their masters are in a state of brutal ignorance in this respect? A parish minister* in the West-Indies saith, that he "drew up plain and easy instructions for the slaves, invited them to attend at particular hours on Lord's-day, appointed hours at home, and exhorted their masters to encourage their attendance. But inconceivable was the listlessness with which he was heard, and bitter the censure heaped on him in return. It was suggested, that he aimed to render them incapable of being good slaves by making them Christians—some who approved of the plan, did not think themselves obliged to co-operate: I stood," says he, "a rebel convict against the interest and majesty of plantership."

When Archbishop Secker asked what success the missionaries "had in baptizing and converting negro slaves? how the catechist at Codrington college in Barbadoes proceeded with those slaves that belonged to the college estate," and whom he presumed had been instructed in Christianity? He was answered, "I found one old negro, who told me he could say all his catechism. I asked him, if he did not find himself much happier and better since he became a Christian, than he was before? Why, sir, said he, I am old man, and as a driver am not put to common labour; but Christian not made for negro in this country. How so? What is your duty towards God? He repeated it. What is your duty towards your neighbor? Ah, master, I don't say that no more. Why so? Because, master, I can't say it from my heart, if I think of white man."

Had African slaves the means of Christian instruction, had they been treated with humanity, still the making slaves of them hath been no more than *doing evil that good may come.* Christianity and humanity would rather have dictated the sending books and teachers into Africa, and endeavors for their civilization. Have they been treated as children of the same family with ourselves? as having the same Father, whose *tender mercies are over all his works?* as having the same

* Mr. Ramsay.

natural prerogatives with other nations? Or have they been treated as outcasts from humanity?*

The Greeks and Romans, amidst their improvements in philosophy, arts and sciences, established slavery as far as they extended their conquests. Their rage for conquest had the world for its object. They made war without having received any injury. Captives taken in war were exposed to sale. And indeed all the ancient nations considered conquest as a just foundation for slavery. Some moderns have undertaken to defend the same principle. In an age and country so well acquainted with the rights of men, this kind of reasoning merits very little attention. It is, moreover, wholly inapplicable to the case

* The committee of the society in London, instituted in 1787, for the purpose of effecting the abolition of the slave trade, reported to the society, January 15, 1788, "that sundry specimens evince that a trade of great national importance might be opened by once establishing the confidence of the natives." The sentiments and reasoning of a great commercial writer on this subject are just and forcible.

"If once a turn for industry and the arts was introduced [into Africa], a greater quantity of the European produce and manufactures might be exported thither, than to any other country in the whole world. No country is richer in gold and silver. Here is a prodigious number of elephants, which would not only facilitate the inland intercourses of commerce, but also, in the teeth of these notable animals, afford a very beneficial branch of commerce. The fruitful rich lands, every where to be found upon the coasts and within the country, upon the banks of the rivers near the gold-coast and the slave-coast, would produce all the richest articles of the East and West-India commerce. It is melancholy to observe, that a country which has 10,000 miles sea-coast, and noble, large, deep rivers, should yet have no navigation; streams penetrating into the very centre of the country, but of no benefit to it; innumerable people, without knowledge of each other, correspondence, or commerce—Africa, stored with an inexhaustible treasure, and capable, under proper improvements, of producing so many things delightful as well as convenient, seems utterly neglected by those who are civilized themselves, and its own inhabitants quite unsolicitous of reaping the benefits which nature has provided for them. What it affords in its present rude, unimproved state, is solely given up to the gain of others, as if not the people only were to be sold for slaves to their fellow-creatures, but the whole country was captive, and produced its treasures merely for the use and benefit of the rest of the world, and not at all for their own. Instead of making slaves of these people, would it not rather become nations, who assume the name and character of Christians, to give them a relish for the blessings of life, by extending traffic into their country in the largest extent it will admit of, and introducing among them the more civilized arts and customs? While the slaving trade continues to be the great object of" other nations, and these "promote the spirit of butchery and making slaves of each other among the negro princes and chiefs, their civilization, and the extension of trade into the bowels of the country, will be obstructed."

(Postlethwait, vol. I. p. 686; 727.)

of African slavery. Whatever just dominion conquerors may claim over the conquered must be founded in this, that the latter were the aggressors. Did the Africans first invade the rights of the nations who have carried on the slave trade? or give them a foundation of complaint? Were they ever conquered by their foreign invaders?

But the reasoning is not less unjust than inapplicable. The objects of a just war are the security of national rights, and indemnification for injuries. Superior force may enslave, but gives no right. It is inglorious, savage and brutal to insult a conquered enemy, and reduce him to the lowest servility.

"But did not the Jews make slaves of the Canaanites by the express command of God?" They did indeed. Those nations had *filled up their measure of iniquity*. The Supreme Sovereign devoted them to destruction, and commissioned Israel to be the executioners of his justice. "Thou mayest not," said God, "consume them at once, lest the land become desolate, and the beasts of the field increase against thee. By little and little will I drive them out from before thee." Of those nations, remaining in the land, they might purchase bond-servants, and transmit them as an inheritance to posterity. The Gibeonites, one of these devoted nations, obtained a league of peace with Joshua, under pretence that they were a very remote people. When their stratagem was detected, he saved them alive, because of his league; but he made them all bond-men, hewers of wood, and drawers of water (Lev. 25. 44, 45, 46. Joshua chap. 9th). When a like warrant can be produced, it will authorize a like practice.

"But Ishmael was the son of a bond-woman. His posterity therefore can have no claim to freedom." This is not a just consequence; nor is this objection supported by history. The prophecy concerning Ishmael was, "He will be a wild man; his hand will be against every man, and every man's hand against him." His posterity, the Arabians, have lived in war with the world. The Egyptians, Assyrians, Persians, Greeks, Romans, Tartars and Turks have in vain attempted to subjugate them. They have been and are free and independent.

That the heathen have no right to any possession on earth, is an article of the Roman faith. The charters of Britain to her late colonies held out the same language. But is this the language of him, whose is "the world, and they that dwell therein"? who "hath made of one blood all nations of men to dwell on all the face of the earth; and determined the bounds of their habitation"? In enslaving the pagans of Africa, have the Christians of Europe and America proceeded on this principle, that the author of their religion, whose *kingdom is not of this world*, hath commissioned them to seize on the possessions, and, what is more, on the persons, of those heathen? Among the enumerated articles of commerce in mystical Babylon in the day of her fall, *slaves and souls of men* closeth the account—intimating that this kind of commerce was the consummation of her wickedness. Let such as imitate the example, consider the consequence.

> Man's obdurate heart does not feel for man.
> He finds his fellow guilty of a skin
> Not colour'd like his own; and having pow'r
> T' enforce the wrong, for such a worthy cause
> Dooms and devotes him as his lawful prey.
> Thus man devotes his brother, and destroys;
> And worse than all, and most to be deplor'd,
> As human nature's broadest, foulest blot,
> Chains him, tasks him, and exacts his sweat
> With stripes, that mercy with a bleeding heart
> Weeps when she sees inflicted on a beast.
> Then what is man? And what man seeing this,
> And having human feelings, does not blush,
> And hang his head, to think himself a man?*

Our late warfare was expressly founded on such principles as these: "All men are created equal: They are endowed by their Creator with certain unalienable rights; among these are life, liberty, and the pursuit of happiness." Admitting these just principles, we need not puzzle ourselves with the question, whether a black complexion is a token of God's wrath? If attempts to account for the color of the blacks, by ascribing it to climate, or the state of society, or both, should not be perfectly satisfactory (and perhaps they are not), shall we therefore conclude, that they did not spring from the same original parents? How then shall we account either for their origin or our own? The Mosaic, which is the only account of the origin of mankind, doth not inform us what was the complexion of Adam and Eve.

*Cowper.

If we admit the Mosaic account, we cannot suppose that the Africans are of a different species from us: If we reject it, we have no account whence they or we sprang. Let us then receive the Mosaic history of the creation, till another and better appears. According to that, the Africans are our brethren. And, according to the principles of our religion, they are *children of the free-woman as well as we*. This instructs us, *that God is no respecter of persons, or of nations—hath put no difference between Jew and Greek, barbarian and Scythian*. In Christ Jesus, in whom it was foretold "all nations shall be blessed," those "who sometimes were far off, are brought nigh, and have access by one Spirit unto the Father." So that they "are no more strangers and foreigners, but fellow-citizens with the saints, and of the houshold of God." The heathen will all be given him for his inheritance, and the uttermost parts of the earth for a possession.

Why then should we treat our African brethren as the elder son in the parable treated the younger, offended at the compassion of their common parent towards him? Why place them in a situation incapable of recovery from their lost state? their state of moral death? Did Jesus come to redeem us from the worst bondage? Shall his disciples then enslave those whom he came to redeem from slavery? who are the purchase of his blood? Is this *doing to others*, as he hath commanded, *whatsoever we would that they should do to us?* Is it to *love our neighbour as ourselves?*

On a view of the wretched servitude of the Africans, some may suspect, that they must have been *sinners above all men*, *because they suffer such things*. This way of reasoning, however common, our Lord has reproved—particularly in the instance of the blind man; of those who were slain by the fall of the tower in Siloam; and of those whose blood Pilate mingled with the public sacrifices. All mankind are *the offspring of God*. His government over them is parental. Children may have the fullest proof that the government of their father is not capricious and tyrannic, but most wise and kind: At the same time, they cannot explain many parts of it; but unreservedly submit to his pleasure, having the fullest confidence in his superior wisdom, his paternal care and affection.

That such as have been educated in slavish principles, justify and practise slavery, may not seem strange. Those who profess to understand and regard the principles of liberty should cheerfully unite to abolish slavery.

Our middle and northern states have prohibited any further importation of slaves. South-Carolina passed a prohibitory act for a limited time. Consistently with the federal constitution the traffic may be stopped in seventeen years; and a duty of ten dollars may be laid on every slave now imported. By an act of the legislature of Connecticut, all blacks and mulattoes born within the state from March 1784, will be manumitted at the age of 25 years. The act of Pennsylvania liberates them at the age of twenty eight years. Such provision hath been made for the gradual abolition of slavery in the United States. Could wisdom and philanthropy have advanced further for the time?

In the northern division of the United States, the slaves live better than one quarter of the white people. Their masters are possessed of property; nor is harder labor required of the slaves, than a great part of the masters perform themselves. Might the estate of the masters be exempt from the maintenance of their slaves, but very few would hesitate to manumit them.

In co-operating with the wise measures and benevolent intentions of the legislature of Connecticut, we shall do as much as can be desired to ease the condition of slavery, and extinguish the odious distinction. Humane masters, requiring no more than is just and equal, and affording to their servants the means of moral and religious instruction, take the only sure course to make them faithful. Many receive such kind treatment, and have such affection to their masters, that they wish to abide with them. Nor is it to be doubted but many others, who may wish to be manumitted, would soon repent their choice. Still the term slave is odious, be the master's yoke ever so light. And it is very questionable whether any servant can be profitable who is not a voluntary one.

The revolution in the United States hath given free course to the principles of liberty. One ancient kingdom, illuminated by these principles, and actuated by the spirit of liberty, hath established a free constitution. The spirit will spread, and shake the throne of despotic princes. Neither an habit of submission to arbitrary rule in church and state, nor the menaced interference of neighboring kingdoms, could prevent, or counterwork, a revolution, propitious in its aspect on the rights of other nations, and of mankind. No combination of European potentates can impede the progress of freedom. The time is hastening, when their subjects will not endure to be told, that no government shall exist in any nation but such as provides for the perpetuation of absolute monarchy, and the transmission of it to the families in present possession. The time is hastening, when no monarch in Europe shall tell his subjects, *Your silver and your gold are mine.*

The present occasion will be well improved, if we set ourselves to banish all slavish principles, and assert our liberty as men, citizens and Christians. We have all one Father: He will have all his offspring to be saved. We are disciples of one master: He will finally *gather together in one the children of God.* Let us unite in carrying into effect the purpose of the Saviour's appearance. This was to give *peace and good will to man*, and thus bring *glory to God on high.*

Being "one body in Christ, and every one members one of another"; we should take care "that there be no schism in the body." They who separate themselves, or separate others, without cause, are schismatics. Christ is not divided. A religious party is of all others the most odious and dangerous. The terms express a palpable contradiction. The dire effects of proselyting zeal in Romish, and even in Protestant, countries would have been prevented, had Christian liberty been understood, and the exercise of it permitted.

Whether ignorance or learning, weakness or craft, have bound the heaviest burthens in religion, we need not enquire. Each of them hath done much in this way in ages past. Happily for the present age of light and liberty, the spirit of bigotry and domination cannot encumber and debase Christianity as heretofore. The exercise of private judgment, an appeal to the scriptures, and the cultivation of Christian charity and philanthropy, will display the excellency of our religion.

To conclude: In vain do we assert our natural and civil liberty, or contend for the same liberty in behalf of any of our fellow-creatures, provided we ourselves are not made free from the condemnation and dominion of sin. If there is such a thing as slavery, the servant of sin is a slave—and self-made. The captive, prisoner and slave, in an outward respect, may be free in Christ, free indeed; while he who enjoys full external liberty, may, in regard to his inward man, be under the power of wicked spirits: These enter and dwell in an heart garnished to receive them. Jesus Christ, and no other, saveth from sin and wrath. The spirit of life quickeneth those who are dead in trespasses, and looseth those whom Satan hath bound. "If we be dead with him, we believe that we shall also live with him."

The new Jerusalem is free in a more exalted sense than the church on earth. True believers, "sealed with the holy Spirit of promise, have the earnest of their inheritance, until the redemption of the purchased possession." In that day of complete redemption, of glorious liberty, may God of his infinite mercy grant that we may meet all the ransomed of the Lord, with songs and everlasting joy, saying: "Blessing, and honour, and glory, and power, be unto him that sitteth upon the throne; and unto the lamb who was slain, and hath redeemed us to God by his blood, out of every kindred, and tongue, and people, and nation. Amen."

36

A SERMON DELIVERED AT THE ANNUAL ELECTION

Israel Evans

CONCORD

1791

ISRAEL EVANS (1747–1807). A contemporary of James Madison at the College of New Jersey, Evans was graduated in 1772 and was ordained a Presbyterian minister in 1776. As a chaplain throughout the Revolutionary War with the New Hampshire brigade commanded by General Enoch Poor, he was involved in the Battle of Saratoga in 1777, in the campaign of 1779 against Joseph Brant's Iroquois Indians, and in the victory at Yorktown in 1781, where he preached to the combined American and French forces under Lafayette. He became the second settled minister of Concord, New Hampshire, serving from 1789 until 1797, when he resigned. He remained in the town until his death. Dartmouth College awarded Evans an A.M. degree in 1792.

An animated and patriotic preacher, Evans saw the wonder-working hand of Providence in every event of the Revolutionary War and in the national glory looming beyond the triumph over British tyranny, a glory that would blend with the fulfillment of God's plan for the world. The election sermon reprinted here was preached in Concord in 1791 before the General Court of the state of New Hampshire.

A

SERMON,

DELIVERED AT *CONCORD*,

BEFORE

The Hon. General Court

OF THE STATE OF

NEWHAMPSHIRE,

AT THE

ANNUAL ELECTION,

HOLDEN ON THE *FIRST* WEDNESDAY IN JUNE,
M.DCC.XCI.

BY THE REV. ISRAEL EVANS, A. M.
PASTOR OF THE CHURCH IN CONCORD.

CONCORD:

PRINTED BY GEORGE HOUGH, FOR THE HONOURABLE GENERAL COURT.

M. DCC. XCI.

Stand fast, therefore, in the liberty wherewith CHRIST *hath made us free, and be not entangled again with the yoke of bondage.*

Galatians V. 1.

riends and Fellow-Citizens,

We have numbered more than twenty-seven years since your opposition to a foreign system of heavy oppression began. The year 1764 has been rendered memorable, on the one side by the folly and injustice of a hated stamp-act, and, on the other, by the resisting energy of the patriot sons of freedom. From that period, the genius of American liberty, by combating distress, misery, and hosts of enemies, waxed strong in her own defence, and hath crowned more than three millions of mankind with national independence. Instructed in the school of freedom, the inhabitants of these confederate states combined their strength in the protection of the rights of men. *They knew and they felt that freemen will be free.* By their exertions, under the favour of a righteous providence, they have established a wise constitution of federal government: they have reached the consummation of every patriot's wish, the glory and felicity of their country; and now enjoy a free system of political happiness, such as gives pleasure, and even transport, to the enlightened patriots of many nations; and has made, perhaps, no small advancement of joy among the benevolent hosts of heaven: for, to every benevolent and virtuous being, the freedom and happiness of the human race is a most pleasing consideration. But there are some men, with the means of public prosperity in their possession, who do not realize the value of freedom; they partake of the common blessings of a free people, and yet are not conscious of national felicity. This, however, does not lessen the real worth of liberty; for in every situation of life, it is the richest inheritance. In true liberty is included, freedom, both moral and civil; it has nothing in contemplation but the happiness of mankind, and therefore it is the principal glory of man; and, in this world, there can be nothing more dignified, or more exalted. Without civil and religious liberty, man is indeed a poor, enslaved, wretched, miserable creature; neither his life, nor his property, nor the use of his conscience, is secured to him; but he is subjected to some inhuman tyrant, whose will is his law, and who *presumes to govern men without their consent.* But let not this gale of honest zeal carry us beyond the recollection of our text.

In the discussion of the text, it may be observed, that the word *liberty*, in this place, does principally imply a freedom from the injunctions of the ceremonial law. This freedom our Saviour purchased for all Christians; and in this freedom the apostle Paul exhorted the Galatians, and all the followers of Christ, to *stand fast.* When we consider the age, and state of the world, in which the Jews lived, and their fondness of show, idolatry, and superstition, we shall find that their religion was well suited to their genius and temper. The religion of the Jews had a very pointed allusion to the character and office of the Messiah, and was therefore wisely enjoined. But those typical and ritual services, after the coming of Christ, having fulfilled their design, became unnecessary. "These, said the apostle Paul, were a shadow of things to come; but the body is of Christ, who hath abolished the law of commandments contained in ordinances." Without the external pomp and show of the Jewish religion, the gospel recommends the worship of God in spirit and truth. The doctrines of the gospel are calculated to promote good will and liberty among men; and where their genuine influence has been extended, mankind have been rendered more happy: they have been instructed, civilized, humanized, and made free. "The wisdom that is from above is first pure, then peaceable, gentle, and easy to be entreated, full of mercy and good fruits, without partiality and without hypocrisy." *The true spirit of the Gospel contains the true spirit of liberty.* We may be assured, that under this benevolent institution, useful liberty of every kind is recommended by the spirit of our text.

Altho my text, in the original meaning, did not respect civil so much as religious liberty, yet I hope I shall not seem to misuse it by making it the foundation of a discourse on liberty in general.

A few observations on the nature of religious liberty, shall constitute the first part of this discourse.

I. Religious liberty is a divine right, immediately derived from the Supreme Being, without the intervention of any created authority. It is the natural privilege of worshipping God in that manner which, according to the judgment of men, is most agreeable and pleasing to the divine character. As the conscience of man is the image and representative of God in the human soul; so to him alone it is responsible. In justice, therefore, the feelings and sentiments of conscience, and the moral practice of religion, must be independent of all finite beings. Nor hath the all-wise Creator invested any order of men with the right of judging for their fellow-creatures in the great concerns of religion. Truth and religion are subjects of determination entrusted to all men; and it is a privilege of all men to judge and determine for themselves.

Religious liberty secures every man, both in his person and property, from suffering on account of his peculiar sentiments in religion; and no practice which flows purely from this fountain of natural right can justly be punished. But when a man adopts such notions as, in their practice, counteract the peace and good order of society, he then perverts and abuses the original liberty of man; and were he to suffer for thus disturbing the peace of the community, and injuring his fellow-citizens, his punishment would be inflicted not for the exercise of a virtuous principle of conscience, but for violating that universal law of rectitude and benevolence which was intended to prevent one man from injuring another. To punish men for entertaining various religious sentiments, is to assume a power to punish them for doing what God gave them an unalienable right to do. For neither the principles of reason, nor the doctrines of the gospel, which are the perfection of reason, have empowered any man to judge for himself and for another man also: this is religious tyranny; this is to controul another man's conscience: and to controul any man's conscience is to contradict that true principle of eternal justice which Jesus Christ published to the world: *Therefore, all things whatsoever ye would that men should do to you, do ye even so to them.*

Suffer me a little to illustrate this maxim of primitive justice. We will suppose, that some man should endeavour to prove, that he had a right to determine what our religious principles and sentiments ought to be; but how would he be pleased when his own arguments should be turned against himself? Should this man, who was unwilling to allow us the free exercise of rational, accountable creatures, be forced, in the change of human affairs, to reside among a people very different from him in matters of religion; he however behaving himself as an honest and peaceable man, and, as a good subject of civil society, serving the interest of the country; would he not think it very unjust and tyrannical to be persecuted for his religious opinions—imprisoned, deprived of his property, and finally condemned to die, only because he could not with a clear conscience worship as they did? Only the Supreme Governour of mankind has a perfect right to receive the homage of the human mind; it is his peculiar prerogative to controul the consciences of men by his infinitely wise and equitable laws. True religion must therefore be founded in the inward persuasion and conviction of the mind; for without this it cannot be that reasonable service which is pleasing to God. The human understanding cannot be convinced by external violence of any kind; nor can the immaterial spirit be influenced by the laws of men, unless they correspond with the goodness, justice, and mercy, of our blessed Creator, our most bountiful Benefactor, and our all wise and righteous Judge. Here joy and gratitude prompt me to say, Oh happy people, who live in this land and in this age of religious liberty! here every man has equally the freedom of choosing his religion; and may *sit every man under his vine, and under his figtree*, and, on the account of religion, *none shall make them afraid.* Let us, my friends and fellow-citizens, *stand fast, therefore, in the religious liberty wherewith God and Christ hath made us free.*

II. With submission to the professional knowledge of my political fathers, I will now venture to make some observations on the nature and principles of civil liberty. These observations shall be included within the following particulars.

1. In this happy land of light and liberty, it is a truth fully established, that all men are by nature equally free. From this principle of natural liberty we derive an indefeasible right of being governed by our own civil constitutions. *We the people* are the source of all legislative authority. Upon this just, benevolent, pleasing, and even delightful principle, the constitutions, the laws, and the governments, of these federal states, will stand fast. All men who understand the nature, and feel the spirit, of such principles, are self-instructed to be their own legislators, either in one collected body, or by representation. When all the people can assemble, and personally contribute their aid in framing constitutions and laws for the government of themselves, then their liberty is most natural and most perfect. But since great loss of time, much expense, and many inconveniences, would attend this mode of legislation, the people have agreed, in free states, to select from the whole body, some of their brethren, whom

they invest with legislative power. What shall be transacted by these delegates or representatives, consistently with the constitution of the people, must be acknowledged as the act of the people. In conformity to this plan, the people keep as near the possession of natural liberty, as is convenient and really useful; and while they are truly virtuous, they will enjoy as much perfect liberty as is necessary to preserve peace, establish justice, and secure political happiness. I shall only add further, under this particular, that when a free people have, according to their constitution, determined to legislate by representatives, they should take great care that the representation may be fully adequate to the importance and welfare of the people; the elections should also be perfectly free, and sufficiently frequent.

2. The elections should be conducted agreeably to the principles of justice and honour. The privilege of electing freely, or being freely elected, is one of the fairest features in the pure image of natural liberty. A free and unbiassed election of the best and the wisest men, is a certain evidence of the flourishing state of liberty. On the other hand, when elections are under dishonest influence, and men can be sold and bought, it is a most lamentable sign that liberty is either in a deep sleep, or in a dangerous decay. When this birth-right of the people is bartered for something as mean as a mess of pottage—when they neglect and despise this natural and constitutional right—they then lose their share and influence in that government of which they were the original foundation. Having neglected that security which at first existed in themselves, and having counteracted the very design of that social compact which was intended to secure them from every species of political injury, they turn traitors to their God who made them free; and for want of exercising that natural power which their Creator gave them, their glory will depart: and, having the hearts of slaves, they will wear the livery and endure the misery of slaves. But I am not willing to spend time in representing this horrible image of slavish misery. This assembly is the image and representation of a free state. I have the honour, I have the felicity, of speaking before men who are too well acquainted with the blessings of liberty to neglect or despise any of the natural or constitutional rights of freemen.

3. The public happiness of a people is promoted, not only by the freedom of elections, but also by the wisdom and goodness of the laws. A wise and a good representation will produce good laws.

Good and wise men, who are clothed with the natural power of their constituents, will study to unite closely the interest of the country and the power of the laws; and where the representation is good, the laws will appear to carry with them the voice and common consent of the people. The laws made after this manner, are the laws of the people, and prove that they are free, and that they virtually legislate for themselves. I leave this particular, after observing, that the public happiness should be the first duty and the prime object of all legislators; and that, in every free and virtuous state, this is the pole-star of legislation.

4. It is the duty of the people, in conformity to the principles of liberty, to choose men to superintend the executive department of the nation: for no man, in a free state, can justly claim the authority of an executive magistrate, without the voice and consent of the people. In the exercise of their own natural power, by their constitution, they must appoint their chief magistrate to this place of honour and trust. In this respect, it may be said, that the people do not only make their laws, but they also execute them, and govern themselves. These considerations should have a tendency to discourage all officers of government from feeling themselves independent of their brethren, the people. With these proper views, they will be more likely to pay that attention to the wants and feelings of the people, which is necessary to increase the public happiness. When, therefore, the most exalted characters in authority feel themselves connected to the whole community by a brotherly, benevolent attachment; then the lives and the estates of the nation are most secure. In addition to this, it may also be said, that the administration of men in power will then be the most useful and honourable, when the affairs of government are conducted with moderation and justice: for the people have not appointed men to insult and injure them, but to promote their best interest. Violence & compulsion will never advance the happiness of freemen. They will know when they are governed agreeably to their constitutions and laws: they will know when they enjoy a portion of that civil prosperity which they are entitled to by their rights and privileges: and they will easily know when they are treated with civility and kindness. The people should have reason to believe, that men in office have nothing more at heart than the felicity of the nation.

5. The best measures should be adopted to establish esteem and

confidence between the people and their rulers; for without this favourable impression, there will be but little peace and satisfaction in the public mind. Great care should be taken not to disturb and irritate the temper of the people; their patience should never be tortured; but they should have as many reasons to be pleased with the transactions of government, as possible, consistent with the public welfare: for good humour and satisfaction greatly contribute to the peace and happiness of government and mankind. When the people have reasonable satisfaction and rest of mind, they will be more industrious, and consequently more virtuous: the produce of the land will be more plentiful; and the strength and resources of the nation will be in proportion to the pleasure and encouragement of the mind. A free, willing, industrious, and virtuous people, well united and well pleased, are the strength of a nation; while the great wealth of a few luxurious, idle drones, are the great bane of liberty. A people with that happy temper of mind which I have described, will be cheerfully obedient to their laws; they will respect and esteem all their good civil officers; and peace and harmony will be pleasant and lasting. The man, whom every benevolent, free and virtuous citizen respects and loves, suffer me to adorn my humble page with the name of Washington, hath declared, that *the best way to preserve the confidence of the people durably is to promote their truest interest.*

6. The principles of a free people are directly opposed to taxation without their own consent by representation. Money should never be extorted by violence, but received as the gifts and free will offerings, or contributions of the people, to pay for the security of their persons and property. Let them be convinced, that the public demands are reasonable and necessary, not merely for the benefit of civil officers, but for the general advantage of the nation; and then as a free, enlightened, generous, virtuous people, they will take pleasure cheerfully to defray the necessary expenses of government. They will be pleased when they recollect, that for a very small portion of their property they can be secured in the real possession of all the blessings of true liberty. But how will their pleasure rise still higher, when they consider, that by doing justice to their brethren, to whom they have committed the toils and dangers of public business; when they consider, I say, that by their contributions they advance not only the great prosperity of the nation, but include also their posterity in the

general happiness. But here let it be observed, that no requisitions should be made but such as are really and absolutely necessary for the support and contingencies of government; and of the expenditure of money the people should have an account. Much the greater part of mankind toil severely for what property they acquire: it would therefore be very unjust and cruel to use it for the gratification of pampered pride and luxury. In a word, that government which improves the interest and happiness of the people, and manages their public affairs consistently with the principles of a generous œconomy, as well as a just and magnanimous policy, free from a prodigal and dishonest waste of the public wealth; such a government will furnish the most reasonable satisfaction, and will be the most valued and the most bravely defended.

III. Under this head of discourse, I will endeavour to shew when it may be said that a people *stand fast in the liberty wherewith they are free.* With the prosecution of this design, I will attempt to intermix the spirit and freedom of an application.

1. The people are in the habit and exercise of liberty, when they resort to the first principles of government, and trace their rights up to God the Creator: when they exercise their natural power of framing any social compact conducive to the common interest: feel independent of all human power but that which flows from themselves: disdain the subjection of their consciences to any authority but the will of God: refuse to be controuled by the will of any man who claims an independent power of disposing of their lives and estates: recollect that they entered into society to have their natural rights, which are the basis of civil rights, secured. To maintain such principles of original justice, is to stand fast in the righteous liberty of man. True liberty suffers no man to be injured in his person, estate, or character: it encourages and enables him to improve his happiness; and, within the limits of the public good, insures to him every blessing to which imperfect human nature can attain. All the toils, sufferings, treasure and blood of men, are not lost, when they are the price and purchase of liberty. Without religious and civil liberty, we can have no security of life, or of any of the good things of God: we cannot practice the sentiments of our consciences: but where the rights of man are equally secured in the greatest degree, there is the greatest happiness—*and that is our country.*

2. When you carefully regard the election of your representatives and officers of government, you will stand fast in your liberty. It is a darling privilege of all freemen to elect the best qualified men to represent them in a state or national assembly. But do a people stand fast in the discharge of their duty—are they in the exercise of their civil rights, when they neglect to choose men of established principles of virtue and liberty? Do they wish to have good laws, and yet neglect to choose men who have proved themselves friends to the rights of their brethren? Can they reasonably expect that good laws will proceed from men who *fear not God nor regard man?* Will men, who feel no obligations of love and duty to their Creator, be good examples to their constituents? Will they add any weight to the laws they assisted to make, when they are so prompt to violate them? Do they not, as far as their influence will reach, defeat the very laws they voted for? Will a public and patriotic spirit originate from vicious principles? Is it natural for noble and generous sentiments to flow from vice? Do not bad principles make men selfish, narrow the mind, and banish all benevolent propensities of doing good to men? Will not the very knowledge which unprincipled men may have, degenerate into selfish low cunning, and serve only to embarrass and perplex the honesty and good common sense of men who are able and willing to promote the interest of society? I need not tell you, that men under the influence of selfish passions, will sacrifice the best interest of their country, whenever they can greatly advance their own importance; and, like a Dean and an Arnold, by the most infamous and horrible treason, betray that liberty which they once pretended to defend. Do any of the people ask me, as one of their brethren, who are the men we must choose, in order to stand fast in our liberty? First, separate, in your minds, the most wicked and unprincipled men, from being objects of your choice; and then, out of the rest, select men of understanding, for of such there will enough remain, who are actuated by principles of love and obedience to God, and animated by a generous benevolence to mankind; who really love to see their brethren free and happy: for in this every benevolent man must take pleasure. Benevolent principles will produce the noblest acts of public and patriotic good; they will enable men to discern easily the advantage of the people. "For when private interest and private views are removed, it will be easy to know what is the public good." Let me beseech all the

people to remember, that their safety and happiness in society depends upon the election of good and wise representatives. Under the smiles of providence, the prosperity of a free people is in their own hands; for they have knowledge enough, if well improved, to advance and secure their welfare. In a few words, choose the men to manage your public affairs, to whom you would not fear to entrust the most important concerns of a private nature. This is the way to stand fast in your liberty.

3. The example of civil officers has great influence on the minds of mankind. They ought to be punctual in their observation of the laws of the country. As public men, or private citizens, they should be uniform in the practice of virtue, and the defence of liberty. The people call them fathers: we are willing to be their political children, as long as they are good parents. But, should not fathers be examples of goodness to their children? Will children do well, if the parents are wicked and do wrong? Will the children be obedient to the public laws, if the parents violate them? Will the children love freedom, if the parents disregard it? Will the children cultivate a public spirit, if the parents are selfish? Do fathers love their children, and not strive in all respects to promote their felicity? It is most reasonable, therefore, to conclude, that it is the great and indispensible duty of rulers to encourage the practice of religion by their own influence and example: and I venture to declare, that no civil officer does the half of his duty, unless he endeavours to suppress vice and disorder, and so prevent the necessity of punishment. Mankind very quickly and justly exclaim against the absurdity of allowing those men to be teachers of religion, who live in the habitual practice of vice and wickedness: Shall we not, with equal justice, condemn the practice of those men who break through those restraints which were intended to suppress vice, and consequently encourage virtue? Should they not be *ministers of God for good* to the people, in every possible way? Every man of common sense acknowledges, that religion is very useful to mankind; and especially the precepts and truths of the gospel. It is also allowed, that public worship is of particular and national advantage. To favour and practice virtue is therefore to increase the public happiness, and to answer the intention of government: and by these means their own importance and authority will be increased.

4. When the people are submissive to their laws and rulers, upon

the principles already mentioned, their liberties will be permanent. Where the true spirit of religion is united to the free and generous spirit of liberty, obedience will be a pleasing duty. The author of our benevolent religion hath commanded us to *render unto Cæsar the things which are Cæsar's; and unto God, the things that are God's.* The apostles also say, *Submit yourselves to every ordinance of man for the Lord's sake. Render to all, their dues: tribute, to whom tribute is due; custom, to whom custom; fear, to whom fear; honour, to whom honour.* Men who are under the influence of reason and religion, will not blame the necessary measures of government. They will not be factious and turbulent, but of a reasonable and complying disposition. They will be influenced by such generous sentiments as the following: *Look not every man on his own things, but every man also on the things of others.* We must endeavour to render ourselves extensively useful, and promote the good of our country; in which, not only our own happiness, but the happiness of millions, is included.

5. The liberties of a people cannot be lasting without knowledge. The human mind is capable of great cultivation. Knowledge is not only useful, but it adds dignity to man. When the minds of men are improved, they can better understand their rights—they can know what part they are to act, in contributing to the welfare of the nation. Freemen should always acquire knowledge; this is a privilege and pleasure unknown to slaves; this elevates the mind of man; this creates a conscious dignity of his importance as a rational creature, and a free agent. The happiness of mankind has been much advanced by the arts and sciences; and they have flourished the most among freemen. Slavery blots the image of the Creator, which was at first impressed upon man: it banishes knowledge, and courts misery. But men, enlightened, pursue with ardour the knowledge and recovery of their rights. Liberty is enlightened by knowledge; and knowledge is nurtured by liberty. Where there is wisdom, virtue, and liberty, there mankind are men. In all the dark ages of the world, tyranny has been established upon the slavish ignorance of mankind. Tyrants, in time past, secured their domination by darkening the minds of their subjects. In the present day, they tremble at the approaching light of knowledge and liberty. They turn indignant from the glorious illuminations of America and France. They hear with horrour the sound of freedom and the rights of men. They would still imbrute the human

race, and make mankind forget that they are men. Be assured, my dear countrymen, knowledge is absolutely necessary to secure the blessings of freedom. If you wish to see your country not only free in your day, but also to feast your imaginations with the pleasing prospect of a free posterity for many ages to come; let me entreat you, to encourage and promote that knowledge which will enable the people successfully to watch all the enemies of liberty, and guard against the designs of intriguing men. Unless the people have knowledge, they may be imposed upon by men who are always lying in wait to disturb the peace of society, create disorder and confusion, and, in the tumult, overturn the liberties of the country. Be always awake to your own interest, and you will have nothing to fear: but if you sleep, the enemies of liberty will awake: sleep, and by your death-like slumbers you will give them life: for liberty has never yet appeared upon the face of the earth without meeting enemies to contend with. There have been men in America, who have reprobated what they were pleased to call the inquisitive sauciness of the people, when they wished to know how the public affairs of the country were conducted, and how justice and liberty might be secured. Nay, some men, still more unjust and tyrannical, have ventured to say—blush! ye degenerate sons of free parents! that the people, when in the possession of liberty, are unable to use it for their own advantage, and therefore they ought to be governed against their wills, and without their choice, by men, to be sure, much wiser than themselves, and more disposed to do them good. This is as much as to say, that the people ought to be robbed of their natural rights for their own advantage and happiness. But whoever is acquainted with the history of despotic power, need not be informed, that a free people will always use their freedom more consistently with the principles of justice and reason, than any men with uncontrouled power. It is a truth, and it is now too late to deny it, that no man, or body of men, are fit to be entrusted with unlimitted power. This power they would most certainly abuse, whenever their unjust wills were in the least opposed. Let the youth be well educated in wisdom and virtue; let them be instructed in the true principles of freedom, and they will improve their liberty most agreeably to the rational happiness of mankind. In this free country, knowledge is peculiarly necessary, where no other qualifications are requisite, for the most important offices of government, but virtue and ability. I again say, let the children and youth be well educated. In the earliest stages of life, let a free and public spirit be infused into the youthful mind. This is the way to exclude from their young breasts all oppressing and cruel passions. Unless the doors of education are open to all the youth of the country equally, advantages may be taken by some men of cunning, to tyrannize over the rest, and become masters of their property. Every parent, and every friend to the freedom of his country, ought to be solicitous for the improvement of our youth in the principles of freedom and good government, and then the people will stand fast in their liberty for a long time; yes, as long as such principles are in their true exercise; and, with submission to the divine will, as long as they please. But what! Shall I doubt the attention and exertions of my fellow-citizens to this all-important cause of public prosperity? Shall the children and youth of a free people be suffered to grow up ignorant of the value of those liberties you intend to commit to their trust? Shall they be unfit to take care of those political blessings which have been secured for them at the great expense of much toil, treasure, and precious blood? Oh! Liberty, thou friend to mankind, forbid it; justice, thou guardian of the rights of men, forbid it; ye patriots and fathers of your country, forbid it: but rather let me say, Oh! thou blessed God, who takest no pleasure in the misery of thy children, forbid it, for the sake of him who *hath made us free.*

6. The principles and practice of our peaceable and benevolent religion, are the foundation on which all the blessings of life and liberty must stand fast. *Righteousness exalteth a nation.* True religion will incline a people to love and honour the Most High who *ruleth among the children of men.* The LORD hath said, *Them that honour me, I will honour.* Religion is intended to unite men together in the bonds of brotherly love and good will; to prevent bad habits; to suppress disorder; to calm factious spirits; and to put an end to the shedding of brothers' blood. The influence and importance of religion should be felt by men both in their family and national connections. Without it, they can neither be happy in this world nor in a future state. May the benevolent efforts of all public teachers of true religion, be united with the affectionate influence of parents, to promote the personal and national welfare of our country. By instilling good sentiments into the tender minds of children and youth, you will teach them to

stand fast in their liberty. Good impressions, made in early life, are very frequently of lasting benefit both to individuals and the public. *Train up a child in the way he should go, and when he is old he will not depart from it.* But, in addition to all your pious exertions, let me entreat you, never to forget to beseech the Father of mercies and the God of all grace, to implant in the hearts of our youth, by the divine Spirit, the true principles of holiness.

I hope it has been evident, that, in the whole body of this discourse, I have endeavoured to interweave sentiments of religion and virtue. I cannot, therefore, suppose it necessary at present, to prosecute this particular article any farther. Permit me, however, to assure you, that I have not ventured nor wished to recommend liberty without virtue; for this would have been a recommendation of licentiousness. True liberty may be summed up in this declaration: that we have a right to do all the good we can; but have no right to injure our fellow-men: we have a right to be as happy as we can; but no right to lessen the happiness of mankind.

Thus far I have attempted to comply with the appointment of the civil fathers of this state. In this compliance, my diffidence and fear have given me no small anxiety, lest I should not answer the design of their appointment. I have not, therefore, been influenced by a presuming expectation of communicating to this honourable political body, any new information. I feel, nevertheless, in my mind, a pleasing persuasion, that my fathers in government will not be displeased with any sincere and humble attempt to inspire their younger sons with a just sense of the blessings and privileges they enjoy under the present legislative and executive authority. In a few years, some of the youth of the present day must be called to fill the places of the fathers now in office. The thought is serious! Who knows the consequence? Is it not then of the utmost importance that the minds of young men should be impressed with the best sentiments of equal liberty? Shall we not exhort them to stand fast in their liberty, that their country may be free? Shall we not animate the rising generation, to transmit to their posterity that invaluable inheritance of freedom, which they must soon receive from the present race of patriots when they shall rest from their labours? This is a day of joy: it reminds you of one of the great privileges of freemen: it should be a day of gratitude also. Oh! that you did but feel and realize your happy situation, that you might send up to heaven the warmest gratitude of hearts glowing with love and praise to that blessed Saviour *who hath made us free!*

Fathers, brethren, and fellow-citizens, with the happy feelings of a brother freeman, I congratulate you on the enjoyment of that liberty which I have been describing: it involves in it every thing most conducive to your peace and prosperity on earth: clasp it to your bosoms, and religiously swear, that you will live freemen, or die bravely. I rejoice, that it is in your power, under God, to stand fast in your liberty. Shall I contrast your present situation with the deplorable state of man in ages past? Would not this draw a cloud of grief over the bright sunshine of your happy feelings? We rejoice, that the earth hath been delivered from the hands of those inhuman butchers, whose unrelenting murders have filled so many bloody pages of history; who slaughtered millions of the human race, for no other purpose but to extend their cruel and ambitious power, and oppress and lay waste the world. Tyrants, who, instead of being transmitted down to us with illustrious names, for being the most successful destroyers of their fellow-creatures, should be named after the most furious beasts of prey; and, on account of the mischief they have done to mankind, be classed with tempests, earthquakes, and plagues. We rejoice, with thankful hearts, that we are not under the power of such plagues of the human race, who wage war with the peace and happiness of mankind; who think it is an act of heroism to depopulate whole countries to gratify private revenge. We now see that the patriotic resolutions of our countrymen have not been in vain: we now see that the treasures expended in the defence of liberty, have realized a national interest of more value than ten thousand per cent: we now see that the inexpressible trials and sufferings of a patriot army, have been productive of the richest fruits; and that the blood of our heroes has been the seed of liberty. But, we commiserate the deplorable condition of many of our fellow-men, who now groan under the heavy chains of despotism: we wish the rights of men may be soon restored to them.

But I return from this digression. I find political happiness not abroad, but at home. Happy age and country in which we live! We remember no æra since the creation of the world, so favourable to the rights of mankind as the present. The histories of mankind, with only a few exceptions, are the records of human guilt, oppression, and misery. Although some shadow of rude liberty was contended for by a few small uncivilized tribes of men, yet they were subjected by those nations who were more powerful. At the beginning of the Christian æra, almost two thirds of mankind were in the most abject and cruel slavery. The Grecian and Roman nations, notwithstanding their boasted love of liberty, were not acquainted with the true principles of original, equal, and sentimental liberty. Though an imperfect civilization had made some progress among them, yet they neither understood the nature, nor practised the duties, of humanity. They who are acquainted with the true history of Greece and Rome, need not be informed, that the cruelty they exercised upon their slaves, and those taken in war, is almost beyond the power of credibility. The proud and selfish passions have always endeavoured to suppress the spirit of freedom. Even Rome herself, while she pretended to glory in being free, endeavoured to subject and enslave the rest of mankind. But no longer shall we look to antient histories for principles and systems of pure freedom. The close of the eighteenth century, in which we live, shall teach mankind to be truly free. The freedom of America and France, shall make this age memorable. From this time forth, men shall be taught, that true greatness consists not in destroying, but in saving, the lives of men; not in conquering, but making them free; not in making war, but making peace; not in making men ignorant, but making them wise; not in firing them with brutal rage, but in making them humane; not in being ambitious, but in being good, just, and virtuous. Of France, it may be said, in the language of scripture, *Who hath heard such a thing? Who hath seen such things? Shall the earth be made to bring forth in one day? Or, Shall a nation be born at once?* Behold a nation of freemen, rising out of a nation of slaves! This gratifies the feelings of humanity and benevolence. We wish to see all men independent of all things but the laws of God, and the just laws of their country. And will any man blame me for saying, that, in America, every friend to justice and the rights of men wishes prosperity to that generous nation, who are allied to these United States, and who so powerfully aided them in securing their independence and peace. In the name of the Lord of hosts, let us pray, *that no weapon that is formed against their freedom, shall prosper.*

I once more invite you to join me in gratitude to that best of Beings, by whose providential goodness and power *the lines are fallen unto us in pleasant places; yea, we have a goodly heritage.* Here harvests grow for the free and cheerful husbandman: here, neither awed by lordly and rapacious injustice, nor dejected by beholding idleness high fed and fattened on the labours of other men, they reap and enjoy the pleasing fruits of their honest industry. *Ye shall eat your bread to the full, and dwell in your land of safety.* Here the people dwell together as brethren; peace, harmony, industry, and health, unite their various gifts to make this life a blessing: here poor human nature, in other parts of the world long depressed by ignorance and enslaving power, seems to reclaim the primitive blessings of creation, and to rejoice that it was made *in the image of* GOD: here conscience assumes her first authority; religion is no longer enslaved to the wills and laws of men; public and private happiness are guarded by the laws and government of the people. *Stand fast, therefore, in the liberty wherewith Christ hath made us free, and be not entangled again with the yoke of bondage.* Let us determine to be free from the unjust power of men, and free from the slavery and tyranny of sin, and we shall then be truly free. *If the Son, therefore, shall make you free, ye shall be free indeed.*

With the words of a celebrated French writer, this discourse will be concluded.

> Ye people of Northamerica, let the example of all nations who have gone before you, and above all that of Greatbritain, serve you for instruction. Fear the affluence of gold, which brings with luxury the corruption of manners, the contempt of laws. Fear a too unequal distribution of riches, which exhibits a small number of citizens in opulence, and a great multitude of citizens in extreme poverty; whence springs the insolence of the former, and the debasement of the latter. Secure yourselves against the spirit of conquest. The tranquillity of an empire diminishes in proportion to its extension. Have arms for your defence; have none for offence. Seek competency and health in labour; prosperity in the culture of lands, and the workshops of industry; power in manners and virtue. Cause arts and sciences, which distinguish the civilized from a savage man, to flourish and abound. Above all, watch carefully over the education of your children. It is from public schools, be assured, that come the wise magistrates, the capable and courageous soldiers, the good fathers, the good husbands, the good brothers, the good friends, the good men. Wherever the youth are seen depraved, the nation is on the decline. Let liberty have an immoveable foundation in the wisdom of your laws, and let it be the indestructible

cement to bind your states together. Establish no legal preference amongst the different forms of worship. Superstition is innocent, wherever it is neither persecuted nor protected; and may your duration, if it be possible, equal the duration of the world!

AMEN

37

THE RIGHTS OF CONSCIENCE INALIENABLE

John Leland

NEW-LONDON

[1791]

John Leland (1754–1841). A key figure in the rise of religious liberty in America, the Baptist minister John Leland had two careers, one in Massachusetts, the other in Virginia. His only formal education was in the elementary schools of Grafton, Massachusetts, his birthplace, yet he became well educated and widely read. Having experienced a "sign from God," he became a minister and went to preach in Orange County, Virginia, in 1776. During his fourteen years in Virginia, he led the fight to disestablish the Episcopal Church, to secure religious freedom, and to ratify the Constitution. He became a friend, constituent, and important ally of James Madison and made indispensable contributions to Madison's election to the first United States Congress in 1789. Madison, particularly in fulfillment of a campaign promise to Leland, George Eve, and other Baptists (and with George Washington's support) insisted upon adoption of the Bill of Rights as amendments to the Constitution. Leland's views and importance are comparable to those of Isaac Backus.

In 1791 Leland returned to Massachusetts, where he spent most of his last fifty years. There and in Connecticut he proposed that the state constitutions be changed as he fought for disestablishment of the Congregationalist Standing Order and for religious liberty for Baptists and others deprived of constitutional protection. Religious liberty was secured in Connecticut in 1820, and Leland finally saw the Congregational system in Massachusetts overthrown in 1833. Leland was a liberal in politics, as well as in religion; he supported the Jeffersonian Republicans—and, later, the Jacksonian Democrats—and strongly opposed slavery and the slave trade. In 1811 he was elected on the Republican ticket to the Massachusetts legislature, his second public office, for he had served as an Orange County delegate to the Virginia convention that ratified the federal Constitution in 1788.

Leland's nineteenth-century biographer L.F. Greene appraised him this way: "Through a long life, Elder Leland sustained, with uniform consistency, the two-fold character of the *patriot* and the *Christian*. For his religious creed he acknowledged no directory but the Bible. He loved the pure, unadulterated word of truth. . . . His political creed was based upon the 'sufficient truths' of equality, and of inherent and inalienable rights, recognised by the master spirits of the revolution . . ." (*Writings of Elder John Leland* [1845] pp. 50–51). Leland's 1831 autobiographical sketch hardly mentions politics, for his mission

THE

CONNECTICUT DISSENTERS'

STRONG BOX:

NO. I.

CONTAINING,

The high-flying Churchman ſtript of his legal Robe, &c. By the rev. JOHN LELAND, Paſtor of the Baptiſt Church in Cheſhire, Maſs.

The Diſſenters' Petition.

Connecticut Eccleſiaſtical Laws.

American Conſtitutions (Extracts from). *Sixteen* of which recogniſe the Rights of Conſcience— and *Three* the doctrine of Church and State.

Some remarks.

LORD! LAY NOT THIS SIN TO THEIR CHARGE!

SAUL! SAUL! WHY PERSECUTEST THOU ME?

COMPILED BY A DISSENTER.

Printed by Charles Holt, New-London.
1802.

was evangelism, and he calculated the thousands of miles he had traveled, tabulated his 1,515 baptisms, and wrote as his epitaph: "Here lies the body of JOHN LELAND, who labored ________ to promote piety, and vindicate the civil and religious rights of all men." (We can fill the blank with "67 years.") In 1834 he wrote: "The plea for *religious liberty* has been long and powerful; but it has been left for the United States to acknowledge it a right inherent, and not a favor granted: to exclude religious opinions from the list of objects of legislation" (ibid., pp. 38–39).

Leland was "as courageous and resourceful a champion of the rights of conscience as America has produced," according to Lyman H. Butterfield. "In his very individualism Leland was a representative American of his time. Self-reliant to the point of eccentricity and a tireless fighter for principle, he was without arrogance, and the reminiscences of those who knew him speak most often of his humor, his gentleness, and his humility. . . . John Leland therefore has a place in our history as well as in our folklore" ("Elder John Leland, Jeffersonian Itinerant," *Proceedings of the American Antiquarian Society*, Oct. 15, 1952).

This 1791 sermon was probably written shortly after Leland returned to New England from Virginia; it was reprinted several times. Its original full title was *The Rights of Conscience inalienable; and therefore Religious Opinions not cognizable by Law: Or, The high-flying Churchman, stript of his legal Robe, appears a Yaho[o].*

There are four principles contended for, as the foundation of civil government, viz. birth, property, grace, and compact. The first of these is practised upon in all hereditary monarchies, where it is believed that the son of a monarch is entitled to dominion upon the decease of his father, whether he be a wise man or a fool. The second principle is built upon in all aristocratical governments, where the rich landholders have the sole rule of all their tenants, and make laws at pleasure which are binding upon all. The third principle is adopted by those kingdoms and states that require a religious test to qualify an officer of state, proscribing all non-conformists from civil and religious liberty. This was the error of Constantine's government, who first established the christian religion by law, and then proscribed the pagans and banished the Arian heretics. This error also filled the heads of the anabaptists in Germany (who were re-sprinklers): they supposed that none had a right to rule but gracious men. The same error prevails in the see of Rome, where his holiness exalts himself above all who are called gods (i.e. kings and rulers), and where no protestant heretic is allowed the liberty of a citizen. This principle is also plead for in the Ottoman empire, where it is death to call in question the divinity of Mahomet or the authenticity of the Alcoran.

The same evil has twisted itself into the British form of government; where, in the state-establishment of the church of England, no man is eligible to any office, civil or military, without he subscribes to the 39 articles and book of common-prayer; and even then, upon receiving a commission for the army the law obliges him to receive the sacrament of the Lord's supper; and no non-conformist is allowed the liberty of his conscience without he subscribes to all the 39 articles but about 4. And when that is done his purse-strings are drawn by others to pay preachers in whom he has no confidence and whom he never hears.

This was the case with several of the southern states (until the revolution) in which the church of England was established.

The fourth principle (compact) is adopted in the American states as the basis of civil government. This foundation appears to be a just one by the following investigation.

Suppose a man to remove to a desolate island and take a peaceable possession of it without injuring any, so that he should be the honest inheritor of the isle. So long as he is alone he is the absolute monarch of the place, and his own will is his law, which law is as often altered or repealed as his will changes. In process of time from this man's loins ten sons are grown to manhood and possess property. So long as they are all good men each one can be as absolute, free, and sovereign as his father; but one of the ten turns vagrant, by robbing the rest; this villain is equal to if not an overmatch for any one of the nine—not one of them durst engage him in single combat: reason and safety both dictate to the nine the necessity of a confederation to unite their strength together to repel or destroy the plundering knave. Upon entering into confederation some compact or agreement would be stipulated by which each would be bound to do his equal part in fatigue and expence; it would be neccessary for these nine to meet at stated times to consult means of safety and happiness; a shady tree or small cabin would answer their purpose; and in case of disagreement four must give up to five.

In this state of things their government would be perfectly democratical, every citizen being a legislator.

In a course of years, from these nine there arises nine thousand; their government can be no longer democratical, prudence would forbid it. Each tribe or district must chuse their representative, who (for the term that he is chosen) has the whole political power of his constituents. These representatives, meeting in assembly, would have power to make laws binding on their constituents; and while their time was spent in making laws for the community each one of the community must advance a little of his money as a compensation therefor. Should these representatives differ in judgment the minor must submit to the major, as in the case above.

From this simple parable the following things are demonstrated:

1. That the law was not made for a righteous man, but for the disobedient. 2. That righteous men have to part with a little of their liberty and property to preserve the rest. 3. That all power is vested in and consequently derived from the people. 4. That the law should rule over rulers, and not rulers over the law. 5. That government is founded on compact. 6. That every law made by the legislators inconsistent with the compact, modernly called a constitution, is

usurpive in the legislators and not binding on the people. 7. That whenever government is found inadequate to preserve the liberty and property of the people they have an indubitable right to alter it so as to answer those purposes. 8. That legislators in their legislative capacity cannot alter the constitution, for they are hired servants of the people to act within the limits of the constitution.

From these general observations I shall pass on to examine a question, which has been the strife and contention of ages. The question is, "*Are the rights of conscience alienable, or inalienable?*"

The word *conscience* signifies *common science*, a court of judicature which the Almighty has erected in every human breast; a *censor morum* over all his actions. Conscience will ever judge right when it is rightly informed, and speak the truth when it understands it. But to advert to the question—"Does a man upon entering into social compact surrender his conscience to that society to be controled by the laws thereof, or can he in justice assist in making laws to bind his children's consciences before they are born?" I judge not, for the following reasons:

1. Every man must give an account of himself to God, and therefore every man ought to be at liberty to serve God in that way that he can best reconcile it to his conscience. If government can answer for individuals at the day of judgment, let men be controled by it in religious matters; otherwise let men be free.

2. It would be sinful for a man to surrender that to man which is to be kept sacred for God. A man's mind should be always open to conviction, and an honest man will receive that doctrine which appears the best demonstrated; and what is more common than for the best of men to change their minds? Such are the prejudices of the mind, and such the force of tradition, that a man who never alters his mind is either very weak or very stubborn. How painful then must it be to an honest heart to be bound to observe the principles of his former belief after he is convinced of their imbecility? and this ever has and ever will be the case while the rights of conscience are considered alienable.

3. But supposing it was right for a man to bind his own conscience, yet surely it is very iniquitous to bind the consciences of his children; to make fetters for them before they are born is very cruel. And yet such has been the conduct of men in almost all ages that

their children have been bound to believe and worship as their fathers did, or suffer shame, loss, and sometimes life; and at best to be called dissenters, because they dissent from that which they never joined voluntarily. Such conduct in parents is worse than that of the father of Hannibal, who imposed an oath upon his son while a child never to be at peace with the Romans.

4. Finally, religion is a matter between God and individuals, religious opinions of men not being the objects of civil government nor any ways under its control.

It has often been observed by the friends of religious establishment by human laws, that no state can long continue without it; that religion will perish, and nothing but infidelity and atheism prevail.

Are these things facts? Did not the christian religion prevail during the three first centuries, in a more glorious manner than ever it has since, not only without the aid of law, but in opposition to all the laws of haughty monarchs? And did not religion receive a deadly wound by being fostered in the arms of civil power and regulated by law? These things are so.

From that day to this we have but a few instances of religious liberty to judge by; for in almost all states civil rulers (by the instigation of covetous priests) have undertaken to steady the ark of religion by human laws; but yet we have a few of them without leaving our own land.

The state of Rhode-Island has stood above 160 years without any religious establishment. The state of New-York never had any. New-Jersey claims the same. Pennsylvania has also stood from its first settlement until now upon a liberal foundation; and if agriculture, the mechanical arts and commerce, have not flourished in these states equal to any of the states I judge wrong.

It may further be observed, that all the states now in union, saving two or three in New-England, have no legal force used about religion, in directing its course or supporting its preachers. And moreover the federal government is forbidden by the constitution to make any laws establishing any kind of religion. If religion cannot stand, therefore, without the aid of law, it is likely to fall soon in our nation, except in Connecticut and Massachusetts.

To say that "religion cannot stand without a state establishment" is not only contrary to fact (as has been proved already) but is a contradiction in phrase. Religion must have stood a time before any law could have been made about it; and if it did stand almost three hundred years without law it can still stand without it.

The evils of such an establishment are many.

1. Uninspired fallible men make their own opinions tests of orthodoxy, and use their own systems, as Procrustes used his iron bedstead, to stretch and measure the consciences of all others by. Where no toleration is granted to non-conformists either ignorance and superstition prevail or persecution rages; and if toleration is granted to restricted non-conformists the minds of men are biassed to embrace that religion which is favored and pampered by law (and thereby hypocrisy is nourished) while those who cannot stretch their consciences to believe any thing and every thing in the established creed are treated with contempt and opprobrious names; and by such means some are pampered to death by largesses and others confined from doing what good they otherwise could by penury. The first lie under a temptation to flatter the ruling party, to continue that form of government which brings the sure bread of idleness; the last to despise that government and those rulers that oppress them. The first have their eyes shut to all further light that would alter the religious machine; the last are always seeking new light, and often fall into enthusiasm. Such are the natural evils of establishment in religion by human laws.

2. Such establishments not only wean and alienate the affections of one from another on account of the different usages they receive in their religious sentiments, but are also very impolitic, especially in new countries; for what encouragement can strangers have to migrate with their arts and wealth into a state where they cannot enjoy their religious sentiments without exposing themselves to the law? when at the same time their religious opinions do not lead them to be mutinous. And further, how often have kingdoms and states been greatly weakened by religious tests! In the time of the persecution in France not less than twenty thousand people fled for the enjoyment of religious liberty.

3. These establishments metamorphose the church into a creature, and religion into a principle of state; which has a natural tendency to make men conclude that bible religion is nothing but a trick of state. Hence it is that the greatest part of the well informed in literature are

overrun with deism and infidelity: nor is it likely it will ever be any better while preaching is made a trade of emolument. And if there is no difference between bible religion and state religion I shall soon fall into infidelity.

4. There are no two kingdoms or states that establish the same creed or formularies of faith (which alone proves their debility). In one kingdom a man is condemned for not believing a doctrine that he would be condemned for believing in another kingdom. Both of these establishments cannot be right—but both of them can be, and surely are, wrong.

5. The nature of such establishments, further, is to keep from civil office the best of men. Good men cannot believe what they cannot believe; and they will not subscribe to what they disbelieve, and take an oath to maintain what they conclude is error: and as the best of men differ in judgment there may be some of them in any state: their talents and virtue entitle them to fill the most important posts, yet because they differ from the established creed of the state they cannot —will not fill those posts. Whereas villains make no scruple to take any oath.

If these and many more evils attend such establishments—what were and still are the causes that ever there should be a state establishment of religion?

The causes are many—some of them follow.

1. The love of importance is a general evil. It is natural to men to dictate for others; they choose to command the bushel and use the whip-row, to have the halter around the necks of others to hang them at pleasure.

2. An over-fondness for a particular system or sect. This gave rise to the first human establishment of religion, by Constantine the Great. Being converted to the christian system, he established it in the Roman empire, compelled the pagans to submit, and banished the christian heretics, built fine chapels at public expence, and forced large stipends for the preachers. All this was done out of love to the christian religion: but his love operated inadvertently; for he did the christian church more harm than all the persecuting emperors did. It is said that in his day a voice was heard from heaven, saying, "Now is the poison spued into the churches." If this voice was not heard, it nevertheless was a truth; for from that day to this the christian reli-

gion has been made a stirrup to mount the steed of popularity, wealth, and ambition.

3. To produce uniformity in religion. Rulers often fear that if they leave every man to think, speak and worship as he pleases, that the whole cause will be wrecked in diversity; to prevent which they establish some standard of orthodoxy to effect uniformity. But is uniformity attainable? Millions of men, women and children, have been tortured to death to produce uniformity, and yet the world has not advanced one inch towards it. And as long as men live in different parts of the world, have different habits, education and interests, they will be different in judgment, humanly speaking.

Is conformity of sentiments in matters of religion essential to the happiness of civil government? Not at all. Government has no more to do with the religious opinions of men than it has with the principles of the mathematics. Let every man speak freely without fear—maintain the principles that he believes—worship according to his own faith, either one God, three Gods, no God, or twenty Gods; and let government protect him in so doing, i.e. see that he meets with no personal abuse or loss of property for his religious opinions. Instead of discouraging of him with proscriptions, fines, confiscation or death; let him be encouraged, as a free man, to bring forth his arguments and maintain his points with all boldness; then if his doctrine is false it will be confuted, and if it is true (though ever so novel) let others credit it. When every man has this liberty what can he wish for more? A liberal man asks for nothing more of government.

The duty of magistrates is not to judge of the divinity or tendency of doctrines, but when those principles break out into overt acts of violence then to use the civil sword and punish the vagrant for what he has done and not for the religious phrenzy that he acted from.

It is not supposable that any established creed contains the whole truth and nothing but truth; but supposing it did, which established church has got it? All bigots contend for it—each society cries out "The temple of the Lord are we." Let one society be supposed to be in possession of the whole—let that society be established by law—the creed of faith that they adopt be so consecrated by government that the man that disbelieves it must die—let this creed finally prevail over the whole world. I ask what honor *truth* gets by all this? None at all. It is famed of a Prussian, called John the Cicero, that by one oration he reconciled two contending princes actually in war; but, says the historian, "it was his six thousand horse of battle that had the most persuasive oratory." So when one creed or church prevails over another, being armed with (a coat of mail) law and sword, truth gets no honor by the victory. Whereas if all stand upon one footing, being equally protected by law as citizens (not as saints) and one prevails over another by cool investigation and fair argument, then truth gains honor, and men more firmly believe it than if it was made an essential article of salvation by law.

Truth disdains the aid of law for its defence—it will stand upon its own merits. The heathens worshipped a goddess called truth, stark naked; and all human decorations of truth serve only to destroy her virgin beauty. It is error, and error alone, that needs human support; and whenever men fly to the law or sword to protect their system of religion and force it upon others, it is evident that they have something in their system that will not bear the light and stand upon the basis of truth.

4. The common objection "that the ignorant part of the community are not capacitated to judge for themselves" supports the popish hierarchy, and all protestant as well as Turkish and pagan establishments, in idea.

But is this idea just? Has God chosen many of the wise and learned? Has he not hidden the mystery of gospel truth from them and revealed it unto babes? Does the world by wisdom know God? Did many of the rulers believe in Christ when he was upon earth? Were not the learned clergy (the scribes) his most inveterate enemies? Do not great men differ as much as little men in judgment? Have not almost all lawless errors crept into the world through the means of wise men (so called)? Is not a simple man, who makes nature and reason his study, a competent judge of things? Is the bible written (like Caligula's laws) so intricate and high that none but the letter-learned (according to common phrase) can read it? Is not the vision written so plain that he that runs may read it? Do not those who understand the original languages which the bible was written in differ as much in judgment as others? Are the identical copies of Matthew, Mark, Luke and John, together with the epistles, in every university, and in the hands of every master of arts? If not, have not the learned to trust to a human transcription, as much as the unlearned have to a translation? If these questions and others of a like nature can be confuted, then I will confess that it is wisdom for a conclave of bishops or a convocation of clergy to frame a system out of the bible and persuade the legislature to legalise it. No. It would be attended with so much expence, pride, domination, cruelty and bloodshed, that let me rather fall into infidelity; for no religion at all is better than that which is worse than none.

5. The ground work of these establishments of religion is clerical influence. Rulers, being persuaded by the clergy that an establishment of religion by human laws would promote the knowledge of the gospel, quell religious disputes, prevent heresy, produce uniformity, and finally be advantageous to the state, establish such creeds as are framed by the clergy; and this they often do the more readily when they are flattered by the clergy that if they thus defend the truth they will become nursing fathers to the church and merit something considerable for themselves.

What stimulates the clergy to recommend this mode of reasoning is,

1. Ignorance—not being able to confute error by fair argument.

2. Indolence—not being willing to spend any time to confute the heretical.

3. But chiefly covetousness, to get money—for it may be observed that in all these establishments settled salaries for the clergy recoverable by law are sure to be interwoven; and was not this the case, I am well convinced that there would not be many if any religious establishments in the christian world.

Having made the foregoing remarks, I shall next make some observations on the religion of Connecticut.

If the citizens of this state have any thing in existence that looks like a religious establishment, they ought to be very cautious; for being but a small part of the world they can never expect to extend their religion over the whole of it, without it is so well founded that it cannot be confuted.

If one third part of the face of the globe is allowed to be seas, the earthy parts would compose 4550 such states as Connecticut. The American empire would afford above 200 of them. And as there is no religion in this empire of the same stamp of the Connecticut standing order, upon the Saybrook platform, they may expect 199 against 1 at home, and 4549 against 1 abroad.

Connecticut and New-Haven were separate governments till the reign of Charles II when they were incorporated together by a charter, which charter is still considered by some as the basis of government.

At present (1791) there are in the state about 168 presbyterial, congregational and consociated preachers, 35 baptists, 20 episcopalians, 10 separate congregationals, and a few of other denominations. The first are the standing order of Connecticut, to whom all others have to pay obeisance. Societies of the standing order are established by law; none have right to vote therein but men of age who possess property to the amount of 40*l*, or are in full communion in the church. Their choice of ministers is by major vote; and what the society agree to give him annually is levied upon all within the limits of the society-bounds, except they bring a certificate to the clerk of the society that they attend worship elsewhere and contribute to the satisfaction of the society where they attend. The money being levied on the people is distrainable by law, and perpetually binding on the society till the minister is dismissed by a council or by death from his charge.

It is not my intention to give a detail of all the tumults, oppression, fines and imprisonments, that have heretofore been occasioned by this law-religion. These things are partly dead and buried, and if they do not rise of themselves let them sleep peaceably in the dust forever. Let it suffice on this head to say, that it is not possible in the nature of things to establish religion by human laws without perverting the design of civil law and oppressing the people.

The certificate that a dissenter produces to the society clerk (1784) must be signed by some officer of the dissenting church, and such church must be protestant-christian, for heathens, deists, Jews and papists, are not indulged in the certificate law; all of them, as well as Turks, must therefore be taxed to the standing order, although they never go among them or know where the meeting-house is.

This certificate law is founded on this principle, "that it is the duty of all persons to support the gospel and the worship of God." Is this principle founded in justice? Is it the duty of a deist to support that which he believes to be a threat and imposition? Is it the duty of a

Jew to support the religion of Jesus Christ, when he really believes that he was an impostor? Must the papists be forced to pay men for preaching down the supremacy of the pope, whom they are sure is the head of the church? Must a Turk maintain a religion opposed to the alcoran, which he holds as the sacred oracles of heaven? These things want better confirmation. If we suppose that it is the duty of all these to support the protestant christian religion, as being the best religion in the world—yet how comes it to pass that human legislatures have right to force them so to do? I now call for an instance where Jesus Christ, the author of his religion, or the apostles, who were divinely inspired, ever gave orders to or intimated that the civil powers on earth ought to force people to observe the rules and doctrine of the gospel.

Mahomet called in the use of law and sword to convert people to his religion; but Jesus did not, does not.

It is the duty of men to love God with all their hearts, and their neighbors as themselves; but have legislatures authority to punish men if they do not? So there are many things that Jesus and the apostles taught that men ought to obey which yet the civil law has no concerns in.

That it is the duty of men who are taught in the word to communicate to the teacher is beyond controversy, but that it is the province of the civil law to force men to do so is denied.

The charter of Charles II is supposed to be the basis of government in Connecticut; and I request any gentleman to point out a single clause in that charter which authorises the legislature to make any religious laws, establish any religion, or force people to build meeting-houses or pay preachers. If there is no constitutional clause, it follows that the laws are usurpasive in the legislators and not binding on the people. I shall here add, that if the legislature of Connecticut have authority to establish the religion which they prefer to all religions, and force men to support it, then every legislature or legislator has the same authority; and if this be true, the separation of the christians from the pagans, the departure of the protestants from the papists, and the dissention of the presbyterians from the church of England, were all schisms of a criminal nature; and all the persecution that they have met with is the just effect of their stubbornness.

The certificate law supposes, 1. That the legislature have power to establish a religion: this is false. 2. That they have authority to grant indulgence to non-conformists: this is also false, for religious liberty is a *right* and not a *favor*. 3. That the legitimate power of government extends to force people to part with their money for religious purposes. This cannot be proved from the new testament.

The certificate law has lately passed a new modification. Justices of the peace must now examine them; this gives ministers of state a power over religious concerns that the new testament does not. To examine the law part by part would be needless, for the whole of it is wrong.

From what is said this question arises, "Are not contracts with ministers, i.e. between ministers and people, as obligatory as any contracts whatever?" The simple answer is, Yes. Ministers should share the same protection of the law that other men do, and no more. To proscribe them from seats of legislation, &c. is cruel. To indulge them with an exemption from taxes and bearing arms is a tempting emolument. The law should be silent about them; protect them as citizens (not as sacred officers) for the civil law knows no sacred religious officers.

In Rhode-Island, if a congregation of people agree to give a preacher a certain sum of money for preaching the bond is not recoverable by law.*

This law was formed upon a good principle, but, unhappy for the makers of that law, they were incoherent in the superstructure.

The principle of the law is, that the gospel is not to be supported by law; that civil rulers have nothing to do with religion in their civil capacities. What business had they then to make that law? The evil seemed to arise from a blending religious right and religious opinions together. Religious right should be protected to all men, religious opinion to none; i.e. government should confirm the first unto all—the last unto none; each individual having a right to differ from all others in opinion if he is so persuaded. If a number of people in Rhode-

* Some men, who are best informed in the laws of Rhode Island, say, that if ever there was such an act in that state there is nothing like it in existence at this day; and perhaps it is only cast upon them as a stigma because they have ever been friends to religious liberty. However, as the principle is supposable I have treated it as a real fact; and this I have done the more willingly because nine tenths of the people believe it is a fact.

Island or elsewhere are of opinion that ministers of the gospel ought to be supported by law, and chuse to be bound by a bond to pay him, government has no just authority to declare that bond illegal; for in so doing they interfere with private contracts, and deny the people the liberty of conscience. If these people bind nobody but themselves, who is injured by their religious opinions? But if they bind an individual besides themselves, the bond is fraudulent, and ought to be declared illegal. And here lies the mischief of Connecticut religion. My lord, major vote, binds all the minor part, unless they submit to idolatry, i.e. pay an acknowledgment to a power that Jesus Christ never ordained in his church; I mean produce a certificate. Yea, further, Jews, Turks, heathens, papists and deists, if such there are in Connecticut, are bound, and have no redress: and further, this bond is not annually given, but for life, except the minister is dismissed by a number of others, who are in the same predicament with himself.

Although it is no abridgment of religious liberty for congregations to pay their preachers by legal force, in the manner prescribed above, yet it is antichristian; such a church cannot be a church of Christ, because they are not governed by Christ's laws, but by the laws of state; and such ministers do not appear like ambassadors of Christ, but like ministers of state.

The next question is this: "Suppose a congregation of people have agreed to give a minister a certain sum of money annually for life, or during good behaviour, and in a course of time some or all of them change their opinions and verily believe that the preacher is in a capital error, and really from conscience dissent from him—are they still bound to comply with their engagements to the preacher?" This question is supposable, and I believe there have been a few instances of the kind.

If men have bound themselves, honor and honesty call upon them to comply, but God and conscience call upon them to come out from among them and let such blind guides* alone. Honor and honesty are amiable virtues; but God and conscience call to perfidiousness. This shows the impropriety of such contracts, which always may, and

*The phrase of *blind guides*, is not intended to cast contempt upon any order of religious preachers; for, let a preacher be orthodox or heterodox, virtuous or vicious, he is always a blind guide to those who differ from him in opinion.

sometimes do lead into such labyrinths. It is time enough to pay a man after his labour is over. People are not required to communicate to the teacher before they are taught. A man called of God to preach, feels a necessity to preach, and a woe if he does not. And if he is sent by Christ, he looks to him and his laws for support; and if men comply with their duty, he finds relief; if not, he must go to his field, as the priests of old did. A man cannot give a more glaring proof of his covetousness and irreligion, than to say, "If you will give me so much, then I will preach, but if not be assured I will not preach to you."

So that in answering the question, instead of determining which of the evils to chuse, either to disobey God and conscience, or break honor and honesty, I would recommend an escape of both evils, by entering into no such contracts: for the natural evils of imprudence, that men are fallen into, neither God nor man can prevent.

A minister must have a hard heart to wish men to be forced to pay him when (through conscience, enthusiasm, or a private pique) they dissent from his ministry. The spirit of the gospel disdains such measures.

The question before us is not applicable to many cases in Connecticut: the dissenting churches make no contracts for a longer term than a year, and most of them make none at all. Societies of the standing order rarely bind themselves in contract with preachers, without binding others beside themselves; and when that is the case the bond is fraudulent: and if those who are bound involuntarily can get clear, it is no breach of honor or honesty.

A few additional remarks shall close my piece.

I. The church of Rome was at first constituted according to the gospel, and at that time her faith was spoken of through the whole world. Being espoused to Christ, as a chaste virgin, she kept her bed pure for her husband, almost three hundred years; but afterwards she played the whore with the kings and princes of this world, who with their gold and wealth came in unto her, and she became a strumpet: and as she was the first christian church that ever forsook the laws of Christ for her conduct and received the laws of his rivals, i.e. was established by human law, and governed by the legalised edicts of councils, and received large sums of money to support her preachers and her worship by the force of civil power—she is called the *mother of harlots*: and all protestant churches, who are regulated by law, and force people to support their preachers, build meeting-houses and otherwise maintain their worship, are daughters of this holy mother.

II. I am not a citizen of Connecticut—the religious laws of the state do not oppress me, and I expect never will personally; but a love to religious liberty in general induces me thus to speak. Was I a resident in the state, I could not give or receive a certificate to be exempted from ministerial taxes; for in so doing I should confess that the legislature had authority to pamper one religious order in the state, and make all others pay obeisance to that sheef. It is high time to know whether all are to be free alike, and whether ministers of state are to be lords over God's heritage.

And here I shall ask the citizens of Connecticut, whether, in the months of April and September, when they chuse their deputies for the assembly, they mean to surrender to them the rights of conscience, and authorise them to make laws binding on their consciences. If not, then all such acts are contrary to the intention of constituent power, as well as unconstitutional and antichristian.

III. It is likely that one part of the people in Connecticut believe in conscience that gospel preachers should be supported by the force of law; and the other part believe that it is not in the province of civil law to interfere or any ways meddle with religious matters. How are both parties to be protected by law in their conscientious belief?

Very easily. Let all those whose consciences dictate that they ought to be taxed by law to maintain their preachers bring in their names to the society-clerk by a certain day, and then assess them all, according to their estates, to raise the sum stipulated in the contract; and all others go free. Both parties by this method would enjoy the full liberty of conscience without oppressing one another, the law use no force in matters of conscience, the evil of Rhode-Island law be escaped, and no persons could find fault with it (in a political point of view) but those who fear the consciences of too many would lie dormant, and therefore wish to force them to pay. Here let it be noted, that there are many in the world who believe in conscience that a minister is not entitled to any acknowledgment for his services without he is so poor that he cannot live without it (and thereby convert a gospel debt to alms). Though this opinion is not founded either on reason or scripture, yet it is a better opinion than that which would force them to pay a preacher by human law.

IV. How mortifying must it be to foreigners, and how far from conciliatory is it to citizens of the American states, who, when they come into Connecticut to reside must either conform to the religion of Connecticut or produce a certificate? Does this look like religious liberty or human friendship? Suppose that man (whose name need not be mentioned) that fills every American heart with pleasure and awe, should remove to Connecticut for his health, or any other cause —what a scandal would it be to the state to tax him to a presbyterian minister unless he produced a certificate informing them that he was an episcopalian?

V. The federal constitution certainly had the advantage, of any of the state constitutions, in being made by the wisest men in the whole nation, and after an experiment of a number of years trial, upon republican principles; and that constitution forbids Congress ever to establish any kind of religion, or require any religious test to qualify any officer in any department of the federal government. Let a man be pagan, Turk, Jew or Christian, he is eligible to any post in that government. So that if the principles of religious liberty, contended for in the foregoing pages, are supposed to be fraught with deism, fourteen states in the Union are now fraught with the same. But the separate states have not surrendered that (supposed) right of establishing religion to Congress. Each state retains all its power, saving what is given to the general government by the federal constitution. The assembly of Connecticut, therefore, still undertake to guide the helm of religion: and if Congress were disposed yet they could not prevent it by any power vested in them by the states. Therefore, if any of the people of Connecticut feel oppressed by the certificate law, or any other of the like nature, their proper mode of procedure will be to remonstrate against the oppression and petition the assembly for a redress of grievance.

VI. Divines generally inform us that there is such a time to come (called the Latter-Day Glory) when the knowledge of the Lord shall cover the earth as the waters do the sea, and that this day will appear upon the destruction of antichrist. If so, I am well convinced that Jesus will first remove all the hindrances or religious establishments, and cause all men to be free in matters of religion. When this is effected, he will say to the kings and great men of the earth, "Now see what I can do; ye have been afraid to leave the church and gospel in my hands alone, without steadying the ark by human law; but now I have taken the power and kingdom to myself, and will work for my own glory." Here let me add, that in the southern states, where there has been the greatest freedom from religious oppression, where liberty of conscience is entirely enjoyed, there has been the greatest revival of religion; which is another proof that true religion can and will prevail best where it is left entirely to Christ.

F I N I S

38

A SERMON FOR THE DAY OF GENERAL ELECTION

David Tappan

BOSTON

1792

DAVID TAPPAN (1752–1803). The son of a Congregational minister, Tappan was born in Manchester, Massachusetts, and was graduated in 1771 from Harvard. In 1774 he was ordained pastor of the church in the third parish of Newbury, where he remained for eighteen years. He then became Hollis Professor of Divinity at Harvard, serving in that post until his death. Theologically, he was a moderate Calvinist; politically, he was an American patriot during the Revolution and a Federalist afterward. "One of the most prolific authors of the eighteenth century" (John F. Berens in *American Writers Before 1800*, p. 1410), Tappan published numerous sermons. His *magnum opus*, entitled *Lectures on Jewish Antiquities*, was published posthumously in 1807.

Noted for a plain preaching style, Tappan at first welcomed the French Revolution as a continuation of the American Revolution, clearing the way for the coming of the millennium through the destruction of popery. But he soon turned against the French revolutionists as diabolical and atheistic and joined with Timothy Dwight in a fierce denunciation of the movement. Tappan steadily taught the vital relationship of virtue and republicanism, a theme well-developed in the election sermon printed here, preached in Newbury before Governor Hancock, Lieutenant Governor Samuel Adams, and the Massachusetts legislature on May 30, 1792.

A SERMON

PREACHED BEFORE

HIS EXCELLENCY JOHN HANCOCK, Esq.
GOVERNOUR;

HIS HONOR SAMUEL ADAMS, ESQ.
LIEUTENANT-GOVERNOUR;

THE HONOURABLE THE
COUNCIL, SENATE, AND HOUSE OF
REPRESENTATIVES,
OF THE
COMMONWEALTH
OF
MASSACHUSETTS,

MAY 30, 1792.

BEING THE DAY OF

GENERAL ELECTION.

By DAVID TAPPAN, A. M.

PASTOR OF A CHURCH IN NEWBURY.

PRINTED IN *BOSTON*, MASSACHUSETTS:
AT THE State Press, BY THOMAS ADAMS,
PRINTER TO THE HONOURABLE, THE GENERAL COURT.

M,DCC,XCII.

Thou leddest thy People like a Flock, the Hands of Moses and Aaron.

Psalm 77, verse 20

How various and transcendent are the excellencies of the sacred writings! They combine all the different species of literary composition in their highest perfection, and consecrate them to the moral improvement, the present and future happiness of man. They furnish the best summary precepts, models, and incentives, for producing the good citizen and statesman, for effecting an orderly and prosperous state of things in the civil and temporary combinations of this world: Whilst their primary object is, to prepare men for the far nobler, the everlasting community of the blessed.

These observations are eminently illustrated by that part of the inspired volume, which relates to GOD's ancient people. The words just recited, look back to the infancy of that favoured nation. They introduce the GOD of Israel under the beautiful figure of a shepherd leading his flock; which expresses in a very lively and endearing manner, the singular tenderness and care, with which heaven had conducted that people from the bondage of Egypt, to the promised Canaan. The latter part of the verse, presents the subordinate and united agency of Moses and Aaron, in accomplishing that memorable series of events. These two celebrated characters had been early and closely linked together, by the ties of nature, of religion, and of common sufferings. They were afterwards united by the more awful bond of a divine commission, which constituted them plenipotentiaries from Jehovah, the king of Israel, to the Egyptian court, which employed them as instrumental saviours of their oppressed countrymen, as their guides and protectors through the dangers of the wilderness, and the prime ministers of their civil and ecclesiastical polity. Whilst the one was chief magistrate in the commonwealth, the other was high priest, or first officer in the church. And the institution and combined influence of these two orders in that community, were a most wise and salutary provision both for its public and individual happiness.

The divine appointment, then, and concurrent agency of the civil and ecclesiastical ruler, in leading the ancient people of GOD, naturally invite our attention to the importance and utility of political and religious guides in a christian state, and to that union of affection and of exertion for the common good, which ought to characterize and cement them. To explain and enforce this union, without confounding the church and the commonwealth, or blending the different provinces of their respective ministers, is a truly delicate task. The speaker hopes, however, that his well-meant endeavours to explore such a field, before an audience so respectable, will not be deemed either vain, or impertinent to the occasion. He flatters himself that the seasonable and momentous complexion of the subject, which cannot fail to strike every intelligent eye, will procure to the discussion and application of it a candid reception.

This joyful anniversary collects our civil and sacred leaders from various parts of the state, to one consecrated spot. It unites them, methinks, into one happy brotherhood. It brings them together to the altar of GOD, their common founder, master, and judge. It makes them joint partakers in a kind of yearly festival, sacred to liberty and to religion—a festival, which seems to renew and to seal mutual friendship, and their harmonious ardent affection to the general interest. Is it not congenial then with the spirit of the day, as well as decent and useful on other accounts, that these two orders should sometimes be the united object of its public addresses from the word of GOD; that their reciprocal influence, and their conjunct operation to the common good, should be clearly defined, and forcibly urged?

Under the solemn impression of these ideas, we will endeavour to mark out the two different provinces of Moses and Aaron, or of the ruler and the priest; the beneficent influence of each upon the public welfare; and the several ways, in which they may and ought to befriend and assist each other in leading the people of GOD.

The discriminating genius of the two departments may be thus defined. The one has for its immediate object, the temporal interest of mankind; the other, their spiritual and everlasting. The one aims to regulate their outward behaviour, so far as to restrain them from injuring one another or the public, and engage their contributions to the common welfare: The other contemplates the due regulation of the heart, as well as the overt-acts which issue from that source. The one enforces its addresses by sanctions merely civil and worldly; the other by motives which chiefly respect the soul and the life to come.

Let us now turn our attention to the important and happy influence of each department upon the public interest.

The importance of such an officer in society as the civil magistrate, is immediately seen and felt by all. It grows out of the present weakness and corruption of mankind. It is suggested by the social feelings belonging to our frame, joined with a sense of mutual dependence and common danger. Accordingly, when such officer possesses the spirit of his station, and with intelligence and fidelity pursues its leading design, the effects on the community will be equally benign and diffusive. A ruler of this character, like the central orb of the planetary world, enlightens and animates, cements and beautifies the whole political system. With a skilful, steady, yet gentle hand, he moulds a confused mass of discordant materials into one regular and harmonious compound, and holds it together with a silken, yet invincible chain. By a strictly righteous, equal, and paternal administration, he spreads the blessings of justice, freedom, tranquillity, public and private prosperity, through all classes of the people. The advantages of such a magistracy transcend description. To use the delicate and splendid figures of inspiration. It resembles "the light of the morning, when the sun riseth, even a morning without clouds; like the tender grass springing out of the earth by clear shining after rain."

But it is needless to expatiate on this branch of our subject. The beneficent influence of good civil rule stands confessed to the eye of reason. It is inscribed, as with a sun-beam on the face of our happy country. It has been delineated with superiour ability and address, on these anniversary solemnities.

Let us then direct our attention to the other object before us, namely, the importance and benefit to society, of the christian priesthood, or of public religious instructors. To set this point in a just and easy light, let us consider at large, the necessity of religion to the well-being of a community, and then inquire, what are the best means of diffusing and maintaining it.

The necessity of religion to public order and happiness, has been generally acknowledged by discerning minds in all countries and ages, yea, by enlightened infidels and atheists. But a set of philosophers and free-thinkers, who boast of their superiour reason and liberality, have appeared on the stage, in these days of modern refinement, who have employed all the powers of metaphysical sophistry and licentious ridicule to shake the foundations of religion: And some of them have even denied its political importance and utility, and have proposed in its stead a kind of philosophical or civil morality, as fully competent to the purposes of general order and security. A system of ideas, or at least of practical feelings, very similar to this, seems growing into fashion in various parts of the American Union; a system, which considers all religious principles, observances and instructors, as the remains of old monkish ignorance, superstition and bigotry, or the antiquated offspring of worldly policy, begotten in the early and ruder stages of society; but which are wholly unsuitable and useless, if not a heavy tax upon the public, in this more enlightened and mature period of human affairs! But let us meet these refined politicians upon their own ground; and ask them, what they have to substitute in the room of religion, as an adequate prop to their own favourite scheme of morality.

Will they say, that civil laws and institutions, planned with wisdom, and executed with vigour, will completely answer the purpose? But these human provisions can embrace only the visible actions of the subject. They can prevent or punish those offences only, which may be known and legally proved. They consequently, leave out of their jurisdiction all secret crimes; as well as those numberless immoralities, which human laws can never distinctly define, but which operate as the poison both of private and social felicity. Civil regulations proclaim their own incompetency, even in the judicial procedures submitted to their authority: For no general rule can accommodate itself to an infinite diversity of circumstances: And therefore the aid of religious principle seems absolutely necessary to supply the defect. This will teach the legislator to construct, and the judge to interpret and apply the laws, upon so just and liberal a plan, as will present the best advantages in every case, for discovering the truth, and so for protecting the innocent, as well as chastising the wilful offender. This will induce a conscientious, a filial and generous obedience, on the part of the subject, to the reasonable authority of the magistrate and the laws. At the same time it will prevent a cowardly, degrading submission to the claims and measures of imperious despots, or a fawning, idolatrous, prostration at the feet of a dignified fellow-worm. In short, whilst human laws punish criminal actions, it is the glory of religion to prevent them, to tear up the roots from which they grow. Whilst law is deaf and unrelenting to the cries of penitent guilt, religion pardons and comforts the suppliant, returning offender, and hereby encourages and fortifies his purposes and efforts of future obedience. Whilst the one enforces strict justice only, the other inculcates the whole train of gentle and beneficent virtues: It inspires an intercourse of humane, generous kindness, and grateful attachment and fidelity, between the higher and lower classes in society; an intercourse, which like the vital fluid diffuses chearful health through the whole political body. Thus civil institutions and measures, even in their best state, require the succours of religion, to supply their deficiencies, to soften their rigour, to enforce and to sweeten their observance.

"But a sense of honour, the desire of esteem and praise, and fear of their opposites, joined to the efficacy of salutary laws, will certainly form a sufficient security of the general order and welfare." We answer, the good influence of this principle will not bear a comparison with that of religion. For the praise or censure of the world, exerts its principal force within a very small circle, upon more splendid or public characters; whilst the great majority of the people, concealed under humble roofs, feel little of its efficacy. But religion applies its stimulating or withholding influence to the ignorant, the obscure, and the weak; as well as to the wise, the noble and the mighty. The world does not bestow its palm, till men have almost reached the goal; but religion applauds and cherishes the first virtuous desire, intention, or effort. The world often mistakes in its judgment of characters and actions; but religion places an unerring witness and judge in our very bosoms. In a word, even the esteem of men in the case before us, ultimately derives its force from religion. For if the social or moral virtues of mankind, were once stripped of the lustre, the stability, and the majesty, which religious principles communicate, the respect paid to them, would suffer an immediate shock: The idea of honour and disgrace, connected with their performance or omission, would be greatly enfeebled: And the opinion of the world, left without a steady guide, would grow too fluctuating and capricious, to restrain or to actuate human conduct.

"But the connexion between the interest of the public and of individuals, lays a sufficient bond upon the latter to contribute to the order and welfare of the former." We reply, this connexion is not always so immediate and striking, as to influence the unthinking, the poor and the wretched, to pay homage to the order and beauty of the social system, whilst there is nothing for them individually, but apparent deformity and misery; whilst those very principles and rules, which secure harmony to the public, wealth, power and magnificence to some of their fortunate neighbours, seem to bind them down to perpetual poverty and toil; and when a violation of these laws promises instant relief or benefit to themselves, and at the same time, perhaps threatens no direct injury to the community at large. There are some cases too, in which the more opulent ranks, or the governing powers of the state, may with reason consider the public interest and their own, as separate objects: And if their minds are not enlightened and regulated by religion, they will often view these two interests as distinct, when they really unite. They will also be supremely inclined to pursue private advantage, at the expence of every rival claim. In such instances, what is there effectually to restrain such elevated characters from sacrificing the public, at the shrine of their adored, though paltry idol? There is nothing which promises a sure and perpetual guard against these evils, but religious principles, the sentiment of a deity, and of a future state of recompence, early planted in the minds, and deeply rooted in the hearts both of the high and the low.

"But some infidel and irreligious characters have conducted well in a social and political view." We answer, religious ideas early taught and imbibed, will secretly influence the conscience and practice, long after the understanding has begun to question, and even to reject the arguments, on which they are founded. Besides, a habit of order and propriety in conduct, once formed, is not easily subdued by after speculations; especially when an adherence to it is connected with the marks of public esteem and favour, or enforced by the commanding motive of private interest. Not to add, that there are some, who affect a superiority to the common mass of mankind, by talking like infidels, who yet feel themselves constrained to think and act, in many instances, like vulgar believers.

"But if religion be the main prop of social order, why does not the latter always relax and decline with the former?" The answer is, religion still keeps her hold of men, through the medium of natural conscience, of early habit, and some awful controlling impression of a future retribution, even when their hearts do not feel her transforming power, nor their lives display her peculiar and most attractive charms. If then religious principles have such salutary effects on society, even when their influence is feeble, and when they manage the human mind by the inferiour and precarious handle of fear; what would be their fruits, if they reigned in full glory, and commanded the free and steady services of love? If love to GOD and men, which is the life of religion, pervaded all classes in the community, what a copious and excellent harvest would it quickly produce! This would ensure the universal practice of all those virtues, which nourish and exalt a nation; whilst it directly promoted the interest and comfort of all ages, conditions and stations; it would, as the great law of moral attraction, draw the affections and efforts of all to one common center, the good of the whole. Must not such a spirit and conduct immediately advance the respectability, the vigour, the temporal and spiritual prosperity of a people? Must they not draw down the approving smiles, the guardian care, the rewarding munificence of the Supreme Ruler of nations? On the other side, must not irreligion, and its natural offspring, vice, equally tend, both by a direct and a judicial operation, to disjoint, to enfeeble, to destroy a community? Does not the universal experience of public bodies from the beginning to this day, seal the truth of these observations? Is it not one mighty practical demonstration of the salutary fruit of piety and virtue, or the baneful influence of their opposites, upon the order, the liberty, the general welfare of nations?

The necessity of religion to public happiness being sufficiently proved, an interesting question arises; what are the best means of diffusing and maintaining in a community this precious and fundamental blessing? This inquiry brings up to view the importance of public religious instructors. The political necessity of such an order of men, directly results from that of religion itself, when compared with the ignorance, dulness, and depravity of the human mind, the spiritual and sublime nature of religious truths, the want of leisure as well as ability in the bulk of mankind, for studying and familiarizing them, and the influence of surrounding objects of worldly cares and amusements to intercept their view, to efface or weaken their impression. ["]In this dark and impure region," how apt are even the most contemplative and virtuous characters to lose sight of moral and spiritual objects, and to get out of the sphere of their attractive and regulating influence! How greatly then do we all need the friendly voice of stated monitors, to recal our forgetful, wandering feet; and to enlighten and warm our hearts afresh with the divine principles and motives of religion! Those in high station need to be frequently reminded, that there is a Being above them, to whom they are accountable, equally with the lowest of the people. Persons of great genius and learning, require to be often admonished that their obligations to serve GOD and the public, are proportioned to their superiour talents. The worthy and good in society, need a frequent and lively inculcation of those truths, which tend to nourish and fortify their virtues, to enliven and extend their efforts of usefulness. How much more needful, then is public religious instruction to the inferiour members of the community, to the numerous class of laborious poor, to the grossly ignorant, the careless, and the vicious! Without this, how shall they obtain a competent knowledge, or an abiding practical impression of their various relations and duties to GOD, to man, to civil society?

In this view, the public worship of the Deity, and stated instructions in religion and morality, appear as necessary and beneficial to the state, as they are to the souls of individuals: And the institution of a weekly sabbath, devoted to those purposes, is the offspring of profound and generous policy, if viewed merely in its aspect upon our present social condition. For the decent and united observation of it, by the members of each corporation, is, an eminent mean of promoting useful knowledge, civilization and good neighbourhood; of strengthening the cords both of political and christian union; of bringing seasonable rest and refreshment to the body and mind, after the fatigues of worldly care and toil; and of keeping alive in the minds of all ranks, an awful commanding sense of Deity, of moral and religious obligation: Agreeably, the public benefits of this institution are distinctly visible on the face of those communities, which carefully support and observe it; whilst the contrary features equally distinguish those, which despise or neglect it.

The preacher cannot do full justice to this part of his theme, or to his own profession as a gospel minister, without adding, that the christian religion, properly stated and enforced by its teachers, has a peculiarly favourable influence upon the present social state of mankind: For, it is the volume of revelation only, that fully illustrates and confirms, and with due authority presses, those great religious principles, which we have shown to be the basis of virtue and of order. At the same time it superadds a new scheme of truth, suited to the lapsed state of mankind, which at once encourages, directs, assists and constrains to universal goodness; it presents the Deity, in the full orbed lustre of his perfections; it displays the matchless philanthropy, the generous expiation and intercession of his Son; it offers and conveys the needed succours of his spirit; it ascertains and describes the future joys and sorrows of immortality. Must not these discoveries, suitably realized, powerfully tend to check transgression—to kill the seeds of vice, and to produce, to enoble, and improve every branch of a virtuous character? The moral system too, which christianity builds upon these principles, is an eminent friend to our present felicity. For it inculcates the most extended, the most active, the most self-denying benevolence; it links us to the great brotherhood of man; yea, it unites us to the universe, to eternity, and to GOD, the head and sum of both. It levels all the haughty feelings of superiour rank or abilities, and places true greatness in humble, condescending, elevated goodness. By this, as well as by constantly pointing us to those two great levellers, death and an endless retribution, it introduces a kind of generous republican equality among the different orders and conditions in society. It equally regards and secures the interest of all the members of the community, by that great rule of equity, "whatever ye would that men should do unto you, do ye even so to them." By presenting the same motives and rewards of virtue to the weak and the strong, and by urging both to secret acts of goodness, from a regard to the approving eye, and final recompence of the Supreme Judge; it provides a steady support, a constant opportunity, a universal engagement to the practice of virtue. We may add, it regulates and refines those important social connexions and duties, the conjugal, parental and filial, in a manner highly favourable to the order and happiness of human society. In a word, the spirit of our religion, is uniting and peaceable: It is loyal, patriotick, and free: It is the life and support of good government and of rational liberty. Even the positive, ceremonial rites of christianity, properly administered, are important out-works, which guard the public welfare: For by striking upon the senses and imaginations of men, they bring affecting truths with peculiar force to their hearts, and hereby operate to produce a decent and regular outward deportment.

What an engine of public usefulness, then, does the christian institution put into the hands of its ministers! And how important is it to the common good, that such an order of men should be spread out over the whole community! What unspeakable aid may they afford to, as well as receive from, the civil magistrate! Whilst the people at large reap a plentiful harvest from the united labours of both! Which brings us more distinctly to point out the several ways in which the ruler and priest may and ought to combine their influence, or to assist each other, in leading the people of GOD.

We mean not to advocate such a union or cooperation of the two orders, as involves a heterogeneous mixture of civil and spiritual objects; as places the magistrate upon CHRIST's throne, in the church, and invests the christian minister with the honors and the powers of the state: Such motley alliances are the offspring of political and priestly ambition, aided by equal cunning; are the main pillar both of civil and religious tyranny; and the source of infinite mischiefs to the intellectual and moral character as well as the temporal condition of mankind. They infect the best religion under heaven, its professors and ministers, with the spirit of this world, with a proud, cruel, persecuting and immoral disposition. As a celebrated writer observes, "persecution is not an original feature in any religion; but is always the strongly marked feature of all law, religion, or religions established by law. Take away the law-establishment, and religion re-assumes its original benignity. In America a Catholic priest is a good citizen, a good character, and a good neighbour; an Episcopalian minister is of the same description; and this proceeds from there being no law-establishment in America."

But whilst we execrate such treasonable conspiracies between rulers and priests, against the dearest rights and interests of man, we may consistently recommend to the two orders, a liberal and patriotick combination for the general good. There is indeed, in many respects, a natural alliance between intelligent, virtuous magistrates and ministers, in a free and christian state.

And first, the magistrate may and ought to cooperate with the christian instructor, by throwing the weight of his personal example and private influence into the scale of christian piety and virtue. The efficacy of example, when arrayed in all the splendour of high office, is not to be described. As religion adds grace and dignity to the most exalted station, so she derives a superiour charm and majesty from it.

When the great political characters in a community, give their uniform sanction to religion, by exhibiting her fairest features in their daily deportment; when they openly revere the name, the sabbaths, the temple, and all the sacred institutions of the Most High; when they liberally and zealously contribute to the settlement and support, the reputation and success of a learned and virtuous priesthood, to the extensive propagation of christian knowledge, and to the pious education of the rising age; when they are eminent patterns of virtue themselves, and are careful to cherish and honour it in others; how unspeakably do such examples confirm and extend the credit and influence of religion! What animation and confidence, what superiour respectability and success, do they give to its teachers! What authority and energy must the inward consciousness, and open lustre of such virtue impart to rulers themselves, in their official proceedings; especially those which have for their object, the suppression of wickedness, and the encouragement of the opposite interest! Which leads us to observe, that rulers efficaciously concur with christian ministers, when they carry the spirit of religion into their public conduct: When all their political measures are regulated by the everlasting maxims of natural justice, of christian equity and benevolence: When they accordingly distribute the burdens, apply the resources, fulfil the engagements and discharge the debt of the public, with the scrupulous fairness, the exact economy, the assiduous attention required by those rules, in the similar transactions of private citizens: When they detest and scorn the idea of sanctioning by their public authority, any measure, which they would blush to avow or to practise in their individual capacity: In short, when the whole system of their public conduct appears to be prompted and guided by a supreme regard to the example and laws, the approbation and honour of the infinite Ruler and the good of his moral family: What a glorious attestation is here of the reality, the commanding force of religious obligation! Such a train of political measures is pregnant with various and almost inconceivable good. It inculcates various sentiments upon the public mind, with all the authority and force of the highest, the most conspicuous, and unequivocal example. It also directly and efficiently contributes to the general prosperity: For it proceeds upon principles, which are as essentially necessary and conducive to social union and happiness, as the laws which govern the material world, are to the harmony and welfare of nature.

Further, the magistrate may greatly strengthen the christian teacher, by directing his public attention to the advancement of religion and virtue as an immediate and primary object; by so arranging his measures for the increase of temporal good, as to render them in the best manner subservient to that which is spiritual and eternal; by enacting and executing laws for the prevention or punishment of profaneness and immorality; by promoting virtuous characters to offices of honor and usefulness; by neglecting and dispising the vicious; by lessening and removing the temptation to iniquity; by augmenting and multiplying the encouragements to goodness; by giving birth and efficacy to public and private means of learning, so essential to rational piety; by effectually providing for the support and decent observance of public religious worship and instruction so necessary, as we have seen, to the virtue, the civilization, and happiness, of the community. Such a legal provision for the maintainance of religious institutions, obviously falls within the province of the magistrate, on account of their transcendent importance to civil government and society: Nor does such provision adjusted upon an equal and liberal plan, make the least approach to a political establishment of any particular religious profession, nor consequently involve any invasion of the prerogative of CHRIST, or the sacred rights of conscience. On the other hand,

Secondly. The christian minister may and ought to strengthen the hands of the civil ruler. If he possesses those qualities of head and heart, which suit his benevolent and comprehensive office, he must have the most tender and ardent feelings for the interest of the state, as well as the church. He must perceive an important connexion between them, as well as the friendly aspect of the christian doctrine upon both. He must consequently feel a double stimulus to a prudent and faithful discharge of his trust. He therefore endeavours, both in his public ministrations, and in his private conversation and example, so to represent and enforce the christian system, as that it may, under the divine blessing, have its full effect upon the character and condition of mankind, in reference to this world and the next. He takes particular care not to make this beneficent and peaceable religion, an engine of civil or spiritual tyranny, confusion, malignant strife, or in any respect, an instrument of increasing, instead of lessening human depravity and wretchedness. He feels himself peculiarly united to the worthy magistrate, by the ties of personal esteem and public affection. He studies that his whole deportment respecting the rulers and the laws, may express and promote a spirit of decent subjection and obedience, and he enforces such submission by all the authority and sanction of religion. His social intercourse with his family and flock, his daily prayers in private and in public, tend to kindle and to nourish the sentiments of loyalty and patriotism. He loves to mention in the ears of the rising race, the names and services of patriot rulers, of eminent public benefactors; and hereby to charm the tender mind to the love of virtue, of country, of mankind, as well as to a due veneration for, and grateful submission to such ministers of divine benevolence. His public discourses too, all tend either directly or remotely, to form his hearers into good citizens and subjects, as well as holy christians. That such a reciprocation of services between the two orders, falls within the line of propriety and important duty, is too obvious to the eye of discernment, to require a formal illustration.

It is with great satisfaction, that we appeal to the historic page of our own country, for a striking comment upon the preceeding discourse. Our fathers were led out of the house of bondage in Britain, into the wilderness of America, and planted here, as in the land of promise, by the same divine Shepherd, who led ancient Israel from deep oppression and misery, to the joys of freedom and plenty. The same good spirit, which inspired Moses and Aaron, to undertake and conduct so arduous an enterprize, evidently guided and animated the leaders in that great attempt, which gave birth to New-England. The same union of friendship, of counsel and exertion in the public cause, which characterized the Hebrew lawgiver and high-priest, distinguished the political and religious fathers of Massachusetts. The rulers of the state, were at the same time members and pillars of the church. The religion which they thus solemnly professed, was the rule of their public and private conduct, and the advancement of its interests, a main object of both. For this purpose, they readily co-operated with the schemes and endeavours of worthy clergymen, and contributed their best efforts for their comfort, reputation and success.

The advice and influence of the priesthood were likewise ever at hand, to aid and succeed the operations of the magistrate, and to promote the civil, as well as religious interests of the people. It is granted, indeed, that our ancestors carried this union of church and state, to an unwarrantable length. But this was not their peculiar fault: It was the complexion of the age. And shall we, their children, who owe so much to their generous services and sufferings, shall we, like undutiful and cursed Ham, take pleasure in exposing their nakedness? No, my fellow-citizens; whilst we spread a veil of filial piety over their imperfections, let [us] with the most grateful emotions, celebrate that united agency of Moses and Aaron, which, under GOD, laid such early and noble foundations of freedom and order, of science and religion; which in the feeble infancy, and great poverty of the settlement gave birth to a public seminary of learning; a seminary, which from its foundation, to this day, has borne on its front the united inscription of the ruler and the priest, in the names of its founders, and benefactors, of its governors and sons! But passing over the intermediate stages of our history; you will permit me modestly to ask, does not the inscription just mentioned, appear very conspicuous on the face of our late glorious revolution? Did not these two orders remarkably unite their efforts to keep the public mind in a posture of vigilance, of information, of patriotic ardour? In those times which tried men's souls, did not the public prayers and discourses, the private influence and example of the great body of the clergy, firmly and successfully co-operate with the civil and military measures of the country? Did not the same zealous concurrence of the two departments, procure the adoption of the excellent constitution of Massachusetts, and of the present federal system, which gives union, order, and happiness to America? Did not the same virtuous and unshaken combination eminently mark that perilous and alarming crisis, which a few years since passed over this commonwealth? Do not these striking facts evince, that the spirit of the clerical office at least, in this enlightened and free country, is an important friend to the liberty, government and happiness of society? On the other hand, it becomes us gratefully to acknowledge the support which religion and its ministers have received from the civil government of this state, from the authority and example of some of the first political characters in it; the additional reputation and success which they have instrumentally derived from that source; and the consequent face of superiour union and order, civilization and virtue, which adorns a great part of our community. These advantages would strike us with much greater force, were we allowed to contrast our situation in these respects, with that of some other parts of the Union: But decency forbids the invidious comparison.

When we look over this numerous and respectable assembly, a cloud of witnesses rushes upon our senses and hearts, in support of the ideas now advanced.

Our eye is first caught by the chief magistrate of this commonwealth, who has had a large share in the great political drama, that has been acted on the stage of the new world, and covered it with glory. The presence of his Excellency restrains the lips of delicacy from paying him a formal tribute of praise. But while his distinguished political services are engraven on every American bosom, justice to a different part of his character, constrains us to observe, that he has ever treated religion, its institutions and ministers, with a respect becoming the enlightened, consistent patriot, and ruler, in a christian state. The clergy within his jurisdiction, feel the animating influence of his attention and patronage, and wish him in return, a large experience of the comforts of our divine religion, amidst that trying scene of bodily infirmity, with which he has so long been afflicted. It is also our united prayer to GOD, that his Excellency may ever form his whole private and public conduct upon the divine model proposed in the life and precepts of the christian lawgiver. That so his personal example and official measures may unite their influence to spread piety and virtue as well as every temporal blessing, through the community. To this, he will feel himself urged by every motive, which can operate upon a heart of sensibility; in particular, by the interesting prospect of death and endless retribution, to which the highest earthly god is equally bound with the lowest of his subjects. May conscious fidelity chear the solemn hour of dissolution, inspire boldness before the decisive tribunal, and be crowned with superiour glory in the kingdom of heaven.

His Honour, the lieutenant-governour, merits our tribute of respect, on account of that distinguished union of political wisdom, patriotic virtue, and christian piety, which has long dignified his character. Notwithstanding the eminence of his reputation among the civilians of the age, he has not been ashamed of the cross of CHRIST, but has long been inlisted under that despised, but heavenly banner. May he still continue an ornament and pillar, both of the church and commonwealth, till his hoary head shall come down to the grave in peace.

The Honourable council claim our regards, on account of their important share in the executive department, and worthy personal qualities, which pointed them out to the suffrages of their enlightened fellow-citizens. Whilst their elevation to this office reflects on them a ray of glory, it obliges them to a correspondent dignity of sentiment and conduct: It invites them to a noble imitation of the governing wisdom, justice and mercy of him, who is the wonderful Counsellor, the King of righteousness and of peace. It particularly calls them to advise and consent to the appointment of such characters only, to interpret and execute the laws, as are exemplary themselves for the observance of human and divine injunctions, and endowed with talents and dispositions suited to the important trust. In this way they may unspeakably promote the civil and moral interests of all parts of the commonwealth.

The gentlemen who compose the two branches of the Honourable legislature, will permit our congratulations on the fresh mark of esteem and confidence, with which their constituents have honoured them. They will likewise remember that the trust, with which they are charged, is very solemn and momentous; that it is rendered still more awful, by the declarations and oaths, with which they have recently entered on its execution. As we cannot doubt their sincerity in those professions and appeals to heaven, we entertain a chearful hope that all their transactions on this day and through the year, will be regulated by the excellent principles of that religion, and of those civil constitutions which they have publicly taken for their guide. We reasonably expect that all their laws and proceedings will be so many branches growing out of the stock of equal justice and comprehensive benevolence; that they will be strongly marked with the same integrity, virtue and honor, which suit and adorn the rational and christian character in a private capacity. They will ever remember that the same practical principles, must form the basis both of public and individual happiness and glory; and that the policy of those who would rear the fabrick of national prosperity upon a different foundation is equally unphilosophical and iniquitous. As human art, in order to produce certain useful effects must conform to the principles of nature, or the established laws of its great Architect; so the politician must build the order and welfare of society upon those moral principles and connexions, which the same Almighty Ruler, has instituted in the rational system. If he act an opposite part, he virtually, attempts a new creation: Yea, like the man of sin, he exalts himself above all that is called GOD; for it is the glory of the Deity himself, though he be an absolute Almighty Sovereign, that he cannot govern upon any other plan than that of inviolable truth, justice, and goodness; that he cannot lie to any of his subjects, or trifle with their reasonable petitions, expectations or claims. It will be the glory of our rulers, to copy after this divine original. No idea therefore of omnipotence or uncontrolled sovereignty, will be permitted to infect their deliberations and decisions; but their whole conduct, as it respects particular citizens, the commonwealth in general, and the great American republic, will, we trust, exhibit a fair picture of honest, enlarged and federal policy.

Honored fathers: As you do not remove out of the sphere of religious obligation, by entering the circle of politicks; as you, have all this day professed the christian belief, and many of you are complete visible members of the Redeemer's family; you will feel under the most sacred ties, to devote the superiour powers and advantages of your present stations, to the christian interest. Whilst therefore you tenderly guard the rights of conscience, and afford equal protection to all peaceable citizens, you will make and enforce every needful provision for the general diffusion of religious and moral sentiments, and for the maintenance and observation of those christian and literary institutions, which are requisite to that end. Among such institutions, the neighbouring university has a distinguished claim to your liberal patronage. It has been one of the grand nurseries of civilization, liberty, good government and religion. Our very existence, as a respectable community, is, under GOD, greatly derived from that source. Filial gratitude then, as well as every sentiment of public virtue, press our rulers to nurse and cherish this their ancient parent, with a tender and generous care.

In a word, let me respectfully call upon all our civil officers, in every department, to consecrate their authority, influence and example to the greatest good of the community. You, gentlemen, collectively considered, are the moving and regulating principle of the whole political machine. If you jointly and strenuously pursue a virtuous train of conduct, it will operate like a powerful charm upon all parts of the system, and call up a new creation of beauty, virtue and happiness. Let it then be your first ambition and endeavour, to make mankind wiser, better and happier; to raise up the drooping head of virtue; to tread down irreligion and vice; to enlarge the empire of knowledge and righteousness; to augment as much as possible, the sum of created good, and of creating and redeeming glory.

And since the advancement of these great interests lies very much between you and the standing teachers of religion, let gentlemen in these different orders cultivate a friendly and patriotic alliance, by all the methods which prudence and generous virtue suggest.

Ye venerable leaders of our civil and ecclesiastical tribes; how many and how forcible are the ties which bind you together! In this land of political and religious freedom, you both derive your election to office from one source; you are fellow-labourers in one great and benevolent cause; you are important members of one civil body, and by visible profession and sacred obligation, of one christian family; in the due performance of your several offices, you display the same leading excellent talents and virtues, and mutually give and receive the most important support. Certainly then, there can be no strife, no jealous distance between you; for ye are brethren. We congratulate the people of Massachusetts, on the liberal and virtuous union, which at this moment subsists between you, and which is particularly exemplified in those numerous laudable incorporations, which embrace many of your first characters; and which have for their object, the interests of science, of arts, of education, of humanity, of christian knowledge and piety. To perpetuate this union and render it still more operative to the general good, and not the low selfishness or vanity of exalting and strengthening his own profession, considered as a separate interest, has been the preachers governing motive in this discourse; and with a view to the same grand object, he modestly submits to the candour of both departments, a few monitory hints, suggested by the present aspect of society and of religion.

In the first place: Our leading characters in the civil and the literary line, will feel the peculiar importance, at this degenerated period of animating their clerical brethren, in every method dictated by wisdom and virtue; and particular, by encouraging them to calculate their public ministrations upon principles of the most extensive usefulness. They will consider, that many of us are connected with societies, which are chiefly composed of the labouring and more illiterate class; that these peculiarly need the privileges of a weekly sabbath and public religious instruction; and that many of them require very plain, and very pungent applications, in order to enlighten their ignorance, to rouse their stupidity, or to check their vicious career. Our christian patriots, therefore far from despising, will generously aid those teachers, who frequently endeavour, by all the methods of familiar, pathetic, or alarming address, to reach and refine these rougher parts of the community. The enlarged knowledge and experience of our learned civilians will also inspire sentiments of candour towards the priesthood, in regard to that variety of speculation, of gifts, and address, by which it is diversified; they will view this diversity as naturally resulting in great measure from the spirit of free inquiry and improvement, which characterizes the present day. They will consider too, that it furnishes public teachers suited to the various capacities, tastes and prejudices, and all the grades of character and condition, which at this period mark the face of society. They will further consider, that the operation of republican equality and religious freedom, will sometimes introduce a christian instructor not perfectly agreeable to the relish or the speculations of a few superiour members of a corporation, but perhaps very acceptable and beneficial to the general mass of the people. In such cases, does not a regard to social order, to equal rights, to the greatest moral and political good, require a generous and peaceable acquiescence?

On the other hand it becomes the clergy at this day studiously to hold up their office, and the religion which they teach, in the most respectable and pleasing light. A special attention to this object, is rendered important, by the present improved state of society; by the learning and politeness, which adorn many of our religious assemblies; by the rapid progress of loose sentiments and manners, and the consequent disrelish or contempt of christian doctrines, institutions, and teachers. To check these spreading evils it becomes the sacred order to pay great attention both to the private and public duties of their function; it becomes them, in the performance of the latter, to display a force of reasoning, a propriety of thought, of method and expression, a decency of style and address, which may at once bear down the scoffs and the sophistry of libertinism, justly please the taste of literary refinement, and at the same time exhibit the plain, the affectionate, the evangelical preacher. It becomes them both in their ministrations and personal example, to represent the christian institution and ministry, as friendly to human happiness in both worlds; as breathing a social and courteous, a candid and forbearing, a loyal, uniting, and public spirit; a spirit, which whilst it supremely attaches us to the service and rewards of the life to come cherishes a proper sensibility of our rights, duties, and enjoyments as inhabitants of the earth. It becomes them in every consistent method, to support the civil interests of the community, the respectability of its rulers, and the efficacy of its laws. And whilst law speaks to the public ear, in one uniform, inflexible tone, it is ours, my reverend fathers and brethren, to bring home the addresses of religion to the bosoms of individuals; and by a pertinent and forcible application of her peculiar truths and sanctions, to seize their consciences, their imaginations, their hearts; to possess and command their inmost feelings. By this process, under the influence of the all creating spirit; we are first to mould them into good men, and then by an easy transition into good citizens, rulers and subjects. Above all, let us ever keep in our own realizing view, and endeavour to enforce upon our people, the primary, the infinitely weighty object of our religion and ministry, viz. the spiritual, everlasting salvation of immortal beings, and the glory of GOD and his Son, shining forth in the wondrous contrivance, and accomplishment of it. Whilst our rulers are pushing forward our temporal prosperity and glory, let us labour to establish and to complete that glory, by a corresponding advancement of this most important object. Into this channel let us endeavour to draw all the civil and literary, as well as religious advantages, which come within our reach. Let the united efforts of the clergy and laity, be especially employed in diffusing christian knowledge and virtue, through those vast territories of our country, whose poverty, and remote situation have precluded the stated enjoyment of religious institutions; and in promoting a more general and effectual attention to the private means of education, in various parts of the commonwealth. By such a union of public exertion, our leading characters in church and state, will resemble the two olive-trees, which the Prophet saw in vision, emptying their golden oil into the candlestick of Zion.

Fellow-citizens of this great assembly,

I felicitate you and our common country, on the natural, civil and religious advantages, by which we are so eminently exalted; and especially on the prosperous train of our national affairs, under the auspices of indulgent heaven, and its favourite minister, the President of the United States. When we mention this beloved citizen and benefactor of America, every bosom present, feels the endearing and forcible illustration, which his example gives to the leading sentiment of this discourse. For the charm of his piety, of his public and private virtue, as well as political wisdom, has been a principal cement of our national union, and so a prime source of all its attendant blessings. What then is wanting to complete the glory and happiness of our country? Nothing but the general prevalence of the same excellent spirit; a spirit of sublime virtue, corresponding to the natural grandeur and extent of America, and to its noble constitutions of government and religion. Virtue enlightened and invigorated by political and christian knowledge, is eminently the soul of a republic. It is necessary to direct, to enliven, to guard the election of its rulers, and to secure to them, the generous confidence, submission and co-operation of the people. It is peculiarly requisite in a community like ours, spread out over such an immense continent, divided by so many local governments, prejudices and interests: A people so circumstanced, can never be firmly and durably united, under one free and popular government, without the strong bands of religious and moral principle, of intelligent and enlarged patriotism. Liberty planted in such a soil, will be perpetually tending to unbridled licentiousness, distracting jealousies, and popular confusion. Let us then set up a vigilant guard against these encroaching evils. Let us not imagine that the exercise of civil liberty, consists in ignorant or envious abuse of public characters and measures; nor that religious freedom will justify careless neglect or wanton contempt of the truths, the ordinances, and ministers of that religion, which was sent down from heaven to guide us, to present and future happiness. Though we are not accountable to the civil magistrate for our religious sentiments and worship; yet we certainly are to the Deity; and he has given us no liberty in this enlightened country, either to think with deists and sceptics, or to live like atheists; nor will the prostitution of his Sabbaths, to idleness or amusements in defiance of human and divine laws, pass in his account for a mark of superior politeness or liberality. In opposition to these wicked, but too modish abuses of liberty, let us remember that energetic government, is the guardian of freedom, and that religion, especially the christian, is the pillar of both. Let us then properly respect, support, and concur both with our civil and religious ministers. Let us exercise the most scrupulous care in the election of both, and be rationally satisfied, that their heads and hearts, their principles and morals, comport with the spirit of their several offices. But having chosen them, let us treat their persons and administrations with that confidence and honour, which become a wise and magnanimous people, and which may, by the blessing of GOD, give the greatest effect to their benevolent labours.

Finally: As the crown of all, let us become pious towards GOD, humble and obedient believers in his Son, conscientiously submissive to the government and laws of our country, sober, frugal, and diligent in our several employments, just and kind to one another, unitedly and zealously attached to the great interests of America, and of the whole human fraternity. Then we shall hold out an inviting example to all the world, of the propitious operation of a free government; we shall encourage and accelerate the progress of reason, and of liberty, through the globe. Already has the new world diffused the light and warmth of freedom across the Atlantic, into the old; which has given birth to a surprising and glorious revolution. Let us be nobly ambitious, by our future conduct, to feed and extend the generous flame; and thus to realize the wishes and hopes of all benevolent spirits in heaven and earth. Let us especially labour and pray, that these political struggles and changes, may, under the divine agency, introduce new and brighter scenes of christian knowledge and piety, till the whole world shall be covered with divine glory and human bliss. And may we in particular, after having filled our departments in society here, with usefulness and honor, be united to the more glorious community of the righteous; where the official distinctions of Moses and Aaron, are known no more; where all the followers of the Lamb, shall form one royal priesthood, one mighty combination of perfect and happy immortals; and GOD the original source of being and blessedness, shall be all in all.

A M E N

39

A SERMON PREACHED BEFORE THE ARTILLERY COMPANY

Peter Thacher

BOSTON

1793

PETER THACHER (1752–1802). Thacher, the great-grandson of Reverend Peter Thacher (d. 1727), graduated in 1769 from Harvard with highest honors. He later had conferred upon him a doctor of divinity degree from the University of Edinburgh. He was pastor at the Congregational Church in Malden, Massachusetts, from 1770 to 1784, and then moved to the Brattle Street Church in Boston, where he remained until his early death from tuberculosis (in Savannah, Georgia). Regarded by George Whitefield as the ablest preacher in the colonies—he called Thacher the "young Elijah"—his oratorical powers were much valued by Massachusetts patriots, who gave him special "beating orders" to organize the coastal defense. Chaplain to the General Court, he was the probable author of the Resolutions of Malden to its General Court representative. He later represented the town in the convention that framed the 1780 state constitution. After the Revolution, he was active in a number of affairs, including the Society for the Propagation of the Gospel Among the Indians, the Society for Promoting Christian Knowledge, the Humane Society, the Charitable Fire Society, and the American Academy of Arts and Sciences. He was also a founder (in 1791) and a trustee of the Massachusetts Historical Society.

Thacher published twenty-two sermons, a list of which is given in William Emerson, *A Sermon on the Decease of the Reverend Peter Thacher, D.D.* (1803).

A

SERMON,

PREACHED BEFORE

THE

ANCIENT AND HONORABLE

ARTILLERY COMPANY,

JUNE 3, 1793;

BEING THE DAY

OF THEIR

Annual Election of Officers.

BY PETER THACHER, D. D.

PASTOR OF A CHURCH IN BOSTON.

PRINTED AT *BOSTON*,

BY MANNING AND LORING,

IN QUAKER LANE.——MDCCXCIII.

Then the five men departed and came to Laish, and saw the people that were therein, how they dwelt careless, after the manner of the Zidonians, quiet and secure; and there was no magistrate in the land, that might put them to shame in any thing; and they were far from the Zidonians, and had no business with any man.

Judges XVIII.7.

All scripture is written for our instruction. It is intended not only to reveal to us the purposes of God's mercy and the requisitions of his will, but to furnish our minds with the wisdom which is profitable to direct us in the various situations to which by Providence we are called. The history of the Bible contains a lively picture of human life and manners. It paints the various feelings which agitate the heart of man at different periods. It describes the manner in which individuals and bodies of men have conducted in different circumstances. It points out the motives of their conduct, and the consequences which resulted from it. And thus the word of GOD furnishes us with maxims of wisdom, and lessons of experience, without our paying the dear price at which they are sometimes purchased. From this history we find that mankind have been much the same in all ages; that the same passions and principles have actuated them all; and that the same effects have generally resulted from the same causes.

Modern philosophers are ready to suppose that they have made great improvements in the knowledge of mankind, and in the various systems by which human governments may be formed and supported with the most happy success. But if we read the history of the Bible, we shall be ready to conclude with Solomon, "The thing that hath been, it is that which shall be; and that which is done is that which shall be done; and there is no new thing under the sun." In this history we shall find the same general principles laid down which are now considered as the basis of free and happy states, and the same methods prescribed to preserve and increase them when they are formed. It is difficult to find any situation now to which there cannot be found some parallel in the sacred volume.

The maxim, "that it is necessary in peace to prepare for war," is now adopted by every human government. Founded in reason and good sense, this maxim will be questioned by no one who does not doubt the lawfulness of war in all cases. Experience decides positively upon its truth, and the conduct of mankind proves their conviction of its expediency. And a striking example of the truth of this maxim is given us by the words of the text. The men of Laish were careless and secure; they had no order nor government; they considered themselves as at a distance from any enemy, and in no danger of an invasion; and these very causes operated to incite the Danites to invade them, and rendered their conquest easy and certain.

"Laish," say commentators,* "afterwards called Caesarea Philippi, was placed in a very pleasant situation between the rivers Jor and Dan, almost at the foot of mount Libanus. This town was the extreme border of Judea to the north, as Beersheba was to the south. The inhabitants dwelt after the manner of the Zidonians. The city of Zidon was nearly surrounded by the sea; it was strongly fortified, and thus its citizens felt perfectly secure. The Zidonians were a very powerful people, and had little to dread from any of the nations around them. This occasioned them to feel perfectly at ease; and the men of Laish, who were probably a colony from Zidon, catched the manners of the parent state, and without the same reason felt the same security. They were distant a day's journey from Zidon, which was sufficient to prevent them from receiving thence immediate assistance and support, in an attack suddenly commenced and finished. When the history says that they had no business with any man, it probably means that they did not carry on trade and commerce with any people, and lived entirely by themselves; or else, that they had so little care of their safety, and so high an opinion of their own abilities, as to form no league or alliance with any other people."

The history to which the text relates is briefly this: The tribe of Dan had not conquered the whole portion of land assigned to them in Canaan; and being straitened for room, they determined, by a vigorous exertion, to procure to themselves the accommodation which they needed. They acted prudently and wisely in the prosecution of this design; for, they did not at once commence an emigration without having any certain object before them, but detached a small party to

* Pool's Synopsis

find out a place adapted to their views, and a people that could be easily conquered. Laish presented itself to them as calculated to answer both these purposes. The motives which induced the children of Dan to attack the place, and the reasons which made the conquest so easy, are briefly recounted in the report of the spies: "Arise, that ye may go up against them; for we have seen the land, and behold it is very good: And are ye still? Be not slothful to go and to enter to possess the land. When ye go, ye shall come unto a people secure, and to a large land; for GOD hath given it into your hands—a place where there is no want of any thing that is in the earth." The fertility of the soil, and the pleasantness of the situation, animated their wishes to possess the land. The perfect security in which the people dwelt, and their total unpreparedness to defend themselves, calmed their fears of any formidable resistance. They came, they saw, they conquered. And the people of Laish fell, a melancholy proof of the danger of security, and a striking demonstration of the necessity of preparing against violence and invasion, even in a time of the most profound peace, and at the greatest distance from any enemy.

This lesson, so strikingly delineated in the history before us, is the lesson of the day. We are now met in the house of GOD to assist the devotions of an ancient and respectable military corps, founded by our ancestors, to guard against the very error which proved fatal to the existence and independence of Laish. This corps was intended as a nursery for the officers who should command the militia of the colony, and who might thus train them up to "fight for their brethren, their sons and their daughters, their wives and their houses." Deeply as these good men were impressed with the peaceful religion of JESUS CHRIST, they still believed the lawfulness and necessity of defending the liberty and property which GOD had given them. Brave and hardy, like the wilderness which they subdued, they could not endure the idea of yielding their independence even to the boldest invader; and therefore by vigilance and exertion, by order and discipline, they guarded against the danger, or prepared themselves to repel it. They founded therefore this company, in which the principal men among them cheerfully enrolled themselves, and where the man who had commanded armies did not feel his honor injured, or his dignity impaired, by being commanded in his turn.

The occasion therefore, and the sentiment of the text, lead me[:]

In the first place, to remark upon the folly which a people discover, and the danger to which they expose themselves, when they live in a state of security, unprepared to resist an invasion, or defend themselves against the attacks of an enemy.

But how are we to defend ourselves when our country is invaded, and we are threatened with the loss of every thing we hold dear, by the violence and fury of an enemy? By declaring, with the honest Quaker, that we will not resist any force which may come against us, because our holy religion forbids us to fight? By long and learned and critical orations upon the injustice and cruelty of invasion, and its inconsistency with the rights of man? Shall we send the ministers of religion to meet an army of invaders, and to tell them that they are not doing as they would be done by; that they act inconsistently with the religion of CHRIST, and that GOD will punish them for their injustice? Or, shall we spread out our supplicating hands to them, and beg them not to shed brethren's blood, nor deprive us of the liberty, the property and independence which GOD has bestowed upon us, and which we desire to transmit to our children?

Were all mankind actuated by the peaceful religion of JESUS CHRIST (as they will be at some future period) then these methods would be effectual; but under the present circumstances of human nature they would be the subject only of derision. So deeply is the human heart depraved, so strongly do ferocious passions operate upon mankind, as that the still small voice of reason and religion cannot be heard. The loud calls of ambition and avarice drown their feeble whispers, and a torrent of violence and oppression sweep away their warmest advocates.

In these circumstances, our only method is to resist force with force, to repress the violence which we do not provoke, and to let men know that we will defend with our lives the liberty and the happiness which GOD has given us.

But it is strange, some will observe, that doctrines of this nature should be preached by a minister of peace, who professes a religion which breathes the warmest benevolence, and teaches mankind to live and love as brethren! Our master, will they say, "came not to destroy men's lives, but to save them"; he strictly prohibits every degree of wrath and envy, and enjoins us to follow ["]peace with all men."

The lawfulness of defensive war has been so often proved from this place, upon these occasions, as that many observations upon the subject will be needless. We must take mankind as they are, because they will not be what they ought. We know that there are men, and many men, who are totally destitute of moral principle, and care not whom they wound or destroy, if they can enrich and aggrandize themselves. We know that there are nations who wish to assume universal authority, and subjugate their neighbours to their will. Can any man, in the exercise of common sense and reason, suppose that the Gospel prohibits us to resist such violence? Am I obliged to deliver my purse to an highwayman, or my life to a murderer, when I am able to defend myself? Does the religion of CHRIST enjoin its votaries to submit to the violence of the first ruffian nation which will attack them; to give up their liberty, and the liberty of their children, to those who would make them "hewers of wood and drawers of water?" If my brother, agitated with a delirium, attempts to injure me, or take away my life, am I to yield myself a quiet victim to his distraction? These questions carry their own answer with them, and must strike conviction to every unprejudiced mind; for to act in this manner will be to present our throats to the butcher, and to court our own destruction.

Wars undertaken to gratify the lust of power, differences excited by those "lusts from whence come wars and fightings among men," are decidedly contrary to the law of GOD. Every good man mourns over those fatal contentions where kindred blood is shed; and where brethren of the same family, children of the same father "bite and devour one another." But where a people contend not for glory or conquest; where they take every method to avoid an alternative so disagreeable; yet where they cannot preserve their lives, their liberties, their estates and their religion, without "resisting unto blood," they are to do so. If they do it not, they offend against GOD, and voluntarily sacrifice the birthright which he has given them. GOD of old commanded his people to resist such attempts, and to make war upon those who attacked them; and would he have done this had war been unlawful in all cases, and directly contrary to the nature and reason of things? I am aware that he permitted many things under former dispensations "because of the hardness of men's hearts," because the state of human nature would not permit them to be different; but then he never expressly enjoined men to do what was morally wrong? War he has enjoined; and Meroz was cursed by divine command, because they "came not to the help of the Lord, to the help of the Lord against the mighty."

If it is lawful thus to defend ourselves, and if we have reason to expect the divine protection and support only in the use of proper means, then it is certainly wrong to neglect these means, and to live in a state of supineness and security; because discipline and military knowledge are absolutely necessary to successful war; and such discipline cannot be attained at once. All knowledge is progressive, and military skill is to be acquired in the same way, by the same exertions and perseverance which make us eminent in any other science. True it is, that native bravery and ardent enthusiasm will do much to animate men to heroic deeds in defence of their country; but with how much greater advantage do these principles operate, when they are tempered with discretion, and guided by experience! The first is the courage of a mastiff, who shuts his eyes, and runs into the very jaws of destruction, but who sometimes bears all before him; the second is the fortitude of a man, who knows the nature of his object, and the means by which it may be accomplished. A nation free and brave cannot be conquered; but its defence must cost more dearly, and its distresses must be greatly protracted, if its subjects are not acquainted with the art of war. Absurd and foolish then it is, for any people to live in security, to flatter themselves that their tranquillity shall not be interrupted, and to remain ignorant of military discipline! They act unwisely when they do not learn the art of defending themselves, until that defence is immediately necessary; and when they trust to their enemy's beating them into skill, and instructing them to be soldiers, as the "men of Succoth were taught with briers and thorns."

It is certainly unwise, again, for a people to live in security, without preparing against invasion until that invasion takes place, because exertions for defence suddenly made will not be so effectual, nor answer the same purpose with those which are made coolly and with time. If fortresses are suddenly erected, they will want strength and firmness. If an army is raised, and they are called to fight before they have been instructed in the first rudiments of war, they will probably be defeated. Haste is no friend to wise counsels or to effectual defence. The spur of the occasion may animate to vigorous exertions for a short time, and despair may lead a rude and undisciplined multitude to do wonderful things; but their violence will soon put them out of breath, and a cool and wary enemy will be able gradually to defeat and disperse them. In these cases, as in all others, skill and knowledge will make hard things easy, and will save much labour and pains. By a wise and judicious mode of defence, not hastily adopted, but carefully adjusted in all its various parts, much damage may be prevented, and many valuable lives may be saved. What wise people then will neglect, even in the bosom of tranquillity, to guard against every surprise, and prepare themselves to resist the first bold intruder who may attack them!

No people can have any ground for security while they are destitute of the means of defence. They lie open to every danger, and are liable to be insulted, abused and conquered, by any nation which may think them worthy of their attention. Such a state ought to excite alarm, and no people should be easy while they are exposed to danger so imminent. But their listlessness, like that of a man in a lethargy, commonly increases with their disease, and generally terminates in the death of their liberty.

But, preparations made in peace, and an ability to resist invasion are, thirdly, the most effectual means to prevent it. Their neighbours will esteem it madness and folly to expose themselves to such a formidable resistance; and a people thus prepared and disciplined will be an object, not only of veneration, but of fear. Marauders, tyrants who wish to carry their despotism into foreign countries, or to fatten on their spoils, will not choose for their objects those hardy and skilful nations, who stand ready to defend themselves and their country. Such men will look, as did the tribe of Dan, for some people who dwell quiet and secure, without vigilance, without discipline or the means of resistance. Such a people court invasion, they invite an attack, and beckon to those who delight in spoil to "come and take away their place and nation." Wary and prudent commanders will consider long before they attack a fortress strongly fortified and well garrisoned; and they will count the cost before they invade a country whose inhabitants are all trained to discipline, and "know how to use the sword and the bow." But the weakness of a fortress, the ignorance or security of a people, mark them as proper subjects to be attacked and conquered.

Respectability always attends the vigilance and discipline which I am recommending. It is a proof of wisdom to look forward and prepare for futurity, to guard against any danger which may arise, and to provide remedies for every disaster which may happen. Such conduct is a proof of a healthy and vigorous state; it discovers energy in council, and an elastic well braced government. This people will stand high in the estimation of the world. Their alliance will be courted, and this will give them new strength and new defences. The saying of our Lord, alluding however to a more important circumstance, will in this case be fully accomplished—"Unto him that hath shall be given, and he shall have abundance, but from him that hath not shall be taken even that which he seemeth to have."

The history of mankind will furnish us with numberless instances wherein the truth of these observations has been exemplified. Scarcely a page of this history can be opened which does not contain full conviction of it. But we need not go from our own age or our own times to find this conviction. The people of America have proved it to the world, and have reaped the happy consequences of vigilance and discipline, as well as of personal bravery. At the commencement of our late controversy with one of the most formidable nations upon earth, we had not the means of defence which other nations enjoy. We were without ammunition, without money, and without allies; but we had an hardy yeomanry, zealous in the cause of liberty, and versed from their infancy in the use of arms. Every man had been more or less trained and disciplined; and we had a general acquaintance with military science. We proved the benefit of this preparation, when we met the embattled legions of Britain, and spread terror through hosts commanded by their ablest generals. The heights of Charlestown witnessed the bravery of our citizens, and furnished a convincing evidence of the wisdom of those institutions which made the people of New England soldiers from their cradle. Superior as were our foes in equipments, "in all the pomp and circumstance of war," yet still they paid so dearly for their victory as that the acquisition of one or two more such victories would have ruined them.

And how deplorable would have been our situation, had we not been thus instructed and prepared for defence! Attacked by an enemy who claimed a right to "bind us in all cases whatsoever," and whose high toned spirits were exasperated at the idea of resistance, we must have fallen a prey to their violence, and bidden an everlasting farewell to liberty and its blessings. Taskmasters, worse than Egyptian, would have been set over us, and our children must have toiled to support the luxury of their oppressors.

But when resistance had taken place, and we had declared ourselves independent, what miseries, what exquisite distresses would have been the probable consequences of our subjugation! An incensed soldiery would have given way to their unhallowed lusts, and disregarded the laws of GOD and man to gratify their cravings! Alas! —what sound is this which pierces my heart? It is the shrieks of a tender wife, wrested from the arms of a beloved husband, to gratify the appetitie of a lordly master! But whence are those soft complainings, those deep drawn sighs? They are the lamentations of injured innocence, of violated virtue, of the defiled virgin, who has fallen a victim to brutal force! But why does busy imagination transport me to a scene still more painful? Why does it hurry me to the field of blood, the place of execution for the friends of American liberty? Whom does it there call me to see led to the scaffold with the dignity of Cato, the fortitude of Brutus, and the gentleness of Cicero marked deeply on his countenance? It is the gallant Washington, deserted by his countrymen, and sacrificed because he fought in their defence! Of whom consists yonder group of heroes? It is an Hancock, an Adams one and the other, a Franklin, a Rutledge!—but I repress the bursting sentiment—the bare imagination bows my soul with unutterable grief!

Thanks to the GOD of armies, and to the vigilance and bravery of our countrymen—these distressing scenes were never realized! Freedom, peace and independence have blessed our land; and the very nation whom we opposed, laying aside the bitterness of civil contention, has extended to us a friendly hand, and now declares herself happy in our alliance. A recurrence to past scenes should not therefore excite our resentment; it should only animate us to the vigilance, the bravery, and the active preparation which proved, under GOD, the means of our deliverance.

I proceed to remark, fourthly, on the necessity of government to the existence and defence of any people.

One reason assigned for the easy conquest of Laish is, "that there was no magistrate in the land, who might put them to shame in any thing,"—who could punish them for doing wrong, or make any man ashamed of his want of virtue or patriotism. Such a people must fall an easy prey to an invader; for without government no people can remain in security, nor can any nation be defended from its enemies.

By restraining vice, the magistrate prevents men from contracting habits of effeminacy. He guards them from weakness of mind, and excites them to hardihood and patriotism. The great and noble principles of love to our country, of sacrificing private interest to public happiness, of guarding the rights of posterity, and disseminating universal felicity, cannot subsist in a mind narrowed and depraved by criminal indulgence. Vice makes cowards of mankind. It contracts and stifles the noblest principles of human action, and renders men abject in their sentiments and conduct. As far as vice is discountenanced, as far as men are made ashamed of doing base and unworthy actions, so far general security is increased, and the aggregate of national strength is enlarged.

The design of good government is to form a focus to which all the diverging rays of power in a community may be collected, and which may enable a people to bring the force of the whole to one point. This accumulated power protects every individual in his rights; it guards the weak from the violence of the strong, and the few from the oppression of the many. The same power is competent to defend the whole from invasion or other injury. Nothing can be done by way of defence where there is no government. Money cannot be raised. Men cannot be disciplined—nor can any great object be steadily pursued. When a people without government are invaded, every man will propose and pursue his own mode of defence. A thousand different schemes will be thrown out. The people will be distracted in their views; and before this distraction can be calmed, a final conquest may save them the trouble of defending themselves for the future. A nation rent with divisions, destitute of law, of subordination and rulers, presents a proper object for an attack, because it promises an easy if not a valuable conquest. The very people themselves who have been agitated by different scenes, who have no rest for the soles of their feet, who find their lives, their liberties and estates afloat, and exposed to the lawless violence of any who may be pleased to seize them, this people themselves will join an invading army, and prefer any security, any protection to none at all. Without government, indeed, without law and order, there is no liberty, no security, no peace nor prosperity. Men ought to guard their rights; they ought to resist arbitrary power of every kind; they ought to establish a free government; but no people can be safe, no nation can be happy where "every man does what is right in his own eyes," and the people are driven about by the whirlwind of their passions.

If, again, a government is free and just, they will be cheerfully supported by the people in defending their country. Wars too often arise from the ambition or other passions of princes and great men, and the justice of them may be properly doubted. Where an interest exists in the government separate from that of the people, the latter will always feel a jealousy, and will not be ready to give them effectual support. But where "our rulers are from among ourselves, and our governors proceed from the midst of us"; where every man, elevated as his station may be, returns at stated periods to the mass of the people; where our rulers cannot injure us without hurting themselves, we may cheerfully acquiesce in their calls to defend ourselves, and may be sure that they will not wantonly engage in a war, which exposes them as well as us to heavy expense and grievous misfortune. The conscientious soldier, who will not support a war which he does not believe to be lawful, may here feel his mind perfectly at ease, and may discover his skill and his fortitude in defending his injured country, or supporting its just claims. Happy people, who are blessed with such a government! Happy land, shadowed all around with the tree of liberty, and yet strengthened and united by a firm and vigorous government! No wonder that thou art envied by other nations, who are either crushed by arbitrary power, or distressed by confusion and anarchy!

The reasons against indulging to security, and neglecting to provide for defence, I observe once more, operate with peculiar force upon a people whose distant situation prevents their receiving assistance from their allies. The people of Laish were far from the Zidonians, and had no business or connexion with any man. The sacred historian informs us also, that the Danites came "unto Laish, unto a people that were at quiet and secure, and they smote them with the edge of the sword, and burnt the city with fire, and there was no deliverer, because it was far from Zidon." If a people dwelling thus remotely do not defend and help themselves, no one can help them. Before their friends and allies can hear of their distress, it may be complete; and they may be subdued and ruined before the least assistance can be given them. This consideration should operate strongly upon a nation thus situated, and induce them to keep themselves in a constant state of defence; to cultivate military skill and discipline among the inhabitants; to be provided with all the means of defence; to keep a vigilant eye upon the state of all nations, so that they may not be surprised on a sudden; and to put all their fortresses into such a condition, as that they may be able to check a sudden attack, and give time for the people, the natural bulwarks of the state, to assemble and resist their daring invaders.

The past discourse, you must be sensible, hath had a respect to the situation of this country, and the duty of this day. We, my fellow citizens, dwell in a distant part of the world, far removed from any allies, and very little interested in the politics of Europe. This circumstance should not only operate to excite us to pay a close attention to the state of our militia, and the means of our defence, but it should prevent us from engaging in their quarrel, or adopting their wars. Our assistance can be of very little benefit to them, but it may essentially injure us. Our country is young, and cannot bear the loss of men, which is the certain consequence of war. It is free, and does not wish its citizens to mix with the slaves of Europe, and catch their servile manners. It venerates religion, and will find no advantage, should its people associate with those who despise religion, and trample upon every divine law. In case of a war, we cannot be supported or assisted by any European power as they can support one another; and America may be essentially injured before our allies in Europe can know that an enemy has attacked us. GOD in his providence has placed us in a remote part of the world, and if our brethren in other countries "fall out by the way," we will endeavour to reconcile them, but we will not become partners in their quarrels. They have a right to choose their own governments, and manage their own affairs, without our interference. GOD does not call us to war. We are not attacked nor endangered; until we are, we have no right to spill our own blood, or that of our children. Let us then "study the things that make for peace." Let us unite in repressing those restless spirits who cannot see a quarrel going on without inserting themselves in it. Let us be ready constantly to exert our good offices in bringing about peace; and let us devoutly pray that GOD would hasten the time when "wars shall cease from the earth," and the peaceful kingdom of

JESUS CHRIST, which breathes nothing but good will to men, shall universally prevail.

Through the goodness of GOD, America now enjoys a great degree of peace. She has passed through an arduous contest, and having struggled long with formidable distress, she is effectually relieved; and while she breathes the pure and fragrant air of liberty, her prosperity rapidly increases, and her branches extend far and wide. On our frontiers indeed a cloud, not bigger than a man's hand, has arisen, and has extended to a formidable and distressing degree. Our armies have been defeated, and we mourn the brave men who have fallen in the wilderness, and whose bones are now whitening in the sun. It is not for me to determine upon the necessity or expedience of this war. As a minister of religion, I can only wish and pray for peace, and anticipate the time when "the sword of the wilderness" shall destroy no more.

If, my brethren, we mean to guard ourselves from invasion, and to lengthen out our tranquillity, we must cultivate a good government; we must reverence the laws, and support the magistrate in "putting to shame those that do evil." It is a duty enjoined by our holy religion to submit to such government, and it is a maxim founded in eternal truth, that no people can be conquered or destroyed who are united in supporting a free and good constitution. A consciousness of being freemen, of being protected in the enjoyment of life and property, by laws which know not the rich from the poor, or the great from the small; this consciousness will give men elevation of sentiment; it will inspire them with fortitude and perseverance, and make them superior to all the slaves and sycophants upon earth.

While we support our various constitutions of government, and guard against intestine divisions, we ought to pay a strict attention to the state of our militia, and the other means of defence. Americans will never suffer a standing army among them in time of peace. The militia are the natural defenders of this country. They have a stake in it. They have a share in its sovereignty; and they fight for their wives, their children, their liberty, and their all. Such men cannot be cowards; they must be brave and determined; and when any of these blessings are taken from them, or threatened to be done away, they will be "like a bear robbed of her whelps," and will determine to conquer or die.

But this very ardor and impetuosity may be fatal to them, unless they are under the direction of judgment and discipline. These are necessary to check their effervescences, and lead their efforts to such points as may be most beneficial. Our militia then should be disciplined. Our young men should be early instructed in the art of war, and every one should hold himself in readiness to "play the man for his people, and the cities of his GOD." Let us have our fortresses in good repair, and be ready at all points to resist an invasion; and this is the most likely method to prevent it.

Your institution, gentlemen of the Ancient and Honorable Artillery Company, is designed to answer this important purpose, and is a striking proof of the wisdom and foresight of our ancestors. Venerable men! My heart warms when I view the schools, the colleges, the churches which they founded; and when I see this company assembled, so admirably adapted "upon all our glory to create a defence." Methinks I see them looking down from the seats of bliss, smiling to behold this favourite institution flourishing and increasing; delighting themselves in the good of which they thus laid the foundation, and charging us to transmit the freedom and happiness which they have given us, a fair and a large inheritance to the latest posterity!

You are citizens, gentlemen, as well as soldiers, and you know the necessity of order and government. These you will feel it your duty to support and preserve, while you value and defend the liberty of your country. You know that these duties do not interfere. You know that without government freedom cannot subsist, because government alone can protect the helpless individual, or restrain the lordly tyrant. You know also that a free government is necessary to animate and direct the efforts of a people in their own defence, and that the tree of liberty never flourishes, unless it is preserved from rude violence by the sacred barriers of law and justice.

Countenanced by the commander in chief, who himself formerly led a corps in some respects similar to your own, and encouraged by the good wishes and plaudits of your fellow citizens, you are becoming every year more useful and respectable. The choice which you have made of men to command you, who have known not only the parade, but the reality of war, and have bravely defended the liberties of America, has done you and your country honor. Men of the first abilities have been heretofore the objects of your choice; and I hope that the elections of this day will prove, that you are still governed by the same wisdom and prudence, which in this respect have heretofore marked your conduct.

Should you be called to defend your country, or protect its rights, I have no doubt but that you would prove your military skill to be no impediment to brave and valorous exertions. Sure I am, that you would never turn your backs to an enemy, or suffer yourselves to be defeated. You are Americans. You are descendants of men, who sacrificed every thing to assert their liberty. Many of you have "jeoparded your lives on the high places of the field," and your bosoms glow with genuine patriotism. Such men are invincible. Nothing can subdue them but the power of that Being who hath declared, "that the race is not always to the swift, nor the battle to the strong."

Go on, gentlemen, and prosper. In peace prepare for war. Cultivate in your own breasts, and impress upon your children, an ardent love to civil and religious liberty. And while you discharge your duty to society, forget not the Being who has made you what you are, at whose tribunal you must all stand, and whose "favour is better than life." If you submit to his Gospel, and are governed in heart and in life by its precepts, you shall be made "more than conquerors"; your brows shall be adorned with unfading laurels, and your triumphs shall be complete and eternal!

We live, my brethren of this assembly, in a day when grand and important scenes are acting upon the theatre of the world. We have seen "kings led in chains, and nobles in fetters of iron." We have seen the towers of despotism, erected in dark ages, and sacred to the uses of tyranny and oppression, tumbling to the ground, and razed to their foundations. We hear "of wars and rumours of wars." Mankind "bite and devour one another." "Brother is pursuing brother unto death," and the earth is crimsoned, deeply crimsoned, with Christian blood. Humanity sheds a tear over the folly of her sons, but faith lifts her keen and humble eye from earth to heaven, and anticipates the good which shall come out of this evil: She expects the fulfilment of those precious promises which speak of the future peace and happiness of man; and teaches us to exclaim, "amidst the wreck of nature and the crush of worlds," Alleluia, the Lord GOD omnipotent reigneth."

A M E N

40

A SERMON ON THE ANNIVERSARY OF THE INDEPENDENCE OF AMERICA

Samuel Miller

NEW-YORK

1793

SAMUEL MILLER (1769–1850). A native of Delaware, Miller was educated at home by his father, Reverend John Miller, and his brothers, followed by a year at the University of Pennsylvania and theological training with Reverend John Nisbet, principal of Dickinson College. He was ordained a Presbyterian minister in New York City in 1793 (the year of the sermon reprinted here) and eventually became pastor of the Wall Street congregation that later became First Presbyterian Church. He was appointed professor of church history and government at Princeton Theological Seminary, which he had helped to found in 1813. Under Miller, Archibald Alexander, and George Hodge, the seminary dominated Princeton for over fifty years.

A man of great energy, Miller published dozens of books and pamphlets on a wide range of subjects, from suicide, to slavery, to the theater. His *Brief Retrospect of the Eighteenth Century* (2 vols., 1803) won him honorary D.D.s from Union College and from the University of Pennsylvania. He was a founder of the New York Bible Society, a corresponding member of the Philological Society of Manchester, England, corresponding secretary of the New Historical Society, a trustee of both Columbia College and the College of New Jersey, historian and later moderator of the Presbyterian General Assembly, and chaplain of the first regiment of the New York State artillery.

Although Miller was not a striking preacher, he was a good one, and the quality of his mind and depth of learning are reflected in the sermon from July 4, 1793, published here.

A SERMON,

PREACHED IN NEW-YORK, JULY 4th, 1793.

BEING THE

ANNIVERSARY

OF THE

INDEPENDENCE OF AMERICA:

AT THE REQUEST OF THE

TAMMANY SOCIETY, OR COLUMBIAN ORDER.

BY SAMUEL MILLER, A. M.

ONE OF THE MINISTERS OF THE UNITED PRESBYTERIAN CHURCHES, IN THE CITY OF NEW-YORK.

NEW-YORK—PRINTED BY THOMAS GREENLEAF.

And where the Spirit of the Lord is, there is Liberty.

II. Corinthians, iii. 17.

In contemplating national advantages, and national happiness, numerous are the objects which present themselves to a wise and reflecting patriot. While he remembers the past, with thankfulness and triumph; and while he looks forward, with glowing anticipation, to future glories, he will by no means forget to enquire into the secret springs, which had an active influence in the former, and which, there is reason to believe, will be equally connected with the latter.

These ideas naturally arise, in the mind of every American citizen, especially on this anniversary of our country's natal hour. While we review, with gratitude and exultation, the various steps which have paved the way for our political advancement, we are obviously led to search for the happy principles, which laid at the foundation of these —and while we suffer fancy to draw aside, for a moment, the veil which covers futurity, and to disclose its bright scenes, we cannot overlook the same objects, on the extension and farther influence of which, we are to build our hopes.

We have convened, indeed, principally to celebrate the completion of another year of freedom to our western world. We are to keep this day as a memorial of the time which gave rise to the precious privileges we enjoy, as a sovereign and independent people. It may, therefore, be imagined, that our only proper employment, on the present occasion, is, to take a retrospect of the interesting scenes, which that glorious æra presented to the mind, and to recount the noble atchievements, which, under the direction of infinite wisdom, laid the foundation of our prosperity and happiness. But why should our chief attention be directed toward these objects? They are objects, indeed, upon which to gaze, delight and elevate the patriotic mind. They are objects, which, to lose sight of, is to forfeit the character of a faithful citizen. But, at the same time, they are objects too familiar to all present to need the formality of repetition. I address many of those who were near witnesses of these stupendous transactions; and not a few who were agents in the important work. Whose hearts burn within them, at the recollection of events, which the world beheld with amazement: and who view with transport, the political greatness which these events were the means of ushering in, and establishing in our country.

In an audience of this description, then, where is the necessity of my trespassing on your patience, by a bare recital of what is so well known, and so feelingly remembered? Where is the need of my attempting, with minute care, to call up to your view, the patriotic and wise management of our counsels, in those trying times—the fortitude and enthusiastic ardor of our heroes—the splendor of our conquests—or the dignity and glory to which we are exalted by the supreme Arbiter of nations? Rather let us turn our attention to the grand Source, from which we are to expect the long continuance, and the happy increase of these invaluable gifts of heaven.

And to this choice of a subject I am also led by the recollection, that the respectable society to which this discourse is, in a particular manner, addressed, hold up, as the great object of their attention, every thing that may tend to promote the progress of civil liberty, and to transmit it, pure and undefiled, to the latest posterity. They profess to stand as guardians over those inestimable rights and privileges, which have been so dearly purchased, and, in general, to seek, in every form, the advantage of their country. To an association established upon such laudable principles, nothing that is included in these great outlines of their system, can be considered either as foreign to their plan, or beneath their attention. Nothing can be considered entirely inapplicable to their designs, in celebrating this auspicious day, that is, in any degree, connected with the promotion of public dignity and happiness.

It is under this impression, my fellow citizens, that I propose, on the present occasion, to offer you a few general remarks on the important influence of the Christian religion in promoting political freedom. And, as the foundation of these remarks, I have chosen the words which have just been read in your hearing.

I am well aware, that these words, taken in their proper sense, have a principal reference to liberty of a different kind from that to which I would accommodate and apply them. They refer to that glorious deliverance from the power, and the ignoble chains of sin and satan, which is effected by the Spirit of the Lord, in every soul, in which his special and saving influences are found. They point out, also, that release from the bondage of the legal administration, which the gospel affords to all who receive it in sincerity and truth. But, as I am persuaded the proposition contained in our text is equally true, whether we understand it as speaking of spiritual or political liberty, we may safely apply it to the latter, without incurring the charge of unnatural perversion.

The sentiment, then, which I shall deduce from the text, and to illustrate and urge which, shall be the principal object of the present discourse, is, *That the general prevalence of real Christianity, in any government, has a direct and immediate tendency to promote, and to confirm therein, political liberty.*

This important truth may be established, both by attending to the nature of this religion, in an abstract view; and by adverting to fact, and the experimental testimony with which we are furnished by history.

That the corrupt passions and the vices of men, have, in all ages of the world, been the grand source and support of tyranny, and of every species of political and domestic oppression, is a truth too well known, and too generally admitted, to require formal proof, on the present occasion. A moment's reflection on the nature of tyranny, and of those dispositions in the constituent members of society, which lead to its origin and advancement, is sufficient to convince every unprejudiced mind, that human depravity is the life and the soul of slavery. What was it that first raised this monster from the infernal regions, and gave him a dwelling among men, but ignorance, on the one hand, and on the other, ambition and pride? These his complotters and associates, proceeding in a state of indissoluble connection, have always held up his deformed head, and wielded his iron rod. Together they have invariably come into being—together they have lived and flourished—and into one common grave have they sunk at last.

The truth is, that political liberty does not rest, solely, on the form of government, under which a nation may happen to live. It does not consist, altogether, in the arrangement or in the balance of power; nor even in the rights and privileges which the constitution offers to every citizen. These indeed, must be acknowledged to have a considerable effect in its promotion or decline. But we shall find, on a close inspection, that something else is of equal, if not of greater importance. Cases may easily be conceived, where, without a single material or glaring deficiency in any of these, true and desirable liberty may be almost unknown: and, on the other hand, where, under the most wretched organization of government, the substance of freedom may exist and flourish. Human laws are too imperfect, in themselves, to secure completely this inestimable blessing. It must have its seat in the hearts and dispositions of those individuals which compose the body politic; and it is with the hearts and dispositions of men that Christianity is conversant. When, therefore, that *perfect law of liberty*, which this holy religion includes, prevails and governs in the minds of all, their freedom rests upon a basis more solid and immoveable, than human wisdom can devise. For the obvious tendency of this divine system, in all its parts, is, in the language of its great Author, to bring *deliverance to the captives, and the opening of the prison to them that are bound; to undo the heavy burthens; to let the oppressed go free; and to break every yoke*. But to be more particular—

The prevalence of real Christianity, tends to promote the principles and the love of political freedom, by the doctrines which it teaches, concerning the human character, and the unalienable rights of mankind; and by the virtues which it inculcates, and leads its votaries to practice. Let us take a hasty view of each of these—

Can oppression and slavery prevail among any people who properly understand, and are suitably impressed with, those great gospel truths, that all men are, by nature, equal—children of the same common Father—dependent upon the same mighty power, and candidates for the same glorious immortality? Must not despotism hide his head in those regions, where the relations of man to man are distinctly realized—where citizens, of every rank, are considered as a band of brethren, and where the haughty pretensions of family and blood, are viewed in all their native absurdity, and in those odious colours in which this sublime system represents them? In short, must not every sentiment, favorable to slavery, be forever banished from a nation, in which, by means of the benign light of the glorious sun of righteousness, all the human race are viewed as subject to the same great laws, and amenable to the same awful tribunal, in the end.

Christianity, on the one hand, teaches those, who are raised to places of authority, that they are not intrinsically greater than those whom they govern; and that all the rational and justifiable power with which they are invested, flows from the people, and is dependent on their sovereign pleasure. There is a love of dominion natural to every human creature; and in those who are destitute of religion, this temper is apt to reign uncontrouled. Hence experience has always testified, that rulers, left to themselves, are prone to imagine, that they are a superior order of beings, to obey whom, the ignoble multitude was made, and that their aggrandizement is the principal design of the social compact. But the religion of the gospel, rightly understood, and cordially embraced, utterly disclaims such unworthy sentiments, and banishes them with abhorrence from the mind. It contemplates the happiness of the community, as the primary object of all political associations—and it teaches those, who are placed at the helm of government, to remember, that they are called to preside over equals and friends, whose best interest, and not the demands of selfishness, is to be the object of their first and highest care.

On the other hand, Christianity, wherever it exerts its native influence, leads every citizen to reverence himself—to cherish a free and manly spirit—to think with boldness and energy—to form his principles upon fair enquiry, and to resign neither his conscience nor his person to the capricious will of men. It teaches, and it creates in the mind, a noble contempt for that abject submission to the encroachments of despotism, to which the ignorant and the unprincipled readily yield. It forbids us to call, or to acknowledge, any one master upon earth, knowing that we have a Master in heaven, to whom both rulers, and those whom they govern, are equally accountable. In a word, Christianity, by illuminating the minds of men, leads them to consider themselves, as they really are, all co-ordinate terrestrial princes, stripped, indeed, of the empty pageantry and title, but retaining the substance of dignity and power. Under the influence of this illumination, how natural to disdain the shackles of oppression—to take the alarm at every attempt to trample on their just rights; and to pull down, with indignation, from the seat of authority, every bold invader!

But again—The prevalence of Christianity promotes the principles and the love of political freedom, not only by the knowledge which it affords of the human character, and of the unalienable rights of mankind, but also by the duties which it inculcates, and leads its votaries to discharge.

The fruits of the spirit are, justice, love, gentleness, meekness, and temperance: Or, in other words, these are among the distinguished graces and duties, which the Christian system not only commands us constantly to regard, but which it creates in the mind, and which are found to prevail, in a greater or smaller degree, in all who sincerely adopt it. Now these are unquestionably the grand supports of pure and undefiled liberty—they stand equally opposed to the chains of tyranny, and to the licentiousness of anarchy.

It is a truth denied by few, at the present day, that political and domestic slavery are inconsistent with justice, and that these must necessarily wage eternal war—so that, wherever the latter exists in perfection, the former must fly before her, or fall prostrate at her feet. What, then, would be the happy consequence, if that golden rule of our holy religion, which enjoins, that we should do unto all men whatever we would wish that they should do unto us, were universally received and adopted? We should hear no more of rulers plundering their fellow citizens of a single right; nor of the people refusing that obedience to equitable laws, which the public good requires. We should see no oppressor claiming from his equals, a subjection which they did not owe; nor should we see the latter lifting up their lawless hands, to resent the reasonable requisitions of an authority constituted by themselves. In short, were this principle universally to predominate, we should see nothing, on the one side, but demands founded on a sincere regard to the general interest; and, on the other, that ready compliance, which promotes the peace and happiness of society.

No less extensively beneficial in its effects on civil liberty, is that pure and refined benevolence, which the Christian system inculcates, and establishes in the minds of those who are under its government. Though the constitution of a country be ever so defective; yet if every rank of citizens be under the habitual influence of that universal charity and good will, which is one of the distinguished glories of our holy religion, there will freedom substantially flourish. To suppose that oppression, with the numerous hell-born woes, which follow in his train, can be cherished in regions, where the mild spirit of benevolence and love reigns, is to suppose that the most discordant principles are capable of uniting; that demons of darkness, and angels of light can dwell together in harmony. Impossible! Wherever that heavenly temper is found, which, like the Deity himself, delights in showering down blessings, both on enemies and friends; there will the unalienable rights of men be acknowledged, and every infringement of them will be viewed with abhorrence.*

Nor let us omit to take notice of the peculiar temperance and moderation, which the gospel system enjoins. These are of no less importance, with respect to their influence on political happiness, in general, and especially as they affect the interest of civil liberty. It is an observation as old as the fact upon which it is founded, that nothing more certainly tends, to subvert the principles of freedom, and abate a laudable enthusiasm for republican equality, than a departure from that simplicity of manners, and that prevailing moderation, which our religion inculcates and promotes. Ever since the establishment of civil society, the words of the Roman poet, when speaking of his own country, have been applicable to most great empires—

Sævior armis
Luxuria incubuit, victumque ulcisitur orbem.

Juv.

But for this evil, there is no preventive that promises so much success, no cure so effectual, as that which is here presented. Christianity, more powerful than human strength, and more efficacious than human law, regulates the passions, and roots out the corruptions of men. It not only tames the savage breast, and gives a deadly blow to barbarity of manners; but also tends to quench every extravagant thirst for power; to beat down every high thought, that exalteth itself

*Here it will, perhaps, be objected, that however just these remarks may appear in theory, yet their force is not a little weakened, by adverting to the numerous persecutions and wars, to which Christianity has given rise. But let it be remembered, that Christianity has been more frequently the mere pretext, than the true motive, of those mutiplied acts of cruelty and intolerance, which sully the pages of history. Generally have the offspring of ambition, revenge, or some equally corrupt principle, been attributed to religion, and supposed to have nothing else for their origin. But admitting for a moment, that Christianity has in reality, been the cause of much mischief of this kind; yet it was Christianity shamefully misunderstood, and impiously perverted. It was not the pure and benevolent system of the gospel, but blind zeal and mad fanaticism.

against the general good; and to render men contented with those rights which the God of nature gave them. While these dispositions prevail, slavery must stand at an awful distance, bound in chains, and

> Liberty, fair daughter of the skies!
> Walk in majestic splendor o'er the land,
> Breathing her joys around—

Having thus contemplated, in an abstract view, the native tendency of the Christian religion, to promote civil liberty; let us now take our stand with history, that mistress of wisdom, and friend of virtue, who from her exalted station, causes human events to pass in review, before her impartial tribunal.

When we compare those nations, in which Christianity was unknown, with those which have been happily favored with the light of spiritual day, we find ample reason to justify the remarks which have been made. It may be asserted, with few exceptions, that there never was a regularly organized government, since the foundation of the world, where the true religion was not received, in which political slavery did not hold a gloomy reign.* It has been generally found, indeed, that in proportion as the faint glimmerings of the light of nature, with which pagan nations were favored, gathered strength, and grew in brightness, in the same proportion has something like social freedom been promoted and extended. But these glimmerings have still proved inadequate to the desirable purpose, of imparting to their liberty a consistent and permanent character.† As examples of this truth, you will readily recur to the African and Asiatic kingdoms, not excepting some in other quarters of the globe.

On the other hand, it may be observed, with equal confidence, and with fewer exceptions, that there never was a government, in which

*To relate the enormities of despotism, and the consequent degradation and wretchedness to which human nature has been reduced, in many parts of the globe, would be equally shocking and incredible to an American ear. How must the lives and fortunes of men have been trampled upon, among the Mexicans, when, at the dedication of their great temple, we are told they had 60 or 70,000 human sacrifices; and that the usual amount of them, annually, was about 20,000! See Clavigero's History of Mexico, vol. I, page 281.

†The republics of Greece and Rome must be acknowledged, in some degree, exceptions to this general remark. But even among them, numerous were the instances in which the aspect of their political affairs bore testimony to their sad want of Christian knowledge.

the knowledge of pure and undefiled Christianity prevailed, in which, at the same time, despotism held his throne without controul.* It is true indeed, that in the Christian world, during those centuries wherein gross superstition reigned, and the truth was buried in darkness, slavery reared his head, and scattered his poison among men. It is true, that then, the cloud of oppression sat thick and deep over the nations, and the world was threatened with a relapse into ancient barbarity. But when, at the auspicious æra of the reformation, the great source of day rose again upon the benighted world; when the true knowledge of the Lord revived, the truth speedily made men free. When, in this splendid and glorious light, they began to see what they were, and what they ought to be; they delayed not to cast off their chains, and to assert their rights, with dignity and independence. This is the light, which ever since those days, has been gradually undermining the throne of tyranny in Europe.† This is the light, which, gathering strength and refinement, by its passage over the mighty deep, hath kindled a flame in this western world, which, we trust, will continue to blaze, with encreasing brightness, while the sun and moon shall endure.

Nor is it political slavery alone, that yields to the mild and benign spirit of Christianity. Experience has shewn, that domestic slavery also flies before her, unable to stand the test of her pure and holy tribunal. After the introduction of this religion into the Roman em-

*"Christianity, says Baron Montesquieu, has prevented despotism from being established in Ethiopia, notwithstanding the heat of the climate, the largeness of the empire, and its situation in the midst of African despotic states."

†One of the bitterest enemies of Christianity, Mr. Hume, observes, that "the precious sparks of liberty were kindled and preserved by the Puritans in England; and that, to this sect, whose principles appear so frivolous, and whose habits so ridiculous, the English owe the whole freedom of their constitution." The unfounded and malicious reflection which this passage contains, deserves no comment. The concession is worthy of notice, as it is the concession of an adversary.

It may also be mentioned, in this place, that out of the 17 provinces of the Low Countries, which groaned under the tyranny of Philip II. only the 7, now called the United Provinces, which admitted and established the principles of the reformation, succeeded in their attempts to throw off the Spanish yoke. The rest, indeed, made a faint effort to gain their liberty, but failed; and are not, to this day, a free people. A remarkable testimony, that Christianity can only be expected to exert her native influence, and produce the happiest effects, when she appears in her beautiful simplicity, stripped of that gaudy and deforming attire, with which corrupt and ambitious men have ever been disposed to clothe her.

pire, every law that was made, relating to slaves, was in their favor, abating the rigors of servitude, until, at last, all the subjects of the empire were reckoned equally free.*

Humanity, indeed, is still left to deplore the continuance of domestic slavery, in countries blest with Christian knowledge, and political freedom. The American patriot must heave an involuntary sigh, at the recollection, that, even in these happy and singularly favored republics, this offspring of infernal malice, and parent of human debasement, is yet suffered to reside. Alas, that we should so soon forget the principles, upon which our wonderful revolution was founded! But, to the glory of our holy religion, and to the honor of many benevolent minds, this monster has received a fatal blow, and will soon, we hope, fall expiring to the ground. Already does he tremble, as if his destruction were at hand. With pleasure do we behold many evident presages of the approaching period, when Christianity shall extend her sceptre of benevolence and love over every part of this growing empire—when oppression shall not only be softened of his rigours; but shall take his flight forever from our land.

That happier times, and a more extensive prevalence of liberty, are not far distant, there are numerous reasons to believe. If so signal and glorious has been the influence of Christianity, in promoting political and domestic freedom, notwithstanding her restrained and narrow operation among men, what may we not expect, when her dominion shall become universal? If such have been her trophies, amidst so much opposition, and the continual struggles of contrary principles, what may we not indulge the hope of seeing, when her empire shall be coextensive with terrestrial inhabitants—when *the knowledge of the Lord shall cover the earth, as the waters cover the depths of the sea?*

Then, may we not conclude, that universal harmony and love, and

*When Pope Gregory the great, who flourished toward the end of the 6th century, gave liberty to some of his slaves, he offered this reason for it—"Cum Redemptor noster, totius Conditor naturæ, ad hoc propitiatus, humanam carnem volueret assumere, ut divinitatis suæ gratia, dirempto (quo tenebamur captivi) vinculo, pristinæ nos restitueret libertati: salubriter agitur, si homines, quos ab initio liberos natura protulit, et jus gentium jugo substituit servitutis, in eá, quá nati fuerant, manumittentis leneficio, libertati reddantur." Gregor : Magn : ap. Potgiess : lib. iv. c. I. sect. 3. What a triumph is here exhibited, of Christian principles, over the sordid dictates of pride and selfishness! Would to God we could more frequently hear this language, and see corresponding practice, in Christians of the present day!

as the necessary consequence of these, universal liberty, shall prevail? Then, may we not confidently hope, that oppression shall be as much abhorred, and as much unknown, as freedom is, at present, in many parts of the globe? That the name of man, of whatever nation, or kindred, or people, or tongue, shall then be the signal of brotherly affection: When the whole human race, uniting as a band of brethren, shall know no other wishes, than to promote their common happiness, and to glorify their common God: When *there shall be nothing to hurt nor destroy in all the holy mountain of God—when the desart shall rejoice, and blossom as the rose; and when the kingdoms of this world, shall become the kingdoms of our Lord, and of his Christ?*

Imagine not, my fellow citizens, that these are the flights of a vain and disordered fancy. The sacred volume teaches us to *comfort one another with these words*, and to triumph in the glorious prospect. The Author of truth himself, bids us look forward, with joy and gladness, to—

The blest Immanuel's gentle reign;

—when, *from the rising of the sun, to the going down thereof, his name shall have free course and be glorified.*

To the introduction of these happy days, it seems as if the present time afforded many hopeful preludes. Can we turn our eyes to the European states and kingdoms—can we behold their convulsive struggles, without considering them as all tending to hasten this heavenly æra? Especially, can we view the interesting situation of our affectionate allies, without indulging the delightful hope, that the sparks, which are there seen rising toward heaven, though in tumultuous confusion, shall soon be the means of kindling a general flame, which shall illuminate the darkest and remotest corners of the earth, and pour upon them the effulgence of tenfold glory?

The splendor of their prospects is, indeed, not altogether unclouded. But, we trust, that every difficulty and disorder will speedily vanish, and give place to harmony, and efficient government. We trust, that *He who rides in the whirlwind, and directs the storm*, will wield their fierce democracy with his mighty arm—hush the rude noise of war in their borders—breathe propitious upon their counsels—and, in the end, crown their exertions with abundant success.

The glorious structure, which this once oppressed people are employed in erecting, has been assailed by numerous malignant foes. Black, and awfully threatning clouds have hung over it—the rains have descended—the floods have poured forth—the winds have blown —they have all beat violently upon it; but, as if founded upon a rock, it has yet stood. And we hope it will stand. We hope that, bidding calm defiance to the fury of every tempest, it will continue to rise with increasing greatness, until time shall be no more. Cease, then! ye shortsighted sons of ambition, who would oppose this important work; ye who delight in oppression, and who feed on the miseries and debasement of men; cease to imagine, that by your feeble arm, you shall be able to withstand the Mighty One of Israel! Remember, that if this cause be of the Lord, you cannot overcome it; and if, haply, you be found fighting against God, your labors, like those of the unhappy sufferer of old, will but revert upon your own heads.

Let the haughty kings of the earth, then, set themselves, and the rulers take counsel together, against the Lord, and against the work of his hands;—He that sitteth in the heavens will laugh—the Lord will have them in derision. If this wonderful Revolution be, as we trust, a great link in the chain, that is drawing on the reign of universal harmony and peace; if it be occasioned by christian principles, and be designed to pave the way for their complete establishment, however it may appear to be sullied by irreligion and vice,* it is the cause of God, and will at last prevail.

*The author is well aware, that, in offering his sentiments, thus freely, on the French Revolution, he stands upon controverted ground. It would, therefore, ill become his inexperience, and more particularly his profession, to enter into the details, or the warmth of this argument. He cannot help thinking, however, that the great pillars of this Revolution rest upon those natural rights of men, which are assumed by the best writers on government; and upon those fundamental principles of religion which the Author of our natures has revealed.

It is objected to this revolution, that it has been stained by violence and inhumanity of the most attrocious and unnecessary kind. Wherever a life has been wantonly destroyed, or other severities unnecessarily inflicted, no one should withhold his censure. But shall we make no distinction between the crimes of an enraged multitude, and the decisions of constituted authorities? or, between the precipitancy of a popular assembly, at the crisis of a struggle, and the deliberations of settled government? When a nation, so long distressed, lifts her avenging arm, and breaks her chains on the heads of her oppressors; when a people make a violent effort, to overturn the mountains of despotism under which they are buried, can we expect perfect wisdom, prudence, and moderation to guide all their exertions? While man remains such a creature as he is, this would be a miracle indeed!

But it will be further asked—Why, since the great object of this discourse is to establish a natural connection between christianity and political liberty; why, in France,

Having thus commented, in a general manner, on some of the leading objects, which presented themselves from the passage of scripture which was chosen, the first emotions which naturally arise, both from the preceding remarks, and this interesting occasion, are those of gratitude and of praise. Here, happily, our thankfulness as patriots, and our thankfulness as christians, perfectly coincide, and are inseparably connected together.

Let us unite, then, in offering our grateful acknowledgments, to the Sovereign Dispenser of all blessings, that, while many nations are covered with the mantle of darkness and superstition; and in consequence of this, are groaning under the yoke of servitude; the Sun of righteousness hath risen upon us, with healing in his wings; and hath taught us, in a political view, to know, and to maintain our proper character. Let us bless his holy name, that, under the influence of this light, we have been led to assert the dignity of human nature—to throw off the chains of oppression—to think and act for ourselves, and to acknowledge no other king than the *King of the universe*. Let us bless his name, that, under the guidance of the same light, we have been led to frame a constitution, which recognizes the natural and

amidst the prevalence of the latter, does the former appear to be so little respected and acknowledged, especially among the principal friends and promoters of the revolution? Why do we not see a remarkable attention to real religion, amidst so many exertions to secure the rights of men? The answer is, that Christianity, considered as a system of principles, in theory, may produce extensive effects, where its special and saving influence is extremely small. Nay, every attentive observer of human affairs, has doubtless discovered a secret but important operation of these principles, on minds actually despising and rejecting them. The one half of that light, in which infidels boast, as the splendid result of reason alone, is, in fact, the light of revelation; and while they contemn its grand Source, they adopt and use it, in all their religious creeds, and in many of their daily actions. A small extension of this thought, will, perhaps, when applied to the French nation, and to all similar cases, go far toward solving the difficulty in question—that people may be acting in the light of christian principles, though they know it not, neither regard them. A deliverance from the darkness of superstition, may have led them, at once, to cast off the chains of tyranny, and to renounce even the just restraints of real Christianity.

But, after all; is there not reason to hope, that many of the accounts which have been circulated in America, respecting the disorder, vice, and contempt of all sacred things, prevalent in France, are totally groundless? Is it not possible, that there is much more regularity, decorum, and real religion, in that struggling Republic, than her neighboring enemies, so fond of misrepresentation and calumny, are willing to allow? That many shameful instances of exaggeration have been detected is well known.

unalienable rights of men; which renounces all limits to human liberty, but those which necessity and wisdom prescribe; and whose great object is, the general good. *O give thanks unto the Lord! for he is good; for his mercy endureth forever. Let the redeemed of the Lord say so, whom he hath redeemed from the oppressor, and delivered from all their destructions. O that men would praise the Lord, for his goodness, and for his wonderful works to the children of men!*

Again; if it be a solemn truth, that the prevalence of Christianity, has a natural and immediate tendency to promote political freedom, then, those are the truest and the wisest patriots, who study to encrease its influence in society. Hence it becomes every American citizen to consider this as the great palladium of our liberty, demanding our first and highest care.

The Lord hath done great things for us, whereof we are glad. The lines are fallen unto us in pleasant places, yea, we have a goodly heritage. We possess an extensive, noble country. Fertility and beauty vie with each other, in favor of our ease, accommodation, and delight. Every avenue to national importance, and the felicity of individuals, is opened wide. Let it, then, in addition to all these advantages, and to complete its glory, let it be Immanuel's land. This will refine, and inconceivably appreciate your freedom. This will render you at once the pattern, and the wonder of the world.

To each of you, then, my fellow citizens, on this anniversary of our independence, be the solemn address made! Do you wish to *stand fast in that liberty, wherewith* the Governor of the universe *hath made you free?* Do you desire the encreasing prosperity of your country? Do you wish to see the law respected—good order preserved, and universal peace to prevail? Are you convinced, that purity of morals is necessary for these important purposes? Do you believe, that the Christian religion is the firmest basis of morality? Fix its credit, then, by adopting it yourselves, and spread its glory by the lustre of your example! And while you tell to your children, and to your children's children, the wonderful works of the Lord, and the great deliverance which he hath wrought out for us, teach them to remember the Author of these blesssings, and they will know how to estimate their value. Teach them to acknowledge the God of heaven as their King, and they will despise submission to earthly despots. Teach them to be Christians, and they will ever be free!

And O, thou exalted Source of liberty! not only grant and secure to us political freedom; but may we all, by the effectual working of thy mighty power, and through the mediation of Christ Jesus, be brought into the glorious liberty of the sons of GOD; that when this world, and all that is therein, shall be burnt up, we may become citizens of a better country, that is an heavenly.

AMEN

41

AN ORATION IN COMMEMORATION OF THE INDEPENDENCE OF THE UNITED STATES OF AMERICA

Enos Hitchcock

PROVIDENCE

1793

Enos Hitchcock (1745-1803). A 1767 graduate of Harvard College, Hitchcock was a minister in Beverly, Massachusetts, and Providence, Rhode Island. He saw extensive action as chaplain during the Revolution. He was first appointed chaplain in 1776 to serve with the Third Massachusetts Continentals on their way to Crown Point and Ticonderoga. The following year he was at Ticonderoga and Saratoga when, just after the defeat of Burgoyne, captured Tories wearing Indian war paint were driven through the streets. He spent much of 1778 with his brigade at Valley Forge. At West Point the following year, the circumstances were nearly as bad as they had been at Valley Forge. And so it went through the rest of the war.

He had been home in Beverly off and on between campaigns, but finally he resigned his post there in 1780 and moved to the First Congregational Church in Providence, where he remained. His theology moved from Arminian to Unitarian over the years, but in the many disputes over doctrine, he always took a reconciling line; he would, for instance, baptize by immersion those who asked for it. He apparently had wealth, independent of his minister's salary, perhaps from his wife's family's property in Maine. He raised a fine parsonage and lived well. He was a friend of Dr. Ezra Stiles, president of Yale, who conferred an M.A. on him in 1781. He received a D.D. from Brown University in 1788, where he had been a trustee since 1782. He campaigned for the abolition of slavery and, advocating free public education, he warned: "What will be the state of American government, if they are not nurtured by general education, and strengthened by public virtue, let the fate of many fallen republics tell!" (*A Discourse on Education* [Providence, 1785], p. 10).

Hitchcock was a popular participant in patriotic events, was first chaplain of the Society of the Cincinnati in Rhode Island, and went to Philadelphia in 1787 for the constitutional convention. He campaigned for Rhode Island's ratification of the Constitution, which he regarded as the plan for a perfect government, while the alternative to federalism was anarchy.

These views can be seen in the Fourth of July, 1793, oration reprinted here, delivered at the Baptist meeting-house. Hitchcock kept extensive diaries during the war, the surviving ones being in the hands of the Rhode Island Historical Society and largely published in their *Collections* (vol. 7). He published a number of sermons and pam-

A N

O R A T I O N,

IN COMMEMORATION OF

The INDEPENDENCE of the UNITED STATES of *America.*

DELIVERED

In the *Baptist* Meeting-House in PROVIDENCE, *July* 4th, 1793.

By ENOS HITCHCOCK, D. D.

Printed by J. CARTER.

phlets on patriotic themes and two large works on domestic matters: *Memoirs of the Bloomsgrove Family* (2 vols., 1790); and *The Farmer's Friend, or the History of Mr. Charles Worthy* (1793). The former work, dedicated to Martha Washington, addressed the problems of child-rearing (some of it not quite to modern taste, perhaps, such as punishing children by dipping their little heads in ice water.)

The return of this anniversary hath reminded us, my respected fellow-citizens, of an event full of wonders, and pregnant with consequences important, not to this country only, but to mankind. Called again to felicitate you on this memorable day, I feel myself secure in your candour to those sentimental effusions which the occasion may suggest. There is a pleasure in the idea of addressing a free and an enlightened people, on the blessings they enjoy, and on the happiness of their condition. Americans! this day recognizes your emancipation. It is your jubilee. It is the birth-day of your independence, of your national existence! Let it never be forgotten, that, on the fourth day of July, one thousand seven hundred and seventy-six, forth issued from the illustrious and patriotic Congress the following magnanimous declaration:

"We, therefore, the Representatives of the United States of America, in Congress assembled, appealing to the Supreme Judge of the World for the rectitude of our intentions, do, in the name and by authority of the good people of these Colonies, solemnly publish and declare, that these *United Colonies* are, and of right ought to be, *free and independent States*."

This declaration was accompanied with the reasons which compelled them to make it, and which were deemed sufficient to justify the measure in the view of the world. It was nobly made at the most eventful period of the war, when your country was bleeding at every pore, without a friend among the nations of the earth. God alone was her friend! The justice of her cause was registered in the high chancery of heaven. The stars fought in their courses for her; and the event justified a step which had so astonished the world.

To retrace the steps which led to the accomplishment of the revolution, and the causes which prepared the way for it, would be to enter into a field of discussion too large for the present occasion. It would be to repeat what has already been done in a thousand forms. Historians have collected and arranged the great mass of materials. Orators have marked, in polished periods, the great outlines of the revolution. Poets have sung its praises, and, stretching forward on the prophetic wing, the vocal muse hath assigned to it every good of which so great an event can be productive. The subject, however, is not exhausted. Sentimental gleanings still remain to be gathered through the extending field, by those whom you shall annually appoint to celebrate "this memorable event."* New subjects will be continually arising out of the improving condition of our own country, the progress of society, government and manners, in the world, which will result from the revolution, and from the establishment of our independence.

Our oration now turns to view the advantages of the natural situation, and political freedom, which we, as a people, enjoy.

These are suggested to us by a recognition of the independency of the American Republic. To what purpose could be the possession of the former, without the enjoyment of the latter? In both respects, our lines have fallen in pleasant places; and we have a goodly heritage. What nation on earth can boast of such a territory, in extent and fertility of soil, situation and variety of climate? The situation and extensive territory of the United States are favourable for a great variety of productions, and convenient for commerce. Extending from the thirty-first to the forty-sixth degree of north latitude, and averaging at more than one thousand miles in breadth, they comprehend such a variety of soil and climate, as to be capable of almost every kind of production, either necessary or convenient to man. The prolific soil will reward the cultivator's labour, and furnish an ample supply for its increasing inhabitants. It is not usual for any of the casualties, whereby the fruits of the earth are at any time cut off, to pervade so extensive a space at the same time. While one part is pinched with drought, or devoured by insects, others have a superabundance to supply their demands. Bounded on the Atlantic ocean

*_At a town-meeting of the freemen of the town of Providence, held on the seventh day of April,_ A.D. 1793.

Resolved, that his excellency the governor, Messrs. Joseph Nightingale, Ephraim Bowen, jun., Jeremiah Olney, and Welcome Arnold, be a committee to make choice of a person to deliver a suitable oration on the fourth day of July next, to commence at twelve o'clock at noon, in commemoration of the independence of the United States: that said committee provide a place for the delivery of such oration; and that an oration on said memorable event be continued annually.

A true copy:

Witness, Daniel Cooke, town-clerk

by a vast extent of coast, they enjoy every advantage of foreign and domestic commerce. Intersected by many rivers, at distances favourable for internal navigation, or to supply artificial canals, the inhabitants enjoy an easy transportation for the exuberant growth of their fertile banks.

This soil is distributed in such portions amongst the inhabitants, and holden by such a tenure, as afford the greatest security to the continuation of a free government. "Most free states have studied to find out means of preventing too great an inequality in the distribution of landed property. What tumults were occasioned at Rome, in its best times, by attempts to carry into execution the agrarian law? Among the people of Israel, by direction of heaven, all estates which had been alienated during the course of fifty years, returned to the original owners at the end of that term." It is beyond a doubt, that the fee simple of the soil generally resting in the cultivators of it, and that general mediocrity of condition which follows from it, are circumstances most favourable to a republican form of government. Virtue and industry, talents and knowledge, will form the principal distinctions; and the motives to these will be increased, while the opportunities for vice are rendered fewer.

In such a state, the hereditary demagogue, and the cringing sycophant, are alike unknown. Protected by laws of their own framing, the people cannot be oppressed. Enjoying an equal government, which has no lucrative sinecures to bestow, there will be no great scope for ambitious intrigue. Such generally is the state of this country, whose inhabitants consist principally of independent and hardy yeomanry, mostly trained to the use of arms, instructed in their rights—reaping and enjoying the fruits of their own industry. Happy the people that are in such a state! all the blessings of secular and political enjoyment lie within their reach, unendangered from the rapacious hand of neighbouring powers, jealous of their growth, envious at their prosperity, and avaricious of their spoils. It is among the principal advantages of our situation, that we are not surrounded by such petulant and encroaching neighbours. Of the evil of such a situation, we may form some idea from what we suffer by the vicinity of the savage tribes.

From the natural situation of this country, and the peculiar circumstances of its inhabitants, arise many political advantages; for the enjoyment of which we are indebted to the revolution. The features of our policy have a strong resemblance to the magnificent and well-proportioned features of our country. No longer do we subscribe to the absurd doctrine of the divine right of kings, no longer bow our necks to the galling yoke of foreign legislation. Independent of these servilities, we enjoy the divine right of governing ourselves. In the exercise of this right, we have seen a complete political revolution, unawed by surrounding enemies, and uninfluenced by their intrigues. We have seen a constitution of civil government formed under the influence of reason and philanthropy, which meets the approving voice of the ablest politicians. Much has been said of its excellence by the greatest civilians. It is granted on all hands, [“]that the safety of the nation is the object of all government; and that the will of the people is the supreme law in all republican governments. But the arbitrary power of the many will produce anarchy, as that of an individual does despotism. It is necessary, therefore, that the social will be collected, and concentrated in one form or constitution of government; no state having yet appeared, where the people at once govern themselves without representation. This constitution, like the combination of organs that form the constitution of the human body, must contain within itself sufficient force and energy to carry on the necessary functions.” “The head dictates the laws, and the other members execute. It is essential that the head, which represents the legislative and judicial powers, should be calm and deliberate in its decrees; and that the arm, representing the executive, should have promptitude and force.”

Every good government must exist somewhere between absolute despotism, and absolute democracy. In either of these extremes, neither liberty nor safety can be enjoyed. It will follow, that a constitution wherein the three powers, legislative, executive and judicial, are most perfectly combined for the prosperity of the people, is the best. Indeed, the great Montesquieu has made it appear, that these three powers exist, in some degree, in every form of government, even the most absolute. As these powers display their cooperative influence, in a greater or less degree, in the governmental machine, they have received their name or stile. The name of aristocracy is given to the government of those states, where a permanent senate governs all, without ever consulting the people. “Such is Venice, which is also called a republic; it is a pure aristocracy in this sense, that the three powers are in the hands of the nobles. That state, in which the will of an individual is most frequently a law, and decides on the life or death of the subject, is called a despotic state. Such is the Turkish empire. But it is not true, that the sultan is absolute master; his power finds limits at every step he advances, and he is obliged to respect them. This empire, then, is between aristocracy and despotism; but inclines towards the latter. The state in which the will of an individual is sometimes absolute, but where co-legislative bodies always join in the exercise of power, is called a monarchy. This species of government is between despotism and aristocracy, but inclines towards the latter. The state where the people choose their magistrates for a fixed period, and often assemble to exercise the sovereignty, is a democracy, and is called a republic; such were Athens and Rome, and such are the United States of America."

Amidst the various shades between the primitive colours in which different governments have been cast, these United States have wisely cast their's in that mild form which is most congenial to the rights of man, and the enjoyment of equal liberty—that liberty, which to independence unites security—which to *the most ample elective powers, unites strength and energy in government*. You will permit me here to felicitate you on the re-election of two of the first political characters in the world, to the two first offices in the American Republic; and on the honour your electors have done themselves by their unanimity in the election.

The present flourishing condition of these states, affords the best comment on the excellence of our constitution. All useful theories are practicable. The most perfect model of government that imagination can form will be useless, if the state of mankind renders it impracticable. Already has experience taught us, that our government is fraught with many blessings. The same internal causes that led to independence, and national existence, have guided the people of these states to a wise and deliberate choice of persons, to whom the powers of government might safely be entrusted. To the wisdom of their elections, and to the judicious appointment of officers to the several departments of state, are they to ascribe their present flourishing condition. Under the happy influence of their wisdom, fidelity and industry, we see our credit restored abroad, and established at home

—our deranged finances reduced to system, and made productive beyond the calculations of the most sanguine. Although the revenue laws may, in some respects, operate unequally at present, yet the object of the government being the distribution of equal justice, such alterations and reforms will doubtless take place, as to produce all that equality which the nature of the case will admit. Who does not see reason to rejoice in the provision making for the current of justice to run pure through the Union, who but the dishonest and fraudulent debtor, or the criminal offender? The dignity, candour and impartiality, displayed from the judicial bench, augur well to the rights of individuals, and to the peace of society.

Here property is rendered secure, by the equality of law to all; and every man, being master of the fruits of his own labour, enjoys the right of property—no arbitrary imposition of taxes or of tythes, no lordly exactions of rents, chill the heart of industry, nor repress the cultivator's exertions—no mercantile corporations, with exclusive rights, damp the ardent spirit of enterprize. Hence we see a trackless wilderness, in the short space of one hundred and seventy years, converted into a fruitful field; and, in the space of ten years, we see trade and commerce, no longer limited by parliamentary restrictions, nor distressed by war, extending to all parts of the globe, from the straits of Magellan to the inhospitable regions of Kamskatka. Hence also we see the American genius springing forward in useful arts, projecting great and astonishing enterprizes, *tearing down mountains and filling up vallies*,* and making efforts unknown in those countries where despotism renders every thing precarious, and where a tyrant reaps what slaves have sown.

A polite and ingenious European traveller (Dr. Moore), tells us, "The chilling effects of despotic oppression, or the benign influence of freedom and commerce, strike the eye of the most careless traveller." And, speaking of the disorders incident to free governments, says, "The temporary and partial disorders which are the conse-

* Mr. John Brown, merchant, of this town, has already gone far, since March last, towards removing a hill of about 400 feet in length, 180 in breadth, and 60 in height—amounting to 150,000 tons of earth; which, when completed, will raise useless flats into 6 acres of useful building-ground, which will be connected with the Massachusetts by an elegant bridge, now building by the same gentleman.

The author hopes Mr. Brown will pardon this liberty, as reference was evidently had to it.

quence of public freedom, have been greatly exaggerated by some people, and represented as more than an equivalent to all the advantages resulting from a free government. But if such persons had opportunities of observing the nature of those evils which spring up in absolute governments, they would soon be convinced of their error. The greatest evil that can arise from the licentiousness which accompanies civil liberty, is, that people may rashly take a dislike to liberty herself, from the teasing impertinence and absurdity of some of her real or affected well-wishers; as a man might become less fond of his best friend, if he found him always attended by a snappish cur, which without provocation was always growling and barking.

"What are the disorders of a free government, compared to the gloomy regularity produced by despotism? in which men are obliged to the most painful circumspection in all their actions; are afraid to speak their sentiments on the most common occurrences; suspicious of cherishing government spies in their household servants, distrustful of their own relations and most intimate companions; and at all times exposed to the oppression of men in power, and to the insolence of their favourites. No confusion, in my mind, can be more terrible than the stern disciplined regularity and vaunted police of arbitrary governments, where every heart is depressed by fear, where mankind dare not assume their natural character, where the free spirit must crouch to the slave in office, where genius must repress her effusions, or, like the Egyptian worshippers, offer them in sacrifice to the calves of power; and where the human mind, always in shackles, shrinks from every generous effort."

There is a point of depression, as well as exaltation, from which human affairs naturally return in a contrary direction, and beyond which they seldom pass, either in their decline or advancement. The present is a crisis, in human affairs, that teems with great and interesting events. Long, long has the old world been sunk in ignorance, superstition and bondage. But the period of her emancipation appears to be rapidly approaching. What a mighty combination of events is now conspiring to the general spread of knowledge and freedom! Judging from what we have seen and experienced, we may conclude that the measures now taken to crush the rights of mankind, and to overturn the altar of freedom, will be productive of the contrary effect. Indeed a dark cloud at present vails the fair countenance of liberty in France. Inexperienced in the science of a free government, and unprepared for the enjoyment of it by a previous course of education, of intellectual improvement, and moral discipline, they have tarnished their glory by excesses; and, in the paroxysms of their zeal, have carried excess to outrage.

It is the misfortune of men struggling for liberty, that they are apt to be carried too far, *as we have been taught by experience*. The more the human mind hath been depressed, the greater will be its extravagancies, when it bursts forth from the shackles of tyranny into the full light of freedom. Like the vibrating pendulum, it flies from one extreme to another; and, like that, must have time to regulate itself. Shall we reject the cause of human liberty, because anarchy attends the first efforts of a people to gain it, or because ferocity marks some of their steps towards it? Or shall our confidence in its progress be overthrown, because threatened by hostile confederacies? As Americans, we must either renounce that which is our boast and glory, or warmly wish success to the great principles of the French revolution—principles founded on the equal liberty of all men, and the empire of the laws. As rational beings, and as Christians, we should recollect, that from partial evil, it is the glory of the Supreme Ruler to bring forth general good; and that, as inspiration expresseth it, "He makes the wrath of man to praise him; but the remainder of wrath will he restrain."

The present war in Europe has a further object than the subjugation of France. It is a war of kings and despots, against the dearest rights and the most invaluable privileges of mankind. Should the combined powers succeed against France, and the re-establishment of monarchy there exist among possible events, what security have we, that the same attempt will not be made to restore monarchy in this country? Has not united America led the way? And may she not boast, with an honest pride, of the influence of her example in exciting the attention of many nations to their natural and civil rights? With what freedom of thought—with what enlightened and ardent philanthropy, has she inspired many of the nations of Europe! What would be her condition, if subjugated by the confederates against freedom, we may learn from the state of Poland, lately made free by a voluntary compact with its king; but now subdued by the ferocious power of the north, divided among her jealous neighbours, and the people sold with the soil, like the animals that graze upon it. Let the generous feelings of human nature rise indignant at the abhorrent idea of part of itself being thus degraded. Whatever may be the fate of France in the present contest, the great principles of the revolution will eventually find advocates in every part of the world, even among those who are now most inveterate against the conduct of the French. The doctrines of hereditary powers—of the divine right of kings—of their inviolability, and incapacity to do wrong, are fast declining, and will soon be exploded. They are solecisms of the same nature with their divine right to do wrong; and will, in future, more enlightened and liberal days, be read of with astonishment.

How often doth a hand unobserved shift the scene of the world! The calmest and stillest hour precedes the whirlwind; and it hath thundered in the serenest sky. The monarch hath drawn the chariot of state, in which he had been wont to ride in triumph; or been dragged to a scaffold, by the misguided zeal of his late admirers; and the greatest who ever awed the world, have moralized at the turn of the wheel. Such, O Louis, has been thy untimely fate! At thy urn, let pitying nature drop a sympathetic tear! Cease, thou sanguinary demon, any longer to support thy bloody standard! May the milder genius of true liberty, and more enlightened policy, speedily pervade the councils, and bless the people of France!

Our attention now returns with delight to contemplate that portion of religious and scientific freedom which our country enjoys. To the early care of our ancestors to establish literary, and encourage religious institutions, are we much indebted for the accomplishment of the late revolution, which shows us the vast importance of paying great attention to the rising sons and daughters of America, by giving them an enlightened and a virtuous education. Here the human mind, free as the air, may exert all its powers towards the various objects laid before it, and expand its faculties to an extent hitherto unknown. It has been the policy of all monarchical governments, and of some religious institutions, to keep the people in ignorance, the more easily to dazzle them into obedience by external marks of greatness, and of native superiority. Knowledge and true religion go hand in hand. When the former is obscured, the latter is mutilated, and enveloped in the shades of superstition and bigotry. And whenever the civil power has undertaken to judge and decide concerning truth and error, to oppose the one, while it protected the other, it has invariably supported bigotry, superstition and nonsense.

"Anaxagoras was tried and condemned in Greece, for teaching that the sun and stars were not deities, but masses of corruptible matter. Accusations of a like nature contributed to the death of Socrates. The threats of bigotry, and the fear of persecution, prevented Copernicus from publishing, during his life time, his discovery of the true system of the world. Galileo was obliged to renounce the doctrine of the motion of the earth, and suffered a year's imprisonment for having asserted it." Many other instances of a similar nature, and much later date, might be mentioned; the tendency of which has been to cramp the human powers, to destroy in some measure the end of education, by directing the current of thought into a narrow channel. Hence the doctrine of the revolution of the earth round the sun, would have been as great "a stumbling-block to the prejudiced Jews, and as apparent foolishness to the learned Greeks, as that of a crucified Jesus to be the Saviour of the world."

By the constitution of the United States, no man is abridged of the liberty of enquiry—no religious test is required—no bait is thrown out by government to encourage hypocrisy, or exclude the honest and deserving. In this respect it possesses a liberality unknown to any people before. It must give pleasure to every generous mind, to hear "the children of the stock of Abraham" thus addressing our beloved president: "Deprived as we have heretofore been of the invaluable rights of citizens, we now (with a deep sense of gratitude to the Almighty Disposer of all events) behold a government erected on the majesty of the people—a government which to bigotry gives no sanction, to persecution no assistance, but generously affording to all liberty of conscience, and immunities of citizenship—deeming every one, of whatever nation, tongue or language, equal parts of the governmental machine. This so ample and extensive federal union, whose basis is philanthropy, mutual confidence, and public virtue, we cannot but acknowledge to be the work of the great God, who ruleth in the armies of heaven, and among the inhabitants of the earth."*

* Extract from an address presented President Washington by the Jews at Newport, when on his tour through the eastern states, August 1790.

In this view of the subject, may we not consider these as the dawn of brighter days, of a brighter sun than ever blessed the world before; as a commencement of the golden age, that introduces a better system of religion than most of those which have been hitherto professed in the world; a religion that enforces moral obligations, not a religion that relaxes and evades them; a religion of peace and charity, not of strife and party rage? The importance of religion to the peace and order of society, is unspeakably great. Every thing is replaced and established by religion. It surrounds the whole system of morality, resembling that universal force of physical nature, which retains the planets in their order, and subjects them to a regular revolution. But as to all decent modes and outward expressions of it, the rights of conscience remain untouched. Here all religious opinions are equally harmless, and render men who hold different opinions equally good subjects, because there are no laws to oppose them, no force to compel them. The use of arms, and the military art, of which we have this day so agreeable and elegant a specimen, are directed to a very different object, the defence of freedom, and as a bulwark of the state.

May we ever show ourselves worthy of the blessings we enjoy, and never tarnish the bright lustre of this day, by any unbecoming excesses. Americans! think of the many privileges which distinguish your condition. Be grateful for your lot; and let your virtue secure what your valour, under God, hath obtained; and transmit to latest posterity the glorious inheritance. May the political edifice erected on the theatre of this new world, afford a practical lesson of liberty to mankind, and become in an eminent degree the model of that glorious temple of universal liberty which is about to be established over the civilized world.

42

THE NECESSITY OF THE BELIEF OF CHRISTIANITY

Jonathan Edwards, Jr.

HARTFORD

1794

JONATHAN EDWARDS, JR. (1745-1801). The son and namesake of one of the great American minds of the eighteenth century (Jonathan Edwards the elder died in 1758), Edwards was himself an outstanding personality. He was born in Northampton, Massachusetts, and at the age of six went with his family to live with the Mohican Indians for seven years while his father did missionary work. The family then moved in early 1758 to Princeton, New Jersey. A short time afterward, young Jonathan was orphaned by the death of his father and then of his mother, Sarah Pierpont Edwards.

Edwards was graduated from the College of New Jersey in 1765. He had experienced a powerful conversion during his college days and thereafter went to Bethlehem, Connecticut, to study theology with his father's friend Joseph Bellamy. In 1769 he became pastor of the White Haven Church in New Haven, where he remained until 1795, when he was dismissed because of doctrinal disputes and the decline of the church. After serving briefly as pastor of the church in Colebrook, he was elected president of Union College in Schenectady, New York. He died within two years. This was reminiscent of his father's fate, even more so when it is noted that both father and son chose to preach, on the first Sunday of their final years, on the same text, "This year thou shalt die" (Jeremiah 28:16).

While lacking the imagination and originality of his father, the younger Edwards had a powerful mind and wrote important works advancing a "governmental" theory of the Atonement, a defense of his father's theory of the will, and an elaborate study of the Mohican language (published in 1788). He was active in charitable and missionary endeavors and vigorously opposed slavery and the slave trade. His writings are collected in *The Works of Jonathan Edwards, D.D., . . . with a Memoir of His Life* (2 vol., 1842).

The sermon reprinted here was given on the anniversary of the election in Hartford on May 8, 1794.

The Necessity of the Belief of Christianity by the Citizens of the State, in order to our political Prosperity;

ILLUSTRATED IN A

SERMON,

PREACHED BEFORE HIS EXCELLENCY

SAMUEL HUNTINGTON, Esq. L. L. D.

GOVERNOR,

AND THE HONORABLE THE

GENERAL ASSEMBLY

OF THE

STATE OF *CONNECTICUT,*

Convened at Hartford on the Day of the Anniversary Election.

May 8th, 1794.

By JONATHAN EDWARDS, D. D.

Pastor of a Church in New-Haven.

HARTFORD:

PRINTED by HUDSON and GOODWIN.

MDCCXCIV.

Yea, happy is that people whose God *is the Lord.*

Psalm CXLIV. 15.

In this passage of sacred scripture, that people is pronounced happy, whose God is the Lord. But what is the meaning of the expression, "whose God is the Lord?" or when may it be truly said, that the God of any people is the Lord? The answer is, when they believe, worship and obey the Lord or Jehovah, as the only true God, and that according to his revealed will. The Lord was the God of the Israelites, when they complied with the dispensation, under which they lived; and he is our God, when we cordially believe and comply with the gospel. If we do so, the text pronounces us happy; and it plainly implies, that we cannot be happy on any condition short of this.

Therefore the subject, which I beg leave to propose from our text for present consideration, is this, The necessity of a belief of christianity by the citizens of this state, in order to our public and political prosperity. This proposition is plainly implied in the text. For if that people only be happy or prosperous, whose God is the Lord; and if to believe and comply with christianity be implied in having the Lord for our God; it follows, that the belief of christianity by the citizens of this state, is necessary to our political prosperity.

Political prosperity requires the general practice of a strict morality. But this cannot be so well secured by any other means, as by a belief of christianity. Motives of a religious kind appear to be necessary to restrain men from vice and immorality. Civil pains and penalities alone are by no means sufficient to this end; nor are civil honours and rewards sufficient encouragements to the practice of virtue in general. The civil magistrate does not pretend to reward virtue in general according to its moral excellency. He does indeed reward some particular acts of virtue, which are highly beneficial to the public. But the many virtues of private life pass without any other reward from him, than the bare protection, which is afforded in common to the persons who practise those virtues, and to all who are free from gross crimes.

Nor does the magistrate pretend to punish vice in general. He does undertake to punish those gross vices, which consist in the violations of the perfect rights of men, and in those cases only, in which the violations are both manifest and are manifestly proved before a proper tribunal. But all violations of even these rights which are perpetrated in private, or which, though perpetrated publicly, are not legally proved, pass entirely free from civil pains and penalties. The same is true of all violations of the imperfect rights, as they are called, which are violated by ingratitude, selfishness, neglect of kind offices, &c. Yet these vices are in their consequences, often as hurtful to the public good, as injustice, fraud or robbery; and indeed the former are the source of the latter. Now to restrain from vices of this latter description, from all vices practised in private, and from vice in general, nothing is so useful as a full belief of a final judgment, and of a subsequent state of rewards and punishments, in which all sin not renounced by sincere repentance, shall be punished, and every man shall receive according to that which he does in the body, whether it be good or evil.

Let us suppose a citizen restrained from vice by the fear of civil penalties only. Such a person will feel himself under no obligation to pay either public or private debts, unless he expects legal judgment and execution; and under no obligation to speak the truth, unless he fears a prosecution for fraud or defamation. He will feel himself at liberty to live in idleness, profusion, intemperance and lust, and to take every advantage consistent with law, to defraud and oppress his fellow citizens. He will requite no kind offices, as he has no motive to gratitude. He will have no motive to the greater part of his duty to his own children, and in a thousand instances may neglect them, when he is bound by the strictest moral obligation, to assist and do them good. He may indulge himself in passion and ill nature, in contention and violence, so far as not to expose himself to the law; and of course will take no pains to preserve peace among his neighbours; but will rather, as his humour happens to be, foment by words and actions, animosities, law-suits and contentions in every form. Ever complaining under the mildest and justest government, he will in numberless ways oppose measures, and especially expences, subservient and necessary to the public good; and will excite and spread discontent among others. Now is this a good citizen? What if the whole state consisted of such citizens? Could it enjoy political prosperity?

The best and perhaps the only remedy for such diseases, is a full belief of the divine universal providence, of the accountableness of all men to God for all their conduct, and of a future equal retribution.

Some religion then, and some belief of a future state is necessary to our political prosperity. But what religion shall we adopt? and what system concerning a future state is most useful to the state? It is not possible to introduce and give a general spread through the state, to Mahometanism or paganism; and it would be a work of time and of great difficulty, to lead the citizens in general into the belief of deism or what is called the philosophical religion. Therefore we seem necessitated to have recourse to christianity: and this is most excellently adapted to the ends of restraining men from vice and promoting that general practice of strict morality, which is so essential to the political prosperity of any people. It is adapted to these ends by its precepts; by the moral character of the author of those precepts; by his absolute supremacy and sovereignty; by the motives of reward and punishment with which those precepts are enforced; by the facts which it relates, and by the examples which it exhibits. It is enforced not by the bare authority of our feeble reason, but by the authority of our creator, our judge, and our all-perfect God. It depends not on the obscure investigations, subtil refinements and uncertain conclusions of human intellect; but on the omniscience, the veracity, the justice, the goodness and the will of God: And thus it is excellently adapted to the principles and feelings which are common to human nature, and which exist in the weakest and most ignorant, as well as the most intelligent and learned. A man who cannot follow the shortest and most easy chain of reasoning on the nature of things and the tendency of human actions, and who will not from such reasoning feel his obligation to virtue in general or to particular virtues, will at once feel the force of the positive and authoritative declarations and requisitions of the Almighty: and where is the man, learned or unlearned, of weak or strong powers, who does not see and feel the difference between the advice and directions of some learned and acute philosopher, and *thus saith the Lord*? Above all, the motives arising from the doctrines of the final judgment and a future state, lay an inconceivably greater restraint on the depravity of human nature, than any thing that is or can be suggested by the philosophical religion.

Let us compare this religion with christianity in a few particulars, which immediately relate to our present subject.

It is a maxim of infidelity to follow nature. Now to follow her, is to follow all the appetites and passions of which we are naturally the subjects; and this will lead to all kinds of vice. But it is a maxim of christianity, to follow the divine law, the precepts of the gospel and the example of Christ: and whether these lead to vice or virtue, I need not inform you.

Another maxim of infidelity is, that man was made for his own happiness; that is, that every man was made for his own individual happiness. This then is to be the supreme object of every man; and this object is to be pursued, as infidels themselves teach, by gratifying his natural appetites and passions, which brings us just where we were before, to all vice and wickedness: And if an infidel deny his appetites and passions, he must be governed by other motives than any which his system of morality suggests. But christianity teaches, that we were created for an end, which so far as we pursue, we cannot fail of sincere piety and strict morality.

Infidels are divided into two classes, those who deny a future state of existence, and those who allow such a state. The former deny all moral government of God, and that we are at all accountable to him; and some of the most noted among them deny any evidence of his moral perfections. Now it is manifest, that according to this system mankind can be under no restraint from vice, by the consideration of a future state of rewards and punishments, or by the consideration of their accountableness to God, or of his commands or prohibitions. Nor does this system admit of any motives derived from these sources, to the practice of virtue. Yet these motives, with respect to mankind in the gross, are the most powerful. The authors and abettors of this system seem to rely on a sense of honour, as the great motive to virtue and restraint from vice. And what is this sense of honour? If it be a sense of shame in doing wrong, and a sense of the honourableness of doing right, it is a mere sense or knowledge of right and wrong; and this so far as it is founded on truth, is undoubtedly a proper rule of conduct, and a man who is disposed to virtue, will practise according to this rule. But how are men in general, without the aid of revelation, to attain, in all cases, to the knowledge of right and wrong, of virtue and vice? It is manifest by abundant experience both antient and modern, that mere human reason is insufficient for this.

If by this sense of honour be meant, as I imagine is generally meant, a sense of our own supposed personal dignity, a pride naturally arising from this sense, and a disposition to resent and revenge every thing which is grating to our pride; this in many cases is so far from a motive to virtue and restraint from vice, that it is itself a vice. Let this sense of honour be ever so well limited and explained, it cannot be a motive to virtue and a restraint from vice to all men; because it does not reach and cannot influence all men. How many are there in every nation and country, who have very little sense of their own dignity, and very little elevation of soul in a consciousness of it? How many are there, who in a prospect of gain, would not scruple to betray their friends, to steal their neighbours property or to betray their country?

It is manifest therefore, that this philosophical religion, could it be generally introduced and established among us, would be a very great political evil, as it would weaken and even annihilate those motives to virtue and restraints from vice, which are most powerful on the minds of men in general.

Besides: this system so far as it denies the evidence of the moral perfections of God, not only cuts off the motives to virtue, drawn from a future state and from those divine perfections; but even suggests motives to vice. If it be a matter of uncertainty, whether God be a friend to virtue or a friend to vice, it may be, that we shall please him most by an unrestrained indulgence of vice, and by the practice of virtue shall provoke his malice and vengeance. Nay, if it be a matter of uncertainty, whether the deity be a benevolent or malicious being, we can have no certainty, but that he will give us an existence in a future state, on purpose to gratify his malevolence in our everlasting torment. And to be consistent, the advocates for the system now under consideration should not say a word against the christian doctrine of endless punishment, on the ground of its supposed injustice or opposition to grace and mercy; because they acknowledge, that they know not, that God is just, gracious or merciful.

Thus this scheme, which was invented to avoid the fears of future punishment, defeats itself; and while it attempts to deliver us from a just punishment, leaves us exposed to any punishment ever so unjust, cruel and malicious.

As to that kind of infidelity, which allows the divine moral perfections and a future state of rewards and punishments; though this is more plausible than the former; yet the motives to virtue and restraints from vice, which it affords, are not to be compared with those of the gospel. Agreeably to the gospel all men are to be rewarded according to their works done in the body, whether they be good or evil. Some are to be beaten with few stripes, some with many stripes, according to their several aggravations of guilt. But in the future punishment which infidels admit, there is nothing vindictive, nothing therefore which is intended to support law and government. The only punishment which they admit, is that which is designed for the good of the person punished;* and therefore as soon as the person punished repents, he is released. Now it is manifest on the slightest reflection, that the motive to avoid sin and vice on this plan, is exceedingly diminished from what it is on the plan of the gospel. On the plan of the gospel the motive is endless misery, proportioned in degree to the demerit of the person punished. On the infidel plan it is a merciful chastisement, which is to continue no longer than till the subject shall repent. And as every sinner will naturally flatter himself, that he shall repent as soon as he shall find his punishment to be intolerable; so all the punishment, which on this plan he will expect, is one that shall continue but for a moment, after it shall have become extreme or intolerable. And whether this momentary extreme punishment be an equal restraint on vice, as the endless misery threatened in the gospel, let every man judge. It is plain, that in a comparative view it is as nothing. Therefore as even this, the most plausible scheme of infidelity, cuts the sinews of morality and opens the floodgates of vice; the prevalence of it in our state would be a very great political evil.

If we take the pains to compare christianity with antient paganism, we shall find, that the former has, even in a political view, the like advantage over the latter, which it has over infidelity. If in the ac-

* See Blount and Tyndal.

count, which I shall now give of the pagan religion, some things shall be mentioned, which will be grating to those of the most delicate feelings; I think I shall be entitled to the pardon of my hearers, as otherwise it will be impossible for me to do justice to this important subject.

Paganism, though it taught a future punishment of wicked men of certain descriptions; yet indulged and even encouraged vice in a variety of ways. It taught that there were many gods, some male and some female; some comparatively good, others exceedingly evil; but all and even the chief god, on many occasions acting a most wicked part and indulging the vilest lusts. Some of their female deities were deceased women of most abandoned characters. Jupiter, whom they called *the father of gods and men*, was himself the son of Saturn who according to some, was king of Crete; according to others, was Ham the son of Noah; according to others, was Adam; but on every hypothesis was a mere man. This man, the antient heathens believed, had a number of children, and was wont to devour them as soon as they were born: but Jupiter was saved by an artifice of his mother. He, grown to maturity, rebelled against his father, who till then was supposed to be the supreme God, drove him from his throne, and seized his authority and dominions. When Jupiter had by these means raised himself to the place of supreme deity, he was wont to transform himself into various visible shapes, to facilitate his designs of criminal intercourse with women here on earth. Now how destructive of the interests of virtue and morality must necessarily have been these ideas of the gods; and especially these ideas of the character and conduct of the supreme god, *Jupiter the greatest and the best!*

In like manner destructive to morality must have been almost all their other ideas of their gods; as of their animosities and contentions among themselves; of their intrigues and lusts; and the vicious and most abominable practices by which, in many instances, they were worshipped. The goddess Venus was openly worshipped by whoredom;* and the feasts called Saturnalia and Bacchinalia were celebrated by the practice of every lewdness and debauchery. The vices of

* Every woman among some nations was obliged, at least once in her life, to prostitute herself to any person, even the greatest stranger, who would accept her favour. This done in honour to Venus.

drunkenness and whoredom in these cases were accounted, instead of moral evils, the highest acts of virtue and piety.

Now as all these ideas and practices tended to a general depravity of morals; so their effects abundantly appeared in the vicious lives of the heathen world.

I am well aware, that it has been said, that christianity has depraved the morals of mankind; that vice is far more predominant among christians, than ever it was among the antient heathens; and that therefore we may justly conclude, that christianity is less subservient to virtue and a moral life, than paganism. This has been urged as an argument against the divine original and the truth of christianity; and may be urged as an argument against the good policy of encouraging and supporting it in any state. The consideration of this objection then is pertinent and necessary to the discussion of the subject now before us.

In answer to this objection I beg leave to observe in the first place, that if vice were more predominant in christian nations, than it was among the heathens, it would not certainly follow, that this increase of vice is the effect of christianity. Christianity prevails in civilized nations only; and in such nations there is much more opportunity for many vices and much more temptation to them, than among those who are not civilized. Nay, in civilized nations only, is there a possibility of the prevalence of many vices. In proportion as civilization is promoted, the wants of men are increased. Their food, their drink, their apparel and the education of their children, must be more expensive, and more expence is in every respect required to their living in fashion among their neighbours. And in proportion to the increase of their wants, the temptation to covetousness, extortion, oppression, deceit and fraud, is increased. Again, in proportion as civilization is promoted, the means of luxury of every kind are increased, and with the means, the temptations to luxury and luxury itself are increased. No wonder a savage, who wishes for nothing more than what he may take in hunting and fishing, and who has furnished himself with this, does not steal, rob or extort his neighbour's property; no wonder he attempts not to obtain it by falsehood or fraud. Nor is it any wonder, that living on such a low and scanty diet as he generally does, he is very rarely guilty of a rape, of adultery or other lewdness. Nor ought it to be matter of wonder, that all these vices are far more prevalent in civilized nations, than among barbarians. But the prevalence of these vices in such nations, is not owing to christianity, but to civilization and its usual attendants. They were at least as prevalent among the antient Greeks and Romans, as they are among us. Persecution does not usually obtain among [the] heathen, because either they have no religion themselves to instigate them to persecution; or there is no religion different from their own, to be the object of their persecution; or if there be a different religion, it makes no opposition to that which they have chosen, and therefore their religious zeal is not excited against it.

This affords an answer to an objection to christianity much insisted on by some, that the heathens do not persecute; but that christians do most virulently persecute even one another; and therefore that christianity makes men worse instead of better. The answer to this objection is, that the different religious sentiments and forms of worship among the antient heathens did not in general oppose each other. They rather justified each other, as the heathens maintained an intercommunity of gods and religions. Though every nation had its own gods and religion; yet whenever the individuals went into another nation, they joined in the worship of the gods and in the observance of the rites of the nation in which they then were. Therefore there was no opportunity for persecution. But the nature of christianity is very different. It condemns and opposes all other religions as false and ruinous. Therefore as it touches the pride of those whom it condemns, it provokes opposition and the persecution of itself, merely because it tells the truth. And the professors of christianity too, by a misguided zeal, have been often led into the spirit and practice of persecution.

Now this persecution of christianity by those of other religions, is not the effect of christianity, but of opposition to it; and the persecuting spirit which has appeared in some christians, is not the effect of christianity, but of the abuse and perversion of it; and for neither of these is christianity itself answerable. The best institution in the world may be opposed and persecuted; and the best institution in the world may be abused and perverted. But christianity never gave any just occasion for either the persecution or perversion of itself.

Besides, the charge of persecution may justly be retorted. For no sooner did christianity make its appearance in the world, than it was violently opposed and virulently persecuted, by those very heathens, who in the objection now before us are said not to have been guilty of persecution. And as long as they had the power in their hands, this opposition was continued or repeated, under various Roman emperors, for ten successive and bloody persecutions, in which thousands and hundreds of thousands were martyred in various ways, the most malicious and cruel.

Nay, the heathens showed a disposition to persecute not only christians, but one another, whenever there was opportunity. No sooner did Socrates oppose the religion and polytheism of his countrymen, than they began a persecution of him, which ended in his death. And Cambyses, the Persian monarch, in contempt of the Egyptian god Apis, not only stabbed him with his dagger, but ordered the priests of Apis to be severely whipped, and all the inhabitants of Memphis to be slain, who should be found rejoicing on the occasion of the appearance of that god.* These things demonstrate, that the ancient heathens did possess an high degree of the spirit of persecution, and not only toward the christians, but toward one another. The like spirit hath been manifested by heathens of modern times. Passing other instances, I shall mention one which took place in our own country. By the exertions of our ancestors, the first European settlers of this country, a considerable number of the aborigines were converted to the christian faith. The pagan Indians were displeased with this, banished from their society all the converts, and when they could do it with safety, put them to death, and would have massacred them all, had they not been restrained by the fear of our ancestors.†

The facts concerning Socrates and Cambyses, furnish an answer to that part of the objection under consideration, which urges that christians persecute not only heathens, but one another; whereas heathens did not persecute one another. It appears by the facts just mentioned, that heathens have persecuted one another. Besides, the same reason is to be assigned for christians persecuting one another, as for the heathens persecuting christians. The protestants say, that the religion of the papists is fundamentally wrong; on the other hand, the papists

* Prideaux's connection.

† Neal's Hist. New-England.

assert the same concerning the protestants. Thus by a mutual renunciation, condemnation and excommunication of each other, the false zeal of these and other different sects among christians is kindled into persecution, on the same grounds on which persecution is begun and carried on, between christians and heathens. But by reason of the forementioned intercommunity of gods and religions among the antient heathens, these grounds of persecution did not exist among them in general, though in some cases they did both exist and produce their usual fruits.

Let us now more directly attend to the charge brought against christianity, that vice is more prevalent among christians, than it was among the antient heathens.

Christians indeed have no virtue to be the ground of boasting; on the other hand they have great reason to be ashamed and humbled on account of their vices and their depravity of manners. Still I maintain, that open vice is not so prevalent in christian nations, as it was among the antient heathens. Let us compare those antient heathens, of whom we know the most and who were the most improved and polite, with the christians of whom we know the most; the antient Greeks and Romans with the citizens of the United States.

Here it is to be observed, that we labour under great disadvantage. We know our own country and its predominant vices, both public and private. In order to this we need but open our eyes and look around us. We have not the same advantage to know the antients. We are entirely dependent on history for information concerning them and their vices; and this generally relates the public transactions of nations only, as their wars and treaties, their laws and public judgments; but is mostly silent concerning the morals and private lives of individuals or of the people considered collectively; and so far as we are ignorant of the antients we have no right to charge them with vice. However, with all this disadvantage, I fear not to proceed to the comparison.

Let us then institute the comparison with respect to the principal moral virtues, as temperance, chastity, truth, justice and humanity.

1. As to temperance; though this was reckoned among the virtues by the pagan moral writers, yet it is plain from their writers in general, that drunkenness was exceedingly common among them, and among all ranks, among magistrates, philosophers and priests, as well

as others. Their priests in some of their religious feasts were always intoxicated. Even Cato, though a Stoic philosopher, one of their strictest moralists and a principal magistrate, was remarkably addicted to this vice. So was Zeno, the founder of the sect of the Stoics; and Chrysippus, another Stoic philosopher died in consequence of excessive drinking at a sacrifice.* The character of their principal magistrates, priests and philosophers, does not appear to have suffered much, if at all, by this vice. It must therefore have been considered by the people, as a very venial fault, if any at all. Indeed this is evident by all their writers. But how it is esteemed among us, and what would be the effect of it on the reputation of our principal magistrates and divines, I need not inform you.

2. As to chastity, it is manifest from the whole current of pagan writers, that they considered fornication as no crime, and therefore ran into it without reserve. Not only is this observable of Homer's heroes, but even the modest Virgil's pious Aeneas, who was meant to be a perfect character, had an amour with Dido, without the least shame or sense of indecency. Simple fornication was not only commonly practised without restraint; but was allowed by all their philosophers, and was positively encouraged by some of them.† Many of the customs of the Greeks and Romans promoted lewdness. The manner of the appearance of women in some of their public exercises, was such as directly tended to that vice; and the ideas of the lawfulness and expediency of a community of wives so far prevailed and had such an influence on practice, as not only implied the violation of chastity, but had a most baleful general tendency with respect to that virtue.‡ Though it is hardly credible, yet unnatural vices had too

* Priestley's Institutes.

† "None of the philosophers ever represented simple fornication, especially on the part of the man, as any vice at all. Cato commended a young man for frequenting the public stews; and Cicero expressly speaks of it, as a thing that was never found fault with." *Priestley's Institutes.* All that was enjoined by Epictetus, who of all the philosophers, is perhaps the most celebrated for his strict maxims of morality, was, "that people should abstain from fornication before marriage as far as they could; and that if they did not abstain, they should use it lawfully, and not be severe in reprehending those who did not abstain." Enchiridion, Chap. 47.

‡ "At Sparta, young women appeared naked in the public exercises; and when married women had no children, their husbands were encouraged to consent to a free intercourse between them and other men; a custom which Plutarch vindicates. This was also agreeable to the doctrine of the Stoics; and it is well known, that that rigid Stoic,

much the sanction of some legislators and philosophers, and were countenanced by many of them. Xenophon informs us, that the sin of Sodom was encouraged by the public laws of several of the states of Greece. It was more especially so among the Cretans, in order to prevent too great an increase of the people. Solon, one of the seven wise men of Greece, and the celebrated law-giver of Athens, forbad this practice to slaves, which necessarily conveys the idea of his thinking it fit for free men only. According to Cicero, the Greek philosophers not only generally practised, but even gloried in this vice: And Plutarch informs us, that many parents would not suffer their children to keep the company of those philosophers, who pretended to be fond of them. Diogenes was remarkable for indulging himself in the most abominable practices openly, and without a sense of shame; affecting, according to the maxim of the Cynics, to live according to nature.* These unnatural vices were increased in a most astonishing manner, about the time of the promulgation of christianity. Seneca says, that in his time they were practised ["]openly and without shame at Rome."† These accounts given by heathen writers, fully justify the charges thrown out on this head against the heathens, by the writers of the New Testament, especially by the apostle Paul, in his first chapter to the Romans: Though to christians the inspired writers need no authority, but do of themselves sufficiently prove the amazing depravity of the heathen world in this respect.

3. Truth is a moral virtue, the obligation and necessity of which are perhaps as evident as those of any virtue whatever. Yet the Stoic philosophers taught that lying was lawful, whenever it was profitable; and Plato allowed, that a man may lie, who knows how to do it at a proper time.

4. Let us inquire how far justice was maintained and practised among the antients. I now mean justice in matters of property. For that kind of justice which is opposed to oppression and cruelty, will

Cato of Utica, consented to such an intercourse between his own wife and his friend Hortensius. Plato in his book of laws, recommends a community of women; and he advises, that soldiers be not restrained with respect to any kind of sinful indulgence, even the most unnatural species of it, when they are on an expedition." *Priestley.*

* Does not the forementioned deistic maxim of following nature directly lead to the same abominable practices?

† Priestley.

come into view, when we shall consider the humanity of the antients. It is well known to have been a maxim at Sparta, that probity and every thing else was to be sacrificed to the good of the state. The Spartans encouraged their children to steal, but punished those who were taken in the fact, as not being dextrous in the business.

> We may judge of the state of Greece, with respect to the kind of justice of which we are now speaking, from that passage in a dialogue of Xenophon—in which he humourously shows the advantages of poverty and the inconveniencies of riches; and by what Tacitus says, that the temples were full of debtors and criminals, as churches and monasteries used formerly to be in popish countries. Rome and the neighbourhood of it, in the most interesting period of its history, viz. in the time of Cicero, abounded with robbers. Sallust says, that Cataline's army was much augmented by the accession of highwaymen about Rome. Cicero observed, that had Milo killed Clodius by night, it might have been imagined, that he had been killed by highwaymen, and that the frequency of such accidents would have favoured the supposition, though he had with him thirty slaves completely armed and accustomed to blood and danger. By the law of the twelve tables, possession for two years formed a prescription for land, and of one year for moveables; an evident mark of frequent violences, when such a law was necessary to secure a title to property.*

How different our situation is from this, and how much more secure our persons and property are, I need not mention in this auditory.

5. We proceed now to inquire how far the antient heathens practised the duties of humanity, and how far they violated those duties by outrage, oppression and cruelty. The Stoics condemned all compassion. No wonder then that they imbibed and practised inhumanity. Some philosophers, particularly Democritus, recommended revenge; and Plato owns that forgiveness of injuries was contrary to the general doctrine of the philosophers. These ideas seem perfectly to coincide with those among the moderns, who are the great advocates for a sense of honour. And how far these ideas are consistent with scripture, with reason or with humanity, I leave you to judge.

It was common with the Romans to make war on other nations for the end of enlarging their own dominions, and aggrandizing their empire. Generally they had no better motive to their wars than this. But

* Priestley's letters on general policy.

what is such a war, but a complication of downright robbery, cruelty and murder? They practised equal injustice in the manner in which they carried on their wars. They enslaved their captives or put them to death in cold blood, as they pleased. Their triumphs were most oppressive and cruel. The conquered kings and generals, loaded with chains, were driven into the city, and to the capitol before their conquerors, and were followed by mimicks and buffoons, who insulted over their misfortunes. When they arrived at the forum, they were led back to prison and there strangled; and this under the pretence of taking full revenge of their enemies. What better is this, than the treatment which our savage Indians give their captives?

The treatment which they gave those captives whose lives they spared, was correspondent to this cruelty toward those whom they put to death. As has been observed, they absolutely enslaved them; and by law, slaves were considered not as men, but as mere things, the mere property of their masters, and were treated, punished, and put to death at any time and in any manner, as their masters pleased, whether by beating, starving, torture, or otherwise. "The Spartans having conquered a neighbouring nation, the Helots, enslaved them, frequently butchered them in cold blood, and applauded their youths, when they killed them by surprise." "The Romans were not ashamed to suffer their old and useless slaves, when worn out in their service, to starve on an island in the Tyber, as was their common practice. Vidius Pollio used to throw his slaves, who had disobliged him, into his fish ponds, to be preyed upon by his mullets."*

Though to our shame, to the shame of humanity and the scandal of christianity, a slavery and a treatment of slaves similar to what existed among the Romans, exist and are tolerated in some parts of America; yet this scandal cannot be thrown on christendom in general. Such a slavery did indeed once generally obtain in Europe; but the benevolent and humane spirit of the gospel and the principles of justice taught there, have long since generally abolished it from that quarter of the world.

The proscriptions and assassinations, which were so common among the antients, are a further proof of their injustice, violence and inhumanity. It is well known that during the contests of Marius and

* Priestley.

Sylla, and during the triumvirate of Octavianus, Anthony and Lepidus, nothing was more common than to advertise a certain price for any man's or any number of men's heads; which was no other than hiring any cut-throat, and even a man's own domestics, to murder him and bring in his head. In this way the best men of Rome were murdered, and among the rest Cicero the great orator, philosopher and ornament of Rome. Amidst all the vices justly imputable to christians, they are not guilty of such barbarity and outrage as this. Such is the salutary influence of christianity, that even kings, who among the antients no sooner fell into the hands of their rivals or opposers, than they were assassinated, are now not put to death without a formal trial; which is a clear demonstration among many others, of our improvement in civilization and humanity, beyond any thing which existed among the most enlightened heathens.

Another instance of the barbarity and inhumanity of the antients, is their treatment of their children. "The antient Roman laws gave the father a power of life and death over his children, upon this principle, that he who gave, had also the power to take away. And a son could not acquire any property of his own during the life of his father; but all his acquisitions belonged to his father, or at least the profits, for life."* Thus children, during the life of their fathers, were perfect slaves, and in a worse condition than the slaves in this state; for the master in this state has not the power of life and death over his slaves. Nor were these mere speculations of the Romans; but their practice was correspondent. Hence the custom of exposing children; that is, of laying them, as soon as born, in the streets, on the banks of rivers, or in other frequented places, and unless some compassionate person should take them up and provide for them, leaving them there to perish and to be devoured by dogs. The motive to this horrid practice was, that the parents might be free from the trouble and expence of their education. Both Plato and Aristotle say, that there should be laws to prevent the education of weak children. Accordingly among the other Greeks, beside the Thebans, when a child was born, it was laid on the ground, and if the father designed to educate it, he immediately took it up. But if he forbore to do this, the child was carried away and exposed. The Lacedemonians indeed had a different cus-

* Blackstone.

tom; for with them all new born children were brought before certain triers, who were some of the gravest men in their own tribes, by whom the infants were carefully viewed; and if they were found lusty and well favoured, they gave orders for their education; but if weakly and deformed, they ordered them to be cast into a deep cavern in the earth, near the mountain Taygetus, as thinking it neither for the good of the children nor for the public interest, that defective children should be brought up. [“]It was the unhappy fate of daughters especially to be thus treated, as requiring more charges to educate and settle them in the world than sons.”*

In several nations, not only infants, but also the aged and the infirm, were exposed and left to perish.

Another horrid inhumanity, prevalent among the antient heathens, was the practice of sacrificing captives and slaves at the funerals of the dead. Thus Achilles sacrificed twelve young Trojans to the manes of Patroclus; and Aeneas sent captives to Evander, to be sacrificed at the funeral of Pallas. This was first practised with respect to persons of great eminence only, but at length it was done at the funerals of all persons of property, and became a necessary part of the ceremony.

Another practice as horrid as any I have mentioned, was that of exhibiting gladiators, trained to fencing and the use of the sword, spear, &c. on purpose that they might fight and kill one another on the stage, for the mere entertainment of the spectators, as some people now bait bulls and set dogs to fighting. “These poor wretches were made to swear that they would fight unto death; and if they failed of this, they were put to death by fire or sword, clubs, whips, or the like.”†

Those who have not attended to history, are apt to imagine, that the exhibition of gladiators was a rare thing, and that when it happened, a few pairs only were engaged. But it was far otherwise. Under the Roman emperors this inhuman entertainment cost innumerable lives. Cesar when edile, gave three hundred and twenty gladiators. Gordian in the time of his edileship, exhibited twelve entertainments, that is, one in each month. In some of these were five hundred champions, and in none of them less than one hundred and fifty. Taking it at a medium, he must have exhibited at the very least, three thousand. Titus exhibited these cruel shows for an

* Encyclopedia.

† Chambers Dictionary.

hundred days together. The good and moderate Trajan continued these spectacles for an hundred and twenty three days; and in that time gave ten thousand. When we consider how many different ranks of people gave these entertainments, ediles, pretors, questors, consuls, emperors and priests, besides private persons at funerals (which become so common a practice, that it was an article in a last will) we must be convinced, that the numbers were vast. What adds to the inhumanity of this custom, is, that it was designed for a gay entertainment and was attended as such. This horrible custom grew to such an extravagance, that it was found necessary to moderate it by law, in the time of the heathen emperors. Constantine first prohibited it altogether. But so violent was the taste for it, that it crept in again. The emperor Honorius entirely suppressed it.*

I shall take notice of only one more vice of the antient heathens, that is suicide. This was recommended by many philosophers, as an heroic act of virtue, and was practised by some of the highest fame, as by Zeno the founder of the sect of the Stoics, by Cato of Utica, and by Brutus. No wonder if under such instructors and such examples, suicide was very common among the antients. Beside the wickedness of this in the sight of God, the ruinous tendency of it in a political view is manifest on the slightest reflection. By this one vice not only any man may deprive the state of his aid and throw his family and dependents on the public; but the most important citizens, by throwing away their own lives in the most important and critical moment, may greatly endanger and entirely overthrow the commonwealth. What if our Washington, or the most wise and influential members of our congress, had destroyed themselves in the most critical periods of the late war?

From this brief survey of the vices of the antient heathens, I leave my hearers to judge how well founded the objection against christianity is, that it has depraved the morals of mankind.

I have now finished the observations which I intended, on the subject proposed, which was, the necessity of a belief of christianity by the citizens of this state, in order to our public and political prosperity. In subserviency to this general design I have endeavoured to show, that some religion is necessary to our political prosperity; that no other religion than the christian, can be generally received and established in this country; and that if some other religion could be

* Doct. Leachman's Sermon I. Cor. i. 21.

established among us, it would by no means be so useful in a political view, as the christian. I have endeavoured to illustrate the last observation by a comparison of christianity with the philosophical religion of infidelity and with antient paganism. I now beg leave to make two or three inferences from what has been said.

1. If christianity be more useful than any other religion, even for political purposes, we may presume that it is still more useful for the other purposes, which are indeed its immediate objects, piety and true virtue, and peace and comfort in them. The great foundations of religion and virtue are, the moral perfections of God, his moral government, the rule of our duty, a future state of retribution, the possibility of pardon and the end of our creation. Let us in these several particulars compare christianity with the philosophical religion, which is the only rival of christianity with any among us.

1. As to the moral perfections of God, christianity certainly teaches them more clearly than they can be learnt from any light afforded by the philosophical religion. The scriptures assure us, that holy, holy, holy is the Lord of hosts; that he is a God of truth and without iniquity, just and right is he; that he is the Lord, the Lord God merciful and gracious, long suffering, and abundant in goodness and truth, keeping mercy for thousands, forgiving iniquity and transgression and sin, and that will by no means clear the guilty. Yea, they assure us, that God is love. They clear up the difficulty arising from the evil in the world, by informing us of the end of all things, and that all things shall finally be overruled for good. But the philosophical religion gives no clear evidence at all of the moral perfections of God. This is acknowledged by some of the principal writers on that system. Hume, the most acute of all infidels, says we ought to infer from the works of God, intermixed as they are with good and evil, that God is of a mixed character, partly good and partly evil. Also Lord Bolingbroke, another principal deistical writer, holds, that there is no evidence of the moral perfections of God.

2. The like advantage have we by the scriptures as to the evidence of the reality and nature of the moral government of God. On the pretence that we are under the influence of a necessity of coaction, it is denied by some infidels that we are moral agents, and that we are capable of either virtue or vice. Now not only is this matter cleared up by revelation, but it is to be observed, that to be consistent, such

infidels ought also to deny, that we are capable of any crime in civil society.

If we be not moral agents, we are no more capable of murder, than a stock or a stone; and a man who from malice prepense kills another, no more deserves punishment, than the stone or the tree, which falls on a man and crushes him to death; and the man who from a wish to introduce and establish arbitrary government in his country, now a free and happy republic, betrays its ships and fortresses, no more deserves punishment, than the tempests which sink the former, or the fire which consumes the latter.

Some deny, that God at all concerns himself with human affairs or actions. But this is not only not reconcileable with the scriptures, but not with the moral perfections of God. If we be capable of virtue, and yet he neglect us, so as not to set before us proper motives to it, and not to show by proper rewards and punishments his approbation of the virtuous, and disapprobation of the vicious; this cannot be reconciled with his moral perfection.

It is further urged, that we are not in any case punishable, as all things are right, or as the poet expresses it, *whatever is, is right.* If by this observation be meant, that things are by the all-wise and all-governing providence of God, overruled to answer a good purpose, though in many instances directly contrary to their natural tendency; this is granted. But if it be meant, that all things in their own nature tend to good, this is not true. Malice has no natural tendency to good but a natural tendency to evil. On the other hand, benevolence has a natural tendency to good. Nor will it be pretended, that if malice reigned through the universe, the universe would be as happy, as if benevolence universally reigned. It is the natural tendency of a rational action, which determines its moral quality, and not the consequence produced by Almighty God, contrary to its natural tendency.

If all human actions were in a moral view indifferent, we should no more deserve punishment for murder, than we should for saving our country from ruin.

This scheme shuts all moral good out of the universe, as well as all moral evil. For if all the tempers and actions of men, are as to morality alike, it must be because there is no morality in any of them. If there be moral good in any of those tempers or actions, there must be moral evil in the directly opposite; and if there be no moral evil in the latter, there is no moral good in the former: as if there were no natural evil in pain there would be no natural good in pleasure.

But while infidels confound themselves and the principles of reason, in their discourses concerning the moral government of God; the scriptures assure us of the reality of that government, and of our accountableness to God.

3. The scriptures give us a plain and excellent rule of duty, pointing out our duty not only in general, but in all the most important particulars. How extremely deficient in this instance also, is the philosophical religion? It is indeed said, that the rule of our duty is right reason and the law of nature, and that virtue is a conformity to them. But this is saying no more than virtue is virtue, and that the rule of our duty is the rule of our duty. For right reason in this case means what is reasonable and right in a moral sense; and duty and what is right in a moral sense are the same thing: and it is just as difficult to find out the law of reason and of nature, as to find out our duty.

4. The scriptures give us the most positive assurance of a future state. But the philosophical religion can never assure us of this, because it cannot assure us of the moral perfections of God, by which alone he is disposed to reward the righteous and punish the wicked. Therefore infidels are greatly divided among themselves on this subject. Some as was before observed believe a future state, some disbelieve it. Those who believe such a state, believe that God made all men for their own personal happiness, and that therefore he will make them all happy in the future world. But all this depends on the moral perfections of God, of which they, as their principal writers confess, have no evidence. And if there be no evidence of God's moral perfections, there is no evidence, that he designs the happiness of his creatures either here or hereafter: nor is there any evidence but that he designs the final misery of all his creatures. Or if infidels had evidence of the moral perfections of God, they would not have evidence, that God made every man for the end of his personal happiness. The perfect goodness of God doubtless implies, that he made all things with a design to promote good on the whole or on the large scale. So that taking the system of intelligent creatures together, there shall be the greatest possible happiness in it. But this does not imply, that every individual creature shall be completely happy. There is no

accounting for the calamities and sufferings of this life on any other supposition, than that they will all finally issue in the greatest happiness of the system: and to suppose that they conduce to the good of the system, by making the persons themselves who suffer them here, more happy hereafter, is a mere conjecture unsupported by any argument. Therefore to indulgc it and to build upon it, is altogether unreasonable and unphilosophical.

On the whole, there is no evidence but that the good of the general system may be promoted by the exemplary punishment of the wicked in the future world. And if it would be promoted by such a punishment, infinite goodness not only admits of it, but requires and demands it.

5. The scriptures assure us of a way of pardon and acceptance with God; but the philosophical religion gives no such assurance. Infidels do indeed expect to be pardoned on their bare repentance. But the expectation of pardon on repentance, implies an acknowledgment, that they deserve punishment even though they repent, and that such punishment would be just: otherwise there could be no pardon in the case. To pardon is to exempt from punishment not an innocent man, but a guilty one: and to pardon a penitent implies that he deserves punishment, and that his punishment would be just. But if the punishment of the penitent would be just, the interest of the kingdom of God, the great community against which he has sinned, requires his punishment. The very idea of a just punishment is of one which, (there being no atonement or substitution), is due to the community or to the public good of the community, against which the crime punished was committed. But if the public good of God's kingdom, which is the universe, require the punishment of the sinner, it is not consistent with divine goodness to pardon him. What ground then has the infidel to expect pardon, when both justice and goodness require his punishment?

6. Christianity informs us of the end of our creation. It is generally holden by infidels, as was before observed, that we were made for our own personal happiness. But if this were true, it would prove, that God does concern himself with human actions, and that he aims to prevent those which tend to our destruction. It would also prove, that those rational actions which tend to destroy our happiness, are

morally evil, and that all actions are not in the same sense right. The evidence that God created us for our own happiness, must depend on the evidence of God's moral perfections. But as has been observed, the infidel has no evidence of these. Besides, if God really created us all for the end of our own personal happiness, it seems that he has in this world obtained his end, in a very imperfect degree only; and on the plan of infidelity there is no evidence of a future state. Therefore on that plan there is no evidence, that God will ever obtain his end in our creation.

Or if infidels should grant, that we were made for the general good of the system of intelligences, this would be to give up the chief object of infidelity; because the general good may admit of our misery in the future world, as it does of our misery in this.

But christianity clearly informs us, that God made all things for his glory, implying the greatest happiness and perfection of the creation as a system; or for the glorious exercise and display of his power, wisdom and goodness in raising his kingdom, which is the creation, as a system, to the highest degree of perfection and happiness.

Thus we see in what darkness, as to the most essential principles of religion, we should have been involved, had we not been favoured with the light of divine revelation, and in what darkness they are involved, who embrace the philosophical religion of infidelity. And thus we have further proof how happy that people is, whose God is the Lord, not only as this circumstance lays a foundation for their political good, but especially as it lays a foundation for true virtue and piety, for peace and comfort here and eternal happiness in the favour of God hereafter.

2. A second inference from this subject is, that since christianity appears to be necessary to the public good of the state, it ought to be encouraged by magistrates and rulers of every description. They are appointed to be the guardians of the public good; of course it is their duty to protect and promote every thing tending to it, and especially every thing necessary to it. Therefore as christianity is necessary to the public good, they are bound to encourage, promote and inculcate that, by their example and profession, by speaking and acting in favour of it both in public and private, by supporting christian ordinances and worship, and by promoting to places of trust and profit

those who profess it and live agreeably, and who are otherwise properly qualified. Magistrates are called to do all this on the ground of the soundest policy.

3. For the same reasons the citizens in general are obligated to encourage and promote christianity, by being themselves christians and that not only in profession, but in heart and life, and by giving their suffrages for those who are of the same character. It is indeed to be confessed, that not all professed christians are good men or real christians; yet among professed christians are many men, who possess good abilities and a proper share of information, who are strictly moral and upright, and who expect to give an account of their conduct to God. Such are the men to be promoted in the state; and the citizens by promoting such men, will encourage and promote christianity, and at the same time promote the good of the state.

I beg the further patience of the auditory, while I close the discourse, with the addresses usual on this occasion.

In the first place I beg leave to address myself to his Excellency the Governor.

May it please your Excellency,

In obedience to your command I appear in the desk this day; and I could think of no subject more important and at the same time more suitable to the present occasion, than the happiness of that people whose God is the Lord. I have therefore endeavoured to illustrate the necessity of the christian faith and practice, to the prosperity of the state. I may appeal to your Excellency how far this faith and practice have hitherto contributed to our political prosperity. Had not our ancestors been firm and exemplary in this faith and practice; had they not taken pains to hand them down to us; had they not in all their towns and settlements instituted schools, in which the principles of christianity, as well as other things were taught; had they not provided for the support of public worship, for the due observance of the Lord's day and for the public teaching of christianity on that day; had they not provided for the support of a studious and learned ministry, who being themselves men of knowledge, should be able to instruct others; I appeal to your Excellency, whether our political affairs would not at present have worn a very different aspect. And if our supreme magistrates had not been, both by profession and apparent practice, christians, it would doubtless have had a very baleful influence on the christian and moral character of the people at large, and consequently on our political prosperity. But we are happy in that we have had from the beginning, even to the present day, a series of governors, who have been not only an honour to the state, but ornaments to our churches. May such a series be still kept up without interruption. This, as it will be a proof of our christian character, will also be a proof of our public prosperity in every successive period, and a pledge of our subsequent prosperity. May God grant, that your Excellency shall effectually contribute to this prosperity in every way, in which your eminent situation affords opportunity. And when earthly states and empires shall be no more, may your Excellency, in that series of excellent men and excellent governors, and among all real christians, "shine forth as the sun in the kingdom of your Father."

2. The discourse addresses itself to his Honour the Lieutenant Governour, to the legislative council of the state, and to the representatives of the towns in general assembly.

Honourable legislators,

Since the belief and practice of christianity are so necessary to the political good of our state, and since you are appointed to be the guardians of our political good, I thought it not impertinent to suggest to you some important means, by which you may obtain the end for which you are appointed. Opposition to christianity both in faith and practice was never, at least in our country, so great and so increasing, as at the present day. It lies with you, gentlemen, by a steady belief, profession and practice of christianity; by your conversation and weight; by the appointments which you shall make to the various offices, civil and military, and by all your public proceedings, to withstand this opposition, and to guard against the danger to the public good, arising from the depravity of manners which opposition to christianity naturally induces. It is your province, in conjunction with his Excellency the Governour, to appoint all our executive civil authority and to confer the higher military honours. When men of licentious principles and practice are promoted either in the civil or military line, it gives a dignity and an influence to vice and irreligion. And "one sinner destroys much good," especially when exalted to a high station of honour and authority. Now, if you give this advantage to vice, you will thereby injure the state; but more immediately you will injure religion and the kingdom of Christ. And let me beseech you to remember, that you also have a master in heaven, to whom you, as well as the rest of men, must give an account. The only way to gain his approbation is, to keep a conscience void of offence, and in your political transactions not to act from party attachments and private connections, not to practice intrigue to serve your own interests or those of your friends; but to endeavour to serve the public in the best manner according to your capacity and opportunity. In so doing you will appoint to the several executive offices, men of knowledge and discretion; men that fear God and hate covetousness; men who will be just and rule in the fear of God. By the promotion of such men, virtue will be encouraged and vice will be restrained; by their official proceedings, law and justice will be executed, and "judgment will run down as waters, and righteousness as a mighty stream," even that righteousness which exalteth a nation. Then shall our political interests be in a prosperous state; then shall we be that happy people whose God is the Lord.

3. The reverend pastors of the churches, who are present, will suffer the word of exhortation.

My fathers and brethren,

We who are employed in the work of the ministry, are deeply interested in this subject. We are interested in the prosperity of the state, and are peculiarly interested in this mean of prosperity on which I have been insisting. It is our business to study and teach christianity, and thus to promote the political good of the state, as well as the spiritual good of the souls of our hearers. This is a noble employment, to fidelity and zeal in which, not only the motives of religion call us, but even those of patriotism. Therefore if we have any love to religion and the souls of men; nay if we have any public spirit and love to our country, let us diligently study the evidences, the nature, the doctrines and duties of christianity, and inculcate them with all plainness, assiduity and perseverance, giving line upon line and precept upon precept. This is to be done,

1. By instruction. Without communicating instruction and information concerning the truth, we can expect to do nothing in our

work to any good purpose. Knowledge and not ignorance is the mother of real devotion. The rational mind is to be led by the exhibition of the truth only.

2. By every motive to persuade, drawn from reason and revelation, from time and eternity; and among others this motive of the public good of the state and our general happiness, liberty and prosperity as a people, is not to be omitted.

3. By a christian life and conversation. If we do these things; if we thus instruct, persuade and live, we shall at last stand in our lot, and shall be owned as his, when Christ our Lord and judge "shall make up his jewels."

4. I shall, in the last place, address myself in a very few words to this numerous auditory collectively. Men and brethren, this subject nearly concerns you all. How happy would you be, if the Lord were indeed your God? Nor can you be truly happy on any other condition. However prosperous you may be in your private concerns, in your property, your business and your reputation; yet unless you are the objects of the favour of God and the heirs of eternal life, you are truly in a miserable situation. You have not only the motive of eternal happiness to choose the Lord for your God; but the motives of the peace, good order, and happiness of the people as a body politic, and the general prosperity of the state. You all feel a firm attachment to your liberties and to the privileges of a republican government. Of all forms of government a republic most essentially requires virtue and good morals in the great body of the people, in order to its prosperity and even its existence. But the way to virtue and good morals is to choose the Lord for your God. Nor is this all; you not only have to choose and serve the Lord yourselves, but by the same reasons by which you are obligated to choose the Lord for your God, you are obligated to seek out and by your suffrages to promote to legislative authority, such as are of the same character. In a republic all authority is derived from the people: and such as they generally are, we may expect their representatives, legislators and all their civil authority will be. If you have the Lord for your God, you will elect those of the same character with yourselves, to be your legislators; you will encourage and support them and other faithful rulers in the thorough discharge of their duties of civil government, and you will withhold your suffrages from those who acknowledge not the Lord as their

God and regard not his law. Nor can you consistently and innocently give your suffrages to men of this last discription: for thus you would give a sanction and influence to sin and vice, would be partakers of their wickedness and would do an injury to the state.

But if you and the good people of the state in general shall unite to practise virtue and christianity, and to promote the wisest and best men among us, we shall doubtless be that happy people described in the text, and as so many instances of our happiness "judgment shall dwell in the wilderness and righteousness remain in the fruitful field. And the work of righteousness shall be peace, and the effect of righteousness quietness and assurance for ever."

THE END

43

THE WONDERFUL WORKS OF GOD ARE TO BE REMEMBERED

David Osgood

BOSTON

1794

DAVID OSGOOD (1747-1822). Osgood left the fields of his father's farm at the age of nineteen, mastered a Latin grammar, and sixteen months later was admitted to Harvard, where he was graduated in the class of 1771. The Arminians complained that he was a Calvinist, and the Calvinists that he was Arminian. Eventually, on a controversial vote, he became the third minister of the First Congregational Parish of Medford, Massachusetts, and he remained there the rest of his life. A rough-cut man, short on the social amenities, he was a moderate patriot during the Revolution. He socialized little, catechized once a year, and never visited parishioners except on such formal church occasions as weddings and funerals. In later years he took to memorizing his sermons and repeating them now and again, a process restricted by one retentive congregation member who would raise his hand during a sermon to indicate with a number of fingers how many times he had heard it.

Osgood was an incandescent orator, however, sufficiently so to impress Daniel Webster, who commented on one sermon that "it was the most impressive eloquence it had ever been his fortune to hear" (*Sibley's Harvard Graduates*, 17:574). Osgood was preeminently a political preacher: Of twenty-two published sermons, several of them widely reprinted, eleven were on political subjects. This Thanksgiving Day sermon brought Osgood instant celebrity for its attack on Governor Samuel Adams for failing to mention the federal government, whose 1789 Thanksgiving Proclamation (by President Washington) was being observed. Osgood detected a Republican conspiracy—he even suspected secession—in this, and the hand of the Jacobins at work. The sermon went through six pamphlet reprintings (the second edition is given here), as well as newspaper reprintings, and it engendered a response covering the entire front page of a Republican newspaper, the *Independent Chronicle* (April 3, 1795), along with a number of other replies. A Federalist newspaper commented that Reverend Osgood knew "by the roaring of the Jacobins, that he [had] bitten them in a sore place" (Ibid., p. 575).

When asked about his practice of reading the text, closing the Bible, then removing his glasses and discoursing from memory, Osgood gave two reasons for this: "One, that he believed he could give his discourse greater effect by looking his auditors in the face—the other, that he wished to shew the Methodists and Baptists (of whom

The Wonderful Works of GOD are to be remembered.

A

SERMON,

DELIVERED

ON THE DAY

OF

ANNUAL THANKSGIVING,

NOVEMBER 20, 1794.

BY DAVID OSGOOD, *A. M.*
PASTOR OF THE CHURCH IN MEDFORD.

Publiſhed at the Requeſt of the Hearers.

The Second Edition.

Printed by SAMUEL HALL, No. 53, Cornhill, BOSTON,
MDCCXCIV.

it seems he has a number in his own parish) either that preaching without notes was no proof of inspiration, or, that he was as much inspired as themselves" (Ibid., p. 577). An unknown commentator wrote:

> There were passages in some of the sermons that we heard from the "old man eloquent," that thrilled through our frames, and such as could not easily be resisted or forgotten. And when in the midst of what seemed commonplace he laid aside his spectacles and turned away from his manuscripts, we were sure that it would be followed by a burst of fiery eloquence, and we were not mistaken. He held the audience for some minutes in rapt attention, and we hardly knew whether we were in the body or out of the body, so completely were we entranced and caught up, as it were, into the third heaven (Ibid., p. 578).

Osgood died of angina pectoris on December 12, 1822. A 469-page volume of his sermons was published in 1824.

He hath made his wonderful works to be remembered.

Psalm CXI. 4.

The works of God are usually distinguished into those of creation, and those of providence. By the former, we understand the stretching forth and garnishing of the heavens, the forming and replenishing of the earth, and the originating of the present order and course of nature. By the latter, are meant the continued preservation, the upholding and governing of all these things; and the superintending of all events, both in the natural and moral world. All these are great and wonderful works, worthy to be had in constant remembrance by every rational spectator. They make God to be remembered; nay, they are so many memorials of him, witnessing his eternal power and godhead, his overflowing benignity, and his care of, and kindness towards, his creatures.

They who have any taste for intellectual and moral pleasures, who are capable of relishing what is grand and sublime, will delight in prying into, and contemplating these great and wonderful works of creation and providence. To this purpose it is observed in the context, that the works of the Lord being great, honourable and glorious, they will be *sought out* or investigated *by all them who have pleasure therein*. By these works the Psalmist has special reference to the more signal dispensations of Providence in his dealings with his covenant people, the descendants of Abraham his friend. In these dispensations he set before them the most striking illustrations of his character and glorious perfections. They often saw him, on one occasion and another, triumphing over the false gods of the heathen around them, executing judgment upon their vain idols, and confounding their stupid worshippers. They saw his infinite power displayed in an almost continued series of miraculous operations; his justice in the exemplary punishment of cruel oppressors; his mercy in numberless affecting instances towards themselves; and his truth and faithfulness in the exact fulfilment of his promises and predictions. These things were intended to make lasting impressions on their minds—such as might not be easily or speedily effaced. The wonderful works of Providence are wrought for this very purpose, that, by beholding them, men may be so affected, as to have God continually in their thoughts, and thereby be led to fear and serve him.

The text may teach us, that the more signal mercies of heaven towards us, and those more remarkable deliverances which, at any time, have been wrought in our favour, ought to be gratefully remembered, and thankfully acknowledged by us. These things are some of the chief beauties and most brilliant pages in that book of Providence, which it highly concerns us daily to read and study. This book indeed contains the whole history of God's dealings with mankind, from age to age; in which he displays his moral perfections to the view of his rational offspring. The clear light of eternity will show every part of this volume to be full of meaning; and such an explanation will then be given to those passages, which are now esteemed dark and mysterious, as will induce enraptured saints, with astonishment, to exclaim, *O the depth of the wisdom and knowledge of God!* But while we dwell in this land of shadows and obscurity, we see only a small proportion of what God does; and having such limited views of his dispensations, it is no wonder if we be unable to comprehend the meaning of particular events.

There are many, however, which contain such striking illustrations of the divine attributes, especially of the divine mercy and goodness, that we can be at no loss about them. Not a few of these have fallen within our own observation; and many others our ears have heard, and our fathers have told us. God expects and requires, that we gather them up as a treasure, and carefully preserve them in our memories. They are in themselves memorable; and he hath done them, that they might be remembered by us. Of course, he is highly offended when men *forget his works and the wonders which he hath shewed them.* Such behaviour reflects upon the Divine Majesty, as though his method of governing the world, and his dealings with his creatures, were not worthy of our attention. The misery and destruction of men are, in some instances, attributed to their not *regarding the work of the Lord, nor considering the operation of his hands.* And it is certain, that the frequent review of the more striking dispensations of Providence is of excellent use to confirm us in the belief, and to excite us to the practice, of true religion. Through the weakness and darkness of their minds, and the strength of their corruptions, mankind are prone to unbelief. Some, under every advantage for light and conviction, do, notwithstanding, indulge to sceptical opinions: And they would generally, perhaps, be in danger of such opinions, and of calling in question the first principles and fundamental articles even of natural religion, the being, perfections, and moral government of the Deity; were it not for those less common appearances of his Providence, by which they are awakened to consider the manifold proofs of a Supreme Almighty Ruler working in the midst of them, and sitting as Governor and Judge among the nations.

At certain periods of time, through the several ages and among the different nations of the world, God breaks forth in signal and remarkable dispensations for the relief of the righteous, or for the punishment of the wicked. His providence is seen justifying its own procedure in vindicating and delivering oppressed innocence, or in precipitating prosperous guilt from its lofty seat. On these occasions, God is known by the glory that surrounds him. Beholding these extraordinary proofs of his presence and power, men are constrained to say, *Verily there is a reward for the righteous: verily he is a God that judgeth in the earth.*

And when we are once established in the belief of such a great and glorious Being, this faith will naturally prompt us to fear and serve him. Convinced of his power and justice by the awful manifestations of them in his works, we shall be led to stand in awe of him, and heedfully to shun whatever we apprehend to be offensive in his sight. Struck with the more signal displays of his mercy and goodness, and excited by them to the more fixed contemplation of his unbounded beneficence; we shall be satisfied, that our happiness must consist in the enjoyment of his favour. This persuasion will render us anxious to know *what the Lord our God requires of us;* and solicitous to approve ourselves to him, by a patient continuance in well-doing.

Our present trust in the divine mercy is also encouraged by the remembrance of former favours and deliverances. For this purpose, among others, the Israelites were enjoined to teach "their children the praises of the Lord, his strength, and his wonderful works—that the generation to come might know them—even the children which should be born: who should arise and declare them to their children; that they might set their hope in God."

The honour of God, the interests of religion, and the comfort and consolation of good men, being all promoted by the memory of the divine dispensations; it is highly agreeable to reason, and consonant to scripture, that public days should be set apart, on which a whole people may unite in celebrating the goodness of God; recollecting the instances of his providential care of, and kindness towards, them; and talking of his wonderful works in their favour. Such institutions serve as *pillars of remembrance*, to revive and perpetuate a sense of our obligations to heaven. The thoughts of the great body of the people are so taken up about their own private affairs, that they are prone to pay but little attention to the concerns of the public. After the first impression is worn off, they soon forget, at least practically, national mercies and deliverances, as well as national judgments. They need to have their minds stirred up by way of remembrance. And when God, by a long and continued series of remarkable interpositions, has multiplied, blessed, and prospered any people—has, on one occasion and another, repeatedly rescued them from great and threatning dangers—put them in full possession of their rights and liberties, laws and religion; and from year to year continues them in the quiet enjoyment of these privileges, together with the usual bounties of his munificent providence; they cannot too frequently recollect, nor too fervently and gratefully acknowledge, these signal instances of the divine benignity. It surely becomes christian magistrates, and is a duty they owe to God, to call upon their subjects to unite in commemorating these wonderful works of heaven in their favour.

Our forefathers, from the first settlement of the country, esteemed certain seasons of the year as highly proper for special acts of devotion. At the opening of the spring, they judged it fit and suitable, to set apart a day for humiliation and prayer; that they might implore the divine blessing on the affairs of the ensuing season—that it might be rendered fruitful, healthy and prosperous. And after the reception of these mercies, at the close of the season, another day was set apart for public thanksgiving. To this custom of our pious and renowned ancestors the proclamation for the observance of this day expressly refers. To the friends of religion among us it must be highly agreeable, to join in making this day a grateful memorial of God's providential kindness towards us; and especially, in recording the more signal mercies of the last revolving season.

He hath, says the proclamation, *been pleased to favour us with a good measure of health, while others, whom we ought to pity and pray for, have been visited with contagious and mortal sickness.* In the West-India Islands, in some of the southern states, and even in the neighbouring state of Connecticut, we have heard of an unusual mortality. But among ourselves, the instances of it have, as yet, fallen considerably short of the average number for the last twenty years. It is rare, indeed, that a year passes over us in which health is more generally enjoyed. Life is the basis of all our enjoyments in this world; and health is the balm of life. It sweetens and enhances all the comforts of life. It enables us to bear our part in the affairs of the world, and to partake of that rich profusion of good which a bountiful Providence sets before us. When therefore we see, or hear of, others from whom this blessing is withdrawn, it ought to excite our gratitude afresh, that to us it is still continued. On this day it becomes us, with increased love and thankfulness, to pay our vows to that Being who is the health of our countenance and the God of our lives; whose kind visitations uphold us in the land of the living, while many others, cut off by pining sickness, are continually sinking into the grave.

Next to the blessing of health, the proclamation mentions those of harvest: *He hath smiled on our agricultural labours, and caused the earth to yield her increase.* For the space of some weeks, at the opening of the spring, our prospect was melancholy. An early drought and a late frost, unusually severe, alarmed our apprehensions. But, from that period, we have rarely known, in this vicinity, a more fruitful season. Refreshing showers succeeding each other at short intervals, preceded and followed with a warm sun, have furnished a continued supply of grass for the cattle, and rendered the latter harvest, and the various productions of autumn, plentiful and abundant. In this respect also we record the rich bounty of Providence, and are constrained gratefully to acknowledge, that still "he leaveth not himself without witness, in that he continueth to do us good, to give us rain from heaven and fruitful seasons, filling our hearts with food and gladness."

With the blessings already recounted the proclamation goes on to inform us, that *He hath prospered our fishery, and in a great measure our merchandise, notwithstanding the depredations of unreasonable despoilers.* The attack of these despoilers upon our commerce has undoubtedly been infamous, and such as ought to be execrated by all civilized nations. And were we to judge of the extent of the mischief which they have done us, from the representations in some of the public papers, and in the resolves of certain self-created societies, we might be led to conclude, that the trade of the country was annihilated, and all its merchants bankrupts. It is therefore, after such continued alarms through the season, some consolation to hear, from so high an authority, that, notwithstanding all our losses, disappointments and vexations, a great measure of commercial prosperity has been enjoyed. Of this, indeed, we have yet further evidence even ocular demonstration, in the splendid and princely appearance of many of our mercantile citizens, and in the high price of our country produce, enhanced to a degree, which (though oppressive and ruinous to a few individuals whose sole dependence is upon a fixed stipend) is yet exceedingly gainful to the great body of the community. Such prodigious exportations would not, and could not, be continued, did not the merchant, notwithstanding every risk, find his account in them.

What a claim upon our gratitude then is this, that, through the mercy of heaven, we are allowed to increase in wealth, in numbers and strength, at a time, when the nations of Europe are madly wasting, impoverishing and destroying each other. There the awakened jealousy of tyrants, tenacious of their usurped powers, and the ferocious zeal, the desperate fury of a mighty, though long oppressed nation, have set the world in a flame. These lusts consume the abundance of the seas and the treasures of the dry land, the productions both of nature and art: They lay waste the works and improvements of ages, and, so far as their power extends, render all the elements subservient to misery and ruin. What a blast do the follies and vices of men bring upon the rich blessings of heaven? For our continued exemption from these scenes of devastation and ruin, how fervent should be our gratitude to the supreme Disposer: In times past we have experienced them; and may heaven grant, that we may know them no more! As yet we hail each of the contending nations as our friends; and while they are mutually suffering such complicated evils from one another, these states present a common asylum for the distressed of all parties, who are almost daily arriving on our peaceful shores.

The enumeration of blessings in the proclamation concludes with adding, *He hath continued to us the inestimable blessing of the Gospel, and our religious, as well as civil rights and liberties*. For the former of these

—the rich blessings of the gospel and our religious privileges—as they are primarily a supernatural grant from heaven, and comprise all our hopes and prospects for eternity; so no period, short of that endless duration, will be sufficient for adequate returns of adoration and praise. For the latter, our civil rights and liberties, we are, under Providence, and as the mean by which heaven has granted and continues them to us, indebted to a cause or source which, I am sorry to observe, is not mentioned, nor even referred to, in the proclamation —I mean the general or federal government. This omission is strange and singular, beyond any thing of the kind that I recollect to have seen since the first union of the states in the memorable year 1775. It has, to say the least, a strong appearance of disconnection with the general government, and an air of separate sovereignty and independence, as though we enjoyed not our civil rights in union with the other states under one common head.

Here then, I think it my duty, to remind you, that of all our political blessings for which we ought, on this day, to make our grateful acknowledgments to the divine goodness, our federal government is the greatest, the chief, and, in fact, the basis of the whole. Its form and constitution are by wise men universally admired. The wisdom, integrity, ability and success of its administration have commanded the respect and applause of the world. Its happy effects and consequences to ourselves, which we have known and experienced, have been great and estimable, beyond any other political good which we have ever enjoyed. By guarantying to each of the states a republican form of government, and the enjoyment of every right consistent with the rights of the whole, it becomes to them all their greatest security against the attempts both of internal faction and external invasion. In this view, it is their main pillar of support and bulwark of defence.

Previous to the adoption of this most excellent form of government —under the old confederation, these states presented to the world a many-headed monster, frightful and alarming to all the lovers of peace and good order. Each state claimed a negative on the resolves of the whole in Congress assembled; and the regulations of the several states respectively were continually interfering and clashing with each other. From this foundation for discord, parties and divisions were inevitable. In almost every state, many were disaffected towards their own immediate government. In some of the states, open rebellions existed. Things went on from bad to worse, till the administration of justice was suspended, the laws silenced—all public and private faith left without a support, and the obligation of promises and contracts set aside. Men could neither confide in the public, nor in one another. Industry wanted encouragement—trade languished—a general uneasiness prevailed; and we tottered on the brink of the most dreadful convulsions.

The federal government was no sooner organized, than it speedily rescued us from this eminently hazardous situation. It gave fresh vigor to each of the state governments; awed into submission the factious through all the states; restored the course of justice, and thereby established peace and good order among the citizens at large. It recovered the sinking credit of the nation, together with that of the respective states; and gave such a spring to commerce, agriculture, manufactures, and all those useful arts which supply the necessaries and conveniencies of life, that they have flourished to a degree incomparably beyond what had ever been known in this country before. In promoting these important ends of every good government, it exceeded the most sanguine expectations of its friends and patrons. So striking and manifest were its beneficial effects, that even its restless enemies were compelled to silence. This tide of public prosperity continued rising even after the commencement of the present troubles in Europe: The current of our trade flowed for a while with but little interruption, and with accumulated profit to our merchants and farmers.

In this prosperous situation of our affairs, a foreign incendiary appeared among us; the object of whose mission was, at all events, to draw us in for a share in the war of Europe. By fair negociation with the existing government, he had no hope of success. It was therefore necessary, that the government should be overthrown; or, at least, that the wise and good men entrusted with its administration, should be driven from the helm. Materials for either or both of these purposes were ready to his hand.

In every country there are some who envy the abilities of their superiours, and covet their stations; some constitutionally turbulent and uneasy, who can have pleasure in nothing but scenes of tumult and confusion; some who can make themselves conspicuous on no other occasions; and some in desperate circumstances, whose only hope of bettering them is in revolutions of government. Besides a proportion of all these, there has been in this country a large party, from the beginning, ill affected toward the federal government; and with these may be reckoned numbers of ignorant, though honest, people, who think the period arrived when the debt of gratitude ought to be paid to our allies. The passions, prejudices and opinions of these several classes of people prepared their minds to receive the impressions of an insidious minister.

He immediately put in practice the arts which had proved so dreadfully efficacious in his own country. His intrigues were suddenly and surprisingly extended. His very breath seemed to kindle the smothered embers of sedition from Georgia to Newhampshire. Presses through the states were engaged to forward his designs, by conveying torrents of slander and abuse against the great officers of government. Popular societies, unknown to the laws, were recommended and actually formed under the influence of demagogues well skilled in the business of faction. The British councils, as though in league to aid the attempts of Genet, perfidiously seized upon our trade, and thereby furnished (what as yet had been wanting) a plausible occasion for clamour to those who were seeking it, and a just ground of resentment and indignation to the most peaceable and well disposed. The passions of men were worked up to a degree of fury. Rash and violent measures were proposed and strenuously urged. Favoured by these circumstances of embarrassment to the government, the western counties in Pennsylvania embraced the opportunity to rise in rebellion.

Such, my hearers, have been the trials and dangers to which our peace, liberty, and all our political happiness, have been exposed. That the consequences have not, as yet, been more pernicious, we have abundant reason, this day, to thank and praise the Supreme Disposer. Our general government, with all our rights and privileges embarked, has been steering between Scylla and Charybdis: That we have not been dashed upon either, is owing to the good hand of God, influencing and directing the pilots.

The prospect is now more favourable. Through the wise and good conduct of the president, his ministers, and the men of sober judgment in Congress, we seem to have escaped many rocks and quicksands. With dignity and firmness they resisted the intrigues and machinations of an unworthy ambassador, till, at length, they obtained his removal. With respect to the nation from whom we have received unprovoked injuries, while they have been preparing for the dernier resort, by putting the country into a state of defence; they have sent forward to them the remonstrance of reason, truth and justice, that (if possible) they might prevent the dreadful calamity of war. A degree of success has already attended the negociation. The offending power now appears half ashamed of the wrongs which it hath committed against us; and is constrained to promise restitution. They have also, the present year, been successful against the hostile tribes of savages: And to suppress rebellion, have sent forth an army so numerous and powerful as affords the hopeful prospect of effecting the purpose without the effusion of blood. To the several democratic societies through the states, who have incessantly censured, misrepresented and calumniated all these measures of our federal rulers, they have opposed a dignified patience and moderation, worthy of their high stations and great abilities.

But as those societies, and the spirit of faction which they engender, nourish and spread among the people, are, in my view, the greatest danger which, at present, threatens the peace and liberties of our country, I shall close this discourse with a few strictures upon them.

In every country the men of ambition, who covet the chief seats in government, exert all their abilities to ingratiate themselves with the source of power. Under a monarchy they are the most servile courtiers at the levee of the prince. In a republic, the same men appear in the character of flaming patriots, profess the warmest zeal for liberty, and call themselves the friends of the people. In monarchies, their intrigues and factions are endless. But as the monarch himself is the main object of all their attempts, over whom they endeavour to extend their influence; their factions are usually limited to the precincts of the court, and rarely occasion any general convulsion in the empire. In a republic, the case is widely different: thousands and millions are the object whom they would influence. Of course, the more popular any government is, the more liable it is to be agitated and rent by parties and factions. Our's is not the first republic which the world has seen. Some centuries before the christian era, the states of ancient Greece and Rome were so many republics. But through the intrigues of ambitious and designing men, influencing each one his party, they became so many hot beds of faction and dissention. Their worthiest and best characters, when such chanced to hold the reins of government, were soon hunted down; and the vilest of men took their places, and this in continual rotation. Civil wars frequently occurred; and as either party prevailed, proscriptions, banishments and massacres ensued. Precisely the same scenes are now exhibited in France. We all rejoiced at the downfall of despotism in that country: We considered it as the dawn of liberty to the world. But how soon was the fair morning overcast? They had no sooner adopted a popular government, than all the violence of faction broke out. A constitution, which the collected wisdom of the nation had been two years in framing, was, in a day or an hour, overset and demolished. From that time to this, their civil government has been nothing but a contest of parties, carried on with all the ferocity of barbarians. Previous to the revolution, it was said of the French, that so refined was their sensibility, so abhorrent of every appearance of cruelty, that they would not suffer tragedy to be acted at their theatres. Is it not astonishing, how so great a change in the morals and manners of a nation could be so suddenly effected? Faction alone accounts for it. Had the representatives of the nation been left to act their own judgment, uncontrouled by the leaders of faction, they would never have been guilty of those excesses and cruelties which chill all humane minds with horror. But how came those factious leaders by such a controuling power over the convention? Solely by means of those popular societies in which they presided, or over which they first gained an influence. These gave to faction its whole force.

On the same principles with those in France are founded the democratic societies in this country; and should they become numerous here, as they are there, they will infallibly have a similar effect. Their pretence is, to watch government—they mean the federal government. But this, like each of the state governments, is chosen by the nation at large; and, of course, every man in his individual capacity has an equal right and an equal interest in watching its measures. What presumption then is it, and what an usurpation of the rights of their brethren, for private associations, unauthorized by the laws, to arrogate this charge to themselves? Admitting the propriety of setting a watch upon Congress and the president; are not the state legislatures fully competent to the business? Is not their interest at stake, and their jealousy always awake, ready to notice any fault or error in the general government? What then is there for these private associations to do? Good they cannot do; and if they do any thing, it must be evil. And that they have done evil already, and are, in fact, the support of a pernicious and inveterate faction against the general government, among many other unquestionable proofs, the omission of our chief magistrate, just mentioned, is, to my mind, not an improbable one. For unless we suppose him to have fallen under the baneful influence of those societies, we know not how to account for his having hazarded a proclamation in which we are directed, neither to give thanks for any advantages enjoyed by means of that government, nor even to ask the blessing of heaven upon it.* As though its destruction were already decreed, it is treated as no longer the subject of prayer.

Should so melancholy an event as its overthrow ultimately take place, no cause at present appears so probable, as those ill-judged associations. To pull down and destroy good governments as well as bad, is their only tendency. In the nature of things they can have no other effect. In such a country as this, therefore, where, through the distinguishing mercy of heaven, we have obtained a government so admirably adapted to promote the general happiness, these irregular and unwarrantable associations ought to be guarded against and suppressed with a vigilance like that with which we extinguish a fire when it is kindling in a great city. Their meetings are so many collections of combustibles; and should they be generally extended, the whole country will be in a flame. The members of those societies, by virtue of this relation, necessarily become the mere tools and dupes of

* This must appear the more extraordinary when we reflect, that at the time of issuing the proclamation, war with the savages raged on our frontiers, rebellion in the bosom of the country, and our situation, with respect to the powers of Europe, had become so critical, that we were actually fortifying and forming a numerous army.

their artful leaders, who have their own ends to serve by all their professions of patriotism.

> The moment a man is attached to a club, his mind is not free: He receives a bias from the opinions of the party: A question indifferent to him, is no longer indifferent, when it materially affects a brother of the society. He is not left to act for himself; he is bound in honour to take part with the society—his pride and his prejudices, if at war with his opinion, will commonly obtain the victory; and rather than incur the ridicule or censure of his associates, he will countenance their measures, at all hazards; and thus an independent freeman is converted into a mere walking machine, a convenient engine of party leaders.

In this way a few ambitious individuals are enabled to extend their influence; and as they rise in power and consequence, to infringe upon the liberty of the public.

> Each individual member of the state should have an equal voice in elections; but the individuals of a club have more than an equal voice, because they have the benefit of another influence; that of extensive private attachments, which come in aid of each man's political opinion. And just in proportion as the members of a club have an undue share of influence, in that proportion they abridge the rights of their fellow citizens. Every club therefore, formed for political purposes, is an aristocracy established over their brethren. It has all the properties of an aristocracy, and all the effects of tyranny. It is a literal truth, that the democratic clubs in the United States, while running mad with the abhorrence of aristocratic influence, are attempting to establish precisely the same influence under a different name. And if any thing will rescue this country from the jaws of faction, it must be either the good sense of a great majority of Americans, which will discourage private political associations, and render them contemptible; or the controling power of the laws of the country, which, in an early stage, shall demolish all such institutions, and secure to each individual, in the great political family, equal rights and an equal share of influence in his individual capacity.
>
> But let us admit that no fatal consequences to government, and equal rights, will ensue from these institutions, still their effects on social harmony are very pernicious, and already begin to appear. A party spirit is hostile to all friendly intercourse; it inflames the passions; it sours the mind; it destroys good neighbourhood: it warps the judgment in judicial determinations: it banishes candor and substitutes prejudice; it restrains the exercise

> of benevolent affections; and in proportion as it chills the warm affections of the soul, it undermines the whole system of moral virtue. Were the councils of hell united to invent expedients for depriving men of the little portion of good they are destined to enjoy on this earth, the only measure they need adopt for this purpose, would be, to introduce factions into the bosom of the country. Faction begets disorder, force, rancorous passions, anarchy, tyranny, blood and slaughter.*

May the God of order and peace preserve us from such dreadful calamities! and to him shall be the glory forever.

AMEN

* *The Revolution in France, by an American*: a judicious and instructive pamphlet.

44

THE REVOLUTION IN FRANCE

Noah Webster

NEW-YORK

1794

NOAH WEBSTER (1758–1843). Son of the Congregational deacon Noah Webster, Sr., the author of this discourse on the French Revolution was the great lexicographer who gave birth to *An American Dictionary of the English Language*. The younger Noah received his preparatory training for college from Reverend Nathan Perkins in West Hartford, Connecticut. He entered Yale but then briefly served in the Revolutionary War; he resumed his studies at Yale and was graduated in 1778. Intent upon a legal career, he was in due course admitted to the bar in Hartford, only to give up law practice in 1793. From 1782 onward, he had been increasingly drawn to his true career, the study and teaching of the English language in its distinctive and patriotic modes. His grammars, readers, and spellers began to be published in 1784 and were issued and reissued well into this century. Webster estimated that fifteen million copies of *The American Spelling Book* had been printed by 1837 and, in all, a hundred million (running through four hundred editions) of the blue-backed speller had been printed by the twentieth century.

Webster agitated throughout the country for a copyright law to protect his publications and eventually saw one passed. A strong Federalist, he campaigned for the adoption of the Constitution. He also lectured far and wide on the English language and collaborated with Benjamin Franklin in devising a phonetic alphabet. Though Franklin's version proved too radical for full adoption, his and Webster's efforts helped shape the American language.

In New York, Webster edited magazines and newspapers off and on over a ten-year period. By 1803—having moved to New Haven, Connecticut, in 1798—he had abandoned that line of work and turned to his chief concern, the study of language. Beginning with the publication of a preparatory lexicon in 1806, he brought forth the *Dictionary* in two quarto volumes in 1828. The most ambitious publishing project in America up to that time, this work demonstrated a great advance in the field of lexicography.

Webster spent most of his later years in Amherst, Massachusetts, and in New Haven, and in that period he published five revisions of the *Dictionary*, a revised translation of the King James Version of the Bible, and many essays and addresses. Captured by the inspirations of the Second Awakening, he became a strong Calvinist and Congregationalist, especially after 1808.

THE

Revolution in France,

CONSIDERED IN RESPECT TO ITS

Progress and Effects.

BY AN AMERICAN.

Harum ego religionum nullam unquam contemnendam putavi ; mihique ita persuasi, Romulum auspiciis, Numam sacris constitutis fundamenta jecisse nostræ civitatis ; quæ nunquam profecto sine summa placatione Deorum Immortalium tanta esse potuisset.

CICERO DE NATURA DEORUM LIB. III.

The motto may be thus rendered in English : "I never thought any religion to be despised : I have always considered the foundation of our State to be laid in religious institutions ; and that without the favor of heaven, the Republic would never have arrived to its present flourishing condition."

OLD FASHIONED PHILOSOPHY OF CICERO.

" *Religion in no Country is founded in Truth.*"

" *Death is an everlasting Sleep.*"

MODERN PHILOSOPHY, LATEST FRENCH FASHION.

NEW-YORK:

[*Printed and Published according to act of Congress.*]

BY GEORGE BUNCE, and Co. No. 64 Wall-Street.

M,DCC,XCIV.

In *The Revolution in France*, Webster brilliantly reflects on the religious and philosophic implications of the upheaval. Always concerned to find a balance between virtue and liberty, this piece marked Webster's departure (in the words of William F. Vartorella) "from his tenets espousing the rights of man to self-enhancement. The indiscriminate use of the guillotine made him shudder; his philosophical foundation crumbled under the strain and man, a sullen being, emerged as depraved" (*American Writers Before 1800*, p. 1534).

PREFACE

In the progress of the French Revolution, candid men find much to praise, and much to censure. It is a novel event in the history of nations, and furnishes new subjects of reflection. The end in view is noble; but whether the spirit of party and faction, which divided the National Assembly, sacrificed one part, and gave to the other the sovereign power over the nation, will not deprive the present generation of the blessings of freedom and good government, the objects contended for, is a very interesting question. Equally interesting is it to enquire what will be the effects of the revolution on the agriculture, commerce, and moral character of the French nation. The field of speculation is new, and the subject curious.

The writer of the following remarks came into society, during the late war with Great-Britain; his heart was very early warmed with a love of liberty; his pen has often advocated her cause. When the revolution in France was announced in America, his heart exulted with joy; he felt nearly the same interest in its success, as he did in the establishment of American independence. This joy has been much allayed by the sanguinary procedings of the Jacobins, their atheistical attacks on christianity, and their despicable attention to trifles. He is however candid enough to believe much of the violence of their measures may be attributed to the combination of powers, formed for the most unwarrantable purpose of dictating to an independent nation its form of government. Perhaps other circumstances, not known in this country, may serve to palliate the apparent cruelty of the ruling faction. But there are some proceedings of the present convention, which admit of no excuse but a political insanity; a wild enthusiasm, violent and irregular, which magnifies a mole-hill into a mountain; and mistakes a shadow for a giant.

A just estimate of things, their causes and effects, is always desireable; and it is of infinite consequence to this country, to ascertain the point where our admiration of the French measures should end, and our censure, begin; the point, beyond which an introduction of their principles and practice into this country, will prove dangerous to government, religion and morals.

With this view, the following strictures are offered to the American public. Freedom of discussion is a privilege enjoyed by every citizen; and it is presumed that some degree of severity will be pardoned, when it has truth for its support, and public utility for its object.

INTRODUCTION

Men of all descriptions are frequently asking the questions, what will be the fate of France? What will be the consequences of the revolution in France? Will France be conquered? and others of a like nature.

These questions are extremely interesting, as they respect every thing which concerns the happiness of men in the great societies of Europe and America; government, liberty, arts, science, agriculture, commerce, morality, religion.

It would be an evidence of daring presumption to attempt to open the volume of divine determinations on these momentous questions. But it is highly proper, at all times, to exercise our reason, in examining the connection between causes and their effects; and in predicting, with modesty, the probable consequences of known events.

It is conceived to be the duty of the historian and the statesman, not merely to collect accounts of battles, the slaughter of the human race, the sacking of cities, the seizure and confiscation of shipping, and other bloody and barbarous deeds, the work of savage man towards his fellowmen; but to discover, if possible, the causes of great changes in the affairs of men; the springs of those important movements, which vary the aspect of government, the features of nations, and the very character of man.

The present efforts of the French nation, in resisting the forces of the combined powers, astonish even reflecting men. They far exceed every thing exhibited during the energetic reigns of Francis Ist. and Louis XIVth. To ascertain the true principles from which have sprung the union and the vigor which have marked this amazing revolution, is a work of no small labor, and may be of great public utility.

JACOBIN SOCIETY

It is conceived the first principle of combination in France, was the establishment of the Jacobin Society. The members of this association might not originally have foreseen the extent of the revolution, or the full effect of their own institution. At the time it was formed, there might have been many persons in it, who were friends to the monarchy of France, under the control of a constitution, and an elective legislative assembly. But the interest of the ancient court, the nobility and clergy was then considerable, not only in Paris, but in every department of France. It was necessary, in the view of the leaders of the republican party, to circumscribe or destroy the court-influence by direct legislative acts; or to raise throughout France, a combination of republicans, who, by union and concert, might oppose it with success. The public mind was not ripe for the first expedient, the direct invasion of the privileged orders; the republicans therefore, with a discernment that marks great talents, resorted to the last expedient, the institution of popular societies in every department of that extensive country. These societies are all moved by the mainspring of the machine, the Jacobin Society in Paris; and by the perfect concert observed in all their proceedings, they have been able to crush every other influence, and establish over France a government as singular in its kind, as it is absolute in its exercise.

COMMISSIONERS

In pursuance of the same principle of combination, tho not cotemporary in its adoption, was the plan of conducting both civil and military operations in all parts of the republic, by commissioners from the National Convention. It was found that, altho the Jacobin societies had a very extensive influence in seconding the views of the republican party; yet this was the influence of opinion, and private exertion merely; an influence too small and indirect, to answer every purpose. These societies were voluntary associations, unclothed with any legal authority. To conduct the intended revolution, it was necessary there should be persons, in all parts of the country, vested with full powers to execute the decrees of the convention, a majority of whom were Jacobins; and whose measures were only the resolutions of the Jacobin Society in Paris, clothed with the sanction of a constitutional form. To supply the defect of legal authority in the several popular societies, commissioners were deputed from the convention, invested with the most absolute powers to watch over the civil and military officers employed in responsible stations, to detect conspiracies, to arrest suspected persons, and in short to control all the operations of that extensive country. These commissioners, being usually taken from the Jacobin Society at Paris, and having a constant communication with the convention, which was ruled by them, were enabled to carry all their measures into full effect. A single club, by this curious artifice, gave law to France. An immense machine, by the most extraordinary contexture of its parts, was and is still, moved by a single spring.

To unclogg this machine from all its incumbrances, and give vigor to its active operations, it was necessary to displace all its enemies. For this purpose, all suspected and disaffected persons were to be removed. Under pretence of guarding the public safety, and delivering the republic from traitors, insiduously plotting its destruction, a court was established, called the Revolutionary Tribunal, consisting of men devoted to the views of the Jacobins, and clothed with powers that made their enemies tremble. The summary jurisdiction, assumed or exercised by this tribunal, together with its executive instrument, the guilotine, have filled France with human blood, and swept away opposition.

The commissioners in the several departments and municipalities have renewed the tyranny of the decemvirs of Rome. The writer is informed that while they affect the pomp and the manners of Roman consuls, they exercise the powers of a dictator. The two commissioners at Bourdeaux, imitating as far as possible the Roman habit, ride in a car or carriage drawn by eight horses, attended by a body of guards, resembling the pretorian bands, and preceded by lictors with their battle-axes.

The authority of all the commissioners is nearly dictatorial. They arrest, try and condemn, in a most summary manner. Not only difference of opinion, but moderation and especially the possession of money, are unpardonable crimes, punishable with death, in the view of these delegates of dictatorial power.

By this principle of combination, has a party, originally small, been enabled to triumph over all opposition.

In the mean time, a numerous and ignorant populace were to be amused, united, won to their party, and fired with enthusiasm for liberty. These people, who little understand the principles of government, were to be rendered subservient to the views of the republican party; and as their reason could be little affected by arguments, their passions were to be roused by the objects of sense. As the most of them cannot read, particular persons were employed in the towns and villages to read to them, the inflammatory writings which flowed from the Parisian presses. These readers collected the people in crowds, read to them such pieces against the king, queen, nobility and clergy, as were calculated to irritate their passions and inspire them with implacable hatred against these orders. They were taught to believe them all tyrants, traitors and oppressors. These public readers would also harrangue extemporaneously on the same subjects: such artifices had a prodigious effect in changing the attachment of the people for their king and their priesthood, to the most violent aversion. This hatred soon discovered itself in the destruction of a great number of noblemen's chateaus; the busts of ancient kings, pictures and other ensigns of the royal government. At the same time a number of patriotic songs were composed as *Ca ira*, *Carmagnole*, and the *Marseillais Hymn*; which were soon spread over France, and have had a more extensive influence over the soldiers, seamen, and the peasantry of that country, in reconciling them to the hardships of war, and firing them with an enthusiasm for what they call liberty, than the world in general will believe; an influence perhaps as powerful as that of all other causes combined.

Interrupted as our intercourse is with France, and agitated as the public mind must be with passing scenes, it cannot be expected that we should obtain from that country a dispassionate and minute detail of causes and their consequences; but I believe the facts I have mentioned will go far to account for the unprecedented union of the people of France, notwithstanding the operation of the usual causes of discord, and the influence of foreign gold very liberally exerted to disunite them, and perplex their measures. It has however been necessary for the convention to resort to the terrors of the guillotine, and of death and the destruction of whole cities, to awe the spirit of opposition to their system. Very numerous and most terrible examples of punishment have had a powerful temporary effect, in subduing their internal dissensions. How far the people will bear oppression, is a point on which we cannot decide.

NATIONAL TREASURY

The measures taken by the convention to prolong the resistance of France, are no less singular, bold and decisive. It was found that immense sums of money would be necessary to maintain the vast body of men and military apparatus, requisite to oppose the combined forces of more than one half of Europe. To furnish the funds necessary for this purpose, the convention very early adopted the plan of issuing *assignats* or bills of credit, an expedient practised with great success in America, during her late revolution. This paper however was issued on safer ground than the American paper; as confiscated property to a vast amount was pledged for its redemption.

It was found however that this paper would depreciate; as the funds pledged for its redemption were exhausted, or proved inadequate to the enormous demands made upon the nation, in consequence of a great augmentation of their military establishment, after opening the last campaign. To supply the deficiency, and to put it out of the power of chance or enmity to drain the republic of its specie, the convention adopted the following desperate expedients. They exacted from moneyed men whatever specie they possessed, by way of loan. This is called *emprunt force*; a forced loan. And to make sure of this specie they contracted with certain bankers in Paris to advance 12 millions sterling of the money, paying them a large commission for the risk and forbearance. The amount of the specie to be thus bro't into the national treasury, may be 20 millions sterling. This measure, together with the proceeds of confiscations, has accumulated a great proportion of the current specie of the country, in the treasury.

Not satisfied with these measures, the convention have taken possession of all the plate of the churches, which, in all Roman Catholic countries, must be very considerable, but in France, amounts to an immense value. It is estimated by gentlemen well acquainted with this subject, that this public plate, which is carried to the mint, will amount to 25 millions sterling; a sum nearly equal to the whole current specie of that rich commercial country, England.

It was estimated by Mr. Neckar and others, just as the revolution commenced, that the current coin of France was at least 80 millions sterling; a sum equal to one third, perhaps one half, of all the specie of Europe. Allowing large sums to have been carried out of the country by emigrants, and some to be buried for safety, but taking into the account the accession of 25 millions coined from plate; and we may estimate the amount of specie in possession of the convention, to be from 60 to 70 millions sterling.

Having thus collected all the precious metals in that country, the convention, instead of using specie freely to furnish supplies for the army, expend it with great œconomy. They hold it in reserve, for times and exigencies when all other expedients fail. At present they compel every person whatever to take assignats for provision, clothing and other articles, at a certain price fixed by a valuation. They sieze whatever grain or other articles a man has, beyond an estimated supply for his own family, and pay him in paper at the stated price. In this manner they seem determined to make their paper answer every purpose as long as possible, and when this fails, they will still have specie enough at command, with the aid of some taxes, to prosecute the war for three or four years.

PROBABLE EVENT OF THE WAR

It may be doubtful whether the body of people will long sit easy, under such severe regulations. An enthusiasm for liberty will do much; the guilotine, and an irresistable army will do more, towards preserving peace and order. But there is nothing dearer to a man than the liberty of making his own bargains; and whether the forcible means employed to procure from people their produce or manufactures, will not at least check industry and limit the exertions of laborers to a bare supply of their own wants, is a point very problematical. But whatever may be the wants of France, there is little danger, while her specie is at the command of government, that her provisions will fail. Her rich soil will furnish the principal mass of food;

and should distress call for foreign supplies, her own shipping will supply her from abroad.

If these ideas are well founded, France is able to sustain a war of many years. She can supply men enough to resist the combined powers forever. Her natural population will forever repair her annual loss of men; and the longer a war lasts, the more soldiers will she possess. The whole country will become an immense camp of disciplined veterans.

While policy, aided by the strong arm of absolute power, is thus furnishing France with the means of defence, what prospect have the combined powers of effecting their purposes? France may defend herself until England is a bankrupt, and Austria is beggared. Possibly England and Holland may sustain the war another campaign; and more than this, they unquestionably will not. The states of Italy, which have been compelled to renounce their neutrality, will yield a cold, reluctant, feeble assistance, and embrace the first favorable moment to renounce the confederacy. Portugal is nothing in the contest. Spain, it is an equal chance, will be overrun and plundered by a French army; will itself be disabled and its riches only furnish the French with additional means of defence. Prussia has gained her principal object in obtaining a large division of Poland; she now demands a considerable debt of the empire, which the diet is not well able to discharge. The empress of Russia is encouraging the controversy, while she laughs at the combination, and is adding to her dominions. Austria is powerful, but she is exhausting her resources; and by reason of the distance which great part of her supplies are to be transported, her means must fail, before those of France. Already the emperor calls for voluntary aids from his subjects in Flanders. In this situation where is the hope of conquering France!

It is more probable that France will not only resist all this force, but will retain strength sufficient to commence an offensive war, when the confederacy of her enemies shall be dissolved, and the resources of each exhausted. Her enemies will waste their strength in making France a garrison of disciplined soldiers, impregnable within, and terrible to surrounding nations. The moment the combination is broken, and the army now investing France, disabled, half a million of hardy exasperated French warriors, inured to service, and fired with victory, will be let loose upon defenceless Europe; and in their mad enthusiasm to destroy, not despotism merely, but all the works of elegance and art, they may renew the desolations of the 6th and 7th centuries. Already has France experienced a revolution in property, in manners, in opinions, in law, in government, that has not been equalled in the world since the conquests of Attila and Genseric. The ravages of Genghis Khan, of Tamerlane and the Saracens were extensive, they were attended with slaughter and devastation. But the conquered nations only changed masters and remained unchanged themselves. The revolution in France is attended with a change of manners, opinions and institutions, infinitely more singular and important, than a change of masters or of government.

Of the two possible events, a conquest of France, and a total ultimate defeat of the combination against the republic, I am free in declaring my opinion, that the *former is less probable* than the latter. And should victory finally declare for France, her armies may prove formidable to Europe. Italy and the Netherlands must inevitably fall under her dominion, unless prevented by a timely pacification.

Such being the origin and progress of this astonishing revolution, let us examine its probable effects.

DEBTS

The effects of war upon the hostile nations are always to exhaust their strength and resources and incur heavy debts. Should France succeed in baffling her foes, an immense debt will be contracted, which must be paid, funded or expunged. An immediate payment is not to be expected; it will be impracticable. It may be justly questioned, whether the best administration of her finances will, for many years, discharge the interest. Such a general war, which involves in it a diversion of laborers from their usual occupations, a destruction of manufacturing towns and villages, a limitation of commercial intercourse, and especially a loss of capital among all descriptions of citizens, must dry up the sources of revenue, and occasion a deficiency that will materially affect the credit of the nation. If therefore the government should be disposed to fund the national debt, its inability to pay the interest, must, for some years, cause a depreciation in the value of the receipts or evidences of that debt. This depreciation will renew the speculations of John Law's administration—or rather the scenes exhibited in America in 1790, 1791 and 1792. Should this be the case, immense fortunes will be made; a new species of aristocrats, as they will be called, will arise out of the equality of *sans-culottism*, and unless a change of sentiment shall take place in the people, these new-fledged nabobs will be considered as noxious weeds in society, that are to be mown down with that political scythe, the all-levelling guillotine.

But the funding of debts is at present not an article in the national French creed. On the other hand, the revolutionists execrate the system that entails on posterity the debts of the present generation, and fills a country with negociators and stock-jobbers. If then the nation cannot pay the principal, and will not pay the interest, the remaining alternative is to expunge the whole debt.

We cannot however suppose that the same administration of the government will continue for a long period. The probability is that when danger of external foes shall be removed, the nation will elect a new convention of a very different complection. Too many good citizens will be public creditors, to suffer the debts of the nation to be wiped away with a spunge. It is more probable that efforts will be made to discharge them; and as the proceeds of confiscations will be soon exhausted, and there are no wild lands in France, the government must resort to the usual modes of raising money, by customs, and taxes, with loans or anticipations of revenue. So that after all the fine philosophy of France, she will probably be obliged to submit to some of the old schemes of finance, which her wise legislators now execrate. We have therefore no great reason to apprehend that her government will be able to expunge her debts, nor can we suppose that absolute freedom from debt will constitute a part of her promised millenium of reason and philosophy.

AGRICULTURE

The important changes in the tenure of lands in France will produce the most distinguishable effects. The feudal system was calculated for no good purpose, except for defence among a barbarous people. It was every way formed to check the exertions of the great mass of people, whose labor, in all countries, is the principal source of wealth. That must always be a bad system of tenures which deprives the laboring man of the great stimulus to industry, the prospect of enjoying the reward of his labor. Such was the feudal system throughout Europe, and it is observable that agriculture and manufactures have made slow progress in every part of Europe where that system has been suffered to prevail in its ancient vigor. The principal cities of Italy and Germany first regained their freedom and revived industry. The abolition of military tenures in England may be considered as the epoch of her wealth and prosperity. Under the old government of France, the feudal system had lost much of its severity. There were many laboring men who enjoyed small freeholds; too small however for the purpose of improving in cultivation. But two thirds of the lands were leased to the peasantry, the landlord furnishing the stock of the farm, and receiving half the produce. This mode has ever been found less beneficial to a country, than leases on fixed rents in money.

But by the late revolution, a vast proportion of the lands will change hands; and much of them become freehold estate, subject to no rent or none that shall be oppressive. The laboring people, becoming proprietors and cultivating for their own benefit, will feel all the motives to labor that can influence the human heart in that particular. The mind, unfettered and prompted to action, will exert its faculties in various kinds of improvement and when the distresses of war shall cease, the French nation will push improvements in agriculture to a length hitherto unknown in that country. Previous to this however, property must be placed under the protection of law; and the laws must receive an energy from a well-constituted executive power, that shall ensure a due execution.

MANUFACTURES

The same circumstances which will invigorate industry in one branch of business, will extend their influence to every other. For some years indeed the desolating effects of war will be visible. The destruction of some manufacturing towns, the loss of capital, and the diversion of laborers from their employment, will be severely felt for many years.

But the active genius of the French nation, unfettered from the imposing prejudices of former times, when it was held degrading to engage in manual occupations, will surmount these difficulties; and the immense wealth of the emigrant nobles, the national domains, or other property which had been monopolized and sequestered from employment, under ancient institutions, will be brot into action in every branch of business. After the ravages of war shall be repaired, a greater mass of capital will be employed in useful arts, and rendered productive. All the plate of the churches, now converted into coin, and immense sums formerly squandered by a profligate nobility, or withheld from employment by cloistered monks, will be brought into circulation, and become the means of encouraging industry. Add to these circumstances, the amazing increase of enterprize, which must follow a revolution, that has awakened a nation from the slumbers of ignorance and inaction, and roused into life the dormant faculties of its citzens.

COMMERCE

Simular circumstances will forward the growth and extension of commerce. France has long been respectable for its commerce and its navy. But the increase of agriculture and manufactures, which will necessarily follow the downfall of the feudal distinctions, and the more general diffusion of property, will produce also a correspondent increase of commerce. This commerce will require the use of shipping, and the late navigation law of France, will recal to her some of the advantages of the carrying trade, heretofore enjoyed by the English and the Dutch, and be the means of augmenting her navy.

ARTS AND SCIENCE

Free governments are the soil best fitted to produce improvements in the arts and sciences. All history testifies this. France indeed, under her old government, had been distinguished for a cultivation of the sciences, and many of the most useful and elegant arts. In many respects, the lover of philosophy was free, and full scope was given to human genius. In other respects, freedom of writing was restrained by the hand of power, and the bold writers of that nation were compelled to retire beyond the reach of it.

The universal freedom of writing, which we may expect to prevail, when the present storm subsides, will be among the most conspicuous blessings of that nation. The arts will receive new encouragement, and the sciences new luster, from the active genius of renovated France.

RELIGION

The progress of the revolution in France, with respect to morals and the religion of the nation, affords a most interesting spectacle to reflecting men. The hierarchy of Rome had established, over the minds of its votaries, a system of errors and superstition, that enslaved their opinions and plundered their purses. Long had nations been the victims of papal domination, and spiritual impositions. Accustomed from childhood to count their beads, to bow to the host, and chant *te deum*, men supposed that ceremony was devotion; while an artful priesthood availed themselves of their weakness and errors, to spunge from the deluded multitude, a great portion of the fruits of their honest labor.

For three centuries past, the reason of man has been removing the veil of error from his mind. In some countries, the veil has been rent asunder: and human reason, aided and directed by revelation, has assumed its native dignity. But in France, science and education, while they had illuminated a portion of its inhabitants, had not dissipated the gloom that was spread over the mass of the nation. Inquisitive men had searched for truth, and astonished at the monstrous absurdities of the national religion, their minds, starting from the extreme of superstition, vibrated to the extreme of scepticism. Because they found religion, clothed with a garb of fantastical human artifices, they rejected her as a creature of human invention, pronounced her ceremonies a farce, and derided her votaries. Hence sprung a race of literary men, denominated philosophers, who, under their illustrious champions, Voltaire, and Rousseau, attempted, by secret undermining or open assault, to demolish the whole fabric of the national religion, and to erect upon its ruins, the throne of reason.

Before the present revolution commenced, this philosophy had spread among the literati of France; and Paris exhibited then, what Italy does now, the two most irreconcileable extremes, of atheism and profound superstition; the most scandalous vices mingled with the most scrupulous observance of religious rites; the same persons retiring immediately from their mock-devotions at Notre Dame, to the revels of prostitution.

In this situation of the moral and religious character of the French nation, began the revolution of 1789. The philosophical researches of Voltaire, Rousseau and the Abbe Raynal, had long before unchained the minds of that part of the French nation who read; a respectable class of men. These men understood the errors of their government and the nature of liberty. They were prepared to second the operation of those political causes, which hastened the crisis of a revolution. The first attentions of the reformers were occupied with the correction of political evils, rather than those of religion. But when the first national assembly came to examine the system of their government with minute inspection, they found it a complicated machine, in which the ecclesiastical state was so interwoven with the political, that it would be impossible to retrench the corruptions of the one, without deranging the whole fabric. It became neccessary therefore (and the philosopher rejoiced at the neccessity) to take down the whole machine of despotism, involving all the privileged orders in the proposed renovation.

The first assembly proceeded as far as they durst, in laying their hands upon the immense possessions of the clergy, and abolishing the monastic institutions; making provision, at the same time, for maintaining the clergy by granting them annual salaries, suited to their former ranks in the church. This step was bold, and gave umbrage to many of the higher dignitaries. But as the assembly had the policy to augment the salaries of most of the inferior clergy, the curates or vicars, who were the most numerous body, and had most influence over the people, this measure insted of endangering, rather strengthened the cause of the revolution.

Upon the election of the second assembly, a new scene was to be presented. A party of violent republicans, not satisfied with the constitution of 1791, and resolved to exterminate monarchy, and with it all the privileged orders, after a violent contest with their adversaries, the Fuillans, in which the latter were defeated, assumed the government of France; and from the full establishment of the Jacobins, with a decided majority in the convention, we date many important changes in the customs and institutions of that country. The progress of these changes in detail is left for the historian: my limits confining me to sketches only of these great events. In general, however, I may observe, that the ruling party in France, have waged an inveterate war with christianity; and have endeavored to efface all the monuments by which it has been perpetuated. They have abolished not only the sabbath, by substituting one day in ten as a day of rest and amusement in lieu of one day in seven; but they have changed the mode of reckoning time, substituting the foundation of the republic as the vulgar era, instead of the christian era. They have not indeed prohibited any man from believing what religion he pleases: but as far as their decrees can reach, they have established, not deism only, but atheism and materialism. For these assertions I have their own decrees. In their decree respecting burials, they say, they "acknowlege no other doctrine, except that of national sovereignty and omnipotence." If I understand this, it denies the being of a God. They ordain, that deceased persons shall be carried to the place of burial, covered with a pall, on which shall be depicted sleep, under the shade of the trees in the field, a statue shall be erected, representing sleep—and on the gate of the field, this inscription—"death is an everlasting sleep." This is an explicit denial of the immortality of the soul, and in effect the establishment of materialism by law.

The church of Notre Dame is converted into the temple of reason; a colossal monument is erected in honor of the day, when reason triumphed over what they call fanaticism; and festivals are ordained to celebrate the memorable epoches of important changes in the government and religion of France. A great number of the clergy have publicly renounced their profession declaring their belief that their ancient religion was superstition and error, and that the only true religion is the practice of justice and moral virtue.

This account of the proceedings in France exhibits, in a luminous point of view, the singular contexture of the human mind; now depressed with chimerical horrors; demons, ghosts, and a God in terrors, armed with vengeance, and hurling nine tenths of mankind to the bottomless pit; now, elevated on the pinions of a subtle philosophy, men soar above all these bug-bears; revelation, piety, immortality, and all the christians hopes are rejected as phantoms; the Supreme Jehovah is reasoned or ridiculed out of existence, and in his place is substituted the *omnipotence of national sovereignty.*

Vain men! idle philosophy! I will not attempt to expatiate on the pernicious effects of such mistaken and misdirected reason. A sorrowful prediction of woes that must fall upon the nation, thus set afloat on the wide ocean of doubt, and tossed between the ancient hopes of immortality, and the modern legislative assurance of everlasting sleep in annihilation, would be derided as the cant of bigotry; the whining lamentations of interested priest-craft. But I will meet your philosophy upon your own ground; and demonstrate, by the very decrees which demolish the ancient superstition, that you yourselves are the most bigotted men in existence.

It is the remark of a great philosopher, whose opinions I am sure you will respect, that the mind of man is subject to certain unaccountable terrors and apprehensions, proceeding from an unhappy situation of affairs, from ill health, or a melancholy disposition. This is the origin of superstition and priestcraft. The mind of man is also susceptible of an unaccountable elevation and presumption, arising from success, luxuriant health, strong spirits, or a bold confident disposition. This is the source of enthusiasm. Hume's Essays, Vol. I. 75.

I will not controvert this explanation of the two most remarkable principles in the mind. Nor will I wholly deny the conclusion he draws, that superstition is most favorable to slavery, and enthusiasm, to liberty. But I will go farther in this question than he did, and farther than you will at first admit to be just—but it is a position warranted by all history and perpetual observation, that if superstition and enthusiasm are not essentially the same thing, they at least produce effects, in many respects, exactly similar. They always lead men into error.

Superstition and enthusiasm operate by different means and direct the mind to different objects; but they agree in this respect, they imply or produce an excessive improper attachment to certain objects, usually objects of little real consequence. They are equally the humble votaries of some deity, tho each has a different one and worships him in her own peculiar mode. From the only regular body of deists in the universe, as Mr. Hume calls the disciples of Confucius; from the exalted philosophers of Greece and Rome, Plato, Pythagoras and Cicero: or from the still more refined philosophers, the noble disciples of reason, the members of the National Convention of France, down to the lowest bigot that drones out a lifeless existence over his beads and his crucifix in some dark monastic cell, there is one single principle of the human mind operating steadily to produce these different characters: this principle is a strong, universal and irresistable disposition to attach itself to some object or some system of belief which shall be a kind of idol to be worshipped in preference to all others. The object only is varied; the principle eternally the same. The principle springs from the passions of the mind, and cannot be annihilated without extinguishing the passions; which is impossible. When a gloomy mind clings to its priest or its altars, it is called superstition. When a bold mind, and ardent spirits rise above grovelling objects, and embrace spiritual delights, with raptures and transports, it is called enthusiasm or fanaticism. When a long series of reflection and reasoning has cooled or moderated the passions, the mind is governed less by feeling and more by argument; the errors of superstition and enthusiasm are perceived and despised; the mind fixes itself upon a theory of imaginary truth, between the extremes of error; and this is pronounced reason and philosophy. That this reason is not truth itself nor an infallible standard of truth, is obvious: for no two men agree what it is, what its nature, extent or limits. No matter; superstition and enthusiasm are beat down; reason is exalted upon a throne, temples are erected to the goddess, and festivals instituted to celebrate her coronation. Then begins the reign of passion; the moment reason is seated upon her throne; the passions are called in to support her. Pride says[:] I have trampled down superstition, that foe to truth and happiness—I have exalted reason to the throne; I am right—every thing else is wrong. Obey the goddess reason, is the great command: and woe to the man that rejects her authority. Reason is indeed the nominal prince, but the passions are her ministers, and dictate her decrees. Thus what begins in calm philosophy, ends in a most superstitious attachment to a particular object of its own creation. The goddess *reason* is at last maintained by pride, obstinacy, bigotry and to use a correct phrase, a blind superstitious enthusiasm.

The history of men is one tissue of facts, confirmatory of their observations. The Egyptians adored certain animals; and to injure a cat in Egypt, was a crime no less enormous than to pull down a liberty cap, to use the christian era, or wear abroad the robes of a priest in France; it was sacrilege. When we are told by credible historians that the Egyptians, when a house was on fire took more pains to save the cats, than the house, we stare and wonder how men could ever be so weak and stupid as to regard a cat, as a sacred animal. But is not the cap of liberty now regarded with a similar veneration? Would not an insult offered to it be resented and call down the vengeance of its votaries? How is this? Why the answer is easy—the Egyptians venerated a cat and a cow, and our modern idolaters venerate a liberty cap. The passion of the Egyptians will be called superstition perhaps; the passion of our people, enthusiasm. But it is the object that is changed, and not the principle. Our people are perpetually exclaiming "*Liberty is the goddess we adore*," and a cap is the emblem of this goddess. Yet in fact there is no more connection between liberty and a cap, than between the Egyptian deity Isis, and just notions of God; nor is it less an act of superstition to dance round a cap or a pole in honor of liberty, than it was in Egypt to sacrifice a bullock to Isis.

The Greeks were a learned nation: but they had their Delphic oracles, whose responses were regarded as inspiration. The Romans, were more superstitious, and were governed in public and private affairs, by the appearances of the entrails of beasts, the flight of birds, and other omens. Both these nations were superstitious; that is, they believed their fate to be connected with certain religious rites; they placed confidence in certain supposed deities or events; when in fact there was no connection at all between the cause and effect, but what existed in opinion. The Pythian god in Greece knew nothing of future events; the auspices in Rome had no connection with the fate of those who consulted them, but the people believed in these consultations, and according to the result, were inspired with confidence or depressed with apprehensions. There were philosophers indeed in those enlightened nations who rejected the authority of their divinities. Cicero says, in his days, the Delphic oracle had become contemptible. Demosthenes declared publicly, the oracle had been gained over to the interest of Philip. These and many others were the deists of Greece and Rome; the Humes and Voltaires of antiquity. But they never had the courage or the inclination to abolish the religion of their countrymen—they treated the fabled divinities of their country with more respect than the Jacobin club has paid to the founder of christianity. At the same time, while they indulged their fellow citizens in their own worship, they wrought out of their own imagination, some airy deity; some fine subtle theory of philosophy, which they adored with the superstition of bigots. It is idle, it is false that these philosophers had refined their ideas above all error and fanaticism—they soared above the absurdities of material deities, the lares and penates of the vulgar; but they framed etherial divinities, and spent their lives in paying homage to these fictions of imaginations.

In short the only advantage they had over vulgar minds was, that common people were content to worship the gods of the country, already framed to their hands; while the pride of each philosopher was busy in creating deities suited to his particular fancy.

When christianity became the religion of Rome, many of the pagan rites were incorporated, and some of the temples and deities, brot into use in the christian religion. The use of incense or perfumes, holy water, lamps, and votive offerings in churches, are pagan ceremonies retained in the Romish church. In lieu of the images of heathen deities Jupiter, Hercules or Bacchus, the christians substituted the statues of saints, martyrs and heroes; or else preserved the old images, giving them only a different dress. The pantheon of ancient Rome was re-consecrated by Boniface IVth, to the Virgin Mary, and all the saints.

What is all this? the christians pretended to abolish and exterminate pagan superstition—they only changed the name, and the objects to which veneration was to be paid. Instead of worshipping and sacrificing to Bacchus, the new converts adored the figure of a saint.

The Romans had a celebrated festival, called Saturnalia in honor of Saturn; this festival found its way into antient Scandinavia, among our pagan ancestors, by whom it was new-modelled or corrupted, being kept at the winter solstice. The night on which it was kept was called mother-night, as that which produced all the rest; and the festival was called Iuule or Yule. The christians, not being able to abolish the feast, changed its object, gave it the name of Christmas, and kept it in honor of Jesus Christ, altho the ancient name yule was retained in some parts of Scotland, till within a century. Mallet North Antiq. Vol. I. 130, Cowel. voc. Yule. What is the deduction from these facts? This certainly, that men have uniformly had a high veneration for some person or deity real or imaginary: the Romans for Saturn: the Goths for the mother-night of the year; and the christians for the founder of their religion. The christians have the advantage over the pagans in appropriating the feast to a nobler object; but the passion is the same, and the joy, the feasting, and the presents that have marked the festival are nearly the same among pagans and christians.

Let us then see whether the national convention of France have succeeded in exterminating superstition and fanaticism; and with them, their offspring, persecution.

They have indeed abolished the christian sabbath, because it was one of the institutions of superstition and the support of error, bigotry and priestcraft. But with the absurdity and inconsistency that ever accompanies fanaticism, they have established a similar institution, under a different name; instead of a christian sabbath once in seven days, they have ordained a political sabbath once in ten days. The object only is changed, while the uses of such a day are acknowledged by the convention themselves: and in spite of their omnipotence, the nation will appropriate that or some other day to nearly the same purposes.

They have abolished the christian era, and substituted the epoch of the abolition of monarchy, or what is the same thing, the *foundation of the republic*. And what do they gain by this change? Merely the trouble of introducing confusion and perplexity into their own mode of reckoning time, during the present generation, and into their negociations with other powers, forever. The era itself is a thing of no kind of consequence; it is not of the value of a straw; but when this indifferent thing is established, as a common point of reckoning time, among a great number of surrounding nations, it becomes of great moment, and the change of it marks a contempt of common utility and a superstitious regard to the period of the revolution, or rather the era of their own triumph over their opposers, that is equal to the ancient respect for the Delphic oracle, or the modern veneration for a papal bull. The object only is changed; the passion is the same.

They have also annihilated the national worship, and of course a great number of holidays. But they have decreed a most magnificent and splendid festival, to be celebrated once in four years, in honor of the republic. What is this but a superstitious veneration for a new era, instead of the old ones? But what is singular in this institution is, that it is professedly copied from the celebration of the Olympic games in Greece. What then is become of the convention's reason and philosophy, which was to buoy them above vulgar prejudices? Do they, in this instance, exhibit proofs of exalted reason? Is it less a prejudice to venerate the Greek Olympiads, than the christian sabbath, or christian era? Let Danton and Robespiere answer this question, or blush for their philosophy.

The convention have also rejected the national faith, and sanctioned, with a decree, the doctrines of deism and materialism. This is another sublime effort of their Grecian philosophy to annihilate superstition and bigotry. But in the moment they are shunning Scylla, they are shipwrecked on Charybdis. It was not sufficient to destroy one faith; but they proceeded to establish another. They erect a statue to sleep, and on the gates of their burying fields, ordain this inscription, "Death is an everlasting sleep." Laugh not, ye refined sages, at the poor ignorant Greeks, who, lost and bewildered in the mazes of doubt, with more honesty than yourselves, acknowledged their ignorance, and erected an altar to the unknown god. St. Paul informed that venerable body of sages, the Athenian Areopagus, that this was superstition; yet the inscription on the altar at Athens, and that on the gates of the burying places in France, proceeded from equal ignorance, and the devotion paid to the statue of sleep will be as blind, as head-strong, and as marked with superstition, as the worship of the unknown god in Athens.

The convention, in their zeal for equalizing men, have with all their exalted reason, condescended to the puerility of legislating even upon names. That they should abolish titles of distinction, together with the privileges of the nobility and clergy, was natural; but that the common titles of mere civility and respect should be attacked was astonishing to indifferent spectators, who had expected their proceedings to be marked with dignity. The vulgar titles of address, *monsieur* and *madame*, whatever might have been their original sense, had become mere names of civility, implying no distinction, and applied equally to all classes of people. They were literally terms of equality; for when *A* addressed *B* with the appellation, *Monsieur*, *B* answered him with the same address; denoting an equality of standing and a mutuality of respect.

Yet these harmless titles, which had no more connection with government, than the chattering of birds, became the subject of grave legislative discussion, and the use of them was formally abolished. And what did the convention substitute in their place? Why the awkward term *citizen*, which is in fact a title of distinction, denoting a man who is free of a city, and enjoys rights distinct from his fellow inhabitants; or at least one that has a legal residence in a country, and in consequence of it, enjoys some rights or privileges, that are not common to all its people. In proof of this I need only suggest, that in the United States and I believe in all other countries, certainly in France, legal provision is made for acquiring the rights of citizenship.* Reflect, ye philosophic legislators, and be ashamed of your contradictions.

The convention have also abolished the insignia of rank, civil and ecclesiastical. Even a priest cannot wear his robes, except in the temples. But it was not sufficient to reduce all ancient orders; they established another distinction, which was represented by the cockade of liberty. Enthusiasm had only taken down one order, to put up another; and no sooner was the order of liberty instituted, than its members assumed an arrogant imperious behavior: they esteemed themselves better than their fellow-citizens; the cockade became a badge of despotism; every one who would not join the order, and go to every excess in their measures, was denounced as a traitor, and a man must wear the national cockade, or be massacred. Yet there is not the smallest connection between a cockade and liberty, except what exists in the fanaticism of the order. It is superstition of the

* By the present constitution of France, citizenship is lost by naturalization in a foreign country. If Danton himself should come to America and be naturalized, he would no longer be a French citizen. Mr. is a mere title of civility, applicable to all men, in all places, and under all circumstances; the most equalizing title in the French or English language.

rankest kind; and precisely of the same nature as that which fired millions of bigots to rally under the banners of the cross, in the 12th and 13th centuries, and march, under Peter the hermit, to recover the holy land from infidels. The cross in one case had the same effect in inspiring enthusiasm, that a cockade has in the other. Peter the hermit, and the Jacobins of France equally acknowledged the principles and the passions of the human heart. To accomplish their purposes they made use of the same means; they addressed themselves to the passions of the multitude, and wrought them up into enthusiasm.

To complete the system of reason which is to prevail in France, in lieu of ancient errors and absurdities, all the statues of kings and queens, together with busts, medalions, and every ensign of royalty, nobility or priesthood, are ordered to be annihilated. Even the statue of Henry IVth on the new bridge; a monument erected to the most patriotic prince that ever graced the royal diadem; who had projected a plan of universal peace in Europe, and who, had he not fallen prematurely by the hand of an assassin, would perhaps have done more for the happiness of society, than all the philosophers France ever produced; even his statue could not escape the philosophic rage for innovation. The statue is annihilated, and in its place, at the motion of David the painter, a colossal monument is decreed to be raised on the bridge, to transmit to posterity the victory of nations over kings, and of reason over fanaticism. Yes, philosophers, a noble victory this! But you forget that this very decree is the height of political fanaticism. The monument is changed with the object of fanaticism; and this is all the difference between you and the admirers of Henry IVth who erected the statue which you have demolished.

Marat also has a monument erected to his memory, in the pantheon! And who was Marat? A Prussian by birth; by profession, a journalist, who lived by publishing libels on the moderate men who opposed the Jacobin Club: by nature, a bloodthirsty wretch, the instigator of massacres, whose cruelty and baseness inspired a woman with courage to assassinate him. To such a pitch has the fanaticism of these philosophers carried them in this instance, that they have actually dispensed with the decree which denies the honors of the pantheon to patriots, until they have been dead ten years, and in favor of his extraordinary merits, Marat was deified a few months after his death.

The refined imitators of the Greek philosophers have gone beyond their predecessors, in a stupid veneration for departed heroes; and if the present fanaticism should continue a few years, they will fill their new pantheon, with canonized Jacobins.

The same blind devotion to every thing ancient has led these superstitious reformers into the most ridiculous changes of names. Church is a relic of christian bigotry—the name therefore is rejected and in its place, the Latin word *temple* is substituted. This in France is philosophical! But what is more extraordinary, is, that in the moment when the modern calendar was abolished, and new divisions of time instituted, and even the harmless names of the months changed because the old calendar was the work of a pope and a relict of priestcraft: nay, at the time these wise and sublime reformers were abolishing, not only superstition, but even a belief in any superior being; they themselves sequestered a building for the express purpose of immortalizing men, and even gave it the Grecian name, *Pantheon*, which signifies the *habitation of all the Gods*. Such perpetual contradictions, such a series of puerile innovations, are without a parrallel in the history of revolutions: and while these regenerators of a great nation believe themselves the devotees of reason and philosophy and exult in their supereminent attainments, they appear to the surrounding world of indifferent spectators, as weak, as blind and as fanatical, as a caravan of Mahometan pilgrims, wading thro immense deserts of suffocating sands, to pay their respects to the tomb of the Prophet.

It is remarkable also, that with professions of the most boundless liberality of sentiment, and with an utter abhorrence of bigotry and tyranny, these philosophers have become the most implacable persecutors of opinion. They despise all religious opinions; they are indifferent what worship is adopted by individuals; at the same time, they are establishing atheism by law. They reject one system to enforce another. This is not all; they pursue with unrelenting cruelty, all who differ from them on political subjects. The friends of a limited monarchy, to the constitution of 1791, to a federal government, however honest, fair and candid, all fall before the Jacobins. The Marquis La Fayette, that unimpeachable hero and patriot, fell a sacrifice to his integrity. He had sworn to maintain the constitution of 1791—he respected his oath—and was driven into exile and a dungeon. The Jacobins also swore to maintain that constitution—they perjured themselves—and now rule triumphant. Dumourier, the ablest general that has figured in France this century, after a series of unexampled victories, fell a sacrifice to Jacobin jealousy. The moment the Jacobin club felt their superiority, they commenced tyrants and persecutors; and from the execution of Mr. Delassart, the first victim of their vengeance, to that of Mr. Brissot and his adherents, a series of persecution for mere difference of opinion has been exhibited in France, that has never before been equalled. The Jacobins differ from the clergy of the dark ages in this—the clergy persecuted for heresy in religion—the Jacobins, for heresy in politics. The ruling faction is always orthodox—the minority always heterodox. Totally immaterial is it, what is the subject of controversy; or in what age or country the parties live. The object may change, but the imperious spirit of triumphant faction is always the same. It is only to revive the stale plea of necessity; the state or the church is in danger from opinions; then the rack, the stake or the guillotine must crush the heresy—the heretics must be exterminated.

It was the language of the pagan emperors who persecuted the christians; "these sectaries must be destroyed—their doctrines are fatal to our power." It was the language of the popes and cardinals, who instigated the persecution of the Hussites, Wickliffites, Lutherans and Calvinists; "these reformers are heretics who are dangerous to the true church, they must be destroyed; their doctrines must be exterminated; it is the cause of God." It is the same language, which the barbarous followers of Mahomet employed and still employ to justify the enslaving of christians. The same is the language of the British acts of Parliament which lay all dissenters from the established church, under severe restraints and disabilities. It is the present language of the court of inquisition in Spain and Portugal—it is the language of the Jacobin faction in France, with the change only of the word *liberty* for *church.* The mountain exclaim, "liberty is in danger from traitors." But when we examin the proofs, nothing appears to warrant the charge, but the single circumstance that these dangerous men *belonged to another party*; they were acknowledged republicans, but differed in opinion, as to the precise form of government, best calculated to secure liberty. Yet being Girondists, another party, they are wrong; they are dangerous; they must be exterminated. This is merely the result of faction; for it is now, and probably will forever remain a mere speculative point, whether Danton or Brissot was right; that is, whether a federal or an indivisible republic is the best form of government for France. But power and not argument or experience, has decided the question for the present. It is the precise mode in which the Roman emperors decided christianity to be dangerous—the precise mode in which the Chinese emperors reasoned to justify thc cxpulsion of christians from their dominions; and a mode which a violent ruling faction always employs to silence opposition. As a temporary measure, it is always effectual: But I will venture to affirm, that such vindictive remedies for political and religious contentions are, in every instance, unwarrantable. In religious affairs, they proceed from bigotry, or a blind zeal for a particular creed. In political contests, an indiscriminate denunciation of opposers, and the infliction of death upon slight evidence, or mere suspicion can proceed only from savage hearts, or the mad rancor of party and faction.

MORALITY

However necessary might be the revolution in France, and however noble the object, such great changes and a long war will have an effect on the moral character of the nation, which is deeply to be deplored. All wars have, if I may use a new but emphatic word, a demoralizing tendency; but the revolution in France, in addition to the usual influence of war, is attended with a total change in the minds of the people. They are released, not only from the ordinary restraints of law, but from all their former habits of thinking. From the fetters of a debasing religious system, the people are let loose in the wide field of mental licentiousness; and as men naturally run from one extreme to another, the French will probably rush into the wildest vagaries of opinion, both in their political and moral creeds. The decree of the convention authorizing divorces, upon the application of either party, alleging only unsuitableness of temper, hereby offering allurements to infidelity and domestic broils, is a singular proof of the little regard in which the morals of the nation are held by the ruling party. The efforts made by the convention to exterminate every thing that looks like imposing restraint upon the passions, by the fear of a supreme being and future punishments, are a most extraordinary experiment in government, to ascertain whether nations can exist in peace, order and harmony, without any such restraints. It is an experiment to prove that impressions of a supreme being and a divine providence, which men have hitherto considered as natural, are all the illusions of imagination; the effect of a wrong education. It is an experiment to try whether atheism and materialism, as articles of national creed, will not render men more happy in society than a belief in a God, a Providence and the Immortality of the soul. The experiment is new; it is bold; it is astonishing.

In respect to manners also the effects of the war in France must be deplorable. War, carried on between foreign nations, on the most humane principles, has a powerful tendency to decivilize those who are immediately concerned in it. It lets loose the malignant passions of hatred and revenge, which in time of peace, are laid under the restraints of law and good breeding. But in addition to the ordinary decivilizing tendency of war, the present contest in France is carried on with the implacable fury of domestic rage, and the barbarity of assassination. Hostilities have raged in almost every part of that extensive republic, and have been inflamed by faction, insurrection and treason. The Parisians, aided by the Marsellois, massacred thousands on the 10th of August, and 2d and 3d September 1792; and great part of the victims of popular fury fell, merely because they were suspected, without the slightest proof of guilt. The like scenes were exhibited on a smaller scale, at Lyons, and in some other parts of the country. The summary vengence taken on the insurgents in various parts, and especially on the rebels at Lyons and Toulon, must have accustomed great bodies of people to scenes of cruelty, and rendered them unfeeling towards their enemies. But the sanguinary executions of persons condemned by the revolutionary tribunals, at Paris, and in various cities of France, must have rendered the populace extremely ferocious. In many of the calamitous proceedings of the triumphant party in France, there has been displayed a rancor of malice and cruelty, that reminds us of savages: and we can scarcely believe these things done by a nation unquestionably the most polite in the world. The facts however cannot be denied; and they illustrate my remarks, as to the effects of war on the moral character of men.

If these remarks then are just, it is to be supposed that the French nation, will for a few years, be so ferocious and licentious, as to render it extremely difficult to reduce them to a subordination to law.

The virulence of party we know in America; but in France, the spirits of men are still more exasperated against each other; and party-rage will not, for a long time, be repressed, without frequent bloodshed. If the odious distinction of whig and tory, still exists in America, and frequently calls forth abuse; how much more will party spirit prevail in France, during the present generation!

It then naturally occurs as a question, what will be the consequences of the abolition of christianity, or the national worship of France?

The general answer appears to me not difficult—atheism and the most detestable principles will be the fashion of the present age; but peace, education, and returning reason will at length prevail over the wild ideas of the present race of philosophers, and the nation will embrace a rational religion.

The nation is now so totally demoralized by the current philosophy of the age, and the ferocious spirit of war and faction, that atheism is a creed perhaps most adapted to the blind and headstrong genius of the present generation. But I am yet one of the old fashioned philosophers, who believe that, however particular men under particular circumstances may reject all ideas of God and religion, yet that some impressions of a Supreme Being are as natural to men, as their passions and their appetites, and that nations will have some God to adore and some mode of worship. I believe some future legislature of France will be obliged to tread back some of the steps of the present convention, with respect to the establishment of a chimerical reason in lieu of religion.

GOVERNMENT

I am of the same opinion respecting their constitution of government. France cannot enjoy peace or liberty, without a government, much more energetic than the present constitution would be, without the aid of danger without and a guillotine within. The moment France is freed from external foes, and is left to itself, it will feel the imbecillity of its government. France now resembles a man under the operation of spasms, who is capable of exerting an astonishing degree of unnatural muscular force; but when the paroxism subsides, languor and debility will succeed. This observation applies to its political force; and when the war shall cease, the military will be strong, while the civil power is weak. The consequences of disbanding half a million of soldiers at once, I will not attempt to predict. Should any dissatisfaction prevail in the army at the moment of peace, on account of pay, provisions, or any other cause, the nation will have to contend with more formidable foes, than the military machines of Austria and Prussia. Great caution and policy will be necessary in dispersing such a number of soldiers and bringing them back to habits of industry and order.

The seeds of faction, that enemy of government and freedom, are sown thick in the present constitution of France. The Executive Council, to be composed of twenty-four members, will be a hot-bed of party; and party spirit is violent, malignant and tyrannical. The French could not have fallen upon a more effectual expedient to create and perpetuate faction, with its train of fatal evils, than to commit the execution of the laws to a number of hands; for *faction is death to liberty*.

The Republic of France is to keep an army in pay, in time of peace as well as war. This army will always be at the command of the executive. When the minister at war is a man of talents and a wicked heart, he may make use of the army for the purposes of crushing his competitors. A standing army in America is considered as an engine of despotism; and however necessary it may be in the present state of Europe, it will or may prove dangerous to the freedom of France.

REMARKS

Let it not be thought that the writer of these sheets is an enemy to liberty or a republican government. Such an opinion is wholly unfounded. The writer is a native American; born in an independant republic. He imbibed a love of liberty with his first ideas of government; he fought for the independance of his country; he wishes to see republican governments established over the earth, upon the ruins of despotism. He has not however imbibed the modern philosophy, that rejects all ancient institutions, civil, social and religious, as the impositions of fraud; the tyranny of cunning over ignorance, and of power over weakness. He is not yet convinced that men are capable of such perfection on earth, as to regulate all their actions by moral rectitude, without the restraints of religion and law. He does not believe with the French atheist, that the universe is composed solely of matter and motion, without a Supreme Intelligence; nor that man is solely the creature of education. He believes that God, and not education, gives man his passions; and that the business of education is to restrain and direct the passions to the purposes of social happiness. He believes that man will always have passions—that these passions will frequently urge him into vices—that religion has an excellent effect in repressing vices, in softening the manners of men, and consoling them under the pressure of calamities. He believes in short that, notwithstanding all the fine philosophy of the modern reformers, that a great part of mankind, necessitated to labor, and unaccustomed to read, or to the civilities of refined life, will have rough passions, that will always require the corrective force of law, to prevent them from violating the rights of others; of course, he believes government is necessary in society: and that to render every man free, there must be energy enough in the executive, to restrain any man and any body of men from injuring the person or property of any individual in the society. But as many of the preceding remarks appear to be a severe reprehension of the ruling party in France, it is necessary to explain myself more freely on this subject.

The cause of the French nation is the noblest ever undertaken by men. It was necessary; it was just. The feudal and the papal systems were tyrannical in the extreme; they fettered and debased the mind; they enslaved a great portion of Europe. While the legislators of France confined themselves to a correction of real evils, they were the most respectable of reformers: they commanded the attention, the applause and the admiration of surrounding nations. But when they descended to legislate upon names, opinions and customs, that could have no influence upon liberty or social rights, they became contemptible; and when faction took the lead, when a difference of opinion on the form of government proper for France, or a mere adherence to a solemn oath, became high treason punishable with death, the triumphant faction inspired even the friends of the revolution, with disgust and horror. Liberty is the cry of these men, while with the grimace of a Cromwell, they deprive every man who will not go all the lengths of their rash measures, of both liberty and life. A free republic, is their perpetual cant; yet to establish their own ideas of this free government, they have formed and now exercise throughout France a military aristocracy, the most bloody and despotic recorded in history.

But, say the friends of the Jacobins, "this severity is absolutely necessary to accomplish the revolution." No this is not the truth. It is necessary to accomplish the views of the Jacobins; but a revolution was effected before the Jacobins had formed themselves into a consistent body, and assumed the sovereign sway. This first revolution did not proceed far enough in changes of old institutions to satisfy the atheistical part of the new convention. The first constitution had abolished the distinction of orders—it had stripped the nobles and clergy of their titles and rank—it had stripped the church of her possessions—it had taken almost all power from the king—but it had left untouched the two relics of monarchy most odious to little minds, the name of king and his hereditary descent. This furnished the violent members of the convention with a pretext for a further reform, in which, not royalty alone, for this is a matter of little consequence, but even the customary modes of speech, and the sublime truths of christianity, have fallen equally a prey to the regenerating enthusiasm of these profound philosophers.

What had *liberty and the rights of men* to do with this second revolution? If, on experiment, it had been found that the limited monarchy of the first constitution, which except its civil list, had scarcely the powers of the executive of the United States, was productive of real evils and real danger to the freedom of the government, the nation would have seen the danger, and by general consent, in a peaceable manner, and without the violence of party rage, monarchy would have been abolished. The progress of reason, information and just notions of government was ripening the nation fast for an event of this kind.

But admit what the Jacobins will say, that there was a necessity for removing the king; that he was a traitor, and a plot was forming to replace the monarchy with all its prerogatives; and that there is a foundation for a suspicion of this kind, no man can doubt; yet what shall we say to the trial and condemnation of the Brissotines? Brissot, Le Brun and their followers were the more moderate party, but unquestionably republicans. So far as evidence against them has appeared in the trials published, there is not an iota of proof to warrant the charge of treason. Their great crime was, they were federalists —they believed so extensive a country as France, would be best governed by a constitution similar to that of America, each department* having a local legislature to regulate the interior police of the department, and all the departments confederated under a general government for the purpose of regulating the great concerns of the nation. Whether right or wrong, this was a mere question of speculation; and Brissot had precisely the same right to plan, to urge, and if possible, to establish his system, as Danton and Robespiere had to establish theirs. Each had the same rights, the same freedom of debate (or ought to have had) the same privilege of proposing forms of government, and the inviolability of the legislative character ought to have afforded to each the same protection. The outrages committed upon this inviolability are the work of detestable faction, that scourge of almost every free government, and the disgrace of the French Revolution. The Brissotines were charged with "conspiring against the unity and indivisibility of the republic"; that is, against a theoretical form of government; and all the other charges appear to be invented by the malice of party, as they are not supported by any credible proof whatever. But let us go farther and admit, what is probably not true, that all these sacrifices were necessary; what shall we say to the impious attempts to exterminate every part of the christian religion, and substitute Grecian philosophy and atheism as a nation creed? Is this also necessary to maintain liberty and a free government? What shall we say to the legislature of a great nation, waging a serious war with mere names, pictures, dress and statues? Is this also necessary to the support of liberty? There is something in this part of their legislative proceedings that unites the littleness of boys, with the barbarity of Goths.

Let us then separate the men from the cause; and while we detest the instrument, let us admire and applaud the end to be accomplished. We see roses growing among thorns, and we know a Judas, in betraying his Lord, was a vile instrument of man's redemption. I

* I say, each department; but I do not know the extent of the subdivisions contemplated by the federalists.

am an old fashioned believer in a divine intelligence, that superintends the affairs of this world, always producing order out of confusion. So far as the experience of three thousand years, and the present knowledge of men, will furnish data for reasoning on political subjects, we may safely conclude that the affairs of France are in a state of vacillation, moving from extreme to extreme by the impulse of violent causes: and that in a few years those causes will be removed, the vibration will cease, and the legislature, tracing back some of the steps of their predecessors, will take the middle path in government, religion and morals which has ever been found practicable and safe. *In medio tutissimus ibis*, is a maxim that never yet deceived the man, the legislator or the philosopher. Monarchy can never be restored in France, until the people are exterminated. A republican government in some shape or other, will maintain its ground; and I trust and hope, the defeat of the combined powers will teach them the observance of the law of nations, "that one power has no right to interfere with the government of its neighbor."

I would only suggest further that the present war is weakening the feudal system in Europe, and the whole fabric must soon tumble to the ground. Austria and Prussia are exhausting themselves, and Russia is gaining strength. It is not impossible that the Russian power may swallow up the residue of Poland; Prussia and Austria may share the same fate; and the republicans of France may hereafter prove the only barrier that can successfully resist the arms of those modern Scythians. The ancient balance of power in Europe is evidently suffering a material change; when that is destroyed, a general convulsion must succeed, which may shake every throne, and give a new aspect to the political horizon of Europe.

APPLICATION

The revolution of France, like that of Rome, is fruitful in lessons of instruction, of which all enlightened nations should avail themselves, and which may be of great use to the United States of America.

The most important truth suggested by the foregoing remarks is, that party spirit is the source of faction and *faction is death to the existing* government. The history of the Jacobins is the most remarkable illustration of this truth. I will not undertake to say that there did not exist in France a necessity for a combination of private societies, because I do not know whether it was not necessary to exterminate the remains of royalty and nobility, before a free government could be established and rendered secure and permanent. On this point I am not qualified to determin. But that it was this league of Jacobins, combining the individuals of a party scattered over a vast extent of country, into a consistent body, moved by a single soul, that produced the second revolution in France, is a point of which there can be no question. Their opposers, the moderate party impliedly acknowledged this truth, when they attempted to resist their force by the same means; and formed themselves into a society, called, from their place of meeting, *Fuillans.* But it was too late. The Jacobins were organized; they had already gained over the populace of Paris to their interest, and had, by caresses, and alarming their fears by the cry of despotism, won over a great part of the peasantry of the country. The Rubicon was passed; party had become faction; the Jacobins and the Fuillans were the Cesar and the Pompey of France; one or the other must fall; the Jacobins were the most powerful; they employed a body of armed men to disperse their opposers; the Fuillans were crushed; and the Jacobins, like Cesar, were seated on the throne. Admit the necessity of such a confederacy in France, or in any country where it is expedient and proper to overthrow the existing government; yet it becomes a most serious question, what is the use of such a combination of societies in the United States. When government is radically bad, it is meritorious to reform it; when there is no other expedient to rid a people of oppression, it is necessary to change the government; but when a people have freely and voluntarily chosen and instituted a constitution of government, which guarantees all their rights, and no corruption appears in the administration, there can be no necessity for a change; and if in any particular, it is thought to require amendment, a constitutional mode is provided, and there is no necessity for recurring to extraordinary expedients. In America therefore there can exist no necessity for private societies to watch over the government. Indeed to pretend that a government that has been in operation but five or six years, and which has hitherto produced nothing but public prosperity and private happiness, has need of associations in all parts of the country to guard its purity, is like a jealous husband who should deem it necessary, the day after his nuptials, to set a centinel over his wife to secure her fidelity.

If the government of America wants a reform, the best mode of effecting this, is the constitutional mode. If it is become absolutely necessary to overthrow it, the most direct mode of doing it, is to organize a party for the purpose, by condensing its scattered forces into union and system. But if the point is admitted, that the government does not require any essential alteration, which cannot be effected in a legal way, it follows of course that the establishment of private societies is not necessary. For the same reason that such societies were found useful in France, they ought to be avoided like a pestilence in America; because a total renovation was judged necessary in that country; and such a total renovation is judged not necessary in America—because a republican government was to be established in that country; and in this, it is already established on principles of liberty and equal rights.

As the tendency of such associations is probably not fully understood by most of the persons composing them in this country, and many of whom are doubtless well-meaning citizens; it may be useful to trace the progress of party-spirit to faction first, and then of course to tyranny.

My first remark is, that contentions usually spring out of points which are trifling, speculative, or of doubtful tendency. Among trifling causes I rank personal injuries. It has frequently happened that an affront offered by one leading man in a state to another, has disquieted the whole state, and even caused a revolution. The real interest of the people has nothing to do with private resentments, and ought never to be affected by them, yet nothing is more common. And republics are more liable to suffer changes and convulsions, on account of personal quarrels, than any other species of government; because the individuals, who have acquired the confidence of the people, can always fabricate some reasons for rousing their passions —some pretext of public good may be invented, when the man has his own passions to gratify—the minds of the populace are easily enflamed—and strong parties may be raised on the most frivolous occasions. I have known an instance in America of a man's intriguing for and obtaining an election to an important trust; which he immediately resigned, and confessed he had done it solely to gratify his own will and mortify his enemies. Yet had the man been disposed, he might have used his influence to strengthen a party, and given trouble to the state.

Another cause of violent parties is frequently a difference of opinion on speculative questions, or those, whose real tendency to secure public happiness is equivocal. When measures are obviously good, and clearly tend to advance public weal, there will seldom be much division of opinion on the propriety of adopting them. All parties unite in pursuing the public interest, when it is clearly visible. But when it is doubtful what will be the ultimate effect of a measure, men will differ in opinion, and probably the parties will be nearly equal. It is on points of private local utility, or on those of doubtful tendency, that men split into parties.

My second remark is, that a contention between parties is usually violent in proportion to the trifling nature of the point in question; or to the uncertainty of its tendency to promote public happiness. When an object of great magnitude is in question, and its utility obvious, a great majority is usually found in its favor, and vice versa; and a large majority usually quiets all opposition. But when a point is of less magnitude or less visible utility, the parties may be and often are nearly equal. Then it becomes a trial of strength—each party acquires confidence from the very circumstance of equality—both become assured they are right—confidence inspires boldness and expectation of success—pride comes in aid of argument—the passions are inflamed—the merits of the cause become a subordinate consideration—victory is the object and not public good; at length the question is decided by a small majority—success inspires one party with pride, and they assume the airs of conquerors; disappointment sours the minds of the other—and thus the contest ends in creating violent passions which are always ready to enlist into every other cause. Such is the progress of party-spirit; and a single question will often give rise to a party, that will continue for generations; and the same men or their adherents will continue to divide on other questions, that have not the remotest connection with the first point of contention.

This observation gives rise to my third remark; that nothing is more dangerous to the cause of truth and liberty than a party-spirit. When men are once united, in whatever form, or upon whatever occasion, the union creates a partiality or friendship for each member of the party or society. A coalition for any purpose creates an attachment, and inspires a confidence in the individuals of the party, which does not die with the cause which united them; but continues, and extends to every other object of social intercourse.

Thus we see men first united in some system of religious faith, generally agree in their political opinions. Natives of the same country, even in a foreign country, unite and form a separate private society. The Masons feel attached to each other, tho in distant parts of the world.

The same may be said of Episcopalians, Quakers, Presbyterians, Roman Catholics, federalists, and antifederalists, mechanic societies, chambers of commerce, Jacobin and democratic societies. It is altogether immaterial what circumstance first unites a number of men into a society; whether they first rally round the church, a square and compass, a cross, or a cap; the general effect is always the same; while the union continues, the members of the association feel a particular confidence in each other, which leads them to believe each others opinions, to catch each others passions, and to act in concert on every question in which they are interested.

Hence arises what is called bigotry or illiberality. Persons who are united on any occasion, are more apt to believe the prevailing opinions of their society, than the prevailing opinions of another society. They examin their own creeds more fully (and perhaps with a mind predisposed to believe them), than they do the creeds of other societies. Hence the full persuasion in every society that theirs is right; and if right, others of course are wrong. Perhaps therefore I am warranted in saying, there is a species of bigotry in every society on earth—and indeed in every man's own particular faith. While each man and each society is freely indulged in his own opinion, and that opinion is mere speculation, there is peace, harmony, and good understanding. But the moment a man or a society attempts to oppose the prevailing opinions of another man or society, even his arguments rouse passion; it being difficult for two men of opposite creeds to dispute for any time, without getting angry. And when one party attempts in practice to interfere with the opinions of another party, violence most generally succeeds.

These remarks are so consonant to experience and common observation, that I presume no man can deny them; and if true, they deserve the serious attention of every good citizen of America.

The citizens of this extensive republic constitute a nation. As a nation, we feel all the prejudices of a society. These national prejudices are probably necessary, in the present state of the world, to strengthen our government. They form a species of political bigotry, common to all nations, from which springs a real allegiance, never expressed, but always firm and unwavering. This passion, when corrected by candor, benevolence and love of mankind, softens down into a steady principle, which forms the soul of a nation, true patriotism. Each nation of the world is then a party in the great society of the human race. When at peace, party spirit subsides, and mutual intercourse unites the parties. But when the interest of either is attacked, a war succeeds, and all the malignant and barbarous passions are called into exercise.

Admit national prejudices to be in a degree, necessary; let us see what other prejudices exist in the United States, which may prove pernicious to ourselves. The American nation is composed of fifteen subordinate states. I say subordinate; for they are so in all national concerns. They are sovereign only in their internal police.

The states were erected out of British colonies; and it was the policy of Great Britain, rather to foment, than to allay or eradicate, colonial prejudices. She knew that such prejudices weakened the strength of the colonies, and kept them in subjection to the mother-empire. Even the manners, the language and the food of the people in one colony were made the subjects of ridicule by the inhabitants of another. Ridicule is accompanied or followed by a degree of contempt; and hence sprung a dissocial turn of mind among the people of different colonies, which common interest and common danger have not yet converted into perfect harmony.

Since the revolution, a jealousy between the states has sprung from the superior wealth, magnitude or advantages of some, which the small states apprehended would enable the large ones to swallow them up in some future time. This jealousy is mostly removed by the present constitution of the United States; which guarantees to each state, its independence and a republican form of government. This guarranty is the best security of each.

Another source of apprehension has been and still is, the danger of what is called consolidation. The states are constantly asserting their sovereignty, and publishing their fears that the national government will gradually absorb the state governments. Their jealousy on this head is alive, and alarmed at every breeze of air. I am clearly of opinion, that if peace and harmony can be preserved between the general and particular governments, the purity of our national government will depend much on the legislatures of the several states. They are the political guardians, whose interest is constantly impelling them to watch the progress of corruption in the general government. And they will always be the more attentive to their duty, as they entertain not only a jealousy of the general government, but a jealousy of each other.

But I differ from many people who fear a consolidation. So far as my knowledge of history and men will enable me to judge on this subject, I must think our danger mostly lies in the jealousy of the several states. Instead of a probable annihilation of the state governments, I apprehend great danger from the disuniting tendency of state jealousy, which may dismember the present confederacy. That the states have the power to do this, I have no doubt; and I consider our union, and consequently our strength and prosperity as depending more on mutual interest, and mutual concession, than on the force of the national constitution. Consolidation is with me a bugbear, a chimera, as idle and insignificant, as the medallion of a king. But from the disorganizing tendency of state jealousy, there appears to be a well founded apprehension of danger.

But the principal danger to which our government is exposed will probably arise from another quarter; the spirit of party, which is now taking the form of system. While a jealousy and opposition to the national constitution exist only in the legislatures of the several states, they will be restrained and moderated by the public dignity of those bodies, and by legal or constitutional forms of proceeding. Opposition thus tempered loses its terrors.

But opposition that is raised in private societies of men, who are self-created, unknown to the laws of the country, private in their proceedings, and perhaps violent in their passions, the moment it ceases to be insignificant, becomes formidable to government and freedom. The very people who compose these societies, are not aware of the possible consequences that may flow from their associations. They are few of them persons of extensive historical knowlege; and they do not perceive, that under pretence of securing their rights and liberties, they are laying the foundation of factions which will probably end in the destruction of liberty and a free government. They do not consider, that when men become members of a political club, they lose their individual independence of mind; that they lose their impartiality of thinking and acting; and become the dupes of other men. The moment a man is attached to a club, his mind is not free: He receives a biass from the opinions of the party: A question indifferent to him, is no longer indifferent, when it materially effects a brother of the society. He is not left to act for himself; he is bound in honor to take part with the society—his pride and his prejudices, if at war with his opinion, will commonly obtain the victory; and rather than incur the ridicule or censure of his associates, he will countenance their measures, at all hazards; and thus an independant freeman is converted into a mere walking machine, a convenient *engine of party leaders*.

It is thus that private associations may always influence public measures; and if they are formed for the express purpose of discussing political measures, they may prove pernicious to the existing government.

The Society of Jesuits, formed at first without any intention of influencing government, became at last formidable to the civil power, wherever they were established and the society was finally dissolved by the arm of power, on account of the danger of its intrigues. The society was at first small and insignificant; but its influence was increased and strengthened by such means as I have described, till a small part of the inhabitants of a country, became dangerous to its government!

The masonic societies do not often intermeddle with politics; tho I have known an instance or two, in a different state, in which their influence was exerted for the brethren, and to a very bad effect. But were the masons in this or any European country, to unite their efforts for the purpose of governing the politics of the country, they might insensibly assume a great share of influence. To the honor of the craft be it mentioned, they have generally avoided any abuse of their power in this respect. But should that society or any other make it a business to unite their opinions and influence the measures of government, the society would establish an aristocracy in the country, and it would be necessary that the institution should share the fate of the Jesuits.

Private associations of men for the purposes of promoting arts, sciences, benevolence or charity are very laudable, and have been found beneficial in all countries. But whenever such societies attempt to convert the private attachment of their members into an instrument of political warfare, they are, in all cases, hostile to government. They are useful in pulling down bad governments; but they are dangerous to good government, and necessarily destroy liberty and equality of rights in a free country. I say necessarily; for it must occur to any man of common reflection, that in a free country, each citizen, in his private capacity, has an equal right to a share of influence in directing public measures; but a society, combined for the purpose of augmenting and extending its influence, acquires an undue proportion of that general influence which is to direct the will of the state. Each individual member of the state should have an equal voice in elections; but the individuals of a club have more than an equal voice, because they have the benefit of another influence; that of extensive private attachments which come in aid of each man's political opinion. And just in proportion as the members of a club have an undue share of influence, in that proportion they abridge the rights of their fellow citizens. Every club therefore formed for political purposes, is an aristocracy established over their brethren. It has all the properties of an aristocracy, and all the effects of tyranny. It is only substituting the influence of private attachments, in lieu of the influence of birth and property among the nobility of Europe; and the certain effect of private intrigue in lieu of the usurped power and rights of feudal lords; the effects are the same. It is a literal truth, which cannot be denied, evaded, or modified, that the democratic clubs in the United States, while running mad with the abhorrence of aristocratic influence, are attempting to establish precisely the same influence under a different name. And if any thing will rescue this country from the jaws of faction, and prevent our free government from falling a prey, first to civil dissensions, and finally to some future Sylla and Marius, it must be either the good sense of a great majority of Americans, which will discourage private political associations, and render them contemptible; or the controling power of the laws of the country, which in an early stage, shall demolish all such institutions, and secure to each individual in the great political family, *equal rights and an equal share of influence* in his individual capacity.

But let us admit that no fatal consequences to government, and equal rights will ensue from these institutions, still their effects on social harmony are very pernicious, and already begin to appear. A party-spirit is hostile to all friendly intercourse: it inflames the passions; it sours the mind; it destroys good neighborhood: it warps the judgment in judicial determinations: it banishes candor and substitutes prejudice; it restrains the exercise of benevolent affections; and in proportion as it chills the warm affections of the soul, it undermines the whole system of moral virtue. Were the councils of hell united to invent expedients for depriving men of the little portion of good they are destined to enjoy on this earth, the only measure they need adopt for this purpose, would be, to introduce factions into the bosom of the country. It was faction that kept the states of Greece and Rome in perpetual perturbation; it was faction which was an incessant scourge of merit; it was faction which produced endless dissension and frequent civil wars; it was faction which converted a polite people, into barbarous persecutors, as it has done in France; and which finally compelled the brave republicans of Rome to suffer a voluntary death, or to shelter themselves from the fury of contending parties, beneath the scepter of an emperor.

APPENDIX

ON FACTION

The following short account of the disputes between Sylla and Marius in Rome, is too applicable to my purpose to be omitted.

Sylla and Marius were competitors for the command of the army destined to act against Mithridates in Asia. Sylla obtained the appointment. Marius, to revenge himself, and if possible, displace his rival, had recourse to P. Sulpicius, a popular tribune, of considerable talents, but daring and vicious. This man made interest with the people, sold the freedom of the city to strangers and freemen, with a view to strengthen his party, and proposed a number of popular laws, in direct violation of the Roman constitution—some of which artifices are exactly similar to those employed by the Jacobins in France and their disciples.

The consuls attempted to defeat these projects; but the tribune, collected a multitude of the people, went to the senate house, and commanded the consuls to comply with their wishes. This is precisely the mode of proceeding adopted by the Jacobins in Paris.

The consuls refused; the populace drew their daggers; the son of the consul, Pompeius, was killed, but Sylla escaped. This answers to the manner in which the Jacobins destroyed their enemies, the Fuillans, by employing an armed body of ruffians.

Sylla however was brought back and compelled to comply with the demands of the tribune. He was therefore left in possession of the consulship, and soon after joined the army. His colleague, Pompeius, was degraded, and Sulpicius obtained the laws he had proposed. Sylla was displaced and Marius appointed to the command of the army. Just so the Jacobins proceeded, till they had filled all public offices with their own partizans.

Now the factions were ripe, and they ended as other factions end, in *repelling force with force.* Sylla would not resign his command to a faction. (La Fayette and Demourier had the spirit of Sylla, in like circumstances, but their troops would not support them.) He marched his army of 35,000 men towards Rome. The city was in confusion. The senate, by order of Sulpicius and Marius, the Marat and Barrere of Rome, sent a deputation, forbidding the approach of the army. The deputies were insulted by the soldiers. Other ambassadors were dispatched by the senate, requesting Sylla not to proceed. He answered he would stay where he was; but he detached a body of men to take possession of one of the gates of the city. The people drove them back, but Sylla arrived in time to support them; and he set fire to the adjacent houses. Marius resisted, and promised freedom to the slaves that would join him. But he was forced to flee and Sylla, assembling the senate, proposed the banishment of Sulpicius, Marius, and ten of their principal adherents. The edict was passed, and Sylla set a price upon their head, and confiscated their estates. Sulpicius was taken by the treachery of a slave and put to death. To reward the slave, Sylla gave him his freedom, and then ordered him, for the treachery, to be thrown from the Tarpeian rock (the method of rewarding and punishing modern traitors is much similar—giving them a round sum of money and consigning them to infamy).

Sylla convened the people, annulled the new laws of Sulpicius, created three hundred senators to strengthen his interest, and soon set out for Asia, with his army. I cannot detail the whole history of this business—suffice it to say, this pitiful question, which of two able generals (either of them fit for the purpose, and not of a straw's value to the public which gained the appointment), should command the army in the Mithridatic war, gave rise to two parties or factions, which pursued each other with implacable enmity, till they brot their forces into the field, and an action was fought, which cost the lives of ten thousand men.

Marius, the conqueror of the Cimbri, and savior of Rome, an exile, took shipping, was cast away, taken by his foes, escaped, suffering incredible hardships; finally arrived in Asia, where he was maltreated—at last recalled by Cinna the consul, he returned to Italty, and embodying a number of slaves, he entered Rome, and filled it with slaughter; his party putting to death every man, whose salutation Marius did not return.* Marius grew daily more blood-thirsty, and at

* Who does not see the same tragedy acted in France, where a picture of a king is a signal for rallying, and a cockade or other signal of party is necessary to secure a man's life? And who does not see the beginnings of a similar tragedy, in the infamous practice of setting the marks of party upon the peaceable citizens of America? The people who make this attempt may be well meaning—they may not foresee to what lengths faction will carry men, when opportunities favor; but peace and happiness forbid all such odious distinctions.

last put to death every person of whom he had the least suspicion. Who does not see the guillotine in ancient Rome?

Marius soon after died: but his son headed an army and supported his faction. Sylla, having defeated Mithridates and reduced him to terms of peace, returned to Italy; fought the Marian party, and in two actions, it is said, twenty thousand men were slain in each. Finally Sylla crushed his rival's party, and put to death the leaders, filling Rome with slaughter, as Marius had done before him. Sylla's cruel proscriptions fill the reader with horror. Nearly five thousand of the best citizens of Rome were proscribed and massacred. Sylla's assassins roamed thro Italy to find the adherents of Marius, and put them to indiscriminate slaughter. When the senators appeared alarmed at such outrages, Sylla answered them coolly, "Conscript fathers, it is only a few seditious men, whom I have ordered to be punished" precisely the language of the ruling faction in France, and precisely the language of party in all countries.

It is remarkable also that the pretext for these violences is always the same "to rescue the state from tyranny—to destroy despotism—to exterminate traitors." This was the perpetual cant of Sylla and Marius, while they were butchering each other's adherents with merciless cruelty. This was the pretence of Cromwell in England—and it is the present language of the ruling men in France. The state must be saved, and to save it, our party must prevail; liberty must be secured; but to secure it, we must be absolute in power, and of course liberty is crushed. A republic must be established; but to do this, a few commissioners, with dictatorial power, seconded by an irresistable military force, must govern the country. Our government shall be a *republic, one and indivisible*; and to effect this, it is necessary to put to death the representatives of one half the republic, that the whole may be governed by the other half. Freedom of debate is a constitutional right; but we must have a Paris mob to hiss down our enemies.

Sylla crushed his enemies, with the blood of nearly one hundred thousand citizens and soldiers; and after he had thus delivered Rome from tyrants, as he pretended, he ordered the people to elect him perpetual dictator. He treated the people just as all popular leaders treat them; first courting them, with the cry of liberty; making them the instruments of their own elevation; then trampling on them as slaves. Just so in England, Cromwell destroyed the tyranny, of Charles I, by the cant of liberty and religion, then saddled the English with his own despotic power. Just so Danton, and Barrere are now dictators in France; without the name, but with all the powers; and who will succeed them, God only knows.

I beg the reader to consider these facts, as intended solely to set in a strong point of light the danger of faction. I will not say that the tyranny and corruptions of the old governments in Europe will not warrant men in hazarding all possible temporary evils, to effect a renovation. I would, with candor, believe such violences, in some degree, unavoidable. But nothing short of most palpable corruption, the most unequivocal proof of necessity, can warrant men in resorting to irregular bodies of the people, for a redress of evils. While law and constitution are adhered to, the remedy will always be safe. But when tumultuous meetings of people, unknown to the laws, and unrestrained by legal modes of procedure, undertake to direct the public will, faction succeeds; and faction begets disorder, force, rancorous passions, anarchy, tyranny, blood and slaughter.

JACOBIN CLUB

At the beginning of the late revolution in America, the people of this country had recourse to a similar mode of combining all parts of the continent into a system of opposition to the existing government. In most of the colonies, the British crown, by its officers, had considerable influence. To resist this influence, the leaders found it necessary to call in the aid of the great body of the people; to rouse their passions, inflammatory publications were circulated with great industry; and to unite, condense and direct the opinions and passions of an immense people, scattered over a great extent of territory, associations were formed, under the denomination of Committees of Safety, which had a correspondence with each other, and moulded the proceedings of the people into uniformity and system. The first Congress grew out of the same system; and then followed union, concert and energy in prosecuting the revolution.

It has been an inexplicable mystery to many very judicious men, how the Americans should have been brot to unite in opposing the usurped claims of Great-Britain, when the evils of slavery were not in reality felt, but only expected by the people. In short, why such a number of illiterate men should be prevailed upon to resist tyranny in principle, and risk the evils of war, when the effects of the British claims were but slightly felt by the mass of people. All parties however agree in ascribing this amazing union, to the good sense of the Americans.

The truth is, discernment and talents were necessary to form and direct the system; but the multitude were managed more by their passions than by their reason. The committees of safety were the instruments of union; and the passions of the populace the instruments of action. The presses teemed with publications addressed to the passions; the horrors of slavery were presented to the imagination in striking colors: and the men who wrote intended, when they wrote, to exaggerate real facts for the purpose of rousing the passions of resentment and dread of evils, which reason told them, were not to be expected. These matters are now known. And it appears very clear from history and observation, that in a popular government, it is not difficult to inflame the passions of a people with imaginary as well as real evils. In Europe, the people have real evils to extirpate. The passions of Americans are inlisting on one side or the other of the present contest in France. We feel no loss of personal liberty as yet, in consequence of the combination against France; but artful men address the passions of our citizens; they teach them to fear, that if France should be reduced, the combined powers will attack liberty in America. Cool men who reflect upon the difficulties of such an attempt, consider all such apprehensions as groundless and idle. But two or three hundred men collected, might have their passions so wrought upon by an artful or noisy declaimer, as to believe the danger real. They then grow violent, and denounce as enemies, all who are cool or moderate enough to entertain no such fears. Thus two parties are formed on a mere imaginary evil, and when the parties are formed, some badge of distinction, a button or a cockade is assumed, to widen the breach, and create disaffection, suspicion and hostile passions. All this is very visible in America; and because some men are too rational to be alarmed at chimeras, too temperate to commit themselves hastily, or too respectable not to despise little badges of distinction, the livery of faction, they are insulted as enemies to the rights of the people: And whenever opportunities offer, they fall a prey to the fury of popular passion. This is the triumph of passion over reason; of violence, over moderation. Should the present controversy in Europe continue two or three years longer, I should not be surprized to see party spirit in America, which grew originally out of a mere speculative question, proceed to open hostility and bloodshed. People are easily made to believe their government is bad, or not so good as they might expect from change; they may be made to fear corruption, which they do not see, and which does not exist: and to risk real evils at the present moment, to guard against possible evils, a century hence. All this may be done, if restless daring men will take pains to manage popular passions.

[FUILLANS]

It may seem strange that moderation should be deemed a crime; but it is a literal truth. In the sittings of the Jacobin Club Dec. 26th. 1793, Robespiere was under the necessity of vindicating himself from the charge of being a moderate, a Fuillant.

Nor is it less singular that some of the charges against their opposers should consist of mere trifles or suspicion, or were so indefinite as not to be capable of proof. One of the charges against Le Brun, was, that he christened a daughter by the name of "Victoire Demourier Jamappe." This was done while Demourier was in full career of glory; yet his enemies, from this circumstance, deduced proof of Le Brun's conspiracy with Demourier. He was convicted of conspiring against the unity and indivisibility of the republic; that is, of attempting to form a federal government in France, like that of America.

[THE TEMPLE OF REASON]

There is no instance of idolatrous worship recorded in history, that displays more blind superstition, than the celebration of the Festival of Reason. The idol adored, is not the same as those worshipped by the ancient Druids, or modern Hindoos; but it is still an idol, and the pagan world cannot furnish a more striking instance to prove that men will forever worship something, whether a cat, a bird, an oak, the sun, the moon, fire, or the Temple of Reason. Totally immaterial is it, what the idol is; the deity of the day has no connection with men's happiness, otherwise than as he is visible; he strikes the senses; he rouses the passions of the multitude, and they believe he is propitious to them—how or in what manner they never know or enquire. The oak of the Druids was just as good and powerful a deity, as the temple or altar of reason. The oak inspired its votaries with superstition and enthusiasm; and that is precisely the effect of the French festival of reason; for of all fanatics that ever existed, the French appear, in all that respects what they call philosophy, to be the least rational. The following is the account of the festival.

> Paris, Nov. 12.
>
> A grand festival dedicated to reason and truth was yesterday celebrated in the ci-devant cathedral of Paris. In the middle of this church was erected a mount, and on it a very plain temple, the facade of which bore the following inscription; *A la Philosophie*. Before the gate of this temple was placed the Torch of Truth in the summit of the mount on the Altar of Reason spreading light. The convention and all the constituted authorities assisted at the ceremony.
>
> Two rows of young girls dressed in white, each wearing a crown of oak leaves, crossed before the Altar of Reason, at the sound of republican music; each of the girls inclined before the torch, and ascend[ed] the summit of the mountain. Liberty then came out of the Temple of Philosophy towards a throne made of grass, to receive the homage of the republicans of both sexes, who sung a hymn in her praise, extending their arms at the same time towards her. Liberty descended afterwards to return to the temple, and on re-entering it, she turned about, casting a look of benevolence on her friends. When she got in, every one expressed with enthusiasm the sensations which the goddess excited in them, by songs of joy, and they swore never to cease to be faithful to her.

How little men see their own errors. All this ceremony and parade about reason and liberty; at a time when the governing faction were wading to the altar thro rivers of innocent blood; at a time when the tyranny, imprisonments, and massacres of a century are crouded into a single year.

One absurdity more must be noticed. The Jacobins have displayed an implacable hatred of royalty and every thing that belongs to it. Even devices of kingly origin on coins and rings have not escaped their vengeance, yet these same people have borrowed the principal emblem of royalty themselves; to adorn this festival: and two rows of young girls are furnished with crowns of oak leaves.

OF ARISTOCRACY

There is not a word in the English or French language so much bandied about by disigning men, and so little understood by their echoing agents, as the word aristocrat. A few days ago an honest man, by no means the least informed, was asked if he knew the meaning of it; he replied very ingenuously, "he did not understand it, but he supposed it some French word." Yet this word is used with great effect to excite party prejudices.

Aristocracy in Europe denotes a distinction of men, by birth, titles, property, or office. In America this distinction does not exist with respect to hereditary titles or office; nor with respect to birth and property, any farther than the minds of men, from nature or habit, are inclined to pay more than ordinary respect to persons who are born of parents that have been distinguished for something eminent, and to persons who have large estates. This propensity, whether natural or habitual, exists—no man can deny it; and this is all Mr. Adams, in his defence, means by the words well-born; an expression that has rung a thousand changes from New-Hampshire to Georgia. Yet the very declaimers who fill our ears with a perpetual din on this subject, are exemplifying the truth of this natural aristocracy, in almost every negociation of their lives. The most noisy democrat in this country, who feasts upon the words liberty and equality, cannot put a son apprentice to business, without searching for a respectable family to take him; nor marry a son or daughter, without enquiring particularly into the family, connections and fortune of the proposed partner. It may be said, this propensity to pay respect to such things is wrong and vitious—be it so—the propensity exists—these things are true—they cannot be contradicted. And Mr. Adams, instead of advocating aristocracy and its exclusive privileges, makes it a main point in his defence, to explain the nature and tendency of this principle in men, and to point out cautions and expedients for guarding against its pernicious effects in government. His labors to check this spirit of aristocracy in America, entitle him to the character of a firm intelligent republican.

If the word aristocracy is applicable to any thing in America, it is to that personal influence which men derive from offices, the merit of eminent services, age, talents, wealth, education, virtue, or whatever other circumstance attracts the attention of people. The distinguishing circumstances of nobility in Europe, are hereditary titles, estates and offices, which give the possessor some claims or rights above others. In this country, most of the circumstances which command particular respect, are personal, accidental or acquired, and none of them give the possessor any claims or rights over his fellow citizens. Yet the circumstances which do actually give this personal influence, which forms a kind of natural or customary aristocracy, exist universally among men, savage or civilized, in every country and under every form of government. The circumstances are either natural, or arise necessarily out of the state of society. Helvetius and other profound philosophers may write as much as they please, to prove man to be wholly the *creature of his own making*, the work of education; but facts occur every hour to common observation, to prove the theory false. The difference of intellectual faculties in man is visible almost as soon as he is born, and is more early and more distinctly marked than the difference of his features. And this natural difference of capacity originates a multitude of other differences in after-life, which create distinctions; that is, they give rise to those circumstances of talents, wit, address, property, and office to which men invariably pay a kind of respect. This respect gives personal influence to the possessor, in some circle, either small or great, and this personal influence is the natural aristocracy of men, in all countries and in all governments. It exists among the native Indians; it has existed in every republic on earth: From the president of the United States, to the humble apple-dealer at the corner of Fly-market, every person enjoys a portion of this personal influence among his particular acquaintance. It exists in government, in churches, in towns, in parishes, in private societies and in families.

It is this insensible aristocracy of opinion and respect that now forms the firmest band of union between the states. The long and eminent services of our worthy President have filled all hearts with gratitude and respect; and by means of this gratitude and respect, and the confidence they inspire in his talents and integrity, he has a greater influence in America than any nobleman, perhaps than any prince, in Europe. This respect has hitherto restrained the violence of parties: whatever be the difference of opinion on subjects of government, all parties agree to confide in the president. This is the effect of his personal influence; and not a respect for the laws or constitution of the United States. Americans rally round the man, rather than round the executive authority of the union. And it is a problem to be solved, after his leaving the office, what energy, or force really exists in the executive authority itself.

If my ideas of natural aristocracy are just, the president of the United States, is a most influential, and most useful aristocrat: and long may America enjoy the blessings of such aristocracy!

A similar personal influence is observable in other men. In every state, in every town, there are some, who, by their talents, wealth, address or old age and wisdom, acquire and preserve a superior share of influence in their districts. This influence may do good or hurt, as it is coupled with good or bad intentions. But that when confined to small districts, as towns and parishes, it has most generally a good effect, there is no doubt. An old respected citizen has a thousand opportunities of correcting the opinions, settling the quarrels, and restraining the passions of his neighbors. This personal influence in small districts is most remarkable in some parts of New-England; wherever it exists, peace and concord distinguish the neighborhood; and where by any accident, it does not exist, society is distracted with quarrels and parties, which produce an uncommon depravity of morals.

One remark further. The people who contend most for liberty and equality, and who are most alarmed at aristocracy, are, in America, the greatest dupes of this aristocracy of personal influence. Federal men not only respect the president, but they make the constitution and laws of the United States, their standard; at least they aim to do it. On the other hand, their opposers rally round the standard of particular men. There are certain leading men in the antifederal interest, who have more absolute authority over the opinions of that party, than is possessed by any man in America, except the president of the United States. As the aristocracy of America consists in this personal influence, the men, who in private associations, have the most of this influence, are, in their sphere, the most complete aristocrats. And at this time, certain influential men in the democratic clubs, are the most influential aristocrats there are in America among private citizens.

While this personal influence is governed by good motives, or limited to small districts, it is not dangerous and may be useful. When it extends far, it may be useful or dangerous, according as it is directed by good or vitious men. It is always to be watched—in public affairs, it is controled by the laws; in clubs and private citizens, it has no restraint but the consciences of men; and it is to be watched with double vigilance, as its danger is in proportion to its extent.

[CONTEMPT FOR RELIGION]

It is remarked that the Estates General, on their first assembling May 5, 1789, commenced their important labors with a solemn act of devotion. Preceded by the clergy and followed by the king, the representatives of the nation repaired to the temple of God, accompanied with an immense croud, and offered up vows and prayers for success.

Contrast this with the late severe laws respecting the clergy, and the abolition of christianity. Some of the convention pretend to entertain a respect for morality; yet as early as 1791, before they had proceeded to publish atheism as a national creed, one of the members in debate declared it "impossible for a society to exist without an immutable and eternal system of morality"; and this declaration was followed with *repeated and loud busts of laughter*. This is an instance selected from thousands to show their contempt of every thing that looks like the obligations of religion and morality. Moniteur 15 November, 1791.

[ON JACOBIN SUBVERSION]

The following remarks of Mr. Neckar, who was in France and observed all the arts invented by the Jacobins to get command of the people, are [too] much in point to be omitted.

It was an artful contrivance, the success of which was certain, to involve the constitution in two words, liberty and equality. Men of sense would perceive that between these ideas, and a just conception of a political institution there was a vast distance. But the people are to be acted upon only by reducing things to a small compass; it is by restricting their ideas to the narrow circle of their feelings, and absorbing their passions in a phrase, that we become their masters. This object accomplished, a watchword, or in its stead, an outward token, a mark of distinction, the color or fold of a ribbon, has greater effect than the wisdom of a Solon or the eloquence of a Demosthenes. Such are the multitude—such the description of the empire that may be obtained over them; and criminal indeed are those who take advantage of their weakness, and practice arts to deceive them, rather than to render them happy by the sole authority of reason and morality.

Neckar on Exec. Power Vol. 2. 269.

The emissaries of the Jacobins are attempting to make themselves masters of the people in America by the same means—by clubs and a button, or other badge of distinction. Detestable is the artifice, and may confusion be the portion of the Jesuitical incendiaries, who are thus secretly planting enmity and sedition in our peaceful country!

[ON FACTIONAL SAVAGERY]

Of the ferociousness of civil war, history furnishes innumerable proofs; and the people of France are daily presenting new examples of the sanguinary spirit of all parties in that distracted country. The following official letter offers a specimen.

Letter from the president and members composing the military committee with the Army of the West, to the commonalty of Paris, dated Saumur, 6 Nivose, (Dec. 25.)

We have to communicate to you the interesting news of the total destruction of the banditti on the right banks of the Loire. There are here and there yet some small remains of these monsters in the interior part of La Vendee, but as our armies are no longer obliged to divide themselves, they will undoubtedly soon clear the whole country. Those who solicit the convention to prevent the great measures of public welfare, and try to inspire them with a false compassion, are either traitors or egotists. If you had seen like me, what this fanatic herd is capable of! Patriots thrown into the fire alive, others cut and chopped to pieces. Two days before the siege of Angers, in a country which was supposed to be all sacred to liberty, three hundred soldiers were assassinated by these monsters, in the neighborhood of Chemeville, and nevertheless the evening before they had cried Vive la Republique! and declared that they sincerely repented of their errors: and in different parts of this unhappy country similar events have taken place.

(Signed) Felix & Millie.

It is surprizing that men will be guilty of the most direct and palpable contradictions, and yet they will not see them—they cannot be convinced of them. The military committee call the insurgents a banditti, a fanatic herd: accuse them of throwing patriots into the fire alive, and chopping them to pieces. Yet with the same breath, they declare the news of their total extirpation by shooting, drowning, and beheading them in cool blood. Besides[,] who began these scenes of carnage? The patriots, so called; the Jacobins and their adherents. The massacre of the 10th of August and 2d and 3d of Sept. were the first scenes of the bloody drama that has been exhibiting for two years in that populous country. In the first scenes of the tragedy several thousand men fell victims—many of them not even suspected of disaffection to the cause of liberty. Who does not see the massacre of St. Bartholomew revived in all its horrors? Change but the names of Catholics and Protestants, to Jacobins and Royalists, and the same scene is presented. The apparent motives are different, but analagous. The catholics put to death the protestants in 1572, because they opposed the power of the Catholics. They opposed Catherine of Medicis, and the Duke of Guise; and the latter, thinking them troublesome, pronounced them traitors and heretics, a scheme of universal assassination was formed, and the King Charles IXth, gave his assent to it. On that dreadful night, the sound of a bell was the signal for rallying, and the assassins were let loose upon the unsuspecting protestants. Five thousand in Paris, and twenty-five or thirty thousand in France, fell victims to the savage fury of the dogs of faction. All this was to *serve God and religion.*

Draw a parrallel between this scene and the massacre of August and September 1792. The popular party suspected treason in their opposers. Without trial or proof they must be exterminated. A banditti is prepared, from Paris and Marseilles. At midnight the bell gives the signal for rallying; the populace collect and the bloody work is begun—the Swiss guards, all suspected persons, priests and prisoners fall a sacrifice, in the indiscriminate slaughter. In these massacres, six or seven thousand persons are murdered—and for what? Why the old stale plea of necessity is called in to justify it—and liberty in this case, as religion in the massacre of St. Bartholomew is made the stalking horse to drive the trade of butchering their fellow men. The truth is, religion in one case and liberty in the other directly forbid all such outrages. It is faction. Men are always the same ferocious animals, when guided by passion and loosed from the restraints of law. Let parties grow warm—let their passions be inflamed—let them believe one man is the enemy of another—let opposition exasperate them—and it is only for some daring demagogue to cry, your religion, or your liberty is in danger—your enemies are heretics or traitors—they must be exterminated—and the murderous work begins, and seldom ends till one party crushes the other. In all cases of this kind, without one solitary exception on record, faction ends in tyranny—the victorious party, even with the word liberty incessantly on their tongues, never failing to exercise over the defeated party, the most cruel vengeful acts of domination.

This is a most interesting subject to Americans; as the seeds of faction, that bane of republics, seem to be sown by an industrious party in America, and God only knows what will be the fruit of these things. So strong is the impression on my mind, that the present situation of Europe, and our attachment to the French cause require all the caution and vigilance of government and good sense, to save this country from running mad in theories of popular constitutions, and plunging itself into the evils of faction and anarchy, that I beg leave to subjoin the following facts and remarks on this subject.

The manner in which the reports to the National Convention, mention the destruction of the rebels at La Vendee, many of them honest deluded country people, fills the reader with horror. "Our soldiers, hand to hand, cut them down in front of their cannon. Streets, roads, plains and marshes were encumbered with the dead; we marched over heaps of the slain." "This banditti, these monsters—this army of robbers is destroyed." "This war of rogues and peasants." "It would have done your heart good to see these soldiers of Jesus and Louis XVII, throwing themselves into the marshes, or obliged to surrender." "Five hundred rebels were brot in; they implored pardon, which was refused—they were all put to death." "Six hundred were brot to Acenis; 800 to Angers and a great number to Saumer—the representatives of the people would rid the earth of them by ordering them to be thrown into the Loire." "The late actions on the Vendee have cost the lives of 40,000 persons." "The civil war the last summer is supposed to have cost France two hundred thousand lives." These are the accounts we have received from France. "The rebels have been nearly all killed—the royalists have been all massacred—the prisoners are so numerous that the guillotine is not sufficient—I have taken the method, says Garrier, of having them all shot to death." These are the words of the triumphant republicans. Nay, two brothers finding a third brother among the rebels, demanded he should be tried by the military committee.

But what exceeds all the descriptions of barbarity hitherto known in America, is the speech of Collot D'Herbois in the National Convention. "Jacobins! Some persons wish to moderate the revolutionary moment; take care of it; never forget what Robespiere told you on this subject. Some persons wish to make you establish a committee of clemency—No clemency!—be always Jacobins and mountaneers, and liberty shall be saved."

Such are the terrible effects of civil war, the offspring of faction. Foreign wars are conducted with more humanity: it is in civil wars only that men turn savages, and exult over the mangled carcases of their fathers, brethren and fellow citizens.

[ON TREASON]

It is said that Brissot and his party went farther than I have admitted in the text; and actually attempted to exite the people to arms in support of their proposed federal government. The charge on trial was, that "they had conspired against the unity and indivisibility of the republic," and this was held treason. Admit this to be proved; yet it is also admitted that they were republicans; they were all enemies of monarchy. The only circumstance then that fixes the charge of criminality on this party, is, that they were less numerous than the Jacobins: for the Jacobins had recourse to the same means to destroy their opposers, the Fuillans—they employed an armed populace and actually dispersed them by force. This is a public fact. Had the Fuillans, the moderate party, been more numerous (and a few additional members would have turned the scale), they would have crushed the Jacobins, and their ideas of a republican government would have been right—the Jacobinic system of an indivisible republic would have been wrong; and the Jacobins would have been traitors for attempting to maintain it by force. This is a fair statement of the question between the parties.

When the public will of a nation has instituted a government, and that government is in exercise, the constitution is the standard of right; the men who adhere to it are *faithful to their country*; they are good citizens. When during a revolution, the old government is, by the representatives of the nation, abolished in legal form, and a new one is not yet established, there is a kind of interregnum, a period when the representatives are at liberty to propose any form of government they please. No peaceable act of any representative, to establish his own system, can be called treason. There is no constitution against which an act of treason can be committed—no law, no standard by which it can be defined or proved. If any man attempts to use force and compel his countrymen to receive his system, in preference to others, it is an unwarrantable act—a high misdemeanor—an invasion of liberty—perhaps it may be treason: tho it would be difficult to punish it in a course of legal justice, for there is no law by which it can be determined.

This was nearly the situation of France, when the controversy between the parties in the second convention originated. The constitution of 1791 was abolished with great unanimity, on the first day, if I mistake not, of the session. No new constitution was digested. The members of the convention divided upon the form of government most proper for France. The Jacobins were the first to employ force. They established their power by violence. This cannot be denied. If the employment of force then, was treason, the Jacobins were first guilty. They were the aggressors. The dispersion of the Fuillans, and the horrid massacres of August 10th and Sept 2d and 3d were occasioned by a banditti of the populace of Paris and Marseilles, instigated by some of that party. The party succeeded, and success has decided their cause to be just. It is this success alone, which has given the name of patriotism to the violences of the Jacobins—it is defeat alone which has given the epithet of treason to the efforts of the Brissotines. The mere question, "whose proposed system of government is best for France" is a mere speculative point, on which people will have different opinions; and to entertain this or that opinion, can never be justly denominated treason.

I go farther, and declare my own private opinion, that in the course of a few years, a change will take place in France; and it is an equal chance that the Jacobins will be denounced as traitors, by a majority of the nation; and the statute of La Fayette or Brissot will be erected on the ruins of the statue of Marat. Factions are playing the same game that Sylla and Marius played at Rome—the same game that York and Lancaster played in England—the man who is exiled to day as a traitor, will to-morrow be recalled, and hailed as the protector of liberty. When party spirit subsides and factions lose their violence, then and not before, will tyranny give way to freedom, and the capricious sway of men, to the mild steady dominion of law.

CONCLUSION

Those who suppose France now in possession of a free government are most egregiously mistaken. At no period has France experienced a despotism so severe and bloody, as the present authority of the convention, backed by a full treasury and more than a million of disciplined troops. This severe tyranny has imprisoned and executed more French citizens in 18 months past, than had been thrown into the Bastile for three centuries, preceding its demolition.

Nor are the French now fighting for internal liberty; they are fighting against external foes; a vile league of tyrants that have unwarrantably attempted to control the internal affairs of France. God grant that they may be defeated, and severely chastized for their insolence!

It is this unprecedented league of princes that now gives union and energy to the French nation. It is perhaps the sole principle of union. When this combination shall be dissolved, and France left to *act only upon herself*, more than half the revolution will still remain to be effected. France will then have to conquer the *errors of her legislators* and the *passions of a turbulent populace*. She will find a defective constitution and feeble laws—she will find violent parties, strong prejudices, unbridled licentiousness to be subdued. Instead of one tyrant or a convention of tyrants, she will find a multitude of little tyrants in each of her forty-five thousand towns and villages. Anarchy, disorder, and proscriptions will afflict her for some years; and probably the present convention and their successors will be buried in the ruins of the present paper constitution of government.

But society cannot exist without government. Experience and severe calamities will ultimately teach the French nation, that government immediately in the hands of the people, of citizens collected without law, and proceeding without order, is the most violent, irregular, capricious and dangerous species of despotism—a despotism, infinitely more terrible than the fixed steady tyranny of a monarch, as it may spring up in a moment, and unexpectedly spread devastation and ruin, at any time, in any place, and among any class of citizens. The tyranny of a monarch is the steady gale, which gives time to prepare for its ravages; it enables the seamen to clear his decks and hand his sails—the farmer to leave his field, to shut his doors and shelter himself and his herds from the impending storm. But popular despotism is a whirlwind, a tornado of passions; it collects in a moment; a calm clear sky is instantly darkened, and furious winds, bursting on their affrightened victims while helpless and unguarded, sweep away the fruits of their labor, and bury them in the ruins.

The French will learn this important truth, that the assembly of representatives, who are to govern twenty-six millions of people, is not to be a company of stage-players, whose speeches are to be regulated by the hisses and acclamations of a promiscuous collection of men in the galleries. They will learn that a Paris mob is not to govern France, and that the galleries of the convention must be silenced, or France will be enslaved. In short the French people must learn that an enthusiasm, necessary to animate her citizens in time of war, will be a source of infinite disorder in time of peace; that passions, essential to them when engaging a foreign enemy, will be fatal to their own government: that in lieu of private wills, the laws must govern; and that parties must bend their stubborn opinions to some conciliatory plan of government on which a great majority of citizens can coalesce and harmonize. When all this is done, they must learn that the executive power must be vested in a single hand, call him monarch, doge, president, governor, or what they please; and to secure liberty, the executive must have force and energy. They must also learn a truth, sanctioned by numerous experiments, that legislative power, vested in two houses, is exercised with more safety and effect, than when vested in a single assembly. The conclusion of the whole business will be, that civil war and the blood of half a million of citizens, will compel the nation to renounce the idle theories of upstart philosophers, and return to the plain substantial maxims of wisdom and experience. Then, and not before, will France enjoy liberty.

Americans! be not deluded. In seeking liberty, France has gone beyond her. You, my countrymen, if you love liberty, adhere to your constitution of government. The moment you quit that sheet-anchor, you are afloat among the surges of passion and the rocks of error; threatened every moment with ship-wreck. Heaven grant that while Europe is agitated with a violent tempest, in which palaces are shaken, and thrones tottering to their base, the republican government of America, in which liberty and the rights of man are embarked, fortunately anchored at an immense distance, on the margin of the gale, may be enabled to ride out the storm, and land us safely on the shores of peace and political tranquillity.

Chronology

1795–1805

1795 MANIFESTATIONS OF THE BENEFICENCE OF DIVINE PROVIDENCE TOWARDS AMERICA, Bishop James Madison

Jay's Treaty with Great Britain is narrowly ratified by the Senate (June 24). Bitter opposition has consolidated Jefferson's Democratic-Republican Party as a political power and alienated the French First Republic. The two countries are on the brink of war by the following spring.

Timothy Pickering succeeds Edmund Randolph as Secretary of State after the latter, accused of corruption, resigns (Dec. 10). A completely reorganized cabinet now includes only Federalists, with Hamilton out but still a potent influence; John Adams will retain this cabinet when he becomes second president.

Pinckney's Treaty with Spain opens up the entire Mississippi River, including New Orleans at its mouth, to American trade.

Oliver Evans, a prolific and successful inventor, publishes the first textbook of mechanical engineering, *The Young Mill-Wright's and Miller's Guide.*

1796 Tennessee is admitted as the sixteenth state (slave-holding), with John Sevier as Governor (June 1).

British forces evacuate Detroit and other Great Lakes strongholds, as agreed in Jay's Treaty (July-Aug.).

France refuses to receive Charles C. Pinckney as James Monroe's replacement as American minister until "grievances have been redressed" (Aug. 22).

Washington's Farewell Address, never delivered orally, is published in the Philadelphia *Daily American Advertiser* (Sept. 17).

The United States signs a treaty with Tripoli to pay annual tribute, commissions, and ransom for the release of American seamen captured by Barbary pirates and for the security of U. S. vessels (Nov. 4).

Andrew Jackson is chosen by Tennessee as the state's first Congressional Representative (Nov.).

John Adams is elected President (71 electoral votes) and Thomas Jefferson Vice President (68 electoral votes) (Dec. 7).

Thomas Paine publishes *The Age of Reason*, the most influential publication of a number that attack religion as superstition.

1797 SERMON BEFORE THE GENERAL COURT OF NEW HAMPSHIRE AT THE GENERAL ELECTION, Stephen Peabody

President John Adams and Vice President Thomas Jefferson are inaugurated (Mar. 4).

The first special session of Congress is called by President Adams after the French expulsion of Pinckney, the U. S. minister (May 15).

A treaty with Tunis is signed, similar to that signed with Tripoli, with even higher sums being paid to protect American ships and seamen from Barbary pirates (Aug. 28; not ratified until Jan. 10, 1801).

In the "XYZ Affair" Talleyrand in Paris seeks a forced loan of $240,000 to France and a personal bribe to smooth things between his country and the United States. He detains the diplomat Elbridge Gerry when American commissioners refuse (Oct. 18). Undeclared naval war results, lasting until 1800.

The U. S. S. Constitution ("Old Ironsides"), a 44-gun frigate, is launched and put into highly effective service by the U. S. Navy against the French and Barbary pirates (Oct. 21).

1798 A DISCOURSE, DELIVERED AT THE ROMAN CATHOLIC CHURCH IN BOSTON, John Thayer

THE DUTY OF AMERICANS, AT THE PRESENT CRISIS, Timothy Dwight

War fears produce a variety of measures aimed at strengthening the federal government, including four laws known as the Alien and Sedition Acts outlawing political opposition (June–July); these are applied against Democratic-Republican spokesmen, editors, and printers.

The Marine Corps is established (July 11).

The Kentucky Resolutions, drafted by Jefferson, assert the power of sovereign states to determine the constitutionality or nullity of the Alien and Sedition Acts (Sept. 12). The Virginia Resolutions, composed by Madison, are similarly enacted to oppose the unconstitutional exercise of federal power in Virginia (Dec. 24).

Eli Whitney invents the basic techniques for mass production and builds an assembly line for the production of army muskets on a government contract.

1799 A new peace commission is sent to Paris by Adams upon Talleyrand's assurance that they will be respectfully received (Feb. 25).

A new Kentucky Resolution, also drafted by Jefferson, is enacted against the rebuttal that only the federal judiciary can decide on the constitutionality of laws. The resolution insists that states may nullify congressional enactments (Nov. 22).

The Sixth Congress meets, the last to have a Federalist majority (Dec. 2).

Washington suddenly dies (Dec. 14). Napoleon Bonaparte proclaims a week of mourning in France, and honors are paid him in England (Dec. 14).

1800 A SERMON OCCASIONED BY THE DEATH OF WASHINGTON, Henry Holcombe

ON THE EVILS OF A WEAK GOVERNMENT, John Smalley

THE VOICE OF WARNING TO CHRISTIANS, John Mitchell Mason

A SOLEMN ADDRESS TO CHRISTIANS AND PATRIOTS, Tunis Wortman

The Second Great Awakening begins.

The federal government moves from Philadelphia to Washington, D.C. (June).

With the Treaty of Morfontaine ("Convention of 1800"), naval war between the United States and France is ended (Sept. 30).

Congress convenes in Washington and John and Abigail Adams occupy the new presidential residence, the White House (Nov. 17).

1801 OVERCOMING EVIL WITH GOOD, Stanley Griswold

John Marshall, appointed by Adams and confirmed by the Senate, takes the oath of office as Chief Justice of the United States (Jan. 20–Feb. 4).

Electoral ballots from the 1800 election are finally counted and, after an all-night session and 36 rounds of voting to break a deadlock, Jefferson (with Hamilton's help) is elected President, Aaron Burr Vice President (Feb. 11).

War against Barbary pirates results as the Pasha of Tripoli declares war on the United States (May 14). The struggle lasts until 1805.

The Great Revival of the West, part of the second Great Awakening, begins at a Presbyterian camp meeting in Cane Ridge, Kentucky (Aug. 6).

1802 AN ORATION IN COMMEMORATION OF THE ANNIVERSARY OF AMERICAN INDEPENDENCE, William Emerson

1803 The Supreme Court *Marbury* v. *Madison* decision establishes judicial review by declaring an act of Congress null and void (Feb. 24).

Ohio becomes the seventeenth state, the first in the Union in which slavery is illegal from the beginning (Mar. 1).

The Louisiana Purchase treaty with France for $15 million doubles the nation's land area, from which thirteen new states will be created (May 2).

The three-year Lewis and Clark expedition to the Pacific coast begins (Aug. 31).

New England Federalists (including some clergy) secretly connive with New Yorkers and Vice President Burr to secede and form a Northern or Northeastern Confederacy. In the New York gubernatorial race, Hamilton opposes Burr, who intends to become president of the confederacy.

1804 Democratic-Republican Party leaders set out to impeach and remove Federalist judges, such as Federal District Judge John Pickering of New Hampshire and Supreme Court Justice Samuel Chase (Jan.-Mar.).

Aaron Burr kills Alexander Hamilton in a duel at Weehawken, New Jersey (July 11).

Jefferson is re-elected for a second term (162 electoral votes), with George Clinton of New York elected as Vice President (Dec. 5).

1805 A SERMON, ON THE SECOND COMING OF CHRIST, John Hargrove

Jefferson is inaugurated for a second term, with Vice President Clinton (Mar. 4); Madison continues as Secretary of State, Albert Gallatin as Secretary of the Treasury.

A treaty is signed ending the Tripolitanian War (June 4).

The Lewis and Clark expedition arrives at the mouth of the Columbia River (Nov. 7) and builds Fort Clatsop (near present-day Astoria, Oregon) for winter quarters.

The Ninth Congress convenes with decisive Democratic-Republican majorities in both House and Senate (Dec. 9).

The University of South Carolina is opened.

Mercy Otis Warren publishes the three-volume *The Rise, Progress and Termination of the American Revolution.*

45

MANIFESTATIONS OF THE BENEFICENCE OF DIVINE PROVIDENCE TOWARDS AMERICA

Bishop James Madison

RICHMOND

1795

Bishop James Madison (1749-1812). A cousin of President James Madison, Madison was educated as a lawyer under George Wythe after graduation with high honors from the College of William and Mary in 1771. He became a professor of philosophy and mathematics at the college but soon decided upon the ministry. He was ordained in England in 1775 as an Anglican priest. Two years later he became president of William and Mary and held that position until his death. A strong advocate of independence, he went so far, we are told, as to speak of the republic—rather than kingdom—of heaven. He served as the captain of a militia company of his students and saw considerable action during the Revolution. After the war, Madison devoted himself to reviving the College of William and Mary; in 1784 he taught political economy using Adam Smith's *Wealth of Nations* as a textbook. As a surveyor and cartographer, he established the boundary between Virginia and Pennsylvania and later drew the map of Virginia commonly called Madison's Map (issued first in 1807 and corrected in 1818). He was a leading scientist of the day and corresponded with Thomas Jefferson about scientific matters.

Madison also devoted himself to the reorganization of the Episcopal Church in Virginia after the war. Consecrated the first Bishop of Virginia (in Canterbury in 1790), he was the third of three American bishops through whom the episcopate came to the United States. Disestablished and with its properties under attack, the church faced formidable problems that, rather than being solved during Madison's tenure, further deepened.

The sermon reprinted here was preached on February 19, 1795, proclaimed a day of national thanksgiving and prayer by President Washington.

MANIFESTATION

OF THE

Beneficence of Divine PROVIDENCE

TOWARDS AMERICA.

A

DISCOURSE,

Delivered on Thursday the 19th of February, 1795, being the day recommended by the PRESIDENT *of the* United States, *for general Thanksgiving and Prayer.*

By BISHOP MADISON.

PUBLISHED *at the request of the* AUDITORS.

RICHMOND:
Printed By THOMAS NICOLSON, 1795.

Only fear the Lord, and serve him; for consider how great things he hath done for you.

[I] Samuel XII. 2[4].

Brethren,

There are few situations more interesting to the human race, than that which the people of America this day presents. The temples of the living God are every where, throughout this rising empire, this day, crowded, I trust, with worshippers, whose hearts, impressed with a just and lively sense of the great things, which he hath done for them, pour forth, in unison, the grateful tribute of praise and thanksgiving. Yes, this day, brethren, "the voice of rejoicing and salvation is in the tabernacles of the righteous"; and with reason, for the history of nations doth not exhibit a people who ever had more cause to offer up to the great author of every good the most fervent expressions of gratitude and thanksgiving. Let, my brethren, the sons of irreligion, wrapped in their dark and gloomy system of fatality, refuse to open their eyes to the great luminous proofs of providential government, which America displays; let them turn from a light, which their weak vision cannot bear; but let the righteous, let those who trust in God, who can trace in that good and glorious being, the relations of father, friend and governor, let them, with eagle eyes look up to that full blaze of salvation, which he hath vouchsafed to this new world. Permit me then, upon this occasion, to turn your attention to those great things, which the Lord hath done for us, to those manifold displays of divine providence, which the history of America exhibits; and let the subject afford an opportunity to revive within us sentiments of lively gratitude, and excite sincere resolutions to fear the Lord, and to serve him; in a word, to increase daily in piety, and in all those noble affections of the soul which dignify the christian and the patriot.

I. Who can tell how many ages had been swallowed up in the all-absorbing gulph of time, before the bold navigator first essayed to visit these distant regions of the earth? Who can tell, how long this western world had been the habitation of the listless savage, or the wild beasts of the forest? At these questions chronology drops her epochs, as incapable of conducting her to periods so remote, and which have escaped her grasp. The ways of heaven must oft appear to us, weak mortals, dark and intricate. But the first suggestion, which here presents itself, is, that providence seems to have thrown a veil over this portion of the globe, in order to conceal it from the eyes of the nations of the east, until the destined period had arrived for the regeneration of mankind, in this new world, after those various other means, which the wisdom of the Almighty had permitted to operate, in the old, had proved ineffectual. In vain had reason, the hand-maid of pure religion, long attempted to convince men of the reciprocal duties, which equality and fraternity impose. Still there would arise some one,

> "of proud ambitious heart, who, not content
> with fair equality, fraternal state,
> would arrogate dominion undeserved
> over his brethren, and quite dispossess
> concord and law of nature from the earth."*

In vain had even thy dispensation of love and peace, blessed Jesus! long essayed to disarm ambition of the ensanguined sword, and to diffuse benevolence, equality and fraternity among the human race. Millions still groaned under the heavy pressure, which tyranny imposed. Yes, even thy gospel of love, of universal fraternity, had been, too often, perverted into the most formidable system of oppression; and mankind, instead of seeing it diffuse the heavenly rays of philanthropy, too frequently beheld it as imposing a yoke, to degrade and enslave them. The princes of the earth sought not for the sacred duties, which it enjoined; but they sought to render it the sanction of their exterminating vengeance, or their deep laid systems of usurpation. Is not the history of almost all Europe pregnant with proofs of this calamitous truth? If you can point to some small portion, where the religion of the blessed Jesus, untrammeled with political usurpations, was left to operate its happy effects upon the passions and the conduct of men; or where toleration extended wide her arms of mercy to embrace the whole family of Christ, the spot appears like a solitary star, which in the midst of night, beams forth alone, whilst

*Milton—*Par. lost.*

clouds and thick darkness obscure the rest of the innumerable host of heaven. Alas! what avails the voice of reason or religion, when the lust of domination has usurped the soul! At the shrine of this fell demon, the human race was sacrificed by thousands. Nay, too many of the sons of Europe are still bound with cords to the altars of ambition, and there immolated, not only by thousands, but by tens of thousands. Do you doubt the assertion, afflictive as it seems to our brethren of the old world? The last four years have, in their flight, scarcely wanted a moment to testify the melancholy truth. I will not add the long catalogue of those innumerable scourges, which, from time to time, have visited Europe; I will not speak of those various tempests, which, by divine command, have so often shaken the guilty nations of the east, but which seem in vain to have uttered the voice of warning and reproof: Domination still rivetted her iron chains; the fangs of governments; avaricious, arbitrary and vindictive, entered even into the souls of the suffering people. The heritage of the Lord were only as sheep destined to be shorn or slaughtered, whilst the unfeeling despot exacted in return, not obsequious obedience only, but even professions of gratitude for the innumerable blessings, which flowed from his hallowed protection. How were these chains to be burst asunder? How was the human race to be restored to their inherent rights, rights, which the God of nature consecrated at the birth of every individual? How was the dignity of man to be vindicated? How were those sentiments of equality, benevolence and fraternity, which reason, and religion, and nature enjoin, to reassume their sovereignty over the human soul, and to dash against the heads of usurpers the chains, the burthens, the oppressions, which had so long brought down the grey hairs of the multitude with sorrow to the grave? How could the principles of a revolution so important, so essential for the happiness of the human species, be generated, but by raising up, as it were, a new race of men, in some remote, some blessed clime, where, from their infancy, unfettered by those errors, which time appears to sanctify, they should be trained not only to a knowledge, but to a just sense of the duty of asserting and maintaining their rights; and above all, where the love of equality, the basis of all rights and all social happiness, should be congenial to man? This favoured region, favoured indeed of heaven, is America. It is here, a knowledge of those political truths, which the immortal Sydneys and the Lockes of former years investigated with philosophic eye, bursts spontaneous forth. It is here, that men, led by the hand of nature, their minds unawed and unobscured by opinions and customs as barbarous and unfriendly to social rights as the dark chaotic ages, which gave them birth, see and acknowledge as axioms, what philosophers have toiled to establish by deductions, long and intricate. It is in America, that the germs of the universal redemption of the human race from domination and oppression have already begun to be developed; it is in America, that we see a redintegration of divine love for man, and that the voice of heaven itself seems to call to her sons, go ye forth and disciple all nations, and spread among them the gospel of equality and fraternity.*

II. These considerations present to our minds the first traces of the beneficent designs of providence in the history of this new world. Nor ought it, in the 2d place, to be here forgotten, that the current, or general tendency of providence is also to be traced back to the source, whence the present free and enlightened race of America sprung. For surely, our fore-fathers, amidst the wreck of human rights, and the convulsive tempests with which ambition had so often overwhelmed the nations of the east, still evinced, at times, no small portion of that etherial spirit, that ardent love of liberty, which glows in the American breast. It was this indomitable spirit, this attachment to the inherent rights of man, stronger infinitely than the fear of those storms, which agitate the immense atlantic, or of the fierce and cruel tenants of the howling wilderness, or the ravages of disease, and famine and death itself, which urged our fore-fathers to these distant shores. Yes, brethren, it was this noble principle, this love of liberty, which defying all dangers, conducted our fore-fathers to America; but who doth not see, that this principle, whilst it only could prompt

* Terms have their days of fashion, like many other things. The term, *equality*, seems to be in the wane; it has its enemies even in America. But whoever will read Dr. Brown's excellent essay upon the *natural equality of men*, will there find this grand principle justly appreciated; he will find, that it is the only basis on which universal justice, order and freedom, can be firmly built; or permanently secured. The view, says the writer, exhibited in this essay, so far from loosening the bands of society, or weakening that subordination, without which no government can subsist, will draw more closely every social tie, and more strongly confirm the obligations of legal obedience, and the rights of legal authority. Certainly this principle is one of the hinges upon which the christian system turns.

to the bold enterprize, was no where to be found so pure, so energetic as in Britain? Who doth not see, that thus to have transported it to America, thus to have incorporated it with the primary social institutions of this country, may be justly deemed an event most fortunate for mankind, nay, most worthy of providence itself? Had this principle been equally transported to the fertile plains of Mexico, or Peru, instead of the *Auri sacra sames*, they also would have had their apostles, nay, their martyrs to liberty. Yes, even Mexico, and Peru, e're this distant period, would have had their Washington, would have unfurled the banners of liberty, and would have fought, and bled, and conquered. If then we dare attempt with mortal eye to trace those causes, by which the Almighty operates, it will not be thought presumptuous, I trust, not only to ascribe to his directive wisdom the introduction of a principle, which here fostered, will redeem the captive nations of the earth; but also, the introduction of it, at a time, when its active, but daily increasing energy should accelerate the great and glorious revolution, which it has already effected in America, which it has commenced in Europe, and which will not be arrested in its progress, until the complete restoration of the human race to their inherent rights be accomplished, throughout the globe. Let the tyrants of the earth set themselves in array against this principle; "they shall be chased as the chaff of the mountain before the wind, and like the down of the thistle before the whirlwind."*

III. But these reflections, pleasing as they are to the friends of piety, of reason and of liberty, give way to others, excited by more obvious dispensations of providence. Suppose, my brethren, when our forefathers here first rested the soles of their feet, delivered from those waters, which seemed almost to cover the face of the whole earth, the guardian angel of America withdrawing the curtain of time, had opened to their view the prospect, which this day presents; had shewn to them, America, free, independent, and holding an eminent rank among the nations of the earth; had shewn to them her sons and her daughters, numerous as the stars of heaven, assembled in the houses of their God, and with one voice, offering up the grateful incense of adoration, praise and thanks-giving, "for the great things that he hath done for them"; had shewn to them the first in-

*Isaiah

stance, which the world has ever exhibited, of written social compacts, together with her plans of government, founded on the eternal basis of wisdom, equality and justice; had shewn to them, the thousand blessings, which peace, from her horn of plenty, scatters round, with the arts and sciences gradually advancing in her train; had shewn to them, her navies, loaded not with the desolating weapons of war, but with the fruits of the earth, vexing with their prows the most distant seas; had shewn to them the bright portrait of that heroic citizen, whose prudence, whose fortitude, and whose wisdom shine equally refulgent in war as in peace; and lastly, had shewn to them, the fairest portion of the old world, by the example of America, by the influence of that energetic principle, which she had nurtured and matured, awaking as from a dream, "putting on strength as in the antient days, in the generations of old," uprooting the deep founded systems of usurpation, and gathering the oppressed under the wings of liberty and fraternity: And whilst he presented the glorious, the animating prospect, should say to them, all these events, my sons, great and astonishing as they are, shall come to pass within the short period, of a patriarchal life; would they not have fallen down upon their faces, and worshipping the God of their fathers, exclaimed[,] "This is the Lords doing, and it is marvellous in our eyes"? We, brethren, fortunate as we are, have lived to see this triumphal day. And is there a soul here present, is there one throughout this rising empire, who doth not trace, in the eventful history of America, the conspicuous displays of the hand of providence? Is there one, who is not ready also to exclaim, "it is the Lords doing"? Where, in what records of mankind, will he discover a progress from infancy to manhood, so accelerated, so astonishing in all its stages, so superior to all those ordinary means, by which empires are matured? I will not call your attention to that heroic contest, which so lately distinguished this country, and which, unequal, bold and hazardous as it appeared in its commencement, soon terminated in the establishment of liberty and independence, soon held aloft to the nations of the earth, the sublime example, which called, and still calls aloud, "awake, awake, put on strength, O nations of the earth; awake as in the antient days, in the generations of old."* I will not retrace those scenes of blood, of

* Jeremiah

horror and desolation, through which the patriot sons of America once triumphant passed. Ministers of the gospel! be it yours to bind up and to heal the wounds, which contentions and wars inflict. But ah! who does not remember, when the fate of this rising empire, nay of mankind, hung trembling between the fury of the oppressor, and the weakness of the oppressed? how many were our prayers to the God of battles! how often did we look forwards upon the mightiness of the adversary; how often backwards upon our own imbecility, upon our wives and our tender infants? In that awful crisis, who does not remember, that in God alone was our trust? Yes, "O people, saved by the Lord, it was his right hand and his holy arm," which rescued thee from the strength of the lion and the bear; it was the same wise and gracious providence, which delivered the youthful unarmed David from the hands of Goliath, accoutred as he was, "with a sword, and with a spear, and with a Shield," which also delivered thee, from the hands of the mightiest of nations.

Do these our conclusions appear to some to savour of presumptive arrogance, or do we discover to the philosophic mind an enthusiastic imbecility in ascribing these events, so peculiar to the annals of America, to the particular direction of providence? Let such bethink themselves, if such there be, that it is a just reliance upon the superintending providence of God, a reliance dictated by the concurrent voice of reason, of philosophy and religion, which compels the humble, the grateful and the wise to consider all those dispositions or events, which so remarkably coincide with the general plan of the moral government of the world, as indications of the design and direction of omnipotence. Causes and effects are, doubtless, in the hands of him who willed their connexion. But his will is the general happiness. They who indulge this idea, so consolatory to man, will therefore consider it as the homage which is due to the creator, regenerator and preserver of the universe, to ascribe to his superior direction, effects so concordant with his goodness, and which so greatly transcend all human means. Yes, brethren, if the effects, which we have, in your hearing, thus slightly traced; if the period of time when America was discovered, the necessity and the consequent production of other means for the restoration of human rights, than those, which had hitherto operated; if her origin, and the consequent possession of a principle, which, nurtured and matured, is now pervading, and will animate and excite the whole family of mankind to vindicate their lost rights; if her astonishing progress from infancy to the station, which she now possesses, a progress, which the opposition of a ten-fold force served only to accelerate: if, become free and independent, having accomplished the most unparalleled revolution, a revolution unstained by fratricide, or the blood of the innocent, she hath given to nations the first lesson by which their rights may be preserved, and men reassume their native dignity, by realizing that sacred compact, which before existed only in idea, and by accurately delineating the boundary beyond which, her servants, whether legislators or magistrates, dare not pass; if she hath established upon a rock, the empire of laws, and not of men; if America, as a tender and affectionate daughter, is ready, from her exuberant breasts, to afford the milk of regeneration to her aged and oppressed relatives; if, in short, from a beginning the most inauspicious, she hath thus outstript all political calculation, thus risen to this day of glory, thus ascended on high, thus triumphed over every obstacle, and if all these be effects worthy of the divine interposition, then we will still cherish the fond idea, we will cling to the full persuasion, that our God hath been, "our strength, our refuge, and our fortress," a God, who, at the birth of creation, destined man for liberty, for virtue and for happiness, not for oppression, vice and misery.

IV. But, my brethren, to rest contented with merely viewing the hand of providence, or in acknowledging the plan of divine wisdom, which is here operating for the general felicity, would be to halt at the threshhold of the temple of God. Gratitude, warm and fervent, united to a sincere resolution "to fear and to serve him," is the return, which the Almighty beneficence claims from every worshipper. It is the first sacrifice of a heart capable of being touched by acts of unbounded love, by deeds of mercy and kindness so eminently extended not to us only, but, through our agency, to the whole human race. I confess to you, brethren, who detest ingratitude even to man, as the sure but melancholy symptom of a heart, dark, gloomy, and void of every virtuous sensibility, when I recall to mind the past, contemplate the present, and pursuing the confederacy of causes, look forward to those blessings of peace, of order, of justice and of liberty, which are daily advancing with an accelerated progress, my soul becomes sublimed with the grand idea of the undeviating love of God to man; I trace in the moral, as well as in the physical world, the evident vestiges of a Providence, all wise, all merciful, and all gracious: my hopes, temporal as well as eternal, instead of fluctuating in the uncertain ocean of those degrading sentiments, which overwhelm the soul with fear and despondency, are anchored even at the footstool of the throne of God. Yes, brethren, struck with the awful image of a goodness so generous and so extended, my heart overflows with gratitude, I form new resolutions to fear and to serve him, I exclaim with the Psalmist—"Let the people praise thee, O God; let all the people praise thee. O let the nations be glad and sing for joy; for thou shalt judge the people righteously, and govern the nations upon earth."

But, brethren, important considerations still demand our attention. Has heaven been thus propitious; are we possessed of all those blessings which flow from governments founded in wisdom, justice and equality; doth the morning of America break forth refulgent with unclouded glory? Then it behoves us, above all things, to inquire, how are these blessings to be preserved? how shall we ensure to her a meridian splendor, worthy of such a morning? This inquiry immediately resolves itself into another. What is there in this sublunary state, that can attract the smiles of heaven, or ensure political happiness, but virtue? Never was there a mortal so depraved, never was there a conscience so deaf to that internal voice, which always whispers truth, but must acknowledge, that virtue only gives a title to hope for the favour of that high and lofty one, who inhabiteth eternity. Fellow-citizens, let virtue then, I entreat you, be the ruling principle, the polar star, which should influence every sentiment, and guide every action, since it alone will conduct us into the haven of felicity. But will you trust, for the diffusion of virtue, to that political morality, which a vain philosophy would substitute in the room of those lessons, which the heavenly teacher delivered? Shall virtue trickle from the oozy bed of political catechisms, or shall it gush, pure and in full stream, from the rock of our salvation? Ah! brethren, the moment that we drop the idea of a God, the remunerator of virtue, but the avenger of iniquity; the moment we abandon that divine system of equality, fraternity, and universal benevolence, which the blessed Jesus taught and exemplified; the moment that religion, the pure and undefiled religion, which heaven, in compassion to the infirmity of human reason, vouchsafed to mortals, loses its influence over their hearts, from that fatal moment, farewell to public and private happiness, farewell, a long farewell to virtue, to patriotism, to liberty! Virtue, such as republics and heaven require, must have its foundation in the heart; it must penetrate the whole man; it must derive its obligations and its sanctions, not from the changeable ideas of the political moralist, or thc caprice of the wisest of human legislators, but from the unchangeable father of the universe, the God of love, whose laws, and whose will we are incited to obey by motives, the most powerful that can actuate the human soul. Men must see and feel, that it is God himself, their maker and their judge, who demands obedience to duties, which constitute their individual, their social, their eternal happiness. Then, and not till then, will virtue reign triumphant in the hearts of citizens; then will she have her sacrifices in the midst of the deepest obscurity, as well as in the open day, in the most private and secret retirements, as well as upon the house tops.

There is, we will grant, a sublime philosophy, which may form her sages, and even her virtuous and heroic sages. But, will her abstract doctrines concerning moral obligation, stript of those awful sanctions, which religion annexes, touch the hearts of an entire nation, the poor, the simple, the unlettered, as well as the learned and the wise? No, brethren, these sages of philosophy will appear, once perhaps, in a century; her lessons of wisdom, admitting them to possess the efficacy contended for, can be extended but to a few; whilst religion diffuses her soul-saving leaven thro' the whole political mass. It is not for the learned and wise only, that she reserves the knowledge of her heavenly precepts; they are addressed to the whole family of mankind; the whole universe is her school. She has, moreover, this distinguishing advantage; she lays her divine hands upon the infant, and whilst she embraces him with the arms of mercy, stamps upon his tender, susceptible mind, the indelible, but just and awful idea of a God, the judge as well as the creator of the universe, a God, whose all-seeing eye delights only in virtue, a God, who has promised thro' Jesus Christ, a glorious and ever blessed immortality as the reward of well-doing, whilst the torturing hour of shame, remorse and misery is shewn to await the impious and the wicked. Thus taught by religion, man becomes acquainted with his real character; instead of being amenable only to human laws, whose utmost vigilance he may and often does elude, he sees himself accountable to a being, as just as merciful, as omnipotent as omniscient. He finds himself destined, not to the narrow range of the beasts that perish, but to immortal life. The bright prospect invigorates his soul; sentiments of conscious dignity elevate him above what is low or mean; his views are fixed upon what is truly great and good, patriotic and brave; no tears appal him, but confident in his God, he evinces himself, whether in adversity or prosperity, the inflexible friend of justice and humanity.

And yet, great God! how many are there among the sons of men, urged, we hope, rather by the delusive phantoms of their imaginations, than by the lust of wicked passions, who would tear from the human heart, prostrate in the dust, nay obliterate from the face of the earth every vestige of that divine, that beneficent system of justice, fraternity and equality, which Jesus Christ delivered! rash, unthinking mortals! listen, at least, to the prayer which that divine system, ever breathing charity and compassion, still offers up for its vindictive enemies; "Father! forgive them, for they know not what they do!"

Fellow-citizens, it is an easy task for those who may have the honour of addressing an American audience this day, to point out the excellencies of our civil governments, to shew their superior aptitude for the promotion of political happiness, to evince that obedience to laws, constitutionally enacted, is the only means of preserving liberty, and that every expression of the public will is obligatory upon every citizen; to prove, that representative republics, instead of being the prolific parents of anarchy and confusion, are, on the contrary, of all the forms of government, under which men have yet associated, either thro' compulsion or choice, the most promotive of private and public happiness, the most susceptible of that energy, which is equally capable of curbing the licentiousness of the multitude, or of frustrating the wicked designs of the ambitious; it is easy for them to shew, that virtue is the vital principle of a republic, that unless a magnanimous spirit of patriotism animates every breast, unless a sincere and ardent love for justice, for temperance, for prudence, for fortitude, in short, for all those qualities, which dignify human nature, pervades, enlivens, invigorates the whole mass of citizens, these fair superstructures of political wisdom must soon crumble into dust. Certainly, my brethren, it is a fundamental maxim, that virtue is the soul of a republic. But, zealous for the prosperity of my country, I will repeat, and in these days, it is of infinite moment to insist, that without religion, I mean *rational religion*, the religion which our Saviour himself delivered, not that of fanatics or inquisitors, chimæras and shadows are substantial things compared with that virtue, which those who reject the authority of religion would recommend to our practice. Ye then who love your country[,] if you expect or wish, that real virtue and social happiness should be preserved among us, or, that genuine patriotism and a dignified obedience to law, instead of that spirit of disorganizing anarchy, and those false and hollow pretences to patriotism, which are so pregnant with contentions, insurrections and misery, should be the distinguishing characteristics of Americans; or, that, the same Almighty arm which hath hitherto protected your country, and conducted her to this day of glory, should still continue to shield and defend her, remember, that your first and last duty is "to fear the Lord and to serve him"; remember, that in the same proportion as irreligion advances, virtue retires; remember, that in her stead, will succeed factions, ever ready to prostitute public good to the most nefarious private ends, whilst unbounded licentiousness, and a total disregard to the sacred names of liberty and of patriotism will here once more, realize that fatal catastrophe, which so many free states have already experienced. Remember, the law of the Almighty is, they shall expire, with their expiring virtue. God of all nature! Father of the human spirit, preserve these prosperous, these happy republics from so dreadful a calamity. May thy gracious providence, which hath hitherto nurtured, protected, and conducted them to this day of praise and thanksgiving, ever be the supreme object of their regard? May the blessings already received, inspire every heart with just sentiments of gratitude, and with the inflexible resolution to perform those duties which become us as christians, and as citizens. May peace and happiness, truth and justice, order and freedom, religion and piety ever proclaim thy praises, thy providential goodness, thy love to man, not only in this land of liberty, but wherever the human race is found. Amen.

— 46 —

SERMON BEFORE THE GENERAL COURT OF NEW HAMPSHIRE AT THE ANNUAL ELECTION

Stephen Peabody

CONCORD

1797

STEPHEN PEABODY (1741–1819). A native of Andover, Massachusetts, Peabody was a Harvard graduate in the class of 1769. As the oldest member of his class, entering at twenty-two, he was nicknamed *Pater Omnium* by classmates. Peabody was a ringleader and cut-up in college, and his diary for 1767 is regarded by Clifford K. Shipton as "the most revealing document relating to colonial education which has come down to us" (*Sibley's Harvard Graduates*, 17:207n). Peabody's extensive diaries, his principal writings, provide a detailed portrait of himself as parson and of his times in New England.

Peabody settled in Atkinson, New Hampshire, in 1772 and remained there as pastor for the rest of his life. He was an orthodox Calvinist who measured his orthodoxy by agreement with the Bible at every point, and he avoided any hint of being a member of this or that theological faction. He was especially critical of emotional preachers (meaning Baptists and Methodists) but was himself an emotional preacher "who wept at his own pathos, or in sympathy with his bereaved hearers" (ibid., p. 212). He served as a chaplain during the Revolution with Colonel Poor's regiment on Winter Hill. Dartmouth College awarded him an honorary A.M. in 1792. Peabody loved to play the fiddle and sing, often serving in the pulpit as a one-man choir, though he was sometimes joined by his household pet, Little Dog. (Little Dog's death received more attention in his diary than that of any human being.) Peabody's swift conquest of the heart of his second wife, the widow Elizabeth Smith Shaw, in 1795, became a classic of New England folklore. His stepson, William Smith Shaw, became secretary to President John Adams, and Reverend Peabody and his wife were frequent visitors to the Adams household in Quincy. In addition to preaching and catechizing, Peabody farmed, and he and Elizabeth kept the Atkinson Academy, admitting girls to it after 1794, to the shock of the community.

This election sermon, preached in Concord, New Hampshire, on June 11, 1797, celebrates republican government as the rule of law in the United States and as a unique improvement over monarchy, aristocracy, and democracy as practiced through the ages.

A SERMON,

DELIVERED AT *CONCORD*,

BEFORE

The Honourable General Court

OF THE

STATE

OF

NEW HAMPSHIRE,

AT THE

ANNUAL ELECTION,

HOLDEN ON THE FIRST WEDNESDAY IN *JUNE*,
1797.

BY THE Rev. Stephen Peabody, A. M.
PASTOR OF THE CHURCH IN ATKINSON.

Published by Order of the General Court.

Concord:
PRINTED BY *GEORGE HOUGH*.

M.DCC.XCVII.

Moreover, thou shalt provide out of all the people, able men, such as fear GOD, *men of truth, hating covetousness; and place such over them, to be rulers of thousands, and rulers of hundreds, rulers of fifties, and rulers of tens.*

Exodus XVIII. 21.

In the great scale of beings, mankind hold a dignified station. The human mind, capable of improvement, under advantageous cultivation, progresses in knowledge and refinements, honourary in their nature, and ornamental in their consequences. Individuals, with privileges of this kind, shine as lights in the world. Societies, composed of characters improved in science and virtue, have every advantage in their social connection.

By long experience, the jarring passions and interests of men, shew the necessity of government. Various have been the forms, by which mankind have enjoyed distinguished privileges. A particular discussion of all the principles of government, will not be expected upon this occasion, as many of this respectable audience are better acquainted with them, than the speaker. An attempt of this, would be a departure from duty.

That ecclesiastical constitution, exhibited in the sacred scriptures, is the foundation upon which the ministers of religion are placed: It contains those rules and regulations which we are called to vindicate, and by it we are furnished with a code of laws and precepts, admirably suited to governors, and governed—rules designed to promote general happiness here, and to prepare for a far more exalted state in the regions of immortality. These are peculiar excellencies in the oracles of truth.

In the early ages of time, government was confined to private families; but when men multiplied, it was consistent with infinite wisdom to point out methods by which there should be a government upon a more extensive scale. This took place with the the people of Israel, while in the land of Egypt. The Egyptians, under a pretence that Israel would increase in numbers and power, treated them in a manner incompatible with humanity. Whereupon the Lord was pleased to provide for them a deliverer—to raise up Moses, remarkably to preserve him in his infancy, to appear unto him in a burning bush, to appoint him a ruler, and to accompany him with such proofs of his divine mission, as were convincing to a mind not clouded with ignorance, or blinded with prejudice.

The good man, with reluctance, modestly accepted the appointment, with Aaron his brother, his assistant in the arduous task. Mutually supporting each other, the Lord was with them. Happy for them, and thrice happy for the people, they were united by the most endearing ties, when placed, the one a political, the other an ecclesiastical leader. Aiming at the same great object, under the particular direction of heaven, they went on, hand in hand, through a series of unexampled trials, conducting and protecting their charge, as faithful shepherds guide their flocks. Connected with an ingrateful people, those worthies met with singular difficulties in their way, were censured when performing the will of God, and exerting every power to advance the best interest of society.

Jethro, the priest of Midian, father-in-law to Moses, anxious for his son's welfare, and sensible that his task was insupportable, proposed some alterations, that a part of the burden might be removed from him, and placed upon others. These we have in the theme under consideration—the manner of executing their several trusts specified—the extent of their power defined—and, in cases of intricacy, an appeal open to the chief magistrate, their last resort. Here the privileges of the people were in a great measure to be secured by the amiable characters of their rulers, and especially by his who was their supreme judge, and under the immediate influence of the king of kings.

This was the form of government then established: It was a theocracy; and its permanency shews it was suited to the genius of the people in that period of the world, as it continued in the days of Moses, Joshua, and till Samuel's time, sanctioned with the approbation of heaven. They were governed by wise judges, given them by a God who was their guardian and friend, till his favour was forfeited by a revolt from him, casting off his authority, and determining to have a king of their own, in imitation of the heathen nations. This conduct proceeding from a factious disposition, was displeasing to God: Yet he granted their request, gave them a king—but a king in judgment.

The oracles of truth are not decisive, respecting any particular, permanent form of civil polity. We are left at liberty to adopt rules and laws agreeable to our inclinations. In a state of ignorance and barbarism, a despotic power may be necessary; but where knowledge is diffused, and reason enlightened, the bastile bars are seen—the shackles eluded.

A republican government, as defined by an eminent writer, "in which all men, rich and poor, magistrates and subjects, officers and people, masters and servants, the first citizen and the last, are equally subject to the laws," is doubtless the most unexceptionable. This is the general principle which supports the government of united America, happily removed from that monarchy, aristocracy, or democracy, which have injured mankind. This form has the public good for its principal object: It rests primarily in the hands of the people; and when delegated, is exercised a limited period, and returns to its origin. A people with a good constitution, judicious laws, in the hands of an executive authority influenced by the maxims of wisdom and goodness, attentive to their true interest, will acquire strength and stability, as they improve in knowledge and virtue.

The directions given in my text, are adapted to any people, under whatever form of government, when wisdom and probity are their guide. And in this view, we trust they are peculiarly applicable to the people of America, and demand attention in all our elections to fill the offices of state, supreme and subordinate. Though under dissimilar forms, electors may be different, yet the characters of the elected should be the same.

The subject before us exhibits the duty of a people in the choice of their rulers, and delineates the leading traits essential to those in public office.

I shall attempt to make some observations upon the several particulars here specified, to form good rulers—speak of the duties of their station—then draw some inferences—and conclude with addresses suited to the present occasion.

The first particular in the choice of rulers, should be natural abilities. Able men, are such as have been distinguished by the God of nature. As in the ecclesiastical department, a novice is excluded; so in the civil, men of sense and judgment are to be preferred: Men of fortitude, of resolution, who fear not the faces of the unprincipled; but when occasion requires, can oppose them with firmness: Men of clear heads, and determined hearts. But it is not enough that men should have natural endowments; more is necessary: The gifts of nature should be improved by study and close application, and truth investigated in the paths of science. There should be a general knowledge of the principles of natural and political law: And without this, men are exposed; they are easily deceived, and led into errors, disgraceful to themselves, and injurious to their constituents. Designing individuals have every advantage of the illiterate, to influence their conduct to the accomplishment of sinister purposes. A good natural understanding, therefore, and decent and liberal acquirements, are necessary ingredients in the able statesman.

Another qualification in an accomplished ruler here recommended, is the fear of GOD. This being granted, an atheist can have no part or lot in this matter. A being who is believed not to exist, cannot be feared. But besides these, there are those in an enlightened age of the world, who acknowledge the being of GOD, and yet are not afraid to offend him by trampling on his authority. Such are poorly qualified for eminent stations in government. An important trait in the character of a good ruler is wanting.

The fear of God is the best guard against temptations to a deviation from the rules of right. By this, human passions are regulated, and men are influenced to "run the ways of God's commandments, rendering to all their dues—tribute to whom tribute is due, custom to whom custom, fear to whom fear, honour to whom honour." A consciousness of his omnipresence to whom we are all accountable, fixes a lasting impression upon the heart, fans every spark of moral rectitude, and calls forth patriotic exertions. The belief of an entire dependance on him, is an impenetrable mound against an inundation of immoralities: It is the best constructed fortress against the savage artillery of the prince of darkness. Shielded with a helmet from the God of armies, the intrepid ruler marches at the head of his battalions, with prudence, fortitude, and perseverance, which insure protection, and lead on to victory. Examples of wisdom and virtue, originating from the fear of God, have a commanding influence upon the human mind; and in all our elections, such qualifications should invariably direct our choice.

We pass on to a third particular essential in Jethro's rulers. They were to be men of truth.

Possessed of a principle opposed to falsehood and deceit, they were to be eminent for their integrity. This was a qualification necessary in the law-givers of Israel. To a man of this description, "his yea, and nay, are Amen." His tongue is a faithful index of his mind. He strictly observes the words of inspiration, "Wherefore, putting away lying, speak every man truth with his neighbour." Sensible that he is always in the presence of the God of truth, he never allowedly deviates from its laws. Such a character, the more it is examined, the more illustrious it will appear: It will be "like the path of the just," pourtrayed by the wise king Solomon, "which as the rising light, shineth more and more unto the perfect day."

One thing more, necessary for accomplished rulers. They should hate covetousness.

However contemptible a covetous disposition may be, in the sight of God and man, we are constrained to acknowledge it is too prevalent to give full liberty for any one class of men to cast a stone at others. Rigid parsimony should not be indulged in a ruler; and it certainly is not in one who fears God, and has a sacred regard to truth. A principle of virtue is discovered, in a generous disregard to personal wealth, when it comes in competition with the interest of the public. When a good ruler is engaged in his office, his duty to the station arrests his first attention; self, has only a secondary place in his mind. When called to act in public, he leaves his private concerns behind him; they drop, till he has faithfully performed his higher engagements. Presuming that the electors in this state for the present year, so far as they have proceeded, have been actuated by the foregoing principles; that they have provided able men, fearers of God, men of truth, haters of covetousness, to compose the present legislative assembly—let us proceed to offer a few thoughts upon the duties annexed to the trust reposed in them.

It was the advice of Jethro to Moses, that the proposed characters should be placed over the people, to be rulers of thousands, rulers of hundreds, rulers of fifties, and rulers of tens. With great propriety this may be applied to the several officers of a republic, in a succession, from the first magistrate. The federal and state governments in America, have furnished us with constitutions and laws, by which the duties peculiar to each office are ascertained. Our laws, however, are not like those of the Medes and Persians, which cannot be altered: The people have always a right to the exercise of their power, as the public interest may require. And may we not affirm, that in theory there is no government so rational as where elections are frequent, the elected under the public eye, and to continue during the people's pleasure? This is a privilege we enjoy. Our annual elections give us an opportunity to select our best citizens to transact our public and most important business, to enact new laws, and make appointments according to the exigencies of the state.

A general assembly to a republic, in many respects stands in the place of a Moses to Israel; the refulgence of whose virtues should resemble the face of Moses, after he had received the law of the Lord on Mount Sinai. The authority of a state is to provide men duly qualified to act in the necessary departments. The reins of government are to be given into their hands for those purposes. Their trust is important, and when they are under the solemnity of an oath, they are bound by the strongest ties! By them, the duties of every office should be contemplated previous to a choice. And any station had better remain vacant, than be improperly filled. Those passages of inspiration will always remain true, "When the righteous are in authority, the people rejoice; but when the wicked beareth rule, the people mourn." "He that ruleth over men must be just, ruling in the fear of God."

A conscientious regard to the principles of rectitude in general, and a strict adherence to the duties annexed to each office, either in the legislative or executive, whether relative to the civil, military, or ecclesiastical departments, instamp upon it a dignity, by which the vicious are restrained, and the virtuous encouraged. In short, the duties incumbent upon mankind, relative to their God and each other, obligatory upon all, and those peculiarly adapted to the various offices in a well regulated government, will be regarded with undiverted attention by every man deserving public confidence.

Permit me to enumerate some of the objects which naturally present themselves to the mind of the wise guardians of a country. The most perfect body of human laws ever framed, have their defects; and these are made obvious by practice. In their operations, they in all respects do not answer the designs proposed. Wise legislators, upon a discovery of imperfections, by which the citizens are embarrassed or wronged, by which any class of men are injured, will exert themselves for a reformation, and not give over the pursuit till it be accomplished. As they are the guardians of the people, fidelity to their trust demands their attention. Laws should be founded upon the principles of reason and justice—should be few in number, perspicuous, and punctually executed. Those which have been made, and are now in force, ought they not to be made plain and intelligible? Might not perplexities, expences, and great injustice, be prevented, and society highly favoured? Explicit laws, binding mankind to the rules of justice, are an admirable security to all branches of society. Under them, contracts are valid, peaceable members of the community are protected in the enjoyment of their interests, the profligate restrained and punished, and in a sense the "wrath of man is made to praise God."

A frequent revision of the laws and constitutions of a country, with such alterations as good policy may suggest, promotes that general utility which cements the various parts of society, and forms a complete harmonious whole.

Again—An important object in the minds of good rulers, is, the increase of useful knowledge.

A foundation placed in the minds of youth, is like "good seed sown in good ground," in its proper season; and gives the fairest prospects of a happy increase to the well being of society. The principles of virtue and knowledge early implanted, naturally take root, and produce a luxuriant harvest. Those who are thus favoured, are "trained up in the way they should go," the best prompter on life's devious journey. Hence the propriety of having able instructors, whose morals and language are worthy of imitation: And hence the necessity of giving ample encouragement, in a business so important and laborious. Though honourable donations have been made for the promotion of literature, yet the fostering hand of our civil fathers may be required for bringing to maturity. May it not then be expected, that every aid and encouragement will be given to education? The views of such as are young, are hereby extended; they are raised above the grovelling vulgarisms too common to that age, which will have a happy influence upon society, in preparing the rising generation to fill with honour the most dignified stations, when they may be called to act upon the theatre of life.

Is there not a third and an important object in the mind of rulers, viz. the increase of virtue and religion?

The ideas which have by some been adopted, that the civil authority should never interpose in matters of religion, are erroneous. It is granted by the most learned politicians, that the religious forms which have been established and supported, have had a powerful tendency to promote civility, to restrain vicious men, to protect the innocent, to countenance worthy pursuits, and to discountenance the immoralities which have contaminated mankind! Sentiments of this nature have flowed from knowledge and experience: And if they be well founded, is it not a truth, that establishments of this kind invite the attention of that civil policy which is the support of government? If, therefore, virtue and religion form the principal pillar which upholds the civil fabrick, it is evidently a duty for wise rulers to contribute something for its support. Upon this principle, many professed deists contribute with cheerfulness and liberality to public teachers of morality; they are patrons to the worship of God in gospel order: They have considered it as a measure wisely adapted to uphold government—and in this they deserve an encomium.

Such as fully believe the Christian religion, and receive the scriptures as the word of God, have additional motives for their utmost exertions that sobriety and goodness may be promoted. It is indisputable, that the more a society live in the practice of virtue, the greater prosperity they enjoy: The more they are under the influence of vicious principles, the more unhappiness they will experience. The sacred oracles give us the best directions: In them, no unreasonable restraints are imposed, no rational enjoyments are forbidden: Excess alone is transgression. So far as the scriptures are strictly regarded, so far every member of the community conducts with propriety: The various propensities and passions peculiar to human nature, are directed to right objects: And there, CHRIST, a most faithful and compassionate legislator, stands, giving law to his subjects. In those records, his character is exhibited, his maxims are registered, his example left for our imitation; and the whole perfectly reconcileable to virtue, religion, and the best policy: Thence may be extracted wisdom and instruction to guide us into the paths of rectitude; to save us from destructive courses of error and delusion: Here is a constitution worthy the particular notice of every man who holds an office in government; that under the influence of its rules, he may be instrumental in diffusing virtuous and benevolent principles: Directed by this, he will give his public testimony in favour of those who are engaged professionally to prepare mankind for blessings in this life, and a glorious future reward.

One farther essential in good rulers, is, that they are themselves exemplary.

There can be no greater burlesque upon the character of rulers, than when, under binding obligations to God, and their constituents, they are making laws which they are the first in violating! But how agreeable are the prospects, when judicious laws are made, are esteemed sacred; and are punctually observed by the enactors! A sanction is hereby placed upon them, which impresses every mind. And societies having their eye upon their rulers, observing their consistency, are led to follow their example, which naturally tends to rectify the vices and to reform the manners of the community. When precept and example are harmonious in rulers, every observer is charmed with the character; when they are at variance, they cannot fail to produce contempt. Of great importance then it must appear, for those who are clothed with authority, to have the qualifications described in my text, to be themselves exemplary, and let their light shine before men, who, aiming at one great object, the best interest of the public, are filled with present animation; and their views, not confined to this life, are extended, and terminate in immortality.

The discourse shall be closed with an improvement—and with addresses suited to the present occasion.

The suggestions which have been given, exhibit the necessity of a government established upon the principles of reason, and guarded by the maxims of justice and virtue. The passions natural to men, indicate that we were formed for society—and they powerfully excite us to enter into social connections. From a state of natural equality, communities are formed. The infirmities of men require protection —their vices, restraints and punishment. A free government, therefore, under which the virtuous are encouraged, and the vicious punished, is the palladium of the rational mind. How important, then, that it should be supported; that every aid should be given to those who are entrusted with authority, so long as they perform their duty. Vigilance respecting rulers, a check to prevent an undue exercise of power, are requisite, to preserve inviolate the liberties and privileges of a people. An unrestrained authority is dangerous; witness Hazael,

Haman, and the unfortunate Charles. Extremes are always attended with consequences most unfavourable: Tyranny and anarchy, equally pernicious! An opposition to good government is inexcusable, as it "resists an ordinance of God." A tame submission to an unjust authority, discovers a pusillanimity derogatory to the human mind. Wherever a just government is wanting, as an "hidden treasure" it should be sought and established: Where it hath been enjoyed, and is become deficient, it should be carefully amended, as was before hinted. Too great efforts cannot be made to uphold and perpetuate a well-founded government—and continued exertions will facilitate its rising in respectability.

From the ideas which have been brought into view, may not the people of America felicitate themselves under our present forms of government, and in the general characters of our rulers, especially those in exalted stations? Though we may not be favoured with supreme magistrates who have an immediate intercourse with heaven, as had Moses the law-giver of Israel; yet we may presume that they have been, and are, favoured with the approving presence of God.

Our constitutions of government, though they may be imperfect, stand high in the estimation of the enlightened and impartial among the nations of the earth: And under them, we have reason to rejoice in a general prosperity. If virtue and attention are not with us dormant, little can be wanting to complete the system.

When we take a retrospect of the scenes through which we have passed, since the commencement of our late contest, our minds upon the recollection are impressed with a trembling, grateful pleasure. In consequence of injuries and insults, with but little more than a sling and stone we encountered the giant, and foiled Britain!

A propitious Providence, like the "pillar of a cloud and of fire to Israel," led the American armies. And not less apparent hath been the hand of God, in our civil operations. The organization of our governments, hath been attended with salutary effects in the increase of property and respectability. After our thankful acknowledgments to God, the great Superintendent, we should not neglect to express gratitude to a Washington, a Franklin, an Adams, a Jay, and to other heroes who have been instrumental in accomplishing those great purposes, so much for the honour and interest of the American states, and for the happiness of future generations.

Shall we not spend a moment in contrasting our present circumstances in a state of peace, with what we experienced when involved in the horrors of war? in contrasting our situation, with many of the European nations whose garments are now stained with human blood? Let us read the history of the French revolution, and we shall have additional reason to rejoice in God for his favours, and in the language of inspiration must say, "hitherto hath the Lord helped us."

Again—from the reflections we have been making, we learn the advantages of a virtuous government. If we look into the sacred history, we find the prosperity of Israel ebbing and flowing with the morality of their sovereigns. When they had good kings, heavy judgments were averted; but when their rulers were vicious, they forsook the Lord, ran into idolatry, exposed themselves, and judgments came upon them like a flood! They became so abandoned, that God said of them by his prophet, "Though Moses and Samuel stood before me, my heart could not be towards this people; cast them out of my sight, and let them go forth."

And hath it not been generally true, that ignorance, a neglect of God and his worship, idleness, luxury, dissolute manners, and factions, have been certain preludes to the destruction of states and empires? Is not this abundantly proved by the histories of ancient times? Was not this verified in the destruction of Sparta, Athens, Rome? And if we may reason from past events, we may safely presume, that like causes will produce similar effects, however we may be involved in the issue.

Though it pleases God not to reward or punish individuals in this life, according to their merit or demerit, as appears by the histories of the prophets and apostles, by the parable of Dives and Lazarus, by the prosperity of Nero, and the misfortunes of Louis; yet heaven hath balanced national virtue by affluence, and vice by a counterpoise of adversity. Nothing, then, can be a greater stimulus to a virtuous government, to adopt the most energetic measures, that religion and every species of virtue may be encouraged: On the other hand, that vice, with its baneful retinue, and whatever may be derogatory to the citizen, the statesman, or the christian, may be discountenanced, and meet with an exemplary punishment! The officers of government have a price put into their hands, to promote the interest of their brethren, and the common cause of virtue. And when they are repeatedly, by the suffrages of their country, called into office, it is an evidence in their favour, and a public declaration, that their past conduct hath been approved.

Many of our civil fathers, upon the present anniversary, have frequently been selected to act as guardians to the people of this state. Their past fidelity hath been a sufficient recommendation to their present promotion; and we trust, the transactions of the ensuing year will, with resplendency, evidence the wisdom and judgment of the people in their choice.

His excellency the governor, the honourable council, senate and house of representatives, will please to accept my cordial congratulations upon the present joyful occasion. Regularly introduced into your several offices, clothed with authority, we cheerfully anticipate the salutary effects of your deliberations, in the advancement of the general prosperity, the safety and interest of every class of citizens. May wisdom, integrity, and unanimity, attend your councils, and concentre in all your decisions. May that spirit which directed Moses in the government of Israel, preside in all your pursuits; that under your administration, order and regularity may be conspicuous, knowledge and undissembled religion may spread their benign influences, illuminating every part of the system.

The present anniversary, which has collected the guardians of our civil rights from the several parts of the state, has brought together numbers in the ecclesiastical department, who wish to be considered as fellow-helpers in the cause of our country. May I be permitted to address my brethren, upon this auspicious day, and rejoice with them under a government, where harmony pervades the various departments, and so happily unites, in one common centre, the civil and ecclesiastical influence?

My brethren and friends,

Every effort of ours, to promote virtue, and to oppose the prevalence of vice, contributes something to strengthen the hands of our civil rulers: Their exertions for the accomplishment of the same purposes, encourage our hearts. With satisfaction we attend upon our annual convention, to unite our best endeavours that religion may be promoted at the season and place of our public elections: And our pleasure is heightened by that generous friendship which has ever appeared in the guardians of the state, to our order, and by that reciprocity of affection which has glowed in every countenance. Ardently wishing the present harmony may be perpetuated, and to unite our efforts in aiding the civil magistrate, we have great confidence in having that assistance and support from the same government, which may terminate in a general increase of mutual happiness.

Something by way of address to this respectable audience, shall finish the present discourse.

My friends and fellow citizens,

After a series of signal interpositions, the inhabitants of this land are placed upon the shores of freedom, with the olive branch flourishing in their hands. Heroes in the field, wise men at the head of the civil polity, with a prevailing intercourse with heaven, have brought on the present æra. For years past, no nation ever experienced greater prosperity. "The voice of joy and health have been heard in our habitations"; the earth hath teemed with a profusion of rich treasures; "the little hills have rejoiced on every side."

Arts and sciences have flourished; and a spirit of enterprize, before unknown in the annals of our country, hath been displayed, not in opening deep waters, that travellers may go through dry shod, but in providing safe passages over them; and also to divert the watery element into different channels, to facilitate the labours of men. Perhaps no period was ever so favourable for the general increase of property, as what we are now experiencing.

This life is a changing scene. Prosperity and adversity await mankind, under the superintendency of unerring wisdom. Though we have been a highly privileged people, this may not continue. Prosperity too often produces luxury, which leads to a decay of virtue, to irreligion, and ruin. May heaven divert our feet from paths so dangerous, and lead us on in the way of truth and safety. This is the course to preferments—it is the high way to honour and happiness, and a prologue to immortal joys.

Let us then cultivate virtue in ourselves—carefully avoid shading the light of reason, counteracting remonstrances of conscience, and what is recorded in God's word. In the steady practice of every duty to God, to society, and ourselves—under the influence of caution, candour, and generosity—we may expect the divine approbation.

When we act as electors, our eyes should ever be upon the "faithful of the land." We shall, no doubt, have frequent calls for elections to the most important offices. This is verified by late experience—by the retirement of our worthy chief magistrate, at a critical period; and the choice of a successor, whose past eminent services have given him the best title to public confidence. Calls of this nature should be improved to awaken our vigilance, that we may obtain a true knowledge of the most deserving, and of those of a contrary description; that our future proceedings may be consonant to the principles of reason and sound policy.

May the great Superintendent give wisdom to our supreme government at their present session, in transactions of the highest moment to the states of America—that prudence, fortitude, and unanimity, may mark every movement, and instamp a dignity upon our national character. With a rational confidence in that authority, under God, we rest our political safety: We rely upon their wisdom and integrity.

Presuming that we shall not be deceived, we shall ever be ready to support government, to reward all who are faithfully discharging the duties of their stations, from those who are rulers of thousands, to such as are only rulers of tens.

Upon a reflection, that we have all a part to act in the drama of life, our minds cannot but be impressed, that our several stations require various exercises! "That though on earth the powers that be are ordained of God," and cannot be disregarded but by incurring the divine displeasure; yet we are accountable to higher powers, and ere long must assemble at the bar of the great Judge of the earth!

Keeping that solemn period ever in view, let us perform our parts in life with a cheerful seriousness, as in the presence of an omniscient God. With lives regulated by the maxims of truth, by the illuminations of the divine spirit, let us "run the ways of God's commandments," disseminating light and knowledge, till we are prepared to enter into a world of glory, where virtue alone will dignify and exalt every immortal spirit, in the immediate presence of God, of the Redeemer, in the society of angelic hosts and innumerable glorified saints—where one chorus of praise shall commence, progress in ceaseless ages, and subordinate power be absorbed in heaven's Sovereign.

AMEN

47

A DISCOURSE, DELIVERED AT THE ROMAN CATHOLIC CHURCH IN BOSTON

John Thayer

BOSTON

1798

John Thayer (1758–1815). Born in Boston and graduated from Yale, Thayer became a Congregational minister and served in the Revolution under John Hancock at Castle William (1780–81). He was the first American divine to convert to Roman Catholicism; while studying in Europe he was ordained a priest by the archbishop of Paris (1787). He returned to America intent upon converting the Puritans to Catholicism and spent the period from 1790 to 1803 in missionary endeavors in New England, Virginia, and on the frontier in Kentucky. He was derided by the American ecclesiastics as "John Turncoat." While the public responded to him well, the usually tolerant Ezra Stiles harshly commented: "Commenced his life in impudence, ingratitude, lying & hypocrisy, irregularly took up preaching among Congregationalists, went to France & Italy, became a proselyte to the Romish church, & is returned to convert America to that [church] . . . of haughty insolence & insidious talents" (*Literary Digest of Ezra Stiles*, 3:416). An estimated 600 Catholics lived in New England by 1785, most of them "improper Bostonians" originally from Ireland (the first Catholic church in New England was founded in Boston in 1788).

Stiles's remarks notwithstanding, Thayer proved an effective missionary while in America, and he continued that work in his retirement in Limerick, Ireland, beginning in 1803. He conceived a plan to organize a convent in Boston, but finding little cooperation and no volunteers, he proceeded to train his own postulants. These became the nucleus of the famous Ursuline Convent in Charlestown (Boston), established in 1819 after Thayer's death. The convent was burned down by a nativist mob in 1834.

This powerful sermon, one of Thayer's finest, was preached in the Boston Catholic Church on May 9, 1798, designated by President John Adams as a day of humiliation and prayer. This observance was proclaimed amidst the furor in the country over the humiliating rebuff of American emissaries in Paris, Elbridge Gerry, John Marshall, and Charles C. Pinckney, by the French Republic, now under radical government by the Directory—the famous "X, Y, Z Affair." Thayer's tenor and his recitation of French atrocities during the Terror is indicative of the climate of opinion. Washington had been recalled as nominal commander-in-chief of the American army, which was being mobilized by Alexander Hamilton at President Adams's direction.

A

DISCOURSE,

DELIVERED,

AT THE ROMAN CATHOLIC CHURCH IN BOSTON,

ON THE 9TH OF MAY, 1798,

A DAY RECOMMENDED BY THE

PRESIDENT,

FOR

HUMILIATION AND PRAYER

THROUGHOUT THE

UNITED STATES.

BY THE

Reverend JOHN THAYER, *Catholic Miſſioner.*

Printed at the preſſing Solicitation of thoſe who heard it.

Printed by SAMUEL HALL, No. 53, Cornhill, BOSTON.

1798.

The fitting out of the navy was accelerated, naval war ensued, and the possibility of full-scale warfare against France loomed. So divided was the country, and so strong was the fear of Jacobin influence, that Washington himself insisted that Republicans be excluded from the army as potentially disloyal. The enactment of the repressive Alien and Sedition Acts, whereby political opposition became a crime, occurred during June and July; it was thus within weeks of Thayer's sermon on May 9, and provides an index of the feverish temper of the times.

Pray without ceasing—give thanks.

I Thessalonians, v. 17, 18.

In the words just read, the inspired apostle inculcates on us the two important duties of prayer and thanksgiving, which the President of the United States invites us all to perform on this day. We have need to pray for the pardon of our sins, as a nation, and as individuals, and to humble ourselves profoundly before God on account of them; and we have need to pray for the continuation of the mercies, both spiritual and temporal, which we have hitherto enjoyed. To the proclamation of our Supreme Magistrate, our Right Rev. Bishop has been pleased to add his strong recommendation, in which, in addition to the objects of humiliation and prayer common to all our fellow-citizens, he urges us to beseech the Lord to put a stop to the dreadful persecution which is now ravaging his own church, and to comfort and strengthen its visible head. But, though the duty of humiliation and prayer be incumbent on us at all times, and *more specifically at the present*, still, seeing the astonishing change that has lately taken place in the public mind, I consider the duty of thanksgiving as yet more pressing—I shall, therefore, at this time, mention to you some of the motives which should excite us all to gratitude and thanksgiving to the great bestower of all good; and, as I proceed, I shall, from time to time, make such reflections as are proper to incline our hearts to prayer and humiliation.

During the whole course of my ministry among you, my brethren, I have never before entered into any details concerning political affairs; nor should I do it now, were it not to teach you to appreciate duly the government under which you live, and to point out your duties towards it.

1. The first blessing which demands our cordial thanks to God is, that we live under the freest and most easy government in the world. The constitution of the United States unites a proper degree of energy with all the liberty which any reasonable person can desire. It is well-balanced, our executive, legislative and judicial authorities being independent of, and mutually checked by, each other. They all emanate from the people at large; who have always the power to put an

end to any real abuses which may take place, by displacing their present representatives and appointing others that have their confidence—and as long as the great body of the people do not see the necessity of a change of men and measures, we may rest assured, that the abuses, however they may be magnified by party-scribblers and declaimers, are not of a very alarming nature. Under such a government as this, every insurrection against the constituted authorities, or opposition to them, is a revolt of a part against the general will, by which those authorities exist, and is highly criminal. Praised be God, that this happy constitution, under which persons of all denominations enjoy entire security for their lives, property, and liberty, whether spiritual or political, is still unimpaired and in full operation; and that all the attempts to overturn, or to weaken it, by concentrating all its powers in the single house of representatives, have only served to throw light upon its principles, and to give it additional strength.

2. Another cause of thanksgiving to God is, that the administration of this most excellent constitution, ever since its first establishment, has been committed to men eminent for their wisdom, firmness, and patriotic services. I need only mention a Washington, that guardian genius, that saviour of his country, that ornament of the human race, to excite in all your hearts the warmest feelings of esteem, gratitude and love. Long may he enjoy the charms of that retirement in which he has chosen to spend the evening of his life: may the blessings of this country and of the universe be yet many years his reward; and at length, enriched with every christian as well as moral virtue, may he enter the realms of everlasting felicity.

We have great reason to be thankful, that, when that approved warrior and admired statesman resigned the helm of state, and sought the repose which his age and health required, God did not permit the intrigues of a foreign, insidious nation to succeed in raising the man of their choice to the presidential chair; but inspired us with sufficient courage to place at our head a statesman and patriot, whose ability and integrity, proved in the most trying times, eminently entitle him to our confidence and affection. Such is the illustrious John Adams, the present president of these states. This great man can have nothing in view but the happiness and prosperity of his fellow-citizens, with whose fortunes his own, and those of his family, are evidently and inseparably connected.

He wishes for no power unwarranted by the constitution, and for no support incompatible with the generous spirit of freedom. Since the publication of his instructions to our messengers of peace, we have learned, better than ever, to appreciate his worth. We are now assured of his moderate and conciliatory temper, as well as of his decisive firmness. Under such a leader we have nothing to fear: never will he sacrifice the honor of his country; never will he relinquish any part of that independence which has long been the object of all his toils and labors, and for the obtaining of which so many of our brave countrymen have spilt their blood and lost their lives. Let us offer up our fervent prayers to heaven, on this day, that his invaluable life may be preserved, and his health continued; that God would give him wisdom to discern what are the best measures to be adopted for the good of his country, and the fortitude to put them into execution, in spite of every obstacle and opposition; and that all those who assist him in council may be men of ability and integrity, so that the public may receive no detriment from incapacity or dishonesty. Let us all resolve to give him a generous and cordial support, and openly avow this resolution by setting our names to the manly and spirited addresses which are now proposed for the signature of all citizens. Let us tell him, that we feel, as we ought, the value of that liberty which we enjoy, and that we pledge our fortunes and sacred honour to defend it with loyalty and fidelity, under the banners of the government which we have chosen. Let us express our indignation at the repeated insults offered to this government, which has sought peace by every possible mean compatible with the dignity and honour of an independent nation. Let us declare, with the firmness and self-respect of freemen, our readiness to unite in every effort, which shall be made, to prevent our being subjected to the degrading conditions which a foreign nation seeks to impose upon us, as preliminary to all negociation for peace, and that we consider war, with all its attendant calamities, as by far the least of the two evils. Let us show, that we love the government which protects us, and that we are not divided from it, either in interest or affection. In fine, let us express our warm and unequivocal approbation of the wise and temperate system which has hitherto been pursued with regard to foreign nations, and our increasing confidence in him who presides over us with so much wisdom and prudence.

3. A third motive, which we have, of the sincerest thanks to heaven is, that, while a spirit of disorganization and disorder has produced such baleful effects in other countries, America, in spite of the effervescence produced among us by the extraordinary exertions of foreign and domestic intriguers, yet remains in a happy state of tranquillity. France appears to have been raised up by God for the chastisement of an impious world. I speak not of France governed by the descendants of St. Louis; it was then the guardian of religion and good morals, and the asylum of the unfortunate. Happy land! where I received the most valuable part of my education, and where I passed my happiest years among esteemed friends and beloved associates! Alas! to me no more! They are all either cruelly butchered, banished, or reduced to wretchedness at home. If I forget thee, O dear, charming abode, *may my right hand forget her cunning; may my tongue cleave to the roof of my mouth.* But now; how changed! My heart sinks within me, my spirits die away, when I recal the fate of some of my dearest inmates. But soon the painful recollection is swallowed up in the consideration of the complicated distresses of that once highly favoured empire.

France revolutionized is more truly the scourge of God, than was ever Attila, or any other barbarous conqueror recorded in history. Its tyrants, like Satan, their father, may be literally said *to go about, seeking whom they may devour.* If we cast an eye over the map of the world, we shall find, in almost every part, most dreadful traces of their destructive plans. The miseries which they have spread throughout the globe are beyond all the powers of calculation; miseries so universal as to have excited the horror of all who have the feelings, or merit the name, of human beings—miseries which will never be effaced from the memory of mankind, and which entire ages of peace and tranquillity will be scarcely able to repair. What unparalleled calamities have they not inflicted on their own wretched country! what wanton cruelties and atrocities have they not committed there! Their own writers confess, that, by the different modes of destruction, the guillotine, shooting, drowning, and the like, upwards of 30,000 persons were killed at Lyons, and that that once magnificent city was in great part levelled to the ground, that, at Nantz, according to the lowest estimate, 27,000 (some say, 40,000) were murdered, chiefly by drowning,* so that the water of the Loire, on which it stands, became putrid, and was forbidden to be drunk, that at Paris, 150,000, and in la Vendee 300,000 were destroyed. They own themselves, that, since the beginning of their execrable revolution, two millions of their nation have been sacrificed, of which 250,000 were women, and 30,000 children: and in this immense carnage are not included the soldiers who have perished in camp and fallen in battle, nor the unborn infants who were destroyed together with their mothers. Look into that country, and examine its present state. Though, by plunder, forced loans, contributions, and other iniquitous means, its lordly rulers have made a very great part of the riches of Europe to concentre there; still, by their narrow policy, by the ruin of all manufactures, commerce, and every other regular source of wealth and revenue, and by the entire subversion of all public confidence, they have reduced the wretched inhabitants to a state little short of actual beggary and starvation. No slavery can be equal to their's: their condition is the most degraded that can be conceived. Every thing they possess, and even their very persons, are in a constant state of requisition; that is, they must be given up at the call of their rapacious masters, under pain of death, if they refuse. No man there dares write, print, speak, or even indicate, by the smallest sign, any disapprobation of whatever measures may chance to be dictated by the faction actually in power. Every press is seized that sends forth the least word in opposition to the mandates of the haughty directors, and the editors are put to death, imprisoned or banished. The people have no stable, fixed laws, by which to regulate their conduct: one edict is scarcely rendered public before it is annulled by another directly contrary; so that what is considered as lawful, and even patriotic, to-day, may to-morrow be accounted a crime worthy of death and confiscation.

Under these accumulated calamities, the wretched slaves might find their yoke less galling, their burdens less insupportable, if they could enjoy, *as it were by stealth*, the consolations of religion, for

* This mode of putting people to death they blasphemously called the national baptism.

which they hunger and thirst. But no; their tyrants have nearly dried up this source of comfort. And here, my friends, what horrid scenes present themselves to our recollection! Many years before the revolution burst forth, the self-styled philosophers, a tribe composed of deists, atheists and materialists, had, by their secret clubs, by impious and obscene publications, and by various other means, suggested by the infernal spirit, attempted, and in part succeeded, to corrupt the different classes of society in France. But never could their system of impiety take effect upon the great mass of the citizens, who found, and ever will find, their happiness in the belief of religion. They had long plotted the utter extirpation of all religion, but, in the first place, of that which, by its greater extension and superior attachment to order and good government, stood more immediately in the way of their nefarious projects: this religion was the Roman Catholic: its overthrow was, therefore, resolved on; and the moment they had trampled down the ancient authorities of the kingdom, they employed every artifice, and made every effort, to effect their purpose. They began their impious attack on the church, by degrading her ministers in the eyes of the populace, by stripping them of those distinctive garments of their order, which, for ages, had rendered them respectable to the faithful. They then deprived them of their livings and other possessions, and represented them as inimical to the true interests of the country, because they would not take oaths which tended to nothing less, than the renunciation of the authority of the sovereign pontiff and of the bishops; in a word, of the catholic religion, which had been transmitted to them through several succeeding centuries. Upon their noble and almost unanimous refusal to apostatize from their faith, one of the most horrible persecutions (and perhaps the most so), that was ever levelled against the ministers of the altar, commenced, and has continued, with almost unabating fury, until the present moment: according to the very last authentic accounts, the priests are still hunted down, and very great rewards are offered for delivering them up. Thousands of these holy men, of these generous confessors of Jesus Christ, have been put to death, by drowning, shooting, and guillotining, or have perished through want and ill treatment. Thousands and tens of thousands of them have been banished from their homes, destitute of all means of subsistence, by the bloody edicts of the monsters of France; or have gone into voluntary exile, and are now wandering in foreign climes, where they either suffer all the horrors of indigence, or prolong their existence by the precarious charities of strangers. I need not inform you, my brethren, that the two excellent priests, who govern this flock with so much profit, and who are so deservedly dear* to you all, are here only in consequence of the terrible vexations in their own country.

But the cruelty of the persecutors was not confined to the different orders of the clergy; it extended even to the poor, innocent, defenceless nuns, who, by almost entire exclusion from exterior conversation, and a consecration to the tranquil exercises of devotion, were become far more timid than the weakest of their sex who live in the world. Bands of armed ruffians were sent into their sacred asylums, who used every species of violence to force them to take the sacrilegious oath to give up their religion. Many of those unoffending virgins expired under the murderous lash, to preserve inviolate fidelity to their vows. Very few of them indeed were terrified, or even seduced, into a compliance with the orders of their tyrants. At length, when all means of perversion had been essayed in vain, a barbarous edict strips them of all their property at one stroke; their convents are declared to belong to the nation; and, in one day, all those helpless victims, to the number of 30,000, are turned out by force to all the miseries attendant on a state of poverty and want. Many of them had grown old in the cloister; many of them were sick and infirm; all of them had given up, under the sanction of former laws, whatever they possessed in the world, and of course found themselves in the utmost distress. No consideration of this kind was capable of touching the more than adamantine hearts of their enemies, who, to aggravate their wretched and forlorn situation, forbad all persons, under the severest penalties, to harbour more than two of them together. All the eloquence that ever fell to the lot of a mortal would be totally inadequate to point out, in their real turpitude, only a small part of those deeds of horror which have taken place in France within these

* The Rev. Messrs. Matignon and Chevrus, who now superintend the catholic congregation in Boston.

We can assert with truth, supported by the whole current of ecclesiastical history, that, in no age or country, have the clergy, as a body, ever conducted themselves with so much prudence, dignity and heroic firmness, as the gallican clergy have done, through a nine years' insidious, violent and bloody persecution.

few years past. The many traits of savage barbarity related in the history of the world, all collected and united together, appear tender mercies, when compared with the refined cruelties of the sanguinary factions of that country; cruelties not committed by a few unlicensed individuals, amid the disorders of a revolution, but by commission from the men in power, and under their immediate eye. Were I to enter into a few details, such as are given by the writers of their own party, the hairs of your heads would stand erect; an involuntary tremor would seize every joint and limb of your bodies; loving husbands and wives, you could not resist the shock; tender mothers, you would faint at the recital; and your modesty, my virgin hearers, would be indeed most sensibly wounded. I, therefore, turn from these abominable scenes.

To all their inhuman deeds, they have added the most horrid impieties and profanations. They have stripped the churches of the holy vessels, vestments and other things consecrated to the worship of God, and have converted them all to common uses. Some of these venerable temples they have turned into play-houses, stores, rope-walks, stables, and the like; and others they have devoted to the worship of impious men and prostituted women, to whom they have paid the most extravagant honours. They have respected nothing that has the least relation to religion. They have commanded all bibles, prayer-books, sacred images, &c. to be brought forth, and have consumed them in one common mass. Nor, in this respect, has one religious profession been more favoured than another; for the dissenting meeting-houses, and even the Jewish synagogues, were emptied also, and their contents committed to the flames. They have spared no one of the sacred institutions of Christianity; and, in order to obliterate it entirely from the memory of mankind, they have made it a crime to pass the first day of the week in exercises of religious worship (a practice co-eval with the existence of the Christian religion), and have introduced, in its stead, the decade, a day wholly devoted to profane amusements.

But the funest effects of the revolution in France have not been limited to that country—it has also proved a sweeping deluge to their West-India colonies: it has carried devastation and ruin into those once flourishing islands, under the pretext of spreading among them the blessings of freedom: the slaves have been let loose upon the whites; the richest towns have been given up to plunder, and burnt; and a war of extermination has been declared, and still furiously rages.

If we look into the European world, and consider the countries which the French have either conquered, or seduced to fraternize with them (as they term it), we shall see every where, that, notwithstanding their most solemn promises of liberty of conscience, of security of life and property, they have uniformly robbed the churches, taken away the lives and estates of those who would not join in all their atrocities, deprived the people of the freedom of religion, plundered them by their armies, levied upon them the most grievous contributions, forced them to give up their strong-holds, and to maintain their conquerors among them for the purpose of keeping themselves in subjection. Holland* was an hive of bees; her sons flew on the wings of the wind to every corner of the globe; and returned laden with the sweets of every climate. Belgium was a garden of herbs, the oxen were strong to labour, the fields were thickly covered with the abundance of the harvest. Unhappy Dutchmen! they still toil, but not for their own comfort; they still collect honey, but not for themselves! France seizes the hive as often as their industry has filled it. Ill-judging Belgians! they no longer eat in security the fruits of their own grounds; France, all-grasping France (whose never-ceasing cry is, "give, give"), finds occasion, or makes occasion, to participate largely in their riches; it is more truly said of themselves than of their oxen, they plough the fields, but not for their own profit.

It would take up far more time than could be possibly given to one discourse, to follow their murdering bands to all the places through which, like destroying angels, they have spread terror and desolation. Wherever they have met with the least resistance, especially if an individual Frenchman was killed in the conflict, whole bodies of respectable magistrates have been made to expiate, with their lives, the pretended rebellion; entire cities have been threatned with extermination for the same offence, and nothing but enormous sums of money have been able to save them from the impending ruin. Like impetuous torrents, in the rapidity of their course, they have borne down every thing before them; and, without distinction of friends and ene-

* Bishop Watson.

mies, they have effaced, from the list of independent nations, Geneva, Genoa, Venice, and the papal territory.

The pope had been for ages, by the liberality of Christian princes, a very considerable temporal sovereign. His dominions had been secured to him by the same solemn treaties, which had hitherto bound kingdoms and states to each other. Yet, in spite of those treaties, no sooner was the National Assembly formed, than it forcibly wrested from him a valuable part* of his possessions, under a pretext, which would sanction every robbery, viz. that it would be a very convenient addition to the French empire. From that first aggression they have never desisted, one moment, from their project of destroying the temporal sovereignty of the Roman pontiff, and, if possible, of putting an end to his spiritual supremacy in the church. And, though our Holy Father has constantly shown himself the most pacific of men, a true disciple of the meek and humble Jesus; though this his disposition has been evident before the eyes of all Europe, as Buonaparte† is obliged to acknowledge; though his unfeigned piety, his firmness and moderation amidst the greatest difficulties, his spirit of sacrifice and concession wherever his conscience and duty were not implicated, have drawn on him the veneration and love of all good men, the admiration and esteem of his enemies, and have created a lively solicitude, among the most judicious dissenters from our faith, for the preservation of his person and temporalities; notwithstanding all this, the terrible and all-devouring republic has, at length, made an occasion to rob him of all his states; and, in order to secure the co-operation of his own subjects, in the iniquitous work, she has flattered their ears with the syren sound of freedom, which will very soon terminate in the most wretched slavery.

Let me here fix your attention, for a few moments, on the common father of all the faithful. Perhaps, while I am now speaking, he is exposed to the most ignominious treatment, is insulted and reviled, as was the Redeemer of the world, whom he represents on earth; perhaps he is now confined to a horrid dungeon, loaded with chains, as was St. Peter, to whom he is a most worthy successor; or, perhaps, he has fallen a victim to the fury of the enemies of God and man, and

* Avignon.

† See his letter to the pope.

has thus become a glorious martyr for the holy catholic faith. Children are obliged to pray for their parents; the church is bound to pray for her head: thus did the primitive Christians for St. Peter, who, on account of their prayers, was delivered from prison by the miraculous interposition of an angel. Our reverend bishop has ordered every priest to pray for the sovereign pontiff, in an especial manner, during six successive months. It is a duty which we most cheerfully undertake. We hope, that each one of you, who has the smallest love for his religion, will unite his prayers to those which are ascending, from every part of the catholic church, for the same important object. But, while we urge you earnestly to pray, we, at the same time, exhort you not to be discouraged at the present gloomy aspect of affairs in the church. Though some fanatics, in the *jacobinic* vehicles of slander and abuse, have lately very much exulted over the misfortunes of the pope, as if the fall of anti-christ* were near at hand; we catholics despise such ranting stuff, knowing, as we do, with the certitude of divine faith, that all their silly forebodings will prove vain; and that the church will stand and triumph, in spite of earth and hell combined against her. God has declared, that *the gates of hell shall not prevail against her*; and his word will be fulfilled. She has past through far more grievous trials: all the powers of the world were leagued against her from her very infancy; and for three hundred years together the greatest part of her chief pastors spilt their blood in her defence. Her past preservation is a pledge of future protection. All her sufferings were foretold by her Divine Founder, who took care to build her upon so solid a rock, that she will ever stand immoveable amidst all the floods and storms of persecution and impiety which may beat against her. Pope Pius the VIth is the successor of St. Peter, the prince of the apostles; he is the vicar of Jesus Christ on earth, and the visible head of his church; and, therefore, whatever may be his fate, yet, as sure as God is true, so sure he will have a

* There are many persons who fancy, and boldly assert, that all the impieties and disorders of the French revolution are so many steps to bring about, what they term, the millenium, a mere chimerical state, which will never have an existence except in their imagination. If such be the prelude, how glorious must be the millenium itself! Strange, that they do not clearly see, that all these things, instead of being signs of the overthrow of anti-christ already established, are the predicted forerunners of his approaching reign!

successor, even until the end of ages. Mighty revolutions shall take place throughout the globe: kingdoms shall be changed into republics, and republics into kingdoms: civilization shall succeed to barbarism, and barbarism to civilization: Amid all these vicissitudes, still the bark of St. Peter, with his successors at the helm, shall sail triumphantly down the stream of time; and never will the pilot appear more venerable, than when he guides the vessel amidst the howling tempest and raging billows. We ought, indeed, to be deeply humbled, that iniquity is permitted to go to such lengths against God's holy church; we ought, each one, to consider our sins as, in part, the causes of this terrible calamity; we ought, therefore, to resolve on a reformation of life, especially at this time, when the charity of very many catholics is become cold, when the enemies of the church are her own favoured children, whom she has brought up with the tenderest care and affection, and fed with the word of God and the sacraments. But, I repeat it; we must not be dismayed, as if all were lost. God's promise will have its full and perfect effect: he is still the strong and Almighty Lord: his arm is not shortened; he will yet protect his church, which he has purchased with his own precious blood: her enemies will all be defeated and confounded; and she, like gold tried in the fire, will be purified from all her dross* in the crucible of tribulation, and will shine more bright and glorious than ever. Let these reflections be your consolation.†

* By dross I mean bad members of the church, whether they be clergymen or laymen. These are separated from her by the fire of persecution. By dross I likewise intend all deviations, in practice, from the holy doctrine and morality of the Catholic church, which we hold to be always infallible and invariable. We believe also, that the church is infallible in her general discipline, that is, that her rules of government for all the societies in her communion, however varied according to circumstances, are always infallibly best, every thing considered—and this triple infallibility, of *doctrine*, *morality and general discipline*, we suppose to be fully implied in Christ's promises, that *he will be always with his church, that the gates of hell shall never prevail against her, and that the Holy Ghost shall teach her all truth and abide with her forever.*

† What is here said, it is hoped, is a sufficient answer to Dr. Belknap's remarks on popery, in his fast-sermon. After "*about twenty years of attentive contemplation, with the best helps,*" he has at length made the ludicrous discovery, that the English and French governments are "*rotten toes of Nebuchadnezzar's image,*" and that *the pope is doubtless a beast and a whore.* Wonderful proficiency in study! Quere. How happens it, that the word *whore*, which the lowest of the vulgar can scarcely utter without a blush, can be em-

All the miseries which the French have occasioned, and are now occasioning, are but the beginnings of what they meditate. Their object now clearly appears to be universal domination; and, without a miraculous interference of divine providence, we have much reason to fear that they will obtain it, at least on the continent of Europe. Spain, Portugal and Switzerland seem just ready to fall within the fraternal embrace of those ministers of divine vengeance. What will be the fate of England, against which their hatred and malice appear principally levelled, or, rather, for whose immense riches they have the most voracious desire, a period, not far distant, must disclose. In the mean time, we ought to wish ardently and pray fervently for the preservation of that magnanimous kingdom, the only remaining bulwark, in Europe, against the inroads of barbarism.

Let us now consider what has been the baseness and injustice of that great nation (as they insultingly call themselves), towards America. At a very early period of their revolution we acknowledged their existence as a republic, and formally received their ambassador; for which act we hazarded the displeasure of the principal powers of Europe then leagued against them, and war with the most formidable

ployed so freely before the most respectable congregations, consisting in great part of modest ladies? I should have thought, Doctor, that, after the observations which I addressed, some years since, to you and to your brother Lathrop, and which, to this day, remain unanswered, mere shame would have prevented your repetition of the same insipid ditty.

Dr. Morse has certainly deserved well of his country for his interesting abridgement of the infernal conspiracy of the Illuminati. From the peculiar hatred which these miscreants bear to the Roman Catholic religion, as directly opposed to their projects of immorality and disorder (of which L'abbe Baruel furnishes abundant proof in his memoirs of illuminatism), he might be led to a better opinion of its High-Priest—notwithstanding which, this respectable personage is so great a bugbear in his eyes, that even he cannot conclude his fast-sermon without twice attacking him. It is curious, that the ministers must be always seeking some occasion of venting their spleen upon the poor pope. If he is falling, in God's name, let him go off the stage in peace. At this moment, when our church is opposing deism, atheism, and every other system of impiety; when our clergy, with the pope at their head, are victims for the common cause of christian morality and good government, as well as for their attachment to their particular dogmas of faith; and when even dissenting ministers, whom I could name, own that they should be incapable of the same courage; is it not carrying insult and outrage to the extreme, to persist in calling anti-christian the church which performs such wonders against all anti-christian doctrines? I really flattered myself, that this canting style was out of date, at least among the ministers of Boston and its vicinity.

of them all. We sent them our bread when their ports were blockaded, and they were in a starving condition. We even went so far as to pay into their hands, and long before it became due, the debt which we had contracted with their good king, whom they had most inhumanly murdered. Our merchants were seduced to carry them the rich produce of our soil; and, to the eternal infamy of that swindling republic, they yet remain entirely unpaid, or else have been obliged to receive depreciated paper. Our vessels have been embargoed in their ports, to the very great damage of their owners; our merchants have been plundered, for years together, to the amount of millions; the stipulations of our solemn treaty with them have been continually violated; and all this injurious treatment was given us under the frivolous pretext of imperious necessity; the sense of which phrase is more intelligibly expressed in the high-wayman's words; *your purse or your life*. The despots of France have continually interfered in the concerns of our government, from which they have endeavoured, by their spies, their bribes, and their nefarious and artful intrigues, to divide the body of the people. They have treated our chief magistrates with the utmost indignity and contempt: they have persuaded the people to despise and vilify their rulers, to controul the authorities constituted by themselves to act in their behalf, and to establish a system of disorganization and a wild, unprincipled, democracy, in place of our present rational liberty, which is supported by law and order. All these aggravated wrongs, all this accumulation of unmerited injury and abuse, we have forborne to resent, still hoping for redress from that generosity and justice which are innate in the human heart. We have used every mean of conciliation compatible with the dignity and honour of an independent, sovereign, people. Our government first sent over to them a gentleman of the highest respectability, with full powers to adjust all existing differences; but he was spurned from their presence, and treated with the most marked contempt. But, duly appreciating the great blessing of peace, our president still persisted in his conciliatory conduct; and, to the gentleman, whom they had already refused, he joined two others of our most distinguished citizens, fondly flattering himself, that this mark of condescension and deference would produce its proper effect. But no sooner do they arrive, than they are treated with the most sovereign indignity. Still they wait with patience: they supplicate: they suffer every degradation to effect a reconciliation,* or even an interview, with the insolent usurpers of despotic power. And what is the answer which their agents return to all these humiliations? It is this, my friends:

> *You must first put into our hands thirty-three millions of dollars, as a free gift and as a loan; that is, more silver than can be carried in a hundred waggons, each loaded with a ton weight: and all this enormous sum only to be admitted into our sublime presence, in order to be told, whether, and on what terms, we will make peace with you; for which peace, if we condescend to make it, you must give us as many millions of dollars as we shall be graciously pleased to demand; and our demand shall not be regulated by the justice of your claims which we acknowledge and laugh at, but by our power to exact and by your ability to pay—and if you refuse these conditions; if you do not give us, as long as you have any thing to give; we will ravage your coasts; we will treat you as we have treated Holland, Geneva, Genoa, and the other republics; nay, we will destroy you as a nation, and parcel you out to whomsoever we please, as we have done with the most ancient republic in the world, Venice, which we had but just before declared free and independent.*

Such is the substance of the answer given to our envoys by the haughty sultans of France—and is there a single freeman in America, whether a native or a foreigner, whose blood does not boil within him at the bare mention of so much insolence, and who does not reply to it, in the language of our envoys; *we will make one manly struggle before we comply?*

Though many may have been misled, in time past, from want of proper information, and from an opinion that France was fighting in the cause of liberty, no one now, since their iniquitous and oppressive conduct towards this country has come to light, unless he be a hired villain, or naturally delight in confusion, bloodshed and rapine, can find the least apology for them. The charm of the word *liberty*, with which they have so long fascinated the ignorant and unwary, is now dissolved. Honest men can now openly and freely express their sentiments, without any dread of that impudent, hectoring faction, which has so long terrified peaceable people into silence, and, in some measure, over-awed our government.

* While this discourse was preparing for the press, the memorial of our envoys made its appearance. Their humble and adulatory language to the tyrants of France can scarcely be excused by the ardent desire of peace which dictated it. In every thing else it must be gratifying to the honest pride of true Americans.

From a review of what has been said, we see great cause of humiliation, before God, for the extreme depravity of the human heart. In the conduct of the usurpers and people of France, we discover what men are capable of, when they renounce their God and religion, and give themselves up to their passions. We should also be humbled, in the divine presence, on considering, that we are, at least, the partial causes of the awful judgments which are abroad in the world: nor must we flatter ourselves with being less guilty than others, because we are less severely chastised. Our situation hitherto has been truly enviable. While we bewail the crimes by which we have merited God's anger, and deprecate his wrath, we ought to give him unfeigned thanks for all our blessings. While a notable part of the civilized, christian, world has, for several successive years, heard nothing but the din of arms and the confusion of war; we have enjoyed the happy effects of tranquillity and peace. While Jacobinism, by which I mean the principles of anarchy, disorganization, plunder and murder, has spread its baleful influence throughout the fairest portions of the universe, it has evidently made but small progress in America, notwithstanding the unwearied efforts which have been made for its propagation. That this is the case, is now very visible from the unanimous determination, which has burst forth, from one end of the Union to the other, to support our happy government, and to sacrifice every thing rather than to submit to national degradation: an unanimity, in my view, far greater than that which prevailed during our revolutionary war. In that war, many of our most respectable and virtuous citizens were on the side of Great-Britain from real motives of loyalty and of conscience; but no American can plead loyalty, religion, conscience, or any other honourable motive, for dissenting, from the body of his countrymen, in the noble stand they are now making against the most unjust, imperious, insulting and impious nation that inhabits the globe. None but the basest and most treasonable of motives can influence such a wretch. I hope, my brethren, there is not an individual among you all, who does not feel the same patriotic enthusiasm which animates the breasts of native citizens. Besides the motives for indignation, which the generality of them have, against the vile miscreants of France who wish to lord it over the world, you, as Catholics, have a motive yet more powerful; which is, that they have profaned and destroyed your churches, barbarously oppressed, banished, and murdered, your bishops, priests, monks and nuns; and have carried their audacity so far, as to lay their sacrilegious, polluted, hands on the Lord's anointed, the visible head of the church, the common father of all the faithful. May we, then, never again hear from the mouth of any Irish Catholic, that he rejoices at every victory, and applauds every action, of the French, because they are the enemies of his English oppressors. Granting the reality of the oppression of which you complain, and that you have suffered it all purely on account of your attachment to the catholic faith, which has been the glory of your nation from St. Patrick to the present day: yet what has this in common with the defence of the constitution, the government and laws of united America? This country has received you into her bosom with the greatest affection: she makes you partakers of the same privileges and* immunities which her native sons enjoy: she takes under her protection your lives, property and religion. The most of you are probably settled here for life: many of you have wives and children, to whom you are tenderly attached, and whose welfare, as well as your own, is intimately connected with the welfare of the country. It is, therefore, evidently your interest, that America remain free and independent, in order that the blessings of liberty and good government may be transmitted to your posterity. It would be the height of baseness and ingratitude not to join heart and hand in defending the land where you earn your bread, and enjoy all the happy advantages which result from social life. England, which you deem your enemy and oppressor, it is true, is grappling with the nation which is now plundering and insulting us. It is not, for that reason, the cause of England that we are called to defend. I know, that, to engage the ignorant and unwary on the side of France, it has been said by her partisans, that she is defending the cause of all the oppressed, throughout the world, against their tyrants, and the cause of republicanism against monarchy: but this language is too stale to pass current, at this time, even with the most uninformed; especially since she has swallowed up all the republics of the old world. France is the great oppressor of the universe; and, therefore, opposition to her is the *common cause of the human race* against their tyrants, plunder-

* I speak here of the federal government; for, in several of the states, as in Massachusetts, Roman Catholics are subjected to certain disqualifications.

ers and murderers: it is the *cause of every regular government, and of all civilized society* against disorganization, anarchy and terror: it is *the cause of all religion and virtue* against deism, atheism and every species of immorality: it is your cause; it is my cause; it is every honest man's cause: it is a cause, in which are deeply interested our lives, our property, our liberty, our conscience, our every thing that is dear to us for time and eternity. Fly, then, to the standard of this country; and oppose, by every mean in your power, all the open or insidious attacks of the enemy. Cheerfully subscribe your names to the address of this town to the president of the Union, in which an offer of life and fortune is made to him for the efficient defence of the country. No neutrality, my brethren: "*he that is not with me, is against me*," is as true with respect to the land that feeds you, as with respect to God himself. Avoid all those men who seek to inflame your passions against England, in order to range you on the side of France. Read none of those seditious, lying, papers, in which our own rulers, the men of our choice, and all their measures, are perpetually villified, calumniated, and misrepresented, and in which every thing that is done by the French, however absurd, inconsistent and infamous, is forever extolled, and held up as the model of perfection; papers which, with truth and liberty for their motto, are always replete with falsehood and with the sentiments of slaves.

If you wish to escape the horrors which jacobinism has produced in France, and wherever else its pestilential maxims have gained ground, you must strive to destroy it in the bud; that is, you must suppress all insubordination, disobedience, or even disrespect, towards your civil rulers, as well as towards your ecclesiastical superiors. You have heard much of *the rights of man*, it is high time now to attend to *the duties of man*. Remember, that no one can ever have a *right to do wrong*, and that obedience and respect to your lawfully established rulers are among your strictest duties. The contrary conduct is extremely wrong and sinful. A spirit of disobedience and revolt is strangely prevalent among children and servants. This is, at present, a very general complaint;* and it is an abundant source of

* Without being a prophet or the son of a prophet, I venture to predict, that proper subordination, among the youth of this town, can never be re-established, until the mode and degree of correction be again placed in the hands of the school-masters. Their situation, at present, is too servile and dependent.

jacobinism in the state. Attend, therefore, to family discipline; keep your dependents in proper subjection, and they will contract those habits of obedience and submission which will render them good citizens, and which will effectually counteract all the attempts of disorganizers to introduce anarchy and confusion into this now peaceful and happy land.

A M E N

48

THE DUTY OF AMERICANS, AT THE PRESENT CRISIS

Timothy Dwight

NEW-HAVEN

1798

TIMOTHY DWIGHT (1752–1817). A native of Northampton, Massachusetts, and a Congregational minister, Dwight was regarded in his mature years as the dominant figure in Connecticut's established order. A prodigy as a boy, he is said to have learned the alphabet in one lesson, to have been reading the Bible at four, and to have become familiar with Latin by six. He entered Yale at thirteen, was graduated in 1769, and returned as a tutor in 1771, a position he kept for six years. He left in 1777 to serve for two years as chaplain in General S.H. Parson's Connecticut brigade. Politically active, Dwight continued in the ministry and in 1783 was ordained pastor of the Greenfield Hill Congregational Church, where he remained for twelve years. He wrote patriotic songs and poems, including a lumbering epic of eleven books in rhymed pentameters, *The Conquest of Canaan* (1785), which was calculated to give America something comparable to Greece's *Iliad* and Rome's *Aeneid.*

Dwight's fame, however, came as Ezra Stiles's successor as president of Yale, a position he held from 1795 to his death. Yale dates its modern history from Dwight's administration. Stiles disliked Dwight extremely, and his later detractors dubbed him Pope Dwight—while his admirers ranked him just behind St. Paul. A rigid Calvinist and a staunch Federalist, he battled with all his considerable energy against the rising tides of infidelity in religion and democracy in politics.

About all that the modern reader will know of Dwight's poetry is the hymn "I Love Thy Kingdom, Lord." The prose exhibited here reflects a far-from-serene Fourth of July in 1798, when the Jacobins were seen as threatening the country from all quarters, not least in the form of Jeffersonian Republicans and their atheistic allies.

THE DUTY OF AMERICANS, AT THE PRESENT CRISIS,

ILLUSTRATED

IN A

DISCOURSE,

PREACHED ON THE FOURTH OF JULY, 1798;

BY THE REVEREND

TIMOTHY DWIGHT. D.D.

PRESIDENT OF YALE-COLLEGE;

AT THE REQUEST

OF THE

Citizens of New-Haven.

NEW-HAVEN;

PRINTED BY THOMAS AND SAMUEL GREEN,

1798.

Behold I come as a thief: Blessed is he that watcheth, and keepeth his garments, lest he walk naked, and they see his shame.

Revelation XVI. xv.

This passage is inserted as a parenthesis in the account of the sixth vial. To feel its whole force it will be necessary to recur to that account, and to examine it with some attention. It is given in these words.

V. 12. "And the sixth angel poured out his vial upon the great river Euphrates; and the water thereof was dried up, that the way of the king of the east might be prepared."

13. "And I saw three unclean spirits like frogs come out of the mouth of the dragon, and out of the mouth of the beast, and out of the mouth of the false prophet.["]

14. "For they are the spirits of * devils, working miracles, which go forth unto the kings of the earth, and of the whole world, to gather them to the battle of that great day of God Almighty."

15. "Behold I come as a thief: Blessed is he that watcheth, and keepeth his garments, lest he walk naked, and they see his shame."

16. "And he gathered them together into a place called in the Hebrew tongue Armageddon."

To this account is subjoined that of the seventh vial; at the effusion of which is accomplished a wonderful and most affecting convulsion of this guilty world, and the final ruin of the Antichristian empire. The circumstances of this amazing event are exhibited at large in the remainder of this, and in the three succeeding chapters.

Instead of employing the time, allowed by the present occasion, in stating the several opinions of commentators concerning this remarkable prophecy, opinions which you can examine at your leisure, I shall, as briefly as may be, state to you that, which appears to me to be its true meaning. This is necessary to be done, to prepare you for the use of it, which is now intended to be made.

In the 12th verse, under a natural allusion to the manner in which the ancient Babylon was destroyed, a description is given us of the measures, used by the Most High to prepare the way for the destruc-

* Gr. Demons

tion of the spiritual Babylon. The river Euphrates surrounded the walls, and ran through the middle, of the ancient Babylon, and thus became the means of its wealth, strength and safety. When Cyrus and Cyaxares,* the kings of Persia and Media, or, in the Jewish phraseology, of the east, took this celebrated city, they dried up, or emptied, the waters of the Euphrates, out of its proper channel, by turning them into a lake, or more probably a sunken region of the country, above the city. They then entered by the channel which passed through the city, made themselves masters of it, and overturned the empire. The emptying, or drying up, of the waters of the real Euphrates thus prepared the way of the real kings of the east for the destruction of the city and empire of the real Babylon. The drying up of the waters of the figurative Euphrates in the like manner prepares the way of the figurative kings of the east for the destruction of the city and empire of the figurative Babylon. The terms *waters*, *Euphrates*, *kings*, *east*, *Babylon*, are all figurative or symbolical; and are not to be understood as denoting real kings, or a real east, any more than a real Euphrates, or a real Babylon. The whole meaning of the prophet is, I apprehend, that God will, under this vial, so diminish the wealth, strength, and safety, of the spiritual or figurative Babylon, as effectually to prepare the way for its destroyers.

In the remaining verses an event is predicted, of a totally different kind; which is also to take place in the same period. Three unclean spirits, like frogs, are exhibited as proceeding out of the mouth of the dragon or Devil, of the beast or Romish government, and of the false prophet, or, as I apprehend, of the regular clergy of that hierarchy. These spirits are represented as working miracles, as going forth to the kings, of the whole world, to gather them; and as actually gathering them together to the battle of that great day of God Almighty, described in the remainder of this chapter, and in the three succeeding ones. Of this vast enterprise the miserable end is strongly marked, in the name of the place, into which they are said to be gathered—Armageddon—the mountain of destruction and mourning.

The writer of this book will himself explain to us what he intended by the word *spirits* in this passage. In his 1st Epistle, ch. iv. v. 1. he says, "Beloved, believe not every spirit; but try the spirits, whether

* The Darius of Daniel

they be of God; because many false prophets are gone out into the world."*

I.E. Believe not every teacher, or doctrine, professing to come from God; but examine all carefully, that ye may know whether they come from God, or not; for many false prophets, or teachers passing themselves upon the church for teachers of truth, but in reality teachers of false doctrines, are gone out into the world.

In the same sense, if I am not deceived, is the word used in the passage under consideration. One great characteristic and calamity of this period is, therefore, that unclean teachers, or teachers of unclean doctrines, will spread through the world, to unite mankind against God. They are said to be three; i.e. several; a definite number being used here, as in many other passages of this book, for an indefinite one; to *come out of the mouths* of the three evil agents abovementioned; i.e. to originate in those countries, where they have principally co-operated against the kingdom of God; to be *unclean; to resemble frogs*; i.e. to be lothesome, clamorous, impudent, and pertinacious; to be *the spirits of demons*, i.e. to be impious, malicious, proud, deceitful, and cruel; *to work miracles*, or wonders; and *to gather great multitudes of men to battle*, i.e. to embark them in an open, professed enterprise, against God Almighty.

Having thus summarily explained my views of this prophecy, I shall now for the purpose of presenting it in a more distinct and comprehensive view, draw together the several parts of it in a paraphrase.

In the sixth great division of the period of providence, denoted by the vials filled with divine judgments and emptied on the world, the wealth, strength and safety of the Antichristian empire will be greatly lessened, and thus effectual preparation will be made for its final overthrow.

In the meantime several teachers of false and immoral doctrines will arise in those countries, where the powers of the Antichristian empire have especially distinguished themselves, by corrupting the truth, and persecuting the followers, of Christ; the character of which teachers and their doctrines will be impure, lothesome, impudent, pertinacious, proud, deceitful, impious, malicious, and cruel.

These teachers will, by their doctrines and labours, openly, pro-

* See also v. 2, 3, 6.

fessedly, and in an unusual manner, contend against God, and against his kingdom in this world, and will strive to unite mankind in this opposition.

Nor will they fail of astonishing success; for they will actually unite a large part of the human race, particularly in Christendom, in this impious undertaking.

But they will only unite them to their destruction; a destruction most awfully accomplished at the effusion of the seventh vial.

From this explanation it is manifest, that the prediction consists of two great and distinct parts; *the preparation for the overthrow of the Antichristian empire; and the embarkation of men in a professed and unusual opposition to God, and to his kingdom, accomplished by means of false doctrines, and impious teachers.*

By the ablest commentators the fifth vial is considered as having been poured out at the time of the Reformation. The first is supposed, and with almost absolute certainty, to have begun to operate not long after the year 800. If we calculate from that period to the year 1517, the year in which the Reformation began in Germany, the four first vials will be found to have occupied about four times 180 years. 180 years may therefore be estimated as the greatest, and 170 years as the least, duration of a single vial. From the year 1517 to the year 1798 there are 281 years. If the fifth vial be supposed to have continued 180 years, its termination was in the year 1697; if 170, in 1687. Of course the sixth vial may be viewed as having been in operation more than 100 years.

You will now naturally ask, What events in the Providence of God, found in this period, verify the prediction?

To this question I answer, generally, that the whole complexion of things appears to me to have, in a manner surprisingly exact, corresponded with the prediction. The following particulars will evince with what propriety this answer is returned.

Within this period the Jesuits, who constituted the strongest branch, and the most formidable internal support, of the Romish hierarchy, have been suppressed.

Within this period various other orders of the regular Romish clergy have in some countries been suppressed, and in others greatly reduced. Their permanent possessions have been confiscated, and their wealth and power greatly lessened.

Within this period the Antichristian secular powers have been in most instances exceedingly weakened. Poland as a body politic is nearly annihilated. Austria has deeply suffered. Venice and the popish part of Switzerland as bodies politic have vanished. The Sardinian monarchy is on the eve of dissolution. Spain, Naples, Tuscany, and Genoa, are sorely wounded; and Portugal totters to its fall. By the treaty, now on the tapis in Germany, the Romish archbishoprics and bishoprics, in that empire, are proposed to be secularized, and as distinct governments to be destroyed. As the strength of these powers was the foundation, on which the hierarchy rested; so their destruction, or diminution, is a final preparation for its ruin.

In France, Belgium, the Italian, and Cis-rhenane republics, a new form of government has been instituted, the effect of which, whether it shall prove permanent, or not, must be greatly and finally to diminish the strength of the hierarchy.

In France, and in Belgium, the whole power and influence of the clergy of all descriptions have, in a sense, been destroyed; and their immense wealth has been diverted into new channels. In France, also, an open, violent, and inveterate war has been made upon the hierarchy, and carried on with unexampled bitterness and cruelty.*

Within this period, also, the revenues of the pope have been greatly curtailed; the territory of Avignon has been taken out of his hands; and his general weight and authority have exceedingly declined.

Within the present year his person has been seized, his secular government overturned, a republic formed out of his dominions, and an apparent and at least temporary end put to his dominion.

To all these mighty preparations for the ruin of the Antichristian empire may be added, as of the highest efficacy, that great change of character, of views, feelings, and habits, throughout many Antichristian countries, which assures us completely, that its former strength can never return.

Thus has the first part of this remarkable prophecy been accomplished. Not less remarkable has been the fulfilment of the second.

* In the mention of all these evils brought on the Romish hierarchy, I beg it may be remembered, that I am far from justifying the iniquitous conduct of their persecutors. I know not that any person holds it, and all other persecution, more in abhorence. Neither have I a doubt of the integrity and piety of multitudes of the unhappy sufferers. In my view they claim, and I trust will receive, the commiseration, and, as occasion offers, the kind offices of all men possessed even of common humanity.

About the year 1728, Voltaire, so celebrated for his wit and brilliancy, and not less distinguished for his hatred of christianity and his abandonment of principle, formed a systematical design to destroy christianity, and to introduce in its stead a general diffusion of irreligion and atheism. For this purpose he associated with himself Frederic the II, king of Prussia, and Mess. D'Alembert and Diderot, the principal compilers of the Encyclopedie; all men of talents, atheists, and in the like manner abandoned. The principal parts of this system were, 1st. The compilation of the Encyclopedie;* in which with great art and insidiousness the doctrines of natural as well as Christian theology were rendered absurd and ridiculous; and the mind of the reader was insensibly steeled against conviction and duty. 2. The overthrow of the religious orders in Catholic countries; a step essentially necessary to the destruction of the religion professed in those countries. 3. The establishment of a sect of philosophists to serve, it is presumed, as a conclave, a rallying point, for all their followers. 4. The appropriation to themselves, and their disciples, of the places and honours of members of the French Academy, the most respectable literary society in France, and always considered as containing none but men of prime learning and talents. In this way they designed to hold out themselves, and their friends, as the only persons of great literary and intellectual distinction in that country, and to dictate all literary opinions to the nation.† 5. The fabrication of books of all kinds against christianity, especially such as excite doubt, and generate contempt and derision. Of these they issued, by themselves and their friends, who early became numerous, an immense number; so printed, as to be purchased for little or nothing, and so written, as to catch the feelings, and steal upon the approbation, of

* The celebrated French Dictionary of Arts and Sciences, in which articles of theology were speciously and decently written, but, by references artfully made to other articles, all the truth of the former was entirely and insidiously overthrown to most readers, by the sophistry of the latter.

† So far was this carried, that a Mr. Beauzet, a layman, but a sincere christian, who was one of the forty members, once asked D'Alembert how they came to admit him among them? D'Alembert answered, without hesitation, "I am sensible, this must seem astonishing to you; but we wanted a skilful grammarian, and among our party, not one had acquired a reputation in this line. We know that you believe in God, but, being a good sort of man, we cast our eyes upon you, for want of a philosopher to supply your place." Brit. Crit. Art. Barruel's Memoirs of the History of Jacobinism. August 1797.

every class of men. 6. The formation of a secret academy, of which Voltaire was the standing president, and in which books were formed, altered, forged, imputed as posthumous to deceased writers of reputation, and sent abroad with the weight of their names. These were printed and circulated, at the lowest price, through all classes of men, in an uninterrupted succession, and through every part of the kingdom.

Nor were the labours of this academy confined to religion. They attacked also morality and government, unhinged gradually the minds of men, and destroyed their reverence for every thing heretofore esteemed sacred.

In the mean time, the Masonic societies, which had been originally instituted for convivial and friendly purposes only, were, especially in France and Germany, made the professed scenes of debate concerning religion, morality, and government, by these philosophists*, who had in great numbers become Masons. For such debate the legalized existence of Masonry, its profound secresy, its solemn and mystic rites and symbols, its mutual correspondence, and its extension through most civilized countries, furnished the greatest advantages. All here was free, safe, and calculated to encourage the boldest excursions of restless opinion and impatient ardour, and to make and fix the deepest impressions. Here, and in no other place, under such arbitrary governments, could every innovator in these important subjects utter every sentiment, however daring, and attack every doctrine and institution, however guarded by law or sanctity. In the secure and unrestrained debates of the lodge, every novel, licentious, and alarming opinion was resolutely advanced. Minds, already tinged with philosophism, were here speedily blackened with a deep and deadly die; and those, which came fresh and innocent to the scene of contamination, became early and irremediably corrupted. A stubborn incapacity of conviction, and a flinty insensibility to every moral and natural tie, grew of course out of this combination of causes; and men were surely prepared, before themselves were aware, for every plot

* The words *philosophism* and *philosophists* may in our opinion, be happily adapted, from this work, to designate the doctrines of the deistical sect; and thus to rescue the honourable terms of philosophy and philosopher from the abuse, into which they have fallen. Philosophism is the love of sophisms and thus completely describes the sect of Voltaire: A philosophist is a lover of sophists. Brit. Crit. Ibid.

and perpetration. In these hot beds were sown the seeds of that astonishing Revolution, and all its dreadful appendages, which now spreads dismay and horror throughout half the globe.

While these measures were advancing the great design with a regular and rapid progress, Doctor Adam Weishaupt, professor of the canon law in the University of Ingolstadt, a city of Bavaria (in Germany) formed, about the year 1777, the order of Illuminati. This order is professedly a higher order of Masons, originated by himself, and grafted on ancient Masonic institutions. The secresy, solemnity, mysticism, and correspondence of Masonry, were in this new order preserved and enhanced; while the ardour of innovation, the impatience of civil and moral restraints, and the aims against government, morals, and religion, were elevated, expanded, and rendered more systematical, malignant, and daring.

In the societies of Illuminati doctrines were taught, which strike at the root of all human happiness and virtue; and every such doctrine was either expressly or implicitly involved in their system.

The being of God was denied and ridiculed.

Government was asserted to be a curse, and authority a mere usurpation.

Civil society was declared to be the only apostasy of man.

The possession of property was pronounced to be robbery.

Chastity and natural affection were declared to be nothing more than groundless prejudices.

Adultery, assassination, poisoning, and other crimes of the like infernal nature, were taught as lawful, and even as virtuous actions.

To crown such a system of falshood and horror all means were declared to be lawful, provided the end was good.

In this last doctrine men are not only loosed from every bond, and from every duty; but from every inducement to perform any thing which is good, and, abstain from any thing which is evil; and are set upon each other, like a company of hellhounds to worry, rend, and destroy. Of the goodness of the end every man is to judge for himself; and most men, and all men who resemble the Illuminati, will pronounce every end to be good, which will gratify their inclinations. The great and good ends proposed by the Illuminati, as the ultimate objects of their union, are the overthrow of religion, government, and human society civil and domestic. These they pronounce to be so good, that murder, butchery, and war, however extended and dreadful, are declared by them to be completely justifiable, if necessary for these great purposes. With such an example in view, it will be in vain to hunt for ends, which can be evil.

Correspondent with this summary was the whole system. No villainy, no impiety, no cruelty, can be named, which was not vindicated; and no virtue, which was not covered with contempt.

The names by which this society was enlarged, and its doctrines spread, were of every promising kind. With unremitted ardour and diligence the members insinuated themselves into every place of power and trust, and into every literary, political and friendly society; engrossed as much as possible the education of youth, especially of distinction; became licensers of the press, and directors of every literary journal; waylaid every foolish prince, every unprincipled civil officer, and every abandoned clergyman; entered boldly into the desk, and with unhallowed hands, and satanic lips, polluted the pages of God; inlisted in their service almost all the booksellers, and of course the printers, of Germany; inundated the country with books, replete with infidelity, irreligion, immorality, and obscenity; prohibited the printing, and prevented the sale, of books of the contrary character; decried and ridiculed them when published in spite of their efforts; panegyrized and trumpeted those of themselves and their coadjutors; and in a word made more numerous, more diversified, and more strenuous exertions, than an active imagination would have preconceived.

To these exertions their success has been proportioned. Multitudes of the Germans, notwithstanding the gravity, steadiness, and sobriety of their national character, have become either partial or entire converts to these wretched doctrines; numerous societies have been established among them; the public faith and morals have been unhinged; and the political and religious affairs of that empire have assumed an aspect, which forebodes its total ruin. In France, also, Illuminatism has been eagerly and extensively adopted; and those men, who have had, successively, the chief direction of the public affairs of that country, have been members of this society. Societies have also been erected in Switzerland and Italy, and have contributed probably to the success of the French, and to the overthrow of religion and government, in those countries. Mentz was delivered up to

Custine by the Illuminati; and that general appears to have been guillotined, because he declined to encourage the same treachery with respect to Manheim.

Nor have England and Scotland escaped the contagion. Several societies have been erected in both of those countries. Nay in the private papers, seized in the custody of the leading members in Germany, several such societies are recorded as having been erected in America, before the year 1786.*

It is a remarkable fact, that a large proportion of the sentiments, here stated, have been publicly avowed and applauded in the French legislature. The being and providence of God have been repeatedly denied and ridiculed. Christ has been mocked with the grossest insult. Death, by a solemn legislative decree has been declared to be an eternal sleep. Marriage has been degraded to a farce, and the community, by the law of divorce, invited to universal prostitution. In the school of public instruction atheism is professedly taught; and at an audience before the legislature, Nov. 30, 1793, the head scholar declared, that he and his schoolfellows detested a God; a declaration received by the members with unbounded applause, and rewarded with the fraternal kiss of the president, and with the honors of the sitting.†

I presume I have sufficiently proved the fulfilment of the second part of this remarkable prophesy; and shewn, that doctrines and teachers, answering to the description, have arisen in the very countries specified, and that they are rapidly spreading through the world, to engage mankind in an open and professed war against God. I shall only add, that the titles of these philosophistical books have, in various instances, been too obscene to admit of a translation by a virtuous man, and in a decent state of society. So fully are these teachers entitled to the epithet unclean.

Assuming now as just, for the purposes of this discourse, the explanation, which has been given, I shall proceed to consider the import of the text.

The text is an affectionate address of the Redeemer to his children, teaching them that conduct, which he wills them especially to pursue

* See Robison's Conspiracy and the Abbe Barruel's Memoirs of the history of Jacobinism.

† See Gifford's Letter to Erskine.

in this alarming season. It is the great practical remark, drawn by infinite wisdom and goodness from a most solemn sermon, and cannot fail therefore to merit our highest attention. Had he not, while recounting the extensive and dreadful convulsion, described in the context, made a declaration of this nature, there would have been little room for the exercise of any emotions, beside those of terror and despair. The gloom would have been universal and entire; a blank midnight without a star to cheer the solitary darkness. But here a hope, a promise, is furnished to such as obey the injunction, by which it is followed; a luminary like that, which shone to the wise men of the east, is lighted up to guide our steps to the Author of peace and salvation.

Blessed, even in this calamitous season, saith the Saviour of men, *is he that watcheth, and keepeth his garments, lest he walk naked and they see his shame.*

Sin is the nakedness and shame of the scriptures, and righteousness the garment which covers it. To watch and keep the garments is, of course, so to observe the heart and the life, so carefully to resist temptation and abstain from sin, and so faithfully to cultivate holiness and perform duty, that the heart and the life shall be adorned with the white robes of evangelical virtue, the unspotted attire of spiritual beauty.

The cautionary precept given to us by our Lord is, therefore,

That we should be eminently watchful to perform our duty faithfully, in the trying period, in which our lot is cast.

To those, who obey, a certain blessing is secured by the promise of the Redeemer.

[I.] The great and general object, aimed at by this command, and by every other, is private, personal obedience and reformation of life; personal piety, righteousness, and temperance.

To every man is by his Creator especially committed the care of himself; of his time, his talents, and his soul. He knows, or may know, better than any other man, his wants, his sins, and his dangers, and of course the means of relief, reformation, and escape. No one, so well as he, can watch the approach of temptation, so feelingly pray for divine assistance, or so profitably resolve on future obedience. In truth no resolutions, no prayers, no watchfulness of others, will profit him at all, unless seconded by his own. No other person can make any useful impressions on our hearts, or our lives, unless by rousing in us the necessary exertions. All extraneous labours terminate in this single point: it is the end of every doctrine, exhortation, and reproof, of every moral and religious institution.

The manner, in which such obedience is to be performed, and such reformation accomplished, is described to you weekly in the desk, and daily in the scriptures. A detail of it, therefore, will not be necessary, nor expected, on the present occasion. You already know what is to be done, and the manner in which it is to be done. You need not be told, that you are to use all efforts of your own, and to look humbly and continually to God to render those efforts successful; that you are to resist carefully and faithfully every approaching temptation, and every rising sin; that you are to resolve on newness of life, and to seize every occasion, as it presents itself, to honour God, and to bless your fellow men; that you are strenuously to contend against evil habits, and watchfully to cherish good ones; and that you are constantly to aim at uniformity and eminency in a holy life, and to "adorn the doctrine of God our Saviour in all things."

But it may be necessary to remind you, that personal obedience and reformation is the foundation, and the sum, of all national worth and prosperity. If each man conducts himself aright, the community cannot be conducted wrong. If the private life be unblamable, the public state must be commendable and happy.

Individuals are often apt to consider their own private conduct as of small importance to the public welfare. This opinion is wholly erroneous and highly mischievous. No man can adopt it, who believes, and remembers, the declarations of God. If "one sinner destroyeth much good," if "the effectual fervent prayer of a righteous man availeth much," if ten righteous persons, found in the polluted cities of the vale of Siddim, would have saved them from destruction, the personal conduct of no individual can be insignificant to the safety and happiness of a nation. On the contrary, the advantages to the public of private virtue, faithful prayer and edifying example, cannot be calculated. No one can conjecture how many will be made better, safer, and happier, by the virtue of one.

Wherever wealth, politeness, talents, and office, lend their aid to the inherent efficacy of virtue, its influence is proportionally greater. In this case the example is seen by greater numbers, is regarded with more respectful attention, and felt with greater force. The piety of Hezekiah reformed and saved a nation. Men far inferior in station to kings, and possessed of far humbler means of doing good, may still easily circulate through multitudes both virtue and happiness. The beggar on the dunghill may become a public blessing. Every parent, if a faithful one, is a public blessing of course. How delightful a path of patriotism is this?

It is also to be remembered, that this is the way, in which the chief good, ever placed in the power of most persons, is to be done. If this opportunity of serving God, and befriending mankind, be lost, no other will by the great body of men ever be found. Few persons can be concerned in settling systems of faith, moulding forms of government, regulating nations, or establishing empires. But almost all can train up a family for God, instil piety, justice, kindness and truth, distribute peace and comfort around a neighbourhood, receive the poor and the outcast into their houses, tend the bed of sickness, pour balm into the wounds of pain, and awaken a smile in the aspect of sorrow. In the secret and lowly vale of life, virtue in its most lovely attire delights to dwell. There God, with peculiar complacency, most frequently finds the inestimable ornament of a meek and quiet spirit; and there the morning and the evening incense ascends with peculiar fragrance to heaven. When angels became the visitors, and the guests, of Abraham, he was a simple husbandman.

Besides, this is the great mean of personal safety and happiness. No good man was ever forgotten, or neglected, of God. To him duty is always safety. Around the tabernacle of every one, that feareth God, the angel of protection will encamp, and save him from the impending evil.

II. Among the particular duties required by this precept, and at the present time, none holds a higher place than the observation of the Sabbath.

The Sabbath and its ordinances have ever been the great means of all moral good to mankind. The faithful observation of the sabbath is, therefore, one of the chief duties and interests of men; but the present time furnishes reasons, peculiar, at least in degree, for exemplary regard to this divine institution. The enemies of God have by private argument, ridicule, and influence, and by public decrees, pointed their especial malignity against the Sabbath; and have expected, and not without reason, that, if they could annihilate it, they should overthrow christianity. From them we cannot but learn its importance. Enemies usually discern, with more sagacity, the most promising point of attack, than those who are to be attacked. In this point are they to be peculiarly opposed. Here, peculiarly, are their designs to be baffled. If they fail here, they will finally fail. Christianity cannot fall, but by the neglect of the Sabbath.

I have been credibly informed, that, some years before the Revolution, an eminent philosopher of this country, now deceased, declared to David Hume, that Christianity would be exterminated from the American colonies within a century from that time. The opinion has doubtless been often declared and extensively imbibed; and has probably furnished our enemies their chief hopes of success. Where religion prevails, their system cannot succeed. Where religion prevails, Illuminatism cannot make disciples, a French directory cannot govern, a nation cannot be made slaves, nor villains, nor atheists, nor beasts. To destroy us, therefore, in this dreadful sense, our enemies must first destroy our Sabbath, and seduce us from the house of God.

Religion and Liberty are the two great objects of defensive war. Conjoined, they unite all the feelings, and call forth all the energies, of man. In defense of them, nations contend with the spirit of the Maccabees; "one will chase a thousand, and two put ten thousand to flight." The Dutch, in defense of them, few and feeble as they were in their infancy, assumed a gigantic courage, and grew like the fabled sons of Alous to an instantaneous and gigantic strength, broke the arms of the Spanish empire, swept its fleets from the ocean, pulled down its pride, plundered its treasures, captivated its dependencies, and forced its haughty monarch to a peace on their own terms. Religion and liberty are the meat and the drink of the body politic. Withdraw one of them, and it languishes, consumes, and dies. If indifference to either at any time becomes the prevailing character of a people, one half of their motives to vigorous defense is lost, and the hopes of their enemies are proportionally increased. Here, eminently, they are inseparable. Without religion we may possibly retain the freedom of savages, bears, and wolves; but not the freedom of New-England. If our religion were gone, our state of society would perish with it; and nothing would be left, which would be worth defending.

Our children of course, if not ourselves, would be prepared, as the ox for the slaughter, to become the victims of conquest, tyranny, and atheism.

The Sabbath, with its ordinances, constitutes the bond of union to christians; the badge by which they know each other; their rallying point; the standard of their host. Beside public worship they have no means of effectual descrimination. To preserve this is to us a prime interest and duty. In no way can we so preserve, or so announce to others, our character as christians; or to effectually prevent our nakedness and shame from being seen by our enemies. Now, more than ever, we are "not to be ashamed of the gospel of Christ." Now, more than ever, are we to stand forth to the eye of our enemies, and of the world, as open, determined christians; as the followers of Christ; as the friends of God. Every man, therefore, who loves his country, or his religion, ought to feel, that he serves, or injures, both, as he celebrates, or neglects, the Sabbath. By the devout observation of this holy day he will reform himself, increase his piety, heighten his love to his country, and confirm his determination to defend all that merits his regard. He will become a better man, and a better citizen.

The house of God is also the house of social prayer. Here nations meet with God to ask, and to receive, national blessings. On the Sabbath, and in the sanctuary, the children of the Redeemer will, to the end of the world, assemble for this glorious end. Here he is ever present to give more than they can ask. If we faithfully unite, here, in seeking his protection, "no weapon formed against us will prosper."

3. Another duty, to which we are also eminently called, is an entire separation from our enemies. Among the moral duties of man none hold a higher rank than political ones, and among our own political duties none is more plain, or more absolute, than that which I have now mentioned.

In the eighteenth chapter of this prophecy, in which the dreadful effects of the seventh vial are particularly described, this duty is expressly enjoined on christians by a voice from heaven. "And I heard another voice from heaven, saying, Come out of her, my people, that ye be not partakers of her sins, and that ye receive not of her plagues." Under the evils and dangers of the sixth vial, the command in the text was given; under those of the seventh, the command which we are now considering. The world is already far advanced in the period of the sixth. In the text we are informed, that the Redeemer will hasten the progress of his vengeance on the enemies of his church, during the effusion of the two last vials. If, therefore, the judgments of the seventh are not already begun, a fact of which I am doubtful, they certainly cannot be distant. The present time is, of course, the very period for which this command was given.

The two great reasons for the command are subjoined to it by the Saviour—"that ye be not partakers of her sins; and that ye receive not of her plagues"; and each is a reason of incomprehensible magnitude.

The sins of these enemies of Christ, and Christians, are of numbers and degrees, which mock account and description. All that the malice and atheism of the dragon, the cruelty and rapacity of the beast, and the fraud and deceit of the false prophet, can generate, or accomplish, swell the list. No personal, or national, interest of man has been uninvaded; no impious sentiment, or action, against God has been spared; no malignant hostility against Christ, and his religion, has been unattempted. Justice, truth, kindness, piety, and moral obligation universally, have been not merely trodden under foot; this might have resulted from vehemence and passion; but ridiculed, spurned, and insulted, as the childish bugbears of drivelling idiocy. Chastity and decency have been alike turned out of doors; and shame and pollution called out of their dens to the hall of distinction, and the chair of state. Nor has any art, violence, or means, been unemployed to accomplish these evils.

For what end shall we be connected with men, of whom this is the character and conduct? Is it that we may assume the same character, and pursue the same conduct? Is it, that our churches may become temples of reason, our Sabbath a decade, and our psalms of praise Marseillois hymns? Is it, that we may change our holy worship into a dance of Jacobin phrenzy, and that we may behold a strumpet personating a goddess on the altars of Jehovah? Is it that we may see the Bible cast into a bonfire, the vessels of the sacramental supper borne by an ass in public procession, and our children, either wheedled or terrified, uniting in the mob, chanting mockeries against God, and hailing in the sounds of Ca ira the ruin of their religion, and the loss of their souls? Is it, that we may see our wives and daughters the victims of legal prostitution; soberly dishonoured; speciously polluted; the outcasts of delicacy and virtue, and the lothing of God and man? Is it, that we may see, in our public papers, a solemn comparison drawn by an American Mother club between the Lord Jesus Christ and a new Marat; and the fiend of malice and fraud exalted above the glorious Redeemer?

Shall we, my brethren, become partakers of these sins? Shall we introduce them into our government, our schools, our families? Shall our sons become the disciples of Voltaire, and the dragoons of Marat;* or our daughters the concubines of the Illuminati?

Some of my audience may perhaps say, "We do not believe such crimes to have existed." The people of Jerusalem did not believe, that they were in danger, until the Chaldeans surrounded their walls. The people of Laish were secure, when the children of Dan lay in ambush around their city. There are in every place, and in every age, persons "who are settled upon their lees," who take pride in disbelief, and "who say in their heart, the Lord will not do good, neither will he do evil." Some persons disbelieve through ignorance; some choose not to be informed; and some determine not to be convinced. The two last classes cannot be persuaded. The first may, perhaps, be at least alarmed, when they are told, that the evidence of all this, and much more, is complete, that it has been produced to the public, and may with a little pains-taking be known by themselves.

There are others, who, admitting the fact, deny the danger. "If others," say they, "are ever so abandoned, we need not adopt either their principles, or their practices." Common sense has however declared, two thousand years ago, and God has sanctioned the declaration, that "Evil communications corrupt good manners." Of this truth all human experience is one continued and melancholy proof. I need only add, that these persons are prepared to become the first victims of the corruption by this very selfconfidence and security.

Should we, however, in a forbidden connection with these enemies of God, escape, against all hope, from moral ruin, we shall still re-

* See a four years Residence in France, lately published by Mr. Cornelius Davis of New-York. This is a most valuable and interesting work, and exhibits the French Revolution in a far more perfect light than any book I have seen. *It ought to be read by every American.*

ceive our share of their plagues. This is the certain dictate of the prophetical injunction; and our own experience, and that of nations more intimately connected with them, has already proved its truth.

Look for conviction to Belgium; sunk into the dust of insignificance and meanness, plundered, insulted, forgotten, never to rise more. See Batavia wallowing in the same dust; the butt of fraud, rapacity, and derision, struggling in the last stages of life, and searching anxiously to find a quiet grave. See Venice sold in the shambles, and made the small change of a political bargain. Turn your eyes to Switzerland, and behold its happiness, and its hopes, cut off at a single stroke: happiness, erected with the labour and the wisdom of three centuries; hopes, that not long since hailed the blessings of centuries yet to come. What have they spread, but crimes and miseries; Where have they trodden, but to waste, to pollute, and to destroy?

All connection with them has been pestilential. Among ourselves it has generated nothing but infidelity, irreligion, faction, rebellion, the ruin of peace, and the loss of property. In Spain, in the Sardinian monarchy, in Genoa, it has sunk the national character, blasted national independence, rooted out confidence, and forerun destruction.

But France itself has been the chief seat of the evils, wrought by these men. The unhappy and ever to be pitied inhabitants of that country, a great part of whom are doubtless of a character similar to that of the peaceable citizens of other countries, and have probably no voluntary concern in accomplishing these evils, have themselves suffered far more from the hands of philosophists, and their followers, than the inhabitants of any other country. General Danican, a French officer, asserts in his memoirs, lately published, that three millions of Frenchmen have perished in the Revolution. Of this amazing destruction the causes by which it was produced, the principles on which it was founded, and the modes in which it was conducted, are an aggravation, that admits no bound. The butchery of the stall, and the slaughter of the stye, are scenes of deeper remorse, and softened with more sensibility. The siege of Lyons, and the judicial massacres at Nantes, stand, since the crucifixion, alone in the volume of human crimes. The misery of man never before reached the extreme of agony, nor the infamy of man its consummation. Collot D. Herbois and his satellites, Carrier and his associates, would claim eminence in a world of fiends, and will be marked with distinction in the future hissings of the universe. No guilt so deeply died in blood, since the phrenzied malice of Calvary, will probably so amaze the assembly of the final day; and Nantes and Lyons may, without a hyperbole, obtain a literal immortality in a remembrance revived beyond the grave.

In which of these plagues, my brethren, are you willing to share? Which of them will you transmit as a legacy to your children?

Would you escape, you must separate yourselves. Would you wholly escape, you must be wholly separated. I do not intend, that you must not buy and sell, or exhibit the common offices of justice and good will; but you are bound by the voice of reason, of duty, of safety, and of God, to shun all such connection with them, as will interweave your sentiments or your friendship, your religion or your policy, with theirs. You cannot otherwise fail of partaking in their guilt, and receiving of their plagues.

4thly. Another duty, to which we are no less forcibly called, is union among ourselves.

The same divine Person, who spoke in the text, hath also said, "A house, a kingdom, divided against itself cannot stand." A divided family will destroy itself. A divided nation will anticipate ruin, prepared by its enemies. Switzerland, Geneva, Genoa, Venice, the Sardinian territories, Belgium, and Batavia, are melancholy examples of the truth of this declaration of our Saviour; beacons, which warn, with a gloomy and dreadful light, the nations who survive their ruin.

The great bond of union to every people is its government. This destroyed, or distrusted, there is no center left of intelligence, counsel, or action; no system of purposes, or measures; no point of rallying, or confidence. When a nation is ready to say, "What part have we in David, or what inheritance in the son of Jesse?" it will naturally subjoin, "Every man to his tent, O Israel!"

The candour and uprightness, with which our own government has acted in the progress of the present controversy, have forced encomiums even from its most bitter opposers, and excited the warmest approbation and applause of all its friends. Few objects could be more important, auspicious, or gratifying to christians, than to see the conduct of their rulers such, as they can, with boldness of access, bring before their God, and fearlessly commend to his favour and protection.

In men, possessed of similar candour, adherence to our government, in the present crisis, may be regarded as a thing of course. They need not be informed, that the existing rulers must be the directors of our public affairs, and the only directors; that their views and measures will not and cannot always accord with the judgment of individuals, as the opinions of individuals accord no better with each other; that the officers of government are possessed of better information than private persons can be; that, if they had the same information, they would probably coincide with the opinions of their rulers; that confidence must be placed in men, imperfect as they are, in all human affairs, or no important business can be done; and that men of known and tried probity are fully deserving of that confidence.

At the present time this adherence ought to be unequivocally manifested. In a land of universal suffrage, where every individual is possessed of much personal consequence as in ours, the government ought, especially in great measures, to be as secure, as may be, of the harmonious and cheerful co-operation of the citizens. All success, here, depends on the hearty concurrence of the community; and no occasion ever called for it more.

But there are, even in this state, persons, who are opposed to the government. To them I observe, That the government of France has destroyed the independence of every nation, which has confided in it.

That every such nation has been ruined by its internal divisions, especially by the separation of the people from their government.

That they have attempted to accomplish our ruin by the same means, and will certainly accomplish it, if they can;

That the miseries suffered by the subjugated nations have been numberless and extreme, involving the loss of national honour, the immense plunder of public and private property, the conflagration of churches and dwellings, the total ruin of families, the butchery of great multitudes of fathers and sons, and the most deplorable dishonour of wives and daughters;

That the same miseries will be repeated here, if in their power.

That there is, under God, no mean of escaping this ruin, but union among ourselves, and unshaken adherence to the existing government;

That themselves have an infinitely higher interest in preserving the independence of their country, than in any thing, which *can* exist, should it be conquered;

That they must stand, or fall, with their country; since the French, like all other conquerors, though they may for a little time regard them, as aids and friends, with a seeming partiality, will soon lose that partiality in a general contempt and hatred for them, as Americans. That should they, contrary to all experience, escape these evils, their children will suffer them as extensively as those of their neighbours; and

That to oppose, or neglect, the defence of their country, is to stab the breast, from which they have drawn their life.

I know not that even these considerations will prevail: if they do not, nothing can be suggested by me, which will have efficacy. I must leave them, therefore, to their consciences, and their God.

In the mean time, since the great facts, of which this controversy has consisted, have not, during the preceding periods, been thoroughly known, or believed, by all; and since all questions of expediency will be viewed differently by different eyes; I cannot but urge a general spirit of conciliation. To men labouring under mere mistakes, and prejudices void of malignity, hard names are in most cases unhappily applied, and unkindness is unwisely exhibited. Multitudes, heretofore attached to France with great ardour, have, from full conviction of the necessity of changing their sentiments and their conduct, come forth in the most decisive language, and determined conduct, of defenders of their country. More are daily exhibiting the same spirit and measures. Almost all native Americans will, I doubt not, speedily appear in the same ranks; and none should, in my opinion, be discouraged by useless obloquy.

5. Another duty, injoined in the text, and highly incumbent on us at this time, is unshaken firmness in our opposition.

A steady and invincible firmness is the chief instrument of great atchievements. It is the prime mean of great wealth, learning, wisdom, power and virtue; and without it nothing noble or useful is usually accomplished. Without it our separation from our enemies, and our union among ourselves, will avail to no end. The cause is too complex, the object too important, to be determined by a single effort. It is infinitely too important to be given up, let the consequence be what it may. No evils, which can flow from resistance, can be so great as those, which must flow from submission. Great sacrifices of property, of peace, and of life, we may be called to make, but they will fall short of complete ruin. If they should not, it will be more desirable, beyond computation, to fall in the honourable and faithful defence of our families, our country, and our religion, than to survive, the melancholy, debased, and guilty spectators of the ruin of all. We contend for all that is, or ought to be, dear to man. Our cause is eminently that, in which "he who seeketh to save his life shall lose it, and he who loseth it," in obedience to the command of his Master, "shall find it" beyond the grave. To our enemies we have done no wrong. Unspotted justice looks down on all our public measures with a smile. We fight for that, for which we can pray. We fight for the lives, the honor, the safety, of our wives and children, for the religion of our fathers, and for the liberty, "with which Christ hath made us free." "We jeopard our lives," that our children may inherit these glorious blessings, be rescued from the grinding insolence of foreign despotism, and saved from the corruption and perdition of foreign atheism. I am a father. I feel the usual parental tenderness for my children. I have long soothed the approach of declining years with the fond hope of seeing my sons serving God and their generation around me. But from cool conviction I declare in this solemn place, I would far rather follow them one by one to an untimely grave, than to behold them, however prosperous, the victims of philosophism. What could I then believe, but that they were "nigh unto cursing, and that their end was to be burned."

From two sources only are we in danger of irresolution; *avarice, and a reliance on those fair professions*, which our enemies have begun to make, and which they will doubtless continue to make, in degrees, and with insidiousness, still greater.

On the first of these sources I observe, that, if we grudge a part of our property in the defence of our country, we lose the whole; and not only the whole of our property, but all our comforts, and all our hopes. Every enjoyment of life, every solace of sorrow, will be offered up in one vast hecatomb at the shrine of pride, plunder, impurity, and atheism. Those "who fear not God, regard not man." All interests, beside their own, are in the view of such men the sport of wantonness, of insolence, and of a heart of millstone. They and their engines will soon tell you, if you do not put it out of their power, as one of the same engines told the miserable inhabitants of Neuwied (in Germany) unhappily placing confidence in their professions. Hear the story, in the words of Professor Robison,

> If ever there was a spot upon earth, where men may be happy in a state of cultivated society, it was the little principality of Neuwied. I saw it in 1770. The town was neat, and the palace handsome and in good state. But the country was beyond conception delightful; not a cottage that was out of repair; not a hedge out of order. It had been the hobby of the prince (pardon me the word) who made it his daily employment to go through his principality, and assist every housholder, of whatever condition, with his advice and with his purse; and when a freeholder could not of himself put things into a thriving condition, the prince sent his workmen and did it for him. He endowed schools for the common people and two academies for the gentry and the people of business. He gave little portions to the daughters, and prizes to the well-behaving sons of the labouring people. His own houshold was a pattern of elegance and œconomy; his sons were sent to Paris, to learn elegance, and to England, to learn science and agriculture. In short the whole was like a romance, and was indeed romantic. I heard it spoken of with a smile at the table of the bishop of Treves, and was induced to see it the next day as a curiosity. Yet even here the fanaticism of Knigge (one of the founders of the Illuminati) would distribute his poison, and tell the blinded people that they were in a state of sin and misery, that their prince was a despot, and that they would never be happy 'till he was made to fly, and 'till they were made all equal.
>
> They got their wish. The swarm of French locusts sat down at Neuwied's beautiful fields, in 1793, and intrenched themselves; and in three months prince's and farmers' houses, and cottages, and schools, and academies, all vanished. When they complained of their miseries to the French general, René le Grand, he replied, with a contemptuous and cutting laugh, "All is ours. We have left you your eyes to cry."

Will you trust such professions? Have not your enemies made them to every country, which they have subjugated? Have they fulfilled them to one? Will they prove more sincere to you? Have they not deceived you in every expectation hitherto? On what grounds can you rely on them hereafter?

Will you grudge your property for the defence of itself, of your families, of yourselves. Will you preserve it to pay the price of a Dutch loan? to have it put in requisition by the French Directory? to label it on your doors, that they may, without trouble and without a tax bill, send their soldiers and take it for the use of the Republic? Will you keep it to assist them to pay their fleets and armies for subduing you? and to maintain their forts and garrisons for keeping you in subjection? Shall it become the purchase of a French fete, holden to commemorate the massacres of the 10th of August, the butcheries of the 3d of September, or the murder of Louis the 16th, your former benefactor? Shall it furnish the means for *representatives of the people* to roll through your streets on the wheels of splendour, to imprison your sons and fathers; to seize on all the comforts, which you have earned with toil, and laid up with care; and to gather your wives, sisters, and daughters, into their brutal seraglios? Shall it become the price of the guillotine, and pay the expense of cleansing your streets from brooks of human blood?

Will you rely on men whose *principles justify falshood, injustice, and cruelty?* Will you trust philosophists? men who set truth at nought, who make justice a butt of mockery, who deny the being and providence of God, and laugh at the interests and sufferings of men? Think not that such men can change. They can scarcely be worse. There is not a hope that they will become better.

But perhaps you may be alarmed by the power, and the successes, of your enemies. I am warranted to declare, that the ablest judge of this subject in America has said, that, if we are united, firm, and faithful to ourselves, neither France, nor all Europe, can subdue these states. Against other nations they contended with great and decisive advantages. Those nations were near to them, were divided, feeble, corrupted, seduced by philosophists, slaves of despotism, and separated from their government. None of these characters can be applied to us, unless we voluntarily retain those, which depend on ourselves. Three thousand miles of ocean spread between us and our enemies, to enfeeble and disappoint their efforts. They will not here contend with silken Italians, with divided Swissers, nor with self-surrendered Belgians and Batavians. They will find a hardy race of freemen, uncorrupted by luxury, unbroken by despotism; enlightened to understand their privileges, glowing with independence, and determined to be free, or to die: men who love, and who will defend, their families, their country, and their religion: men fresh from triumph, and strong in a recent and victorious Revolution. Doubled, since that Revolution began, in their numbers, and quadrupled in their resources and advantages, at home, in a country formed to disappoint invasion, and to prosper defence, under leaders skilled in all the arts and duties of war, and trained in the path of success, they have, if united, firm, and faithful, every thing to hope, and, beside the common evils of war, nothing to fear.

Think not that I trust in chariots and in horses. My own reliance is, I hope, I ardently hope yours is, also, on the Lord our God. All these are his most merciful blessings, and, as such, most supporting consolations to us. They are the very means, which he has provided for our safety, and our hope. Stupidity, sloth, and ingratitude, can alone be blind to them as tokens for good. We are not, my brethren, to look for miracles, nor to expect God to accomplish them. We are to trust in him for the blessings of a regular and merciful providence. Such a providence is over us for good. I have recited abundant proofs, and could easily recite many more. All these are means, with which we are to plant, and to water, and in answer to our prayers God will certainly give the increase.

But I am peculiarly confident in the promised blessing of the text. Our contention is a plain duty to God. The same glorious Person, who has commanded it, has promised to crown our obedience with his blessing; and has thus illumined this gloomy prediction, and shed the dawn of hope and comfort over this melancholy period.

To you the promise is eminently supporting. He has won your faith by the great things he has already done for your fathers, and for you. The same Almighty Hand, which destroyed the fleet of Chebucto by the storm, and whelmed it in the deep; which conducted into the arms of Manly, and of Mugford, those means of war, which for the time saved your country; which raised up your Washington to guide your armies and your councils; which united you with your brethren against every expectation and hope; which disappointed the devices of enemies without, and traitors within; which bade the winds and the waves fight for you at Yorktown; which has, in later periods, repeatedly disclosed the machinations of your enemies, and which has now roused a noble spirit of resistance to intrigue and to terror; will accomplish for you a final deliverance from the hand of those, "who seek your hurt." He has been your fathers' God, and he will be yours.

Look through the history of your country. You will find scarcely less glorious and wonderful proofs of divine protection and deliverance, uniformly administered through every period of our existence as a people, than shone to the people of Israel in Egypt, in the wilderness, and in Canaan. Can it be believed, can it be, that Christianity has been so planted here, the church of God so established, so happy a government constituted, and so desirable a state of society begun, merely to shew them to the world, and then destroy them? No instance can be found in the providence of God, in which a nation so wonderfully established, and preserved, has been overthrown, until it had progressed farther in corruption. We may be cast down; but experience only will prove to me, that we shall be destroyed.

But the consideration, which ought of itself to decide your opinions and your conduct, and which adds immense weight to all the others, is that the alternative, as exhibited in the prediction, and in providence, is beyond measure dreadful, and is at hand. "Behold," saith the Saviour, "I come as a thief"—suddenly, unexpectedly, alarmingly—as that wasting enemy, the burglar, breaks up the house in the hour of darkness, when all the inhabitants are lost in sleep and security. How strongly do the great events of the present day shew this awful advent of the King of Kings to be at the doors?

Turn your eyes, for a moment, to the face of providence, and mark its new and surprising appearance. The Jews, for the first time since the destruction of Jerusalem by Adrian, have, in these states, been admitted to the rights of citizenship; and have since been admitted to the same rights in Prussia. They have also, as we are informed, appointed a solemn delegation to examine the evidences of Christianity. In the Austrian dominions, it is asserted, they have agreed to observe the Christian Sabbath; and in England, have in considerable numbers embraced the Christian religion. New and unprecedented efforts have been made, and are fast increasing, in England, Scotland, Germany, and the United States, for the conversion of the heathen. Measures have, in Europe, and in America, been adopted, and are still enlarging, for putting an end to the African slavery, which will within a moderate period bring it to an end. Mohammedism is nearly extinct in Persia, one of the chief supports of that imposture. In Turkey, its other great support, the throne totters to its fall. The great calamities of the present period have fallen, also, almost exclusively upon the

Antichristian empire; and almost every part of that empire has drunk deeply of the cup. France, Belgium, Spain, Ireland, the Sardinian monarchy, the Austrian dominions, Venice, Genoa, popish Switzerland, the Ecclesiastical State, popish Germany, Poland, and the French West-Indies, have all been visited with judgments wonderful and terrible; and in exact accordance with prophecy have furthered their own ruin. The kings, or states, of this empire are now plainly "hating the whore, eating her flesh, and burning her with fire." Batavia, protestant Switzerland, some parts of protestant Germany, and Geneva, have most unwisely, not to say wickedly, refused "to come out" and have therefore "partaken of the sins, and received of the plagues," of their enemies. To the same unhappy cause our own smartings may all be traced; but blessed be God, there is reason to hope, that "we are escaping from the snare of the fowler."

So sudden, so unexpected, so alarming a state of things has not existed since the deluge. Every mouth proclaims, every eye looks its astonishment. Wonders daily succeed wonders, and are beginning to be regarded as the standing course of things. As they are of so many kinds, exist in so many places, and respect so many objects; kinds, places and objects, all marked out in prophecy, exhibited as parts of one closely united system, and to be expected at the present time; they shew that this affecting declaration is even now fulfilling in a surprising manner, and that the advent of Christ is at least at our doors. Think how awful this period is. Think what convulsions, what calamities, are portended by that great Voice out of the temple of heaven from the Throne—"It is done!" by the voices and thunderings and lightnings, by the unprecedented shaking of the earth, the unexampled plague of hailstones, the fleeing of the islands, the vanishing of the mountains, the rending asunder of the Antichristian empire, the united ascent of all its sins before God, the falling of the cities of the nations, the general embattling of mankind against their Maker, and their final overthrow, in such immense numbers, that "all the fowls shall be filled with their flesh."

"GOD is jealous, and the Lord revengeth; the Lord revengeth and is furious; the Lord will take vengeance on his adversaries, he reserveth wrath for his enemies. The Lord is slow to anger, and great in power, and will not at all acquit the wicked. The Lord hath his way in the whirlwind, and in the storm, and the clouds are the dust of his feet. The mountains quake at him, and the hills melt; and the earth is burnt at his presence, yea the world, and all that dwell therein. Who can stand before his indignation? Who can abide in the fierceness of his anger?"

In this amazing conflict, amidst this stupendous and immeasurable ruin, how transporting the thought, that safety and peace may be certainly found. O thou God of our fathers! our own God! and the God of our children! enable us so to watch, and keep our garments, in this solemn day, that our shame appear not, and that both we and our posterity may be entitled to the blessing which thou hast promised.

AMEN

A SERMON OCCASIONED BY THE DEATH OF WASHINGTON

Henry Holcombe

SAVANNAH
1800

Henry Holcombe (1762–1824). Born in South Carolina, Holcombe received no formal education after the age of eleven. He enlisted in the Revolutionary army early in the war and became an officer by the age of twenty-one. He converted to the Baptist faith about this time and was rebaptized (having been raised as a Presbyterian), and he achieved some fame for delivering fiery sermons to his troops from horseback. He became pastor of the Pine Creek Church in 1785, married the following year, and soon thereafter baptized his wife, her mother and brother, and his own father. In 1795 he became a pastor in Savannah, Georgia, and five years later he received a D.D. from the College of Rhode Island (Brown).

While Holcombe vigorously opposed deism and the theater, he generally mingled his religious and civic concerns by founding an orphanage in Savannah, working to improve the state's penal code, establishing and supporting the Mount Enon Academy near Augusta, and publishing a literary and religious magazine called the *Georgia Analytical Repository*. He became ill in 1810 and moved to Philadelphia, hoping for better health in a different climate, and accepted a pastorate there. He tended toward isolationism of the kind recommended in Washington's famous phrase "no entangling alliances," which to Holcombe translated into a rejection of foreign missions. In his later years he preached against war as contrary to God's revelation.

The sermon reprinted here is one of Holcombe's most famous and one of hundreds preached all over America to mark the passing of "the father of his country," George Washington. It was preached in Savannah on January 19, 1800, and repeated several times elsewhere.

A SERMON,

OCCASIONED BY THE DEATH OF

Lieutenant-General GEORGE WASHINGTON,

LATE

P R E S I D E N T

OF THE

UNITED STATES OF AMERICA;

WHO WAS BORN, FEBRUARY 11TH, 1732, IN VIRGINIA, AND DIED, DECEMBER 14TH, 1799, ON MOUNT VERNON, HIS FAVORITE SEAT IN HIS NATIVE COUNTRY; FIRST DELIVERED IN THE BAPTIST CHURCH, SAVANNAH, GEORGIA, JANUARY 19TH, 1800, AND NOW PUBLISHED, AT THE REQUEST OF THE HONORABLE CITY COUNCIL,

By HENRY HOLCOMBE, *Minister of the Word of God in Savannah.*

> " *Mark the perfect Man, and behold*
> " *the upright: for the end of that Man is peace.*" David.

Printed by SEYMOUR & WOOLHOPTER, on the BAY.

Know ye not that there is a great man fallen?

2d of Samuel, 3d Chap.
and part of the 38th Verse.

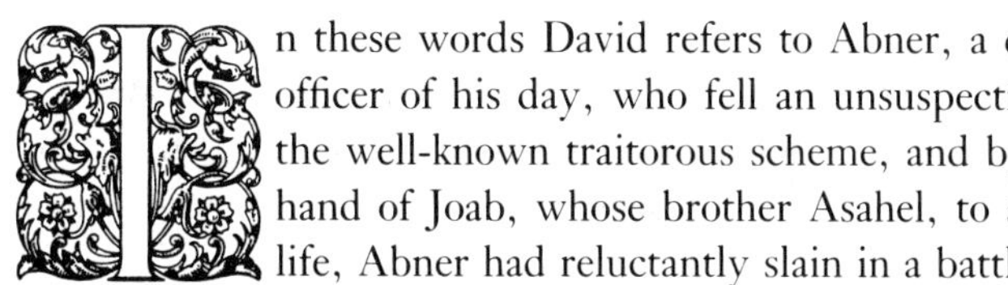

In these words David refers to Abner, a distinguished officer of his day, who fell an unsuspecting victim to the well-known traitorous scheme, and by the bloody hand of Joab, whose brother Asahel, to save his own life, Abner had reluctantly slain in a battle at Gibeon. To awaken a correspondent sense of their great loss in the afflicted tribes, David addressed to them the pathetic inquiry adopted on this melancholy occasion, as applying with the most forcible propriety to the late Lieutenant General George Washington. Know ye not that in him a great man, a much greater than Abner, is fallen? The sufficiently visible effects of this penetrating conviction render a comparison of these great men unnecessary, would the dignity of my subject, and the solemnity which reigns over this unexampled and overflowing concourse admit it. Their coincidence in point of greatness, established by the highest authorities, whatever disparity as to the degrees of it, may exist, is all that is requisite to my purpose. In reliance therefore, on the plenitude of candor to which I am already greatly in arrears, however inadequate to the important service which has unexpectedly devolved on me, and with all the unaffected diffidence which overwhelms me, I shall make immediate advances towards the awful ground on which our greatest orators sink unnerved, and giants in literature stand and tremble! And though I am not about to deliver an oration, nor to pronounce an eulogium; but to preach a sermon, and briefly touch on one of the greatest merely human characters, I am fully apprised of the delicacy of my situation, and too sensibly feel the pressure of difficulties.

My feeble soul take courage! A Demosthenes or a Cicero might fail here without dishonor; and though the famed Cæsars, Alexanders, Pompies and Marlboroughs, must resign their inferior laurels to the more famous American general, he was but a man; all his greatness was derived from his and thy Creator, and thou wilt be assisted in the execution of thy arduous design by the prayers, candid allowances and liberal constructions of thine audience, who will deem it very pardonable on thy theme to be defective. The first doctrinal observation which our text, and the occasion of our assembling, unitedly suggest, is seriously important: Great as Abner was, he fell; and Washington is fallen; it, therefore, undeniably follows *that great men, as well as others, must fall.* Though it would be absurd to attempt a formal proof of this doctrine and have the appearance of an insult on dying man, there is nothing that merits more frequent, or more serious consideration; and a few explanatory remarks on it are so far from being amiss, that they are indispensible. The heathens and deists, of all descriptions, believing the immortality of the human soul, consider their bodies as falling by death into corruption and dust, never to rise; and their notions of the state, exercises, and enjoyments of the soul after death are so vague, indistinct, and unimpressive, that they have little or no visible effect on their practice. Atheists, and such deists as believe the soul of man to be mortal, consider all who are fallen, and our immortal Washington among the rest, as plunged into undistinguished and irretrievable ruin! as consigned to their original nonentity!! Happily for our various interests, few, if any, of these gloomy monsters disgrace, or infest the United States: They are chiefly, if not altogether, confined to the smoke and flame in which they have involved miserable Europe. Let Americans never suffer their nature and its author to be insulted and degraded by the influence, or existence of such detestable sentiments;

> Scorned be the man who thinks himself
> a brute;
> Affronts his species, and his God blasphemes.

But gladly I turn your attention from the cold, lifeless principles, and painful uncertainty of the better sort of heathens and the deists, and especially from the insupportable horrors of annihilation, to what we are to understand by the fall of men in death; and, in a word, it is their fall from this world; from its honors, pleasures, profits; and from the exercise of their mortal powers. By a figure of speech, which puts a part for the whole, or the contrary, and common with inspired, and other writers, in saying that a great man is fallen, David means no more than that his mortal part is dead; but he was better informed than to suppose that even this was dead or fallen, to revive, to rise no more. We not only know from divine revelation, but from an important and well attested fact, gloriously demonstrated at this time by its numerous and happy consequences, that our bodies are not only capable of a resurrection, but shall actually rise! Were the horrible reverse of these exhilirating representations true, inconsiderable indeed would be our cause of triumph in existence, or reason to boast of human excellence! "*Verily every man, at his best state,*" considered merely in his relation to this transitory scene, "*is altogether vanity.*" And the inevitable fall of the greatest, as well as all other men, when viewed in a true light, and considered in its eternal consequences, must fill the enlightened considerate mind with the most serious reflections. It is said,

Xerxis surveyed his mighty host with tears,
To think they'd die within an hundred years:

But judging from past events, what enormous devastations among the inhabitants of the earth must be spread in less than half that time! "Your fathers, where are they? and the prophets, do they live forever?" Where are all preceding generations, and the great men who illuminated and adorned them? Alas! the mighty ruins of mortality! With a few illustrious exemptions, recorded in the oracles of God, the silent, and almost imperceptibly slow, but steady and irresistibly strong current of time, has borne them into the boundless ocean of eternity! And yet Philip of Macedon was far from being alone, in needing daily to be told that he was a mortal man.

That all men must fall, is universally acknowledged; but too few apply this serious truth to their own cases; Doctor Young had reasons for his bold assertion, "All men think all men mortal but themselves." And great men, from a variety of circumstances, are more than others, addicted to this waking dream, this sometimes fatal delusion; and strange as fatal! "*Know ye not that there is a great man fallen?*" and that consequently *great men must fall!* Riches, power, titles, universal applause, to which may be added even virtue and piety, avail nothing in this warfare, "Death enters, and there's no defence." Acknowledge this all do, they must, however inconsiderate and profane, for who can deny it? "*But O, that they were wise, that they understood this, that they would consider their latter end!*" How natural, reasonable, and interesting is this? And one would think it might be added, how difficult to avoid it!

As man perhaps the moment of his breath,
Receives the lurking principle of death;
The young disease that must subdue at length,
Grows with his growth, and strengthens with his strength.

And when these latent seeds of dissolution produce their ultimate effect, our text directs us in what regards our duty to the memories of the just. By fair and obvious implication, it says, *the fall of a great man merits respectful and public attention.*

Know ye not that there is a great man fallen?

This question was not asked for information, and it not only forcibly affirms the fall of a great man; but evidently excites to mourning on account of it, and proper expressions of respect for his memory. *Know ye not*, that is, are ye not apprised, or disposed to consider, as ye should be, and to practically declare, *that* in your judgment, *there is a great man*, a man of worth, and entitled to high and public regard, *fallen?*

And accordingly we find that David said to the people to whom he addressed the words of our text, "Rent your clothes, and gird you with sackcloth, and mourn before Abner." The sacred historian adds, "And king David himself followed the bier. And they buried Abner in Hebron: And the king lifted up his voice, and wept at the grave of Abner; and all the people wept."

The solemnity concludes with an oration by the king, which produced the highest effects of oratory, and closes with an acknowledgment, that he was rendered weak though anointed king, by the loss of that great man. Parellel passages, in great variety, might be recited in confirmation of this doctrine. Instances are numerous in the patriarchal age, of burying persons of eminent piety and worth, with every mark of respect and solemnity.

The venerable founders of the Jewish church and nation, had the tribute of high encomiums, and genuine mourning for many days, paid to their memories and their merits. A beautiful specimen of ancient eulogy, is David's lamentation over Saul and Jonathan. With an ardor and elevation peculiar to himself, he exclaims, "The beauty of Israel is slain in thy high places; how are the mighty fallen! Tell it not in Gath, publish it not in the streets of Askelon, lest the daughters of the Philistines rejoice, lest the daughters of the uncircumcised triumph. Ye mountains of Gilboa let there be no dew, neither let there be rain upon you, nor fields of offerings; for there the shield of the mighty is vilely cast away, the shield of Saul, as though he had not been anointed with oil. From the blood of the slain, from the fat of the mighty, the bow of Jonathan turned not back, and the sword of Saul returned not empty. Saul and Jonathan were lovely and pleasant in their lives, and in their deaths they were not divided: They were swifter than eagles, they were stronger than lions. Ye daughters of Israel weep over Saul, who clothed you in scarlet, with other delights, who put on ornaments of gold upon your apparel. How are the mighty fallen in the midst of the battle!"

This natural and laudable, as well as ancient and universal custom of honoring the pious and eminent dead, may be further justified by quotations from the new testament. At the grave of Lazarous, "JESUS wept"; devout men buried Stephen, who had the honor to be the first martyr in the christian cause, with great lamentation; and Paul mentions a number of the illustrious characters of antiquity, with the highest respect, and warmly recommends their noble and heroic conduct to the imitation of posterity. After bestowing on many the encomiums proper to their respective merits, he adds, "And what shall I more say? For the time would fail me to tell of Gideon, and of Barack, and of Sampson, and of Jepthae, of David also, and of Samuel, and of the prophets; who through faith subdued kingdoms, wrought righteousness, obtained promises, stopped the mouths of lions, quenched the violence of fire, escaped the edge of the sword, out of weakness were made strong, waxed valient in fight, and turned to flight the armies of the aliens." So warm a panegyrist of these great men was the Apostle, that he avers, "*Of them the world was not worthy.*" And though many of these failed of obtaining the attention due to their merits in, and immediately after their respective generations, by having their names and worthy deeds enrolled in the volume of inspiration, GOD has plainly shewn us that the fall of a great good man should excite respectful and public attention. Encouraged, therefore, and in some degree assisted by such precedents, I will proceed to what is finally incumbent on me; and that is, *to evince the applicability of my text to the illustrious deceased.*

It must be acknowledged that the scriptural and consequently rational and becoming custom of praising departed persons, has been shamefully abused. The great among the heathens have, in many instances, been exalted to celestial honors, and idolized to distant generations. And by persons of better information, funeral panegyric has been so indiscriminately bestowed, that it has blended all distinctions of character and become proverbially false. But it is not on these or any other accounts, to be refused on proper occasions, this would be falling into the opposite extreme. And perhaps a more proper occasion than the present for commendation and applause never occurred, or one on which higher might be bestowed, consistently with truth and moderation. Never I believe could it be said of any with more propriety than of General Washington, that what his acquaintances would condemn as below his merit, strangers would consider as the most fulsome adulation, or exaggerated applause. But to proceed: Most obviously does my text apply to this great man, considered as enriched with merely natural endowments. His features, actions, and whole deportment, before he was refined by learning, clothed with power, or known to fame, attracted every eye, fixed attention, and commanded respect. As the immediate effect of divine bounty he possessed the seeds whose blossoms and fruits ultimately rendered him the boast of his country, and the glory of the age. The rich furniture of his mind could receive no assistance from the common rules of art, because by innate strength it rose nobly superior to them, comprehending the true principles, and proper standard of criticism.* His perceptions were prompt, intuitive, clear; and were displayed from earliest youth in the facility and rapidity with which he acquired knowledge, and in the exact order, method and propriety conspicuous in the management of all his affairs. And to the fatal day which put a period to the most valuable of mortal lives, his conduct and atchievements, proclaimed his genius entirely original, superlatively bright, the offspring of the Father of Lights. In his vast mind centered that shining aggregate of excellencies which beamed with such effulgence in his dignified and manly countenance, and were so

* True criticism is the application of taste and of good sense to the several fine arts. Blair.

eminently ornamental, I will not say of his country, nor of this generation, but of human nature. When we consider that all effects must have an adequate cause, we are led to trace the wonders which have appeared in Washington's life, to, at least, an equally wonderful source: This we find in a soul calm and serene as the most delightful summer-evening, more expansive than the ocean, more resplendent than yonder sun, and steady as the poles! These intellectual, and consequently immortal treasures rendered him uncommonly great as the child of nature; and our text applies to him very forcibly as enlarged and enobled by mental acquisitions.

Divine Providence gave him opportunities and dispositions to add great acquired, to the greatest natural abilities. If his education were not classical, it was profound: If he had not the comparatively superficial knowledge of all names, he possessed an universal knowledge of things: And tho' no great proportion of his precious time was spent in the study of dead languages, it was because the beautious objects of all kinds of useful and ornamental knowledge invited his attention and persuit, in all the copious elegance of English attire.

His great mind was occupied with correspondent objects. He had well arranged and distinct ideas of all assentially interesting, and truly important facts, domestic and foreign, antient and modern, temporal and spiritual. Among the subjects which Washington investigated, and the objects which he regarded with an assiduity and seriousness becoming their importance, were science, morality and religion; civil and religious liberty; agriculture commerce and navigation; tactics, and the different forms of civil government; the rise of revolutions, and falls of empires, in connection with their causes and consequences; and the religions, laws, customs, characters and origin of nations.

With a singular felicity of perception, he comprehended the subjects of his knowledge in all their extensions and relations; and we well know, that in his conversation, public speeches, and admirable writings, ease and strength were united with all the beauty and simplicity of precision. But as it would require talents brilliant as his own to do justice to a subject of such extent and sublimity, I shall conclude these imperfect remarks on his great literary merit, by observing that the honor of conferring on him the degree of L.L.D. was reserved for Rhode-Island College:* From the œconomy observable in all the variety and profusion, if I may so express myself of heaven's bounties, we are led to conclude that such mental strength and excellence as Washington possessed, must have been properly deposited, furnished with suitable organs, and intended for appropriate and important purposes: And our expectations are fully answered when we view him as entitled to the application of our text, *by the disposals of an all superintending Providence.*

Born and raised under a free government, he early imbibed, and always cherished, and retained the sacred principles of liberty, his birth right, inviolable. Though of respectable descent, ancestry need not be mentioned, where personal and intrinsic worth is so eminent and conspicuous. Nor does he derive any of his greatness from the large possessions with which his many and distinguished virtues, and services, were to as great a degree as he would permit, but by no means adequately rewarded: he conferred honor on affluence. The complicated organ of his vast and noble mind, a glorious specimen of divine ingenuity, was moderately large, elegantly proportioned, and amply endowed with agility and strength, gracefulness and dignity. In early youth his superior parts and abilities attracted public attention; and by traversing a trackless desert, obtaining the intelligence so

* "Sept. 1st, 1790, the degree of Doctor of Laws, was conferred on George Washington, president of the United States of America." Soon afterwards, it appears from the Baptist annual register for 1791, of which Doctor Rippon of London is the editor, that "In a conversation between several friendly gentlemen, which turned chiefly on the confinement of Lewis the little, who, like an absolute sovereign, had said to five and twenty million of people, I will be obeyed; contrasted with the popularity of Washington the Great—it was mentioned, that the Baptist College, in Rhode-Island, had conferred the degree of Doctor of Laws, on the president of the United States; while it seemed to be the general mind that this distinguished character in the history of man, would prefer the laurels of a college to a crown of despotism, one of the company, it is said, quite impromptu, gave vent to the feelings of his heart, in the following effusion:

When kings are mere sovereigns, or tyrants, or tools,
No wonder the people should treat them as fools;
But Washington therefore presides with applause,
Because he well merits the Doctor of Laws.
I'll ne'er be a ruler till I'm L.L.D.
Nor England, nor Scotland shall send it to me,
I'll have my diploma from Providence Hall,
For Washington had, or I'll have none at all."

interesting to his beloved country, and saving Bradock's army on the Monongahela, from the jaws of a cruel death by merciless savages, he proved himself capable of the most difficult, arduous and perilous services. The sagacity and prowess, promptitude and decision, which he displayed, about this time, on several trying occasions, were strongly indicative of his future elevation. And from the universal rectitude of his conduct in private and public, civil and religious life, as well as from the proofs he had furnished of his great military capacity, President Davis, long before there existed a thought of the late revolutionary war, said from the pulpit, "I may point out to the public that heroic youth, Col. Washington, whom I cannot but hope, providence has hitherto preserved for some important service to his country." And this has since assumed the appearance of a divine prediction: For we feel, and the world knows what an *important service he has rendered his country*. When the unhappy controversy between Great-Britain and her thirteen American provinces, rose so high, and produced such effects, that the dreadful appeal to the sword was no longer dispensible, Washington, whose name can receive no additional lustre from epithets, was unanimosly appointed by the representatives of the American people, to head their undisciplined troops, almost without money or arms against British, well armed and well disciplined veterans. The bloody conflicts which ensued, the prodigies of address, valor and perserverance of the commander in chief, and the glorious result are well known and need not now be repeated. His superiority to difficulties, to all other men embarrassing and insuperable, unconquerable fortitude, well-timed, and well-planned attacks on a superior foe, and splendid victories, are clothed in all the elegance and pomp of language by historians and poets of the first eminence. Uninfluenced by ambition, when he had conducted us seven long years, through fields of blood and carnage, to sovereignty, independance and peace, like another Cincinnatus, he returned to his agricultural employments, and sought repose in the shades of retirement. Through his influence, an army angry and distressed from painful, important, and yet uncompensated services, sheathed their swords, and followed the example of their illustrious chief!

But his well-tried, and sterling merit, united to the splendor of his talents, and the unbounded confidence of his fellow-citizens, soon rendered it necessary, from the inefficacy of our governmental arrangements, that he should again embark on the stormy sea of politics. Summoned by his country, to whom he could deny nothing, to assist in forming, and adopting our present energetic, yet free and happy constitution, he readily obeyed; and after the accomplishment of these important objects, he was called by the unanimous voice, of, at least, three millions of people to preside over these sovereign and independent states. To the presidential chair he continued a noble ornament, by the united wish of his grateful country, who delighted to honor him, eight years, and discharged the important duties of this high station with his usual wisdom and firmness, integrity and rectitude. And after retiring the second time, in full possession of the affections and confidence of the people, to the solitude which he was as capable of enjoying, as of adorning public life, he was prevailed on, tho' hoary with years, and covered with glory, to accept the command of our armies, when the political hemisphere wore a most menacing and wrathful aspect. Behold the greatest general in the world, tho' on the borders of three score and ten, in obedience to his much indebted country, ready, again, to take the field against her insulting foes!

And so obvious was the policy of this appointment, that it was anticipated, as well as ardently wished by every intelligent citizen. His martial and august appearance, the sound of his name and voice, the glance of his experienced eye, and the lightning of his sword at the head of our armies, rendered them gloriously enthusiastic, and absolutely invincible! But great as he was by nature, a liberal education, and the display and perfection of his superior powers, natural and acquired, in spheres of action the most conspicuous, elevated and important, he was still greater by the invaluable *gifts of the* G*OD of grace*. Considered as aggrandized by these, our text applies to him with the utmost propriety and force!

Know ye not that a great man, the greatest of men, *is fallen*?

He would have been equalled by several if he had not shone in the mild majesty of morals and religion. This lustre, when other things are equal, gives a decided superiority. Before, and an essential part of his honor was humility. He had as little of that tumid pride, which in its plentitude goes before destruction, as any man on earth. He always felt his dependance as man; and trusting in the living GOD, whom he served, his boldness and magnanimity, could be equalled by nothing but his modesty and humility. By these radical advantages, he displayed an equanimity through the most trying extremes of fortune, which does the highest honor to the human character. He was the same whether struggling to keep the fragments of a naked army together in the dismal depths of winter, against a greatly superior foe, or presiding under the laurel wreath over four millions of free men!

He was too great to be depressed or elated by any thing that ceases with this life.

> 'Tis moral grandeur makes the mighty man.
> How little they who think ought great below!

Washington's as all true wisdom ever did, and always must, began with the fear, which was the only fear he ever knew, the *fear of the Lord of Hosts*: And this was truly filial, for its transcendently glorious object, was equally the object of his supreme affection.

These divine and immortal principles preserved his tongue from every species of profanity, and not only his actions but his heart from pollution. Alexander conquered the world; but far from ruling his spirit, or being in any respect his own master, he fell an early and loathsome sacrifice to intemperance. Far greater than Alexander the great, was Washington: He ruled his appetites and passions in scenes of the greatest trial and temptation; and will remain forever a bright example, to all men, of temperance and moderation in all things, as well as a striking contrast to all, "*The rational foul kennels of excess.*"

His piety, though like his other shining excellencies unaustentatious, was genuine and exalted. Through the veil of all his modest reserve, it was discoverable in the whole tenor of his conduct, and especially in his admirable and appropriate answers to the numerous addresses of his almost adoring fellow-citizens where he uniformly, and with glowing gratitude ascribes all the glory of his unparralelled successes to GOD.

How high christianity stood in his estimation, and how near its interests lay to his heart, every one may see, who has read his excellent answers to the congratulatory addresses of various religious bodies, on his first election to the chief magistracy of these United States. And his opinion of religion in a political view, I will do myself the honor to give you in his own words; so that though alas! he is dead, he still to his weeping country thus speaketh: "Of all the dispositions and habits which lead to political prosperity, religion and morality, are indispensable supports. In vain would that man claim the tribute of patriotism, who should labor to subvert these great pillars of human happiness, these firmest props of the duties of men and citizens. The mere politician, equally with the pious man, ought to respect and cherish them. A volume could not trace all their connections with private and public felicity. Let it simply be asked, where is the security for property, for reputation, for life, if the sense of religious obligation desert the oaths which are the instruments of investigation in courts of justice? And let us with caution indulge the supposition, that morality can be maintained without religion. Whatever may be conceded to the influence of refined education on minds of peculiar structure, reason and experience both forbid us to expect that national morality can prevail in exclusion of religious principles. 'Tis substantially true, that virtue or morality is a necessary spring of popular government. The rule indeed extends with more or less force to every species of free government. Who that is a sincere friend to it can look with indifference upon attempts to shake the foundation of the fabrick! Promote then, as an object of primary importance, institutions for the general diffusion of knowledge; in proportion as the structure of a government gives force to public opinion, it is essential that public opinion should be enlightened."

Ye winds, wait these sentiments on your swift pinions; and ye sunbeams record them in more than golden characters, throughout the political world!

American, English, French, and all other politicians, hear him who was as famous in the cabinet, as formidable in the tented field! In proportion as he is regarded, will be prevented the effusion of blood; hostilities will cease, and order and confidence between rulers and the ruled, individuals and nations, will ensue.

The essential advantages of religion, in a political light, were discovered clearly, and felt impressively by the American sage, whose eagle eye distinguished plainly betwixt vain pretenders to religion, and its real possessors; and whose cool deliberative sagacity, discerned the difference between genuine religion, as delineated in the holy scriptures, and the empty forms, gross adulterations, and shameful abuses of it. And it is difficult to determine, whether he were most correct and eminent in religious theory or practice. But one thing, and that of vast importance, is evident: Bright as this sun of human glory shone, with the sweetly blended rays of morality and religion, through every stage, and in every condition of life, like the cloudless star of day, gently and with increasing majesty, sinking beneath the western horizon, his mild effulgence was greatest in death!

His mind was tranquil and serene,
No terrors in his looks were seen;
A Saviour's smile dispell'd the gloom,
And smooth'd his passage to the tomb.

O Death! never hadst thou, but in one astonishing instance, such a prisoner before!

A victory, which enraged Britain's cannon, sword and gold, though well tried, could never effect, is thine! But monster! spare thy ghastly smile! Momentary will be thy triumph! As the declining sun, by divine energy, soon ascends with renewed splendors, Washington shall ere long burst thy bands asunder, all immortal! A while venerable shade! we must leave thy precious remains enshrined by trembling hands, with solemn pomp, and thy deathless part under the sublime character, of the spirit of a just man made perfect, in lively and well-founded hope of their re-union, and of the consummation of *thy glory and felicity*! And is a great man fallen? Is Washington no more? Alas is he gone! gone forever! The conqueror of royal armies and their mighty generals, the late president of the United States, and later commander in chief of the American armies, is fallen! The father, friend, benefactor and bulwark of his country, is fallen! Washington is fallen! A scene of action the most brilliant; a life with virtuous and heroic deeds, the most luminous, is now the subject of eulogy! All the respectful, affectionate, and aggrandizing epithets, contained in our language, are employed in vain, to set his exalted merit in an adequately conspicuous point of light: And we anticipate the elaborate productions of rival pens of the first distinction, now moving with celerity and ardor, to give an admiring world the life of Washington: But to draw his true portrait is more than mortal hands can do; "*It merits a divine.*" "When he went out to the gate, through the city, when he prepared his seat in the street, the young men saw him and hid themselves; and the aged arose and stood up; the princes refrained talking, and laid their hand on their mouth; the nobles held their peace and their tongues cleaved to the roof of their mouth. When the ear heard him, then it blessed him; and when the eye saw him, it gave witness to him; because he delivered the poor that cried, and the fatherless, and him that had none to help him. The blessing of him that was ready to perish, camc upon him; and he caused the widow's heart to sing for joy. He put on righteousness, and it clothed him; his judgment was a robe and a diadem. He was eyes to the blind, and feet to the lame; he was a father to the poor, and the cause that he knew not he searched out. And he brake the jaws of the wicked and pluckt the spoil out of his teeth." To this inimitable sketch by the pencil of inspiration, let us add, in silent grief for our irreparable loss, badges of deep mourning, melting eyes and bleeding hearts, which will more emphatically express his worth than the sublimest imagery, and the most glowing encomium in the hands of erudition and art.

And permit me to observe, that the greatest honor of all that we can do to his memory, and the best improvement that we can make of his life and death is to imitate his virtuous and pious examples: And this may be done by those of the tenderest capacities, and in the lowest ranks of society.

Honor and fame from no condition rise,
Act well your part there all the honor lies.

My fair hearers, may I not hope that you will do more than weep? This is natural, it is becoming, it is unavoidable. Many of you could not refrain from tears when, some years ago, you saw the face of the hero who had, for you, endured so many painful years of fatigue, and hardships of all kinds, amidst dangers in all forms: Much more abundantly must your tears flow, now you hear your great friend and benefactor, is no more. Mourn with his venerable relict, sinking under stupendous grief, for him who has slain your enemies, saved your country, "and put on ornaments of gold upon your apparel": But I am persuaded you will do more; you will, like the great and virtuous Washington, in your measure, increase the dignity and happiness of human nature; you will adorn by your solid, though private virtues, social life, of which you were intended to be the brightest ornaments.

War-worn veterans! venerable fathers! you must feel the most pungent grief for him who led you in battle and to victory: And having enjoyed the advantages of his glorious examples, both in the peaceful cabinet, and on the hostile plains, you need not be reminded of your special obligations to patriotic virtue, and genuine piety.

He has taught you how to live and how to die.

Painfully tender, on this solemn occasion, must be the feelings of you, my fellow citizens, who lately, at the appearance of danger stepped forward, with an honorable zeal, in your country's defence. Your great commander in chief, is fallen! I see you feel the shock, and you need not wish to conceal it.

Masculine cheeks bedew'd with tears,
Become the august occasion;
Nor need they blush, should heaving sighs
Escape the manly breast, to day.

We have sustained, our country, and the world have sustained no common loss. Nations should mourn. *Our nation does mourn.* Our venerable and much beloved chief magistrate, the supreme council of the land, our bereaved armies, rising navy, cities, towns and villages, exhibit a widely-extended, endlessly-diversified, and most melancholy scene of deep mourning! All christian and masonic societies with an honest pride and exultation claiming Washington as their brother, are laudably ambitious of making the most emphatical expressions of their fraternal regard and affection. The Cincinnati, after these, in particular, and all other societies in general; and in fine all descriptions of the American people, have variously, and yet as with one voice, testified their high respect, and most cordial affection, for the dear and illustrious object of their common attachment. "*Know ye not that there is a great man fallen?*" Methinks I hear the honorable city council, and the rest of the worthy magistrates present, the officers of all grades, the reverend clergy, the congregation who statedly meet here, and the respectable residue of this vast mourning concourse, reply—Alas! too well we know it! The most callous heart feels it! Washington is indeed fallen! The awful report is propagated in thunder along the North American coast and reverberates in tremendous accents from the distant hills! The shock of Mount Vernon, trembling from the summit to its affrighted centre, shakes the continent from New-Hampshire to Georgia! O fatal, and solitary Mount Vernon is an appellation that no longer becomes thee, and may thine appearance correspond with thy situation! No more let cheerful green array thee!*

Thine august inhabitant is fallen! But words are vain! Come more expressive silence, we resign the unutterable theme to thee!

* As several of the author's friends politely hinted that when the following imprecations on Mount Vernon were delivered from the pulpit, in imitation of David's lamentation over Saul and Jonathan, some thought them liable to an unfavorable construction, he has excluded them from the sermon, but to prevent any mistake as to their matter, amongst the numbers who heard them, they are retained in this place:

When vernal suns return, let vernal showers and dews withhold their wonted influence, and perpetuate thy melancholy hue! Let germinating sap no more ascend thy variegated shrubs and trees! Odoriferous breezes wake there no more! Barren as Gilboa, fatal to Jonathan and Saul, let blasting winds henceforward howl through the desolated mansion of that pale mount!

— 50 —

ON THE EVILS OF A WEAK GOVERNMENT

John Smalley

HARTFORD

1800

JOHN SMALLEY (1734-1820). A Yale graduate in 1756, Smalley studied at first with Eleazar Wheelock and after graduation with Joseph Bellamy, both New Light ministers. Ezra Stiles (later president of Yale) was his tutor. Smalley held a pastorate for fifty years at Farmington (New Britain), Connecticut. Though regarded as a mediocre preacher, he was of first importance as a theologian of his generation, and he possessed a keen mind and a vigorous writing style. These traits are displayed in a number of publications, including forty-eight sermons published in two volumes in 1803 and 1814. He was awarded a D.D. by the College of New Jersey (Princeton) in 1800.

Smalley was at first lukewarm to the cause of independence and came under attack by those who fervently desired it, including the local Committee of the Sons of Liberty. Ezra Stiles attributed Smalley's stance to theological rather than political reasoning, for Smalley firmly believed that the tradition of passive obedience and nonresistance in civil matters was the true biblical teaching.

The piece reprinted here was preached as the Connecticut election sermon in 1800.

ON THE EVILS OF A WEAK GOVERNMENT.

SERMON,

PREACHED ON THE

GENERAL ELECTION

AT HARTFORD, IN CONNECTICUT,

MAY 8, 1800.

By JOHN SMALLEY, A. M.

PASTOR OF A CHURCH IN BERLIN.

HARTFORD:

PRINTED BY HUDSON AND GOODWIN.

1800.

And I will give children to be their princes, and babes shall rule over them. And the people shall be oppressed, every one by another, and every one by his neighbour: the child shall behave himself proudly against the ancient, and the base against the honorable.

Isaiah iii. 4, 5.

When we read and hear such threatening predictions as this; and see our judges as at the first, and our counsellors and governors as at the beginning—equally wise and good; we are ready to bless ourselves, and to say in our hearts, These things shall not come upon us. That the whole of what is here foretold, has not yet come upon us, we have certainly great reason to bless God, and to congratulate one another. But it should be remembered, that neither past mercies, nor present happy circumstances, are any security against evils to come. Surprising changes in this fallen world, have ever been frequent, and are still to be expected. Prosperity and adversity, like sunshine and storms, are wont to follow each other, almost in constant rotation. Communities, as well as individuals, that have been remarkably raised up, are often as wonderfully cast down, in the providence of God, when most exalted. "He blesseth them also," it is said,* "so that they are multiplied greatly, and suffereth not their cattle to decrease. Again they are minished, and brought low, through oppression, affliction and sorrow."

Of such vicissitudes, the chosen people threatened in our text, was a striking and an instructive example. This nation had long been favored, in regard to government, as well as religion, far beyond any other then on the earth. From its earliest infancy, it had been under the peculiar guardianship of heaven. "When Israel was a child," says the most High in Hosea,† "then I loved him, and called my son out of Egypt: I taught Ephraim also to go, taking them by their arms: I drew them with cords of a man, with bands of love; and I was to them as they that take off the yoke."

They had been liberated from powerful oppressors, and cruel taskmasters, by the out-stretched arm of the Almighty. They had been

* Psalm cvii. 38, 39.
† Chap. xi. 1–4.

led like a flock, through the Red Sea, and forty years in a most perilous, howling wilderness, by the hand of Moses and Aaron. Under Joshua, their great and beloved general, they had vanquished mighty armies; and had obtained a peaceful settlement as a free and an independent people, in a land flowing with milk and honey.

Here, when they forgat God their saviour, who had done such great things for them, and so many wonderous works before their eyes, he sometimes left them to have no guide, overseer or ruler; and suffered the heathen around them, to make terrible inroads on their borders. Nevertheless, as often as they cried unto the Lord in their distresses, he raised them up judges—valiant, righteous men, to deliver them out of the hand of their enemies, and to administer justice among them. Afterwards, because of their uneasiness, and the hardness of their hearts, God gave them kings; and these, several of them, were very eminent for wisdom and virtue. Nor was their happiness, in this respect, yet at an end; for Isaiah prophesied no later than the reign of Hezekiah; one of the most amiable and best of princes.

But, from the days of their fathers, they had gone away from God's ordinances; and now, it seems, the measure of their iniquities was almost full. A very awful decree of the holy one of Israel against them is therefore here announced. See the preceding context.

> For, behold, the Lord, the Lord of hosts, doth take away from Jerusalem, and from Judah, the stay and the staff; the whole stay of bread, and the whole stay of water; the mighty man, and the man of war; the judge, and the prophet, and the prudent, and the ancient; the captain of fifty, and the honorable man, and the counsellor, and the cunning artificer, and the eloquent orator. *And I will give children to be their princes, &c.*

From my text, thus connected, the doctrine deducible, which will be our present subject, is this:

> *That to be under a weak government, is one of the greatest calamities, ever sent upon a people.*

This, you observe, is here threatened together with drouth and famine in the extreme—a total want of bread and of water; as well as being bereaved of the most eminent men, in every necessary employment: and it is mentioned last, and most enlarged upon, as the consummation of misery.

But, after explaining the calamity designed, and some of the principal causes of it, I shall attend, more particularly, to the proof and illustration of this doctrine.

There are two senses, in which government is said to be weak: when it is unwise; and when it wants energy. The latter is the more extensive signification of the phrase; and it comprehends the former: this, therefore, is the sense now to be considered. By a weak government will be meant, one that wants energy; whether through the weakness of those by whom it is administered, or by any other means.

To mention, with a little enlargement, some of the most common causes of so great an evil, will not be foreign to the design of this anniversary.

1. That the government of a nation or state has not proper energy, may be the fault of its constitution. A form of government may be such, that, unless the administration of it be arbitrary, it will necessarily be weak.

To give rulers all that power, and reserve to the subjects all that liberty, which is best for the people, is a nice point; very difficult, I imagine, to be exactly hit, by the wisest of men, and men the most disinterested. There is danger of erring, undoubtedly, on either hand; of abridging freedom, as well as of limiting authority, more than is for the greatest general good—of adopting a constitution too despotic, as well as one too feeble. But when it is left to the people at large, what government they will be under, the error most to be apprehended, I believe, is on the side of the inefficiency.

The love of liberty is natural to all mankind; and even to birds, and four-footed animals, and creeping things. Of this celebrated virtue, we lost nothing by the fall of our first parents. Every one, however depraved in other respects, wishes to be free—unboundedly free; to have none above him; to be his own subject, his own governor, his own judge. And when, for obtaining the advantages of social union, individuals give up to the community, or to any constituted authorities, a power over their words and actions, their property and lives; they do it with great reluctance, and as sparingly as possible.

To observe the extreme reluctance of some, on such occasions—to see how strenuously they will dispute every inch of power, vested any where, which might possibly be abused, or turned against themselves; is apt to remind one of the cautious policy of certain ancient pagans, described by Jeremiah, in regard to their gods. Not only would they have gods of their own making, and made of such materials that they must needs be born, because they could not go; but, as wooden gods could fall and might happen to fall upon the makers of them, or on their children, or valuable furniture; for full security, they *fastened them with nails and with hammers.* "Be not afraid of them," says the prophet; "for they cannot do evil; neither also is it in them to do good."

Checks, unquestionably, there ought to be, on every department of a free government: But if such checks be laid upon rulers, that the ruled are under no check at all, harmless, indeed, will such rulers be; but altogether insignificant. These *servants of the people*, must have more power than the child, and the base, who proudly so call them; unless we would have them miserable gods, or *ministers of God to us for good*—their scripture titles. They must have authority to punish treasonable lies against themselves, as well as slanders against the meanest of their subjects; otherwise, who will be afraid of them? Or what protection can they afford?

2. That the government of a people is too weak, may be the fault of those betrusted with its administration. It may be owing to their weakness; or to their indolence, or slowness in doing business; or to their excessive lenity; or to their not being of a virtuous character, or not paying a due attention to the strict regularity of their own lives. These particulars, suffer me cursorily to go over.

When the rulers of a land are children; whether in understanding, or in firmness and stability of mind, we are not certainly to expect that the reins of government will be guided with discretion, and held with sufficient force. To govern well, at least in the higher and more difficult offices, considerable theoretic knowledge, some experience, and more than common natural powers, are altogether necessary. And so is that degree of courage and inflexibility, which will enable a man to maintain his post, and to persevere in what appears to him the plain path of duty; unmoved by noisy opposition—undaunted by popular clamor—undismayed by imminent danger.

To support an efficient government, rulers must likewise be men of vigilance and activity. "He that ruleth," says an apostle,* "with dili-

* Rom. xii. 8.

gence." And of Jeroboam it was said,* "Solomon, seeing the young man that he was industrious, he made him ruler over all the charge of the house of Joseph." A commonwealth, under the superintendency of indolent men, will resemble the field of the slothful which we read of, that was "all grown over with thorns; the face of it covered with nettles, and the stone wall thereof broken down." Or, though rulers be not "slothful in business"; they may be so slow in transacting it, and in bringing any thing to a termination, as very much to lower the tone, and defeat the salutary designs, of civil government. When courts of justice are so dilatory in their decisions, and such endless evasions, and reviews, are admitted; that a man had better lose almost any debt or damage, than commence a legal process for a recovery, the protection of law must be lamentably weak.

Excessive lenity, will have a similar effect. Mercy, is indeed an amiable attribute; to pass over a transgression, is said to be the glory of a man; and being ready to forgive, is a duty much inculcated in the word of God: But in one who sustains any place of authority, whether that of a parent, or master, or civil magistrate; lenity and indulgence may be carried farther than is the glory or duty of a man; unless it be his duty and glory to have no government. Should rulers remit crimes, or pass them over without condemnation, when the public good, or righting an injured individual, requires their punishment; merciful they might be, but not as our Father in heaven is merciful.

Liberality to the poor, out of one's own proper goods, is a capital christian virtue; but of the property of other people, judges and lawgivers, may possibly be over liberal. The persons even of the poor, are not to be respected in judgment. Making provision by law, for supporting such as are unable to support themselves, is doubtless very commendable; but why those who happen to be the creditors of the poor; who have helped them much already, and suffered much by their slackness and breach of promise, should be still obliged to lose ten times more for their relief, or for the relief of their families, than others equally able, it is not easy to conceive. And should courts of law, or courts of equity, cancel the debts of men, whenever they plead a present incapacity to pay them, whether such clemency might not too much weaken government, as a security to every one in his

* 1 Kings XI, 28.

rightful claims, may be a question. Indeed, in any case, to give an insolvent debtor a final discharge from all he owes, without the consent of his creditors, looks like giving him a licence to be an unrighteous man. For can it ever be right, or can any court under heaven make it right, for a man not to pay his promised debts, for value received, when now he has money enough, because once, the payment of them was not in the power of his hands.

Thus to exonerate of a heavy load of old debts, one deeply insolvent, is necessary, it will be said; as without this he could have no courage to commence business anew. And, no doubt, such expected exoneration, will be a mighty encouragement to extravagant adventurers, who have nothing to lose, since, by running the greatest hazards, with the slenderest chance of immense gain, they risk only the property of others. If successful, the profit is their own; if unsuccessful, the loss is their neighbour's. But if the tendency of being thus merciful, were much better than it is; or the urgency for it far greater; would it not be doing evil that good may come. "He that ruleth over men must be just."* The laws of truth and righteousness, are not noses of wax; to be bent any way, as will suit present convenience. It is dangerous to break down, or break over, the fixed barrier of eternal justice, on any pretence of temporary necessity.

One way more was hinted, in which those who govern, may weaken government; and that is, by being men of a vicious character; or by not paying a due attention to the strict regularity of their own lives. Indeed, "a wicked ruler" is often strong, and fierce, and active, as "a roaring lion and a ranging bear"; but rarely for the benefit of "the poor people." He will not be eager to pluck the spoil out of the mouth of the fraudulent villain, or the violent oppressor; unless that he may get it into his own. Nor will authority, in the hands of libertine men, however it may terrify, be much revered. When the makers or judges of laws, are themselves notorious breakers of them, or of the laws of heaven, government will necessarily fall into contempt. It is also to be observed, that advancing to posts of honor, men of loose principles and morals, gives reputation to licentiousness, and stamps it as the current fashion. Their example will encourage evil doers, more than all the punishments they are likely to inflict, will be a

* 2 Sam. xxiii. 3.

terror to them. "The wicked walk on every side when the vilest men are exalted."*

But rulers may be far from being the vilest men, they may be very good men; and yet, by an incautious conformity to common practices, supposed to be innocent, they may too much countenance some things which are of very hurtful tendency. Permit me to instance in one particular. "It is not for kings," we read, "to drink wine, nor for princes strong drink."† And certainly, it is not for the lower classes to drink so much of these as many of them do, if they regard their health, or competence, or peace. I select this instance, because it is directly pertinent to the main subject in hand. Nothing is a greater weakener of government—nothing makes the multitude more heady and high-minded—nothing raises oftener or louder, the cry of liberty and equality—nothing more emboldens and inflames that little member, which boasteth great things, and setteth on fire the whole course of nature—nothing, in a word, makes men more incapable of governing themselves, or of being governed, than strong drink. Now, if rulers drink, though not to drunkenness; not so as quite to "forget the law," or greatly to "pervert the judgment of any"; if they only drink as much as is very universally customary, in polite circles, on great occasions; though they do not hurt themselves, they may too much sanction that which will hurt their inferiors. That divine injunction, "Thou shalt not follow a multitude to do evil,"‡ lies with peculiar weight on civil rulers, as well as religious teachers. They, more than others, are under obligation to lead the multitude, in whatsoever things are sober, wise and good. They, of all men, are bound in duty to abstain from all appearance of any thing, which, improved upon by bungling eager imitators, might grow into a practice pernicious to society. Nor should it be forgotten, that every deviation from rectitude of conduct, lessens the dignity, and lowers the authority of great men. "Dead flies cause the ointment of the apothecary to send forth a stinking savor: so doth a little folly, him that is in reputation for wisdom and honor."§ But,

3. That weakness of government which is a calamity to any people,

* Psalm xii. 8.

† Prov. xxxi. 4.

‡ Exod. xxiii. 2.

§ Eccl. x. 1.

is often principally the fault of the people themselves. It may be owing to their negligence, or to their caprice and folly, in the choice of their rulers; or it may be owing to their ill-treatment of them when chosen. A government most excellent in its constitution, and most wise, just and firm, in its administration, may be enervated, or rendered inadequate, by the ungovernableness of the people: By their revilings and slanders—their haughtiness and insolence—their factions and tumults. David once said, "I am this day weak, though anointed king; and these men, the sons of Zeruiah, are too hard for me."*

Nor must it be omitted, that, besides the immediate natural causes of a weak government, the irreligion, or general wickedness of a people, may be its procuring cause, as a judgment of heaven. "The most High ruleth in the" nations of men; "and giveth" the dominion over them, "to whomsoever he will."† "For promotion cometh neither from the east, nor from the west, nor from the south; but God is the judge; he putteth down one, and setteth up another."‡ When the ways of a people please the Lord—when they fear him, and work righteousness; among other blessings, he gives them good governors, under whose able and equitable administration, they lead quiet and peaceable lives. On the contrary, when they forget him, neglect his worship, and disregard his word; among other modes of punishment, he takes away their wise and faithful magistrates, and gives them weak or wicked ones in their stead; or leaves them to trample all authority under foot. This was the cause of the calamities threatened in our text and context. See the eighth verse, which concludes the paragraph. "For Jerusalem is ruined, and Judah is fallen; because their tongue and their doings are against the Lord, to provoke the eyes of his glory."

Let us now attend, as was proposed, to the proof and illustration of the doctrine laid down: That, of all the calamities ever sent upon a people, being under a weak government, is one of the most deplorable.

It is said,§ "Woe to thee, O land, when thy king is a child." It is

* 2 Sam. iii. 39.

† Dan. iv. 32.

‡ Psal. lxxv. 6, 7.

§ Eccl. x. 16.

also asked,* "If the foundations be destroyed, what can the righteous do?" And if we consider the matter, it may easily be seen, that the people of all characters, and not merely the righteous among them, must be in a very wretched condition, should government be overturned, or have no coercive force.

First; an exposedness to all manner of mutual injuries, without redress, is one obvious evil thence arising. *The people shall be oppressed, every one by another, and every one by his neighbour.*

"Surely oppression maketh a wise man mad," is an observation of the royal preacher.† And many are the accounts in history, of oppression's having had this effect on a multitude of men, the wise among the foolish. How often have whole nations raved and raged, like the fiercest of animals, under the operation of the hydrophobia, at only a distant apprension of this terrible evil?

I am sensible, it is the dread of oppression from government, and not of being oppressed one by another, through the want or weakness of it, that usually occasions this rage, and these ravings. The people are ten times more apt to be afraid of having heavy burdens and grievous restraints laid upon them, by the best men in power, than of any thing they might be in danger of suffering from their equals, however wicked, and however unrestrained. But what can be the reason of this? Is it because there is not really as much mischief to be feared, from individual, as from public oppression? From the oppressions of the many, as of the few? From the unrighteousness of millions, let loose, as from that of one man, or a small number of men?

This, certainly, is not the case; this cannot be the reason. When there is no law, and every one does what he thinks fit, without fear of punishment, the people, I believe, have ever been, and are ever likely to be, much more unhappy than even under a very despotic and oppressive government.

What then *is* the reason? Why are the people, whose voice is said to be the voice of God, so much more ready to sound and take an alarm, when threatened with the latter, than with the former of these evils? Why are they so loud and tumultuous, when their liberties are

* Psal. xi. 3.
† Eccl. vii. 7.

thought to be in any danger; and so quiet and easy, when government is rudely attacked, and ready to be overthrown? Why is the shock of terror so much greater and more universal, at the remotest prospect of tyranny, than at the nearest, and most evident approximation to total anarchy? There may be several reasons.

One, probably, is; when the people are oppressed by each other, their sufferings are separately felt: Whereas, oppression from the higher powers falls upon all in a body. In the former case, every one bears his own different burdens; and divided complaints, though bitter, make but a confused and feeble murmur: in the latter case, all feel or fear the same; all voices, therefore, are united in one tremendous cry.

Another reason may be; under oppression from government, often no other way of relief is seen, than popular combinations and insurrections; but when injuries are done us by individuals, because there is no government to restrain them, a remedy is always near and obvious. If every one is oppressed, every one can be an oppressor. If a man's neighbours all bite and devour him, he can bite and devour all his neighbours. Hence, a dissolution of government, instead of being universally deprecated, appears to many, "A consummation devoutly to be wished."

But there is another cause of the wonderful phenomenon I am accounting for, more influential perhaps with the most, than both the forementioned. It is owing to charity. A kind of charity, not the exclusive glory of modern times; but entirely peculiar to fallen creatures. A kind of charity, which covers a multitude of our own sins, from our own sight. A kind of charity which always begins, and ends, at home; though often extensive in its circuits. From this boasted charity, we are ever inclined to hope all things, and believe all things, in favour of any number, or class, or order of beings, in which we ourselves are included. Thus men, naturally think of mankind, more highly than they ought to think. Frenchmen, of the French: Britons, of the British: Americans, of the people of America: Those of every state and town, of their own state's men and town's men; and men of every calling, of their brethren of the same occupation, collectively considered. In like manner, the common people, think the common people exceedingly honest, harmless, and virtuous; while of those in power, though of their own choosing, and just chosen out of all the people, they have not near so favorable an opinion. That the people should have too much liberty, therefore, they are not at all afraid: that rulers will not have checks enough upon them, is all their fear.

This beam, of selfish liberality of sentiment, it may be impossible for us to cast wholly out of our eye: But that, round the edges of it, we may get some glimpse of real human nature; I know of no better way than to look upon mankind one by one; or in circles not including ourselves. Let us then think of other nations; other states; other towns, and neighbourhoods; or of particular persons among our nearest neighbours. In this separate view, let us search and look; let us impartially examine characters. Where do we find a great predominance of the innocent inoffensive people? Where do we find a nation, or state, or town, or society, except our own, so very virtuous? Where do we find many individuals, besides ourselves, so just and true, temperate and chaste, meek and merciful; so free from coveteousness, pride, envy, revenge, and every unfriendly passion, that we could live safely among them, were they at full liberty from all the restraints of law and government?

Indeed, how great an alteration this would make, in the apparent characters of most men, it is difficult to conceive, without the trial. A very partial trial of it, for a short time, some of us have once seen; when it was made lawful to discharge pecuniary obligations, at the rate of a tenth, a twentieth, and even a fiftieth, of the real value justly due. We then had a convincing evidence, that the external justice of our common honest people, is owing to the expected compulsion of civil law, much more than to uprightness of heart, or feelings of conscience, or any dread of a higher tribunal. From this specimen, and from the sacred story of the behaviour of the men of Benjamin, relative to the Levite from mount Ephraim, when "there was no king in Israel; and every one did that which was right in his own eyes"; we may have some faint idea of the horrid scenes of unrighteousness, lewdness and cruelty, that would every where be acted, were it not for the fear of temporal punishment. From all that we have read of the destruction of mankind by one another, when ever they are at liberty; and from recent indisputable information of the shocking state of things, where government has been overturned; we may well believe that the scripture accounts of the depravity of men, are no exaggeration. Not even the following: "Their throat is an open sepulchre; with their tongues they have used deceit; the poison of asps is under their lips; whose mouth is full of cursing and bitterness; their feet are swift to shed blood. Destruction and misery are in their ways, and the way of peace have they not known."*

But if this be a true portrait of fallen men, when left to themselves, how much are we indebted to the restraint laid upon them, for the little peace we enjoy? And may we not well be convinced, that all the terror of the civil sword, in the most faithful and skilful hands, will not be more than enough to restrain from iniquity, such a race of beings, so that they may dwell together, not in unity, as brethren, but with any tolerable safety? Especially if, as is added to finish the above picture, "There is no fear of God before their eyes"? And that this last trait, is still a part of the character of many, is abundantly evident, both from their avowed principles and open practices. Now this being the case, that while the hearts of men are fully set in them to do evil, they have no fear of the God of heaven to restrain them; were it not for the dread of gods on earth, our civil rulers, what security should we have, for our names, or property, or lives? If we had no other evil to apprehend, from weakness of government, than only this, of lying open to all manner of mutual oppressions, slander, frauds and violences; it would, even then, be evidently one of the greatest calamities that could befal a people.

But a second evil, some what distinct, and worthy of some notice, is suggested in our text: No one in a subordinate station would keep his proper place, or treat his superiors with suitable respect. *The child shall behave himself proudly against the ancient, and the base against the honorable.*

Solomon says, "There is an evil which I have seen under the sun, as an error that proceedeth from the ruler: Folly is set in great dignity, and the rich in low place. I have seen servants riding upon horses, and princes walking as servants upon the earth."† When authority fails, or is obstructed, at the fountain head, its remotest streams must, in a little time, run low. If parents will not obey magistrates, children will be disobedient to parents; if masters refuse subjection to

* Rom. iii. 13–17.
† Eccl. x. 5, 6, 7.

the higher powers, their servants and apprentices will soon pay as little regard to their injunctions. Thus this evil proceedeth from the ruler; or from his not being able to rule. And a serious evil it certainly is. By superiors, in every degree, it will soon be very sensibly felt. They will have none to fear them, none to honor them, none over whom they can have any command. Inferiors, of the very lowest grade, may exult, for a while, in such æras of freedom; and think them glorious times. But even to these—to the child and the base, this turning of things upside down, generally proves fatal in the end. Being under no control, they spend their time in idleness; waste their substance, if they have any, in riotous living; have recourse to pilfering, gambling, and every hazardous expedient, to support their extravagances, and by various foolish and hurtful practices, soon plunge themselves into irrecoverable wretchedness and ruin.

There is yet a third capital evil, arising from too weak a government, which, though not mentioned in our text, should be briefly noticed, when treating of this subject at large. A community in such a situation, will be able to make little defence against a foreign enemy. Like the people of Laish, who had no magistrate in the land to put them to shame in any thing; they will be an easy prey to any handful of enterprising invaders. No resources can be drawn forth —no navies furnished—no armies raised and supplied—no fortifications erected and garrisoned, without energy in government. What Solomon says of a man that has no rule over his own spirit, holds equally true of an ungoverned nation: it "is as a city that is broken down, and without walls."

The doctrine, I conceive, needs no farther illustration or proof. It only remains, that I endeavor to point out some useful inferences from it, applicable to our own times, and to the present occasion.

1. The holy scriptures may hence be vindicated, in their being so much on the side of government; and no more favorable to the insurrection of inferiors.

On these topics, it must be acknowledged, the spirit of the gospel, as well as of the old testament, is somewhat different from the spirit that worketh in the children of disobedience, among whom we have all had our conversation. Our Saviour "went about doing good, and healing all that were oppressed of the devil"; but under the political oppressions of the Jews, his countrymen, he seemed not much to sympathize with them. When it hurt their consciences to pay tribute to a foreign power, and they asked him whether it were lawful; his answer was, "Render to Caesar, the things that are Caesar's, and to God, the things that are God's." He constantly preached peace, meekness, humility and submission. His apostles in like manner, taught children to obey and honor their parents: and servants to be "subject to their own masters, with all fear; not only to the good and gentle, but also to the froward." And, instead of animating their numerous proselytes, at Crete, at Rome, and all over the world, to rise in arms against these rulers of the earth who were their unrighteous and unmerciful persecutors; they would have them "put in mind to be subject to principalities and powers, to obey magistrates":* they exhorted them to "submit themselves to every ordinance of man, for the Lord's sake";† and told them, "Whosoever resisteth the power, resisteth the ordinance of God; and they that resist shall receive to themselves damnation."‡

At this distance of time, and after so many revolutions, such passages as these may seem hard sayings, to some good soldiers, even of Jesus Christ. No wonder that the inculcators of so much poverty of spirit, should be rejected with scorn, and treated with scurrility, in this "age of reason." We are not to wonder, were there no other cause, that infidelity should exceedingly increase, in these times of "illumination."

To the spiritually minded Christian, however, it will readily occur, in favour of the author and finisher of our faith, and his first ministers, that the great object they had in view, was to save the souls of men; and that, teaching them to be meek and lowly in heart, poor in spirit, and contented in whatsoever state they were, was better adapted to this design; than filling the heads of inferiors with exalted notions of the equal "rights of man"; inflaming their hearts with pride and angry passions; and throwing families into envying and strife, and nations into the convulsions of civil war; till every one can be as free as the freest, and as high as the highest.

But, leaving things eternal out of the question; according to the subject to which we have now been attending, if the preachers and

* Tit. iii. 1.

† 1 Pet. ii. 13.

‡ Rom. xiii. 2.

penmen of the New-Testament had aimed only to promote the temporal happiness, of only the lower classes of mankind, they would have done wisely in writing and preaching, on the duties of subordination, exactly as they did. Never can there be peace on earth, or any safety among men, while children are allowed to rise up against their parents, servants against their masters, and subjects against their civil rulers, whenever they think differently from them, or dislike their government. Thus to make the child, the governor of his governors, and the base, the judge of his judges, is the certain way to endless confusion, in all human societies.

2. If the doctrine insisted on be true, it follows, that a ready submission to all those burdens which are necessary for the support of good government, and for national defence, is the wisdom, as well as duty of any people.

The apostle to the Romans, having said, "The powers that be are ordained of God"; having observed that the benevolent end of their ordination was the good of the people; and, on these grounds, having enjoined subjection to them, he adds; "For this cause pay ye tribute also: for they are God's ministers, attending continually upon this very thing."

Public expenses are apt to appear to many, excessively high: but, perhaps, they do not well consider the real occasion there is for great expenditures, in a nation or state of any magnitude.

In order to the support of good government, many rulers, of high and low degree, are absolutely necessary. And it is necessary that those who occupy the higher offices, should be men of superior knowledge, and uncommon natural abilities: such knowledge as is not easily acquired, and such abilities as might procure them a plentiful income in other occupations. If the bramble, or the shrub oak, were adequate to rule over the trees, a cheap government might be expected; but if the vine, the fig-tree, and the olive-tree, must be promoted; we are not to think that these will leave their rich fruits; their sweetness, and fatness, without a suitable compensation. Besides, rulers of high rank, must be at no inconsiderable expense, to support the proper dignity of their stations. It is also to be taken into the account, that the duties of those who rule well, and attend continually upon this very thing, are not only exceedingly laborious, but that some parts of the essential services they have to render must be very disagreeable; if they have any compassionate sensibility. The execution of deserved vengeance, is said to be God's strange work; as being, in itself, most opposite to one whose nature is love, and who delighteth in mercy. And, doubtless, that punishment of evil doers, for which earthly rulers are appointed, and which the public good requires, must be really painful to the feelings of humanity; more painful, in many cases, than the amputation of limbs, and other high operations in surgery, for which, on that account, as well as because of the superior skill and great care requisite, an ample fee to the operator is thought reasonable. Moreover; those who stand in elevated stations, are the marks of obloquy, and exposed to many dangers, much more than men on the level ground of private life. All these things well weighed, the equitable reward of governors, and the necessary cost of supporting good government, must be no inconsiderable burden on the people.

In order to national defence, against hostilities from abroad, still heavier expenses are often indispensible. In perilous times, there must be armies and fleets, forts and garrisons. At the first out set, more especially, when all these things are to be new-created, to a people unused to such vast expenditures, they will naturally appear enormous; and very easily may a popular clamor be raised against them. It is possible, indeed, that more may be laid out in these ways, many times, than the public exigences require; but of this, few of the complainers are competent to judge. A nation that has an extended coast, and an extensive commerce to defend, had better be at immense charges for the security of these, than lie open to those spoliations and invasions, to which, without arming, when all the world is at war, they might inevitably be exposed.

To provide both for the internal and external safety of a numerous people, the burdens laid upon them must often be heavy. These are evils to be lamented; but in the present state of mankind, they are necessary for the prevention of far greater evils; and should therefore be submitted to, without murmuring.

3. The preceding observations may suggest to us, some peculiar advantages of a republican form of government.*

Under every form, there must be orders and degrees; some must

* This inference was passed over in the delivery.

bear rule, and others be subject to tribute. Under every form, there will be duties, imposts, excises, and perhaps direct taxation. All forms of government, however, are not equal. Much advantage hath the republican, many ways.

One advantage is, that the people may always have good rulers, unless it be their own fault. Under a monarchy, or an aristocracy, let the body of the people be ever so virtuous, and ever so vigilant, they may have children for their princes, and babes to rule over them. When power is hereditary, in kings or nobles, not only is there a risk of having the highest seats of government filled by minors; but, if this should not happen, the hazard is great, that those who inherit the first offices of government, will frequently be men of not much knowledge, or of not much virtue. But in elective governments, where the people at large are the electors, and especially where the elections are frequent, they may always have wise and faithful men in all places of authority; if such are to be found, and if such they choose.

It may next be observed; that in republican governments, there is the least occasion for illegal associations, or popular tumults, to obtain a redress of grievances. If there be any mal-administration, or any fault in the constitution, a remedy is provided, without disturbing the public peace.

Another advantage must not be forgotten, which is very great: under this free form of government, the interests of rulers and subjects are so blended—so the same, that the former cannot oppress the latter, without equally oppressing themselves. In an absolute monarchy, the king; and in an aristocracy, the nobles, may "bind heavy burdens, and lay them on men's shoulders," without being obliged to "touch them themselves with one of their fingers": but in democracies, the highest magistrates are subject to the same laws, the same duties, the same taxes, which they impose upon others. At least, those who this year bear rule, the next election may be under law, under tribute. This is a great security against their decreeing unrighteous decrees, and writing grievous things.

Lastly; representative rulers feel themselves so dependent on the people, for their continuance in office, that they are not likely to grow haughty and unreasonably over-bearing, as those naturally will, who have no such dependence.

These are some of the peculiar advantages of a republican government. But then, it is to be well remembered, that the best things may become the worst for us, by being abused. To render democratic governments stable and happy, it is highly necessary that the people should be wise, virtuous, peaceable, and easily governed. For want of these requisites, republics have often been, like "man that is born of a woman, of few days, and full of trouble."

4. In the more particular application of our subject, we are naturally led to a view and conviction, of our own mercies, and privileges, and prospects, and duties.

That the past mercies of heaven towards this country, have been singularly great, every pious observer will be ready devoutly to acknowledge. I have reference, chiefly, to political mercies; or those which relate to civil liberty and government. Hardly another instance can be found, I believe, in all history, of a people's enjoying both these blessings jointly, in so high a degree, for so great a length of time, as they have been enjoyed by several of these united states; and by this state, in particular. The people of Connecticut, from the beginning, have invariably chosen their chief magistrates, and general assembly; and they have had a succession of good governors far beyond the common lot of mankind. Our "officers have been peace, and our exactors righteousness," with as few exceptions, perhaps, as ever were known in any part of the world.

Or, if we confine the retrospect, within the compass of the last five and twenty years; and extend it to the whole union, how wonderful have been the salvations granted us! In this period, we have passed through the Red Sea of a revolutionary war; in which our then friends and coadjutors, assaying to follow us, as most who ever attempted it before us, have been drowned. Here, quite contrary to what usually happens, on such occasions, we had guides eminent for prudence, stability, coolness, and unconquerable perseverance. And one, super-eminent for all those; by the integrity of whose heart, and the skilfulness of whose hands, we were led like a flock, in safety, far surpassing all rational expectation. We have also passed, afterwards, thro the howling wilderness of an almost national anarchy: where were pits, and scorpions, and fiery flying serpents. Here again, our great men, with *the greatest of all* at their head, in a general convention, formed and recommended our present admirable constitution.

And our wisest counsellors and most eloquent orators, in every state, straining every nerve, procured its adoption; whereby we were saved, when on the brink of dissolution. That such men were raised up, and put forward, in these times of need; and their way made prosperous; was certainly "the Lord's doing, and ought to be marvellous in our eyes." In either of these perils, "it was of the Lord's mercies that we were not consumed."

And as past mercies, so our present privileges, are singular, and such as deserve a very grateful acknowledgment. While many other nations are suffering the ravages of a most furious war, still likely to be carried on with redoubled rage; we enjoy the inestimable blessings of peace. While most other nations are under the dominion of hereditary kings and nobles, such as they happen to be born and educated, whether virtuous or vicious, wise men or fools; we have rulers from the highest to the lowest, of our own election. While one other nation, great and highly civilized, after swimming in seas of blood for eight years, and after nearly as many revolutions, in a violent contest for liberty and equality, has at last, nothing more of either than the empty name, we possess the reality of both, as far as is consistent with any order or safety.

Our national expenses are necessarily great: but the burden of them is laid, as much as possible, on those most able to bear it; among whom, the imposers, being of the richer class, have taken a large proportion on themselves. In the nation, and in this state, the policy of government, certainly, is not to "grind the face of the poor." The mildness and gentleness of our administration, it appears to me, is generally very great; and, in regard to its wisdom and firmness, considering the times, I think it deserving of much applause. Respecting rulers, certainly our condition, hitherto, is far different from that described and threatened in our text.

Such have been our mercies; such are our privileges. What then are our prospects? Not altogether fair and promising, after all. As in the blessings of heaven, and the abuse of these blessings, there is a striking resemblance between us, and the land of Judah and inhabitants of Jerusalem, at the time of this prophecy, to which we have been attending; so, in the sequel, it is possible there may be a similitude. Our mountain is not yet so strong, that we have reason, from any quarter, to say in our prosperity, we shall never be moved.

Some may flatter themselves, that, although other republics have frequently been tumultuous, and of short continuance; ours will be peaceful and permanent, because of the greater knowledge and virtue of the people.

It is true, in this part of the union at least, "We know that we all have knowledge." But, I doubt, we have more of the "knowledge which puffeth up," than of that knowledge which promises "stability of times." It is true, we have the light of the gospel; and were we disposed to be guided by this light, we need not fear the fate of ancient republics, that were bewildered in pagan darkness. But, in matters relative to government and subordination; too many choose to take their instructions from heathen philosophy, rather than from the oracles of God. And as the knowledge, so the virtue, of even this happy country, exceedingly wants to be Christianized. It is true, our "charity aboundeth": but I am afraid we have not much of that charity which is "the bond of perfectness, or the bond of peace."

Perhaps some good people are ready to think, we may safely "trust in God; who hath delivered, and doth deliver, that he will yet deliver us." And had we rendered according to the benefits done us, indeed, we might thus securely trust. But has this been the case? On the contrary, have we not sinned more and more, since the almost miraculous deliverances granted us? Has not the worship of God been neglected; his day and name been prophaned, his laws transgressed, and his gospel despised and rejected, of late years, more than ever? Have not infidelity, and all manner of loose principles, and immoral practices, abounded in all parts of the land, since the revolution, and our happy independence, more than at any former period? Shall we then "lean upon the Lord, and say, Is not the Lord among us? no evil can come upon us"?* Or shall we think, "Because we are innocent, surely his anger shall turn from us"? His ancient covenant people thus leaned, and thus said, in times of their greatest degeneracy; but what were the answers of God to them?† "You only have I known, of all the families of the earth; therefore will I punish you for all your iniquities." And, "shall I not visit for these things? shall not my soul be avenged on such a nation as this?"

When we read such solemn divine admonitions as these, and con-

* Micah iii. 11. Jer. ii. 35.

† Amos iii. 2. Jer. v. 9.

sider our own ways and doings, can we confidently expect the continued smiles and protection of the holy governor of the world? Instead of this, may not our flesh well tremble for fear of him? Have we not reason to be afraid of his avenging judgments?

And has he not already begun to testify his righteous displeasure against us, in some terrible instances? For several years past, our capital towns and cities have been sorely visited with a wasting pestilence; little, if at all known before, in these parts. And now, very lately, a most awful breach has been made upon us; and of the very same kind threatened in our context to Jerusalem and Judah. *For, behold, the Lord, the Lord of hosts, hath taken away from America, the stay and the staff: the mighty man, and the man of war. The judge, and the prudent, and the ancient: The captain of all our armies, and our most honorable man.* All these, in one; by a sudden and surprising stroke, hath the Lord taken away. The man who "fought for us, and adventured his life for, and delivered us." The man who gave system to our distracted affairs; united our broken confederacy; and long guided our difficult course, between the whirlpools of European wars. The man, but for whom, very possibly, we should now have been wretched, conquered, rebel colonies; instead of triumphant, free, independent states; and but for whom, afterwards, we might have been as a roap of sand, instead of a strong united nation: The man to whom we are thus indebted—on whom we were thus dependent, is no more.

What farther public calamities the sudden decease of this great Saviour of his country may portend, God only knows. We have reason to apprehend, that as he was ever prosperous in life, so his death, for him, was favorably timed; that he was taken out of the way of evils to come; great evils coming on a land most dear to him; which he could only have seen, to his inexpressible sorrow of heart, without being able to prevent. This lesson, however, we are plainly and most impressively taught, by a providence which has clothed a continent in mourning; that Gods on earth must die like men.* That "no man hath power over the spirit, to retain the spirit; neither hath he power in the day of death; and there is no discharge in that war." We have many great and good men, yet spared to us; nor are we without one, at the head of our national government, who, I presume, has the high

* Psal. lxxxii. 6, 7. Eccl. viii. 8.

veneration of the best judges, and their cordial prayers that he may long live; and long fill the important station which he now possesses. But his breath is in his nostrils; and so is the breath of every other man, most accounted of; in the nation, or in the state. Nor is natural death, the only way whereby our remaining firm pillars, may be removed.

And if we consider the spirit that now worketh, well may we be apprehensive of unhappy changes; and of all the evils threatened in our text. Some of these, we already experience. Though God hath not given children to be our princes, nor many bad men, we hope, to rule over us; yet the people are oppressed one by another, in a degree, I believe, beyond what has been usual heretofore. And certainly it is a remarkable day, for the child's behaving himself proudly against the ancient, and the base against the honorable. Nor is this to be wondered at. Of such scenes as we have lately passed through, it is the natural consequence. In revolutionary times, all expressions of respect are wont to be laid aside, or the application of them reversed. The great lessons inculcated on youth, instead of modesty, dutifulness and subordination; are boldness, self-sufficiency, and self-importance. Children, too young to read the bible, or to be taught their catechism, are mounted on the stage, to act the orator, the patriot and politician: while the parents, the aged and the wise, sit or stand around in low place, wonder and applaud. Brutus and Cassius (not Jesus nor Paul, Peter nor John), are the great models and instructors, of the rising generation of Christians. Such things as these, we have seen; and the effects of them, we still sadly feel. Habits of subordination, always painful to human pride; when once effaced, or much weakened, are not easily restored. On the other hand, habits of haughtiness and disobedience, always congenial to the human heart; when once imbibed, naturally increase to more ungovernableness. One point of freedom gained, another is struggled for with the greater ardor. Licentiousness, like the grave, never says, "It is enough."

In this state, though not near so free as some, great liberties are enjoyed. We have liberty to do every thing that we ought; and a great many things that we ought not. In matters of religion, our liberties are almost unbounded. We may sell, buy and read, what books we please: the best, or the most atheistical and blasphemous. We may worship what god we choose: a just God, or one who has no justice for men to fear. Every creature, has equal liberty to preach the gospel: and to preach what gospel he thinks proper. Those who persuade men by the terrors of the Lord, to stand in awe, and not sin; and those who embolden men in all manner of iniquity, by assurances of no wrath to come, have equal encouragement. Any people may make the firmest legal contract for the support of what minister they will; and any number, or all of them, may break it when they will. In civil matters, our liberty is a little more circumscribed; yet, in these, we have a good deal of elbow-room, to do wrong, as well as right. We may honor all men, or defame the most dignified and worthy characters. We may speak the truth, or assert and propagate falsehoods. Men may fulfil their promises, or not fulfil them; pay their debts, or never pay them, without any restraint, or much danger of compulsion. All these liberties, and a thousand others, if not explicitly by law allowed; are taken, very freely by many, in their worst latitude; and taken with impunity, in a multitude of instances.

Yet, with all this, numbers among ourselves, and much greater numbers in the freer states, it is said, are not satisfied; but are striving, by calumnies, and by intrigues, for new revolutions still further to weaken government. That some men might wish to have their own hands and tongues at greater liberty, provided their neighbours and enemies could be kept fast bound, may easily be conceived: but how any man, on the least sober reflection, should be willing that all others should be under less restraint than they now are, appears almost inconceivable. One would have thought, that the tragedy so long exhibited on the great European theatre of confusion, and especially the last scene; must have opened the eyes of the most blind; and obliged them to see, that overturning and overturning, with a view to break all bonds of society asunder, is not the way to public happiness, or personal safety. Nevertheless, this seems not to have been the case. A majority of the people, however, it may be presumed, are convinced, that our greatest immediate danger, is of having too little government, not too little liberty.

Nor are our duties, if we have this conviction, hard to be understood. Were we in earnest disposed, to stand in the ways, and see, and ask for the old paths, where is the good way? And would we walk therein, rest might be found; and the threatened evils now spoken of, be prevented.

If we would not have the child behave himself proudly against the ancient, and the base against the honorable, greater attention should be paid to the schooling and government of the rising generation. Some attempt towards a reform in this matter has already been made, under the auspices of the general assembly: and, as far as I have had opportunity to observe, it has been attended with encouraging effects. It is necessary that those just weaned from the breast, should have line upon line, and precept upon precept; and it is of importance what those lines and precepts are. Little ones should be learnt their letters, at least; if not a few lines of the New-Testament, before they are learnt to be Grecian and Roman orators and patriots. They should be learnt a little modesty, and a little manners, before they are learnt to govern the nation. They should be made good children, before we attempt to make them great men.

If our legislators would prevent our being oppressed every one by another, the old and good way is, to have a code of laws, as short and plain as possible, and suitably inforced. Obsolete laws; and laws the only tendency of which is to evade, or needlessly delay, the operation of justice; I should think, ought to be repealed. And certainly great care should be taken, by the appointment of capable and faithful judiciary and informing officers, that the laws unrepealed be duly executed.

If our judges of courts, would keep us from oppressing, or being oppressed, they should cause "judgment to run down as waters, and righteousness as a mighty stream." They should see that the old complaint in Isaiah;* "Judgment is turned away backward, and justice standeth afar off; truth is fallen in the street, and equity cannot enter," be not applicable to ourselves. They should see, if possible, that their judgment seats be not environed with so high piles of voluminous fortifications, and such numerous garrisons, armed at all points, and able to defend any thing, that right can hardly be obtained, in the plainest cause, without a siege, as long, and as costly, as the siege of Troy.

If the freemen—the fountain of power, would strengthen government, or guard against its being farther weakened; they should be very punctual in attending their legal meetings, and very careful for

* Chap. lix. 14.

whom they give in their suffrages, as members of Assembly, or of Congress. They should see that they do not vote for weak men, however honest; nor for vicious men, however capable; nor for intriguing men, who are crowding themselves forward, by every popular artifice: who understand perfectly all the duties and faults of their superiors, but see no beam in their own eye, and never mind their own business. Men of real abilities, are generally unassuming and self-diffident. Men sensible of the difficulties and responsibility of important posts of trust, are generally backward to undertake them. Men restless where they are, and troublesome to those above them, are generally haughty and overbearing, if advanced to higher stations. Nor should the freemen be too much given to change; unless they mean to weaken government. Bad men, if in office, cannot be too soon turned out; but those who have ruled well, ought not to be dropped, merely that every man may have his turn; nor merely to show the great power of the people, and to keep their servants, who govern them, more in fear of them.

The ministers of the gospel, are thought to have no concern with the temporal happiness of mankind: doubtless, the good way for them, whether the old way or not, is to confine themselves very much to their spiritual vocation. Doubtless their principal business is, to save the souls of those who hear them. But in order to [do] this, they must warn all, of that "wrath of God which is revealed from heaven, against all ungodliness and unrighteousness of men." They must "convert sinners from the error of their ways," or they cannot "save their souls from death." They must teach their converts to "observe all things whatsoever Christ hath commanded," by himself or his apostles; or they cannot make them "meet to be partakers of the inheritance of the saints in light." And among these instructions, teaching them to "obey those who have the rule over them, and to be cautious how they speak evil of dignities, must not be omitted. Ministers must not "shun to declare all the counsel of God," both to rulers and subjects, if they would be "pure from the blood of all men." In a word, they must do what in them lies to make all their hearers good Christians; for without this they can never get them to heaven; and they need do no more, to make them peaceable and orderly members of society on earth. Thus far, and in this manner, Aaron may still support the hand of Moses, in ministering to the temporal good of men, even in a consistency with the modern line of separation drawn between them.

Lastly; all, of every order, if they would do their part to prevent all the evils threatened in our text and context, from coming upon us, as the righteous judgments of heaven, must see that their tongues and their doings are not against the Lord. Never can we rationally hope that God will be at peace with us, unless we treat his laws and ordinances with greater attention and respect. Unless we cease to do evil, and learn to do well; unless some check be put to those loose principles, and licentious practices, which have over-flowed all our cities, and towns, and villages.

The old paths, then, and the good way, to which we must return, and in which we must walk, would we find rest, are plain before us.

But, it is to be feared, the voice of a majority may now be, as it was in the days of Jeremiah: *We will not walk therein.* Both from the signs of the times, and from several predictions of scripture, I think the probability is, that things are not about to alter for the better, but for the worse. Mankind seem yet combining, and "taking counsel together, against the Lord, and against his annointed, saying, Let us break their bands asunder, and cast away their cords from us"; and God seems remarkably leaving them to strong delusions, to believe strange lies. He seems determined to let them go on, and try the boasted experiment of liberty and revolutions, to the uttermost: designing, it may be supposed, to have a more convictive discovery exhibited, than has ever yet been given, of the madness in the heart of the sons of men, before the general regeneration of the world. The unclean spirits, predicted to come out of the mouth of the dragon, and out of the mouth of the beast, and out of the mouth of the false prophet, as represented in the vision of John; appear evidently to have gone forth over all the earth, and to have been exceedingly busy and successful, in raising and training up their forces for the battle of that great day of God Almighty;* which, according to the common calculation of expositors, is now only commencing. Whether we turn our eyes to the word of prophecy, or to the aspects of providence, we have reason to be very apprehensive, that "this darkness" is yet for a while, to "cover the earth, and gross darkness the people,"† in a

* Rev. xvi. 13, 14.

† Isa. lx. 2.

greater and greater degree, before the expected reign of light and truth, righteousness and peace.

Nevertheless, let not good men despond: not let them relax their exertions to repel, as long and as extensively as they can, the prevalence of error, irreligion and wretchedness. Mightier is he that is with them, than all that are against them. When it is asked in the eleventh psalm: "If the foundations be destroyed, what can the righteous do?" the answer is short, but very emphatical and abundantly sufficient: "*The Lord is in his holy temple; the Lord's throne is in heaven.* Elsewhere, the psalmist, adoring the power and wisdom of the most High, says, "Surely the wrath of man shall praise thee; the remainder of the wrath shalt thou restrain."* It is often said, "Christ is able to support his own church and ministers, without the aid of human laws." This is doubtless true, it is also true, that Christ is able to take care of his church, and to bring the many sons given him to glory, without any ministers at all. And equally true is it, that God is able to govern the nations, without the help of earthly rulers. But, from these premises, the consequence will not follow, without hard drawing, that men may innocently and safely neglect exerting the power they have, for the support, either of good government, or of uncorrupted Christianity. "Those that walk in pride, God is able to abase"; but is there therefore nothing hazardous, nor wrong, in thus walking? A curse was once denounced, on them who "came not to the help of the Lord, against the mighty[")]; though the Lord helped himself, without their assistance. But the foregoing truths, however they may have been perverted to the countenancing of human negligence in the cause of God or Christ, are matter of just consolation to the pious and good, when they walk in darkness and have no light: when they see little probability that their utmost efforts for the support of order, or of undefiled religion, will have any effect.

There will always be some, and some that ought to be leaders and teachers, whose policy it is, to turn with the times; to swim with the tide, and swing with the vibrating pendulum of popular opinion. Who will trim their way to seek love; and "become all things to all men, if by all means they may save" themselves. But a steadfast adherence to truth and duty, however great the apparent danger, is the

* Psal. lxxvi. 10.

only way of real safety. He who thus "loses his life, shall save it"; and he shall lose his life who would save it, by deserting his post, or hiding himself under refuges of falsehood, when evil is foreseen. "The fearful and unbelieving, shall have their part" at last, in the same lake with bolder transgressors. "The fear of man bringeth a snare; but whoso putteth his trust in the Lord shall be safe."* For the encouragement of good men, in perilous times, and particularly of good rulers, it is written: "He that walketh righteously, and speaketh uprightly; he that despiseth the gain of oppressions, that shaketh his hands from holding of bribes, that stoppeth his ears from hearing of blood, and shutteth his eyes from seeing evil; he shall dwell on high; his place of defence shall be the munitions of rocks: bread shall be given him, his waters shall be sure."† On these grounds is the exhortation in Isaiah, a few chapters after our text,‡ with which I shall conclude. "Say ye not, A confederacy, to all them to whom this people shall say, A confederacy: neither fear ye their fear, nor be afraid. Sanctify the Lord of hosts himself; and let him be your fear, and let Him be your dread."

* Prov. xxix. 25.
† Isa. xxxiii. 15, 16.
‡ Chap. viii. 12, 13.

51

THE VOICE OF WARNING TO CHRISTIANS

John Mitchell Mason

NEW-YORK

1800

John Mitchell Mason (1770–1829). Born in New York City and educated both at Columbia College (1789) and, theologically, at the University of Edinburgh (1792), Mason became the pastor of the Scotch Presbyterian Church on Cedar Street, New York City, after the death of his father (Reverend John Mason), who was a longtime pastor there. He later resigned this pulpit for a new congregation at Murray Street Church, his denomination being the Reformed Church of North America. He founded a theological seminary in 1804, which later became Union Theological Seminary, and subscribed support for it while gathering its library in Great Britain. He founded *The Christian's Magazine* in 1806 and wrote much of its content. He served as trustee of Columbia College for two periods totaling twenty-six years, and he was elected first provost of the college in 1811. When his health failed, he decided that a new climate might help him, so he moved to Carlisle, Pennsylvania, where he was president of Dickinson College for three years. In 1822 he left the Associate Reformed Church and became a member of the Presbyterian Presbytery of New York. He returned to New York in 1824 and remained there until his death.

Mason was one of the greatest pulpit orators of his age and had no superior as a preacher during his best years (C. F. Himes, *A Sketch of Dickinson College* [1789], p. 52; John DeWitt, "The Intellectual Life of Samuel Miller," *Princeton Theological Review*, April 1906, p. 175). This sermon of 1800, published anonymously, reflects Mason's view that Thomas Jefferson was a "confirmed infidel" whose "rejection of the Christian religion and open profession of atheism" had disqualified him from being chosen President of the United States.

Regarded as "one of the most noted clerical pamphlets against Jefferson" (Dumas Malone, *Jefferson and His Time*, III:522), the sermon continues the ruinous attack on Jefferson's religion made in an anonymous tract by William Linn, with Mason's assistance (and mentioned herein on the second page of Mason's text, as well as later on), entitled *Serious Considerations on the Election of a President: Addressed to the Citizens of the United States* (Evans No. 37835), also published in 1800.

THE

VOICE OF WARNING,

TO

CHRISTIANS,

ON

THE ENSUING ELECTION

OF

A PRESIDENT

OF

THE UNITED STATES.

[By John Mitchell Mason]

---

*Blow the trumpet in Zion—*WHO IS ON THE LORD'S SIDE?

NEW-YORK:

PRINTED AND SOLD BY G. F. HOPKINS, AT WASHINGTON'S HEAD, NO. 136, PEARL-STREET.

1800.

If a manly attempt to avert national ruin, by exposing a favorite error, should excite no resentment, nor draw any obloquy upon its author, there would certainly be a new thing under the sun. Men can seldom bear contradiction. They bear it least when they are most demonstrably wrong; because, having surrendered their judgment to prejudice, or their conscience to design, they must take refuge in obstinacy from the attacks of reason. The bad, dreading nothing so much as the prevalence of pure principle and virtuous habit, will ever be industrious in counteracting it; and the more candid, rational and convincing the means employed in its behalf, the louder will be their clamor, and the fiercer their opposition. On the other hand, good men are often led insensibly astray, and their very honesty becomes the guarantee of their delusion. Unaware, at first, of their inconsistency, they afterwards shrink from the test of their own profession. Startled by remonstrance, but unprepared to recede; checked by the misgivings of their own minds, yet urged on by their previous purpose and connection, the conflict renders them irritable, and they mark as their enemy whoever tells them the truth. From the coincidence of such a bias with the views of the profligate and daring, results incalculable mischief. The sympathy of a common cause unites the persons engaged in it; the shades of exterior character gradually disappear; virtue sinks from her glory; vice emerges from her infamy; the best and the basest appear nearly on a level; while the most atrocious principles either lose their horror, or have a veil thrown over them: and the man who endeavors to arrest their course, is singled out as a victim to revenge and madness. Such, from the beginning, has been the course of the world. None of its benefactors have escaped its calumnies and persecutions: not prophets, not apostles, not the Son of God himself. To this treatment, therefore, must every one be reconciled, who labors to promote the best interests of his country. He must stake his popularity against his integrity; he must encounter a policy which will be contented with nothing short of his ruin; and if it may not spill his blood, will strive to overwhelm him with public execration. That this is the spirit which has pursued a writer, the purity of whose views is equalled only by their importance—I mean the author of *Serious Considerations on the Election of a President*, I need not inform any who inspect the gazettes. To lay before the people of the United States, proofs that a candidate for the office of their first magistrate, is an unbeliever in the scriptures; and that to confer such a distinction upon an open enemy to their religion, their Redeemer, and their hope, would be mischief to themselves and sin against God, is a crime never to be forgiven by a class of men too numerous for our peace or prosperity. The infidels have risen *en masse*, and it is not through their moderation that he retains any portion of his respectability or his usefulness. But in their wrath there is nothing to deprecate; nor does he deserve the name of a Christian, who, in order to avoid it, would deviate an hair's breadth from his duty. For them I write not. Impenetrable by serious principle, they are not objects of expostulation, but of compassion; nor shall I stoop to any solicitude about their censure or applause.

But do I represent as infidels all who befriend Mr. Jefferson's election? God forbid that I should so "lie against the truth." If I thought so, I should mourn in silence: my pen should slumber forever. That a majority of them profess, and that multitudes of them really love, the religion of Jesus, while it is my terror, is also my hope. Terror, because I believe them to be under a fatal mistake; hope, because they, if any, are within the reach of conviction. I address myself to them. The latter, especially, are my brothers, my dearer ties and higher interests than can be created or destroyed by any political connection. And if it be asked, Why mingle religion with questions of policy? Why irritate by opposition? Why risk the excitement of passions which may disserve, but cannot aid, the common Christianity? Why not maintain a prudent reserve, and permit matters of state to take their own course? I answer, Because Christians are deeply engaged already: Because the principles of the gospel are to regulate their political, as well as their other, conduct: Because their Christian character, profession and prosperity are involved in the issue. This is no hour to temporize. I abhor that coward spirit which vaunts when gliding down the tide of opinion, but shrinks from the returning current, and calls the treason prudence. It is the voice of God's providence not less than of his word, "Cry aloud, spare not; lift up thy voice like a trumpet, and shew my people their transgression, and the house of Jacob their sins." With Christians, therefore, I must expostulate; and may not refrain. However they may be displeased, or threaten, I will say, with the Athenian chief, "*Strike, but hear me.*"

Fellow Christians,

A crisis of no common magnitude awaits our country. The approaching election of a president is to decide a question not merely of preference to an eminent individual, or particular views of policy, but, what is infinitely more, of national regard or disregard to the religion of Jesus Christ. Had the choice been between two infidels or two professed Christians, the point of politics would be untouched by me. Nor, though opposed to Mr. Jefferson, am I to be regarded as a partizan; since the principles which I am about to develope, will be equally unacceptable to many on both sides of the question. I dread the election of Mr. Jefferson, because I believe him to be a confirmed infidel: you desire it, because, while he is politically acceptable, you either doubt this fact, or do not consider it essential. Let us, like brethren, reason this matter.

The general opinion rarely, if ever, mistakes a character which private pursuits and public functions have placed in different attitudes; yet it is frequently formed upon circumstances which elude the grasp of argument even while they make a powerful and just impression. Notwithstanding, therefore, the belief of Mr. Jefferson's infidelity, which has for years been uniform and strong, wherever his character has been a subject of speculation—although that infidelity has been boasted by some, lamented by many, and undisputed by all, yet as it is now denied by his friends, the charge, unsupported by other proof, could hardly be pursued to conviction. Happily for truth and for us, Mr. Jefferson has written; he has printed. While I shall not decline auxiliary testimony, I appeal to what he never retracted, and will not deny, his *Notes on Virginia*.*

In their war upon revelation, infidels have levelled their batteries against the miraculous facts of the scripture: well knowing that if its historical truth can be overturned, there is an end of its claim to inspiration. But God has protected his word. Particularly the universal

* The edition which I use is the second American edition, published at Philadelphia, by Matthew Carey, 1794.

deluge, the most stupendous miracle of the old testament, is fortified with impregnable evidence. The globe teems with demonstrations of it. Every mountain and hill and valley lifts up its voice to confirm the narrative of Moses. The very researches and discoveries of infidels themselves, contrary to their intentions, their wishes and their hopes, are here compelled to range behind the banner of the bible. To attack, therefore, the scriptural account of the deluge, belongs only to the most desperate infidelity. Now, what will you think of Mr. Jefferson's Christianity, if he has advanced positions which strike directly at the truth of God's word concerning that wonderful event? Let him speak for himself:

> It is said that shells are found in the Andes, in South America, fifteen thousand feet above the level of the ocean. This is considered by many, both of the learned and unlearned, *as a proof of an universal deluge.* But to the *many considerations opposing this opinion*, the following may be added: The atmosphere and all its contents, whether of water, air, or other matters, gravitate to the earth; that is to say, they have weight. Experience tells us, that the weight of all these columns together, never exceeds that of a column of mercury of 31 inches high. If the whole contents of the atmosphere then were water, instead of what they are, it would cover the *globe but 35 feet deep:* but, as these waters as they fell, would run into the seas, the superficial measure of which is to that of the dry parts of the globe, as two to one, the seas would be raised only 52½ feet above their present level, and of course would *overflow the land to that height only.* In Virginia this would be a very small proportion even of the champaign country, the banks of our tide-waters being frequently, if not generally, of a greater height. Deluges beyond this extent then, as for instance, to the North mountain or to Kentucky, seem out of the laws of nature. But within it they may have taken place to a greater or less degree, in proportion to the combination of natural causes which may be supposed to have produced them. But such deluges as these, will not account for the shells found in the higher lands. A second opinion has been entertained, which is, that in times anterior to the records either of history or tradition, the bed of the ocean, the principal residence of the shelled tribe, has, by some great convulsion of nature, been heaved to the heights at which we now find shells and other remains of marine animals. *The favorers of this opinion do well to suppose the great events on which it rests to have taken place beyond all the æras of history; for within these certainly none such can be found*; and we may venture to say further, that no fact has taken place either in our own days, or in the thousands of years recorded in history, which proves the existence of any

> natural agents within or without the bowels of the earth, of force sufficient to heave to the height of 15,000 feet, such masses as the Andes.*

After mentioning another opinion proposed by Voltaire, Mr. J. proceeds, "There is a wonder somewhere. Is it greatest on this branch of the dilemma; on that which supposes the existence of a power of which we have no evidence in any other case; or on the first which requires us to believe the creation of a body of water and "its subsequent annihilation?" Rejecting the whim of Voltaire, he concludes, that "*the three hypotheses are equally unsatisfactory, and we must be contented to acknowledge, that this great phenomenon is, as yet, unsolved.*"†

On these extracts, I cannot suppress the following reflections.

1. Mr. Jefferson disbelieves the existence of an universal deluge. "*There are many considerations,*" says he, "*opposing this opinion.*" The bible says expressly, "*The waters prevailed exceedingly upon the earth, and all the high hills that were under the whole heaven were covered.*"‡ Mr. Jefferson enters into a philosophical argument to prove the fact impossible; that is, he argues in the very face of God's word, and, as far as his reasoning goes, endeavors to convict it of falsehood.

2. Mr. Jefferson's concession of the probability of deluges within certain limits, does not rank him with those great men who have supposed the deluge to be partial, because his argument concludes directly against the scriptural narrative, even upon that supposition. He will not admit his partial deluges to rise above 52 1/2 feet above the level of the ocean. Whereas the scripture, circumscribe its deluge as you will, asserts that *the waters were fifteen cubits* (27 1/2 feet nearly) *above the mountains.*§

3. Not satisfied with his argument, Mr. Jefferson sneers at the scripture itself, and at the credulity of those who, relying upon its testimony, believe "that the bed of the ocean has by some great convulsion of nature, been heaved to the heights at which we now find shells and other remains of marine animals." "*They do well,*" says he, "*to suppose the great events on which it rests to have taken place beyond all the æras of history; for within these none such are to be found.*" Indeed! And so

* Jefferson's Notes on Virginia, p. 39–41.

† Jefferson's Notes on Virginia, p. 42.

‡ Gen. vii. 19.

§ ib. v. 20.

our faith in God's word is to dwindle, at the touch of a profane philosopher, into an "opinion," unsupported by either "history or tradition!" *All the fountains of the great deep*, saith the scripture, *were broken up.** Was this no "great convulsion of nature?" Could not this "heave the bed of the ocean to the height at which we now find shells?" But the favorers of this opinion *suppose the great events on which it rests to have taken place beyond all the æras of history*. And they do well, says Mr. Jefferson: the plain meaning of which is, that their error would certainly be detected if they did not retreat into the darkness of fable. Malignant sarcasm! And who are "the favorers of this opinion?" At least all who embrace the holy scriptures. These do declare most unequivocally, that there was such a "great convulsion of nature" as produced a deluge infinitely more formidable than Mr. Jefferson's philosophy can digest. But he will not so much as allow them to be history: he degrades them even below tradition. We talk of times for our flood, he tells us, "anterior to the records either of history or tradition." Nor will it mend the matter, to urge that he alludes only to profane history. The fact could not be more dubious or less deserving a place in the systems of philosophy, from the attestation of infallible truth. And is this truth to be spurned as no history; as not even tradition? It is thus, Christians, that a man whom you are expected to elevate to the chief magistracy, insults yourselves and your bible.†

* Gen. vii. 11.

† Nay, as it is only the scripture which authenticates the popular belief of an universal deluge, Mr. Jefferson's insinuation can hardly have any meaning, if it be not an oblique stroke at the bible itself. Nothing can be more silly than the pretext that he shews the insufficiency of natural causes to effect the deluge, with a view of supporting the credit of the miracle. His difficulty is not to account for the deluge: he denies that; but for *the shells on the top of the Andes*. If he believed in the deluge, natural or miraculous, the difficulty would cease: he would say at once, *The flood threw them there*. But as he tells us, "*this great phenomenon is, as yet, unsolved*," it is clear that he does not believe in the deluge at all; for this "solves" his "phenomenon" most effectually. And for whom does Mr. J. write? For Christians? None of them ever dreamed that the deluge was caused by any thing else than a miracle. For infidels? Why then does he not tell them that the scripture alone gives the true solution of this "great phenomenon?" The plain matter of fact is, that he writes like all other infidels, who admit nothing for which they cannot find adequate "natural agents"; and when these fail them, instead of resorting to the divine word, which would often satisfy a modest enquirer, by revealing the "arm of Jehovah," they shrug up their shoulders, and cry, "Ignorance is preferable to error."‡

‡ Notes on Virginia, p. 42.

4. Mr. Jefferson's argument against the flood is, in substance, the very argument by which infidels have attacked the credibility of the Mosaic history. They have always objected the insufficiency of water to effect such a deluge as that describes. Mr. J. knew this. Yet he adopts and repeats it. He does not deign so much as to mention Moses: while through the sides of one of his hypotheses, he strikes at the scriptural history, he winds up with pronouncing all the three to be "equally unsatisfactory." Thus reducing the holy volume to a level with the dreams of Voltaire! Let me now ask any Christian, Would you dare to express yourself in a similar manner upon a subject which has received the decision of the living God? Would you patiently hear one of your neighbors speak so irreverently of his oracles? Could you venture to speculate on the deluge without resorting to them? Would you not shudder at the thought of using, in support of a philosophical opinion, the arguments which infidels bring against that Word which is the source of all your consolation; much more to use them without a lisp of respect for it, or of caution against mistake? Can he believe the bible who does all this? Can an infidel do more without directly assailing it? What then must you think of Mr. Jefferson?

But it was not enough for this gentleman to discredit the story of the deluge. He has advanced a step farther, and has indicated, too plainly, his disbelief in the common origin of mankind. The scriptures teach that all nations are the offspring of the first and single pair, Adam and Eve, whom God created and placed in paradise. This fact, interwoven with all the relations and all the doctrines of the bible, is alike essential to its historical and religious truth. Now what says the candidate for the chair of your president? After an ingenious, lengthy, and elaborate argument to prove that the blacks are naturally and morally inferior both to white and red men; and that "their inferiority is not the effect merely of their condition of life,"* he observes, "I advance it therefore as a suspicion only, that the blacks, whether *originally a distinct race, or made distinct by time and circumstances*, are inferior to the whites in the endowments both of body and mind."† He had before asserted, that "besides those of col-

* Notes on Virginia, p. 205.

† ib. 209.

or, figure, and hair, there are *other physical distinctions, proving a difference of race.*"* He does, indeed, discover some compunction in reflecting on the consequences of his philosophy. For to several reasons why his opinion "must be hazarded with great diffidence," he adds "as a circumstance of great tenderness," that the "conclusion" to which his observations lead, "would *degrade a whole race of men from the rank in the scale of beings which their Creator may perhaps have given them.*"† Much pains have been taken to persuade the public that Mr. Jefferson by "distinct race" and "difference of race," means nothing more than that the negroes are only a branch of the great family of man, without impeaching the identity of their origin. This construction, though it may satisfy many, is unfounded, absurd, and contradicted by Mr. Jefferson himself. Unfounded: For when philosophers treat of man as a "subject of natural history," they use the term "race," to express the stock from which the particular families spring, and not, as in the popular sense, the families themselves, without regard to their original. A single example, embracing the opinions of two philosophers, of whom the one, M. de Buffon, maintained, and the other, Lord Kames, denied the common origin of mankind, will prove my assertion.

"M. Buffon, from the rule, that animals which can procreate together, and whose progeny can also procreate, are of one species, concludes, that all men are of one race or species."‡ Mr. Jefferson, writing on the same subject with these authors, and arguing on the same side with one of them, undoubtedly uses the term "race" in the same sense. And as the other construction is unfounded, it is also absurd. For it represents him as laboring through nearly a dozen pages to prove what no man ever thought of doubting, and what a glance of the eye sufficiently ascertains, viz. that the blacks and whites are different branches of a common family. Mr. Jefferson is not such a trifler; he fills his pages with more important matter, and with deeper sense. And by expressions which cut off evasion, contradicts the meaning which his friends have invented for him. He enumerates a variety of "distinctions which prove a difference of race." These distinctions he alledges are not accidental, but "physical," i.e.

* ib. 201.

† ib. 203.

‡ Kames's Sketches, vol. i. p. 24.

founded in nature. True, alarmed at the boldness of his own doctrine, he retreats a little. His proofs evaporate into a suspicion; but that suspicion is at a loss to suspect, whether the inferiority of the blacks (Mark it well, reader!) is owing to their being *"originally a distinct race, or made distinct by time and circumstances."* Branches of the same stock originally distinct, is a contradiction. Mr. Jefferson therefore means, by different races, men descended from different stocks. His very "tenderness" is tinctured with an infidel hue. A conclusion corresponding with his speculations, affects him, because it *"would degrade a whole race of men from the rank in the scale of beings which their Creator may perhaps have given them."* So then; the secret is out! What *rank in the scale of beings* have we, obeying the scripture, been accustomed to assign to the injured blacks? The very same with ourselves, viz. that of children of one common father. But if Mr. Jefferson's notions be just, he says they will be degraded from that rank; i.e. will appear not to be children of the same father with us, but of another and inferior stock. But though he will not speak peremptorily, he strongly insinuates that he does not adopt, as an article of his philosophy, the descent of the blacks as well as the whites from that pair which came immediately from the hands of God. He is not sure. At best it is a doubt with him—"the rank which their Creator may perhaps have given them!" Now how will all this accord with revealed truth? God, says the Apostle Paul, *"Hath made of one blood all nations of men, for to dwell on all the face of the earth."** Perhaps it may be so, replies Mr. Jefferson; but there are, notwithstanding, *physical distinctions proving a difference of race.* I cannot repress my indignation! That a miserable, sinful worm, like myself, should proudly set up his "proofs" against the truth of my God and your God, and scout his veracity with a sceptical perhaps! I intreat Christians to consider the sweeping extent of this infidel doctrine of "different races." If it be true, the history of the bible, which knows of but one, is a string of falsehoods from the book of Genesis to that of the Revelation; and the whole system of redemption, predicated on the unity of the human race, is a cruel fiction. I ask Christians again, whether they would dare to speak and write on this subject in the stile of Mr. Jefferson? Whether any believer in the word of the Lord Jesus, who is their

* Acts xvii. 26.

hope, could entertain such doubts? Whether a writer, acute, cautious, and profound, like Mr. Jefferson, could, as he had before done in the case of the deluge, pursue a train of argument, which he knew infidels before him had used to discredit revelation, and on which they still have great reliance—Whether, instead of vindicating the honor of the scripture, he could, in such circumstances, be as mute as death on this point; countenancing infidels by inforcing their sentiments; and yet be a Christian? The thing is impossible! And were any other than Mr. Jefferson to be guilty of the same disrespect to God's word, you would not hesitate one moment in pronouncing him an infidel.

It is not only with his philosophical disquisitions that Mr. Jefferson mingles opinions irreconcileable with the scriptures. He even goes out of his way for the sake of a fling at them. "Those," says he, "who labor in the earth, are the chosen people of God, if ever he had a chosen people, whose breasts he has made his peculiar deposit for substantial and genuine virtue."*

How does a Christian ear relish this "profane babbling?" In the first place, Mr. Jefferson doubts if ever God had a chosen people. In the second place, if he had, he insists they are no other than those who labor in the earth. At any rate, he denies this privilege to the seed of Abraham; and equally denies your being his people, unless you follow the scythe and the plow. Now, whether this be not the lie direct to the whole testimony of the bible from the beginning to the end, judge ye.†

* Notes on Virginia, p. 240.

† Some have been vain enough to suppose that they destroy this proof of Mr. J's infidelity, by representing his expression "the chosen people of God, if ever he had a chosen people," as synonimous with the following: "A. B. is an honest man, if ever there was an honest man," which so far from doubting the existence of honest men, that it founds, in the certainty of this fact, the assertion of A. B's honesty. On this wretched sophism, unworthy of good sense, and more unworthy of candor, I remark,

1. That the expressions are by no means similar. The whole world admits that there are honest men, which makes the proposition, "A. B. is an honest man, if ever there was an honest man," a strong assertion of A. B's honesty. But the hundredth part of the world does not admit that God had a chosen people, and therefore the proposition that "those who labor in the earth are the chosen people of God, if ever he had a chosen people," is, upon this construction, no assertion at all that the cultivators of the soil are his people, because there are millions who do not believe the fact on which it must be founded: viz. that he had a chosen people.

2. That if the expressions were parallel, Mr. J. would still be left in the lurch, because the first asserts A. B. to be as much an honest man as any man that ever lived;

After these affronts to the oracles of God, you have no right to be surprized if Mr. Jefferson should preach the innocence of error, or even of atheism. What do I say! He does preach it. "The legitimate powers of government," they are his own words, "extend to such acts only as are injurious to others. *But it does me no injury for my neighbors to say there are twenty Gods or no God.* It neither picks my pocket nor breaks my leg."*

Ponder well this paragraph. Ten thousand impieties and mischiefs lurk in its womb. Mr. Jefferson maintains not only the inviolability of opinion, but of opinion propagated. And that no class or character of abomination might be excluded from the sanctuary of such laws as he wishes to see established, he pleads for the impunity of published error in its most dangerous and execrable form. Polytheism or atheism, "twenty gods or no god," is perfectly indifferent in Mr. Jefferson's good citizen. A wretch may trumpet atheism from New Hampshire to Georgia; may laugh at all the realities of futurity; may scoff and teach others to scoff at their accountability; it is no matter, says Mr. Jefferson, "it neither picks my pocket, nor breaks my leg." This is nothing less than representing civil society as founded in atheism. For there can be no religion without God. And if it does me or my neighbor no injury, to subvert the very foundation of religion by denying the being of God, then religion is not one of the constituent principles of society, and consequently society is perfect without it; that is, is perfect in atheism. Christians! what think you of this doctrine? Have you so learned Christ or truth? Is atheism indeed no injury to society? Is it no injury to untie all the cords which bind you to the God of heaven, and your deeds to his throne of judgment; which form the strength of personal virtue, give energy to the duties, and infuse sweetness into the charities, of human life? Is it indeed no injury to you, or to those around you, that your neighbor buries his conscience and all his sense of moral obligation in the gulph of atheism? Is it no injury to you, that the oath ceases to be sacred? That the eye of the Omniscient no more pervades the abode of crime? That you have no hold on your dearest friend, farther than the law is

and so Mr. J. asserts "those who labor in the earth" to be as much the "chosen people of God," as any people that ever lived. This is still the lie direct to the whole bible, and the inventors of this lucky shift, must set their wits at work to invent another.

* Notes on Virginia, p. 231.

able to reach his person? Have you yet to learn that the peace and happiness of society depend upon things which the laws of men can never embrace? And whence, I pray you, are righteous laws to emanate, if rulers, by adopting atheism, be freed from the coercion of future retribution? Would you not rather be scourged with sword and famine and pestilence, than see your country converted into a den of atheism? Yet, says Mr. Jefferson, it is a harmless thing. "It does me no injury; it neither picks my pocket, nor breaks my leg." This is perfectly of a piece with his favorite wish to see a government administered without any religious principle among either rulers or ruled. Pardon me, Christian: this is the morality of devils, which would break in an instant every link in the chain of human friendship, and transform the globe into one equal scene of desolation and horror, where fiend would prowl with fiend for plunder and blood—yet atheism "neither picks my pocket nor breaks my leg." I will not abuse you by asking, whether the author of such an opinion can be a Christian? or whether he has any regard for the scriptures which confines all wisdom and blessedness and glory, both personal and social, to the fear and the favor of God?

The reader will observe, that in his sentiments on these four points, the deluge; the origin of nations; the chosen people of God; and atheism, Mr. Jefferson has comprized the radical principles of infidelity in its utmost latitude. Accede to his positions on these, and he will compel you to grant the rest. There is hardly a single truth of revelation which would not fall before one or other of them. If the deluge be abandoned, you can defend neither the miracles, nor inspiration of the scripture. If men are not descendants of one common stock, the doctrine of salvation is convicted of essential error. If God never had any chosen people but the cultivators of the soil, the fabric of the New Testament falls to the ground; for its foundation in the choice of Israel to be his peculiar people, is swept away. And if the atheism of one man be not injurious to another, society could easily dispense not only with his word but with his worship.

Conformable with the infidelity of his book, is an expression of Mr. Jefferson contained in a paragraph which I transcribe from the pamphlet entitled *Serious Considerations*, &c.

When the late Rev. Dr. John B. Smith resided in Virginia, the famous Mazzei happened one night to be his guest. Dr. Smith having, as usual, assembled his family for their evening devotions, the circumstance occasioned some discourse on religion, in which the Italian made no secret of his infidel principles. In the course of conversation, he remarked to Dr. Smith, "Why your great philosopher and statesman, Mr. Jefferson, is rather farther gone in infidelity than I am"; and related, in confirmation, the following anecdote: That as he was once riding with Mr. Jefferson, he expressed his "surprise that the people of this country take no better care of their public buildings." "What buildings?" exclaimed Mr. Jefferson. "Is not that a church?" replied he, pointing to a decayed edifice. "Yes," answered Mr. Jefferson. "I am astonished," said the other, "that they permit it to be in so ruinous a condition." "*It is good enough,*" rejoined Mr. Jefferson, *["]for him that was born in a manger!!*" Such a contemptuous fling at the blessed Jesus, could issue from the lips of no other than a deadly foe to his name and his cause.*

Some of Mr. Jefferson's friends have been desperate enough to challenge this anecdote as a calumny fabricated for electioneering purposes. But whatever they pretend, it is incontestibly true, that the story was told, as here repeated, by Dr. Smith. I, as well as the author of "Serious Considerations," and several others, heard it from the lips of Dr. Smith years ago, and more than once. The calumny, if any, lies either with those who impeach the veracity of a number of respectable witnesses, or with Mazzei himself. And there are not wanting, among the followers of Mr. Jefferson, advocates for this latter opinion. He must have been a wretch indeed, to blacken his brother-philosopher, by trumping up a deliberate lie in order to excuse his own impiety in the presence of a minister of Christ! If such was Mazzei, the philosopher, it is our wisdom to think, and think again, before we heap our largest honors upon the head of his bosom-friend.

Christian reader, the facts and reasonings which I have laid before you, produce in my mind an irresistible conviction, that Mr. Jefferson is a confirmed infidel; and I cannot see how they should have a less effect on your's. But when to these you add his solicitude for wresting the bible from the hands of your children—his notoriously unchristian character—his disregard to all the ordinances of divine worship—his utter and open contempt of the Lord's day, insomuch as to receive on it a public entertainment;† every trace of doubt must vanish. What is a man who writes against the truths of God's word?

* Serious Considerations, p. 16, 17.

† At Fredericksburgh, in Virginia, in 1798.

who makes not even a profession of Christianity? who is without Sabbaths; without the sanctuary; without so much as a decent external respect for the faith and the worship of Christians? What is he, what can he be, but a decided, a hardened infidel?

Several feeble and fruitless attempts have been made to fritter down and dissipate this mass of evidence. In vain are we told that Mr. Jefferson's conduct is modest, moral, exemplary. I ask no odious questions. A man must be an adept in the higher orders of profligacy, if neither literary occupation, nor the influence of the surrounding gospel, can form or controul his habits. Though infidelity and licentiousness are twin sisters, they are not compelled to be always in company; that I am not a debauchee, will therefore be hardly admitted as proof that I am not an infidel. In vain are we reminded, that the "Notes on Virginia" contain familiar mention, and respectful acknowledgment, of the being and attributes of God. Though infidelity leads to atheism, a man may be an infidel without being an atheist. Some have even pretended, that anxiety for the honor of God, prompted them to fix the brand of imposture upon the scripture! But where has Mr. Jefferson, when stating his private opinions, betrayed the least regard for the gospel of our Lord Jesus Christ? In vain is it proclaimed, that he maintains a Christian minister at his own expence. I shall not enquire whether that maintenance does or does not arise from the product of glebe lands attached to many southern estates. Taking the fact to be simply as related, I will enquire whether prudent and political men never contribute to the support of Christianity from other motives than a belief of its truth? Mr. Jefferson may do all this and yet be an infidel. Voltaire, the vile, the blasphemous Voltaire, was building churches, and assisting at the mass, while he was writing to his philosophical confidants, concerning your divine Saviour, *Crush the wretch!* In vain is the "*Act for establishing religious freedom*," which flowed from the pen of Mr. Jefferson, and passed in the Assembly of Virginia, in 1786, paraded as the triumph of his Christian creed. I protest against the credibility of the witness! That act, I know, recognizes "the Holy Author of our religion," as "Lord both of body and mind," and possessing "almighty power"; and by censuring "fallible and uninspired men," tacitly acknowledges both the inspiration and infallibility of the sacred writers. But Mr. Jefferson is not here declaring his private opinions: for these we must look to his Notes, which were published a year after, and abound with ideas which contradict the authority of the scriptures. He speaks, in that act, as the organ of an assembly professing Christianity; and it would not only have been a monstrous absurdity, but more than his credit and the Assembly's too, was worth, to have been disrespectful, *in an official deed*, to that Redeemer whose name they owned, and who was precious to many of their constituents. Such Christianity is common with the bitterest enemies of Christ. Herbert, Hobbes, Blount, Toland, Tindal, Bolingbroke, Hume, Voltaire, Gibbon, at the very moment when they were laboring to argue or to laugh the gospel out of the world, affected great regard for our "holy religion" and its divine author. There is an edict of Frederic the II. of Prussia, on the subject of religious toleration, couched in terms of the utmost reverence for the Christian religion, and yet this same Frederic was one of the knot of conspirators, who, with Voltaire at their head, plotted the extermination of Christianity: and whenever they spoke of its "Holy Author," echoed to each other, *Crush the wretch!* This act, therefore, proves nothing but that, at the time of its passing (and we hope it is so still) there was religion enough in Virginia, to curb the proud spirit of infidelity.

Christians! Lay these things together: compare them; examine them separately, and collectively: ponder; pause; lay your hands upon your hearts; lift up your hearts to heaven, and pronounce on Mr. Jefferson's Christianity. You cannot stifle your emotions; nor forbear uttering your indignant sentence—*infidel!!*

This point being settled, one would think that you could have no difficulty about the rest, and would instantly and firmly conclude, "Such a man ought not, and as far as depends on me, shall not, be President of the United States!" But I calculate too confidently. I have the humiliation to hear this inference controverted even by those whose "good confession" was a pledge that they are feelingly alive to the honor of their Redeemer. No, I am not deceived: they are Christian lips which plead that *"Religion has nothing to do with politics"—that to refuse our suffrages on account of religious principles, would be an interference with the rights of conscience—that there is little hope of procuring a real believer, and we had better choose an infidel than a hypocrite.*

That religion has, in fact, nothing to do with the politics of many who profess it, is a melancholy truth. But that it has, of right, no concern with political transactions, is quite a new discovery. If such opinions, however, prevail, there is no longer any mystery in the character of those whose conduct, in political matters, violates every precept, and slanders every principle, of the religion of Christ. But what is politics? Is it not the science and the exercise of civil rights and civil duties? And what is religion? Is it not an obligation to the service of God, founded on his authority, and extending to all our relations personal and social? Yet *religion has nothing to do with politics!* Where did you learn this maxim? The bible is full of directions for your behaviour as citizens. It is plain, pointed, awful in its injunctions on rulers and ruled as such: yet *religion has nothing to do with politics.* You are commanded "*in all your ways to acknowledge him.*"* *In every thing, by prayer and supplication, with thanksgiving, to let your requests be made known unto God,*"† "*And whatsoever ye do, in word or deed, to do all in the name of the Lord Jesus.*"‡ Yet *religion has nothing to do with politics!* Most astonishing! And is there any part of your conduct in which you are, or wish to be, *without law to God,* and not *under the law of Christ?* Can you persuade yourselves that political men and measures are to undergo no review in the judgment to come? That all the passion and violence, the fraud and falsehood, and corruption which pervade the systems of party, and burst out like a flood at the public elections, are to be blotted from the catalogue of unchristian deeds, because they are politics? Or that a minister of the gospel may see his people, in their political career, bid defiance to their God in breaking through every moral restraint, and keep a guiltless silence because *religion has nothing to do with politics?* I forbear to press the argument farther; observing only, that many of our difficulties and sins may be traced to this pernicious notion. Yes, if our religion had had more to do with our politics; if, in the pride of our citizenship, we had not forgotten our Christianity: if we had prayed more and wrangled less about the affairs of our country, it would have been infinitely better for us at this day.

But you are afraid that to refuse a man your suffrages because he is an infidel, would *interfere with the rights of conscience.* This is a most singular scruple, and proves how wild are the opinions of men on the

* Prov. iii. 3.
† Phil. iv. 6.
‡ Col. iii. 17.

subject of liberty. Conscience is God's officer in the human breast, and its rights are defined by his law. The right of conscience to trample on his authority is the right of a rebel, which entitles him to nothing but condign punishment. You are afraid of being unkind to the conscience of an infidel. Dismiss your fears. It is the last grievance of which he will complain. How far do you suppose Mr. Jefferson consulted his conscience when he was vilifying the divine word, and preaching insurrection against God, by preaching the harmlessness of atheism? But supposing Mr. Jefferson to be conscientiously impious, this would only be a stronger reason for our opposition. For the more conscientious a man is, the more persevering will he be in his views, and the more anxious for their propagation. If he be fixed, then, in dangerous error, faithfulness to God and truth requires us to resist him and his conscience too; and to keep from him the means of doing mischief. If a man thought himself bound in conscience, whenever he should be able, to banish God's sabbath, burn his churches, and hang his worshippers, would you entrust him with power out of respect to conscience? I trow not. And why you should judge differently in the case of an infidel who spurns at what is dearer to you than life, I cannot conceive. But in your solicitude for the conscience of Mr. Jefferson, have you considered, in the mean time, what becomes of your own conscience? Has it no rights? no voice? no influence? Are you not to keep it void of offence towards God? Can you do this in elevating his open enemies to the highest dignity of your country? Beware, therefore, lest an ill-directed care for the conscience of another, bring your own under the lashes of remorse. Keep this clear, by the word of God, and there is little hazard of injuring your neighbor's. But how can you interfere with any man's conscience by refusing him a political office? You do not invade the sanctuary of his bosom: you impose on him no creed: you simply tell him you do not like him, or that you prefer another to him. Do you injure him by this? Do you not merely exercise the right of a citizen and a Christian? It belongs essentially to the freedom of election, to refuse my vote to any candidate for reasons of conscience, of state, of predilection, or for no reason at all but my own choice. The rights of conscience, on his part, are out of the question. He proposes himself for my approbation. If I approve, I give him my support. If not, I withhold it. His conscience has nothing to do with my motives; but to my own conscience they are serious things. If he be an infidel, I will not compel him to profess Christianity. Let him retain his infidelity, enjoy all its comforts, and meet all its consequences. But I have an unquestionable right to say, "I cannot trust a man of such principles: on what grounds he has adopted them is not my concern; nor will his personal sincerity alter their tendency. While he is an infidel, he shall never have my countenance. Let him stay where he is: and let his conscience be its own reward." I could not blame another for such conduct to me; for he only makes an independent use of his privilege, which does me no injury: nor am I to be blamed for such conduct to another, for I only make the same use of my privilege, which is no injury to him. Mr. Jefferson's conscience cannot, therefore, be wronged if you exclude him from the presidency because he is an infidel; and your own, by an act of such Christian magnanimity, may escape hereafter many a bitter pang. For if you elect Mr. Jefferson, though an infidel, from a regard to what you consider the rights of conscience, you must, in order to be consistent, *carry your principle through.* If infidelity is not a valid objection to a candidate for the presidency, it cannot be so to a candidate for any other office. You must never again say, "We will not vote for such a man because he is an infidel." The evil brotherhood will turn upon you with your own doctrine of the "rights of conscience." You must then either retract, or be content to see every office filled with infidels. How horrible, in such an event, would be the situation of your country! How deep your agony under the torments of self-reproach!

But there is no prospect, you say, of obtaining a real Christian, and we had *better choose an infidel than a hypocrite.* By no means. Supposing that a man professes Christianity, and evinces in his general deportment a regard for its doctrines, its worship, and its laws; though he be rotten at heart, he is infinitely preferable to a known infidel. His hypocrisy is before God. It may ruin his own soul; but, while it is without detection, can do no hurt to men. We have a hold of him which it is impossible to get of an infidel. His reputation, his habits, his interests, depending upon the belief of his Christianity, are sureties for his behaviour to which we vainly look for a counterbalance in an infidel; and they are, next to religion itself, the strongest sureties of man to man. His very hypocrisy is an homage to the gospel. The whole weight of his example is on the side of Christianity, while that of an open infidel lies wholly against it. It is well known that the attendance of your Washington, and of President Adams upon public worship, gave the ordinances of the gospel a respectability in the eyes of many which otherwise they would not have had: brought a train of thoughtless people within the reach of the means of salvation: and thus strengthened the opposition of Christians to the progress of infidelity. You can never forget the honorable testimony which Mr. Adams bore, in one of his proclamations, to a number of the most precious truths of Revelation; nor how he was abused and ridiculed for it, by not a few of those very persons who now strive to persuade you that Mr. Jefferson is a Christian. In short, your president, if an open infidel, will be a centre of contagion to the whole continent: If a professed Christian, he will honor the institutions of God; and though his hypocrisy, should he prove a hyprocrite, may be a fire to consume his own vitals, it cannot become a wide-spreading conflagration.

Can you still hesitate? Perhaps you may. I therefore bespeak your attention to a few plain and cogent reasons, why you cannot, without violating your plighted faith, and trampling on your most sacred duties, place an infidel at the head of your government.

1. The civil magistrate is *God's officer. He is the minister of God*, saith Paul, *to thee for good.** Consequently his first and highest obligation, is to cherish in his mind, and express in his conduct, his sense of obedience to the Governor of the Universe. *He that ruleth over men must be just, ruling in the fear of God.*† The scriptures have left you this and similar declarations, to direct you in the choice of your magistrates. And you are bound, upon your allegiance to the God of the scriptures, to look out for such men as answer the description; and if, unhappily, they are not to be had, for such as come nearest to it. The good man, he who shall "dwell in God's holy hill," is one "in whose eyes *a vile person is contemned;* but he *honoreth them that fear the Lord.*"‡ But can you pretend to regard this principle, when you desire to raise an infidel to the most important post in your country? Do you call this *honoring them that fear God?* Nay, it is honoring them who do not fear God: that is, according to the scriptural contrast, honoring a vile

* Rom, xiii. 4.
† Ps. xv. 4.
‡ 2 Sam. xxiii. 3.

person, whom, as Christians, you ought to contemn. And have you the smallest expectation that one who despises the word and worship of God; who has openly taught the harmlessness of rebellion against his government and being, by teaching that atheism is no injury to society, will, nevertheless, *rule in his fear?* Will it shew any reverence or love to your Father in heaven, to put a distinguishing mark of your confidence upon his sworn foe? Or will it be an affront to his majesty?

2. The civil magistrate is, by divine appointment, *the guardian of the sabbath. In it thou shalt not do any work; thou, nor thy son, &c. nor the stranger that is within thy gates.** "Gates," is a scriptural term for public authority; and that it is so to be understood in this commandment, is evident from its connection with "stranger." God says that even the stranger shall not be allowed to profane his sabbath. But the stranger can be controlled only by the civil magistrate who "sitteth in the gate."† It therefore belongs to his office, to enforce, by lawful means, the sanctification of the sabbath, as the fundamental institute of religion and morals, and the social expression of homage to that God under whom he acts. The least which can be accepted from him, is to recommend it by personal observance. How do you suppose Mr. Jefferson will perform this part of his duty? or how can you deposit in his hands a trust, which you cannot but think he will betray; and in betraying which, he will not only sacrifice some of your most invaluable interests, but as your organ and in your name, lift up his heel against the God of heaven? In different states, you have made, not long since, spirited exertions to hinder the profanation of your Lord's day. For this purpose many of you endeavored to procure religious magistrates for this city, and religious representatives in the councils of the state. You well remember how you were mocked, traduced, execrated, especially by the infidel tribe. But what is now become of your zeal and your consistency? I can read in the list of delegates to the legislature, the names of men who have been an ornament to the gospel, and acquitted themselves like Christians in that noble struggle, and yet are expected to ballot for electors, whose votes shall be given to an infidel president. Who hath bewitched you, Christians? or, what do you mean by siding with the infidels to lift into the chair

* Ex. xx. 10.
† Dan. ii. 49.

of state, a man more eminent for nothing than for his scorn of the day, the ordinances, and the worship of your Redeemer; and who did not blush to make it, in the face of the sun, a season of frolic and revel?* Is this your kindness to your friend?

3. The *church of God has ever accounted it a great mercy to have civil rulers professing his name.* Rather than yield it, thousands of your fathers have poured out their blood. This privilege is now in your hands: and it is the chief circumstance which makes the freedom of election worth a Christian's care. Will you, dare you, abuse it by prostituting it to the aggrandizement of an enemy to your Lord and to his Christ? If you do, will it not be a righteous thing with God to take the privilege from you altogether; and, in his wrath, to subject you, and your children, and your children's children, to such rulers as you have, by your own deed, preferred?

4. You are commanded to *pray for your rulers:* it is your custom to pray, that they may be men *fearing God and hating covetousness.* You intreat him to fulfil his promise, that kings shall be to his church *nursing-fathers, and queens her nursing-mothers.*† With what conscience can you lift up your hands in such a supplication, when you are exerting yourselves to procure a president, who you know does not fear God; i.e. one exactly the reverse of the man whom you ask him to bestow? And when, by this act, you do all in your power to defeat the promise of which you affect to wish the fulfilment? Do you think that the church of Christ is to be nurtured by the dragon's milk of infidelity? Or that the contradiction between your prayers and your practice does not mock the holy God?

5. There are circumstances in the state of your country which impart to these reflections, applicable in their spirit to all Christians, a double emphasis in their application to you.

The federal Constitution *makes no acknowledgement of that God* who gave us our national existence, and saved us from anarchy and internal war. This neglect has excited in many of its best friends, more alarm than all other difficulties. The only way to wipe off the reproach of irreligion, and to avert the descending vengeance, is to prove, by our national acts, that the Constitution has not, in this instance, done justice to the public sentiment. But if you appoint an

* The Fredericksb. feast, given on the Sabbath, to Mr. J. 1798.

† Is. xlix. 23.

infidel for your president, and such an infidel as Mr. Jefferson, you will sanction that neglect, you will declare, by a solemn national act, that there is no more religion in your collective character, than in your written constitution: you will put a national indignity upon the God of your mercies; and provoke him, it may be, to send over your land that deluge of judgments which his forbearance has hitherto suspended.

Add to this the consideration, that *infidelity has awfully increased.* The time was, and that within your own recollection, when the term infidelity was almost a stranger to our ears, and an open infidel an object of abhorrence. But now the term has become familiar, and infidels hardly disgust. Our youth, our hope and our pride, are poisoned with the accursed leaven. The vain title of "philosopher," has turned their giddy heads, and, what is worse, corrupted their untutored hearts. It is now a mark of sense, the proof of an enlarged and liberal mind, to scoff at all the truths of inspiration, and to cover with ridicule the hope of a Christian; those truths and that hope which are the richest boon of divine benignity; which calm the perturbed conscience, and heal the wounded spirit; which sweeten every comfort, and soothe every sorrow; which give strong consolation in the arrest of death, and shed the light of immortality on the gloom of the grave. All, all are become the sneer of the buffoon, and the song of the drunkard. These things, Christians, you deplore. You feel indignant, as well as discouraged, at the inroads of infidel principle and profligate manners. You declaim against them. You caution your children against their infection. And yet, with such facts before your eyes, and such lessons in your mouths, you are on the point of undoing whatever you have done; and annihilating, at one blow, the effect of all your profession, instruction, and example. By giving your support to Mr. Jefferson, you are about to strip infidelity of its ignominy; array it in honors; and hold it up with eclat to the view of the rising generation. By this act, you will proclaim to the whole world that it is not so detestable a thing as you pretended; that you do not believe it subversive of moral obligation and social purity: that a man may revile your religion and blaspheme your Saviour; and yet command your highest confidence. This amounts to nothing less than a deliberate surrender of the cause of Jesus Christ into the hands of his enemies. By this single act—my flesh trembles, my blood chills at the thought! by this single act you will do more to destroy a regard for the gospel of Jesus, than the whole fraternity of infidels with all their arts, their industry and their intrigues. You will stamp credit upon principles, the native tendency of which is to ruin your children in this world, and damn them in the world to come. O God! "the ox knoweth his owner, and the ass his master's crib: but thy people doth not know, and Israel doth not consider."*

With these serious reflections, let me connect a fact equally serious: *The whole strength of open and active infidelity is on the side of Mr. Jefferson.* You may well start! But the observation and experience of the continent is one long and loud attestation to the truth of my assertion. I say open and active infidelity. You can scarcely find one exception among all who preach infidel tenets among the people. Did it never occur to you, that such men would not be so zealous for Mr. Jefferson if they were not well assured of his being one of themselves—that they would cordially hate him if they supposed him to be a Christian —or that they have the most sanguine hope that his election to the presidency will promote their cause? I know, that to serve the purpose of the moment, those very presses which teemed with abuse of your Redeemer, are now affecting to offer incense to his religion; and that deists themselves are laboring to convince you that Mr. Jefferson is a Christian; and yet have the effrontery to talk of other men's hypocrisy! Can you be the dupes of such an artifice? Do you not see in it a proof that there is no reliance to be placed on an infidel conscience? Do you need to be reminded that these infidels who now court you, are the very men who, four years ago, insulted your faith and your Lord with every expression of ridicule and contempt? That these very men circulated, with unremitting assiduity, that execrable book of Boulanger, entitled *Christianity Unveiled;* and that equally execrable abortion of Thomas Paine, *The Age of Reason*? That, in order to get them (especially the latter) into the hands of the common people, they sold them at a very low rate; gave them away where they could not sell them; and slipped them into the pockets of numbers who refused to accept them? Do you know that some of these infidels were at the trouble of translating from the French, and printing, for the benefit of Americans, a work of downright, undisguised atheism,

* Is. i. 3.

with the imposing title of *Common Sense*? That it was openly advertised, and extracts, or an extract, published to help the sale?* Do you know that some of the same brotherhood are secretly handing about, I need not say where, a book, written by Charles Pigott, an Englishman, entitled *A Political Dictionary*? Take the following sample of its impiety (my hair stiffens while I transcribe it): "Religion—a superstition invented by the arch-bishop of hell, and propagated by his faithful diocesans the clergy, to keep the people in ignorance and darkness, that they may not see the work of iniquity that is going on," &c.†

Such are the men with whom professors of the name of our Lord Jesus Christ are concerting the election of an infidel to the presidency of the United States of America. Hear the word of the Lord. "What fellowship hath righteousness with unrighteousness? And what communion hath light with darkness? And what concord hath Christ with Belial? And what part hath he that believeth with an infidel?"‡ Yet Christians are uniting with infidels in exalting an infidel to the chief magistracy! If he succeed, Christians must bear the blame. Numerous as the infidels are, they are not yet able, adored be God, to seize upon our "high places." Christians must help them, or they set not their feet on the threshold of power. If, therefore, an infidel preside over our country, it will be your fault, Christians; and your act; and you shall answer it? And for aiding and abetting such a design, I charge upon your consciences the sin of striking hands in a covenant of friendship with the enemies of your master's glory. Ah, what will be your compunction, when these same infidels, victorious, through your assistance, will "tread you down as the mire in the streets," and exult in their triumph over bigots and bigotry.

* The title is a trick, designed to entrap the unwary, by palming it on them through the popularity of Paine's tracts under the same name. The title in the original, is *Le bon Sens, Good Sense*. It was printed, I believe, in Philadelphia; but the printer was ashamed or afraid to own it.

† Pigott's Political Dictionary, p. 132. This work was originally printed in England; but having been suppressed there, the whole or, nearly the whole, impression was sent over to America, and distributed among the people. But in what manner, and by what means, there are some who can tell better than the writer of this pamphlet. It was thought, however, to be so useful, as to merit the American press—for the copy which I possess, is one of an edition printed at New-York, for Thomas Greenleaf, late editor of the Argus: 1796.

‡ 2. Cor. v. 14, 15.

Sit down, now, and interrogate your own hearts, whether you can, with a "pure-conscience," befriend Mr. Jefferson's election? Whether you can do it *in the name of the Lord Jesus?* Whether you can lift up your heads and tell him that the choice of this infidel is for his honor, and that you promote it in the faith of his approbation? Whether, in the event of success, you have a right to look for his blessing in the enjoyment of your president? Whether, having preferred the talents of a man before the religion of Jesus, you ought not to fear that God will blast these talents; abandon your president to infatuated counsels; and yourselves to the plague of your own folly? Whether it would not be just to remove the restraints of his good providence, and scourge you with that very infidelity which you did not scruple to countenance? Whether you can, without some guilty misgivings, pray for the spirit of Christ upon a president whom you choose in spite of every demonstration of his hatred to Christ? Those who, to keep their consciences clean, oppose Mr. Jefferson, may pray for him, in this manner, with a full and fervent heart. But to you, God may administer this dread rebuke: "You chose an infidel: keep him as ye chose him: walk in the sparks that ye have kindled." Whether the threatnings of God are not pointed against such a magistrate and such a people? "Be wise, O ye kings," is his commandment; "be instructed ye judges of the earth: serve the Lord with fear and rejoice with trembling: *Kiss the son*, lest he be angry, and ye perish from the way when his anger is kindled but a little."* What then is in store for a magistrate who is so far from "kissing the son," that he hates and opposes him? "The wicked shall be turned into hell, and all the nations that forget God."† And who forget him, if not a nation which, tho' called by his name, nevertheless caresses, honors, rewards his enemies? The Lord hath sworn to strike *through Kings in the day of his wrath.*‡ Woe, then, to those governments which are wielded by infidels, when he arises to judgment; and woe to those who have contributed to establish them! To whatever influence they owe their determinations and their measures, it is not to the "spirit of understanding and of the fear of the Lord." Do I speak these things as a man; or saith not the scripture the same also?

* Ps. ii. 10–12.
† Ps. ix. 17.
‡ Ps. cx. 5.

> Woe to the rebellious children, saith the Lord, that *take counsel, but not of me*, and that cover with a covering, *but not of my Spirit*, that they may add sin to sin. That walk to go down into Egypt *(and have not asked at my mouth)* to strengthen themselves in the strength of Pharaoh, and to trust in the shadow of Egypt. Therefore the strength of Egypt shall be your shame, and the *trust in the shadow of Egypt your confusion*.*

This is the light in which God considers your confidence in his enemies. And the issue for which you ought to be prepared.

I have done; and do not flatter myself that I shall escape the censure of many professed, and of some real, Christians. The stile of this pamphlet is calculated to conciliate nothing but conscience. I desire to conciliate nothing else. "If I pleased men, I should not be the servant of Christ." I do not expect, nor wish, to fare better than the apostle of the gentiles, who became the enemy of not a few professors, because he *told them the truth*.† But the bible speaks of "children that will not hear the law of the Lord—which say to the seers, See not: and to the prophets, Prophesy not unto us right things: speak unto us smooth things: prophesy deceits."‡ Here is the truth, "Whether you will hear, or whether you will forbear." If you are resolved to persevere in elevating an infidel to the chair of your president, I pray God not to "choose your delusions"—but cannot dissemble that "my flesh trembleth for fear of his judgments." It is my consolation that my feeble voice has been lifted up for his name. I have addressed you as one who believes, and I beseech you to act as those who believe, "That we must all appear before the judgment seat of Christ." Whatever be the result, you shall not plead that you were not warned. If, notwithstanding, you call to govern you an enemy to my Lord and your Lord; in the face of earth and heaven, and in the audience of your own consciences, I record my protest, and wash my hands of your guilt.

Arise, O Lord, and let not man prevail!

* Is. xxx. 1–3.
† Gal. iv. 16.
‡ Is. xxx. 9, 10.

52

A SOLEMN ADDRESS TO CHRISTIANS AND PATRIOTS

Tunis Wortman

NEW-YORK

1800

Tunis Wortman (d. 1822). Wortman's background and activities before the 1790s are unknown. He appears first as a New York City lawyer and man of the Enlightenment, a French-style partisan of liberty, and an apostle of the millennial republic. He viewed the French Revolution as the continuation of the American Revolution and as the European phase of history's progress toward universal peace. By 1801 disillusionment had set in, and Napoleon had shattered the dream. Wortman moved in the intellectual circle that included physician and author Elihu Hubbard Smith, law professor James Kent, and novelist Charles Brockden Brown. He served as the clerk of the city and county of New York from 1801 to 1807. Active in public affairs and in demand as an orator, he was the first secretary of the New-York Democratic Society and a member of both the Manumission Society and the Tammany Society; the latter he turned into a wing of the Jeffersonian Republican Party. Wortman viewed the Federalists as "antirepublican Anglophiles," and he fought the Federalist opposition to the War of 1812 by starting a newspaper, *The Standard of Union*, in New York City; this was an effective organ of his support for President James Madison's policies.

Aside from newspaper editorials, only four specimens of Wortman's authorship survive, but they are ample displays of a fine writer with a powerful, well-educated mind. All were published between 1796 and 1801. In them we find him quoting a range of classical and modern writers including Plato, Cicero, Horace, Shakespeare (of whom he seems particularly fond), Gibbon, Locke, Montesquieu, Priestly, and Reid. The most substantial work is a 300-page book on political and constitutional theory entitled *A Treatise Concerning Political Enquiry and the Liberty of the Press* (New York, 1800; repr. Da Capo Press, 1970 [ed. Leonard W. Levy]). It was published with the help of Albert Gallatin, who sought subscriptions for it among Republican members of Congress. Leonard Levy calls it "Wortman's great book" and "the book that Jefferson did not write but should have." He compares it with Milton's *Areopagitica* and Mill's *On Liberty* and summarizes: "Wortman's treatise is surely the preeminent American classic, because of its scope, fullness, philosophical approach, masterful marshalling of all the libertarian arguments, and uncompromisingly radical view" (Levy, *Emergence of a Free Press* [Oxford, 1985], pp. 328, 331-32).

A

SOLEMN ADDRESS,

TO

CHRISTIANS & PATRIOTS,

UPON THE

APPROACHING ELECTION

OF A

President of the United States:

IN ANSWER TO A PAMPHLET, ENTITLED,

" *Serious Considerations,*" *&c.*

NEW-YORK;

PRINTED BY DAVID DENNISTON.

1800.

A Solemn Address, his fourth piece, Wortman signed "Timoleon," who is emblematic of saintly opposition to tyranny in Plutarch's portrayal. It is a response to *Serious Considerations* (1800), written by Reverend William Linn, with the assistance of Dr. John M. Mason, and contains, according to Joseph Sabin, "stories calculated to ruin Jefferson among all pious people" (*A Dictionary of Books Relating to America* [29 vols., 1868-1936], 10:373; see the note to the preceding sermon by Mason, number 51). Wortman intends to counter the "false, scandalous, and malicious" attack of Jefferson launched by Linn, whom he compares to Judas Iscariot. He begins by quoting the Ninth Commandment: "Thou shalt not bear false-witness against thy neighbor."

DEDICATION

To the Reverend Dr. L——

"Thou shalt not bear false-witness against thy neighbour."
—The ninth commandment.

I am not an admirer of dedications, nor will you, sir, be flatterd by the following. Your present situation, and the nature of the subject upon which I am about to remark, have rendered it proper that the ensuing observations should be particularly inscribed to yourself.

You are not only a divine, but also a party politician. For my own part, I think these two characters absolutely incompatible. From the minister of religion, we have a right expect exemplary purity and sincerity. In the statesman, we constantly discover cunning, intrigue and duplicity: It remains for you to reconcile these opposite characters to each other.

You are a partizan of Mr. Pinckney; in the presence of your maker, I would tell you so. I allow you the rights of opinion as a man, but I cannot permit you, with impunity, to abuse the influence you possess with your congregation.

I am an advocate for religion, in its purity and truth; if I am an unworthy, yet I am, nevertheless, a sincere son of the church: I cannot tamely see that church and its heavenly doctrines prophaned to party purposes; my bosom burns with indignation at the attempts to render christianity the instrument of tyrants.

A pamphlet has lately made its appearance, entitled, "*Serious Considerations.*" I hesitate not, in the language of lawyers, to call it false, scandalous and malicious; it has the clerical mark upon it: Yet, I say not that you are the author, but I firmly declare that, by adopting its sentiments and declarations, you have rendered it your own.*

You are the author of a handbill, which you intended for a prayer;

* Mr. M——, if he pleases, may father the *Sickly Child.*

it recommends the pamphlet to which I have alluded: This handbill, or this prayer you gave to Mr. Van Hook, to be circulated among the consistory. There is a want of openness, in such procedure, unworthy of the upright mind; yet it evinces a sense of shame which I wish you to retain. There was a Judas Iscariot among the apostles; and history has furnished examples of priests who have betrayed their country; yet still there have been many famous pastors, who have maintained the dignity of the church, with zeal and fidelity. Alas! it has been left for you to demonstrate, that every minister is not, necessarily, a patriot and a gentleman.

For the present, sir, adieu! Weak men have believed that this country contains a Cæsar. Thanks to heaven they are deceived. I will not insult the ashes of the noble Julius, by comparing him with the ringleader of a modern party: Be assured, that Cæsar is no more; his mighty spirit sleepeth in the dust. Hope not for the messiah of royalty. The diadem, and mitre, and tiara, cannot be restored, even by the worst man in America.

The following ideas cannot be new to you, at least they ought to be familiar; pardon me if I inform you, that many of your friends have regretted that those ideas have ceased to influence your conduct. From your interest, then, from your prudence, if not from your candor, let me expect an attentive perusal of my sentiments.

Timoleon

TO MY READERS

In the ensuing observations, I shall consider your duties as christians and as patriots. I shall make it my task to establish the following propositions.

1st. That it is your duty, as christians, to maintain the purity and independence of the church, to keep religion separate from politics, to prevent an union between the church and the state, and to preserve your clergy from temptation, corruption and reproach.

2d. That as christians and patriots, it is equally your duty to defend the liberty and constitution of your country.

3d. Although I am a sincere and decided opponent of infidelity, yet as it respects a president of the United States, an enmity to the constitution is the most dangerous evil; inasmuch as christianity is secure by the force of its own evidence, and coming from God, cannot be destroyed by human power; but, on the contrary, the constitution, is vulnerable to the attacks of an ambitious and unprincipled executive.

4th. That Mr. Jefferson is in reality a republican, sincerely attached to the constitution of his country, amiable and irreproachable in his conduct as a man, and that we have every reason to believe him, in sincerity, a christian.

5th. That the charge of deism, contained in such pamphlet, is false, scandalous and malicious—that there is not a single passage in the Notes on Virginia, or any of Mr. Jefferson's writings, repugnant to christianity; but on the contrary, in every respect, favourable to it —and further, that there is every reason to believe the story of Mazzei a base and ridiculous falsehood.

6th. That Mr. Adams is not a republican, agreeably to the true intent and meaning of the constitution of the United States.

7th. That a party has long existed, and still exists, hostile to the constitution, and with reason, suspected of favouring the interests of a foreign power—that Mr. Pinckney is the candidate of that party, and therefore cannot be a republican.

And lastly—that the interest of the people; the preservation of public liberty, and the safety of our present constitution, irresistibly demand that Mr. Jefferson should be elected president of the United States.

Timoleon

Christianity sprung from heaven. Hypocrisy is the offspring of hell. The former is productive of peace, & virtue, and life eternal; but thc latter is an abomination in the sight of Almighty God, and has filled the world with crimes and blood, and misery, and desolation.

I address you upon the most solemn and momentous subjects which can interest the mind—religion and liberty. I consider you in the capacity of believers and patriots, as equally anxious to maintain every inestimable right which appertains to christians & to men. You have a religion which deserves your pious solicitude; but need I to remind you that you likewise have a country! Are you to be told that your duty, as christians, is irreconcilable with the sacred obligations which bind you to the state? Are you at this day to be solemnly and seriously called upon to sacrifice your freedom upon the altars of your GOD? No, my countrymen, your religion is inestimable and worthy of your care. Your civil constitution is also invaluable. It is the palladium of all your social blessings, & the peculiar gift of providence. Your obligations to your children, to your country, and to heaven, command you to defend that constitution. With a voice too powerful to be resisted, they conjure you to cling to, and fasten upon it, "with the last strong hold which grapples into life."

I wish to impress your minds with a solemnity equal to the magnitude of the subject—to inspire you with a resolution to defend both your liberty and your faith. I intreat you to reflect, with equal seriousness, upon the duties which you owe to religion, and those which you owe to your country. In the course of these pages, I shall consider each of these sources of obligation. I shall equally investigate the duties which, as christians, you owe to religion, and those which, as citizens, are to be performed to the state.

First then, what are your principal duties, as christians, with respect to religion?

It is a primary duty to preserve that religion, pure, holy & unadulterated, unmixed with temporal pride and worldly ambition. The great author of christianity most expressly assured his ministers, that his kingdom is not of this world, and that it was impossible for them, at the same time, to serve God and Mammon: his divine wisdom foresaw that if they were led astray by the enticing riches and alluring objects of this world, they would prove but faithless pastors to his people. With the example of the pagan priests before his eyes, he dreaded the pollution of his celestial system, from the connection which he too evidently foresaw, would take place between his own ministers and the secular establishments; such is the obvious import of many of the most impressive precepts of the Saviour. The event has proved that his apprehensions have been too fatally verified.

It was not by precept alone; it was likewise by his illustrious example, that the founder of our religion enforced that salutary lesson. Carefully abstaining from all active agency in political affairs, and exclusively confining himself to the duties of his station, as priest of the most high God, he rendered unto Cæsar the things which are Cæsar's, and unto God, the things which are God's. Meek and unassuming in his deportment, he intended by his life, to afford a standing example of conduct to be pursued by christian divines —disavowing all concerns with the affairs of state, he evidently considered an active agency in politics to be inconsistent with that purity and sanctity of character, which should appertain to ministers of the gospel.

It is essential to the interests of religion, that its teachers should be set apart, to the performance of their sacred duties. I have said it, and I earnestly repeat it; "they cannot serve God and Mammon." The charge of their flocks requires all their pastoral care; their attention should always be directed heavenward; if they mingle too deeply in the affairs of this world, they are apt to become unmindful of the prospects of the next. If they look to temporal rewards, and to the riches of this globe, their minds become poisoned and perverted, and they are immediately reduced to the level of common men. We are in the habit of connecting the character of religion with that of the individuals who profess to be its teachers; however pure or excellent his doctrines, a clergyman, without practical piety, is a stumbling block to the people.

I have always attached the highest respectability to the character of a christian divine. I see and I feel that there is not an order of men in the community capable of rendering such signal services, or of inflicting such extensive injuries. If it is the duty of the clergy to watch over the conduct of their congregations, it is equally incumbent upon congregations, to be mindful of the conduct of their pastors—they should confine their ministers to the duties of their sacred calling, and above all things, beware how they permit them to acquire a political ascendancy.*

Clergymen are but men, in common with ourselves; they partake of every human infirmity and every human passion. If ambition is suffered to insinuate itself into the pulpit, it is more dangerous in proportion, as it has greater powers and opportunities of mischief. Let me ask any pious divine, if he is not sensible of possessing an undue ascendency over the minds of his hearers, if he should be so abandoned as to exercise it?

Let me not be told, that religion is in danger, and that we should therefore increase the powers and influence of the clergy. I say, and am ready to maintain, that religion is in greater danger, by permitting them to intermeddle with political concerns, than by confining them, with the utmost rigour, to the duties of their profession; as men and as citizens, they have an equal right to express their opinions and give their suffrages; but they should never be permitted to carry their politics into the sacred desk, and more especially, they should not be suffered to make religion an engine of politics.

I have ever been convinced, that a political divine is a dangerous character.† The more I read, and the more I reflect, the more thoroughly am I convinced of the truth of that position. There never will be wanting men, who by caresses and flattery & inflaming their passions, will make them the instruments of every crime, and the shameless tools of the greatest ambition; by this means religion becomes a solemn farce, and an impious mockery of God—and liberty, and government, & every thing valuable upon earth prostituted under the pretended mask of piety.

* Why should we read history without profiting by it? Ambition and tyranny have always been fond of assuming the masque of religion and making instruments of judges and divines. Cromwell the usurper was a detestible hypocrite. We have already one judge who rivals Jefferies or Tresilian. We have more than one minister to match a Wolsey or a Laud.

† Dr. D. and Dr. S. and Dr. L. and Mr. M. *cum multus aliis*, will please to attend to this sentiment; indeed I could wish it were possible for them to peruse the whole of my pamphlet with candour.

I am writing to sincere professors, and not to those who make religion a cloak for base and selfish purposes. Men of the latter description, are not to be moved by expostulation or argument; such men will court the "rocking of the battlements" if they could gain by the event; they would sit as unmoved spectators, and with steady eyes behold the destruction of law, and order, and liberty, and of the peace and constitution of their country, or rather they would assist in lighting the firebrand of death and desolation; but such men are not christians, they deserve not that honourable appellation: wherever they exist they are capable of every crime, no reasoning of mine can divert them from their purposes.

If you are real christians, anxious for the honor and purity and interest of the christian church, you will feel a steady determination, to preserve it free from corruption. Unless you maintain the pure and primitive spirit of christianity, and prevent the cunning and intrigue of statesmen from mingling with its institutions; you will become exposed to a renewal of the same dreadful and enormous scenes which have not only disgraced the annals of the church, but destroyed the peace, and sacrificed the lives of millions. It is by such scenes and by such dreadful crimes, that christianity has suffered; by such fatal and destructive enormities which, since the days of Constantine, have been perpetrated without intermission, that the church has become debased and polluted; in language similar to that of Joshua, we have reason to exclaim there is an accursed thing within the tabernacle. The blood of many an innocent Abel has stained the ephod, the vestments and the altar. Religion has suffered more from the restless ambition and impiety of the church of Rome, than from all the writings of a Voltaire, a Tindal, a Volney, or even the wretched blasphemies of Paine.*

We have years and volumes—we have a world of experience before us, in the sufferings and the miseries of ages—we read a lesson too impressive to be resisted: both as christians and as men, we are powerfully conjured to reject all attempts to promote an union between the church and the state—the very idea of such a union is insupportable. Neither directly or indirectly should we suffer it to be effected.

* The reader is only referred to Mosheim's Ecclesiastical History, he will find that no imagination is capable of pourtraying the picture in colours too high or glowing.

Religion and government are equally necessary, but their interests should be kept separate and distinct. No legitimate connection can ever subsist between them. Upon no plan, no system, can they become united, without endangering the purity and usefulness of both —the church will corrupt the state, and the state pollute the church. Christianity becomes no longer the religion of God—it becomes the religion of temporal craft and expediency and policy. Instead of being the sacred guide to lead mankind to heaven, it becomes the prostituted instrument of private cupidity and personal ambition. I am not to be told there is no longer danger in such an alliance; the danger has always existed, and as long as men retain their passions and vices, will exist in all its force. The church of Rome arose from the smallest beginnings. She commenced her career with professions of mildness, clemency and moderation, displaying at first the innocence and the harmlessness of the dove: she afterwards discovered the horrid fangs of the serpent, and exercised the unrelenting barbarity of a crocodile. The successors of St. Peter, no longer spiritual bishops, became a race of tyrants, more ferocious than Nero, a Domitian, and more pampered than Eliogabalus himself. They extended the arms of their authority into every European kingdom, and into every christian church. I need not revive the memory of the inquisition, or usurp the province of the historian, in painting the sufferings of the wretched Hugonots. It is for a moment only that I point to the fires of Smithfield, and to the massacre of St. Bartholomews—did this proceed from religion—from the mild and benevolent spirit of christianity? God of heaven, forbid the rash surmise! rescue thy ministers and thy altars from the odius imputation, and preserve thy church from the pollution and abomination which accompanies a connection with the state.

With the sincerity of a christian, I feel for the honour of religion. I feel for the pious character of christian divines.* I dread lest that character should be tarnished and debased, and deprived of its usefulness, by the unworthy conduct of some of its professors; the present moment is dangerous. Attempts have been made to unite the interests of religion, with the crimes and abuses, and corruptions of governments. There is reason to apprehend the consequences.

Men of weak minds, men of limited researches are apt to be mis-

* Would to God they would feel for themselves with equal sincerity!

guided, they are prone to confound the abuses of the most excellent establishment with the establishment itself. The sincere friend of christianity, should be vigilent and guarded; he should be zealous in vindicating his religion, from the charge of participation in the intrigues and oppression of statesmen; the christian divine should be cautioned to pursue a prudent and temperate conduct, to keep aloof from the coalition of parties, and maintain a steady seat in the sanctuary unmoved and unruffled by the whirlwind and the tempest.

Whatever interested men may tell you, religion is not in danger. It is founded on a rock which has often been assailed, but cannot be shaken. It is a melancholy truth, that christianity has suffered more from the blind zeal and wicked perfidy of pretended friends, than from the open attack of its most inveterate foes. Why should religion have enemies? Let me ask what interest, or what motive mankind can have in opposing a system founded on truth and benevolence? It is no answer to say that such opposition springs entirely from the pride of philosophy, or from the corruption and perversity of our nature!

Experience suggests a more satisfactory but a more fatal reason; the crimes and abuses which have been committed in its name, cruelty and persecution, and intolerance have raised up an host of enemies, and accounts for the zeal, the bitterness and the vehemence of their opposition. It is the departure from the original purity of the system; the alliance with courts; the impurities and prophanity of spurious, amphibious, hermorphredite priests, the innumerable atrocities and persecutions, which have been perpetrated in the name of the most high, that has produced or encouraged the school of infidelity, and occasioned many an honest mind to believe that the establishment of christianity, is incompatible with civil freedom. Let me conjure you, then, to purify the altar, to keep things sacred from intermingling with things prophane, to maintain religion separate and apart from the powers of this world; and then, to use an expression similar to that of the infidel Rousseau, you will hasten the æra when all mankind shall bow at the feet of Jesus.

If I write with warmth, it is because I am interested in the subject, and feel its importance. I am not an unconcerned spectator of the events which distract and agitate the earth; equally a friend to religion and to civil freedom, I cannot endure the attempts which are making to oppose them in hostile array to each other; and to connect the existence of christianity with the safety of corrupt and oppressive establishments of government. I think, that the preservation of religion is separate and independent from all human establishments; its existence depends upon the energy & validity of its own evidence, its testimony both external & inherent speaks powerfully, & pleads irresistibly to the understanding & the heart. Our hopes, & fears, & interests, and reflections, are a sufficient pledge for the continuance of our faith; the moment you place the subject upon a different footing, you lessen its importance and prostitute its dignity, you open a door for every species of corruption, you expose your pastors to temptations incompatible with the integrity and purity of their character, you render religion an engine in the hands of any government for the time being; no matter what, you interpose an insurmountable gulph between piety and patriotism, and reduce the conscientious patriot to the dilemma of chusing between his country and his faith.

It is because I am the friend, and not the enemy of christianity, that I am the advocate of liberality and toleration. I have examined the evidences on both sides of the question, and know that the system is not in danger; it comes from heaven and cannot be shaken, it is proof against all the artillery of infidels, but alas! it is not proof against the mistaken zeal, and persecution, and prejudices of its friends. There was a time when discordant sectaries & churches were hurling their anathemas against each other with invincible jealousy and indignation, but now they are happily united against a common enemy; but still, I see, and deplore the same impolitic spirit, which committed the hapless heretic to the faggot, and plunged the sword of intolerance into the bosom of its unoffending victim. I have said it, and I ever will maintain, that this spirit never has been, and never will be of service to christianity; persecution may generate and multiply hypocrites, but will never produce a single convert; it steels, and irritates, and hardens the heart. It is the power of repulsion which disorganizes and splits asunder, it has not a single charm or attraction.

Mistake me not my readers, these observations are not levelled against any particular individual, or any particular church. Christians are all brethren, fellow labourers in one vineyard, and it is sincerely trusted joint inheriters of one glorious inheritance. I am pleading a great cause, that of civil and religious liberty; my earnestness proceeds not from passion, but from the sincerity of conviction; there may be possibly a mixture of enthusiasm in the manner, but upon such a subject, the want of enthusiasm would be coldness. I charge no one church with intolerance, but I say, that intolerance will creep into every church that becomes vested with temporal power; and, I say further, that almost every clergyman will become intolerant, who is either directly or indirectly connected with the state. I know not how it is, but there is something in the nature of zeal which poisons the mind, and produces the most bitter weeds, unless it is sown in a soil of uncommon urbanity; we need not open the volumes of ecclesiastical history, to prove this position, our own experience and observation of living men, and manners are abundantly sufficient; only observe the conduct of the great Athanasius, how greatly did his inflammatory disposition serve to foment the flares of animosity, which had been kindled in the church; look at the still greater Calvin, even this illustrious reformer, in the exuberance of his zeal, was contented with nothing less than the painful death of the miserable Servetus. If understandings so enlightened, so vast, I will add so sublime, are susceptible of intolerance and persecution, what shall we say of the common race of modern clergymen?

I respect the church of England, as it exists in America, it is my duty to respect it; I have no objections to the harmless title of bishop, disunited from exclusive privileges and baneful powers. But, how has that church persecuted every other denomination, that refused to conform with her religious rites and ceremonies. In America she is mild, and peaceable, and benevolent, because she is not a component part of the state, because she is unarmed with the destructive weapons of secular power. In England she had totally disfranchised the whole body of dissenters; before the revolution she pursued them to this, their last best refuge; armed with equal authority the demon of spiritual hierarchy, like a gigantic Colossus would have strode across the atlantic; but let such injuries for ever be buried in oblivion, or the recollection of them only revived for instructive and prudential purposes.

Would to God, that my feeble pen could inspire christians with that spirit of forbearance and moderation, which forms so amiable and essential a part of their system. Imbued with that clemency, and moderation, and charity, and love of man, which so eminently characterises the sacred pages of the gospel, religion would be seated upon an adamantine rock, and all mankind irresistibly attracted by her simplicity, her sincerity and her truth. Such is christianity when cloathed in the robes of righteousness, such her lovely, and pure, and dignified character, when arrayed with the smiles, and charms, and glory, and freshness of the morning; she comes blooming from the bosom of her heavenly author. But I cannot disguise my indignation, when I see her altars polluted and disgraced, when I see the sacred religion of truth and heaven, prostituted into a cloak to cover every indecency, every enormity & every crime; when I see men whose worldly ambition should have prevented their approaching even the vestibule of the temple, assuming the character, and officiating in the functions of priests of the most high, descend into the forum or comitia, and engage as political engines to influence the elections of the people; are such men serving the God of heaven, a sacrificing to the carnal and impious mammon? are they promoting the holy cause of religion, or pampering their own ambitious lusts? If I had the spear of Ithuriel, I would transfix them in their hypocrisy, and expose them as spectacles of deformity and guilt.

Believe me, this is not to promote the interests of christianity, nor to defend it against the dangers to which it may be exposed. I have asserted, and I repeat with energy, that the true source of apprehension, is from the corruptions which proceed from an intermingling connection with the states and not from the reasoning, the sophistry, or the ridicule of infidels. I cannot, I will not endure the idea that religion is to be defended by any weapon but argument alone. It is an insult to truth to deny the energy of its powers, or to insinuate a doubt that it is not invincible. This is the work of scepticism—it is the most dangerous species of infidelity. When I hear a man distrust the force of the evidences of christianity, I doubt the sincerity of his profession—I feel persuaded that he is not a christian from conviction. I have heard and examined the argument of infidels. I pity their delusion, but I will not compliment them with the persuasion that they are capable of overthrowing the citadel of the Catholic faith. In my turn, I have perused with no little attention, the writings of their principal champions—The delicate irony of Gibbon—the sarcastic asperity of Voltaire—the flowing eloquence of Rosseau—the arguments and specious subtilty of Hume, and Hobbes, and Tindal—the contemptible philosophy of Volney. Gracious heaven! is it possible that a learned christian can apprehend danger from the attacks of such feeble artillery? Will he dread the assertions of philosophers who have the ignorance and the impudence to declare "that christianity consists in the allegorical worship of the sun, under the cabalistical names of Chrisen, or Yesus, or Jesus"? Such a man will expose a want of magnanimity, and exhibit distrust more prejudicial to the truth and dignity of his cause, than all the feeble efforts of its enemies. An antidote may be found in thousands of invaluable volumes. Even Dr. Linn has asked, "whether that christianity which has withstood the roaring of the lion, shall now be afraid of the brayings of the ass." I could mention only five writers who have refuted every argument which has ever been, or ever will or can be offered against christianity; and, perhaps, I need not inform the reader of research, that I refer to Grotius, Paley and Hartley, to West on the Resurrection, and Littleton on the conversion of St. Paul.

Let me then ask the sincere, the pious christian, whether he thinks his religion stands in need of additional support? and whether he will consent to prop his church, which from its nature, is permanent and eternal, with the transitory things of this world, which pass away like the empty shadow, and vanish like the morning clouds and evening dew? Whether he will corrupt the purity of christianity by a dangerous connection with the affairs of state? Whether he will subject the ministers of his congregation to temptation and reproach, by permitting them to intermeddle with political concerns, and to become the directors of his temporal affairs, as well as his spiritual guides? And lastly, whether he will consent to revive that spirit of intolerance and persecution, which has been the reproach of religion, so long disgraced the church, and occasioned such complicated desolation, misery and imposture?

And thou, O minister of the gospel! consecrated guardian of the honour and purity of the church! canst thou, with hands unclean, officiate in the sacred temple; and with mind unholy, approach the altars of thy God? The external appearance of sanctity—the lifeless image of religion, may deceive the world, but thou shalt tremble before the omniscient eye of the Almighty. Let not then the cross of thy Saviour be prostituted to the works of darkness and ambition, and to the ruin of thy country! weak and wretched mortal, the reward of thy iniquity will avail thee not: for in a few fleeting years, thou shalt be numbered with the dead. O, keep the leaven of unrighteousness from mingling with the Eucharist, and the bitter waters of Mara from poisoning the sacred cup!

I feel already that I am trespassing upon your attention; yet before I leave this part of my address, let me conjure you in the name of your country—in the name of liberty & the constitution—in the name of religion, & every principle that is sacred on earth or in heaven—I conjure you to beware how you permit your faith and attachment as christians, from interfering with your duties as citizens. The inevitable consequence of an union of the church with the state, will be the mutual destruction of both. Religion, instead of remaining an active and efficient director of faith and conduct, will be converted into an engine to promote the ruin of the constitution. Ambitious and aspiring men, who wish to subvert the liberties of the people, will represent their political opponents as atheists and infidels, and fasten upon your honest prejudices to render you the instruments of your own undoing. This is not the language of speculation. I see with indignation, that it has already been done. The pulpit and the press are at this moment engaged to effect the base designs of a political party. Is this the way to promote the interests of the church, by connecting it with party views and party operations? to unite its prosperity with the election of Jefferson, or Adams, or Pinckney? To render it obnoxious to those, who, from honest and patriotic views, espouse the part of the former candidate? Will you tell the patriot whose understanding convinces him that the liberty of the people, and the very existence of the constitution, depends upon the election of Mr. Jefferson, that he is placed in a dilemma in which he must either abjure his country or his religion? Yet all this and more, he has been told in a pamphlet, which, I am sorry to say, bears every inherent mark of having been written by a clergyman. It is a disgrace to the author, and a scandal to the church; and unless such practices are prevented for the future, the cause of christianity will suffer more from such mischievous attempts to connect it with politics, than from all the evils which the writer of it pretends to apprehend from the election of Mr. Jefferson.

Hitherto, then, I have only considered you in the character of christians, and endeavoured to discuss some of your principal duties, as it respects the preservation of religion; arguments and examples without number might be multiplied to prove to you the danger which would arise from the connection of the church* with the state; those which have been adduced, are sufficient to weigh with candid and unprejudiced minds, and I have already said that readers of another description are above the reach of either argument or example.

Such then, Americans, are some of your principal duties with respect to the church—but as christians, it is equally your duty to guard the state, to watch as well as to pray. I maintain it to be the sacred and imperious duty of every religious man, to preserve the rights, and liberties, and constitution of his country. *If your civil privileges are once gone, my countrymen, what shall protect your religious ones?* What shall prevent one domineering church from becoming the favourite, & like the rod of Aaron, devouring all the others? Such things have been, and nothing but the wisdom and virtue of the people can prevent them from happening again. I do not believe that Mr. Jefferson is a deist—there is nothing in the wretched pamphlet of ——, to convince me of that fact. It is a groundless calumny. If it was truth, it could be supported by better evidence. I shall presently bestow a few observations upon that contemptible production; but let us barely, for the sake of argument, imagine a case. Suppose, for a moment, that there are three candidates for the presidency—Mr. Jefferson, Mr. Adams, and Mr. Pinckney—that Mr. Jefferson was in reality a deist, but a decided friend to the republican constitution of his country—that the two others were very pious & sincere christians, but secretly friends to aristocracy or monarchy, & hostile to the spirit of the present constitution, *which of the three would be the most dangerous man*? Mr. Jefferson, in such case, even if he had the intentions, could not be of the smallest disservice to religion: thanks to heaven, christianity has taken too deep a root to be capable of being shaken by the opinions, or even the enmity of any president. I know of no other method by which religion can be injured by any government in this country, except by its setting one powerful church above the heads of the rest.

* When a church becomes directly or indirectly connected with a state, it may still retain its external form and appearance, but Christianity no longer remains, the heavenly virtues become extinct, and the pure spirit of piety disgusted by its avarice, ambition and impiety takes wings and flies to heaven. Nothing, nothing is left but a state without liberty and a church without religion.

But this Mr. Jefferson is incapable of doing; for according to such position; he would be equally indifferent to all; in this sense, strange as it may appear, christianity would have much more to apprehend from a bigot than an infidel. But let us imagine for a moment, that an enemy to the constitution should be elected president of the United States. Gracious heaven! I shudder when I contemplate the picture! Our liberties prostituted—our religion at the mercy of one intolerant church—for every tyranny must & will have its establishment. Our civil constitution abandoned, or what is worse, mutilated, and distorted, and deformed into every protean shape; and the fruits of our glorious revolution—of the blood of our fathers, of the miseries of our families and our children—of the burning and ravaging of our towns, and of the desolation of our villages gone—gone forever!! These are serious—these are impressive considerations. Tell me christian! which of these alternatives is the most pregnant with calamity?

I am not a friend to the empty fripperies, and badinage, and extravagancies of modern philosophy, nor am I an advocate of the excesses and abuses of that revolution which now convulses France, and astonishes the civilized world. I declare to God, that I have no confidence in a nation which can change its government and its religion in a moment, and see the wear and tear of consciences and constitutions with the same apathy and unconcern as if they were suits of cloathes. I love my own government, because I see in it a liberal, rational and practicable form, not springing up by accident, like a mushroom in the night, but growing out of the habits, manners and ancient institutions of the people. I see in it a system of regular political architecture, modelled in the best order, proportioned in perfect symmetry, containing unity of design, and divested of every species of false ornament. It is the workmanship of a master in the art. It is the property of a people who are deserving of its blessings, because they know how to use and appreciate them. Such a people should not, and they will not be trifled with—they reverence their magistrates and pastors—they yield a generous, and noble, and willing obedience to the laws—they are conscious of the masterly beauties of their civil constitution, and determined to preserve them. Such a people uniformly acting from the bias of the judgment and understanding, with a wise, discretionate and sagacious subordination, can readily distinguish between the legitimate exercise, and the unwarrantable abuse of authority. I speak not only of the temporal, but also of the spiritual powers. My observations are equally applicable to statesmen and divines.

I know, and I feel, that there is a powerful conflict between old and new governments, and old and new philosophy, and that religion has been pressed and dragged into the warfare. I wish that the conflict may be confined to Europe, where it has originated. As it regards the collision between governments, I have very little prediliction either for the ancient or the new. To me they appear almost equally abominable. My blood should never be wasted in behalf of the Bourbons or the consuls. I know not how it happens that French and American liberty have been confounded: they have scarcely a common attribute. There is just as much analogy between an hospitable winters fire and the destructive flames and lava of Etna and Vesuvius. The liberty and religion of Washington is not the liberty and religion of Marat and Robespierre, and Anarchalis Cloots, that flaming "orator of the human race." I make these observations, because some admirers of the Corinthian columns and capitals of the British constitution have endeavoured to trace a resemblance between French and American liberty. I abjure and renounce and anathematize all affiliation with the bacchanalian liberty of the great republic. Let it resist the ancient monarchies of Europe, and monster encounter monster, until they mutually perish. I love and admire that sober and rational liberty which exists in America, defined and established in an organized and regular constitution. It is the duty of religion to protect that liberty and that constitution. In the character of Christians, I solemnly call upon you to remember the obligations which bind you to your country.

Thus far I have addressed you in your religious characters, not because I suppose the duties of a christian and a patriot are incompatible with each other, but because the author of the pamphlet to which I allude, affects to consider a political subject exclusively in a theological view. Only attentive to the fancied interests of his church, he seems to have forgotten the existence of truth, of conscience, of country, and of God. To the attainment of his favourite object, and in the presence of heaven, I tell him, that the election of Mr. Pinckney is that object. He is willing to sacrifice every consideration, for the smiles of that great man, or for the mess of pottage from his table, this inglorious Esau is willing to barter his birthright, his freedom, and his country. But I am too proud to dwell upon personal restrictions. Let me in future consider you in the united relation of patriots and friends of religion. I call your serious attention to the situation of your country.

There are three candidates for the presidential chair—Mr. Jefferson, Mr. Adams, and Mr. Pinckney. Originally the two former were usually considered as the only candidates; the last was viewed as a candidate for the office of vice-president, and for that only. But there was always a schism among the federalists upon that subject. The leaders most devoted to British politics intended from the beginning to take advantage of the principal defect in our constitution, which confers the presidency upon the candidate having the greatest number of votes, without designating the office for which they were intended, and by their intrigues to give their favourite the ascendency. Mr. Pinckney must therefore be considered as the third candidate, and as the candidate of the British party.

We are now to consider the character and opinions of each of those candidates; let us execute our task with impartiality, and confer the palm upon him to whom it is justly due.

As a learned and experienced statesmen, Mr. Jefferson rises superior to the level of his rivals; he is the author of the declaration of independence, which in point of energy, as a composition, is equal at least to the Philippics of Demosthenes; as a negociator, his abilities are universally acknowledged. His letters to Genet and Hammond, when secretary of state, are master-pieces, & elegant models of diplomatic correspondence. In those letters he vindicates the rights of his country, with the firmness of a patriot, the acuteness of a profound logician, & the extensive research of a scholar deeply read in the history and in the laws of nations, and possessing an intimate knowledge of the interests of his country; his talents, as a statesman are equal to any emergency; as a proficient in general science, the name of Jefferson would reflect a lustre upon any age or country. Such is the sage of Monticelli.

But, Mr. Jefferson is an invincible patriot, equally attached to the constitution of his country, and to the liberties of the people. In every situation of life, he has evinced the most unshaken fidelity. Mr. Jefferson is an American republican, and a federalist in the true and unadulterated sense of the term. Faithful to the original principles of our revolution, his conduct has been steady, uniform and consistent. Times and circumstances have changed, but he has ever remained, and still remains the same; he has not the versatility of little minds, which like the lightest feather are driven before the gentlest breeze; it is his political virtue and his unshaken attachment to the liberty and happiness of his country, which constitutes the principal glory of his character, and which has deservedly rendered him the favorite of the people.

When the little butterflies of party, have ceased to flutter, and the noisy puppies of the day, are choaked with rage and disappointment, to the honor of Mr. Jefferson, it will be remembered, that in this licentious age, when morality hath almost become an empty sound, the bitter and vigilant malevolence of his enemies, has not dared to cast a stigma upon the purity of his character. Believe me, my countrymen, their only sincere objection is, that he is a republican and a patriot; if he would only forsake his country, and enter into their plans of government, he might be a deist or an adulterer* or any thing else, with perfect impunity.

I have seen nothing to convince me that Mr. Jefferson is a deist. On the contrary from information, at least, as respectable as that of the author of the pitiful pamphlet, which I shall presently condescend to notice, my information is that he is a sincere professor of christianity—though not a noisy one. But, I will candidly confess to you, that if I had ever so sincere a conviction of his infidelity; my prejudices, if you will permit me to call them so, are not so strong as to sacrifice my country to their operation; believing as I do, that public liberty and the constitution, will not be safe under the administra-

* What are we to think of the religion of those divines, who are the advocates of Mr. H——— of the man who had the cruelty publicly to wound and insult the feelings of his family, and to publish and glory in his shame? The confessions of J.J. Rosseau, the philosopher and citizen of Geneva, are nothing to those of our American youth. Our hero's apology for adultery stands unrivaled in ancient or modern language. Nathan the prophet had the courage to rebuke the Lord's anointed for a similar offence; but some of our clergymen generously excuse the frailties of their favourite party ringleader. There are some books which should never get out of print: The pamphlet detailing the love of Alexander and the fair Maria should stand as an eternal monument of the licentious manners of the age. Remember reader, that Alexander is a husband and a father and some people say a Christian. *Sed quere debit.* Nothing can prove the insincerity of such reverend defenders of religion more demonstrably than their advocating this man.

tion of Mr. Adams or Mr. Pinckney; I cannot see that the christianity of either of them will atone for the loss of my political freedom. There may be some merit in sacrificing every thing to the sign or external symbol of the cross; but it is a merit to which I do not aspire. If the other candidates were republicans, and Mr. Jefferson a deist, then the religion of the former would turn the scale of opinion in their favor; but, I never will be duped by the christianity of any man that meditates the ruin of the constitution. I am not prepared to surrender my liberty civil and religious, the future happiness of my children, the prosperity of my country, the welfare of millions of human beings yet unborn, and every possession and enjoyment that is valuable to men, and patriots, and christians. I know, that my GOD requires not such a sacrifice; he that would not permit Abraham to give his son Isaac as a burnt offering, demands not that my country should be prostrated on the altars of his religion; the infernal rites of Moloch required human victims, and a priest of Moloch would delight in the sacrifice of hecatombs. But christianity is the religion of grace, & mercy, and justice, and liberty.

I shall now proceed to enter into a more critical examination, of the pamphlet entitled "Serious Considerations, &c." and I request to be accompanied with a careful and patient attention. Be assured my readers, that politics and not religion is the object of the writer of that pamphlet, he writes as a partizan of Mr. Pinckney, and not as the advocate of evangelical purity and truth; he is not animated by a fervent love of religion, but excited and propelled by a deadly hatred to Mr. Jefferson. Such is the man, and such the character of his production.

Quiequid Græcia mendax,
Audet in historia.

Is surpassed by this *caput mortuum* of stupidity, frivolity and malice.

The professed intention of the pamphlet, is to prove Mr. Jefferson a deist; its real object, to ensure the election of Mr. Pinckney; assurances to the contrary are only evidences of depravity and falsehood; are you seriously to be told, that, if Mr. Jefferson is rejected, any other man except Mr. Adams or Mr. Pinckney, can possibly be appointed?

If Mr. Jefferson is a deist, and his rivals are enemies to the constitution, most unfortunate is our alternative; our views are confined, and our choice is limited. At this election, no other individual in existence can by the remotest possibility become your president; you would be driven to elect between an infidel and an enemy to the constitution. Has this writer dared to assure you, that Mr. Adams & Mr. Pinckney are republicans? Has he even attempted to prove that they are attached to public liberty, and determined to support our present happy and excellent constitution? Has he told you, that Mr. Adams has never expressed and written sentiments strongly favouring aristocratical orders, and distinctions in the state? Has he had the presumption to state, that Mr. Pinckney is not the candidate of the Anglo-federal, or, if you please, the British party in America? These are facts, which like the ghost of Banquo, have terror in their aspect; you cannot look upon them with a steady eye, unmoved. One of these men must be elected, one of them inevitably is destined to be your president; you have no other choice, no other alternative. If Mr. Adams and Mr. Pinckney are not republicans, then cease your songs to liberty, hang your harps upon the willows, and mourn the loss of departed freedom, gone for ever; professions of religion will avail you not; neither Moses, nor the prophets, nor the fathers, will protect your civil constitution.

But, what reason have we to believe that Mr. Jefferson is a deist? Nothing but the misrepresentation of his avowed and interested enemies. Remember that

Trifles light as air
Are to the jealous confirmation strong,
As proof of holy writ.

Let us examine the subject with candor.

In order to establish the infidelity of this enlightened statesman and patriot, the author of the pamphlet relies upon certain inutilated passages of the "notes on Virginia," and a pretended conversation, or rather a particular expression used in conversation with Mr. Mazzei.

Several passages in the notes upon Virginia, have been the subjects of animadversion; the first respecting the deluge, the second concerning the origin of the aborigenes of this country, the third relating to the Africans, or negroes, and the last, supposed to contain sentiments disrespectful to divine revelation. I shall proceed to examine those subjects in their order.

In the first place, Mr. Jefferson is supposed to deny the existence of an universal flood, such as Moses describes, and jews and christians equally believe. This is not the fact.

I do aver, that there is not a sentence in the notes upon Virginia, which either expressly, or even by implication denies the existence of such flood. By a recurrence to that work, we will readily perceive that the deluge is a topic collateral to the principal subject of discussion. In answer to questions either actually made, or supposed to have been asked by a learned foreigner, Mr. Jefferson is proceeding to describe the principal productions of his native state; while employed in this task; a remarkable and an interesting phenomenon arrests his attention, that is, the existence of petrified shells, or calcareous substances on the tops, or near the surfaces of the highest mountains. That circumstance "is considered by many both of the learned and the unlearned as proof of an universal deluge." Mr. Jefferson, on the contrary, is inclined to believe that such fact alone, unsupported by higher authority, would not amount to proof of a deluge.

He then proceeds to state a reason, why the ordinary laws or common operations of nature are insufficient to produce an universal flood, that if the whole contents of the atmosphere were water, "it would cover the globe but 35 feet deep, but as these waters as they fell would naturally run into the seas, the superficial measure of which, is to that of the dry parts of the globe as two to one, the seas would be raised only 52½ feet above their present level, and of course would overflow the lands to that height only." He supposes that deluges beyond such extent, are out of the ordinary laws of nature, and he supposes right.

This is the only passage in the work of Mr. Jefferson relating to the Deluge—he concludes, "there is a wonder somewhere, and that it requires us to believe the creation of a body of water and its subsequent annihilation."

Mr. Jefferson is writing in the character of a philosopher, and endeavouring, as a collateral point to his principal subject, to ascertain whether an universal deluge can be accounted for by the ordinary laws of nature? finding it impossible, how does he conclude? by denying it, by even insinuating a doubt? No—by terming it a "wonder," or, in other words, a miracle.

The reasoning of Mr. Jefferson so far from being repugnant to the holy scriptures, or from expressing a disbelief of the fact which is there related, strongly demands an opposite interpretation. Philosophy, who is blind to many of the common occurrences in nature, can never account for the extraordinary or miraculous interpositions of Almighty power. It is for this reason that Mr. Jefferson, after attempting to investigate the subject wisely, abandons every hypothesis and confesses his own ignorance—in this sense he exclaims, that "Ignorance is preferable to error; and that he is less remote from the truth who believes nothing, than he who believes what is wrong."

No sentiment can be more correct or prudent than that which I have last quoted; but even this sentiment has been distorted into a proof of infidelity. Mr. Jefferson confines the sentiment to philosophical subjects—he by no means extends it to the truth of revelation—he does not assert that it is best to disbelieve the existence of the Deluge; but that it is better to disbelieve every human hypothesis which would presumptuously endeavour to account for it, than to believe what is wrong.*

Yet, the Deluge is a wonder! a miraculous, a stupendous exertion of sovereign power! Who can account for it? Can man, weak man, conceive the manner in which it was effected? It would seem to require the creation of oceans of water and their subsequent annihilation! In the sense of Mr. Jefferson I make the exclamation, "*Ignorance is better than error*," and with respect to every hypothesis which philosophy would introduce, "He is less remote from the truth who be-

* To shew that this is his meaning, let us take his own words, together with the other parts of the sentence connected with them, "The establishment of the instance cited by M. de Voltaire (says Mr. Jefferson) of the growth of shells unattached to animal bodies, would have been that of his theory. But he has not established it. He has not left it on ground so respectable as to have rendered it an object of enquiry to the literati of his own country. Abandoning the fact therefore, the three hypotheses are equally unsatisfactory; and we must be contented to acknowledge that this great phenomenon is as yet unsolved, ignorance is preferable to error, and he is less remote from the truth who believes nothing, than he who believes what is wrong." Now to what does such observation relate? To philosophical theories and hypotheses, and not to the deluge or any other truth of revelation. By the same mode of juggling I could extract deistical sentiments from the writings of the apostles.

lieves nothing, than he who believes what is wrong." But God, who created the heavens and the earth, can create an universe of water and destroy it at his pleasure.

I do therefore confidently aver, that there is not a single expression in that passage which furnishes a fair implication of "disrespect for divine revelation." The position to be gathered from it is, that an universal flood cannot be accounted for from general laws. Had Mr. Jefferson on the contrary attempted to account for it from the ordinary operations of nature, and in the pride of philosophy exclaimed, "*There is no wonder*," then there would have been reason to suspect his sentiments—but no, it was a wonder, it was an extraordinary miracle. It was one of those stupendous acts of power which the Deity upon peculiar occasions performs for the wisest purposes. Had it been an ordinary event it would have ceased to be a miracle. Could it have been accounted for from universal laws, it would no longer have been miraculous; and, unless we consider it in the light of a miracle, then I assert that we oppose the true intent and meaning of the holy scriptures. Mr. Jefferson therefore very wisely rejects every philosophical hypothesis upon the subject, and rests it upon its proper basis of testimony, to wit, the authority of the sacred writings. That such is the correct interpretation of the passage of Mr. Jefferson, I appeal to the decision of the learned and unprejudiced reader; and I earnestly request that the notes upon Virginia may be perused with the most critical attention. The text is before us—let us decide for ourselves —we have no manner of necessity for a commentary.

Secondly—with respect to the question—from whence did the first inhabitants of America originate? The sentiments of Mr. Jefferson have been most criminally misrepresented. The author of the pamphlet has omitted every passage in which a positive opinion is given, and states the sentiments of Mr. Jefferson to be diametrically opposite from what he himself has declared them. At this moment that wretched author shall stand convicted of the *suppressio veri* with the criminal intention of deceiving the people. Let the culprit be exposed. Mr. Jefferson shall speak for himself. In the name of truth I demand that he may be heard.

> Great question (says Mr. Jefferson) has arisen from whence came those original inhabitants of America? Discoveries long ago made were sufficient to shew that a passage from Europe to America was always practicable,

> even to the imperfect navigation of ancient times. In going from Norway to Iceland—from Iceland to Greenland—from Greenland to Labrador—the first traject is the widest; and this having been practised from the earliest times, of which we have any account of that part of the earth. It is not difficult to suppose that the subsequent trajects may have been sometimes passed. Again—the late discoveries of Captain Cook coasting from Kamschatka to California have proved, that if the two continents of Asia and Africa be seperated at all, it is only by a narrow streight, so that from this side also inhabitants may have passed into America; and the resemblance between the Indians of America and the eastern inhabitants of Asia would induce us to conjecture that the former are the descendants of the latter, or the latter of the former, excepting indeed the Eskimaux, who from the same circumstance of resemblance and from identity of language, must be derived from the Greenlanders, and those probably from some of the northern parts of the old continent. (Notes on Virginia p.106 & 107—Phil. edition.)

Such are Mr. Jefferson's own words upon the subject, it is the only passage in which he expressly declares his sentiments with respect to that important question. It is therefore evident that his opinion is diametrically opposite to what is attributed to him by that disingenuous and designing writer. From the decisive circumstances of resemblance, from the proximity, if not the junction of the two continents, and from similarity of language, he concludes, that the inhabitants of each continent proceeded from a common origin—why was this remarkable passage so carefully concealed? Most evidently for the purpose of imposing upon the reader. A writer who is capable of such unworthy subterfuges, possesses a weak head as well as a bad heart —he becomes entitled to no credit. No honest man would betray such fraud and insincerity, or voluntarily expose himself to degradation.

It is true that the great question, whether all mankind have proceeded from one common origin? has divided the learned world. The human species exhibit so great a variety in intellect, complexion and form, that it has often been doubted whether climate and education, or any moral or physical laws could have produced that diversity. Philosophers have considered the subject as open to discussion, and that they might safely venture to advocate either position without a violation or impeachment of theological faith—thus one side of the proposition has been maintained by Dr. Smith, and an opposite by Lord Kame: but we find that Mr. Jefferson, in supposing that the inhabitants of America and those of the old continent have proceeded from a common origin, has, in reality, adopted the opinion most accordant with the scriptures.

It is also true, that when viewing the subject entirely upon philosophical grounds, Mr. Jefferson supposes that similarity of language is the best human test from which we can trace the affinity of nations; for this reason he laments that the languages of so many Indian tribes have been suffered to expire—but we must remember that Mr. Jefferson had already expressed his sentiments in favour of a common origin in the most decisive terms—we cannot readily imagine that an author of his reputation would palpably contradict himself in the very next passage. What he afterwards advances is entirely a matter of speculation, and not the declaration of any contrary opinion; for even if we were to believe that a greater number of radical languages was an infallible test of antiquity, and that the Americans possessed a greater number and variety of such radical languages than the Asiatics, that postulate could only give rise to a contest for superior antiquity, and by no means decide the principal question of identity of origin.

It might further be remarked, that neither of those positions can be considered as an infallible *indicium* of the faith or infidelity of its advocates; divines themselves have differed with respect to their sense of inspiration, or rather as to the extent in which it is to be taken; thus some have been the advocates of plenary inspiration, others of partial inspiration only, & others again consider certain parts of scripture as entirely historical. I mention this circumstance, not as disbelieving the doctrine of plenary inspiration, not as questioning the decisive authority of Moses, but to shew that the subject has not been placed upon fair ground. If the writers assertions were true instead of false, still they would prove nothing; instead of believing that the Americans and Asiatics have proceeded from a common stock, Mr. Jefferson might have advocated a different opinion, and still have been a christian.

"Gallileo was sent to the inquisition, for affirming that the earth was a sphere"; there was a time, when Sir Isaac Newton would have provoked the horrors of an *auto da fe*, for believing that the sun is stationary. In the book of Joshua (chapt. 10, verses 12, 13 & 14), it is writen that the Israelitish captain commanded the sun to stand still on a particular day, that is to suppose it moves on every other occasion, otherwise the passage would have no meaning; yet all the learned world coincide in opinion with Gallileo and Sir Isaac notwithstanding the apparent authority of the scriptures to the contrary. Galileo and Sir Isaac Newton were both christians, still they pursued their philosophical speculations; if the adversary of Mr. Jefferson, believes the sun to be stationary, by adopting his own mode of reasoning, he is proved to be an infidel.

So far then Mr. Jefferson stands completely exculpated from the charge of infidelity; but a third passage occurs, upon which peculiar stress appears to have been laid—it is that which respects the distinction which nature or circumstances have interposed between black and white men: an expression as correct as it is innocent, has given rise to the accusation; but it vanishes at the first approach of liberal investigation.

The existence of negro slavery has long been considered as one of our greatest political evils; like all other crimes by the righteous dispensations of providence it has been inseparably accompanied by its own calamities. The day of retribution is rapidly approaching—slavery must have an end—but what is to become of the slaves? When I consider the situation of the southern states—when I perceive how numerous a proportion of their population is composed by black men —my mind misgives me—the most terrifying reflections rush upon my understanding: The evil exists within our bosom—how shall it be removed?

Shall slavery be continued for ever? that idea is equally debasing to the master and the slave—justice, humanity, and even policy forbid it —besides, the population of the negroes is nearly equal to that of the whites; and notwithstanding the hardships under which they labour, the former multiply as fast as the latter—what then shall secure the perpetual submission of the slave? But suppose that they are restored to freedom, what shall be their destiny? Shall they be banished to foreign climes? Whither shall they become transported? Will they quietly submit? In what region of the globe will they be received without resistance? Send them to Africa, from whence their fathers have been dragged, and you render them completely wretched. You impose upon them a sentence, if possible, more severe than slavery itself; you have changed their languagc, manners and religion; in Africa they would meet with beings similar indeed in complexion, but radically different in every other respect. Will you surrender to them a portion of your own territory separated by metes and bounds, and establish an independent empire in the neighbourhood of your republic? Or lastly, when they are free shall they continue among us; shall they be placed upon an equality with their former masters, and admitted to partake of all our privileges? More than all, shall they marry and co-habit, and intermingle with our sons and daughters, and the inhabitants of America become a motley and degenerate race of mulattoes?

It is against this last idea that Mr. Jefferson reasons with energy and sensibility. Incorporate the blacks into the state, and you incorporate eternal misery and degradation. "Deep rooted* prejudices entertained by the whites; ten thousand recollections by the blacks of the injuries they have sustained; new provocations; the real distinctions which nature has made; and many other circumstances, will divide us into parties, and produce convulsions which will probably never end, but in the extermination of the one or the other race." (Notes on Virginia.)

Reason, justice and religion require that negroes should be free. But they require not that we should expose ourselves to degeneracy: We may sincerely advocate the freedom of black men, and yet assert their moral and physical inferiority. It is our duty to assert their liberties, but it is not our duty to blend our form and colour and existence with theirs. Education and habit, nay, nature herself recoils at the idea. It is against this shocking idea that Mr. Jefferson reasons with all his powers; he calls them a different race of men, and with justice he terms them so. It is in the same sense that we are in the daily habit of terming the Eskimaux, the Hottentots, and the Arabs a different race from the inhabitants of Europe.

But does Mr. Jefferson deny that negroes are men? does he deny them the sacred privileges of humanity? He says with truth, that there is now a physical difference which interposes an insuperable barrier between us; my own feelings powerfully dictate that such is the case. The idea of intermingling is insupportable. We cannot intermingle without injury—I may add, without prostitution. Mr. Jeffer-

* I would tell Mr. Jefferson they are not "prejudices."

son says, that there is a difference at present, but he has pretended to account for it by denying that they sprang from a common origin with ourselves? Does he introduce any hypothesis upon the subject hostile to divine revelation? Does he pretend to deny that the force of climate and cultivation through the lapse of centuries is insufficient to account for the dissimilarity? No, he does not—I defy all the tergiversation of his adversaries to fix the stigma upon him.

In justice to Mr. Jefferson, it must be mentioned, that though he contends for the inferiority of the blacks, he only argues against their cohabiting with us, and not against their freedom—his position, evident as it is, is advanced with exemplary diffidence and tenderness. In a subsequent passage he exclaims, with generous warmth,

> *Can the liberties of a nation be thought secure when we have removed their only firm basis, a conviction in the minds of the people, that these liberties are of the gift of* GOD*? That they are not to be violated but with his wrath? Indeed I tremble for my country when I reflect that* GOD *is just, that his justice cannot sleep for ever!**

Is this the language of an infidel! this the zealous exclamation of an enemy to God? O fye sir, shame upon your head! How dare you attempt to deceive your congregation! Mr. Jefferson has reasoned against the universal prostitution of his countrymen—and would you, sir, with all your meekness and piety, and humility, mingle your blood with that of the blacks?

Black spirits and white;
Blue spirits and grey,
Mingle, mingle, mingle,
You that mingle may.

O doctor, doctor, what a hopeful progeny would you produce!

It is upon the expression "difference of race" that the "baseless fabrick" of sophistry has been erected, by confounding the term "race" with the word "genus," or even "species." Mr. Jefferson is represented to have stated the negroes as originally a distinct order of beings; but the expression "race" *ex vi termini* by no means conveys that idea; still less so, when its sense is regulated by the general intentions of Mr. Jefferson, the manner in which it is used, and the

* Notes on Virginia, p. 173.

other parts of the passage into which it is incorporated.* The term in strictness signifies "a family, a generation, or a particular breed"; and in common parlance it is frequently used, if possible, in a more restricted sense. Thus every family may be correctly denominated a distinct race. The house of York and that of Lancaster formed a different race or dynasty of princes. The whole censure upon Mr. Jefferson is built upon an idle cavil with respect to this word. I appeal to the judicious reader, and refer to the work itself, whether the term race is not applied in the correct and limited sense in which I consider it, not as implying an original difference of ancestry, but as refering to the present difference of situation. Nothing is either more common or more proper, than to consider seperate nations, even of white men, as forming a distinct race. Thus the Romans and the Goths are termed a seperate race of men; and thus, from the three sons of Noah, Shem, and Ham, and Japhet, proceeded distinct races. Yet we do not deny their common origin, though time and circumstances have occasioned a total forgetfulness of consanguinity.

I feel that it is unnecessary to dwell any longer upon this passage —instead of impeaching Mr. Jefferson, the writer of the pamphlet has only succeeded in rendering himself ridiculous: there is yet one remaining passage to be discussed before I enter upon the consideration of it—permit me to offer a few remarks upon the base and idle story said to have been communicated by Mr. Mazzei.

It must already have been evident to the discerning reader, that the author of the pamphlet writes with a certain object in view, and that in the pursuit of such object he is regardless of truth or sincerity; he has fastened upon every opportunity to defame his political antagonist, not only by misrepresenting his sentiments, but by concealing the truth; by the manner in which he has conducted his work, he has forfeited all pretensions to credit.

The practice of that writer is not singular. The party to whom he is attached, has been in the constant habit of publishing assertions equally impudent and extravagant; the character of a patriot is so odious in their sight, that every calumny has been invented to blacken and defame it—ten thousand monstrous stories have been circulated and detected—the arrows have as often recoiled upon their masters

* Dr. Johnson.

—and yet they have the hardihood to continue the practice. Thus Mr. Gallatin, who is known to have descended from the most respectable parentage at Geneva, has been represented by turns as an itinerant vagabond, as a strolling fidler, and a shoe-black; such ridiculous tales never answer a good purpose, they disgust every sensible and liberal mind.

If the greatest liar in existence utters the most ridiculous falsehood against the most innocent man, you cannot resist him by reasoning, or refute his assertion by any syllogistical deduction; his tale is a matter of credit and not a matter of argument. The belief of such an allegation must entirely depend upon the general reputation of the parties, and the views and integrity of the relator. If the crime of adultery or seduction, for instance, was laid to the charge of Mr. H——, such a report would be readily believed; but if propagated concerning General Washington, would be absolutely incredible. Again, if a story is circulated by a man whose veracity is not impeachable, and who has no sinister object in view, his relation will be entitled to our confidence; but where a tale is propagated by a man who has already deceived us, and who appears to have a design & an interest in so doing, our credulity must be abject indeed if we suffer ourselves to be imposed upon.

After these preliminary observations, let us attend to this most ridiculous tale. Upon the supposed authority of a Dr. John B. Smith, a Virginia clergyman, it is asserted, that Mr. Mazzei, of whom so much mention has been lately made, related to this Dr. Smith the following anecdote; "That as he (Mazzei) was once riding with Mr. Jefferson, he expressed his surprize that the people of this country take no better care of their public buildings—What buildings? exclaimed Mr. Jefferson—is not that a church? replied he, pointing to a decayed edifice—Yes, answered Mr. Jefferson. I am astonished, said the other, that they permit it to be in so ruinous a condition! It is good enough, says Mr. Jefferson, for him that was born in a manger." Thus far.

Upon this extraordinary relation, let us make the following remarks:

In the first place, you have the story from the third or fourth hand. Jefferson is supposed to have used an expression to Mazzei—Mazzei to Smith—Smith to the writer of the pamphlet—and he to you; a story never loses by travelling: an expression of the most innocent nature may have been misconceived by Mazzei; Dr. Smith may have misunderstood him; as for the writer, his words and intentions are too evident to be mistaken.

Secondly, the story is too particular to be credited; if the conversation did ever take place, it must have happened many years ago. It was never heard by the writer of the pamphlet, or even by Dr. Smith himself. In relating the story, it is next to impossible that Mazzei and Smith and the writer should give the connected chain and particular expressions of the conversation in the order and connection used by the parties. In attempting to do this, like all other inventors, the writer has overshot his mark. It is impossible that he should have heard the particulars of an antiquated conversation with such accuracy and minuteness, as to give it in the form of a dialogue. It is therefore evident, that this dialogue is a recent fabrication of his own. He has all the merit of invention, but no claim to fidelity.*

Thirdly, the character of Mr. Jefferson renders the tale incredible, placing his morality and religion entirely out of sight; it is not probable that as a man of common prudence he would have used so obnoxious an expression.

Fourthly, the tale proceeds from a most suspicious fountain. We should be careful how we receive the character of any man from the mouth of his enemies. Justice requires that we should not judge rashly. It is evident that the author of the pamphlet is the bitter enemy of Mr. Jefferson; it is evident that he writes with the express view of rendering him an injury; it is evident that he is not guided by religious incentives, but by political and party views: And lastly, it is evident that he is generally regardless of truth and sincerity. Conscious that the criticism upon the notes on Virginia was untenable, his only resource was to invent this ridiculous story. When he pretends to reason, his pen trembles in his hand. In the paroxism of

* If Dr. L——— should be the author of the pamphlet, I admire his invention, but cannot commend his sagacity. The next time he writes the tales of ancient times, I would advise him to be less particular as to the minutiæ. His story would have been told better if it had been confined to generals; at present it has not the appearance of plausibility. The colloquial form was rather unfortunate. Such a dialogue could only have been manufactured in the doctors closet—it favours strongly of romance. Man of sin, Belial hath sent unto thee his lying spirit.

despair, he supplies the weakness of his logic by the boldness of assertion. But even this desperate sally has baffled his purpose; for, how is it possible that we can believe a story so improbable in itself; so incredible when applied to a man whose manners are confessedly mild and amiable, and who has ever been distinguished by consummate virtue and prudence: When that story, coming from the third or fourth hand, and in every stage of its passage liable to misconstruction, as well as exposed to misrepresentation, is related by a bitter enemy to serve an interested purpose, and when the relator has, upon every other occasion, been convicted of the base design to injure and deceive us?*

I enter into the examination of the remaining head of accusations which this disingenuous writer has exhibited against Mr. Jefferson. It cannot have escaped the observation of the reader, that the author of the pamphlet has endeavoured to give the sense of Mr. Jefferson from detached and mutilated passages of his work, and, by the suppression of the rest, endeavoured to distort and misrepresent his real sentiments. We have seen, that in the most material instance he has endeavoured, by implication, to represent him as favouring one opinion; when, in the most express and positive language, he has in reality advanced a doctrine diametrically opposite. When a writer will descend to such base and villainous† arts, he becomes altogether unwor-

* The more I reflect upon the subject, the more I am convinced the story is incredible; and yet it is possible, that in the course of conversation, an expression somewhat similar may have been used in the most innocent and laudable point of view. Those who recollect the intolerable avarice of the clergy, and particularly in Italy, of which Mazzei was a native; those who remember the millions and millions which were torn from the wretched people, to purchase baubles to decorate the church of "our Lady at Lorenzo," would not be surprized, if in a conversation between the Italian and the patriot, that the latter should, by an easy association, with honest warmth, and yet without irreverence, have adverted to the circumstance of our Saviour's being laid in a manger. Expressions equally innocent have been tortured into guilt, when laid upon the rack of an enemy.

It was a part of the eternal dispensations of Providence—it was the choice of our blessed Lord to be seen in a manger—it was intended as an everlasting monument of his humility. *Christus habet multos ministros sed paucos imitatores.* The cross of Christ, the stumbling block of the Jews, and foolishness to the Greeks is the Christians glory. What, shall a minister of the gospel be ashamed of the cross, or offended at the mention of the manger!

† Shakespeare says, a man may smile and smile and be a villain; so men may preach and pray and still be liars.

thy of credit; he exposes the wickedness of his own designs, and can no longer be believed. The author, who can wilfully misrepresent the sentiments of another by an easy transition of baseness, can fabricate a story or propagate a groundless tale. It is as criminal to pervert the sentiments of Mr. Jefferson, with a view to render him an injury, as to invent the story of Mazzei from the same unworthy motive; the object is, in both cases, identical, and the instruments not essentially different. If the author should be a clergyman, his offence becomes encreased; from that order of men we have a right to expect examples of fidelity.

The passage to which I now allude, is that which more particularly respects religion. The only object of Mr. Jefferson, is to discountenance political establishments in theology; upon this subject, his adversaries must confess that he reasons with perspicuity, energy & truth. I refer the reader neither to these pages nor to the pamphlet entitled "Serious reflections" but entreat him to peruse the work itself; I aver that upon this subject Mr. Jefferson reasons with the conciseness and nervous energy of Tacitus—he writes with the pen of a master; in no instance does he speak a language, upon no occasion does he betray a sentiment disrespectful to Christianity; he states that by the common law of England heresy was a capital offence punishable by burning, and that until the statute of Elizabeth, its definition was submitted to the ecclesiastical judges—that the execution was by the cruel and infamous writ *de hæretico comburendo*, that by the statute of Virginia antecedent to the revolution, heresy was punishable by the incapacity of holding any office civil, ecclesiastical or military, and on a repetition by disability to sue; to take any gift or legacy, to be guardian, executor or administrator, and by three years imprisonment without bail. I should despair of rendering justice to the sentiments of this excellent writer, without permission to transcribe them in his own forcible language, "This (continues Mr. Jefferson) is a summary view of that religious slavery, under which a people have been willing to remain, who have lavished their lives and fortunes for the establishment of their civil freedom. The error seems not sufficiently eradicated, that the operations of the mind as well as the acts of the body, are subject to the coercion of the laws, but our rulers can have authority over such natural rights, only as we have submitted to them; the rights of conscience we never submitted, we could not submit *we are answerable for them to our God.* The legitimate powers of government, extends to such acts only as are injurious to others; but it does me no injury for my neighbour to say, there are twenty Gods or no God, it neither picks my pocket nor breaks my leg; if it be said, his testimony in a court of justice cannot be relied on, reject it then, and be the stigma on him. Constraint may make him worse by making him a hypocrite, but it will never make him a truer man: it may fix him obstinately in his errors, but will not cure them. Reason and free enquiry are the only effectual agents against error—give a loose to them, they will support the true religion, by bringing every false one to their tribunal, to the test of their investigation; they are the natural enemies of error, and of error only. Had not the Roman government permitted free inquiry, Christianity could never have been introduced. Had not free inquiry been indulged at the æra of the reformation, the corruptions of Christianity could not have been purged away."

Such then are the sentiments inculcated by this invaluable performance, and do these imply a spirit of infidelity? is liberality, and forbearance, and toleration incompatible with the gospel? God forbid, that Christians should believe so. How is Christianity to be infused? by the mild light of reasoning—by the force of conviction, or by the burning fire of persecution? Then abandon preaching, ministers of the Most High, descend from the pulpit—forsake the altar—seize the torch—the firebrand and faggot—grasp the murderers steel—destroy and exterminate—establish the empire of panic—the universal dominion of fear—spare them not—be the ministers not of grace and mercy, and benevolence, but of vengeance—perpetrate dark deeds "without a name," where then will be your converts? in the language of Mr. Jefferson, you will make hypocrites but not true men.

I am bold to say, that those sentiments of Mr. Jefferson are in perfect conformity to the genuine precepts of our religion, as well as the principles of our civil constitution, we have had enough of the kingdom of Anti-christ; hecatombs of human victims have bled and perished, their blood has stained the earth, and their mouldering bones unburied, bleaching by the rain and scorching sun, have called aloud to heaven. Our ancestors also were persecuted—here they fought for and obtained repose; Oh let not their children unmindful of their miseries and wrongs, in their turn become persecutors!

Such then, is the interesting subject which engrossed the attention of our virtuous and learned countryman, impressed with its importance, his language glows with animation; it is upon a single expression used in the warmth of sensibility, and in the ardour of argument, that peculiar reliance has been placed "it does me no injury for my neighbour to say, there are twenty Gods, or no God, it neither picks my pocket nor breaks my leg." The expression is a strong one, but it is strictly true in the sense in which it was applied. Belief indeed may, nay will influence our conduct; the errors of my neighbour may be dangerous, I would distrust the man who would palliate adultery, or endeavour to excuse a theft; but the manner in which Mr. Jefferson applies the sentiment renders it perfectly correct, he distinguishes between our *actions* and our *opinions*, for the former we are amenable to the civil magistrate, for the latter he expressly tells us we "*are answerable to our God.*" Speaking of the rights of conscience, he says, that—"we never submitted them to our civil rulers, we could not submit them, the legitimate powers of government extend to such *acts*, only as are injurious to others"; it is therefore demonstrable that Mr. Jefferson exclusively contemplates civil injuries: that is to say, injuries visible and palpable, and for which human laws afford redress; in this legal sense, the sentiments of my neighbour are no injury to me, his opinions should not be subjected to the coercion of the civil magistrate. For our conduct we are responsible to man; for our opinions only to our God. I sustain no civil injury by the vicinage of an atheist, if it is a damnum in the language of lawyers, it is *damnum absque injuric.* Government has no right to interfere, it cannot interpose without danger, and without a manifest violation of the social compact.

Government is an human institution, introduced for temporal purposes—it was never intended to be the sovereign arbiter of religion, conscience, and opinion. Fearful of committing himself upon the subject, the author of the pamphlet is driven to express the very same sentiment, tho' in language far inferior. Mark his inconsistency! note his palpable contradiction! "It is true (he acknowledges) that a mere opinion of my neighbor will do me no injury, government cannot regulate or punish it, the right of private opinion is inalienable." Mr.

Jefferson has contended for no more. If the sentiment is an evidence of infidelity on the part of the one; it is equally so with respect to the other.*

Throughout the passage in question, Mr. Jefferson has only advocated those doctrines which, with a feebler pen I have attempted to enforce. I wish Christianity to become extended into every region of the globe, but I wish it to prevail by the energy of reason, and not by the terror of persecution, or the power of the sword. I am jealous of the interference of government; I know that it never interposes from a pious zeal towards religion, but from corrupt, ambitious, and interested views. I am conscious that belief is involuntary, that it must flow spontaneously from the dictates of the understanding, and can never be enforced by the engines of tyranny.

The rights of conscience rise superior to the controul of the civil magistrate; why should we be solicitous to multiply hypocrites? let believers be sincere in their professions, or let men continue infidels. I also most cordially unite with Mr. Jefferson in a wish to see, and I do actually perceive "a government in which no religious opinions (whatever) are (officially) held, and where the security for property and social order rests entirely upon the force of law." In the expression of this sentiment I am not apprehensive of being misunderstood; I sincerely wish that every individual concerned in the administra-

* Dr. L—— or whoever is the author of the pamphlet, is determined that Mr. Jefferson shall be a deist or atheist at all events. After exhausting his whole budget with respect to Mr. Jefferson, he asserts, that Mr. Nobody, a pupil of Mr. Jefferson, once upon a time, used an atheistical expression, and sagaciously concludes that Mr. Jefferson is therefore an atheist! Now who is this Mr. Nobody? Mr. Jefferson keeps no school or academy, how can he have pupils? The good doctor is a wonderful logician; admitting that his premises are true, by what singular process does he derive his conclusion?

If any man affronts or opposes the doctor, to be sure he must be a deist. His reverence must find this practice of calling hard names very convenient, as it may stand in the place of argument. Let the following anecdote serve as a specimen of his peculiarity. The doctor, like many other men, being willing to earn his money as cheap as possible, was in the habit of preaching the same sermon very frequently; some of the congregation, wishing to hear something new, petitioned the consistory upon the subject; the doctor, instead of meeting the application openly, endeavoured to parry it, by observing upon the character of the applicants. Such a man was such a thing, and such a man was a deist. One of the proscribed meeting the doctor in the street told him he did not take it kind; the doctor with a very good countenance turned it off by saying, he, good soul, did not mean any harm, and inviting the injured person to his house, assured him they should be very good friends again!!!

tion, in every department and in every station principal or subordinate, from the president to the constable, should be a Christian in earnest, not boasting a nominal, but possessing a zealous, lively and active faith; but as a government, as a body corporate and politic, as an organized artificial systematized corps, it should not have, it cannot have any religion; it should allow to each of its citizens an unlimited exercise of conscience; it should never interfere, unless social law, and order, and morals become invaded—if a contrary doctrine should ever prevail, every fibre of my heart would bleed for the misery of my country. Such as I wish it, is our present constitution, and so may it ever continue; to the people under God I intrust its preservation; unless you my countrymen, are vigilant and circumspect, the time may come when freedom religious and civil, shall be no more, and hope itself expire; and then, O then the solemn warning of that Jefferson, who has been so unworthily traduced will only furnish occasion for unavailing regret! Hear him before it is too late. "The spirit of the times (he almost prophetically exclaims) may alter —will alter; our rulers will become corrupt, our people careless, a single zealot may commence persecutor, and better men be his victims. It can never therefore be too often repeated, that the time for fixing every essential right on a legal basis, is while our rulers are honest and ourselves united. From the conclusion of this war, we shall be going down hill, it will not then be necessary to resort every moment to the people for support, they will be forgotten therefore, and their rights disregarded; they will forget themselves, but in the sole faculty of making money, and will never think of uniting to effect a due respect for their rights; the shackles therefore which shall not be knocked off at the conclusion of this war, will remain on us long; will be made heavier and heavier till our rights shall revive or expire in a convulsion."

But, why should I proceed? with every liberal mind, Mr. Jefferson must stand acquitted from the charge of infidelity; for him I feel not —he enjoys "the eternal sunshine of the spotless mind," for religion I feel not—it stands secure in the sacred majesty of truth—it is for my country that I feel, and for the safety of its constitution that I tremble. I shall offer a few observations with respect to Mr. Adams and Mr. Pinckney, and attempt to explore the prospect which lies before us.

I hold it to be a maxim essential to our safety, that the government of the United States should only be administered by a republican. Whatever may be the virtues or religion,* whatever the talents of Mr. Adams, his principles are not republican, his sentiments are not congenial with the spirit of the constitution, he has published and proclaimed his opinions, they stand as an everlasting record and monument against him; his religion and his piety may possibly be sincere, but they cannot atone for the destruction of the constitution, and the slavery of the people; Mr. Adams is the advocate of privileged orders and distinctions in society, he would willingly engraft the armorial trappings and insignia of aristocracy upon the simple majesty of republican institutions. Mr. Adams would destroy the essential nature and character of a republic; his principles would wrest the government from the hands of the people, and vest its dominion and prerogatives in the distinguished and "well born few"—Mr. Adams is the advocate of hereditary power, and hereditary privileges —has he not told you "that republican government may be interpreted to mean any thing! that the British government is in the strictest sense a republic! that an hereditary president and senate for life, can alone secure your happiness! that in the conflict of political opinions which prevail in our country, it is admissible for one faction to seize the persons of their opponents, and banish them within the lines of an invading enemy!"

Immortal heaven! can we listen to such sentiments with coldness? Let it not be imagined that such opinions are purely speculative, and therefore not dangerous. Speculation always pants and struggles for an opportunity to become ripened into action. Mr. Adams cannot hold such heretical doctrines without being a dangerous president; if he does not admire the constitution in its present shape, depend upon it his influence will be exerted to render it more palatable to himself. If no other evil happens, the temper and opinions of the man will give a tone and character to his administration; he will warp, and

* Hypocrisy has become a fashionable vice. God alone can separate the sheep from the wolves. Who would have believed that an eminent judge would have become a preacher, or Governeur M—— a sincere convert to Christianity. It is said, that a very illustrious personage, when at Philadelphia, was for some time in the habit of hearing Dr. Priestly, until his friends admonished him that he would sacrifice his popularity —there was certainly more policy than sincerity in the discontinuance of that habit.

twist, and torture the features of your infant government, and prostrate your constitution upon the fatal bed of Procrustes, until it loses its original symmetry, proportion and character. Whenever an opportunity arises, by a latitude of construction, by a wanton licentiousness of interpretation, he will multiply and intrench the prerogatives of the executive, and establish his favorite theory upon the ruins of the constitution. Every violation will increase the appetite for power; it will augment the danger by the force of habit and the pretext of example. Encroachments always proceed with an accelerated momentum, "One precedent creates another; they soon accumulate and constitute law; what yesterday was fact to-day is doctrine: Examples are supposed to justify the most dangerous measures, and where they do not suit exactly, the defect is supplied by analogy."* He who maintains the principles and the doctrines of slavery, is "totally unfit to be the ruler of a free people."

The interest of the nation demands that we should have an administration of liberty and justice and œconomy. Our future executive should not be the president of a party but the president of the United States; to speak emphatically, he should be the president of public liberty, the *president of the constitution.* We have seen an alien bill, vesting the executive in certain cases with almost unlimited powers. We have witnessed a sedition law triumphant over the liberty of the press. We have beheld an incessant and restless spirit of persecution multiplying fines, and penalties, and imprisonment. We have seen an itinerant judge not content with exercising his powers unbiassed on the bench of justice, industriously travelling in pursuit of victims. We have seen those records and muniments which were necessary for the vindication of a defendant, sternly denied to him in defiance of that law which has idly stated, that the truth of an allegation shall be a compleat defence in cases of libel. We have heard the judges of the United States prejudge a question, in which the life of a prisoner was concerned, by refusing to listen to the arguments of counsel in a trial for treason. In the case of Robins, we have viewed an attempt to destroy the independence of the judiciary by subjecting them to the controul and directions of the president—we have seen authorities, which the constitution has denied to the government, claimed and

* Junius.

exercised under the dangerous idea that they are given by the common law of England. In the expences of a small army composed of many officers and few soldiers, and never in actual service, we can readily perceive the enormous cost of a permanent military establishment—we have seen an ambassador sent to England for the purpose of procuring satisfaction for the depredations upon our trade, at this moment under the operation of his treaty, recognizing the British debts: We are astonished with the liquidation of a balance of millions against us—we have a national debt increasing and likely to increase, until its annual interest shall exhaust the fruits of laborious industry and taxation, like the leaves of autumn gather and multiply around us. Such, Americans, is the picture of our present prosperity. I shall proceed no farther, volumes would not exhaust the subject. Let us be true to ourselves—let us rally before the genius of liberty and the spirit of the constitution, and let no consideration divert us from the determined resolution of preserving the rights and freedom of our country.

Enough of Mr. Adams. I am impressed with the conviction that he is destined to re-visit the shades of retirement, enjoying literary leisure, he may establish a Tusculum at Braintree, or, like Plato, soothe his imagination by visionary theories; from the Republicans he cannot expect a single suffrage, and it would be folly to rely upon the attachment or fidelity of the Federalists—the wounds of Timothy—insulted honor—disappointed hopes—unsatisfied revenge—powerful incentives, and irresistible passions, have united to give the ascendency to Mr. Pinckney. It is not to be imagined that the quondam secretary will be idle, a single southern vote or a single eastern elector will prevent the re-election of Mr. Adams; and upon the failure of Mr. Jefferson, confer the empire upon his anglo-federal rival. Like Simeon of old, Mr. Adams may repeat the *Nunc dimittis*, and if Mr. Jefferson should be elected, he may justly exclaim "*Quia viderunt oculi mei Salutare tuum.*"

I know not Mr. Pinckney, politically speaking, he is a man whom no-body knows,* but it is perfectly understood that he is contemplat-

* We have the character of the two Mr. Pinckney's from no less a man than President Adams himself—This illustrious personage has written as follows:

"The Duke of Leeds once enquired of me very kindly, after his classmates in Westminster school, the two Mr. Pinckney's, which induces me to believe, that our new ambassador has many powerful old friends in England.

ed as a second† Bibulus who permitted Cæsar to govern. We can judge of the individual from the character of the party by whom he is supported, and the views by which such party is uniformly actuated. It is well known, that at the last election Mr. T. Pinckney was supported by Mr. Hamilton*, in preference to Mr. Adams; and that C. C. Pinckney is now the candidate of the exiled members of the present administration. It is a matter of notoriety, that an explosion has taken place in the cabinet, and that a violent schism has ensued between the leaders of the Federal party. The dismission, or rather the expulsion, of Mr. Pickering, evinces that a convulsion had taken place in our councils, which may probably form a distinguished æra in our history. The president has not thought proper officially to furnish us with his reasons for the dismissal of the secretary, but it is perfectly understood, that his obstinate opposition to the negociation

Again, "*Knowing, as I do, the long intrigue, and suspecting, as I do, much British influence in the appointment*, were I in any executive department, I should take the liberty to keep a vigilant eye upon them," &c.

Two things are plainly observable in this letter, first, that there is actually a British party in this country, and secondly, that the Pinckney's belong to that party. When this appears from the testimony of Mr. Adams himself, whose information must be correct, who can shut his eyes against conviction? And yet one of these men is a candidate for the presidency!

† Most of my readers will recollect the consulship of Julius Cæsar and Bibulus, which was emphatically termed, the consulship of Julius and Cæsar. Buonaparte, or his friend the Abbé, who had so many constitutions, of all shapes, in his pigeon holes, appears to have copied from that period in the Roman history, with the addition of a single cypher. Thus in Rome it stood 01, in France it stands 001—if we should have an American Bibulus, we should, in some measure, approach the Spanish inquisition, where the inquisitor general was concealed. How terrible would be our situation, if our Cæsar should be covered with a mantle of secrecy, and how much more so, if of that Cæsar we might exclaim

Not in the regions
Of horrid hell can come, a devil more damn'd
In ills to top Macbeth.

* It is seldom that we correctly appreciate the talents of a man. I think that those of Mr. H——— though they are respectable, have been overrated. Such circumstance is sometimes dangerous. The vulgar look upon such a man with awe, and he is furnished not only with incentives, but also the opportunity of becoming a leader. I scarcely know a branch of knowledge in which he has not superiors. The late Mr. Duer did, and Mr. Gallatin certainly does surpass him in finance. And as to oratory, in which he is supposed to stand preeminent, he is rather remarkable for circumlocution, than strength or perspicuity—he may boast of the copia verborum—words numerous as the autumnal leaves, which strew the brooks at Vallombrosa. He is not a disciple of the school of Cicero, a Quinctilian—of his elocution it may be said, "Corpus sine pectore."

with France, and his manifest partiality for Mr. Pinckney, were the principal occasions of the variance. Since that period at least, the Federalists have become divided into two parties, actuated by different views, and governed by different leaders. The party of Messieurs Pinckney, Hamilton, and Pickering, is the most desperate and violent; its principal characteristics have been a hatred to France; predilection for England; an inflexible determination for war, and an invincible enmity to freedom and the constitution.

When Tracy proclaimed his war of extermination, it was usually considered as an unmeaning ebullition of the passions; for my own part, I was not disposed to view it as the momentary paroxism of a distempered brain; there was a degree of method and consistency in those ravings which indicated system and design. I saw an earnestness and sincerity in this madness which was the evidence of deliberation—war had been agreed upon in cool and serious moments, and that war was designed for the attainment of no common object.

The enmity to Mr. Adams, and the abuse which has been showered upon his head—the undisguised disappointment of the federal leaders, and the division which has taken place in that party proves much—the Sybilline volumes are opened—we have the key to secrets more mysterious than the grave—the laurels of the general are blasted—for the present ambition has become defeated—but the constitution is saved.

Why should the negociation with France have occasioned so much clamour if nothing but the public prosperity had been in question? What benefit could have been produced by war that will be denied us by negociation? Could the national dignity or the substantial interests of America require more than an honorable satisfaction? Even the spirit of Cato would have been satisfied with an ample concession, if the rivalship of his favorite Rome had not extorted the dreadful sentence "delendum est Carthago." Between us and France there is no such rivalship. It was not the motive of Cato which produced such invincible aversion to peace; an ambitious general at the head of an army, would have been the master of the liberties of his country—this consideration is the clue which enables us to explore the labyrinth, as we enter into its recesses the plot thickens around us—when we unfathom its mysteries we become encompassed with horrors.

Every day and every event furnishes new conviction that the advocates of Mr. Pinckney are not the friends of the constitution: should they ever acquire the ascendency, I would tremble for its fate. There is abundance of testimony to prove that this party is not contented with our present limited government, but that it is their steady and uniform object to introduce a system essentially and radically different. The constitution proposed by Mr. Hamilton in the late general convention, was every thing but federal; it went to the establishment of a permanent executive, and to the total subversion of the states. The governors were to have been appointed by that herculean executive, and united America, ruined by the perfidy of one man, was again to have been prostrated before the throne of a powerful and almost absolute monarch!

That project is far from being abandoned—it has again been revived in another form—the pamphlet of young Fenno, contemptible as it is, in every respect, betrays the object and purpose of his party. This boy, nurtured in the air of a court, and conversant with the designs and opinions of his patrons, has presumed to offer a system of government to the United States. It is true that this system does not possess originality, but is the servile counterpart of the project of Mr. Hamilton; it exhibits the same features and betrays the same views. An alliance offensive and defensive with Great Britain—perpetual war with France and Spain—foreign conquests—permanent naval and military establishments—an eternal, unextinguishable debt—a perpetual system of funding and speculation—the compleat annihilation of states—a division of the country into districts or provinces, to destroy even the memory of their existence—a president with unlimited powers—governors, or prefects of his appointment—a house of lords composed of such prefects—a permanent aristocracy—an enslaved, impoverished and miserable people—such are the detestable propositions with which millions of freemen have been insulted. My bosom burns with indignation—my pen almost drops from my hand—O! America! my country! may heaven preserve thy freedom—may it preserve thee from the designs of thy treacherous sons. Such is the party of Mr. Pinckney—I feel that my powers are inadequate to pourtray the amplitude of their baseness.*

* The friends of a certain great man have lately been fond of comparing him to Buonaparte, for what reason we can readily divine. Of that man the Aurora has publicly said, that on his late visit to New-England, after drinking his favourite toast, "a

I have assigned to you sufficient reasons why neither Mr. Adams nor Mr. Pinckney should be your president—GOD, who knows my heart, knows that I address you from pure and patriotic motives. I am wholly unconnected with any political character either in or out of office. My sentiments are not secret. I profess and will maintain them candidly and openly, in public and in private—yet it is not probable that as the writer of this pamphlet, I shall ever be known to the world. Let the sentiments it contains be appreciated as they merit, their truth and propriety cannot become affected by any personal considerations; for my own part I delight in obscurity, in the shades of retirement, unknown and unnoticed by the great, accompanied with the solaces of private friendship, let me securely tread the paths of liberty and virtue. I belong not to the school of the Jacobins, or the Federalists. I have no blind respect for names alone, claiming the privilege of thinking for myself, I shall always enquire *Quid sit pulchrum, quid turpe, quid utile, quid non.* I am the partizan of Mr. Jefferson, in no other sense than I am the partizan of truth, and freedom, and my country. Christianity I have advocated, and will ever advocate, upon true, sincere and liberal grounds; but I never will tamely permit it to be converted into an engine for the destruction of every privilege and enjoyment, and prospect, which is valuable upon earth. I reverence our civil constitution, because, from the serious dictates of the understanding, I am convinced it is the best and most perfect in the world—to preserve it therefore, I shall ever exercise my limited talents, and, if necessary, sacrifice my life.

At this moment you are called upon to take a stand upon the principles of your constitution; while the world is agitated to its centre, and alarms are heard from every quarter, it would be madness to

strong government" he positively declared, that "if Mr. Pinckney is not elected president, a revolution will be the consequence, and that within the next four years he will lose his head, or be the leader of a triumphant army!!!" There is no other difference between such an expression and treason, than what exists between the meditation and execution of paracide. Such declarations have been copied in the public prints. I have waited for a denial of them, but have never been gratified. Shall the accusation be taken sub silentio[?] Friends of religion—ministers of the gospel, are you content to submit to the sacrifice of your civil constitution, and view the blood of your countrymen smoaking upon the earth? O shame—if there is a villain in America capable of such enormous baseness, by heaven he shall "lose his head." Cataline in the bosom of the Senate, or Cataline concealed is a formidable enemy—driven to desperation he is wretched, imbecile, and contemptible.

loosen the anchor of your safety, this is not a time for speculation, it is not a season for changing your system of government. Scylla lies on the one side, and Charybdis on the other, why should you hazard your security? why should you entrust your political constitution in the hands of men whose fidelity, and whose principles are more than suspected? Jefferson is known, his sentiments—his character—his probity are established; he is not the man of France or of England—but the man of public liberty—the man of the people—the man of the constitution.

I wish not to foment the rage of parties; on the contrary my most ardent desire would be to allay the fervency of their resentments; but in a time like the present, good men cannot remain inactive, neutrality would amount to a criminal abandonment of principles; I have ceased to discriminate parties, by the idle jargon of the day, jacobins and democrats, and old, and new federalists, let them be buried, and upon their prostrated ruins, let us erect the universal party of liberty, and virtue, and the constitution; such men as Mr. Pinckney and Mr. Adams, will never establish harmony, the people cannot, nor should they extend their confidence towards them, they never will believe their liberties secure, in the hands of men deservedly rendered obnoxious. If there is a man in America who at the present crisis, can restore harmony to the empire, and give stability to the constitution—it is Mr. Jefferson.

I have no idea of sacrificing the liberties of my country, to mistaken compliance towards divines; when Philip meditated the destruction of Greece, he commenced his career by corrupting the oracles—such was the insidious policy of the tyrant, who triumphed at Cheronæ; it reads a powerful lesson to the people, and with resistless energy, forbids them to render religion the fatal instrument of ambition. God forbid! that the British party—the sycophants of Liston, and the supporters of the infamous Cobbett* should give as a presi-

* That the British have designs upon the government of this country, is a fact beyond the reach of doubt. When Mr. Jefferson was secretary of state, Lord Auckland had the presumption to recommend the infamous Cobbett as a clerk in his office; for what purpose? as a spy to betray the secrets of it. The wretch went to Philadelphia, buzzed about the government, and filled the country with his detestible effusions. Disappointed at length by the explosion in the cabinet, and ruined by the righteous verdict, in the suit of Dr. Rush, he blackguards the President and runs away. His successor, poor Fenno does a similar thing. Not all the democrats in the community

dent. People of America, patriots and electors, be assured that it is not religion, but the state which is in jeopardy—Jefferson, who has been the object of so much unmanly but unavailing calumny, is one of the strongest bulwarks of its safety; remember that at this moment, your liberty, your constitution, your families, your children, the fate of the empire, depend upon the rectitude of your decision. May the God of heaven, infuse a portion of his grace and wisdom into your hearts, and understandings, and direct you to the final resolution, most conducive to his glory, and to the prosperity of our beloved country.

Timoleon

POSTSCRIPT

Now, Americans, after what you have seen and heard, can you doubt the existence of a British party hostile to your constitution? Only compare facts and circumstances together; if you suffer yourselves to be imposed upon you will deserve the consequences. First, you have seen Mr. Adams openly write in favour of aristocratical principles. Secondly, you have seen Mr. Hamilton propose a real monarchical constitution. Thirdly, the proceedings of that convention have been kept a profound secret. What could have been the reason of that extraordinary measure, except to shut out the light of inquiry? Do you think the dungeons of the Inquisition would have been barred and bolted, if its proceedings had been favourable to the public good? Fourthly, you have seen the British printer, Peter Porcupine, openly countenanced and protected at the seat of government. Fifthly, you have seen his successor, Mr. Fenno, tread in his very footsteps. Sixthly, you have seen this very Fenno, who is privy to the whole secret, openly recommend a British alliance, and a monarchy in substance. Seventhly, you have witnessed the very extraordinary disappointment occasioned by the negociation with France. Can you

have abused Mr. Adams with half the virulence of this young man; it is ludicrous yet somewhat provoking, to see such men as Fenno and Porcupine bedaub each other with praise. Is bene ese. Such is the abominable service in which Christianity is to be pressed.

possibly account for this circumstance, without believing that the British interests are preferred to those of America? Eighthly, you have seen the infamous Cobbett, immediately afterwards, abuse your president and your government, and take his flight. Ninthly, you have seen Fenno join in his abuse, and openly ridicule your independence and your revolution. Mr. Liston goes home, finding that he can be of no service at present. Eleventhly, this very Peter Porcupine was recommended by Lord Auckland as a clerk to Mr. Jefferson, who was at that time secretary of state. Could this have been for any other reason than to give that wretch an opportunity of betraying the secrets of the office to his friends and employers the British; and, Twelfthly, you have the evidence of Mr. Adams himself, that there is a British party in this country, and that the Pinckney's are attached to that party. He tells you expressly, that he had long known the British intrigue, and even inspected it in the diplomatic appointment of Pinckney. Yet Mr. Adams, knowing all these things, remained connected with those men, until there is every reason to believe that they endeavoured to shake him off, to make room for a person upon whom they could place more dependence. But this is not all the evidence, there is more behind the curtain. I recommend the perusal of Fenno's pamphlet, as a correct index to the designs of the British faction. After all this evidence, is it possible that any American whig, should withhold his suffrages from Mr. Jefferson?

53

OVERCOMING EVIL WITH GOOD

Stanley Griswold

HARTFORD
1801

STANLEY GRISWOLD (1763–1815). A Yale graduate in 1786 and Congregational clergyman at New Milford, Connecticut, Griswold led a checkered life and died of a fever at Shawneetown, Illinois Territory. He was expelled from the pulpit in 1797, allegedly because of his disbelief in human depravity and for preaching universal salvation. But his political views were more likely the cause, since he favored democracy and Thomas Jefferson and was even said to support the French Revolution—all of which made him odious to the Connecticut clergy.

Griswold retreated to Walpole, New Hampshire, to edit one of the new Republican papers there, the *Political Observatory*. After two years he was appointed secretary of the Michigan Territory, and he disappeared into the Western wilderness. Later he moved to Ohio, where he served as an appointed United States senator for six months in 1809–1810. The final five years of his life were spent riding a judicial circuit in the Ohio and Wabash valleys, although it is uncertain whether or how he had learned the law.

The sermon reprinted here—which is at once eloquent, profound, and conciliatory—was part of the Wallingford, Connecticut, celebration of the election of Jefferson to the presidency in 1801; it was one of the events that sent Griswold packing out of the ministry and out of Connecticut. The acrimonious flavor of the political religion of the time can be surmised from this and the previous two sermons of John M. Mason and Tunis Wortman. Governor John Reynolds described Griswold as "a correct, honest man—a good lawyer—paid his debts, and sang David's Psalms" (Reynolds, *The Pioneer History of Illinois* [1852], p. 337).

OVERCOMING EVIL WITH GOOD.

A

SERMON,

DELIVERED AT

Wallingford, Connecticut,

MARCH 11, 1801;

BEFORE A NUMEROUS COLLECTION OF THE FRIENDS

OF THE

CONSTITUTION,

OF

THOMAS JEFFERSON, PRESIDENT,

AND OF

AARON BURR, VICE-PRESIDENT

OF THE

UNITED STATES.

BY STANLEY GRISWOLD, A. M.

Of New-Milford.

HARTFORD:

PRINTED BY ELISHA BABCOCK,

—1801.—

My respectable audience,

I came not hither to preach a system of party-politics, nor to excite nor indulge ravings of faction. I came in obedience to what I conceived to be the duty of a Christian and a patriot, to contribute my most earnest endeavors toward healing the unhappy divisions of our country.

Unfortunately some individuals are to be expected to be beyond cure, especially from such remedies as I shall apply, having drank down the poisonous virulence of party too copiously to admit of an easy recovery. But the citizens at large I cannot consider by any means in this predicament. They have ever been honest, are still honest, and desire nothing but to be honest.

If unhappily any individuals be past cure, the lenient remedies of the gospel, which I purpose to apply on this occasion, upon such will be thrown away. And for such nothing seems to remain but the severer applications of reproof and rebuke, which our Saviour occasionally exhibited to some in his day, while he spake to the multitudes with the greatest mildness and affection.

The method I have judged most proper to attain the object suggested, is to address a few considerations more particularly to the injured —those of every denomination and description of sentiment in our country, who may have suffered wrongfully—who have received wounds, and whose wounds have not yet forgotten to smart.

On such the peace and tranquility of our country, I conceive, very greatly depend. Their conduct and the course they adopt are to have no inconsiderable share in determining, whether this country is to settle down in quietness, and harmony to be restored to its citizens —or whether it is yet to be agitated and shaken to its centre by the outrages of party.

Far would I be from impeaching the prudence, the patriotism or the christianity of any who hear me. But it must be confessed, that we are all men, and men of like passions. Hence the necessity of repeatedly calling to remembrance the maxims of sound wisdom and the wholsome precepts of religion. If by suggesting any of these I might contribute in some small degree to the felecity of my country,

I could easily forego the ambition of appearing a political preacher on this occasion, and should consider myself well rewarded for any calumnies which are past, or for any which are yet to come.

For pursuing the object proposed, the gospel of the benevolent Jesus affords themes in abundance. I have chosen that cluster of directions recorded[:]

Bless them who persecute you; bless and curse not. Rejoice with them that do rejoice, and weep with them that weep. Be of the same mind one toward another. Mind not high things, but condescend to men of low estate. Be not wise in your own conceits. Recompense to no man evil for evil. Provide things honest in the sight of all men. If it be possible, as much as lieth in you, live peaceably with all men. Dearly beloved, avenge not yourselves, but rather give place unto wrath: for it is written, Vengeance is mine; I will repay, saith the Lord. Therefore, if thine enemy hunger, feed him; if he thirst, give him drink: for in so doing thou shalt heap coals of fire on his head. Be not overcome of evil; but overcome evil with good.

Romans xii. 14–21.

You will at once recognize these precepts as being peculiar to our holy religion. However different they may be from the suggestions of flesh and blood, however contrary to the habits of unholy men or to the temper and practice of the world, on candid examination they will be found perfectly to consist with reason and sound philosophy, and they bear excellently the test of experience.

If any thing like policy and art may be conceived of the religion of Jesus Christ, the sentiment which runs through the passage we have read and is summed up in the concluding words, has an eminent claim to such a character—*overcome evil with good.* A harmless policy indeed! yet the most effectual to accomplish the purpose designed. If the expression may be used, it is to revenge one's self by benevolence, it is to take vengeance by shewing kindness. Would you melt the obdurate heart of your foe, would you conquer him and lay him completely at your feet, the surest and most effectual way to accomplish it, is to do him good. Heaping upon him acts of kindness will have a similar effect as the smith's *heaping coals of fire* upon a crucible whose obstinate contents he wishes to resolve; they will soften the injurious passions, they will melt down the heart of iniquity and enmity: the first effect will be shame, the next, reconciliation and love.

If this be not the directest way to conquer and get recompense for evil, it is certainly the most noble way. If it is not the most effectual, it is certainly the most godlike. This is the policy which God Almighty pursues toward our wicked race. This is the policy by which he conquers evil. We behold it in every morning's sun which he raises upon our world. We behold it in every shower of rain which he sends upon our earth. We behold it more gloriously still in the face of Jesus Christ, the Saviour. It shines in the redemption he wrought out for sinners. It is conspicuous in the example he set for mankind. It distinguishes the system of morals which he taught. It is the glory of the gospel. Much did he urge it upon men as what alone could make them truly *the children of their Father who is in heaven*, and in pursuing of which only, they could be accounted genuine Christians and be said to *do more than others*.

This divine, this peaceful policy, my hearers, is what I wish now to urge upon you and upon myself; and could my voice extend through my country, it should be urged upon every citizen of America. Would to God! an angel from heaven might descend at this important epoch, that he might fly through our land, and in trains of celestial eloquence impress upon all the injured in it, the glory of *rendering blessing for cursing*, of *overcoming evil with good*. But I hope such have no need of miraculous means to convince them of the excellence of this gospel-policy and of the propriety and urgent necessity of putting it into eminent practice at the present time.

How desirable—what an epoch to be remembered indeed would this be, if the wounds of our country might now be healed!—if henceforth she might bleed no more through intestine divisions, party-virulence, the ravings of faction and the mad acts of blind infatuation! How happy, if mutual good will, heavenly charity and justice might once more be revived among us! How glorious, if the *new order of things*, as it is called (I care not whose order nor what order it is called), might prove but the abolition of hatred, calumny, detraction, rigid discrimination, personal depression and injustice, and instead thereof restore the old order of social felicity, mutual confidence, benevolent and candid treatment which once distinguished the citizens of this country! If one sincere desire is cherished by my soul, it is, that this happy old order of things might be restored, that we might see an eternal end to the little, detestable maxims of party, and that the generous principles of the country might come forward and reign. O genius of America! arise; come in all the majesty of thine ancient simplicity, moderation, justice; re-commence thine equal empire; drive the demon, party, from our land: From henceforth let the order among us be thy order.

To insure such a glorious and most desirable order of things, my hearers, it is absolutely necessary that the injured among us, of whatever sentiment or character, should not think of revenging, should not think of retaining prejudices and a grudge against their fellow-citizens; but if they revenge at all, let it be by benevolence. The only strife should now be, who can shew the most liberality and kindness, who can do an enemy the most good. Let those who have been the most wronged, be the first to come forward and forgive. Let them bury in magnanimous amnesty, all that is past; and let them exhibit an example of what it is to be truly great—great like a Christian—great like God.

In this sublime policy of the gospel it is by no means implied, that we should be stoics, indifferent to good and evil, or that we should be reconciled to abuse, or that we should not rejoice and be thankful to heaven when we are delivered from it. Christianity was never designed to impair the noble sensibilities of our nature.

I profess no great skill as a politician; nor does it belong to me to say, whether the sufferings which have arisen in our country from political causes, be now certainly at an end. But this I say, if there be well-founded reason to think they are at an end, if the present epoch in American affairs may really be considered as a deliverance on all hands from that unparalleled injustice, those overbearing torrents of abuse and accumulations of injuries; which for some time past have been heaped upon worthy and innocent men, and stained, I fear, the annals of our country beyond the power of time to obliterate—if, I say, this be really the case and may be relied on as fact, then I declare the present occasion an occasion of great joy, deserving our most fervent gratitude to God. And if it be an epoch to prevent still greater abuses from coming on, if it is to set back the tide of party-rage from reaching any farther, if it is to say to that boisterous deluge, which was rolling on in such terrible floods and already swept away much that is dear to us, *hitherto hast thou come, but no farther, and here shall thy proud waves be staid*—if it is to prevent a relentless civil war from existing among us, whose flames, alas! lately appeared to be fast kindling, and in the apprehension of many, threatened by this time to have exhibited the awful scene of brother armed against brother—and garments rolled in blood through our land—if henceforth nothing more is to be feared for personal character, liberty, life, the safety of our Constitution and government, the peace of our country and our social happiness, then I declare it an epoch deserving eternal remembrance and the most heart-felt exultation before the God of heaven. God grant, it may prove such an æra, and that our dear country may once more be happy.

But it requires no great political skill to see that all this in a measure depends on conditions: and one principal condition unquestionably is, that the injured forget their wrongs and be above revenge.

This leads me to suggest a few considerations to recommend the precepts in the text, or the gospel-policy of *overcoming evil with good.*

No one can doubt, that this is an eminent and very distinguishing part of the system taught by the author of our religion. Forgiveness of injuries, love to enemies, charity, a mild, inoffensive behavior, and even literally *the rendering of good for evil*, were themes much upon his tongue, continually urged and enforced by him. By the authority of our Lord, then, we are bound to practise these virtues.

And his example was strictly conformable to these his precepts. Never man *endured so much contradiction of sinners against himself*, so much enormous outrage, such monstrous abuse, as Jesus Christ endured. Yet never man behaved so perfectly inoffensive, or so unremittingly persevered in doing good. He was reproached as a glutton and a drunkard, a *friend and associate of publicans and sinners, a petulent fellow in community, an enemy to Cesar and all government, a low-bred carpenter's son, a turner of the world upside down, a foe to religion, a vile heretic, a perverter of the good old traditions of the elders and the commands and institutions of the fathers, a despiser of the sabbath, a blasphemer, a deceiver of the people, an agent of Beelzebub*—but the time would fail me to tell of all the reproaches and all the hard names with which he was reviled.

Nor did his sufferings rest only in what pertained to reputation. His whole walk on earth was amid snares and plots craftily laid to take, not only his liberty, but his life. And every thing was favorable to render those snares successful: they were laid by a powerful hierarchy, seconded by the rulers of the day, and the Evil One must come and render his aid. Much did he suffer: but never did he manifest a single wish to injure them. The people generally were more friendly to him: they frequently flocked in multitudes around him, and often did they form a defence for his life which his foes dared not provoke. But sometimes means were found to inflame them also, and set them against him. In these cases he was left alone to sustain the vengeance of an enraged world. He could not live long. He was too honest and too good for this earth. At an early period of life he fell a victim to the powers combined against him.

But what was his conduct under these sufferings? what was his conduct even in that last trying hour, that hour of darkness, when perfect innocence was about to suffer indignities which should belong only to the foulest guilt? Now we should expect revenge, if ever. Now, that the measure of his injuries was full, might we not look for some capital blow to retaliate for the whole at once? Why did he not shake the earth out of its place and crumble his enemies to dust? Why did he not bid his waiting legions of angels empty the realms of heaven—fly and smite his abusive foes to destruction? Good God! what do we see!—*he goes as a lamb to the slaughter, and as a sheep before her shearers is dumb, so he openeth not his mouth!* His dying breath wafts a tender prayer to the throne of mercy for his murderers, *Father, forgive them, for they know not what they do!*

Shall such an example shine before us, and not ravish us with its glories? Shall we boast such an Author of our religion, and not be ambitious to imitate him? How do all the injuries which we endure and all our sufferings dwindle into nothing compared with those of our Master? And oh! how should all dispositions of vengeance melt away from our souls before the burning lustre of his example?

But let us look at the intrinsic merits of this conduct, thus exemplified by Jesus, and so eminently required by his precepts. This conduct may be justified both on the ground of good policy and of moral obligation.

First, on the ground of policy. The apostle evidently suggests the idea of policy in these words, *for, in so doing, thou shalt heap coals of fire on his head.* We have already explained this figure. It alludes to a smith's heaping coals of fire upon a crucible, or any hard substance which he wishes to soften or solve. A very happy allusion to set forth the power of kind actions upon the hearts of our abusive enemies. If we wish to conquer them most effectually, this is the way to do it. We all, I presume, have witnessed somewhat of this in our intercourse with mankind. If we ourselves have ever unjustly abused another, for him to return us obliging and good actions upon it, makes us ashamed, and we soon desire to forget what we have done. This kind of conduct, well-timed and properly directed, is absolutely irresistible. It puts upon man the appearance of a superior being, and compels regard. To repulse evil with evil, tends only to sharpen the hostile passions and to fix the parties in everlasting hatred. This is not conquest, it is only continuing the battle without ever deciding the victory.

I suppose it likely, that it was on account of this peculiar feature in the character of Christ and his religion, that so many of his crucifiers were afterwards *pricked in the heart* and turned to be his followers, as we are told three thousand did at one sermon of Peter's, on the subject of the crucifixion. And on the same account the religion of Christ made rapid progress in the world, so long as its supporters exhibited this its peculiar feature. But when they assumed the power of the state and the power of armies to assist the power of Christianity, and its advocates became fierce, revengeful, intolerant, then its spread was retarded, and even Mahometanism outstripped it in progress.

But secondly, the gospel-conduct in question, may be justified upon the ground of moral obligation. Our enemies and abusers, be they who they may, have something in them or pertaining to them which deserves our regard, and I will say, our love, notwithstanding the malice and depravity which they may also possess.

In the first place they have existence. And is not existence valuable? Think of annihilation: See how anxious all are to preserve their lives, not excepting the very brutes. What is thus demonstrated to be valuable by every testimony around us, and by our own irresistible feelings, ought surely to be prized at some rate and to be treated accordingly.

They have also rational faculties. And are not these valuable? Look at the idiot or at the delirious wretch! what an afflicting sight is the absence of mental faculties? They are to be regarded, then, where they exist.

Our enemies possess immortal natures. This confers inestimable worth. The fly, that lives and sports a summer, is a being of small value. The brute, that protracts his life to a few years, is more valuable. But man, who is destined to live when the sun and the stars are no more, who is to travel onward and grow in excellence through eternal ages, possesses a value beyond all computation, beyond all conception. Our Saviour estimates a soul above the whole world. Is such an object to be dealt lightly with? Is he rashly to be consigned over to utter hatred, and shall every sentiment be expunged from our hearts which should excite us to consult his welfare?

They also have a *capacity for virtue and happiness.* However depraved at present, yet they are not beyond recovery. If malice now rankles in their hearts, yet their hearts are capable of being receptacles of benevolence. They are salvable creatures, restorable to virtue and felicity. Shall they be thrown away as good for nothing, and all regard be withdrawn from them, when this capacity is in them and they may yet be ranked with ourselves in dignity and bliss? Ought they not rather to be considered as a valuable machine, disordered truly, but capable of repair? Do we throw away our gold and silver utensils, because for the present they may have gotten out of order? Moral evil is but a disorder of the mind, and is removable. The evil should be hated; but the unhappy subject of it is still to be regarded. Our desire and endeavor should be to rectify, not destroy.

The dignified nature of man, and his capability of being restored to virtue and felicity, were what rendered him in his sins an object of regard to his Maker, and procured for him the merciful provision of the gospel. What if God had treated our sinful race according to the dictates of enmity and hatred? Who would ever have found mercy? No, he loved us notwithstanding *we were enemies in our minds by wicked works. God so loved the world, that he gave his only begotten son to die. Herein is love, not that we loved God, but that he loved us, and sent his Son to be the propitiation for our sins. God commendeth his love towards us, in that while we were yet sinners, Christ died for us.* From the example of our Maker, then, as well as by looking directly at the subject, we see there is something in enemies and wicked men, which is a proper foundation for love, and demands benevolent treatment.

Another consideration which should commend our enemies to our affectionate regards is, they are our brethren, children with us of one great Parent, members together of one great family. Their blood is a branch of the same fountain which flows in our veins. They are "bone of our bone and kindred souls to our's." "Pierce my vein," says a poet,

> Take of the crimson stream meandering there
> And catechise it well: apply thy glass,
> Search it, and see now if it be not blood
> Congenial with thine own.

They exercise all the functions which we exercise. They weep as we weep. They feel as we feel. They suffer as we suffer. If some of the family are proud, selfish, disposed to be injurious and trample on the rights of the rest, let them be brought to know their places—but let them still be beloved. What is here suggested is the foundation of philanthropy, or universal benevolence, which unquestionably is the benevolence of the gospel, and what we all ought to entertain.

Thus on the solid basis of moral obligation rests the duty of loving and treating well our enemies.

I shall now mention a few considerations of another kind, which should make us extremely cautious how we indulge revengeful feelings toward those who may have abused us.

First of all, we ourselves are frail, fallible beings, and therefore may mistake the intentions of our fellow-creatures, misapprehend their motives, or may see their actions in a distorted form. Perhaps they are not so guilty as we imagine. Or it may be, through frailty we have offered unwarrantable provocation. In either of these cases revenge would be unjust.

We are further to consider, that our enemies and abusers are also subject to frailties. Great allowances are to be made on this account. The God of nature seems to have created some souls on an extremely little scale. Such are they who, capable only of being actuated by party-spirit, do nothing, think nothing, feel nothing, but just as party-spirit dictates. Some of this description have been known not to be able to hold common good neighborhood, nor Christian fellowship, nor to celebrate an anniversary festival, nor to communicate with their God, no, not even to hear a prayer, with one not of their particular party, be [h]is character as bright as an angel's. Shall we be disposed to revenge upon such little creatures?—pity, pity, nothing but pity is called for.

Others may become enemies and abusers merely because they mistake the intentions, the principles, the views of each other. They may see you through a false medium. Their enmity may be founded on some false report. They may be acted upon by an influence which they do not perceive; may be led by the interested and crafty; may be deluded, deceived, excited by groundless alarm and cajoled in a thousand ways, which they themselves would despise, had they better information. I verily believe, that more than one half of the feuds, animosities and enmities which afflict mankind, flow from these sources, rather than from any real ground of difference, or from downright malice of heart. I am certain this is the case in times of general party, when the people are roused up to oppress and abuse one another. Oh! it is piteous to see the fatal fruits of this frailty, to see honest and well-meaning people made to drink down potions of poisonous prejudice against their brethren for no cause, to see them excited to baleful rage, made to vent reproaches, and ready to whet the sword of destruction, as against cannibals and monsters, when the principles of both are identically the same, and all are seeking the same object, only perhaps some party-name, devised and applied by knaves, with a plenty of misrepresentation, is the whole difference between them! I am bold to say it, this of late years has been afflictingly the case in this country. People, whose real principles differ not one jot nor tittle, have been made most cordially to hate one another. The most genuine patriots have been anathematized by the most genuine patriots, the truest whigs by the truest whigs, the best republicans by the best republicans! It was a pitiable scene. But ought we to be disposed to revenge? Whoever thou art, of whatever party, that hast suffered in this way, if you hate these good people, you hate your best friends, you hate your compatriots and real brethren. Moreover, they never hated you; they hated only a phantom in your stead, a shade, an empty shade, which has been artfully raised up before them and called by your name. The people at large are honest, and all the sin lies at the door of their deceivers. These may be rebuked sharply: they may be spoken to as the mild Jesus spake to the deceivers of the people in his day, *Ye serpents! ye generation of vipers! how can ye escape the damnation of hell?* But to the people we should never speak in this manner. They were never spoken to thus by their friend Jesus. He always addressed the multitudes with respect and tenderness. And even their deceivers should not be devoted to hatred and ill offices. Like our Lord the genuine Christian will pray for them, if he can do no more.

When people are drawn by the designing into deep delusion and high party-rage, it is not to be expected that they all will come out together, that every one so soon as another will have the scales fall from his eyes to see clearly what has been the matter. This depends very much upon accident. The schemes of the crafty are often so deeply laid and so closely hedged about, that it requires years for them to come fairly out and be seen by the greater part of honest people. Often it is true of such schemes, "*Longa est injuria, longæ ambages.*" Many of the honest and unsuspecting will not be undeceived but by the unfolding of the scheme in serious and alarming facts. But to some it may by accident be leaked out beforehand, perhaps from the very mouths of its authors. Or circumstances of a local and particular nature may conspire to convince some long before others. When this is the case, the first who are convinced will be thought hard of, and perhaps be calumniated and abused by their own brethren whose conviction is to come later. The schemers will endeavor to make this the case as much as possible, and will foment it by every means in their power. What is here observed may furnish an answer to those who sometimes ask one who differs from them, "How comes it that you know so much more than every body else?" The true answer is, it comes by accident and various local circumstances, more than from any superiority of understanding or better principles of patriotism. But it will be acknowledged, I think, that in these cases patience ought to be used, a very mild and gentle conduct ought to be observed. To revenge would be to revenge upon honest men.

We may vary a little the statement of this matter. The difference between honest people at the present day (and such I conceive the great body on both sides to be) is merely a difference of belief. Some individuals, to be sure may be most wicked and designing. But, it is idle to say, that the great body of people on either hand are not honest. They are honest, and most sincerely friendly to the Constitution and their country. But one of one party believes there is a design on foot to overturn the Constitution and deprive the country of its liberties. Another of another party believes no such thing. Whereas the latter would equally detest such a design and its authors, could he believe it were so. Now shall men go to revenging upon one another merely for differences of faith, or belief? It would be reviving the worst doctrine of the dark ages.

Another consideration which should make us cautious not to indulge revenge is, that by so doing we pollute and injure our own souls. Revenge is a foul passion. To be overcome with it, is to be overcome with evil. Be it never so justly provoked, it hurts the temper; and if allowed to continue, will stop little short of entirely ruining it. Revenge is very properly pictured as a chief characteristic of the infernals. And the perfection of God is to be ever serene, good and forgiving. When we can sincerely forgive our enemies, bless them and do them good, it is a token of great advancement in grace: for our Saviour considers this as the badge of Christian perfection, who in view of it says, *Be ye therefore perfect, even as your Father who is in heaven is perfect.*

As a further recommendation of this heavenly conduct, let me observe, that whoever finds himself truly disposed to practise it, may have the consolation to think, that most probably he is in the right with respect to those things for which he is abused, and that his oppressors are wrong. The sure signs of error are a rigid, illiberal conduct, persecution and abuse, a disposition to discriminate, depress and keep down by violence whatever is opposed, and to repay tenfold when we have it in our power. This kind of conduct from of old has always distinguished the advocates of error, and is a certain badge of it. Whereas truth never feels a necessity for these things, but is always mild, meek, liberal, generous, friendly to moderation and the utmost fairness, asks only an equal chance to be heard, disdaining violence, sure to conquer by her own charms. The Pharisees and chief-priests on the one hand, and Jesus on the other, were perfect examples of the conduct which error and truth respectively inspire.

When parties exist, perhaps there is no better rule to determine which is nearest the truth, than to recur to the manner of their treating each other, and mark the quantity of abuse offered on either side. And among all the species of abuse, perhaps that of epithet is as sure a standard as any. Whichever party invents and applies odious epithets in the greatest abundance and of the most unfounded and scandalous import, may be presumed to be most out of the way.

The peaceful conduct under consideration may be recommended from the excellent effect which will ultimately attend it, although for the present moment it may be unsuccessful. When men are outrageously abused, they are wont to think, there was never any thing like it before. And if their abusers prosper over them, they are apt to despair, and imagine all to be lost unless they resort to desperate efforts and oppose violence to violence. But this is the short-sighted wisdom of the flesh. We at this late age of the world have reason to know better. Have not worthy men, the just, friends of truth, of righteousness, of liberty, of every the most laudable cause, suffered in every age? To omit the mention of others, did not the immaculate Jesus and his first followers suffer, as men never suffered? Yet, what was the effect? Did not the gospel rise, shake itself from ignominy and run triumphantly through the world; while their outrageous foes soon sank out of repute and out of remembrance? There is something in mankind which favors suffering merit, and will assist it in spite of all opposition, something which approves of moderation and reasonable conduct, and condemns overbearing things. This is a laudable disposition in mankind, and where there is nothing special to repress the public will, it is certain to give eventual triumph to those who under abuse, conduct according to the maxims of Christ; it will in the end bring them, with their cause, out of all their troubles.

Finally, my hearers, if any of you (and I would address those of every description, sentiment and party) if, I say, any of you have experienced the odious effects of a system of conduct the opposite of the one we are considering, if you have experienced those effects in your reputation, business, profession, property or individual freedom, if your indignation has been roused, or your contempt excited at any little, narrow, malevolent acts of men by which you have been attempted to be injured—will you not still continue to detest, and forbear to adopt such a despicable system of conduct for your own? I beg to be considered as addressing all of every sentiment and character, who have been abused by any conduct opposite to the liberal precepts of Jesus. Will you not abominate such conduct as you have been taught to do by your own hard experience? and will you not cleave to the generous, the manly, the godlike deportment prescibed in the gospel? Let me call upon your own sufferings; let me appeal to your own past feelings—your sorrow, your pity, your indignation, your scorn—let me bring them all to your remembrance and conjure you by them; never, never to fall into a line of conduct which you so much disapprove. Never lose sight of those noble sentiments which you so much wished might have been shewn toward you. While they are fresh in your recollection, consecrate them, sanctify them, let them be eternally held sacred. Repay nothing of what you have received: nobly forbear. *All things whatsoever ye would, that men should have done to you, do ye even so to them.*

As it respects the public welfare and peace of the country, let me ask, Has not the monster, party, raged long enough? Has he not marched like a bloody cannibal through our land and glutted sufficiently his abominable maw? Has he not dovoured enough of reputation, enough of honest merit, enough of our social peace and happiness? Has not brother hated brother, neighbor neighbor, citizen citizen, long enough? Is it not time to put an end to the wounds of society and to heal our bleeding country?

I feel the more earnest on this occasion as I consider the present juncture of affairs most important. And I view myself addressing an audience composed in some considerable degree of a description of men through this country on whose prudent and wise conduct, much, very much depends to restore tranquility and happiness to our land.

Let me, then, bring to your view our bleeding country. Let me place her before you in all her deplorable plight, torn and mangled with faction, poisoned with the venom of party, wrecked with intestine hatred, strife, division, discord, and threatened with complete dissolution. Before you she stands. To you she turns her eyes: she implores your consideration: she begs to be restored to her wonted dignity and happiness. "Will you," she cries, "introduce a system of party, personal depression and abuse, and tear my vitals asunder? Oh! remember Jesus, the friend of the world! His precepts will heal me. If you have been *persecuted*, I beseech you to *bless*: if you have been *despitefully used*, *pray for* your abusers: if you have been *reviled*, *revile not again. Render to no man evil for evil, but contrariwise, blessing. Overcome evil with good.* Thus shall my reproach be wiped away: thus shall my wounds be healed: thus shall you and all my children be restored to happiness."

Agreeably to these importunate cries of our country, suffer me to conclude with offering a few particular directions for the observance of all on whom any thing depends relative to our country's peace.

First of all, dropping on all hands every term and epithet of party —I mean such terms and epithets particularly as originated in rancor, and have no foundation in reality—carefully consult the ancient spirit of the country, see what its maxims were formerly, and what now are its genuine principles and wishes. Whatever you find these to be, with them go forward and do the public will. Be not a faction within the country; but be the country itself. Let not your spirit be the passion of party; but let it be the public spirit. Let the genius of America reign.

Give me leave to say, you will not mistake the ancient maxims of this country nor its present wishes if you be stedfast, genuine *republicans.* If we recur to our forefathers we shall find them republican from the beginning. The spirit of freedom drove them from their native land and brought them to this then howling wilderness. Genuine principles of liberty were conspicuous in all their early proceedings. No greater liberty-men were ever seen in America, than Winthrop, Davenport, Hooker, Haynes, and all that band of worthies who, under God, were the means of our being planted here. Much has been said about the forefathers of New-England. The truth is, the leading, most distinguishing traits in their character were these two, *liberty* and *religion.* In both they were sincere, and prized them above all price. With beams extracted from these sources, their souls were illuminated and warmed. They did not set up an outcry about liberty with an insidious view to root out religion and overturn its institutions: neither on the other hand did they make an out-cry about religion and its institutions with a view to cover over an insidious design of departing from the principles of civil liberty. These principles they carefully handed down to their sons, and in every period of the country's progress they have been conspicuous. They broke out in full splendor in 1775 and '76, of which the *Declaration of Independence* is an illustrious proof. Again they shone forth with effulgent lustre in 1787 and '88, and the unparalleled *Constitution of the United States* was their fruit. These ancient, deep-rooted, republican principles of the country must be most sacredly regarded; for, be assured every variation from them will be resisted and bring on convulsions.

To have said thus much in favor of republican principles I hope will not be deemed to favor of party-spirit. For, I am designating the acknowledged principles of my country. And I beg leave to add, that they are principles of eternal rectitude and equity. Republicanism can no more be considered a party, than immutable truth and righteousness can be considered a party. And republicans can no more be called a faction, than nature, reason and scripture with their Author, can be called a faction. For, these principles rest on the solid basis of nature, are clear as the sun to the eye of reason, and the bible is full of them from beginning to end. Nothing ever appeared to me more preposterous than to say the bible favors of monarchy. What did God say to his people, Israel, when they first asked for a king to rule over them? Read the eighth chapter of 1 Sam. and you will see how he resisted their request and set before them all the evils of monarchy.* But when the people were deaf, and said (because they could say nothing better), *Nay, but we will have a king*, then God *gave them a king in his wrath*. And wrath indeed it was! If the public mind at any time become so depraved as that they will have a king, why then there is no help for it; and it becomes the duty of good men to make the best of the evil. Thus did the prophets and good men in Israel. But because they wished to make the best of an evil, shall it be argued that they were in favor of the evil and were its zealous abettors?

When Jesus Christ came, every maxim and every precept he gave, so far as an application can be made, was purely republican. If we had no other saying of his than this, it would be sufficient to determine the matter. *Ye know*, says he, *that the princes of the nations exercise lordship over them, and their great ones exercise authority upon them. But it shall not be so among you: but whosoever will be chiefest among you let him be servant of all.* True he did not come to intermeddle with human governments. But it is plain to see what his real sentiments were. It was not without ground that he was suspected of not being very

* Note. Those who are able to read the original Hebrew will find in this passage, as generally through the old Testament, ideas which can hardly be communicated by a literal translation.

friendly to Cesar. If he paid him his tribute-money, it was on this principle, *lest we should offend them.* He was a friend to order, but he was in favor of righteous order. *Mind not high things, but condescend to men of low estate.*

If there be a privileged order of men known in the bible, it is the poor and the oppressed. Such are in scripture taken to God's peculiar favor, he appears their special protector and avenger, and denounces terrible woes upon the head of their oppressors.

Is not iniquity condemned in the bible? But what is iniquity? The word is from *in* and *æquus*, unequal: not unequal as to property or any other accidental circumstance, or appendage; but unequal as to rights. Thus the thief claims a right to trample on the rights of his neighbor, with respect to property, the slanderer with respect to character, the murderer with respect to life. These will not be subject to laws which subject the rest of community; but must claim privileges above them and peculiar to themselves. The noble lord, who trespasses with impunity upon the inclosures of his neighbors, differs nothing from the thief, except that the iniquitous laws of unequal government protect the one and hang the other. Iniquity surely is hateful to God. He repeatedly appeals to mankind in his word, *Are not my ways equal? are not your ways unequal?*

Thus republican principles are no party-principles, inasmuch as they are founded in nature, reason and the word of God. At any rate, they are the principles of our country; and in exhorting you to abide by them, I am sure I speak the mind of the country, and what she herself would urge with pathetic importunity, were she to rise in my place and address you.

Permit me further to say, you would not mistake the old and genuine maxims of the country, if you should set an inestimable value upon that instrument, called *The Declaration of American Independence.* There her principles are displayed. There they are graven as in adamant, never to be effaced. That was the banner she unfurled when she arose to assert her rights. Under that banner she marched to victory and glory. On that were inscribed the insignia of all she contended for.

Cherish then, that immortal document of what once were declared in the face of the world to be the principles of this country. I firmly believe they are still its principles.

Give me leave to say further, you will not mistake the will and pleasure of the country, if you give all your friendship, all your best wishes, and all the support in your power to the incomparable *Constitution of the United States.* This Constitution was adopted by a fair expression of the public will. It is the government of the country and the ordinance of God. When we examine its merits, we find it but another edition of the genuine principles of republicanism, equal rights its foundation, and the welfare of the people its object. The precious maxims of the Declaration of Independence are transplanted into the Constitution. And as under the former the country marched to victory, so under the latter she may advance to prosperity.

Let the Constitution then, be esteemed the palladium of all that we hold dear. Let it be venerated as the sanctuary of our liberties and all our best interests. Let it be kept as the ark of God. Obey the laws of government. Be genuine friends of order. Take that reproach from the mouths of monarchs, that republicans are prone to rebellion. Dissipate that stigma, if it has been fastened upon any of you, that you are disorganizers, Jacobins, monsters. Let your love of order consist not in profession, but in reality. Let it be manifested, like true religion, in practice. *Love not in word neither in tongue, but in deed and in truth.*

Be not devoted to *men*. Let *principles* ever guide your attachments. To be blindly devoted to names and men's person's, is at once a token of a slavish spirit, and a sure way to throw the country into virulent parties. Be ready to sacrifice a Jefferson as freely as any man, should he become elated with power, exalt himself above the Constitution and depart from republican principles. Our Constitution contemplated independent freemen, men having a mind of their own, when it provided the right of suffrage. If we are to follow a man blindly wherever he leads, and if his coming once into office is to secure him there forever, whatever his conduct be, in the name of common sense let so idle a thing as suffrage be expunged from our Constitution, and save the people the trouble of meeting so often for election. So long as a man in power behaves well and cleaves to your own principles, give him your support and your applause. But the instant he departs from the line prescribed for him by your social compact, peaceably resort to your right of suffrage, and hurl him from his eminence, be he who he may. In the mean time, always be in subjection to *the powers that be.* By thus devoting yourselves to the principles of our excellent constitution and to the existing laws of government, you will be sure to do the pleasure of the country.

Let me say further, the pleasure of our country is to be free from foreign attachments. To be devoted to England or France or any one nation in preference to another, is unjust in itself, and a sure method to convulse the country with parties. We ought to wish well to all nations, desiring their deliverance from evil, and that they may enjoy their rights and happiness, without connecting ourselves intimately with the fortunes of any. One principal purpose for which we should look at other nations is to learn from their miserable experience how to preserve our own liberties, how to secure our own happiness.

Lastly, to be genuinely and truly religious, would not be mistaking the ancient maxims of our nation. As I have endeavored in this discourse to hold up before you one of the chief and most peculiar features of the gospel, and have urged it by various considerations, I shall not now be lengthy. Give me leave to say, the genuine spirit of the gospel is the very perfection of man. Possessing that spirit, *nation would no more rise against nation, nor kingdom against kingdom, the lion would lie down with the lamb, and there would be nothing to hurt or destroy throughout the earth; each one might sit under his vine and fig tree, having none to make him afraid.* Genuine Christianity is a system of complete benevolence. Where it enters with its spirit and power, every relation is rendered kind, and every duty is cheerfully discharged. In no relation would its effects be more excellent than between ruler and people. Not that church and state should be blended in the manner which has so much afflicted the world. Far from it. *Christ's kingdom,* in such a sense, *is not of this world.* But it would be no matter how much the spirit of Christianity were blended with the spirit of rulers, or with the spirit of the ruled. The more the better. If the spirit of rulers were to be perfectly Christian, tyranny would never more be known. And if the spirit of the citizens were perfectly Christian, there would be little or no need of government.

This peaceful religion is the nominal religion of our country. How would she rejoice if it might be the real religion? Then indeed *would she be glad and rejoice and blossom as the rose. She would blossom abundantly, and rejoice with joy and singing. The glory of Lebanon would be given her, the excellency of Carmel and Sharon.* Imbibe, then, into your souls the spirit of this most excellent religion, and bring forth its fruits in your lives.

On the whole, my hearers, take the particulars we have mentioned, and blending them into one character, put that character on; and proceed with it in all its dignity and amiableness, along the course before you. Uniting the principles of liberty with order, and crowning the whole with genuine religion, be *clear as the sun, fair as the moon, and terrible as an army with banners.* Amaze once more the tyrants of the earth when they look toward this land: let them see that men can be free without licentiousness, orderly without needing the shackles of despotism, religious without the impositions of bigotry. By assuming this character, be invulnerable to your foes; baulk the hopes of the envious.

Let this character be invariably maintained. On no occasion and on no account let it sink into the low regions of party. Ah! stoop not —stoop not to the extreme littleness—I was going to mention instances, but the dignity of the pulpit checks me. Far, far from such despicable things be your conduct. Let the American character be borne aloft. Let it soar like the eagle of heaven, its emblem, bearing the scroll of our liberties through fields of azure light, unclouded by the low-bred vapors of faction; and let it not be degraded into a detestable owl of night, to dabble in the pools of intrigue and party and delight itself in the filthy operations of darkness.

Where are our Fathers? where are our former men of dignity, our Huntingtons, Shermans, Johnsons, Stiles's, who in their day appeared like men, gave exaltation to our character, and never descended to a mean thing? It appears to me, in every department we are dwindled, and more disposed to act like children than men.

Let the spirit of our fathers come upon us. Be men: rise: let another race of patriots appear: bring forward another band of sages. Let America once more be the admiration of the world.

Think not that the dignity of a nation can be commuted. Think not that it can be transferred from its only genuine seat, the *mind of its citizens*, and be made to consist in any thing else.

> *Ou lithoi, oude xula, oude*
> *Technee tektoonoon ai poleis eisen:*

All' opou pot' an oosin andres,
Autous soozein eidotes,
Entautha [kai] teichee kai poleis. Alceus.

What constitutes a state?
Not high-raised battlements and lofty towers;
Not cities proud, nor spangled courts.
No—*men*—high-minded *men*;
Men, who their duties know;
But know their rights, and knowing, dare maintain.

Yes, the true and everlasting dignity of a state spurns all commutation. It never can be made to consist in ornamented stone and wood. You must be men, high-minded men, else the national character will unavoidably sink, prop it how you may. What was Greece, what was Rome, when their men disappeared, their high-minded men? Splendor, pomp, luxury indeed, enough of it; but no glory. And soon their pomp was brought down to the grave. What was Egypt after its people became a race of slaves? did their pyramids prop the falling character of the nation? O Americans! be *men*: let the glory of the nation rest in the dignity of *mind*. Be like the pillars which formerly stood under and bore up your honor. It was a goodly range of plain, hardy, independent, republican sages. These are your best props. Put them under again. Many indeed are fallen. And chiefly thee we lament, O Washington, who wast thyself half our glory! What a pillar wast thou in the fabric of our commonwealth? When shall another such arise? But we hope we have others somewhat resembling. Let us all, my friends, endeavor to be such. The way is open before us; and we have the best of models. Be great then, like Washington, be inflexible like Adams, be intelligent and good like Jefferson.

Give me leave on this occasion particularly to point you to Thomas Jefferson as a laudable example of that magnanimous and peaceable conduct which I have recommended to you in this discourse, and which is so peculiarly necessary to be put in practice at the present juncture. That he has been abused, I suppose will be acknowledged on all hands. But have you heard of his complaining? Have you heard him talk of vengeance and retaliation? Do his writings heretofore betray a little soul? Does his late letter to his friend in Berkley, does his answer to the committee of the house of Representatives, does his farewell address to the Senate* breathe the meanness of a spirit bent on revenge? Placid on his mount he seems to have sat, as Washington on his, and beheld the storm of passion among his fellow-citizens with no other sensations than those of extreme pity and deep concern for his country. Like Washington be seems to have looked with an equal eye to the north and to the south, to the east and to the west of the union, and wished them all happiness. Should it come to pass, that he can be so little as to discriminate one half of his fellow-citizens from the other half, and withhold from them all confidence and all respect, brand them for enemies and traitors, deprive them of all offices and honors, and depress and afflict them all in his power —give me leave to say, I shall be one to execrate his conduct most sincerely. What! shall the country be thrown into convulsion and wretchedness, and the conduct which does it, not be abominated?

But at present we are persuaded of better things. At least, every thing which as yet has transpired from him is directly the reverse. And it is for this reason that I point you to him for an example of what ought to be the conduct of all in the present posture of affairs. O my countrymen! those who have any regard for the peace and honor of America!—if you *have been reviled, revile not again*—if *you have been persecuted, bless;* if you *have had all manner of evil spoken against you falsely, recompense to no man evil for evil.* In a word, *be not overcome of evil, but overcome evil with good.* Come, and in this holy sanctuary of God bring all your grievances, all your resentments, and laying them upon the altar of sacrifice, consume and purge them all away. Turning to the golden altar of incense, inhale largely the sweet perfumes of patriotism, charity and every heavenly grace. Let your breasts henceforth glow with nothing but these peaceful, exalted sentiments.

* The inaugural speech of the president had not at this time arrived. Otherwise a reference to that might have been sufficient, without alluding to the communications here mentioned, which had been seen.

The author presumes he shall not differ from the candid part of his fellow-citizens, if he declares this inaugural speech to be a very excellent specimen of fine sentiment, sound policy, and of that magnanimity and moderation which are inculcated in this discourse. And he is happy to observe a very striking resemblance between the writings of President Jefferson and the late illustrious Washington, which augurs well for our country.

Then shall your dear country rejoice over you as her genuine sons —her tears shall be dried, her reproach shall be wiped away, peace shall be restored to her afflicted bosom; you shall be blessed with your own reflections, and generations to come shall rise up and call you blessed. Amen.

54

AN ORATION IN COMMEMORATION OF THE ANNIVERSARY OF AMERICAN INDEPENDENCE

William Emerson

BOSTON

1802

WILLIAM EMERSON (1769-1811). The son of William Emerson—a Congregational pastor at Concord Church who was present at the Battle of Concord—and the father of Ralph Waldo Emerson (the fourth of eight children), Emerson was a Unitarian clergyman and pastor of the First Church in Boston after 1799. A decade earlier he was graduated from Harvard, where he had been ordained as a Unitarian pastor. Interested in the social, literary, and musical life of Boston, as well as its religious affairs, he was criticized for worldliness. Theologically liberal and an eloquent, if formal, preacher, he served as chaplain of the Massachusetts Senate and an overseer of Harvard College. Emerson participated in the Massachusetts Historical Society, edited the *Monthly Anthology* literary magazine, and founded the Anthology Club, from whose library the Boston Athenaeum Library developed. He died at the age of forty-one, leaving as his most substantial work *An Historical Sketch of the First Church in Boston*, published posthumously in 1812.

ORATION

Pronounced July 5, 1802,

AT THE REQUEST OF THE INHABITANTS OF THE

TOWN OF BOSTON,

IN COMMEMORATION OF THE ANNIVERSARY OF

American Independence.

BY THE REV. WILLIAM EMERSON.

Some truths are not by *Reason* to be try'd,
But we have sure EXPERIENCE for our guide.

DRYDEN.

1802

BOSTON:

MANNING & LORING, PRINTERS, NO. 2, CORNHILL.

It is the glory of nations, as it is of individuals, to increase in wisdom, as they advance in age, and to guide their concerns, not so much by the result of abstract reasonings, as by the dictates of experience. But this glory is no more the uniform felicity of ancient states, than of their ancient citizens. In the eighteenth century, the British nation had existed thirteen hundred years; seen ages roll away with wrecks of empires; marked thousands of experiments in the science and the art of civil government; and had risen to a lofty height of improvement, of freedom, and of happiness. It was yet the misfortune and the disgrace of this kingdom, so famous in the annals of modern Europe, to war with the principles of her own constitution, and to tread, with presumptuous step, the dangerous path of innovation and unrighteousness.

This sentiment will be vindicated by considering, as on this occasion we are bound "to consider, the feelings, manners, and principles, which led to the declaration of American independence, as well as the important and happy effects, whether general, or domestick, which have already flowed, or will forever flow, from the auspicious epoch of its date."

In assisting your performance of this annual duty, my fellow-citizens, I claim the privilege, granted to your former orators, of holding forth the language of truth; and I humbly solicit a favour, of which they had no need, the most liberal exercise of your ingenuousness and benevolence.

The *feelings* of Americans were always the feelings of freemen. Those venerable men, from whom you boast your descent, brought with them to these shores an unconquerable sense of liberty. They felt, that mankind were universally entitled to be free; that this freedom, though modified by the restrictions of social compact, could yet never be annulled; and that slavery, in any of it's forms, is an execrable monster, whose breath is poison, and whose grasp is death.

Concerning this liberty, however, they entertained no romantick notions. They neither sought nor wished the freedom of an irrational, but that of a rational being; not the freedom of savages, not the freedom of anchorites, but that of civilized and social man. Their doctrine of equality was admitted by sober understandings. It was an equality not of wisdom, but of right; not a parity of power, but of obligation. They felt and advocated a right to personal security; to the fruits of their ingenuity and toil; to reputation; to choice of mode in the worship of God; and to such a liberty of action, as consists with the safety of others, and the integrity of the laws.

Of rights like these, your ancestors cherished a love bordering on reverence. They had inhaled it with their natal air: it formed the bias and the boast of their minds, and indelibly stamped the features of their character. In their eyes honour had no allurement, wealth no value, and existence itself no charms, unless liberty crowned the possession of these blessings. It was for the enjoyment of this ecclesiastick and political liberty, that they encountered the greatest dangers, and suffered the sharpest calamities. For this they had rived the enchanting bonds, which unite the heart to it's native country; braved the terrour of unknown seas; exchanged the sympathies and intercourse of fondest friendships, for the hatred and wiles of the barbarian; and all the elegancies and joys of polished life, for a miserable sustenance in an horrible desert.

It was impossible for descendants of such men not to inherit an abhorrence of arbitrary power. Numerous circumstances strengthened the emotion. They had ever been taught, that property acquires title by labour; and they were conscious of having expended much of the one for little of the other. They were thence naturally tenacious of what they possessed, and conceived, that no human power might legally diminish it without their consent. They had also sprung from a commercial people; and they inhabited a country, which opened to commerce the most luxuriant prospects. Of course, property with them was an object of unusual importance. Inhabitants of other regions might place their liberty in the election of their governours; but Americans placed it in the control of their wealth: and to them it was a matter of even less consequence, who wore the robes of office, or held the sword of justice, than who had the power of filling the treasury, and appropriating its contents.

The resolves and attempts, therefore, of the British government to raise an American revenue, they viewed as a thrust at their liberties. By these measures, they felt themselves wronged, vilified, and insulted. If they acknowledged the pretended *right of parliament to bind them in all cases whatever*, it cleft, like a ball of lightning, the tree of colonial liberty, giving its foliage to the winds, and its fruit to the dust. There was no joy, which it did not wither; no hope, which it did not blight. An angry cloud of adversity hung over every department of social life. Demands of business, offices of love, and rites of religion, were, in some sort, suspended, and the earliest apprehensions of the American infant were those of servitude and wretchedness.

Such were the feelings, which impelled resistance to Great-Britain, and the rejection of her authority. They were the feelings of men, who were vigilant of the rights of human nature, of freemen, whose liberties had been out-raged, of patriots, determined never to survive the honour of their country.

American independence was also induced by American *manners*. The planters of this western world, especially of New-England, were eminent for the purity and lustre of their morals. They were industrious from choice, necessity, and habit. Their mode of living rendered them abstinent from enervating pleasures, and patient of toil. The difficulties of subduing a rough wilderness, the severities of their climate, and the rigour of paternal discipline, were almost alone sufficient to preserve in their offspring this simplicity of life. It had, however, a yet stronger guard in their military and civil, literary and religious institutions.

Exposed continually to the incursion of hostile and insidious neighbours, they trained their youth to the exercise of arms, to courage in danger, and to constancy in suffering.

The forms of their government were popular. They exercised the right of choosing their rulers; and they chose them from the wisest and best of the people. Virtue and talents were indispensable qualifications for office, and bribery and corruption were unknown and unsuspected.

A deep foresight and an expanded generosity directed their plans of education. Colleges were founded in the midst of deserts; and the means of knowledge and goodness were within the reach of all ranks of the community. Every householder was the chaplain of his family; every village had its instructer of children; every parish its minister of the gospel; every town its magistrate; and every county its court of justice. The study of the law, which is ever conservative of liberty, had a due proportion of followers, among whom it numbered as eminent civilians, as any age or country has produced. The colonists, in short, enjoyed all those advantages, which conduce to intelligence, sobriety, hardihood, and freedom in a people.

Such were the manners, which distinguished Americans for a century and an half. They were the manners of men, who, though poor, were too rich to be venal; though humble in pretension, too proud for servility; and though overlooked in the mass of mankind, as possessing no national character, yet convinced the proudest monarchy in the world, that an attempt to oppress them was dangerous, and to conquer them, impossible.

The impossibility of subjugating America consisted not in the feelings and manners only, but likewise in the political *principles* of her sons. They honestly believed, what they boldly avowed, that the assumption of parliament was a violation of law, equity, and ancient usage.

These colonies originally were composed of men, who were rather ejected from Britain, as nuisances of the state, than fostered as her duteous children. If, when their increasing population and riches became an object of attention, they owed any thing to the parent country, it was to the king, who gave them their charters, and not to the parliament, which had expended neither cost nor concern in their settlement, and taken no part in the management of their internal affairs. Whilst the governour represented the royal authority, the provincial assembly was to each province what parliament was to Britain. It framed laws, levied taxes, and made every provision for the publick exigence. In regard to the single article of commerce, parliament did, indeed, exercise an unquestioned power of monopoly. In all respects else, it was unknown to the colonies. When, therefore, this body, in which the colonists were not represented, asserted the right of colonial taxation, it's claim was unjust; and with the same right in reality, if not in appearance, might the colonial assemblies have gravely maintained the identical supremacy over the people of Britain, which parliament assumed over the people of America.

Was it, then, right in the colonies to resist the parliament, and wrong to resist the king? No. For the king had joined the latter to oppress the former, and thus became, instead of the righteous ruler, the tyrant, of this country, to whom allegiance was no longer due.

Americans called themselves free, because they were governed by laws originating in fixed principles, and not in the caprice of arbitrary will. They held, that the ruler was equally obliged to construct his laws in consonance with the spirit of the constitution, as were the people to obey them when enacted; and that a departure from duty on his part virtually absolved them from allegiance.

Let not this be deemed a licentious doctrine. Who is the rebel against law and order, the legislator ordaining, or the citizen resisting, unconstitutional measures? It is the unprincipled minister, who artfully innovates on the custom of governing; the ambitious senator, whose self is his god; the faithless magistrate, who tramples on rights, which he has sworn to protect; these are the men, who, by perverting the purposes of government, destroy it's foundations, bring back society into a state of war, and are answerable for its mischievous effects. Not those who defend, but those who attack, the liberties of mankind, are disturbers of the publick peace; and not on you, my countrymen, but on thee, O Britain, who killedst thy people with the rod of oppression, be the guilt of all that blood, which was spilt in the revolutionary war!

Here, then, you find the principles, which produced the event, we this day commemorate. They were the principles of common law and of eternal justice. They were the principles of men, who sought not to subvert the government, under which they lived, but to save it from degeneracy; not to create new rights, but to preserve inviolate such, as they had ever possessed, rights of the same sort, by which George III then sat, and still sits, on the throne of England, the rights of prescription.

Hence, through the progress of our revolution, these principles continued their operation. Armed in the uprightness of your cause, you disdained an appeal to those ferocious passions, which commonly desolate society in times of commotion. No man lost his life for resisting the general opinion. Instruction maintained its influence, law its terrours, and religion its divine and powerful authority. Property was secure, and character sacred; and the condition of the country was as remote from a savage democracy, as from a sullen despotism.

Such was the American revolution. It arose not on a sudden, but from the successless petitions and remonstrance of ten long years. It was a revolution, not of choice, but of necessity. It grew out of the sorrows and unacknowledged importance of the country; and having to obtain a definite object by definite means, that object being obtained, was gloriously terminated.

As evidence, that I have not misrepresented the "feelings, manners, and principles," which gave birth to your independence, recollect the early, regular, and effectual methods adopted by the United States, to form a national constitution of civil government.

That continental patriotism, which, in a time of war, was able to bend individual interest to the common benefit, proved sluggish, precarious, and totally inadequate to the purposes of union and order in the season of peace. There lacked a principle of cohesion, springing from the certain tendencies of human passion, which should compel the knowledge, industry, and emulation of every citizen to promote the opulence and power of the country.

Such a cement was recognized in the federal constitution. It's healthful operations, guided by its celebrious framers and friends, revived the languishing spirit of Columbia. Our consequent rapid population had scarcely a parallel in history. Individuals suddenly multiplied into families, families into towns, and towns into populous and flourishing states. What liberty was to the people of Europe in the twelfth and thirteenth centuries, government was now to this country. It patronized genius and learning, gave stimulus to enterprize, and reward to labour. It encouraged agriculture and manufactures; unfurled the sails of commerce; lifted publick credit out of the mire of contempt; and placed America on a dignified eminence among the nations of the earth.

These are among *the important and happy effects of a domestick nature, which have already flowed* from our national independence.

There is, moreover, a *general effect, which will forever flow from the auspicious epoch of July 4, 1776.* As often, as the sun shall enlighten this day, in each successive revolution of our orb, it will admonish the rulers of mankind of the folly and danger of innovations in government.

Sound politicks is ever conversant with expedience and the temper of the age. It is not a science, which may be learned in the closet, and forced into practice against nature and circumstances. An endeavour, therefore, to engraft untried theories, however plausible, upon the usual mode of administering affairs of state, is always an hazardous undertaking. The man, who would rashly change even a government confessedly corrupt, betrays pitiable ignorance and presumption. What then shall be thought of English ministers, who impinged on rights and usages, which, for generations, had strengthened and adorned the ancient empire, and were imparting nourishment to this infant realm; and who expended thousands of lives and millions of money in a fruitless effort to legalize their wrongs?

Although, then, the American revolution must be considered, in regard to this country, the most honourable and felicitous, and in the view of the historian, the most splendid, event the world ever saw, yet to legislators in all climes and periods, it conveys this solemn instruction; it teaches them in a voice, louder than the thunders of heaven, to be just and wise: just in not abridging the freedom and invading the properties of their fellow-men, and wise in not abandoning the measures of a temperate policy for the gairish projects of innovation.

If, however, this revolution contains a monition to rulers against political speculations, a revolution of later date affords similar warning to every description of men. The vicissitudes of France, during the twelve past years, defy the pen of description, and deter the writer, who values his credit with posterity, from essaying the record of truth. See there, ye vaunting innovators, your wild and dreadful desolations! Whatever was visionary in metaphysick, or violent in practice, you greedily adopted; and as hastily destroyed whatever bore the semblance of order, rectitude, and antiquity. You fixed no bounds to either your ambition or cupidity. Not content with banishing faith, and law, and decency from the gallick dominion, your ever changeful and unhinging policy assumed the forms of hostility to other governments, and threatened to bring upon the whole civilized world the decades of disorder and rapine.

Yet what have Frenchmen gained by all this revolutionary errour and phrenzy? After warring with science, they now encourage it; after abolishing christianity, they have restored it; and after murdering the mildest of despots, their present republick is a mere mixture of military despotism and of popular slavery.

In thus animadverting on the conduct and character of a foreign government, I fulfil a painful, but necessary duty. It is a necessary part of this day's solemnity, because the American, has sometimes been confounded with the French, revolution,* when that bears no more resemblance to this, than the movement of a regular and beneficent planet is like the wanderings of a comet, which "from his horrid hair shakes pestilence and war,"† "importing change to times and states."‡ It is necessary, because along with the political innovation, which was ravaging Europe, there came abroad an infidel philosophy, equally subversive of freedom, as of morals. For how shall the liberty of individuals be preserved in a state of universal licentiousness? And after the prostration of religious principle, how can you hope for purity of manners? What shall support the superstructure, when the foundation is removed? Who ever put faith in the national convention of France, after it had denied the existence of God? Or what was ever more farcical, than a report on morals from the mouth of Robespierre, whilst that monster of faction was wading to empire in the blood of his country? It is, finally, necessary, because this unholy spirit of atheism has already deteriorated the political and moral condition of this country, and still menaces our hopes, privileges, and possessions.

Should it be the fate of America to drink still deeper of the inebriating bowl, it's government, whose existence depends on the publick sentiment, must fall a victim to the draught. Should the rulers of our country, especially, ever become intoxicated with the poison; should they deviate from the course prescribed by their wise predecessors, incautiously pulling down what had been carefully built; should they mutilate the form, or impair the strength of our most excellent constitution; should they amuse themselves with ephemeral experiments, instead of adhering to principles of certain utility; and should they despise the religion and customs of our progenitors, setting an example of impiety and dissipation, deplorable will be the consequences. From an head so sick, and an heart so faint, disease will extend to the utmost extremities of the political body. As well may you arrest the

*A very instructive and valuable tract on this topick is found in a pamphlet, printed at Philadelphia, entitled "The origin and principles of the American revolution, compared with the origin and principles of the French revolution, translated from the German of Gentz, by an American gentleman."

† Milton

‡ Shakespeare

flight of time, or entice the moon from her orbit, as preserve your freedom under atheistical rulers, and amidst general profligacy of habit. Libertinism and lethargy, anarchy and misrule will deform our once happy republick; and it's liberties will receive an incurable wound. The soil of America will remain; but the name and glory of the United States will have perished forever. This lovely peninsula will continue inhabited; but "the feelings, manners, and principles" of those Bostonians, who nobly resisted the various acts of British aggression, will be utterly changed. The streams of Concord will flow as formerly, and the hills of Charlestown grow verdant with each return of spring; but the character of the men, who mingled their blood with those waters, and who eternized those heights, will be sought for, but shall not be found.

What execrations shall we merit from posterity, if, with the instruction and example of preceding ages, and our present advantages, we shall tamely suffer this havock from the besom of innovation! Compared with ours, the memory of those Goths who overwhelmed in their conquests the arts and literature of Greece and Rome, will be glorious and amiable. They destroyed the improvements of their enemies; but we shall have abolished the customs of our forefathers, and the worthiest labour of our own hands: they pleaded the necessity of wasting the refinements of civilization to prevent luxury and vice; but the annihilation of our institutions will annihilate all our virtue and all our liberty.

Are we willing, then, to bid farewell to our independence and freedom? Shall we relinquish the bright visions of republican bliss, which, twenty-six years, have feasted our imagination? Upon the trial of only half that period, will we decry a constitution, which is the wonder of the universe? Or, on account of supposed or real injuries, which it may have sustained, will we desert the noble fabrick?

Be such national perverseness and instability far from Americans! The dust of Zion was precious to the exiled Jew, and in her very stones and ruins he contemplated the resurrection of her walls, and the augmented magnificence of her towers. A new glory, too, shall yet overspread our beloved constitution. The guardian God of America, he, who heard the groans of her oppression, and led her hosts to victory and peace, has still an ear for her complaints, and an arm for her salvation. That confidence in his care, which consists in steadfastness to his eternal statutes, will dispel the clouds, which darken her hemisphere.

Ye, therefore, to whom the welfare of your country is dear, unite in the preservation of the christian, scientifick, political, and military institutions of your fathers. This high tribute is due to those venerable sages, who established this Columbian festival, to the surviving officers and soldiers of that army, which secured your rights with the sword, and to the memory of their departed brethren. You owe it to the ashes of him, who, whether considered as a man among men, an hero among heroes, or a statesman among statesmen, will command the love and admiration of every future age. Yes, immortal Washington, amidst all the rancour of party, and war of opinions, we will remember thy dying voice, which was raised against the madness of innovation! "We will cherish a cordial, habitual, and immovable attachment to our national union; accustoming ourselves to think and speak of it, as of the palladium of our political safety and prosperity." You owe it to his great successor, who has now carried into retirement the sublime and delightful consciousness of having been an everlasting benefactor to his country. Enjoy, illustrious man, both here and hereafter, the recompense of the wise and good! And may the principles of free government, which you have developed, and the constitutions which you have defended, continue the pride of America, until the earth, palsied with age, shall shake her mountains from their bases, and empty her oceans into the immensity of space! You owe it to the civil fathers of this commonwealth, and in particular to him, who, thrice raised to it's highest dignity, watches over it's immunities with painful diligence, and governs it with unrivalled wisdom, moderation, and clemency. You owe it, in fine, Americans, to yourselves, to your posterity, and to mankind.

With daily and obstinate perseverance perform this momentous duty. Preserve unchanged the same correct feelings of liberty, the same purity of manners, the same principles of wisdom and piety, of experience and prescription, the same seminaries of learning, temples of worship, and castles of defence, which immortalize the memory of your ancestors. You will thus render yourselves worthy of their names and fortunes, of the soil which they watered with the sweat of their brows, and of the freedom, for which their blood was the sacrifice. You will thus give consistence, vigour, beauty, and duration to the government of your country; and, rich reward of your fidelity! you will witness a reign of such enlightened policy, firmness of administration, and unvaried justice, as shall recal and prolong to your enraptured eyes *the age of Washington and of Adams*.

55

A SERMON, ON THE SECOND COMING OF CHRIST

John Hargrove

BALTIMORE

1805

JOHN HARGROVE (1750–1839). The practice of delivering sermons in the Capitol in Washington began in Thomas Jefferson's administration and continued for decades until after the Civil War (see Anson Stokes, *Church and State in the United States*, 1:499-507). All denominations were included in the invitations to preach, and the President, cabinet members, senators, representatives, and the general public attended. The sermon reprinted here, *A Sermon, on the Second Coming of Christ and on the Last Judgment*, delivered on Christmas Day, 1804, was at least the third sermon preached by John Hargrove in the Capitol. He had preached on the day after Christmas in 1802, with President Jefferson and about forty senators and representatives and sixty other people in attendance. Interest was such that he was invited to preach again the following evening. The mystical and eschatological teachings of the Church of the New Jerusalem, a denomination sprung from the writings of Emanuel Swedenborg (1688–1772), were of evident interest to Hargrove's audience. The Baltimore church where he was pastor was the first of the denomination founded in the country (1792). Dr. Joseph Priestly, Jefferson's mentor in things religious, was attracted to the Swedenborgian doctrines of final things, and the matter of Christ's divinity and resurrection were points of debate between him and Jefferson. (See Robert Hindmarsh, *Letters to Dr. Priestly* [1792]; and D. W. Adams, ed., *Jefferson's Extracts from the Gospels* [1983], pp. 14-25, in *The Papers of Thomas Jefferson*, Second Series.) In general, all this was in line with the newly aroused interest in the relationship between republicanism and religion.

John Hargrove was born in Ireland and came to America in 1769. He worked as a land surveyor and as a master weaver, and he published *The Weavers Draft Book and Clothiers Assistant* (1792; repr. 1979), the first book of its kind published in America. He was ordained a minister in the Methodist Episcopal Church in 1776 and became a member of the first faculty of Cokesbury College in Abington, Maryland, in 1788. While few details of his life are known, it appears that he converted to the Swedenborgian sect after going to Baltimore to study these teachings with the intention of refuting them. In any event, in 1799 he became the first Swedenborgian minister ordained in the United States and was the pastor of the Church of the New Jerusalem in Baltimore until 1830. He died there in 1839.

A

SERMON,

ON THE SECOND COMING OF CHRIST,

AND

ON THE LAST JUDGMENT.

DELIVERED THE 25th DECEMBER, 1804,

BEFORE BOTH HOUSES OF CONGRESS,

AT THE

CAPITOL IN THE CITY OF WASHINGTON.

BY JOHN HARGROVE,

MINISTER OF THE NEW JERUSALEM CHURCH—BALTIMORE.

"The *natural* man receiveth not the things of the spirit of God; for they are *foolishness* to him, *because they are spiritually discerned.*" PAUL.

"I will take no man's liberty of judging from him, neither shall any man take mine from me. I will think no man the worse *man,* nor the worse *christian,* nor love him less for differing in opinion from me. I am fully assured that God *does not,* and therefore man *ought not* to, require any more of any man than this. *To believe the scripture to be God's word, To endeavor to find the true sense of it, and to live according to it.*" CHILLINGWORTH.

"Now it is allowed us to enter *intellectually* into the mysteries of our holy faith." SWEDENBORG.

PRINTED BY WARNER & HANNA—1805.

PREFACE

The numerous and valuable improvements in all the arts and sciences, which have so rapidly succeeded each other during the last half century, contribute to convince the men of the Lord's New Church that a *new order of things* has taken place in the spiritual world, and is thence daily manifesting its happy effects in the natural world; for the natural world is only a world of effects; but the spiritual world is a world of causes.

It is likewise a pleasing and sure presage of increasing knowledge and liberality, that on all such occasions, it is seldom enquired whether these improvements were first suggested by a Whig or a Tory, a Jew or a gentile: To which we may also add, that the bloody and infernal swords of religious intolerance and persecution, are now, probably, for ever sheathed, through the mild, but extensive climates of these United States; for here we have no Inquisition—no Bastile.

And yet it is a fact, that whenever any theological idea or system which is apparently new is announced, or submitted to the consideration of the christian world, "*a hue and cry*" of heretic, and blasphemer is immediately resounded and reverberated; and the most hostile and illiberal opposition manifested against all such annunciations, even by many who positively refuse to examine the premisses!

Such ignorant and bigoted opposers to the growing state of gospel knowledge, should reflect, however, that there is a sure promise left unto the church of God, that "*The path of the just shall be as the shining light, that shineth more and more unto the perfect day*"; or as it is elsewhere expressed, that in the latter days "*The light of the moon shall be as the light of the sun, and the light of the sun shall be seven fold, even as the light of seven days.*" Hence, when he who was the "*Light of the World*" appeared on earth "*in the likeness of sinful flesh,*" he plainly and positively declared that (over and above what he then had revealed) he had "*many more things*" to announce, which, at that period they were "*not able to bear*"; but that nevertheless, the time should come, when a brighter dispensation of gospel truths should be afforded us, particularly respecting the true nature of the holy trinity, or object of Christian worship. (See St. John's Gospel xxi. chapter, 12th and [25]th verses.)

Now this blessed period the men of the New Jerusalem Church are fully persuaded hath already taken place: A period which in its future progress will effect the happy downfall of mystic Babylon; and a full and final judgment and rejection of those principles of superstition and infidelity which have brought the church to the consummation of its first period.

Whatever effect the following discourse may have, towards hastening the progress of the period alluded unto, is not for *me* to determine; but this I can say, that it would not have made its appearance so soon from the press, had I not received the following letter, from a member of congress a few days ago; which on this occasion I have respectfully solicited and also obtained leave to insert, without any alteration.

Washington, 30th January, 1805.

Sir,

I have to lament that when you was lately in Washington, I was unable to procure an introduction to you; and consequently had not the pleasure of a conversation, which might have superceded the necessity of this application: I attended at the Capitol when you preached the last sermon at that place, when I was ravished and delighted with your expositions of the doctrines of the gospel; but being as novel as reasonable, I was unable to impress them on my mind in such a way as to be able to systematize them; I have therefore to request (if it can be done without inconvenience to yourself), that you would furnish me with a copy of the sermon. I shall leave this place about the 4th of March for the southward, previous to which, I should be gratified to hear from you. Meanwhile I beg leave to subscribe myself, with sentiments of high consideration your obedient humble servant,

J. B. Earle

The receipt of this letter, I say, produced in my mind, not only a desire to comply with the request of my honorable though unknown correspondent; but impressed me also, with a presumption, that were I to print off and circulate an ample edition of the discourse alluded to, it would probably prove equally pleasing to many other sincere inquirers after religious knowledge. Such as it is, therefore, it is now presented before a candid and enlightened people; not to court contention however, God is my witness; but with the fond hope that I may contribute, in some small degree, to arrest infidelity, and dissipate superstition; and that it may have this happy influence, is, and ever shall be, the fervent and sincere prayer of

Baltimore, 14th Feb. 1805. The Author

For he cometh, for he cometh, to judge the earth:—He shall judge the world with righteousness, and the people with his truth.

Psalms XCVI. 13

Various and voluminous are the treatises, with which the christian world has been burdened for ages past, respecting the two grand and interesting doctrines evidently involved in the text before us: I say burdened, because it is an acknowledged fact that after all which has been said, or written on the subject, "clouds and darkness" still rest upon it.

And yet, there are few articles, I presume, within the ample and sacred circle of Christian theology, which appear to have a more solemn and irresistible claim to our pious attention than the doctrines here alluded to—viz.

I. The Lord's second advent into the world; and
II. The general or last Judgment.

Feeling, therefore, as I do at present, far more anxious to satisfy the sincere enquirer after truth, than to display any singular talents for extempore oratory, I have concluded to deviate from my usual mode of public speaking, and avail myself of some prepared notes on this occasion, in order to aid a declining memory, and thereby do the more justice to my subject.

The aggregate number of all who are justly entitled to the appellation of believers in divine revelation, may, with considerable propriety, be arranged under three distinct classes: To wit, the Jewish church, the past or former Christian church, and the New Jerusalem church; which latter church, is now forming, by the Lord, in various parts of the earth, through the medium of the theological writings of that profound philosopher and heaven-taught-seer, Baron Emanuel Swedenborg. And, notwithstanding each of these churches, equally and cordially subscribe to the divine authority and inspiration of the book of Psalms; yet it is equally certain that each of them has adopted some leading sentiments upon the subject, now before us, peculiar to themselves and distinct from each other.

The Jews still contend that the Messiah (promised by the antient prophets) has never yet made his appearance in this world; but, at the same time admit, that he will come, at some future period, in all the grandeur of an earthly prince, and prowess of a mighty conqueror: when he will establish the antient city of Jerusalem, as the centre of his future kingdom and glory.

The former Christian church, has always, to the present period, taught, that the promised Messiah did come into the world, in the days of Augustus Cæsar, and, that Jesus Christ, who was crucified on Mount Calvary, near Jerusalem, was that Messiah; who, though now exalted unto the right hand of God in the heavens, will, nevertheless, make his personal appearance again on earth, at some future period —in order to judge all mankind who have ever lived in the world, and assign to each his eternal abode in heaven or in hell according to the deeds done in the body: Immediately after which, the visible universe will be destroyed, and the procreation of the human race cease forever; but that nevertheless, God will afterwards create *a new heaven, and a new earth*, which shall abide to eternity.

The men of the New Jerusalem church, however, differ very considerably, from each of the former churches, in their ideas of the true meaning of the subject now before us—affirming, that the Messiah, not only came into the world, "in the flesh," in the days of Augustus Cæsar, but also, that he has actually effected his second general advent, "in the spirit," not many years ago—by a gracious revelation of the spiritual sense of his holy word, in which, he may be said to have his more immediate residence; and, that he has thereby effected an exploration, and judgment unto condemnation, upon all those evil and false principles, which have too long obtained, and reigned in the world, and have brought the first period of the Christian church to its consummation; and that this is what is signified in the sacred pages, by the destruction of the former heavens, and the former earth, and the creation of new heavens and a new earth in their place.

The Jews have never ceased to express their astonishment and offence, at the former Christian church, for their weakness, or madness (as they call it) in believing that the Messiah ever yet made his appearance in the world, "in the flesh," and that Jesus of Nazareth was he; while on the other hand, the former Christian church, now seem equally astonished and offended at the men of the Lord's new church, for believing that this promised Messiah, or Jesus Christ, hath already effected his second general advent, "in the spirit."

The New Jerusalem church, however, can perceive no good reasons to be astonished or offended, either at the Jews, or former Christians, for not having as yet, adopted the peculiar faith of the new church, on the subject before us—confident, that a great degree of our religious differences on this and other profound passages of the scriptures, originate in the imperfection, and depravity of our nature, in its present lapsed and fallen state; while at the same time they also think it not improbable that part of these differences may be traced up to the order of divine Providence, whose general design seems to be, that every created thing, but especially the human mind, should gradually advance from lesser states of perfection to greater; thus causing "*the path of the just to shine brighter, and brighter unto the perfect day.*"

The progress of gospel knowledge in the world, has long since been predicted by its blessed author, under the familiar representation of "*a grain of wheat,*" which after it is sown in the earth, makes its first productive appearance "in the blade,"—next "in the ear"—and afterwards, "*the full corn in the ear*": But notwithstanding we are inclined to view this spiritual grain of wheat (which was cast into the spiritual earth, or church, at our Lord's first advent) as having already progressed on from the tender blade, to the full corn in the ear; yet we must be permitted to view it, as still inclosed within its chaff, from whence we doubt not, it will soon be well threshed out, by the skillful labors of the men of the Lord's new church; so that when "*He whose fan is in his hand,*" shall more evidently appear, he may gather the pure wheat into his garner, there to be reserved for the daily bread of his future church on earth forever.

The acquisition of genuine truth, particularly if it be of a religious nature, is certainly "*more to be desired than gold, even much fine gold.*" Yea, "*its price is far above rubies*": It restores the image of God unto the human soul, and is the Christian's best shield in all his spiritual conflicts. Hence it is written, "*It is a tree of life to all that lay hold on it, and happy is every one that retaineth it.*"

"*Buy the truth, and sell it not,*" was the advice of the sage and inspired king of Israel; but alas! how few are now willing to purchase it at its stated price, or to seek for it "*as forbidden treasure*"; for it is to be feared, that oft times it lies buried deep, beneath some stupendous and venerable pile of superstition.

Picture to yourselves my respected hearers, Abraham, upon mount Moriah, just about to offer up his son, his beloved son Isaac at the command of God; or Jeptha, in the very act of sacrificing his beautiful and only daughter, in order to accomplish a rash religious vow! How exquisite, how indescribable must then have been their paternal feelings! Yet what if I say, that feelings still more painful, must probably be experienced by many of us, before ever we become possessed of the genuine truths of the everlasting gospel.

Do you ask, "Is it our very lives then that we must first part with?" I answer, Yes—the very life of all our beloved lusts, and of all our darling prejudices, will God first require at our hands—all—all must be relinquished—perish—die!

Had the many pious and learned commentators who have preceeded us upon the present subject, paid more attention to the sacred and peculiar phraseology of the text, and less unto human creeds and systems, we should not have such an enormous heap of mere fallacies (not to say superstitious rubbish) to remove out of the way to day, in order that you might perceive the goodly foundations of "*the holy city, the New Jerusalem*," now descending from God out of heaven; but, as the case now stands, the sooner it is done the better, though probably, while we are engaged in the work, superstition may groan out an "anathema," and infidelity "*laugh us to scorn*": But through the divine mercy of the Lord, these things shall not move or deter us; being prompted by a clear conviction of duty, and viewing it as our peculiar and appointed cross.

And, may I hope my respected hearers, that during our present investigation, and elucidation of the passage now before us, you will not be so much concerned to learn whether what remarks I advance be new or old, as whether they be true or false? In order to this, however, it may be necessary, perhaps, to forget if possible, all our former creeds and catechisms, upon the subject; and while we reject, with manly boldness, all the jargon and learned nonsense of the schools, let us thankfully avail ourselves of the friendly aids of reason and science, which the Almighty hath now so liberally bestowed upon us, as the willing and useful handmaids to true Christian theology;

so shall we be enabled to draw such conclusions upon the subject, as shall be worthy of Christian philosophers, and of American freemen.

As Christians, we dare not suppose that there is any unmeaning expression, or needless tautology in the sacred pages of divine inspiration, as this would be no less than an acknowledgment that their divine dictator did not inspire his own chosen scribes, the prophets and apostles, with so correct and happy a phraseology as some of his more enlightened creatures could have suggested, than which no idea that can possibly enter the mind of a Christian can be more impious and preposterous.

Now if the justice of this last remark be granted, its application to our present subject will be found considerably useful, not only in obtaining just perceptions of the nature and number of our Lord's general advents into the world, but also respecting the nature of those respective and general judgments which are evidently declared in the text to be the inseparable and awful effects of each of the aforesaid advents.

For thus it is written, in the text before us—"*For he cometh, for he cometh, to judge the earth, He shall judge the world in righteousness, and the people with his truth.*"

Here then, we may perceive, as in the pure light of heaven, that (unless we admit there is useless tautology or unmeaning expressions in the sacred pages of inspiration) we have three distinct articles laid before us, most worthy of all our serious consideration.

1st. That there were two grand and distinct advents of the Lord-God into this world, plainly announced, even under the Jewish dispensation.

2dly. That each of these general advents was to be accompanied with a grand or general judgment. And

3dly. That each of these grand or general judgments was to be effected by similar means, to wit, "*By righteousness and truth.*"

Previous however, to our particular and singular observations, upon the true nature of these advents and judgments, it may be proper to remark, that it was no less a person than JEHOVAH-GOD, whose advents into this world were announced in the text.

This will appear irresistibly evident from the whole tenor of the sacred scriptures, particularly the 50th psalm (which indeed seems a literal extract from the 16th chapter of the first book of Chronicles)

—but then, it should be known, that in the Deity, whom we call JEHOVAH-GOD, there exists a divine Trinity; not of persons however, but of essential principles, which principles, when rightly apprehended, we have no objection to call Father, Son, and Holy Ghost; or, to speak more intelligibly, the *Divine Love*, the *Divine Wisdom*, and the *Divine proceeding Power*, which trinity also, corresponds unto that, in every individual man, to wit, his will, his understanding, and their proceeding affections and perceptions; hence therefore, it is written that "*God created man in his own image and in his own likeness.*"

Neither should we forget, that the holy scriptures, in various places, declare and testify, that all the aforesaid principles of Deity; or "*fullness of the Godhead bodily*," dwelleth in Jesus Christ, our Lord and Saviour; hence Isaiah assures us, that the "holy child" should be called, "The Everlasting Father" (though it is an established fact, that the men of the New Jerusalem church alone, are yet willing to recognize him as such). And hence also, it was, that when Philip formerly required Jesus Christ (whom he willingly recognized as the Son of God) to shew him the Father, he received this very remarkable answer from our Lord—"*Have I been so long with you, and yet hast thou not known me Philip? He that hath seen me hath seen the Father; how sayest thou then, shew us the Father?*"

Indeed it would appear, that soon after this (when the disciples were more powerfully illuminated) the sole and supreme divinity of Jesus Christ was cordially recognized by them all; insomuch that St. Jude stiles him, "*The only wise God, our Saviour*"; St. John calls him, "*The true God, and Eternal Life*"; and St. Paul declares him to be, "*The Lord of Glory.*"

And I may add, that even Thomas—the honest but unbelieving Thomas, was at last so overpowered with this divine conviction, that he cried out in a holy extacy, "*My Lord and my GOD!*

To the mere natural man who has never elevated his ideas of the Deity above matter and space, it is probable that this doctrine, of God's descending into this world, and ascending to heaven again, may appear altogether paradoxical, if not futile; such persons, however, with all their boasted attainments in science, and the knowledge of nature, stand in need of still further instruction respecting the God of nature; both as to his divine essence, as well as his divine existence.

For, how silly and absurd would it be, to imagine that the Almighty and Omnipresent Creator of all worlds, is "*such a being as ourselves*," having a fixed residence, or local abode in any one part of the universe which he has made? seeing, that if it be the work of his hands, and the effect of infinite love, wisdom and power, the Creator himself must have existed before *nature, space and time*; consequently, must be altogether distinct from nature and space, as to his divine essence, and from time, as to his divine existence.

And yet, illuminated reason may perceive, that the Deity, at the same time, must exist in, and through all matter, and in and through all space, though distinct from both; even as the human soul exists in, and through flesh and blood, and yet is distinct from both; the latter being composed of material particles, the former of spiritual principles.

The essential principles of the divine nature, are *the divine love*, and *the divine wisdom;* from whence, *the divine power* and all other attributes of the Deity originate and flow. The essential or constituent principles of human creatures, are the will and the understanding, from whence not only all their actions, but also all affections and perceptions originate and flow; so that the essential principles of man correspond to the essential principles of God, and are designed by the Creator to be the recipients thereof: The will of man being the designed recipient of the love of God; and the understanding of man being the designed recipient of the wisdom of God.

From this brief view of the nature of the Deity, as well as of the human soul, as not being composed of material particles; but of spiritual principles; and consequently not limited by space, we may obtain some leading and useful ideas, respecting the true nature of the Lord's advents into this world, more accurate perhaps than have obtained for many ages past.

How common it is to hear pious christians say, that at such and such a time, the Lord GOD graciously drew near, and visited them? By which, they certainly mean nothing more, than that they then experienced a gracious approach and influx of the divine love and wisdom of the Lord into their souls—illuminating their dark understandings, and purifying their corrupt wills; and, whereby also, a judgment was effected, unto condemnation, in the spiritual world of their own mind, upon all those evil and false principles, which had previously reigned there, terminating in their rejection.

Can it be considered unreasonable then, or antichristian, in the men of the New Jerusalem church, to believe, that the general advents of the Lord, alluded to in the text, certainly signify some operations of the divine love and wisdom of the Lord, analogous to those just now alluded to, though carried on upon a more extensive or general scale, in order to effect a more extensive though similar judgment, or blessing unto his church?

For my own part, I freely confess, as a sincere believer in divine revelation, that this opinion has obtained the entire possession of my mind for some years past—as being more consonant to all the adorable attributes of the Deity and the pure principles of uncorrupted reason than, that the second advent of the Lord, should be attended with a total destruction of the visible universe, in order to judge the inhabitants of this little world, and to punish the wicked.

For, I would ask the impartial and scientific Christian, what necessity can there be, in such a case, for all "*this wreck of matter, and this crush of worlds*"? What affinity can there possibly be, between the guilt and punishment of the men of this world, and the destruction of all other worlds in the universe? Or, by what law are all these stupendous worlds which are scattered through the immensity of space, to gravitate towards this? Can the Deity now make better worlds than he has done? No my beloved, the works of creation are all pronounced "very good"; and we have sufficient reason to believe, that they have always answered every purpose which infinite love, wisdom and power, could possibly have in view, in their creation.

One thing is very certain from the text, that each advent of the Lord was to be attended with similar effects, to wit, "*To judge the earth*"—and this by similar means—"*By righteousness and truth.*"

Now we all know that when the Lord GOD was graciously pleased to make his first grand advent into the world, "in the flesh," through that medium or body which he then assumed, it was not to destroy the world, but that "*the world, through him, might be saved,*" in consequence of that powerful and general influx of divine love and wisdom, which was thereby manifested in the world (or the church); so likewise, it is more than probable, it will be at the Lord's second general advent; not to destroy, but again to save; except it be to destroy our superstitious prejudices, and our sectarian and anti-christian divisions, through the medium of righteousness and truth; or a more powerful opening and revelation of his holy word, in its genuine or spiritual sense.

It is likewise evident, from the phraseology of the text before us, that as certain as the Lord's second advent will be attended with a grand or general judgment; so sure also, was his first advent attended with a similar one.

This is a point highly worthy our most profound attention; as it will doubtless lead to, or enable us to form a correspondent or just idea of the true nature of the grand or general judgment which is also to attend the Lord's second advent.

That a grand or general judgment took place at our Lord's first advent, will appear, if we only attend to his own declarations in the Gospel of St. John (ix. chapter, 39th verse) where he thus expresses himself, "*For judgment am I come into this world*"; and lest we should have too limited an idea of the nature and extent of this judgment, hear him again in the xii. chapter and 31st verse of the same gospel, adding, "*Now is the judgment of this world!*" Many passages might also be adduced here, from the prophets, to prove that the first as well as the second advent of the Lord, was to be attended with a grand, or general judgment, but perhaps they might be deemed superfluous.

Yes, my Christian brethren, a grand and general judgment did indeed, and in truth take place at our Lord's first advent and that through the very means predicted in the holy scriptures—"*By righteousness and truth*"; or by the superior light and grace of the blessed gospel; whereby the long established errors of heathenism, with all the vain traditions of the Jews, were explored and detected as fallacious; and a judgment, a general and final judgment of condemnation and rejection, was then passed upon them forever.

And, if the Lord GOD be still mindful of his church on earth: If he hath not "*forgotten to be gracious*["]; and if similar causes will produce similar effects; there is good ground for believing that his second grand or general advent hath already taken place; whereby the true and genuine sense of the holy scriptures, in which the Lord hath his more immediate residence, is now revealed from heaven, in "*power and great glory*"; dissipating the mere fallacies of the letter, and effecting another general and final judgment, even upon the principles of superstition and infidelity for ever more.

O! My beloved, already "*The judgment is set, and the books are opened!*" *Now*, therefore, *every man's works* (or creeds) *shall be made manifest, for the day shall declare them*—for now, behold!—"*He cometh*," making "*the clouds his chariot, and riding upon the wings of the wind*": that is, approaching the intellectual faculties of the members of his true spiritual church, by and through the medium of the literal sense of the holy scriptures, rightly explained by rational doctrine.

I am well aware, however, that many plausible objections against the doctrines of the New Jerusalem church, on the subject in question, can be urged from the mere letter of the sacred pages; for it may be asked, do not the holy scriptures plainly and positively declare, that previous to the Lord's second coming, or concomitant therewith, "*The sun shall be darkened, and the moon turned into blood; and all the stars of heaven fall unto the earth?*" And further, that then also "*The heavens shall pass away with a great noise—the elements melt with fervent heat, and the earth, and all the works that are therein shall be burnt up?*"

To this I answer, that all these things are certainly recorded in the holy scriptures; and all these things, I verily believe have already taken place in the world (or rather in the Christian church)—not in the literal sense, however, but in the spiritual, as every truly illuminated or spiritual Christian may clearly perceive, soon as he looses sight of the mere letter, in the splendor and trancendant glory of its spiritual sense.

I have then to request, upon this particular and solemn occasion, that every impartial and enlightened christian now present, will continue to lend me his entire and most profound attention, while I endeavor to reply to all the most formidable objections that can be urged against us, from the mere surface of the scriptures; after which, I wish no other conclusions to be drawn, than those which your rational faculties, aided by the good spirit of God, may prefer.

In the ii. chapter of the book of Joel we have a very memorable prophecy respecting the first advent of the Lord, and its effects. "*Behold*" (saith the prophet), "*the day of the Lord cometh, it is near at hand: a day of darkness and gloominess, of clouds and thick darkness*," &c. "*Then*" (says he) "*the earth shall quake, and the heavens shall tremble, the sun and the moon shall be dark, and the stars shall withdraw their shining*," &c.

Now let us look into the ii. chapter of the Acts of the Apostles, which relates the singular transactions of the day of pentecost; when the Holy Ghost, or divine influence of the Lord's love and wisdom, flowed down upon, or into the apostles, to the astonishment of the multitude, insomuch that some of them cried out, "*These men are drunken with wine.*" *But Peter standing up with the eleven lifted up his voice and said unto them, Ye men of Judea and all ye who dwell at Jerusalem, be this known unto you, and hearken unto my words; for these are not drunken as ye suppose, seeing it is yet but the third hour of the day; but this is that which was spoken by the prophet Joel, (saying) and it shall come to pass in the last days (saith God) I will pour out my spirit upon all flesh, &c. And I will shew wonders in heaven above, and signs in the earth beneath, blood, and fire and vapor of smoke; the sun shall be turned into darkness, and the moon into blood, before that great and notable day of the Lord come.*"

Here, then, my attentive hearers, you may perceive St. Peter plainly and positively declares that a fulfilment of all the wonderful antecedents and concomitants of the Lord's first advent into the world, as announced by the prophet Joel, actually took place in the true sense of the words, on the day of pentecost: To wit, That in the last days (that is, doubtless, of the Jewish church), "*The sun should be darkened and the moon turned into blood,*" &c. But, I would ask, did these things actually take place then, in the literal sense? No, my beloved, they did not; they certainly did then in the spiritual sense, or the word of the Lord is not true. Yes, my Christian hearers, they did take place then in the spiritual sense, upon those principles of the church which correspond to these bright luminaries of heaven. The love of God, in that church, was then darkened indeed, by self-love, and the love of the world; and there was no true faith then existing, but what was injured and wounded by their foolish and vain traditions; and hence it was, that the divine mercy of the Lord, constrained him to descend at that time into the world, by a powerful influx of his divine love and wisdom (through the medium he was pleased to assume), in order to redeem mankind, and establish a new church.

When, therefore, we are told in another place, by the same apostle, that at the second coming of the Lord, "*The elements shall melt with fervent heat, and the earth and all the works that are therein shall be burnt up*["]; we are not to understand the words in their mere literal sense (for this is forbidden both by the dictates of illuminated reason, and the known principles of science); we can, therefore, only correctly view them in the same sense in which St. Peter understood Joel; to wit, in a spiritual sense.

For, with respect to the natural elements, he could not possibly allude to these; as he must have known, that three out of four, usually called elements, have always been in a fluid state; consequently, there would be no propriety in announcing that air, fire or water should be made to "*melt with fervent heat*," at the second coming of the Lord; no my beloved, the elements that shall then melt, or pass away, must certainly mean those erroneous elements of theology which have too long obtained in the Christian church, and brought it to its consummation: These shall melt away, I verily believe; yea, they are even now melting fast away, before the increasing influence of the sun of righteousness, which, I am happy to believe, is rising with heavenly rapidity, to the meridian of the human mind—and gradually dissipating, in its blessed progress, those dense clouds of superstition and infidelity, which have too long obscured its sacred beams from the spiritual earth, or church of Christ.

As to the natural earth, on which we live, I am far from believing that it is to be burnt up, or destroyed at the second advent of the Lord; this certainly was not the opinion of the royal and inspired Psalmist, or his wise and learned son Solomon. The last observes, that though "*One generation passeth away, and another cometh, yet the earth abideth forever*"; and the former declares, in the 78th psalm, and 69th verse, that "*The Lord hath built his sanctuary* (or church) *like the earth which he hath established for ever*["]: And again, in the 93d psalm and 1st verse, he assures us, that "*the earth is established*," *so, that* "*it cannot be moved*."

Again, what occasion for the heavens "*to pass away with a great noise*," in consequence of the inhabitants of *this* little world having sinned? Or by what medium will the "great noise" which will accompany their dissolution reach us here? And further, if it be the abode of angels that we are to understand by the heavens, it may be asked, where are they to abide when their place of residence is destroyed?

If however, on the other hand, these heavens signify the erroneous principles which have obtained in the Christian church, for many ages past, and from which many fanatics have formed to themselves an imaginary heaven, we may perceive the propriety of the apostle's expression, when he tells us, that they shall pass away "*with a great noise*"; for this great noise will doubtless take place among the different denominations and sects of Christians, while each will endeavor with loud clamor, to contend unto death, for their favorite but superstitious creeds.

It is true, it is also written, that at the second coming of our Lord, "*all the stars of heaven shall fall to the earth*"; but if any christian understands these words in the mere literal sense, he betrays his great ignorance of the vast magnitude and indefinite number of those mighty worlds, and systems of worlds, which the Almighty Creator hath exhibited to our wondering view, as well as of the universal and immutable laws of gravity and attraction.

By the "*stars of heaven*" then, which are to "*fall unto the earth*," previous to the second advent of the Lord, I understand, that at that period, all illumination, respecting the word of the Lord, will fall into its lowest state, so that the sacred pages of divine inspiration, may be said to cease yielding their heavenly light, and be, as it were, extinct in the firmament of the church.

That the above, is actually the true sense of "*the stars of heaven falling unto the earth*," will, I presume, appear sufficiently evident to the candid and pious christian, who is conversant with the sacred pages of divine inspiration.

The prophet Daniel in his viii. chapter tells us that he once saw (in the spiritual world no doubt, and not in the natural world) a "*He-goat, which waxed great, even unto the host of heaven, and cast down some of the host, and of the stars, and stamped on them!!*["]

Again. In the xii. chapter of the Revelations, St. John informs us, that when he was let into the spirit (or spiritual world) he there saw "*A great red dragon, having seven heads and ten horns*"; and that "*his tail drew down the third part of the stars of heaven and did cast them to the earth*."

Now my christian hearers, what are we to think of this "he-goat," and this "dragon"? Or rather what are we to think of these stars, which they were permitted to draw down from heaven unto the earth, and stamp upon? What can we think, or believe them to be, but divine illumination, or the knowledge of the truths of the word of God? which the antichristian principles of error and of evil—of superstition and of infidelity (signified by this he-goat and this dragon) have been long endeavoring (with too much success I fear) to draw down into contempt, and to extinguish—which is here represented by stamping on them.

Yes, my respected audience, this must be the meaning of these passages, and now, even now, are they fulfilled in a very powerful and painful degree; so that, as a certain poet expresses it,

The Sun (of Love) no longer shines,
The Moon withdraws its light,
The Stars (or heavenly truths), decline,
The Church is sunk in night.

Yet I trust it may now also be added with equal truth,

But lo! the mighty God appears,
On clouds behold him ride,
He comes to dry his Zion's tears
And cheer his mourning bride.

Still however, I view the objector to my remarks, advancing with another famous passage from the writings of St. Paul; and which may be considered as his last or dernier resort.

The Apostle, when writing to the Thessalonians, expresses himself as follows.

> *For this we say unto you by the word of the Lord, that we which are alive, and remain unto the coming of the Lord shall not prevent them which are asleep; for the Lord himself shall descend from heaven with a shout, with the voice of the Archangel, and with the trump of* GOD; *and the dead in Christ shall rise first. Then we which are alive and remain shall be caught up together with them in the clouds, to meet the Lord in the air, and so shall we ever be with the Lord.*

Now, says the objector to the doctrines of the New Jerusalem church—We have not, as yet, heard this shout, or trump of God alluded to, neither have any christians been "*caught up in the air*"; therefore it is impossible for us to believe that the Lord's second advent has already taken place in the world, or been effected.

In reply to this, apparently formidable objection, I would beg leave to make the following remarks.

1st. I find that the same Apostle whispers in our ear, in another place, that the mere "*natural man receiveth not the things of the spirit of God, for they are foolishness unto him, because they are spiritually discerned*["]; and I am confident, that every intelligent christian in the world, who can divest himself of the honest prejudices of his former creed, upon this subject, must soon perceive that it is impossible to understand this famous passage of St. Paul to the Thessalonians in its mere natural or literal sense, without first declaring open war against his rational faculty, as well as against the known and acknowledged principles of science.

2dly. As to the trumpet which is to sound an alarm, at the second coming of the Lord, the same Apostle expressly calls it the last trumpet in the 15th chapter of his 1st Epistle to the Corinthians; which evidently implies; that a former or first trumpet had likewise been blown, and also, heard in the world.

But it may be asked, who ever heard this first trumpet, or when was it blown?

The only satisfactory answer that can be given, is, that this first trumpet was not a natural but a spiritual one; which was blown indeed, and in truth, by the first preachers of the everblessed gospel; and heard by thousands, and tens of thousands of pious men and women, who rendered a chearful and humble obedience to its "joyful sound."

Similar to this first trumpet, therefore, do I believe the sound of the last trumpet will be, even a gracious and soul illuminating revelation of the word of God, as to all its profound and holy mysteries, and prophecies; which revelation the Almighty, for wise and gracious purposes, hath hitherto withheld "*from ages and generations*"; but hath now, in mercy revealed, for the salvation of his future church on earth, from infidelity and superstition, forevermore.

3dly. As to our being "*caught up in the air*," in order "*to meet the Lord at his coming*," we all well know that up and down are mere relative terms; and, that the point of the visible heavens, or universe, which is this moment above our heads, will in twelve hours more be beneath our feet; consequently, with respect to space, no part of the heavens or universe can be said, with propriety, to be any more above us, than beneath us.

By a moderate knowledge, however, of the peculiar style of the holy scriptures; or of the science of correspondency, by which they were written, we can easily reconcile this passage of St. Paul to the Thessalonians, with all the principles of reason, analogy and known science.

The antients, were frequently wont to compare the internal and spiritual principles in man, to the external and material universe, calling man, a microcosm, or world in miniature; hence they called the sensual or lowest principle in man, the earth; his rational faculty, the air, and his most internal or spiritual faculty they called heaven.

Agreeably to this peculiar style (which we dare not deny, obtains through all the holy scriptures) by being "*caught up in the air, to meet the Lord at his coming*," we are to understand that at that happy and long-wished for period of the church, the impartial and scientific christian, whose devout and humble mind is diligently engaged in the study of the sacred pages, shall feel, and experience a blessed elevation of all his ideas respecting the Lord and his holy word, from sensual to rational perceptions, whereby he shall be more intimately conjoined unto his God, above the clouds and mists of superstition and infidelity forever.

Lastly. One thing is certain, that if there be no hidden or spiritual meaning involved in that famous passage to the Thessalonians, St. Paul must have been extremely ignorant indeed, respecting the true figure and diurnal motion of the earth—as well as the omnipresence of that Divine Person whose advent he then predicted, and of whom he writes in another place, that "*In him, dwelleth all the fullness of the Godhead bodily*." But for my own part, I have no such mean opinion of the Apostle's knowledge; for, even admitting that his former preceptor Gamaliel suffered him to leave college so very ignorant, I dare not suppose that this ignorance still prevailed after he had received the finishing stroke to his ministerial accomplishments, in the third heavens, which was previous to this.

There, indeed, he informs us that he heard some things, which "*it was not lawful for him to utter*" (that is, to the then infant church of God). May we not presume then, that if Moses, after he was favored with an extraordinary intercourse with God upon Mount-Sinai, was obliged to put "*a vail over his face*," while he rehearsed the particulars of what he heard upon the mount, which vail, the Apostle tells us is "*still untaken away* (from the Jews) *in the reading of the Old Testament*" (and which, doubtless, signifies the literal sense of the holy scriptures, which vails the lustre and glory of the spiritual sense, from mere sensual or natural men)—may we not, I say, presume, that the Apostle also, when writing to the infant church of Thessalonica, was constrained to use a similar vail, which vail, I fully believe is yet as much "untaken away" from the generality of Christians, while reading Paul's Epistles, as Moses' vail is to the Jews while reading the Old Testament.

I trust, however, that there will soon be a blessed and general "*turning unto the Lord*," when this vail of the letter will be taken away, from both Jews and Christians, and when the heaven-inspired pages will again be esteemed "precious," as they were in the days of Samuel.

Yes my beloved, let us indulge the pleasing hope, that God hath at length "*avenged his own elect that cry unto him night and day*"; and that the long expected, and long predicted time, "*even the set time to favor Israel is now come*."

But, I fear I have intruded too much upon the patient attention of my respected audience; and yet my subject is far—very far from being exhausted; I will, however, close it for the present, after having made a few brief remarks by way of application.

As Christians, we are all happily agreed in believing that the first advent of the Lord has actually taken place in the world, even eighteen hundred years ago, though the Jewish church refuse to join us in this article.

Now my beloved, it is worthy your recollection, that at that period, the Jews were the only visible church of God then upon the earth, and the only people who expected and prayed that the Messiah would come: Indeed his coming was particularly described, as to the very time, in the book of Daniel (though in a style peculiar to the prophet). The place of his birth also, together with all the grand or leading circumstances of his life and death; and even of his resurrection are to be found plainly noted down by various prophets; and yet, strange to tell, yet not more strange than true, the Jews were the primary and most powerful rejectors of his first coming!

The reason, (or rather the cause) of this strange conduct in the Jews, is not difficult to point out; for, having then as a church grievously receded and apostatized from the precepts and ordinances of God's holy law; and thereby sunk themselves into the most sensual state, both of affection and perception; they were neither capacitated nor inclined to search out the "*wonders of God's holy law*": Hence, they only dwelt on the mere surface, and rested in the letter; vainly expecting an earthly prince, and mighty general in the person of their Messiah; being far more anxious to be delivered from the Roman yoke, than from the yoke of sin.

When, therefore, he came, even "*the desire of nations*," they could perceive "*no form or comeliness in him that they should desire him*," but rejected all his gracious councils against their own souls.

I cannot now take notice of the wicked conduct of the Jews, on this occasion; suffice it to say, in the language of an Apostle, they ceased not to persecute and defame him, until, at last, "*They crucified the Lord of Glory*."

O! Horrid impiety, do you say? O! miserable, unhappy, infatuated people!

But, I have another word to add, and I trust you will consider it until you pardon me for declaring it; to me, it now appears not improbable that the Christian world at the Lord's second coming will exhibit the second act of the same tragedy.

When this takes place (and as a man of the New Jerusalem church I verily believe it already has), the scenery, and the performers, will be doubtless new, but the grand plot will be the same.

It is true, we can no more crucify him "in the flesh," but we may "in the spirit"; and, whatever Christian rejects the spiritual sense of the word of God, may be truly said to reject that holy spirit which dictated it, and dwells therein.

As to the different sects and denominations of the former Christian church, I bear them witness that "*they have a zeal for God*"; but (I must be permitted to add) "*not according to knowledge*." For, if it was idle and vain in the Jews, to expect, and look for an earthly prince and conqueror; it is no less so for the Christian world to look for, and expect an exterior and personal appearance of the Lord Jesus Christ, in a circumscribed form, or in any particular part of outward creation; in the room of looking for his spiritual and glorious appearance in his church, and the man of his church, by a gracious and powerful descent of his divine principles of love and wisdom therein.

To conclude. Should the honest, but fallacious prejudices of former creeds and teachings, prevent any of my enlightened audience from instantaneously subscribing to the doctrines of the new church upon the present subject, I can assure them they will not thereby offend me; neither shall I the less esteem them on that account. God forbid. The grand point, in my opinion, is, to be obedient and faithful to our best perceptions of God's holy word; the inhabitants of heaven can do no more.

But in order to be faithful, and give every one here "*his portion in due season*," I must be permitted to add one word more: Should there be now before me, any Christian, high or low, rich or poor, whose enlightened and scientific mind compels his interior assent to the doctrines just delivered, and yet—will be such a wretch as to affect to reject or not to believe them, because they are yet unpopular; or, that they fear their candid avowal of them may subject them to some persecution or censure, and perhaps block up their way to some future contemplated and desired perferment; what shall I say to such a character?

I could say much, but I trust that conscience can, and will say much more. O! then conscience, thou agent of the Most High and monitor of man, I adjure thee to do thine office faithfully and impartially in every breast that is before me! That superstition and infidelity, the love of self, and of the world may no more assume the reins of government; but that God may be glorified, in the rational reception *of the spiritual sense of his holy word*, and that precious and immortal souls may be saved, with an everlasting salvation!

"*Now unto the King eternal, immortal and invisible, the only wise God our Saviour, be glory and dominion forever and ever.*" Amen!

FINIS

Anton Janson, a typefounder practicing in Leipzig, Germany, cut this book type which bears his name sometime between 1660 and 1687. In recutting this fine old typeface, Linotype punchcutters have been fortunate in retaining its sharpness and sparkle, which make this one of the finest types now available. Definite information concerning Anton Janson is difficult to obtain. Whether or not he was of Dutch ancestry is not clear. Wolffgang Dietrich Erhardt bought the Janson matrices from the heirs of Edling in Holland. Edling, also a Leipzig typefounder, was Janson's successor and may have been his son-in-law. Whether or not his heirs brought the Janson punches or matrices to Holland is not known, yet the acquisition of these matrices in Holland by Erhardt may explain why the Janson type has been known as a Dutch type.

Editorial services by Harkavy Publishing Service,
New York, New York
Book design by Hermann Strohbach, New York, New York
Typography by Alexander Typesetting Company,
Indianapolis, Indiana
Printed and bound by R.R. Donnelley & Sons Company,
Crawfordsville, Indiana